UNITED STATES ARMY IN WORLD WAR II

The European Theater of Operations

BREAKOUT AND PURSUIT

Whitman Publishing Edition

by

Martin Blumenson

Whitman Publishing, LLC
PUBLISHING SINCE 1934

ATLANTA, GA
2012

Breakout and Pursuit
Whitman Publishing Edition

© 2012 Whitman Publishing, LLC
3101 Clairmont Road • Suite G • Atlanta, GA 30329

Correspondence concerning this book may be directed to Whitman Publishing, Attn: WWII (Breakout and Pursuit), at the address above.

ISBN: 0794837670
Printed in China

If you enjoy this book, you will also enjoy *World War II: Saving the Reality—A Collector's Vault* (by Kenneth W. Rendell).

Each of the following volumes about the European Theater of Operations can be read and enjoyed separately; at the same time, each takes a natural place in the framework of the whole history of the war. *Cross-Channel Attack* • *Breakout and Pursuit* • *The Lorraine Campaign* • *The Siegfried Line Campaign* • *The Ardennes: Battle of the Bulge* • *Riviera to the Rhine* • *The Last Offensive*. For a day-by-day study of all the war's ground actions, see *Chronology: 1941–1945*.

For a complete catalog of history, hobby, sports, and other books and products, visit Whitman Publishing at www.whitman.com.

. . . to Those Who Served

Foreword to the First Printing

The campaign in the summer of 1944 related in this volume included some of the most spectacular ground action of the U.S. Army during World War II. It began with the slow and costly hedgerow fighting against determined German efforts to contain the Normandy beachhead; it entered its decisive stage when the breach of German defenses permitted full exploitation of the power and mobility of U.S. Army ground troops; and it reached the peak of brilliance with successive envelopments of principal German forces and the pursuit of their remnants north and east to free most of France, part of Belgium, and portions of the Netherlands. By late August the war in the west appeared to be almost over, but the tyranny of logistics gave the enemy time to rally at the fortified West Wall and delay surrender for another eight months.

In the European Theater subseries the backdrop for this volume is *Cross-Channel Attack,* which carries the story to 1 July. *Breakout and Pursuit* follows the U.S. First Army through 10 September (where *The Siegfried Line Campaign* picks up the narrative), and the U.S. Third Army through 31 August (where *The Lorraine Campaign* begins). The logistical factors that played so large a part in governing the pace and extent of combat operations are described in much greater detail in Volume I of *Logistical Support of the Armies.*

The tremendous scope of this campaign, and its partially improvised character, have left a heritage of controversies to which no final answers can be given. The author has had free access to the records and to many of the leading players in the drama, and his account should have wide appeal to the general reader as well as to the serious military student of grand tactics.

Washington 25, D.C.
15 June 1960

JAMES A. NORELL
Brigadier General, USA
Chief of Military History

Foreword to the Whitman Publishing Edition

U.S. Army World War II chief of staff General George C. Marshall called it "one of the greatest feats of American Arms"—the late-July through early-September 1944 breakout from the Normandy beachheads and subsequent sweep across France spearheaded by fast-moving U.S. armored and infantry divisions. Marshall's dramatic judgment does not seem like mere wartime hyperbole. Despite an agonizingly slow start in June and July inching their way through the maze of Normandy's formidable hedgerows, expertly used by skilled German defenders to exact an appalling toll, by mid-September (D+100 days) American, British, and Canadian armies had already raced ahead to the border of Germany. This stunningly rapid advance propelled Allied armies about 250 miles *beyond* the pre-invasion OVERLORD D+100 objective of reaching only the line of the Seine River. Paris had been liberated from German occupation by the end of August, and U.S. Seventh Army—after invading southern France that month and driving north up the Rhone River valley—had closed up on the southernmost flank of Supreme Allied Commander General Dwight D. Eisenhower's 400-mile-long front line. Rumors of "Home by Christmas" flew through Allied ranks. The rumors were egregiously premature. Although much had been accomplished, the apparently beaten German army soon proved amazingly resilient—and extremely dangerous.

Unequalled *mobility* was one of the World War II U.S. Army's hallmarks—another was its seemingly limitless amount of deadly firepower—and the Americans' German opponents could only marvel enviously at their enemy's lavishly supplied amount of motor transportation. In one telling incident during the August 1944 pursuit across France, German observers were amazed to watch *ten thousand* U.S. vehicles of an American corps pass through one road during a single 24-hour period—no other army in the world was capable of such feats of mobility. Credit for, in effect, "motorizing" the World War II American army is largely due to the foresight of Lieutenant General Lesley J. McNair (tragically killed in Normandy by Allied bombers, July 25, 1944), who replaced all horse-drawn transport with motor vehicles when he created the U.S. Army that would fight the war. Conversely, throughout World War II most of the German army relied on horses to move artillery and supplies, while nearly all German infantrymen walked.

Before that mobility could be exploited in their dazzling pursuit across France, however, the Allies had to break out of Normandy's fiercely defended hedgerows.

v

From the June 6, 1944, D-Day landings until the key German roadblock at St. Lô was carpet-bombed into rubble July 25, American, British, and Canadian troops fought a grinding, nightmarish war of attrition. German defenders, usually so cleverly sited as to be unseen by their attackers, turned each of the countless hedgerow-enclosed fields into a mini-fortress that required the close tactical cooperation of Allied infantrymen, tankers, artillerymen, and combat engineers to attack and capture—although the weapons employed were modern, the attackers' ordeal was not unlike assaulting and capturing a seemingly endless series of medieval fortresses. The "reward" for those Allied soldiers lucky enough to survive capturing one field—and very many did not survive—was to wearily begin assaulting the next one. From D-Day until late July, the cost to the Allies of the Normandy Campaign exceeded 120,000 casualties. One telling gauge of the ferociousness of hedgerow combat was that soldiers' *minds* were broken as well as their bodies. Although not always included in casualty tallies, an *additional* 25 to 33 percent of the number of physically wounded Allied soldiers was put out of action due to what was then called "combat fatigue"—today recognized as Post Traumatic Stress Disorder (PTSD).

Operation COBRA, July 25–31, 1944, mercifully brought an end to the Allies' hedgerow nightmare, providing the break*through* that propelled the break*out* and subsequent pursuit across France. Despite an initial detour west into Brittany—quickly opening the region's ports had been presumed by OVERLORD planners to be a vital objective—and enduring a sharp August 7–13 German counterattack at Mortain, Allied armies were racing east along France's well-developed road network by mid-August. Two American armies spearheaded the Allied race to the German border: Lieutenant General Courtney H. Hodges's First Army and, notably, Lieutenant General George S. Patton Jr.'s Third Army. Lieutenant General Omar N. Bradley, elevated to U.S. 12th Army Group command upon the August activation of Patton's army, described how the two armies reflected the very different personalities of their commanders: Hodge's "temperamental" First Army "trudged across Europe with a grim intensity," while Patton's Third was notoriously "noisy and bumptious," a "cavalry army" whose unexcelled mobility was boldly exploited by a commander to whom pursuit seemed his natural element. Only when the "tyranny of logistics" caused Allied armies to outrun their logistical support in late August–early September were retreating German armies finally given the breathing space they so desperately needed to regroup, rearm, and rebuild their shattered forces into a cohesive defensive line—their so-called "Miracle in the West." Among American G.I.s later fighting that fall in the mud and misery of Lorraine and battering futilely against German Siegfried Line defenses, the optimistic "Home by Christmas" slogan was replaced by a more cynical but certainly more fervent hope that they would come "Home Alive in '45."

Martin Blumenson (1918–2005)—acclaimed Patton scholar, dear friend and generous mentor to many young historians throughout his life—lived much of the action he brilliantly recounts in *Breakout and Pursuit:* "How the Allies exploited the initial success of their landings and drove from the shores of Normandy to the German border." During the campaigns whose details he describes so expertly, Blumenson served as a U.S. Army historical officer with Patton's Third Army and, later, with Seventh Army. The scope of his 1961 *Breakout and Pursuit* is vast and the action varies widely, covering "the grueling positional warfare of the battle of the hedgerows, the breakthrough of the main enemy positions, exploitation, encirclement, and pursuit, as well as a number of actions falling under the general heading of special operations—an assault river crossing, the siege of a fortress, and night combat, among others."

Only a talented historian with Blumenson's superb insight, skills, and rare gift for crafting a compelling narrative could have written such a comprehensive yet dramatic account—Blumenson proved to be the Chief of Military History's perfect choice to create what remains one of the most popular and widely read volumes of *The United States Army in World War II*. For anyone seeking to truly *understand* how the Allies got from Normandy to the German border, Blumenson's *Breakout and Pursuit* is clearly the "must read" starting point. It is justifiably acclaimed a military history classic.

Jerry D. Morelock, PhD
Colonel, U.S. Army, ret.
Editor in Chief, *Armchair General* Magazine

Jerry D. Morelock, a 1969 West Point graduate, served 36 years in uniform. He is a decorated combat veteran whose military assignments included Chief of Russia Branch on the Pentagon's Joint Chiefs of Staff and head of the history department at the Army's Command and General Staff College. After retiring from the Army, he was executive director of the Winston Churchill Memorial and Library at Westminster College, Fulton, Missouri—the site of Churchill's famous 1946 "Iron Curtain Speech"—and is adjunct professor of history and political science at Westminster College. Since 2004, he has been editor in chief of *Armchair General* magazine, the only military-history magazine selected by the *Chicago Tribune* as one of its "50 Best Magazines" in the world. Among the award-winning historian's numerous publications is his acclaimed book, *Generals of the Ardennes: American Leadership in the Battle of the Bulge*. He is married to the Russian artist Inessa Kazaryan Morelock.

The Author

Martin Blumenson, a graduate of Bucknell University, received M.A.
degrees in History from Bucknell in 1940 and from Harvard University in
1942.   Commissioned in the Army of the United States, he served as a historical officer of the Third and Seventh Armies in the European theater during World War II.   After the war he taught history at the U.S. Merchant
Marine Academy (Kings Point) and at Hofstra College. Recalled to active
duty with the U.S. Army in 1950, he commanded a historical detachment
in Korea before beginning work on *Breakout and Pursuit* in June 1952.   He
wrote the book while on active duty in the Office of the Chief of Military
History.   After a tour of duty as Historian, Joint Task Force SEVEN, he
returned to OCMH as a civilian historian and is writing a volume on the
war in the Mediterranean theater—Salerno to Cassino.   His works include
Special Problems of the Korean Conflict (Washington, 1952); The Atomic
Weapons Tests in the Pacific, 1956 (Washington, 1957); two essays in *Command Decisions* (New York: Harcourt, Brace and Company, 1959); and
numerous articles in military and historical journals.

Preface

Covering the period 1 July to 11 September 1944, *Breakout and Pursuit* takes up the story of the European campaign at the time when the Allies considered their cross-Channel beachhead well established on the Continent. How the Allies exploited the initial success of their landings and drove from the shores of Normandy to the German border is the subject of the volume.

The events of the period comprise a rich variety of military experience. Virtually every sort of major operation involving co-ordinated action of the combined arms is found: the grueling positional warfare of the battle of the hedgerows, the breakthrough of the main enemy position, exploitation, encirclement, and pursuit, as well as a number of actions falling under the general heading of special operations—an assault river crossing, the siege of a fortress, and night combat, among others. In their variety and complexity, these operations frequently bring into sharp focus the delicate problems of coalition warfare.

The point of view is from the top down—how the situation appeared to the commanders and what decisions they made to solve their problems. Though the author has tried to present at some time or other the situation at each command echelon on the Allied side, the most consistent observation post is at the corps level where, because of the nature of the operations, particular independence of judgment and great initiative in action were required.

The emphasis is on the ground combat performed by U.S. Army troops. The activities of the other Allied forces and of the opposing Germans are included to the extent required to bring the American effort into proper perspective. Air support and logistical arrangements have been detailed when necessary for a better understanding of ground operations.

The attempt has been made to fulfill two objectives, each of which has sometimes excluded the other. On the one hand, the author has endeavored to present material of interest to the career soldier, who may seek instruction and who may perhaps be prompted to further study. On the other hand, the author has tried to write an account of interest to the general reader, who may be motivated by curiosity and the hope of learning in some detail about the conduct of the campaign, the expenditure of men and matériel, and the problems that face military leaders engaged in war.

The dates in the volume are all in 1944 unless otherwise noted.

The author has had the privilege and pleasure of working with many who have lightened his task and to whom he is greatly indebted. Mr. Wsevolod Aglaimoff, Deputy Chief Historian for Cartography, gave liberally of his military sophistication, perspective, and wisdom; his contributions to the military content and language of this volume were considerable. Mr. James B. Hodgson did most of the research in the German records; his knowledge of enemy operations was always a tonic to an author struggling to reflect both sides of the same battle in a single mirror. Miss Mary Ann Bacon, the editor, saved the author embarrassment by discovering before it was too late many inconsistencies and contradictions in fact as well as in style. Dr. Kent Roberts Greenfield, the former Chief Historian, by his very presence an inspiration in the cause of scholarship, gave invaluable help in military as well as historical matters during the writing and revision of the manuscript.

Mrs. Lois Aldridge at the Federal Records Center, Alexandria, was never too busy to locate and make available pertinent documents, which otherwise would not have come to the author's attention. Mrs. Helen V. Whittington, copy editor, performed a painstaking task with cheerful patience. Ruth Alexandra Phillips selected the photographs. Nicholas J. Anthony compiled the Index.

Among those to whom the author owes a special debt of appreciation are the present Chief of Military History, Brig. Gen. James A. Norell, as well as Maj. Gens. Orlando Ward, Albert C. Smith, and John H. Stokes, former Chiefs of Military History, and Cols. George G. O'Connor and Ridgway P. Smith, Jr., former Chiefs of the War Histories Division.

The work was undertaken under the guidance of Dr. Hugh Cole and the supervision of Dr. Roland A. Ruppenthal, former chiefs of the European section. It was completed under the direction of Mr. Charles B. Mac-Donald, Senior Historical Adviser of the World War II Branch, whose understanding of military operations, felicity of phrase, and patient and unsparing counsel put him without question first among those who helped to give the volume whatever value it may have.

To these and many more go my sincere thanks.

For the facts presented, the interpretations made, and the conclusions drawn, for inadequacies and errors, I alone am responsible.

Washington, D.C.   MARTIN BLUMENSON
15 June 1960

Contents

PART THREE

Breakthrough

PART FOUR

Breakout Into Brittany

PART SEVEN

Pursuit

Maps

Illustrations

Illustrations are from the Department of Defense files.

PART ONE

IN THE WAKE OF THE INVASION

CHAPTER I

The Allies

Mission

The heart of Germany was still a long way off for the United States and British and Canadian troops battling the Germans on the Channel coast of France on 1 July 1944. The invading armies of the Western Allies, with the help of other United Nations, had crossed the Channel to strike at the heart of Germany and destroy her armed forces. Their purpose: the liberation of western Europe.[1] Two months later, in September, after combat in the hedgerows, breakout, exploitation, and pursuit, the Allies were much closer to their goal. Having carried the battle across France, Belgium, Luxembourg, and the Netherlands to the frontier of Germany—to within sight of the dragon's teeth along the Siegfried Line—the Allies seemed very close indeed.

The cross-Channel attack, launched from England on 6 June 1944, had accomplished the first phase of the invasion by 1 July. Ground troops had broken through the crust of the German coastal defenses and had also established a continental abutment for a figurative bridge that was to carry men and supplies from the United Kingdom to France. At the beginning of July the Allies looked forward to executing the second stage of the invasion: expanding their continental foothold to the size of a projected lodgment area.

Lodgment was a preliminary requirement for the offensive operations aimed toward the heart of Germany. Before the Allies could launch their definitive attack, they had to assemble enough men and material on the Continent to assure success. The plans that had shaped the invasion effort—OVERLORD and NEPTUNE—defined the boundaries of the lodgment area selected.[2] Securing this region was the Allied objective at the beginning of July.

The lodgment area contemplated in the master plan consisted of that part of northwest France bounded on the north and the east by the Seine and the Eure Rivers and on the south by the Loire, an area encompassing almost all of Normandy, Brittany in its entirety, and parts of the ancient provinces of Anjou, Maine, and Orléans. Offering adequate maneuver room for ground troops and providing terrain suitable for airfields, it was within range of air and naval support based in England. Perhaps most important, its ocean coast line of more than

---

[1] Dir, CCS to SCAEF, 12 Feb 44, quoted in Gordon A. Harrison, *Cross-Channel Attack*, UNITED STATES ARMY IN WORLD WAR II (Washington, 1951), App. B.

[2] COSSAC (43) 28, Opn OVERLORD, 15 Jul 43, conveniently digested in Harrison, *Cross-Channel Attack*, App. A; NEPTUNE Initial Jt Plan by the ANCXF, the CinC 21 AGp, and the Air CinC AEAF, 1 Feb 44, NJC 1004, copy 100, SHAEF RG 910.

five hundred miles contained enough port facilities to receive and nourish a powerful military force. The Seine ports of Rouen and Le Havre; Cherbourg; St. Malo, Brest, Lorient, and Vannes in Brittany; St. Nazaire and Nantes at the mouth of the Loire—these and a number of smaller harbors had the capacity to handle the flow of men and matériel deemed necessary to bolster and augment the invasion force. (*See Maps I, VIII, XII.*)

The planners felt that Allied troops could take the lodgment area in three months, and in June the Allies had already secured a small part of it. After seizing the landing beaches, the troops pushed inland to a depth varying from five to twenty miles. They captured Cherbourg and the minor ports of St. Vaast, Carentan, Isigny, and Grandcamp. They possessed a good lateral route of communications from Cherbourg, through Valognes, Carentan, and Bayeux, toward Caen. Almost one million men, about 500,000 tons of supplies, and over 150,000 vehicles had arrived on the Continent.[3]

Despite this impressive accomplishment, certain deficiencies were apparent. According to the planners' calculations, the Allies at the end of June should have held virtually all of Normandy within the confines of the lodgment area; in actuality, they occupied an area scarcely one fifth that size. The amounts of personnel, equipment, and supplies brought

to the Continent lagged behind the planners' expectations, and the 31 air squadrons that operated from 17 continental airfields contrasted with the planners' requirements for 62 squadrons based on 27 fields. In addition, the small Allied beachhead was crammed and congested. Airstrips were so close to the beaches that flight operations sometimes interfered with ground traffic. Carentan, a major communications center on the single lateral road held by the Allies, was little more than three miles from the front, and the city and its small but important highway bridge received periodic shelling from German field artillery. Caen, a D-Day objective, still remained in German hands and blocked the approaches to the Seine over a comparatively flat plain that favored tank warfare and the construction of airfields.[4]

The disparity between plans and reality prompted speculation as to whether the Allies had lost their momentum, whether a military stalemate had already been reached, and whether trench warfare similar to that of World War I was to recur. It also caused revision of the build-up schedules. Additional combat troops were ferried to the Continent at

---

* Maps numbered in Roman are placed in inverse order inside the back cover.

[3] Roland G. Ruppenthal, *Logistical Support of the Armies, Volume I*, UNITED STATES ARMY IN WORLD WAR II (Washington, 1953) (hereafter cited as Ruppenthal, *Logistical Support, I*), 421, 422, 422n.

[4] Air Chief Marshal Sir Trafford Leigh-Mallory, "Despatch, Air Operations by the Allied Expeditionary Air Force in N.W. Europe, November 1944," Fourth Supplement to the *London Gazette* of December 31, 1946 (January 2, 1947) ; PS/SHAEF (44) 13 (Final), SHAEF Plng Staff, Post-NEPTUNE Plng Forecast 1, 27 May 44, and SHAEF (44) 17, Comments on NEPTUNE Initial Jt Plan and Annexes, 12 Feb 44, both in SGS SHAEF File 381, Post-OVERLORD Plng; Annex A to SHAEF/1062/7/GDP, 17 Jun, Summary of Manoeuvre, SHAEF File 307.2, Logistic Studies; CS (44) 16th Mtg (19 May), Min of CofS Conf, SGS SHAEF File 337/3; IX Engr Comd Prog Rpt, 8 Jul, and 5th ESB Tel Rpt, 28 Jun, FUSA G-3 Jnl File; Ruppenthal, *Logistical Support, I*, 415–16.

TYPICAL COTENTIN TERRAIN, *looking westward from UTAH Beach.*

the expense of service units. The disruption of the planned equilibrium of combat and service troops was not serious, for the lines of communication were short and required only a small administrative establishment; but if the Allies suddenly surged forward and overran a large area, the disproportionately small number of service troops might prove unequal to the task of maintaining adequate logistical support. Despite this unpleasant possibility, the Allies had little choice. Their basic need was space—room for maneuver, space for the build-up, and more depth in the beachhead for security.[5]

Tied to the need for space was a corollary requirement for port capacity. Cap-

[5] Ltr, General Dwight D. Eisenhower to Lt Gen Omar N. Bradley, 25 Jun, FUSA G-3 Jnl File; Dwight D. Eisenhower, *Crusade in Europe* (New York: Doubleday & Company, Inc., 1948), pp 245, 265; Answers by Lt Gen Walter B. Smith and Maj Gen Harold R. Bull to questions by members of the Hist Sec. ETOUSA. 14–15 Sep 45, OCMH Files.

ture of Cherbourg had confirmed the expectation that the Germans would destroy the major harbors before allowing them to fall to the Allies. The destruction of the Cherbourg facilities had been so thorough that extensive and lengthy rehabilitation was necessary. Although restoration of the minor ports was practically complete by the beginning of July, their facilities could accommodate only a relatively insignificant portion of the build-up requirements. Consequently, as anticipated by the planners, the Allies were relying on improvisation at the invasion beaches. At the end of June the Allies did not yet appreciate the surprisingly large tonnage capacities developed there. What seemed more important were the effects of a severe Channel storm that had occurred between 19 and 21 June, a storm that had interrupted logistical operations, deranged shipping schedules, diminished the rate of build-up, and destroyed beyond repair one of two artificial harbors. This seemed to indicate beyond doubt the pressing need for permanent installations that would be serviceable in the autumn and winter as well as the summer of 1944.[6] Securing major continental ports to sustain the invasion effort depended on the acquisition of more space, and so the Allies hoped to expand their continental foothold to gain first the ports of Brittany and later those of the Seine.

Though achievement had not kept pace with the blueprint, there was good reason in the summer of 1944 for Allied confidence in ultimate victory. Expect-

ing quick success in their endeavors, the Allies were not aware of the heartbreaking combat that awaited them in Normandy. The difficulty of the campaign in July was to exceed the forebodings of the most pessimistic, even as comparatively rapid advances in August were to surpass the prophecies of the most daring.

The operations in western Europe comprised but one act of the larger performance on the stage of World War II. In widely separated theaters of operations the war against the Axis powers had entered the decisive phase. In the same month that Allied troops invaded western Europe, U.S. forces in the Pacific invaded the Marianas and gained an important naval victory in the Philippine Sea. In Burma and India, the Allies put the Japanese on the defensive. In southern Europe the capture of Rome prompted the Germans to start withdrawing 150 miles up the Italian peninsula toward Florence and Pisa. Only in China was the enemy still conducting offensive operations, but this was to be his last major attack of the war. The Russians broke the Mannerheim Line in Finland and were gathering strength for advances in the Minsk area and western Ukraine, and also in Poland and Rumania. Arrangements were being completed for an Allied invasion of the Mediterranean coast of France in support of OVERLORD.

Of all these actions, the cross-Channel attack was perhaps the most dramatic. It illustrated clearly that the Allies had taken the initiative. By the summer of 1944, Allied strategy rather than Axis aims had become the controlling factor in the bitter struggle.

---

[6] Ruppenthal, *Logistical Support*, I, 406–15; Msg, NCWTF to ANCXF, 28 Jun, FUSA G–3 Jnl File.

GENERAL EISENHOWER *with American field commanders (left to right) Generals Bradley, Gerow, and Collins.*

Forces

Based on the concept of unconditional surrender enunciated by President Franklin D. Roosevelt at the Casablanca Conference in January 1943, Allied strategy had as its object the ultimate occupation of the enemy countries. Before this was possible, the enemy war machines had to be destroyed. With this as the determining motivation, the Allies had embarked on a series of operations in an attempt to reach positions from which they could launch the final crushing blows against the enemy homelands. Against the enemy in Europe, the Allies had set into motion an inexorable march begun in 1942 in North Africa, continued in 1943 in Sicily and Italy, and developed in 1944 in France. Prime Minister Winston S. Churchill promised that the fighting would be kept in constant flame until the final climax, and to many observers the end of the war in Europe seemed near at hand. The invasion of Normandy, "part of a large strategic plan designed to bring about the total defeat of Germany by means of heavy and concerted assaults upon German-occupied Europe from the United Kingdom, the Mediterranean, and Russia," gave hope that the pledge would be fulfilled.[7]   Since the resources

---

[7] NEPTUNE Initial Jt Plan cited in n. 2, above.

GENERAL MONTGOMERY

of Great Britain and the United States in 1944 did not permit maintaining more than one major fighting front in Europe, France was selected as the decisive theater, OVERLORD the decisive campaign.[8]

Directing the invasion of western Europe, General Dwight D. Eisenhower, Supreme Commander, Allied Expeditionary Force, synchronized the joint operations of air, sea, and land forces in a field operation of a magnitude never before attempted. In commanding U.S., British, and Canadian troops—the major components of his force—and contingents representing the governments-in-exile of Norway, Poland, Belgium, Luxembourg, the Netherlands, Czechoslovakia, and the embryo government of the Free French, he was also making coalition warfare work. By temperament and by experi-

ence, General Eisenhower was extraordinarily well qualified for his assignment.[9]

The naval forces under General Eisenhower that participated in the invasion were under the command of Admiral Sir Bertram H. Ramsay. Though the air forces had no over-all commander, General Eisenhower employed Air Chief Marshal Sir Arthur W. Tedder, his deputy commander, as a *de facto* commander to co-ordinate the operations of the strategic and tactical air arms. Strategic air power was the function of the U.S. Eighth Air Force, under Lt. Gen. Carl Spaatz, and the British Bomber Command, under Air Chief Marshal Sir Arthur Harris. Tactical air power in direct support of ground operations on the Continent came from the U.S. Ninth Air Force (under Lt. Gen. Lewis H. Brereton), the 2d Tactical Air Force of the Royal Air Force, and the Air Defence Command of Great Britain, all co-ordinated by the Allied Expeditionary Air Force (AEAF), a headquarters commanded by Air Chief Marshal Sir Trafford Leigh-Mallory. Assigned to render close assistance to U.S. ground troops were the fighter-bombers of Maj. Gen. Elwood A. Quesada's IX Tactical Air Command (TAC), a subordinate unit of the Ninth Air Force.

General Eisenhower reserved for himself the eventual direction of the Allied ground forces, a task he would assume later. His headquarters, SHAEF, was in England, but he was a frequent visitor to the combat zone, and he advised his subordinate commanders through per-

---

[8] See, for example, SHAEF to AGWAR, S–54425, 23 Jun, SHAEF Msg File.

[9] See Forrest C. Pogue, *The Supreme Command*, UNITED STATES ARMY IN WORLD WAR II (Washington, 1954), pp. 33ff.

sonal conversations and tactful letters.[10] Early in July he would establish a small command post in Normandy so that he could remain in close touch with the situation.

For the initial stages of the cross-Channel attack, a period that was to last until September, General Eisenhower had delegated operational control of the Allied land forces to General Sir Bernard L. Montgomery. The ranking British field commander, General Montgomery, was thus the *de facto* commander of all the Allied ground forces engaged in western Europe. As Commanding General, 21 Army Group, General Montgomery directed two armies: the Second British commanded by Lt. Gen. Miles C. Dempsey, and the First U.S. commanded by Lt. Gen. Omar N. Bradley.[11]

The headquarters and subordinate elements of two other armies—Lt. Gen. Henry D. G. Crerar's First Canadian Army and Lt. Gen. George S. Patton, Jr.'s, U.S. Third Army—were in the process of being transported from England to France. Although the elements were incorporated into the active armies as they arrived on the Continent, the more quickly to bolster the fighting forces, the army headquarters were not to become operational until a time to be determined later. When that occurred, the British and the Canadian armies would come under General Montgomery's 21 Army Group, while the U.S. armies would function under an army

group commanded by General Bradley. With two army group headquarters and four armies operational, and with SHAEF presumably active on the Continent by that time, the direct control of all the continental ground troops was to revert to General Eisenhower as Supreme Commander.

To help the armies on the Continent, the Allies were counting on a friendly civilian population in France. At the least, the French were expected to assure safety in Allied rear areas, thus freeing military forces that would otherwise be needed to protect the lines of communication. At the most, the inhabitants might support the Allied effort by armed insurrection, sabotage, and guerrilla warfare against the occupying Germans. Long before the invasion, the Allies began to try to increase anticipated French support by reconstituting the French military forces outside France and by fostering the growth of an effective underground resistance inside the country. By the summer of 1944 one French division was in England and ready to take part in OVERLORD, and an estimated 100,000 men inside France had arms and ammunition for sabotage and diversionary activity.[12]

To regularize the resistance movement and accord its members the same status as that of the armed forces in uniform, SHAEF, in June 1944, recognized General Pierre Koenig of the Free French headquarters in London as the commander of the French Forces of the Interior (FFI). His mission was to delay

---

[10] See, for example, Ltr, Eisenhower to Bradley, 25 Jun, cited in n. 5, above.

[11] For description of General Montgomery's character, personality, and habits, see Major-General Sir Francis de Guingand, *Operation Victory* (New York. Charles Scribner's Sons, 1947), pp. 165–94.

[12] For a detailed account of how the French military forces were reconstituted, see Marcel Vigneras, *Rearming the French*, UNITED STATES ARMY IN WORLD WAR II (Washington, 1957).

the concentration of German forces opposing the invasion by impeding the movement of German reserves, disrupting the enemy lines of communication and rear areas, and compelling the enemy to maintain large forces in the interior to guard against guerrilla raids and sabotage.

By 1 July it was clear that French assistance to OVERLORD was of substantial value. Although no French Regular Army units were yet on the Continent, resistance members were helping Allied combat troops by acting as guides, giving intelligence information, and guarding bridges, crossroads, and vital installations. Far from the fighting front, the presence of armed resistance groups in German rear areas was becoming a demoralizing psychological factor for the enemy, a harassing agent that diverted his troops from the battlefield, disturbed his communications, and shook his confidence.[13]

The Allied combat forces in Normandy at the beginning of July were deployed on a front about seventy miles long. In the eastern sector—the left of the 21 Army Group—General Dempsey's British Second Army occupied positions from the mouth of the Orne River westward to the vicinity of Caumont. During June the British had moved south from three landing beaches toward the general target area of Caen. At the end of the month, with three corps operational, General Dempsey's line formed a semicircle from about three to seven miles from the northern edge of the city. (*Map I*)

In the western sector—the right of the

21 Army Group—General Bradley's U.S. First Army extended from Caumont to the west coast of the Cotentin.[14] In June the Americans had pushed south from OMAHA Beach to Caumont, had driven west from UTAH Beach to isolate Cherbourg, and had moved north and taken that port. At the end of the month, three corps were in the line while a fourth, after capturing Cherbourg, was hurrying south to join them.

The disposition of the Allied forces— the British on the left and the Americans on the right—had been planned to facilitate supply in the later stages of the invasion. Although stocks in the United Kingdom flowed to the troops of both nations over the landing beaches in the summer of 1944, eventually men and matériel in support of the U.S. forces were to come directly from the United States, and the Breton ports were the most convenient points of entry to receive them. Likewise, the continental harbors along the Channel were logical ports of entry for the British forces. This determined not only the deployment of troops but also their objectives from the outset.

Terrain

With the capture of Cherbourg at the end of June marking the close of the first phase of continental operations, General Eisenhower had the choice in the next phase of directing action east toward the Seine ports of Le Havre and Rouen, or south toward the Breton ports, principally St. Nazaire, Lorient, and

---

[13] See Pogue, *Supreme Command*, Chapters VIII and XIII, and below, Chapter XXIX.

[14] Throughout this volume, the term *Cotentin* refers to the area bounded by Cherbourg on the north, Avranches on the south, the Vire River on the east, and the English Channel on the west.

Brest. A move to the Seine ports, a more direct thrust toward Germany, was the bolder course of action, but unless the Germans were already withdrawing from France or at the point of collapse, success appeared dubious. More logical was an American drive southward to capture the Breton ports while the British and Canadians covered American operations by striking through Caen and later toward the Seine. A major impediment to this course of action was the terrain. (*Map 1*)

The ground that was to serve as the battlefield in July was of a diversified nature.[15] On the Allied left was the Caen–Falaise plain, gently rolling open country of cultivated fields and pastures, dry and firm ground suitable for large-scale armored operations and airfield construction. Facing the Allied center between the Orne and Vire Rivers were the northern fringes of a sprawling mass of broken ground—small hills, low ridges, and narrow valleys—gradually rising in height toward the south. West of the Vire River in the Carentan area was a marshy depression crisscrossed by sluggish streams and drainage ditches. On the extreme right of the Allied front, between the marshland and the coast, a cluster of hills dominated the countryside and gave the Germans a solid anchor for their left flank.

With the exception of the Caen–Falaise plain, the battlefield had a compartmentalized character that was bound to impose limitations on the Allies. It restricted maneuver and by the same token favored the German defense. The natural limitations were further aggravated by a man-made feature encountered at every turn, the hedgerow, the result of the practice of Norman farmers for centuries of enclosing each plot of arable land, pasture as well as orchard, no matter how small.

The hedgerow is a fence, half earth, half hedge. The wall at the base is a dirt parapet that varies in thickness from one to four or more feet and in height from three to twelve feet. Growing out of the wall is a hedge of hawthorn, brambles, vines, and trees, in thickness from one to three feet, in height from three to fifteen feet. Originally property demarcations, hedgerows protect crops and cattle from the ocean winds that sweep across the land. They provide the inhabitants with firewood. Delimiting each field, they break the terrain into numerous walled enclosures. Since the fields are tiny, about 200 by 400 yards in size, the hedgerows are innumerable. Because the fields are irregular in shape, the hedgerows follow no logical pattern.

Each field has an opening in the hedgerows for human beings, cattle, and wagons. For passage to fields that do not lie adjacent to a road, innumerable wagon trails wind among the hedgerows. The trails appear to be sunken lanes, and where the hedgerows are high and the tops overarch and shut out the light, they form a cavelike labyrinth, gloomy and damp.

---

[15] Institut National de la Statistique et des Etudes Economiques, *Régions géographiques de la France* (Paris, n.d.), pp. 263–65; British Admiralty, Handbook Series, *France*, 3 vols. (London, 1942), Vol. I, p. 12, fig. 7, and p. 18, Vol. II, *passim; Atlas Bottin*, 2 vols. (Paris, 1951), II, 145; Opn Plan NEPTUNE (20 May 44); First U.S. Army, *Report of Operations, 20 October 1943–1 August 1944*, 7 vols. (Paris, 1945), I, 124–25. In footnotes through Chapter XXII, all references cited as First U.S. Army, *Report of Operations*, are to the 20 October 1943–1 August 1944 report. See also footnote 13, Chapter XXIII.

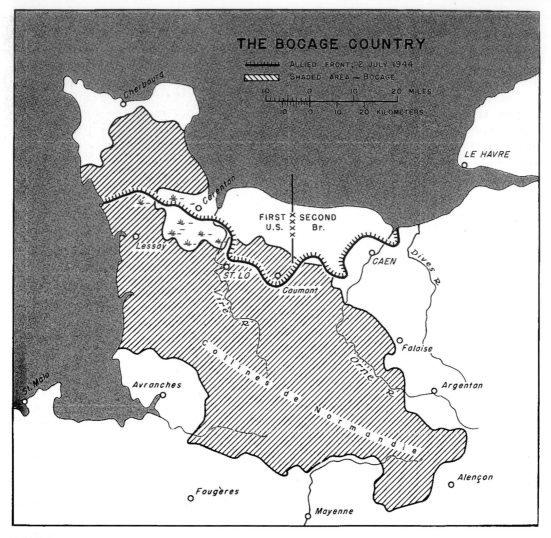

MAP 1

From a tactical point of view, each field is a tiny terrain compartment. Several adjoining fields together form a natural defensive position echeloned in depth. The abundant vegetation and ubiquitous trees provide effective camouflage, obstruct observation, hinder the adjustment of artillery and heavy weap-

ons fire, and limit the use of armor and the supporting arms.

The hedgerow is the most persistent feature in the Cotentin. Unimpressed by fine terrain distinctions, American soldiers called the whole area the hedgerow country, often simply "this goddam country." Many troops had already become familiar with it in June, and before long many more would come to know and detest it.

Tactics

The OVERLORD and NEPTUNE plans had been so concerned with the scope and complexity of the problem of getting troops ashore on the Continent that the bulk of the invasion preparations had pointed only toward the initial assault. In comparison to the wealth of material on the physiography of the coastal region, little attention had been given to the hedgerows inland. Operational techniques had not been developed, nor had special equipment been devised. The combat units had devoted little time in England to training for hedgerow tactics.

HEDGEROW POSITION *in the Cotentin.*

Looking beyond the landing, some British officers, particularly those who had withdrawn across France toward Cherbourg in 1940, were convinced that the Allies could not wage effective warfare in the hedgerows against a strongly established enemy. Such leaders as Field Marshal Sir Alan Brooke, Chief of the British Imperial General Staff, and Lt. Gen. Sir Frederick E. Morgan, the chief COSSAC planner, were among those who anticipated serious difficulties.[16] They remembered also the poorly armed Chouans, who in the last decade of the eighteenth century had utilized the hedgerows to fight an effective guerrilla war of ambush against the superior armies of the Republic.[17]

Other invasion planners had found argument to support the contrary contention. They felt that the natural defensive features of the hedgerow country would aid the Allies in maintaining their initial continental foothold during the critical early period of the build-up. They believed that the Germans would be unable to stop an attack mounted across a wide front. And they expected enough progress to be made by the British through Caen, the gateway to the Seine, to outflank the Cotentin.[18]

Failure to secure Caen by 1 July was

---

[16] COSSAC formed the initials of the Chief of Staff, Supreme Allied Commander (designate), whose organization formulated the OVERLORD plan in 1943 before the appointment later that year of General Eisenhower as Supreme Allied Commander.

[17] Intervs, Pogue Files.

[18] Interv, Col S. L. A. Marshall with Gen Eisenhower, Detroit, 3 Jun 46, and Interv, Pogue with Lord Tedder, London, 13 Feb 47, Pogue Files; see Lieutenant-General Sir Frederick Morgan, *Overture to OVERLORD* (New York: Doubleday & Company, Inc., 1950), pp. 157–58.

the greatest single disappointment of the invasion. A vital communications center, Caen was the key to operations eastward to the Seine and southeastward to the Paris–Orléans gap. Held by the Germans who blocked the comparatively flat plain that invited the use of armor and the construction of airfields, Caen also offered harbor installations for small ships. Three groups clamored for the capture of Caen: the proponents of armored warfare, who were in search of mobility; the tactical air force engineers, who were looking for airfield sites; and the logistical organizations, which were seeking port facilities. In addition, continued German occupation of Caen seemed to be dramatic evidence of Allied impotence. Without Caen, the Allies were vulnerable to an enemy armored thrust to the sea, a drive that would, if successful, split the Allied foothold and imperil the entire invasion effort. To some observers, the failure to take the city savored of hesitation and excessive caution.[19]

Conspicuously untroubled about Caen, and apparently unaware of the concern the situation was causing, General Montgomery directed the tactical operations on the Continent with what might have seemed like exasperating calm. For Montgomery, the commander of the Allied ground forces, the important factors at this stage of the campaign were not necessarily the capture of specific geographical objectives, or even the expansion of the continental

foothold. Retaining the initiative and avoiding setbacks and reverses were the guiding principles that determined his course of action.[20]

These aims were paradoxical. Retaining the initiative was possible only by continued offensive operations; yet this course was often risky because the Germans had massed the bulk of their armor in front of the British sector of operations.[21] If in trying to maintain a balance between offense and defense General Montgomery seemed to give more weight to preventing Allied reverses, he was motivated by his belief that holding the beachhead securely was more important at that time. By directing General Dempsey to make a series of limited objective attacks with his British Second Army during June, however, General Montgomery had prevented the Germans from regrouping their forces for a major counterattack and thus had denied them the initiative.[22]

From the equilibrium that General Montgomery established, a corollary principle was evolved. Unable to move through Caen for the moment, General Montgomery reasoned that if he could "pull the enemy on the Second Army," he would facilitate the U.S. First Army advance to the south. General Eisenhower had come to the same conclusion and expressed the hope that General Bradley could attack south while Montgomery had "got the enemy by the

---

[19] Lewis H. Brereton, Lieutenant General, U.S.A.; *The Brereton Diaries* (New York: William Morrow and Company, 1946), p. 287; Captain Harry C. Butcher, USNR, *My Three Years With Eisenhower* (New York: Simon and Schuster, Inc., 1946), p. 581.

[20] 21 AGp Dir, M–502, 18 Jun, Pogue Files.

[21] See below, Ch. II.

[22] Field Marshal the Viscount Montgomery of Alamein, *Normandy to the Baltic* (Boston: Houghton Mifflin, 1948), pp 86, 108; see also Field Marshal the Viscount Montgomery of Alamein, *Despatch* (New York: The British Information Services, 1946), p. 6.

throat on the east." [23]   Both men were harking back to the OVERLORD concept, which had proposed that the British institute operations toward the east in order to cover American operations to the south.   Attracting the bulk of the enemy strength was a dangerous game, but the Germans, for other reasons, had already concentrated a larger part of their power in front of the British sector. General Montgomery thus had little alternative but to contain these forces. He had begun to do so even before the Americans were ready to attack to the south.   While the U.S. First Army was driving north toward Cherbourg, General Montgomery had planned an attack by the British Second Army to insure, as he later wrote, "the retention of the bulk of the enemy armour on the Second Army front." [24]

Originally set for 18 June, the British attack had been postponed because certain essential units were still unloading on the beaches and artillery ammunition was temporarily in short supply. Not until a week later, on 25 June, had the British Second Army jumped off—its objective the capture of Caen and bridgeheads across the Orne River south of that city.   Rainy weather and determined enemy resistance balked the British of gaining their objectives, and Caen remained in enemy hands.   Yet the nearness of the British to Caen threatened the city, and on 29 June, in order to insure retention of it, the Germans launched a large-scale counterattack. The British dispersed by massed artillery

fire what turned out to be un-co-ordinated thrusts. [25]   The situation then became relatively calm.

The results of General Montgomery's activity were clear in retrospect.   He had held the eastern flank firmly and had continued to keep a great part of the German strength on the British front.   But if this had been General Montgomery's basic intention, his apparent determination to take Caen had obscured it.   Even General Eisenhower seemed bewildered, particularly since Montgomery had informed him that the British offensive launched on 25 June was to be a "blitz attack." [26]

General Montgomery had certainly wanted Caen.   That he had not secured it led to inevitable comparison and contrast of the British and the American operations.   On 18 June General Montgomery had given the Americans the "immediate task" of seizing Cherbourg and the British the "immediate task" of capturing Caen.   He had quickly changed the British task after judging the difficulties too great for immediate execution.   The Americans had secured Cherbourg on schedule. [27]

Debate had already arisen over General Montgomery's intentions, a debate that was to grow as time passed.   Did Montgomery, from the beginning of the invasion, plan to attract and contain the bulk of the German power to facilitate an American advance on the right? Or did he develop the plan later as a rationalization for his failure to advance

[23] Montgomery to Eisenhower, M–30, 25 Jun, SGS SHAEF File 381, OVERLORD, I (a) ; Eisenhower to Montgomery, 25 Jun, Pogue Files.

[24] Montgomery, *Normandy to the Baltic,* p. 94.

[25] Montgomery, *Normandy to the Baltic,* pp. 94, 97, 101; see below, Ch. II.

[26] Montgomery to Eisenhower, M–30, 25 Jun, SHAEF Incoming Msgs.

[27] 21 AGp Dirs, M–502 and M–504, 18 and 19 Jun, Pogue Files; Pogue Intervs.

through Caen? Was he more concerned
with conserving the limited British manpower and was his containment of the
enemy therefore a brilliant expedient
that emerged from the tactical situation
in June? [28] The questions were interesting but irrelevant, for the Germans had
massed their power opposite the British
without regard for General Montgomery's original intentions.

Whatever Montgomery's intent—
which was obviously not clear to other
Allied commanders at the time—the British seemed to be stalled before Caen.
Denied access to the desirable terrain
east of Caen and to the main approaches
to the Seine and Paris, the Allies
looked to General Bradley's U.S. First
Army for operational progress. Thus it
came about that, although the British

sector offered terrain more favorable for
offensive operations, American troops in
July were to undertake the unenviable
task of launching a major attack in the
Cotentin through terrain ideally suited
for defense.

Romans, Franks, Bretons, and Nor-
mans had fought on the Cotentin, and
innumerable skirmishes had occurred
there between the English and the
French. But since the devastating civil
wars of religion and revolution, little
had disturbed the tranquillity and
prosperity of the inhabitants. Even the
German occupation had had little effect
on the habits of people who were mainly
concerned with the problems of cattle
breeding and the production of butter
and cheese. Although they had "prayed
for an Allied landing," they had "hoped
that it would take place far from
them." [29] They were not spared. Where
megalithic monuments of prehistoric
times lay beside the remains of medieval
monasteries, the armies of World War
II marked the land in their turn, creating
their own historic ruins to crumble with
the others.

---

[28] Pogue Intervs; Memo, Eisenhower for Pogue,
10 Mar 47; 21 AGp CinC Notes, 15 Jun 44; 21 AGp
Dirs, M-502, 18 Jun, M-505, 30 Jun; Photostatic
copy of Gen Montgomery's address, Brief Summary
of Opn OVERLORD, 7 Apr 44; Statement concerning
British manpower strength, no title, n.d., in folder
labeled CALA Docs, Cables and Dirs, etc. All six
in Pogue Files. Montgomery, *Normandy to the
Baltic*, pp. 21–24; Chester Wilmot, *The Struggle
for Europe* (New York: Harper & Brothers, 1952),
pp. 336–41; Harrison *Cross-Channel Attack*, p. 181;
Pogue, *Supreme Command*, pp. 183ff; Omar N.
Bradley, *A Soldier's Story* (New York: Henry Holt
and Company, Inc., 1951), pp. 325–26.

---

[29] Robert Patry, *St.-Lô* (St. Lô, 1948), page 14
of Eugene Turboult's English translation.

CHAPTER II

The Enemy

At the beginning of July 1944, Germany was the target of military operations on four fronts: the Soviet drive in the east, the partisan warfare in the Balkans, the Allied operations in Italy, and the Allied offensive in western France. Only in Scandinavia did German military forces enjoy the quiet of a relatively static situation.

Of the four fronts, the Balkan battlefield was of minor importance, and the Italian sector, where the Germans fought a delaying action as they fell back, was of secondary significance. The Eastern Front, engaging the preponderance of German resources, was of most concern to the Germans, although the cross-Channel attack had posed a more direct threat to the homeland, and for a brief time—until the Russians launched their summer offensive late in June—the Normandy front was more important. From July on, the Eastern and Western Fronts received nearly equal attention from those directing the German war effort, though far from equal resources.

Exhausted by almost five years of war, its Navy powerless, its Air Force reduced to impotence, and able to offer serious resistance only on the ground, Germany seemed on the verge of defeat.

The Machinery of War

Adolf Hitler was directing the war. In addition to the responsibility and the nominal command borne by all heads of states, Hitler exercised a direct control over military operations. He determined the military strategy on all fronts and supervised closely the formulation of plans and their execution. Increasingly, as the struggle continued, he controlled the tactical operations of the troops. This close control of the military was perhaps inevitable. The pyramidal hierarchy of command reached its ultimate in him.

With an active and bold imagination, and often displaying an astute grasp of military matters, Hitler could coordinate his military objectives and his political goals far better than anyone else in Germany. Though by 1944 Hitler had delegated to others many of his governmental functions, he felt that he could not afford to do so in the military realm. The urgency of the life and death struggle with the Allies, he was convinced, compelled him to give his personal attention even to relatively minor problems, and his self-assumed commitments overworked him.

As head of the state, Hitler bore the title of *Fuehrer*.[1] As such, he was also

---

[1] The following account is based on: Harrison, *Cross-Channel Attack*, pp. 128ff; Pogue *Supreme Command*, pp. 175ff; James B. Hodgson, The German Defense of Normandy. OCMH MS R-24; Capt.

HITLER *with (from left to right) Gross-admiral Erich Raeder and Field Marshals Keitel and Goering.*

the Supreme Commander in Chief of the Armed Forces—the *Oberster Befehlshaber der Deutschen Wehrmacht.* His staff was the Armed Forces High Command, the *Oberkommando der Wehrmacht* (OKW), headed by Generalfeldmarschall Wilhelm Keitel. Theoretically, OKW was the highest military echelon under Hitler, and to it belonged the prerogatives of grand strategy and joint operations. On a lower echelon, Reichsmarschall Hermann Goering headed the Air Force High Command, the *Oberkommando der Luftwaffe* (OKL); Gross-

James F. Scoggin, Jr., ed., *OB WEST, a Study in Command,* containing MS # B–308 (Zimmerman), MS # B–672 (Buttlar), MS # B–718 (Speidel), MS # B–633 (Rundstedt), and MS # B–344 (Blumentritt), Hist Div, Dept of the Army (German Report Series, 3 vols, n.d.).

admiral Karl Doenitz headed the Navy High Command, the *Oberkommando der Kriegsmarine* (OKM); while Hitler himself headed the Army High Command, the *Oberkommando des Heeres* (OKH).

In theory, the chief of the OKW, Keitel, received the reports and co-ordinated the activities of the OKL, OKM, and OKH. But Goering outranked Keitel and therefore reported directly to Hitler. Doenitz felt that Keitel had little interest in and understanding of naval matters, and he also reported directly to Hitler. Since Hitler himself was chief of the OKH, there seemed to be no practical need for the OKW. Yet because the war against the Soviet Union required all the attention of the OKH, the OKW assumed the direction of the other theaters.[2] OKW and OKH were thus reduced to agencies directing the ground campaigns and, together with OKL and OKM, were directly subordinate to and dominated by Hitler, the Supreme Commander in Chief.

Although the chain of command was unified at the top in the person of Hitler and although spheres of activity seemed clearly defined among the high commands, staff functions in actual practice were often confused. OKW, for example, had no intelligence section or logistical apparatus. For information about the enemy and for administration, including replacements, it relied on the OKH. OKL organized and controlled antiaircraft artillery units, Luftwaffe field divisions, and paratroopers, which in American doctrine were ground force

[2] These included the areas of western Europe, Scandinavia, and the Mediterranean. See Harrison, *Cross-Channel Attack,* pp. 133ff.

units. Competition over such matters as replacements caused friction among the services. Goering exploited his political power, while Reichsfuehrer Heinrich Himmler complicated the command structure because he headed the *Schutzstaffel* (SS), an elite corps of infantry and armored units.[3]

Similar inconsistencies appeared in the field. Commanders exercised control over assigned troops but not over strictly defined geographical areas. Except in designated fortress cities, the three military services were independent branches, expected to co-operate but not functionally organized to insure complete co-ordination of effort. The result, perhaps not so surprisingly, redounded to Hitler's personal advantage.

In western Europe, *Navy Group West* was the field command of the OKM, and the *Third Air Fleet* was the field command under OKL. The ground force field command under the OKW was *Oberbefehlshaber West (OB WEST)*, and within the limits of the German command system it functioned as the theater headquarters. Unlike General Eisenhower, who in comparison had virtual carte blanche for the conduct of the war, the German theater commander operated under the close personal supervision of Hitler, who directly or through the Operations Staff of OKW, the *Wehrmachtfuehrungsstab (WFSt),* a planning section directed by Generaloberst Alfred Jodl, did not hesitate to

GENERAL JODL

point out what he deemed errors of judgment and maneuver.

The theater commander did not control the naval and air force contingents in his sector. France, Belgium, and the Netherlands, though under the nominal control of *OB WEST,* each had a military governor who exercised responsibility for internal security of the occupied territory; yet for tactical action against an invading enemy, *OB WEST* had operational control over the troops assigned to the military governors. OKW maintained direct contact with each military governor and supervised *OB WEST* supply and administration.

For tactical operations *OB WEST* controlled two army groups. These had the mission of defending the Channel and Atlantic and the Mediterranean coast lines of the *OB WEST* area. Their

---

[3] Founded in 1925 to protect Hitler, the SS evolved from a small bodyguard to a vast organization that formed military units called the *Waffen SS*. Regiments and divisions were gradually organized from *Waffen SS* battalions.

zones of operations were the Netherlands and Belgium and those French administrative and political departments touching the sea. The boundary between the army groups was an east–west line across France from the Loire River to the Swiss border near Lake Geneva, although there was always a lack of clarity as to whether *OB WEST* or the military governor exercised authority over tactical troops in central France. *(Map 2)*

South of the boundary was the sector of *Army Group G,* a headquarters that controlled the *First Army,* which defended the Atlantic coast of France south of the Loire, and *Nineteenth Army,* which held the Mediterranean shores of France. The *Replacement Army,* which trained units in the interior of France, furnished troops for security duties against the FFI and was ready to undertake operations against airborne landings.

North of the Loire–Geneva boundary line was *Army Group B.* Under this headquarters, *LXXXVIII Corps* occupied the Netherlands, *Fifteenth Army* defended the coast of Belgium and of northern France to the Seine River, and *Seventh Army* had responsibility for that part of northwest France between the Seine and the Loire Rivers.

The chain of command, then, that had functioned to meet the Allied invasion of western Europe consisted of Hitler; the OKW, which transmitted Hitler's orders; *OB WEST,* the ground force headquarters in the west that operated as the theater command; *Army Group B,* which had tactical control of the troops along the Channel coast; and *Seventh Army,* which had found itself responsible for the area invaded.

The Changing Strategy

German strategy in July was rooted in the events of June. When the Allies landed on the Normandy beaches on 6 June 1944, the Germans were without a firmly enunciated policy of defense.[4] The *OB WEST* commander, Generalfeldmarschall Gerd von Rundstedt, and the *Army Group B* commander, Generalfeldmarschall Erwin Rommel, were in vague but basic disagreement on how best to meet the expected Allied invasion. Rundstedt tended to favor maintaining a strong strategic reserve centrally located, so that after he determined the main invasion effort he could mass the reserve and destroy the Allies before they could reinforce their beachhead. Sometimes called the concept of mobile defense, this was a normal operational technique. Rommel presupposed Allied air superiority, and he argued that the Germans would be unable to move a centrally located reserve to the battlefield since the Allies would control the air in that area; he believed it necessary to defeat the Allied invaders on the beaches. Sometimes called the concept of static defense, this theory gave impetus to the construction of the Atlantic Wall.[5]

Hitler never made a final decision on which method of defense he preferred. Consequently, neither method was established as a distinct course of action. By

---

[4] See Harrison, *Cross-Channel Attack,* pages 151–57 and 243–58 for a detailed discussion of the changes in German strategic concepts.

[5] See *OB WEST, a Study in Command,* pages 49ff. for a description of the divergence in the operational views of Rundstedt and Rommel.

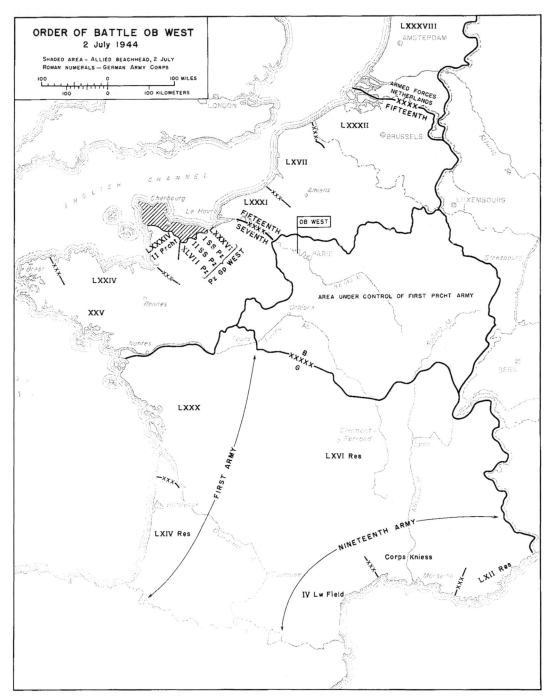

MAP 2

FIELD MARSHAL ROMMEL

inference, it appeared that Hitler favored defense on the beaches since he had charged Rommel with specific responsibility for coastal defense even though the task might logically have belonged to the theater commander, Rundstedt. Although Rommel was subordinate to Rundstedt, he thus had a certain favored status that tended to undermine the chain of command. This was emphasized by the fact that he had direct access to Hitler, a privilege of all field marshals.

Despite a lack of cohesion in the command structure and an absence of coherence in defensive planning, the three commanders acted in unison when the Allies assaulted the beaches. Rommel gave battle on the coast, Rundstedt began to prepare a counterattack, and

Hitler approved the commitment of theater reserves.

Their actions stemmed from traditional German military thought and training, which stressed the ideal of defeating an enemy by a decisive act rather than by a strategy of gradual and cumulative attrition.[6] As a consequence, the German military leaders, although fighting essentially a defensive battle, searched for a bold counterattack that would destroy the Normandy beachhead and drive the Allies back into the sea. While Rommel fought the tactical battle of the beaches, Rundstedt designated a special headquarters (which he had organized in 1943 to train armored units) to plan and launch a counterattack of decisive proportions. Under the command of the *OB WEST* armor specialist, General der Panzertruppen Leo Freiherr Geyr von Schweppenburg, *Panzer Group West* assumed this function.[7] An Allied bomber struck Geyr's headquarters on 10 June, killed several key members of the staff, and obliterated immediate German hopes of regaining the initiative.

To take the place of *Panzer Group West*, which could not be reorganized quickly after the bombing, the Germans planned to upgrade the *LXXXIV Corps* headquarters to an intermediate status pending its eventual elevation to an army headquarters. On 12 June, however, its commander, General der Artil-

---

[6] Herbert Rosinski, *The German Army* (Washington: Infantry Journal, Inc., 1944), 185ff; Fuehrer Dir 40, quoted in translation in Harrison, *Cross-Channel Attack*, App. A.

[7] See Harrison, *Cross-Channel Attack*, pp. 247, 348-49, 373-74. The commander of *Panzer Group West* is hereafter referred to as Geyr.

lerie Erich Marcks, was also killed by an Allied bomb.[8]

By mid-June Rommel was inclined to believe that the Allies had gained a firm foothold in France.[9] Experience in Sicily and Italy seemed to indicate that when Allied assault troops succeeded in digging in on shore, it was very difficult to dislodge them. On 12 June Hitler appeared to accept the validity of the danger, for on that date he recalled an SS panzer corps of two SS armored divisions—about 35,000 men—from the Eastern Front and dispatched them with highest transportation priority to the west. The mission of these units was to take part in the vital counterattack that was to destroy the Allied beachhead.

While the SS panzer corps and other reinforcements hurried toward Normandy, German troops on the Western Front were sustaining serious losses. Allied air superiority was hampering and delaying the movement of German men and supplies to the battle area, and Allied ground troops were swarming ashore with increasing amounts of equipment. As early as three days after the invasion, officers of the OKH intelligence section and of the OKW operations staff discussed the probable loss of Cherbourg.[10] Five days later, on 14 June, Rundstedt and Rommel agreed to leave only light German forces in defense of the port if the Americans should cut the Cherbourg peninsula and isolate the

FIELD MARSHAL VON RUNDSTEDT

northern portion of it. Thus, only a few troops would be sacrificed in the north while the bulk of the German forces on the peninsula would withdraw and form a defensive line near its base to oppose an expected American attack toward the south. Two days later, on 16 June, as the field commanders, upon learning that the Americans were about to cut the peninsula, prepared to put the withdrawal plan from Cherbourg into effect, OKW transmitted Hitler's refusal to permit them to evacuate the port.[11]

Although Field Marshals Rundstedt and Rommel considered a strong and costly defense of Cherbourg useless, Hitler was not interested in conserving several thousand soldiers when he could expend them and perhaps keep the Allies

---

[8] *AGp B* Telecon, 2115, 11 Jun. There was some talk of having the upgraded corps take responsibility for the entire active front. *OB WEST KTB,* 12 Jun and *Anlagen* for period.

[9] Rommel to Keitel, *Beurteilung der Lage am 11.6.1944,* 12 Jun, *AGp B KTB Ia Tagesmeldungen; OB WEST, a Study in Command,* I, 3.

[10] Telecon, 1105, 9 Jun, *Handakte, Chef Abt. Fremde Heere West;* see MS # B–784 (Criegern).

[11] *Seventh Army KTB,* 14 and 16 Jun; *AGp B KTB,* Annex 52a to *Anlage 32;* Harrison, *Cross-Channel Attack,* pp. 413–14.

from gaining a major port, at least until the counterstroke, now planned for 25 June, was launched. While the master counterattack was being prepared to oust the Allies from Normandy, Hitler was unwilling to yield cheaply what he correctly judged to be an important link in the projected chain of Allied logistics.

Despite Hitler's wishes, the defense of Cherbourg was disappointing.[12] German troop confusion, inadequate provisioning of the fortress, and the vigor of the American attack were disheartening to the Germans. The field marshals concentrated their efforts on mounting the still pending major counterattack, even though Hitler continued to recommend counterattacks designed to aid the Cherbourg defenders.[13]

Conferring with Hitler at Soissons on 17 June, the field commanders agreed to launch through Bayeux what they all hoped would be the decisive counterattack.[14] A reorganized *Panzer Group West,* under the control of *Army Group B,* was to direct the tactical operation, which would now be launched no earlier than 5 July. The purpose of the attack was to split the Allies on the coast and dispose of each separately.

As tactical plans for the Bayeux offensive were being readied and troops and supplies assembled, the British launched their attack toward Caen on 25 June.[15] Almost at once the local commander defending Caen judged that he would have to evacuate the city. To retain Caen the *Seventh Army* on 26 June prepared to employ the troops assembling for the Bayeux offensive, not in the planned offensive mission but for defensive reasons, to counterattack the British. Before the commitment of this force, however, the situation eased and became somewhat stable. Nevertheless, German apprehension over the possibility of continued British attacks in the Caen sector did not vanish.

At this time not only the commanders in the west but also OKW passed from thinking in terms of offensive action to an acceptance of a defensive role.[16] "No matter how undesirable this may be," Rundstedt informed OKW, "it may become necessary to commit all the new forces presently moving up—in an effort to stop and smash . . . the British attack expected to start shortly southeast from

---

[12] After capture of the city, the American corps commander asked, but the German commander (who had been taken prisoner) refused to answer, why he had defended the high ground around Cherbourg, good outer defensive positions, instead of retreating to the better inner ring of forts to make his stand. Maj William C. Sylvan, former senior aide to Lt Gen Courtney H. Hodges, Deputy Comdr, First Army, Personal Diary (hereafter cited as Sylvan Diary), entry of 27 Jun. Major Sylvan kept his diary, dealing primarily with General Hodges' activities, with the approval of General Hodges. A copy is on file in OCMH through courtesy of Major Sylvan.

[13] Harrison, *Cross-Channel Attack,* pp. 411–12, 442; *AGp B KTB,* 17 Jun; *OB WEST KTB,* 24 Jun, *Anlage 295,* 27 Jun, *Anlage 355,* and 28 Jun, *Anlage 375; Der Westen* (Schramm); for a more detailed explanation, see Martin Blumenson and James B. Hodgson, "Hitler versus his Generals in the West," *United States Naval Institute Proceedings* (December, 1956).

[14] Ecksparre Min, *AGp B KTB, Anlagen,* Fall 1940–Sep 1944, Annex 17; Notes in the Jodl Diary,

17 Jun; *Der Westen* (Schramm); Hans Speidel, *Invasion 1944* (Chicago: Henry Regnery Company, 1950), pp. 92–99.

[15] Ltrs, Rommel to Rundstedt, and Speidel to *OQu West,* 21 Jun, *AGp B Ia Operationsbefehle;* see above, Ch. I.

[16] *OB WEST KTB,* 25 Jun, *Anlage 306.* The best evidence of the changing attitude is found in *OB WEST KTB,* 26 Jun.

Caen." [17] So serious had the British threat appeared on 25 June that Rundstedt and Rommel fleetingly considered withdrawing to a line between Avranches and Caen.[18]

By withdrawing to an Avranches–Caen line the Germans would have good positions from which to hold the Allies in Normandy. Yet such an act might also be interpreted by higher headquarters as the first step in a complete withdrawal from France. Keitel and Jodl had agreed soon after the invasion that if the Germans could not prevent the Allies from breaking out of their beachhead, the war in the west was lost.[19] The point in question was a definition of the term *beachhead*. Would not a withdrawal from the lines already established give the Allies the space and maneuver room to launch a breakout attempt?

The alternatives facing the German field commanders late in June seemed clear: either the Germans should mount the Bayeux offensive and attempt to destroy the Allied beachhead in a single blow, or they should abandon hope of offensive action and defend aggressively by counterattacking the British near Caen.[20] The British, by acting first, had temporarily nullified the possibility of offensive action, and this seemed to crystallize a growing pessimism among the German commanders in the west.

Rundstedt had long been convinced that if only a defensive attitude were possible, it would be hopeless to expect ultimate success in the war.[21] Rommel, too, became persuaded that the German chance of victory was slim.[22] More than Rundstedt perhaps, Rommel felt that the Allied naval guns employed as long-range artillery would prevent the Germans from ever regaining the invasion beaches, and significantly he had plotted the first objectives of the Bayeux attack just outside the range of Allied naval gun fire.[23] By 15 June Rommel had admitted that the front would probably have to be "bent out" and Normandy given up because the danger of an Allied attack toward Paris from Caen was worse than a possible threat to Brittany.[24]

Hitler nevertheless remained firm in his resolve. Even though Rundstedt insisted that the focal point was Caen, Hitler kept thinking in terms of an attack west of the Vire River to save or regain Cherbourg. He cared little whether the reserves gathered near Caen were used for offensive or defensive purposes.

Tactical developments in the Caen sector bore out the apprehensions of the field marshals. There seemed to be no alternative but to commit additional reserves against the doggedly persistent British. The only troops available were

[17] Rundstedt to Jodl, 1800, 26 Jun, *OB WEST KTB, Anlage 340.*

[18] Telecon, Blumentritt to Speidel, 1610, 25 Jun, *AGp B KTB.*

[19] *ONI Fuehrer Conferences on Matters Dealing With the German Navy* (Washington, 1947), .12 Jun (also published as Doc 175–C, *Trial of the Major War Criminals Before the International Military Tribunal* (Nuremberg, 1949), XXXIV.

[20] *Der Westen* (Schramm).

[21] Guenther Blumentritt, *Von Rundstedt, the Soldier and the Man* (London: Odhams Press Limited, 1952), pp. 184, 198; Harrison, *Cross-Channel Attack*, p. 443.

[22] See B. H. Liddell Hart, ed., *The Rommel Papers* (London: Collins, 1953).

[23] *Pz Gp W KTB, Anlagen 10.VI.–9.VIII.44,* Annexes 6, 7, and 8.

[24] Telecon, Rommel to Pemsel, 2150, 15 Jun, *Seventh Army KTB, Anlagen Ferngespraeche und Besprechungen, 6.–30. VI. 44.*

those of the *II SS Panzer Corps* with-drawn from the Eastern Front and slated to initiate the Bayeux offensive. The corps jumped off on 29 June in an attack that, if successful, would disrupt the British beachhead, but it was in no sense the contemplated decisive master blow.

On that day, 29 June, Rundstedt and Rommel were at Berchtesgaden, where they listened as Hitler enunciated his strategy.[25] Acknowledging that Allied air and naval supremacy prevented a large-scale German attack for the mo-ment, Hitler deemed that, until an attack could be launched, the Germans had to prevent the development of mobile war-fare because of the greater mobility of the Allied forces and their supremacy in the air. The German ground troops must endeavor to build up a front designed to seal off the beachhead and confine the Allies to Normandy. Tac-tics were to consist of small unit actions to exhaust the Allies and force them back. In the meantime, the German Air Force and Navy were to disrupt Allied logistics by laying mines and attacking shipping. More antiaircraft protection against Allied strafing and bombing was to permit the German Army to regain a freedom of movement for troops and supplies that would en-able the field forces to launch a decisive offensive sometime in the future.

Thus, the ground troops in Normandy were to assume a defensive role tem-porarily, while the Air Force and Navy

tackled the important problems of logis-tics and mobility. Goering and Doenitz were to hamper Allied logistics and deny the Allies mobility; they were to give the German ground forces a measure of protection for their supply system, there-by assuring them a certain degree of mobility. Until these missions were executed, the ground forces had to hold every inch of ground in a stubborn de-fense. Unless Hitler could insure for his troops at least temporary protection from Allied planes, offensive maneuvers on a large scale were out of the question. Until he could secure a more favorable balance of supply, he could not launch the decisive action designed to gain a conclusive victory.

Whether or not Hitler believed that Goering and Doenitz with the obviously inadequate forces at their disposal could give him what he wanted, he proceeded on the assumption that they might.

When Rundstedt and Rommel re-turned to the west on 30 June, they learned that the German counterattack north of Caen had bogged down. The brief presence, for once, of German planes over the battlefield, until dis-persed by Allied air forces, had been ineffective. The larger situation in Normandy resembled an intolerable im-passe. While the Allied build-up pro-ceeded smoothly, the Germans were hav-ing great difficulty reinforcing the battle-field; destroyed bridges and railroads and Allied air strafing during daylight hours made this task nearly impossible. With the balance of force in Normandy swinging in favor of the Allies, continued German defense seemed a precarious course of action. Such was the basis on which the field marshals now formally

[25] Wolfram's Min, 1 Jul, in *AGp B KTB,* Annex 33; Jodl Diary, 29 Jun; *ONI Fuehrer Confs; Der Westen* (Schramm); Harrison, *Cross-Channel Attack,* pp. 445ff.

recommended a limited withdrawal in the Caen area.[26]

Hitler refused. To withdraw, even in limited fashion, seemed to him to admit defeat in Normandy, acknowledgment that the Germans had failed against what he estimated to be only one third of the strength that the Allies would eventually be able to put on the Continent. He saw that because there were no prepared defensive lines in the interior of France, no fortified positions that could be occupied by withdrawing troops, defeat in Normandy meant eventual evacuation of France. The only possible place where the Germans could resume a defensive effort would be at the German border, and this made necessary rehabilitating and manning the unoccupied West Wall, the Siegfried Line.

Hitler had prohibited the erection of fortified lines of defense in France because he believed that their presence would tend to weaken the front by acting as a magnet for weary combat troops and for what he termed "defeatist" commanders. Furthermore, Hitler appreciated that, when troops withdrew, personnel tended to straggle and abandon equipment, actions Germany could ill afford. He was also aware that the Allies, with their superior mobility, would be able to advance more rapidly than the Germans could withdraw. Finally, he underestimated neither the damage to morale a withdrawal would occasion nor the ability to harass that the FFI and a hostile French population possessed.[27]

On the other hand, the German troops in Normandy occupied excellent and extremely favorable positions for defense. If the Germans contained the Allies and prevented the expansion of the beachhead, they would retain advantageous ground from which Hitler could launch the decisive action that could turn the course of the war. And yet to remain in Normandy and seek the decision there meant the acceptance of the risk of losing the entire committed force. If the Allies broke through the German defenses and developed a war of movement, the result would bring catastrophe to German hopes. Air power and mobility would enable the Allies to institute a blitzkrieg. Unlike that on the Eastern Front, where tremendous space cushioned the effect of breakthrough, mobile warfare on the Western Front was sure to bring the Allies quickly to the border of Germany.[28]

On the afternoon of 1 July Hitler announced his position unequivocally and declared his willingness to gamble: "Present positions are to be held," he ordered. "Any further enemy breakthrough is to be hindered by determined resistance or by local counterattack. The assembly of forces will continue. ..." [29] The Germans were to take advantage of the terrain, prevent the expansion of the Allied beachhead, and remain as close to the coast as possible.

This seemed logical to the *OB WEST* operations officer, who felt that a return

---

[26] *AGp B KTB*, 1830, 29 and 30 Jun; Harrison, *Cross-Channel Attack*, p. 446.

[27] *ONI Fuehrer Confs*, 12 Jun; Harrison, *Cross-Channel Attack*, pp. 411, 412, 447; *OB WEST, a*

Study in Command, I, 46–47; *Der Westen* (Schramm).

[28] *Der Westen* (Schramm).

[29] *OB WEST Ia KTB*, 1 Jul.

to the position warfare tactics of World War I was desirable. The Germans needed "to build an insurmountable barrier in front of the enemy along the tactically most adantageous line, from which the enemy numerical and materiel superiority must be beaten down with every conceivable means." If the Germans could fight a war of attrition over a long period of time, using all the guns in their arsenal, antiquated or not, they would perhaps be able some time in the future to launch a counterattack with specially chosen and trained troops to inflict a defeat on the Allied forces on the Continent.[30]

In complete disagreement, Rundstedt called Keitel, chief of the OKW, and stated that he did not feel up to the increased demands. Whether he meant the increased demands placed on him by higher headquarters or the increased demands of an impossible situation was perhaps a deliberate ambiguity.[31] Reading Rundstedt's message as a request for relief, as an admission of defeat, or simply as an expression of disagreement, Hitler relieved his commander in chief in the west on 2 July. Two days later, Hitler also relieved Geyr, the commander of *Panzer Group West,* who had had the temerity to initiate a report criticizing the "tactical patchwork" in the west—a report endorsed and transmitted up the chain of command to Hitler.[32] Of the field commanders who had met

the Allied invasion three weeks before, only Rommel remained in command, and even he had supposedly asked Hitler at Berchtesgaden how he still expected to win the war.[33]

Hitler was not impressed with the professional abilities of his senior officers in the west. The Germans had failed in June. The Allies had established a firm beachhead in Normandy. Cherbourg had fallen. A major German counteroffensive had failed to materialize. A fresh armored corps had been committed with no apparent result.

The Germans had massed troops for a decisive counterattack that did not get started. When the German frame of reference changed from an offensive to a defensive cast, it seemed fortunate to find the bulk of the German strength in Normandy opposite the British. For the Caen sector appeared to lead directly to Paris, and that was where the Germans figured the Allies intended to go.

As the German ground action became defensive in character, Hitler placed his main reliance on air and naval effort and hoped that Goering and Doenitz would correct the balance of power then unfavorable to the Germans. Until this occurred, the German ground troops were to hold fast and preserve a vital condition—a restricted Allied beachhead—for the offensive action that was eventually to "throw the Anglo-Saxons out of Normandy." [34]

---

[30] *"Ia Notitz fuer Chef,"* 1 Jul, *OB WEST KTB, Anlage 415.*

[31] *Taetigkeitsberichte des Chefs des Heerespersonalamtes,* 1 Jul; Harrison, *Cross-Channel Attack,* pp. 446–47. *OB WEST KTB,* 3 July, clearly states that Rundstedt requested relief for reasons of health and age. This contrasts with his later denials of ever having requested relief.

[32] *Der Westen* (Schramm) ; Rommel to Rundstedt, 2400, 30 Jun, *AGp B Ia Operationsbefehle; Pz Gp W KTB, Anlagen,* Annex 33a; Harrison, *Cross-Channel Attack,* p. 445, n.880. Headquarters have been personalized as much as possible in the citations in the interest of brevity.

[33] Liddell Hart, *The Rommel Papers,* pp. 480–81.

[34] *Handakte Chef Abt. Fremde Heere West,* Jun.

Tactical Dispositions

While the higher commands were preoccupied with offensive planning, the tactical units facing the Allies were occupied with the practical necessity of fighting a defensive war.

When the Allies landed in France, the German *Seventh Army* controlled Normandy and Brittany from the Orne River to the Loire. Commanded since September 1939 by Generaloberst Friedrich Dollman, who had led it to victory over the French in 1940, the army had its headquarters in comfortable buildings at le Mans. The long peacetime occupation duty had apparently dulled the headquarters' capacities, for even after the invasion it seemed to carry on business as usual. Subordinate commands complained of its bureaucracy in handling supplies, while higher headquarters sometimes felt a lack of personal initiative among its members.[35]

Doubts as to the efficiency of the *Seventh Army* headquarters had led to discussion of relieving the army of responsibility for the Normandy battlefield and of relegating it to Brittany. The commitment of *Panzer Group West* and the plan to upgrade a corps were attempts to replace the *Seventh Army* command, but because of the destruction of the *Panzer Group West* headquarters and the death of General Marcks, both by Allied bombings, the *Seventh Army* at the end of June still directed combat operations.[36] *(See Map I.)*

By then the task had become exceedingly complicated. From one corps in contact with the Allies at the time of the invasion, the subordinate headquarters in contact and under the *Seventh Army* had increased to six. Initially, the *LXXXIV Corps,* commanded by Marcks, had met the Allies. The *I SS Panzer Corps,* under General der Panzertruppen Josef Dietrich, had moved forward from the OKW reserve to assume on 8 June a portion of the front near Caen. Several days later the *II Parachute Corps,* under General der Fallschirmtruppen Eugen Meindl, had traveled from Brittany to the St. Lô sector. On 13 June the *XLVII Panzer Corps,* commanded by General der Panzertruppen Hans Freiherr von Funck, had come forward from the *Army Group B* reserve to the vicinity of Caumont. In midmonth, General der Infanterie Hans von Obstfelder had moved his *LXXXVI Corps* from the Bay of Biscay to take the front between Caen and the Seine River. The *II SS Panzer Corps,* commanded by Generaloberst Paul Hausser, had arrived in the Caen sector near the end of the month after having been recalled from the Eastern Front.[37]

These seemed too many corps for one army to handle. Consequently, on 28 June the Germans divided the Normandy front into what amounted to two army sectors. On that date *Panzer Group West* took control of the four corps on the right, while *Seventh Army*

---

[35] *AGp B KTB,* 12, 13, 28 Jun; Interv by Hodgson with former Generalmajor a.D. Rudolf-Christoph Freiherr von Gersdorff, *Seventh Army* Chief of Staff, Washington, 28 Jul 53, OCMH Files.

[36] *AGp B KTB,* 12 Jun; *OB WEST, Anlage 101,*

12 Jun.

[37] James B. Hodgson, The Germans on the Normandy Front, 1 July 1944, OCMH MS R–49; see also James B. Hodgson, Command and Staff Roster, Western Command, June to September 1944, MS R–24a.

retained control of the two on the left.[38] The boundary lay just west of Caumont and almost corresponded with the boundary that separated the British and American fronts. On 1 July the corps that faced the Allies lined up from east to west in the following order: *LXXXVI, I SS Panzer, II SS Panzer, XLVII Panzer, II Parachute,* and *LXXXIV.*

Each of the two sectors facing the Allies at the beginning of July had about 35,000 combat troops in the line, but there was a great difference in tactical strength because of armament.[39] *Panzer Group West,* opposite the British, had approximately 250 medium and 150 heavy serviceable tanks, the latter including quite a few Tigers and King Tigers.[40] Opposite the Americans the *Seventh Army,* in contrast, had only 50 mediums and 26 heavy Panthers.[41] Of antiaircraft artillery in Normandy, *Panzer Group West* controlled the deadly dual-purpose guns of the *III Flak Corps* and had at least three times the quantity of the other antiaircraft weapons possessed by the *Seventh Army.* It had all three rocket projector brigades available in the west—the *Nebelwerfer,* which fired the "screaming meemies." It also had the preponderance of artillery.[42]

The imbalance of strength evolved from the nature of the battlefield terrain. In the western sector, where the Americans operated, the hedgerowed lowlands inhibited massed armor action and were ideal for defense. In the eastern sector, facing the British, the terrain was favorable for armored maneuver. Having hoped to launch a major counterattack in June, the Germans had concentrated the bulk of their offensive power there. At the end of the month, when the Germans were passing from an offensive to a defensive concept in Normandy, the presence of stronger forces on the eastern sector seemed fortuitous to them since Caen blocked the route to Paris.[43]

Hitler expected the Allies to make the capture of Paris their principal objective. He figured that the British Second Army would carry the main weight of the attack, while the U.S. First Army would protect the open flank. In this belief, he anticipated that the Allies would try to gain control of the middle reaches of the Orne River as a line of departure. From there he expected British forces totaling twenty or twenty-two divisions to strike toward Paris and to seek to meet and defeat the German Army in open battle west of the Seine.[44]

In order to forestall the anticipated action, the Germans planned to withdraw the armored divisions—all of which were under *Panzer Group West*—from front-line commitment and replace them

---

[38] *Seventh Army* exercised operational control over *Panzer Group West* until 1 July, when *Panzer Group West* came directly under *OB WEST.* Until 5 July *Panzer Group West* depended on the *Seventh Army* for supply; on 6 August *Panzer Group West* became the *Fifth Panzer Army.*

[39] See detailed estimated totals in Hodgson, R-49.

[40] For the characteristics of the German tanks, see below, Chapter III.

[41] *OKH Generalinspekteur der Panzertruppen Zustandsberichte, SS-Verbaende, XII.43–VII.44.*

[42] Ltr, I6/Stoart/Ia #3748/44, 21 Jun, *AGp B Ia Opns. Befehle;* MS # B-597 (Pickert) ; see Hodgson, R-24.

[43] *OB WEST KTB,* 25 and 26 Jun, and *Anlagen 315* and *340.*

[44] Estimate of Allied Capabilities and Intentions, Sitrep for 30 Jun, dated 1 Jul, *OKW/WFSt, Lágeberichte, 1–7.VII.44;* Hitler Ltr of Instr, 8 Jul, quoted in full in *OB WEST* Ltr of Instr, 8 Jul, *AGp B Fuehrerbefehle; OB WEST, a Study in Command,* I, 38.

with infantry. On 1 July some 35,000 combat infantrymen were moving toward the front to make this substitution. When the infantrymen eventually supplanted the armor in defensive positions during the month of July, *Army Group B* hoped to have two army sectors nearly equally manned. Nine armored divisions, most relieved by the infantry, would be in immediate reserve.[45]

To obtain this hoped-for disposition, the Germans had reinforced the battle area in Normandy by virtually depleting by 1 July their reserves in the west. The *First Parachute Army,* under OKL control, was only a small headquarters theoretically performing an infantry training mission in the interior of France and could, in extreme emergency, be counted as a reserve force. OKW controlled only one parachute regiment; *OB WEST* had no units in reserve. *Army Group B* had an armored division and an armored regiment still uncommitted. The *Seventh Army* had not yet committed one SS panzer division and one parachute division. *Panzer Group West* had nothing in reserve.[46]

To get troops to the battlefield in Normandy, the *Seventh Army* had stripped its forces in Brittany of four divisions and two regiments, and a fifth division was to come forward early in July.[47] The commander of the Netherlands forces had furnished one division. *Army Group G* had contributed from its relatively meager forces in southern France six divisions—four infantry, one panzer grenadier, and one armored—all under orders or marching toward Normandy at the end of June.

Only the *Fifteenth Army* remained untouched. The few divisions it had sent to Normandy had been replaced by units brought from Norway and Denmark. At the beginning of July the *Fifteenth Army,* deployed between the Seine and the Schelde, still had seven divisions under direct control and directed four subordinate corps that controlled eleven additional divisions.

The Germans had refused to divert this strong force into Normandy because they expected a second Allied invasion of the Continent in that area. German estimates throughout June had considered an Allied invasion of the Pas-de-Calais—the *Kanalkueste*—a strong possibility.[48] They were convinced that launching sites of a new weapon—the V-1—on the coast of northern France and Belgium constituted a challenge the Allies could not ignore. The Pas-de-Calais was the section of continental Europe nearest to England, and an Allied assault there could be supplied most easily and supported by air without interruption. The fact that this Channel coast area also offered the shortest route to the Rhine and the Ruhr was not ignored.[49]

[45] See James B. Hodgson, "Counting Combat Noses," *Combat Forces Journal* (September, 1954), pp. 45–46, for a definition and explanation of German combat effectives.

[46] Hodgson, R–24, Order of Battle, 6 Jun and 3 Jul, Apps. D and F; MS # P–154.

[47] James B. Hodgson, German Troops Withdrawn from Brittany, 6 June to 15 July 1944, OCMH MS R–34.

[48] The term Pas-de-Calais is here and hereafter used in the loose sense as designating the coast line between the Somme River and Gravelines (near Dunkerque). See Harrison, *Cross-Channel Attack,* p. 450.

[49] Hitler Ltr of Instr, 8 Jul, cited n. 44; *OB WEST, a Study in Command,* I 37; JIC (44) 276 (O) (Final) and JIC (44) 287 (O) (Final), German Appreciation of Allied Intentions in the West, 26 Jun and 3 Jul, Pogue Files. For the V–1, see below, p. 34.

The Germans expected an Allied invasion of the Pas-de-Calais because they believed that the Allied divisions still in the United Kingdom belonged to "Army Group Patton." They speculated that the future mission of these troops was an invasion of the Continent in the Pas-de-Calais area, this despite the fact that German intelligence rated the troops as capable of only a diversionary effort.[50]

"Army Group Patton" was in reality an Allied decoy, a gigantic hoax designed to convince the Germans that OVERLORD was only part of a larger invasion effort. Practiced under the provisions of Operation FORTITUDE, the Allied deception was effective throughout June and most of July. Naval demonstrations off the Channel coast, false messages intercepted and reported by German intelligence, and other signs of impending coastal assault kept the Germans in a continual state of alert and alarm and immobilized the considerable force of the *Fifteenth Army*.[51]

That Operation FORTITUDE was a powerful deterrent to committing the *Fifteenth Army* in Normandy was clearly illustrated by the fact that casualties among troops in contact with the Allies, which mounted alarmingly, were not promptly replaced. By the beginning of July, casualties were outnumbering individual replacements. Yet other factors also accounted for the growing short-age of manpower on the Western Front, among them a complicated replacement system and difficulties of transportation.

German ground units on the Western Front consisted of a variety of types. The regular Infantry division, with between 10,000 and 12,500 men, had six battalions of infantry organized into either two or three regiments. The specialized static division of about 10,000 men, basically a fortress unit designed to defend specific coastal sectors, had a large proportion of fixed weapons, little organic transportation, no reconnaissance elements, and few engineers. The panzer grenadier division, 14,000 strong, was a motorized unit with one tank battalion and two infantry regiments of three battalions each. The armored division, with 14,000 troops, had two tank battalions; its armored infantrymen were organized into two regiments of two battalions each. The SS panzer division, with 17,000 men, had two tank battalions and two regiments of armored infantry of three battalions each. The Luftwaffe also had ground units because German industry could not manufacture enough planes for the manpower allocated and because Goering had ambitions to have a land army of his own. There were two types of Luftwaffe ground units, both somewhat weaker in fire power than the regular Infantry division. The parachute division had 16,000 paratroopers who were in reality infantrymen; the units accepted only volunteers who received thorough infantry training. The Luftwaffe field division, about 12,500 men, contained miscellaneous surplus personnel from the antiaircraft artillery, from air signal units, from aircraft maintenance crews, from administrative units, and a certain number of recruits and foreigners.[52]

To replace combat losses in the various units in the face of competition between Himmler and Goering for the limited German manpower was no easy task. In late 1942 the Germans had set up training, or reserve, divisions designed to furnish replacements for units in combat. Originally these divisions had had an occupation role, which had not impaired their training function, but later they became garrison troops, and when occupying coastal sectors they were upgraded to field divisions. Thus, instead of existing for the purpose of supplying replacements to the combat forces, they were themselves eventually in need of replacements.[53]

Although diversity of units, competition between services, and a defective replacement system prevented the Germans from maintaining combat formations at authorized strengths, the difficulties of transportation comprised the most important reason for manpower shortages on the front. By the end of June, when the railroads were badly damaged by Allied air atttack and all the Seine River bridges except those at Paris had

been destroyed, barges moving on the Seine from Paris to Elbeuf and an eighty-mile overland route for trucks and horse-drawn wagons from Elbeuf to Caen formed perhaps the most dependable line of communications. All highways and other supply routes were overcrowded and in constant danger of Allied air attacks during daylight hours. Units traveling to reinforce the front had to move in several echelons, reload several times en route, and march a good part of the way on foot, mostly at night.

Transportation difficulties also created supply and equipment shortages. At the beginning of July, the deficit in fuel amounted to over 200,000 gallons per day. Of daily requirements figured at 1,000 tons of ammunition, 1,000 tons of fuel, and 250 tons of rations, only about 400 tons of all classes of supply could be brought to the front.[54] That the quartermaster general of the west had to borrow fifteen machine guns from the military governor of France in order to fill a request from the Cherbourg garrison illustrated into what straits German supply had fallen.[55] For lack of dependable and long-distance railroad routes, armored divisions wore out valuable equipment on the highways before getting to the combat area. The major highways to Normandy were littered with wrecked vehicles. Movement was possible only during darkness, and that at a snail's pace.[56]

Conspicuous by their absence from the battlefield were the planes of the *Third Air Fleet*. German ground troops grimly joked that Allied aircraft

---

[52] Behind the front the Organization Todt, a paramilitary formation of German and foreign laborers, both hired and impressed, was an auxiliary construction force. Formed in 1938 to build the West Wall, Todt helped Army engineers repair roads, build bridges, and construct fortifications. Order of Battle Annex 9, Semi-Mil Servs, XV Corps G–2 Per Rpt 25, 28 Aug.

[53] WD TM–E 30–451, *Handbook on German Military Forces* (Washington, 15 March 1945); SHAEF Intel Notes of 24 Aug 44, German Replacements to the Normandy Battle Area, FUSA G–2 Jnl and File; Order of Battle Annex 2, 17 Luftwaffen Feld Division (Air Force Field Div), 18 Aug, XV Corps G–2 Per Rpt 16, 19 Aug.

[54] Hodgson, R–24.

[55] *OB WEST OQu WEST KTB*, 21 and 24 Jun.

[56] *OB WEST, A Study in Command*, I, 91ff.

were painted silver, while German planes in contrast were colorless and invisible: "In the West they say the planes are in the East, in the East they say they're in the West, and at home they say they're at the front." Of an authorized 500 aircraft in the west, the Germans had about 300 planes, of which only about 90 bombers and 70 fighters could get off the ground at any one time because of shortages of spare parts and fuel. This small number could not challenge the Allied air supremacy.[57]

By July there was, however, a new weapon in operation that gave the Germans hope of redressing their discouraging situation. Air missiles called the V–1 (originally after *Versuchmuster,* meaning experimental model, later *Vergeltungswaffe,* translated vengeance weapon) and launched for the most part from the Pas-de-Calais area had on 13 June begun to fall on England in a campaign that was to last eighty days. Admittedly a terror agent directed at the civilian population, the V–1's were intended as a reprisal for Allied air attacks on German cities. The campaign reached its greatest intensity during the seven-day period ending 8 July, when a total of 820 missiles were counted approaching the English coast. The Germans soon began to launch some V–1's from medium bombers. Though they were not to appear until early September, the Allies learned in July that V–2 weapons, supersonic rockets deadlier than the V–1's, were almost ready for operational use.

Allied bombers had since 1943 been attacking V-weapon installations, particularly those diagnosed as ground

launching sites. Despite air force protests that the bombardment (Operation CROSSBOW) diverted planes from their primary offensive mission, and despite the fact that air bombardment of the sites was an inadequate defense against the reality of the V–1 attack and the potentiality of the V–2, General Eisenhower on 29 June ordered the air attacks to "continue to receive top priority." Without effective defenses to combat either the V–1 or the V–2, the Allies could only hope that ground forces on the Continent would soon overrun the launching sites. Though the guided missile attacks caused widespread death and destruction in England, they had no effect on Allied tactical or logistical operations. Yet in late June and early July the V–1's and the V–2's were a "threat of the first magnitude" to the Allied command, for "no member of the Allied forces, at any level, knew exactly what the new German weapons might accomplish." [58]

Though many difficulties and disadvantages faced the German ground soldiers, morale was generally high. Dis-

[57] MS #C–017 (Speidel).

[58] Royce L. Thompson, Military Impact of the German V-weapons, 1943–1945, MS, OCMH; Lt Col Melvin C. Helfers, The Employment of V-weapons by the Germans during World War II, OCMH Monograph; Magna Bauer, The German Withdrawal From the Ardennes (May 1955), R–59; Wesley Frank Craven and James Lea Cate, eds., *The Army Air Forces in World War II,* Vol. III, *Europe: Argument to V–E Day* (Chicago: The University of Chicago Press, 1951) (hereafter cited as *AAF III*), p. XXV, Chs. IV and XV; Eisenhower, *Crusade in Europe,* pp. 259–60; SGS SHAEF File 381, CROSSBOW. Allied concern over German jet-propelled planes, another new development, prompted warnings to the ground forces that any jet aircraft that were shot down were to be guarded so that AEAF personnel could make a technical examination of the remains. VII Corps Opns Memo 36, 13 Jul.

cipline continued to be an effective cohesive power. Leadership, though often not entirely unified at the higher echelons of command, was excellent at the combat levels. Career and reserve officers and men, as well as conscripted personnel, professed to be uninterested in politics and concerned only with performing their duty. SS officers and noncommissioned leaders were hard-bitten Nazis who were literal minded about their pledge to fight until they died.

Paratroopers were excellent soldiers. Only the volunteer foreign troops serving with German units were undependable under fire, and they constituted but a small part of the entire German force.

Despite complaints of impotence due to Allied air superiority, despite a shortage of replacements and supplies, despite the harassing operations of the FFI that slowed the movement of reserves to the battlefield, the Germans in the west had yet to be beaten.

CHAPTER III

The Situation

American

General Bradley was responsible for the conduct of American operations in Normandy. His mild and modest manner might easily have led those who did not know him to underestimate his qualities as a commander in combat. But General Eisenhower judged that he had "brains, a fine capacity for leadership, and a thorough understanding of the requirements of modern battle."[1] General Bradley was to prove more than equal to his tasks.

During most of his early career General Bradley had alternated between assignments at the U.S. Military Academy and the Infantry School, both as student and instructor. After Pearl Harbor, as a division commander, he directed in turn the training activities of two divisions. He received his first overseas assignment as deputy commander of General Patton's II Corps, in North Africa. When General Patton relinquished the corps command in order to form the Seventh U.S. Army headquarters for the invasion of Sicily, General Bradley became the corps commander for the remainder of the North African

campaign and the operations in Sicily. In the fall of 1943 he was called to England to command both the U.S. 1st Army Group and U.S. First Army. As commander of the 1st Army Group, General Bradley supervised the planning of the U.S. ground units that were to participate in OVERLORD.[2] As commander of the First Army, he directed the American elements in the invasion assault.[3] Under the control of General Montgomery, temporarily the Allied ground commander, General Bradley, as the senior American field commander on the Continent, enjoyed a far wider latitude of action than would normally have been granted him had he been directly under an American commander.[4]

The land force that General Bradley commanded at the beginning of July consisted of four corps headquarters and thirteen divisions—nine infantry, two armored, and two airborne. Not all the units had been tested and proved by

---

[1] Ltr, Gen Eisenhower to General George C. Marshall, 24 Aug 43, as quoted in parchmented MS by Forrest C. Pogue, The Supreme Command, Ch. I, p. 73, OCMH Files.

[2] 12th AGp AAR, I, 5.

[3] The First Army staff assisting General Bradley on the Continent was formed about a nucleus of veterans. One tenth of the headquarters officers, over 30 individuals, had had combat experience in the Mediterranean. Maj. Gen. William B. Kean, the chief of staff, Col. Joseph J. O'Hare, the G–1, Col. Benjamin A. Dickson, the G–2, Col. Truman C. Thorson, the G–3, and Col. Robert W. Wilson, the G–4, belonged in this category. First U.S. Army, Report of Operations, I 14–15.

[4] Bradley, Soldier's Story, pp. 209–10, 350.

combat, but except for one armored and two infantry divisions all had had some battle experience during June. Scheduled to lose both airborne divisions in the near future, General Bradley momentarily expected the arrival of two additional infantry divisions and soon thereafter several armored divisions.

Even while the focus of the U.S. First Army effort had been directed north toward Cherbourg in June, General Bradley had tried to get an American attack to the south started. General Montgomery had urged him not to wait until Cherbourg fell before extending his operations southward toward la Haye-du-Puits and Coutances. General Eisenhower had reminded Bradley to "rush the preparations for the attack to the south with all possible speed," before the Germans could rally and seal off the First Army in the Cotentin.[5]

The attack had depended on the arrival in France of the VIII Corps, a headquarters assigned to the U.S. Third Army but attached temporarily to the First. Operational on the Continent on 15 June, the VIII Corps had assumed control of those forces holding a line across the base of the Cotentin Peninsula and had protected the rear area of the troops driving toward Cherbourg. General Bradley had instructed the VIII Corps commander to attack to the south on 22 June, but the Channel storm of 19–21 June disrupted logistical operations and caused a temporary shortage of artillery ammunition. Because the Cherbourg operation and the attack to the south could not be supported simultaneously, the VIII Corps offensive was postponed.[6]

On the day that Cherbourg fell—26 June—General Bradley had again directed the advance south toward Coutances, this time to begin on or about 1 July, VIII Corps moving out first and the other corps following on army order. Once more the operation had to be delayed because tactical regrouping and logistical arrangements were not completed in time.[7]

On the last day of June General Bradley received from General Montgomery the formal instructions that were to govern his action in July. Montgomery took his cue from the NEPTUNE plan, which had projected a wheeling movement, as opposed to a north–south axis of advance in the OVERLORD plan, and directed the U.S. First Army to pivot on its left in the Caumont area. Wheeling south and east in a wide turn, the First Army was to find itself, upon completion of the maneuver, facing east along a north–south line from Caumont, through Vire and Mortain, to Fougères, its right flank near the entrance into Brittany. At this point in the operations General Patton's Third U.S. Army was to become operational and move south and west to seize Brittany, while the First Army, in conjunction with the British and Canadian forces on the left, was to advance east toward the Seine and Paris. Desiring "drive and energy," General Montgomery wanted General

[5] 21 AGp Dir, M–504, 19 Jun, Pogue Files; Ltr, Eisenhower to Bradley, 25 Jun, FUSA G–3 Jnl File.

[6] First U.S. Army, *Report of Operations*, I, 82; VIII Corps AAR, Jul; Montgomery to Eisenhower, M–30, 25 Jun, SGS SHAEF File 381, Opn OVERLORD, I (a) ; Bradley, *A Soldier's Story*, pp. 303–04.
[7] FUSA FO 1, 26 Jun; First U.S. Army, *Report of Operations* I, 82.

Bradley, once started, to continue without pause.[8]

General Bradley's revised and final order disclosed his intention to accomplish his mission in several phases. He named the Coutances–Caumont line as the immediate objective of the First Army attack that was to start on 3 July. The main effort was to be made in the Cotentin.[9]

Not all of the U.S. troops were in the Cotentin. In the left portion of the army sector, east of the Vire River, Americans lightly held a salient in *bocage* terrain, where the small hills, while not particularly favorable for offensive action, were not discouragingly adverse. Since the middle of June, while the major portion of the American strength had been operating against Cherbourg on the army right, the troops near St. Lô and Caumont had remained inactive because General Bradley had been unwilling to divert to them resources needed for the drive on Cherbourg, and because offensive activity on the left could have extended the salient and perhaps opened a gap between the American and the British forces.[10] It was this latter factor that prompted General Bradley to initiate the attack to the south across the damp spongy ground of the Carentan plain. (*See Map I.*)

At the conclusion of the attack on the right, and with his troops holding the Coutances–St. Lô–Caumont line, General Bradley would have his entire army on firm dry ground, terrain suitable for offense by mechanized forces. At that time, as the elements on both sides of the Vire River would be on similar terrain, he would be able to deliver an attack with equal effectiveness from either his left or his right. Then he would be ready to begin another operation in further compliance with General Montgomery's directive to wheel on his left to the Fougères–Mortain–Vire–Caumont line. But first Bradley had to move the forces on his right across the waterlogged area west of Carentan.

This swampy terrain was a natural position for defense. There, in 1940, the French had established a line and had endeavored to prevent the Germans from capturing Cherbourg. In 1944 the Germans were holding approximately the same positions they had occupied four years earlier, but this time they were on the defensive.[11] The area was excellent for defense because of the *prairies marécageuses.* Large marshes sometimes below sea level, the *prairies* appear to be ancient arms of the sea, land partially reclaimed from the ocean. Open spaces that seem absolutely flat, they are breaks in the hedgerow country providing long vistas across desolate bogs.

There are five of these large swamps on the Carentan plain. Four are located along rivers draining into the Carentan bay—the Merderet, the Douve, the Taute, and the Vire. The river beds are so close to sea level that the water does not flow at a discernible rate of speed but rather oozes toward the ocean; often the streams appear stagnant. The fifth marsh or bog, called

[8] 21 AGp Dir, M–505, 30 Jun, Pogue Files.

[9] FUSA FO 1 (rev), 1 Jul.

[10] See Harrison, *Cross-Channel Attack*, pp. 374, 376–77; First U.S. Army *Report of Operations*, I, 72–73.

[11] See Jacques Mordal, "La Defense de Cherbourg," *La Revue Maritime,* New Series No. 76 (August, 1952), 963–80.

the Prairies Marécageuses de Gorges, is about twelve square miles in size and lies southwest of Carentan. These major swamps and many smaller marshes comprise nearly half the area of the Carentan plain.

From the height of an adjacent hill the *prairies* seem at first glance to be pastureland, though the grass is neither bright nor lush. A base of brown dims the lustre of the vegetation like a blight. This is peat, semicarbonized vegetable tissue formed by partial decomposition in water, plant masses varying in consistency from turf to slime. Impassable in the winter when rain and snow turn them into shallow ponds, the *prairies* in the summer are forage ground for cattle. Because the land is treacherously moist and soft, crossing the bogs on foot is hazardous, passage by vehicle impossible. In addition to numerous streams and springs that keep the earth soggy, mudholes and stagnant pools, as well as a network of canals and ditches, some intended for drainage and others originally primitive routes of transportation, close the marshland to wheeled traffic except over tarred causeways that link settlements together.

Adjacent to the marshes and comprising the other half of the Carentan plain is hedgerowed lowland suitable for farming. Barely above the level of the swamps, the lowland frequently appears to consist of "islands" or "peninsulas," wholly or partially surrounded by marshland.

Because swamps comprise so much of the region, the arable land is divided into tiny fragments of ownership. Since the fields are smaller than those in the *bocage,* the hedgerows are more numerous. The excessive moisture of the lowlands stimulates growth to the point where the luxuriant vegetation is almost tropical in richness, and the hedgerows are higher and thicker. The ground is hardly less soft than the neighboring marshes because of a high water table.

Since the swamps are impassable to a modern mechanized army, the hedgerowed lowland of the Carentan plain, even though of precarious consistency, had to sustain General Bradley's pre-existence of lowland and marsh projected operations in July. But the co-sented him with strictly limited avenues of advance. To proceed through the Cotentin, U.S. troops had to advance within well-defined corridors blocked by huge hedgerows.

The Germans had emphasized this natural condition by flooding much of the moist swampland and transforming it into lakes. They had constructed concrete dams to keep fresh-water streams from reaching the sea and had reversed the automatic locks of the dams originally constructed to hold back the sea at high tide. In the summer of 1944 the marshland was covered with water.[12] The insular or peninsular character of

[12] VIII Corps AAR, Jul; (British) Inter-Service Information Series (I.S.I.S.), *Report on France,* Vol. II, *Normandy, West of the Seine,* Pt. III (C), "Waterways" (Inter-Serv Topographical Dept Jan, 43); Abbé Paul Levert, "Le Front Allemand est Brisé," in René Herval, ed., *Bataille de Normandie,* 2 vols. (Paris: Editions de "Notre Temps," 1947). Vol. I, p. 159n; Le Capitaine de Vaisseau Delpeuch, *Le Mur de l'Atlantique,* 10 vols., Vol. III *La Côte de la Manche, de la Seine au Mont St. Michel* (Bordeaux, 1952) (MS in possession of the Hist Sec, Ministry of the Navy, Republic of France), p. 95; Robert Bethégnies, *Le Sacrifice de Dunkerque (1940)* (Lille, 1947), pp. 225–26. I am indebted to Médecin en Chef Hervé Cras of the Historical Section, Ministry of the Navy, Republic of France, for the two latter references.

the corridors of advance was thereby intensified.

The U.S. forces by the beginning of July had secured jump-off positions on the dry land of the Carentan plain. These were obvious to the Germans, who held superior ground on the *bocage* hills that ring the Cotentin marshes. With excellent observation of American movements, the Germans were able to mass their fires with such accuracy that American commanders warned drivers against halting their vehicles at crossroads, near bridges, or in towns; drivers were to proceed briskly through intersections, to take cover during a forced halt, and, if not able to camouflage their vehicles when stopped, to get clear without delay.[13]   Even far behind the front, care had to be exercised.   When a tank destroyer unit disregarded the warnings of military police and crossed a bridge on a main route three miles behind the front line, a division provost marshal renounced his "responsibility" for the safety of that unit.[14]

Three corridors of advance lead through the Carentan plain, each marked by a road.   One goes along the west coast of the Cotentin from la Haye-du-Puits to Coutances.   Another runs from Carentan southwest to Périers.   The third goes south from Carentan to St. Lô.   General Bradley decided to make his main effort along the coastal road, for that corridor is the widest and the ground the most firm.   Along this axis, but in reverse, the Germans had broken through the French defenses in 1940 and gained Cherbourg.

The VIII Corps, which comprised the army right flank on the west coast of the Cotentin, was to advance through la Haye-du-Puits to Coutances, a longer distance than that down the corridors leading south from Carentan to Périers and St. Lô.   By having VIII Corps begin its advance first, General Bradley expected all the army elements to reach the objective line at the same time.   The VII Corps, alerted to advance along the Carentan–Périers axis, and that part of the XIX Corps west of the Vire River, positioned for an advance from Carentan toward St. Lô, were to go into action in turn, from right (west) to left (east).

Although General Bradley thus exposed himself to criticism for piecemeal commitment, he had no other logical choice.[15]   The VII Corps headquarters, which had hurried south from Cherbourg to take a sector at Carentan, needed time for orientation.   The XIX Corps required troops that were in the process of arriving from the landing beaches.   But with higher headquarters impatiently demanding that the offensive to the south get underway at once, and with the attack having been postponed twice before, General Bradley felt that he could not delay.   Furthermore, waiting until all units could attack simultaneously would give the enemy more opportunity to prepare his defenses, an opportunity the Germans had certainly exploited during the previous two-week period of inactivity.

Although most of the Americans facing the hedgerow and marshy terrain of the Cotentin were aware of the difficulties to come, the opposite had been

---

[13] 1st AGp Observers Gp Ltr, 1 Jul, VIII Corps G–3 Jnl File.
[14] 82d Abn Div G–3 Jnl, 0130, 2 Jul.

[15] See VIII Corps AAR, Jul.

true before the invasion. American officers for the most part had known little of the hedgerow country. Few had seen the hedgerows, and air photos gave no real appreciation of what they were like. If most American commanders had not been able to visualize hedgerow fighting, most of the soldiers had not even been able to imagine a hedgerow. Not until the U.S. troops entered the hedgerows in June had they begun to have an idea of how effectively the terrain could be used for defense.[16]

The hedgerow fighting in June had been so difficult that many units made special studies of the problem. Most concluded that the principles of tactics taught at The Infantry School at Fort Benning, Georgia, applied in this terrain as elsewhere. The task was to pin the enemy down with a base of fire and maneuver an element along a covered approach to assault from the flank. In Normandy the lateral hedgerows marked not only the successive lines of advance and the positions for a base of fire but also the enemy defensive positions; hedges parallel to the line of advance could be made to serve as covered approach routes.

As this technique developed in June, a refinement emerged. The tank-infantry team operating toward a short objective and with a simple plan proved to be effective. The objective was always the same, the next hedgerow. The plan was to provide for simultaneous advance of armor and infantry and their mutual support. As it usually worked out, a tank platoon supporting an infantry company fired through the lateral hedge that marked the line of departure and

sprayed the flank hedgerows and the far side of the field to be taken with covering fire. The infantry advanced along the flank hedges to the next lateral row and cleared the enemy out at close range. With the field thus secured, one section of tanks moved forward, while the other remained temporarily at the rear to eliminate enemy troops that might suddenly appear from a concealed point or from an adjacent field. White phosphorus shells from 4.2-inch chemical mortars and artillery could be brought to bear on stubborn enemy groups.[17]

Advancing from one field to the next and clearing out individual hedgerows was a costly and slow procedure. It exhausted the troops and brought a high rate of casualties, but the slow plodding technique seemed necessary since "blitz action by tanks" was usually unsuccessful. A rapid armored advance generally resulted in only bypassing enemy groups that held up the infantry that was following.[18]

Several drawbacks complicated the simple type of small unit attack developed in June. One difficulty was moving armor through the hedgerows. The openings that already existed in the enclosures for wagons and cattle were well covered by German antitank gunners, and the appearance of an American tank prompted an immediate reaction. Although it was possible for a tank to climb the smaller hedgerow banks, the tank's most vulnerable part, the relatively lightly armored underbelly, was

---

[16] Answers by Gens Smith and Bull, 14–15 Sep 45.

[17] XIX Corps, The Tk-Inf Team, 24 Jun, VIII Corps G–3 Jnl File, Jul; 507th Parachute Inf AAR, Jun and Jul.
[18] FUSA Armd Sec Memo 1, Lessons from Combat in Normandy, 19 Jun, 30th Div G–3 Jnl File.

thus exposed.[19] Consequently, before a tank could protrude its guns and advance through a hedgerow, it was necessary for accompanying engineers to blast a hole through the hedgerow wall and open a passage for the tank. The explosion immediately attracted German attention to the point where armor was to breach the hedgerow, and enemy antitank weapons were not slow in covering the new opening.

The old sunken roads between the hedgerows were another hazard. So deep that they screened men and light vehicles from observation, these lanes, one observer said, "might have been made for ambush." [20] The highways of the region, narrow tarred roads, were adequate for mechanized forces, but the hedgerows that lined them gave excellent concealment to hostile troops.

The fields were so small and the hedgerows consequently so numerous that the opposing forces fought at close range. U.S. troops armed with the M1 rifle, a weapon more effective at long ranges, were somewhat at a disadvantage. Submachine guns, more useful for clearing hedgerows at short ranges, and riflegrenade launchers, particularly suitable for firing over the hedges at short distances, were in too short supply to be made available to all troops. There was also a shortage of white phosphorus shells, effective in clearing hedgerow corners of enemy strongpoints.[21]

A serious hindrance to American operations in hedgerow country was the lack of observation posts in the flat area of irregularly shaped fields, where it was impossible to anticipate the pattern of the hedgerow enclosures. Hedgerows and fields all resembled each other. There were few terrain features to serve as general objectives, as geographical markers, or as guiding points for small units. Consequently, small units had difficulty identifying their map locations with accuracy. Directional confusion often existed. Constant surveillance and frequent regrouping were necessary to maintain correct orientation.

Because the Germans occupied superior terrain in the surrounding *bocage,* American offensive movement brought immediate enemy artillery and mortar fire, deadly fire that had been carefully registered in advance. American counterbattery fire was difficult, for the hedgerows limited observation and prevented accurate adjustment of fire from the ground. Scaling ladders were in demand to place observers in trees, but forward observers were loath to climb trees for vantage points because of the danger of being shot by nervous Americans (many Americans were not yet experienced in battle and tended to be overalert to the possibility of enemy snipers). So extreme had this situation become in June that one division forbade its troops in the rear of the assault elements to fire into trees unless a hostile act had been committed; the division

[19] There was feeling in some quarters that the lack of emphasis on hedgerow operations during the preinvasion period had prevented the development of an infantry support tank heavily armed in front and in the bowels. Interv, Col C. H. Bonesteel, III (formerly in the 12th AGp G–3 Plans Sec), 18 Jun 47, Washington, Pogue Files.
[20] 314th Infantry Regiment, *Through Combat* (Germany, n.d.), an unofficial history, p. 18.

[21] First U.S. Army, *Report of Operations,* I, 80; FUSA (Ord) Ltr, Supply of WP for 105-mm. and 155-mm. howitzers, 1 Jul, FUSA G–3 Jnl File.

recommended that forward observers place red streamers in the foliage and a guard at the base of any tree they used for observation purposes.[22] Small cub planes, organic equipment of artillery units, were excellent for reconnaissance, observation, and adjustment of artillery fire, but rain and overcast skies frequently kept them grounded in the Cotentin.

Another complication was the general absence in combat units of smooth-working tank-infantry-engineer-artillery teams. Preinvasion training had not developed such teams, and instructions during combat, however exact, could not produce proficient units in short order. The most obvious weakness of the American ground attack during June was the tank-infantry team. Many infantry commanders did not know how to use tanks properly in support, and many tank commanders did not realize how best to render assistance in a given situation. "The development of operational procedures and techniques between the infantry and close support tanks must not be left until the arrival in the combat zone," an army report stated, but that was the situation exactly.[23] The infantry divisions had not had sufficient training with separate tank battalions, even though the latter units were normally division attachments. To remedy this situation, a tank battalion attached to a division in Normandy continued, insofar as possible, to be associated with that division throughout the campaign. Eventually, this devel-

oped mutual confidence and an awareness on the part of both of the individual peculiarities, the limitations, and the strengths of each. By the beginning of July, sufficient time had not elapsed to produce smoothly functioning tank-infantry teams.

The greatest problem in achieving adequate tank-infantry co-ordination was that of communication. The difficulty of on-the-spot co-ordination between an infantry platoon leader taking cover in a ditch and a commander buttoned up in his tank was a continual complaint that plagued the operations of tank-infantry teams, a universal problem not limited to Normandy.[24] Because voice command could not always be heard above the sounds of battle and the noises of tank motors, hand signals had to be worked out and smoke signals and pyrotechnic devices prearranged. Riflemen guiding tanks sometimes had to get in front and jump up and down to get the attention of a driver. Eventually a tanker would stick his head through a turret hatch and take the message.[25] Because armor and infantry radios operated on different channels, division signal companies in Normandy installed in the tanks infantry-type radios that could be tuned to the infantry radio net. To avoid the frustration that sometimes compelled infantrymen to pound their fists on tanks in vain efforts to claim the attention of tankers peering through tiny slits, Signal companies attached to the outside of tanks microphones or telephones connected with the tank in-

---

[22] Maj Gen Leonard T. Gerow to Gen Bradley, 0905, 27 Jun, and 90th Div Operational Memo 8, 2 Jul, FUSA G–3 Jnl File.

[23] First U.S. Army, *Report of Operations*, I, 121–22.

[24] See, for example, John Miller, jr., *CARTWHEEL: The Reduction of Rabaul*, UNITED STATES ARMY IN WORLD WAR II (Washington, 1959).

[25] See CI 47 (8th Div).

tercommunication system. Nevertheless, the development of smoothly functioning combinations had to attend the
evolution through combat of elements
accustomed to working in unison in mutual confidence and with a minimum of
overt direction.[26]

While infantry platoons trained with
tanks as much as possible in Normandy,
engineers made up explosive charges to
blast tank-sized openings in hedgerows.
Engineers in those divisions facing water
obstacles assembled sections of bridging
for future river and canal crossings.
Above all, commanders tried to indoc-
trinate the individual soldier with the
idea that continuous and aggressive advance was the best assurance of safety in
the hedgerow terrain.

At the beginning of July, those Americans who had fought in the hedgerow
country during the preceding month had
no illusions about instituting a major
drive through that type of terrain.
Added to the difficulties of the terrain
was the weather. In June clammy cold
rain had kept the swamps flooded, slowed
road traffic, neutralized Allied air superiority, concealed enemy movements and
dispositions, and left the individual soldier wet, muddy, and dispirited. During the first weeks of July almost incessant rain was to continue.

In addition to problems of terrain and
weather, Americans were facing a meticulous and thorough enemy, troops well
dug in and well camouflaged, soldiers

holding excellent defensive positions.
Bolstering the defenses were tanks superior in protective armor and in fire
power to those available to the Americans.

The German tank employed in large
numbers in western Europe was the
Mark IV, a medium tank of 23 tons with
a 75-mm. gun.[27] The standard combat
vehicle of tank battalions in armored
divisions, it presented no frightening aspect of invulnerability. The Mark V
or Panther, on the other hand, weighing
45 tons and carrying a high-velocity 75-
mm. gun, had appeared in Normandy
during June in limited numbers and
with good effect. Panthers were beginning to be distributed to tank battalions
organic to armored divisions. Although
the Allies had not yet made contact in
Europe with the Mark VI or Tiger,
knowledge acquired in North Africa of
its 56-ton weight and 88-mm. gun was
hardly reassuring. This tank was reserved for separate battalions distributed
on the basis of one to an armored corps.
Reports of a modified Mark VI, the King
or Royal Tiger, weighing 67 tons, mounting an improved 88-mm. gun, and be-

[26] First U.S. Army, *Report of Operations*, I,
121–22; see Robert L. Hewitt, *Work Horse of the
Western Front, the Story of the 30th Infantry
Division* (Washington: Infantry Journal, Inc.,
1946) (hereafter cited as Hewitt, *Story of 30th Division*), pp. 21–22.

[27] The following is based on Colonel C. P.
Stacey, *The Canadian Army, 1939–1945* (Ottawa:
King's Printer, 1948), p. 183n.; G. M. Barnes,
Major General, United States Army (Ret.), *Weapons of World War II* (New York: D. Van Nostrand
Company, Inc., 1947), *passim;* Constance McLaugh-
lin Green, Harry C. Thomson, and Peter C. Roots,
*The Ordnance Department: Planning Munitions
for War*, UNITED STATES ARMY IN WORLD
WAR II (Washington, 1955), Chs. X–XIII; Wilmot, *The Struggle for Europe*, pp. 294, 309; Ruppenthal, *Logistical Support*, I, 443; WD TM–E 30–
451, *Handbook of German Military Forces* (Washington, 15 March 1945); *OKH Generalinspekteur
der Panzertruppen Fuehrervortragsnotzigen, Band
II, VI.–IX.44.*

ginning to appear in the west, increased Allied concern.[28]

In contrast, the heaviest British tank used in Europe, the Churchill, was not quite 40 tons, while the all-purpose Sherman, the American medium tank used by the British as well, weighed only 30. Most of the Shermans mounted the relatively low-powered 75-mm. gun at this time, although a few carried a 76-mm. gun or a 105-mm. howitzer. The primary weapon of the American light tank was the 37-mm. gun, although a few were beginning to be equipped with the 75-mm. gun.

Though German tanks were more heavily armed and armored than Allied tanks, they had the disadvantages of being less mobile and less dependable mechanically. Also, in contrast with Allied armor, they lacked a power-driven traversing turret; the German hand-operated firing turrets could not compete with those of the Allied tanks, but they were more than adequate for long-range action.

American antitank weapons and ammunition were not generally effective against the frontal armor of the heavier German tanks. It was necessary to attack enemy tanks from the flanks, and the restricted terrain and narrow roads of the hedgerow country made this difficult. Even from the flanks, American weapons were not wholly effective. Only the 2.36-inch rocket launcher, the bazooka carried by the individual soldier, could be employed with any hope of consistent success.

Although experiments were being made in the United States to improve the armor-piercing quality of ammunition, General Eisenhower in early July wrote to General George C. Marshall, Chief of Staff, U.S. Army, "We cannot wait for further experimentation." [29] The 90-mm. guns, organic at this time to the antiaircraft artillery gun battalions, seemed to offer a means to improve antitank defense and armor capabilities in the attack. But greater numbers of this weapon were needed, both for tank destroyers and for tanks. So urgent was this need that General Eisenhower sent a special representative to the United States to expedite not only delivery of the 90-mm. guns but also research on improved armor-piercing ammunition. At the same time, in the field General Bradley was attaching 90-mm. antiaircraft artillery gun battalions to ground combat elements for defense against armor, since the weapon of this unit was the only one "sure to penetrate" the front of the heavier German tanks.[30]

At the end of June the apparent superiority of German tanks seemed particularly serious. Searching for evidence of a forthcoming enemy counterattack against the Allied foothold, Allied intelligence estimated that 230 Mark IV, 150 Mark V (Panther), and 40 Mark VI (Tiger) tanks faced the Allies. To these could be added the tanks of three elite

---

[28] See XIX Corps AAR, Jul, for a descriptive sheet on enemy armor circulated to the troops. This sheet lists the dimensions of the enemy tanks and has photographs of the Mark IV and V. Opposite the Mark VI listing there is a large question mark and the inscription: "None met yet—will YOU get the first?"

[29] Ltr, Eisenhower to Marshall, 5 Jul, Pogue Files.

[30] Ltr, Gen Bradley to Maj Gen J. Lawton Collins, 6 Jul, FUSA G-3 Jnl File.

GENERAL HAUSSER

divisions assembling one hundred miles west of Paris—about 200 Mark IV, 150 Panther, and 80 Tiger tanks. These constituted a sizable armored force, especially if, as seemed likely, the Germans were to employ them in a massive counterattack.[31]

Impressed by the "formidable array" of German panzer divisions on the British front, eight definitely identified and more on the way, 21 Army Group warned that a "full blooded counterattack" seemed imminent. In agreement, First Army pointed to the British-American boundary and to the Périers–Carentan area as the two most likely places for an enemy counterattack.[32]

The First Army G–2, Col. Benjamin A. Dickson, was disturbed by the postponements of the First Army attack to the south in June. He felt that the *II SS Panzer Corps* (controlling the *9th* and *10th SS Panzer Divisions*), arriving in Normandy from the Eastern Front, might not be fully assembled by 1 July, but that it was certain to be entirely assembled two days later, when American operations in the Cotentin were scheduled to start. An immediate First Army attack, on 1 July, might force the commitment of the German armored units in defense rather than in a counterattack. Furthermore, a panzer division and two infantry divisions were moving into Normandy from the *Fifteenth Army* Pas-de-Calais area. If the Americans attacked at once, they might prevent the Germans from deploying these forces in orderly defensive dispositions. Other elements of the *Fifteenth Army*, still immobilized by the threat of FORTITUDE, could not possibly reach the First Army battle area by 1 July, but they might conceivably do so by 3 July. Finally, delaying the attack until 3 July allowed the enemy two more days to improve his positions, perfect his communications, and establish a sound supply situation in the "rather good natural defensive line" selected in front of the U.S. forces.[33] Despite these disadvantages of postponing the attack beyond 1 July, General Bradley's offensive was not to get underway for two more days.

This then was the situation of the U.S. First Army just before it began its July offensive, an attack pointed through a

[31] FUSA G–2 Per Rpt, 28 Jun.

[32] 21 AGp Div, M–505, 30 Jun; FUSA G–2 Est 7, 29 Jun.

[33] FUSA G–2 Spec Est 4, 29 Jun.

flooded pastoral region of ten thousand little fields enclosed by hedgerows. Through this region made for ambush, where the German defenders had dug into the hedgerow banks and erected strong defenses, the Americans were to fight from field to field, from hedgerow to hedgerow, measuring the progress of their advance in yards. Over it all a steady rain was to pour, and the odors of the Normandy soil were to mingle with the smell of decaying flesh and become part of the war.

German

At the beginning of July the Germans in the west were in the midst of important command changes. Generalfeldmarschall Guenther von Kluge, who had commanded an army group on the Eastern Front for two and a half years, was arriving to replace Rundstedt as commander in chief in the west. General der Panzertruppen Heinrich Eberbach, formerly a corps commander on the Eastern Front and an outstanding armor officer, was about to relieve Geyr as commander of *Panzer Group West*. Hausser, formerly commander of the *II SS Panzer Corps* had recently become commander of the *Seventh Army*, taking the place of Dollman, who had died of a heart attack. Of the high-ranking officers who had met the Allied invasion less than a month earlier, Rommel, commander of *Army Group B*, remained as the single veteran with experience against the British and Americans.

Deeply impressed by the Allied success and the German failure in June, Rommel felt that errors in tactical deployment and in handling reserves had

FIELD MARSHAL VON KLUGE

contributed to a large extent to the situation at the beginning of July.[34] He also believed that *OB WEST*'s lack of certain command prerogatives had been detrimental to the German effort; he recommended that *OB WEST* be given command over all the elements in the theater, including Navy and Air, "like Montgomery's" headquarters.[35]

Aware of Rommel's capacity for enthusiasm and despair, Hitler had alerted Kluge to the possibility that Rommel might be a difficult subordinate. But when Kluge visited Rommel soon after his arrival in the west, he found that they were agreed on the course of action

---

[34] The major source for this section is James B. Hodgson, Battle of the Hedgerows, R–54.

[35] Rommel Memo, 3 Jul, *AGp B Operationsbefehle 19.VI–31. VIII.44.*

to be followed: "Unconditional holding of the present defense line. . . . Improvement of the present lines forward, i.e. by attack after most careful preparation where it appears profitable. Fortification of the sector behind the front by all means available." [36]

The two sectors of the army group front were dissimilar. Eberbach, who had the mission of keeping Montgomery from getting across the Caen plain toward Paris, deepened the defense of *Panzer Group West*. He feared that if his troops occupied a shallow line of resistance in dense concentrations they would be destroyed by British artillery. He therefore planned to keep one third of his infantry on a lightly held outpost line and on his main line of resistance. The remainder of the infantry was to hold successive positions behind the main line to a depth of about 2,000 yards. Rear echelon troops and reserves were to construct alternate positions from 1,000 to 6,000 yards behind the front. These defenses, plus interlocking firing positions backed up by the antiaircraft artillery of the *III Flak Corps* in a ground role, were to prevent British armor from making a breakthrough. Behind the static defense positions, emergency reserves consisting of tank-infantry teams were to be ready to move to threatened points of penetration. Finally, if the British nevertheless broke through the defenses, panzer divisions in operational reserve were to be prepared to seal off the openings.

This was deep-zone defense and effective utilization of resources for a defensive mission. During July, Eberbach was to attempt with partial success to replace his armor on the front with infantry units arriving to reinforce the sector. [37]

Hausser, in command of the *Seventh Army*, with fewer troops but better defensive terrain than Eberbach, organized what in comparison appeared to be a shallow defense. Behind the outpost line and the main line of resistance, both sparsely manned in order to bolster the reserves, the bulk of the troops were grouped into local reserves capable of launching counterattacks with the support of tanks and assault guns. Although Hausser's *Seventh Army* lacked the fire power of Eberbach's *Panzer Group West*, it had plenty of assault guns. Superior to tanks in fire power, they were effective weapons that Americans habitually mistook for tanks.

In the *Seventh Army* sector the Germans expected a type of combat they called "bush warfare." Battle in the hedgerows was to be fought according to the pattern of active defense. Anticipating that the Americans would advance in small parallel tank-infantry columns, the Germans planned to meet them by having a reserve commander lead his small unit in a counterattack against the American flank—if he could find it. "We cannot do better," the Germans reported, exactly as their American adversaries often stated, "than

[36] *OB WEST KTB,* 3 Jul; Memo for Record, 2 Jul, *Pz Gp W KTB, Anlage 35;* Min of Hitler Confs, Fragment 46, p. 3, published in Felix Gilbert, *Hitler Directs His War* (New York: Oxford University Press, Inc., 1950), pp. 102–04.

[37] Telecons, 1 Jul, *AGp B KTB;* Memo for Record, Rommel and Geyr, 2 Jul, *Pz Gp W KTB, Anlage 35;* Hitler Ltr of Instr, 8 Jul, quoted in full in Kluge Ltr of Instr, 8 Jul, *AGp B Fuehrerbefehle; Pz Gp W* SOP's, 6 Jul, *Pz Gp W KTB Anlagen 71* and *72;* MS # B–840 (Eberbach) .

to adopt the methods of combat of the enemy with all his ruses and tricks." [38]

Because of the planning for offensive action in June, the bulk of German strength was still concentrated in the Caen sector under *Panzer Group West*. In comparison, the *Seventh Army*, with a defensive mission of preventing the Americans from driving south, was expecting the imminent arrival of a single armored division. The army had three relatively fresh infantry-type divisions four composite units of battered troops that were divisions in name alone, one detached parachute regiment, and three kampfgruppen. Of two sorts, kampfgruppen were mobile combat teams of regimental size formed from static of infantry divisions with organic or requisitioned transport to meet the crisis of the invasion, or they were improvised field formations used to organize remnants of combat units. The kampfgruppen in the *Seventh Army* sector at the beginning of July were of the first type; during July many were to become the second sort.

The *Seventh Army* had two corps, the *II Parachute* and the *LXXXIV*. The *II Parachute Corps*, which had moved from Brittany in mid-June, held a sixteen-mile sector between the Vire and the Drôme Rivers. Responsible for the St. Lô–Caumont area, the corps controlled two divisions and two kampfgruppen.

On the extreme left (west) of the German positions in Normandy, the *LXXXIV Corps* faced the Americans in the Cotentin. The initial corps com-

mander, Marcks, had been killed early in June, and OKW had appointed Generalleutnant Dietrich von Choltitz to take his place. While Choltitz was traveling from the Italian front to take up his new post, General der Artillerie Wilhelm Fahrmbacher had temporarily left his corps command in Brittany to lead the *LXXXIV Corps* in the Cotentin. Choltitz assumed command on 18 June, and Fahrmbacher returned to Brittany.

Responsible for the area west of the Vire River to the Cotentin west coast, Choltitz in reality had two sectors separated by the Prairies Marécageuses de Gorges. A panzer grenadier division, reinforced by an infantry kampfgruppe and a separate parachute regiment, defended on the right (east). On the left, elements of five infantry divisions were deployed in an outpost position and on a main line of resistance. Desiring a deeper defense, Choltitz had on his own initiative delineated additional lines of defense in the rear, lines he had not divulged to higher headquarters for fear of appearing to controvert Hitler's instructions to hold fast. In the center and to the rear, a parachute regiment, under OKW control, constituted the corps reserve.

The strength of the German defenses in the Cotentin stemmed not so much from the quality or the number of the troops as from the nature of the terrain occupied. The soldiers of the static coastal divisions that had met the initial onslaught of the Allied invasion were older personnel, many of limited duty, equipped for the most part with a variety of weapons that were not the most modern. These units, as well as others that had arrived later, had sustained very heavy losses during the June fighting.

---

[38] Report of combat experience, "*Erfahrung der Panzer-Bekaempfung an der Invasionsfront Normandie,*" Sonderstab Oehmichen, z. Zt. Oberbefehlshaber West Ic/Pz. Offz., 25 Jun, *AGp B KTB Anlage,* 29 Jun; MS # B–731 (Fahrmbacher).

Yet the ground they held in the Cotentin was so favorable for defense that the Germans could look forward with confidence to the forthcoming American attack.

American preoccupation with Cherbourg in June and the German decision to contest not that main effort but the anticipated drive to the south had resulted in a two-week respite in the Cotentin that the Germans had used to advantage. They had fashioned a coherent defense.[39]

Despite excellent defensive preparations—Eberbach facing the British with a deep-zone defense, Hausser facing the Americans and utilizing the terrain to advantage—holding the line in Nor-

mandy was a gamble. As Rundstedt and Rommel had pointed out, if the Allies succeeded in penetrating the German positions, the absence of defensive lines between Normandy and the German border meant that the Germans would have to withdraw from France. Lacking mobility comparable to that of the Allies meant that the withdrawal would probably turn into retreat and rout. Yet the fact was that the German troops held the best positions they could hope for in France. The line was relatively short; the terrain was naturally strong; the battlefield imposed serious restrictions on Allied deployment. Only a small sector of open ground near Caen was difficult to defend. With reserves on the way, the Germans could reasonably hope to hold out until the decisive counterattack or the miracle promised by Hitler turned the course of the war.

---

[39] MS # B–418 (Choltitz); Dietrich von Choltitz, *Soldat unter Soldaten* (Konstanz–Zurich–Wien: Europa Verlag, 1951).

PART TWO

THE BATTLE OF THE HEDGEROWS

CHAPTER IV

The Offensive Launched

The Preparations

Designated to lead off in the U.S. First Army offensive to the south, VIII Corps was to advance twenty miles along the Cotentin west coast, secure high ground near Coutances, and form the western shoulder of a new army line extending to Caumont. The line was to be gained after VII, XIX, and V Corps attacked in turn in their respective zones. A quick thrust by VIII Corps promised to facilitate the entire army advance. By threatening the flank of enemy units opposing U.S. forces in the center, the corps would help its neighbors across the water obstacles and the mire of the Cotentin. At the conclusion of the offensive action across the army front, the Americans would be out of the swampland and on the dry ground of Normandy *bocage*.

The VIII Corps held a fifteen-mile front in a shallow arc facing a complex of hills around the important crossroads town of la Haye-du-Puits. Athwart the Cherbourg–Coutances highway and dominating the surrounding countryside, these hills formed a natural defensive position on which the Germans anchored the western flank of their Normandy front. Just to the south of the hill mass, the firm ground in the corps zone narrowed to seven miles between the Prairies Marécageuses de Gorges and

the tidal flats of the Ay River. This ground was the VIII Corps' initial objective. *(Map 3)*

Charged with the task of unhinging the German line at its western end was Maj. Gen. Troy H. Middleton, a soldier with a distinguished and extensive combat career. He had enlisted in the Regular Army in 1910 and had risen during World War I to regimental command and the rank of colonel. He had demonstrated his competence in World War II as a division commander in Sicily and Italy. Several months before the invasion of western Europe he had assumed command of the VIII Corps, and nine days after the continental landing the corps headquarters had become operational in France with the mission of protecting the rear of the forces driving on Cherbourg. The terrain that had been of great assistance to the VIII Corps in June now inversely became an aid to the enemy.

Looking south across hedgerowed lowland toward la Haye-du-Puits, General Middleton faced high ground between sea and marsh, heights that shield the town on three sides. On the southwest, Hill 84 is the high point of the Montgardon ridge, an eminence stretching almost to the sea. On the north, twin hills, 121 and 131 meters in height, and the triplet hills of the Poterie ridge rise abruptly. To the east, Mont Castre lifts

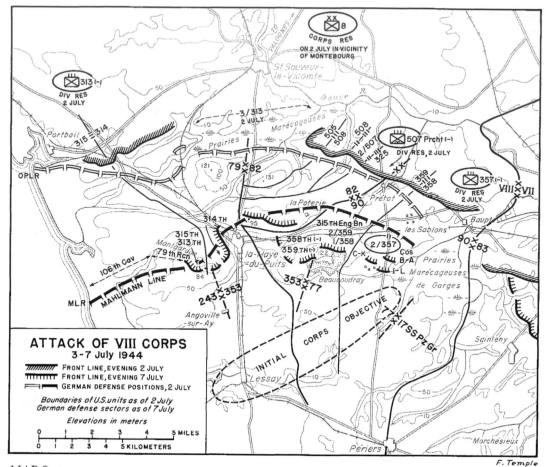

MAP 3

F. Temple

its slopes out of the marshes. The
adjacent lowlands make the hill masses
seem more rugged and steep than they
are. To reach the initial objective, VIII
Corps had first to take this commanding
terrain.

General Middleton had three divisions, veterans of the June fighting. All
were in the line, the 79th Infantry on
the right (west), the 82d Airborne in
the center, and the 90th Infantry on the
left. Because the 82d was soon to be
returned to England to prepare for pro-

jected airborne operations, General
Middleton assigned the division only a
limited objective, part of the high
ground north of la Haye-du-Puits. The
79th Division on the right and the 90th
on the left were to converge and meet
below the town to pinch out the airborne infantrymen. Thus, the corps
attack was to resemble a V-shaped thrust,
with the 82d clearing the interior
of the wedge. The terrain dictated
the scheme of maneuver, for the
configuration of the coast and the

westward extension of the *marécage* narrowed the corps zone south of la Haye-du-Puits. To replace the airborne troops, the 8th Division was to join the corps upon its arrival in France. Expecting to use the 8th Division beyond the initial objective, staff officers at corps headquarters tentatively scheduled its commitment to secure the final objective, Coutances.

Thus the VIII Corps was to make its attack with three divisions abreast. Each was to secure a portion of the heights forming a horseshoe around la Haye-du-Puits: the 79th was to seize the Montgardon ridge on the west and Hill 121; the 82d Airborne was to capture Hill 131 and the triplet hills of the Poterie ridge in the center; and the 90th, making the main effort, was to take Mont Castre on the east. With the commanding ground about la Haye-du-Puits in hand, the 79th Division was to push south to Lessay. There, where the tidal flats of the Ay River extend four miles inland and provide an effective barrier to continuing military operations southward, the 79th was to halt temporarily while the 90th continued with the newly arrived 8th.[1]

Two problems confronted VIII Corps at the start of the attack: the hedgerow terrain north of la Haye-du-Puits and the German observation points on the commanding ground around the town. To overcome them, General Middleton placed great reliance on his nine battalions of medium and heavy artillery, which included two battalions of 240-mm. howitzers; he also had the temporary assistance of four battalions of

the VII Corps Artillery. Only on the afternoon before the attack did he learn that he was also to have extensive air support. In accordance with routine procedure, the air liaison officer at corps headquarters had forwarded a list of five targets considered suitable for air bombardment—suspected supply dumps and troop concentration areas deep in the enemy rear. A telephone call from First Army headquarters disclosed that General Eisenhower had made available a large number of aircraft for employment in the VIII Corps zone. When assured "You can get all you want," the corps commander submitted an enlarged request that listed targets immediately in front of the combat troops.[2]

Allied intelligence was not altogether in agreement on the probable German reaction to the American offensive. Expecting a major German counterattack momentarily, higher headquarters anticipated strong resistance.[3] On the other hand, the VIII Corps G–2, Col. Andrew R. Reeves, thought either a counterattack or a strong defense most unlikely. Because of the inability or reluctance of the Germans to reinforce the Cherbourg garrison, because of their apparent shortage of artillery ammunition and their lack of air support, and because of the

---

[1] VIII Corps AAR, Jul.

[2] VIII Corps G–3 Jnl File, 2 Jul. Requests for air support usually came from the G–3 Air Section of a division and were funneled through the corps and army G–3 Air Sections to the IX TAC, which fulfilled the requests according to the availability of planes. For a detailed study of air-ground liaison, see Kent Roberts Greenfield, Army Ground Forces and the Air-Ground Battle Team Including Organic Light Aviation, AGF Study 35 (Hist Sec, AGF, 1948), particularly pp. 69ff.

[3] 21 AGp Dir, M–505, 30 Jun, Pogue Files; FUSA G–2 Est 7, 29 Jun.

LA HAYE-DU-PUITS. *Road at top leads south to Périers and Coutances.*

probable low morale of their soldiers, he considered an immediate counterattack improbable. Nevertheless, he recognized that if the Germans were to keep the Allies from expanding their bridgehead, they would eventually have to counterattack.   Until they could, it was logical that they try to keep the Allied beachhead shallow by defending where they stood. Colonel Reeves believed, however, that they lacked the strength to remain where they were.   He expected that as soon as they were driven from their main line of resistance near la

Haye-du-Puits, they would withdraw through a series of delaying positions to the high ground near Coutances.[4]

That VIII Corps would drive the enemy back was a matter of little doubt, since it was generally believed on the lower levels that the corps had "assembled a force overwhelmingly superior in all arms. . . ."[5] Below the army echelon, intelligence reports exaggerated the

---

[4] VIII Corps G–2 Est 2, 28 Jun.

[5] 82d Abn Div G–2 Est, 1 Jul. The G–2 reports of the 82d are typical of those published by the other divisions of VIII Corps.

fragmentary nature of German units and underestimated German organizational efficiency and flexibility. The First Army G–2 cautiously estimated that the German infantry divisions in Normandy averaged 75 percent of authorized strength and lacked much equipment. But the VIII Corps G–2 judged that among the enemy forces on his immediate front "the German divisional unit as such . . . has apparently ceased to exist." [6] Perhaps true in the last week of June, the latter statement was not accurate by the first week in July.

For all the optimism, combat patrols noted that the Germans had set up an exceptionally strong outpost screen, replenished their supplies, reorganized their forces, and resumed active reconnaissance and patrolling. It was therefore reasonable to assume that the enemy had strengthened his main line of resistance and rear areas. Morale had undoubtedly improved. On the other hand, intelligence officers judged that enemy morale and combat efficiency had risen only from poor to fair. Germans still lacked aggressiveness when patrolling; critical shortages of mines and wire existed; and artillery fired but sporadically, indicating that the Germans were undoubtedly conserving their meager ammunition supplies to cover delaying action as they withdrew.[7]

Confidence and assurance gained in the Cherbourg campaign led most Americans to expect no serious interruption in the offensive to the south. A schedule of artillery ammunition expenditures allotted for the attack revealed temporary removal of restrictions and a new system of self-imposed unit rationing. Although ammunition stocks on the Continent were not copious, they appeared to be more than adequate. Even though officers at First Army warned that unreasonable expenditures would result in a return to strict controls, the implicit premise underlying the relaxation of controls for the attack was the belief that each corps would have to make a strong or major effort for only two days. Two days of heavy artillery fire by each corps was considered adequate to propel the army to the Coutances–Caumont line.[8]

In the two days immediately preceding the attack, U.S. units on the VIII Corps front noted a marked change in enemy behavior. German artillery became more active; several tanks and assault guns made brief appearances; small arms, automatic weapons, and mortar fire increased in volume; infantrymen seemed more alert. American patrols began to have difficulty moving into hostile territory. Only in the corps center could reconnaissance patrols move more freely into areas formerly denied them. From these indications, corps concluded that the enemy was preparing to make a show of resistance before withdrawing.[9]

Commanders and troops making last-minute preparations for the jump-off watched in some dismay a few minutes after midnight, 2 July, as a drizzling rain began to fall. The early morning attack hour was fast approaching when the rain became a downpour. It was

---

[6] FUSA G–2 Est 7, 29 Jun; VIII Corps G–2 Est 2, 28 Jun.

[7] 82d Abn Div Rev Intel Annex to FO 7 (Rev), 28 Jun, and G–2 Est, 1 Jul.

[8] FUSA Ltr, Fld Arty Ammo Expenditures, 2 Jul, VIII Corps G–3 Jnl File; 83d Div G–2, G–3 Jnl and File, 2 and 3 Jul.

[9] VIII Corps Weekly Per Rpt, 1 Jul.

obvious that the heavy air program promised in support of the offensive would have to be canceled.[10] As events developed, not even the small observation planes, invaluable for locating artillery targets in the hedgerow country, were able to get off the ground.

Despite this early disappointment, the attack otherwise began as scheduled. American troops plodded through the darkness and the mud toward the line of departure. At 0515, 3 July, the artillery started a 15-minute preparation.

The Defenses

The Germans had no intention of falling back. From the high ground near la Haye-du-Puits, so dominating that observers on the crests could watch Allied shipping off the invasion beaches, Germans studied the preparations for the attack they had been expecting for almost two weeks. They were ready. Yet despite their readiness, they were almost taken by surprise. The state of affairs harked back to the development of the *LXXXIV Corps* defenses west of the Prairies Marécageuses de Gorges.

In June, just before American troops had cut the Cherbourg peninsula and isolated the port, Rundstedt, Rommel, Dollman, and Fahrmbacher had decided to divide the *LXXXIV Corps* forces into two groups—one in the north to defend Cherbourg, the other to block American movement south. Their intention had been to leave weak forces in defense of

Cherbourg and to build a strong line across the Cotentin from Portbail to the Prairies Marécageuses de Gorges.[11] By insisting on compliance with original plans for a forceful defense of Cherbourg, however, Hitler had disrupted the German commanders' plan. As a result, the troops in the south were weaker than had been hoped. The designated chief of the forces in the south (Generalleutnant Heinz Hellmich of the *243d Division)* was killed in action on 17 June, and Col. Eugen Koenig (the acting commander of the *91st Infantry Division,* whose general had died on 6 June) became the local commander responsible for erecting a defense to halt the expected drive to the south.

Koenig had had available a total of about 3,500 combat effective soldiers of several units: remnants of the *91st* and *243d Divisions,* a kampfgruppe of the *265th Division* (from Brittany), and miscellaneous elements including *Osttruppen,* non-German volunteers from eastern Europe. Together, the troops composed about half the effective combat strength of a fresh infantry division. With these few forces, but with adequate artillery in support, Koenig had fashioned a line that utilized marshland as a defensive barrier.

When Choltitz had taken command of the *LXXXIV Corps,* he had soon come to the conclusion that he could not depend on Koenig to hold for long. American paratroopers of the 82d Airborne Division had actually penetrated the marsh line as early as 12 June.[12] Koenig's forces were too weak to

---

[10] FUSA G-3 Jnl, 0340, 3 Jul. *Note:* The hours of the day in this volume are British Double Time when used in connection with Allied activities, one hour earlier for the Germans—so that 1300 for the Allies is the same as 1200 (noon) for the Germans.

[11] Harrison, *Cross-Channel Attack,* pp. 413ff; Hodgson, R-24, R-34, and R-49.

[12] Harrison, *Cross-Channel Attack,* p. 402.

eliminate the penetration or to hold the positions already seriously threatened. The *Osttruppen* were not always reliable.[13] Besides, Choltitz felt that the high ground near la Haye-du-Puits was better defensive terrain. He therefore had his reserve units—the *353d Division,* which had just arrived from Brittany, and remnants of the *77th Division*—establish positions on the Montgardon ridge and on Mont Castre. The ridge defenses, sometimes called the Mahlmann Line after the commander of the *353d,* were hastily organized because of anxiety that the Americans might attack at any moment. When the positions were established, Choltitz regarded them as his main line of resistance. Thinking of Koenig's troops as manning an outpost line, he expected them to resist as long as possible and eventually to fall back to the ridge line.

In contrast with Choltitz's idea, Rundstedt had recommended that the main line of resistance be established even farther back—at the water line formed by the Ay and Sèves Rivers. Although Choltitz did not place troops there, he considered the water line a convenient rally point in case withdrawal from the la Haye-du-Puits positions became necessary.[14] Hitler, who disapproved of all defensive lines behind the front because he feared they invited withdrawal, wanted Koenig's positions to be held firmly. To inculcate the idea of holding fast, he had Koenig's defenses designated the main line of resistance. With

Koenig's marsh line marked on maps as the main defenses in the area, the fresh troops of the *353d Division* seemed unoccupied. In order to use them, OKW ordered Hausser to have Choltitz move the *353d* to replace the panzer grenadiers in the eastern portion of the corps sector. The panzer grenadiers were to disengage and become a mobile reserve for the *Seventh Army.* With the *353d* scheduled to depart the high ground around la Haye-du-Puits, Choltitz had to reduce the Mahlmann Line to the reality of a rally line manned entirely by the *kampfgruppe* of the *77th.*

By 3 July the *77th Division* troops had moved to the eastern part of Mont Castre, while the *353d* was moving from ridge positions to assembly near Périers. The VIII Corps attack thus occurred at a time of flux. Members of the *LXXXIV Corps* staff had correctly assumed, from the noise of tank motors they heard during the night of 2 July, that an American attack was in the making, and they had laid interdictory fires on probable assembly areas. But judging that the rain would delay the jump-off—on the basis that bad weather neutralized American air power—the *Seventh Army* staff mistakenly labeled the VIII Corps offensive only a reconnaissance in force with tank support. The real American intention soon became apparent to both headquarters, however, and Hausser and Choltitz recalled the *353d Division* from Périers and repositioned the men on the high ground about la Haye-du-Puits.[15] Hitler's desires notwithstanding, these positions became the main line of resistance.

---

[13] Telecon, Choltitz to Hausser, 30 Jun, *Seventh Army* Tel Msgs.

[14] *Pz Lehr Div Ib KTB, Allg. Anlagen,* Annex 241; see MS # B–418 (Choltitz) for an account of *LXXXIV Corps* activity, 18 Jun to 15 Jul. Choltitz, *Soldat unter Soldaten,* p. 187 is rather confused.

---

[15] *Seventh Army* and *AGp B KTB's,* 3 Jul; *Tagesmeldungen, OB WEST KTB, Anlage 433.*

As a result of the last-minute changes that occurred on 3 July, the Germans opposing VIII Corps were able to defend from positions in depth. Fanned out in front was *Group Koenig,* with parts of the *91st,* the *265th,* and the *243d Divisions* on the flanks, and east European volunteers (including a large contingent of Russians) generally holding the center. Artillery support was more than adequate—the entire division artillery of the *243d,* plus two cannon companies, five antitank companies, a complete tank destroyer battalion, and an assortment of miscellaneous howitzers, rocket launchers, antiaircraft batteries, captured Russian guns, and several old French light tanks. Behind *Group Koenig,* the *353d* and a kampfgruppe of the *77th* were to defend the high ground of the Montgardon ridge and Mont Castre. The *2d SS Panzer Division,* assembling well south of St. Lô in *Seventh Army* reserve, was able to move, if needed, to meet a serious threat near la Haye-du-Puits.[16] Even closer, in the center of the *LXXXIV Corps* sector, south of Périers, was one regiment (the *15th*) of the *5th Parachute Division* (still in Brittany). Although under OKW control, it could probably be used in an emergency to augment the la Haye-du-Puits defenses. All together, the German forces were far from being a pushover.

Poterie Ridge

In the VIII Corps attack, the 82d Airborne Division had the relatively modest role of securing a limited objective be-fore departing the Continent for England. Having fought on French soil since D Day, the airborne division had lost about half its combat strength. Yet it still was an effective fighting unit, with three parachute infantry regiments and one glider infantry regiment forming the principal division components.

The troops had been carefully selected for airborne training only after meeting special physical and mental standards. The division had participated in World War II longer than most units in the European theater, and its members regarded with pride their achievements in Sicily and Italy. To an *esprit de corps* that sometimes irritated others by its suggestion of superiority, the aggressive veterans added a justifiable respect and admiration for their leaders. Maj. Gen. Matthew B. Ridgway, the division commander, displayed an uncanny ability for appearing at the right place at the right time. His inspiring presence, as well as that of the assistant division commander, Brig. Gen. James M. Gavin, was responsible in no small degree for the efficiency of the unit.[17]

In the center of the VIII Corps sector, the 82d Airborne Division held a line across the tip of a "peninsula" of dry ground. In order to commit a maximum number of troops at once, General Ridgway planned to sweep his sector by attacking westward—between marshland on the north and the la Haye-du-Puits–Carentan road on the south—to take the hills just east of the St. Sauveur-le-Vicomte–la Haye-du-Puits road, which separated the airborne division's zone

---

[16] *AGp B Id* Memo, 4 Jul, *AGp B Ia Op. Befehle.*

[17] The division journals and other records give ample evidence of the high regard the men had for their leaders.

from that of the 79th Division. The terrain was hedgerowed lowland, with half a dozen tiny settlements and many farmhouses scattered throughout the countryside; there were no main roads, only rural routes and sunken lanes.

In the early hours of 3 July, even before the artillery preparation that signaled the start of the First Army offensive, a combat patrol made a surprise thrust. Guided by a young Frenchman who had served similarly in the past, a reinforced company of the 505th Parachute Infantry (Lt. Col. William Ekman) slipped silently along the edge of the swamp and outflanked German positions on the north slope of Hill 131. At daybreak the company was in the midst of a German outpost manned by *Osttruppen*. Startled, the outpost withdrew. The main body of the regiment arrived by midmorning and gained the north and east slopes of the hill. Four hours later the 505th was at the St. Sauveur-le-Vicomte–la Haye-du- Puits road and in possession of the northern portion of the division objective. The regiment had taken 146 prisoners and had lost 4 dead, 25 wounded, and 5 missing.[18]

The 508th Parachute Infantry (Col. Roy E. Lindquist) had similar success in gaining the southeast face of Hill 131, and a battalion of the 507th Parachute Infantry (Col. Edson D. Raff) cleared its assigned sector. The leading units moved so rapidly that they bypassed enemy troops who were unaware that an attack was in progress. Though the U.S. follow-up forces had the un-

expected and nasty task of clearing small isolated groups, the leading units were at the base of the objective by noon and several hours later were ensconced on the slope. Casualties were few.

On the left the story was different. Making the main division effort, the 325th Glider Infantry (Col. Harry L. Lewis) was to move west to the base of the Poterie ridge, then up and down across each of the triplet hills. After a slow start caused by enemy mines, the regiment moved rapidly for a mile. At this point the advance stopped—two miles short of the eastern slope of the Poterie ridge. One supporting tank had hit a mine, three others were floundering in mudholes, and German fire rained down from the slopes of Mont Castre, off the left flank.

It did not take long for General Ridgway to recognize the reason for easy success of the regiments on the right and the difficulty of the 325th. While the parachute regiments on the right were rolling up the German outpost line, the glider men had struck the forward edge of the German main line of resistance. At the same time, they were exposed to observed enfilading fire from Mont Castre.

To deal with this situation, Ridgway directed the 325th commander to advance to the eastern edge of the Poterie ridge. Using this position as a pivot, the other regiments of the division were to wheel southward from their earlier objectives and hit the triplet hills from the north in frontal attacks.

Colonel Lewis renewed the attack during the evening of 3 July, and although the glider men advanced over a mile and a half, they were still 600 yards short of

---

[18] The account of operations is taken from the official records of the division and the regiments.

their objective when resistance and darkness forced a halt two hours before midnight. When another effort on the morning of 4 July brought no success, General Ridgway ordered the wheeling movement by the other regiments to begin. Each battalion of the 508th was to attack one of the triplet hills while the 505th moved south along the division boundary to protect the open right flank.

Problems immediately arose when two battalions of the 508th and the glider regiment disputed the use of a covered route of approach. Because of the delay involved in co-ordinating the route and because of withering fire from both the Poterie ridge and Mont Castre, the two battalions made little progress during the day. The third battalion, on the other hand, had by noon gained a position from which it could assault the westernmost eminence, Hill 95. Following an artillery preparation reinforced by corps guns, two rifle companies made a double envelopment while the third attacked frontally. The battalion gained the crest of the hill but, unable to resist the inevitable counterattack that came before positions could be consolidated, withdrew 800 yards and re-formed.

Meanwhile, troops of the 505th moved south along the division boundary, advancing cautiously. Reaching the base of Hill 95 that evening, the regiment made contact with the 79th Division and set up positions to control the St. Sauveur-le-Vicomte–la Haye-du-Puits road.

His battalions now in direct frontal contact with the German positions but operating at a disadvantage under German observation, General Ridgway ordered a night attack. As darkness fell on 4 July, the men moved up the hedgerowed and unfamiliar slopes of the Poterie ridge. The 325th Glider Infantry secured its objective on the eastern slope of the ridge with little difficulty. The battalion of the 508th Parachute Infantry that had taken Hill 95 during the afternoon only to lose it walked up the slope and secured the crest by dawn. A newly committed battalion of the 507th Parachute Infantry, moving against the easternmost hill, had trouble maintaining control in the darkness, particularly after making contact with the enemy around midnight. Withdrawing to reorganize, the battalion commander sent a rifle company to envelop the hill from the east while he led the remainder of his force in a flank approach from the west. Several hours after daylight on 5 July the two parties met on the ridge line. The Germans had withdrawn.

Another battalion of the 507th moved against the center hill of the Poterie ridge, with one company in the lead as a combat patrol. Reaching the crest without interference and assuming that the Germans had retired, the advance company crossed the ridge line and formed a defensive perimeter on the south slope. Daybreak revealed that the men were in a German bivouac area, and a confused battle took place at close range. The remainder of the battalion, which had stayed on the north slope, hurried forward at the sound of gunfire to find friend and foe intermingled on the ridge. Not until afternoon of 5 July did the battalion establish a consolidated position.[19]

---

[19] Pfc. James L. Geach of the 325th Glider Infantry, though he had never handled a rocket

During the afternoon the 82d Airborne Division reported Hill 95 captured and the Poterie ridge secure. Small isolated German pockets remained to be cleared, but this was a minor task easily accomplished. Maintaining contact with the 79th Division on the right and establishing contact with the 90th Division in the valley between the Poterie ridge and Mont Castre on the left, the 82d Airborne Division assumed defensive positions.

In advancing the line about four miles in three days, the airborne division had destroyed about 500 enemy troops, taken 772 prisoners, and captured or destroyed two 75-mm. guns, two 88-mm. antitank guns, and a 37-mm. antitank weapon. The gains had not been without serious cost. The 325th Glider Infantry, which was authorized 135 officers and 2,838 men and had an effective strength of 55 officers and 1,245 men on 2 July, numbered only 41 officers and 956 men four days later; the strongest rifle company had 57 men, while one company could count only 12. Casualties sustained by this regiment were the highest, but the depletion of all units attested to the accuracy of German fire directed from superior ground.

By the morning of 7 July, all enemy pockets had been cleared in front of the airborne division. Lying in the rain-filled slit trenches, the men "began to sweat out the much-rumored trip to England." [20] The probability appeared good: two days earlier the 79th Division had briefly entered la Haye-du-Puits, the 90th had moved up the slopes of Mont Castre, and the 8th was almost ready to enter the lines.

Mont Castre

The action at the Poterie ridge was not typical of the VIII Corps attack launched on 3 July, for while the 82d Airborne Division swept an area relatively lightly defended, the 79th and 90th Divisions struck strong German positions in the la Haye-du-Puits sector. Trying to execute the V-shaped maneuver General Middleton had projected, the infantry divisions hit the main body of the *LXXXIV Corps* on two major elevations, the Montgardon ridge and Mont Castre. Their experience was characteristic of the battle of the hedgerows.

The ability of the 90th Division, which was making the corps main effort on the left (east), was an unknown quantity before the July attack. The performance of the division during a few days of offensive action in June had been disappointing. The division had lacked cohesion and vigor, and its commanding general and two regimental commanders had been relieved. Maj. Gen. Eugene M. Landrum, with experience in the Aleutian Islands Campaign the preceding year, had assumed command on 12 June and had attempted in the three weeks before the army offensive to reorganize the command and instill it with aggressiveness. [21]

---

launcher, seized a bazooka and fired several rounds, forcing two enemy tanks to withdraw. He was awarded the DSC.

[20] William G. Lord, II, *History of the 508th Parachute Infantry* (Washington: Infantry Journal, Inc., 1948), p. 37.

[21] [Maj. Roland G. Ruppenthal], *Utah Beach to Cherbourg,* AFA Series (Washington, 1947), p. 129; Harrison, *Cross-Channel Attack,* pp. 402–03.

To reach his assigned portion of the corps intermediate objective, General Landrum had to funnel troops through a corridor a little over a mile wide—a corridor between Mont Castre on the west and the Prairies Marécageuses de Gorges on the east. His troops in the corridor would have to skirt the edge of the swampland and operate in the shadow of Mont Castre, a ridge about 300 feet high extending three miles in an east–west direction. The western half of Mont Castre, near la Haye-du-Puits, was bare, with two stone houses standing bleakly in ruins on the north slope. The eastern half, densely wooded and the site of an ancient Roman encampment, offered cover and concealment on a height that commanded the neighboring flatland for miles. No roads mounted to the ridge line, only trails and sunken wagon traces—a maze of alleys through the somber tangle of trees and brush. If the Germans could hold the hill mass, they could deny movement to the south through the corridor along the base of the eastern slope. Possession of Mont Castre was thus a prerequisite for the 90th Division advance toward Périers.

Reflecting both an anxiety to make good and the general underestimation of German strength, General Landrum planned to start his forces south through the corridor at the same time he engaged the Germans on Mont Castre. The division was to attack with two simultaneous regimental thrusts. The 359th Infantry (Col. Clark K. Fales), on the right, was to advance about four miles through the hedgerows to the thickly wooded slopes of Mont Castre, take the height, and meet the 79th Division south

of la Haye-du-Puits. The 358th Infantry (Col. Richard C. Partridge), on the left, was to force the corridor between Mont Castre and the *prairies*. In possession of the high ground, in contact with the 79th Division, and holding the corridor east of Mont Castre open, General Landrum would then commit the 357th Infantry (Col. George H. Barth) through the corridor to the initial corps objective.

To provide impetus across the hedgerowed lowlands, General Landrum ordered the 357th, his reserve regiment, to mass its heavy weapons in support and the attached tanks and tank destroyers also to assist by fire. In addition to the organic artillery battalions, General Landrum had a battalion of the corps artillery and the entire 4th Division Artillery attached; the 9th Division Artillery had been alerted to furnish fires upon request.

The driving, drenching rain, which had begun early on 3 July, was still pouring down when the attack got under way at 0530. At first it seemed that progress would be rapid. Two hours later resistance stiffened. By the end of the day, although American troops had forced the Germans out of some positions, the *Seventh Army* commander, Hausser, was well satisfied. His principal concern was his supply of artillery ammunition.[22]

The 90th Division advanced less than a mile on 3 July, the first day of attack, at a cost of over 600 casualties.[23] The

---

[22] *Seventh Army* and *AGp B KTB's*, 3 Jul.

[23] The account of tactical operations is based upon the official records (the After Action Reports, operations orders, periodic reports, and journals) of the units involved.

Germans demonstrated convincingly, contrary to general expectation, that they intended and were able to make a stand. The 90th Division dented only the outpost line of resistance and had yet to make contact with the main defenses. "The Germans haven't much left," an observer wrote, "but they sure as hell know how to use it." [24]

If the Germans had defended with skill, the 90th Division had not attacked with equal competence. Tankers and infantrymen did not work closely together; commanders had difficulty keeping their troops moving forward; jumpy riflemen fired at the slightest movement or sound.

The experience of Colonel Partridge's 358th Infantry exemplified the action along the division front for the day. One of the two assault battalions of the regiment remained immobile all day long not far from the line of departure because of flanking fire from several German self-propelled guns. The other battalion moved with extreme caution toward the hamlet of les Sablons, a half-dozen stone farmhouses in a gloomy tree-shaded hollow where patrols on preceding days had reported strong resistance. As infantry scouts approached the village, enemy machine gun and artillery fire struck the battalion command post and killed or wounded all the wire communications personnel. Unable to repair wire damaged by shellbursts, the unit commanders were without telephones for the rest of the day.

Judging the enemy fire to be in large

volume, Colonel Partridge withdrew the infantry a few hundred yards and requested that division artillery "demolish the place" with white phosphorus and high-explosive shells. The artillery complied literally, and at noon riflemen were moving cautiously through the village. Ten minutes later several enemy tracked vehicles appeared as if by magic from behind nearby hedgerows. A near panic ensued as the infantrymen fled the town. About twelve engineers who were searching for mines and booby traps were unable to follow and sought shelter in the damaged houses.

To prevent a complete rout, Partridge committed his reserve battalion. Unfortunately, several light tanks following the infantry became entangled in concertina wire and caused a traffic jam. Anticipating that the Germans would take advantage of the confusion by counterattacking with tanks, Partridge ordered a platoon of tank destroyers to bypass les Sablons in order to fire into the flank of any hostile force. He also called three assault guns and three platoons of the regimental antitank company forward to guard against enemy tanks. The 315th Engineer Combat Battalion contributed a bazooka team to help rescue the men trapped in the village.

The Germans did not attack, and in midafternoon Partridge learned that only one assault gun and two half-tracked vehicles were holding up his advance. It was late afternoon before he could act, however, for German shells continued to fall in good volume, the soft lowland impeded the movement of antitank weapons, and the presence of the American engineers in les Sablons in-

---

[24] Penciled ltr to Brig Gen Claude B. Ferenbaugh (n.d.), 83d Div G–2, G–3 Jnl and File.

hibited the use of artillery fire. After the engineers had worked their way to safety, Partridge at last brought co-ordinated and concentrated tank, artillery, and infantry fire on the area, and a rifle company finally managed to push through les Sablons that evening. Colonel Partridge wanted to continue his attack through the night, but an enemy counterthrust at nightfall, even though quickly contained, convinced General Landrum that the regiment had gone far enough.

The excellent observation that had enabled the Germans to pinpoint 90th Division activity during the day allowed them to note the American dispositions at dusk. Through the night accurate fire harassed the division, rendering re-organization and resupply difficult and dangerous.

Resuming the attack on 4 July, the 90th Division fired a ten-minute artillery preparation shortly after daybreak. The German reaction was immediate: counterbattery fire so intense that subordinate commanders of the 90th Division looked for a counterattack. Not wishing to move until the direction of the German thrust was determined, the regimental commanders delayed their attacks. It took vociferous insistence by General Landrum to get even a part of the division moving. No German counterattack materialized.

Colonel Fales got his 359th Infantry moving forty-five minutes after the scheduled jump-off time as a surprising lull in the German fire occurred. Heading for Mont Castre, the infantry advanced several hundred yards before the enemy suddenly opened fire and halted further progress. Uneasy specu-

lation among American riflemen that German tanks might be hiding nearby preceded the appearance of three armored vehicles that emerged from hedgerows and began to fire. The infantrymen withdrew in haste and some confusion.

Through most of the day, all attempts to advance brought only disappointment. Then, at dusk, unit commanders rallied their men. Unexpectedly the regiment began to roll. The advance did not stop until it had carried almost two miles.[25]

The sudden slackening of opposition could perhaps be explained by several factors: the penetration of the airborne troops to the Poterie ridge, which menaced the German left; the heavy losses sustained mostly from the devastating fire of American artillery; and the lack of reserves, which compelled regrouping on a shorter front. With great satisfaction the Germans had reported that their own artillery had stopped the 90th Division attack during the morning of 4 July, but by noon the *LXXXIV Corps* was battling desperately. Although two battalions of the *265th Division* (of *Group Koenig*), the *77th Division* remnants, and a battalion of the *353d Division* succeeded in denying the approaches to Mont Castre throughout 4 July, the units had no local reserves to seal off three small penetrations that occurred during the evening. Only by getting OKW to release control of the

---

[25] Capt. Leroy R. Pond, a battalion commander, and Pvt. Barney H. Prosser, who assumed command of a rifle company (upon the loss of all the officers) and two leaderless platoons of another company, were key figures in the advance. Both were awarded the DSC.

15th Parachute Regiment and by committing that regiment at once was the *Seventh Army* able to permit the *LXXXIV Corps* to refashion its defensive line that night.[26]

Despite their difficulties, the Germans continued to deny the 90th Division entrance into the corridor between Mont Castre and the swamp. German fire, infiltrating riflemen, and the hedgerows were such impediments to offensive action that Colonel Partridge postponed his attack several times on 4 July. Most of his troops seemed primarily concerned with taking cover in their slit trenches, and American counterbattery fire seemed to have little effect on the enemy weapons.

When part of the 358th Infantry was pinned down by enemy artillery for twenty minutes, the division artillery investigated. It discovered that only one enemy gun had fired and that it had fired no more than ten rounds. Despite this relatively light rate of fire, one rifle company had lost 60 men, many of them noncommissioned officers. The commanding officer and less than 65 men remained of another rifle company. Only 18 men, less than half, were left of a heavy weapons company mortar platoon. A total of 125 casualties from a single battalion had passed through the regimental aid station by midafternoon, 90 percent of them casualties from artillery and mortar shelling. Tired and soaking wet from the rain, the riflemen were reluctant to advance in the face of enemy fire that might not have been delivered in great volume but that was nonetheless terribly accurate.

Although German fire continued, the 358th Infantry got an attack going late in the afternoon toward the corridor. With the aid of strong artillery support and led by Capt. Phillip H. Carroll, who was wounded in one eye, the infantry moved forward several hundred yards to clear a strongpoint.[27] By then it was almost midnight. Because the units were badly scattered and the men completely exhausted, Colonel Partridge halted the attack. Long after midnight some companies were still organizing their positions.

On its second day of attack, 4 July, the 90th Division sustained an even higher number of casualties than the 600 lost on the first day.[28] Mont Castre, dominating the countryside, "loomed increasingly important." Without it, the division "had no observation; with it the Boche had too much." [29]

More aware than ever of the need for Mont Castre as a prerequisite for an advance through the corridor, General Landrum nevertheless persisted with his original plan, perhaps because he felt that the Germans were weakening. Judging the 358th Infantry too depleted and weary for further offensive action, he committed his reserve regiment, the 357th, on 5 July in the hope that fresh troops in the corridor could outflank Mont Castre.

The 357th Infantry had only slight success in the corridor on 5 July, the

---

[26] *OB WEST KTB,* 1330, 4 Jul; *Seventh Army KTB,* 4 Jul, and *Tagesmeldungen,* 5 Jul.

[27] Captain Carroll was awarded the DSC.

[28] 90th Div AAR, Jul. FUSA Daily Estimated Loss Reports, July, gives 549 casualties sustained by the organic units on 4 July as contrasted with 382 reported for the previous day, but the figures for both days were incomplete.

[29] 90th Div AAR, Jul.

third day of the attack, but on the right the 359th registered a substantial gain. Good weather permitted tactical air support and observed artillery fires, and with fighter-bombers striking enemy supply and reinforcement routes and artillery rendering effective support, the regiment fought to the north and northeast slopes of Mont Castre in a series of separate, close-range company and platoon actions. Still the Germans continued to resist aggressively, launching repeated local counterattacks.[30] The failure of the 357th Infantry to force the corridor on the left and the precarious positions of the 359th on the slopes of Mont Castre at last compelled General Landrum to move a battalion of the 358th Infantry to reinforce his troops on Mont Castre, the beginning of a gradual shift of division strength to the right.

Colonel Fales on 6 July sent a battalion of his 359th Infantry in a wide envelopment to the right. Covered by a tactical air strike and artillery fire and hidden by hedgerows on the valley floor, the infantry mounted the northern slope of Mont Castre. At the same time, the other two battalions of the 359th and a battalion of the 358th advanced toward the northeastern part of the hill mass. Diverted by the wide envelopment that threatened to encircle their left and forced to broaden their active front, the Germans fell back. The result was that by nightfall four battalions of U.S. infantry were perched somewhat precariously on Mont Castre. Not only did General Landrum have possession of the high ground, he also owned the highest point on the ridge line—Hill 122.

Success, still not entirely certain, was not without discomfiture. The wide envelopment had extended the 90th Division front. A roving band of Germans on the afternoon of 6 July had dispersed a chemical mortar platoon operating in direct support of an infantry battalion, thus disclosing gaps in the line, and had harassed supply and communications personnel, thus revealing the tenuous nature of the contact between the forces in the valley and those on the high ground.[31] To fill the gaps and keep open the supply routes, General Landrum committed the remaining two battalions of the 358th Infantry in support of his units on Mont Castre, even though concentrating the weight of his strength on the right deprived the troops on the left of reserve force. Two complete regiments then comprised a strong division right.

The decision to reinforce the right did not entirely alleviate the situation. The terrain impeded efforts to consolidate positions on the high ground. Underbrush on the eastern part of the hill mass was of such density and height as to limit visibility to a few yards and render movement slow. The natural growth obscured terrain features and made it difficult for troops to identify their map locations and maintain contact with adjacent units. The incline of the hill slope, inadequate trails, and entangling thickets made laborious the task of bringing tanks and antitank guns forward.[32]

Evacuation of the wounded and supply of the forward troops were haz-

---

[30] *Seventh Army KTB* (Draft), 5 Jul.

[31] 90th Div G–3 Jnl, 0255, 7 Jul.
[32] 90th Div G–3 Jnl, 2330, 6 Jul; Lt Col Charles H. Taylor's Notes on Mont Castre, ML–1071.

ardous because obscure trails as well as the main routes were mined and because many bypassed or infiltrating Germans still held out in rear areas. The understrength infantry battalions were short of ammunition, water, and food. Seriously wounded soldiers waited hours for transportation to medical installations. One regiment could hardly spare guards or rations for a hundred German prisoners. Vehicles attempting to proceed forward came under small arms and artillery fire. Much of the resupply and evacuation was accomplished by hand-carry parties that used tanks as cargo carriers as far as they could go, then proceeded on foot. A typical battalion described itself as "in pretty bad shape. Getting low on am and carrying it by hand. Enemy coming around from all sides; had 3 tks with them. Enemy Arty bad. Ours has been giving good support. No report from [the adjacent] 1st Bn." [33] General Landrum relieved one regimental commander, who was physically and mentally exhausted. About the same time the other was evacuated for wounds.

Rain, which began again during the evening of 6 July, added to General Landrum's concern. Conscious of the enemy's prior knowledge of the terrain and his skillful use of local counterattack at night as a weapon of defense, General Landrum drew on the regiment engaged in the corridor to shift a battalion, less one rifle company, to reinforce Mont Castre and alerted his engineers for possible commitment as infantry.

General Landrum's anxiety was justified, for the enemy counterattacked repeatedly during the dark and rainy night, but on the morning of 7 July the 90th Division still possessed Hill 122 and the northeast portion of the ridge. One battalion summed up the action by reporting that it was "a bit apprehensive" but had "given no ground." [34]

Continuing rain, deep mud, and the difficulty of defining the enemy front hindered further attempts on 7 July to consolidate positions on Mont Castre. Judging the hold on the high ground still to be precarious, General Landrum placed all three lettered companies of the engineer battalion into the line that evening.[35] With the division reconnaissance troops patrolling the north edge of the Prairies Marécageuses de Gorges to prevent a surprise attack against the division left flank and rear, one battalion of the 357th Infantry, less a rifle company, remained the sole combat element not committed. During the night of 7 July General Landrum held onto this battalion, undecided whether the situation on Mont Castre was more critical than that which had developed during the past few days in the corridor on the left.

In the corridor, Colonel Barth's 357th Infantry had first tried to advance along the eastern base of Mont Castre on the morning of 5 July. Shelling the regimental command post, the Germans delayed the attack for an hour and a half. When the fire subsided, Colonel Barth sent a battalion of infantry in a column of companies, supported by

[33] 90th Div G-3 Jnl, 2340, 6 Jul; Engr Opns, 2000, 5 Jul, 90th Div G-3 Jnl File; 315th Engr Combat Bn Jnl, 1530, 6 Jul, and 0020, 7 Jul; 358th Inf Jnl, 7 Jul.

[34] 90th Div G-3 Jnl, 0425, 7 Jul.
[35] 90th Div Sitrep 58, 8 Jul; 315th Engr Combat Bn Jnl, Jul.

tanks, toward the hamlet of Beaucoudray, the first regimental objective.

Between the regimental line of departure and Beaucoudray, a distance of about a mile, a tar road marked the axis of advance along a corridor bordered on the east by encroaching swamps, on the west by a flat, grassy meadow at the foot of Mont Castre. Near Beaucoudray, where the ruins of a fortified castle indicated that the terrain was tactically important a thousand years earlier, a slight ground elevation enhanced the German defense. The position on the knoll was tied in with the forces on Mont Castre.

Aided by artillery, infantry and tanks entered the corridor on 5 July, knocked out a German self-propelled gun, and moved to within 1,000 yards of Beaucoudray before hostile artillery and mortar fire halted further advance. With inadequate space for the commitment of additional troops, the battalion in the corridor sought cover in the hedgerows while the enemy poured fire on the men. A platoon of 4.2-inch chemical mortars in support became disorganized and returned to the rear.

On 6 July, early morning mist and, later, artillery and mortar smoke shells enabled a rifle company to advance through Beaucoudray and outpost the hamlet.[36] This displacement created room for part of the support battalion. While two rifle companies north of Beaucoudray covered by fire, two other companies advanced several hundred yards south of the village. The result gave Colonel Barth good positions in the corridor—with three rifle companies

south of Beaucoudray, two immediately north of Beaucoudray, and one at the entrance to the corridor, the regiment at last was ready to drive toward the division objective.

The achievement was actually deceptive. The troops were in a defile and in vulnerable positions. As nightfall approached and with it the increasing danger of counterattack, Colonel Barth moved his regimental antitank guns well to the front. His defense lost depth when General Landrum decided to move the battalion that constituted Barth's regimental reserve to reinforce the Mont Castre sector. Fortunately, Landrum left one company of the battalion in position north of the corridor as a token regimental reserve.

The Germans, meanwhile, had reinforced their positions in the la Haye-du-Puits sector with the *15th Parachute Regiment* and had been making hurried attempts since 5 July to commit part of the *2d SS Panzer Division,* the last of the *Seventh Army* reserve, in the same sector. To maintain their principal defenses, which were excellent, and allow reinforcements to enter them, the Germans had to remove the threat of encirclement that Colonel Barth's 357th Infantry posed in the corridor. Remnants of the *77th Division* therefore prepared an attack to be launched from the reverse slope of Mont Castre.[37]

At 2315, 6 July, enemy artillery and mortar fire struck the right flank of the U.S. units in the corridor as a prelude to an attack by infantry and tanks. The American antitank weapons deployed generally to the front and south were for the most part ineffec-

[36] The 357th Inf AAR, Jul, contains the following account in detail.

[37] *Seventh Army KTB* (Draft), 5–7 Jul.

tive.[38] One of the three rifle companies south of Beaucoudray fell back on the positions of a company north of the village. The other company north of Beaucoudray fell back and consolidated with the company at the entrance to the corridor. The six rifle companies of the two battalions became three two-company groups, two of them—those immediately north and south of Beaucoudray—in close combat with the enemy. Fused together by the pressure of the German attack, the consolidated two-company units inside the corridor fought through a rainy, pitch-black night to repel the enemy. When morning came the group north of the village appeared to be in no serious danger, but the group south of Beaucoudray had been surrounded and cut off.

To rescue the isolated group, Colonel Barth on 7 July mounted an attack by another rifle company supported by two platoons of medium tanks. Despite heavy casualties from mortar fire, the infantry reached the last hedgerow at the northern edge of Beaucoudray. There, the company commander committed his supporting tanks. A moment later the commander was struck by enemy fire. As the tanks moved up, the Germans launched a small counterattack against the right flank. By this time all commissioned and noncommissioned officers of the company had been either killed or wounded. Deprived of leadership, the infantrymen and tankers fell back across the muddy fields. Difficulties of reorganizing under continuing enemy fire prevented further attempts to relieve the encircled group that afternoon.

In quest of ammunition, a small party of men from the isolated group reached safety after traversing the swamp, but the battalion commander to whom they reported deemed the return trip too hazardous to authorize their return. In the early evening, radio communication with the surrounded companies ceased. Shortly afterward a lone messenger, after having made his way through the swampy *prairies*, reported that one company had surrendered after enemy tanks had overrun its command post. Although Colonel Barth made his reserve company available for a night attack to relieve any survivors, the ineptitude of a battalion commander kept the effort from being made.

Sounds of battle south of Beaucoudray ceased shortly after daylight on 8 July. When six men, who had escaped through the swamp, reported the bulk of both companies captured or killed, Barth canceled further rescue plans.[39] Apprehensive of German attempts to exploit the success, he formed his regimental cooks and clerks into a provisional reserve.

After five days of combat the 90th Division had advanced about four miles at a cost of over 2,000 casualties, a loss that reduced the infantry companies to skeleton units. Though this was a high price, not all of it reflected inexperience and lack of organization. The division had tried to perform a difficult mission in well-organized and stubbornly defended terrain. The German defenders were of equal, perhaps superior numbers —approximately 5,600 front-line combat-effective troops of the *91st, 265th, 77th,*

---

[38] 357th Inf Jnl, 16 Jul.

[39] The Germans took 250 men and 5 officers prisoners. *Seventh Army KTB* (Draft), 8 Jul.

and *353d Infantry Divisions*, the *15th Parachute Regiment,* and lesser units. The pressure exerted by the 90th Division alone had forced *LXXXIV Corps* to commit all its reserve, *Seventh Army* to commit certain reserves, and OKW to release control of the parachute regiment, its only reserve in the theater. Wresting part of Mont Castre from the enemy had been no mean achievement. Though fumbling and ineptitude had marked the opening days of the July offensive, the division had displayed workmanship and stamina in the fight for Mont Castre.

To commanders at higher echelons, possession of undeniably precarious positions on Mont Castre and failure to have forced the Beaucoudray corridor seemed clear indications that the 90th Division still had to learn how to make a skillful application of tactical principles to hedgerow terrain. The division had demonstrated continuing deficiencies, hangovers from its June performance. Some subordinate commanders still lacked the power of vigorous direction. Too many officers were overly wary of counterattack. On the surface, at least, the division appeared to have faltered in July as it had in June. The conclusive evidence that impressed higher commanders was not necessarily the failure to secure the initial objectives south of la Haye-du-Puits in five days, but the fact that by 8 July the division seemed to have come to a halt.

Montgardon Ridge

While the 90th Division had been attacking Mont Castre and probing the corridor leading toward Périers, the 79th

Division, on the VIII Corps right, had made its effort along the west coast of the Cotentin. On the basis of the attack on Cherbourg in June, the 79th was considered a good combat unit.[40] Imbued with high morale and commanded by the officer who had directed its training and baptism of fire, Maj. Gen. Ira T. Wyche, the division was in far better shape for the July assignment than was the 90th.

During the first phase of the VIII Corps drive to Coutances, General Wyche was expected to clear his zone as far south as the Ay River estuary, seven miles away. He anticipated little difficulty.[41] To reach his objective, he had first to secure the high ground in his path near la Haye-du-Puits—the Montgardon ridge and its high point, the flat top of Hill 84. Capture of the height would give General Wyche positions dominating la Haye-du-Puits and the ground descending southward to the Ay, would make la Haye-du-Puits untenable for the Germans, and would permit the 79th to meet the 90th approaching from the corps left.

To take the Montgardon ridge, the 79th Division had to cross six miles of hedgerowed lowland defended by remnants of the *243d Division* and under the eyes of a battalion of the *353d Division* entrenched on the ridge. Only a frontal assault was possible. The division was also to seize the incidental objective of Hill 121, a mound near the left boundary that provided good observation toward la Haye-du-Puits and

---

[40] Ltr, Eisenhower to Marshall, 5 Jul, Pogue Files.

[41] 79th Div Intel Annex 2 to FO 5, 1 Jul.

Montgardon. General Wyche planned to send the 314th Infantry against Hill 121 on the left while the 315th moved toward the Montgardon ridge on the right.

Attempting to outflank Hill 121, the 314th Infantry (Col. Warren A. Robinson) drove toward la Haye-du-Puits on the rainy morning of 3 July with a rifle company on each side of the main road.[42] Machine gun and mortar fire from a railway embankment parallel to the road stopped the leading units after a half-mile advance, but the heroic action of a single soldier, Pfc. William Thurston, got the attack moving again. Charging the embankment and eliminating the enemy machine gunners in one position with rifle fire, Thurston penetrated the German line and unhinged it.[43] His companions quickly exploited the breach, and by the end of the afternoon they had gained about three miles. There, the leading battalion halted and set up blocking positions to protect a separate advance on Hill 121. Another battalion that had followed was to turn left and approach the hill in a flanking maneuver from the southwest.

A large bare mound, Hill 121 was adorned by a small ruined stone house reputed to be of Roman times, a romanesque chapel, and a water tower.

---

[42] Records of the 79th Division are sketchy. The After Action Report is in reality a daily summary of each regimental effort. The G–3 Journal is thin. Combat Interviews 153 contains only fragmentary material. The unofficial history of the 314th Infantry, *Through Combat*, is helpful, and General Wyche has kindly made available his personal journal.

[43] Thurston was awarded the DSC.

Also visible were German fortifications of sandbagged logs. Spearheaded by a twelve-man patrol, the battalion started toward the base of the hill at dusk. As the men disappeared into the hedgerows, the regimental commander lost communications with the command party. At 2300, when General Wyche instructed his regiments to halt for the night, no acknowledgment came from the men moving on Hill 121. Not until 0230, 4 July, when an artillery liaison officer who apparently possessed the only working radio in the command reported the battalion closing on the objective did any word emerge. An hour later the same officer provided the encouraging news that the battalion was on the hill.

Upon receipt of the first message, Colonel Robinson, the commander of the 314th, had immediately dispatched his reserve battalion to assist. At daybreak both forces were clearing the slopes of Hill 121. The Germans had held the hill with only small outposts. By midmorning of 4 July Hill 121 was secure. The division artillery had an excellent observation post for the battle of the Montgardon ridge and la Haye-du-Puits. On 4 July the 314th Infantry moved to within two miles of la Haye-du-Puits and that evening established contact with the 82d Airborne Division on the left. Because heavy German fire denied the regiment entry into la Haye-du-Puits, the infantry dug in and left the artillery to duel with the enemy.

The artillery would be needed on the Montgardon ridge because the 315th Infantry (Col. Bernard B. McMahon) still had a long way to go toward that objective, despite encouraging progress

during the morning of 3 July. With
two battalions abreast and in columns
of companies, the third echeloned to the
right rear, and a company of tanks in
close support, the regiment at first advanced slowly but steadily; self-assurance
and optimism vanished just before noon
when three concealed and bypassed German armored vehicles on the coastal
flank opened fire. The loss of several
tanks promoted panic, and infantrymen
streamed to the rear in confusion.

Because artillery and antitank weapons reacted effectively, the disruption to
the attack proved only temporary, although not until midafternoon were
tanks and infantry sufficiently reorganized to resume the attack. By nightfall
the 315th had advanced a little over a
mile.

Movement through the hedgerows toward Montgardon was slow again on the
second day of the attack until the observation provided by the 314th Infantry's
conquest of Hill 121 began to show effect. Such good progress had been made
by afternoon that the division artillery
displaced its battalions forward.

Not until evening, when the infantry
was two miles short of Hill 84 and taking
a rest, did the Germans react with other
than passive defense. Enemy infantry
supported by armored vehicles suddenly
emerged from the hedgerows. Two rifle
companies that had halted along a
sunken road were temporarily surrounded, but 50 men and 4 officers held firm
to provide a bulwark around which the
dispersed troops could be reorganized.
As the division artillery went into action with heavy fire, the regiment built
up a solid defensive perimeter. The
Germans had counterattacked to cover

a withdrawal of the 243d to the main
line of defense on the Montgardon ridge.
During the action the Germans took
64 prisoners.[44]

Temporarily checked in the drive on
the Montgardon ridge, General Wyche
ordered the 314th Infantry to enter la
Haye-du-Puits the next morning, 5 July,
in the hope of outflanking the German
positions on the high ground. Moving
down mined and cratered roads to the
northeastern outskirts of town, one company formed a base of fire while another
slipped into the railroad yard. The success was short-lived, for enemy artillery
and mortar fire soon drove the company
back.

By midmorning of 5 July General
Wyche had decided on a new, bold move,
which he hoped might explode the division out of its slow hedgerow-by-hedge-
row advance and perhaps trap a sizable
number of Germans north of the Ay
River. He committed his reserve, the
313th Infantry (Col. Sterling A. Wood),
in a wide envelopment to the right, to
pass across the western end of the Montgardon ridge and drive rapidly downhill
to the Ay.

Starting at noon on 5 July, the 313th
Infantry moved toward the ridge with a
two-company tank-infantry task force in
the lead. Marshy terrain and lack of
adequate roads slowed the movement.
By late afternoon the task force was
still several hundred yards short of the
ridge. As the troops reached a water-
filled ditch running through the center
of a flat grassy meadow, they came under
such a volume of artillery fire that the

---

[44] *Seventh Army KTB*, 5 Jul; MS # A–983 (Mahlmann).

advance stalled. Just before dark the enemy counterattacked twice and drove the task force and the rest of the regiment several miles back in confusion. Before daybreak, 6 July, few would have attested either to the location or the integrity of the regiment. Mercifully, the Germans did not exploit their success. The regiment found time to regroup.

Disappointed in the results of the 313th Infantry advance even before the counterattack, General Wyche late on 5 July had again sent the 315th, supported by tanks and tank destroyers, directly against Hill 84. This time the regiment reached the north slope of the hill. The 79th Division at last had a toehold on the highest part of the Montgardon ridge.

To reinforce this success and prepare for final conquest of the ridge, General Wyche on 6 July jockeyed his other two regiments. He ordered the 314th to swing its right around la Haye-du-Puits and gain a foothold on the eastern slope. The regiment accomplished its mission during the morning. He turned the 313th eastward from its location on the division right rear to positions in support of the troops on Hill 84. By noon of 6 July, the fourth day of the attack, the 314th and 315th Regiments were on the northern and eastern slopes of Montgardon, while the 313th was echeloned to the right rear at the base of the ridge.

In ordering all three regiments to attack during the afternoon to carry the crest, General Wyche bowed to the compartmentalizing effect of the hedgerow terrain and told each commander to attack alone when ready. The technique worked. Although the 313th Infantry on the right gained no ground against

strong positions protected by wire and mines, the 315th in the center overran Hill 84, and the 314th on the left completed occupation of the eastern portion of the main ridge. By daybreak of 7 July the 79th Division could note that la Haye-du-Puits was outflanked, that the Germans ought now to abandon the town, and that as soon as earlier advances were extended to cover the entire ridge, the division might head south toward the Ay River.

It did not take long on 7 July for General Wyche and his subordinate commanders to realize that this kind of thinking was premature. The Germans held doggedly to the rest of the high ground. They also stayed in la Haye-du-Puits; an American patrol accompanied by a German prisoner who was recruited to talk the garrison into surrender could not even get past the first houses. The Germans not only refused to budge from the high ground and the town, they prepared to attack. Having hurriedly reinforced the la Haye-du-Puits sector with a small portion of the *2d SS Panzer Division,* Choltitz launched his counterattack on the afternoon of 7 July as armored contingents in about two-battalion strength assaulted the Montgardon ridge.[45]

The German armored troops struck with such violence and behind such a volume of supporting fire that the first blow almost pushed the 79th Division off the ridge. In an attempt to achieve better co-ordination between the two regiments on the main ridge, General Wyche placed both under one com-

---

[45] *Seventh Army KTB,* 7 Jul.

mander. The expedient worked. Soon the infantry, artillery, tanks, and tank destroyers began to execute a co-ordinated defense. Destruction of three German tanks appeared to extinguish the spark of the German drive.[46] By nightfall the Germans were stopped, but gone was the optimistic belief that a quick drive to the Ay would be possible.

In five days of hedgerow fighting, the 79th Division had attained the crest of the Montgardon ridge but was still short of the intermediate objective. Though the division casualties in the hedgerows had not been consistently high, the fighting on the high ground on 7 July alone resulted in over 1,000 killed, wounded, and missing. The cumulative total for five days of battle was over 2,000.[47] Seriously depleted in numbers, its remaining troops badly in need of rest, and some units close to demoralization in the face of seemingly incessant German shelling, the 79th Division was no longer the effective force that had marched to Cherbourg the preceding month. For the moment the 79th seemed no more capable of effective offensive combat than did the 90th.

Initiating the First Army offensive, the VIII Corps had failed to achieve the success anticipated. The Germans had indicated that they were prepared and determined to resist. They had given up little ground, defended stubbornly, and utilized the hedgerows and observation points with skill. They had employed their weapons on a scale not expected by the Americans and had inflicted a large number of casualties. Although the VIII Corps took 543 prisoners on 3 July, 314 on 4 July, 422 on 5 July, and 203 on 6 July, they were inferior troops for the most part, non-Germanic eastern Europeans, and the corps could look forward to no sudden enemy collapse.

The rain had been a severe handicap to the Americans. Although limited visibility gave the troops some measure of concealment and protection from the German fire, the weather had denied the corps the full use of its available resources in fire power and mobility. Not until the third day of the offensive had tactical air been able to undertake close support missions, and two days later recurring poor weather conditions again had forced cancellation of extensive air support. Operations of the small artillery observation planes were also limited by weather conditions. Finally, the rain had transformed the moist fields of the Cotentin into ponds of mud that immobilized in great part the motorized striking force of the American tracked and wheeled vehicles.

The 82d Airborne Division had swept across an area for the most part lightly defended and had displayed a high degree of flexibility and effectiveness in meeting the problems of hedgerow warfare. If the 79th and 90th Divisions seemed less adaptable and less professional than the airborne troops, they had met enemy forces at least numerically equal in strength who occupied excellent defenses. The two infantry divisions had nevertheless by the end of 7 July breached the German main line of defense. By then, replacements untested by battle comprised about 40 percent of

---

[46] FUSA G-3 Jnl, 7 Jul.
[47] FUSA Daily Estimated Loss Rpt, Jul.

their infantry units. With both the 79th and the 90th Division needing rest and the aggressive 82d Airborne Division about to depart the Continent, its place to be taken by the inexperienced 8th Division, VIII Corps could expect no sudden success. On the other hand, the Germans could anticipate no respite, for to the east the U.S. VII Corps in its turn had taken up the battle.

CHAPTER V

The Offensive Broadened

The Carentan – Périers Isthmus

In keeping with the desire of Generals Eisenhower and Montgomery to get the American offensive to the south under way, General Bradley had lost no time in redeploying the VII Corps from Cherbourg. As the Cherbourg operation was ending on the last day of June, Bradley ordered the VII Corps headquarters to move to Carentan immediately to assume responsibility for an area on the left (east) of the VIII Corps.[1]

The new VII Corps sector, between the Prairies Marécageuses de Gorges and the flooded Taute River, covered the shallowest part of the Allied beachhead. Through Carentan passed the only highway linking the U.S. troops in the Cotentin with the Allied forces east of the Taute River. The area was considered the weakest and most sensitive part of the entire First Army front. (Map 4)

A road center and small seaport, Carentan was extremely vulnerable to German attack. The VII Corps positions, facing southwest toward Périers, were only three and a half miles from the center of Carentan. A German counterattack in mid-June had come to within 500 yards of retaking the town, and German field artillery continued to interdict the town and the highway bridge across the Taute River.[2] The First Army staff did not rule out the possibility that a determined German attack might overrun Carentan, cut the Allied beachhead in two, and deny the Allies lateral communication by land.[3] Advancing the front line south of Carentan would eliminate these dangers and the nuisance of German shelling.

More important than these defensive considerations was the offensive motivation. The VII Corps objective was a portion of the Coutances–St. Lô highway. To reach the objective the corps had to pass through a narrow and well-defined corridor constricted by adjacent marshes. Resembling an isthmus two to three miles wide, the corridor between Carentan and Périers severely limited the amount of strength that corps could bring to bear. Only after reaching the Périers–St. Lô highway would VII Corps have adequate room for deploying its forces, and there, south of the Prairies Marécageuses de Gorges, the VII Corps

---

[1] Upon the request of the VII Corps commander, the corps rear area at Carentan was enlarged to give his artillery and other supporting troops necessary movement space and sufficient roadways. Sylvan Diary, 27 Jun.

[2] [Ruppenthal], *Utah Beach to Cherbourg*, pp. 90–93.

[3] German action would also threaten to bring unloading operations to a halt at Isigny, a minor port receiving supplies seven miles east of Carentan. FUSA G–2 Est 7, 29 Jun.

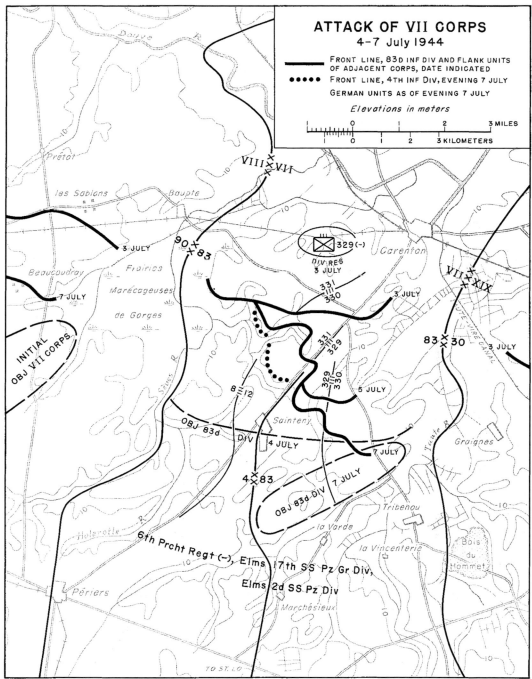

ATTACK OF VII CORPS
4–7 July 1944

▬▬▬ FRONT LINE, 83D INF DIV AND FLANK UNITS
OF ADJACENT CORPS, DATE INDICATED

●●●●● FRONT LINE, 4TH INF DIV, EVENING 7 JULY

GERMAN UNITS AS OF EVENING 7 JULY

Elevations in meters

6th Prcht Regt (−), Elms 17th SS Pz Gr Div,
Elms 2d SS Pz Div

D. Holmes, Jr.

MAP 4

would be at a juncture with the VIII Corps. Continuing south, the two corps would come abreast at the Coutances–St. Lô highway, the final army objective. Should resistance disintegrate before the final objective was reached, General Bradley could use an armored division that he had in the army reserve to exploit the American success.[4]

General Bradley had thought of launching the VII Corps attack on 3 July, at the same time the VIII Corps jumped off, but he had decided to help VIII Corps on its first day of operations by giving it temporary control of the VII Corps Artillery. He therefore postponed the VII Corps effort until 4 July, when VII Corps was to regain control of its own artillery support. A battalion of 8-inch howitzers and several battalions of medium artillery from army were to reinforce the fires of the corps pieces.[5]

The VII Corps commander was Maj. Gen. J. Lawton Collins, who as a lieutenant colonel three years earlier had been the corps chief of staff. In the Pacific he had commanded the 25th Division on Guadalcanal and New Georgia. The division code name, LIGHTNING, seemed to describe General Collins' method of operation. As VII Corps commander, his direction of the invasion landings on UTAH Beach and his vigorous prosecution of the Cherbourg campaign had reinforced the suitability of his nickname, "Lightning Joe." Flushed with success and generating unbounded confidence, General Collins and his staff enthusiastically accepted the challenge presented by the new task assigned to the VII Corps.

The first problem that General Collins faced was how to use to best advantage in the constricted corps zone the three infantry divisions available to him. Retaining the 4th and 9th Infantry Divisions, which had participated in the Cherbourg operation, Collins on 2 July took control of the 83d Infantry Division, which was manning the Carentan sector. Little more than three miles from Carentan, one fourth of the way to Périers, the 83d Division held defensive positions across the narrow isthmus. Directing the 83d to advance a little over two miles to Sainteny, which was half way to Périers, Collins set the stage for committing at least part of another division. Hoping that the 83d Division would reach Sainteny in one day, he planned to have elements of the 4th Division go on to Périers on the second day. If on reaching Sainteny the 83d did not make contact with the VIII Corps attacking along the western edge of the Prairies Marécageuses de Gorges, surely the 4th Division would meet the VIII Corps near Périers. At that point, if the 83d Division made a similar advance, crossed the Taute River, and gained its assigned portion of the Périers–St. Lô highway, enough terrain would be available to employ the 9th Division.

Though General Collins wanted the 83d Division to reach Sainteny in a day, he nevertheless recognized that the width of the Carentan–Périers isthmus might enable comparatively few enemy troops to hold up forces of superior numbers. To reach Sainteny, the 83d Division had to squeeze through the narrowest part, a neck scarcely two miles wide. Hedgerows restricted mechanized units to well-defined channels and gave

[4] [2d Lt. David Garth], *St.-Lô*, AFA Series (Washington, 1946), p. 5.
[5] VII Corps AAR, Jul; 83d Div AAR, Jul.

the enemy ideal cover and concealment for delaying action. Except for the tarred highway to Périers and a lateral route between causeways, the roads on the isthmus were little better than wagon trails. American observers had detected neither antitank ditches nor permanent fortifications, but they felt sure that the Germans had organized their positions to a depth of several miles and were covering all road junctions with machine guns.[6]

The Germans in the Périers sector, comprising part of the right (east) wing of the *LXXXIV Corps,* were under the local operational control of the headquarters of the *17th SS Panzer Grenadier Division,* a tough, well-trained unit. The division had one of its two regiments holding positions below Carentan. Attached to it was the separate *6th Parachute Regiment,* a veteran though somewhat depleted unit. The leadership of these forces was especially strong and experienced.[7]

Aware of the German units that faced the 83d Division, General Collins did not underestimate their fighting ability. He also realized that early morning marsh mist and the promise of continuing rain would reduce the effectiveness of artillery support and diminish the help offered by tactical air. But he had no alternative to striking the Germans frontally—terrain, unit boundaries, and the First Army plan made a frontal attack by the 83d Division inevitable.

Though the primary aim was a short advance to allow the commitment of a second division, Collins, with characteristic confidence, ordered the 83d to maintain the momentum of its attack; if the division destroyed the German defenses at once, it was to advance as far as the Taute River in the left (east) portion of the corps zone.

The 83d Division had arrived in Normandy in the latter part of June and under VIII Corps control had relieved the 101st Airborne Division (Maj. Gen. Maxwell D. Taylor) at Carentan. The airborne troops had moved into the army reserve to prepare for their return to England, but not before boasting of their accomplishments and exaggerating the toughness of the Germans to the novice infantrymen who replaced them. Some members of the new division became jittery.[8] Highly conscious of the division's inexperience, General Collins was to supervise its activities closely.

The 83d Division commander, Maj. Gen. Robert C. Macon, who had commanded a regiment in North Africa, had the problem of advancing units in terrain that could hardly have been less favorable for offensive action. The almost incessant rain of the previous weeks had soaked the isthmus beyond saturation. As the drainage ditches swelled into streams and the swamps turned into ponds, the surface of the fields became a potential sheet of mud. Progress for foot troops would be difficult; cross-country movement by vehicles virtually impossible; movement of armor in close support most difficult; good direct fire support by tanks and tank destroyers

---

[6] VII Corps AAR, Jul, and FO 4, 3 Jul, with Intel Annex, 2 Jul.

[7] *OKH Generalinspekteur der Panzertruppen, Zustandberichte, SS Divisiones,* Jun 43–Jul 44; MS # B-839 (von der Heydte); Harrison, *Cross-Channel Attack,* pp. 356–65.

[8] Lt Col Henry Neilson, Hosp Intervs, III, GL-93 (238).

a noteworthy accomplishment; supply hazardous.

To gain the greatest shock effect commensurate with his constricted zone, General Macon decided to commit two regiments abreast in columns of battalions. To advance down the Carentan –Périers road, the 331st Infantry (Col. Martin D. Barndollar, Jr.) was to attack along the right of the highway, while the 330th Infantry (Col. Ernest L. McLendon) attacked on the left. Col. Edwin B. Crabill's 329th Infantry (minus one battalion) was to constitute the division reserve. One battalion of the 329th was to clear a small area on the right flank at the edge of the Prairies Marécageuses de Gorges. Division fire power was to be augmented by the 9th Division Artillery, the 746th Tank and the 802d Tank Destroyer Battalions, the 4.2-inch mortars of two companies of the 87th Chemical Battalion, and the quadruple .50-caliber machine guns of the 453d Antiaircraft Artillery Automatic Weapons Battalion. Eager to prove its competence and nervous about its impending trial in battle, the 83d Division celebrated the Fourth of July by firing a ten-minute artillery preparation and then jumping off at daybreak.[9]

Mishaps plagued the division from the start. Tanks in close support immediately "messed up" wires, and General Macon lost touch with his assault formations soon after they crossed the line of departure. Two hours later, the commander of the 331st, Colonel Barndollar, was dead with a bullet below his

heart. Soon afterwards, engineers attempting to clear paths through enemy mine fields were being picked off by enemy rifle fire. At midmorning, enemy infantrymen on the division right flank temporarily surrounded several tanks that were trying to advance over soft and muddy marshland. The division moved but a short distance toward Sainteny, 200 yards at most, before German mortar and machine gun fire, from hedgerows and from log pillboxes reinforced by sandbags, halted the attack.

Following the action of the division from his corps command post, General Collins in midmorning became impatient with the slow progress. He had assured General Macon that he would not interfere with the conduct of operations, but when one infantry battalion waited for others to come abreast, Collins phoned the division headquarters and informed the chief of staff, "That's exactly what I don't want." What he did want was the battalion in the lead to cut behind the Germans who would then be forced to withdraw. "Don't ever let me hear of that again," General Collins warned, "and get that down to the regimental and battalion commanders and tell Macon about it." But telephonic exhortation, no matter how pertinent, could not blow down the defended hedgerows—nor, apparently, could the personal endeavors of General Macon and his assistant division commander, Brig. Gen. Claude B. Ferenbaugh, who had gone down to the regiments to press the attack.

On the division right flank the battalion of the 329th Infantry attempting to clear the small area near the Prairies Marécageuses de Gorges had managed to advance about 1,000 yards. Two

---

[9] The following account is taken from official unit records. All quotations, unless otherwise noted, are from the valuable record of telephone conversations in the division G–2, G–3 Journal.

rifle companies had crossed a stream swollen by rain and overflowing its banks. The adjacent terrain had become virtual swamp, with some mudholes waist deep. When the battalion commander tried to get his heavy weapons company across the stream just before noon, enemy mortars and machine gun fire forced the men to hug the ground. Commitment of the reserve rifle company produced no effect since the riflemen could do no better than the machine gunners of the weapons company in the face of the enemy fire. Taking heavy casualties, unable to maneuver in the swampy terrain, and fearing attack from the rear by the same infiltrating Germans who had earlier isolated several tanks, the battalion commander ordered a withdrawal. The men moved back to their original line of departure. Upon reorganization, the battalion discovered that one rifle company was almost a total loss; another could muster only one third of its strength.[10] Large numbers of stragglers intensified the impression of extreme losses. About fifty men of the battalion entered the division artillery positions during the afternoon and caused short-lived consternation by claiming to be the only survivors. Having lost most of its equipment in the swamp, the battalion remained on its line of departure to protect the division right flank. That evening it arranged a truce with the enemy, without authorization from higher headquarters, to collect its dead and wounded.

Impatient over the division's lack of progress, General Collins was infuriated when he learned of the battalion withdrawal on the division right. "Tell the CG," he informed the division chief of staff by telephone, "that I want the withdrawal investigated." Why make it necessary, he demanded, to lose more lives in forcing a crossing of the stream a second time? And when, he wanted to know, was the division going to launch a co-ordinated attack down the corridor?

For all the strenuous efforts of the division and assistant division commanders, the regiments were not ready for a concerted attack until late afternoon. After two postponements, General Macon finally got it started. The division artillery fired a preparation, and the two regiments attacked again down the Carentan–Périers road. They had made only minor advances before heavy artillery fire forced one regiment to pull back; a counterattack just before dark pushed back the other.

The terrain and stubborn resistance had soured the Fourth of July celebration and had thwarted the 83d Division in its attempt to advance beyond its outpost lines. "If the going is good, and it should be," General Macon had said, "we will have them rocked back, and will go right on." The going had not been good. Prepared defenses, active mortar fire, and extensive use of automatic weapons had been too effective. Only six German prisoners had been taken.

A count of personnel in the front-line positions of the 331st Infantry revealed only 300 men. The commander of the German parachute regiment in opposition, Col. Friedrich A. Freiherr von der

---

[10] 2d Battalion, 329th Infantry, *Combat Digest* (Germany, n.d.), p. 15.

Heydte, returned medical personnel his forces had captured, with a note stating that he thought General Macon needed them.[11] He was right. In its first day of combat the 83d Division had lost almost 1,400 men. An accurate breakdown of casualty figures was impossible. One regiment reported a total of 867 casualties without attempting further classification. On the basis of such incomplete information, the division arbitrarily categorized the total casualties and reported 47 killed, 815 wounded, and a surprising 530 missing in action. Many of the missing were stragglers and isolated troops who were later to rejoin the division, but at the end of the first day the division had suffered a more than 10 percent loss.[12]

Although the 83d Division had failed to achieve its mission of allowing the VII Corps to commit a second division in the isthmus after the first day's action, General Collins had no alternative but to keep pushing. He ordered the attack to secure Sainteny to continue on 5 July. General Macon changed his dispositions but slightly. The 331st Infantry, now commanded by Lt. Col. William E. Long, was to try again on the right of the Carentan–Périers road. Colonel McLendon's 330th Infantry, which had

sustained the highest number of casualties, was to relinquish part of its zone to two battalions of Colonel Crabill's 329th Infantry. The third battalion of the 329th would remain on the division's extreme right as flank protection.

The attack on 5 July began on a disheartening, if exaggerated, note. During the ten-minute artillery preparation, the executive officer of one of the regiments phoned division headquarters that the division artillery was "slaughtering our 3d Battalion." In reality, the regiment had received only a few short rounds.

The division jumped off on schedule. Unfortunately, the attack that morning repeated the unsuccessful pattern of the previous day. The troops made little progress.

Restless and impatient in a situation that denied use of available strength, General Collins ordered General Macon to make room "or else." Since there was no place to go except forward, Macon had to insist on continuation of a costly frontal attack. That afternoon he began to apply more pressure on his subordinate commanders. "You tell him," General Macon ordered, "that he must take that objective and go right on down regardless of his flank; pay attention to nothing, not even communication." An hour later he instructed a regimental commander, "Never mind about the gap; keep that leading battalion going."

When a battalion commander protested that he had only about 400 men, General Macon assured him, "That is just what I need, 400 men; keep driving." In midafternoon a regimental commander reported infiltrating enemy. "They won't hurt you any," Macon promised. "They shoot us," the regi-

---

[11] With caution, von der Heydte added that if the situation were ever reversed in the future, he hoped that General Macon would return the favor. Ltr, Ferenbaugh to OCMH, 20 May 53; MS # B–839 (Heydte).

[12] By 7 July the consolidated figure of those missing in action declined to 243 (83d Div G–2, G–3 Jnl). Casualty figures in the sources available (FUSA Daily Estimated Loss Rpts, Jul; the 83d Div G–2, G–3 Jnl; the 83d Div G–4 Daily Rpts, G–4 Jnl; and the 83d Div G–1 AAR, Jul) are constantly at variance. Figures chosen for the text represent an estimate compiled from all sources. Discussions recorded in the telephone journal are valuable contemporary estimates.

mental commander explained. When he protested that one of his battalions consisted of only one and a half rifle companies and the heavy weapons company, or about 300 men, the general sent the assistant division commander and two platoons of tanks to help the regiment clear the area.

When another battalion commander reported what looked like a counterattack, the general ordered, "Do not pay any attention to it; you must go on down [in attack.]" To a third battalion commander's protest that he had no reserve left, General Macon answered, "You go on down there and they [the enemy] will have to get out of your way."

By evening the general was shouting. "To hell with the [enemy] fire, to hell with what's on your flank, get down there and take the area. You don't need any recon. You have got to go ahead. You have got to take that objective if you have to go all night."

All seemed in vain when General Collins telephoned that evening. "What has been the trouble?" he asked. "[You] haven't moved an inch." The trouble was the same: mud, canalized routes of advance, and strong resistance.

Just before dark the division did succeed in reaching a hamlet half way to Sainteny, but the Germans would permit no celebration of the achievement. When accurate mortar and artillery fire battered the troops after dark, each of the two regiments lost contact with one of its battalions for several hours. When finally located during the early morning hours of 6 July, the battalions needed water, food, ammunition, litters, ambulances, and reinforcements. Nev-

ertheless, the troops held on to their hard-won gains.

In two days the 83d Division had displayed almost all the weaknesses and made virtually all the mistakes of a unit new to combat. Poor reports from subordinate units, incorrect map locations, and weak communications made accurate artillery support almost impossible and effective aid from the few tactical planes in the air on the second day difficult. Lax command control and discipline resulted in an inordinately large number of stragglers. Regimental and battalion commanders did not seem able to coordinate their attached units, institute reconnaissance in time, or press their attacks with vigor. Tank-infantry cooperation was especially bad, and mutual complaint and recrimination resulted. Infantrymen accused tankers of refusing to work at night and of disobeying orders with the excuse that they were only attached units, and at least one infantry commander threatened to shoot a tank officer for declining to advance in support. On the other hand, the tankers had little confidence in the ability of the infantry to protect them from close-range counterattack, and at least one tank commander threatened to shoot infantrymen who seemed on the verge of running to the rear and abandoning the tanks. The inexperience of the division was apparent on all echelons. When General Macon remarked that the commander of another division used his antiaircraft guns to mow down the hedges facing him, the artillery commander of the 83d Division asked, "How does he get them into position?" "I don't know," General Macon answered.

Despite its deficiencies, the division

had managed by sheer persistence to advance over a mile down the Carentan–Périers road. As a result, the division was at the southern end of the narrow neck and was ready to debouch into wider terrain just north of Sainteny. But in making the advance, it had suffered an additional 750 casualties. With these losses, many among key personnel, the future effectiveness of the division had been seriously impaired.

Although the advance of the 83d still did not permit commitment of a second division, General Collins, already delayed one day, decided to wait no longer. The depletion and exhaustion of the 83d must have been a factor in his decision. He ordered General Macon to confine his efforts to the left of the Carentan–Périers road and to shift his direction from the southwest toward Périers to the south toward the bank of the Taute River. Collins then instructed the 4th Division commander to take temporary control of the battered and depleted 331st Infantry on the right of the Carentan–Périers road, commit one of his own regiments through it, and drive toward Périers. Responsibility for the isthmus on the right of the road passed to the 4th Division.

The 4th Division was an experienced unit. It had taken part in the D-Day invasion of the Continent and had participated effectively in the Cherbourg operation. In the process, however, the division had lost about 5,400 men. Only five of the rifle company commanders who had made the D-Day landing were with the division three weeks later. Though many key individuals remained to steady the 4,400 replacements who partially refilled the division's

ranks, Maj. Gen. Raymond O. Barton, who had commanded the unit since 1942, remarked with regret, "We no longer have the division we brought ashore." [13]

General Barton planned to commit the 12th Infantry (Col. James S. Luckett), with a company each of the 87th Chemical, the 70th Tank, and the 801st Tank Destroyer Battalions, and a platoon of the 377th Antiaircraft Artillery Automatic Weapons Battalion. To support the attack, Barton regained control of his division artillery and an additional battalion of medium field artillery, which for three days had been operating with the 90th Division. At the same time that the 12th Infantry moved into position to make the main division effort toward Périers, elements of Col. James S. Rodwell's 8th Infantry were to relieve the battalion of the 329th Infantry still on the extreme right flank of the corps.

Early on 6 July the 12th Infantry began to relieve the 331st. It was a difficult relief since strong enemy fire and local counterattack harassed the troops. When the 12th Infantry had finally passed through and attacked to gain a favorable line of departure for the coordinated effort planned with the 83d Division, the regiment met firm resistance that halted the advance at once. Further attack for that day was canceled.

In the meantime, the enemy maintained heavy fire on the 83d Division and launched minor counterattacks, inflicting about 700 additional casualties. Under

---

[13] CI 30 (4th Div).

punishing pressure, the division nevertheless held its positions.

The lack of success during the third day of action along the Carentan–Périers axis, this time involving a veteran unit, must have confirmed General Collins' suspicions that the inexperience of the 83d Division had not been the principal factor in holding back its advance. He concluded that the cost of bulldozing through the lowlands with conventional tactics was too high and turned to an ally, the IX Tactical Air Command. During the previous few days, as the weather had permitted, fighter-bombers of the IX TAC had attacked targets of opportunity and struck enemy positions located by ground observers. General Collins now asked for more. He wanted a mass dive-bombing effort by more than a hundred planes to pummel the enemy in front of the 4th and 83d Divisions for forty-five minutes before renewal of the ground attack on 7 July.[14] With this assistance and a co-ordinated attack by the two divisions, General Collins hoped that the 83d Division would reach Sainteny by dark on 7 July and that the 4th Division would move far enough forward toward Périers to allow the 9th Division to be committed. Expecting this to be fulfilled, General Collins alerted the 9th Division for a move to an assembly area near Carentan.[15]

Two events marred the beginning of the attack on 7 July. The first occurred after General Barton had decided to obliterate the resistance in the small area on the right near the Prairies Marécageuses de Gorges. The area had

bothered the 83d Division, which had made an unsuccessful effort to clear it on the first day of its attack. The main obstacle to success was the stream, which was difficult to cross. Deciding that it could best be crossed during darkness, General Barton had instructed the commander of the 8th Infantry to make a surprise move during the night of 6 July. By sending two battalions over the stream at night, the units would be in position to clear the area at daylight, 7 July, thus eradicating a potential nuisance to the division rear that might hold up the advance should the division break through to Périers.

Though the regimental commander complied with instructions, one of his battalions could not cross the stream even at night because of enemy fire. The other battalion, after having picked its way through the marsh during the night and made the crossing, found itself in an untenable position at daybreak and was forced to withdraw after taking more than a hundred casualties.[16]

The second disappointment was a drizzling rain on the morning of 7 July that resulted in cancellation of the strong air support. "Disappointing news," General Collins reported to the divisions prepared to jump off. "But go right ahead with your attack."

General Macon attempted to swing his 83d Division gradually southward to the bank of the Taute River. His new axis of advance was the secondary road that crossed the Carentan–Périers isthmus laterally and led to the causeway over the flooded Taute. Despite the

---

[14] VII Corps Opns Memo 30, 6 Jul.
[15] [VII Corps] Notes for the CofS, 7 Jul, VII Corps G–3 Jnl and File.

[16] 4th Div and VII Corps AAR's, Jul; Telecon *Seventh Army* to *AGp B*, 1050, 7 Jul, *AGp B KTB.*

new direction of advance, the right flank elements of the division were still to take Sainteny. As the division endeavored to move forward during the morning of 7 July, it repelled five counterattacks, local in nature but fierce in intensity. Strong fire from the division artillery, effective use of bazooka teams, and direct fire from tanks and tank destroyers finally defeated the enemy efforts, though one battalion, isolated by German infiltrators, had to hold out until jeeps escorted by light tanks brought ammunition and food and restored communications. In the late afternoon Colonel McLendon's 330th Infantry made effective use of the division artillery, chiseled a narrow penetration through the enemy positions, and gained several hundred yards on the east flank. The achievement was hailed as substantial, raising hopes that the enemy defense was deteriorating, but the enemy quickly recovered as the reconnaissance battalion of the SS panzer grenadiers sealed off the penetration.[17] The 83d Division captured only seventeen prisoners that day. The German paratroopers and SS soldiers fought stubbornly, refusing to surrender when outnumbered and overpowered and giving ground only with desperate reluctance. The 83d Division failed to reach either Sainteny or the bank of the Taute River during the day.

The 12th Infantry of General Barton's 4th Division had even less success. Improved weather conditions during the afternoon permitted several fighter-bombers to operate over the VII Corps front, where they bombed enemy positions opposing the regiment. The 4th

Division Artillery followed the bombardment with a preparation, and the regiment jumped off once more. Unfortunately, the strenuous efforts resulted in hardly any gain.

In their attack on 7 July the two committed regiments of the 4th Division sustained almost 600 casualties. The 12th Infantry moved forward but slightly; the 8th, on the right flank, advanced not at all. Even for an experienced division, the stubborn and skillful resistance of the Germans in the Cotentin was proving too much. The swamps and the mud were themselves formidable enemies, but the most important obstacle insofar as the 4th Division was concerned was the old problem of the hedgerows. To take an average-size field required an entire infantry company, for there was no way of telling along which row or on which side of the hedge the Germans would be, and therefore there was no way of knowing the best approach.[18]

As the 4th Division rediscovered the problems of waging offensive warfare in Normandy, the 83d Division began to show signs of improvement. The men who had survived the early fighting began to feel like veterans and to act as such. Command control tightened, communications improved, and the division began to utilize its attached units with confidence. When requesting replacements for the 83d Division from the First Army on 7 July, General Collins remarked that the division was coming along pretty well.

The improvement was a bright spot in an otherwise bleak situation. Although the 83d Division was beginning to gain experience, each of its regiments was ap-

---

[17] *Seventh Army KTB* (Draft), 7 Jul.

[18] CI 30 (4th Div).

proximately 600 men understrength, and the men remaining were exhausted after four days of combat. While the 4th Division had not sustained such high casualties, it was not fully committed. Nor was it possible yet for General Collins to employ the 4th Division in full force. Early commitment of the 9th Division appeared unlikely. The VII Corps had failed to move even to Sainteny, an advance of only two and a half miles. The combination of German resistance and the Cotentin marshes and hedgerows had stymied the Americans, at least for the moment in the Carentan–Périers isthmus. Continuation of the attack meant costly frontal effort with little promise of rapid success.

Unknown to the Americans, their offensive action was more successful than the results seemed to indicate. The aggressive defense of the Germans—tactics to seal off local penetrations by counterattack and to encircle American spearheads—was unable to function properly under effective artillery fire and fighter-bomber attack. Despite skillful ground defense, the Germans were gradually being forced back, their reserves were being used up, and their defensive line was dangerously stretched. With the two regiments on the isthmus being increasingly depleted, the SS panzer grenadier division committed in defense of Périers part of its regiment that had been east of the Taute River.[19]

Despite the impact of the VII Corps thrust, the *Seventh Army* looked upon it as it had done when judging the adjacent VIII Corps attack on the previous day— as merely a reconnaissance in force. Although depreciating the American in-

tention, the *Seventh Army* urgently called for help. With two U.S. Corps exerting pressure, the Germans began to be concerned over their relatively meager forces in reserve.[20] Anticipating by 5 July that the Americans might break through to Périers and cut off the *LXXXIV Corps* forces in the la Haye-du-Puits sector, Hausser, the *Seventh Army* commander, had demanded additional reserves. The *2d SS Panzer Division* had been moved westward from the *II Parachute Corps* sector to meet the American attack, and by 7 July its troops were strung across the Cotentin and battling both VIII Corps at la Haye du-Puits and VII Corps on the Carentan– Périers isthmus.[21]

The VII Corps attack had thus robbed the German sectors on both sides of the corridor; it had prevented the Germans from employing all their available armor at la Haye-du-Puits; it also had weakened the St. Lô sector just to the east. Instead of massing the armored division for a strong counterattack, the Germans had had to meet American pressure by committing the armored unit piecemeal in defense. The panzer division's striking power was thus dissipated across the active front. To meet the need for still more reserves, Rommel and Kluge prevailed upon OKW and Hitler to release the *5th Parachute Division* from its station in Brittany, and on 7 July the paratroopers began to move toward the Cotentin battlefield.[22]

If General Bradley surmised these

---

[19] *Seventh Army* and *AGp B KTB*'s 5–7 Jul.

[20] *Seventh Army KTB*, 4 Jul; Telecon, *Seventh Army* to *AGp B*, 1300, 4 Jul, *AGp B KTB*.
[21] *Seventh Army KTB* (Draft), 5 Jul; Telecon *Seventh Army* to *AGp B*, 1610, 7 Jul, *AGp B KTB*.
[22] Telecons Hausser to Rommel, 1930, 7 Jul, and Rommel to Kluge, 2020, 7 Jul, *AGp B KTB*.

developments, he could not have been entirely dismayed by the fact that the VII Corps attack on the isthmus had been halted at the same time as that of the VIII Corps. Also, on the same day, 7 July, operations immediately to the east, in the XIX Corps zone, seemed to show an opportunity for rapid success. Shifting his hopes eastward, General Bradley looked to the region between the Taute and the Vire Rivers, where additional American pressure seemed to promise a swift penetration of the enemy defenses.

The Vire and Taute Bridgehead

The XIX Corps held positions straddling the Vire River, which split the corps zone into equal parts of dissimilar terrain—Cotentin lowland on the west and rolling country on the east. The difference was accentuated by the fact that the troops on the left (east) were along a front that was several miles in advance of the line on the right. *(Map 5)*

The corps portion of the First Army objective lay astride the Vire River along the Coutances–St. Lô–Bayeux highway—between the villages of St. Gilles and St. André-de-l'Epine, about four miles southwest and northeast of St. Lô, respectively. The objective included not only the high ground adjacent to the highway but also the city of St. Lô.

In compliance with the dictates of the terrain, the corps attack was to take place in two steps—first west of the Vire River, the second east of it. The initial effort (on 7 July) was to get troops across the Vire et Taute Canal and the Vire River and push the corps right flank to that part of the objective west of the Vire. Such action would protect the lateral coastal highway between Carentan and Isigny, which was still under occasional hostile fire; but more to the point, it would place troops on the high ground along the Périers– St. Lô highway, which was part of the First Army's Coutances–Caumont objective line. U.S. forces there would outflank St. Lô on the west and threaten the city from that direction. Reaching Pont-Hébert, about half way to the objective, would be enough to indicate this menace to the Germans, and at that point the troops on the corps left were to launch their attack east of the Vire.[23]

The XIX Corps was commanded by Maj. Gen. Charles H. Corlett. A West Pointer whose quiet manner inspired confidence and who had a knack of getting the most from sometimes difficult subordinates, General Corlett had participated in operations on Attu and had led the 7th Division in the successful Marshall Islands campaign in the Pacific. Sent to the European theater as an expert in amphibious warfare, he had brought the XIX Corps from England to France in June.[24]

General Corlett controlled two divisions: the 30th Infantry on the corps right was to make the attack on 7 July to seize the high ground immediately west of St. Lô; the 29th Infantry was to attack later east of the Vire and directly toward St. Lô. The 35th Infantry Divi-

---

[23] Ltr, Corlett to OCMH, 19 Jan 54; XIX Corps FO 4, 2 Jul (rescinding FO 4, 28 Jun).

[24] Ltr, Corlett to OCMH, 2 Sep 53; see Philip A. Crowl and Edmund G. Love, *Seizure of the Gilberts and Marshalls*, UNITED STATES ARMY IN WORLD WAR II (Washington, 1955).

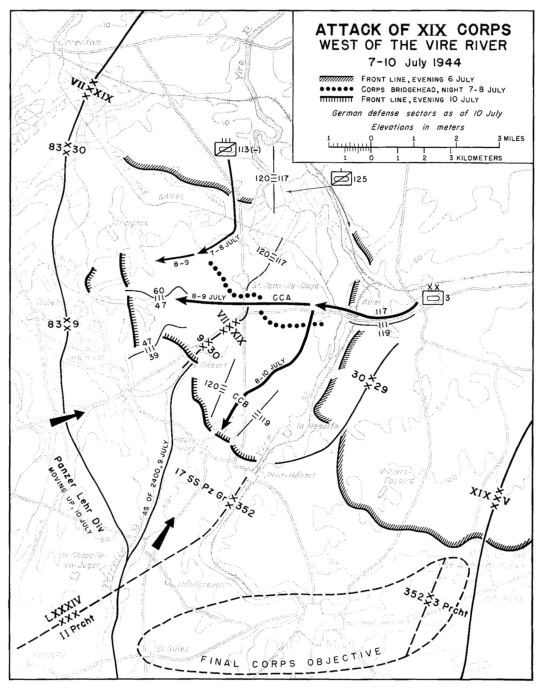

ATTACK OF XIX CORPS
WEST OF THE VIRE RIVER
7-10 July 1944

⬚⬚⬚⬚⬚	FRONT LINE, EVENING 6 JULY
••••••	CORPS BRIDGEHEAD, NIGHT 7-8 JULY
⫿⫿⫿⫿	FRONT LINE, EVENING 10 JULY

German defense sectors as of 10 July

Elevations in meters

VII XXIX

83 X 30

113 (−)

120 ☰ 117

125

7-8 JULY

8-9

120 ☰ 117

St. Jean-de-Daye

60 ⫼⫼⫼ 47

8-9 JULY   CCA

XX 3

83 X 9

47 ⫼⫼⫼ 39

VIII XXIX

9 X 30

8-10 JULY

117 ⫼⫼⫼ 119

120 ☰ CCB ⫼⫼⫼ 119

30 X 29

Panzer Lehr Div
MOVING UP, 10 JULY

AS OF 2400, 9 JULY

17 SS Pz Gr X 352

Pont-Hébert

XIX X V

LXXXIV
XXX
II Prcht

352 X 3 Prcht

FINAL CORPS OBJECTIVE

MAP 5

sion, in the process of arriving in France, was soon to join the XIX Corps for commitment either east or west of the Vire, depending upon the development of the offensive. It was rumored that Corlett was also to receive an armored division for employment west of the Vire, but no confirmation had come through by 7 July.[25]

To bring up his right, General Corlett had to take a large and difficult step. His forces had to advance about nine miles across moist bottomland rising gradually toward the ridge west of St. Lô. The operations were to take place in an area six miles wide, between the Taute and Vire Rivers, which flow north in parallel channels to Carentan and Isigny, respectively. Connecting the two rivers was the Vire et Taute Canal, a shallow east–west waterway joining Carentan and Airel. The canal marked the forward positions at the beginning of July.

The 30th Division, which held these positions, had arrived in Normandy in mid-June. Most of the division was still untested in battle. Its commander, Maj. Gen. Leland S. Hobbs, who had led the division since 1942, was known to be intensely intolerant of persons he suspected of inefficiency.

All three regiments of the 30th Division were in the line and deployed in an arc along the Vire et Taute Canal and the Vire River. The 120th Infantry held the north bank of the canal, the 117th and 119th Regiments the east bank of the river near Airel. The first problem facing General Hobbs in the forthcoming attack was how to get across the

GENERAL CORLETT

water barrier and establish a bridgehead easily reinforced and expanded.

The gently sloping banks of the Vire et Taute Canal were only twenty feet apart, and the water in some places was shallow enough to be waded. Nevertheless, a muddy bottom made fording treacherous, and the adjacent terrain was completely open marshland. North of the canal the soft ground between Carentan and Isigny was not suitable for concentrating heavy equipment and large numbers of supporting troops. Two roads had originally crossed the canal, a country road near the Taute River and a tarred highway closer to the Vire, but the bridges had been destroyed.

The Vire River south of the juncture with the canal, at Airel, had steep banks eight feet high. The river in July was 60 feet wide and the water from 9 to 14 feet deep. Low, flat, and exposed fields

400 yards in width bordered the Vire on each side, but the land was relatively dry. East of the river the ground was firm and had a well-surfaced road network. Where a highway crossed the river near Airel, an arched stone bridge was only slightly damaged.

Although the size of the canal made it a less obvious obstacle, the river offered several positive advantages for an assault crossing. Getting across the 60-foot river in assault boats was likely to be quicker and less costly than wading the canal. The Germans had flooded both waterways, but their efforts at the Vire were less efficacious. The road network east of the river was better than that north of the canal, and the damaged stone bridge at Airel could be easily repaired. There was little cover and concealment in either of the two areas.

The logical immediate objective of forces establishing a bridgehead was a road intersection near St. Jean-de-Daye, a crossroads equidistant—about three miles—from the canal and the river. The fact that artillery and infantry weapons could support a crossing of either the river or the canal with equal effectiveness influenced General Hobbs' decision to make a two-pronged attack across both water barriers. The division was to move from the north across the canal and from the east across the river to seize a bridgehead defined by the roads that intersected south of St. Jean-de-Daye. Once in possession of the bridgehead, the division would move south to the high ground west of St. Lô.

To cross the Vire River in the division main effort, General Hobbs selected the 117th Infantry (Col. Henry E.

Kelly), a regiment that had demonstrated river crossings at The Infantry School, Fort Benning, Georgia. The 117th Infantry was to move across the open terrain at the edge of the river just before daybreak and at dawn was to embark in assault boats several hundred yards north of the Airel stone bridge. Three assault waves were to be ferried across the river on a 400-yard front while bridges were being prepared to accommodate the rest of the troops. If the bridges were not ready at the end of the third assault wave, the infantry was to continue crossing in boats until enough bridges were placed to permit foot and vehicular passage. Upon reaching the far shore, the infantry was to clear the hamlet at the western end of the Airel bridge, get astride the road leading west, and move uphill toward the St. Jean-de-Daye crossroads. As soon as the entire regiment was across the river, Col. Alfred V. Ednie's 119th Infantry was to follow.

At the canal, Col. Hammond D. Birks was to send the 120th Infantry across the water on foot in the early afternoon of the day of attack. The crossing site was to be at the destroyed bridge on the highway leading south to St. Jean-de-Daye. The land was sufficiently dry for about 400 yards on each side of the bridge site to permit deploying two battalions abreast. After wading the canal, the battalions were to drive south. In the wake of the infantry, Col. William S. Biddle's 113th Cavalry Group was to cross and turn west toward the Taute River to protect the 30th Division's right flank. The third battalion of the 120th Infantry was to remain on the north bank of the canal at the country road near the Taute

River. Designated as the corps reserve, the battalion was to support the regimental crossing by fire, make a crossing feint of its own, and check any German attempt to make a countercrossing.[26]

As in almost all opposed bridgehead operations, much depended upon the work of the division engineers, in this case the 105th Engineer Combat Battalion (Lt. Col. Carroll H. Dunn). In addition to assisting the infantry with demolitions, flame throwers, and mine removal, the engineers had major assignments at both the river and the canal.[27]

At the river the engineers were to blow gaps for infantry passage through the last hedgerow before the water. They were to supply 40 assault boats and crews of four men per boat. Three men of each crew were to paddle the boats across while the fourth remained on the east bank to pull the boat back by rope for the next wave. To help the infantrymen mount the steep bank on the far side, the engineers were to build scaling ladders with special hooks.

In addition, the division engineers, with the help of corps engineers, were to span the river with a variety of bridges. First priority was given to a footbridge; next, a ponton infantry support bridge was to be placed across the river to permit the organic division vehicles to cross. Afterwards, a floating treadway was to be installed and the stone bridge at Airel was to be repaired for the heavy vehicular traffic of the armor and artillery units. When all

three vehicular bridges were in operation, General Hobbs planned to use the stone structure and the treadway for one-way traffic moving west into the bridgehead, the ponton bridge for traffic moving east out of it.

At the canal the engineers were to lay duckboards as footbridges for the men of the heavy weapons companies and also for the litter bearers evacuating casualties. Medical planners expected long hand-carry hauls at both the river and the canal because the lack of existing vehicular bridges and the absence of cover in the areas bordering the water precluded the use of jeeps fitted with litter racks.[28] For eventual vehicular passage at the canal the engineers were to install a section of treadway bridging and repair the destroyed structure at the crossing site.

American G-2 officers expected both crossings to meet strong resistance. Intelligence indicated three regimental-sized organizations deployed between the Taute and Vire Rivers: a regiment of the *17th SS Panzer Grenadier Division,* three battalions of the *275th Division* formed into *Kampfgruppe Heinz,* and elements of the *266th Division* supported by troops of the *352d Division* organized into *Kampfgruppe Kentner*— all under the local operational control of the panzer grenadiers, which in turn functioned under *LXXXIV Corps.* German tanks had not been noted in the region, but an assault gun battalion with about three dozen 75-mm. and 105-mm. pieces in support of the infantry had been observed. Occupying ground that rises gradually toward the south, the Germans had good observa-

[26] Field orders of the division and the regiments in the 30th Div G-3 Jnl File.

[27] 105th Engr C Bn Plan "C," 29 Jun, 30th Div G-3 Jnl File; 105th Engr C Bn Traffic Circ Plan and Overlay, 5 Jul, AAR, Jul; 105th Engr C Bn Hist, Feb 42–15 Nov 45, Vol. II.

[28] XIX Corps Office of the Surgeon AAR, Jul.

tion of the entire area. They had rested, reorganized, and increased their supply levels during several weeks of inactivity, and had maintained a strong counterreconnaissance screen that inhibited American patrolling. Their probable course of action, as judged by intelligence, was to be a tenacious defense employing strong local counterattacks.[29]

This estimate, in marked contrast with the optimistic appraisals made several days earlier by the VII and VIII Corps, was in error. Whereas the two U.S. corps on the First Army right had underestimated the opposition, the XIX Corps overestimated the German strength.

The XIX Corps had actually faced strong German forces on 3 July. An attack between the Taute and the Vire on that date would have met a considerable force of German reserves. The SS panzer grenadier regiment in full force, supported by *Kampfgruppe Heinz,* would have opposed the water crossings; the *353d Division* would have contributed units for a counterattack; and the *15th Parachute Regiment* near Périers and the *2d SS Panzer Division* near St. Lô would have been available for commitment.

By 7 July, however, almost the entire SS panzer grenadier division was fighting on the Carentan–Périers isthmus. The *353d Division* and the *15th Parachute Regiment* were engaged on Mont Castre and at la Haye-du-Puits. The *2d SS Panzer Division* was largely committed at la Haye-du-Puits and north of Périers. *Kampfgruppe Kentner* was east of the

Vire and a part of the *II Parachute Corps.* Thus, the only units ready to oppose the 30th Division between the Taute and the Vire were *Kampfgruppe Heinz* and a small part of the SS panzer grenadiers. These forces nevertheless possessed positive advantages in superior observation and terrain readily adaptable to defense.[30]

To overcome the expected resistance, General Hobbs called upon a tremendous amount of fire power. Dive bombers were to blast the German positions and potential routes of reinforcement. An elaborate artillery plan (drawn by Brig. Gen. George Shea, the XIX Corps Artillery commander) utilized the division artillery, the corps artillery, and the artillery of a nearby armored division. In all, eight field artillery battalions, including one of 8-inch howitzers, were to augment the organic division artillery. In addition, the 92d Chemical and the 823d Tank Destroyer Battalions were to deliver indirect fire. All buildings suspected of housing enemy strongpoints were to be destroyed. A rolling or creeping barrage was to precede the foot troops, the fire to advance 100 yards every five minutes. "Hug the artillery barrage," General Hobbs instructed his subordinate commanders, "it will carry us through."[31]

In preparing to execute the plan, the division applied itself to perfecting the techniques of getting across the water. The 117th Infantry conducted practice

---

[29] XIX Corps AAR, Jul, G-2 Per Rpt 22, 6 Jul, and Intel Annex to FO 5, 7 Jul.

[30] Hodgson, R-54.

[31] 30th Div, Notes for Div and Unit Comdrs, 2 Jul, 30th Div G-3 Jnl File; 30th Div AAR, Jul; 30th Div Arty AAR, Jul; the division and the regimental field orders; 3d Armored Div G-3 Per Rpt 13, 7 Jul.

crossings, and each officer and noncommissioned leader in the regiment studied the terrain and the plan on a large sand table model of the area. The engineers practiced the details of bridge construction, made ready the assault boats, and assembled the required equipment. At the same time, the bulk of the division studied and practiced hedgerow tactics. General Hobbs emphasized the necessity of achieving close infantry, armor, and engineer co-ordination. He stressed the need to keep moving. Since bunching up or building up a firing line along a hedge or a landmark was an "invitation for casualties," he insisted on extended formations.

During their training period the men found that the light machine gun was not the best weapon to support infantry attacks in the hedgerows. They discovered that two 15-pound charges of TNT in burlap bags opened a gap in a hedgerow bank large enough for a tank. Learning that without demolition 50 percent of the hedgerow dikes could be breached by engineer tank dozers, the division attached dozers to the tank units. The men were reminded that the Germans particularly feared white phosphorus shells, which were highly effective against hedgerow positions. They were instructed to use the bazooka as more than a antitank weapon since its rocket head, when employed in high-angle fire and against a hard object, was almost as effective against personnel as the 60-mm. mortar shell.

The division also studied the lessons of its first minor combat action a few weeks earlier. The troops determined that the proper way to advance was to locate the enemy's main line of resistance, then drive to it and roll it up from

the flank, neutralize it, or bypass it. This would eliminate the necessity of feeling out every hedge in the kind of slow deliberate advance that increased the effectiveness of the enemy's prearranged fires. But applying the technique was not easy. The excellent German camouflage made it extremely difficult to find the enemy positions. So inclement was the weather between 25 June and 7 July that not one aerial photographic mission could be flown.[32]

The 30th Division completed its attack preparations during the first days of July. The attached 743d Tank Battalion reported all its tanks—52 mediums and 17 light—ready for combat; the engineers made known their readiness; the infantry seemed to be set. General Hobbs was satisfied that the division would make a good showing.[33]

On the morning of 7 July it rained. All air strikes were canceled. The artillery observation planes remained on the ground.

At 0300 one battalion of the 117th Infantry moved out of its assembly area one mile east of the Vire River.[34]   Low

---

[32] 30th Div Memo, Inf Tk Coordination, 2 Jul, 30th Div G–3 Jnl File; XIX Corps Draft Memo, 4 Jul, XIX Corps G–3 Jnl File; G–2 Sec, German Organization of Defense, Villiers-Fossard, 4 Jul, XIX Corps AAR, Jul; [Garth], St.-Lô, p. 7.

[33] 743d Tk Bn Msg, 2 Jul; 105th Engr C Bn Rpts, 1 and 2 Jul; Telecons, Corlett and Hobbs, 4 Jul. All in 30th Div G–3 Jnl File.

[34] The following account is taken from the official records of the division. The division G–3 Journal is a rich source of recorded telephone conversations and has been used extensively. [Garth], St.-Lô, pp. 9–14, and Hewitt, Story of 30th Division, pp. 26ff, give good detailed accounts of the action, the former from the point of view of the small units involved, the latter from that of the division headquarters. Also of use were: XIX Corps Msgs to FUSA, 7 Jul, FUSA G–3 Jnl File; 30th Div AAR, Jul; and CI 94 (30th Div).

clouds obscured the moon. A drizzling rain fell. Fog hovered over the ground. The brush dripped moisture, and the earth became mud. The corps artillery began its preparation at 0330 by firing on distant targets. Forty-five minutes later the division artillery, tank destroyers, and 4.2-inch mortars began to fire at close-in enemy installations and troop concentration areas. At the line of departure—the last hedgerow before the river—engineer guides met the two infantry assault companies at 0430. Picking up their rubber assault boats and scaling ladders, the infantrymen and engineers moved through holes already blasted in the hedgerow and walked along prepared paths to the water. Organized into groups of twelve, the men carried their craft in addition to their weapons, ammunition, and combat packs. They slid down the slick clay bank and lowered their boats into the stream. Because of the sharp angle of launching, most of the craft shipped some water. The riflemen climbed aboard; the men of the weapons platoons placed their mortars and machine guns in the boats and swam alongside to avoid swamping them.

Shortly after 0430, as artillery shells slammed into the ground ahead, the first assault wave of thirty-two boats crossed the Vire River. Ten minutes later the men were scrambling up the bank on the far side and heading for the first hedgerow in enemy territory. A single hostile machine gun opened fire. As the engineers on the east bank of the river began pulling on their ropes to haul the boats back, enemy artillery and mortar shells began crashing into the stream. Under this shelling the second

and third infantry assault waves paddled across the river.

As the first assault wave pulled away from the near shore, the first critical task of the supporting engineers began—installing a footbridge. Having carried preconstructed sections of the footbridge to the edge of the water, a platoon of engineers had installed six bays when enemy artillery struck the bays and a group of engineers carrying additional duckboard sections. The shells killed four men and wounded four. Though the platoon repaired the bays and set them in place again, enemy artillery tore the bridge loose from its moorings and wounded several more men. Doggedly, the engineers swam into the river to secure the bridge again. About 0600 the footbridge at last was in. Assault boats no longer were needed for the crossing. In the process, the engineer platoon had lost about twenty men, half its strength.

On the far shore, the two leading rifle companies moved quickly to the southwest across the hedgerowed fields for a thousand yards. A rifle company that had landed in the second wave moved south against the hamlet on the west side of the Airel bridge and took it after a short, sharp engagement. By about 0830, the first battalion of the 117th Infantry to cross had met strong but scattered resistance and was astride its axis of advance, ready to drive west to the St. Jean-de-Daye road intersection.

On the near bank of the Vire, engineers continued their bridging efforts. At 0700 they removed bodies and a wrecked truck from the Airel bridge and began demining the stone structure and its eastern approaches. Harassing rifle

STONE BRIDGE AT AIREL

fire ceased after American infantrymen cleared the hamlet across the river. An engineer officer and six men began to repair the two large holes in the bridge roadbed. Though this provided sufficient space for jeeps to make a careful crossing, the bridge had to be capable of bearing heavier traffic—the tank battalion attached to the division had been given first priority for use of the bridge. Under fire from enemy mortars and artillery, which smoke shells fired by the division artillery failed to discourage, a small engineer group maneuvered two trucks fitted with special Brockway bodies to the river. These vehicles not only carried treadway sections but also had hydraulic booms to lift the tread-

ways off and set them in place. Heaving and prying six tons of steel into place, the engineers laid the treadways over the damaged span and by 0900 had covered the gaps in the roadway. The operation took thirteen minutes. Five minutes later a bulldozer crossed the stone bridge and cleared rubble from the streets of the hamlet while engineers swept the western approaches for mines. Vehicles soon began to cross.

At 0730 another group of engineers had started constructing an infantry support bridge for the vehicles organic to the division. They completed it in an hour at a cost of fifteen casualties from enemy artillery fire. Another engineer crew commenced work at 0845 on a floating treadway bridge, which was in place by noon.

The efforts of the engineers gave the division one footbridge and the three planned vehicular entrances into the bridgehead, two of which were capable of sustaining heavy traffic. Without these bridges, the infantry on the far bank might have been unable to sustain offensive operations for long.[35]

All three battalions of Colonel Kelly's 117th Infantry were across the Vire River before 1000 on 7 July. Meeting scattered delaying action from *Kampfgruppe Heinz,* the regiment advanced west toward St. Jean-de-Daye.[36] At 1015 a battalion of Colonel Ednie's 119th Infantry crossed the Airel bridge and moved to protect the left flank of the bridgehead. Tanks and tank destroyers began rolling across about noon.

As the Vire River bridgehead broadened, Colonel Birks prepared to launch the 120th Infantry across the Vire et Taute Canal at 1330. When artillery turned an increased volume of fire on the German positions along the canal just before the scheduled jump-off time, plans temporarily went awry. Instead of wading the canal as instructed, the assault companies decided to wait for engineers to install footbridges. The engineers, having miscalculated the width of the waterway, found it difficult to lay their duckboards. Confusion developed at the line of departure, an occurrence furthered by incoming enemy artillery, mortar, and small arms fire.

About fifteen minutes late, the leading men of the two attacking battalions finally plunged into the canal to launch their advance south along the highway toward St. Jean-de-Daye.

During the afternoon all six battalions on the far side of the water obstacles— three from the 117th Infantry, one from the 119th, and two from the 120th— attempted to establish mutual contact and set up a consolidated position at the crossroads. New to the hedgerow fighting, the men of the 30th Division found that attaining their objectives was no simple task. The men soon discovered how difficult it was in actuality to locate the enemy positions, how hard it was to maintain communications, how easy it was to get lost, how much depended on the individual initiative of the commanders of small units.

Rain added to problems of restricted observation in the hedgerows, and there was little effective infantry-artillery coordination on 7 July. Early in the morning General Hobbs himself canceled the rolling artillery barrage when he noted that the infantry could not keep pace with it. Inspection later revealed that the barrage was wasteful. Firing for five minutes each on lines arbitrarily drawn a hundred yards apart meant that rounds struck the enemy hedgerow positions only by chance. The 4.2-inch mortars, participating in the barrage, fired about 2,100 shells, so much ammunition that expenditures were restricted for the remainder of the month.[37]

---

[35] Engr Sitreps and Engr Sec Jnl, XIX Corps AAR, Jul; 105th Engr C Bn Annual Hist, 1944, Incl 3 (photographs of typical bridge installations); ETOUSA Engr Hist Rpt 10, Combat Engineering (Aug 45), pp. 106–08.

[36] *Seventh Army KTB* (Draft), 7 Jul.

[37] Although there had been some discussion of attaching heavy mortar companies to the infantry regiments for better close support, the use of chemical mortars to support an infantry attack was judged to be "a most unusual role." The

All afternoon Colonel Birks kept calling for commitment of the third battalion of the 120th Infantry into the bridgehead. The corps commander would not release the battalion from reserve positions on the north bank of the Vire et Taute Canal until Colonel Biddle's 113th Cavalry Group had crossed the canal and secured the 30th Division right flank. The cavalry could not cross the canal until the engineers spanned the water with a treadway bridge. The engineers could not put in the bridge because the site was under constant enemy artillery fire. After waiting impatiently for several hours, General Hobbs finally commanded the engineers to disregard the enemy fire and set the bridge in place. Less than an hour later the bridge was in. Pleased, General Hobbs remarked that he "knew it could be done if they had guts." He ordered Colonel Birks to "pour that cavalry over." [38]

Before the cavalry could cross, a traffic jam developed as three tank platoons entered the bridgehead to support the infantry. Not until two hours later, at 2030, could Colonel Biddle begin to move his 113th Cavalry Group across the bridge, an operation that took five and a half hours. Enemy harassing fire and intermingling vehicles of several units impeded the crossing. The narrow roads, originally in poor condition, worsened under the rain and the weight of the heavy vehicles. The single bridge across the canal was inadequate for the main supply route where reinforcements and supplies flowed in one direction while casualties moved in the other. Using bulldozers to fill the canal with earth, the engineers completed a second vehicular crossing site just before midnight. [39]

The traffic congestion at the Vire River was worse. The division had planned to use the stone bridge and the treadway for one-way traffic into the bridgehead, the infantry support bridge for casualties and traffic moving east. Early in the afternoon, as a half-track and trailer were crossing the infantry support bridge, an enemy shell scored a direct hit. The half-track and trailer sank and fouled the ponton structure, and efforts to raise the vehicles and repair the bridge during the afternoon and evening were unsuccessful. This left but two vehicular bridges at Airel, both targets of interdictory shelling. Under the direction of impatient commanders, personnel and supplies trickled across the structures while the roads became more and more congested and the bridge approaches jammed. As engines labored, tires churned and men cursed.

The six battalions in the bridgehead paused to rest and reorganize several hundred yards short of the crossroads in the late afternoon of the rain-soaked day. During the evening they established mutual contact, a continuous line, and a consolidated position overlooking the

heavy mortar companies remained for the moment under artillery control, but by August opinion definitely characterized the heavy mortar as an area weapon that "should be employed in close support of infantry troops." 30th Div Arty AAR, Jul; XIX Corps Cml Sec Jnl, XIX Corps AAR, entries 8, 13, 14, 18 Jul; 12th AGp Immed Rpts 26 and 29, 10 and 28 Aug.

[38] Telecons, Corlett, Hobbs, Birks, and Dunn, 7 Jul, 30th Div G–3 Jnl File; 120th Inf S–3 Rpt, 7 Jul; Msg from Lt Col Walter M. Johnson, 2215, 7 Jul, XIX Corps G–3 Jnl and File.

[39] XIX Corps Engr Sec Msg, 2230, 7 Jul, and 113th Cav Gp Msg, 0245, 8 Jul, XIX Corps G–3 Jnl and File.

road intersection. Although General Corlett wanted the division to continue the attack after nightfall to secure the crossroad objective, General Hobbs persuaded him that exerting pressure by active and aggressive patrolling would suffice.[40]

The 30th Division had failed to take its objective, but it had made a significant advance on its first day of attack with less than 300 casualties.[41] So successful was the river crossing that even before the assault was made across the canal it was rumored that the armored division earlier predicted for the XIX Corps would be forthcoming for employment in the bridgehead. That afternoon General Corlett thought that if he did get the armored division, he would put it across the Vire, pass it through the infantry, and direct it south to the corps objective, the ridge west of St. Lô.[42]

That evening the rumor became fact. General Bradley had decided that if only a light enemy screen protected the ground between the Vire and the Taute Rivers, as seemed likely, armored commitment in the bridgehead was in order.[43] Ten minutes after General Corlett learned that General Bradley had attached the 3d Armored Division to XIX Corps, Corlett was telling the armored division commander to cross the Vire River at Airel, move southwest through the 30th Division, and make a "powerdrive" toward the high ground west of St. Lô. The 30th Division was to follow rapidly in support.[44]

Not long afterwards, contingents of armor were moving toward the stone bridge at Airel. Although the two corps on the First Army right wing appeared halted, it looked as though the XIX Corps between the Taute and the Vire had only begun to advance. If this development were exploited adroitly, the entire First Army offensive might pick up speed.

---

[40] Telecon, Corlett and Hobbs, 7 Jul, 30th Div G-3 Jnl File.

[41] Lt. Col. Arthur H. Fuller of the 117th Infantry received the DSC.

[42] Telecons, Corlett and Hobbs, 1255 and 1725, 7 Jul, 30th Div. G-3 Jnl File.

[43] Telecon, Col Charles W. West and Col Richard W. Stephens, 1750, 7 Jul; FUSA Msg to XIX Corps, 1815, 7 Jul, XIX Corps G-3 Jnl File; [Garth]. St.-Lô, p. 17.

[44] XIX Corps FO 5, 1900, 7 Jul (confirming verbal orders), and Special Map "A"; Ltr, Corlett to OCMH, 19 Jan 54, OCMH Files.

CHAPTER VI

The Attempt To Exploit

The comparative ease with which the bridgehead between the Taute and the Vire Rivers was established on 7 July indicated to Americans and Germans alike the existence of a soft spot in the German defenses. With only *Kampfgruppe Heinz* and a small part of the *17th SS Panzer Grenadier Division* defending the area, the Americans were close to achieving a breakthrough. Hausser, the *Seventh Army* commander, shifted a mobile (bicycle) brigade of light infantry and a reconnaissance battalion westward across the Vire River out of the *II Parachute Corps* sector. This could be only an expedient, a stopgap measure, for obviously the troops were not strong enough, nor the defensive attitude that their commitment implied sufficient, to stop expansion of the bridgehead. What the Germans needed was a counterattack by strong forces to demolish the bridgehead and restore the positions along the canal and the river.

Panzer Lehr, an armored division recently in defensive positions near Caen, seemed to Kluge and Rommel an obvious choice. Having just been replaced by a newly arrived infantry division, *Panzer Lehr* was scheduled to go into the *Panzer Group West* reserve and strengthen Eberbach's zone defense. The division was the only strong force available for transfer to the *Seventh Army* front to counterattack the American bridgehead.

Since shifting the division across the front from the vicinity of Caen to the area west of St. Lô would take several days, the Germans had to preserve the conditions that still made a counterattack feasible. They had to find strong forces that were closer to the threatened area and available for immediate commitment. They settled on the *2d SS Panzer Division,* most of which already was battling the VII and VIII Corps. Although Kluge realized that drawing part of the SS armored division away from the *Seventh Army* left might weaken the west flank defenses beyond repair, Rommel pointed out that the Taute and Vire situation was much more critical. American success between the two rivers had created a minor penetration that, if exploited, might well invalidate the German policy of holding fast. Kluge reluctantly agreed. He approved the plan to send part of the *2d SS Panzer Division* eastward across the Taute to hold until the *Panzer Lehr Division,* moving westward across the Vire, could arrive to counterattack and demolish the bridgehead.[1]

The Americans, for their part, having judged the probable German course correctly, hastened to exploit their success

---

[1] Telecons, 1610, 1910, 1930, 2005, and 2020, 7 Jul, *AGp B KTB; Seventh Army KTB* (Draft), 7 Jul.

GERMAN BICYCLE BRIGADE

before the enemy could act.[2] Hopeful that the First Army offensive was at last about to move with dispatch, but also looking to the lesser goal of shoring up the bridgehead against counterattack, General Bradley gave XIX Corps the 3d Armored Division, which had been in the army reserve.[3] Unwilling to dictate the details of commitment, General Bradley simply instructed General Cor-

lett to support the 30th Division with the armored division.

General Corlett had definite ideas of his own. He wanted to get the 3d Armored Division across the Vire, pass it through the 30th Division, and advance rapidly to the south to seize and hold the high ground west of St. Lô. Unfortunately, it was difficult to translate the desire into action, for General Corlett was severely ill and confined to bed at his command post for several days. He telephoned the armored division commander, Maj. Gen. Leroy H. Watson, in the late afternoon of 7 July and instructed him to cross the Vire River as soon as he could and then drive south. "How far do you want me to go?" General Watson asked. "The Germans have little or nothing over there," the corps commander replied, "just keep going."

---

[2] See, for example, the 3d Armd Div CCB G-2 Daily Narrative, 7–16 Jul.

[3] The official records of the units involved have been supplemented by letters to OCMH from General of the Army Omar N. Bradley, 16 Mar 54; Maj Gen Charles H. Corlett (Ret.), 19 Jan 54; Maj Gen Leroy H. Watson (Ret.) (CG, 3d Armd Div), 22 Feb 54; Maj Gen Leland S. Hobbs (Ret.), 5 Mar 54; and Brig Gen John J. Bohn (Ret.) (CG, CCB, 3d Armd Div), 14 Jan 54. All in OCMH Files. [Garth], St.-Lô, presents an excellent narrative of the events described below.

Thus, at the beginning of the new phase of action between the Taute and the Vire, clarity of aims was lacking. The army commander envisioned a build-up of the bridgehead forces with armor; the corps commander foresaw a limited exploitation to the ridge west of St. Lô; the armored division commander understood that he was to make an unlimited drive to the. south. The incompatibility of intent led to some confusion that was the beginning of increasing disorder.

Although General Corlett had known for some time that the armored division might be attached to his corps, illness prevented him from personally directing its commitment. To help him with the operation, Maj. Gen. Walton H. Walker, commander of the XX Corps, which had not yet been committed to action, temporarily acted as Corlett's representative.

General Watson was surprised by the sudden news of his impending commitment. He had not been informed beforehand of the corps objectives and plans, nor had he discussed with Generals Corlett and Hobbs such arrangements as co-ordinating artillery fires, constructing additional bridges, facilitating the entry of the division into the bridgehead, providing passage through the 30th Division, or determining routes of advance. Guessing that General Corlett intended to commit the entire armored division, which happened actually to be the case, Watson decided to send one combat command across the river first.

General Watson's force was one of the two "old-type" armored divisions in the European theater. Both had been in England preparing for the invasion when a new table of organization, effective September 1943, had triangularized the armored division and reduced its size to make it less cumbersome and more maneuverable. Because reorganizing the two divisions in England might have delayed their battle readiness, they had retained their original organization. In contrast with the new and smaller armored divisions, the 3d Armored Division possessed two combat commands instead of three, 232 medium tanks instead of 168, and with its attached units numbered over 16,000 men instead of 12,000. Powerful, if somewhat unwieldy, the 3d Armored Division was subdivided into twin combat commands, each a strong force easily detached from the whole. Neither Bradley nor Corlett had specified the size of the armored force to be committed west of the Vire River on 7 July, but Watson's decision to commit one combat command as a start was normal.

The armored division had arrived in Normandy late in June. Early plans for July had caused the division to be tentatively alerted for an attack in the VII Corps sector; but because of increasing danger that the Germans might counterattack the army left, east of the Vire River, the division remained in army reserve. Since Combat Command A (CCA) had taken part in a limited objective attack at the end of June, General Watson decided to give Combat Command B (CCB), headed by Brig. Gen. John J. Bohn, the first mission between the Taute and the Vire. In an assembly area east of the Vire River, CCB had been prepared to execute several potential plans of action, among them one based on the assumption that it would attack south after the 30th Division seized St. Jean-de-Daye—exactly the situation the unit was called upon to implement.[4] (*See Map 5.*)

Having been alerted for movement at 1615, 7 July, and having received the march order at 1830, General Bohn led his column toward the Airel bridge. Although he had asked permission to phone General Hobbs to co-ordinate his river crossing with the infantry—wire had been laid to the 30th Division headquarters in anticipation of this kind of emergency—the 3d Armored Division chief of staff assured him that the division staff would take care of all such details. Bohn was to perform under 3d Armored Division control.

General Bohn had quite a task. He had to get 6,000 men in 800 vehicles and 300 trailers, a column over 20 miles long, across a single bridge that was under enemy fire, enter, partially during the hours of darkness, a bridgehead that belonged to another division, and attack a distant objective in strange territory with inexperienced troops.[5]

Since the time length of a combat command column was normally estimated at four hours, and since the Airel crossing site was but five miles from the combat command assembly area, the unit under normal conditions should have been across the Vire River shortly after midnight, 7 July.[6] Conditions on the night of 7–8 July were far from normal. The combat command could use only one road to approach the river, a road that was narrow, rain-soaked, and heavily burdened with other traffic. Maintaining radio silence, the armored force proceeded slowly toward an area that was receiving intermittent enemy artillery fire and becoming increasingly congested with vehicles. The 30th Division alone, attempting to reinforce, supply, and stabilize the bridgehead, was having difficulty maintaining a continuous flow of traffic across the river. Of the three vehicular bridges constructed near Airel, the ponton structure had been knocked out during the afternoon by enemy shells. Of the two remaining—the permanent stone bridge and the floating treadway—one had to carry traffic moving east from the bridgehead. A single bridge was all that was available for CCB, and even that had to be shared with the 30th Division, which was in the process of moving an additional infantry battalion into the bridgehead. With vehicles of both organizations intermingling, the enemy fire falling near Airel further retarding the flow of traffic, and blackout discipline increasing

---

[4] Plan 5 of an undated draft ltr, Bohn to Watson, in compliance with 3d Armd Div FO 2, 2 Jul, 3d Armd Div CCB S–3 Jnl File. Subsequent letters omitted Plan 5. See 3d Armd Div Opn Plan 1, 6 Jul.

[5] CCB consisted of a reconnaissance company and three tank battalions of the 33d Armored Regiment; one battalion and the headquarters of the 36th Armored Infantry Regiment; the 54th and 391st Armored Field Artillery Battalions, each with an attached battery of antiaircraft artillery; a company each of the 83d Reconnaissance Battalion, the 23d Armored Engineer Battalion, the 703d Tank Destroyer Battalion, the 45th Armored Medical Battalion, and the division Maintenance Battalion; and an additional battery of antiaircraft artillery. 3d Armd Div FO 3, 7 Jul; 3d Armd Di-CCB AAR, 7–16 Jul.

[6] This was an estimate given by CCA of the 3d Armored Division on 10 July, based on a speed of 8 miles per hour at night and 12 miles per hour, but with a longer interval between vehicles, during the day. 9th Div G–3 Jnl, 10 Jul; see also CCB March Table, 29 Jul, 3d Armd Div CCB S–3 Jnl File.

the difficulties, the combat command did not get its last vehicle across the bridge until long after daybreak on 8 July.

Across the river, the combat command had to find lodgment in a small area crowded with 30th Division troops and closely hemmed in by an active enemy. A tank battalion received enemy small arms and mortar fire as it moved into assembly just south of the Airel–St. Jean-de-Daye road. A reconnaissance company scouting several hundred yards south of the same road ran into a roadblock guarded by enemy infantrymen with machine guns. During the night, minor enemy forces attacked and drove one small armored unit back to the main road. As the men sought places where they could park their tanks and other vehicles west of the Vire, they were harassed by enemy mortar and artillery fire.[7]

To pass one major element through another is always a delicate procedure. Passing the combat command through the 30th Division was to be a frustrating experience. Without reconnaissance on the part of the armored unit and without co-ordination between the combat command and the infantry division, misunderstanding was inevitable.

On the night of 7–8 July the 30th Division had the bulk of its combat troops west of the Vire. One battalion of the 119th Infantry held the left flank, which rested on the Vire River, and another battalion of that regiment was moving into the bridgehead. The three battalions of the 117th Infantry, in the center, occupied positions just short of the

St. Jean-de-Daye crossroads. Two battalions of the 120th Infantry were echeloned to the right along the road between St. Jean-de-Daye and the canal. West of that road as far as the Taute River, about four miles away, the area still had to be cleared by the 113th Cavalry Group, which had followed the 120th Infantry across the canal.

As soon as General Hobbs had learned that the combat command was to enter the bridgehead, he had ordered his troops to clear the main road west of Airel of all unnecessary traffic and give the armor priority of movement. He envisioned the advance of the combat command to the St. Jean-de-Daye road intersection, where the armor would turn left and drive rapidly south along the good highway toward the corps objective, the high ground west of St. Lô. The first part of this action, the advance to the crossroad, would secure the bridgehead objective, which the 30th Division had not taken. The second part, the drive to the south, would provide the infantry division with an armored spearhead. But General Hobbs did not have operational control of Combat Command B.

General Watson, the armored division commander, gave some consideration to this course of action but decided against it. An advance along the Pont-Hébert highway would present an open flank to the enemy between the highway and the Taute, and taking the crossroads and establishing adequate flank protection would involve the armored unit in a task that might delay the movement southward. General Watson therefore directed General Bohn to turn left immediately after crossing the Airel bridge,

---

[7] Msgs, 2337 and 2338, 7 Jul, 3d Armd Div CCB S–3 Jnl and File.

move southwest over a network of un-improved roads and trails, and reach the main highway leading south at a point three miles below the St. Jean-de-Daye crossroads. The division field order and overlay subsequently showed a short arrow pointing generally southwest from the Airel bridge.

There was nothing unusual in send-ing armor over secondary roads or cross-country to outflank or bypass resistance before resuming an advance along the main axis, and General Watson did not think that the combat command would be unduly delayed. The distance to the main highway was between four and six miles. Although the combat com-mand had not made a prior reconnais-sance, the ground was believed lightly held by the enemy. The risk of getting the tanks involved in hedgerow tactics of fighting from one field to the next seemed slight, and the potential compli-cations of pointing the command di-agonally across the zones of two regi-ments of the 30th Division seemed mi-nor.

Another factor that contributed to General Watson's decision on the route of advance was the framework of refer-ence that governed the employment of armor in the Cotentin at this time. The knowledge that German antitank guns were superior to American armor plate produced among American troops an unwholesome respect of all enemy antitank weapons. Perhaps the most effective was the German 88-mm. anti-aircraft gun, which was used also against ground targets. Just as Americans tend-ed to confuse assault guns with tanks, it became general practice to refer to all German antitank guns as 88's—the 75's

as well as the lighter weapons, whether towed or self-propelled. The experi-ence of CCA of the 3d Armored Division at the end of June had specifically indi-cated that tanks could escape the deadly enemy antitank fire by avoiding the roads and trails and advancing cross-country. Directives and memoranda from higher headquarters endorsed the view. The 3d Armored Division train-ing had stressed the techniques of field-to-field movement; rapid advance along the narrow and restricted highways of the hedgerow country and under the sights of well-sited zeroed-in enemy weapons was considered rash, reckless, and ill advised.[8]

General Bohn had divided his com-mand into three task forces—each formed around a reinforced tank battalion—and an administrative element. They were to deploy in column on a thousand-yard front and attack in normal armored manner, the leading task force advancing in two columns along parallel routes. Shortly after daybreak, 8 July, even be-fore all the combat command's units were across the Vire, the leading task force commenced the attack. Without artillery preparation, men and tanks be-gan to move southwest in an area trav-ersed by country roads and hedgerowed lanes.

Almost at once the task force met and destroyed five Mark IV tanks attached to *Kampfgruppe Heinz*. In the ex-change of fire the task force lost one tank. Through this auspicious begin-ning augured well, the task force soon

---

[8] See, for example, XIX Corps Ltr, Notes on Com-bat Experience, 5 Jul, 30th Div G-3 Jnl and File. Unless otherwise noted, the documents cited in this chapter are in the 30th Div G-3 Jnl and File.

CONGESTION AT AIREL BRIDGE

became involved in the kind of tortuous advance that had become typical of offensive action in the hedgerow country. The armor overflowed the narrow trails and entered the fields, making it necessary for demolition teams and engineer bulldozers to breach the hedgerows. Though the task force received two additional dozers and encountered only light resistance, the day's gain totaled only about a mile and a half.[9]

The limited advance was disappointing, particularly since only minor units had come to the aid of *Kampfgruppe Heinz* during the day. General Watson informed General Bohn that the prog-

ress of the combat command was unsatisfactory. Pointing out the "great opportunity" that faced the command and the "good chance of a break through," he urged Bohn to fit his method of advance to the situation. If he found it impossible to go ahead on the roads, he was to move cross-country; if his tanks bogged down in the fields, he was to dispel among his subordinate commanders the "inflexible idea that cross-country progress is essential."[10] Although there was no real difference between methods of advance in this area, General Bohn had emphasized to his

[9] 3d Armd Div CCB S-3 Jnl and File, entries 1100 and 1128, 8 Jul.

[10] On General Watson's lack of clarity over the advantages of cross-country versus road advance, see 12th AGp Immed Rpt 24, 9 Aug.

task force commander the need for speed and had insisted that he use the roads wherever possible. The task force commander had been reluctant or perhaps simply unable to move his men and vehicles out of the fields.

Meanwhile, in the rear areas of the bridgehead there was a disheartening spectacle of confusion, a confusion throttling an orderly development of the bridgehead and the attack. Seven infantry battalions, one tank battalion, and an artillery battalion of the 30th Division; one infantry battalion, three tank battalions, and two artillery battalions of CCB; plus an almost equal number of supporting troops of both units jammed an area of hedgerowed labyrinths scarcely four miles wide and less than three miles deep. To the tankers the fields seemed full of riflemen; to the infantrymen the terrain appeared covered with armor. In this overpopulated morass of mud, tank treads chewed up wire and destroyed communications, while unemployed combat units jostled supply personnel attempting to carry out their functions. Infantrymen ignorant of the armored commitment were surprised by the appearance of tanks, while tankers were indignant when they found infantrymen occupying fields useful as armored assembly areas. Experienced troops might have surmounted the difficulties engendered by restricted space, but both infantrymen and tankers were novices. Nervous soldiers of both units aggravated conditions by firing their weapons wildly in rear areas and on the flanks. Each organization accused the other of stifling the advance.

By striking southwest immediately

after crossing the Vire, the combat command had impinged on the sector of the 119th Infantry. Only after moving forward several miles would the armored unit have created a zone for itself between the 119th and the 117th Regiments. Agreement on this procedure was reached by representatives of armor and infantry at a special conference for co-ordination during the afternoon of 8 July. At the same time, the artillery commanders of the 3d Armored and 30th Divisions were meeting to keep the artillery of one from firing on the troops of the other.[11]

General Hobbs complained bitterly of the presence of the combat command in the bridgehead. He protested that the armor was cluttering up his sector and bogging down his advance. The presence of tanks in his regimental rear areas, he was sure, was preventing artillery, supplies, and men from reaching his forward areas quickly. Promiscuous tank fire, he reported, had caused sixteen casualties in his division. It was impossible, he contended, to protect his troops with artillery fire for fear of striking armored elements. So incensed was he that he ordered his artillery to give the infantry the fire requested "wherever they are, irrespective of armor or anything else." He felt that either the combat command or the infantry division had to be halted, for both could not operate in the restricted area. He was convinced that the 30th Division without CCB would reach the corps objective rapidly, but that CCB without the 30th Division would "never get any-

[11] Memo by Brig Gen William K. Harrison, jr., Coordination CCB, 117th, 119th Inf, 8 Jul, 3d Armd Div CCB S-3 Jnl File.

place." The armored force commander had been "sitting on his fanny all day, doing nothing" and had not "turned a track in 95% of his vehicles all day long." The 3d Armored Division commander had "only a hazy idea" of what was happening. And there were "too many people in the party," too many commanders giving un-co-ordinated orders.[12]

In hope of resolving the situation and introducing unity of command, General Corlett placed the responsibility of the bridgehead operations on General Hobbs. Attaching CCB to the 30th Division on the evening of 8 July, Corlett directed Hobbs to get the armor and the infantry to make a co-ordinated effort to the south. By this time, Hobbs did not want the combat command. He had his own attached tank battalion and tank destroyers, he asserted, and with them he could exploit the breakthrough his infantry had achieved. When Corlett advised that he would have to keep the combat command because it "could not go any place else," Hobbs agreed to let the armor "just trail along." [13]

The combat command was not entirely at fault. While it had not displayed the daring and dash expected of armor, the principal reason for the failure was the hasty, ill-planned, and un-co-ordinated commitment into a bridgehead of inadequate size. Its route of access into the bridgehead had been sharply restricted, its operational space was small, its routes of advance were poorly surfaced and narrow. The road network was deficient, the hedgerows pre-

sented successive, seemingly endless obstacles, and the swampy Cotentin lowland had become even more treacherous and soft because of rain. Operating in a zone that seemed to belong to another unit, men and commanders of the combat command felt like intruders. When they called for fire support from their organic artillery, they had to wait for clearance from the 30th Division Artillery. Attacking on a narrow front, the combat command held the bulk of its strength, useless, in the rear. Separated from its parent headquarters, the armored force received little guidance and encouragement.

Concern over the minor advance and the disorder in the bridgehead had not detracted from another potential hazard. General Corlett had apparently supposed that crossing the Vire et Taute Canal and taking St. Jean-de-Daye would compel the Germans on the east bank of the Taute to withdraw. Counting on light delaying resistance, the corps commander had given Colonel Biddle's 113th Cavalry Group the mission of clearing the area between the 30th Division right flank and the Taute, but opposition on 8 July was so determined that the cavalry troops had had to dismount from their light tanks and armored cars and fight through the hedgerows like infantrymen.[14] Although elements of the 30th Division secured the St. Jean-de-Daye crossroads on 8 July, they did not take le Désert, a few miles to the west. Anticipating the possibility of a counterattack from the Taute River area, General Corlett directed General Watson to send CCA into the bridgehead to protect the right flank. Specifi-

[12] Hobbs Telecons, 2045, 2100, and 2112, 8 Jul.
[13] Telecons, Corlett and Hobbs, 2207 and 2210, 8 Jul.

[14] See [Garth], St.-Lô, pp. 19–20, for the details.

cally, the combat command was to reinforce the calvalry group.

On the afternoon of 8 July, Brig. Gen. Doyle O. Hickey's Combat Command A crossed the Vire and moved west along the main road toward the Taute. Its passage through the bridgehead intensified the congestion. To add to the confusion, the last battalion of the 120th Infantry entered the bridgehead after being replaced along the north bank of the Vire et Taute Canal by a suddenly available battalion of the arriving 35th Division. The battalion of the 120th moved south through St. Jean-de-Daye. When the infantry met and crossed the CCA column, which was moving west, inevitable delays occurred. "Every road is blocked by armor," Hobbs complained.[15]

Although General Hobbs had said he would let CCB trail along after the 30th Division in his attack south on 9 July, General Corlett insisted that he use the armor to spearhead his advance. The objective was no longer the high ground west of St. Lô, which General Corlett felt could not be attained by a quick armored thrust, but instead Hill 91 at Hauts-Vents, a little more than three miles ahead of the combat command.

About 300 feet above sea level and aptly named for the high winds that sweep across it, Hauts-Vents overlooks the Cotentin lowlands as far north as Carentan. It dominates the St. Jean-de-Daye–Pont-Hébert road and commands the Vire River crossing to the east that leads to St. Lô. It would serve as a compromise objective. If CCB

gained Hauts-Vents quickly, General Corlett thought he might then attack St. Lô from the northwest, or perhaps drive farther south to the original corps objective. With these intentions of the corps commander in mind, General Hobbs ordered General Bohn to resume his attack on 9 July, continuing southwest across the St. Jean-de-Daye–Pont-Hébert highway to Hauts-Vents and Hill 91.

On the second day of the attack, 9 July, General Bohn passed his second task force in column through the first. Passage was difficult because of the terrain, but by midmorning the task force was making slow progress across muddy fields and along narrow roads and trails. Only occasional harassing artillery fire came in. The opposition seemed slight. This prompted Hobbs to order Bohn to get the task force out of the fields and on to the roads.

In part, the order was virtually meaningless. The roads in the area were little better than trails—narrow, sunken in many places, and frequently blocked by trees and overhanging hedges. Movement along these country lanes was not much different from cross-country advance, and possibly worse. A fallen tree or a wrecked vehicle could easily immobilize an entire column. Floundering in the mud, fighting the terrain rather than the enemy, the tankers could not advance with true armored rapidity.

The meaning of the order lay not in General Hobbs' directive to get onto the roads but rather in his judgment that the combat command was not acting aggressively enough to get out of the repressive terrain. Although General

---

[15] Telecons, Hobbs and Walker, 1615, 8 Jul, Corlett and Hobbs, 2210, 8 Jul; XIX Corps G–3 Per Rpt 32, 9 Jul.

Bohn had ordered the attacking task force to use the roads in the same sense that Hobbs had meant it, the task force commander had instructed his units to use the "hedgerow method of advance." When Bohn repeated his order and when the task force commander seemed hesitant about carrying it out, Bohn started forward to expedite personally a change in the manner of attack.

Traffic congestion, intensified by intermittent rain, so delayed General Bohn that he did not reach the task force command post until an hour after noon. Reiterating his orders, he told the task force commander to get on the roads and move. In response, the officer demanded with some heat whether General Bohn realized that he was "asking him to go contrary to General Corlett's directives, General Watson's directives, and the rehearsals . . . of the tank-infantry teams." At this point, General Bohn himself took charge of the task force.

While Bohn was attempting to get through the traffic congestion to the task force, General Hobbs was becoming increasingly dissatisfied with the slow progress. Unwilling to suffer longer what appeared to him a clear case of inefficiency, Hobbs sent Bohn an ultimatum: either reach the objective, Hauts-Vents, by 1700, or relinquish command.

General Corlett had also become dissatisfied. Learning at 1400 that the leading task force had advanced only 600 yards in eight hours but had lost not a man or a tank to German fire, Corlett had come to the conclusion that Bohn was not pressing the attack with sufficient vigor. He requested

General Walker, who was assisting because of Corlett's illness, to inform Bohn that if Bohn's relief were recommended, he, Corlett, would have to concur. Walker transmitted the message shortly after Hobbs' ultimatum arrived.

Still impatient to know why CCB was not getting underway, General Hobbs sent his assistant division commander, Brig. Gen. William K. Harrison, jr., to find out. General Harrison reached the task force about 1500; an hour later he was satisfied that General Bohn had the situation well in hand.

With the task force commander still muttering that "it was fatal to get on the roads . . . after all the indoctrination by the Division Commander," General Bohn finally succeeded in reorganizing the task force so that it could move in column along parallel routes without the delay of plowing abreast through the fields. Anxious to give higher headquarters some sign of progress, he directed a tank company to proceed without delay and without pause southwest to the objective. The tank company was to disregard communications with the rear, move to the St. Jean-de-Daye–Pont-Hébert highway, cross the highway, and continue on to Hill 91 at Hauts-Vents.

Eight tanks of the company moved ahead down a narrow country lane in single file, spraying the ditches and hedges with machine gun fire as they advanced. They soon vanished from sight.

One reason higher commanders were so insistent upon getting CCB rolling was their knowledge of the approach of substantial enemy forces: from the west a part of the *2d SS Panzer Division,* an infantry battalion supported by a tank company; from the east the full power of the *Panzer Lehr Division*. Since early morning intelligence officers had been expressing considerable concern about what appeared to be a strong enemy effort in the making, particularly after aerial reconnaissance confirmed the movement of enemy tanks toward the Taute and Vire sector.[16] General Corlett suggested that a screen of bazookas and antitank guns be thrown up close behind the forward troops, and that all artillery units be alerted for action against enemy armor. A rash of rumors spread through the ranks as everyone became acutely conscious of the probability of counterattack. An incipient cloudiness turning into mist and later into drizzling rain obscured the ground, denied further observation, and thwarted air attack on the enemy columns.

Later in the morning on 9 July, small probing elements of a tank-infantry task force of the *2d SS Panzer Division* struck the 30th Division right flank near le Désert. The threat was contained by noontime, and the 30th Division became satisfied that the anticipated German effort had been stopped. Secure in this belief, the division artillery was displacing its headquarters early that afternoon when enemy infantry, tanks, and self-propelled guns again struck the right flank. For more than an hour, during the critical early stages of the German attack, the division artillery operated from its old command post with limited means of communication. Not until the fire-direction center opened at its new location could un-

qualified co-ordination with XIX Corps be achieved. Despite some uncertainty as to the positions of several U.S. infantry units, eighteen artillery battalions took the Germans under fire. The artillery was chiefly responsible for checking the German thrust.[17] More reassuring was the imminent arrival on that day of the 9th Division, which was to secure the 30th Division right flank.[18]

Though beaten back, the counterattack was not without consequences. Pursuing two Mark IV tanks down a country road, a company of the 743d Tank Battalion (attached to the 30th Division) fell into an ambush. German armor with screaming sirens attacked from the flank at close range, and in fifteen minutes the tank company had lost most of its equipment. Three damaged tanks were abandoned; nine tanks and a dozer were destroyed; five men were dead, four wounded, and thirty-six missing. Having lost two tanks to enemy action the previous day, the company now was virtually destroyed.[19]

Although the 30th Division's infantry generally held firm, a few overt acts were enough to cause hysteria among some individuals. Occupying positions several hundred yards ahead of the units on its flanks, an infantry company withdrew to improve its lateral liaison and communications. About the same time, a limited withdrawal by a nearby battalion prompted the erroneous report that an entire regiment was surrounded.

---

[16] See, for example, 83d Div G–2, G–3 Jnl, 1140, 9 Jul.

[17] 30th Div Arty AAR, Jul; XIX Corps Msg 1815, 9 Jul, FUSA G–3 Jnl; *AGp B KTB*, 8, 9, 10 Jul; Telecon, Pemsel to Speidel, 2350, 8 Jul, *AGp B KTB*; *Seventh Army KTB*, 9 Jul.

[18] See below, Ch. VII.

[19] 743d Tk Bn Rpts, 5 and 6, 8 and 9 Jul.

This exaggeration was typical of the uncertainty and the rumors of disaster that spread through the bridgehead during the afternoon. News of the destruction of the tank company fed the apprehension and contributed to a panic that touched about 200 soldiers who were performing close support missions. As soldiers streamed toward St. Jean-de-Daye in small, disorganized groups, two medical collecting stations, a cannon company, and an infantry battalion headquarters, becoming convinced that the enemy had made a penetration, also withdrew, but in good order, to the vicinity of St. Jean-de-Daye. On the basis of these withdrawals, front-line units became concerned about the integrity and disposition of adjacent troops. Several headquarters complained that subordinate units of other headquarters were fleeing in disorder.[20]

At the height of the counterattack, the eight tanks dispatched by General Bohn were proceeding toward the St. Jean-de-Daye–Pont-Hébert highway. Several miles ahead of CCB's leading task force, and angling southwest toward the highway, the tanks were to turn left when they reached the main road. They were then to go several hundred yards south before turning right on a secondary road to the objective, Hauts-Vents. Spraying the hedges and ditches continuously with machine gun fire, the tankers reached the north–south highway. Instead of turning left and south, the company commander in the lead tank turned right and north toward

St. Jean-de-Daye. The other seven tanks in column followed.[21]

In the meantime, just south of the St. Jean-de-Daye crossroads, a company of the 823d Tank Destroyer Battalion had emplaced its 3-inch guns along the main highway. Stragglers falling back on the crossroads told the tank-destroyer crewmen of a breakthrough by German armor, which, the stragglers said, was just a short distance over the hill. Air bursts exploding in the vicinity from unidentified guns seemed to substantiate the reports. A short while later the reports took on added credence when one of the 30th Division's regiments passed on the erroneous information that fifty enemy tanks were moving north on the highway from Pont-Hébert toward St. Jean-de-Daye. Manning their guns and outposting them with bazookas, the tank-destroyer crewmen peered anxiously through the drizzling rain of the foggy afternoon and listened for the sound of tank motors.

They were fully alert when the silhouette of a tank hull nosed over the top of a small rise a thousand yards away. Although there was little doubt that this was the enemy, a tank-destroyer officer radioed his company to ask whether any American tanks were in the area. The reply came at once: nearby armor was German. By then several other tanks had come into view. Firing machine guns and throwing an occasional round of high explosive into the adjacent fields, the tanks moved

---

[20] 30th Div G–3 Jnl, entry 1749, 9 Jul; 3d Armd Div CCB S–3 Jnl, entry 1830, 9 Jul; XIX Corps IG Ltr, Rpt of Investigation of Incident . . . , 13 Jul.

[21] An element of CCA had made a similar mistake at the end of June "because one TF got mixed up on proper use of Slidex and Map Lay." (Penned note, n.d., 3d Armd Div CCB S–3 Jnl and File.) Slidex was a slide-rule type of decoding device.

steadily toward the tank-destroyer positions. There could be no doubt that these were anything but the long-awaited enemy. The tank-destroyer guns opened fire at a range of 600 yards. The first round scored a direct hit on the lead tank.

At this moment General Bohn at the task force command post was trying to get in touch with the tanks he had sent ahead. On the open radio channel he heard a cry of anguish and the voice of the tank-company commander say with awful clarity, "I am in dreadful agony."

Before mutual identification could be established, crews of the tanks and tank destroyers together had sustained about ten casualties. Two tanks were knocked out.[22]

Reversing direction, the six remaining tanks began rolling back down the highway toward Hauts-Vents. Again they disappeared, again they lost communication with Bohn's headquarters. Although the tank radios could transmit, they perversely failed in reception.

General Bohn subsequently succeeded in getting the bulk of his leading task force to the St. Jean-de-Daye–Pont-Hébert highway. By evening the task force was advancing toward the objective. The third task force, having moved west and cross-country in the rear, debouched on the main road and rolled rapidly to the south.

Just as it began to appear that CCB might complete its mission that night, General Hobbs ordered a halt. General Bohn was to set up defensive positions astride the Pont-Hébert road

about a mile short of Hauts-Vents. Although Bohn requested permission to continue—on the consideration not only of weak opposition but also that the armor was at last free of the constricting terrain and could reach Hauts-Vents before dark—Hobbs refused.

General Hobbs had based his decision upon the likelihood that the Germans might continue to counterattack after dark. If the combat command took Hauts-Vents, the division would have to advance in a strong supporting effort. Although the division had sustained less than 300 casualties that day, most of them from enemy artillery fire, Hobbs felt that he needed to reorganize before attempting to attack. He judged that strong defensive positions were more important. Without a supporting advance by infantry, he believed that Combat Command B would be too far in advance at Hauts-Vents for adequate flank and rear protection in an area where enemy strength was manifest. He told Bohn to direct his troops to "button up along the line I gave them and get a good night's rest." [23]

As the combat command assumed the defensive, General Bohn tried to call back the six tanks that had disappeared. Shortly before darkness, the tankers had reported being on the hill objective at Hauts-Vents. A moment later, an air mission, requested earlier but delayed by the bad weather, struck Hauts-Vents in the fading light. Though American pilots strafed the six tanks, the tanks luckily escaped losses. Unable to receive on their faulty radio sets, and ignorant of the order that had halted

---

[22] 2d TD Gp Ltr, Rpt of Investigation, 11 Jul; 823d TD Bn Rpt 15, 9 Jul.

[23] Telecon, Gen Bohn and Lt Col Harold E. Hassenfelt, 2015, 9 Jul.

the main force of CCB, the tankers formed a perimeter in a field at darkness and awaited the arrival of General Bohn and the rest of the force.[24]

The news that six tanks of Combat Command B were on the objective was received at headquarters of both the 30th Division and the XIX Corps with some skepticism. After forty-eight hours of disappointment, it was difficult to believe that the armor had finally reached Hauts-Vents. But since the possibility existed and because there was further uncertainty about the precise positions of the rest of the combat command, the corps and the division artillery had difficulty planning and executing their harassing and interdictory fires for the night. This was the final blow of another day of frustration in the attempt to achieve co-ordination between armor and infantry.[25]

Having warned General Bohn of relief if he did not reach his objective by 1700, General Hobbs removed him from command five hours later. His grounds: the extreme caution that the combat command had displayed in conducting an attack against relatively light opposition. For the lack of aggressiveness throughout the command, he held the senior officer personally responsible. Although Bohn's efforts on the afternoon of 9 July were commendable, he had not secured the co-operation of his subordinate commanders. Even though the limited roads and trails available to the combat command had intensified the problem of regrouping from a

"hedgerow-to-hedgerow" advance to one "down roads and trails," the failure appeared essentially that of command. "I know what you did personally," General Hobbs assured General Bohn, "[but] you're a victim of circumstances." [26]

Under Col. Dorrance S. Roysdon, CCB resumed the attack toward Hauts-Vents soon after daybreak on the third day, 10 July. The six tank crews, after waiting vainly all night for the combat command to join them on the objective, returned at dawn. Had they remained at Hauts-Vents, they would have facilitated the advance of the main body. As it was, congestion on the sunken roads and enemy antitank fire hampered the command almost at once. A destroyed enemy tank blocked movement until bulldozers, maneuvering tortuously on the narrow road, cleared a bypass. The column continued until the destruction of the lead tank by enemy fire again blocked the way. The roads were so jammed with traffic and movement was so slow that Colonel Roysdon requested permission to use the main highway south to Pont-Hébert instead of the minor country roads leading southwest to Hauts-Vents. General Hobbs denied the request, for he wanted to keep the highway open for the 30th Division to attack south once the armor took Hill 91. After a co-ordination conference attended by General Hobbs, General Watson, Colonel Roysdon, and an infantry regimental commander, the combat command, by midmorning, seemed to be moving ahead. "Whatever confusion we had with the armor is reason-

---

[24] 3d Armd Div CCB S–3 Jnl File, entry 2145, 9 Jul; 30th Div G–3 Jnl, Evening Msgs, 9 Jul.

[25] 30th Sig Co Rpt 21, 9 Jul; Telecons, Hobbs and Bohn, 1140, 9 Jul, Hobbs and Ednie, 1910, 9 Jul.

[26] XIX Corps IG Rpt of Investigation in the Relief of Brig Gen John J. Bohn, Jul 44.

ably well ironed out," Hobbs reported. "Roysdon is kicking them along." [27]

The honeymoon was short lived. That afternoon, as the hedgerow terrain and German fire continued to retard the advance, General Hobbs again became discontented. "If Colonel Roysdon doesn't do what he can do, and should have done by noon today," he threatened, he too would have to be relieved of command. Roysdon's "only trouble" was that he "wasn't doing anything." "Please get them out of our hair," Hobbs begged.[28]

In the evening General Corlett decided to detach CCB from the 30th Division as soon as Hill 91 at Hauts-Vents was secured. The infantry division alone would continue to the ridge west of St. Lô, the final corps objective.[29]

By this time, *Panzer Lehr* was moving into the area. Hauts-Vents was no longer undefended and waiting to be occupied. A contingent of CCB did reach the top of Hill 91 on the evening of 10 July, but strong enemy artillery and mortar fire forced withdrawal. Though unsuccessful in seizing and holding the ground, the contingent nevertheless disrupted *Panzer Lehr* preparations for an attack that had been planned to start shortly after midnight.[30]

Combat Command B jumped off again on the morning of 11 July. Enemy antitank guns east of the Vire River knocked out six tanks immedi-ately, but the attack continued. Reaching the crest of Hill 91 once more, men and tanks again had to give way. A second assault, led personally by Colonel Roysdon, finally secured Hauts-Vents during the afternoon. The accomplishment caused Roysdon to characterize the morale of his exhausted troops as "amazing"; his words of praise: "Enough cannot be said." [31]

Earlier in the afternoon General Hobbs had refused an offer by General Corlett of an additional tank battalion. He already had three battalions of CCB, he said, "sitting on their fannies." Not until a day later, with Hill 91 in hand, could Hobbs look at the matter differently. He agreed with Roysdon that the combat command had done a good job, and he regretted his relief of General Bohn. "If he [Bohn] had had a little more of a chance," Hobbs admitted, "he probably would have done the same thing [as Roysdon]." [32]

The entrance of CCB into the bridgehead had resulted in another frustration similar to those on the other active portions of the First Army front. Five days of combat had advanced the XIX Corps right wing only halfway to the ridge west of St. Lô. Great promise of quick success had turned into failure primarily because of the un-co-ordinated commitment of the combat command into restricted operational space. Whether General Bradley had intended only a reinforced tank battalion to enter the

[27] Telecon, Corlett and Hobbs, 1025, 10 Jul.

[28] Telecons, Corlett and Hobbs, 1750 and 1935, 10 Jul.

[29] XIX Corps Ltr of Instrs, 10 Jul; 3d Armd Div CCB FO 5, 11 Jul.

[30] *Seventh Army KTB*, 10 Jul; *Panzer Lehr* FO, 10 Jul, *Pz Lehr Ib KTB*; see below, Ch. VII, for the *Panzer Lehr* attack.

[31] XIX Corps G–3 Per Rpt 35, 12 Jul; 3d Armd Div G–3 Per Rpt 17, 11 Jul, and CCB S–3 Per Rpt, 11 Jul. Capt. George T. Stallings of the 33d Armored Regiment received the DSC for his actions between 8 and 11 July.

[32] Telecons, Hobbs and West, 1310, 11 Jul, Hobbs and Corlett, 0830, 12 Jul.

bridgehead on 7 July, as was later claimed, was an academic question by the morning of 8 July.[33] The entire combat command had crossed the Vire and was on the ground, and that fact was unalterable. Little more could be

done than to hope that the armor would disentangle itself from the congestion and the terrain. An opportunity to make a deep penetration had been missed, for by the time the combat command got free of its external repressions and its internal inhibitions, the Germans had plugged the gap. *Panzer Lehr* was ready to attack.

[33] Interv of Capt Franklin Ferriss with Gen Bohn, 14 Jul 44, in CI 259; Ltr, Eisenhower to Marshall, 27 Jul 44, S–56328, Pogue Files.

CHAPTER VII

The Offensive Continued

By the end of the first week in July events on the battlefield of Normandy had modified German policies to some extent. Hitler, who had depended on the Air Force and the Navy to regain for the German ground forces a favorable balance of build-up and mobility, realized that his reliance on Goering and Doenitz had been misplaced. He turned to his minister of production, Albert Speer, for increased industrial output of war matériel. With more heavy tanks and guns in the field, and with new weapons mass manufactured and distributed—jet-propelled planes, for example, and long-distance snorkel submarines—Hitler felt he might yet smash the Allied beachhead. Still hopeful, he counted on the Army in the west to stall for time, denying the Allies maneuver room and major ports, until eventually the new weapons might be brought to bear. Until then, German commanders in the west were to improve their defenses, disengage their armor from the front and replace tanks with infantry, and mount limited objective attacks and night operations to keep the Allies off balance. Planning for offensive warfare was temporarily discontinued.[1]

The Battle for Caen

In the first week of July the Allies had command of the air, their ground build-up was proceeding favorably, and enemy reinforcements moving toward the front were being delayed. General Eisenhower nevertheless was highly conscious of the unfulfilled need for greater maneuver room, additional ports and airfield sites, and open country "where our present superiority can be used." Troubled by the "slow and laborious" advance of the First Army in the Cotentin—due, he realized, to terrain and weather conditions as much as to enemy resistance—he was worried more by the shallowness of the British sector, where one of the invasion beaches, a reception point for supplies and personnel coming from England, was still under enemy fire. He questioned whether General Montgomery, in his professed zeal to attract enemy forces to his front and away from the American sector, was making sufficient effort to expand the British part of the beachhead. "We must use all possible energy in a determined effort," General Eisenhower wrote Montgomery, "to prevent a stalemate" and to insure against "fighting a major defensive battle with the slight depth we now have" on the Continent.[2]

---

[1] Hitler Ltr, 8 Jul, quoted in *OB WEST* Ltr, 8 Jul, *AGp Ia Fuehrer Befehle;* ONI Fuehrer Conf, 9 Jul; MS # P–069 (Kreipe) ; *OB WEST KTB,* 10 Jul.

[2] Eisenhower to Montgomery, 7 Jul, SGS SHAEF File 381, OVERLORD, I (a) .

"I am, myself, quite happy about the situation," General Montgomery replied. He had maintained Allied initiative, prevented reverses, and set into motion "a very definite plan." Three needs determined Montgomery's operations—the Breton ports, space for maneuver, and destruction of German forces. "Of one thing you can be quite sure," General Montgomery promised; "there will be no stalemate." [3]

While the Americans were struggling in the Cotentin, the British had mounted another effort against Caen. Because in earlier attempts to take the city the British had been unable to mass sufficient artillery to destroy the strong defenses, the planners discussed the use of heavy bombers to deliver preparatory fire for the ground action. In February and March 1944 heavy bombers had launched attacks at Cassino in Italy to assist ground troops, but without notable success, and during June heavy bombers had rendered occasional close support in France by attacking targets that the chief of the RAF Bomber Command sarcastically termed of "immediate and fleeting importance." [4] But there had been no large-scale use of heavy bombers in direct support of the ground troops.

Use of bombers in a direct support role hinged upon the answer to two major questions: Was it justifiable to divert heavy bombers from their main strategic role? Could the planes bomb close enough to the forward line to facilitate the ground advance without unduly exposing the troops to the hazards

of accidental bomb spillage and inaccurate aim? General Eisenhower resolved the first question. He favored using strategic air for tactical ends whenever those ends were important and profitable. Caen, he believed, was important and profitable. [5] Ground and air planning staffs worked out a solution to the second question. A bomb line 6,000 yards (about three and a half miles) ahead of the leading units, they decided, would minimize the danger to friendly ground troops.

For the July attack on Caen, heavy bombers were to saturate a rectangular target, 4,000 by 1,500 yards, on the northern outskirts of the city. The purpose was to destroy both infantry and artillery positions, cut off forward troops from supply, demoralize enemy soldiers in and out of the target zone, and, finally, boost British ground force morale. Field artillery was to cover the gap between the British line and the air target with normal preparation fires. (*Map 6*)

Canadian troops initiated the offensive on 4 July with a preliminary attack designed to secure the western exits of Caen. Three days later, at 2150 on 7 July, 460 planes of the RAF Bomber Command dropped 2,300 tons of high explosive bombs in forty minutes. Six hours later, just before dawn on 8 July, three British and Canadian divisions attacked directly toward the objective with three armored brigades in immediate support and a fourth in reserve. Though the British found many Germans stunned, some units cut off from ammunition and gasoline supplies, and

---

[3] Montgomery to Eisenhower, 8 Jul, SGS SHAEF File 381, OVERLORD I (a).

[4] Bradley, *Soldier's Story*, p. 339; Marshal of the RAF, Sir Arthur Harris, *Bomber Offensive* (London: Collins, 1947), p. 210.

[5] Capt Butcher (USNR), Diary, 29 Jun 44, Pogue Files.

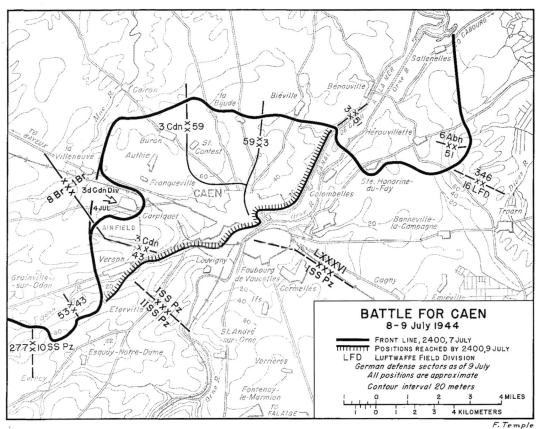

BATTLE FOR CAEN
8-9 July 1944

FRONT LINE, 2400, 7 JULY
POSITIONS REACHED BY 2400,9 JULY
LFD   LUFTWAFFE FIELD DIVISION
German defense sectors as of 9 July
All positions are approximate

Contour interval 20 meters

0   1   2   3   4 MILES
0   1   2   3   4 KILOMETERS

F. Temple

MAP 6

one regiment virtually decimated, resistance did not collapse, the fighting was bitter, casualties heavy. Widespread debris and tremendous craters further obstructed a rapid ground advance.[6]

The full force of the air bombardment had struck the *16th Luftwaffe Field Division*, recently arrived in Normandy from the Pas-de-Calais to replace an armored division in the *Panzer*

Group West line. With one regiment of the *16th* destroyed and quickly overrun, Eberbach committed without result the powerful *21st Panzer Division*, which had just been moved out of the line and into reserve. The attack of the *21st* "did not have much point," according to Rommel, "because of the strong enemy artillery fire." The air bombardment had also fallen on the excellent *12th SS Panzer Division*, still not relieved from front-line defensive duty as had been hoped. Though some strongpoints in this unit's main line of resistance held until burned out by

---

[6] Montgomery, *Normandy to the Baltic*, pp. 113ff; Stacey, *The Canadian Army*, pp. 187ff; [Robert W. Ackerman], Employment of Strategic Bombers in a Tactical Role, 1941–1951, USAF Hist Study 88 (Maxwell Air Force Base, Alabama, Air University, 1953), p. 86; Harris, *Bomber Offensive*, p. 211.

flame-throwing British tanks, the division eventually was forced to give way. On the evening of 8 July, Rommel and Eberbach decided to prepare to evacuate Caen. They began by directing that all heavy weapons be moved across the Orne River, which flows through the city.[7]

The Luftwaffe field division lost 75 percent of its infantrymen and all of its battalion commanders in those units in contact with the British. No longer able to fight as an independent unit, the division was attached to the *21st Panzer Division.* The *12th SS Panzer Division* lost twenty medium tanks, several 88-mm. pieces, all its antitank guns, and a high percentage of its troops. All together, Rommel estimated losses as the equivalent of four battalions of men. Eberbach moved the *1st SS Panzer Division* to positions southeast of Caen to forestall a British breakthrough, but Kluge, by refusing to permit its commitment, accepted the eventual loss of Caen.[8]

On the morning of 9 July British and Canadian troops entered Caen from the flanks and reached the Orne River. The bridges across the river had been destroyed or were blocked by rubble, and there the troops halted.[9]

The Allied ground commander, General Montgomery, had not moved much

closer toward the Breton ports, he had not gained much maneuver space, nor had he captured all of Caen. But he had inflicted heavy losses on the Germans. With *Panzer Lehr* moving to the *Seventh Army* sector to counter the breakthrough threatened by American troops between the Taute and the Vire, *Panzer Group West,* after meeting the British attack, was in difficult straits.

On 10 July Montgomery directed the British Second Army to drive south between Caumont and Caen in order to broaden the beachhead and open lateral routes of communication. Subsequently, the army was also to advance across the Orne River at Caen toward Falaise, if it could do so "without undue losses," in order to position its armor for a drive in strength farther south or toward the Seine. The First U.S. Army was to continue its offensive to the south.[10]

Vitally interested in maneuver room and the Breton ports, General Bradley had been attempting to move out of the Cotentin swamps to dry land along the Coutances–Caumont line, where he could mount an attack toward Brittany. But after nearly a week of bitter fighting, both the VIII and the VII Corps on the army right seemed to be halted, and the XIX Corps had been unable to develop and extend its bridgehead between the Taute and the Vire. Since the Germans were defending with unexpected determination, making excellent use of the terrain, and inflicting considerable losses, prospects of continuing a frontal attack along the well-defined corridors leading through the Cotentin

[7] *OB WEST KTB, Anlagen 536* and *537.*

[8] Conf, Rommel and Eberbach, 2100, 8 Jul, and Telecon, Rommel and Gause, 1115, 9 Jul, *Pz Gp West KTB;* Telecons, Rommel to Kluge, 0655, 9 Jul, Speidel to Blumentritt, 0950, 9 Jul, Eberbach to Tempelhoff, 0910, 11 Jul, *AGp B KTB;* Eberbach to Rommel, 10 Jul, *Pz Gp W KTB, Anlage 104;* Map dated 10 Jul, *OKW WFSt Op (H), Lage West, Stand 9.VII.44; OB WEST KTB,* 9 Jul.

[9] Ltr, Eisenhower to Montgomery, 10 Jul, SGS SHAEF File 381, Opn OVERLORD, I (a) .

[10] 21 AGp Dir, M–510, 10 Jul; Montgomery, *Normandy to the Baltic,* p. 120.

BRITISH TROOPS *clearing away rubble in Caen, 9 July.*

marshes appeared to assure only a repetition of painful progress at prohibitive cost. Getting to the first objective, the Coutances–Caumont line, would so weaken the army that a delay would have to preface a subsequent effort to get to Brittany.

Searching for a different way to gain the Coutances–Caumont line, General Bradley began to consider that a powerful attack on a very narrow front might dissolve the hedgerow stalemate. Yet before he could mass forces on a narrow front, he had to get at least partially out of the Cotentin lowlands. He decided

that ground near the Lessay–St. Lô–Caumont highway might serve his purposes. A compromise objective, it would perhaps give sufficient dry land for the attack to the Coutances–Caumont line.

While General Bradley was bringing his idea to maturity, the slow and painful advance through the hedgerows continued.[11]

Toward Lessay

After five days of attack in July, Gen-

---

[11] Bradley, *Soldier's Story*, p. 329; FUSA Opns Instrs, 8 Jul.

eral Middleton's VIII Corps had moved only to the high ground near la Haye-du-Puits. General Wyche's 79th Division, on the right, occupied most of the Montgardon ridge; General Ridgway's 82d Airborne Division had taken the Poterie ridge in the corps center; and General Landrum's 90th Division, on the left, held precarious positions on the northeast portion of Mont Castre. The infantry divisions were to have met just south of la Haye-du-Puits to pinch out the airborne troops and allow them to return to England, but by the evening of 7 July the divisions on the flanks were still more than three miles apart. (*Map II*) They had each sustained casualties of close to 15 percent of original strength. To give the attack impetus, General Middleton committed the newly arrived 8th Division.

To make room for the new unit, General Middleton redrew the division boundaries. He restricted the 79th Division to a narrow sector along the west coast of the Cotentin, where it was to perform a clearing mission as far south as the Ay River estuary. He reoriented the 90th Division from a south by southwest direction to an axis of advance generally south by southeast; at the Sèves River near Périers the 90th was to be pinched out on its left by the VII Corps in the Carentan–Périers isthmus and on its right by the 8th Division. To the fresh troops of the 8th Division, General Middleton gave the mission of making the main effort of the corps: moving to the Ay River between Lessay and Périers and securing a bridgehead over the river.[12]

Although la Haye-du-Puits was in the

8th Division zone, General Middleton directed the 79th Division to take it, probably because the 79th had already started the job.[13] The town was held by only about 150 Germans, who lacked antitank weapons but defended with machine guns, small arms, and mortars. Virtually surrounded, shelled almost constantly by artillery and tanks, the Germans had mined the approaches to the town and refused to capitulate. The 79th therefore made a thorough plan of attack; artillery, armor, and tank destroyers were to support an assault battalion of infantry.

Late in the afternoon of 8 July, as heavy fire crashed overhead, infantrymen moved toward German mine fields strung with wire in checkerboard patterns about a foot off the ground. As the riflemen tried to high-step over the wire, enemy mortar bursts bracketed them. Machine gunners in trenches that the Americans had not even suspected of being in existence opened fire. Taking many casualties, three rifle companies advanced. Engineers placed their white tapes across mine-swept areas, while bulldozers cut avenues through the hedgerows for the supporting tanks. The infantry reached the northwest edge of la Haye-du-Puits by evening. One rifle company by then was without commissioned officers, but its men methodically cleared the railroad yards and inched toward the center of town. After a bloody house cleaning by the light of flaming buildings, the 79th Division turned la Haye-du-Puits

---

[12] VIII Corps FO 7, 7 Jul, and AAR, Jul.

[13] 79th Div Telecon, 2330, 7 Jul, VIII Corps G–3 Jnl File; Msg, 28th Inf to 8th Div, 0705, 8 Jul, 8th Div G–3 Jnl and File.

over to the 8th Division at noon, 9 July.[14]

Except for taking la Haye-du-Puits, the VIII Corps made no advance during 8 and 9 July. The temporary stalemate resulted from the last German attempts to retake the heights near the town—the Montgardon ridge and Mont Castre. Although the Germans failed to reach the high ground, they did prevent progress toward Lessay–Périers.

At the time it appeared that the failure to move for forty-eight hours rested squarely on the 8th Division, which was exhibiting the usual faults of a unit new to combat. Commanded by Maj. Gen. William C. McMahon, the 8th was rated one of the best-trained U.S. divisions in the European theater. Nevertheless, hesitation, inertia, and disorganization marked its first attempts to advance. Inaccurate reporting of map locations, large numbers of stragglers, and poor employment of attached units were usual symptoms of inexperience, but the division also demonstrated a particular ineptness in the realms of organization and control. When the 90th Division insisted that a regimental commander take responsibility for a sector assigned to him, he reported, "We explained we could not do so tonite or tomorrow morning. Must have time." After the division had struggled for a day to attain a measure of organization, a neighboring unit noted, "Everyone was more or less confused. . . . They didn't seem to be operating according to any particular plan." The deputy army commander, Lt. Gen. Courtney H.

Hodges, visited the division commander and learned that "the 8th had made no known progress, for reasons not very clear." [15]

The commitment of the division coincided with vigorous local counterattacks launched by the enemy. Nevertheless, even after the enemy was repelled or contained, the subordinate units failed to press forward. General McMahon confessed more than once that he did not know exactly what was holding up his troops.[16] The solution he applied was to relieve the commanders of both committed regiments. About the same time the energetic assistant division commander, Brig. Gen. Nelson M. Walker, was killed as he attempted to organize an infantry battalion for an attack.[17] Finally, four days after committing the 8th Division, General Middleton relieved the commander.

Brig. Gen. Donald A. Stroh, formerly assistant commander of the 9th Division, assumed command. Advocating side-slipping and flanking movements, he committed his reserve regiment immediately in hope of gaining his objective quickly. Without special hedgerow training, the division learned through its own errors how to solve the problems of attack and soon began to manifest that steady if unspectacular advance that was feasible in the hedgerows. The troops moved with increasing confidence, maintaining momentum by by-

---

[14] 314th Infantry Regiment, *Through Combat*, p. 22; Wyche Diary; 79th Div AAR, Jul; VIII Corps G–3 Jnl File, 7 and 8 Jul; 8th Div G–3 Jnl, 8 and 9 Jul.

[15] 8th Div G–3 Jnl, 8 Jul, and entry 2400, 9 Jul; 90th Div Msg, 1105, 8 Jul, and VIII Corps Msg, 0940, 9 Jul, VIII Corps G–3 Jnl and File; CI 47 (8th Div); 357th Inf Jnl, entry 1017, 9 Jul; Sylvan Diary, 10 Jul.

[16] 8th Div G–3 Jnl, entries 1810, 8 Jul, and 1540, 9 Jul.

[17] General Walker was posthumously awarded the DSC.

passing small isolated enemy groups.[18] Despite continuing resistance, the division occupied the ridge overlooking the Ay River on 14 July and began to reconnoiter for crossing sites.

The 79th Division, which had attempted to advance south of the Montgardon ridge, had sustained heavy casualties and had moved not at all during 8 and 9 July.[19] A typical rifle company had one officer and 94 men on 7 July, only 47 men two days later.

When German pressure lessened on 10 July, General Wyche again moved the division toward the Ay estuary, a blue blob of water shimmering tantalizingly three miles away in the midst of the green lowland. Jockeying his subordinate units in a series of apparently unrelated moves, short jabs that took advantage of local enemy weakness, General Wyche pressed his advance down the terrain that sloped toward Lessay. A fortunate mistake that occurred in the late afternoon of 11 July facilitated progress. Bombing inadvertently 4,000 yards inside the safety line, American planes rendered unexpected close support. As a result, the division easily took Angoville-sur-Ay. The re-

maining distance to the Ay River was marked by decreasing resistance.

The 79th Division reached the Ay River on 14 July. Although Lessay remained in German hands, General Wyche had cleared the coastal sector between la Haye-du-Puits and the estuary. The effort might have seemed easy in retrospect, but it had cost close to 2,000 men.[20]

On the corps left, the 90th Division, which had been brutally handled by the Germans while taking Mont Castre and trying to push through the Beaucoudray corridor, clung doggedly to positions on the northeast portion of Mont Castre. As the enemy launched strong and repeated attacks on 8 and 9 July, General Landrum reinforced his infantry not only by committing his engineers but also by forming and employing miscellaneous groups of cooks, drivers, and clerks, as well as dismounted cavalry, to guard lines of communications and fill gaps in the infantry positions. To perform the normal engineer functions in the division area, the corps temporarily attached one of its battalions to the 90th Division. The 82d Airborne Division also helped. One enterprising officer set up a consolidated observation post in a château stable tower and on 8 July massed the fires of his regimental mortars on a counterattack in the 90th Division zone. This was a last burst of exuberance for the airborne unit; three days later the troops moved to the beach for transport to England.[21]

As the German pressure diminished

---

[18] VIII Corps Msg, 1430, 12 Jul, 8th Div Msg, 1800, 12 Jul, and Jnl, entry 1900, 12 Jul, 8th Div G–3 Jnl File; CI 47 (8th Div). Capt. Harry L. Gentry, an artillery officer who took command of leaderless infantry soldiers during an attack, 1st Lt. William L. Pryor, who singlehandedly covered the withdrawal of his company, and Pfc. Leo T. Zingale were awarded the DSC for their actions on 10 July. Pfc. Walter S. Wanielista, for his actions on 11 July, and Sgt. Harry Weiss (posthumously), for his singlehanded capture of a pillbox on 13 July, also received DSC's.

[19] T/5 John G. Prentice of the 125th Cavalry Reconnaissance Squadron, for remaining in his tank though it had been set ablaze by an enemy shell and continuing to fire his gun until killed by a second direct hit, was awarded the DSC.

[20] 79th Div AAR, Jul; Wyche Diary; FUSA Daily Estimated Loss Rpt.

[21] 315th Engr C Bn Jnl, Jul; 82d Abn Div AAR, Jun and Jul.

on 10 July, the depleted regiment on the 90th Division left, the 357th Infantry, attacked in the Beaucoudray corridor. Enemy machine gun, mortar, and artillery fire brought disorganization at once. The previous loss of commissioned and noncommissioned officers made effective control difficult. When two rifle companies broke ranks and fled, the regiment canceled further offensive effort for the day.

At the same time, a battalion of the 358th Infantry pushed through the dense thickets of Mont Castre and put to rout platoon sized groups of Germans at close range. In the late afternoon the leading company with the help of six tanks reached the edge of the woods and the south slope of Mont Castre. As they left the concealment of the trees, German self-propelled guns opened fire on them. Flat-trajectory shells destroyed the tanks immediately and forced the infantry company, reduced to one officer and twenty-four men, back into the forest.[22]

Despite this local success, the Germans at the end of 10 July at last virtually abandoned Mont Castre. On the following day the 358th Infantry descended the south slope of the hill mass against little opposition.[23] The situation eased; General Landrum relieved the division engineers of their infantry role. On 12 July the 357th Infantry moved through Beaucoudray against no more than perfunctory opposition.

By this time the division strength was so diminished that small German delaying groups exacted proportionately higher prices for local objectives. No company totaled more than a hundred men. Operating as a single battle group of but 122 men and 4 officers, the rifle components of the 3d Battalion, 358th Infantry, suffered 40 casualties, including all of the officers, at a crossroad ambush on 12 July.[24]

Reduced ranks and fatigue, the hedgerow terrain, and tactical, supply, and communication difficulties combined to deny the 90th Division a rapid advance in pursuit of a withdrawing enemy. It was 14 July when the division reached the Sèves River and established contact with the VII Corps on the left. General Landrum was finally at his objective, three miles north of Périers, but the move across the few miles from Mont Castre had cost almost 2,000 casualties.[25]

After twelve days and over 10,000 casualties, the VIII Corps had moved across seven miles of hedgerows to the banks of the Ay and the Sèves River. Early hope that the Germans would break quickly had long been dispelled. The enemy had given ground only grudgingly. Not until 10 July had the Germans weakened even slightly. Not until 13 July had they begun a genuine withdrawal to positions south of the Ay and the Sèves.

For all the lack of encouragement from an American viewpoint, Choltitz,

---

[22] Taylor Notes on Mont Castre, ML–1071. Lt. Col. Jacob W. Bealke, Jr., and Capt. John W. Marsh received the DSC, the latter posthumously, for their actions this day.

[23] Pfc. Theodore G. Wagner, who crawled forward alone to destroy a key machine gun emplacement with grenades, was awarded the DSC.

[24] 1st Lt. Hubert G. Miller, a company commander who though wounded took command of a leaderless battalion, and Lt. Col. Frederick H. Loomis, who led four tanks and ten men in a successful attack, received the DSC.

[25] 90th Div AAR, Jul; FUSA Daily Estimated Loss Rpts, Jul.

the *LXXXIV Corps* commander opposing the VIII Corps, had been increasingly concerned. He had suffered a minor brain concussion, and what was worse, he had seen all the reserves in his sector committed by 12 July, even the new arrivals from Brittany. The *Panzer Lehr* commander had threatened simply to take off with his tanks if he did not get reinforcements. Without reinforcements to send, Kluge on 13 July authorized the corps to fall back to the south banks of the two rivers. The withdrawal begun that evening was gradual and orderly.[26]

For the Americans, the Lessay–Périers line was only about one third of the distance to Coutances, the original VIII Corps objective. When the grinding attack through the hedgerows ceased, at least temporarily, on 14 July, Coutances, fourteen miles to the south, seemed as unattainable for the moment as Berlin. Yet a new army operation was being contemplated, an operation hopefully designed to gain Coutances more easily than by continuing a purely frontal assault.

Toward Périers

From a one-division limited objective attack, the VII Corps effort had become a two-division attack in the Carentan–Périers isthmus. By 8 July the 83d and 4th Divisions had made such small gains, despite strenuous action, that there was still no space to employ the available 9th Division. The narrow zone of operations and the terrain had inhibited

---

[26] Telecons, Pemsel to Speidel, 1315, 13 Jul, and Choltitz to Pemsel, 1930, 13 Jul, *Seventh Army* Tel Msgs; Telecons, Speidel and Zimmerman, 1635 and 1700, 13 Jul, *AGp B KTB; OB WEST KTB,* 13 Jul, and *Anlagen 611* and *612.*

maneuver. Numerous streams and marshes and the hedgerows had broken large-scale attacks into small, local engagements. A resourceful enemy—the *6th Parachute Regiment,* more and more units of the *17th SS Panzer Grenadier Division,* and artillery and tank elements of the *2d SS Panzer Division*— had felled trees to block the roads, used roaming tanks in mobile defense, and covered crossroads with devastating fire. Though depleted and battered by superior numbers, the Germans had shuffled their units skillfully and continued to make expert use of the terrain. They had revealed no signs of cracking suddenly under the weight of the corps attack.

Because of improved weather conditions, over a hundred planes of the IX Tactical Air Command on 8 July attacked along the VII Corps front only a few hundred feet ahead of a front line marked by artillery. The assistance had small effect. Even more discouraging was evidence that the Germans were bringing more tanks into the Carentan–Périers isthmus. Enemy patrols, each composed of a tank and fifteen to thirty infantrymen, probed the front and made local penetrations, two of which overran battalion aid stations of the 83d Division.

The forward positions of the corps were about five miles below Carentan and still a mile short of Sainteny. Twelve air miles due south of Sainteny was the final corps objective, a portion of the high ground extending generally from Coutances to Caumont. At the rate of advance made the preceding week, the final objective was at least a month and a half distant, but General

Collins kept his interest focused on it. The 4th Division was to secure high ground near Périers, then move south to cut the Lessay–Périers highway. The 83d Division was to gain the west bank of the Taute River, cross the stream, and move south to cut the Périers–St. Lô road. The 9th Division would have to be employed outside the Caretan–Périers isthmus.[27]

On the right (western) half of the Carentan–Périers isthmus, General Barton was finally able on 8 July to bring all three regiments of his 4th Division into the sector available to him, but only the 22d Infantry (Col. Charles T. Lanham) was directed toward Périers. Deployed on the narrowest portion of the isthmus, squeezed by the Prairies Marécageuses de Gorges on the right, the regiment was on the verge of leaving the narrow neck of land that ends near Sainteny. Even this prospect meant little, for the area southwest of Sainteny offered small hope of rapid advance. Dry ground suitable for military operations was nonexistent. The sluggish Sèves and Holerotte Rivers were swollen with rain, transforming the six miles of approach to Périers into a desolate bog scarcely distinguishable from swamp. The division not only had to fight the soggy crust of the land and the high water table, it also had to cross innumerable drainage ditches, small streams, and inundated marshes in an area without a single hard-surfaced road. The terrain alone would have been a serious obstacle; defended by Germans it was almost impassable.

Restricted by inadequate maneuver space, hindered by soft marshland, handicapped by the difficulties of observation, General Barton was unable to concentrate the power of his infantry and supporting arms in a sustained effort. Even the four battalions organic to the division artillery and the additional attached battalion of medium artillery were rarely able to mass their fires effectively. Because of the compartmentalizing effect of the terrain, General Barton attacked with regimental combat teams that pursued quite independent actions. Some measure of co-ordination in the attack could be attempted at the regimental level; more often it was feasible only at the battalion echelon.

While the 22d Infantry fought through the narrowest neck of the isthmus and the 12th rested in reserve, the 8th was trying to clear in a slow and methodical operation the small area on the division right rear, the area just north of the corridor and adjacent to the Prairies Marécageuses de Gorges. Four separate attacks since 8 July had failed. But on 10 July the Germans launched a counterattack; with enemy soldiers in the open for the first time, American artillery and mortar fire decimated their ranks. Striking quickly, the 8th Infantry caught the enemy off balance. Infantry and tanks swept the area, collecting 49 prisoners, burying 480 German dead, and incurring 4 casualties in return. On 11 July the 4th Division was ready to add the 8th Infantry to its effort toward Périers and attempt to blast through the corridor just north of Sainteny.

Still there was no sudden propulsion forward. The 22d Infantry moved into swampy terrain on the right for about

[27] VII Corps AAR, Jul, FO 5, 9 Jul (and Annex 2).

two miles against diminishing opposition; patrols crossed the Holerotte and the Sèves Rivers on 11 and 12 July and sought to make contact with the 90th Division, which was descending along the western edge of the great marsh. The other two regiments in columns of battalions fought toward Périers against strong resistance. Aided by occasional dive-bombers during the infrequent days of good weather, the division had advanced about two miles below Sainteny by 15 July. At the end of that day, still four miles short of Périers, General Barton received the order to halt.

The 4th Division was to be relieved and sent into reserve. In ten days of combat it had sustained approximately 2,300 casualties, including three battalion commanders and nine rifle company commanders.[28] Progress at this cost was prohibitive. The division was to rest for a vital role in the forthcoming First Army operation hopefully designed to end frontal attack.

Hampered by similar conditions, the 83d Division on the left in the meantime had been trying to advance south along the road that crosses the isthmus laterally to the Taute River. The division was to secure the western bank of the river where a mile-long causeway traverses the Taute River flats; it also had to secure its original objective, Sainteny, which was now on its extreme right flank.

The 83d Division's major problem at first centered around German tanks. Increasing numbers of them were becoming apparent, not in concerted offensive action, but individually, backing up the defensive line. The 83d Division

used tank, artillery, tank destroyer, and bazooka fire effectively to destroy them. Nevertheless, so many tanks were in evidence that subordinate commanders found it difficult to think beyond the necessity of eliminating them. Weakened by attrition and fatigue, the units failed to press toward their objectives even after eliminating the tanks that barred the way.

Thinking in the broader terms of taking the main objectives, General Macon exercised close supervision. When the 330th Infantry failed to advance during the morning of 9 July, he could see no reason for it.[29] Just some tanks, the regimental commander explained, but he had a plan to eliminate them; just as soon as he accomplished this, his attack would get under way. General Macon suggested that with bazooka teams well forward and tanks in close support the regiment could attack and thereby accomplish both purposes, but the regimental commander insisted that he had to send out the bazookas before he moved his infantry forward.

"If you just send a [small] party down there," General Macon warned, "you will be fooling around all day."

"Yes, sir," the regimental commander agreed. But first he had to make certain that the enemy tanks were destroyed.

General Macon patiently explained that it was "awfully bad for the morale of the troops" to wait in place "hour after hour; you've got to keep moving," he insisted.

When General Macon phoned three

[28] CI 30 (4th Div); 4th Div AAR, Jul.

[29] The following is taken from the telephone messages in the 83d Division G–2, G–3 Journal.

hours later, the regimental commander admitted that progress had been negligible. Aware of how physically and mentally tired all the subordinate commanders were, General Macon made his next move with reluctance. "I'll have to send someone down there to take over," he said. "We have got to take that objective."

Ten minutes later General Ferenbaugh, the assistant division commander, was on his way to assume temporary command of the regiment. That evening General Macon relieved the regimental commander.

The objective was the Taute River west bank, but the 330th failed to reach it on 9 July. The 331st, on the other hand, finally took Sainteny on that day, assisted by several fighter-bombers and by an adjacent unit of the 4th Division. In terms of real estate, the objective had little to offer, for it had been gutted by white phosphorus shells; it was nevertheless an important milestone on the road to Périers.

With the 4th Division assuming the task of driving toward Périers, the 83d Division turned its entire effort to reaching the west bank of the Taute. The immediate objective was the western point of the mile-long Tribehou causeway across the Taute River flats. When reached, the causeway would provide a crossing site for part of the division, which was to join other units that were sweeping the east bank of the Taute. The remainder of the 83d Division was to clear the west bank of the Taute to another causeway and cross there to the east bank.

Continuing toward the west bank of the Taute, the men found that enemy tanks and assault guns, often dug into the ground and employed as pillboxes, dominated the few trails in the area. Neither dive-bombing nor artillery and tank-destroyer fire appeared to have any effect on them. Although antiaircraft guns of 90-mm. caliber were brought forward, they too appeared powerless to dislodge or destroy them.[30] Only bazooka teams of infantrymen, approaching by stealth to close range before firing their rockets, were capable of taking out the tanks and assault guns.

Prisoners, who said that cooks and bakers were acting as riflemen, gave the 83d hope that the German defenses were cracking, but the enemy had some butchers too, and optimism vanished as the Germans continued to defend with the skill of trained infantrymen. Nevertheless, at the end of 13 July, the 330th Infantry reached the west bank of the Taute near the causeway. To make the advance, the regiment had destroyed over twenty tanks in four days. On 14 July the 330th Infantry crossed the Tribehou causeway and joined other units in sweeping the east bank of the Taute. The regiment was temporarily detached from 83d Division control.

The remaining two regiments of the 83d attacked to reach the other causeway south of the Tribehou crossing site but made little progress. On 13 July several enemy tanks advanced boldly and sprayed a battalion position with machine gun fire, causing the unit to withdraw from a hard-won objective. Cruising tank-infantry teams surrounded the 3d Battalion, 331st Infantry, that night and isolated 126 men for two days before adjacent units could come for-

---

[30] VII Corps Msg, 1020, 10 Jul, FUSA G-3 Jnl.

SHELLED CHURCH IN SAINTENY, *World War I memorial in foreground.*

ward in relief. In vain the 83d Division strove to plow the few miles to the projected crossing site.

During twelve days, the 83d Division had sustained a staggering total of 5,000 casualties. Indeed, had it not been for progressive integration of replacements as the fighting developed, the division would have been little more than a skeleton. As it was, the units were far from first-rate fighting forces. The 331st Infantry had five commanders in one week, and only when Col. Robert H. York arrived on 13 July to become the seventh commander did the regiment achieve a measure of stability.

The attached tank battalion had lost half its tanks to enemy fire by 10 July.[31]

The failure of the 83d Division to make gains in mileage was not due to inherent deficiency. General Collins made a personal test on 11 July when he arrived at the division command post at a time when General Macon was visiting a subordinate unit. In an attempt to get the division moving, the corps commander issued specific attack instructions and directed the subsequent attack, but he could not free the division from

[31] 331st Inf AAR, Jul; 746th Tk Bn Rpt, 10 Jul, 83d Div G–2, G–3 Jnl File.

the frustration of advancing, at most, at the rate of several hedgerows per day.

At midnight on 15 July, the 4th and 83d Divisions (the latter less the 330th Infantry) passed to control of the VIII Corps as part of a reorganization along the entire army front. The 83d began to relieve portions of the 4th Division. Several days later, the newly arrived 4th Armored Division completed the relief.[32]

Terrain and the enemy had brought the VII Corps to a halt on the Carentan–Périers isthmus by 15 July. "The Germans are staying in there just by the guts of their soldiers," General Barton remarked. "We outnumber them ten to one in infantry, fifty to one in artillery, and by an infinite number in the air."[33] The VII Corps attack nevertheless had achieved several ends: by moving the front line a few miles farther from Carentan, the corps had eliminated the nuisance shelling of the town and its vital highway bridge; it had prevented the Germans from launching a counterattack in the sector considered the weakest along the entire American front; and it had inflicted serious losses on the German forces.[34]

Counterattack

While the Germans defended stubbornly and adroitly in the zones of the VII and VIII Corps, they directed their greatest effort against the XIX Corps between the Taute and Vire Rivers. This was the sector where the 30th Division and Combat Command B of the 3d Armored Division were attacking toward the high ground west of St. Lô.

If the U.S. troops reached their objective, the Germans reasoned, they might unhinge the German line in the Cotentin and outflank not only those units defending la Haye-du-Puits and Périers but also the *II Parachute Corps* in the St. Lô–Caumont sector. To reinforce *Kampfgruppe Heinz* and the small portion of the *17th SS Panzer Grenadier Division* resisting between the Taute and the Vire, the *II Parachute Corps* sent part of its reserves, light forces organized around a mobile brigade, to close the gap opened by the American attack. But these troops were obviously too few to dissipate the danger of a serious breakthrough, and the *2d SS Panzer Division* consequently added a tank-infantry task force, which attacked the American flank on 9 July.[35]

Deciding two days earlier that they needed a strong force between the Taute and the Vire, Kluge and Rommel obtained the *Panzer Lehr Division* from the *Panzer Group West* front in order to mount a major counterattack.[36] While the division traveled westward across the Normandy front toward the Taute and Vire region, the inexperience and errors of the U.S. units as much as firm resistance offered by the relatively small German combat groups—the armored task forces and the remnants of *Kampfgruppe Heinz*, reinforced by the parachute corps reserves—prevented a genuine

---

[32] VIII Corps G–3 Per Rpt 33, 18 Jul.

[33] CI 30 (4th Div).

[34] See Brereton, *Diaries*, p. 307.

[35] MS # B–455 (Ziegelmann); Telecons, Pemsel and Meindl, 1800, 7 Jul, Hausser and Rommel, 1935, 7 Jul, Criegern and Pemsel, 1945, 7 Jul, *Seventh Army* Tel Msgs; Pemsel and Meindl, 1910, 7 Jul, *AGp B KTB*.

[36] Telecons, Rommel and Hausser, 1930, 7 Jul, unidentified, 2005, 7 Jul, Kluge and Rommel, 2020, 7 Jul, and Pemsel and Speidel, 2350, 8 Jul, *AGp B KTB*; *OB WEST KTB*, 7 and 8 Jul.

American breakthrough.[37] The arrival of advance elements of *Panzer Lehr* on 10 July was to seal off the penetration, while the projected *Panzer Lehr* counterattack threatened to reverse the situation completely and throw the Americans on the defensive.

General Corlett on 8 July had sent Combat Command A of the 3d Armored Division across the Vire to reinforce the 113th Cavalry Group on the right flank. Adding further to the strength of the already considerable force in the XIX Corps bridgehead, and arriving accidentally in time to meet the attack of *Panzer Lehr,* came the 9th Division, the unit that General Collins had been unable to employ with the rest of his VII Corps on the Carentan–Périers isthmus.

Upon General Hodges' suggestion, General Collins persuaded General Bradley on 8 July that committing the unemployed 9th Division along the east bank of the Taute River would fulfill two useful functions. By outflanking the German resistance on the Carentan–Périers isthmus, the division would help the VII Corps and provide strong protection to the XIX Corps right flank. Bradley decided that the 9th Division's attack would be related more properly to the VII Corps action than to the XIX Corps advance toward St. Lô, so he let Collins retain control of the division. Moving the VII Corps boundary to the east and giving Collins a slice of the XIX Corps zone, General Bradley split the Taute and Vire area between the VII and XIX Corps, the new boundary to be effective as soon as the 9th Division crossed the Vire et Taute Canal and was ready to attack. General Collins ordered the division to attack westward—between the canal on the north and the St. Jean-de-Daye–le Désert road on the south—toward the Taute River. After making contact with the 83d Division, the 9th was to turn south to cut the Périers–St. Lô highway.[38]

The 9th Division was thoroughly battle trained. It had participated in the North African invasion and the Sicilian campaign and in June had played a prominent part in the capture of Cherbourg. General Eisenhower considered it one of the two he rated "tops" in the European theater.[39] The division commander, Maj Gen. Manton S. Eddy, had organized his headquarters in a fashion that resembled German practice. So that he might be free to visit the line units, Eddy kept the assistant division commander at the command post to make emergency decisions and to supervise the "operational group"—the G–2 and G–3 Sections—while the chief of staff supervised the "administrative group"—the G–1 and G–4 Sections.[40] The division had considerable potential fire power and mobility. In addition to controlling two extra battalions of artillery, one light and one medium, the 9th Division assumed control of Combat Command A of the 3d Amored Division and also of the 113th Cavalry Group. To keep the mobile armor and cavalry available for emergency use, General Eddy planned to hold them in reserve. At first he would employ his three in-

[37] Hodgson, R–54, contains a detailed account of the German resistance.

[38] FUSA Opns Instrs, 8 Jul; VII Corps FO 5, 9 Jul; Ltr, Corlett to OCMH, 19 Jan 54; Sylvan Diary, 8 Jul.

[39] Ltr, Eisenhower to Marshall, 5 Jul, Pogue Files.

[40] 12th AGp Immed Rpt 23, 9 Aug.

fantry regiments abreast, attacking westward toward the Taute.

The 9th Division crossed the Vire et Taute Canal on 9 July and was ready on the following morning to meet again the challenge of fighting in the hedgerows. A preparation by dive-bombers and artillery preceded the attack. Two regiments met opposition immediately and to their consternation advanced but several hedgerows. The third regiment had better success clearing the corner formed by the juncture of the Taute River and the Vire et Taute Canal. Resistance was light and enemy artillery conspicuous by its silence. A reconnaissance patrol, however, moving toward Tribehou Island in the Taute River flats, was turned back by mortar and machine gun fire.

That night, as the 9th Division reorganized for attack on the morning of 11 July, enemy fire increased and small groups of tanks and infantry attempted to infiltrate the lines. German tank motors sounded in the distance. From just beyond the division positions came the noise of infantrymen digging in. The 9th Division staff officers depreciated these signs, for they believed that the Germans were merely covering preparations for a general withdrawal during the night. Although the 30th Division on the left reported heavy enemy traffic moving toward the Taute River, the 9th Division staff preferred to accept as more valid an announcement from the 4th Division that the enemy was falling back. This judgment coincided with the view held at First Army headquarters. The army G–2 had interpreted the noisy march across the American front by *Panzer Lehr*, which had

repeatedly broken radio silence en route, as a demonstration of German bluff, an action presaging in reality a general withdrawal.[41]

The Germans were not bluffing. Generalleutnant Fritz Bayerlein, the commander of *Panzer Lehr*, had received his march order on 8 July and had moved at once, though poor roads and strafing by Allied planes had hampered the division march. Not until the night of 10 July was the division in position to attack—too late, Rommel thought. *Kampfgruppe Heinz*, which had suffered approximately 30 percent casualties and had virtually disintegrated as an organized unit, was withdrawn to the southwest as artillery of the *17th SS Panzer Grenadiers* gave covering fire and the *30th Mobile Brigade* and the tank-infantry teams of the *2d SS Panzer Division* launched local counterattacks. Hausser, the *Seventh Army* commander, attached these elements to *Panzer Lehr*, visited the division command post, and talked over the details of the attack with Bayerlein. With Rommel pushing for speed, *Panzer Lehr* was to attack at once—that night. *(Map 7)*

Bayerlein planned to attack with two regimental combat teams abreast. The regiments were to converge on the St. Jean-de-Daye crossroads from the southwest and the south. With the high ground at the crossroads in his possession, he would have command of the American crossing sites over the canal and the river, north and east of St. Jean-de-Daye. Hoping that the night attack would easily achieve a breakthrough,

[41] 9th Div G–3 Jnl, 0005, 0040, 11 Jul, and AAR, Jul; FUSA G–3 Jnl, 0600, 11 Jul, and G–2 Per Rpt 31, 11 Jul.

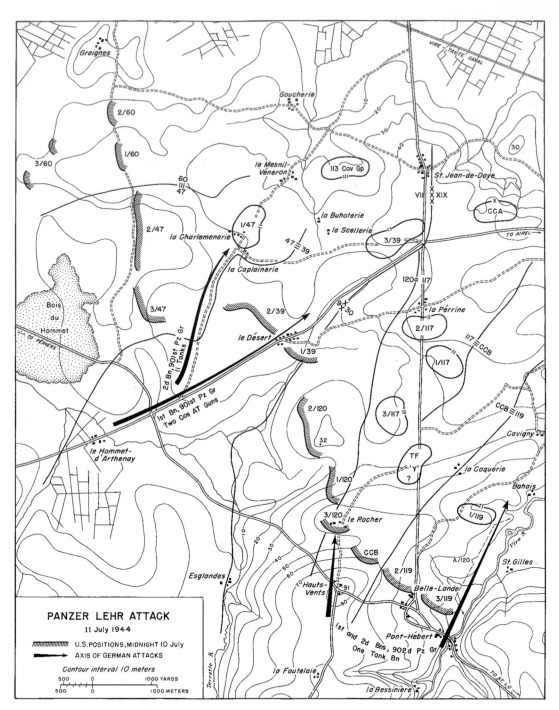

Graignes

2/60

1/60

3/60

Goucherie

le Mesnil-
Véneron

113 Cav Gp

60
III
47

1/47

2/47

la Charlemenerie

47 ≡ 39

la Caplainerie

3/47

2/39

le Désert

9 + 30

1/39

Bois
du
Hommet

TO PERIERS

2d Bn, 901st Pz Gr
II Tanks

1st Bn, 901st Pz Gr
Two Cos AT Guns

2/120

32

le Hommet-
d'Arthenay

1/120

3/120

le Rocher

Esglandes

Hauts-
Vents

91

CCB

la Foutelaie

1st and 2d Bns, 902d Pz Gr
One Tank Bn

la Bessinière

VIRE-TAUTE CANAL

30

30

St. Jean-de-Daye

VII
X X XIX
X X

X
CCA

TO AIREL

3/39

120 ≡ 117

la Buhoterie

la Scellerie

la Pérrine

2/117

117 ≡ CCB

1/117

3/117

CCB ≡ 119

Cavigny

TF
'Y'
?

la Coquerie

Bahais

Vire R.

1/119

A/120

St. Gilles

2/119

Belle-Landel

3/119

Pont-Hébert

TO ST-LO

Terrette R.

MAP 7

Bayerlein envisioned the infantry riding tanks to the objective. The *II Parachute Corps* was to launch a feint directly north from St. Lô in a limited objective attack along the east bank of the Vire River.[42]

The jump-off was scheduled for 0145, 11 July. Unfortunately for *Panzer Lehr*, Combat Command B of the 3d Armored Division in driving toward Hauts-Vents had jostled and delayed the leading panzer elements getting ready to attack. Still in firm possession of Hauts-Vents, *Panzer Lehr* jumped off just before dawn, 11 July, after a short artillery preparation. The routes of attack passed on both sides of CCB. The regiment on the right, moving close to the Vire River through Pont-Hébert, aimed for the Airel bridge and struck the 30th Division. The regiment on the left, moving through le Désert, struck the 30th and 9th Divisions.[43]

In the 9th Division sector, the division staff still was not seriously perturbed even after receiving reports at 0300 of German infiltration along the left flank. Two hours later the fact that Germans were making noise, were firing a great deal, and appeared "to be all around now" occasioned little more than nonchalance mixed with some incredulity. Not until the division artillery reported some confusion because German infantrymen were approaching the gun positions did the staff realize that a counterattack was under way. About the same time an infantry battalion command post was overrun. As reports began to indicate that enemy tanks were throughout the division area, telephone lines from all the regiments went out. Still the situation did not seem serious enough to wake the division commander.[44]

Panzer Lehr's leading elements on the left—two battalions of armored infantry, a company of tanks, and two companies of self-propelled guns—had actually made two shallow penetrations of the U.S. lines near le Désert, one along a regimental boundary of the 9th Division, the other between the 9th and 30th Divisions. The penetrations prompted confusion and some withdrawal before subordinate American commanders could begin to control their troops in close-range fighting.

After daylight brought some amelioration of the confusion, and after wiremen by 0900 had restored communications to the regiments, General Eddy got a coordinated defense into action. Infantrymen cut behind German spearheads to seal routes of withdrawal, while tanks, tank destroyers, and infantry bazooka teams stalked the isolated enemy armor.[45] Tank destroyers alone claimed destruction of at least one Mark IV and twelve Mark V (Panther) tanks. The division artillery pounded enemy tanks parked along the road west of le Désert. American planes flying other missions

---

[42] *Pz Lehr* FO, 10 Jul, in *Pz Lehr Div Ib KTB; Seventh Army KTB,* 10 Jul; 3d Armd Div CCB G–2 Daily Narrative, 7–16 Jul.

[43] See below, Chapter VIII, for the *II Parachute Corps* feint down the east bank of the Vire River.

[44] 9th Div G–3 Jnl, 0305, 0515, 0525, 11 Jul.

[45] Capt. James D. Allgood and 1st Lt. William F. Squire of the 47th Infantry received the DSC for their efforts in repelling the counterattack. T/3 Henry J. Kucharski of the Medical Detachment, 47th Infantry, when unable to render aid because of fire, ripped off his Red Cross armband and waved it in front of him as he advanced toward wounded men. The enemy recognized his mission and halted fire. When a German officer approached, Kucharski sued for and secured a thirty-minute truce, time for him to treat and evacuate American casualties. He received the DSC.

were diverted to counter the *Panzer Lehr* threat, and one formation dropped twenty-two 500-pound bombs on a German armored column.

By the middle of the afternoon of 11 July, the 9th Division had contained the enemy attack. General Eddy was then able to launch his own counterattack and regain ground abandoned earlier in the day. Because of the possibility of further enemy armored action, Eddy established a strong defensive line, giving particular attention to antitank precautions. The 9th Division had sustained little more than a hundred casualties. The only effect of the *Panzer Lehr* effort was to delay the 9th Division attack twenty-four hours.

Along the boundary between the 9th and 30th Divisions, confusion had at first also prevailed among men of the 30th. At a roadblock on a secondary route, guards heard tanks approaching, but were told by higher headquarters that American tanks were in the vicinity. The men let a column of tanks and infantry pass before noticing that the soldiers in the column were speaking German. They immediately alerted troops in the rear who engaged the column with antitank rifles and bazookas. Individual groups of infantrymen spontaneously and with little coordination or direction destroyed five enemy tanks and four armored scout cars, two of the latter mounting flame throwers. Machine guns emplaced earlier that evening for all-around security fired into the ranks of enemy infantry. As the night exploded into sound and flash, the noise of withdrawing tanks gradually became discernible. In the morning it was obvious that the point

of the enemy armored column had been blunted and the main body forced to withdraw.

At the same time, units of the 30th Division near the west bank of the Vire River were repelling the other regimental column of *Panzer Lehr*. Before noon of 11 July, U.S. troops had contained the enemy attack in that area and had cleared German stragglers from the division rear.[46] Though General Hobbs launched his own attack, it ran into resistance at once and made only slight gain.

The effect of the *Panzer Lehr* attack was not confined to the front line. At the still inadequate crossing sites over the Vire, military policemen had been driven from their traffic control posts by the increased enemy shelling. Traffic quickly coagulated. To relieve the congestion and reduce the possibility of embarrassment if a direct shell hit destroyed a bridge, a Bailey bridge was erected and completed late on 12 July; it took somewhat longer than normal because of continuing German fire.[47]

The 30th Division estimated that, with CCB, it had destroyed about 20 Mark IV tanks on 11 July. General Collins judged that the VII Corps had destroyed over 30 German tanks, most of them in the 9th Division sector. Three tactical air squadrons, which had bombed Ger-

---

[46] 2d Lt. Richard A. Kirsting of the 246th Engineer Combat Battalion was awarded the DSC for heroic action that resulted in the capture of forty Germans.

[47] As army engineers manipulated the Carentan locks on 14 July in an attempt to drain the flooded areas of the Cotentin, the Vire River water level descended so rapidly that it endangered the temporary bridge and made additional trestling necessary. XIX Corps Engr Sec Jnl and Sitreps, XIX Corps AAR, Jul.

GERMAN PANTHERS *knocked out near le Désert, 11 July.*

man armored columns, claimed 19 tanks destroyed, 2 probably destroyed, and 7 damaged; 2 half-tracks destroyed and 6 damaged.[48] Perhaps more important, at the height of the counterattack, CCB of the 3d Armored Division had been attacking Hauts-Vents and Hill 91, objectives the unit secured at 1730, 11 July. Without this commanding terrain, *Panzer Lehr* was in the situation of having had the prop knocked out from under its effort; an immediate resumption of the counterattack was out of the question.

The effect of the American action was considerable. *Panzer Lehr* had lost a quarter of its effective combat strength. One task force had started out with 6 infantry officers, 40 noncommissioned officers, and 198 enlisted men (with 36 light machine guns, 5 heavy machine

guns, and 10 bazookas), plus a company of tanks (10); only 7 noncommissioned officers and 23 men had returned with their individual small arms and 6 light machine guns. The *Panzer Lehr* counterattack had been a dismal and costly failure.[49]

Prompt American reaction was only part of the story. More important was the presence of the 9th Division, which the Germans had not known was there. Hastily executing an attack that had come too late, Bayerlein had tried a blitzkrieg in the hedgerows against a numerically superior American force. He had also courted defeat in detail by committing his two assault columns along routes that turned out to be too far apart for mutual support.

Judging the attack to have been an attempt to cut through to Isigny and

---

[48] VII Corps Msgs, 1100, 1230, 1505, 2300, 11 Jul, FUSA G–3 Jnl File; 3d Armd Div CCB G–2 Daily Narrative, 7–16 Jul.

[49] Telcon, Pemsel to Tempelhoff, 1000, 15 Jul, *Seventh Army* Tel Msgs; Rommel to Kluge, 15 Jul, *OB WEST KTB, Anlage 646.*

divide the Allied beachhead, the Americans disparaged the German plan as carelessly conceived, hastily organized, and imperfectly directed. This appraisal overestimated the importance of the effort. As far back as 13 June, when German troops had failed to retake Carentan, tactical commanders had abandoned all hope of regaining Isigny and the coast in that sector, even though as late as 24 June Hitler talked about the possibility of recovering Carentan. From the *Panzer Lehr* attack the Germans had expected little more than limited success, but even that came to naught. By 12 July *Panzer Lehr* was entirely committed in passive defense. Its only accomplishment was having "stopped the American drive to St. Gilles," the high ground west of St. Lô. Bayerlein congratulated his troops for that.[50]

If *Panzer Lehr* had not succeeded in eliminating the U.S. positions south of the Vire et Taute Canal, it was at least in position to block American attempts to continue quickly to the south. Nor was it by this time alone. The original decision to move *Panzer Lehr* from the *Panzer Group West* front had been made at least partially because units outside Normandy that were to reinforce the front still had not arrived. *OB WEST* had wanted to move the *5th Parachute Division* from Brittany to Normandy but needed Hitler's permission to do so. Hitler delayed because the division had been rated in June as suitable only for defensive missions. As various echelons discussed the question of whether the

parachutists' training was sufficiently advanced for the unit to be committed in Normandy, the troops of the division sat idle along the roads in Brittany. After much lobbying of OKW by *OB WEST* staff members, Kluge on 7 July, finally wheedled Hitler's reluctant consent and ordered the paratroopers to march on foot to Normandy. Young troops under inexperienced commanders, they moved into the Taute and Vire area behind *Panzer Lehr* during the night of 11 July. Behind them came the additional forces of the *275th Infantry Division*.[51] Bolstering the *Panzer Lehr* defenses, they were in position to hamper the 9th and 30th Division efforts to move south to the Périers–St. Lô highway.

Although General Bradley felt that his troops had "pretty well chewed up the *Panzer Lehr*," that the Germans were "on their last legs," and that the American offensive "should open up," subordinate commanders were of the opinion that the *Panzer Lehr* soldiers were "great big, husky boys, and arrogant . . . not beaten at all."[52]

Toward the Périers–St. Lô Road

Although the ground between the Taute and Vire Rivers was intrinsically suitable for the application of a unified command, General Bradley had split the

---

[50] 90th Div G–3 Jnl File, 11 and 12 Jul, and AAR, Jul; [Garth], *St.-Lô*, pp. 36–42; Hodgson, R–54; *Pz Lehr* FO, 11 Jul, *Pz Lehr Div Ib KTB*.

[51] *Seventh Army KTB*, 12 Jul; *OB WEST KTB*, 6 Jul; Telecons, 1030, 5 Jul, *AGp B KTB*; Msg, 1900, 5 Jul, *AGp B Op. Befehle*; Telecons, Helmdach and Tempelhoff, 1000, 6 Jul, Zimmerman and Tempelhoff, 2345, 6 Jul, *AGp B KTB*; Telecons, Tempelhoff and Helmdach, 0015, 7 Jul, Pemsel and Zoeller, 0630, 7 Jul, Hausser and Rommel, 2245, 11 Jul, *Seventh Army* Tel Msgs.

[52] Telecons, Corlett and Hobbs, 1422, 1507, 1614, 11 Jul.

region in two. The 9th Division on the right (west) thus could operate with the VII Corps and toward the objectives of that corps. The 30th Division on the left (east) carried the XIX Corps attack toward the high ground west of St. Lô.

On 10 July, when the 9th Division first had been committed between the Taute and the Vire, General Eddy was supposed to have secured the east bank of the Taute River before turning south to cut the Périers–St. Lô highway. To secure the river bank, he had attacked westward toward four specific objectives adjoining the stream: the corner formed by the juncture of the Taute River and the Vire et Taute Canal; the island of Tribehou, a hedgerowed mound of earth the possession of which would enable the 83d Division to make an administrative rather than an assault crossing of the Taute; the Bois du Hommet, a scrub forest that the Germans were using as an assembly area for troops and supplies; and the peninsula of Vincenterie. With these objectives cleared and a portion of the 83d Division across the Taute and operating on the 9th Division's right flank, General Eddy could then turn south to cut the east–west highway between Périers and St. Lô. *(See Maps 5 and II.)*

General Eddy had secured only one of his objectives, the corner formed by the river and the canal, when the *Panzer Lehr* attack disrupted his plans. To forestall a recurrence, Eddy oriented the 47th Infantry (Col. George W. Smythe) toward the south so as to be ready to swing west to outflank and isolate the spearhead of any counterattack. The 39th Infantry (Col. Harry A. Flint) was to drive along the axis of the highway

west of le Désert against what appeared to be the main German defenses. The 60th Infantry (Col. Jesse L. Gibney) was to secure the three remaining objectives that adjoined the east bank of the Taute.

Attacking on 12 July, the 60th Infantry met little opposition. While the 24th Reconnaissance Squadron of Colonel Biddle's 113th Cavalry Group blocked Tribehou on the northeast, the 60th bypassed it. Patrols found the northern portion of the Bois du Hommet unoccupied, and after an artillery preparation fired by eight battalions, the regiment moved through the forest in force against light resistance. Another artillery preparation that evening preceded an infantry move into Vincenterie, which was occupied by midnight. The reconnaissance squadron cleared Tribehou of weak forces on the following day, 13 July.

The 60th Infantry's quick success found no counterpart in the other regimental sectors. Battling west and south of le Désert, the 39th and 47th Regiments met an obdurate enemy. The Germans had shifted their forces to strengthen their positions near le Désert, and they were aggressive. Small tank-infantry combat teams provided a roving defense employing tactics of surprise.[53] As the 39th Infantry fought from hedgerow to hedgerow astride the le Désert road, a small German force, with mortars and self-propelled guns, worked around the flank of a rifle company late in the afternoon of 12 July. Sudden German fire inflicted heavy casualties, including all the company

[53] *Panzer Lehr* FO, 11 Jul, *Panzer Lehr Div Ib KTB; Seventh Army KTB* (Draft), 11–13 Jul.

officers. As the American riflemen began to fall back in confusion, a tank destroyer officer, 1st Lt. Jack G. Hubbard, who was nearby, quickly assumed command and held the men in place until another infantry company came forward and dispersed the Germans.[54] Rain on 13 July nullified air support, and the two regiments again registered inconclusive gains.

When the 330th Infantry of the 83d Division crossed the Tribehou causeway over the Taute River to Vincenterie and was attached to the 9th Division at noon, 14 July, General Eddy set his sights on the Périers–St. Lô highway. He lined the four infantry regiments abreast along an east–west line between Vincenterie and le Désert with the intention of driving quickly across the four miles to the objective. As the attack began, the major problems became evident: an excessively broad front, terrain that canalized offensive action, an infinite number of hedgerows, and an enemy who infiltrated in stubborn groups. All three battalions of the 60th Infantry fought through the night of 14 July against enemy troops that cut wire communications between the battalions and the regimental headquarters. A German company with captured Sherman tanks boldly approached a 47th Infantry roadblock and shot up the outpost. Mines, earth and log obstructions, wrecked vehicles, and debris impeded the division attack. The Germans blew craters in roadbeds and felled trees across the narrow country lanes. While the engineers devoted the bulk of their efforts to keeping the channels of communication and advance open, opera-

tions became "a succession of difficult frontal attacks from hedgerow to hedgerow." By the end of 15 July, after six days of combat, even the seasoned and battle-trained 9th Division had advanced scarcely six miles.[55]

The situation was somewhat similar for the 30th Division. While the infantry had met the *Panzer Lehr* attack, the attached CCB had secured Hill 91 at Hauts-Vents and organized defensive positions about a thousand yards to the south. CCB was to have been released from attachment after capturing Hauts-Vents, but for four days the armor held the most advanced point of the 30th Division line, sitting "on a hot spot" and receiving artillery fire from front and flanks, plus occasional strafing and bombing from American planes. Formerly anxious to be rid of the combat command, General Hobbs now argued to keep it because, as he said, he feared the armor in pulling out might "mix up the roads" and because his own attached tank battalion was a 60 percent loss.[56] The simple truth was that General Hobbs needed the combat command to insure retention of Hauts-Vents.

By the end of 11 July, its fifth day of battle, the 30th Division had sustained 1,300 casualties, and the men who remained were "dead on their feet." Tankers who fought all day long and serviced their vehicles a good part of the night frequently reported, "Tanks need maintenance, men need rest." Four

---

[54] 899th TD Bn Opn Rpt, Jan–Dec 44.

[55] 9th Div G–3 Jnl, 0415, 15 Jul, and AAR, Jul; 15th Engr C Bn Opns Rpts 25 and 26, 14 and 15 Jul; VII Corps AAR, Jul.

[56] Hobbs Telecons, 1657 and 1853, 15 Jul, Collins and Hobbs, 1250, 16 Jul, 30th Div G–3 Jnl and File; see 30th Div G–3 Jnl, 13 Jul.

days later, after fighting to come abreast of the combat command, the 30th Division had taken even heavier losses, almost another 2,000.[57]

In coming virtually abreast of the combat command at Hauts-Vents by 14 July, the 30th Division was in advance of units on its flanks and found itself compressed into a narrow zone. Hauts-Vents is at the northern tip of a narrow ridge leading directly to the Périers–St. Lô highway. Scarcely two miles wide and rising between the Vire River on the east and the Terrette River on the west, this ground sharply defined the 30th Division's zone of advance. The division positions represented a kind of peninsula in an enemy sea that had to be defended as much on the flanks as at the tip. Because the narrow ridge denied maneuver room, the troops had no choice but to operate on the exposed eastern and western slopes. The men on the faces of the ridges presented good targets to German enfilading fire from the flanks. German artillery pieces emplaced across the Vire River in defense of St. Lô inflicted 90 percent of the casualties incurred by the 119th Infantry on the division left flank. For effective counterbattery fire, the 30th Division on at least one occasion directed missions fired by U.S. artillery battalions east of the Vire. The division suddenly became highly conscious of the importance of camouflage, though measures undertaken seemed to improve the situation but little.[58]

Although the Vire River was an effective barrier to enemy infiltration on the left flank, the Terrette was not large enough to deny movement. The primary requirement on the right thus was a closely tied-in series of defensive strongpoints. Compressed into a narrow zone, the 30th Division could do little but hold doggedly to its positions, concentrate on preserving its defensive integrity, hope fervently that the adjacent units would soon come abreast, and advance whenever possible in the slow, tedious process of moving frontally from one hedgerow to the next.

On 14 July, in conjunction with an attack launched on the east bank of the Vire River, the 30th Division, after several days of effort, finally secured the bridge at Pont-Hébert. Possession of the bridge plus the presence of the combat command at Hauts-Vents constituted a threat to St. Lô from the west. Although the Germans defending St. Lô were by this time fighting off an attack by the XIX Corps directly toward the city, they were sufficiently concerned with the indirect threat to increase their artillery fire against the 30th Division. They became very much aware of the fact that continued American progress in the Taute and Vire sector would outflank the entire *LXXXIV Corps.*[59]

Delayed by both the *Panzer Lehr* counterattack and a combination of enemy and terrain, the 9th and 30th Divisions still were short of fulfilling their

[57] Telecon, Corlett and Hobbs, 1507, 11 Jul; 3d Armd Div CCB S–3 Rpt 1, 11 Jul; 743d Tk Bn Unit Rpts 7 and 8, 10 and 11 Jul. All in 30th Div G–3 Jnl and File. FUSA Daily Estimated Loss Rpt, Jul. Capt. John S. Milligan, Jr., of the 197th Field Artillery Battalion was awarded the DSC.

[58] 35th Div Arty Unit Rpt 4, 35th Div Arty AAR, Jul; 30th Div G–3 Jnl and File, 11–14 Jul.
[59] Est of Situation, 12 Jul, *Seventh Army KTB.*

missions when a new factor emerged to modify General Bradley's earlier split of the Taute and Vire River area. As his new plan to get out of the Cotentin approached maturity, the ground near the Périers–St. Lô highway became a vital necessity. To make possible a joint effort by the 9th and 30th Divisions toward the new objective—the Périers–St. Lô highway—General Bradley shifted the corps boundaries again. At midnight on 15 July, General Collins' VII Corps relinquished the Carentan–Périers isthmus to the VIII Corps and assumed control of the area between the Taute and the Vire.

When General Collins surveyed his new VII Corps sector on 16 July, he saw a discouraging prospect. The divisions, although excellent, battle-proved units, were making no more than painfully slow progress toward the Périers–St. Lô highway. On the right, sudden and repeated incursions by small groups of enemy troops on the flanks and in the rear of the 9th Division were disturbing. On the left, the 30th Division's advance along a narrow ridge line with its flanks exposed to fire and infiltration looked less than comforting. Although both divisions had combat commands of armor attached and could have used them, developing plans for the new First Army attack required that the combat commands be withdrawn and reunited under parental control. General Collins detached the armor on 16 July, though he retained two tank companies with the 30th Division and three with the 9th.[60]

The attack then continued as before. Believing that the 9th Division had made

a minor breakthrough on 16 July, General Eddy optimistically hoped to be astride the objective by dusk that day.[61] The hope was premature. The soft terrain of the Terrette River valley and the ubiquitous hedgerows virtually stultified maneuver. The 30th Division was reluctant to abandon the high ground of its ridge sector to clear the valley of the Terrette, while the 9th Division was occupied all along its front and unable for a time to make a special effort on its left flank.

Not until 17 July, when the 330th Infantry finally gained positions close to the Périers–St. Lô road and thereby insured the 9th Division a secure right flank, could General Eddy begin a systematic sweep of the river valley. While the 330th Infantry reverted to its parent 83d Division, the organic regiments of the 9th Division took up the new assignment. At the same time, the 30th Division captured two small bridges and eliminated the possibility of enemy infiltration on the division's right flank.

Four days after the VII Corps assumed control of the sector, the 9th and 30th Divisions reached ground that overlooked the Périers–St. Lô highway between the Taute River and the Vire. The Germans continued to deny the road itself. Although "resistance remained undiminished," the VII Corps attack ceased.[62] The troops held a line adequate, General Bradley believed, for initiating the new First Army operation.

In moving eight miles from the Vire et Taute Canal to the Périers–St. Lô highway, the 30th Division between 7

---

[60] 9th and 30th Div AAR's, Jul.

[61] FUSA Msg, 2015, 16 Jul, XIX Corps G–3 Jnl and File.
[62] 9th Div AAR, Jul.

and 20 July lost over 3,000 men; the 9th Division between 10 and 20 July sustained about 2,500 casualties.[63] Although the divisions were several hundred yards short of the highway, they dominated the road by fire. The VII Corps was abreast of the positions attained several days earlier by the VIII Corps, which dominated the same highway between Lessay and Périers.

In the meantime, the First Army offensive had again been broadened, this time by an attack east of the Vire River, where the XIX Corps was trying to take St. Lô.

---

[63] FUSA Daily Estimated Loss Rpts, Jul; 30th Div G–3 Jnl, 1935, 15 Jul, 2335, 17 Jul; Telecon, Collins and Hobbs, 1600, 17 Jul, 30th Div G–3 Jnl and File.

CHAPTER VIII

The Battle for St. Lô

The Objective

Before the summer of 1944 the provincial city of St. Lô—primarily a market town but also a political and administrative capital—enjoyed a prosperity common to most agricultural centers and reflected a touch of more than rural elegance imparted by the society of officialdom. By the middle of June 1944 this once "charming and serene little city" had become "no more than a heap of smoking rubble." On the day the Allies invaded the Continent, 6 June, Allied planes had bombed the power plant and railroad station and then made concentrated and repeated attacks that seemed to the inhabitants to have been motivated by the sole intention of destroying the city. Almost 800 civilians lay dead under the ruins by the morning of 7 June, and Allied bombers returned every day for a week to increase the devastation.[1]

Although German propaganda pointed to St. Lô as an example of how the Allies were liberating France, the inhabitants apparently harbored less resentment than the Allies had expected. The French exhibited a "pathetic eagerness" to understand why the Allies had

selected St. Lô as an air force target long before the ground troops were near the town. There were several reasons: hope of hindering German troop movements by making a roadblock of the town itself, "a choke-point"; desire to destroy the *LXXXIV Corps* headquarters, located in a suburb until 16 June; and plans to take St. Lô nine days after the invasion.[2]

The Americans' unsuccessful efforts to capture St. Lô in June only stimulated desire for it. Although destroyed, the city at the beginning of July remained a place of vital interest both to the Americans who had helped demolish it and to the Germans who still held it. St. Lô had prestige value, and its continued retention by the Germans or its seizure by the Americans would have a strong effect on the morale of the opposing forces. The capital of the De-

---

[1] Robert Patry, *St.-Lô*, pp. 15–16 (English translation); see also J. de Saint-Jorre, "Saint-Lô sous les Bombes," and A. Legoy, "Exode de Saint-Lô," in Herval, *Bataille de Normandie*, I, 85–101, 102–04.

[2] XIX Corps AAR, Jul; FUSA Psychological Warfare Div Ltr, Bombing of St. Lô, 4 Jul, FUSA G–3 Jnl; Rpt of the Supreme Commander, p. 7; *Seventh Army KTB, Anlagen, Lagenkarten, 6.VI.–30. VI.44.* Cities bombed on 6 and 7 June to produce "choke-points" were Caen, Villers-Bocage, St. Lô, Pontaubault, Coutances, Thury-Harcourt, Lisieux, Falaise, Vire, and Argentan. General Omar N. Bradley and Air Effects Committee, 12th Army Group, *Effect of Air Power on Military Operations in Western Europe* (Wiesbaden, Germany, 1945) (hereafter cited as Bradley, *Effect of Air Power*), p. 28; *Sunday Punch in Normandy: the Tactical Use of Heavy Bombardment in the Normandy Invasion*, Wings at War Series, No. 2 (Washington, 1945), p. 19.

partment of the Manche, St. Lô was politically and psychologically important
to the French. A Norman road center
rivaling Caen, St. Lô would give the
Allies additional lateral communications
and routes to the south. The Americans felt that their possession of St. Lô
would correspondingly deny the Germans the ability to move troops and
supplies easily from one side of the Vire
River to the other immediately behind
the front.

By mid-July, the prestige factor and
the value of the city as an access point
to roads leading south gave way to a
more important reason. Because of its
location at the apex of the Coutances–
St. Lô–Lessay road triangle, the city was
specifically important to General Bradley's emerging plan for achieving more
rapid advance in the Cotentin. A premise of the new plan was American possession of St. Lô, a need that by mid-July
imparted a sense of urgency to the battle
for the city.[3]

The Germans had anchored their
positions on the hills north and northeast of St. Lô, advantageous terrain for
defense. At first they fought not so
much to hold St. Lô as to maintain their
line. The city was useless to them for
lateral communications because it was
within range of U.S. artillery, and their
troop and supply movements were taking place far to the south. But in July,
just before the Americans opened their
attack toward the city, the Germans captured an American field order. With
St. Lô revealed as a major U.S. objective,
the Germans reappraised its worth and

determined to challenge the effort to the
extent of their strength.[4]

German strength appeared adequate.
St. Lô was the responsibility of the *II
Parachute Corps,* which held the sector
between the Vire and the Drôme Rivers.
On the left (west) were three kampfgruppen—one each from the *353d,* the
266th, and the *352d Divisions*—under
the operational control of the *352d*
headquarters. On the right was the *3d
Parachute Division.* In support was the
12th Assault Gun Brigade. Although
the troops in the line were spread thin
across a wide front, they were veterans.
The corps commander, Meindl, though
concerned with what amounted to a
manpower shortage for his wide front,
felt certain that the defensive skill of
his troops and the excellent positions
would offset to a great extent the rather
sparse dispositions. He was confident
he could keep the Americans out of St.
Lô.[5]

The old part of the city of St. Lô occupied a rock bluff that was crowned
by ancient ramparts, a tower, and the
graceful double spires of a fifteenth century church. Surrounding the bluff,
modern St. Lô spreads across the lowlands and up the slopes of encircling
hills. The Vire River, flowing generally northward, enters the city from the
southwest, executes a horseshoe loop,
and leaves to the northwest. The
greater part of the city lies east of the
river and outside the horseshoe. (*Map
III*)

The western suburb of St. Lô, inside

[3] Answers by Gens Smith and Bull to questions,
14–15 Sep 45.

[4] *Seventh Army KTB* (Draft), 11 Jul.
[5] *Seventh Army KTB* (Draft), 11 Jul; Telecons,
Pemsel to Hausser, 1220, 11 Jul, and Pemsel to
Tempelhoff, 1245, 11 Jul, *Seventh Army* Tel Msgs;
OB WEST KTB, 11 Jul; MS # B–401 (Meindl).

the horseshoe loop, is on the high ground that extends westward to Coutances. The northern part of St. Lô rises steeply toward the plateau-like top of Hill 122. On the east, the city spreads toward the base of the Martinville ridge, an eminence that ascends in a gentle slope for four miles to Hill 192. The southern portion climbs very briefly toward high ground that dominates the southern approaches.

Two main highways intersect at St. Lô, and five blacktop roads converge on the city. On the west, the highway from Coutances and the road from Lessay and Périers merge inside the river loop before crossing the stream into town. From the north two routes arrive, one the highway from Carentan through Pont-Hébert and along the western slope of Hill 122, the other the road from Isigny along the eastern edge of the hill. From the east, the road from Caumont merges with the highway from Bayeux and Caen at the Bérigny fork (seven miles from St. Lô) and the resultant single large highway runs along the south face of the Martinville ridge and into town. From the south one highway and two roads enter the city.

At the time of the invasion, St. Lô had been in the V Corps zone. Commanded by Maj. Gen. Leonard T. Gerow, who had directed the landings on OMAHA Beach and the drive to Caumont, the V Corps in June had anchored the American left flank firmly on Caumont and in mid-June had surrendered the St. Lô region to the XIX Corps, under General Corlett. Yet the configuration of the terrain—specifically, the location of Hill 192—is such that both corps had

to participate in the direct attack toward the city.[6] Hill 192 is the culminating point of the high ground that straddles the Bérigny–St. Lô road four miles northeast of St. Lô. In the V Corps zone of operations, Hill 192 gave the Germans observation not only of the V Corps sector as far to the rear as the invasion beaches but also of all the approaches to St. Lô. Capture of the height thus was a prerequisite to the XIX Corps attack on the city. The XIX and V Corps consequently planned co-ordinated action for simultaneous attacks east of the Vire River on 11 July.[7]

Hill 192

As the offensive east of the Vire began, the focal point of the operations initially developed on Hill 192 and involved the right (west) flank unit of the V Corps. While the 2d Armored and the 1st Infantry Divisions on the left (east) of the V Corps sector defended Caumont and held the pivot point of the projected First Army wheeling movement, the 2d Infantry Division attacked on the right to secure Hill 192 in conjunction with the XIX Corps attack toward St. Lô.[8] (Map 8)

Under Maj. Gen. Walter M. Robertson, division commander since 1942, the 2d Division had arrived in Normandy

---

[6] FUSA Ltr, Timing of Attack as Set Forth in FO 1, rev as of 1 Jul, 2 Jul, FUSA G–3 Jnl File.

[7] XIX Corps Memo, 7 Jul, XIX Corps G–3 Jnl; Air Plan for Support of the 29th Div and Ltr of Instr, 10 Jul, 30th Div G–3 Jnl.

[8] V Corps Operations in the ETO, 6 Jan. 1942–9 May 1945 (G–3 Historical Sub-Section; n.p., n.d.), pp. 101ff. This is an excellent source containing a narrative account, reproductions of important documents, and annexes detailing the activities of the supporting services.

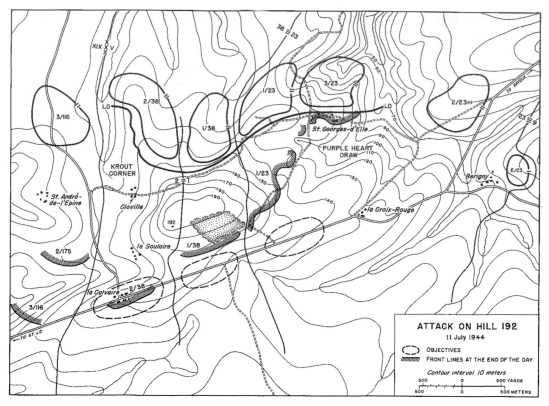

MAP 8

the day after the invasion and had participated in the early drive from OMAHA Beach.   Considered a good unit, the division had no illusions about taking Hill 192 easily, for an attempt in June had cost over 1,200 casualties within three days.[9]   The division awaited the inevitable order to attack the hill again; and while in physical contact with the enemy at distances varying from several yards to a few hedgerowed fields, the division shelled the hill thoroughly, drew up elaborate plans of attack, and conducted training specifically designed for

the assault.   The training emphasized tank-infantry-engineer proficiency in applying the tactics of demolition, fire power, and speed in the hedgerow terrain.   To achieve speed in the attack, troops scooped holes, large enough for tanks to drive through, in the hedgerow embankments that served as the line of departure—holes that left a thin shell of earth on the side facing the enemy; when the attack order came, the tanks would be able to crash through under their own power.   Bursting through the hollowed-out hedgerows, the tankers hoped to be upon the Germans in the next row before antitank weapons could be brought to bear.

---

[9] See Ltr, Eisenhower to Marshall, 5 Jul, Pogue Files.

Hill 192 had been "so pounded by artillery that aerial photographs showed it as a moth-eaten white blanket."[10] Yet it was a strong position. The slopes of the hill rise gradually to a rather flat top, and the small fields bordered by hedgerows and the scattered woods that surface the slopes provided concealment for the defenders. Hedgerows presented natural defensive lines in depth. Sunken lanes provided excellent lines of communication easily protected by a few carefully sited weapons. Several hamlets and occasional farmhouses offered shelter for crew-served weapons and centers of resistance. A tower concealed in a diamond-shaped patch of woods, earlier destroyed by U.S. artillery fire but rebuilt by the Germans, gave the defenders a good observation post. A battalion of the *3d Parachute Division* occupied the hill and had fortified it with an intricate system of mutually supporting positions.

The Germans maintained a tight counterreconnaissance screen, made maximum use of sunken roads and hedges, and employed roadblocks, wire entanglements, and mine fields. Although the main defensive positions were judged shallow—perhaps only two or three hedgerows in depth—the Americans expected the Germans to defend with determination and vigor and to employ local counterattacks to retain their positions. There seemed to be few if any German tanks in the area, and intelligence officers estimated that the *II Parachute Corps* did not have an impressive amount of artillery. The Americans were sure, however, that prior registration would enable the Germans to cover

the approaches to St. Lô and also the slopes of Hill 192 with precision fire.

The "top of the hill is the big thing," General Gerow said, but to make it secure the 2d Division had to advance beyond it and occupy a two and a half mile stretch of the Bérigny highway between the Calvaire road and the Bérigny fork. The other corps units were to make a strong demonstration; air support was arranged; the corps artillery and four artillery battalions of the other divisions in the corps sector were to reinforce the 2d Division fires.[11]

The 38th Infantry (Col. Ralph W. Zwicker), on the right (west) and less than a thousand yards north of the crest of Hill 192, was to make the main assault with three tank companies and two heavy mortar companies attached. The 23d Infantry (Lt. Col. Jay B. Loveless), in the center, was to send one battalion across the eastern slope of the objective. The 9th Infantry (Col. Chester J. Hirschfelder), in position east of the Bérigny fork, was to support the division attack with fire.

Since a haze limited visibility on the morning of 11 July, the planned air support was canceled. The artillery fired a heavy preparation for twenty minutes, and shortly after 0600 the division jumped off.[12]

The preceding night Colonel Zwicker's 38th Infantry had withdrawn several hundred yards for safety during the anticipated air strike, and when the regiment jumped off the troops immediately

---

[10] Sylvan Diary, 11 Jul.

[11] 2d Div G-3 Jnl, 0925, 11 Jul, FO 5, 6 Jul, and G-3 Per Rpt 33, 12 Jul; V Corps FO 10, 4 Jul.

[12] [Garth], *St.-Lô,* pp. 58–60. This American Forces in Action booklet contains an excellent detailed account of the battle for St. Lô with emphasis on small unit action.

met a heavy volume of enemy fire that temporarily prevented them from reaching their line of departure. The Germans had discovered the slight withdrawal, had moved forward, and had thus escaped the full force of the twenty-minute artillery preparation. During the first half hour of the attack, they disabled with *panzerfaust* fire or forced to retire all six tanks in the first wave of one of the assault battalions. The stratagem of scooping out hedgerow banks to gain a surprise forward bound had thus been nullified.

American infantrymen advanced slowly with the help of heavy and accurate artillery fire. Twenty thousand rounds were fired by the division artillery alone; a total of 45 tons of high explosive came from all the artillery in support. Tanks and bazooka teams knocked out assault guns concealed in the rubble of a village. A dozen riflemen enveloped by stealth an enemy position known as "Kraut Corner," reached grenade distance, and destroyed the enemy weapons. Fifteen German paratroopers surrendered. Three who refused to capitulate were buried alive by a tank dozer.

"We have a battle on our hands," General Robertson said, "[but] things are breaking a little, a hundred yards here and a hundred yards there." [13] This was the pattern of the slow, vigorous advance that by noon got the 38th Infantry to the top of Hill 192. The Germans then disengaged and withdrew, and only scattered groups opposed the descent on the south slope. Part of the 38th Infantry dug in on a defensive perimeter just short of the highway and covered the road with fire; the other elements slipped

across the road in small groups and organized the high ground immediately to the south.

Meanwhile, a battalion of the 23d Infantry outflanked a gully called "Purple Heart Draw." Tanks placed direct fire on houses suspected of concealing German strongpoints. Several lucky shots by rifle grenades struck enemy-held hedgerows just right to achieve the effect of air bursts over enemy crew-served weapons. By late afternoon the battalion had crossed the east slope of Hill 192 and gained positions overlooking the Bérigny highway.

That evening Hausser, the *Seventh Army* commander, ordered Meindl, the *II Parachute Corps* commander, to hold Hill 192 at all costs. [14] It was already too late. As U.S. artillery placed harassing fires south of the Bérigny road during the night, the infantry repelled small and ineffective counterattacks. It became obvious to the Americans that the Germans were establishing a new line of defense in the hills south of and overlooking the St. Lô–Bérigny highway.

On 12 July the 2d Division advanced little, spending the day consolidating its new positions south of the Bérigny road. The Germans were relieved when the American attack halted, for with their troops tied down by the XIX Corps attack toward St. Lô, German commanders felt that if the 2d Division had continued its attack toward the south, the Americans would have accomplished a clean breakthrough. [15]

The 2d Division had nonetheless

---

[13] 2d Div G–3 Jnl, 0925 and 0955, 11 Jul.

[14] Telecon, Pemsel and Meindl, 1900, 11 Jul, *Seventh Army* Tel Msgs.

[15] Telecon, Blauensteiner to Helmdach, 1140, 12 Jul, *Seventh Army* Tel Msgs.

achieved a notable success. Although it had taken only 147 prisoners and sustained heavy losses—69 killed, 328 wounded, and 8 missing—it had captured the best observation point in the St. Lô sector, a point from which the Americans could look down the Martinville ridge toward the XIX Corps objective.

Down the Martinville Ridge

The attack directly toward St. Lô, by that part of the XIX Corps east of the Vire River, should logically have followed soon after the successive corps attacks in the Cotentin—those of the VIII Corps on 3 July, the VII on 4 July, and the XIX Corps bridgehead operation launched on 7 July. Although General Bradley had tentatively extended the pattern of his offensive by scheduling the direct attack toward St Lô for 9 July, considerations twice caused him to postpone the effort, each time for twenty-four hours. The first was his hope that commitment of armor west of the Vire would promote quick capture of the high ground west of St. Lô. The second was his feeling that additional troops were needed east of the Vire. Though the 29th Division, regarded as a good outfit, had formed the left of the XIX Corps early in July, Bradley believed, on the basis of combat experience in June, that a single division deployed on a wide front was not strong enough to take St. Lô. At least one additional division would be necessary in order to mount an attack that could be supported in depth.[16]

Whether the 35th Division, designated

for attachment to the XIX Corps, would reach France in time to participate at the beginning of the attack was the question. Though advance elements of the division had relieved portions of the 30th Division and freed them for their bridgehead operations on 7 July, it would take "very strenuous efforts" to get all of the division's men and equipment into position to take over the right portion of the 29th Division zone. Not until 11 July was the 35th Division ready to attack.[17] (*See Map III.*)

A scant four miles north of St. Lô, the 29th and 35th Divisions held positions across an eight-mile front—from la Meauffe through Villiers-Fossard to the Couvains–Calvaire road. St. Lô was in the center of the projected corps zone of operations. In order to secure St. Lô, the divisions would have to advance to the river line west of the city and to the Bérigny road, the eastward exit from the city.

The divisions were to attack abreast in narrow zones. The boundary separating them ran from Villiers-Fossard along the western base of Hill 122 to the loop of the Vire River. The 35th on the right was to move to the two-mile stretch of the Vire immediately northwest of St. Lô; the 29th was to take the city. While one battalion of medium artillery supported the XIX Corps attack west of the Vire, the remainder of the corps artillery—four battalions of 155-mm. howitzers and a battalion each of 4.5-inch guns and 8-inch howitzers—was to assist the attack on St. Lô. General Corlett attached an additional battalion of medi-

---

[16] Telecon, Corlett and Gerhardt, 0825, 8 Jul, 29th Div G–3 Jnl; Ltr, Eisenhower to Marshall, 5 Jul, Pogue Files.

[17] 35th Div CofS Memo, 9 Jul, 35th Div G–3 Jnl; XIX Corps Ltr of Instrs, 7 Jul; XIX Corps and 29th Div Msgs, 0712 and 1200, 10 Jul, XIX Corps G–3 Jnl.

um artillery to the 29th Division, which was to make the main effort of the corps.[18]

The 29th Division was a veteran unit with D-Day experience on OMAHA Beach. Commanded by Maj. Gen. Charles H. Gerhardt, it had taken Isigny and attempted to capture St. Lô in June. While awaiting the reopening of offensive operations, General Gerhardt had organized small tank-infantry-engineer teams and rehearsed their co-ordinated action according to a plan that assigned an infantry squad and one tank to each hedgerowed field and an engineer squad to each infantry platoon or three fields. He directed the division ordnance company to weld iron prongs to his tanks so that they could ram holes in the hedgerow banks to facilitate the placing of demolitions. He also experimented with the technique of infantry crossing the center of the fields rather than moving along hedgerows.[19] By these means, and with heavy artillery support, he hoped—even though replacements had not brought all of his infantry battalions back to authorized strength—to make a rapid, sustained advance.

Bombed from the air and shelled from the ground, St. Lô was in ruins. To avoid not only the costly fighting involved in rooting Germans from the crumbling houses but also the task of clearing the rubble-clogged streets, General Gerhardt designated high ground near the city rather than St. Lô itself as the immediate objectives: Hill 122 north of the town and just inside the division right boundary, the Martinville ridge to

the east, and the heights southeast of St. Lô. With these in his possession and with the 2d Division holding Hill 192, Gerhardt hoped that by threatening to encircle the city he could compel the Germans to evacuate.

Two of the three heights General Gerhardt deemed necessary for his purpose were within striking distance—Hill 122 and the Martinville ridge. Although possession of Hill 122 would give the 29th Division a more direct avenue of approach to the city—the Isigny–St. Lô highway, which enters St. Lô from the northeast—Gerhardt preferred not to attack it directly. Second only to Hill 192 in importance in the St. Lô area, Hill 122 was a bastion of the German defensive line, a position that anchored fortifications on a two-mile ridge extending north to Carillon. The Germans were sensitive to a threat against this height, since its plateaulike crest ends abruptly at a steep slope near the edge of the northern outskirts of St. Lô. From the top of the slope, the city lies exposed and vulnerable.

General Gerhardt preferred to make his main effort on the left (east). He therefore deployed the 115th Infantry (Col. Godwin Ordway, Jr.) across a broad front, north and northeast of Hill 122, on the division right. Even though all three infantry battalions were in the line, a gap of several hundred yards separated two of them. The reason for such thin deployment was Gerhardt's plan to make his main effort to secure the Martinville ridge. By holding this eminence east of St. Lô, U.S. troops would threaten the Germans on Hill 122 with encirclement and isolation from the south. In a potentially untenable

---

[18] XIX Corps Arty AAR, Jul.
[19] The Div Comdr's After Combat Battle Notes, 29 Div AAR, Jul.

MARTINVILLE RIDGE

position, the Germans on Hill 122 would have to withdraw through St. Lô before the Americans entered the city and cut their route of escape. As the Germans withdrew the Americans could decimate them with artillery fire. Occupation of both Hill 122 and the high ground southeast of St. Lô would then be a simple matter.

Assuming that the 2d Division would take Hill 192 and thus secure his flank and rear, General Gerhardt directed the 116th Infantry (Col. Charles D. W. Canham) to slip south on a narrow front near the division left boundary to the Martinville ridge. There the regiment would turn right (west) and descend the ridge toward the eastern edge of town. The 115th Infantry was to make a diversionary effort down the Isigny–St. Lô road toward Hill 122 and protect the division right flank. The 175th Infantry (Col. Ollie W. Reed) was to be prepared to exploit success—either on the Martinville Ridge or, if despite contrary expectation the 115th met little

resistance from Hill 122, along the Isigny–St. Lô axis.[20]

General Gerhardt's scheme was almost disarranged just before daybreak on 11 July when the *II Parachute Corps* launched a diversionary feint in support of the *Panzer Lehr* attack west of the Vire.[21] A German patrol cut the communication wires of the 115th Infantry. Enemy artillery and mortars opened fire. Two paratroop companies supported by engineers struck the thinly deployed troops of the 115th, overran the American lines, encircled part of an infantry battalion, and drove a company of 4.2-inch mortarmen from their positions. Without communication and direction from higher headquarters, heavy mortar support, or knowledge of the extent of the German effort, small groups fought isolated engagements in the early morning light. At 0730, judging that they had done their duty by *Panzer Lehr*,

---

[20] 29th Div FO 18, 4 Jul; 29th Div Arty FO 2, 4 Jul; 116th Inf FO 10, 5 Jul.
[21] See above, Ch. VII.

the German assault companies broke contact and withdrew to their former positions. What was essentially a raid alerted the 29th Division to the possibility that German reserves had been massed in depth for counterattack and would be in position to make a strong defense of St. Lô. The raid also inflicted more than a hundred casualties on the 115th and disrupted its scheduled jump-off. Regimental reorganization took the remainder of the morning, and Colonel Ordway did not launch his attack down the Isigny–St. Lô road until afternoon. As anticipated, little advance was made in the face of strong enemy fire directed from Hill 122.[22]

Meanwhile, General Gerhardt had been able to get his main effort under way on the division left flank early that morning when two battalions of the 116th Infantry jumped off in column behind a heavy artillery preparation. The hedgerows made it difficult to locate the exact sources of enemy fire, and progress was slow against determined resistance. As 4.2-inch mortars fired on the Martinville ridge and tanks knocked out a self-propelled gun on the Calvaire road, the infantry finally got past its first major obstacle, a sunken road heavily protected by antipersonnel mines. The regiment still had gained only six hedgerows in five hours when, suddenly, as the 2d Division secured the crest of Hill 192, the German opposition gave way. The 116th Infantry then moved rapidly south to the Martinville ridge, turned right (west), and began to move down the ridge toward St. Lô.

As soon as the assaulting troops surged forward, Colonel Canham, the regimental commander, committed his reserve battalion. By the end of the day this battalion, with a company of tanks in close support, had set up blocking positions on the division left flank. Entrenched on the south slope of the Martinville ridge, the battalion overlooked the Bérigny road.

Toward the end of the first day General Gerhardt's effort to outflank Hill 122 from the east and south promised success. The 2d Division had captured Hill 192 and was protecting the strong 116th Infantry positions on the Martinville ridge. Apparently ready to close in on St. Lô and threaten Hill 122 with isolation, Gerhardt alerted his reserve regiment, the 175th, to pass through the 116th on the following day and drive into the city from the east.

The plan had one drawback. As soon as the 116th had turned the axis of attack from the south to the west, its left flank had become exposed; men moving across the open fields and orchards of the southern face of the Martinville ridge came under observed German fire from high ground south of the Bérigny road. Having in effect sought defilade from the fires of Hill 122 against the north face of the Martinville ridge, the Americans had come under enfilading fire from the south, shelling that harassed movement and depleted ranks. As a result the 29th Division on 11 July lost almost 500 men.

If Gerhardt persisted with his original scheme of maneuver and brought the bulk of the division down the Martinville ridge, he would send his men through a gantlet of German fire. But because control of the southern face of

[22] 29th Div AAR, Jul and Extract from the Battle Report of the *3d Parachute Division* Operations, 10–20 Jul; XIX Corps Cml Sec Rpt, XIX Corps AAR, Jul.

the Martinville ridge would protect his flank against attack across the Bérigny highway and because an approach to St. Lô from the east still held out the promise of quickly dislodging the Germans on Hill 122, General Gerhardt decided to continue. He became convinced, however, that as long as the Germans had control of the hills north and south of St. Lô, they were not likely to give up the city. Thus he had to take St. Lô by direct assault and occupy the town. On the evening of 11 July he instructed Colonel Canham to "push on, if possible take St. Lô."[23] Encroaching darkness helped to thwart the attempt.

With the American scheme of maneuver revealed by a captured field order, German commanders during the morning of 11 July had been unworried by the American attack. By noontime the outlook had changed. They had lost the top of Hill 192, and the *Panzer Lehr* attack west of the Vire River had fizzled. The considerable American pressure, not only in the St. Lô region but all across the Cotentin, was having a cumulative effect that could not be wished away. Trying to retain possession of the St. Lô defenses, the *II Parachute Corps* reported that its entire front had "burst into flame." A strong volume of effective artillery fire had by nightfall of 11 July reduced the *3d Parachute Division* to 35 percent of its authorized strength. The kampfgruppe of the *353d Division*, fighting alongside the paratroopers, had shrunk from almost 1,000 men to 180. Approving commitment of the last reserve battalion of the *3d Parachute Division*, Meindl, the

corps commander, requested that a regiment of the *5th Parachute Division*, arriving at this time from Brittany, be sent to reinforce his sector. Hausser, the *Seventh Army* commander, refused, judging that the *Panzer Lehr* defeat made the region west of St. Lô more critical. Hausser insisted, nevertheless, that the Martinville ridge be held at all costs. In response, Meindl remarked that someone was soon going to have to come up with a brilliant plan if they were to counter the American pressure. Meanwhile, Meindl established a new line during the night. The positions extended north across the Bérigny highway and over the Martinville ridge to tie in with Hill 122, and faced eastward to meet the threat that had developed on the Martinville ridge.[24]

On the second day of attack, 12 July, the 29th Division made little progress. On the right the 115th Infantry, extended over a broad front, without a reserve, and under the eyes of the Germans on Hill 122, did little more than maintain pressure and sustain casualties. On the left, the 175th Infantry was unable—because of German artillery fire—to pass through the 116th and get into position for a drive down the Martinville ridge. German artillery and mortar fire immobilized the division and again inflicted almost 500 casualties.

Losing nearly 1,000 men in two days was a serious drain on the division, which had not been up to strength at the beginning of the attack. A battalion of the 175th Infantry, even before

---

[23] [Garth], *St.-Lô*, p. 58.

[24] Telecons, Pemsel to Meindl, 1900, 11 Jul, and Blauensteiner to Helmdach, 1140, 12 Jul, *Seventh Army* Tel Msgs; *Seventh Army KTB* (Draft), 11 Jul; Daily Sitrep, 12 Jul, *AGp B Tagesmeldungen*; MS # B-455 (Ziegelmann).

commitment, had only 225 men in its three rifle companies. Several hours after the jump-off another battalion commander had replied, when General Gerhardt asked him how he stood in strength, "On one leg, sir." German fire depleted the division at an alarming rate, and the hedgerow fighting wore out the survivors.   On the evening of 12 July a regimental commander understated the case when he informed Gerhardt, "I think everybody is enthusiastic about taking up a strong defensive position right now and I would recommend it too." [25]

After two days of battle the corps and division commanders, Generals Corlett and Gerhardt, both came to the conclusion, "Hill 122 is SOP"—they needed Hill 122 before they could take St. Lô.   By 13 July, however, General Gerhardt no longer had the strength to seize the hill.   The bulk of the 29th Division, the 116th and 175th Regiments, was inextricably committed in the left portion of the division zone, the Martinville ridge; the 115th Infantry, facing Hill 122 and in position to assault the height, remained stretched across a broad front.   Gerhardt tentatively proposed to envelop and bypass the German strongpoint on Hill 122, but he did not press the point since he did not feel it was a satisfactory solution.[26]

General Corlett held the solution to the problem of Hill 122.   He could commit his corps reserve against it. Yet before doing so, he wanted to give Gerhardt's original plan of maneuver—

continuation of the effort down the Martinville ridge—one more day.   To support the attack he requested particularly heavy air bombardment of Hill 122.[27]

By morning of 13 July the two regiments on the Martinville ridge had managed to assume definite regimental zones abreast and facing west, the 116th generally holding the ridge line, the 175th occupying positions across the southern face of the ridge to the Bérigny road.   In compliance with the corps commander's decision, General Gerhardt directed the 175th Infantry to drive down the Bérigny highway to St. Lô behind a spearhead of tanks.   With dive bombers blasting ahead of the ground troops and neutralizing Hill 122, artillery giving close protection, and tanks driving the point down the road, there was reason to hope that the city might fall.

The hope was short lived.   Hardly had daylight come before hindrances developed.   Not only did bad weather nullify the air effort, but lack of proper co-ordination prevented the tanks from refueling and immobilized them for the duration of the attack.   Deprived of both armor and air support, the infantry, although aided by strong artillery fire, advanced but 500 yards under the pounding of German artillery and mortar shells directed from the ridge south of the highway.

Late in the afternoon the regimental commander, Colonel Reed, requested permission to commit his reserve battalion against the high ground south of the Bérigny road.   When General Ger-

[25] 29th Div G-3 Jnl, 1215 and 1558, 11 Jul, and 1707, 12 Jul.
[26] 29th Div G-3 Jnl, 0955, 13 Jul.

[27] 29th Div FO 20, 12 Jul; 29th Div Arty AAR, Jul.

hardt relayed the request to the corps commander, General Corlett refused for fear it might promote a dispersal of effort. Also, he had by then decided to take action against Hill 122 by committing his reserve, a regiment of the 35th Division, and he needed the reserve battalion of Reed's regiment to constitute a new corps reserve. Ordering General Gerhardt to rest his troops and reorganize his positions on the following day, 14 July, General Corlett turned his main attention to the 35th Division, the unit on the right that had also been attacking since 11 July and would now have to take Hill 122.

Hill 122

Commanded by Maj. Gen. Paul W. Baade, the 35th Division, though well trained, was handicapped by the haste with which it had to be committed. The troops had taken over part of the active front without extensive ground reconnaissance; their knowledge of the enemy was limited to the general idea of where the German forward line lay, the impression that the Germans were defending with vigor, and the immediate realization that the Germans had excellent observation of all movement, particularly in the open fields. Only when the division launched its attack did the men learn how thoroughly the Germans had organized the terrain.[28]

From a line of departure running between la Meauffe (on the Vire) and Villiers-Fossard, the 35th Division faced hedgerow country. The objective, four miles away, was the two-mile stretch of the Vire River between the loop and the bend. The division's right flank was fairly well protected by the Vire River; but on the left, just outside the boundary, Hill 122 dominated the entire zone.

For his attack on 11 July, the same day that the 2d and 29th jumped off, General Baade planned to commit two regiments abreast—the 137th (Col. Grant Layng) on the right adjacent to the river, the 320th (Col. Bernard A. Byrne) on the left. The 134th Infantry (Col. Butler B. Miltonberger) was to be held as corps reserve. After a thirty-minute artillery preparation, the division moved forward at 0600.[29]

The right flank elements of both assault regiments advanced a mile and a half in two hours and straightened the division front, but then the attack stalled. Meeting strong resistance in the hedgerows, the troops encountered many of the same difficulties that plagued nearly all inexperienced divisions in the hedgerows. Communications went out almost immediately. Gaps soon developed between units. The men seemed surprised to find strong opposition from machine guns in sunken roads and behind hedges. With astonishment they noted that it was "hard to put down [artillery] fire behind hedges close to our tr[oop]s."[30] Though the troops had been informed while in England that the Cornish countryside was somewhat like Normandy, neither planning nor training to overcome the terrain obstacles of the hedgerows had gone far

---

[28] Interv with Lt Col Beckley by Capt Franklin Ferris, CI 106; 35th Div G–3 Jnl, 9 Jul.

[29] 35th Div FO 2, 10 Jul, and AAR, Jul.
[30] 35th Div G–3 Jnl, 1820, 11 Jul.

SUNKEN ROAD NEAR CARILLON

beyond speculation.[31] German mortar
and automatic weapons fire was particularly heavy, and one of the wounded was
a regimental commander, Colonel Layng.
The first day of action did little more
than give the troops their baptism of
fire and rudely introduce them into
the complexities of hedgerow warfare.
Across the Vire River General Hobbs
clamored for the 35th Division to advance and cover the 30th Division
flank.[32]

On the second day of attack, 12 July,
the 35th Division employed a 45-minute
artillery preparation to try to soften the
German defenses. This helped to
achieve success against a fortified posi-

tion in a church and cemetery on the
right flank, where machine gunners in
concrete emplacements behind the cemetery walls had been an immovable obstruction since early the preceding day.
A battalion cleared the obstacle shortly
before noon; no prisoners were taken—
all the Germans were dead. The infantry then proceeded to take the next
strongpoint, a fortified château that had
been set ablaze the previous night by
artillery shells.

Despite this advance, the 35th Division made only slight gains on 12 and
13 July. Inexperience and the hedgerows were partly responsible, but more
important was the strong German position at Carillon, which was in the center
of the division zone and backed by the
forces on Hill 122.

Though envelopment looked like the
answer at Carillon, every attempt was
thwarted by a lack of maneuver room
and by the dominating German positions on Hill 122. It became obvious
that if the 35th Division was to progress,
Hill 122, in the 29th Division zone, had
to be in American hands. Only then
did it seem that General Baade would
be able to advance his right flank sufficiently to cover the 30th Division on
the other side of the river.

The situation was partially resolved
on 14 July. While the 29th Division
rested and reorganized, General Baade
sent out part of the 35th in an attack
along the east bank of the Vire. Helped
by a strong 30th Division drive on the
other river bank, the 137th Infantry,
commanded now by Col. Harold R.
Emery, advanced in rain through mine
fields and heavy mortar and artillery
fire to the Pont-Hébert–St. Lô highway.

---

[31] James A. Huston, *Biography of A Battalion*
(Gering, Nebraska: Courier Press, 1950), p. 14.
The volume gives an excellent account of operations as seen from the point of view of a battalion
staff officer.

[32] See Telecon, 12 Jul, 35th Div G–3 Jnl File.

With all three battalions committed and with tanks, tank destroyers, and artillery giving strong support, the 137th secured part of the ridge road. The regiment lost 125 men and 11 medium tanks and took 53 prisoners.

The results of the advance were important. The *352d Division*, which defended the ground adjacent to and east of the Vire River, had always been troubled by its potentially precarious positions. The Vire River defined its left (west) flank and also crossed the unit rear. Since no permanent structures bridged the Vire between Pont-Hébert and St. Lô, if American troops drove to St. Lô or to the loop of the river, the division was trapped. To maintain lateral communications across the Vire, the Germans built an underwater bridge at Rampan, south of Pont-Hébert, but it could not support a wholesale exodus from the sector. The loss of Pont-Hébert so threatened the Rampan crossing site that German engineers hurriedly began to build a temporary bridge just northwest of St. Lô.[33]

Thoughts of withdrawal were becoming stronger as the battle proceeded. During the first three days of the American effort in July, the *352d Division* computed that it had borne 40 attacks— 2 in regimental, 12 in battalion, and 26 in company strength. The effect of the incessant thrust over a three-day period had forced the Germans back. If the U.S. infantry attacks had been effective, their artillery had been devastating. During the first two days, the German division had sustained 840 wounded, most from artillery fire, and was unable to count its dead. American counter-

U.S. SOLDIER IN GERMAN POSITION

battery fire was particularly impressive, destroying in one instance six of the twelve guns of one battalion.

The rapid decline in the effectiveness of the *352d Division* had serious connotations for the Germans defending St. Lô. Should the *352d* collapse, Hill 122 would be lost. The loss of Hill 122 meant eventual withdrawal to the high ground south of St. Lô. Meindl therefore reinforced the forces on Hill 122 with *266th Division* troops he had held in reserve and with the *30th Mobile Brigade*, which had just returned to *II Parachute Corps* control after being relieved by *Panzer Lehr* in the sector west of the Vire.[34]

Unaware of the exact effect the 35th Division was having on the opposition, General Corlett was nevertheless conscious that Pont-Hébert, secured in con-

[33] MS # B-439 (Ziegelmann)

[34] MS # B-455 (Ziegelmann); Hodgson, R-54.

junction with the 30th Division attack on the other side of the river, gave the 35th a favored position. With a foothold on the ridge road, the Americans held an excellent approach to St. Lô from the northwest. Having outflanked the German strongpoint at Carillon, they also threatened Hill 122. Though the 320th Infantry, which was echeloned to the left rear for two miles, could do little more than exert unavailing pressure against Carillon, the 137th had fashioned an enveloping pincer against the Carillon–Hill 122 complex from the west. A similar pincer from the east would form a double envelopment of Carillon and Hill 122. Because the 29th Division, with the bulk of its forces on the Martinville ridge, did not have enough troops in position to assault Hill 122 from the northeast, Corlett shifted the division boundary to the east, to the Isigny–St. Lô highway, giving the 35th Division more maneuver space and Hill 122 as an objective. Corlett released the 134th Infantry from the corps reserve and directed Baade to take the height. In preparation for the attack, the 134th on 14 July replaced two battalions of the 115th Infantry that were west of the Isigny–St. Lô highway, thereby getting into position to strike for Hill 122 while at the same time bringing relief to the overextended 29th Division.[35]

General Baade's intention was to attack with both flank regiments. While the 320th contained the Germans at Carillon, the 137th, on the right, was to advance across the Pont-Hébert–St. Lô ridge road. The 134th, on the left, was to move forward in direct assault

against Hill 122. Success on the flanks would neutralize the Carillon position, eliminate Hill 122, and open the way for an easy advance to the final division objective, the stretch of the Vire River between the loop and the bend.

A need to diverge from this plan became obvious on 15 July soon after the 137th Infantry attacked on the right to cross the Pont-Hébert–St. Lô ridge road. Artillery and mortar fire directed from Hill 122 inflicted 117 casualties and stopped the regiment cold. The 137th could not advance, General Baade deduced, until the 134th Infantry took Hill 122.

Colonel Miltonberger's 134th Infantry also had attacked early on 15 July. The axis of advance was a country road, dirt-surfaced and narrow, from Villiers-Fossard through Emélie to the hardly discernible flat top of the hill. The road parallels the Isigny–St. Lô highway, a mile to the east, and rises slightly for almost three miles as it mounts the gentle northern incline of Hill 122, then drops down the precipitous descent into the northern edge of St. Lô. On both sides of the road typical *bocage* terrain offered advantages to the defenders—impressive hedgerows and sunken lanes that are veritable caves.

The 134th Infantry moved toward the cluster of farm buildings at Emélie behind a rolling artillery barrage. Almost immediately the men became enmeshed in a tangle of hedgerowed lanes and a shower of enemy fire. The threat of confusion hovered over the battlefield as small units fought for individual fields. Although the regiment suffered high casualties in severe splinter actions, it had the hamlet of Emélie by noon.

---

[35] 35th Div AAR, Jul.

Encouraged by this success, General Baade told Brig. Gen. Edmund B. Sebree, the assistant division commander, to form a task force and lead it in the remaining thrust to the crest of Hill 122. Uniting the 134th with two companies of the 737th Tank Battalion, a company of the 60th Engineer Battalion, and a platoon of the 654th Tank Destroyer Battalion, General Sebree completed his preparations by evening.[36] At 2030, after planes bombed German positions around St. Lô and as the 29th Division attacked in its sector, the task force of the 35th Division jumped off.

In the deceptive illumination of twilight, the task force moved swiftly. Advancing up the north slope of Hill 122, General Sebree called on direct fire support from one artillery battalion, parts of two others, and the entire 82d Chemical Battalion. It was a mile to the crest of the hill, and the task force was there by midnight. While the infantrymen dug in, engineers hauled sandbags, wire, and mines up the incline to bolster defensive positions against counterattacks that were sure to follow. The Germans still had sufficient maneuver room north of St. Lô to launch counterattacks, but the integrity of the German strongpoint had been at least temporarily cracked.

The expected counterthrust came in the early hours of 16 July and drove the infantry back slightly until a newly committed reserve battalion helped restore the line.[37] Later that day the Germans launched another attack, supported by heavy mortar and artillery fire. This time American infantrymen gave way in sizable numbers—some stragglers fled back to Emélie—but a counterassault picked up momentum and troops of the 35th Division crossed the crest of Hill 122 despite heavy artillery fire.[38] As German artillery and mortar shells continued to fall on the hill, American troops had an astonishingly clear view of St. Lô, barely a mile away.

Capture of Hill 122 foreshadowed the end of the battle. With this bastion lost, the German defenses around St. Lô began to crumble. On 17 July, the 137th Infantry on the division right was finally able to break across the Pont-Hébert–St. Lô ridge road. Driving south toward the Vire River, the regiment encountered diminishing resistance. Meanwhile, the 320th Infantry prepared to mop up the Carillon area, which the Germans had virtually abandoned.[39]

"Come Hell or High Water"

Although the end of the battle for St. Lô could be foreseen on 17 July, capture of the city had not seemed imminent on 14 July when the 29th Division had paused to reorganize and prepare to renew the attack. Though the city was but 3,000 yards away, it remained in many respects almost as elusive as it had through the first three days of the battle.

Narrowing the 29th Division front to

---

[36] Memo, 15 Jul, 35th Div G-3 Jnl.

[37] 35th Div G-3 Jnl, 1145, 16 Jul. 1st Lt. Vernon W. Pickett was awarded the DSC for his defensive action.

[38] XIX Corps Msg, 1720, 16 Jul, FUSA G-3 Jnl; 35th Div Rpt of Situation, 0930, 17 Jul, XIX Corps G-3 Jnl and File. T. Sgt. Joseph P. Fuller and Pfc. Buster E. Brown received the DSC for heroic action.

[39] S. Sgt. Carl J. Frantz, T. Sgt. Irvin F. Conley, and T. Sgt. Harold D. Snyder were awarded the DSC for actions on 11, 13, and 17 July, respectively.

exclude Hill 122 had provided the troops a fresh hope when they resumed the attack on 15 July. After a day of reorganization and rest, the 115th Infantry moved out along the Isigny–St. Lô road, the 116th made the main effort along the crest of the Martinville ridge on a 600-yard front, and the 175th Infantry gave fire support from positions echeloned to the left rear along the Bérigny road.

For all the expectations, the attack on 15 July began to show signs of dismal failure. The 116th immediately lost seven medium tanks to enfilading enemy fire from the south. Despite diversionary attacks launched by the 175th Infantry and air strikes by the IX Tactical Air Command, the main effort did not get rolling.[40] On the division right, the 115th lost several hundred yards as the result of confusion. Intermingling battalions and misplaced tanks disrupted regimental control. Lack of proper coordination with the 35th Division caused misunderstanding and an exchange of fire among U.S. troops. The firm action of an artillery liaison officer, who took command of an infantry company and restored order and discipline, prevented a panicky withdrawal. A tank platoon nearby might have helped the regiment to regain the lost ground, but the tank commander could not locate a key infantry officer. While the tankers waited for instructions, the tanks remained idle.[41]

The division commander, General Gerhardt, was at first cautiously optimistic. "Looks like we are maybe going to roll," he said. His optimism later changed to stubborn determination. "We're going to keep at this now," he announced, "come hell or high water." Since the day passed with little more than an exchange of counterbattery fires and reorganization of some units, General Gerhardt planned a night attack. "We might do it tonight," he said. Several hours later he admitted, "We . . . did not make the grade."[42] The 115th and 175th Regiments had made no appreciable gain, while the 116th Infantry, commanded now by Col. Philip R. Dwyer, had made what looked like no more than a minor initial advance.[43]

Unknown to the division commander at the time, an event had taken place during the night that was to exercise a significant and fortunate influence on the battle of St. Lô. Two assault battalions of the 116th Infantry had been making good progress along the Martinville ridge when the division headquarters, evidently lacking accurate knowledge of the situation and fearing an overextension of lines, had ordered a halt. One battalion stopped and consolidated a gain of about 500 yards. The other continued to move, for the battalion commander, Maj. Sidney V. Bingham, Jr., had received the order to halt while he was checking his supply lines in the rear. Lacking communication at that particular moment with his advance units, Bingham went forward to stop the advance. When he reached

---

[40] 29th Div G–3 Jnl, 1130, 15 Jul.
[41] 29th Div G–3 Jnl, 0920, 15 Jul.

[42] 29th Div G–3 Jnl, 1357, 2055, and 2225, 15 Jul; 29th Div Msg, 1201, 15 Jul, XIX Corps G–3 Jnl and File.
[43] Colonel Dwyer replaced Colonel Canham, who was promoted to brigadier general and transferred to the 8th Division as the assistant division commander.

his leading troops, he found that they were more than 1,000 yards beyond the regimental front and were organizing positions astride the Bérigny highway. Having met little opposition, they had angled down across the face of the Martinville ridge to a point less than 1,000 yards from the eastern edge of St. Lô.

German artillery and mortar fire directed at the main body of the 116th Infantry fell behind and isolated Bingham's comparatively small unit. Lacking half a rifle company, a squad of the heavy weapons company, the 81-mm. mortars, and the battalion staff—all of which were with the bulk of the regiment—the battalion formed a defensive perimeter. Reporting the gain to the regimental commander, Major Bingham said he thought he could hold even though he had little ammunition.

Separating the isolated force from the 116th and 175th Regiments were gaps of 1,000 and 700 yards, respectively. So strong was enemy fire from artillery, mortars, and automatic weapons that attempts by both regiments to reach the isolated battalion were blocked. So vulnerable was the position that some thought the entire battalion would be annihilated. On the other hand, the battalion's position constituted the closest American approach to St. Lô. Eventually, the latter condition was to prove a significant indication to Germans and Americans alike that the city's defenses were in reality disintegrating.

That this was the case seemed far from plausible at midnight, 15 July, when General Corlett turned over to the VII Corps his sector west of the Vire River and devoted his entire attention

AFTER SECURING HILL 122, *17 July.*

to the situation east of the Vire. The situation at St. Lô was hardly encouraging. On the right, the 35th Division was halted before the Pont-Hébert–St. Lô ridge road and had then only a precarious hold on Hill 122. On the left, the 29th Division was in even worse straits: one regiment unable to advance down the Isigny–St. Lô highway and the other two stopped on the Martinville ridge, apparently incapable either of driving the short distance into the city or of establishing physical contact with an isolated battalion. Yet more than ever the Americans needed St. Lô. General Bradley needed to control the Vire River crossing site at St. Lô in order to block German threats against the flank of his new operation. It was vital to bring the battle of St. Lô swiftly to an end, yet there seemed little alternative to the slow costly pattern of yard-by-yard advances already so familiar.

There was little improvement on 16 July. While the 35th Division fought to retain Hill 122, the 29th Division seemed virtually paralyzed. The 115th Infantry advanced about 300 yards down the Isigny–St. Lô highway and came abreast of the 35th Division forces on Hill 122, but the regiments on the Martinville ridge could not relieve the isolated battalion.

Six days of fighting had brought the 29th close to its goal, but with considerably weakened forces. Two days earlier, 125 replacements had restored one battalion of the 116th Infantry to only 60 percent of its authorized strength; during the night of 16–17 July another battalion received 250 enlisted replacements, bringing its total strength to 420. On 16 July a battalion of the 115th had only a platoon of riflemen remaining in each rifle company. On 17 July 200 men comprised the three rifle companies of a battalion of the 175th, and most of the commissioned and noncommissioned officers had been killed or wounded. Although these were extreme cases, the other infantry battalions were also seriously depleted.[44]

For the final assault on St. Lô at the opportune moment, General Gerhardt turned to the supporting arms. He instructed Brig. Gen. Norman D. Cota, the assistant division commander, to form a task force of tank, reconnaissance, tank destroyer, and engineer troops. They were to be assembled in the division rear area at a location that would enable them to attack toward St. Lô from either

the northeast—by way of the Isigny–St. Lô highway—or the east—down the Martinville ridge. Because Hill 122 was not yet entirely secure, General Gerhardt still expected to make his climactic drive into St. Lô from the east, but he wanted to be ready to drive from the northeast should capture of Hill 122 prove in reality to be the decisive factor in the battle for St. Lô.

A Legend is Born

On 17 July, the seventh day of attack, the 29th Division struck before dawn. Maj. Thomas D. Howie, commanding the 3d Battalion, 116th Infantry, led his men in a column of companies in a silent march toward Major Bingham's isolated unit. Suspicious Germans increased their artillery and mortar fire and played grazing machine gun fire across the slope of the Martinville ridge. Howie's men resisted the impulse to return this fire and crept forward through an early morning mist, still undetected. Several hours after daybreak, they reached Bingham's isolated force.

The regimental commander, Colonel Dwyer, had hoped that the two battalions together would be able to enter the city, but Bingham's men were exhausted. Howie informed Dwyer by telephone that they were incapable of further effort. When Dwyer asked whether Howie could move his battalion alone to the eastern edge of town, Howie replied, "Will do." Several minutes later an enemy shell killed him.

Taking command of Howie's battalion, Capt. William H. Puntenny tried to mount the attack on St. Lô along the Bérigny highway, but the Germans

---

[44] 29th Div G–3 Jnl, 1335, 16 Jul, and 1256, 17 Jul.

threw up such a heavy curtain of mortar fire that the men could not move. All through the day the German fire denied an advance. Late that afternoon a counterattack with tank support started from St. Lô to eliminate the Bingham-Puntenny force. Only the fortuitous presence of American dive bombers saved the day. While the planes strafed and bombed the German column, the division artillery placed a protective screen of fire about the American positions.[45] Disorganized, the Germans withdrew their assault force, but now two American battalions were isolated.

All efforts of the 1st Battalion, 116th Infantry, to open a route to Bingham and Puntenny on 17 July and to bring forward ammunition, food, and medical supplies failed. Half-tracks and tank destroyers, escorted by quadruple .50-caliber machine guns, found the sunken roads about Martinville so clogged with debris, dead horses, and wrecked German vehicles that an advance under continuing enemy artillery fire was impossible. The 175th Infantry also attempted to reach the isolated men by attacking down the Bérigny highway, but the regiment sustained severe losses and made little advance. The only relief was that brought by light planes of the division artillery, which dropped sufficient blood plasma for 35 wounded men.

On the night of 17 July a carrying party of about forty men of the 1st Battalion, 116th Infantry, finally reached the isolated units. The next morning, 18 July, a rifle company—which had

been reduced to 23 veterans but replenished with 85 replacements—opened a supply route to Bingham and Puntenny across the thousand-yard gap. Advancing in two columns along the axial hedgerows one field apart, maintaining visual contact between columns, and leaving four men in each field to hold the supply line open, the company met only light rifle fire. Supplies were brought forward and the wounded were evacuated. The few Germans, in small and disorganized groups, who blundered into the supply route during the day were either killed or captured.

By the time contact was firmly established with the two isolated battalions, the Martinville ridge had lost importance in the battle of St. Lô. The explanation had its basis in the condition that for seven long days had plagued the attacks along the ridge.

In full view of the Germans south of the Bérigny highway, every American movement along the south face of the Martinville ridge had brought deadly fire. Though the two regiments on the ridge had constituted a threat to the town, they had been unable to make the threat good. Attempts to impress the troops with the fact that the German positions were worse than their own had not succeeded. "Tell them that Jerry is in a wedge," the division G–3 had ordered a liaison officer. "Jerry doesn't seem to realize it," had come the reply.[46] So it seemed, for in spite of the wedge exerting pressure from the north—Hill 122—and from the east—the Martinville ridge—the Germans had obstinately refused to release their hold on the city. With the passage of time it had become

---

[45] [Lt. Col. Robert H. George], Ninth Air Force, April to November 1944, USAF Hist Study 36 (Maxwell Air Force Base, Alabama, Air University, 1945), p. 118.

[46] 29th Div G–3 Jnl, 1216, 17 Jul.

a matter of increasing certainty that the forces on the ridge lacked the strength to make the final drive to the objective.

On the afternoon of 17 July, after the 35th Division had firmly established its control over Hill 122, General Gerhardt concluded that the 115th Infantry and not the regiments on the Martinville ridge really held the key to St. Lô. To insert the key, General Gerhardt had somehow to get the regiment to the gates of the city. He therefore directed Colonel Ordway to advance the 115th to the northeast outskirts of St. Lô. The advance depended almost wholly upon the battalion in the regimental center. "Expend the whole battalion if necessary," General Gerhardt ordered, "but it's got to get there." An hour later he repeated the same order.[47] By nightfall of 17 July the troops of the entire 115th Infantry were near the northeastern fringe of the city, but getting there had brought them to the point of almost complete exhaustion.

Convinced beyond doubt that the only feasible point of entry to St. Lô was the northeastern gate, General Gerhardt changed his week-long scheme of maneuver. For operations on 18 July, he ordered the two regiments on the left—those on the Martinville ridge—to hold in place while the 115th made the main effort into the city.[48]

Early on 18 July, General Gerhardt phoned to ask General Baade what he was planning to have the 35th Division do that day. General Baade replied that he would "probably sit tight." As

an afterthought he asked, "Are you going in?"

"I'm going to try," General Gerhardt answered.

"In that case," General Baade said, "so will I."

"You can help on your left," General Gerhardt suggested.

General Baade promised he would "look into it."

Three minutes later General Gerhardt was telling the corps commander that he thought the 35th Division should be ordered to attack to aid the 29th and not be allowed to attack "just because someone else [the 29th] is doing it."

General Corlett's reaction was sharp: "You had better just take on what I said in your order." Apparently realizing Gerhardt's fatigue, he added, "Just take St. Lô and secure it." [49]

If these conversations revealed a tension among American commanders, those occurring among German officers disclosed even greater concern. *Seventh Army* had called *Army Group B* in the midafternoon of 17 July, and Hausser requested not only permission to withdraw in the St. Lô sector but also an answer by 1800 that day. There was some double talk about withdrawing to a line north of St. Lô, but this was not feasible in terms of the terrain. A withdrawal meant retirement to the heights just south of the city, though combat outposts could be retained north of St. Lô.[50]

The request was rather surprising because under Hitler's standing order to hold fast, permission to withdraw was

[47] 29th Div G–3 Jnl, 1456 and 1545, 17 Jul.
[48] XIX Corps Msg 2245, 17 Jul, XIX Corps G–3 Jnl and File; Ltr of Instr, 2300, 17 Jul.

[49] 29th Div G–3 Jnl, 0638 and 0641, 18 Jul.
[50] Telecon, Pemsel to Tempelhoff, 1520, 17 Jul, *AGp B KTB*.

a prerogative of OKW. Yet more surprising was the army group reply to the *Seventh Army*. The operations officer of *Army Group B* stated that, after discussion, the staff had decided that forwarding Hausser's request to *OB WEST* for further transmittal to OKW was not practical. "You take whatever measures you think are necessary," the operations officer advised; "if you have to withdraw, go ahead; just report to us afterwards that the enemy penetrated your main line of resistance in several places and that you barely succeeded in re-establishing a new line to the rear."[51]

Several reasons made a withdrawal necessary. American capture of Hill 122 and the attrition of the German troops in that sector exposed St. Lô from the north. The shortage of troops along the entire St. Lô front made it impossible for the *II Parachute Corps* to re-establish a defensive line north of the city. Underscoring the difficult, even hopeless, situation at St. Lô were the events that had occurred on the other side of the Vire: the 30th Division advance through Pont-Hébert to Rampan, the failure of the abortive *Panzer Lehr* counterattack on 15 July that did no more than delay the 30th Division advance, and the mistaken notion that U.S. troops had crossed the river at Rampan to infiltrate the rear of the *352d Division*. All added up to the uncomfortable threat of American encirclement of St. Lô from the west.

As though this was not bad enough, Rommel, the *Army Group B* commander, while driving forward to visit the front on the afternoon of 17 July,

incurred a severe skull fracture in an automobile accident brought on by strafing from an Allied plane. That evening, when the news became known to the Germans, the *OB WEST* commander, Kluge, assumed command of *Army Group B* as well.

By this time, *Army Group B* had passed Hausser's withdrawal request to *OB WEST*, which informed Jodl at OKW that troops were pulling back to hills north of St. Lô. Kluge tried to avert a complete withdrawal, but though he ordered Hausser to keep the Americans out of the city, he could find no reserves to reinforce the St. Lô sector.[52] The *5th Parachute Division*, which had arrived from Brittany several days earlier, was already committed to reinforce *Panzer Lehr*. The *275th Division*, which was following the paratroopers, would not arrive in the St. Lô region for another day. *Panzer Group West*, which might have furnished troops, was expecting a strong British attack in the Caen area, and Kluge dared not disturb Eberbach's dispositions. Reluctantly, Kluge permitted Hausser to withdraw.[53] Undetected by the Americans, the main forces retired that night leaving strong combat outposts north of St. Lô.

On the American side, General Gerhardt completed his preparations for assault on the morning of 18 July. Though the 115th Infantry had made the drive possible, Gerhardt replaced the regimental commander. "You did your best," Gerhardt told him. Colonel

---

[51] Telecon, Tempelhoff to Pemsel, 1750, 17 Jul, *Seventh Army* Tel Msgs, and 1755, *AGp B KTB*.

[52] Telecon, Speidel to Pemsel, 2155, 17 Jul, *Seventh Army* Tel Msgs; Hodgson, R–54.

[53] Telecons, Kluge and Rommel, 2040, 16 Jul, *OB WEST KTB*, and Speidel to Pemsel, 2200, 17 Jul, *AGp B KTB*.

INFANTRYMEN HIT THE GROUND ON A STREET IN ST. Lô

Ednie, who had come from the 30th Division to understudy the assistant division commander, took his place. Ednie's mission was to open the northeast entrance to the city for the passage of General Cota's task force. Unaware of the German withdrawal, General Gerhardt was cautious. "We may go into St. Lô," he informed the corps commander, "but we don't want anyone to get cut off in there." [54]

After an artillery preparation, the 115th Infantry attacked. Since Hill 122 was no longer a point of embarrassment, the regiment made good progress. At noon Colonel Ednie was hammering on

the gate. "I believe this is the time to alert that Task Force," he advised General Gerhardt. The division commander no longer doubted. "Everything's shaping up now," he informed General Cota, "so I think you'd better get moving." [55]

Forty minutes later General Gerhardt transmitted another order to General Cota. He wanted the body of Major Howie to accompany the first U.S. troops into town.[56] The act was to be not only a gesture of honor and respect to the fallen but also a visible reminder to the members of the task force of all their comrades who had given their lives in a

---

[54] 29th Div G–3 Jnl, 0725 and 0901, 18 Jul.

[55] 29th Div G–3 Jnl, 1147 and 1149, 18 Jul.
[56] 29th Div G–3 Jnl, 1236, 18 Jul.

RUINS OF ST. Lô

task not yet completed. The choice of Major Howie's body was particularly apt, for Howie, who had taken command of a battalion only three days before his death, represented the qualities of courage and sacifice that had made the drive to the gates of St. Lô possible. The triumph belonged to the dead as well as to the living, and through Major Howie the fallen were to participate in the culmination of the effort.

At 1500, 18 July, General Cota's Task Force C departed its assembly area near the division left boundary, crossed the division zone, and began to roll down the Isigny–St. Lô highway. Like a left halfback making a wide run around right end, the task force picked up its interference as it approached the line of scrimmage—the 1st Battalion, 115th Infantry, which was closest to the goal. Silencing an antitank gun just outside the town, passing through harassing artillery and scattered rifle fire, and breaking through a roadblock, the task force entered the northeast portion of St. Lô at 1800 of the eighth day of the battle. Quickly seizing a square near the cemetery and organizing it as a base of operations, Task Force C moved rapidly through the rubble-choked streets to points of importance. Small groups occupied key road junctions, squares, and bridges. One hour after the task force entered the town it was apparent that only scattered German resistance remained to be cleared. The bridges over the Vire were still intact.[57]

About the time the 29th Division task force began its drive into St. Lô, the 35th Division completed its assignment. Colonel Byrne's 320th Infantry mopped up bypassed enemy in the center of the division zone, Colonel Emery's 137th Infantry reached the bank of the Vire River between the loop and the bend, and Colonel Miltonberger's 134th Infantry moved down the south slope of Hill 122 to the northern edge of St. Lô. Because the division boundary did not permit the 35th to enter into town, General Baade requested a boundary change. The XIX Corps G–3 first checked with General Gerhardt: "We have another division crying for part of St. Lô," he reported.

"OK," General Gerhardt said, "let them go to it."

Despite General Gerhardt's largess, the corps commander was reluctant to condone the possibility of confusion and lack of control that might result from intermingling troops of the two divisions in the city. He decided not to shift the boundary, yet some 35th Division troops inevitably entered St. Lô and moved a short way into town.[58]

What had caused St. Lô to fall was the weight of two divisions pressing forward relentlessly for eight days. But if specific events have direct causal relation, two were mainly responsible. The capture of Hill 122 was the more ob-

vious, for its seizure the day before the fall of St. Lô had deprived the Germans of a vital point in their line of defense. The other event was of more subtle significance. At the same time that the 35th Division was securing a hold on Hill 122, the 29th Division was penetrating the enemy defensive line across the Martinville ridge by means of Major Bingham's accidental advance of 1,000 yards. Although temporarily encircled and isolated, Bingham's battalion, less than 1,000 yards from St. Lô, presented a serious menace to the defenders—"an enemy battalion behind our lines."[59] Major Howie's relief force had strengthened the threat. Although the 29th Division troops on the Martinville ridge did not have the power to take the city, their positions constituted a containment force, a base or anchor for the *coup de grâce* delivered by Task Force C. The original scheme of maneuver had thus been reversed. The intended maneuver force, the 116th and 175th Regiments, had become the base, while the 115th Infantry, earlier designated the holding force, had become, with Task Force C, the assault element.

If speed was a fundamental requirement of General Gerhardt's mission, the question of whether the corps attack had been the most expeditious manner of securing St. Lô remained a lingering doubt. Other U.S. units advancing with the same slow rate of speed in the hedgerow country obscured the possibility that the corps might have secured its objective more rapidly had it attacked Hill 122 at the same time that the V Corps had attacked Hill 192. Had the

[57] 29th Div G–3 Jnl, 0517, 19 Jul.

[58] 29th Div G–3 Jnl, 1615, 18 Jul; Penciled note, n.d., 35th Div G–3 Jnl File, 18 Jul; 134th Infantry Regiment, *Combat History of World War II*, compiled by Butler Buchanan Miltonberger (Baton Rouge, Louisiana: Army and Navy Publishing Company, 1946), p. 44.

[59] Telecon, Pemsel to Tempelhoff, 2110, 17 Jul, *Seventh Army* Tel Msgs.

SYMBOL OF ST. LÔ. *The flag-draped coffin of Major Howie rests on the rubble-buried steps of Ste. Croix church.*

Americans controlled Hill 122, the 29th Division would have been able to make its thrust to St. Lô across the north slope of the Martinville ridge and have been shielded from the German fire south of the Bérigny road.

General Gerhardt had a formal message prepared to announce the capture of St. Lô. At 1830, half an hour after Task Force C entered the streets of the town, he confidentially released the message to his special services officer in time to make that evening's edition of the division mimeographed newspaper. "I have the honor," the message read, "to report to the Corps Commander . . .,"

but before General Gerhardt could proclaim the achievement, General Corlett telephoned to inform him that he had already heard the news on a radio broadcast. "NBC beat you to it," General Corlett announced.[60]

Although St. Lô was taken, it was by no means safe. German artillery smashed into the town. Surprised and embarrassed by the speed with which the Americans had taken the city, Hausser ordered Meindl to have the *352d Division* retake the town, but refused

---

[60] 29th Div G-3 Jnl, 1830, 2028, 2048, 18 Jul, and Msg, 2100, 18 Jul, XIX Corps G-3 Jnl and File; FUSA, Spec Sitrep, 0045, 19 Jul.

Meindl's request for part of the *275th Division,* which had just arrived from Brittany and was in the *Seventh Army* reserve behind *Panzer Lehr.* The *352d Division,* which had tried to hold the Vire bridges by fighting in St. Lô with too few men, mounted a counterattack but was too weak to expel the Americans. Hausser and Meindl both later blamed an announcement by the Wehrmacht on the afternoon of 18 July of the withdrawal as the stimulus that had caused the final American assault. Actually, however, they had been unable to secure additional troops and they had feared that U.S. forces west of the Vire would outflank St Lô from the west; both commanders in reality had been forced by American pressure to pull the *II Parachute Corps* back.[61]

To maintain contact and determine the extent of the withdrawal, General Corlett instructed the 113th Cavalry Group to pass through the city. The cavalry received such a volume of antitank, mortar, and artillery fire 500 yards south of St. Lô that it became evident at once that the Germans had retired only to the high ground less than a mile to the south. The *352d Division* counterattack launched that evening confirmed the fact that the enemy had not gone far.[62]

The XIX Corps completed its task

on the morning of 19 July. The 29th Division finished clearing the city, and the 35th Division reported no active enemy troops in its sector.[63]

In capturing St. Lô the divisions had sustained the high losses that had become typical of the battle of the hedgerows. The 35th Division lost over 2,000 men; the 29th Division suffered over 3,000 casualties. On 19 July, in compliance with corps instructions, the 35th Division relieved the 29th, and General Baade deployed his troops across the entire corps front from the Vire River east to the Couvains–Calvaire road.

By the time the men of the 29th Division marched out of St. Lô on 20 July, the body of Major Howie had become a symbol. Task Force C had carried the flag-draped corpse as a battle standard into town on a jeep.[64] Placed on a pile of rubble before the rather plain Romanesque church of Ste. Croix and surrounded by empty, gaping houses, the body had become a shrine, a universal symbol of sacrifice. When the men of the division removed the body and departed the town, the symbol remained in St. Lô. St. Lô itself, disfigured and lifeless, had become a memorial to all who had suffered and died in the battle of the hedgerows.

---

[61] Telecon, Hausser to Pemsel, 1950, 18 Jul, *Seventh Army* Tel Msgs; *Seventh Army KTB* (Draft) and Tel Msgs, 17 and 18 Jul; Hodgson, R–54.

[62] XIX Corps Memo, 19 Jul, XIX Corps G–3 Jnl and File.

[63] 35th Div Msg, 1019, 19 Jul, XIX Corps G–3 Jnl; Huston, *Biography of A Battalion,* pp. 23–46.

[64] A legend had also been born. In 1953 a roadside sign in St. Lô read: " . . . This martyred city [was] liberated the 26th [*sic*] of July 1944 by Major Howie, killed at the head of his troops. . . ."

CHAPTER IX

The Conclusions

The American Point of View

The First Army's July offensive came to an end on 19 July, the day after the capture of St. Lô. Despite the fact that the operations had moved U.S. troops to the southern edge of the Cotentin swampland—along the Lessay–Périers–St. Lô–Caumont line—the results were disappointing.

Heroic exertion seemed, on the surface, to have accomplished little. With twelve divisions, the First Army in seventeen days had advanced only about seven miles in the region west of the Vire and little more than half that distance east of the river. Not only was the distance gained disappointing, the newly established Lessay–Caumont line was less than satisfactory. The VIII Corps physically occupied neither Lessay nor Périers; the VII Corps did not actually possess the Périers–St. Lô highway; and the city of St. Lô remained under enemy artillery and mortar fire for more than a week after its capture by the XIX Corps.[1]

To reach positions along the Lessay–Caumont line, the First Army had sustained approximately 40,000 casualties

during July, of which 90 percent were infantrymen. A rifle company after a week of combat often numbered less than one hundred men; sometimes it resembled a reinforced platoon. Casualties among infantry officers in the line companies were particularly high in the hedgerow country, where small-unit initiative and individual leadership figured so largely. Of all the infantry company officers in one regiment that had entered Normandy shortly after D Day, only four lieutenants remained by the third week in July, and all four by then were commanding rifle companies.[2]

The majority of the casualties were caused by shell fragments, involving in many cases multiple wounds.[3] Many other men suffered combat fatigue. Not always counted in the casualty reports, they nevertheless totaled an additional 25 to 33 percent of the number of men physically wounded. All the divisions made informal provision for treating combat fatigue cases, usually at the regimental collecting stations, and several divisional neuropsychiatrists established exhaustion centers. Work-

---

[1] The XIX Corps civil affairs detachment could not become operational in St. Lô until 29 July, and only then did the French civilian administration begin again to function. XIX Corps AAR, Jul.

[2] FUSA Daily Estimated Loss Rpts, Jul, KCRC; Ruppenthal, *Logistical Support*, I, 460; 30th Div G–3 Jnl, entries 1615 and 1935, 15 Jul, and 2335, 17 Jul; VIII Corps IG Ltr, Rpt of Investigation of 358th Inf Regt, 90th Inf Div, 11 Aug.

[3] The 8th Division, for instance, recorded 2,080 battle casualties between 8 and 31 July as having sustained 3,050 wounds. 8th Div AAR, 8 Jul–4 Aug.

ing with improvised facilities and without personnel specifically assigned for
this purpose, the doctors returned a
large percentage of fatigue cases to duty
after 24 to 72 hours of rest and sedation.
Patients who did not respond were
evacuated to one of two First Army combat exhaustion centers—250-bed hospitals
eventually expanded to 750 and 1,000
beds.[4]

"We won the battle of Normandy,"
one survivor later said, "[but] considering the high price in American lives, we
lost."[5]   Not a bitter indictment of the
way warfare was conducted in the hedgerows, the statement revealed instead the
feeling of despair that touched all who
participated.   Frustration was the clearest impression.   The "working day" was
determined by daylight, usually from
about 0500 to the final wisp of visibility
an hour or two before midnight.   Patrol action and preparations for the morrow meant that even the few hours of
darkness were full of activity.   A new
morning meant little, for little changed
in the dreary landscape of the Norman
battleground.[6]

Over a stretch of such days, you became
so dulled by fatigue that the names of the
killed and wounded they checked off each
night, the names of men who had been your
best friends, might have come out of a
telephone book for all you knew.   All the
old values were gone, and if there was a
world beyond this tangle of hedgerows . . . ,
where one barrage could lay out half a

company like a giant's club, you never expected to live to see it.[7]

It seemed incredible that only a few
days and a few miles separated the water-
filled foxholes from the British pubs, the
desolate Cotentin from the English countryside, the sound of battle from the
noise of Piccadilly.   The hedgerows that
surrounded the rectangular Norman
fields seemed to isolate the men from all
past experience and oppress them with
the feeling that they were beings inhabit-
ing another planet.   Units separated by
a single hedgerow were frequently unaware of each other's presence.   Each
small group knew only of its own efforts
and had but a vague impression that
other individuals were similarly engaged.[8]

The transition from training for war
to the reality of battle was difficult and
often rapid.   Some units incurred casualties before they actually entered combat, as when ships on their way to France
occasionally struck mines or when long-
range German guns found a mark.[9]   Artillery gun crews frequently unloaded
the ships that had brought them to the
Continent and proceeded at once, even
though they were already weary, to support an attack.[10]   The experience of
four and a half newly arrived divisions
underscored the problems of transition.
In addition to the mistakes made by
units, many individuals temporarily forgot the lessons of basic training and
failed, for example, to use cover and concealment properly.   After a week of ac-

---

[4] First U.S. Army, *Report of Operations*, I, 95;
8th Div and XIX Corps AAR's, Jul; CI 84 (29th
Div).

[5] Raymond J. Goguen, *329th "Buckshot" Infantry Regiment* (Wolsenbuettel, Germany: Ernst
Fischer, 1945), p. 36.

[6] PERAGIMUS—"*We Accomplish*" (n.p., n.d.) a
brief history of the 358th Infantry; 358th Inf Jnl, 9
Jul.

[7] 314th Infantry Regiment, *Through Combat*, p.
19.

[8] Typewritten MS, Comment on 82d Div Opn,
82d Abn Div AAR, Jul.

[9] Hewitt, *Story of 30th Division*, p. 16.

[10] See, for example, 174th FA Gp S–3 Rpt, 3 Jul,
VIII Corps G–3 Jnl and File.

tion one tank battalion was "not available for any employment whatsoever because of losses in personnel," and the division to which it was attached used instead three 105-mm. self-propelled guns and three 81-mm. mortars mounted on half-tracks. The intricate maze of sunken roads between matted hedgerows emphasized the sense of bewilderment that afflicted those new to the terrors of combat. It was easy to get lost, and some tank crews found it necessary to designate a man to act as navigator. After the initial shock, however, the sights and sounds of life and death in Normandy became familiar. Dulled by fatigue and habit, the men soon accepted their lot as normal.[11]

Behind . . . [the battalions] the engineers slammed bulldozers through the obstinate hedgerow banks, carving a makeshift supply route up to the forward elements, and everywhere the medics were drafting litter bearers to haul the wounded the long way back.[12]

Several features distinguished combat in Normandy during July 1944 from combat elsewhere. Very soon General Eisenhower had concluded that three factors were making the battle extremely tough: "First, as always, the fighting quality of the German soldier; second, the nature of the country; third, the weather."[13]

The fighting quality of the enemy troops encompassed a great range. Russians and Poles employed in combination with Germans formed an "alloy" that withstood little pressure despite the exceptional leadership of German commissioned and noncommissioned officers. Non-Germanic troops, who comprised the bulk of the prisoners of war taken by the First Army, seemed to be convinced that Germany could not continue the war much longer, and Americans wondered when all the Germans would come to this realization. But the German troops, as distinguished from the *Osttruppen,* were good. Not invincible, the regular Wehrmacht units nevertheless had "staying power," while SS forces and paratroopers were a breed apart: "Elite troops, with an unshakable morale, they asked no quarter and made certain that they gave none. . . ."[14]

The Germans had conducted an active defense, mounting local counterattacks with local reserves supported by small groups of tanks. Well-employed mortars and machine guns and roving artillery pieces characterized their stubborn delaying tactics. Generally, during the early part of the month, the Germans seemed reluctant to employ their artillery in volume, but as the month progressed they increasingly used battery and battalion volleys to obtain mass and concentration on fewer targets. When forced to withdraw, the Germans broke contact during darkness and covered their withdrawal with large numbers of automatic weapons in order to delay the advance by forcing the Americans to commit additional units. By the time American attacks made the covering force break contact, another covering force had set up another delaying posi-

---

[11] 329th Inf AAR, Jul; 314th Infantry Regiment, *Through Combat,* p. 22; 9th Div G-3 Jnl, entry 1430, 17 Jul; XIX Corps Ltr, Notes on Combat Experience, 5 Jul, VIII Corps G-3 Jnl.

[12] 314th Infantry Regiment, *Through Combat,* p. 20.

[13] Ltr, Eisenhower to Marshall, 5 Jul, Pogue Files.

[14] 314th Infantry Regiment, *Through Combat,* pp. 20-21; Telecon, Corlett and Gerhardt, 1833, 1 Jul, 29th Div G-3 Jnl.

tion, and U.S. troops seemed "unable to find the solution to this problem." [15]

American commanders had been alert for evidence that would indicate a penetration of the German defenses. Short-lived pursuit had occurred, for example, in the VIII Corps sector when the Germans withdrew in good order from la Haye-du-Puits to the Ay and the Sèves Rivers. But the only real opportunity to exploit a penetration came after the bridgehead was established between the Taute and the Vire Rivers, and this had been muffed. Capture of Hill 192 by V Corps forces had also pierced the German defensive line, but the projected First Army wheeling maneuver on Caumont precluded a deep thrust in the eastern sector of the First Army line. The advance all along the army front had been painful. The Germans gave way so slowly that the July offensive seemed to have failed. The nature of the country favored the Germans. The marshes of the Cotentin canalized American attacks into well-defined corridors. Soggy ground in large part immobilized the mechanized power of U.S. ground forces. The hedgerows subdivided the terrain into small rectangular compartments that the Germans had tied together to provide mutual support. The result was a continuous band of strong-points in great depth all across the front. Handicapped by lack of observation, by the difficulty of maintaining direction, and by the limited ability to use all supporting weapons to maximum advantage, the Americans adopted a form of jungle or Indian fighting in which the individ-

ual soldier played a dominant role. Units were assigned frontages according to specific fields and hedgerows rather than by yardage, and distances and intervals between tactical formations were reduced.[16] The battleground reminded observers of the tiny battlefields of the American Civil War.

Feeling out each hedgerow for the hidden enemy was a tense affair performed at close range. "Must go forward slowly, as we are doing," a regimental commander reported; "take one hedgerow at a time and clean it up." This was standing operating procedure much of the time. At that slow rate, often a single hedgerow per day, the troops "could see the war lasting for twenty years." "Too many hedges" and not the enemy was the real deterrent to rapid advance.[17]

The weather helped the enemy. The amount of cloud, wind, and rain in June and July of 1944 was greater than that recorded at any time since 1900. It nullified Allied air superiority on many days. Although the IX Tactical Air Command flew over 900 air missions for the First Army between 26 June and 24 July, approximately 50 percent of the potential air support could not be employed because of adverse weather conditions.[18] The rain and the sticky, re-

[15] 30th Div G–2 Est 2, 20 Jul (Incl 2 to Intel Annex 3); VII Corps G–2 Est, 17 Jul; Observations of the Div Comdr, 2d Div AAR, Jul.

[16] First U.S. Army, *Report of Operations*, I, 122–23.

[17] 30th Div G–3 Jnl, entry 1935, 15 Jul; 2d Battalion, 329th Infantry, *Combat Digest*, p. 16; First U.S. Army, *Report of Operations*, I, 86; Sylvan Diary, 29 Jun.

[18] First U.S. Army, *Report of Operations*, I, 91; SHAEF Draft Note for submission to SHAEF G–3 for Release to Public Relations, Meteorological Forecast for Allied Assault on France, June 1944 [14 Aug], SHAEF File GCT 000.9/Ops (A), Meteorological Matters.

pulsive mud it produced made the ground troops wonder whether they would ever be warm and clean and dry again.

Since the depth of the continental beachhead was not much greater in July than it had been in June, the problem of congestion was still acute. Allied army and corps headquarters that had become available on the Continent could not be utilized because of lack of room for the troops they would command. With a single regiment requiring between 14 and 20 miles of road for movement, traffic flowed at a pedestrian rate, often with vehicles bumper to bumper. Macadam roads, the best in Normandy, were few; the great majority of the roads were of gravel. They were all difficult to keep in good repair under the wheels and tracks of heavy military vehicles. In wet weather they were slippery or muddy; during the infrequent periods of sunshine, they quickly became dusty.[19]

Despite the difficulties of ground transportation, the actual delivery of supplies to the combat forces was generally satisfactory. Short lines of communications, lower consumption rates in gasoline and oil, the absence of the Luftwaffe over the combat zone, and the large volume of supplies brought over the open beaches resulted in a relatively stable logistical situation. Artillery ammunition expenditure was heavy between 4 and 15 July, even though control was

being exercised and unrestricted firing forbidden. To compensate for the lack of observation in Normandy, deeper and wider concentrations than normal were fired. Although reserve stocks of ammunition sometimes dropped to low levels on certain types of shells, particularly for the 105-mm. howitzer, the troops were seldom obliged to curtail their firing because of shortages. While artillery, tank destroyer, and antiaircraft personnel replacements were available in unnecessarily large quantities, infantry replacements, particularly riflemen, were in short supply because of the unexpectedly high casualty rates. By the middle of the month the deficiency in infantrymen became so serious that 25,000 rifle replacements were requested from the zone of interior by the fastest transportation possible. Weapons losses—Browning automatic rifles, grenade launchers, bazookas, mortars, and light machine guns—were also higher than anticipated, but replacements arrived through normal channels of resupply from stocks in England. Also, in combat that measured gains in yards rather than in miles, many more small-scale maps were needed. Air shipments of 1:25,000 maps from England remedied the deficiency.[20]

Since the Allies needed to expand the continental foothold in order to gain room for maneuver, airfields, and the increasing quantities of troops and supplies of the build-up, and also to acquire ports of entry, the battle of the hedgerows, in geographical terms, was hardly successful in either the American zone in the Cotentin or the British zone

---

[19] 8th Div G-3 Jnl, entry 0815, 30 Jul; 1st Div G-3 Jnl and File, 15–22 Jul; Annex B to SHAEF/1062/7/GDP, 17 Jun 44, Topography and Communications, and SHAEF/6876/E, SHAEF Engr Div Ltr, Effect of Postponing D-Day for OVERLORD, 10 Apr 44, SHAEF File 370.2, Logistic Studies; Talk to Directors of QMG's Dept on Visit to Normandy, n.d., SGS SHAEF File 381; Stacey, *The Canadian Army*, p. 187.

[20] Ruppenthal, *Logistical Support*, I, 439, 442, 461; First U.S. Army, *Report of Operations*, I, 93–94; FUSA G-4 Daily Summary Rpt, 11 Jul, FUSA G-3 Jnl.

around Caen. Space and port facilities remained the most serious Allied concern. Fulfilling the requirement of Operation OVERLORD—securing adequate lodgment in northwest France—seemed a long way off.

In the third week of July, as the First Army regrouped for a new attempt to gain the Coutances–Caumont line, there was little realization that the July offensive had achieved results of vital significance. Allied preoccupation with geography and the undiminished German resistance had combined to obscure the fact that in pressing for geographical gain the Allies had been fulfilling a precept of Clausewitz: destroying the enemy military forces. Allied pressure along a broad front had prevented the enemy from building strong mobile reserves and concentrating them in offensive action against any one point; it had also thinned the forces in contact.[21] How close the Germans in Normandy had been brought to destruction was to become apparent with surprising clarity in the next few weeks of warfare.

The German Point of View

To the Germans, even more than to the Americans, the July operations had been hard. Only the skillful defensive tactics in the hedgerow terrain plus the pattern of the American offensive had averted complete disintegration of the German defenses in Normandy. The successive nature of the American corps attacks had enabled the Germans to shift units from one threatened portion of the front to another, a course of action perhaps impossible had the First Army been

able to launch simultaneous attacks all across the front.

The activity of the 2d SS Panzer Division, located south of St. Lô and constituting the entire Seventh Army reserve, exemplified German flexibility. The division had on 5 July dispatched a kampfgruppe to la Haye-du-Puits and a battalion of tanks to St. Lô while the main body of troops moved toward Périers. The tank battalion near St. Lô marched onto the Carentan–Périers isthmus on 7 July. Two days later a regiment entered the battle between the Taute and the Vire. The regiment fought there until relieved by Panzer Lehr, and then, together with the kampfgruppe near la Haye-du-Puits, helped the 17th SS Panzer Grenadier Division in defense of Périers.[22]

The units rushed to Normandy had performed a similar function. By the time the 5th Parachute Division arrived from Brittany, on 12 July, the 15th Regiment, which had earlier been detached, was already fighting on Mont Castre. Seventh Army plans to commit the entire division in the la Haye-du-Puits sector were abandoned when the Panzer Lehr attack miscarried, and one of the new regiments was immediately committed between the Taute and the Vire.[23]

On the other hand, such fragmentary commitment led to the dispersal of German units. Goering, whose headquarters had administrative control of Luftwaffe ground forces, soon threatened to stop the flow of replacements to the 5th Parachute Division if the scattered elements were not immediately reassembled

---

[21] First U.S. Army, Report of Operations, I, 89.

[22] Seventh Army KTB (Draft), 5–10 Jul.
[23] Seventh Army KTB, 12 Jul.

and the division used as a unit.[24]   The *275th Division,* which had arrived in the Cotentin by mid-July, could not be employed *in toto* because one of its regiments was already battered by the fighting near la Haye-du-Puits.   Thus the strength of three divisions—each of which, if employed as a powerful unified force, might have turned the course of the battle in any one sector—had been dissipated by the more urgent need to hold back the American pressure.

Plagued by the necessity of committing their reserves piecemeal, the Germans were also concerned by the decline of aggressiveness among their troops. The mounting reluctance of armored divisions to make a wholehearted effort seemed particularly serious.   The classic example of too little too late, at least in Rommel's opinion, had been the *Panzer Lehr* attack on 11 July.   Even in the earlier fighting about Caen, there was dissatisfaction at the higher command echelons with panzer effectiveness. Spirit was a vital prerequisite for success, and signs that spirit was subsiding on the troop level were evident.[25]

The Germans faced shortages in both men and munitions, but the latter was the more significant.   Against an estimated British expenditure of 80,000 artillery rounds around Caen on 10 July, the Germans had been able to fire a scant 4,500 shells in return.   "Although our troop morale is good," a German officer protested, "we cannot meet the enemy matériel with courage alone." The Germans could not meet the Allied

rate of fire because their transportation network had been systematically bombed by Allied planes and sabotaged by the French Resistance.   Efforts to expedite the flow of supplies by increasing the use of the Seine River barges failed to meet the battlefield demands.[26]

That much needed to be replaced and resupplied was obvious from the matériel losses sustained in Normandy.   Between 6 June and 9 July, the Germans had lost 150 Mark IV tanks, 85 Panthers, and 15 Tigers, 167 75-mm. assault and antitank guns, and almost 30 88-mm. pieces—more than enough to equip an entire SS armored division.[27]

Casualty figures were even more depressing.   Between 6 June and 11 July the losses in the west totaled almost 2,000 officers and 85,000 men.   The *243d Division* had lost over 8,000 men in the Cotentin, the *352d Division* almost 8,000 men in the Cotentin and St. Lô sectors, the *716th Division* more than 6,000 near Caen.   The *12th SS Panzer Division,* with casualties numbering 4,485, had seen its infantry components reduced to the strength of a single battalion—one sixth of its authorized strength.   The *21st Panzer Division* had taken 3,411 casualties; *Panzer Lehr* 3,140.[28]   To replace these losses, only 5,210 replacements, or 6 percent of the casualties, had arrived at the front, though another 7,500 or 9 percent were promised or on the way.   By 17 July German casualties in Normandy had risen to about 100,000, of which 2,360 were officers.   Replacements promised

---

[24] Report of Kluge-Jodl Telecon in Zimmerman Telecon, 1245, 16 Jul, *AGp B KTB.*

[25] Report of Rommel's inspection of the front (signed Ecksparre), 16 Jul, *AGp B KTB, Anlagen,* Fall 40–Sep 44.

[26] Conference, Rommel and Gause, 10 Jul, *AGp B KTB, Anlagen,* Fall 40–Sep 44.

[27] *OB WEST KTB,* 10 Jul.

[28] *OB WEST KTB,* 12 Jul.

to fill the depleted ranks would total about 12 percent of the losses.[29]

To Choltitz, who commanded the *LXXXIV Corps,* it seemed that the battle of the hedgerows was "a monstrous blood-bath," the like of which he had not seen in eleven years of war.[30] Yet there seemed to be no way of stopping it except to commit units arriving from quiet sectors in the west to reinforce the sagging Normandy defense. The suggestion by Eberbach, who commanded *Panzer Group West,* that it was time to close most military specialist schools and send the students to the battlefield at once bespoke an impending bankruptcy of manpower resources.[31]

To Kluge, the *OB WEST* commander, the Normandy front was on the verge

of developing into an *ungeheures Kladderadatsch*—an awful mess—and he wondered whether OKW appreciated "the tremendous consumption of forces on big battle days." In view of the heavy losses, he told Jodl, Hitler's order for inflexible defense necessitated an expenditure of troops the Germans could no longer afford. Because Kluge believed that the infantry would not hold much longer, he wanted tanks, more tanks, "to act as corset stays behind the troops." He also wanted Hitler to know that the Normandy situation was "very serious." "If a hole breaks open, I have to patch it," he said. "Tell this to Hitler."[32]

Whether Jodl told Hitler or not, Allied leaders were conceiving an operation that would soon make strikingly evident exactly how serious the situation in Normandy actually was.

---

[29] *OB WEST KTB,* 11 and 17 Jul.

[30] Telecon, Choltitz to Pemsel, 2350, 15 Jul, *Seventh Army* Tel Msgs.

[31] Telecon, Eberbach and Rommel, 1225, 11 Jul, *AGp B KTB.*

[32] Telecon, Kluge and Jodl, 1828, 13 Jul, *OB WEST KTB, Anlage 615.*

PART THREE

BREAKTHROUGH

CHAPTER X

The Breakthrough Idea

In Search of a Panacea

The dramatic divergence between the phase lines projected by the OVERLORD plan for certain dates and the actual extent of the OVERLORD beachhead on those dates led to inevitable discussion in the Allied camp on how to dissolve the apparent stalemate.[1] Having considered even before the invasion the possibility that the Germans might contain the OVERLORD forces, SHAEF planners had formulated various proposals on how to break out of a stabilized front. In mid-July ideas of this nature became extremely pertinent. Attaining maneuver room and the Breton ports remained objectives as valid as they were elusive.

An obvious solution for dissolving the stalemate was to launch a subsidiary amphibious operation outside the OVERLORD beachhead area either by seaborne or by air-transported troops. Yet neither impressed the planners with prospects of success. If the original OVERLORD assault failed to achieve the desired results, how could a smaller force—four divisions was the maximum force immediately available—do better?[2] The necessity of heavy naval involvement (including the use of carriers), difficult and long naval approaches, strong coastal defenses, and the improbability of achieving tactical surprise also discouraged recommendations for amphibious assaults outside the OVERLORD beachhead.[3]

The same was true of plans for airborne operations to dissolve an OVERLORD stalemate. The airborne divisions, committed on the Continent in June, had been delayed in their return to the United Kingdom, and their dispersed locations there, which made unit training difficult, plus a lack of suitable training areas, hindered preparations for immediate commitment. The demands on troop carrier units for air supply prevented effective troop carrier exercises. The need at the end of July to divert almost 400 transport aircraft to the Mediterranean for the invasion of southern France (scheduled for 15 August) made a large-scale airborne operation in support of OVERLORD impossible before late August or early September. Finally, airborne troops dropped outside a sta-

---

[1] Guingand, *Operation Victory*, p. 397. Maps showing the planned phase lines for certain dates and the actual beachhead established are to be found on pages 358 and 391. General Bradley was not in favor of dating phase lines, a British custom. Interv by author with Gen Collins, Washington, 30 Mar 56.

[2] SHAEF/17100/40/Ops (Third Draft), Strategic Reserves for OVERLORD, 17 May 44, SHAEF Air Staff File.

[3] PS SHAEF (44), 21 (Final), 10 Jun 44, NEPTUNE, Stabilization of the NEPTUNE Area, and App. A, SGS SHAEF File 381, Post-OVERLORD Plng.

bilized beachhead might possibly require amphibious reinforcement.[4]

Despite the disadvantages and difficulties of amphibious and airborne operations in support of OVERLORD, Allied planners in June and July continued to explore the possibilities because no other solution was discernible. Since the basic planning already completed for future Allied operations beyond the OVERLORD lodgment area assumed Allied possession of the Breton ports, the planners of subsidiary operations to break the stalemate invariably looked toward Brittany.[5] Of four major combat plans considered by the U.S. 1st Army Group, three focused on Brittany as the target area.[6] Invasion of Brittany was also the central theme of the U.S. Third Army planning in June and July.[7] General Eisenhower gave impetus to this planning by indicating his specific interest in airborne and amphibious operations "involving every likely objective" in Brittany.[8] Yet all the proposed operations seemed to present hazards incommensurate with potential gains.[9]

The search for a panacea to relieve the stalemate came to an end soon after 21 Army Group planners began to press Allied naval sections for definite amphibious assault plans against Quiberon Bay and Brest. Because Quiberon and Brest were Breton ports vital to the American build-up, the U.S. 1st Army Group raised few objections to the British pressure. Admiral Sir Bertram H. Ramsay, the Allied naval commander, thus found himself obliged to consider operations he was unwilling to recommend because formidable enemy coastal defenses and the presence of German U-boat bases would subject naval vessels to unacceptable risk. Ramsay reminded Eisenhower that, before the invasion, ground commanders had rejected the idea of subsidiary airborne operations because they might weaken the main OVERLORD effort. Amphibious operations, he suggested, might have the same result. Accepting the implicit recommendation, General Eisenhower decided, "The principal pressure is to be kept on buildup in the beachhead, with sideshow excursions to be held down to those which will show profit with small investment."[10] It was already apparent that

---

[4] James A. Huston, Airborne Operations, OCMH MS, p. 278; Memo, Eisenhower for Smith, 6 Jul, SHAEF G–3 File 24533/Ops, Future Opns.

[5] See, for example, PS SHAEF (44) 11, Post-NEPTUNE Courses of Action After Capture of Lodgment Area, 3 May 44, SGS SHAEF File 381, Post-OVERLORD Plng; SHAEF Msgs to AGWAR for JPS, 22 Jun, 3, 13, 20, and 27 Jul, SHAEF G–3 File 381-2, 17264/1, SHAEF Weekly Plng Cables; SHAEF/17409/Ops, Status of Plng, 21 AGp, 16 Jun, SHAEF File GCT/322–17/Ops (A), 21 AGp, Gen; PS SHAEF (44) 20, SHAEF G–3 Div, Outline Plan for Air Landing Opn in the Brittany Peninsula, 13, 16, and 19 Jul, and AEAF/T3.22536/ Air, Final Draft, App. B, both in SHAEF G–3 File 24533/Ops, Future Opns; AEAF, Airborne Opns to Further 'OVERLORD,' 6 Jul, and SHAEF/24500/3/ Ops, 14 Jul, both in SGS SHAEF File 373/2, Employment of Airborne Forces in Opn OVERLORD; Montgomery, *Normandy to the Baltic*, p. 124.

[6] LUCKY STRIKE: to exploit eastward in Normandy; SWORDHILT: to secure port facilities in Brittany; BENEFICIARY: to seize the Breton port of St. Malo; HANDS UP: to seize the Quiberon Bay area in Brittany with airborne troops and Ranger/ Commando forces, assisted by the FFI. 12th AGp Rpt of Opns, V, 11.

[7] TUSA AAR, I, Chs. 1 and 2.

[8] Memo, Eisenhower for Smith, 6 Jul, SGS SHAEF G–3 File 24533/Ops, Future Opns.

[9] SHAEF G–3 Div Ltr, Opn in Brittany, 29 Jun, SHAEF G–3 File 24533/Ops, Future Opns; Ruppenthal, *Logistical Support*, I, 468.

[10] Butcher Diary, 11 Jul; Huston, Airborne Opns, pp. 198–99.

no sideshow investment promised a reasonable profit.

Although planning for subsidiary operations did not cease, two events indicated that a final decision had been made against them: the movement of a division from England to the Continent and the publication of a new plan of action. The 28th Division, trained for amphibious operations and originally scheduled for the OVERLORD assault, had remained in England in SHAEF reserve, ready to execute a subsidiary amphibious operation if necessary. The only amphibiously trained force still uncommitted twenty days after the invasion, the 28th Division was released by SHAEF to the 1st U.S. Army Group on 26 June with the condition that it be used only in an amphibious assault. On 13 July SHAEF withdrew the restriction, and ten days later the division moved to the Continent to augment the land forces already committed.[11]

The release of the 28th Division coincided with the appearance of a new operational plan presented by General Bradley and enthusiastically received by General Eisenhower. Bradley proposed to break out of the German containment and obtain maneuver room and eventually the Breton ports through a ground offensive supported by massive air power. A project that would concentrate on the main OVERLORD operation, Bradley's plan followed the advice of SHAEF planners, who had concluded long before that the best way to break a stalemate was by marshaling air power in support of a land offensive mounted from within the stabilized beachhead.[12]

Having searched for a new idea since the second week in July, when the First Army had begun to display definite signs of bogging down in the Cotentin, General Bradley had begun to envision an operation that combined concentrated land power and an overwhelming bombardment from the air. By 11 July General Bradley had conceived the idea; two days later the idea became the First Army's plan. It was called COBRA.[13]

The outstanding feature of COBRA (a name eventually applied to the operation as well as the plan) was the use of a heavy air bombardment to destroy an enemy defensive position of tactical significance. An unusual employment of air power, it was not novel. General Montgomery had used heavy bombers on 7 July in his attack against Caen. Although the bombardment had helped the British gain several miles of ground and part of Caen, the results of the attack had not been particularly spectacular or sufficiently decisive to warrant the expectation that a similar operation, such as COBRA, might achieve more than a limited advance.

That COBRA stirred hope of more than a limited advance—indeed, of a dissolution of the stabilized condition of OVERLORD—was attributable to the planners' belief that they could eliminate two fac-

---

[11] SHAEF/17160/44/Ops, Strategic Reserves for OVERLORD, 6 Jun, and SHAEF/17100/44/Ops (A), SHAEF G-3 Div, Release of 28th Inf Div, 26 Jun and 13 Jul, both in SHAEF File GCT 322-12/Ops (A), SHAEF Reserve; Ruppenthal, *Logistical Support*, I, 457.

[12] PS SHAEF (44) 21 (Final), 10 Jun, NEPTUNE, Stabilization of the NEPTUNE Area, SGS SHAEF File 381, Post-OVERLORD Plng.

[13] FUSA Outline Plan Opn COBRA, 13 Jul.

GENERAL DEMPSEY

As a hush fell over the American front after the capture of St. Lô, intense activity began in the British sector. The Second Army launched a strong attack (GOODWOOD) that promised the Allies an excellent chance of achieving a breakthrough. Had it succeeded, COBRA would probably have been unnecessary.

GOODWOOD had grown indirectly out of the situation on the American front. At a conference on 10 July General Bradley had admitted to General Montgomery that he was discouraged about the offensive in the Cotentin and that he was thinking of the new COBRA idea, not yet completely formulated. General Montgomery had advised him to "take all the time he needed" in the Cotentin. To assist, the British would continue the basic Montgomery pattern of action: attempt to draw the German strength away from the American sector, hold the eastern part of the front firmly, keep the enemy forces opposite the British engaged and off balance by limited objective attacks. Immediately after the conference General Dempsey, the commander of the Second British Army, suggested that the British might take a more positive role in the campaign and launch a strong attack of their own. Montgomery's first reaction was negative, but on reflection he ordered planning started that same day. He alerted Dempsey to hold a corps of three armored divisions in reserve for a "massive stroke" east of the Orne River from Caen to Falaise. By 13 July three ar-

tors that had hampered the Caen operation: the obstructions that bomb craters and debris had placed in the path of ground troops and the long time interval between the air bombardment and the ground jump-off.

Optimistically assessed, if COBRA could co-ordinate the blast effect of a heavy air bombardment with an overwhelming ground attack, the Americans might smash the German ring of containment. Even if COBRA achieved only limited success, the ground gained would give the Allies additional maneuver room. The operation seemed worth a trial. It at least offered a prospect of relief from the painful type of advance that characterized the battle of the hedgerows.

mored divisions were ready under control of the British 8 Corps.[14]

Loath to abandon the idea that the eastern flank was "a bastion" on which not only the U.S. main effort but also the whole future of the European campaign depended, General Montgomery directed Dempsey to maintain balance and a firm base by continuing to exert pressure and destroying German equipment and personnel.[15] Nevertheless, Montgomery found the idea of a British breakthrough attempt increasingly intriguing. He began to think in terms of possibly making a double breakthrough effort—attacks by both British and American troops. By launching GOODWOOD, the British would throw a left hook at the Germans; by following quickly with COBRA, the Americans would strike with a right cross. Whether the primary intention of GOODWOOD was to aid COBRA by forcing the Germans to engage their mobile reserves and the secondary intention to achieve a breakthrough, or whether the reverse was true—though perhaps unimportant in the final analysis and perhaps even unknown to General Montgomery at the time—later became a matter of doubt and controversy.[16]

Like COBRA, GOODWOOD was to have heavy air support. Because the air forces could not support the two attacks simultaneously in the strength desired, GOODWOOD and COBRA were to take place two days apart. Though General Bradley had originally set 18 July as the COBRA target date, the slow advance in the Cotentin caused him to postpone it one day. General Montgomery selected 17 July for GOODWOOD, but adverse weather conditions and the need for extensive regrouping forced a delay. As finally decided, GOODWOOD was to take place on 18 July, COBRA three days later.

The two major deficiencies of the air bombardment launched earlier at Caen were to be corrected for GOODWOOD. Only fighter-bombers were to attack in the zone where armored divisions were to make the main effort, and thus the extensive cratering that had slowed armor at Caen would be avoided. The ground troops were to attack immediately after the air strike in order to capitalize on the paralyzing effect of the bombardment on the Germans.

The ground attack was to involve three corps. On the left (east), from a small bridgehead east of the Orne and northeast of Caen, the 8 Corps was to send three armored divisions in the direction of Falaise in the main effort. In the center, the Canadian 2d Corps was to secure the southern half of Caen (that part of the city beyond the Orne River) and nearby high ground. The British 12 Corps on the right was to launch preliminary attacks several days ahead of

---

[14] 21 AGp Dir, M–510, 10 Jul; Pogue Interv with Gen Bradley, Washington, 14 Oct 46, Pogue Files; "The Aims of Operation 'GOODWOOD,'" a draft extract from B. H. Liddell Hart, *The Tanks* (a history of the Royal Tank Regiment and its predecessors, parts of which have appeared in *The Tank*, the journal of the Royal Tank Regiment).

[15] 21 AGp CinC Notes, 15 Jul, Pogue Files.

[16] Dept of the Scientific Adviser to the Army Council, Mil Operational Research Unit, Rpt 23, Battle Study Opn GOODWOOD, Oct 46; Pogue Interv with Gen Bradley, Washington, 14 Oct 46, and Ltrs, Montgomery to Eisenhower, 12 and 13 Jul, Pogue Files; Montgomery, *Normandy to the Bal-*

tic, p. 130; Bradley, *Soldier's Story,* p. 343; Liddell Hart, *The Tanks,* "The Aims of Operation 'GOODWOOD.'"

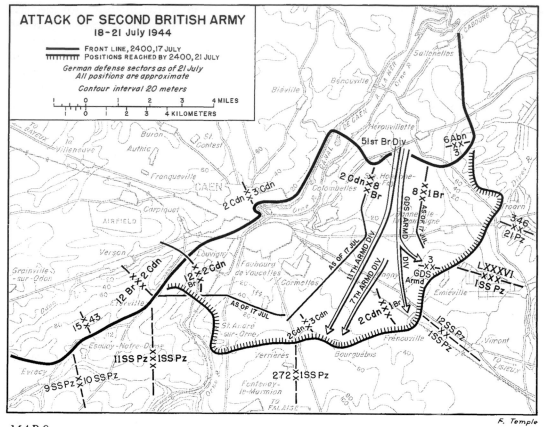

MAP 9

the actual GOODWOOD effort to create a
diversion. The immediate objective of
GOODWOOD was the plain southeast of
Caen, rolling terrain rising toward Falaise. Though neither Montgomery nor
Dempsey mentioned Falaise specifically
in their orders, they and other commanders were thinking of Falaise and
even of Argentan as objectives perhaps
quickly attainable if the battle developed
favorably.[17] *(Map 9)*

Promising General Eisenhower that

his "whole eastern flank" would "burst
into flames," General Montgomery requested the "whole weight of air power"
to bring about a "decisive" victory.
General Eisenhower was enthusiastic,
"pepped up concerning the promise of
this plan," which he termed a brilliant
stroke calculated to knock loose the
shackles that bound the Allies in Normandy. Air Chief Marshal Tedder assured Montgomery that the air forces
would be "full out" to support the "far-
reaching and decisive plan." [18]

[17] Liddell Hart, *The Tanks,* "The Aims of
Operation 'GOODWOOD'"; Rpt 23, Battle Study
Opn GOODWOOD.

[18] Ltrs, Montgomery to Eisenhower, 12 and 13
Jul, Montgomery to Tedder, 14 Jul, Eisenhower

While British naval units fired from the Seine Bay in support, bombers in the largest concentration yet utilized in direct support of a single ground attack loosed their explosives near Caen at daylight, 18 July. Almost 1,700 planes of the RAF Bomber Command and the U.S. Eighth Air Force, plus almost 400 medium and fighter-bombers of the U.S. Ninth Air Force, dropped more than 8,000 tons of bombs to open a path for British ground forces.[19]

Before the bombers came, a quiet had pervaded most of the *Panzer Group West* front since 9 July. Under the control of four corps, eight divisions had manned the 70-mile defensive line, and five divisions had been in reserve. Of the thirteen divisions that comprised *Panzer Group West,* a single division had held twenty miles of marshy coast land on the east flank; two divisions had guarded fifteen miles of *bocage* on the west flank; and ten divisions—five in the line and five in reserve—had covered the critical Caen sector of about thirty-five miles in the center.

To protect the open country around Caen, Eberbach, the commander of *Panzer Group West,* had established a zone defense composed of infantry positions echeloned in depth and covered by antitank fire. The main battle positions,

about 1,200 yards deep, consisted of three lines, while local reserves had organized another defensive line about a mile to the rear. Dual-purpose 88-mm. guns of the *III Flak Corps,* ample artillery pieces, and a rocket launcher brigade in each corps sector supported the infantry positions. Behind the support weapons, four of the reserve divisions had been assembled from two to seven miles in the rear; the fifth reserve division, the *12th SS Panzer,* was undergoing rehabilitation farther to the rear.[20]

Principally from prisoner of war interrogations, Eberbach had learned that Montgomery was planning a three-pronged attack from Caen.[21] Accepting Eberbach's expectation as valid and respecting Montgomery's large number of divisions in reserve, Kluge had dared not weaken the *Panzer Group West* defenses. No further withdrawal from the Caen region seemed possible without inviting disaster.

Although Kluge had not wished to disturb Eberbach's zone defense around Caen, Hitler was not so reluctant. Signs and portents, the Allied deception plan, and weather conditions had convinced the Fuehrer that the Allies were about to make another continental landing near the Seine Bay. The presence of Allied vessels to support GOODWOOD by naval fire added to the conviction. Despite agreement by Kluge and Rommel that they had not seen anything to justify suspicion of another Allied landing and despite their "discomfort" with the Coutances–St. Lô sector, they were forced

to Montgomery, 13 Jul, Pogue Files; Ltr, Tedder to Montgomery, 13 Jul, SGS SHAEF File 381, OVERLORD, I (a).

[19] Leigh-Mallory, Despatch, Fourth Supplement to the *London Gazette* of December 31, 1946, pp. 64–65; Montgomery, *Normandy to the Baltic,* pp. 130–31; FUSA Sitrep 86, 19 Jul; Harris, *Bomber Offensive,* p. 212; [Ackerman], Employment of Strategic Bombers in a Tactical Role, 1941–1951, p. 87; Battle Study Opn GOODWOOD. The figures on the number of tons of bombs dropped differ slightly from source to source.

[20] James B. Hodgson, The Eve of Defeat, OCMH MS R-57.
[21] Telecon, Kluge and Eberbach, 2158, 17 Jul, *OB WEST KTB Anlage 694.*

by Hitler's thinking to consider sending a panzer division from the Caen front to Lisieux, not far from the Seine Bay.[22]

Before actually dispatching a division toward the Seine Bay, Kluge protested to higher headquarters. He asked General der Artillerie Walter Warlimont, Jodl's assistant, what made Hitler insist on sending mobile troops to Lisieux.

"The expectation that in the next couple of days, because of weather conditions . . . ," Warlimont began.

"Oh, the usual reports," Kluge interrupted.

". . . another landing can be made that will put pressure on the weakly held coastal front," Warlimont concluded.

Well, Kluge said, he felt that the Allies were more dangerous in the area where they already were. "We aren't strong enough there," he said. And since he did not have enough troops to cover adequately his entire area of responsibility, he preferred to take his chances where the Allies had not yet appeared. Thus, as to sending troops to Lisieux, he told Warlimont, "I don't like what you say."

"I'll transmit your opinion to the Fuehrer," Warlimont suggested.

"Never mind," Kluge said hastily. "You don't have to tell him anything more. I just wanted to talk it over with you." Still trying to make it clear to Warlimont that he wasn't pleased by the shift at all, he nevertheless agreed to move the *12th SS Panzer Division* to Lisieux.[23] The weakest division in the

Panzer Group West sector, the *12th SS Panzer Division* had started to move to Lisieux when recalled to meet the threat of GOODWOOD.

The SS armored division was recalled partly because Eberbach no longer had a strong reserve. Since the night of 15 July, the British had attacked on the 12 Corps front using flame-throwing tanks and artificial moonlight, which was created by pointing searchlights at the overcast sky. The limited objective attacks, designed to mask the main effort to be launched on 18 July, forced the *II SS Panzer Corps* and part of the *XLVII Panzer Corps* to pull back slightly. Not only did the corps have to commit their local reserves, Eberbach had to commit two of his reserve divisions. If the *12th SS Panzer Division* completed the move to Lisieux, Eberbach would have only two divisions left in reserve.[24]

On the British side, the 8 Corps of the Second British Army, eventually employing three armored divisions, closely followed the air bombardment of 18 July and advanced over three miles in little more than an hour. Tactical surprise and the effect of the bombardment were responsible. Eberbach had not expected Montgomery, who had a reputation for caution, to make a major attack out of the narrow bridgehead he possessed east of the Orne. Even after the attack got under way, Eberbach could not really believe that it was the British main effort. Montgomery had achieved surprise by moving his assault divisions across the Orne only a few hours before the jump-off. With German troops destroyed or dazed by the

---

[22] Telecon, Kluge and Speidel, 1645, 16 Jul, *OB WEST KTB Anlagen 667, 668,* and *671.*

[23] Telecon, Kluge and Warlimont, 1708, 16 Jul, *OB WEST KTB, Anlage 669.*

[24] Hodgson, R–57.

bombardment, the divisions manning defensive positions in the bombed corridor were momentarily paralyzed. Despite valiant efforts to reorganize, they were unable to offer real resistance to the British armored attack.

From about 0900 to noon, the 8 Corps was on the verge of achieving a clean penetration. Only when the British hit the enemy's antitank and *flak* guns on the last defensive line was the advance halted. The heavy antitank screen and the efforts of individual German gun crews and bazooka teams contributed greatly to delaying an immediate exploitation of the potential breakthrough. More important perhaps, the congested battlefield prevented rapid British maneuver, restricted approaches through British mine fields hindered follow-up forces, and subordinate commanders were hesitant to bypass defended villages.

Recovering from the surprise by noon, Eberbach mobilized and committed four tank battalions and four infantry battalions of the *1st SS* and *21st Panzer Divisions* in a counterattack, which dispelled British hope of further immediate penetration.[25] Despite Eberbach's ability to block a clean penetration, his counterattack failed to regain the lost ground, primarily because German tanks moving forward to counterattack "sank into a field of craters and had to be pulled out by tractors." With all of Eberbach's forces committed and with the *12th SS Panzer Division*, which had

turned back from Lisieux, hardly sufficient to affect the situation, Kluge requested and received permission to bring the *116th Panzer Division* from the *Fifteenth Army* sector across the Seine River. "We have to get tanks," Kluge insisted. "We have to let higher headquarters know without misunderstanding that we must have more tanks."[26]

Though the British had lost 270 tanks and 1,500 men on the first day of attack, GOODWOOD continued on 19 July as the British endeavored to extend their gains by limited local attacks. Resistance continued strong, and the British that day lost 131 tanks and incurred 1,100 casualties. Further attempts to advance on 20 July, at a cost of 68 tanks and 1,000 casualties, resulted in little progress. When a heavy thunderstorm on the afternoon of 20 July turned the countryside into a quagmire, GOODWOOD came to an end. An ineffective German counterattack on 21 July signaled the close of the operation.

During the four-day attack, 8 Corps had secured thirty-four square miles of ground and the Canadian 2d Corps had captured the remainder of the city of Caen and part of the plain immediately to the southeast. The 8 Corps lost 500 tanks and over 4,000 men; tank losses in the entire operation totaled 36 percent of all British tanks on the Continent. Although territorial gains were small, particularly when compared with losses and with the expenditure of the air bombardment, Montgomery's attack by 20 July had exhausted Eberbach's

[25] Hodgson, R–57; Rpt 23, Battle Study Opn GOODWOOD; Telecon, Kluge and Blumentritt, 2340, 18 Jul, *OB WEST KTB, Anlage 725;* B. H. Liddell Hart, *Strategy, the Indirect Approach* (New York: Frederick A. Praeger, 1954), p. 316.

[26] Telecons, Kluge and Blumentritt, between 2350, 18 Jul, and 0055, 19 Jul, *OB WEST KTB, Anlagen 725* and *728.*

reserves. Eberbach had to resort to small task forces detached from armored and infantry divisions to operate under the direct control of *Panzer Group West* as "fire-fighting forces." [27]

At a conference with subordinate commanders on 20 July, Kluge reviewed the battle. There was no recrimination, for the troops had fought well. "We will hold," Kluge promised as he attempted to inspire his subordinate leaders, "and if no miracle weapons can be found to improve our basic situation, then we'll just die like men on the battlefield." [28]

While the Germans, despite discouragement, were content that they had fought as well as they could, the Allies were far from happy. General Eisenhower had expected a drive across the Orne from Caen and an exploitation toward the Seine Basin and Paris.[29] Montgomery had been more cautious in his anticipations. On the afternoon of 18 July, the first day of the attack, General Montgomery had been "very well satisfied" to have caught the enemy off balance. The effect of the air support seemed "decisive." The Second British Army had three armored divisions operating in the open country southeast of Caen, and armored cars and tanks, he thought, were threatening Falaise.[30] Two days later, Montgomery judged

that the purpose of the attack had been accomplished. The 8 Corps had advanced nearly six miles and taken 2,000 prisoners, all of Caen had been secured, and the Orne bridgehead had been more than doubled in size. General Montgomery on 20 July instructed General Dempsey to withdraw his armored troops into reserve and replace them with infantry.[31]

To those in the Allied camp who had expected a decisive breakthrough and exploitation, expressions of satisfaction seemed hollow. A profound disappointment swept through the high levels of command. At SHAEF there was much feeling that the 21 Army Group and the Second British Army had not pushed as hard as they might have. "The slowness of the battle, . . . [and] inward but generally unspoken criticism of Monty for being so cautious" brought unusual gloom to General Eisenhower's features. Impatient critics pointed out that Montgomery had gained less than a mile for each ton of high explosives dropped from the planes. Gossips speculated on "who would succeed Monty if sacked." [32]

Later, General Montgomery attempted to explain the reason why "a number of misunderstandings" had arisen. He had been concerned on his eastern flank, he stated, only with "a battle for position," a preliminary operation designed to aid the projected American attack, Operation COBRA. Being a major operation, although important only as a

[27] Hodgson, R–57; Rpt 23, Battle Study Opn GOODWOOD; FUSA Sitrep 86, 19 Jul; Brereton, *Diaries,* p. 310.

[28] Tempelhoff Conf Min, 21 Jul, *AGp B Op. Befehle,* pp. 169–78; Meyer-Detring Conf Min, 22 Jul, *OB WEST KTB, Anlagen Ic Anlageband IV,* Annex 25; Rothberg Conf Min, n.d., *Pz Gp W KTB, Anlagen,* Annex 165.

[29] See Eisenhower, *Crusade in Europe,* pp. 243ff.

[30] Ltr, Montgomery to Eisenhower, 18 Jul, M–60, Pogue Files.

[31] Rpt 23, Battle Study Opn GOODWOOD; FUSA Sitreps 85 and 89, 18 and 20 Jul; Montgomery, *Normandy to the Baltic,* pp. 130–33.

[32] Butcher Diary, 19 and 20 Jul; Liddell Hart. *The Tanks,* "The Aims of Operation 'GOODWOOD.'" The Pogue Files, OCMH, offer abundant evidence of the widespread disappointment and discontent.

preliminary, Operation GOODWOOD had suggested "wider implications than in fact it had." [33]

Apologists could claim that there had been no thought of a breakthrough at the 21 Army Group headquarters, merely hope of a threat toward Falaise to keep the enemy occupied. Critics could claim that Montgomery had tried for a breakthrough with one hand while with the other he had kept the record clear in case he did not succeed. Although General Montgomery had in fact referred in July 1944 to GOODWOOD and to COBRA as parts of an over-all breakthrough plan, he had also, perhaps inadvertently, or perhaps to insure all-out air support, promised that his eastern flank would "burst into flames" and that he would secure a "decisive" victory there. [34] Eisenhower had interpreted Montgomery's intentions for the 8 Corps armored attack as a promise of a plunge into the vitals of the enemy. "I would not be at all surprised," General Eisenhower had written Montgomery, "to see you gaining a victory that will make some of the 'old classics' look like a skirmish between patrols." [35] When the British attack failed to achieve a spectacular breakthrough, disappointment was natural.

Disappointment led General Eisenhower to write Montgomery on 21 July to question whether they saw "eye to eye on the big problems." He reiterated that the Allied needs were the Breton ports; increased space for maneuver, administration, and airfields; and the destruction of German military forces. He remarked that he had been "extremely hopeful and optimistic" that GOODWOOD, "assisted by tremendous air attack," would have a decisive effect on the battle of Normandy. "That did not come about," he wrote, and as a result, he was "pinning our immediate hopes on Bradley's attack." Nevertheless, because the recent advances near Caen had partially eliminated the necessity for a defensive attitude, and because the Allies had sufficient strength and supplies to support major assaults by both British and American armies, he urged General Montgomery to have Dempsey's army launch an offensive at the same time that COBRA began. Eventually, he reminded Montgomery, the U.S. ground strength would be greater than that of the British, but "while we have equality in size we must go forward shoulder to shoulder, with honors and sacrifices equally shared." [36]

On that day General Montgomery was instructing General Dempsey to continue operations "intensively" with infantry to make the enemy believe that the Allies were contemplating a major advance toward Falaise and Argentan. [37] Referring to these instructions, General Montgomery told the supreme commander that he had no intention of stopping offensive operations on the east flank. Nevertheless, as a result of General Eisenhower's letter, Montgomery gave Dempsey more specific instructions to

---

[33] Montgomery, *Normandy to the Baltic*, pp. 127–30; see also Wilmot, *Struggle for Europe*, pp. 353–54, 361–62.

[34] Ltrs, Montgomery to Eisenhower and Tedder, 12, 13, 14, and 18 Jul, cited above, n. 18 and n. 30; Liddell Hart, *The Tanks*, "The Aims of Operation 'GOODWOOD.'"

[35] Ltr, Eisenhower to Montgomery, 13 Jul, cited above, n. 18.

[36] Ltr, Eisenhower to Montgomery, 21 Jul, Pogue Files.

[37] 21 AGp Dir, 21 Jul, M–512, 12th AGp File 371.3, Mil Objectives.

supplement the rather general provisions
of his original directive and thereby
"fattened up" the attack on the east
flank designed to supplement the American effort in the west.[38]

Reassured, General Eisenhower wrote,
"We are apparently in complete agreement in conviction that vigorous and
persistent offensive effort should be sustained by both First and Second Ar-

mies." [39]   But again, as in June when
the U.S. First Army had driven toward
Cherbourg, and as at the beginning of
July when the Americans had commenced their offensive toward the
south, the Allies, and particularly General Eisenhower, had their immediate
hopes pinned on General Bradley's attack.

[38] Ltr, Montgomery to Eisenhower, M–65, 22 Jul,
Pogue Files; Butcher Diary, 25 Jul.

[39] Ltr, Eisenhower to Montgomery, 23 Jul, Pogue
Files.

CHAPTER XI

COBRA Preparations

The perspective within which Operation COBRA was conceived was essentially the same as had bounded General Bradley's July offensive. The objectives remained unchanged: Brittany was the eventual goal, the first step toward it the Coutances–Caumont line.

According to General Montgomery's instructions of the end of June, repeated in July, the First U.S. Army was to pivot on its left at Caumont and make a wide sweep to a north–south line from Caumont to Fougères so that U.S. troops would eventually face east to protect the commitment of General Patton's Third Army into Brittany.[1] To set the First Army wheeling maneuver into motion, General Bradley decided to breach the German defenses with a massive blow by VII Corps on a narrow front in the center of the army zone and to unhinge the German defenses opposing VIII Corps by then making a powerful armored thrust to Coutances. With the basic aim of propelling the American right (west) flank to Coutances, COBRA was to be both a breakthrough attempt and an exploitation to Coutances, a relatively deep objective in the enemy rear—the prelude to a later drive to the southern base of the Cotentin, the threshold of Brittany.[2]

The word *breakthrough*, frequently used during the planning period, signified a penetration through the depth of the enemy defensive position. The word *breakout* was often employed later somewhat ambiguously or as a literary term to describe the results of COBRA and meant variously leaving the hedgerow country, shaking loose from the Cotentin, acquiring room for mobile warfare—goodbye Normandy, hello Brest.

Reporters writing after the event and impressed with the results stressed the breakout that developed rather than the breakthrough that was planned. Participants tended later to be convinced that the breakout was planned the way it happened because they were proud of the success of the operation, perhaps also because it made a better story. In truth, Operation COBRA in its original concept reflected more than sufficient credit on those who planned, executed, and exploited it into the proportions it eventually assumed. COBRA became the key maneuver from which a large part of the subsequent campaign in Europe developed.

During the twelve days that separated the issuance of the plan and the commencement of COBRA, command and staff personnel discussed in great detail the possible consequences of the attack. "If this thing goes as it should," General Collins later remembered General Brad-

---

[1] 21 AGp Dir, M–510, 10 Jul, FUSA File, 21 AGp Dirs.

[2] First U.S. Army, *Report of Operations*, I, 96ff.

ley saying, "we ought to be in Avranches in a week." [3] Certainly it was reasonable to hope that COBRA would precipitate a breakthrough that might be exploited into what later came to be called the breakout, but a justifiable hope did not prove a firm intention—particularly when considered in relation to the stubborn German defense in the hedgerows. Perhaps in their most secret and wildest dreams American planners had visions of a COBRA that would slither across France, but as late as 18 July there were "still a few things that [First] Army has not decided yet." One of those "few things" was that COBRA was to be synonymous with breakout. [4]

Perhaps the best a priori evidence of how difficult it would be to achieve even a breakthrough was the result of two

limited objective attacks launched by the VIII Corps a week before COBRA.

Preliminary Operations

A basic feature of the COBRA plan was the encirclement and elimination of the Germans facing the VIII Corps on the Cotentin west coast. For an effective execution of this concept, VIII Corps had to advance its front quickly toward Coutances at the proper time. Yet two German strongpoints in the corps zone of advance threatened to block a speedy getaway by a portion of the corps. To have to destroy them during the COBRA operation would retard the initial momentum of the COBRA attack. To eliminate them before COBRA commenced, to move the corps front closer to a more desirable line of departure, and to get the entire corps out of Cotentin swampland became the objectives of two preliminary operations.

Because the German strongpoints were virtually independent positions, the preliminary operations initiated by the 83d and 90th Divisions of VIII Corps were separate, local attacks. The actions were remarkably alike in the assault problems they posed, in the nature of the combat, which resembled the earlier battle of the hedgerows, and in the results attained.

The 83d Division attacked first. Since its original commitment on 4 July, the division had fought in the Carentan–Périers isthmus, had gained the west bank of the Taute River near the Tribehou causeway, and had sent the 330th Infantry across the Taute to operate with the 9th Division on the east bank. The remainder of the 83d Division had

---

[3] Interv by author with Gen Collins, 30 Mar 56, Washington, D.C.

[4] 30th Div G–3 Jnl File, 18 Jul; see also VIII Corps AAR, Jul. The only reference in writing found by the author that expresses the breakout idea before the actual operation got under way is in Brereton, *Diaries*, page 306. General Brereton recorded in his notes, dated 11 July (two days before First Army published the COBRA plan) that he had discussed with General Bradley and three corps commanders the matter of air support for COBRA. He added parenthetically that the COBRA attack was designed to break out of the Cotentin and complete the liberation of France, but he did not state whether this was his idea or General Bradley's. Since portions of the diary were written later than the dates ascribed to the entries, the diary is not a reliable contemporary document.

More suggestive is General Bradley's response to General Montgomery's suggestion that airborne troops be dropped in the Avranches area to aid COBRA. General Bradley said he thought that airborne troops might be more suitably used in future operations, perhaps in Brittany (FUSA Msg, 23 Jul, FUSA G–3 Jnl). Since General Bradley was not usually receptive to the idea of airborne operations (as evidenced by his behavior later in the campaign), his remark probably has little significance in connection with what he expected from COBRA.

attacked along the west bank of the Taute toward Périers and had reached a causeway leading to la Varde. In its pre-COBRA assignment, the division was to attack across the la Varde causeway to the east bank of the Taute. In possession of la Varde and near the Lessay–Périers highway, the division would have a water-and-swamp obstacle behind it and be in position to threaten encirclement of Périers from the east. At this point it would also regain control of the 350th Infantry. (*See Map II.*)

The Germans did not hold la Varde in strength. A reinforced company was sufficient since the flat ground around la Varde provided open fields of fire for more than a thousand yards in all directions. Only five machine guns were at la Varde, but they were able to fire as though "shooting across a billiard table." [5] From nearby positions at Marchésieux, German assault guns could provide effective support.

In contrast to the excellent assistance the terrain furnished the defense, there were no natural features to aid the attack. Between the 83d Division on the west bank and the Germans holding la Varde on the east bank stretched the gray-brown desolation of the Taute River flats. The Taute River, at this point a stream fifteen feet wide and two feet deep with about a foot of soft mud on the bottom, flowed along the western edge of the marsh. The causeway that crossed the swamp was a tarred two-lane road little higher than the open area of stagnant marsh and flooded mudholes. Over a mile long, the causeway ran straight and level through borders of

regularly spaced trees that gave the appearance of a country lane. The road in fact was the approach—the driveway—to a small château on the west bank of the swamp. The small bridge over the Taute near the château had been destroyed by the Germans. Along both edges of the swamp, lush banks of trees and hedges concealed the château, which was the jump-off point, and the hamlet of la Varde, the objective. In between, there was no cover. Foxholes in the flats would quickly fill with water. The only feasible method of attack was to crawl forward and then charge the enemy machine guns with grenades and bayonets. The swamp was mucky, and vehicles could not cross the causeway unless the bridge near the château was repaired. [6]

The division commander, General Macon, decided that an attack launched around 1800 would give engineers five hours before darkness to lay temporary bridging across the stream. Thus, build-up and consolidation of a bridgehead established at la Varde could be accomplished during the night. Colonel York's 331st Infantry was to make the assault, Colonel Crabill's 329th Infantry a diversionary attack. A strong artillery preparation was to include considerable smoke. Though the division tried to get tracked vehicles capable of carrying supplies across the swamp in the event engineers could not repair the bridge over the Taute, their efforts

---

[5] Telecon, Macon and York, 0110, 18 Jul, 83d Div G–2, G–3 Jnl and File.

[6] Min of Mtg, 1330, 21 Jul, 83d Div G–2, G–3 Jnl File. The following account has been taken from the 83d Div AAR, Jul, and G–2, G–3 Jnl and File, 16–19 Jul; 331st Inf AAR, Jul; Sgt. Jack M. Straus, *We Saw It Through, 331st Combat Team* (Munich, Germany: F. Bruckmann K.-G., n.d.), p. 19; FUSA Sitreps 84, 85, and 86, 18 and 19 Jul; VIII Corps G–3 Per Rpt 34, 19 Jul.

failed. First Army headquarters, after much prodding, agreed to lend the division eight "Alligators" for one day but refused to furnish drivers.[7] Normally used on the Normandy invasion beaches to handle supplies unloaded from ships, the Alligators arrived in the division area too late for use in the la Varde attack.

In the afternoon of 17 July, shortly before the main attack, reconnaissance troops of the 330th Infantry, on the east side of the river, attempted to approach la Varde from the east. Enemy machine gun fire stopped the effort. The diversionary attack on the west bank, launched by the 329th Infantry in company strength, turned out to be little more than a demonstration that "just pooped out" after taking thirteen casualties.[8] At 1830, half an hour after the diversion commenced, Colonel York sent one battalion of his 331st Infantry toward la Varde in the main effort.

Because the causeway was the natural crossing site and because the flat straight road would obviously be swept by German fire, Colonel York sent his assault battalion through the spongy swamp. Using prefabricated footbridges, the infantry struggled across muck and water sometimes neck deep. At nightfall the battalion reached la Varde and established an insecure bridgehead. Many infantrymen who had crawled through the swamp found their weapons clogged with silt and temporarily useless. The mud, the darkness, and enemy fire discouraged weapons cleaning. Though the regiment had planned to reinforce

the battalion during the night over the causeway, engineers had been unable to erect a temporary bridge because of heavy enemy tank destroyer fire on the bridge site. Unable to get supply vehicles, tanks, and artillery over the flats to support the battalion at la Varde, and deeming it impossible either to transport a sufficient supply of ammunition by hand or to send reinforcements across the treacherous swamp, General Macon reluctantly agreed to let the battalion at la Varde—which shortly after daylight, 18 July, reported it was unable to remain on the east bank—fall back.

The 331st Infantry tried again at dawn, 19 July, in an attack keyed to fire support from the 330th Infantry on the east bank of the Taute and to concealment by smoke and an early morning haze. Eschewing the swampy lowlands, the assault battalion advanced directly down the causeway. Against surprisingly light enemy fire, the troops again established a foothold at la Varde. Engineers in the meantime installed a Bailey bridge across the Taute near the château. Unfortunately, a normal precaution of mining the bridge so it could be destroyed in case of counterattack backfired when enemy shellfire detonated the explosives. The bridge went up with a roar. Since tanks again could not cross the swamp, the foothold at la Varde was once more precarious. When the enemy launched a small counterattack that afternoon, the troops retired.

The failure of this attack ended the attempts to take la Varde. The participating rifle companies had taken casualties of 50 percent of authorized strength, and one battalion commander was missing in action. Difficult terrain and plain bad luck had contributed to

---

[7] Alligator was the nickname given to an unarmored, tracked landing vehicle, the LVT (1).

[8] Telecon, Macon and Crabill, 1920, 17 Jul, 83d Div G–2, G–3 Jnl and File.

the failure, but more basic was the ineffectiveness of the 83d Division. The division earlier that month had incurred more casualties and received more replacements in its short combat career than any other U.S. unit in Normandy in a comparable span of time. The loss of trained leaders and men in the combat echelons and their replacement by the large influx of relatively untrained personnel had diminished the division's efficiency. "We have quite a few new men and they are really new," Colonel York explained; "[they] don't know their officers . . . and the officers don't know their men." [9]

Recognizing the condition of the division, Generals Bradley and Middleton saw no purpose in continuing the futile pattern at la Varde. They saw more hope in revising the VIII Corps role in COBRA. In the meantime the 83d Division was to train and try to assimilate its replacements.

In the same way, the results of the 90th Division's attempts to execute a pre-COBRA mission also contributed to a modification of the VIII Corps role in COBRA. After twelve days of sustained action at Mont Castre and Beaucoudray, the 90th Division had also seen its ranks depleted in the wearing battle of the hedgerows. Less than six weeks after commitment in Normandy, the division's enlisted infantry replacements numbered more than 100 percent of authorized strength; infantry officer replacements totaled almost 150 percent. In comparison to the veterans who had fought in the hedgerows, the replacements were poorly trained and undependable, as soon became obvious in the division's new assignment.

The pre-COBRA objective of the 90th Division was a low hedgerowed mound of earth surrounded by swampland. Athwart the division zone of advance, the island of dry ground held the village of St. Germain-sur-Sèves. Possessing the island and across the Sèves River, the division would be in position not only to threaten Périers but also to get to the Périers–Coutances highway.

Only a weak German battalion held the island, but it had excellent positions dug into the hedgerowed terrain, good observation, and a superb field of fire. Several assault guns and a few light tanks supported the infantry; artillery was tied into the strongpoint defenses. [10]

Two miles long and half a mile wide, the island had been more than normally isolated by the heavy rainfall in June, which had deepened the shallow streams along its north and south banks. Linking the hamlet of St. Germain to the "mainland" was a narrow, tarred road from the western tip of the island. The Germans had destroyed a small bridge there, the only suitable site for engineer bridging operations. Several hundred yards away, a muddy country lane gave access to the island from the north, across a ford. How to cross level treeless swamps that offered neither cover nor concealment was the assault problem. Although a night attack seemed appropriate, the division commander, General Landrum, quickly abandoned the idea. With so many newly arrived replacements he dared not risk the prob-

---

[9] Telecon, Macon and York, 0110, 18 Jul, 83d Div G–2, G–3 Jnl and File; 83d Div G–3 Per Rpt 22, 18 Jul.

[10] Hodgson, R–54.

lem of control inherent in a night operation.[11]

To help overcome the terrain difficulties, General Landrum arranged for
heavy fire support. Since his was to be
the only attack in progress in the corps
zone, more than normal fire power was
available. He received the assistance
of the entire VIII Corps Artillery. Because the 83d Division had found the la
Varde operation so difficult, preparatory
bombardment by tactical air was promised for the 90th Division. To make
certain of a preponderance of fire power,
Landrum directed all nonparticipating
infantry units to support the attack by
fire.

General Landrum selected the 358th
Infantry to make the attack. The regimental commander, Lt. Col. Christian
E. Clarke, Jr., planned to attack with
two battalions abreast, each advancing
along one of the roads to the island.
Once on the island, the two battalions
were to form a consolidated bridgehead.
Engineers were then to lay bridging so
that tanks and assault guns could cross
the Sèves and support a drive eastward
to clear the rest of the island.

Initially scheduled for 18 July, the
operation was postponed several times
until artillery ammunition problems—
matters affecting the COBRA preparations—were settled. The attack was finally set for the morning of 22 July.
Poor visibility that morning grounded
not only the fighter-bombers that were
to make an air strike on the island but

ADVANCING TOWARD ST. GERMAIN

also the artillery observation planes.
Though in great volume, the artillery
preparation thus was unobserved.

Since no other actions were occurring
in the area, the Germans, like VIII
Corps, were able to utilize all their fire
resources within range to meet the American attack. Enemy fire prevented the
assault troops from advancing beyond
the line of departure. A battalion of
the 90th Division not even taking part
in the attack sustained forty-two casualties from enemy shelling.[12] American
counterbattery fires plotted by map
seemed to have no real effect.

Three hours after the designated time
of attack, one battalion moved forward
along the muddy country lane. Taking
50 percent casualties in the assault companies, men of the battalion crossed the
swamp, waded the stream, and reached

---

[11] This account has been taken from: 90th Div
AAR, Jul; FUSA IG Ltr, Failure of Elements of
the 358th Inf, 90th Div, to Resist a German Counterattack, 26 Jul; VIII Corps IG Ltr, Rpt of Investigation of 358th Inf Regt, 90th Inf Div, 11
Aug.

[12] 357th Inf Jnl, entry 1210, 23 Jul.

the island. The momentum of their advance carried them 200 yards into the interior. Colonel Clarke quickly ordered the other assault battalion to take the same route, but only one rifle company managed to reach St. Germain in this manner. Though Colonel Clarke replaced the battalion commander with the regimental executive officer, the new battalion commander had no more success in reinforcing the foothold. The Germans pounded the approaches to the island with artillery and mortars and swept the open ground with machine gun fire. The only practical method of crossing the exposed area was by infiltration, and most men sent toward the island lost their way.

By dark of the first day of attack, at least 400 men were on the island. One battalion reduced to half strength by casualties and stragglers, less its mortar platoon, plus little more than one company of another battalion, formed a horseshoe line on the island about 200 yards deep and a thousand yards wide, with both flanks resting on the swamp. The troops repelled a small German counterattack, and the positions seemed quite stable. Still, efforts to reinforce the bridgehead failed. Because enemy fire prevented engineers from bridging the stream, neither tanks nor tank destroyers could cross.

With the descent of darkness, the troops on the island began to experience a sense of insecurity. Lacking mortars, tanks, and antitank guns, the men withdrew to a defiladed road along the north edge of the island. In the pitchblack darkness, some of the demoralized troops began furtive movement to the rear. Stragglers, individually and in groups,

drifted unobtrusively out of the battle area. Soldiers pretended to help evacuate wounded, departed under the guise of messengers, or sought medical aid for their own imagined wounds. German fire and the dark night encouraged this unauthorized hegira and added to the problems of unit commanders in recognizing and controlling their recently arrived replacements.

Shortly after nightfall, Colonel Clarke discovered that the battalion commander of the forces on the island had remained on the near shore. When he ordered him to join his men, the officer did so, but neglected to take his staff. Learning this later, Colonel Clarke dispatched the staff to the island, but the officers lost their way and did not reach St. Germain.

At daylight, 23 July, the German shelling subsided, a prelude to the appearance of three German armored vehicles on one flank of the American positions and an assault gun on the other. As these began to fire, a German infantry company of about platoon strength—perhaps thirty men—attacked. Only a few Americans in the bridgehead fired their weapons. Panic-stricken for the most part, they fell back and congregated in two fields at the edge of the island. Hedgerows surrounded each of these fields on three sides; the fourth, facing the swamp, was open and invited escape. Continuing German fire across the open ground provided the only restraint to wholesale retreat.

Officers at regimental headquarters on the "mainland" had begun to suspect that the situation was deteriorating when unidentified cries of "cease firing" swept across the two fields. A shell landed in a corner of one field, inflicting heavy casualties on men huddling together in fear. At this moment, despite little firing and few Germans in evidence, a group of American soldiers started toward the enemy, their hands up, some waving white handkerchiefs. That was the end. The rest of the men either surrendered or fled across the swamp.

At the conclusion of the fight for St. Germain, about 300 men were missing in action. A later check revealed that approximately 100 men had been killed, 500 wounded, and 200 captured.

The causes for failure were clear. Weather, terrain, a resourceful enemy, command deficiency at the battalion level (caused perhaps by combat exhaustion during the preceding battle of the hedgerows) had contributed to the result. The main cause, however, was the presence of so many inadequately trained replacements. The 90th Division had not had enough time to fuse its large number of replacements into fighting teams.

It seemed as though the performance of the 90th Division at St. Germain was but a logical extension of earlier unsatisfactory behavior. General Eisenhower remarked that the division had been "less well prepared for battle than almost any other" in Normandy, for it had not been "properly brought up" after activation.[13] Judging that the division needed new leadership, a commander not associated with experiences of the hedgerow battle, higher headquarters decided to relieve the division commander. "Nothing against Landrum," General Eisenhower remarked, adding that he would be glad to have General Landrum in command of a division he himself had conducted through the training cycle.[14]

Failure in the preliminary operations was in many ways depressing, but American commanders still were hopeful that COBRA would not bring another recurrence of the difficult hedgerow fighting. The First Army that was to execute COBRA was not the same one that had launched the July offensive. Battle had created an improved organization, and a continuing continental build-up had strengthened it. What the army needed was the opportunity to get rolling, and COBRA might well provide just that.

The Troops

The hedgerow fighting that had exhausted and depleted the ranks had also made the survivors combat wise. Common mistakes of troops entering combat were "reliance on rumor and exaggerated reports, failure to support maneuvering elements by fire, and a tendency to withdraw under HE [high-explosive] fire rather than to advance out of it."[15] Each unit now had a core of veterans who oriented and trained replacements. Most combat leaders had taken the test of ordeal by fire. The great majority of divisions on the Continent were battle trained.

An assurance had developed that was particularly apparent in dealings with

[13] Ltr, Eisenhower to Marshall, 5 Jul, Pogue Files; see Harrison, *Cross-Channel Attack*, p. 403; Robert R. Palmer, Bell I. Wiley, William R. Keast, *The Procurement and Training of Ground Combat Troops*, UNITED STATES ARMY IN WORLD WAR II (Washington, 1948), p. 459, n. 19.

[14] Ltr, Eisenhower to Marshall, 2 Aug, Pogue Files.

[15] 12th AGp Immed Rpt 41, Misc Comment, 29 Aug.

enemy armor. Earlier, when a regiment had blunted a tank-infantry counterattack, the significant and gratifying result was that it had stopped German armor. "Glad to know they can hold their own against tanks," was the comment.[16] But such experience was becoming increasingly common, and definite identification of a knocked-out Mark VI Tiger proved conclusively that even the German tank with the strongest armor was vulnerable to American weapons. Artillery, tanks, bazookas, tank destroyers, and tactical aircraft could and did destroy German tanks. By 11 July the First Army Ordnance Section had accumulated in collecting points 36 Mark III's and IV's, 5 Mark V's and VI's. The hedgerowed terrain had neutralized to a great extent the ability of the Tiger's 88-mm. gun and the Panther's 75-mm. gun to penetrate an American tank at 2,500 yards. Tanks generally engaged at distances between 150 and 400 yards, ranges at which the more maneuverable Sherman enjoyed a distinct superiority.[17]

Though a tank destroyer crew had seen three of its 3-inch armor-piercing shells bounce off the frontal hull of a Mark V Panther at 200 yards range, a fourth hit had penetrated the lower front hull face and destroyed the tank.[18] A soldier who had met and subdued an enemy tank later reported, "Colonel, that was a great big son-of-a-bitch. It looked like a whole road full of tank. It kept coming on and it looked like it

was going to destroy the whole world." Three times that soldier had fired his bazooka, but still the tank kept coming. Waiting until the tank passed, he had disabled it with one round from behind.[19]

The ability to destroy German armor generated a contagious confidence that prompted some units to add a two-man bazooka team to each infantry battalion, not principally for defense but to go out and stalk enemy armored vehicles.[20] With this frame of reference becoming prevalent, the troops displayed a decreasing tendency to identify self-propelled guns as tanks. Even such a battered division as the 83d manifested an aggressiveness just before COBRA when it launched a reconnaissance in force that developed spontaneously into a coordinated limited objective attack. Not the objective gained but the indication of a spirit that was ready to exploit favorable battle conditions was what counted.[21]

One of the major problems that had hampered the First Army—how to use tanks effectively in the hedgerow country—appeared to have been solved just before COBRA. The most effective weapon for opening gaps in hedgerows was the tank dozer, a comparatively new development in armored warfare. So recently had its worth been demonstrated that a shortage of the dozers existed in Normandy. Ordnance units converted ordinary Sherman tanks into dozers by

---

[16] 83d Div G–2, G–3 Jnl, entry 1209, 8 Jul.

[17] XIX Corps Msg, 1800, 8 Jul, FUSA G–3 Jnl; Annex 1 to FUSA G–2 Per Rpt 48, 28 Jul; XIX and VII Corps AAR's, Jul.

[18] Notes, XIX Corps AAR, Jul; VII Corps AAR, Jul.

[19] CI 30 (4th Div). The soldier was Pvt. Eugene Hix of the 22d Infantry, who was posthumously awarded the DSC for destroying three tanks in three days with his rocket launcher.

[20] See, for example, 356th Inf Jnl, 24 Jul.

[21] 83d Div AAR, 23 Jul; Confirmation of Oral Instrs, 22 Jul, 83d Div G–2, G–3 Jnl and File.

RHINO TANK *with hedgerow cutter crashing through a hedgerow.*

mounting a blade on the front. Some hedgerows, however, were so thick that engineers using satchel charges had first to open a hole, which the dozers later cleared and widened.[22]

Because the use of demolitions and tank dozers was time consuming, the tanks in offensive activity had often remained on the roads, and when cross-country movement became necessary, progress was inevitably slow. In order to speed up the movement of armor, Ordnance units and tankers throughout the army had devoted a great deal of thought and experimentation to find a device that would get tanks through the hedges quickly without tilting the tanks upward, thereby exposing their under-

bellies and pointing their guns helplessly toward the sky. The gadgets invented in July 1944 were innumerable.

As early as 5 July the 79th Division had developed a "hedgecutter," which Ordnance personnel began attaching to the front of tanks. Five days later the XIX Corps was demonstrating a "salad fork" arrangement, heavy frontal prongs originally intended to bore holes in hedgerow walls to facilitate placing engineer demolition charges but accidentally found able to lift a portion of the hedgerow like a fork and allow the tank to crash through the remaining part of the wall. Men in the V Corps invented a "brush cutter" and a "greendozer" as antihedgerow devices.

The climax of the inventive efforts was achieved by a sergeant in the 102d Cavalry Reconnaissance Squadron, Curtis G. Culin, Jr., who welded steel scrap from a destroyed enemy roadblock to a tank to perfect a hedgecutter with several tusklike prongs, teeth that pinned down the tank belly while the tank knocked a hole in the hedgerow wall by force. General Bradley and members of his staff who inspected this hedgecutter on 14 July were so impressed that Ordnance units on the Continent were ordered to produce the device in mass, using scrap metal salvaged from German underwater obstacles on the invasion beaches. General Bradley also sent Col. John B. Medaris, the army Ordnance officer, to England by plane to get depots there to produce the tusks and equip tanks with them and to arrange for transporting to France by air additional arc-welding equipment and special welding crews.

Every effort was made to equip all tanks with this latest "secret weapon," for it enabled a tank to plough through

---

[22] ETOUSA Engr Hist Rpt 10, Combat Engineering, Aug 45, pp. 30–33.

a hedgerow as though the hedgerow were pasteboard. The hedgecutter sliced through the earth and growth, throwing bushes and brush into the air and keeping the nose of the tank down. The device was important in giving tankers a morale lift, for the hedgerows had become a greater psychological hazard than their defensive worth merited.

Named Rhinoceros attachments, later called Rhinos, the teeth were so effective in breaching the hedgerows that tank destroyer and self-propelled gun units also requested them, but the First Army Ordnance Section carefully supervised the program to make certain that as many tanks as possible were equipped first. By the time COBRA was launched three out of every five tanks in the First Army mounted the hedgecutter. In order to secure tactical surprise for the Rhinos, General Bradley forbade their use until COBRA.[23]

Not the least beneficial result of the July combat was the experience that had welded fighting teams together. "We had a lot of trouble with the tanks," an infantry commander had reported; "they haven't been working with us before and didn't know how to use the dynamite."[24] Co-operation among the arms and services had improved simply because units had worked together. Part of the developing confidence was generated by the fact that increasing numbers of medium tanks had received the newer and more powerful 76-mm. gun to replace the less effective 75-mm. gun, and thus were better able to deal with the enemy.[25]

Perhaps the most significant improvement in team operations was the increasing co-ordination that was developing between the ground forces and the tactical airplanes. In addition to performing the primary mission of trying to isolate the battlefield by attacking enemy lines of communication, the IX Tactical Air Command had employed a large portion of its effort in direct and close ground support. The pilots had attacked such targets as strongpoints retarding the ground advance, troop concentrations, gun positions, and command posts. They had also flown extensive air reconnaissance for the ground troops.[26] On a typical day of action the fighter bombers of the IX TAC exerted 40 percent of their air effort in close support of the First Army, 30 percent in direct support of the Second British Army, 10 percent against rail lines and communications 50 to 70 miles behind the enemy front, and 20 percent in offensive fighter activity and ground assault area cover.[27]

[23] 79th Div G-4 Jnl, 5 Jul; XIX Corps G-4 (Rear Echelon) Jnl, 10 and 19 Jul; XIX Corps Ord Sec Jnl, 24 Jul; 30th Div G-3 Jnl, 1405, 19 Jul; Bradley, *Soldier's Story*, p. 342; Eisenhower, *Crusade in Europe*, p. 269; First U.S. Army, *Report of Operations*, I, 122; V Corps Operations in the *ETO*, pp. 120–21; [Lt Col Glenn T. Pillsbury *et al.*], Employment of 2d Armored Division in Operation COBRA, 25 July–1 August 1944, a research report prepared by Committee 3, Officers' Advanced Course (Fort Knox, Ky., The Armored School, May, 1950) (hereafter cited as [Pillsbury], 2d Armd Div in Opn COBRA), p. 8; Guingand, *Operation Victory*, p. 395; Sylvan Diary, 14 and 17 Jul.

[24] Telecon, Stephens and Kelly, 1225, 15 Jul, 30th Div G-3 Jnl and File; 30th Div Ltr of Instrs, 15 Jul.
[25] [Pillsbury], 2d Armd Div in Opn COBRA, p. 19.
[26] First U.S. Army, *Report of Operations*, I, 91; [Robert F. Futrell], Command of Observation Aviation: A Study in Control of Tactical Air Power, USAF Hist Study 24 (Maxwell Air Force Base, Ala., Air University, 1952), *passim*.
[27] FUSA and IX TAC Air Opns Summary for 18 Jul. 30th Div G-3 Jnl and File.

Ground-air communications were being improved. "Wish you would tell the Air Corps we don't want them over here," an irate division staff officer had pleaded early in July after a few strafing planes had struck an American artillery battalion and wounded several men. "Have them get out in front [and] let them take pictures [but] no strafing or bombing." [28] Complaints of this nature were decreasing. Pilots of a tactical reconnaissance group attended courses of instruction in artillery fire adjustment, and as a result high performance aircraft began to supplement the small artillery planes with good effect. [29] Particularly interested in developing a practical basis for plane-tank communications, General Quesada, the IX TAC commander, had very high frequency (VHF) radios, used by the planes, installed in what were to be the lead tanks of the armored column just before COBRA was launched. Tankers and pilots could then talk to each other, and the basis for the technique of what later became known as armored column cover was born. The success of the technique in August was to exceed all expectations. [30]

The development of new air operational techniques and weapons such as rocket-firing apparatus and jellied gasoline, or napalm, also promised more effective support for the ground troops. Experiments with radar-controlled blind dive bombing and with the technique of talking a flight in on target indicated that night fighter operations might soon become more practical. Since no fields for night fighters were operational on the Continent, the craft were based in England. Employment of night fighters in tactical support was not usually considered profitable even though ground forces requested it. [31] In July work with radar-controlled night flights and projects for eventually basing night fighters on continental airfields promoted hope of round-the-clock air support.

Fighter-bomber groups in direct tactical support of the First Army were moving to continental airfields at the rate of about two each week. By 25 July twelve had continental bases. Their nearness to the battle zone eliminated the need to disseminate ground information across the channel to airfields in England as prerequisite for ground support. American ground units desiring air support channeled their requests to the First Army joint air operations section, which secured quick action for specific missions. [32]

During July, the American ground build-up proceeded steadily. Four infantry and four armored divisions reached the Continent during the month

[28] 1st Div G-3 Jnl, entry 1717, 7 Jul.

[29] First U.S. Army, *Report of Operations*, I, 124; Ltr, Corlett to OCMH, 1956.

[30] Brereton, *Diaries*, 21 Jul, p. 311; Bradley, *Effect of Air Power*, p. 41; Bradley, *Soldier's Story*, pp. 337–38; Leigh-Mallory, "Despatch," Fourth Supplement to the *London Gazette* of December 31, 1946, pp. 65–66. Artillery often marked ground targets for the aircraft. Interv by author with Gen Collins, 30 Mar 56, Washington, D.C.

[31] 83d Div G-2, G-3 Jnl, 8 Jul; 1st Div G-3 Jnl, entries 1326, 5 Jul, 0008 and 0012, 6 Jul. Two American night fighter squadrons operated under British control, mainly against guided missiles. In September P-38's of one IX TAC fighter group operated by radar control against German night troop movements, but they were not very successful. [Joe Gray Taylor], Development of Night Air Opns, 1941–1952, USAF Hist Study 92 (Maxwell Air Force Base, Ala., Air University, 1953), pp. 26–27, 116–17. See Leigh-Mallory, "Despatch," Fourth Supplement to the *London Gazette* of December 31, 1946, p. 89.

[32] First U.S. Army, *Report of Operations*, I, 91.

before COBRA. The arrival in England early in the month of the 80th Division brought the theater total of U.S. divisions to 22: 14 infantry, 6 armored, and 2 airborne. Four more were expected in August. During the first twenty-five days of July, almost half a million tons of supplies were brought into France, the bulk across the beaches. Although the Cherbourg harbor began to be used on 16 July, port operations there were not to become important until the end of the month.[33]

To launch COBRA, the First Army had four corps controlling fifteen divisions actually on the army front.[34] General Patton's Third Army headquarters had assembled in the Cotentin during July and was ready to become operational. Similarly awaiting the signal for commitment, two additional corps headquarters were in France at the time COBRA was launched and another was to reach the Continent soon afterward. An infantry division and an armored division, not in the line, were available for use by the First Army in COBRA; another armored division was scheduled to land on the Continent before the end of the month. The First Army also was augmented by many supporting units that belonged to the Third Army: engineer and tank destroyer groups, evacuation hospitals, and Quartermaster railhead, general service, gas supply, graves registration, and truck companies. The Forward Echelon of the Communications Zone headquarters was established at

Valognes by 22 July, and the entire Communications Zone headquarters would soon arrive.[35]

Obviously, one field army, the First, could not much longer effectively direct the operations of such a rapidly growing force. To prepare for the commitment of General Patton's army and to meet the necessity of directing two field armies, the U.S. 1st Army Group headquarters began to displace from England to the Continent on 5 July, a move completed one month later.[36] In order to maintain the fiction of Operation FORTITUDE, the Allied deception that made the Germans believe a landing in the Pas-de-Calais might take place, ETOUSA activated the 12th Army Group under the command of General Bradley. Transferred to the 12th Army Group were all units and personnel that had been assigned to the U.S. 1st Army Group "except those specifically excepted," in actuality, none. The 1st U.S. Army Group, under a new commander, thus became a nominal headquarters existing only on paper until its abolition in October 1944. The 12th Army Group became the operational headquarters that was to direct U.S. forces on the Continent.[37]

The presence of uncommitted headquarters in Normandy proved an embarrassing largess. General Montgomery did not utilize General Crerar's First Canadian Army headquarters until 23 July, when it assumed a portion of

---

[33] Ruppenthal, *Logistical Support, I,* 449, n. 58; 457, 464–65.

[34] One of these corps and seven divisions (plus the 90th Division, which had been attached to the First Army since March) belonged to the Third Army.

[35] FUSA Ltr, Attachment of Third U.S. Army Units, 17 Jul; TUSA Msg, 17 Jul; Forward Echelon, COMZ, ETOUSA Memo, 22 Jul. All in FUSA G–3 Jnl. TUSA AAR, I, 12; XV Corps G–3 Jnl and File, Jul (particularly Telecons 12, 20, and 21 Jul).

[36] 12th AGp AAR, I, 40.

[37] 12th AGp AAR, I, 6; ETOUSA GO 73, 14 Jul, quoted in 12th AGp AAR.

the Second British Army front.[38]   And, on the American side of the beachhead, General Patton's Third Army, along with several corps headquarters, was still not employed in combat.   Since Brittany had been selected as the stage for General Patton's initial operations, the U.S. First Army had to reach the base of the Cotentin peninsula to provide the Third Army a means of ingress.   A successful COBRA was a vital step toward this achievement.

General Eisenhower on 25 July gave General Bradley authority to change the existing command structure of the U.S. forces and erect the organization envisioned by the OVERLORD planners.   At General Bradley's discretion in regard to timing, the 12th Army Group headquarters was to become operational, assume control of the First Army, and commit under its control the Third Army.[39]

Between the end of the earlier July offensive and the launching of COBRA, there was a lull for about a week.   Not only did the period of inactivity permit plans to be perfected and the troops to be better organized for the attack, it also gave the men some rest and time to repair the equipment damaged in the battle of the hedgerows.   Units were able to integrate replacements.   By the time COBRA got under way, all the divisions on the Continent were close to authorized strength in equipment and personnel and most had undergone a qualitative improvement.[40]

The quiet period before COBRA also made possible increased comforts such as hot meals, showers, and clothing changes. Even though B rations—a nonpackaged food affording a variety of hot meals— had reached the Continent early in July and were ready for issue to the troops, the battle of the hedgerows had prevented their being substituted for combat 10-in-1, K, and C rations until later in the month.   With kitchens set up to serve hot meals, "it was amazing how many cows and chickens wandered into minefields . . . and ended up as sizzling platters."[41]

As Allied leaders searched rain-filled skies for a break in the clouds that might permit the air bombardment planned for COBRA, a phrase of the Air Corps hymn came to mind: "Nothing can stop the Army Air Corps."   Nothing, they added, except weather.   While impatient commanders waited anxiously for sunshine, and while General Bradley facetiously assumed the blame for having "failed to make arrangements for proper weather," the First U.S. Army rested and prepared for the attack.[42]

The Plot Against Hitler

During the lull over the battlefield in the west that followed GOODWOOD and preceded COBRA, and while defeats in the east gave the Germans increasing worry over the eventual outcome of the war, a dramatic attempt was made on Hitler's life on 20 July.   In a speech

[38] Stacey, *The Canadian Army*, pp. 187, 194.
[39] 12th AGp AAR, I, 6.
[40] See, for example, 9th Div Jnl, 1525, 17 Jul; 743d Tk Bn Rpt 14, 18 Jul, 30th Div G–3 Jnl and File; FUSA Daily Strength Rpt; First U.S. Army, *Report of Operations*, I, 99.

[41] 314th Infantry Regiment, *Through Combat*, p. 23; 357th Inf Jnl, entry 1900, 15 Jul; 2d Div AAR, Jul, Observations of the Div Comdr; 79th Div G–4 Jnl, 14 and 18 Jul.
[42] Bradley, *Effect of Air Power*, p. 53; Ltr, Bradley to Leigh-Mallory, 23 Jul, OCMH Files.

the following day, Hitler himself released the news to the world. "A very small clique of ambitious, unscrupulous and stupid officers" he announced, "made a conspiracy to kill me, and at the same time to seize hold of the German Supreme Command."[43] Within a short time Allied intelligence officers had pieced together a remarkably accurate account of the occurrence: a cabal of high-ranking Army officers had tried to assassinate Hitler with a bomb in order to seize political power in Germany. The bomb had inflicted only minor wounds on Hitler, and the Fuehrer moved swiftly to suppress the revolt. He named Heinrich Himmler—already Reich Minister of Interior, Reichsfuehrer of the SS (and *Waffen-SS*), and Chief of the Gestapo and German Police—Commander of the Home Forces and gave him control of the military replacement system. Hitler replaced the ailing Generaloberst Kurt Zeitzler, chief of staff of OKH and vaguely implicated in the conspiracy, with Generaloberst Heinz Guderian. High-ranking officers of Army, Air Force, and Navy were quick to reaffirm their loyalty to Hitler. The immediate result of the conspiracy was to tighten centralized control of the military in Hitler's hands.[44]

Allied intelligence had not only the facts but a plausible interpretation. The cause of the *Putsch* was "undoubtedly the belief . . that Germany had lost the war."[45]

That a "military clique," as Hitler calls them, should have been plotting to liquidate him is encouraging; that they should have chosen this moment is exhilarating. . . . The very fact that plotters reckoned that the time was ripe for a venture so complicated as the assassination of the Fuehrer argues that they had good reason to hope for success. . . . There seems . . . no reason to disbelieve Hitler's assertion that it was an Army *Putsch* cut to the 1918 pattern and designed to seize power in order to come to terms with the Allies. For, from the military point of view, the rebels must have argued, what other course is open? How else save something, at least, from the chaos? How else save the face of the German Army, and, more important still, enough of its blood to build another for the next war? [46]

Colonel Dickson, the First Army G–2, believed that the Hitler government would remain in office by suppressing all opposition ruthlessly. He saw no evidence to suppose that the existing German Government would be overthrown by internal revolution or by revolt of one or more of the German field armies. He was certain that only the military defeat and the surrender of the German armies in the field would bring about the downfall of Hitler. The first step toward that goal was to intensify "the confusion and doubt in the mind of the German soldier in Normandy" by "an Allied break-through on the First Army front at this time, which would threaten to cut him off from the homeland, [and which] would be a decisive blow to the German *Seventh Army*." [47] On its knees, the *Seventh Army* had no future "save in the fact that so long as the battle

[43] Hitler Speech, 21 Jul, FUSA G–3 Jnl File, 23 Jul.

[44] FUSA G–2 Est 11, 24 Jul; see Hodgson, R–57, for a detailed bibliographical account of the *Putsch* and also for the reaction in the west; see Wilmot, *Struggle For Europe*, pp. 366ff., for a good account of the revolt.

[45] FUSA G–2 Est 11, 24 Jul.

[46] Hitler and His Generals, App. B to 15 (S) Inf Div Intel Summary 30, n.d., reprinted in SHAEF Weekly Intel Summary 18, n.d., V Corps G–3 Jnl File.

[47] FUSA G–2 Est 11, 24 Jul.

continues the miracle may still take place. Buoyed up by accounts of what V1 had done, no less than by the promise of V2, and still imbued with a discipline that has been impaired only by the substitution of apathy for enthusiasm, the German soldier is still on the [Nazi] party's side." [48]

The fact was that very few officers in the west were implicated in the plot against Hitler. A small but important group in the headquarters of the Military Governor of France at Paris staged a coup that was successful for several hours, but except for isolated individuals who knew of the conspiracy, and rarer still those who were in sympathy with it, the military elsewhere on the Western Front were overwhelmingly loyal to Hitler, even though some might be doubtful of the eventual outcome of the war. Those who did play some small role in the plot had not deliberately or unconsciously hindered field operations by treasonable conduct. The conspiracy had virtually no effect on the military situation in the west. The combat soldier in the "you-or-me" life-and-death struggle was too busy trying to remain alive.[49] The higher officers pledged their continuing loyalty to Hitler. All Germans were more or less impressed with the miracle that had saved Hitler's life.[50]

As a result of the *Putsch,* the effi-ciency of the German war machine under Hitler increased, for Himmler took immediate steps to unify the military replacement system and eventually improved it. The *Putsch* also intensified Hitler's unfounded suspicion that mediocrity among his military commanders might in reality be treason. Rommel, recuperating at home from an injury received in Normandy, was eventually incriminated and forced to commit suicide. Speidel, the *Army Group B* chief of staff, was later imprisoned on evidence that indicated involvement. Kluge, the principal commander in the west, fell under suspicion nearly a month later when battlefield reverses in Normandy seemed to give substance to whispered accusations of his friendliness with known conspirators. Thus the *Putsch,* while giving Hitler the opportunity to consolidate military control even more in his own hands, pointed a blunt warning that the symptoms of military defeat were spreading an infectious distrust and suspicion among the higher echelons of the German military organization.[51]

On the battlefield in Normandy the half-hearted planning for an offensive action near Caen in August came to an end. Even before GOODWOOD had violently disrupted German operational planning, Rommel, just before his near-fatal accident, had estimated that the Germans could hold the Normandy front only a few more weeks at the maximum.[52] Several days later Kluge en-

---

[48] Hitler and His Generals, cited above, n. 46.

[49] See XIX Corps G–2 Per Rpt 55, Annex 3, Study of the Morale of the German Troops on XIX Corps Front, 9 Aug.

[50] See Constantine FitzGibbon, *20 July* (New York: W.W. Norton & Co., 1956) and John Wheeler-Bennett, *The Nemesis of Power* (London: Macmillan & Co. Ltd., 1953) for accounts of the *Putsch.*

[51] Hodgson, R–57; *OB WEST, a Study in Command,* I, 123ff; MS # B–272 (Blumentritt).

[52] Wilhelm Ritter von Schramm, *Der 20, Juli in Paris* (Bad Woerishofen, Germany: 1953), p. 77; Speidel, *Invasion 1944,* pp. 113–17.

dorsed Rommel's view. In a letter to Hitler he stated the hard facts clearly:

In the face of the total enemy air superiority, we can adopt no tactics to compensate for the annihilating power of air except to retire from the battle field. . . . I came here with the firm resolve to enforce your command to stand and hold at all cost. The price of that policy is the steady and certain destruction of our troops. . . . The flow of matériel and personnel replacements is insufficient, and artillery and antitank weapons and ammunition are far from adequate. . . . Because the main force of our defense lies in the willingness of our troops to fight, then concern for the immediate future of this front is more than justified. . . . Despite all our efforts, the moment is fast approaching when our hard-pressed defenses will crack. When the enemy has erupted into open terrain, the inadequate mobility of our forces will make orderly and effective conduct of the battle hardly possible.[53]

When Goodwood seemed to confirm Rommel's and Kluge's opinions, OKW became doubtful of the value of planning an offensive. Until the Germans learned where Patton was, they could not dispel their uncertainty about Allied intentions and consequently could not intelligently plan offensive action or weaken the Pas-de-Calais forces to bolster the Normandy front. On 23 July, immediately upon receipt of Kluge's letter, Jodl proposed to Hitler that it might be time to begin planning for an eventual withdrawal from France. Surprisingly enough, Hilter agreed.[54] But before anything came of this conversation, Cobra raised its head.

The Breakthrough Plan

The persons most intimately connected with Cobra were General Bradley, who conceived it, and General Collins, who executed it. These officers, warm personal friends, each of whom seemed to be able to anticipate what the other was about to do, worked together so closely on the plans and on the developing operations that it was sometimes difficult to separate their individual contributions. Their teamwork was particularly effective within the American concept of command where the higher commander often gives his subordinate great leeway in the detailed planning of an operation. On the basis of reconnaissance, terrain study, road conditions, and photo analysis, the subordinate commander could recommend modifications that might alter quite basically the original idea. With fine communications at their disposal, the American commanders at both echelons (indeed at all levels of command) could and did exchange information and suggestions, and measures proposed by the subordinate could be approved quickly by the higher authority. Where mutual confidence abounded as it did in the case of Generals Bradley and Collins, the closest co-operation resulted, with great credit to both.

General Bradley presented the Cobra idea at a conference with his staff and his corps commanders on 12 July. He characterized the battle of the hedgerows as "tough and costly . . . a slugger's match . . . too slow a process," and spoke of his hope for a swift advance

---

[53] Ltr, Kluge to Hitler, 21 Jul, *OB WEST Ia Nr. 5895/44* and *5896/44 g.Kdos. Chefs,* and enclosure, *Betrachtungen zur Lage,* signed Rommel, 15 Jul, *AGp B Lagebeurteilungen und Wochenmeldungen.*
[54] *Der Westen* (Schramm), pp. 68–69; Speidel, *Invasion 1944,* pp. 115–16; Gestapo Rpt to Bor-

mann, 30 Jul, *EAP 105/22,* 275–76; Hodgson, R–54 and R–57.

made possible by "three or four thousand tons of bombs" from the air. He stated that aggressive action and a readiness to take stiff losses if necessary were the keys to the success of COBRA. "If they [the Germans] get set [again]," he warned, "we go right back to this hedge fighting and you can't make any speed." He insisted, "This thing [COBRA] must be bold." [55]

Requisites for the COBRA operation were many and complex, and General Bradley could only estimate that they in fact were fulfilled. He assumed that the Germans in the Cotentin, under the pressure of the July offensive, would withdraw to an organized and stable defensive line. He had to determine where they would be likely to erect their defense. He had to be certain that the Americans were in contact with the main line of resistance when the operation commenced. He had to be sure that the enemy line would not be so strongly fortified as to defy rapid penetration. He had to have firm ground beyond the Cotentin marshes that would not mire and delay mobile columns. He had to have a region traversed by a sufficient number of roads to permit quick passage of large numbers of troops. Finally, he had to be reasonably sure he could shake his armor loose before the Germans could recuperate from the penetration. [56]

Reasoning that the Germans would withdraw to the vicinity of the Lessay-

St. Lô highway, General Bradley chose that road as the COBRA line of departure. The COBRA battleground—the Coutances–St. Lô plateau—was to be south of the highway. It was a region of typical *bocage,* an area of small woods and small hills, land bounded on the west by the ocean, on the east by the Vire River. The sombre hedgerowed lowland gave way to rolling and cheerful terrain, the swamps disappeared, arable land was more plentiful and fertile, the farms more prosperous, the hedgerowed fields larger. Pastoral hillsides replaced the desolation of the *prairies* and the over-luxuriant foliage of the Carentan lowlands. Roads were plentiful, for the most part tarred two-lane routes. There were several wider highways—four main roads leading south and three principal east–west roads across the Cotentin. Road centers such as Coutances, Marigny, St. Gilles, le Mesnil-Herman, and Notre-Dame-de-Cenilly assured an adequate communications network. Streams were relatively small.

A jumble of small ridge lines and low hills at first glance, the Coutances–St. Lô plateau contains a series of east–west ridges that rise toward the south for about eight miles from the Lessay–St. Lô highway. Forming cross-compartments that would hinder an advance to the south, the ridges favored lateral movement across the First Army front. When in July the VII Corps had attacked down the Carentan–Périers isthmus toward the plateau, General Collins had indicated awareness of the advantages of swinging the offensive to a lateral axis in that region. He had pointed out that if infantry forces reached Marigny, armored troops might well drive west-

[55] FUSA G–3 Conf Notes, 12 Jul, FUSA G–3 Misc File; Garth, Battle for Normandy, pp. 156, 171.

[56] FUSA G–3 Conf Notes, 12 Jul; FUSA Outline Plan, Opn COBRA, 13 Jul; Bradley, *Soldier's Story,* p. 318.

ward along the highway from St. Lô to Coutances in exploitation.[57] General Bradley's COBRA plan took advantage of the terrain in the same way. After air force bombs facilitated the infantry penetration, mobile troops were to veer westward and drive to the Coutances, thereby encircling the Germans on the west coast of the Cotentin.

General Bradley called upon the VII Corps to make the main effort. He therefore changed the corps boundary to reduce the corps zone to a width of four and a half miles. He also enlarged General Collins' force to a total of three infantry and two armored divisions. (*Map 10*)

As outlined by the army plan, COBRA would start with a tremendous air bombardment designed to obliterate the German defenses along the Périers–St. Lô highway opposite the VII Corps. Two infantry divisions, the 9th and the 30th, were to make the penetration and keep the breach open by securing the towns of Marigny and St. Gilles, thereby sealing off the flanks of the breakthrough. Two armored divisions, the 3d and the 2d (the latter after being moved from the V Corps sector), and a motorized infantry division, the 1st (also after having been moved from the V to the VII Corps zone), were then to speed through the passageway—the three-mile-wide Marigny–St. Gilles gap—in exploitation. Tactical aircraft were to have already destroyed river bridges around the limits of the projected COBRA area to isolate the battlefield, and the exploiting forces on the left were to establish blocking positions on the eastern flank and along

the southern edge of the battlefield to prevent the Germans from bringing in reinforcements. The forces in the main exploiting thrust, on the right (west), were to drive toward the Cotentin west coast near Coutances and encircle the enemy opposite VIII Corps. The VIII Corps in turn was to squeeze and destroy the surrounded enemy forces. At the conclusion of COBRA, the First Army would find itself consolidating on the Coutances–Caumont line. If the air bombardment and ground attack paralyzed German reaction completely, the troops were to be ready to exploit enemy disorganization still further by continuing offensive operations without consolidation.[58]

Since the larger and basic American maneuver defined by Montgomery was to be a sweep through the Cotentin around a 90-degree arc with the pivot at Caumont, the U.S. troops east of the Vire had the subsidiary role of containing the enemy forces. While XIX Corps remained in place and supported the VII Corps effort, V Corps was to make a diversionary attack on the second day of the COBRA operation. Both corps

---

[57] VII Corps Tactical Study of the Terrain, 28 Jun.

[58] FUSA Outline Plan COBRA, 13 Jul, with artillery and tank destroyer fire support plans, overlays, and amendments; FUSA Msg, 2055, 14 Jul, and IX TAC Msg, 17 Jul (Amendment 1 to IX TAC Order 84). Both in FUSA G–3 Jnl. Annex 2 (Overlay) to VIII Corps FO 8, 15 Jul; VII Corps Opns Memos 38 and 44, 15 and 20 Jul.

Bombardment on 17 July rendered eight bridges around the COBRA battlefield unserviceable and damaged five; seven bridges escaped damage. Collins Msg, 1230, 23 Jul, 30th Div G–3 Jnl and File.

For the British-American boundary changes that permitted the movement of the 2d Armored and 1st Division from the V Corps to the VII Corps sector, see FUSA Msgs, 14 and 17 Jul, and V Corps Msg, 23 Jul, FUSA G–3 Jnl; 21 AGp Dir, M–510, 10 Jul; Bradley, *Soldier's Story*, pp. 326–28.

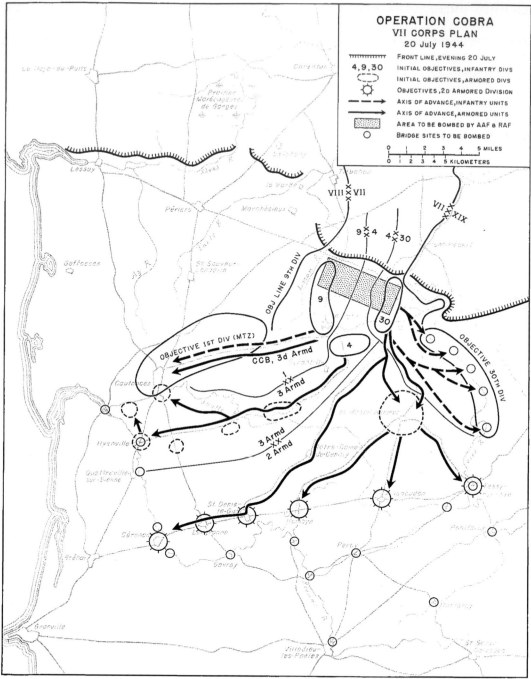

MAP 10

were to tie down German troops that might otherwise be moved to seal off a COBRA penetration. The XIX Corps was also to be ready to displace west of the Vire River and assume a new zone; as VII Corps veered westward toward Coutances, XIX Corps was to be prepared to take over the left portion of the VII Corps zone and drive to the south along the west bank of the river.[59]

The rather general concept expressed in the army outline plan was developed into a detailed course of action by the VII Corps. Corps planners also made two major modifications that affected the weight of the infantry assault and the routes as well as the relative strengths of the exploiting units.

Because the 9th and 30th Divisions were near exhaustion from their battle in the Tautc and Vire region, General Collins requested and received the 4th Division as well, and assigned to it a role in the initial infantry assault. Though General Bradley had planned to retain the 4th in army reserve, he acceded to Collins' request in order to insure a quick follow-up of the air bombardment and a speedy penetration.[60]

More important was the modification

of the exploitation, which virtually changed the character of COBRA. According to the army plan, the mobile forces were to use two main highways leading south, the Marigny–Carantilly road on the right (west) and the St. Gilles–Canisy road on the left. One armored division, presumably the 3d, after moving south for six miles to Carantilly, was to swing in a wide arc for eleven miles—southwest, west, and northwest—to encircle Coutances in the corps main effort. The other armored division, the 2d, after pushing five miles south to Canisy, was to split into three columns and drive southeast, south, and southwest in order to protect the main effort developing toward Coutances. At the conclusion of its advance, the 2d Armored Division was to set up blocking positions across the fronts of both the VII and the VIII Corps—at Bréhal, Cérences, Lengronne, St. Denis-le-Gast, and Hambye, also inferentially at Villebaudon and Tessy-sur-Vire—and thereby across the entire Cotentin. In advance of the forces actually encircling and destroying the enemy near Coutances, the blocking positions were to prevent the Germans from bringing in reinforcements from the southeast and from the south. The motorized 1st Infantry Division was to provide reserve strength to reinforce either armored thrust, or both.[61]

Less concerned with the possible arrival of enemy reinforcements than with the strength already facing the VII and VIII Corps in the Cotentin, General Collins redistributed the power available to him. He re-formed and strengthened

---

[59] FUSA Outline Plan COBRA, 13 Jul; Corlett to OCMH, 19 Jan 54. Plans at the beginning of July had envisioned the eventual displacement of the XIX Corps west of the Vire. These plans had projected an easy capture of St. Lô, and the displacement was to have occurred south of that city. Map Overlay to accompany V Corps FO 9, 1 Jul, in *V Corps Operations in the ETO*, p. 103.

[60] First U.S. Army, *Report of Operations*, I, 98; VII Corps G–3 Ltr, Info Relative to Opn COBRA, 29 Oct 45, and Ltr, Gen Collins to Maj Kenneth W. Hechler, 13 Nov 45, both cited on p. 27 of Hechler's VII Corps in Operation COBRA, a preliminary MS, Hist Div, USAFET, OCMH Files. The Hechler manuscript has been used extensively in the chapters dealing with the breakthrough.

---

[61] FUSA Outline Plan COBRA, 13 Jul; see also Annex 2 (Overlay) to VIII Corps FO 8, 15 Jul.

the main attack force and rerouted it along a more direct approach to Coutances. He transformed the drive along the original and longer route to Coutances into a subsidiary and protective effort. He consolidated the blocking force on the left from three dispersed columns into two compact thrusts.

As formulated by Collins, the plan of exploitation assigned the main encirclement to the motorized 1st Division, with Combat Command B of the 3d Armored Division attached. Armor and infantry, after driving south to Marigny, were to attack westward along the excellent highway directly to Coutances in order to block and help destroy the Germans facing the VIII Corps. The 3d Armored Division, less CCB, was to follow the original and more roundabout route to Coutances; it was to seize the southern exits of Coutances and provide flank protection on the south for the main effort. The 2d Armored Division, strengthened by the attachment of the 22d Regimental Combat Team of the 4th Division, was to drive along the left (east) flank of the corps. One thrust was to go directly to le Mesnil-Herman to cover the movement of the other exploiting forces and prepare for further movement to Villebaudon and Tessy-sur-Vire, two critical points of entry for possible German reinforcements from the southeast. Another 2d Armored Division force was to be ready to go southwest from Canisy through Notre-Dame-de-Cenilly to block German reinforcement from the south, but instead of driving all the way to Bréhal near the Cotentin west coast it was to stop at Cérences. The armor was to halt at Cérences in order to provide a coastal corridor for an advance to the south by

the VIII Corps, to avoid "a hell of a scramble" likely to come if VII and VIII Corps units intermingled south of Coutances, and to prevent the 2d Armored Division from being "strung out too badly." [62]

The COBRA plan in final form thus called for three infantry divisions, the 9th, 4th, and 30th, to make the initial penetration close behind the air bombardment and create a "defended corridor" for exploiting forces, which were to stream westward toward the sea. The motorized 1st Division, with CCB of the 3d Armored Division attached, was to thrust directly toward Coutances. The reduced 3d Armored Division was to make a wider envelopment. The 2d Armored Division, with the 22d Infantry attached, was to establish blocking positions from Tessy-sur-Vire to the Sienne River near Cérences and, in effect, make a still wider envelopment of Coutances.[63]

The VII Corps plan expressed a concept quite different from the army idea. The corps plan reinforced the initial infantry assault. It massed more power against Coutances. It strengthened blocking positions. It projected three encircling columns across the Cotentin and around Coutances. Instead of cutting across the VIII Corps zone of advance, it provided a corridor for the VIII Corps to exploit further a successfully completed COBRA. As a result of these changes, COBRA was no longer a plan designed primarily to encircle Coutances after penetration; it had be-

---

[62] VII Corps FO 6 (rev), 20 Jul; FUSA G–3 Conf Notes, 12 Jul; Ltr, Collins to Hechler, 9 Dec 45, quoted in Hechler, VII Corps in Opn COBRA, p. 27.

[63] Annex 1 (Overlay) to VII Corps FO 6 (rev), 20 Jul.

come a plan to encircle and secure Coutances, disrupt the German defenses west of the Vire River, and set up a situation suitable for further exploitation, presumably by the VIII Corps.

Expecting the VII Corps ground attack to complete the penetration six hours after the bombardment, General Bradley originally scheduled the VIII Corps attack for that time. The failure of both preliminary operations in the VIII Corps zone caused him to modify this arrangement. If the German resistance to the pre-COBRA operations at la Varde and St. Germain was typical of what the Americans could anticipate in COBRA, then six hours was not enough time. General Bradley consequently postponed the VIII Corps attack. If COBRA were launched in the morning, VIII Corps would attack at dawn of the following day; if COBRA were launched in the afternoon, VIII Corps would attack on the morning of the third day.[64]

One other change in plan came as a result of the preliminary operations. Instead of reverting to control of the 83d Division, the 330th Infantry east of the Taute River flats remained a separate unit. Although still considered formally under control of the VIII Corps, the regiment was to begin the COBRA attack with the VII Corps.

Since COBRA's success depended essentially on VII Corps progress, General Collins had six divisions under his control, virtually an army. The armored units augmented the corps strength still more since both were "old type" or "heavy" armored divisions, the only ones in the theater. All the divisions sched-

uled to make the VII Corps COBRA attack were combat experienced; three—the 2d Armored, the 1st, and the 9th—had fought in North Africa and Sicily. While the 9th and 30th manned the corps front in mid-July, the other divisions slated for commitment in COBRA assembled in the rear, careful to avoid contact with the enemy lest their identity be revealed. Tactical surprise was to be as important in COBRA as was the concentration of strength.

In keeping with the mission of VII Corps, First Army gave the corps a large part of its artillery: 9 of its 21 heavy battalions, 5 of its 19 mediums, and all 7 of its nondivisional lights. Nondivisional artillery pieces of all types under corps control totaled 258.[65] For the anticipated duration of the attack—five days—the army allocated the VII Corps almost 140,000 rounds of artillery ammunition.[66] Because ammunition restrictions made all-inclusive prearranged fires difficult, the VII Corps Artillery (Brig. Gen. Williston B. Palmer) did not draw up an over-all fire plan. Attaching to the divisions all seven of the light battalions the army had made available, the corps suballocated to the divisions the greater part of its supply of ammunition.[67] The division fire plans included

---

[64] FUSA Msg to VIII Corps, 24 Jul, FUSA G-3 Jnl.

[65] VIII Corps had 108, XIX Corps 100, V Corps 98. Draft MS, Arty in Opn COBRA, App. C to Gen Bd Rpts, ML-2229.

[66] Ibid. VIII Corps received about 42,000 rounds, XIX Corps 31,000, and V Corps 27,000, for 105-mm. howitzers, 155-mm. howitzers and guns, 4.5-inch guns, 8-inch howitzers and guns, 240-mm. howitzers, and 90-mm. guns.

[67] Each armored division received two self-propelled battalions, the 9th Division received two towed battalions, and the 30th Division received one towed battalion. The 30th also received the 92d Chemical Battalion, less one company. VII Corps Opns Memo 45, 22 Jul.

concentrations on known or suspected enemy installations, some to strike as far as 3,000 yards south of the Périers–St. Lô highway, most to fall on the main enemy defenses near the road. All fire plans emphasized striking specific targets rather than furnishing general support.[68] The VII Corps Artillery was to control 174 pieces of medium and heavy caliber, plus the artillery of the divisions initially in reserve. Adjacent corps artillery units were to assist.

The major preattack bombardment was to come from the air. Planes were to assume the normal artillery missions of disrupting the enemy's communications, neutralizing his reserves, and reducing his will to fight. Far beyond the resources of the artillery available to the First Army, the air bombardment that General Bradley had in mind encompassed terrifying power. To be certain that air commanders appreciated the extent of the support desired, General Bradley went to England on 19 July to present his requirements to the air chiefs in person.

Bradley's primary desire was to obtain "blast effect" by the use of heavy bombers.[69] He wanted the air attack concentrated in mass, the planes to strike in a minimum duration of time. To avoid excessive cratering, which might impede the ground troops, and to prevent the destruction of villages located at critical road junctions, he requested that only relatively light bombs be used.[70] He designated a rectangular target immediately south of the Périers–St. Lô highway, 7,000 yards wide and 2,500 yards deep. To prevent accidental bombing of VII Corps front-line troops, Bradley planned to withdraw them 800 yards from the bomb target. Though 800 yards left no real margin of safety, General Bradley wanted the ground troops close enough to the target for immediate exploitation after the bombardment. To provide additional protection for the ground forces, General Bradley recommended that the planes make their bomb runs laterally across the front, parallel to the front lines, instead of approaching over the heads of American troops and perpendicular to the front. Recognizing that pilots preferred a perpendicular approach to minimize antiaircraft interference, he suggested that the planes use the sun for concealment—if the attack occurred in the morning, the bombers could fly from east to west; in the afternoon, they could attack over a reverse course. In either case, the straight road between Périers and St. Lô would be an unmistakably clear landmark as a flank guide.

For their part, the air chiefs were unable to meet all the requirements. Although they promised blast effect by a mass attack, agreed to use comparatively light bombs, and concurred in the choice of the target, they demurred at making lateral bomb runs and objected to the slender 800-yard safety factor.

A lateral bomb run, the air chiefs

---

[68] VII Corps Letters, Primary Target List—Operation COBRA—Artillery and Air, and Secondary Target List . . . , both dated 20 July, list 42 primary targets and 75 secondary targets.

[69] FUSA G–3 Conf, 12 Jul; Garth, Battle for Normandy, p. 165.

[70] FUSA G–3 Conf, 12 Jul; Ltrs, Leigh-Mallory to Bradley, 19 Jul, and Bradley to Leigh-Mallory, 23 Jul, OCMH Files; Bradley, Soldier's Story, p. 341.

pointed out, meant approaching the target area on its narrow side, that is to say along a narrow corridor. In an operation on the scale requested by General Bradley, this would cause congestion over the target and make the completion of the attack impossible in the brief time desired. To gain the effect of mass, the bombers had to approach from the north over the heads of the ground troops. Admitting that this posed some dangers to the ground troops, the air chiefs noted that the highway would serve as a clearly distinguishable "no bomb line." In addition, the less effective enemy aircraft interference during a perpendicular approach would enable pilots and bombardiers to bomb more accurately.[71]

Despite the fact that the highway made an excellent landmark, the air chiefs wished a true safety ground factor of 3,000 yards. They nevertheless agreed, in light of General Bradley's desire to get the ground troops to the target area quickly, to reduce the safety factor to 1,500 yards. Bradley, for his part, refused to withdraw his troops more than 1,000 yards from the highway.[72] The final result was a further compromise. The ground troops were to withdraw only 1,200 yards, but the heavy bombers were to strike no closer to the ground troops than 1,450 yards. The interval of 250 yards was to be covered by fighter-bombers, which attacked at lower altitudes than the heavies and thus could bomb more accurately.

Participating units in the COBRA air attack were to include all the heavy bombers of the Eighth U.S. Air Force and all the medium bombers and fighter-bombers of the Ninth U.S. Air Force. Fighter planes from the Eighth U.S. Air Force and from the RAF 2nd Tactical Air Force were to fly cover. The RAF Heavy Bomber Command, with planes equipped to carry only large bombs, were excluded because of Bradley's desire to avoid excessive destruction and cratering.[73] Air Chief Marshal Tedder, Deputy Supreme Commander, provided top-level supervision. Air Chief Marshal Leigh-Mallory, commander of the AEAF, was to set the time and the date of the operation. General Brereton, commanding the Ninth U.S. Air Force, was to plan the attack of the bombers. General Quesada, commander of the IX Tactical Air Command, was to co-ordinate the air attack with the ground forces.[74]

The air bombardment was to begin eighty minutes before the ground attack with a twenty-minute strike by 350 fighter-bombers. Most fighter-bombers were to attack the narrow target strip immediately south of and adjacent to the road, although several flights were to bomb and strafe six enemy strongpoints north of the Périers–St. Lô highway.[75]

---

[71] Eighth AF Draft Ltr, Summary of Plng and Execution of Missions 24 and 25 Jul 44, n.d., Rpts of Bombing Errors Made on 25 Jul, 8 Aug 44, USAF Hist Sec Files.

[72] Some commanders, notably General Eddy of the 9th Division, later protested any withdrawal to General Bradley, for they were reluctant to give up terrain acquired with much difficulty. Bradley Soldier's Story, pp. 340–41.

[73] Ltr, Leigh-Mallory to Bradley, 19 Jul; Eighth AF, Spec Rpt on Opns 24 and 25 Jul, USAF Hist Sec Files.

[74] Eighth AF, Tactical Mission Rpts, Operations 492 and 494, 24 and 25 July, USAF Hist Sec Files, give a most straightforward account of the air operation.

[75] VII Corps Opns Memo 45, 22 Jul.

Following immediately, 1,800 heavy bombers, in an hour-long strike, were to blast the main target area, a rectangular "carpet" adjacent to and south of the narrow strip. Upon conclusion of the heavy bomber attack—the beginning of the ground attack—350 fighter-bombers were to strafe and bomb the narrow strip again for twenty minutes. Ten minutes after the completion of this strike, 396 medium bombers were to attack the southern half of the rectangle for forty-five minutes. Throughout the duration of the bombardment, 500 fighters were to fly bomber cover.[76]

For the ground troops, the narrow strip was the threshold, the target area the entrance to the Marigny–St. Gilles gap. To blast open a passageway on the ground, approximately 2,500 planes in a bombardment lasting two hours and twenty-five minutes were to strike a target area of six square miles with almost 5,000 tons of high explosive, jellied gasoline, and white phosphorus.

This kind of air power, many times the equivalent of available artillery, required careful co-ordination to avoid striking U.S. troops, particularly since the employment of heavy bombers intensified the usual problems and dangers of close air support. The size of the individual plane bomb load gave each bomber a considerable casualty-producing potentiality, but since heavy bombers attacked in units, with a lead

bombardier controlling the bomb release of a dozen or so planes, an error in computation or a failure to identify a landmark properly could easily result in disaster. The absence of direct radio communication between the troops on the ground and the heavy bombers in flight made reliance on visual signals necessary. To define the northern limit of the heavy bomber target area during the air attack, artillery was to place red smoke every two minutes on the narrow fighter-bomber strip.[77] This precaution was far from foolproof, for strategic aircraft bombed from high altitudes, and ground haze, mist, dust, or a sudden change of wind direction might render visual signals worthless. Ground troops on the front were to withdraw one hour before the air attack, leaving a protective shell of light forces in position until twenty minutes before the air bombardment, when they too were to withdraw. After the withdrawal, the ground troops were to mark their locations with fluorescent panels. All units participating in COBRA were to have repainted the Allied white-star insignia on their vehicles and tanks.[78]

In the same way that infantry failure to follow an artillery preparation closely tends to cancel the effect of a well-delivered concentration, the inability of the COBRA ground attack to take quick advantage of the bombardment would waste the blast effect of the bombs on the enemy. The ground troops were to cross the three quarters of a mile that

[76] AEAF Opn COBRA, 20 Jul, AEAF/TS.13165/Air, USAF Hist Sec Files, set the planning in motion; IX TAC Opns Order 88 and 89, 19 and 20 Jul, and Annex 4 to VII Corps FO 6, 20 Jul, are the basic planning documents. See also Leigh-Mallory, "Despatch," Fourth Supplement to the London Gazette of December 31, 1946, p. 65; Bradley, Soldier's Story, p. 341; AAF III, pp. 231–32.

[77] VII Corps Opns Memo 45, 22 Jul; Annex 3 to 30th Div FO 13, Air Support Plan, 22 Jul.

[78] Sketch showing prebombardment withdrawal, n.d., 9th Div G–3 Jnl and File; VII Corps Opns Memo 43, 20 Jul; Bradley, Effect of Air Power, p. 104.

separated them from the air target at the conclusion of the heavy bomber strike while fighter-bombers still were strafing and bombing the narrow strip immediately south to the Périers–St. Lô road. The arrival of the infantry at the line of departure and the conclusion of the fighter-bomber strike were to be simultaneous. Medium bombers were then to commence attacking the southern half of the carpet and to continue until the ground troops were across the road and the narrow strip. To insure coordination, the units on the ground were to move forward at the rate of one hundred feet a minute.[79] Artillery was to deliver normal preparatory fires, reinforced by tank destroyer concentrations and antiaircraft artillery ground fire, on the area between the troops and the bombarding planes.

One hour after the ground attack jumped off, all the fighter-bombers of the IX Tactical Air Command and one group of RAF Typhoon planes were to be available to support the First Army for the rest of the day with assault area cover, offensive fighter operations, armed reconnaissance, and air support request missions. Six hours after the ground attack, medium bombers, after having returned to England for refueling and reloading, were to become available for additional missions as necessary. Dive bombers were to be ready for missions on one hour's notice. If the infantry divisions made rapid progress and the exploiting forces were employed at once, fighter-bombers were to furnish column cover by flying protection and reconnaissance for the armored spearheads.[80]

This was the plan on which the Allies counted so much, and on 23 July Allied weather experts expressed a cautious hope that COBRA might soon be launched. Predicting that a slight overcast might break in the late morning of 24 July and that morning haze and light fog would disappear later that day, the forecasters reported that the weather on 24 and 25 July would be favorable for ground operations and moderately favorable for air activity.[81] After a week of waiting, the Allies found the prospect tempting. With Caen and St. Lô in Allied hands, the arrival of fresh infantry and armored divisions on the Continent, mounting stocks of supplies and equipment increasingly available, and the Germans suffering from attrition, a lack of supplies, and an absence of air support, the situation appeared favorable for the breakthrough operation. Air Chief Marshal Leigh-Mallory gave the green light, and the dormant body of COBRA prepared to strike.

[79] Misc Notes, n.d., 30th Div G–3 Jnl and File; Overlay, Amendment 1 to Incl 1, Annex 3 to 30th Div FO 13, 22 Jul; VII Corps Opns Memo 43, 20 Jul.

[80] IX TAC Opns Order 90, 20 Jul, IX TAC Opns COBRA, USAF Hist Sec Files.

[81] 21 Weather Squadron Msg, 23 Jul, 30th Div G–3 Jnl and File.

CHAPTER XII

COBRA

The Opposition

While awaiting the signal for COBRA to begin, intelligence officers pondered some troublesome questions.[1] Did the enemy defenses on the Lessay–St. Lô road represent the actual main battle position? Were there enough mobile German reserves assembled locally to counter the attack successfully? What major reserves were available to the Germans? Where were they? Where were they likely to be committed? Was the Luftwaffe capable of intervention? Would the Germans employ the V–1, V–2, or some other secret weapon against COBRA?

Barring the appearance of miracle weapons and a miraculous resuscitation of the German Air Force, the enemy was thought capable of only defensive action. Neither the *LXXXIV Corps* nor the *II Parachute Corps* seemed to have local reserves capable of intervening with effect. Nor did either *Seventh Army* or *Panzer Group West* appear to have excess troops that might be committed against COBRA. Even if the Germans somehow assembled a reserve for a coun-

terattack from the base of the Cotentin, they would need more time to concentrate sufficient forces than the Americans thought they themselves needed to achieve the success they expected of COBRA. Though the Germans might attempt a rigid defense of the Périers–St. Lô line, deficiencies in manpower and supplies made an effective defense doubtful. The most likely course of enemy action, then, seemed to be a gradual withdrawal accompanied by strong delaying action in terrain favorable to defense, probably along three successive natural defensive lines: between Coutances and Canisy, in the Gavray area, and at the base of the Cotentin near Avranches.

The Americans estimated that the enemy troops facing VII and VIII Corps numbered no more than 17,000 men with less than 100 tanks in support—a slight force to resist the power of more than five times that strength assembled for COBRA. Since captured letters and documents and prisoner-of-war interrogations indicated that the German soldier was weary of war and had no real hope of victory, the fierce resistance met in the hedgerows seemed inexplicable. Perhaps the Germans would suddenly give way during COBRA. Similarly, on the strategic level, it seemed impossible that Germany could hold out much longer. A shortage of oil had become

---

[1] Material on intelligence is from: FUSA Intel Annex to Opn Plan COBRA, 16 Jul; FUSA G–2 Est 9 and 10, 10 and 18 Jul; Annex 2 to VII Corps FO 6, 17 Jul; VII Corps G–2 Est, 17 Jul; VIII Corps G–2 Est 4, 15 Jul; JIC (44) 301 (O) (Final), Weaknesses in Germany's Capacity to Resist, 20 Jul 44, JIC Papers, 1944, Pogue Files; TUSA G–2 Per Rpt 35, 16 Jul.

the major factor limiting strategic and operational efficiency both in the air and on the ground. Deficiencies in heavy armament had dropped the tank strength of panzer divisions to an average of about 70 percent of tables of equipment. A scarcity of drivers, as well as of oil, had intensified a shortage of motor transport that was further increased by wastage far exceeding vehicle replacements and captured matériel. All types of ammunition had deteriorated in quality and quantity. The same could be said for manpower. Propaganda inside Germany seemed to be losing its force and influence. Yet there was no evidence to suggest that anything but invasion of Germany proper would produce a collapse of the home front. Both at home and on the battlefield, the Germans refused to accept the defeat that from the Allied point of view seemed inevitable and only a matter of time.

The significant factors on the battlefield appeared to be the continued lag in infantry build-up and the piecemeal employment of reserves as they reached the battle area. As a result, instead of massing reserves for a co-ordinated counteroffensive, the Germans had dissipated them. The Germans had been compelled to assume a purely defensive attitude, and were forced to fight a constant delaying action from one hastily prepared line or position to another while mounting local counterattacks in company or battalion strength. Without a strategic reserve, the Germans were stripping their Breton defenses and denuding their French Mediterranean coastal positions to meet Allied pressure in Normandy. Only the continued fear of another Allied amphibious assault in

the Pas-de-Calais kept strong forces immobile there. It was reasonable to suppose that the Germans would probably maintain an aggressive defensive attitude along the entire battle front in Normandy and try to amass reserves for a major counterattack sometime in the future, but not in time to affect COBRA.

Allied estimates were quite correct, even though Kluge, commander in chief in the west who had also formally taken command of *Army Group B*, had had some success in building up the front in Normandy. Kluge had managed to secure four infantry divisions from southern France and the Pas-de-Calais (more were promised him), and he was using them to replace armored divisions on the *Panzer Group West* front. His motive was twofold: to keep the panzer divisions from being "ground to pieces," because if that happened "there won't be anything left"; and to create a mobile reserve. Eberbach, the *Panzer Group West* commander, helped Kluge by taking drastic steps to assemble transport and thus speed the arrival of the infantry divisions. Eberbach also feared that if the infantry divisions arriving as replacements came too slowly, little of the panzer divisions would be left to be relieved. Between 10 and 22 July, the four newly arrived infantry divisions replaced five panzer divisions.[2] Operation GOODWOOD virtually nullified this

---

[2] The *277th Division* replaced the *9th SS Panzer Division* on 10 July; the *272d* relieved the *1st* and the *12th SS Panzer Divisions* during the night of 13 July; the *271st* replaced the *10th SS Panzer Division* on 17 July; and the *326th* relieved the *2d Panzer Division* on 22 July. Telecon, Kluge and Jodl, 1828, 13 Jul. *OB WEST KTB, Anlage 615;* "*Unterrichtung ueber die Arbeitsweise des Stages Ob. West . . . ,*" 20 Jul, *OB WEST KTB, Anlage 773;* Hodgson, R–54.

achievement by forcing the recommitment of armor.

The reason for Kluge's primary concern with the *Panzer Group West* portion of the front—that part facing the British—was the terrain around Caen. Montgomery's pressure, climaxed by the GOODWOOD attack, indicated that both Montgomery and Kluge were acting according to the dictates of the terrain. The little offensive planning on higher German echelons during July turned about the idea of launching an attack in the Caen region some time in August.[3] As a result of preoccupation with both the vulnerability of the *Panzer Group West* sector and its excellence for offensive operations, the Germans virtually overlooked the *Seventh Army* front. (*Map IV*)

Dissatisfied with the strength of the Cotentin defenses, Kluge advised Hausser, the *Seventh Army* commander, that his mission was to avoid being pushed back into the interior of France, where the Allies could swing wide and outflank the German positions near Caen. Specifically, Hausser was to remove the two armored divisions on his front—the *2d SS Panzer Division* and *Panzer Lehr*—and concentrate them under army control to be used flexibly against threatened penetrations. Hausser's only immediate move in this direction was to detach two tank companies from the *2d SS Panzer Division* and place them in the army reserve. Before complying further, he awaited the arrival of the *363d Infantry Division* (coming from the *Fifteenth Army*), which was not to reach the *Seventh Army* sector until August. Haus-

ser might have taken *Panzer Lehr* out of the line by substituting for it the *275th Infantry Division*, which he retained under army control immediately behind *Panzer Lehr*. He might have replaced the entire *2d SS Panzer Division* with the *353d Infantry Division*, which Choltitz, the *LXXXIV Corps* commander, withdrew to form a reserve of his own. But Hausser hesitated to pull armor out of the front line because he felt that "the defensive capabilities of an infantry division are less" than those of an armored division. Apparently believing that the type of terrain furnished adequate reason for maintaining the static defense already erected, Hausser did little more than clamor for battlefield replacements, additional artillery and supplies, and the sight of air cover.[4]

Yet Hausser was concerned. The battle of the hedgerows had worn down his forces at an alarming rate. The little that remained of the static units that had fought since the invasion lacked transport, adequate equipment, and even weapons.[5] The more recently arrived units in the Cotentin were also suffering the ravages of attrition. Had the Americans continued their pressure, a decisive result would probably have occurred within a month. But Hausser and other German commanders expected that the Americans would be too impatient to await this kind of decision, and they looked for signs of a big new U.S. offensive. Hausser watched where it seemed more likely to begin—east of the Vire—and in doing so he failed to per-

---

[3] Ltr, Rommel to Kluge, 15 Jul, *Seventh Army KTB, Anlagen, Chefsachen;* see Hodgson, R-57.

[4] *Seventh Army KTB,* 20 Jul; Zimmerman Telecon, 1320, 15 Jul, and Telecon, Helmdach and Tempelhoff, 2240, 25 Jul, *AGp B KTB;* Hodgson, R-57.

[5] See MS # B-731 (Fahrmbacher).

ceive the build-up west of the Vire. He could not conceive of a major attack in strength taking place between St. Lô and Coutances because the terrain there was not conducive to a massive effort. Although Choltitz on 23 July reported a concentration of strong armored forces near the Cotentin west coast, the *Seventh Army* headquarters denied categorically that any indications of an immediately impending attack existed.[6] Part of the reason for the lack of perception at higher headquarters was an overawareness of the importance of the terrain, a feeling that the menacing strength of the British and Canadian units encouraged. It was this that made the German surprise even greater when COBRA came.

Facing the U.S. troops poised to execute COBRA and holding positions generally along the Lessay–St. Lô highway, the *LXXXIV Corps* controlled many units but relatively few troops. In the coastal sector, near Lessay, were the battered remnants of the *243d Division* and beside it the *91st,* with control over remaining elements of the *77th Division* and the exhausted kampfgruppe of the *265th Division* (the depleted *15th Parachute Regiment* of the *5th Parachute Division* had moved east of the Vire River to provide a reserve for the *3d Parachute Division* in the St. Lô sector). The still-strong *2d SS Panzer Division* (augmented by the separate (independent) *6th Parachute Regiment*) and the considerably weakened forces of the *17th SS Panzer Grenadier Division* defended in the Périers area. Immediately to the east was the *5th Parachute Division,* recently arrived from Brittany and controlling

only one regiment. *Panzer Lehr* (augmented by 450 combat troops of the badly damaged *Kampfgruppe Heinz* of the *275th Division* and by 500 partially trained combat troops of an inexperienced regiment of the *5th Parachute Division,* plus some elements of the *2d SS Panzer Division*), occupied the greater part of the ground between the Taute and the Vire, but its right boundary was two miles short of the Vire River. On the right (east) of the *LXXXIV Corps* boundary and adjacent to *Panzer Lehr,* 650 battle-fatigued combat troops of the *352d Division* plus some attached units, all under the control of the *II Parachute Corps,* occupied a two-mile front on the west bank of the Vire.

Each of these units held a portion of the front. In immediate reserve were infantry, reconnaissance, and engineer battalions in the process of rehabilitation. Forming the *LXXXIV Corps* reserve, the tired *353d Division* was assembled south of Périers and behind the *5th Parachute Division.* In *Seventh Army* reserve the *275th Division,* newly arrived from Brittany and controlling two regiments, was stationed behind *Panzer Lehr.* Two infantry companies and two tank companies of the *2d SS Panzer Division* were also under the *Seventh Army* control as a mobile task force in reserve.[7]

The troops directly opposing the U.S.

---

[6] Maj. Kenneth W. Hechler, The Enemy Build-up Prior to Operation COBRA, MS, OCMH Files.

[7] *Panzer Lehr Division* Monthly Status Rpts for Jun and Jul 44, *OKH Generalinspektor der Panzertruppen, Zustandsberichte, Heer,* Jun–Aug 44; *AGp B KTB, 15.1–4.X.44; AGp B Ia Letztemeldungen, 8.VI.–10.VIII.44,* and *Ia Tagesmeldungen, 6.VI.–31.VIII.44; Seventh Army KTB* (Draft) *6.VI–16.VIII.44;* MS # A–902 (Bayerlein); MS # A–973 (Schmidt); MS # A–975 (Schmidt); MS # B–820 (Wilke); Hodgson, R–54; Hechler, The Enemy Build-up Prior to Operation COBRA.

VII Corps on the morning of 24 July totaled about 30,000 men, quite a few more than the Americans estimated. The actual number of combat effectives on or near the front between the Taute and the Vire was much less, perhaps only 5,000. Of these, approximately 3,200 combat effectives of *Panzer Lehr* and its attached units were directly in the path of COBRA.

Authorized almost 15,000 men, *Panzer Lehr* was seriously reduced in strength. Its losses had been almost entirely among its combat elements. Its two regiments of armored infantry, its tank regiment, and its tank destroyer battalion had totaled slightly more than 7,000 combat effectives and over 200 tanks and tank destroyers at full strength; on 24 July only about 2,200 combat troops and perhaps 45 serviceable armored vehicles held the main line of resistance. These organic troops of *Panzer Lehr* and its attached units were to receive the full force of the COBRA bombardment.

The *Panzer Lehr* front extended about three miles along the Périers–St. Lô highway. Several small infantry groups formed centers of resistance on an outpost line north of the highway, but most of the troops were deployed just south of the road. On the left (west) the attached parachute regiment had formed a strongpoint and roadblock near the road to Marigny. On the right (east) *Kampfgruppe Heinz,* near the village of Hébécrevon, had organized five strongpoints, each in the strength of a reinforced infantry platoon with a few tanks or tank destroyers and light anti-tank guns. In the center, organic infantry and tanks had erected three strongpoints, each in battalion strength, between Marigny and St. Gilles, and three

smaller roadblocks to cover the highway to St. Gilles and secondary roads near the village of la Chapelle-en-Juger. If the Americans succeeded in crossing the Périers–St. Lô highway, Bayerlein was prepared to commit regimental reserves— several companies of infantry and a few tanks—located along a country road just south of and parallel to the main highway.

Except for the combatants, the battlefield was deserted. Most of the French inhabitants had evacuated their homes and departed the battle zone. The few who remained in the COBRA area took refuge in isolated farmhouses, most of them, fortunately, outside the air bombardment target.[8]

Bombardment

Air Chief Marshal Leigh-Mallory had set the COBRA H Hour at 1300, 24 July, and on the morning of 24 July he went to Normandy to observe the operation. He found the sky overcast, the clouds thick. Deciding that visibility was inadequate for the air attack, he ordered a postponement. Unfortunately, he was too late. The message announcing his decision reached England only a few minutes before the actual bombing was to commence in France. Although the planes were ordered to return without making their bomb runs, it was impossible to get them all back.

In accordance with the original planning, six groups of fighter-bombers of the IX TAC and three bombardment di-

---

[8] Joseph Toussaint, *La Percée Américaine à l'Ouest de Saint-Lô (La Chapelle-Enjuger dans la Bataille)* (Coutances, France: Editions Notre-Dame, n.d.) , pp. 75ff.

visions (about 1,600 heavy bombers) of the Eighth U.S. Air Force had departed their bases in England and headed toward France. Only the medium bombers, scheduled to bomb last, had not left the ground when the postponement order came. Of the six groups of fighter-bombers in the air, three received the recall order before they dropped their bombs. The other three bombed the general target area, the narrow strip, and certain targets north of the Périers–St. Lô highway, with no observed results. The postponement message to the heavy bombers stayed only a few planes in the last formation.

Ignorant that COBRA had been postponed, pilots of the great majority of the heavy bombers guided their big craft on toward the target. Because no precise radio channels had been designated for emergency communication, there was no certain means of transmitting the news to the planes. While air force personnel in France attempted to get word to the craft aloft, the first formation of 500 planes arrived over the target area. Fortunately, they found visibility so poor that no attack was made. The second formation found cloud conditions so bad that only 35 aircraft, after making three bomb runs to identify the target, released their loads. Over 300 bombers of the third formation, with slightly improved weather conditions, dropped their bombs—about 550 tons of high explosive and 135 tons of fragmentation—before the postponement message finally got through to cancel the remainder of the strike.[9]

The 24 July bombing was unfortunate,

not only because of the likelihood of negating the surprise planned for COBRA, but also because it killed 25 men and wounded 131 of the 30th Division.[10] The tragedy was the result of one accident. The lead bombardier of a heavy bomber formation had had difficulty moving his bomb release mechanism and had inadvertently salvoed a portion of his load. The fifteen aircraft flying in the formation followed his example and released their bombs. The bomb load fell 2,000 yards north of the Périers–St. Lô highway.[11]

On the ground, VII Corps had executed the initial part of the COBRA attack by withdrawing the front-line troops of the 9th and 30th Divisions several hundred yards to the north. The poor weather conditions had prompted commanders to wonder whether the lack of visibility would cancel the air bombardment, but General Collins was characteristically optimistic. He believed that the planes would get through the haze. Even if the heavy bombers were not able to take part in the air attack, he felt that the fighter-bombers would be on hand

---

[9] *AAF III*, 228–30; Eighth AF Tactical Mission Rpt. Opn 492, 24 Jul, USAF Hist Sec Files.

[10] The death of a liaison officer who was sent from the 8th Infantry (4th Division) to the 120th Infantry (30th Division) is included in these figures, which are taken from F. P. Halas' Notes, ML–2244. General Collins' Talk cites the same figures. *ARGUMENT to V-E Day*, page 230, gives the casualty figures as 16 killed and 64 wounded.

[11] *AAF III*, 230. Other short bomb releases did not affect the ground troops: one fighter-bomber pilot made a mistake in landmark identification and dropped his bombs on an American ammunition dump; when another plane was hit by enemy flak, a bombardier in a reflex action touched the toggle switch, released his load on an American airfield, and thereby destroyed two bomb-loaded and manned aircraft on the ground and damaged others. Enemy antiaircraft artillery fire destroyed three heavy bombers that participated in the attack.

ADVANCING TOWARD PÉRIERS–ST. LÔ ROAD. *4th Division advance patrol passes tanks awaiting orders to move up.*

and that their bombardment would give sufficient impetus for the attack. He therefore told his subordinate commanders to go ahead. If the fighter-bomber effort proved insufficient, he expected the heavy bombers to return on the following day.[12]

Notice that the air bombardment had been postponed reached the ground troops a short time before the bombardment actually commenced. What then was the meaning of the bombs that were dropped? What was the mission of the ground troops? Was COBRA delayed? Or were the ground troops to initiate COBRA on the basis of the incomplete air effort?

[12] Telecon, Collins and Hobbs, 1115, 24 Jul, 30th Div G–3 Jnl and File.

While discussion took place at higher headquarters, General Collins decided that the VII Corps had to attack. Withdrawal of the 9th and 30th Divisions had created a vacuum that the Germans would fill unless the infantry returned to the vicinity of the Périers–St. Lô highway. If COBRA was to start without benefit of the full air preparation, the infantry could simply continue the attack, cross the line of departure at the highway, and attempt to pry open the Marigny–St. Gilles gap. If, on the other hand, postponement in the air meant postponement on the ground, then the same conditions on which the COBRA plan was based had to be restored. General Collins therefore told the 9th, 4th, and 30th Divisions, the units scheduled to initiate the COBRA offensive, to make a limited objective attack to the Périers–St. Lô highway. Maybe they would continue beyond the highway, maybe not.[13]

Half an hour later General Collins learned that COBRA was postponed on the ground as well as in the air, but to prevent the enemy from moving north of the Périers–St. Lô highway, the three infantry divisions were to attack at 1300 as though COBRA were going into effect. In reality, the divisions were to restore the front line that had existed before the air bombardment.[14] If the incomplete air bombardment had not forewarned the Germans and destroyed the tactical surprise on which General Bradley counted so heavily, the German main line of resistance would be unchanged for another COBRA effort on the following day. Until COBRA kicked off as planned, the divisions in the VII Corps exploiting force were to remain in their concealed bivouacs.[15]

The abortive air bombardment on 24 July had obviously alerted the Germans to the American ground attack that followed. Enemy artillery fire began to fall in large volume. All three assault divisions had a difficult time that afternoon.

On the corps right, the 9th Division committed its three regiments: the 60th Infantry battled enemy troops that had infiltrated behind the withdrawal; a reinforced battalion of the 47th Infantry struggled until dark to gain a single hedgerow; two battalions of the 39th Infantry fought eight hours to reduce a strongpoint and took 77 casualties, among them the regimental commander, Col. Harry A. Flint.[16] In the corps center, the 4th Division committed the 8th Infantry, which attacked in a column of battalions with tank support; after two hours of heavy fighting and a loss of 27 killed and 70 wounded, the regiment reached a point 100 yards north of the highway. On the corps left, the 30th Division did not advance at once because the assault elements were stunned and demoralized by the bombardment accident. It took almost an hour for the units to recover and reorganize, by which time enemy artillery fire had subsided. The division then advanced and reoccupied its original lines.

The bombardment accident released a flood of controversy. Having expected a lateral approach to the target area, General Bradley was astonished and shocked when he learned that the planes had made a perpendicular bomb run. Using a perpendicular approach, Bradley said later, was an act of perfidy on the part of the Air Forces, "a serious breach of good faith in planning."[17] Other ground commanders had also anticipated a lateral approach, and their surprise was deepened by the horror that the news of casualties brought.[18] Even General Quesada, the commander of the

---

[13] Telecons, Collins and Hobbs, 1205, 24 Jul, and Stephens and Hassenfelt, 1207, 24 Jul, 30th Div G–3 Jnl and File; 4th Div Msg (Gen Barton), 1200, 24 Jul, 4th Div G–3 Jnl and File.

[14] Telecon, Collins and Hobbs, 1227, 24 Jul, 30th Div G–3 Jnl and File; Ltr, Collins to Hechler, 7 Jul 45, OCMH Files; FUSA Msg, 1235, 24 Jul, FUSA G–3 Jnl; 4th Div Msg, 1315, 24 Jul, 4th Div G–3 Jnl and File.

[15] VII Corps Opns Memo 47, 24 Jul.

[16] Colonel Flint was posthumously awarded the Bronze Oak Leaf Cluster to the DSC he had earlier received.

[17] Bradley, Soldier's Story, pp. 341, 346–48.

[18] Hobbs Telecons, 1330 and 1412, 24 Jul, 30th Div G–3 Jnl and File; Sylvan Diary, 24 Jul.

155-MM. HOWITZER, *north of Périers–St. Lô highway, blasts German lines.*

IX TAC, dispatched a telegram of in-dignant protest on the direction of the heavy-bomber approach (his fighter-bombers had made a lateral approach). Quesada demanded whether "another plan" had actually been employed.[19] Obviously, something was wrong. Per-haps something was inexcusably wrong, since COBRA had been conceived and planned, not hastily, but thoroughly over a period of almost two weeks.

At the conference between General Bradley and air representatives on 19 July, when the COBRA air arrangements

were being worked out, the direction of the bombing approach had "evoked con-siderable discussion." General Bradley had insisted on his parallel plan, while all the Air Forces representatives had argued that perpendicular runs were more suitable.[20] At the end of the con-ference the question had not been set-tled formally, though General Bradley must have assumed that his recommen-dation for lateral bomb runs would be accepted. The Air Forces representa-tives had understood that General Brad-ley "was aware of the possibility of gross [bombing] errors causing casualties"

---

[19] Red Line Msg, Quesada to Brereton, 24 Jul, Rpts of Bombing Errors Made on 25 Jul, 8 Aug, USAF Hist Sec Files.

[20] Eighth AF Spec Rpt on Opns 24 and 25 Jul, n.d., USAF Hist Sec Files; Halas Notes, ML–2244.

among his troops, and they thought he had said "that he was prepared to accept such casualties no matter which way the planes approached." [21]   Unaware of this conception, General Bradley had considered the conference "very satisfactory."   Even though Air Chief Marshal Leigh-Mallory had had to "rush off" before its conclusion, General Quesada had remained throughout.[22]   The result of what in reality had been an unsatisfactory conference was an absence of firm understanding and mutual agreement.

The approach route was not the only difficulty. General Bradley recalled after the war that he had gained the impression that the air forces would use bombs no heavier than 100 pounds and was surprised when larger bombs were dropped.[23]   Yet during Bradley's conference at the First Army command post on 12 July, General Collins had asked, "Do we get heavy or medium bombs or both?" and Bradley had replied, "Both." The 260-pound bomb in Bradley's estimation did not "make too big a crater." Collins, who wanted to take a chance on the cratering, had voted for "bigger and better bombs," even 500-pound bombs, while General Quesada had suggested that 260-pound bombs would be large enough.   The discussion had not cleared up the matter, and when the conference ended the question was still not settled.[24]

Despite the absence of agreement, the basic planning documents of the air strike plainly indicated that 450 fighter-bombers and medium bombers were each to carry two 500-pound general purpose bombs as well as 260-pound general purpose and fragmentation bombs.[25] Although 70 percent of the heavy bombers were to carry 100-pound general purpose bombs, the remaining 30 percent were to use 260-pound fragmentation bombs to the extent of their availability and heavier bombs when no more 260-pound bombs could be had.[26]

There was no time for recrimination on 24 July, for an immediate decision had to be made.   Should General Bradley agree to another bombardment under the same terms and thereby indirectly condone the possibility of additional American casualties?   Or should he insist on changing the pattern of air attack, which would mean postponing COBRA for several days at least?   With higher headquarters anxious for action, General Bradley had little choice.   The ground attack on the afternoon of 24 July had re-established the necessary COBRA conditions.   Prospects for good weather on 25 July were improving.   The question whether the premature bombing had lost the Americans tactical surprise was to be resolved at once: the Allies would launch COBRA again at 1100, 25 July.

For the second COBRA bombardment several alterations were made in an attempt to avoid a repetition of the bombing errors.   Air bombardment targets north of the Périers–St. Lô highway—

---

[21] Eighth AF Draft Ltr, Summary of Plng and Execution of Missions 24 and 25 Jul, n.d., Rpts of Bombing Errors Made on 25 Jul, 8 Aug, USAF Hist Sec Files.

[22] Ltrs, Leigh-Mallory to Bradley, 19 Jul, and Bradley to Leigh-Mallory, 23 Jul, OCMH Files.

[23] Bradley, *Soldier's Story*, p. 341.

[24] FUSA Conf Notes, 12 Jul, FUSA G–3 Misc File; Halas Notes, ML–2244.

[25] IX TAC Opns Order 88, 19 Jul; [George], Ninth Air Force, p. 124.

[26] Eighth AF FO's 913 and 917, 23 and 24 Jul, Eighth AF Spec Rpt on Opns 24 and 25, n.d., USAF Hist Sec Files.

WAITING FOR THE COBRA BOMBARDMENT, *8th Infantrymen look skyward.*

six in all—were relegated to the artillery.[27] A special weather reconnaissance plane was to enter the assault area early in the morning to obtain exact atmospheric data and find out if there was adequate visibility for the bombardment. The heavy bombers were to fly as low as safety would permit, and, if possible, bomb visually.[28]

Again on the morning of 25 July the planes came. Flying in groups of twelve, over 1,500 B–17's and B–24's dropped more than 3,300 tons of bombs

in the COBRA area, and more than 380 medium bombers dropped over 650 tons of high explosives and fragmentation bombs. In groups of four, over 550 fighter-bombers dropped more than 200 tons of bombs and a large amount of napalm.[29] The earth shook.

Bombing heights had been fixed around 15,000 feet, but the presence of clouds forced readjustment in flight. Most bombardiers had to recompute their figures en route. Some planes

[27] Lt. Col. Orlando C. Troxel, Jr., Telecon, 2257, 24 Jul, and VII Corps Msg, 0155, 25 Jul, 30th Div G–3 Jnl.

[28] *AAF III,* 232.

[29] *AAF III,* 232–33; Eighth AF Tactical Mission Rpt Opn 494, 25 Jul, USAF Hist Sec Files; Leigh-Mallory, "Despatch," Fourth Supplement to the *London Gazette* of December 31, 1946, p. 65; Sylvan Diary, 25 Jul.

AFTER THE COBRA BOMBARDMENT *men dig out from the short bombings.*

bombed from the relatively low altitude of 12,000 feet, which brought them closer to the enemy antiaircraft fire and thus added to pilot strain, loosened flight formations, and increased the hazards of crowded air over the target. Artillery smoke markers proved of little value because they were not visible until the smoke drifted to high altitudes, and by that time the wind had dispersed and displaced it. Once the attack began, great clouds of dust and smoke obscured not only markers but terrain features as well. Furthermore, the red smoke of artillery markers could hardly be distinguished from shell and bomb bursts and from muzzle flashes of American and German artillery. Because it was impossible to keep bomb formations tight and because the crew members had been impressed with the necessity of avoiding short bombing, a good portion of the bombs landed south of the target area or west and east of it. Some bombs, however, again fell north of the Périers–St. Lô highway and on American positions.[30]

The bombs fell north of the highway because of human error. The lead bombardier of one heavy bomber forma-

---

[30] *AAF III*, 232–34; First U.S. Army, *Report of Operations*, I, 121.

tion had trouble with his bombsight and released visually with bad results. Another failed to identify landmarks properly. The lead pilot of a third formation prematurely ordered bombs away, and all the planes in his unit released their loads. Fragmentation bombs and high explosives from 35 heavy bombers and the bombs of 42 medium bombers dropped within American lines.[31]

This relatively light bombardment north of the road killed 111 of the American troops and wounded 490.[32] In addition some spectators, official observers, and newspaper reporters were hit. Lt. Gen. Lesley J. McNair, commanding general of the Army Ground Forces and *pro tem* commander of the 1st U.S. Army Group, was killed. General McNair had been placed in command of the army group in order to give continuing verisimilitude to the Allied deception maintained by Operation FORTITUDE. Because the news of General McNair's death might compromise FORTITUDE, he was buried secretly, with only senior officers in attendance. The news was suppressed until Lt. Gen. John L. DeWitt reached the theater to become nominal commander of the fictitious army group.[33]

As news of the second short bombing spread across the battle area on 25 July, the sense of elated anticipation that had come with the appearance of the COBRA bombardment fleet vanished. Resentment that the air force "had done it again" and grimness over the prospects of successful ground action spread throughout American ranks.[34] Dismayed and dejected over the nearly 900 U.S. casualties sustained from the bombings in the two days, General Eisenhower resolved that he would never again use heavy bombers in a tactical role.[35]

Near the vicinity where the short bombs had fallen, troops were disorganized and in some cases attack plans were disrupted. The entire command group of the 3d Battalion, 47th Infantry, had been destroyed with the exception of the battalion commander; 30 men were killed or wounded, and the unit had to

[31] *AAF III*, 232–34. On the problems of direct support bombing, see Roswell Wing's pertinent Comment on the Medium Bombardment Effort to Support the 30th Division's West Wall Assault, MacDonald Files, OCMH, and Harris, *Bomber Offensive*, p. 213.

[32] USSTAF In Europe, Report of Investigation, 14 Aug, USAF Hist Sec Files, lists the following casualties: 47th Infantry, 9th Division: 14 killed, 33 wounded; 15th Engineer Battalion: 15 killed, 23 wounded; 60th Field Artillery Battalion: 4 wounded; 84th Field Artillery Battalion: 1 killed, 2 wounded; 4th Division: 10 killed, 27 wounded; 30th Division: 61 killed, 374 wounded. In addition, the 39th Infantry of the 9th Division lost 16 wounded, and the 957th Field Artillery Battalion lost 10

killed and 11 wounded. (See 9th Div G–3 Jnl, 25 Jul.) General Collins in his Talk agreed with the figures of 111 killed and 490 wounded. *AAF III*, page 234, states that a total of 102 were killed and 380 were wounded. Eighth Air Force Special Report on Operations 24 and 25 July, USAF Hist Sec Files, gives a very complete report including plans, maps, photos, bomb damage assessment, and prisoner of war interrogations on the effect of the bombing. [Ackerman], Employment of Strategic Bombers in a Tactical Role, pp. 89ff, does not give a particularly good account.

[33] Bradley, *Soldier's Story*, p. 349; Brereton, *Diaries*, pp. 313–15; Ltrs, Eisenhower to Marshall, 26 and 27 Jul, Pogue Files; ETOUSA Ltr, Assignment of Comd, 21 Jul, AG 322/011 MPM, and SHAEF Ltr, Orders, 9 Aug, AG 211–3 (Generals), SHAEF AG File 322–3 (FUSAG).

[34] *AAF III*, 234.

[35] Bradley, *Soldier's Story*, p. 349. He later changed his mind.

9TH DIVISION TROOPS ADVANCE, IGNORING DUST *kicked up by the Cobra bombardment, 25 July.*

be replaced in the assault. The fire direction center of the 957th Field Artillery Battalion was obliterated. The communications wire between the 9th Division Artillery command post and the firing battalions was cut, and initial preparations had to be controlled by radio. All four assault companies of the 8th Infantry were bombed. Because of extremely high casualties in the 119th and 120th Infantry Regiments, the commanders were as much concerned about securing ambulances for their wounded as about starting the attack. Many individuals who suffered no visible physical injuries sustained concussion and shock. The 30th Division, for example, reported 164 cases of combat exhaustion attributable to the short bombing on 25 July.[36] "The dive bombers came in

beautifully," a company commander related afterward,

and dropped their bombs right . . . where they belonged. Then the first group of heavies dropped them in the draw several hundred yards in front of us. . . . The next wave came in closer, the next one . . . still closer. The dust cloud was drifting back toward us. Then they came right on top of us. . . . We put on all the orange smoke we had but I don't think it did any good, they could not have seen it through the dust. . . . The shock was awful. A lot of the men were sitting around after the bombing in a complete daze. . . . I called battalion and told them I was in no condition to move, that everything was completely disorganized and it would take me some time to get my men back together, and asked for a delay. But battalion said no, push off. Jump off immediately.[37]

The feeling of profound discouragement temporarily overshadowed questions of more immediate importance.

---

[36] 30th Div AAR, Jul; University of Oklahoma Research Institute, Technical Memo, ORO–T–202, Disaster in Battle, 25 Aug 52, *passim.*

[37] Interv with CO, Co B, 8th Inf CI 30 (4th Div).

Had the bombardment neutralized the German defenses in the COBRA area? Had the bomb errors paralyzed American mobility on the ground by demoralizing the assault troops? The answers were soon to be revealed. Short bombing or not, COBRA had been launched; for better or for worse, the ground attack had to go on.

Effect on the Enemy

Not only the main bombardment on 25 July but also the premature bombing on 24 July terrified the Germans and civilians on the other side of the Périers– St. Lô highway. Around noon of 24 July, it must have seemed that the motors of the approaching COBRA armada were like an orchestra of bass viols tuning up. The crash of bombs announced the overture, the premature bombardment. Even the relatively few bombs that were released were enough to create an awesome effect. At least one person believed that the end of the world had come. Others thought that the Allies had developed a new weapon of overwhelming power.[38]

To Bayerlein, commander of *Panzer Lehr,* the bombardment on 24 July obviously signaled the beginning of a major American ground attack. Yet Bayerlein was able to influence the battle little.

The disruption of his communications to forward units and the confusion that resulted made it difficult to organize a co-ordinated defense against the ground attack that followed the bombing. Consequently, Bayerlein was more than gratified by the situation at the end of the day. Ignorant of the fact that Allied plans had gone awry and that the Americans had mounted only a limited objective attack, Bayerlein congratulated himself on the achievement of his troops. They had apparently repelled a major American effort and prevented the troops from crossing the Périers–St. Lô highway. *Panzer Lehr* had flinched under the weight of the bombardment, but it had not given way; the front line remained intact and neither corps nor army reserves had been committed. However, losses from the bombing and the ground attack numbered about 350 men and perhaps 10 tanks and tank destroyers. Ammunition had been expended liberally, and stocks at firing batteries were rather low. Expecting a renewed attack on the following day, Bayerlein requested and received 200 replacements from the regiments of the *275th Division* assembled behind him. He also withdrew the bulk of his outpost line to locations south of the Périers–St. Lô highway, leaving only very lightly manned positions north of the road, where he anticipated strong American artillery fire.[39]

The premature bombing and the limited objective attack on 24 July had thus had the effect of a ruse. They nourished German self-confidence; Bay-

---

[38] Toussaint, *La Percée Américaine à l'Ouest de Saint-Lô,* p.77n. "The bombardment of 24 July," Toussaint, who observed it, later wrote, "was hardly noted in the official reports. However, if its volume did not equal the infernal agitation of the following day, it was nevertheless terrifying." See also J. de Saint-Jorre, "Journal d'un Saint-Lois pendant la Bataille de Normandie," *Mémoires de la Société d' Archéologie de la Manche,* LV, 47, and Saint-Jorre, "Saint-Lô sous les Bombes," in Herval, *Bataille de Normandie,* I, 85ff.

[39] Telecon, Tempelhoff and Helmdach, 1320, 24 July, *AGp B KTB*; James B. Hodgson, Thrust— Counterthrust, the Battle of France, R–58.

erlein had no reason to believe that his division could not repeat its performance and turn the Americans back again. For the real COBRA bombardment that was to come on 25 July, *Panzer Lehr* was deployed substantially as on the preceding day. The only difference was advantageous to the Americans: Bayerlein had thinned his outpost line north of the highway and moved more troops directly into the area scheduled for saturation bombing.

Bayerlein's self-confidence was shared by Hausser, the *Seventh Army* commander, but not by Kluge. When Kluge learned the Allies had bombed front-line positions, he thought immediately the strike must have occurred in the *Panzer Group West* sector, for that was the area he considered of primary importance to the integrity of the entire Normandy front. He lost no time in telephoning Eberbach and asking in alarm what had happened. Nothing new, Eberbach replied; everything very quiet.[40]

Discovering that it was *Panzer Lehr* in the *Seventh Army* sector that had been bombed, Kluge telephoned Hausser and asked for "a quick run-down on the situation."

Hausser complied. He began a calm recital of facts. "Strong fire and patrol activity on the right wing; artillery fire on the Vire bridges; reorganization of the [American] army front."

"Reorganization for what?" Kluge interrupted.

"To insert another corps," Hausser explained. Then after waiting a moment, he continued. "On the left flank

very strong air activity; attacks in the form of bomb carpets three kilometers behind the MLR. Attack against the middle of the left sector. Only limited attacks; no concerted assault recognizable."

"In other words," Kluge pressed for an interpretation, "as weather improves we can expect increasingly severe fighting around St. Lô and westward. Isn't that about it?"

Hausser agreed. "On the extreme left wing also," he added.

"I'd like to ask you again," Kluge insisted, "do you get the impression that you're heading for heavy fighting?"

"We've got to expect it somewhere," Hausser allowed. He revealed little concern or worry.

"Have you created appropriate reserves?" Kluge asked.

Hausser reminded him that the *353d Division* had been pulled out of the line.

But Kluge seemed already to be thinking of something else. "Without any doubt," he said, as though talking to himself, "there's something new in all this air activity. We have got to expect a heavy enemy offensive somewhere."[41]

Kluge's hunch was right, but his guess was wrong. Still assuming that the Allies would make their main effort against the eastern sector, Kluge spent the following day, 25 July, inspecting the forward positions of *Panzer Group West*.[42] He was on hand to witness the reaction to an attack near Tilly launched

---

[40] Telecon, Kluge and Eberbach, 1800, 24 Jul, *OB WEST KTB, Anlage 828.*

[41] Telecon, Kluge and Hausser, 1810, 24 Jul, *OB WEST KTB, Anlage 829.*

[42] *AGp B KTB, Anlagen, Fall, 40–X.44,* Annex 40.

by the 2d Canadian Corps. The Canadians gained a mile or two until the *9th SS Panzer Division* was committed to stop the advance.[43] But there was no real cause for concern on the *Panzer Group West* front. The dangerous sector was across the Vire in the *Seventh Army* area, where COBRA had struck again.

If the previous day's commotion had seemed like Armageddon, the bombardment of 25 July was even worse.[44] Bombs buried men and equipment, overturned tanks, cut telephone wires, broke radio antennas, sent messengers fleeing for foxholes or the nearest crater. Communications with forward echelons were completely disrupted. The bombardment transformed the main line of resistance from a familiar pastoral *paysage* into a frightening landscape of the moon. Several hours after the bombing, the village priest of la Chapelle-en-Juger, near the center of the target area, walked through the fields and thought he was in a strange world.[45]

No less than a thousand men must have perished in the COBRA bombardment. About one third of the total number of combat effectives manning the main line of defense and assembled on the immediate reserve line were probably killed or wounded, the survivors dazed. Perhaps only a dozen tanks or tank destroyers remained in operation. Three battalion command posts

of *Panzer Lehr* were demolished. The attached parachute regiment virtually vanished. Only local and feeble resistance was possible against attacking American infantrymen.[46]

Kamfgruppe Heinz on the *Panzer Lehr* right was the sole unit larger than a battalion that was capable of effective combat. By the end of 25 July that kampfgruppe no longer existed—it had apparently been annihilated in ground action near Hébécrevon. The *II Parachute Corps,* trying to re-establish contact with *Panzer Lehr* that evening, dispatched an infantry battalion to the sector previously occupied by the kampfgruppe. The battalion found only Americans.

Continued Allied air activity in *Panzer Lehr* rear areas during the afternoon of 25 July thwarted efforts to reorganize and build up a new line of defense. One regiment of the *275th Division,* ordered to move up from Marigny and counterattack through la Chapelle-en-Juger, lost all semblance of organization and counted only 200 survivors at the end of the day.

"As of this moment," Kluge reported that evening, "the front has . . . burst." The Americans had made a penetration three miles in width and from one to three miles in depth. Not yet sealed off, the hole was inhabited by isolated units, by bewildered individuals, and by departed souls. The *353d Division* and the remainder of the *275th Division* had been committed, but it was highly questionable whether they could restore the front or even re-establish a defensive line. Kluge nevertheless felt there was

---

[43] 21 AGp Msg, 25 Jul, FUSA G–3 Jnl; Telecons, Speidel to Zimmerman and Zimmerman to Friedel, 2315 and 2335, 25 Jul, *OB WEST KTB, Anlage 849.*

[44] An observer called it "the most imposing aerial parade I have seen since the beginning of this long war." Saint-Jorre, "Saint-Lô sous les Bombes," in Herval, *Bataille de Normandie,* I, 97.

[45] MS # A–902 (Bayerlein); Toussaint, *La Perceé Américaine à l'Ouest de Saint-Lô,* p. 144.

[46] *Seventh Army KTB,* 25 Jul; Liddell Hart, *The Rommel Papers,* pp. 489–90; *Pz Lehr Div Ib KTB,* Annex 247; MS # B–489 (Ziegelmann).

still hope of stopping the Americans. Although "we must fight for every yard on the right wing [*Panzer Group West* sector]," Kluge stated, he had freedom of movement and of withdrawal on the left, west of the Vire. If he could decrease the length of his line west of St. Lô by withdrawal and thereby extricate the *2d SS Panzer Division* and use it as a mobile reserve, he might salvage something from the discouraging situation, but he needed "a free hand in his decisions about *Seventh Army*." Would Hitler give him a free hand? Shortly after midnight, Hitler said he would.[47]

Ground Attack

Hopeful that the COBRA bombardment on the morning of 25 July had caused widespread devastation on the German main line of resistance but not at all sure that it had, infantrymen of the VII Corps moved out in attack at 1100. Despite the disorganization that the bombing errors had prompted, only two units, a regiment of the 9th Division and a battalion of the 30th Division, were unable to attack on the hour, and these jumped off after only a slight delay.[48]

The infantry units initiating the COBRA ground attack were to create a protected corridor for those troops scheduled to follow and exploit a breakthrough. The infantry, therefore, had the mission of securing specific geographical objectives as rapidly as possible. Critical terrain features such as high ground and crossroads that meant

control of the corridor had been carefully assigned to each small unit participating in the attack, and the assault troops were to drive to their objectives without regard to the rate of advance of adjacent units. They were to bypass enemy strongpoints, leaving their reduction to others who would come later. Engineers were to assist forward movement by hastily repairing the roads and removing obstacles. All unnecessary traffic was to stay off the roads in the assault area. The attacking units had been stripped of nonessential equipment to reduce column time lengths. The troops carried extra rations to keep supply traffic to a minimum. They were to hold wounded men and prisoners in place whenever possible. They had been issued enough ammunition to last until the exploiting armor passed through them. Commanders or responsible staff officers were to be at unit radios at all times and tuned to the command net for word that the mobile columns were about to begin their exploitation. When that was announced, the infantry was to clear the main roads and allow the exploitation to get under way without impediment.[49] (*Map V*)

The towns of Marigny and St. Gilles were the main infantry objectives. Their capture would signify a penetration of three miles in depth, and their retention would give the VII Corps control of the road network needed for the exploitation. If the air bombardment had destroyed the German defenses, the

---

[47] Telecons, Speidel to Zimmerman, Zimmerman to Friedel, Friedel to Zimmerman, 2315, 2335, 25 Jul, and 0045, 26 Jul, *OB WEST KTB, Anlage 849.*
[48] VII Corps Sitrep 98, 25 Jul.

[49] VII Corps Opns Memo 43, 20 Jul; 9th Div FO 10, 20 Jul; 4th Div FO 11, 20 Jul; 30th Div FO 13, 20 Jul; 117th Inf FO 10, 20 Jul; 119th Inf FO 5, n.d.; 120th Inf FO 12, 20 Jul; 30th Div Administrative Order 20, 23 Jul; 105th Engr C Bn FO 3, 21 Jul; Misc Notes, n.d., 30th Div G–3 Jnl and File.

infantry would reach and secure Marigny and St. Gilles without great difficulty. General Collins would then catapult his armor forward.

On the VII Corps right (west), the 330th Infantry (detached from the 83d Division) was to seize a part of the Périers–St. Lô highway, including a vital road intersection, and block to the west in order to hamper any German attack from Périers against the corps right flank. In effect, the regiment was to secure and hold the pivot on which the VII Corps main effort was to swing in its turn toward Coutances. Eventually, the 330th Infantry was also to turn westward and join its parent unit and VIII Corps.[50]

The immediate regimental objective was near the Taute River flats, marshy hedgerowed lowland that was outside the COBRA bombardment area. Because the 83d Division had been unable a week earlier to force a crossing of the Taute River over the la Varde causeway, Germans still occupied the la Varde peninsula and constituted a threat to the regimental right flank.[51] Dispersed over a large area, without strength in depth, facing hedgerowed lowlands, about to attack enemy troops that had not been affected by the COBRA bombardment, and harassed by tank destroyer fire from the right rear near Marchésieux, the regiment had a mission as difficult as it was vital.

The advance was rapid so long as fighter-bombers and medium bombers were still striking the COBRA target area southeast of the regimental positions.

In forty minutes the assault battalion advanced 800 yards. When the planes left, the Germans raised their heads from their foxholes, discovered that the saturation bombing had taken place several miles away, and realized that they were not at all hurt. Opening fire from their hedgerow positions and quickly repairing breaks in communication wires caused by a few stray bombs, the soldiers of the regiment that the *5th Parachute Division* controlled soon achieved a coordinated defense that stopped the 330th Infantry. At the same time, shells from Marchésieux began to fall on the 330th's right flank.

The 330th Infantry could get no farther than a point several hundred yards short of its objective. Counterbattery fire by the 83d Division Artillery seemed to have little effect in reducing the volume of enemy shells. Unless a bombing attack destroyed the Marchésieux emplacements and thus eliminated the threat to the regimental right rear, there seemed little hope that the 330th Infantry would attain its immediate COBRA objective.[52]

The 9th Division was to attack to Marigny, along the main highway, which was later to serve the principal exploiting thrust. General Eddy's regiments were to peel off to the west in order to uncover the highway and form a strong protective line facing west. The terrain in the zone of advance—low ridges and small marshes—was rather difficult.

After some confusion occasioned by the bombing errors, the assault units moved rather quickly through the hostile outpost line north of the Périers–St.

---

[50] Min of Mtg (on COBRA), 21 Jul, 83d Div G–2, G–3 Jnl and File; 330th Inf (COBRA) Attack Plan, n.d., 9th Div G–3 Jnl and File.

[51] See above, Ch. XI.

[52] 83d Div G–2, G–3 Jnl and File, 25 Jul, and AAR, Jul.

Lô highway, containing and bypassing several strongpoints that were still active. Once across the line of departure, the troops were surprised to find increasingly troublesome centers of resistance. Despite the saturation bombing, groups of enemy soldiers were still fighting stubbornly. When the 9th Division shifted its weight to the west and met Germans who had been outside the bombardment carpet, the infantry made little progress.

The assault units of the 9th Division, with several exceptions, did not reach their initial objectives. One battalion that did arrive at its objective was prohibited by division order from continuing lest it get too far ahead of the others. Another battalion, which had advanced a thousand yards down the Marigny road, also received the order to halt and consolidate for the night even though it had encountered only sporadic small arms and long-range artillery fire. The caution that General Eddy was demonstrating illustrated American surprise at the tenacity of the German opposition. Enemy troops that had escaped the bomb blast seemed not at all affected by what had happened to nearby units that had been obliterated in the bombardment.

In the center of the VII Corps sector, General Barton had committed only one regiment of the 4th Division. With but slight disorganization because of the short bombing, the 8th Infantry attacked with two battalions abreast on a 2,000-yard front on good terrain for offensive action. One assault battalion immediately bypassed a German strongpoint north of the Périers–St. Lô highway, the line of departure, and moved rapidly south for a mile and a half against scattered opposition; at nightfall the leading troops were just east of la Chapelle-en-Juger. The other assault battalion struck an orchard full of Germans who had such effective fields of fire that the battalion could not sideslip the obstruction. After a two-hour delay, eighteen supporting tanks, which had temporarily lost contact with the infantry, arrived and blasted the orchard. The resistance disintegrated. The battalion crossed the Périers–St. Lô highway and encountered no opposition for 700 yards, but then two German tanks and a line of enemy soldiers along a sunken road again stopped the battalion. Once more the supporting Shermans had become separated from the infantry. The battalion made a double envelopment of the enemy strongpoint and knocked out the two enemy tanks with bazooka fire. Still the enemy held. After the Shermans finally rumbled up, a few rounds of tank fire destroyed the defense. Receiving a sudden order to seize la Chapelle-en-Juger, the battalion changed direction and gained the edge of town. American artillery fire falling nearby brought the attack to a halt.

On the corps left, oriented toward St. Gilles, the 30th Division recovered with amazing quickness from the demoralizing effect of the short bombing.[53] Soon after the infantry started forward American planes bombed and strafed the troops again, driving them into ditches and bomb craters. More angry than scared, the men advanced once more.

They had a twofold mission. The 30th Division was to clear the road to

---

[53] The assistant division commander, General Harrison, who later was awarded the DSC, was on hand to inspire men who appeared to be on the verge of panic.

St. Gilles for the armored thrust to follow and was also to establish roadblocks at the bridges across the Vire River south of St. Lô. The bridges across the Vire had been bombed by tactical aircraft in pre-COBRA operations, and although some structures were damaged or destroyed, actual possession of the bridge sites by 30th Division infantrymen would enhance the security of the COBRA east flank.[54] As the 30th Division veered eastward and uncovered the road to St. Gilles, an armored column, alerted to follow, would drive south to foil German reinforcement from the southeast. General Hobbs thus mounted a two-pronged attack, one thrusting toward St. Gilles, the other pointing toward the high ground inside the horseshoe loop of the Vire River at St. Lô. The minimum assignment for the division was capture of Hébécrevon.

Just across the Périers–St. Lô highway, 30th Division troops met a roadblock built around three Mark V tanks. A frontal three-company attack, supported by Shermans, failed to dislodge the roadblock and resulted in the loss of three American tanks. An attempted double envelopment brought infantrymen into contact with additional German centers of resistance. Aggressive reconnaissance and excellent tank-infantry co-ordination were finally responsible for knocking out a dozen armored vehicles and uprooting the German defense.

In attacking Hébécrevon, the 30th Division had to cross a valley, using an unpaved and mined road with precipitous banks, and make a frontal assault against commanding terrain. Because German fire prevented American en-

gineers from clearing the road of mines, tanks could not accompany the infantry. Lack of alternate roads, absence of stream-crossing sites, closeness of adjacent units, and troop congestion precluded maneuver. An air strike seemingly had no effect on the volume of enemy fire. In the early evening the regimental commander of the 119th Infantry sought clarification of what appeared to be a paradoxical mission: was he to seize Hébécrevon or was he to bypass enemy resistance? Both, replied General Hobbs; "The important thing was to gain control of the crossroad in the town."[55] But not until darkness fell were infantrymen and tanks able to move against Hébécrevon. Soldiers acting like seeing-eye dogs led Shermans around bomb craters and through mine fields into positions for direct fire. Their shelling soon had the desired effect. Around midnight American troops entered Hébécrevon.

The ground attack following the COBRA bombardment on 25 July moved the VII Corps across the Périers–St. Lô highway but not much farther. Although crossing the highway was no mean achievement, the prevailing American attitude was far from elation. The immediate verdict of American commanders judging the effectiveness of the COBRA air strike was virtually unanimous: the bombardment had had almost no effect on the enemy. German artillery fire on 25 July had been light when compared to that of the previous day, but still the volume had been strong. The difference could be ascribed to low ammunition stocks or to

---

[54] [George], Ninth Air Force, p. 118.

[55] Hobbs, Telecons, 1750, 1917, and 2225, 25 Jul, 30th Div G–3 Jnl and File.

the disruption of communications: the "enemy artillery," Americans believed, "was not touched by our bombing." [56] Admittedly, the planes had damaged and destroyed equipment and had inflicted personnel losses in the bombed area, but the "effect of the bombing on the elimination of infantry resistance was negligible." Had not the Germans continued to contest every inch of ground? [57] General Hobbs was more blunt: "There is no indication of bombing," he stated, "in where we have gone so far." [58]

The truth of the matter was that "saturation" bombing had not saturated the entire target. Some American units had moved rapidly through areas in which the German defenses had obviously been neutralized by the bombardment.[59] Others had met resistance they had not expected.

The disappointment resulted in the main from overanticipation and overconfidence in the results of the bombardment. Many American troops had expected the bombardment to eliminate resistance in the target area; they thought that all the Germans would be killed or wounded; they had looked forward to the prospect of strolling through the bomb target area. The fact that some enemy groups had survived and were able to fight seemed to prove that the air bombardment had failed to achieve its purpose. The troops apparently had not realized that air bombardment and artillery fire, even under the most favorable conditions, do not completely

destroy the enemy, but by inflicting heavy losses weaken him physically and morally, disorganize his defenses, and make him vulnerable to infantry attack.[60]

The bombing errors that had taken American lives heightened the sense of discouragement. Comparatively few bombs had produced heavy casualties. Only gradually did the attitude of depression change. The bombing of American troops, it developed, "was not as bad as it seemed at first." [61] It had not materially disrupted the ground attack. The bombardment had, after all, knocked a hole in the German defenses. German prisoners were visibly shaken and dazed. Steel bomb fragments had shredded light vehicles, perforated heavy equipment, cut tank treads, splintered trees, smashed houses, and shattered communications in the enemy sector.[62]

Judged from the point of view of geographical advance, the ground attack had nevertheless gained relatively little terrain. The VII Corps had advanced the line only about a mile south of the Périers–St. Lô highway. That this was the case, even though only isolated and un-co-ordinated German groups remained to contest the advance, could be explained partially by the fact that the initial disappointment itself had nullified to a large extent General Bradley's injunction to be bold. The battle of the hedgerows during the preceding weeks had inflicted its psychological toll on the combat forces. Habits of caution

[56] 30th Div G–2 Per Rpt, 25 Jul; 9th Div Arty AAR, Jul.

[57] 9th Div G–2 Per Rpt, 0030, 26 Jul.

[58] Telecon, Collins and Hobbs, 1550, 25 Jul, 30th Div G–3 Jnl and File.

[59] See, for example, 47th Inf S–3 Per Rpt, 26 Jul.

[60] 12th AGp Immed Rpt 20, 8 Aug.

[61] 9th Div G–3 Jnl, entry 1201, 26 Jul.

[62] See Brereton, *Diaries*, pp. 316–17; Wilmot, *Struggle for Europe*, pp. 390ff.

could not be dissipated by an air strike or by an order. The presence of German defenders *per se* implied stubborn and skillful opposition.

The ground attack had actually succeeded better than anyone supposed. The VII Corps infantrymen had destroyed almost all the Germans who survived the bombardment, but the Germans knew this better than the Americans. It would have been hard to convince the 330th Infantry, for example, which had not yet crossed the Périers–St. Lô highway, that a yawning hole existed before the VII Corps. The 9th Division also was far short of Marigny; the committed regiment of the 4th Division had not secured la Chapelle-en-Juger; and the 30th Division had had great difficulty taking Hébécrevon and uncovering a small part of the road to St. Gilles.[63] In the opinion of American commanders, a clean penetration had not been made by the end of 25 July. They could not believe that once the troops broke through the main line of resistance, which in actuality they already had, there was "nothing in back to stop us." [64]

For his part, General Collins noted the absence of co-ordination in the German defense. If this meant that the enemy main line of resistance had been smashed, Collins reasoned, then the Germans must not be permitted to refashion another and he should commit his mobile reserves immediately. On the other hand, if the Germans had been forewarned by the premature bombing of 24 July, had withdrawn their main line, and escaped the full force of the main bombardment, then the sporadic nature of their defense possibly presaged a counterattack. If the German defenses had not been pierced, or if the Germans had erected another line, committing additional forces to the attack might promote a congestion that could prove fatal.

To General Collins a decision either to commit or to withhold his mobile striking force was a gamble. The infantry had not secured the minimum objectives deemed prerequisite for commitment of the armor. Nevertheless, he noted that the vital roads south to Marigny and to St. Gilles appeared to have been uncovered sufficiently to permit at least the commencement of the armored thrusts. Collins chose to move. During the afternoon of 25 July he decided to commit the armor on the following morning.[65]

---

[63] VII Corps Sitrep 99, 26 Jul.

[64] VII Corps G–2 Memo, 25 Jul, VII Corps G–3 Jnl and File.

[65] The earliest indication discovered of Collins' decision is a telephone conversation at 1745, 25 July, in 30th Division G–3 Journal and File.

CHAPTER XIII

The Breakthrough

Although the armored phase of COBRA was about to begin, the infantry on the morning of 26 July still had much to do. While getting out of the paths of the armored columns, they had to broaden the penetration achieved after the big bombardment and insure its permanence.[1] This was no minor assignment; the infantry found that, even though the Germans were considerably disorganized, enemy morale had not been "shaken to the point where the individual soldier will not carry out his mission, which still is to defend every inch of ground and inflict . . . as many casualties as possible." [2] *(See Map V.)*

German Reaction

The first report to give German higher headquarters any picture of what had happened after the COBRA bombardment revealed that the Americans had penetrated the main line of defense. German commanders learned at 1600, 25 July, that American troops were south of the Périers–St. Lô highway, in Montreuil, and on the road to Marigny.[3] Choltitz immediately committed part of

his *LXXXIV Corps* reserve, a reinforced regiment of the *353d Division*. From an assembly area south of Périers, the regiment moved eastward to secure la Chapelle-en-Juger and thereby seal off the penetration. Not long afterward, Hausser committed part of his *Seventh Army* reserve, a regiment of the *275th Division,* which, from its assembly area near Canisy, also moved toward la Chapelle-en-Juger. Thus, Choltitz and Hausser, acting on the same idea, sent two converging columns to deny the Americans the vital road network controlled by the village in the center of the attack zone.

Hausser hoped that retention of la Chapelle-en-Juger would permit him to re-establish a main line of resistance eastward to Hébécrevon, but he was unaware of the extent of the disaster that had overcome his troops. His command channels had been disrupted by the COBRA bombing and were saturated with overdue messages. Counting on the *5th Parachute Division,* which controlled one regiment, to hold its positions near the Taute River and prevent the Americans from broadening their breach, he was not disappointed, for the paratroopers checked any genuine advance by the 330th Infantry. But Hausser also counted on the *352d Division* (under *II Parachute Corps*) to hold the west bank of the Vire River and prevent

---

[1] 3d Armd Div Ltr of Instrs, 26 Jul (issued orally by CG VII Corps, 25 Jul).

[2] 9th Div FO 11, 26 Jul.

[3] Telecon, Helmdach and Tempelhoff, 1600, 25 Jul, *AGp B KTB*; see also Morning and Daily Sitreps, 25 Jul, *LXXXIV Corps Meldungen; Seventh Army KTB,* 25 Jul.

an American penetration near Hébécrevon. What he did not know was that *Panzer Lehr* had lost the bulk of its organic infantry, at least fourteen of its assault guns, and ten of its few remaining tanks; that *Kampfgruppe Heinz* and the other regiment of the *5th Parachute Division,* both attached to *Panzer Lehr,* had been demolished; and that the regiment of the *275th Division* moving up from Canisy was about to be crushed by American fighter-bombers and infantry. The result was an open left flank for the *352d Division,* and in that condition the unit was simply too weak to hold Hébécrevon, much less seal off a penetration.

Ignorant of these developments and of the loss of Hébécrevon, which opened the route to St. Gilles, the German army and corps commanders in the Cotentin exuded optimism on the morning of 26 July. Choltitz committed the remainder of the *353d Division* eastward toward the Montreuil–Marigny line to slow the efforts of the 9th Division. Hausser, while waiting for the destroyed and virtually nonexistent regiment of the *275th Division* to move northwest from Canisy, decided to launch a counterattack with the company of tanks and the company of infantry of the *2d SS Panzer Division* that he still had in army reserve. He committed this force in the Marigny area, where it met American armor and infantry.

Kluge, who had been diverted to the Caen sector on 25 July by the Canadian attack, thought the situation in the Cotentin might be worse than his subordinates suspected. He suggested that Hausser withdraw the left of the *LXXXIV Corps* slightly in order to shorten the front. This would make it

possible to disengage the entire *2d SS Panzer Division* for a counterattack. By this time, however, U.S. troops on the Cotentin west coast were attacking and tying down the *LXXXIV Corps* left. Hausser could not disengage the entire panzer division; by evening he had succeeded in freeing only one tank battalion and one infantry battalion from the battle. He moved these units eastward toward the breakthrough sector.[4]

Hausser's difficulty with the panzer division was only part of the story. By late afternoon on 25 July he had counted seven distinct American penetrations of his Lessay–St. Lô defensive line. He had also received Bayerlein's report that *Panzer Lehr* had practically no infantry left and that the division was about to cease to exist as an organized unit. Hausser therefore proposed a general withdrawal to Coutances of those *LXXXIV Corps* units in the coastal sector of the Cotentin. Still hoping that la Chapelle-en-Juger was not entirely lost, he thought of manning an outpost line between that village and Geffosses, the latter near the west coast.

Suspecting that a withdrawal might turn into a rout, Kluge insisted on restraint. He ordered Hausser to prepare a main line of resistance from Pirou through Millières to Périers in order to keep the Geffosses–St. Sauveur-Lendelin–Marigny road in German hands. He instructed Hausser to place all his available personnel on the front (rather than echeloning his defense in depth) in order to prevent immediately further American advances. He also repeated

---

[4] Telecons, Kluge and Hausser, 1010, 26 Jul, Pemsel and Tempelhoff, 1830, 26 Jul, *AGp B KTB.*

Penetration

a request, which he had been making to OKW since 13 July, that OKW permit the *9th Panzer Division* to be brought up from southern France to reinforce the *Seventh Army* at once.[5]

Penetration

On the morning of 26 July, the situation from the American point of view did not appear very bright. On the right of VII Corps, the 330th Infantry, which was to safeguard the flank of the COBRA main effort by cutting the Périers–St. Lô highway, securing a road intersection, and turning gradually westward, was hopeful of accomplishing its missions early on 26 July, for the tank destroyer fire that had been harassing the regiment from Marchésieux ceased.[6] But it soon became evident that the German paratroopers in opposition were as determined as ever. Not until late in the evening was the 330th Infantry able to cross the Périers–St. Lô highway, and even then the Germans continued to deny the regiment its crossroads objective.[7]

Instructed to permit the principal COBRA armored column to pass through his 9th Division zone, General Eddy on 26 July had to clear both enemy troops and his own from the Marigny road.

He had to prevent the enemy from cutting the road and thereby blunting the main COBRA thrust. Restricted to a narrow zone of operations and facing German forces unharmed by the COBRA bombardment, General Eddy maneuvered his units so that the 9th Division by the end of the day was two and a half miles south of the Périers–St. Lô highway and almost two miles west of the Marigny road. The division had sustained almost 200 casualties and had captured somewhat fewer prisoners. Although General Eddy had prevented his own troops from hampering an armored column moving south and had kept the Marigny road clear of enemy fire to the extent of his penetration, he faced the opposition of the *353d Division*, which, in trying to retake la Chapelle-en-Juger, threatened the VII Corps right flank.[8]

The 8th Infantry of the 4th Division took la Chapelle-en-Juger in the early morning of 26 July. Combat patrols had entered the village during the night, but the village crossroads was not secured until morning.[9] Continuing south, the regiment moved slowly, clearing isolated enemy groups. Commitment of the reserve battalion in the afternoon provided enough added weight for a three-mile surge that overran part of the *353d Division* and put *Panzer Lehr* artillery units to flight. Early that evening the leading troops engaged what seemed like the remnants of a German battalion, captured about a company of miscella-

[5] *Seventh Army KTB*, 26 Jul; *LXXXIV Corps Daily Sitrep*, 26 Jul, in *LXXXIV Corps Meldungen*; Kluge Order, 1935, 26 Jul, *AGp B Op. Befehle*; Telecons, Kluge and Jodl, 1828, 13 Jul, and Kluge and Zimmerman, 1750, 26 Jul, *OB WEST KTB, Anlagen 615, 860*, and *862*.

[6] Overlay to accompany 9th Div G–3 Per Rpt, 2400, 25 Jul; 83d Div G–2, G–3 Jnl, entry 0915, 26 Jul.

[7] 83d Div AAR, Jul, and G–3 Per Rpt 30, 26 Jul; 9th Div G–3 Jnl, entries 1100, 1145, 2025, and 2100, 26 Jul.

[8] 9th Div G–3 Jnl, entries 1140, 1145, 1406, 1545, 2040, 26 Jul; 39th Inf S–3 Rpt, 26 Jul; VII Corps Sitreps 100 and 101, 26 Jul.

[9] Telecon, Collins and Hobbs, 2215, 25 Jul, 30th Div G–3 Jnl and File; 8th Inf Msg, 1020, 26 Jul, 4th Div G–3 Jnl File.

neous troops, and destroyed or dispersed the others. The regiment cut the Coutances–St. Lô highway and at the end of the day was about five miles south of the COBRA line of departure.[10]

On the corps left, the 30th Division had not only to protect the COBRA flank but also to permit an American armored column to pass through the division zone for exploitation beyond St. Gilles. Enemy artillery fire from what was estimated to be one medium and three light battalions, as well as from several 88-mm. guns, checked any real advance during the morning of 26 July; but counterbattery missions delivered by the artillery units of the 30th Division, the VII Corps, and the XIX Corps produced the desired effect early that afternoon. As the division began to advance against diminishing artillery and mortar fire, an armored column passed through the division zone and drove toward St. Gilles.[11]

The 117th Infantry, attacking toward the loop of the Vire River, was stopped at a steep ravine where a well-positioned line held by part of the *352d Division* was supported by *II Parachute Corps* artillery firing from the high ground south of St. Lô. The regiment made five different attempts to overcome the resistance, but without success. Though close support by fighter-bombers might have aided the attack, General Hobbs was reluctant to request it because he feared a repetition of bombing errors. Accepting the apprehension as valid, General Collins did not press for the employment of tactical air. Not until

evening, after a heavy 4.2-inch mortar preparation that coincided with a German withdrawal, did the regiment cross the ravine and move quickly to the entrance of the loop, less than two miles west of St. Lô.[12]

The 119th Infantry, the other assault regiment, moved rapidly in the afternoon for two miles south of Hébécrevon and cut the Coutances–St. Lô highway. Given a new mission at once—cutting the Canisy–St. Lô highway two miles to the south—the regiment was half way to its objective by nightfall. At this point the leading troops of the 30th Division were more than three miles south of the pre-COBRA positions.

By late afternoon of 26 July, General Collins no longer doubted that his forces had achieved a clear penetration of the enemy defenses. Deeming that the situation demanded speed rather than caution, he told the infantry divisions to continue their attacks through the night.[13]

General Collins' directive coincided with a German order to make a slight withdrawal. During the night of 26 July the German units west of the Taute River—those comprising the left of the *LXXXIV Corps*—withdrew slightly along the coast and took up a new line of defense anchored on Périers and Marchésieux. The *6th Parachute Regiment* passed into the corps reserve at St. Sauveur-Lendelin. Just to the right of the corps boundary, the *352d Division* of the *II Parachute Corps*, already out-

---

[10] 4th Div AAR, Jul.

[11] 30th Div G–2 Per Rpt, 26 Jul, and G–3 Jnl, 26 Jul.

[12] Telecon, Hobbs and Kelly, 1535, 25 Jul, 30th Div G–3 Jnl and File; 30th Div FO 14, 25 Jul; MS # B–489 (Ziegelmann).

[13] VII Corps Opns Memo 49, 27 Jul (confirming oral orders, 26 Jul).

flanked, also withdrew from the loop of the Vire and along the west bank of the Vire River—in order to try to re-establish contact with *Panzer Lehr*.[14] This could be no more than a hope, for by that time there was virtually no organized resistance between the *352d* and the *5th Parachute Divisions,* though the German higher commands did not seem to know it.

Although the 330th Infantry on the extreme right flank of the VII Corps again struck stonewall resistance, all the other infantry units advanced during the night of 26 July. The 9th Division secured a road junction of local importance. The 8th Infantry of the 4th Division, leaving its vehicles and antitank guns behind, moved unencumbered for several miles, outflanked both the *Panzer Lehr* artillery and the remaining reserves of the regiment of the *275th Division* at Marigny, and, at dawn, hastened the flight of a withdrawing enemy column. Some troops of the 30th Division moved easily into the loop of the Vire River while others cut the Canisy–St. Lô road.

Except on the extreme right flank of the VII Corps where the 330th Infantry was denied for the third day the crossroads on the Périers–St. Lô highway that constituted its original objective, developments after daylight on 27 July indicated that the infantry was nearing fulfillment of its COBRA aims. The 9th Division, in a regimental attack against some 200 Germans, who were on a small ridge and were supported by four tanks and several antitank guns, destroyed the bulk of this force and dispersed the re-

mainder.[15] The 4th Division sent its reconnaissance troop ahead to screen a rapid advance.[16] Strong resistance from enemy positions hastily erected during the night melted away. The 8th Infantry cut the Carantilly–Canisy road and proceeded to a point more than seven miles south of the Périers–St. Lô highway. To clear small pockets of bypassed Germans, General Barton committed portions of the 12th Infantry, which had been in division reserve since the commencement of COBRA. Contingents of the 30th Division moved all the way into the loop of the Vire River and established physical contact with the 35th Division at the St. Lô bridge. Other units secured the two Vire River bridges on the main roads south of St. Lô. General Hobbs committed his reserve regiment, the 120th, which drove south along the Vire River for almost six miles against little opposition.

"This thing has busted wide open," General Hobbs exulted. He was right. Evidence of German disintegration was plentiful. Some German soldiers were walking into command posts to surrender; other were fleeing south or across the Vire River.[17]

On the morning of 28 July, the 330th Infantry at last was able to move against virtually no resistance to rejoin its parent unit, the 83d Division. In the 9th Division sector, only an occasional round

---

[14] MS # P–159 (Stoeckler) ; MS # B–839 (Heydte) ; MS # B–439 (Ziegelmann) .

[15] Leading his platoon in an assault across open ground in view of the enemy, 2d Lt. Edward F. Koritzke was killed but inspired his men to overrun the hostile positions. Koritzke was posthumously awarded the DSC.

[16] 4th Div Msg, 1015, 27 Jul, 30th Div G–3 Jnl and File.

[17] Telecon, Hobbs and Birks, 2300, 27 Jul, 30th Div Jnl and File; 30th Div G–3 Jnl, entries 0725, 2033, and 2100, 27 Jul.

of artillery or mortar fire was falling by noon; small arms fire had ceased. Having fulfilled its COBRA assignment, the 9th Division passed into reserve for rest and reconstitution. The 4th Division mopped up isolated enemy remnants and prepared to move south in a new operation. The 30th Division, advancing south along the west bank of the Vire River, passed from control of the VII Corps.

For the infantry units that had run interference, Operation COBRA had ended. General Hobbs perhaps typified infantry sentiment when he stated, "We may be the spearhead that broke the camel's back." [18] There was no doubt that the camel's back was broken and that the infantry had helped break it. But the armored forces of Operation COBRA also played their part.

Commitment of Armor

For the Americans, the critical day of the COBRA operation was 26 July, when General Collins had gambled. He committed some of his forces assembled for the exploitation before the situation was unquestionably ripe for an exploitation maneuver. Specifically, the infantry had not captured the towns of Marigny and St. Gilles, road centers considered prerequisite to an uninhibited exploitation by mobile armored reserves.[19]

The fact that COBRA on 26 July was to become a three-corps offensive actually made it impossible for General Collins to wait for the infantry to seize Ma-

rigny and St. Gilles. The success of the larger effort depended basically on a VII Corps breakthrough. Emphasizing this fact, General Bradley assigned to VII Corps all the air support available on 26 July, thus obliging Collins to step up the attack. The only way to do this was to commit the armor.

The basic gamble involved was the possibility that armored columns would congest the VII Corps battlefield. "The only doubtful part of it [the original COBRA plan] to my mind," General Collins had said two weeks earlier, "is we shouldn't count too much on fast movement of armored divisions through this country; if we make a break-through it is OK but until them . . . [the armored divisions] can't move any faster than the infantry." [20] To minimize congestion, General Collins called upon only part of his reserve, two armored columns instead of the three that were ready.

The commitment of the mobile units on 26 July was not so much the start of the exploitation as an effort to deepen the penetration. Instead of assigning exploitation objectives, Collins told one of the armored columns to take Marigny, the other St. Gilles. Two hundred fighter-bombers were to attack each town in advance of the thrusts.[21] Only after these original infantry objectives were secured was the true exploitation phase of COBRA to begin.

Having expected the COBRA air bombardment to obliterate the German defenses and the infantry to clear the routes of advance, the commanders of the mobile forces had planned to move

[18] Telecon, Hobbs and Birks, 2300, 27 Jul, 30th Div Jnl and File.

[19] See Ruppenthal Notes, ML–2185.

[20] FUSA Conf Notes, 12 Jul, FUSA G–3 Misc File.

[21] 1st Div G–3 Jnl and File, entries 0500 and 0550, 26 Jul.

at least as far as Marigny and St. Gilles with reconnaissance squadrons ahead of their main spearheads. Now a semiadministrative road march of this type was out of the question. The commanders replaced their reconnaissance units with assault troops and retained their artillery under centralized control rather than parceling it out to subordinate combat teams.[22]

Clearing the road to Marigny became the responsibility of Maj. Gen. Clarence R. Huebner, who commanded the 1st Infantry Division and the attached Combat Command B of the 3d Armored Division. Alerted on the afternoon of 25 July to pass through the 9th Division the next day and capture Marigny, General Huebner ordered CCB (Col. Truman E. Boudinot) and the reinforced 18th Infantry (Col. George Smith, Jr.) to attack abreast astride the road. Not quite certain whether the 1st Division, which had motorized its infantry troops, was embarking on exploitation, a VII Corps staff officer in a routine telephone call to transmit the bomb safety line remarked somewhat facetiously that his message was unnecessary if "you are going someplace and are going fast." [23] General Huebner, who commanded one of the two divisions General Eisenhower had characterized as "tops" in the theater, was planning to go somewhere fast all right.[24] He hoped to take Marigny quickly and proceed at once to exploit westward from Marigny to Coutances.

The 1st Division made its approach march to the vicinity of the Périers–St. Lô highway during the night of 25 July without incident. Shortly after daybreak, 26 July, the leading units bypassed an enemy pocket of 150 men still north of the COBRA line of departure. Leaving the reduction of this small force to the reserve battalion of the 18th Infantry, the advance troops drove toward Marigny.[25]

With the combat command on the right (west) of the road and the infantry regiment on the left, the 1st Division troops moved cautiously against small arms fire. Bomb craters in the roads and defended hedgerows bounding the fields were the principal deterrents to a rapid advance. Small roadblocks also slowed the attack. Artillery and tank fire eliminated most of the opposition, but only after the infantry components had received heavy casualties, particularly among key personnel.

Near Marigny, the troops encountered the increasing resistance of the *353d Division* and the two companies of the *2d SS Panzer Division*. Several Mark IV tanks and a few 75-mm. antitank guns north of the town halted progress early in the afternoon. Under cover of an extended tank fire fight, CCB attempted an envelopment to the right but achieved no success. A tactical air strike late in the afternoon enabled armored elements to reach the northern edge of the town; the enveloping forces buttoned up for the night about a mile west of Marigny.[26]

[22] 1st Div FO's 38 and 39, 19 and 25 Jul; G–3 Jnl, entry 1700, 25 Jul; Arty S–3 Per Rpt 38, 26 Jul; [Pillsbury], 2d Armd Div in Opn COBRA, p. 18; 3d Armd Div Arty Annex to 3d Armd Div FO 5, 19 Jul.

[23] 1st Div G–3 Jnl, entry 2155, 25 Jul.

[24] Ltr, Eisenhower to Marshall, 5 Jul, Pogue Files.

[25] 1st Div AAR, Jul, G–3 Jnl, 25 and 26 Jul, Situation Overlay, 2400, 25 Jul, and Msgs, 0725 and 1010, 26 Jul; 1st Div Arty S–3 Per Rpt 39, 26 Jul; 9th Div G–3 Jnl, entries 0130 and 0210, 26 Jul.

[26] 3d Armd Div CCB AAR, Jul, Action 25 Jul–31 Jul.

The presence of American tanks in the northern outskirts of Marigny and the abortive envelopment led the 18th Infantry to the erroneous belief that the combat command had taken the town. Acting on this mistaken impression, the regiment sent a battalion to bypass the town on the east during the evening and take high ground south of Marigny. The battalion took some high ground shortly before midnight and reported completion of its mission. Unfortunately, the battalion had become lost in the darkness; not only was it on the wrong objective, its actual location was a mystery.

The belief that Marigny had been captured was one of the factors leading to General Collins' order to continue the attacks during the night of 26 July. Specifically, Collins instructed General Huebner to commence his exploitation toward Coutances. To provide additional elbow room for the 1st Division, General Collins redrew the boundary between the 1st and 9th Divisions.[27]

General Huebner for his part dared not carry out the order. He was not sure exactly where all his front-line units were, for reports of their locations and dispositions had confused his headquarters throughout the day; he was not certain that his troops had really secured Marigny; he was concerned by continuing resistance near Marigny; and, finally, he feared that large-scale movement during darkness would promote congestion and confusion.[28]

Still without Marigny after two days, the VII Corps had yet to launch its main exploiting effort westward to Coutances. As discouraging as this seemed to be, the success achieved on the other flank of the corps was quite the opposite.

On the left (east) flank, Maj. Gen. Edward H. Brooks, commanding the 2d Armored Division, had what was essentially a protective mission: guarding the COBRA flank on the south and southeast. Yet if General Brooks realized that his mission was defensive in nature, he gave no indication of it. So far as he was concerned, he was going to move. With the 22d Infantry (Col. Charles T. Lanham) attached, he was to attack in a column of combat commands, which eventually were to split and make independent thrusts. Brig. Gen. Maurice Rose's Combat Command A, with the 22d Infantry attached, was to be the leading unit.[29] Rose's troops were to pass through the 30th Division zone and secure St. Gilles.

Effecting the passage of lines without difficulty, CCA drove south early on 26 July in a single column.[30] Almost immediately after the troops crossed the Périers–St. Lô highway, an enemy antitank gun destroyed one Sherman, but this was a blow not soon repeated. Brooks told Rose to get moving, and Rose complied. As the column began to roll, only scattered artillery and antitank fire and an occasional defended hedgerow or ditch provided any genuine

---

[27] VII Corps Sitrep 101, 27 Jul, and Opns Memos 48 and 49, 25 and 27 Jul (the latter confirming oral orders 26 Jul) ; 9th Div G–3 Jnl, entry 1900, 26 Jul.

[28] 1st Div Arty S–3 Per Rpt 39, 26 Jul; VII Corps Tactical Study of the Terrain, 17 Jul.

[29] Other elements of CCA were: 66th Armored Regiment, 702d Tank Destroyer Battalion, 14th Armored Field Artillery Battalion, and engineer, antiaircraft, medical, and maintenance detachments.

[30] 2d Div AAR, Jul; see [Pillsbury], 2d Armd Div in Opn COBRA, p. 18.

resistance. When combined with the problem of bomb craters dotting the countryside, this was nevertheless sufficient to preclude a rapid advance. In the early afternoon a defended roadblock several hundred yards north of St. Gilles held up progress for a short time, but tank fire and an air strike that destroyed four Mark IV tanks and a self-propelled gun soon eliminated the opposition.

In midafternoon CCA rolled through St. Gilles. By this act, the combat command launched the exploitation phase of COBRA. There was no longer any doubt that the German line had definitely been penetrated. The VII Corps had achieved its breakthrough.[31]

Limited Exploitation

South of St. Gilles, CCA of the 2d Armored Division, with the 22d Infantry still attached, headed for its initial objective in the exploitation: the high ground five miles beyond St. Gilles, ground commanding an extensive network of roads leading into the COBRA zone from the east and south. There, at St. Samson-de-Bonfossé, le Mesnil-Herman, and Hill 183, the armor would find good defensive positions from which to halt a possible German counterattack from across the Vire River. To reach the area, CCA had to pass through Canisy, not quite two miles south of St. Gilles.

Proceeding steadily against mortar, artillery, and antitank fire interdicting the Canisy road, CCA had more difficulty with bomb craters, mine fields, and hedgerows than with the occasional

TROOPS ROLLING THROUGH CANISY

enemy resistance. In late afternoon General Rose reported opposition in his zone negligible and estimated that the rear of his column would soon clear St. Gilles.[32] Rose's optimism contributed materially to General Collins' decision to continue the corps attack during the night.

Part of the reason why the opposition was negligible lay in the clearing operations of the 30th Division. Another part lay in the fact that the St. Gilles–Canisy road was the boundary separating the *LXXXIV* and *II Parachute Corps* sectors. *Panzer Lehr* was specifically responsible for the highway. The virtual destruction of *Panzer Lehr* left the road open. The *352d Division*, manning the sector between the road and the river,

---

[31] FUSA G–2 Per Rpt 47, 27 Jul.

[32] 2d Armd Div Msgs, 1730 and 1830, 26 Jul, 30th Div G–3 Jnl and File.

was thus continually outflanked as Rose's combat command drove down an excellent route of advance, threatened solely by occasional flanking fire.

Only as CCA neared the first buildings in Canisy was there any real resistance. At a railroad embankment north of Canisy where a bombed railway overpass had tumbled across the highway, a few Germans tried to make a stand; the combat command outflanked the position from the east and raked the defenders with enfilading fire.[33] Coincidentally, dive bombers struck Canisy and set half the town ablaze. The armor rolled through the burning town that evening.

Just beyond Canisy, General Rose split his command into two columns. One moved southeastward toward St. Samson-de-Bonfossé, the other southward toward le Mesnil-Herman. Although division headquarters assumed that the combat command had halted for the night, Rose drove his men forward with single-minded purpose and determination in compliance with General Collins' and General Brooks' orders.[34] An hour before midnight one column entered St. Samson-de-Bonfossé without a fight. Three hours later the other seized the road intersection just north of le Mesnil-Herman. Only then, with part of the initial objective in hand, did General Rose sanction a halt.

The next morning, 27 July, as batteries of the 14th Armored Field Artillery Battalion leapfrogged forward to give continuous fire support, the combat command engaged enemy tanks and antitank guns before taking and securing

le Mensil-Herman.   Hill 183 fell during the afternoon.   With that, CCA completed its initial mission.[35]

In two days Combat Command A had lost less than 200 men, 3 medium tanks, and 2 small trucks.   Not only the weakness of the opposition but the dispatch with which General Rose had secured his objective had prevented higher casualties.   Even so, Rose was not satisfied with his accomplishment; he complained that the poor condition of the roads, the absence of road bypasses, and the hedgerowed terrain had slowed his movement.[36]

As General Rose prepared to reconnoiter in force toward Villebaudon and Tessy-sur-Vire on the morning of 28 July, word came that CCA's role in COBRA was over.   The combat command and the attached infantry regiment were soon to pass from the control of the VII Corps.

While General Rose's attack had moved smoothly against light opposition, General Huebner had met unexpected difficulty at Marigny on 26 July. The 1st Division, with Combat Command B of the 3d Armored Division attached, had been unable to start the main effort of the exploitation—its thrust westward from Marigny to Coutances to slash across the rear of the German troops facing north against the VIII Corps. Since the VIII Corps had begun to exert pressure from the north on 26 July, it became vital for the 1st Division to get to Coutances at once in or-

---

[33] 2d Armd Div Msgs, 1930 and 2030, 26 Jul, 30th Div G–3 Jnl and File.

[34] 2d Armd Div G–3 Per Rpt 4, 27 Jul.

[35] 2d Armd Div Msg, 1130, 27 Jul, 30th Div Jnl and File. Lt. Col. Lindsay C. Herkness, Jr., was awarded the DSC for his heroic leadership of armored troops; Capt. Mario T. DeFelice, a medical officer, was awarded the DSC for heroism.

[36] 2d Armd Div Msg, 0730, 27 Jul, 30th Div Jnl and File.

der to execute the squeeze play that was part of the basic COBRA idea.

Even though General Huebner did not possess a secure pivot point at Marigny, he felt impelled to begin his exploitation on the morning of 27 July. He ordered Colonel Boudinot's CCB to initiate the westward thrust toward Coutances. In the meantime, Colonel Smith's 18th Infantry was to attack Marigny and high ground south of the town in order to secure the road network required for sustaining the exploitation.

Getting CCB on the way to Coutances conformed with the original 1st Division plan, a plan devised to employ as the axis of advance the east–west Coutances–St. Lô highway, which passes through rolling *bocage* country. West of Marigny the highway runs along the southern slope of a ridge line formed by a complex of three hills—the highest rising 580 feet—a mile or so north of the highway. This prominent terrain feature dominating the approaches to Coutances from the north and east provided an excellent natural blocking position astride the routes of withdrawal of the German forces facing the VIII Corps, and together with Coutances was the 1st Division's objective.

Of the three hills forming the ridge line, the first, five miles west of Marigny, is near Camprond. The second, two miles farther to the west, is near Cambernon. The third is near Monthuchon. To General Huebner the early capture of these hills was of double importance, for they dominated also his own route of approach to Coutances.

General Huebner had selected his attached armored command to spearhead the attack both because a rapid advance along the highway was essential for suc-cess of the COBRA scheme of maneuver and because the highway between Marigny and Coutances was excellent. CCB was to seize the first objective, Camprond, then the third objective, Monthuchon. Motorized infantry regimental combat teams of organic 1st Division troops were to follow in column. The 18th Infantry was to relieve CCB first at Camprond, then at Monthuchon. In turn, the reinforced 16th Infantry (Col. Frederick W. Gibb) was to relieve the 18th at Camprond. The reinforced 26th Infantry (Col. John F. R. Seitz) was to follow secondary roads on the left flank of the other units and seize the second objective, Cambernon. In the end, all three infantry regiments would be lined up on the three objectives to the rear of the German line.

After being relieved at Monthuchon, CCB had a further mission, which was determined by the location of Monthuchon on the north–south Périers–Coutances highway, one of the main escape routes for Germans withdrawing before VIII Corps. The combat command was to be prepared to do one of two things: if the VIII Corps had not pushed back the Germans, CCB was to attack northward toward Périers; if the Germans were trying to escape to the south, CCB was to proceed southwestward from Monthuchon to high ground a mile or so north of Coutances in order to block the three main highways leading into Coutances from the north.[37]

---

[37] 1st Div FO 38, 19 Jul; Annex 1 to 3d Armd Div FO 4, 19 Jul. There was some question on the final mission of the combat command. The 3d Armored Division CCB Field Order 5 of 20 July states that the combat command was to prepare to attack north toward Périers only after blocking the roads above Coutances.

Because of the unexpected resistance at Marigny, General Huebner changed his plan of maneuver on the morning of 27 July. Since continued German possession of Marigny denied the 1st Division an adequate road net, General Huebner withheld one regiment, the 26th, in order to reduce the hazard of traffic congestion. CCB was to secure Camprond, the first objective. Instead of following the armor, the 18th Infantry was to capture Marigny, then send a battalion to free the armor at Camprond. The 16th Infantry, instead of relieving the 18th at Camprond, was to make a wider swing to the west, echeloned to the left rear of CCB, and move all the way to the blocking positions on the highways just north of Coutances. Meanwhile, CCB was to attack and secure in turn all three hill objectives.[38]

The 18th Infantry cleared Marigny on the morning of 27 July, and that afternoon two battalions attacked to the south against strong opposition in an attempt to seize the high ground needed to secure the town.[39] The reserve battalion in midafternoon moved westward along the Coutances highway to relieve CCB at Camprond.

Early that morning CCB had lunged down the Coutances highway.[40] Spearheaded by the reconnaissance battalion and divided into three balanced teams or task forces (a company each of medium tanks and armored infantry), the combat command advanced with two teams abreast. Against disorganized opposition, the attack carried four miles

in four hours. Shortly after midday the task force on the right turned to the north and struck cross-country for the hill near Camprond, two miles away. By midafternoon the task force held the objective.

The advance along the highway had been virtually a road march except for casual encounters with German motorcyclists, ambulances, and staff cars. Progress on the flanks had been more difficult, for the presence of hedgerows enabled scattered enemy groups to form hasty defenses and resist with determination. The result was a gain on a narrow front scarcely wider than the width of the highway.

Moving to relieve the force at Camprond, the battalion of the 18th Infantry encountered virtually no opposition on the Coutances highway, but when it moved off the road toward the hill small enemy groups supported by random tanks began to cause trouble. With the help of fighter-bombers, the battalion gained the hill shortly before midnight.

Meanwhile, the 16th Infantry, which was to make a parallel advance on the left and move swiftly to Coutances, was unable to pass through Marigny until late afternoon of 27 July. Against scattered opposition and sporadic fire, the regiment advanced in a column of battalions immediately south of the Coutances highway. Shortly before midnight the leading battalion came abreast of CCB at a point directly south of Camprond.

Thus at midnight, 27 July, the 1st Division had advanced on a front not quite three miles wide to a point about five miles west of Marigny.[41] Though no

---

[38] 1st Div AAR, Jul.

[39] VII Corps Msg, 0930, 27 Jul, VII Corps G-3 Jnl and File.

[40] 3d Armd Div CCB Opns Overlay and FO, 26 Jul.

[41] 1st Div Situation Overlay, 2400, 27 Jul, 9th Div G-3 Jnl and File.

organized enemy opposition was apparent, small enemy groups supported by an occasional tank or antitank gun formed islands of resistance, floating and static, in the American sea of advance, endangering both supply and evacuation. When twenty-one supply trucks loaded with rations, gasoline, ammunition, and military police went forward from Marigny, a company of medium tanks accompanied them to give protection. The column reached Camprond without incident, but, returning after dark with two truckloads of prisoners, the column had to fight its way back to Marigny.[42] The attempt of a reconnaissance platoon to cross the Lozon River three miles west of Marigny stimulated a counterattack by about a hundred Germans supported by a medium tank and an antitank gun. The platoon had to call for infantry and armor reinforcements from the 9th and 1st Division before dispersing the enemy group.[43]

The result of the main COBRA effort produced disappointment. "Generally, we are not being able to push very fast," the VII Corps G-3 admitted.[44] General Huebner had hoped to rip into the rear of the German defense line. His troops were to have cut German telephone wires, disrupted communications, and in general produced confusion and disorganization.[45] But instead of raising havoc in a slashing exploitation, the 1st Division had not yet secured Marigny and was only half way to Coutances.

The reason for the disappointing advance by the forces carrying the main COBRA effort was to be found in the German dispositions. The *LXXXIV Corps* left had made a withdrawal along the Cotentin west coast during the night of 26 July with the intention of establishing a new main line of resistance. Yet on 27 July the contemplated positions of this line were becoming untenable even before they were established because of the VII Corps threat developing west of Marigny toward the German right (east) flank. When Hausser and Choltitz suddenly became aware that American armored columns were moving through the Marigny–St. Gilles gap, they realized that they would have to move fast to avoid encirclement from the east. There was no alternative to continuing the withdrawal along the Cotentin west coast. To insure escape from encirclement, they erected a north–south defensive line facing eastward. Units manning the line included elements of the depleted *17th SS Panzer Grenadier Division*, reluctantly withdrawing paratroopers, the *353d Division*, and small elements of the *2d SS Panzer Division*.

During the early afternoon of 27 July Choltitz learned that American troops— CCB of the 3d Armored Division, attached to the 1st Division—seemed to have clear sailing toward Coutances. American scouting parties on minor roads had made contact with artillery units of the *353d Division* and the *LXXXIV Corps,* and German artillerymen were fighting as infantry. Discovering also that American troops had reached Guesnay, Choltitz ordered the engineer battalion of the *17th SS Panzer*

---

[42] 3d Armd Div CCB AAR, Jul.
[43] 4th Cav Recon Sq (Mechanized) Unit Rpt 1, 27 Jul, 1st Div G-3 Jnl and File.
[44] VII Corps Msg, 0930, 27 Jul, VII Corps G-3 Jnl and File.
[45] 1st Div FO 38, 19 Jul.

Grenadier Division to "proceed immediately via Montcuit and Cambernon to the railroad junction and seal off the front to the east if you are not [now] engaged in battle.[46]

Harassed continuously by fighter-bombers, the engineer battalion marched eight miles and took positions along the railroad that night. Just to the north, the battalion found a company of the *2d SS Panzer Division* defending Cambernon with ten Panther tanks. This north–south defensive line facing eastward, though far from strong, was efficacious in slowing the 1st Division attack toward Coutances on 27 July. Farther south, hastily organized positions between Carantilly and Quibou held up another American armored column, this one driving toward Montpinchon.

Hausser, meanwhile, had requested permission to withdraw the *LXXXIV Corps* to the Geffosses–St. Sauveur-Lendelin line. Soon afterward he wanted authorization to withdraw even farther, to Coutances. In both cases, he planned to make the withdrawal under the protection of the *2d SS Panzer Division,* which was moving into the Cambernon sector.[47] However, all plans were held in abeyance because Kluge, somewhat inexplicably to those in the Cotentin who awaited his advice, was inspecting the *Panzer Group West* front near Caen. Deciding they could wait no longer, Hausser and Choltitz agreed to withdraw to Coutances and hold it as the anchor point of a new line—an

arc through Cambernon, Savigny, and Cerisy-la-Salle. Unfortunately for their plan, they were unaware that *Panzer Lehr* for all practical purposes no longer existed, and they were counting on *Panzer Lehr* to hold the Soulle River line at Pont-Brocard.

When Kluge returned from the Caen sector late on the afternoon of 27 July, he received a detailed report of a badly deteriorating situation. The salient points were that the *353d Division* was presumed cut off and lost; the *352d Division* on the west bank of the Vire was badly battered and holding a shaky security line facing northwestward into a yawning gap; and remnants of *Panzer Lehr* and the *275th Division,* reinforced by what was hoped was a tank battalion of the *2d SS Panzer Division,* were supposedly holding a line at Quibou and westward. The Americans were running wild; details were not clear, but some troops were known to have reached the village of Dangy, near the vicinity of the *Panzer Lehr* and the *275th Division* command posts.

In this situation, Hausser recommended that Kluge permit him to restore order by straightening the *Seventh Army* front. Hausser proposed to have the *II Parachute Corps* withdraw the *3d Parachute Division* (east of the Vire) "platoon by platoon" and have the *LXXXIV Corps* pull back to the banks of the Soulle and Sienne Rivers.[48] Actually, this maneuver relied on using the nonexistent *Panzer Lehr* to hold a six-mile gap between Pont-Brocard and the shaky *352d Division* on the west bank of the Vire. Furthermore, it

---

[46] *17th SS Pz Gren Div* Msg, 1415, 27 Jul, *17th SS Engr Bn KTB*; see also Telecon, Helmdach and Speidel, 1310, 27 Jul, *AGp B KTB,* and Choltitz, *Soldat Unter Soldaten,* pp. 205–06.

[47] Telecons, Pemsel and Speidel, 1400, 27 Jul, and Hausser and Speidel, 1530, 27 Jul, *AGp B KTB.*

[48] Telecon, Kluge and Pemsel, 1700, 27 Jul, *AGp B KTB.*

counted on a tank battalion of the *2d SS Panzer Division* at Quibou that in reality had but fourteen tanks.

Still primarily concerned with the Caen sector held by *Panzer Group West*, Kluge refused to countenance the withdrawal by the *II Parachute Corps*, which might expose the *Panzer Group West* flank. He instead ordered the *II Parachute Corps* to defend in place in the St. Lô–Caumont sector while the *LXXXIV Corps* anchored its forces on Coutances and executed a fighting withdrawal to the Soulles–Sienne river line. Meanwhile, he was assembling an experienced and somewhat rested armored division in the Caumont area for action in the Cotentin. Aided by whatever could be found of *Panzer Lehr*, the *275th Division*, and the *2d SS Panzer Division*, the experienced armored division was to launch a counterattack to close the gap between the *LXXXIV* and *II Parachute Corps* of the *Seventh Army*.

In addition to the *9th Panzer Division*, which Kluge had requested on the previous day, he asked OKW to send a total of four infantry divisions to Normandy from the *Fifteenth* and *Nineteenth Armies*. Still concerned with the Allied threat to invade southern France, yet realizing that Kluge's situation was serious, Hitler approved release of the *9th Panzer Division* for commitment in Normandy. On the following day, 28 July, he authorized the movement to Normandy of three infantry divisions, the *84th*, the *331st*, and the *708th*.[49]

Meanwhile, in the Cotentin those *LXXXIV Corps* units still north of the St. Lô–Coutances highway infiltrated

south through the VII Corps column or moved around the western end of the American point during the night of 27 July. Covered by a reinforced regiment of the *2d SS Panzer Division*, which held a defensive arc from Cambernon to Savigny, the units on the Cotentin west coast continued to move south on 28 July. The units were the depleted *243d Division*, the kampfgruppe of the *265th Division*, and elements of the *77th Division* and of the *5th Parachute Division*, all apparently under the operational control of the *91st Division*. The *17th SS Panzer Grenadier Division* moved in broad daylight, though harassed from the air, to Cerisy-la-Salle in time to meet an American armored column there. At the same time the *6th Parachute Regiment*, together with *2d SS Panzer Division* tanks and the engineer battalion of the *17th SS*, covered the rear of the withdrawal and protected Coutances from positions near Ouville.

These moves reflected and contributed to the changing situation. Already, on the evening of 27 July, General Bradley had altered plans by assigning General Huebner's last two objectives—Monthuchon and the high ground north of Coutances—to the VIII Corps.[50] But since Huebner saw no certainty that the VIII Corps could reach these objectives ahead of the 1st Division, he proceeded on the tentative assumption that they might still be valid for him. Huebner thus ordered a continuation of his attack on 28 July. CCB was to take Cambernon, the 16th Infantry to capture Monthuchon, the 18th Infantry to remain in the Marigny area, and the 26th

---

[49] *AGp B* and *OB WEST KTB*'s, 27–28 Jul; *OB WEST KTB, Anlage 878*.

[50] FUSA FO 2, 28 Jul; see below, Ch. XIV.

Infantry to relieve CCB at Cambernon. After relief, CCB would be free to drive to the high ground north of Coutances if the VIII Corps was nowhere in evidence.[51]

Developments on 28 July illustrated the discrepancy between the results of COBRA as planned and as executed. North of the St. Lô–Coutances highway, CCB met little opposition on the move toward Cambernon. After knocking out two Mark V Panther tanks with bazookas, reconnaissance troops took the objective, securing it by noon. When Colonel Boudinot asked permission to continue westward to Monthuchon, General Huebner approved after a check with General Collins. (*Map VI*)

Almost immediately word came that VIII Corps had already captured Monthuchon. Still anxious to take a part of his original objective, Boudinot ordered his troops to bypass Monthuchon and take the high ground north of Coutances. Huebner could not sanction a crossing of the north–south Périers–Monthuchon–Coutances highway because it had been reserved for the VIII Corps, and he countermanded Boudinot's order. Although reconnaissance elements were already infiltrating across the road and outposting the high ground north of Coutances, the main body of CCB stopped in time to prevent serious intermingling with the VIII Corps.[52] Forced to halt, the tankers could see the city of Coutances less than two miles away.

Although Combat Command B had found little to obstruct its advance, the 16th Infantry, attacking westward toward Monthuchon in a zone south of the St. Lô–Coutances highway, advanced only slightly before reaching a well-organized defensive line. "Any contact with the enemy?" a division staff officer asked on the telephone. "Three hundred and sixty degree contact," came the somewhat exaggerated reply.[53] The regiment made no further progress during the afternoon, even though regimental attacks brought severe casualties and the loss of fifteen tanks, seven of them mediums. Tactical aircraft, which might have helped, were grounded because of cloudy weather.

Shortly before nightfall General Huebner told CCB to go to the aid of the 16th Infantry. Turning to the southeast and attacking, the combat command pinched the rear of the enemy position. Caught in a trap, the German defense disintegrated. Before midnight CCB and the 16th Infantry made contact.

Committed last, the 26th Infantry executed the 1st Division's final COBRA action. Having passed through Marigny during the morning of 28 July, it moved westward to take Cambernon. CCB's quick seizure of Cambernon and the cancellation of Monthuchon and Coutances as objectives for the VII Corps prompted General Huebner to change the regimental mission to that of sweeping the left flank of the division. Advancing through terrain infested by stragglers and remnants of German units, the 26th Infantry executed what was essentially a mop-up operation. In the early evening the leading battalion turned and faced south to exert pressure

---

[51] 1st Div AAR, Jul, and G–3 Jnl, 28 Jul.

[52] 1st Div G–3 Jnl, entries 1450 and 1537, 28 Jul; 3d Armd Div CCB AAR, Jul.

[53] 16th Inf S–3 Jnl, 28 Jul.

on the rear of German troops trapped near the village of Savigny.[54]

Like CCB's shift to the south, the 26th Infantry's turn to the south was a consequence of the changing situation developing out of COBRA. According to the plan, the main battle was to have occurred in the triangular region formed on the Cotentin west coast between Lessay and Coutances by the highways from Lessay and Coutances to St. Lô. As the VIII Corps exerted pressure south from the Lessay–Périers road, the main exploiting force of the VII Corps was to have raced to Coutances to cut off German escape. "Did we lose the big fish in the trap?" a 1st Division officer asked. "Yes, probably," came the reply.[55] The division had lost two big fish: the prestige of capturing Coutances and the opportunity of trapping large numbers of Germans north of the St. Lô–Coutances highway. In three days, the division had taken only 565 prisoners.[56] The bulk of the Germans, by escaping the VII Corps main effort, had slipped through the COBRA noose. As a result, the fighting shifted to the region south of the Coutances–St. Lô highway. The 1st Division had little alternative but to face south and assume the role that the VIII Corps had earlier played, the role of a pressure force.

---

[54] 1st Div AAR, Jul, and Situation Overlay, 2400, 28 Jul. S. Sgt. George E. Jackson received the DSC for heroic action that day.

[55] 16th Inf Jnl, 28 Jul.

[56] 1st Div G–2 Per Rpt 39, 28 Jul.

CHAPTER XIV

The Breakthrough Developed

The Second Thrust Toward Coutances

When night came on 26 July, the second day of Operation COBRA, General Collins still had one uncommitted unit, the 3d Armored Division (less CCB). Although scheduled to enter the fight on 26 July along with the other two armored columns, the 3d Armored had been withheld because of the uncertainty about the extent of the COBRA penetration. It was located in the VII Corps center where it might be used either to defend against counterattack or to reinforce success at any point within the corps.[1]

When operations on 26 July left no doubt that a clear penetration had been made, General Collins told the commander, General Watson, to begin executing his original mission the next morning, 27 July. (*See Map V.*) Employing General Hickey's Combat Command A (with a battalion of the 1st Division's 26th Infantry attached), the 3d Armored Division was to attack through the middle of the Marigny–St. Gilles gap to the vicinity of Carantilly and Canisy. At Cerisy-la-Salle the division was to turn to the west, secure

Montpinchon, cut the north–south highway about half way between Coutances and Gavray, and set up blocking positions south of Coutances on high ground overlooking the roads leading south to Gavray and Bréhal.

This was basically a defensive mission. In making a wide envelopment en route to Coutances, the 3d Armored Division was to thwart the northward movement of German reinforcements against the 1st Division and its attached CCB. On the other hand, should COBRA thoroughly disorganize the Germans and force their withdrawal, the 3d Armored Division would be in position to block the southern exits from Coutances. If the VIII Corps reached Coutances ahead of the 3d Armored Division, General Watson was to halt at the Coutances–Gavray road in order to circumvent traffic congestion between VII and VIII Corps forces in a subsequent exploitation of COBRA. Because on 26 July a deep exploitation hardly seemed likely, General Collins told General Watson to destroy all bridges over the Sienne River not previously knocked out by air bombardment.[2]

---

[1] 3d Armd Div Ltr of Instrs, 26 Jul (confirming oral orders issued by the corps commander on the evening of 25 July).

[2] FUSA Outline Plan COBRA, 13 Jul; VII Corps FO 6 (rev), 20 Jul; 3d Armd Div Amendment to FO 4, 20 Jul; Ltr, Destruction of Bridges, 22 Jul; Memo, 23 Jul (an extract of VII Corps Msg, 23 Jul); Ltr of Instrs, 24 Jul.

Dividing CCA into three task forces—each basically a battalion of tanks and one of armored infantry—General Hickey sent the comand across the Périers–St. Lô highway in column early on 27 July. The troops were to drive forward aggressively, outflanking or bypassing resistance and avoiding hedgerow fighting. Though the road net was not the best for rapid armored advance, little opposition was expected because the 4th Division already had passed through the area. With Operation COBRA well on the way to success, there seemed no reason why the armored column should not move quickly to the village of Cerisy-la-Salle, then swing to the west.[3]

This line of thought did not take into account certain obstacles—bomb craters, wrecked vehicles, and traffic congestion. The leading task force met a well-organized strongpoint southeast of Marigny around noon of 27 July and lost four of its medium tanks. While the head of the column sought to disengage, the rest of the armor jammed up along the roads to the rear for a distance of almost ten miles. Though the point finally broke contact and bypassed the resistance (which the 12th Infantry of the 4th Division cleared later in the day), another obstacle developed in the Carantilly–Canisy region. Here CCA's advance units encountered several German tanks and antitank guns deployed along a railroad embankment. Prevented from bypassing this resistance because of inadequate roads, the leading task force had no choice but to fight.

Heavy fire from CCA's tanks eventually subdued the defenses, but again the bulk of the column had to wait impotently for several hours along the roads to the rear. Traffic congestion and more enemy pockets prompted a halt shortly after dark.

The advance had been disappointing. The third task force in the column was still far back in the vicinity of Marigny and St. Gilles, the second was in the Carantilly–Canisy area, and the head of the combat command was more than three miles short of Cerisy-la-Salle, the pivot point for the westward thrust toward Coutances.[4]

The villages of Cerisy-la-Salle, on a hill almost 400 feet high, and Montpinchon, on a mound about 425 feet high two miles to the west and on the other side of a steep-walled valley, dominate the surrounding terrain in general and in particular the road net westward to Coutances. The 3d Armored Division commander, General Watson, had assumed that COBRA would develop so rapidly that CCA would occupy Cerisy-la-Salle without difficulty. Plans had thus been prepared for operations only in the area west of that village—along the Montpinchon–Coutances axis.

On the evening of 27 July, the situation demanded a change. CCA had started a day late, and its approach march had been disappointingly slow. In addition, there were indications that the Germans were in the process of establishing a front line facing eastward to cover a withdrawal through Coutances. Should they institute a full-scale withdrawal, they would inevitably try to pass through the Montpinchon–

[3] 3d Armd Div CCA AAR, Jul, and Warning Order, 19 Jul; 3d Armd Div FO 4, 19 Jul, FO 5, 20 Jul, and G–3 Per Rpt 34, 28 Jul.

[4] 3d Armd Div G–3 Per Rpt 33, 27 Jul.

Cerisy-la-Salle region and hold the commanding terrain. If CCA followed the original plan and passed through Cerisy-la-Salle in column, it would continue to move across the German front and be exposed to flanking fire. It might even get involved in an engagement at Cerisy-la-Salle or Montpinchon that might prevent the armor from reaching Coutances in time to block German withdrawal through that important road center. Thus, a quicker way to Coutances had to be found, but at the same time Cerisy-la-Salle and Montpinchon had to be seized and secured to deny the Germans dominating terrain, which in their hands would facilitate their escape from the Coutances area.

General Hickey's solution, which General Watson approved, was to start his turn westward toward Coutances at once and to move on a broad front. The leading task force was to turn west from Canisy, bypass Cerisy-la-Salle on the north, and drive to Montpinchon. The second task force in the CCA column was to continue to Cerisy-la-Salle and capture the high ground there. The last task force in the column was to assume the CCA main effort, swing westward from Carantilly, and head straight for Coutances. (See Map VI.)

Despite hopes for success, CCA was due for another day of disappointment on 28 July. Because of traffic congestion, the main effort from Carantilly did not get started until midafternoon. Even then terrain broken by hedgerows and small hills as well as a dearth of good roads slowed the advance markedly. Clearing isolated resistance, the task force in late afternoon reached a point about five miles west of Carantilly only

to run into a German pocket near Savigny, part of the same one that the 1st Division's 26th Infantry had encountered a few hundred yards to the north. Together, the 26th Infantry and CCA eliminated the pocket, but not until the following day.

In the meantime, the task forces moving on Cerisy-la-Salle and Montpinchon had made few gains. Troops of the *17th SS Panzer Grenadier Division* held the commanding terrain tenaciously and, from good positions on the hedgerowed slopes of both hills, refused to give way, even in the face of bombing and strafing by sixteen planes. The resistance at Cerisy-la-Salle and Montpinchon weakened only when night afforded the Germans concealment for withdrawal. The next day, 29 July, when the two task forces of CCA renewed their attacks, the opposition had virtually vanished. Moving together, the task forces continued with little difficulty to the north–south Coutances–Gavray highway.

Like the 1st Division, CCA had not crossed the Cotentin in time to ensnare the German forces. The Germans had escaped and thus had thwarted the original COBRA intent. The Americans were not sure whether their threat of encirclement had made the Germans pull out or whether the pressure of the VIII Corps had driven them out before the trap could be sprung.

The Pressure Force

As "the direct pressure force," VIII Corps was to tie down the Germans to prevent their disengagement and withdrawal before the completion of the VII Corps envelopment. While the VII

Corps was supposed to block the escape routes of the Germans opposing VIII Corps, VIII Corps was to cross the Lessay–Périers highway on a broad front, advance half way to Coutances (to the lateral highway from Geffosses through St. Sauveur-Lendelin to Marigny), and apply pressure to crush the trapped German forces.[5]

With four experienced infantry divisions, a recently arrived armored division, and a two-squadron cavalry group, and with nine battalions of corps artillery (five heavy and four medium) and a sufficient quantity of ammunition and supplies for a major operation, General Middleton planned to attack with his four infantry divisions abreast.[6] His difficulty was the terrain on the VIII Corps front.

Theoretically, the VIII Corps zone was a fifteen-mile portion of the Cotentin between the west coast and the Lozon River, but since the 330th Infantry of the 83d Division was attacking in conjunction with VII Corps, General Middleton's sector actually stopped at the Taute River. The troops of the VIII Corps facing south toward the Lessay–Périers–St. Lô highway held an irregularly shaped front of from one to five miles north of the highway The line followed the north banks of the Ay estuary and the Ay and Sèves Rivers and cut across the Carentan–Périers isthmus. (*See Map V.*)

On the coast, the 106th Cavalry Group looked toward the Ay estuary. The 79th Division was opposite the town of Lessay and faced the Ay River, which meanders across an open, swampy flood plain that offered the Germans superb fields of fire. The Germans had destroyed the only bridge across the Ay, the one to Lessay, and had mined the only good ford. Between the Ay and the Sèves, the 8th Division held a narrow front where hedgerows constituted natural defensive obstacles in depth. Along the Sèves, the 90th Division looked across a flood plain to the island of St. Germain, still held by the German forces that had turned back the division a week earlier. The 4th Armored Division occupied the western portion of the Carentan–Périers isthmus, and the 83d Division held the eastern part.

Two good highways lead south—one from Lessay, the other from Périers—and converge at Coutances. The terrain between these roads was in the 8th Division zone. Between the Ay and Sèves Rivers it was thick with hedgerows, though the least unfavorable on the corps front for offensive action. General Middleton chose to make his main effort there with the 8th Division, which was to attack frontally to the south and effect a penetration. The 79th Division was to follow through the gap, turn west to outflank the enemy positions south of the Ay, and seize Lessay. The 90th Division was to bypass the St. Germain area on both sides and advance on Périers, while the 83d Division was to attack southwest along the west bank of the Taute and eventually cross the river. When all four divisions were south of the Lessay–St. Lô highway, they were to move to the objective line, the Geffosses–St. Sauver-Lendelin–

---

[5] FUSA Outline Plan COBRA, 13 Jul; VIII Corps FO 8, 15 Jul, and G–3 Sec Msg, 20 Jul, 8th Div G–3 Jnl File.

[6] VIII Corps G–3 Per Rpt, 25 Jul, and Amendment 1 to FO 8, 15 Jul; Gen Bd Arty Rpt, App. C, Arty Support in Opn COBRA.

ENGINEERS CLEARING MINES IN LESSAY

Marigny road. The 4th Armored Division, pinched out by the advance, was to revert to First Army control.[7]

Early on the morning of 26 July the VIII Corps Artillery delivered twenty-five prearranged missions during a one-hour period, laid down counterbattery fires, and then prepared to fire on call. Though ground observation was limited, the small artillery planes assured effective support. Except in the 83d Division sector, where enemy shelling began immediately, German artillery remained silent for about two hours. As the 4th Armored Division helped by delivering supporting fires, the other divisions of the VIII Corps moved out.[8]

Attacking with two regiments abreast, General Stroh's 8th Division met strong small arms and mortar fire at once. The zone of advance was thick with anti-tank and antipersonnel mine fields, and German tanks contested the attack. By sideslipping and outflanking, by employing tanks and tank destroyers to enfilade hedgerow defenses, and by engaging enemy armor with bazookas and antitank grenades, the 28th Infantry, on the right (west), advanced more than a mile and by evening secured the high, wooded ground just north of the Lessay–Périers highway.[9]

The other assault regiment, the 121st Infantry, on the left (east), attacked along the axis of the main road to Périers. If the troops cleared the road for one mile, tanks could use a small bridge over the Sèves River. The stream was only a dozen feet wide and easily fordable, but it ran through such flat, marshy ground that a tank-crossing seemed a dubious proposition except at the bridge. During the regimental attack, two infantry battalion command posts received direct enemy artillery hits. At the height of the crisis German tanks appeared. A tank platoon, called forward to challenge the German tanks, lost one Sherman to a mine and two others to the mud of a marshy bog. Blocked in their advance, unable to cross the river, and without observation of the battlefield, the remaining tanks were unable to help. Taking heavy casualties from small arms and mortar fire, the infantry fell back.

The 90th Division meanwhile mounted a two-pronged attack designed

---

[7] VIII Corps FO 8, 15 Jul, and Annex 2 (Overlay), and G–3 Sec Memo, 18 Jul.

[8] Gen Bd Arty Rpt, App. C; VIII Corps AAR, Jul, and Amendment 1 to FO 8, 17 Jul; Arty Rpt, 26 Jul; 4th Armd Div G–3 Per Rpt 7, 24 Jul; Annex 4 (Arty) to 8th Div FO 4, 16 Jul.

[9] 709th Tk Bn and 28th Inf AAR's, Jul; 8th Div G–3 Jnl, 26 Jul.

to bypass and isolate the St. Germain area. On the right, a battalion of the 359th Infantry crossed the Sèves River in a rapid assault, traversed open, marshy ground, and overran a German trench dug along a fringe of woods. The momentum of the assault carried the battalion a hundred yards beyond the trench to a sunken road. As the soldiers climbed the road embankment to continue south, they met a burst of small arms and mortar fire. A German counterattack supported by tanks and artillery soon followed, driving the infantry out of the sunken road and back to the trench. There the battalion held. Bazooka fire, destroying one German tank, discouraged others from closing in. In the rear, part of the 358th Infantry began a demonstration by fire to distract enemy attention, and the division artillery placed smoke shells ahead of the assault battalion of the 359th. Engineers attempted to construct a ford across the stream for supporting tanks, but German artillery and tank fire barred the only approach route to the stream and prevented not only tanks but also infantry reinforcements from coming forward.

Four and a half miles to the east, the 357th Infantry, comprising the left prong of the 90th Division attack, entered the Carentan–Périers isthmus and tried to advance toward the southwest to make eventual contact above Périers with the main body of the division on the right. At the same time, the 329th and 331st Regiments of the 83d Division attacked along the west bank of the Taute River toward the southwest. Although the three committed regiments had at least twice the strength of the enemy forces that opposed them—in troops, tanks,

mortars, and artillery—and although the 83d Division alone fired more than 300 individual missions before noon, the committed regiments "didn't do a thing." They advanced no more than 200 yards. The Germans fought resourcefully from entrenched positions along hedgerows and sunken roads, using their mortars and few available tanks effectively and keeping their limited artillery active all day.[10]

American intelligence officers had earlier considered that the Germans facing the VIII Corps had two alternatives of equal plausibility. The Germans could, they judged, defend in place or make a strong pretense of defending while withdrawing to the high ground north of Coutances.[11] There seemed no question by the end of 26 July but that the Germans had chosen to take the former course of action. The VIII Corps had succeeded in making a small penetration to the Lessay–Périers highway, but in so doing its divisions had incurred more than 1,150 casualties while capturing less than 100 prisoners. Yet General Middleton was satisfied. His troops appeared to be tying down the enemy and holding him in place for the VII Corps encirclement.[12]

During the early evening of 26 July, General Middleton instructed his subordinate commanders to resume the attack the following morning. Several hours later, after receiving reports that the German opposition on other fronts seemed to be disintegrating and after

---

[10] Telecon, Middleton and Macon, 2100, 26 Jul, 83d Div G–2, G–3 Jnl and File; VIII Corps Arty Per Rpt, 26 Jul.

[11] VIII Corps G–2 Est 4, 15 Jul.

[12] Telecon, Middleton and Macon, 2100, 26 Jul, 83d Div G–2, G–3 Jnl and File.

learning that General Collins had ordered the VII Corps to continue the attack during the night, Middleton alerted his commanders to possible German withdrawal. He told all units to patrol vigorously. If a withdrawal were discovered in any sector, the unit in that sector was to attack at daylight, 27 July, in close pursuit.[13]

Patrols all along the front found not only extensive mine fields but also evidence that appeared to indicate that the enemy lines were being maintained in place. Rain and haze during the early morning hours of 27 July obscured visibility and made further investigation fruitless. On the premise that the Germans were still going to defend in strength, the units made careful, comprehensive attack plans.

Soon after the attack commenced, it became apparent that little more than a profusion of mine fields opposed the assault troops all across the corps front. Artillery preparations proved to have been a waste of ammunition. The 8th Division eliminated insignificant resistance and advanced more than a mile beyond the Lessay–Périers road. Two battalions of the 79th Division crossed the Ay River in single file, each man stepping carefully into the footsteps of the soldier ahead to avoid mines, and against slight harassing small arms fire took Lessay. Division engineers bridged the stream at the ford, and by the end of the day all three regiments were south of the river and abreast of the 8th Division. The 106th Cavalry Group crossed the Ay estuary that evening at low tide

and moved south to protect the coastal flank. The enemy had disengaged.[14]

In the 90th Division zone, after the enemy withdrawal was discovered, the division reconnaissance troop moved out ahead of the 359th Infantry in search of Germans. A destroyed Sèves River bridge on the main road to Périers delayed the advance until early afternoon and extensive mine fields on the roads slowed the leading troops by forcing them to proceed dismounted. By the middle of the afternoon, however, the reconnaissance unit was in the badly battered and deserted town of Périers.[15]

A mile south of Périers, on the highway to St. Sauveur-Lendelin, when troopers encountered a roadblock defended by infantry and tanks, members of the 359th Infantry, following the reconnaissance troop, moved against the opposition. Unable to bring antitank weapons and tank destroyers into range until evening because of mines, the regiment attacked shortly after nightfall, knocked out four German tanks, and then dug in for the night.

On the Carentan–Périers isthmus, the 357th Infantry had suspected an enemy withdrawal because German artillery had ceased early that morning, 27 July.[16] When the troops attacked, they found only mines hampering their advance. Late that evening the regiment crossed the Taute River, overwhelmed German delaying positions just north of the Périers–St. Lô highway, and dug in along the highway for the night. The 358th

---

[13] VIII Corps Fragmentary Orders, 1815 and 2050, 26 Jul, VIII Corps G–3 Jnl; Msg, 2130, 26 Jul, 8th Div G–3 Jnl.

[14] 79th Div AAR, Jul, FO 7, 19 Jul, and G–3 Jnl, 26 Jul; Wyche Diary; VIII Corps G–2 Per Rpt 43, 27 Jul.
[15] 8th Div G–3 Jnl, entry 1542, 27 Jul; VIII Corps Msg, 1415, 27 Jul, FUSA G–3 Jnl.
[16] 375th Inf Jnl, 27 Jul.

Infantry, after sending patrols into the St. Germain area and finding that the Germans had withdrawn, moved south to the vicinity of the Périers–St. Lô highway.

The 83d Division also advanced against light resistance and encountered many mines. Early in the afternoon of 27 July resistance vanished, and the division extended its control over the entire west bank of the Taute River in zone. Just before dark troops crossed the Taute and advanced almost a thousand yards into the Marchésieux and la Varde area.[17]

In possession of the Lessay Périers highway by the end of 27 July, the VIII Corps had made a significant gain, but had captured hardly more than 100 prisoners. The enemy had disengaged and moved behind a strong protective shell. Though small delaying forces and isolated pockets of resistance had hampered American pursuit, the biggest problem to the Americans had been mines—antitank and antipersonnel mines, Teller mines, Schu mines, mustard pot mines, box mines, and all types of booby traps rigged in buildings, hedgerows, ditches, fields, along the roads, and at road junctions and intersections. Behind this screen, the Germans had escaped the COBRA pressure force.[18]

After engineers laid a treadway bridge across the Ay at Lessay, the VIII Corps continued to advance on 28 July. The absence of opposition prompted General Bradley to revoke the original objective line—the Geffosses–St. Sauveur-Lende-

lin–Marigny highway—and to permit the troops to proceed beyond it.[19] The 79th and 8th Divisions met no resistance as they moved about ten and seven miles, respectively, to the vicinity of Coutances. The 90th and 83d Divisions proceeded to the proximity of the Coutances–St. Lô highway, where the 1st Division of the VII Corps lay athwart their zones of advance. The unopposed advance of the VIII Corps and the sense of victory that it engendered were somewhat empty achievements. The number of prisoners taken by all the divisions on 28 July, for example, was little more than 200.

Aided by the terrain, the weather, the darkness, the absence of Allied night fighter planes, and the extreme caution of American troops, who had come to respect the ability of the Germans to fight in the hedgerows, the German troops facing the VIII Corps had neatly slipped out of the trap set by COBRA. American commanders had begun to suspect an impending withdrawal and had noted evidence of it. Operations in the adjacent VII Corps sector had confirmed it. Plans had been changed to anticipate it.[20] Yet despite precaution, warning, and suspicion on the part of the Americans, the Germans gave them the slip.

The Germans, on the other hand, though they had escaped the VIII Corps pressure force and had avoided entrapment by the first and second thrusts of

---

[17] 83d Div G–3 Per Rpt 31, 27 Jul, and G–2, G–3 Jnl, 27 Jul.

[18] VIII Corps G–2 Per Rpt 43, 27 Jul, and G–3 Per Rpt 43, 28 Jul.

[19] VIII Corps Msg, 1515, 28 Jul; 83d Div G–2, G–3 Jnl, entry 1620, 28 Jul; ETOUSA Engr Hist Rpt 10, Combat Engineering, Aug 45, pp. 35, 36; Hosp Intervs, IV, GL–93 (317); XV Corps G–3 Memo, Conf at G–3 Office, Hq Third U.S. Army, 281600 Jul, 29 Jul, XV Corps G–3 Jnl and File.

[20] 79th Div and VIII Corps AAR's Jul; Wyche Diary.

the VII Corps toward Coutances, were not yet safe. They still had to reckon with a third thrust by the VII Corps.

COBRA Completed

The 2d Armored Division, commanded by General Brooks, had the mission of erecting a fence around Operation COBRA. With General Rose's CCA driving along the west bank of the Vire River toward the ultimate objective of Tessy-sur-Vire and with the remainder of the division driving southwestward from Canisy toward Bréhal, General Brooks was to set up a series of blocks along the Cérences–Tessy-sur-Vire line.[21] Although protective by motivation, the armored attack was exploitive by nature. By traversing the comparatively large distances involved, the armored units would arrive in the rear of the German defenses, contribute to enemy disorganization, and shield the VII Corps main effort westward to Coutances.

North of the Périers–St. Lô highway on 26 July and in position for commitment behind General Rose's CCA, CCB (Brig. Gen. Isaac D. White) was prepared to reinforce the CCA attack to the south or the 1st Division drive to Coutances. If neither action proved necessary, CCB was to execute its own planned role in COBRA by following CCA as far as Canisy and then turning to the southwest. With the aim of protecting the COBRA operation against a possible German counterthrust from the south, CCB was to set up blocking positions on the main road between Notre-Dame-de-Cenilly and Lengronne.

By the evening of 26 July, with the road to Canisy clear of CCA troops and COBRA giving cause for optimism, General Brooks made ready to commit CCB on the morning of 27 July in its originally planned role. Because the road network between the Périers–St. Lô highway and Canisy needed extensive repairs, division engineers worked through the night and during the morning to fill craters, remove wrecked vehicles, and construct bypasses. Shortly before noon, 27 July, CCB crossed the Périers–St. Lô highway. Three hours later, after having ruthlessly barred other units from the roads assigned to him, General White had his leading units through Canisy and headed southwest.[22]

At that time General White received a change in mission: "Move at once," General Brooks, the division commander, ordered, "on Cérences and Bréhal." The enemy forces facing the VIII Corps were withdrawing, and CCB was to cut off the withdrawal.[23] Instead of halting at Lengronne, at the Sienne River, in order to leave a coastal corridor for an VIII Corps advance beyond Coutances, CCB was to drive all the way to the Cotentin west coast. General Bradley's original COBRA maneuver had thus been reinstated. The primary concern of CCB was no longer to prevent German reinforcement from the south; the combat command attack had become the main thrust of the VII Corps pincer movement westward.[24] Inheriting the

---

[21] 2d Armd Div FO 3 (Rev 1), 20 Jul, and Annex 3 to FO 3, 18 Jul.

[22] 2d Armd Div G–3 Jnl, entries 1735, 26 Jul. 0859 and 1405, 27 Jul, and Msg, 0030, 27 Jul 30th Div G–3 Jnl and File.

[23] 2d Armd Div G–3 Jnl, entries 1454 and 1600, 27 Jul.

[24] Ltr, Collins to Hechler, 13 Nov 45, quoted in Hechler, VII Corps in Opn COBRA, p. 188.

mission earlier held by the 1st Division, General White was to speed his troops to the coast to intercept and trap the Germans withdrawing toward the south. The altered mission involved no change in route but rather an extension of the drive as originally planned. Speed became even more important. The combat command was to race an opponent who had a head start.

CCB was divided into two columns, but the absence of parallel roads made it necessary to advance the columns alternately.[25] The 82d Reconnaissance Battalion in the meantime sped forward ahead of the main body. Two miles southwest of Canisy, at Quibou, the reconnaissance troops struck an enemy roadblock. While they engaged the German force, the advance guard outflanked the resistance. A battery of the 78th Armored Field Artillery Battalion, traveling with the advance guard, took firing positions on the side of the road and opened fire on self-propelled guns and mortar emplacements half a mile distant. A flight of dive bombers performing armed-column cover struck an enemy-held ridge nearby. Before this smooth-working team, the German defense disintegrated.

Once more on the highway, reconnaissance troops raced through the hamlet of Dangy, unaware that Bayerlein, the division commander of *Panzer Lehr,* was conducting a staff meeting in one of the houses. Overrunning isolated opposition, the fast-moving reconnaissance battalion quickly covered the four miles to Pont-Brocard, a village where the highway crossed the Soulle River. Antitank and small arms fire from the village halted progress briefly, but the advance guard soon arrived, deployed, attacked, and seized Pont-Brocard. The advance continued.

Two hours after midnight, 27 July, the combat command without difficulty secured Notre-Dame-de-Cenilly, a village seven miles southwest of Canisy.

This swift advance during the afternoon and evening of 27 July illustrated more than anything else the penetration achieved by COBRA. There was nothing between the *LXXXIV* and *II Parachute Corps* to stop the American forces rolling through the Marigny–St. Gilles gap. Positions at Quibou had proved ineffective and illusory. Soon after American tanks at Dangy unknowingly passed within a few yards of a joint command post of the *275th Division* and *Panzer Lehr,* a shocked Bayerlein reported *Panzer Lehr* "finally annihilated." Units of the *275th Division* had been out of contact with headquarters during the entire afternoon and by evening were considered lost. Remnants of the *Lehr* and *275th Divisions* retired toward Pont-Brocard and Hambye, carrying with them miscellaneous troops in the area. Realizing the extent of the defeat, Bayerlein placed the blame on higher headquarters. "All calls for help have been ignored," he complained, "because no one [on the upper echelons] believed in the seriousness of the situation." [26] This was hindsight, of course, but the serious situation was about to become worse.

---

[25] The following account is based on [Pillsbury], 2d Armored Div in Opn COBRA, pp. 47–66; Hechler, VII Corps in Opn COBRA, pp. 187–216; 2d Armd Div AAR, Jul.

[26] Bayerlein's Est of the Situation, 2215, 27 Jul, *AGp B Op. Befehle;* see also Liddell Hart, *The Rommel Papers,* p. 490, and MS # A–973 (Schmidt) .

In place at Notre-Dame-de-Cenilly to begin its final drive to the Cotentin west coast, CCB of the 2d Armored Division received word of another change in mission. To prevent overextension, CCB, instead of pushing all the way to the coast, was to move only as far as Lengronne and set up blocking positions between that village and Notre-Dame-de-Cenilly. (*See Map VI.*)

To carry out his blocking mission, General White sought to seize the critical traffic control points that lay southwest of Notre-Dame-de-Cenilly and also the bridges across the Sienne River, which bounded his zone of operations on the south and on the west. All the important bridges across the Sienne were to have been destroyed by air bombardment before COBRA, but some had survived intact. To make certain that none provided escape exits for German units, General White planned to outpost those west of Hambye and prepare them for demolition.

Darting through surprised Germans manning hasty defensive positions, streaking past enemy antitank guns at 50 miles an hour, CCB reconnaissance troops on 28 July secured more than the required number of bridges. With the exception of one at Gavray, held by a strong German force that defied the troopers, detachments took the Sienne bridges on the south and outposted the three bridges north of Cérences. Dispersing the reconnaissance battalion to the limits of the combat command sector and beyond was a feat of daring in the best cavalry tradition.

Though the rapid thrust had revealed the absence of serious German opposition and had brought confusion and hopelessness to the few Germans encountered, General White still could not be sure whether he had arrived too late to spring the trap. Concerned not only with blocking the bridges but also with obstructing the important crossroads, he sent one of his main columns southwest from Notre-Dame-de-Cenilly. The troops mopped up isolated pockets of resistance—hastily assembled elements of the *353d Division* that occupied blocking positions between Notre-Dame-de-Cenilly and St. Denis-le-Gast—and detached small task forces to guard the significant road intersections. A reconnaissance troop outposted the final combat command objective, the Lengronne crossroads. A small task force (a company each of tanks and infantry, reinforced by engineers, medical personnel, and a tactical air control party) guarding the right flank was unable to halt several German tanks that crossed the front and moved south toward St. Denis-le-Gast and eventual escape, but it cut the Coutances–Gavray highway near Cambry, set up defensive positions, and waited for other German troops to appear.

Germans had already put in an appearance early that morning of 28 July near Pont-Brocard. On the right of the *17th SS Panzer Grenadier Division,* which had organized positions at Montpinchon and Cerisy-la-Salle, the regiment controlled by the *5th Parachute Division* was to have anchored the right (south) flank of the north–south line established by Choltitz to mask his withdrawal on the Cotentin west coast. The parachute regiment was nowhere in sight. In its place, a Panther battalion of the *2d SS Panzer Division* under the control of *Panzer Lehr* officers, small units of the

275th Division, and assorted stragglers found themselves trying to re-form a front at Pont-Brocard, where Americans had passed the previous evening.[27] Early on 28 July some of these German troops overran part of the 183d Field Artillery Battalion, a VII Corps Artillery unit supporting the 2d Armored Division from positions near Pont-Brocard. Fortunately, the Division Reserve (Col. Sidney R. Hinds) was on the road from Canisy, and it quickly restored American control in the Pont-Brocard–Notre-Dame-de-Cenilly area.

This and other evidence made it apparent on 28 July that a large German force was bottled up near Montpinchon and Roncey. CCB gradually turned its major attention to the north and northwest to contain it. The combat command, then, had not, after all, arrived too late.

On the German side, confusion in the *LXXXIV Corps* coastal sector on 28 July was appalling. Communications were virtually nonexistent. The corps headquarters had some contact with some divisions but could not exercise effective control. The regiment of the *2d SS Panzer Division* that was covering the withdrawal of the *91st Division* had no knowledge of how the withdrawal was proceeding, and the *91st* had no information about its covering force. Some withdrawing troops found to their discomfiture that the Americans that had crossed the Soulle River at Pont-Brocard were already behind them. Hausser was fired on by an American armored car near Gavray. Tychsen, the commander of the *2d SS Panzer Division,*

was killed close to his command post by an American patrol.[28]

Late in the afternoon of 28 July, when communications between the *LXXXIV Corps* and the *2d SS Panzer Division* ceased, Col. Friedrich von Criegern, the corps chief of staff, went forward to make personal contact with the division. He found that Lt. Col. Otto Baum, the commander of the *17th SS Panzer Grenadier Division,* had also assumed command of the *2d SS Panzer Division* upon Tychsen's death. Baum and Criegern together concluded that American troops had probably already reached the Cotentin west coast and had thereby encircled the German forces still in the Coutances region. They agreed that an immediate withdrawal to the south was in order. They planned to gather all the troops they could find into an all-around defensive cordon, then make a strong attack southward to reach the ground below the Bréhal–Hambye road. While Baum busied himself with the preparations for this course of action, Criegern rushed back to inform Choltitz.[29]

Choltitz had just received an order from Hausser to break out of the Coutances region by attacking not to the south toward Bréhal but to the southeast toward Percy. Hausser wanted to get those forces that broke out of the American encirclement to join troops that Kluge was assembling east of the Vire River for a counterattack west of the

---

[27] MS # A–984 (Mahlmann).

[28] Telecons, Pemsel and Tempelhoff, 0845, 28 Jul, Helmdach and Tempelhoff, 1555, 28 Jul, and Hoehne and Zimmerman, 1030, 28 Jul, in *AGp B KTB;* MS # A–984 (Mahlmann); MS # B–839 (Heydte); MS # P–195 (Wisliceny).

[29] Choltitz, *Soldat Unter Soldaten,* p. 209; *17th SS Engr Bn KTB,* 28 Jul; MS # P–159 (Stueckler); Sitrep, 29 Jul, in *AGp B Tagesmeldungen.*

Vire to seal off the COBRA penetration. A good meeting point for the two forces moving toward each other, Hausser figured, would be Percy. Choltitz protested that an attack southeast from Coutances would leave only weak forces to anchor the entire Normandy front on the Cotentin west coast. But Hausser insisted, and Choltitz complied. He transmitted the order forward—the troops that were virtually encircled south of Coutances were to attack to the southeast, and not to withdraw to the south.[30]

Hausser of course notified Kluge of the instructions he had issued through Choltitz, and when Kluge learned that Hausser had virtually stripped his coastal positions and thereby jeopardized the entire Normandy defenses by inviting American encirclement of the German left flank, he nearly became violent. He told Hausser to send an officer courier to Choltitz at once to cancel the order for the southeastward attack to Percy. Instead, Choltitz was to mount a holding attack to enable the main LXXXIV Corps body to escape south along the coast. The withdrawal was to be made under the protection of outposts that were to hold positions along the north–south railroad between Coutances and Cérences. Meanwhile, a counterattack, to be launched now by two fresh panzer divisions, would strike westward across the Vire toward Percy to act as a diversion for the withdrawal. Once south of Cérences, the LXXXIV Corps was to occupy a new ten-mile-long main line of resistance from Bréhal through St. Denis-le-Gast to Gavray.[31]

Kluge's instructions did not reach the LXXXIV Corps units. Unable to phone Choltitz, Hausser transmitted a message to the corps rear command post. There, the corps quartermaster took a bicycle and rode forward to give the message to Choltitz. He arrived about midnight of 28 July. Without communications to subordinate units and therefore lacking control of their operations, Choltitz did nothing. Satisfied that the units under the control of the 91st Division were withdrawing south along the coast, he allowed the rest of the situation to develop as it would. The corps headquarters moved to the south and escaped intact. Meanwhile, the other units along the coast prepared to attack southeast in compliance with Hausser's original order. The effect would be to storm the blocking positions that the 2d Armored Division had stretched across the Cotentin.

The American commanders, Generals Brooks and White, guessing that the Germans would try to break out during the night of 28 July, called in their dispersed and exposed detachments late in the afternoon. Reinforced by the Division Reserve and by an infantry battalion of the 4th Division that came into Notre-Dame-de-Cenilly that evening, the armored troops took strong defensive positions along a seven-mile line between Pont-Brocard and St. Denis-le-Gast, alert to the possibility that the Germans might try to break out from the Montpinchon–Roncey area to safety.

Meanwhile, Hausser's original order transmitted by Choltitz had brought dis-

---

[30] Choltitz, *Soldat Unter Soldaten*, p. 208; see MS # B–179 (Hausser).

[31] Telecons, Kluge and Hausser, 2000 and 2130, 28 Jul, and Pemsel and Tempelhoff, 2000, 28 Jul,

---

AGp B KTB; see MS # B–179 (Hausser) for a candid account of the command confusion and the conflicting orders.

may to Baum. Baum had been proceeding on the assumption (made by him and Criegern) that he could easily get the two divisions under his control—the *2d SS Panzer* and the *17th SS Panzer Grenadier*—to safety by way of a southern exit. He had become even more confident when he learned that the 2d Armored Division had pulled in its troops to St. Denis-le-Gast, thereby leaving open a ten-mile-wide corridor between that village and the coast. Furthermore, Baum had already pulled his units back from the eastern edge of the pocket, and he no longer had a firm hold on the area northwest of Notre-Dame-de-Cenilly. Without that sector as an assembly area, he could not launch an attack to the southeast through Notre-Dame-de-Cenilly to Percy. Baum compromised. He withdrew southward across the Sienne River, then turned eastward to Percy and thereby achieved the desired result by different means.

The other German troops north of Cérences that were covering the *LXXXIV Corps* withdrawal drifted south in the meantime and gathered near Roncey to attempt to break out to the southeast. The main components of this force that could be identified included parts of the *2d SS Panzer Division* and the *17th SS Engineer Battalion*, most of the *6th Parachute Regiment*, and what remained of the *17th SS Panzer Grenadier Division*. By striking toward Hambye and Percy, these and other troops were to demonstrate that the defensive efforts on the part of the 2d Armored Division had not been wasted.

Shortly before dawn, 29 July, about thirty enemy tanks and vehicles, led by an 88-mm. self-propelled gun, approached a crossroads about three miles southwest of Notre-Dame-de-Cenilly, where a company of armored infantry and a company of tanks were deployed. German infantrymen crawled along the ditches on both sides of the road as half a dozen enemy tanks and armored vehicles assaulted frontally to force open an escape route. The self-propelled gun in the lead overran the American defensive line and was about to make a breakthrough when rifle shots killed the driver and gunner. With the gun carriage blocking the road, individual American and German soldiers battled for the crossroads until daybreak, when the Germans withdrew, leaving 17 dead and 150 wounded. The motor of the undamaged self-propelled gun carriage was still running, the gun still loaded. The Americans sustained less than 50 casualties and lost a tank and a half-track.[32]

About the same time, not far away, about fifteen German tanks and several hundred troops overran an outpost manned by a company of the recently arrived battalion of the 4th Division. The American company commander was killed at once and the infantrymen fell back half a mile into the positions of the 78th Armored Field Artillery Battalion. Two artillery batteries in direct fire, a third in indirect fire, and four guns of the 702d Tank Destroyer Battalion held off the Germans for thirty minutes until nearby armored infantrymen arrived to re-establish the outpost line. They found seven destroyed Mark IV tanks and counted more than 125 enemy dead. Some Germans had

---

[32] S. Sgt. James J. Cermak of the 41st Armored Infantry Regiment was awarded the DSC for heroism.

WRECKED GERMAN ARMOR BULLDOZED OFF A ROAD NEAR RONCEY

escaped in these two actions. Others escaped by filtering through American lines in small groups. In general, however, the CCB cordon proved effective. Troops all along the line had collected enemy stragglers and demoralized remnants of small German units.

Quite certain that Allied fighter-bombers would prevent a German escape in strength during daylight, General White again pushed his defensive line to Lengronne on the morning of 29 July. He re-established the roadblocks at intersections and sent outposts to the Sienne River bridges. General Brooks moved the Division Reserve to St. Denis-le-Gast to keep an eye on German movements south of the Sienne River. Though the Germans maintained their control over the bridge at Gavray, elsewhere only small enemy groups offered half-hearted resistance.

German hopes for an eventual concerted breakout attempt were largely destroyed on 29 July by Allied tactical aircraft. The destruction that occurred went far beyond Allied anticipation. On the afternoon of 29 July pilots of the IX Tactical Air Command discovered a "fighter-bomber's paradise" in the Roncey area—a mass of German traffic, stationary, bumper to bumper, and "triple banked." Pilots estimated at least 500 vehicles jammed around Roncey, and for six hours that afternoon the planes attacked what became known as the Roncey pocket. As squadrons of fighter-bombers rotated over the target, American artillery, tanks, and tank destroyers pumped shells into the mélange. More than 100 tanks and over 250 vehicles were later found in various stages of wreckage, other vehicles had been abandoned intact. Though American intelligence officers guessed that a fuel shortage had caused the Germans to abandon their equipment, the fact was that the Germans had fled on foot in the hope of escaping the devastating fire rained down upon them.[33]

By the evening of 29 July, the 2d Armored Division (less CCA) was the only unit still actively engaged in Operation COBRA. General Bradley had initiated a new attack but the mission of eradicating the isolated German forces trapped in the Cotentin remained with General Brooks. His method was to erect a cage and let the Germans beat against the bars. The armored division was to hold its defensive lines and destroy the survivors of the Roncey disaster who surely would again attempt to escape during the night of 29 July.

As expected, German groups struck the armored defensive line at various points during the night. Some fought desperately to break through, others battled half-heartedly, still others surrendered after a cursory exploration that satisfied the requirements of honor. In the last category belonged the 150 Germans who stumbled into the bivouac area of the 62d Armored Field Artillery Battalion near Lengronne and gave themselves up after a short engagement.

At least two skirmishes reached the proportion of minor battles. The first occurred shortly before midnight, 29 July. As German forces launched a demonstration and a diversionary attack from the vicinity of Gavray with rockets and flares and with a small infantry-tank task force that engaged American outposts near St. Denis-le-Gast, two columns descended from the Roncey pocket and smashed against St. Denis-le-Gast from the north. About a thousand men and nearly a hundred armored vehicles in a well-organized attack penetrated the American line. A Mark V poked its gun through a hedgerow, destroyed the command half-track of a U.S. tank battalion, and set vehicles at the command post ablaze. Disorganized, the Americans fell back, relinquishing St. Denis-le-Gast. Had the Germans been interested in exploiting their success, they might have thoroughly disrupted the defensive cordon. Instead, they wanted only to flee south. Once the spearhead had pierced the American lines, it was every man for himself. The U.S. troops rallied, and an intense, confused battle took place at close range.[34] In the morning the Americans again had a firm hold on St. Denis-le-Gast and its road intersection. They had killed 130 Germans, wounded 124, taken over 500 prisoners, and destroyed at least 25 vehicles, of which 7 were tanks. American losses were almost 100 men and 12 vehicles.

Eleven vehicles of the German force

---

[33] *AAF III*, 242; VII Corps AAR, Jul; First U.S. Army, *Report of Operations*, I, 107; FUSA G-2 Per Rpt 50, 30 Jul.

[34] Lt. Col. Wilson D. Coleman of the 41st Armored Infantry, who was killed while rallying his troops, and S. Sgt. William B. Kolosky of the Division Reserve headquarters, who organized and led a group of heterogeneous headquarters personnel in a defensive position, were awarded the DSC.

that had attacked St. Denis-le-Gast got through the village, but instead of driving south they moved westward toward Lengronne, toward the bivouac of the 78th Armored Field Artillery Battalion. Earlier that night U.S. artillerymen manning guard posts around their howitzers had killed or captured individual soldiers and small groups of men, but the small German column entered the American lines undetected. Moving rapidly, the column passed an antitank gun guarding the road. Perhaps the sentries assumed that the vehicles were American, perhaps they were too startled to open fire. Well inside the artillery bivouac area, an American officer stopped the column and challenged the driver of the lead truck. *"Was ist?"* came the surprised and surprising reply. Mutual astonishment quickly vanished and the battle commenced. Machine guns chattered. Howitzers at pointblank range, some from distances of less than a hundred yards, opened fire. A tank destroyer crew at the side of the road making emergency motor repairs began to fire 3-inch shells into the rear of the German column. With the leading and rear vehicles of the column destroyed, the Germans tried to flee on foot. Silhouetted by the flames of burning vehicles, they made excellent targets for the small arms of the artillerymen. The battle was short. In the morning, the artillerymen counted 90 enemy dead, over 200 prisoners, and all 11 vehicles destroyed. The Americans had lost 5 killed and 6 wounded.[35]

---

[35] Among those killed was Capt. Naubert O. Simard, Jr., who manned an exposed machine gun though he knew that to do so was certain death. Captain Simard was posthumously awarded the DSC.

At the same time the small task force that had established an outpost on the Coutances–Gavray road near Cambry finally saw action after two days of patient waiting. Shortly after midnight, 29 July, about 2,500 Germans made an organized break for safety. The point of the German attack overran a tank roadblock and threatened to crush the entire outpost force. Sgt. Hulon B. Whittington, of the 41st Armored Infantry, jumped on an American tank, shouted through the turret to direct its crew, and maneuvered it through enemy bullets to a place where its point-blank fire destroyed the momentum of the German attack.[36]

Its attack stalled, the German force fell apart. Some panic-stricken Germans fled or surrendered, others battled at close range near burning vehicles. U.S. artillery battalions gave excellent supporting fires without prior registration and without clearance from the division artillery. As a result of the six-hour engagement, 450 Germans were killed, 1,000 taken prisoner, and about 100 vehicles of all types destroyed. American losses were about 50 killed and 60 wounded.

As day broke on 30 July, hundreds of destroyed vehicles and wagons, innumerable dead horses, and the miscellaneous wreckage of defeat lay scattered over the countryside, grim testimony to the extent of the debacle that the Germans had suffered in the Cotentin. The 2d Armored Division alone had killed an estimated 1,500 enemy and captured about 4,000, while losing not quite 100 dead and less than 300 wounded. CCB,

---

[36] Sgt. Whittington received the Medal of Honor.

General Collins felt, had done "a magnificent job." [37]

The fact that the action was over by 30 July became apparent as reconnaissance troops combing the region rounded up 250 prisoners and killed nearly 100 other Germans still trying to escape. Shortly before noon, a group of 100 enemy soldiers walked into a command post of the armored division and surrendered.

Thus ended Operation COBRA on the Cotentin west coast in a final action not unlike the last twitch of a lifeless snake. Even as COBRA was expiring, the battle was passing beyond the limits contemplated for the action. With the Germans reduced to impotence, the offensive was becoming quite different from the original conception.

Despite German losses in the Cotentin, a rather large force escaped in the confusion. Among the units that fought or fled to safety were a battalion of Mark IV tanks of the *2d SS Panzer Division,* and sizable contingents of the *17th SS Engineer Battalion,* the *6th Parachute Regiment,* and the *17th SS Panzer Grenadier Division.* Many individual soldiers had also reached refuge. Quite a few who had abandoned their vehicles in the congested mass of traffic around Roncey and left them to Allied air force bombardment organized themselves into haphazard command groups, some effective, some not, and made their way south. Though a sufficient number of troops gathered to man a line from Percy westward to the sea, the difficulty was that the men were exhausted. As they attempted to establish a defense they fumbled about in various stages of wakefulness. One unit commander, von der Heydte, brought his *6th Parachute Regiment* into a concealed bivouac and there, hidden from Americans and Germans alike, permitted his men to sleep for twenty-four hours before reporting his location to higher headquarters. [38]

From Gavray west to the sea the front was held largely by remnants gathered under the banner of the *91st Division.* Although these forces had had a relatively easy time in withdrawing south along the coast, they had nevertheless been bombed and strafed and had lost troops, equipment, and supplies. Unable to form a continuous, strong, or stable line of defense, they were destined to be overrun in the midafternoon of 30 July.

Learning that little existed to oppose an American sweep down the Cotentin west coast, the German naval coast artillery battery in Granville destroyed its guns and retreated toward Avranches. By nightfall, 30 July, headquarters of the *LXXXIV Corps* and the advance command post of the *Seventh Army* were behind American lines. The only contact that *Army Group B* had with the combat troops along the Cotentin west coast was that maintained by the crew of a telephone relay station in Avranches, at the base of the Cotentin. Just before dark on 30 July, the signal crew reported the approach of U.S. troops. [39]

[37] Ltr, Collins to Hechler, quoted in Hechler, VII Corps in Opn COBRA, p. 216; [Pillsbury], 2d Armored Div in Opn COBRA, p. 85; VII Corps AAR, Jul.

[38] MS # P-159 (Heydte).
[39] *AGp B KTB,* 30 Jul.

CHAPTER XV

Exploiting the Breach

Strictly considered, Operation COBRA lasted only three days. By evening of 27 July, the situation had so evolved that General Bradley could conclude that a successful penetration of the enemy defenses had been achieved. He consequently issued oral instructions that were embodied in a field order distributed on the following day.[1] While the 2d Armored Division (less CCA) completed its COBRA mission in action that continued through 30 July, the other units of the First Army carried out the new orders to exploit the COBRA results.

The forces east of the Vire River that were to have assignments in the exploitation had performed a subsidiary role in COBRA. Their activity, essentially an act of diversion, had influenced General Bradley's decision on how to direct the offensive growing out of the COBRA breakthrough.

The COBRA Diversion

The diversion east of the Vire River was predicated upon a desire to pin down enemy troops and prevent their dispatch westward across the river against the main forces in Operation COBRA. Exactly how this was to be accomplished General Bradley had left rather vague

while awaiting developments in the main attack. Thus the commanders of the two corps east of the Vire, Generals Corlett and Gerow, had to plan their operations on the basis of several contingencies and in the face of a number of question marks.

General Corlett was to be prepared either to displace his XIX Corps to the west bank of the Vire and assume a portion of the VII Corps zone for a drive south or to remain east of the Vire for a drive south along that side of the river. Until Bradley decided which move was to be made, the XIX Corps was to give fire support to the VII Corps.[2]

The future of General Gerow's V Corps was even less definite. Though V Corps was to attack on 26 July, General Bradley had designated no objectives. Nor could General Gerow count on a firm commitment from the forces on his flanks. If XIX Corps, on his right, displaced to a new zone west of the Vire, Gerow would have to extend his responsibility westward to the river. If the British, who were to his left and whose intentions were uncertain, did not advance, V Corps, by attacking, might expose its own left flank. (*See Map V.*)

The V Corps front formed a curved line about fifteen miles long, with the

[1] FUSA FO 2, 28 Jul; see FUSA Msg, 1100, 28 Jul, FUSA G–3 Jnl.

[2] XIX Corps Ltr of Instr 3, 20 Jul.

right flank on Hill 192, the center at Bérigny, and the left near Caumont. Early V Corps planning for Cobra had projected an advance of about ten miles across the entire front, but in final planning General Gerow directed instead a limited objective attack. Designed to move the corps forward about three miles, the attack was to tie down Germans east of the Vire; retain a measure of flexibility necessary for adjusting to the developing Cobra operation; and eliminate a German salient between St. Lô and Caumont that threatened American possession of St. Lô, denied desirable lateral routes of communications (particularly the St. Lô–Caumont highway), and lengthened the V Corps front.[3]

In the *bocage* east of the Vire River, irregular hills covered by hedgerowed fields formed broken ridge lines and raised barriers against an advance toward the south. In this terrain south of the St. Lô–Bérigny highway and west of the Bérigny–Caumont road, the Germans had excellent defensive positions on commanding ground. On the first ridge south of St. Lô—commonly called Hill 101—the Germans had kept XIX Corps from moving beyond St. Lô; in fact a strong counterreconnaissance screen had denied accurate knowledge of German strength and dispositions. On the second ridge—higher ground between the villages of Ste. Suzanne-sur-Vire and St.

Jean-des-Baisants—the enemy had excellent observation and supplementary defensive positions.

The goal of General Gerow's limited objective attack was the St. Jean-des-Baisants ridge. Its capture would threaten to encircle the Germans on Hill 101 and thereby remove an obstacle hampering the XIX Corps. Once in possession of the St. Jean-des-Baisants ridge, General Gerow could either continue his attack to the south or take advantage of the terrain compartment and move southwest along the ridge line to Ste. Suzanne-sur-Vire and the Vire River. The latter maneuver would encircle the Germans on Hill 101.

General Gerow wanted to drive down the St. Jean-des-Baisants ridge. The maneuver he hoped to execute resembled, in miniature, the main Cobra operation west of the Vire. In the same way that the VII Corps veered to the Cotentin west coast, the V Corps would attack southwestward to the Vire River. Like the VIII Corps, the XIX Corps would act as a holding force. In the same manner that a successful VII Corps envelopment might block subsequent VIII Corps progress along the west coast of the Cotentin, a V Corps drive to the Vire would obstruct an immediate XIX Corps advance. If Cobra west of the Vire made possible an exploitation along the west bank of the Vire, the V Corps envelopment to the Vire would pinch out the XIX Corps and permit its displacement to make the main exploitation. The logic appeared unimpeachable, the opportunity tempting. The boundary between the XIX and the V Corps, tentatively drawn, ran southwest to the Vire River, indicating that the

---

[3] V Corps FO's 12 and 13, 16 and 21 Jul; *V Corps Operations in the ETO*, pp. 113ff; see S. Sgt. Jose M. Topete, Maj. Franklin Ferriss, and Lt. Hollis Alpert, Operations of V Corps, 26 July–15 August (hereafter cited Topete *et al.*, Opns of V Corps), a preliminary MS, Hist Div, USFET, 1946, OCMH Files.

XIX Corps was to be pinched out near Ste. Suzanne-sur-Vire.[4]

General Gerow controlled two infantry divisions. On the right he had an experienced division, the 2d, under General Robertson. The 5th Division on the left, commanded by Maj. Gen. S. LeRoy Irwin, had recently arrived in Normandy and had freed the 1st Division for the main COBRA attack. Together, the divisions on the V Corps front easily outnumbered the Germans they faced. Twenty battalions of artillery were in support, and two tank destroyer battalions were tied in with the corps fire direction center. The relative inactivity of the V Corps before the start of COBRA had enabled adequate stockpiling of ammunition.[5]

Several days before COBRA, in compliance with arrangements made by Generals Montgomery and Bradley, the boundary separating the V Corps and the Second British Army was moved to the west, giving the British responsibility for Caumont and reducing the 5th Division zone to regimental frontage. General Gerow planned to attack with the four regiments already on line, the three of the 2d Division and one of the 5th. Because the corps zone was divided into almost equal sectors by wooded and swampy lowland that separated the interior regiments, Gerow projected two simultaneous two-regiment efforts that would converge on the St. Jean-des-

Baisants ridge. He expected to be in possession of the crest of the ridge in two days, after which he planned to send the 5th Division southwest to the Vire River, to St. Suzanne-sur-Vire.[6]

Shortly after dawn on 26 July, 192 American and 44 British guns fired a twenty-minute artillery preparation to open the attack east of the Vire River. This was the precursor of a heavy artillery effort that by the end of the first day was to consume half the ammunition allocated to the V Corps for a five-day period.[7]

Concerned that two weeks of relative inactivity in this sector had enabled the enemy to prepare extensive defensive positions in considerable depth, the 2d Division commander, General Robertson, had developed novel tactics for his attack. Tanks equipped with hedgecutters and protected by time-fuzed artillery fire advanced buttoned up and without infantry support for several hundred yards to breach a few hedgerows in depth across the front. Achieving surprise and taking no losses from enemy fire, the tankers returned after twenty minutes to the line of departure to pick up infantry support. Together the tanks and infantry moved quickly through the gaps in the hedgerows before the Germans could re-establish their positions.[8]

With the help of these tactics, two of the 2d Division's three regiments made

---

[4] V Corps AAR, Jul, Ltr of Instrs to the 5th Div, 24 Jul, FO 13, 21 Jul, Ltr of Instrs supplementing FO 12, 24 Jul, and G–3 Situation Map, 2030, 25 Jul; Memo, Maj Gen S. LeRoy Irwin to Gen Gerow, 23 Jul, V Corps G–3 Jnl.

[5] FUSA Ltr, Relief of 1st Div by 5th Inf Div, 11 Jul, and Msgs, FUSA G–3 Jnl, 12–14 Jul; V Corps History, p. 124; Gen Bd Arty Rpt, App. C; V Corps Ord Sec Rpt, V Corps AAR, Jul.

[6] Observations of the Div Comdr During Jul, 2d Div AAR, Jul; 2d Div FO 6, 19 Jul; 5th Div FO 2, 17 Jul, and FO 3, 22 Jul; V Corps Ltr of Instrs to 5th Div, 24 Jul.

[7] V Corps History, p. 121; Gen Bd Arty Rpt, App. C; V Corps Ord Sec Rpt, V Corps AAR, Jul.

[8] 9th Inf AAR, Jul; Observations of the Div Comdr During Jul, 2d Div AAR, Jul; 741st Tk Bn AAR, Jul.

notable advances. On the division left, the 9th Infantry used twenty-five .50-caliber machine guns previously emplaced on high ground to deliver flanking fire across the regimental front and advanced steadily for almost two miles. Against artillery, mortar, and slight small-arms fire, the regiment nearly reached the St. Lô–Caumont highway. Comprising one half of the corps right flank pincer force, the 23d Infantry gained almost a mile and reached a lateral country road. There, German artillery and high-velocity weapons placed flanking fire on the road and prevented a crossing in strength. The fire also made it difficult to evacuate casualties and bring up supplies. On the division right, where the 38th Infantry composed the other half of the pincer force, a comparable advance was made except on the extreme right. Stanch resistance and an increasingly exposed right flank forced a halt.[9]

Employing artillery fire to good advantage, the only regiment of the 5th Division to attack, the 2d Infantry, also made a quick initial gain of about a thousand yards. It was making a flanking approach to the St. Jean-des-Baisants ridge when intense and accurate German fire caused considerable disorganization. Nevertheless, by committing all three battalions judiciously, the regimental commander, Col. A. Worrell Roffe, was able to keep the attack going

another 1,500 yards. Cutting the St. Lô–Caumont highway, the regiment made a total advance of two miles.[10]

By the end of the first day, the units of the V Corps had taken about 300 prisoners and advanced half way to the St. Jean-des-Baisants ridge. The drive cost nearly a thousand casualties, chiefly from artillery fire.[11] The assault troops had broken through the crust of the German defenses, though they had been unable to exploit local penetrations because of the terrain, the wide frontages, and, in the case of the 2d Infantry Regiment, a certain amount of disorganization within the battalions.[12] The V Corps clearly appeared to be accomplishing its main mission of containing some of the German forces and preventing them from bringing their strength to bear on the main development of COBRA west of the Vire River.

Resuming the attack on 27 July, V Corps advanced but did not reach its objective. The two regiments of the 2d Division, comprising the right arm of the corps pincer movement, gained about a thousand yards against resistance that was appreciably less deter-

---

[9] S. Sgt. Edward V. Maloney of the 38th Cavalry Reconnaissance Squadron, who though mortally wounded continued to fire the guns of his tank to cover the defensive preparations of his unit, was posthumously awarded the DSC. Pfc. Clifford L. Curry of the same unit walked through fire on the battlefield to rescue a wounded soldier. All fire "ceased in salute" as he carried the wounded man back to safety. He was awarded the DSC.

[10] The intensity of the combat may be judged from the fact that five soldiers of the 5th Division were awarded the DSC, two posthumously: Pfc. Milo J. Flynn, Pfc. Amijan O. Lazar, Pvt. Jack Gill, S. Sgt. Richard F. Heinzelman, and T. Sgt. Lloyd N. Peterson.

[11] V Corps G–2 Per Rpts, 26 and 27 Jul. Losses for the 2d Infantry were officially placed at 147, a low figure produced in compliance with a First Army order that estimates of men missing in action were to be "no higher than absolutely necessary." (5th Div G–1 Jnl, 26 Jul.) To equate its reported figures and its actual losses, the division reported higher losses during the succeeding days. General Irwin, Personal Diary; see also Topete et al., Opns of V Corps, p. 25.

[12] Observations of the Div Comdr During Jul, 2d Div AAR, Jul; Comments, 5th Div AAR, Jul.

mined than on 26 July. The regiments on the left were hampered by continuing disorganization and nervousness among 5th Division units, still new in battle. Neither regiment advanced. At the end of the day, V Corps was still more than a mile short of the crest of the St. Jean-des-Baisants ridge. The real achievement was the contact made by the two interior regiments on the corps front. After bypassing the wooded swampy lowland that separated them, the regiments had turned inward and eliminated what had been the Bérigny salient.[13]

Denied the ridge he wanted, General Gerow changed his plans around midday, 27 July. Dividing the corps zone equally between the 2d and 5th Divisions, he alerted both to the possibility that either or both might be designated to make the attack southwestward to the Vire.[14] The reapportionment of frontage acknowledged the strong resistance in terrain favorable for defense. It also was a precautionary measure predicated upon readying the corps to absorb another division, the 35th.

A possibility that the 35th Division soon might pass to V Corps had become strong on the morning of 27 July when indications developed that the XIX Corps might displace west of the Vire River. Since the 35th was the only division of XIX Corps actually in the line, it might be left behind when the corps moved.

Earlier, the XIX Corps had executed its COBRA mission by placing strong artillery fire on the ridges south of St. Lô.

On 27 July the commander of the 35th Division, General Baade, came to the conclusion that the Germans were withdrawing primarily because of American gains west of the Vire. Deciding that an advance was in order, Baade secured the corps commander's permission to attack during the afternoon to secure Hill 101, the ridge immediately south of St. Lô. As events developed, the attack was well timed. The Germans had begun to withdraw during the morning, and the 35th Division took Hill 101 against no more than light resistance. Several Vire River bridge sites southwest of St. Lô fell in the process.[15]

On the evening of 27 July, a telephone call from First Army headquarters to General Corlett acknowledged the changing situation brought about by COBRA. General Bradley had decided to displace the XIX Corps west of the Vire River. As Gerow had anticipated, Bradley attached the 35th Division to the V Corps and extended Gerow's responsibility westward to the Vire.

COBRA had ended, and a new operation was about to begin.

The Post-COBRA Plan

In the COBRA plan, General Bradley had not tried to forecast how the operation might end. Instead, he was prepared to choose his course of action from the actual COBRA results. He could halt the offensive and consolidate his forces or continue his attack to exploit a breakthrough. By the evening of 27 July it

---

[13] 2d Div G-3 Jnl, 27 Jul, and G-3 Per Rpt, 27 Jul; V Corps G-2 Per Rpt, 27 Jul.

[14] V Corps FO 14, 27 Jul; Gerow Memo, 27 Jul, V Corps G-3 Jnl.

[15] 35th Div AAR, Jul, FO 8, 27 Jul, G-3 Jnl, 27 Jul, G-3 Per Rpt, 27 Jul; XIX Corps Ltr of Instr 3, 20 Jul.

was apparent that the success of COBRA warranted a continuation of the attack, and Bradley decided to exploit his gains and broaden and extend his effort.

Specifically, the enemy withdrawal along the west coast of the Cotentin on 27 July—later judged the decisive consequence of COBRA—seemed to offer an opportunity to hasten the withdrawal and turn it into a rout.[16] The fact that the opposition east of Coutances was so strong appeared particularly significant—the forces there were obviously trying "to hold open the door of retreat for the *LXXXIV Corps*." Even the Luftwaffe put in an appearance—a total of thirty planes made eight daylight and sixteen night raids.[17] The Germans had realized the danger of becoming isolated on the Cotentin west coast and had attempted to escape encirclement by withdrawing. "To say that . . . [we are] riding high tonight is putting it mildly," General Bradley wrote General Eisenhower. "Things on our front really look good."[18]

As judged by American intelligence officers—whose gratification over the COBRA results led to some optimistic exaggeration—the Germans in the Cotentin were in flight by 27 July. The only hope the Germans could have of stemming their retreat was to gain refuge behind the Sée River at Avranches. The "bits and pieces," the "shattered remnants," and the "battered portions" of the units in the Cotentin were hardly in shape to make a stand unless fresh troops came forward to reinforce them, and no fresh troops seemed available.

Thus the German course of action would probably be an attempt to erect a hasty defensive line between Avranches and the town of Vire, a line along the south bank of the Sée River and the high ground south of Villedieu-les-Poëles and St. Sever-Calvados. The possibility was also present that the Germans might counterattack from the east with two panzer divisions, but this hardly seemed likely at the moment. The significant conclusion was that "destruction of *LXXXIV Corps* is believed at hand, and the destruction of *II Parachute Corps* is an immediate possibility."[19]

To give the enemy "no time to regroup and reorganize his forces," General Bradley ordered his subordinate commanders to "maintain unrelenting pressure" on the Germans.[20] His great reliance on the judgment of his corps commanders, as well as the fluidity of the situation, led him to formulate his instructions in rather general terms.[21]

There was no need for specifics. Two immediate tasks lay ahead. The German forces still north of Coutances had to be destroyed, those retreating to the south had to be pursued. Difficulties were apparent.

On the Cotentin west coast, where German disorganization seemed greatest, the VII and VIII Corps still had to complete their COBRA mission of eliminating the German forces trapped near Coutances. At the same time, the VII Corps, which had veered westward toward the coast, now had to turn south. Futhermore, VII Corps threatened to cause confusion by intermingling with VIII

---

[16] First U.S. Army, *Report of Operations*, I, 102.
[17] FUSA G–2 Per Rpt 48, 28 Jul.
[18] Ltr, Bradley to Eisenhower, 28 Jul, Pogue Files.

[19] FUSA G–2 Est 12, 28 Jul.
[20] FUSA FO 2, 28 Jul.
[21] First U.S. Army, *Report of Operations*, I, 104–06.

Corps units. The VIII Corps, in addition to concern over the approach of the VII Corps toward its zone of advance, faced mines and wrecked vehicles, obstacles that were serious hindrances to a rapid advance in the restricted coastal road net. Time would be needed to regroup both corps and clear the roads, minimum prerequisites, it seemed, for effective exploitation south toward Avranches.

East of the Vire River, where only the V Corps remained, General Gerow's offensive was inevitably tied to British efforts on his left flank.

Only the XIX Corps received precise instructions from General Bradley. General Corlett was to displace the XIX Corps west of the Vire River and assume responsibility for what had been part of the VII Corps zone. Corlett was to "attack aggressively" in a drive south along the west bank of the Vire to a "goose egg" Bradley had drawn on a map. The "goose-egg" objective was about twenty miles south of le Mesnil-Herman and encompassed the Forêt de St. Sever and the town of Vire.

If XIX Corps could secure its objective, it would be into and partially through the highest terrain in Normandy—a hill mass extending from Avranches through Vire to Falaise— and would be able to deny the Germans use of the ground as the basis of a new defensive line. Vire, an important road center less than twenty miles from the base of the Cotentin, would provide the First Army an excellent pivot for the wheeling movement projected a month earlier—the turn to the east that would allow other American forces to enter Brittany.

To take the step into Brittany, General Patton's Third Army headquarters was ready to become operational. When the Third Army became actively involved in operations on the Continent, the projected new U.S. command structure was to go into effect: General Bradley would take command of the 12th Army Group and Lt. Gen. Courtney H. Hodges, the Deputy Commander, First Army, would replace him as the First Army commander. It seemed as though the moment for the change might coincide with the end of the exploitation growing out of COBRA.

So that the U.S. forces could slip neatly into the new command organization at the conclusion of the exploitation, General Bradley made a special arrangement. He asked General Hodges "to keep close track of" the three corps on the left. He informally appointed General Patton a second deputy commander and assigned him the mission of supervising the activities of the VIII Corps on the right. The VIII Corps, scheduled to come under control of the Third Army, was to act as a bridge to link the post-COBRA exploitation and the entrance of U.S. troops into Brittany. The Third Army was expected to be committed and pass into Brittany about 1 August.[22]

In the meantime, although COBRA and its consequences were an American responsibility, General Montgomery, as the Allied ground commander, was vitally concerned to promote progress on the American front. To create a diversion for COBRA, he had directed General Crerar to launch a holding attack on the Canadian front from Caen

---

[22] TUSA AAR, I, Ch. 2; Ltr, Bradley to Eisenhower, 28 Jul, Pogue Files.

toward Falaise. In compliance, the 2d Canadian Corps had attacked on the morning of 25 July, at the same time that COBRA jumped off. The Canadian attack met such resistance, and set off such strong German counterattacks east of the Orne by two panzer divisions, that Montgomery halted the attack at the end of the first day. Enemy strength in the Caen sector was obviously too great for anything less than an all-out offensive effort, which Montgomery was unwilling or unable to mount. On the other hand, the presence of formidable enemy forces near Caen made it necessary for the British to exercise caution. Montgomery still considered holding Caen, the pivot of the entire Allied front in Normandy, his principal task, and to that end he set in motion deception measures and air and artillery activity to keep the enemy off balance and prevent him from making a serious threat against Caen. It was this that had brought Kluge to the Caen front on 27 July at the height of the COBRA action.[23]

Despite his preoccupation with Caen, Montgomery endeavored to assist COBRA. Looking elsewhere along the eastern portion of the Allied front, he discovered that there seemed to be little if any German armor in the Caumont sector. He decided that an attack south from Caumont along the British-American boundary by the Second British Army would

take advantage of German weakness and be of value. Not only would it help COBRA by preventing the Germans from dispatching forces westward across the Vire River against the Americans, it would also ameliorate the situation at Caen by drawing German armored reserves away from that sector. With the former intention his avowed purpose, Montgomery ordered General Dempsey to attack south from Caumont on 30 July in an operation code-named BLUE-COAT.

Like GOODWOOD, the attempted breakthrough effort south of Caen earlier in July, which had raised doubts concerning Montgomery's primary and secondary motives, BLUECOAT had its ambiguous aspects. If the original intention was to hold German forces in place, thus keeping them from crossing the Vire and interfering with COBRA, BLUECOAT came too late to influence the panzer division that Kluge was moving from the Caumont region toward the American front. Yet because of the American success, it seemed likely that the Germans would make a general withdrawal in the Cotentin and try to swing their entire left flank back to Avranches. To do so they needed a firmly held pivot point. A dominating hill complex culminating in Mont Pinçon—five to eight miles south of the Caumont–Villers-Bocage line—in the British zone of advance seemed suitable for this purpose. If the British denied the Germans the potential pivot point and got behind those German forces trying to swing west to face the Americans, the German withdrawal might disintegrate. This became the final purpose of BLUECOAT. With the object of moving from Caumont through the Forêt

---

[23] Montgomery, *Normandy to the Baltic*, p. 139; British Army of the Rhine, *Battlefield Tour, Operation BLUECOAT, 8 Corps Operations South of Caumont, 30–31 July 44* (Germany: Printing and Stationery Service, Control Commission for Germany, 1947) (hereafter cited as *Operation BLUECOAT*), p. 1; FUSA G–2 Per Rpt 48, 28 Jul; Stacey, *The Canadian Army*, pp. 190–93.

l'Évêque to the town of Vire, the British were to attack on 30 July. [24]

Out of Operation COBRA thus emerged a plan of exploitation, a plan that sought to intensify German disorganization by relentless pressure on the American front and by a quick thrust south from Caumont on the British front. If the plan succeeded, the Allied turning movement toward the southeast would become a reality, and American troops would be able to enter Brittany. For the plan to succeed, the V and XIX Corps of the First Army and the right flank corps of the Second British Army first had to secure a firm pivot point at the town of Vire.

East of the Vire River

While the British were preparing to join the offensive east of the Vire, the V Corps resumed the attack. Assuming responsibility for all the American-held territory east of the Vire on 28 July by taking control of the 35th Division, General Gerow had free rein to push the V Corps to the south in the general direction of the town of Vire. Though General Bradley had assigned him no specific objectives, Bradley had asked him to keep the army headquarters informed on his intentions and progress. To his three divisions—the 2d, 5th, and 35th—General Gerow stated his mission as he understood it: "We *must* keep going to maintain contact, and not give the Boche a chance to dig in. See that all understand this." [25]

As the opposing *II Parachute Corps* pulled back in the hope of establishing defenses that could be tied in with the line the German units west of the Vire were trying to form, the V Corps on 28 July secured its COBRA objective, the St. Jean-des-Baisants ridge from Ste. Suzanne-sur-Vire to Vidouville. All three divisions advanced against light resistance and captured few prisoners. Although the enemy seemed much weaker as a result of the three-day attack and thus made prospects of a virtually unlimited advance seem possible for the V Corps, General Gerow was reluctant to initiate an unrestrained attack because of the terrain and his left flank. (*See Map VI.*)

The Souloeuvre–Vire river line, eleven miles beyond the St. Jean-des-Baisants ridge, appeared the obvious V Corps objective. Although the water alone constituted an obstacle to vehicular movement, the river runs through a ridge mass more than two miles in depth that presented an even more serious barrier to military advance. Steep-walled hills from 600 to 900 feet high would provide the Germans dominant observation, cover and concealment, fields of fire, and a good communications network. Hoping to secure the area before the Germans could organize it for defense, General Gerow nevertheless felt that the intervening terrain precluded a rapid advance. In the heart of the *bocage* country, the corps sector east of the Vire was a region of small irregular hills, small winding roads, and small hedgerowed fields. Combat there was sure to resemble the earlier battle of the hedgerows in the Cotentin.[26]

---

[24] British Army of the Rhine, *Operation BLUE-COAT*, p. 1; Conf Notes, 1100, 28 Jul, and 1645, 28 Jul, FUSA G–3 Misc File.

[25] V Corps Memo, FUSA FO 2, 28 Jul, and penciled note, V Corps G–3 Jnl.

[26] V Corps G–2 Sec Tactical Study of the Terrain, 30 Jul; XIX Corps G–2 Est of Bocage, 25 Jul.

The second factor working against an unchecked V Corps advance was General Gerow's concern over his left flank. Until the British attacked south from Caumont on 30 July (prevented until then by difficulties of regrouping and deployment) and covered the flank, a headlong advance by V Corps would expose an increasingly vulnerable side to the enemy.

General Gerow's solution for his two problems was to set limits on his advance in order to keep tight control.[27]

The Germans facilitated the V Corps advance when the *II Parachute Corps*, with permission, pulled back again.[28] Moving to the first limit of advance with very little difficulty, V Corps by noon 29 July held a line from Condé-sur-Vire to the British positions near Caumont. When the corps commander ordered the attack continued, troops pushed forward again for several thousand yards against sporadic resistance.[29]

Despite the absence of an organized German defensive line, the V Corps divisions did not have an easy time. The terrain inhibited rapid advance, and ambush lurked around every twist in the road. The *bocage* hills were populated by German rear-guard parties who used artillery, mortars, and small arms fire effectively. One American regimental commander, apparently near exhaustion, reported, "Things are not going very well," and said he "would like to be relieved of command." The division commander was not sympathetic. "I

will relieve you when I get ready to do so," he snapped, but later sought to soothe him: "Do not get discouraged," he said, "this is hedgerow fighting. It is tough."[30]

Receiving word that the Germans were withdrawing all along the First Army front and learning that the British were planning to attack on the following day, General Gerow on 29 July ordered his division commanders into an all-out advance. Instead of merely preventing disengagement, the corps was to "drive strong and hard" in "a relentless pursuit."[31] As translated by General Robertson, the troops were to "by-pass everything. Never mind these little pockets of resistance. . . . Let's get down and take a bath in the Vire."[32] (*Map VII*)

The instructions came too late. Though army headquarters claimed that only some "tired old Austrians" were in opposition, the troops had moved into contact with a defensive line covering an important road net centering on Torigni-sur-Vire. As the 35th Division on 30 July tried to take Torigni and the 2d and 5th Division to occupy high ground east of the village, the Germans inflicted close to 1,000 casualties, halted the ad-

[27] V Corps FO, 29 Jul, and G–3 Situation Map, 2030, 28 Jul; 5th Div Outline Plan, 0230, 27 Jul.

[28] Msg, Kluge to Hausser, 28 Jul, *AGp B Op. Befehle*, p. 195; Telecon, Tempelhoff and Pemsel, 0935, 28 Jul, *AGp B KTB*.

[29] V Corps G–3 Jnl, 29 Jul.

[30] Telecon, Robertson and Hirschfelder, 1930, 29 Jul, 2d Div G–3 Jnl. On the previous day, Colonel Hirschfelder, the 9th Infantry commander, had inspired his assault troops by turning his back to enemy fire and, in full view of the Germans, had removed his helmet, placed his hands on his hips, and asked his men what was holding them up. This display of courage and of psychological inspiration provided the spark for continued attack. Colonel Hirschfelder was awarded the DSC.

[31] V Corps FO 16, 29 Jul, Ltr of Instrs, 29 Jul, and Memos for the Record by the CofS, 1120 and 1250, 29 Jul.

[32] Telecon, Robertson and Hirschfelder, 0920, 30 Jul, 2d Div G–3 Jnl.

vance, and dashed American hopes for an immediate pursuit.[33]

To breach the new line, the subordinate units of the V Corps made detailed attack plans, only to discover as they prepared to launch a co-ordinated offensive on the morning of 31 July that the Germans had disengaged.[34] Kluge had authorized the *II Parachute Corps* to withdraw.[35] In falling back, the Germans abandoned not only the Torigni road net but also terrain that was highly defensible. Only mines and sporadic harassing artillery fire opposed an uninterrupted advance. American troops cheerfully advanced across undefended ground, while their commanders chafed at the thought of the enemy slipping away undetected.[36]

Although all concerned pressed for speedy pursuit, the pace of the V Corps advance slowed during the afternoon of 31 July. Nearing the Souloeuvre–Vire water line, the corps encountered pockets of resistance and delaying forces with increasing frequency. The pursuit again threatened to come to a halt.

The boundaries delineating the corps zone of advance met near the town of Vire, fourteen miles southwest of Torigni. If the British on the left and the

XIX Corps on the right advanced as projected, the V Corps would be pinched out near Vire.[37] Blocking the approach to the V Corps limit of advance was the east–west Vire–Souloeuvre river line and hill mass, seven miles north of Vire.

These factors generally and a conversation with General Bradley specifically governed General Gerow's desire to cross the hills and the water barriers quickly.[38] Earlier on 31 July, Gerow had instructed his division commanders to move only as far as the river line. Later in the afternoon he ordered each division commander to get at least one battalion of each front-line regiment across the river before dark.

On the corps right and in its center, the 35th and 2d Divisions met such strong resistance on the approaches to the water line—and particularly near Tessy-sur-Vire—that it became obvious that they could not comply with instructions.[39] On the other hand, the 5th Division on the left met relatively light resistance, indicating that a hard push might gain a bridgehead across the stream.

Unable to reach General Irwin, the 5th Division commander, personally, Gerow phoned one of Irwin's regimental commanders and told him to mount his infantry on tanks. They were to bypass resistance, use only good roads, and get to the water and across it in at least bat-

---

[33] 35th Div G–3 Per Rpt 22, 31 Jul; Ltr, Brig Gen Ralph W. Zwicker to OCMH, 14 Mar 56, OCMH files. Three members of the 5th Division were awarded the DSC for heroic action that day: 1st Lt. Arthur J. Miller, S. Sgt. Konstanty Gugala, and Pfc. Henry N. Powell, the latter posthumously.

[34] 2d Div G–2 Per Rpt and G–3 Jnl, 31 Jul; 35th Div FO 11, 30 Jul, and G–2 Per Rpt, 31 Jul; 5th Div AAR, Jul, and G–2 Per Rpt, 31 Jul; Gerow Msg, 1930, 30 Jul, 5th Div G–3 Jnl and File.

[35] Telecon, 0030, 31 Jul, *AGp B KTB*; Msg, *AGp B to II Para Corps* (for information to the *Seventh Army* and *Panzer Group West*), 31 Jul, *AGp B Op. Befehle*, p. 206.

[36] See the corps and div G–3 Jnls, 31 Jul.

[37] V Corps G–3 Situation Map, 2030, 29 Jul.

[38] Telecon, Gerow and Irwin, 1710, 31 Jul, 5th Div G–3 Jnl and File.

[39] 2d Lt. John F. Hermanspan, Jr., of the 35th Division, after withdrawing his platoon from a village, discovered that six wounded men had been abandoned there. Hermanspan re-entered the village and created a diversion to cover the evacuation of the casualties. Fatally wounded, Hermanspan was posthumously awarded the DSC.

TESSY-SUR-VIRE. *Road to Torigni crosses Vire River, left center.*

talion strength. "In short," Gerow commanded, "hurry." [40] Half an hour later he explained to Irwin, "I told you before to stop at the river—now I want you to change that." The 5th Division was to cover the more than six miles to the river line in record time. [41]

Less than an hour after Gerow forwarded these instructions, he learned that a British armored division had attacked to the southwest, entered the V Corps zone, and secured two bridges across the river. "Well now, I don't like British walking across our front [and] taking [our] objectives," General Gerow complained. [42] But since the British had already secured a bridgehead he saw no reason why the Americans could not use it, specifically the 5th Division, for a quick drive across the remaining seven miles to the town of Vire. [43]

Unfortunately, the intermingling of British tanks and American infantrymen caused confusion. The opportunity for an immediate exploitation by either the British or the Americans was lost. [44] One regiment of the 5th Division reached the north bank of the Souloeuvre River during the early morning hours of 1 August. There it remained

throughout the day, out of contact much of the time with other division units.

By then, however, after having advanced more than seven miles in six days, the corps had reached the end of what had earlier promised to develop into an unlimited pursuit. On 1 August, as the 35th and 2d Divisions fought near Tessy-sur-Vire to get to the Souloeuvre–Vire line, the boundary separating the British and Americans was moved to the west, thereby narrowing the V Corps sector and pinching out the entire 5th Division.

Part of the reason for the boundary change was the success of the British attack south from Caumont. In compliance with Montgomery's endeavor to deny the Germans the pivot point near Mont Pincon, General Dempsey had launched the 8 Corps in Operation BLUECOAT on 30 July. Following a bombardment by 700 heavy bombers and 500 medium and light bombers that dropped 2,200 tons of high explosive, the British attacked a sector that was lightly defended. Only the bombed and inexperienced *326th Infantry Division* stood in the way. On the first day of the attack, the 11th British Armoured Division advanced six to eight miles to come abreast of the V Corps east of Torigni-sur-Vire. Operations on 31 July were hampered by the terrain: by the pronounced ridges running across the axis of advance; by the streams, which flowed in all directions and which in many cases were tank obstacles because of their width, depth, or marshy approaches; and by the tortuous roads, which were often banked by high hedges. But these difficulties were quickly overcome when the British dis-

---

[40] Telecon, Gen Gerow and Col Charles W. Yuill, 1645, 31 Jul, 5th Div G–3 Jnl and File.

[41] Telecon, Gerow and Irwin, 1710, 31 Jul, 5th Div G–3 Jnl and File.

[42] Telecon, Gerow and Irwin, 1750, 31 Jul, 5th Div G–3 Jnl and File. According to *V Corps Operations in the ETO*, page 150, the British secured permission to move the armored unit on the road net across the 5th Division front. Who gave permission is not stated.

[43] V Corps Msg, 1750, 31 Jul, and Telecon, Gerow and Irwin, 1910, 31 Jul, 5th Div G–3 Jnl and File.

[44] 5th Div G–3 Jnl, entries 1840, 1855, and 2245, 31 Jul.

covered that the Forêt l'Evêque, which was astride the boundary between the *Seventh Army* and *Panzer Group West,* had through oversight been left unoccupied by the Germans. A vital stretch of some 1,500 yards of country was theirs for the taking. Thrusting through the forest, the 11th Armoured Division quickly gained the south bank of the Souloeuvre River and by 1 August occupied high ground immediately east of the Vire.[45]

A Clash of Spearheads

While the V Corps and the British were driving toward Vire from the north and northeast, XIX Corps was thrusting toward Vire from the northwest. The evidence unearthed by COBRA indicated that the Germans had nothing to stop a XIX Corps advance along the west bank of the Vire, and General Bradley had acted on that premise. Unfortunately, Kluge had not been idle.

As early as the evening of 27 July, Kluge had begun to try to plug the spreading gap between *LXXXIV* and *II Parachute Corps.* He seized upon the *2d Panzer Division,* then under *Panzer Group West* control. The panzer division had been relieved from frontline duty on 22 July by the *326th Infantry Division* (which had come from the Pas-de-Calais), and the armored unit had moved into reserve southwest of Caen. Having had a few days of respite from battle, the *2d Panzer Division* was to move westward and across the Vire

River to launch a counterattack designed to close the gap.

Kluge at first thought of using the *II Parachute Corps* to direct the counterattack, but he quickly decided to insert a new corps between the *II Parachute* and the *LXXXIV.* The *LVIII Panzer Corps* headquarters was moving from the *Fifteenth Army* toward the *Panzer Group West* area, and Kluge considered employing the panzer corps in the *Seventh Army* center to handle the *2d Panzer Division* counterthrust already planned to take place toward Marigny and St. Gilles.[46] Kluge soon recognized, however, that the situation was changing too rapidly for him to await commitment of the *LVIII Panzer Corps.* Taking the *XLVII Panzer Corps,* which was not only more experienced but also closer to the Cotentin, and replacing it in the *Panzer Group West* front with the incoming *LVIII,* Kluge ordered the *XLVII* to take control of the *2d Panzer Division.* By then the division was moving to an assembly area directly behind the *352d Division* on the west bank of the Vire.[47]

Though Kluge was obviously concerned by the gap in the middle of the *Seventh Army,* he judged the *Panzer Group West* front still to be the more critical sector. The 2d Canadian Corps had launched an attack south of Caen toward Falaise on 25 July, and, although commitment of the *9th SS Panzer Division* had soon checked the Canadians, continuing activity brought Kluge to that sector again two days later, on 27

---

[45] Opn BLUECOAT, pp. 1–2, 47; Leigh-Mallory, "Despatch," Fourth Supplement to the *London Gazette* of December 31, 1946; see Wilmot, *The Struggle for Europe,* pp. 395–98.

[46] Telecon, Tempelhoff and Zimmerman, 1910, 26 Jul, *AGp B KTB; OB WEST KTB,* 26 Jul.
[47] Telecons, Tempelhoff and Speidel, 1010, 27 Jul, and Kluge and Pemsel, 1700, 27 Jul, *AGp B KTB; OB WEST KTB,* 27 Jul, and *Anlage 875.*

July. While he was there, Hausser and Choltitz were struggling to maintain a semblance of order in the *LXXXIV Corps* sector. When Kluge returned to his headquarters that evening, he learned that the *LXXXIV Corps* sector was in turmoil. When he discovered, on the following morning, 28 July, that three divisions had to be considered lost in the Cotentin and that the gap was larger than had been earlier reported, Kluge realized that the *2d Panzer Division* would not be enough. He needed more troops west of the Vire.

The *363d Division* was en route to the Normandy front but was not immediately available for commitment. The *9th Panzer Division*, released from the *Nineteenth Army* in southern France, would not be on hand for about ten days. With no alternative but to call upon *Panzer Group West* and thereby weaken the front south of Caen, Kluge took the *116th Panzer Division*, a unit that had recently come from the Pas-de-Calais into *Panzer Group West* reserve. Together, the *2d* and *116th Panzer Divisions*, under the command of the *XLVII Panzer Corps*, were to attack north from Percy to close the gap between Notre-Dame-de-Cenilly and the Vire River.[48]

Starting on the night of 27 July, the *2d Panzer Division* crossed the Vire River at Tessy-sur-Vire and assembled near Moyon, three miles northwest of Tessy. On 28 July the *XLVII Panzer Corps* assumed command not only of the *2d Panzer Division* but also of the remnants of the *352d Division* near Beaucoudray and the few remaining

units of *Panzer Lehr* near Percy. The *116th Panzer Division*, making a forced daylight march, was expected to be in position to attack northwest from Percy on the following afternoon, 29 July. On 29 July the *XLVII Panzer Corps* also took command of the *2d SS Panzer Division*, deployed between the Sienne River and a point east of Percy.[49]

Meanwhile, Kluge was satisfied on 28 July that these arrangements were the best that could be made, particularly since Warlimont had promised to request permission from Hitler for the *Seventh Army* to withdraw to the Granville–Gavray–Percy–Tessy-sur-Vire–Caumont line.[50] Kluge felt reasonably certain that he could re-establish a stable defensive line. The *II Parachute Corps* would remain essentially in place, making minor adjustments to conform to the new defenses but keeping the *Panzer Group West* left flank well covered. The *XLVII Panzer Corps* would plug the gap in the *Seventh Army* center. And the *LXXXIV Corps*, it still seemed at that date, would hold Coutances until strong forces withdrawing south had re-established a firm anchor at Granville for the entire German defenses in Normandy. This was Kluge's hope. But first he had to reckon with the XIX U.S. Corps.

General Corlett on 28 July was also displacing troops west of the Vire River. He had hoped to take with him his two experienced divisions, the 35th and 29th,

---

[48] Telecons, Kluge and Warlimont, 0925, 28 Jul, Kluge and Gause, 1303, 28 Jul, and Kluge and Blumentritt, 1645, 28 Jul, *AGp B KTB*.

[49] Telecon, Kluge and his son Guenther, a lt col, 1800, 28 Jul, and Speidel and Pemsel, 1350, 28 Jul, *AGp B KTB*; *AGp B KTB*, 29 Jul, *Darstellung der Ereignisse*; Choltitz, *Soldat Unter Soldaten*, p. 208; MS # P–59 (Stoeckler).

[50] Telecon, Kluge and Warlimont, 0925, 28 Jul, *AGp B KTB*; *Der Westen* (Schramm).

leaving the untested 28th Division (Maj. Gen. Lloyd D. Brown) on a relatively static front at St. Lô. But the need for the 35th Division to advance south of St. Lô on 27 July to maintain pressure on the withdrawing Germans changed Corlett's plans. The 35th Division attack nevertheless provided an assist by securing an additional bridge over the Vire southeast of St. Lô, thereby facilitating the movement of the 28th and 29th Divisions into the new corps zone.[51]

At noon on 28 July, while the displacement was being carried out, General Corlett assumed responsibility for the units already engaged in his new zone—the 30th Division and CCA of the 2d Armored Division, the latter reinforced by the 4th Division's 22d Infantry, plus the 113th Cavalry Group. (See Map VI.)

The XIX Corps mission of driving south about twenty miles from le Mesnil-Herman to the town of Vire in what was hoped would be a virtually uncontested pursuit contrasted with the previous aim of the forces already engaged on the west bank of the Vire River. While under VII Corps and engaged in Operation Cobra, the 30th Division and the reinforced CCA of the 2d Armored Division had driven south to wall off the Vire River against possible German attacks launched from the east. By noon, 28 July, they were completing their Cobra assignments. The 30th Division, after securing three Vire River bridges south of St. Lô, was moving against slight resistance toward a natural stopping

place, a stream south of the villages of Moyon and Troisgots, where General Hobbs hoped to "get a little breather."[52] CCA was in possession of its primary Cobra objective, le Mesnil-Herman, and was probing toward the towns of Villebaudon and Tessy-sur-Vire.

Less concerned with blocking a possible German move across the Vire than with launching a rapid advance to the south, General Corlett believed a quick movement to his objective to be possible. Estimates indicated that the XIX Corps faced fewer than 3,000 German combat effectives—disorganized and battered units suported by only four artillery battalions and scattered batteries of self-propelled guns. Without prepared positions and lacking reserves, the Germans could make a stand at only two places, on high ground south of Tessy-sur-Vire and on commanding terrain near Vire.[53]

One speck blemished this optimistic view. While reconnoitering in force from le Mesnil-Herman toward Villebaudon and Tessy-sur-Vire on 27 July, task forces of CCA had encountered increasing resistance that denied advance of more than two miles in each direction.[54] It became apparent that part of the 2d Panzer Division, believed moving westward, was already west of the Vire River. Although Allied planes were harassing the enemy's approach, the panzer division was judged capable of getting at least a motorized infantry regiment and about twenty tanks in front of the XIX Corps by the morning of 28 July.[55]

[51] FUSA Memo, 23 Jul, and Msg, 0015, 28 Jul, FUSA G–3 Jnl; 28th and 29th Div AAR's, Jul; XIX Corps Ltrs of Instr, 6, 1130, and 9, 2330, 27 Jul, and G–3 Per Rpt 51, 28 Jul.

[52] Telecon, Hobbs, 2210, 27 Jul, 30th Div G–3 Jnl and File.

[53] Intel Annex to XIX Corps FO 8, 0300, 28 Jul.

[54] 2d Armd Div G–3 Jnl, entry 1130, 27 Jul; 30th Div G–3 Jnl, entries 1540, 2100, 2305, 27 Jul.

[55] Intel Annex to XIX Corps FO 8, 0300, 28 Jul.

So long as this estimate remained only a pessimistic possibility, General Corlett saw no reason why he could not advance beyond Tessy-sur-Vire and block off this excellent crossing site before the *2d Panzer Division* and other German units could offer serious resistance. Thus he designated the high ground south of Tessy—along the Percy–Pontfarcy line—as the initial corps objective. With this potential enemy defensive line neutralized and with the 28th and 29th Divisions in place for the attack, he would drive to the town of Vire.[56]

To seize the Percy–Pontfarcy line, General Corlett directed General Hobbs to take Tessy-sur-Vire with the 30th Division and block the river crossing sites. No doubt recalling the confusion that had occurred in the Taute and Vire bridgehead area when the 30th Division and a different combat command had intermingled, the corps commander halted movement of the 2d Armored Division's CCA toward Tessy-sur-Vire.[57] Instead, the reinforced CCA was to concentrate on the right of the corps zone and attack south through Villebaudon to Percy. Counting on the mobility of the armored force and on continuing enemy disorganization, Corlett instructed the armored commander, General Rose, to move from Percy eastward to the Vire River. This would serve to encircle Tessy from the west and isolate the town from the south. Then the 29th Division, and later the 28th, would attack to the south.[58]

As events developed, these arrange-

ments were too late, for on 28 July the *2d Panzer Division* was assembling west of the Vire River on a small plateau around Tessy-sur-Vire. The panzer troops gathered behind an east–west tributary of the Vire River—the stream running south of Moyon and Troisgots—and in the area immediately northwest of Tessy for an attack to the northwest. To protect the assembly of the *2d Panzer Division*, Kluge had instructed Hausser to have the *II Parachute Corps,* which still straddled the Vire River, establish a strong defensive line from Moyon eastward through Condé-sur-Vire and Biéville to Caumont, where it was to tie in with the *LVIII Panzer Corps.*[59] Although the line east of the Vire—from Condé-sur-Vire through Biéville—had successfully delayed the V Corps north of Torigni-sur-Vire, the slashing COBRA attack of the 30th Division and CCA had invalidated positions along that line west of the Vire. CCA had already outflanked the line on the west by reaching Villebaudon on 28 July, and the 30th Division was approaching Troisgots.

The remnants of the *352d Division*, reinforced by elements of the *2d Panzer Division* as they arrived, got set to hold the Moyon–Troisgots line. As troops of the 30th Division descended a naked slope during the afternoon of 28 July and moved toward the stream and a long incline behind it, they came under intense fire. The configuration of the terrain exposed the attackers and gave the defenders defilade. American counterbattery missions seemed to have no effect on enemy fire, and from the

---

[56] XIX Corps FO 8, 28 Jul.

[57] 30th Div G–3 Jnl, entry 1550, 28 Jul; Telecons, Corlett and Hobbs, 1313 and 1937, 28 Jul, 30th Div G–3 Jnl and File.

[58] XIX Corps FO 8, 28 Jul.

[59] Msg, Kluge to Hausser, 28 Jul, *AGp B Op. Befehle,* p. 195; Telecon, Tempelhoff and Pemsel, 0935, 28 Jul, *AGp B KTB.*

ridge just south of the Moyon–Troisgots stream German machine guns, tanks, self-propelled guns, and artillery denied advance.[60]

Although General Hobbs committed his reserve regiment on the following day, 29 July, the forces failed to move forward. Certain internal difficulties were apparent: the troops were exhausted, a shortage of telephone wire hampered communications, and fighter-bombers in close support inadvertently strafed and bombed several 30th Division units. But the principal reason why the 30th Division did not take Troisgots was the presence of the fresh and strong 2d Panzer Division defending advantageous terrain. Two co-ordinated attacks against Troisgots—the bastion of the defensive line—by all three regiments of the 30th Division abreast on 30 July and artillery fire exceeding thrice the amount usually expended still failed to propel the division beyond the line of departure. Enemy shells knocked out six of nineteen tanks supporting one regiment.[61]

By this time General Corlett had changed the division objective from Tessy-sur-Vire to Troisgots.[62] Not only did Tessy seem completely out of reach for the moment, even Troisgots appeared unattainable. The 30th Division was far from getting the "little breather" General Hobbs had hoped for.

For all the indications of failure, the 30th Division to a great extent had prevented the 2d Panzer Division from launching its own counterattack. Hausser had helped the Americans too. Having become convinced that the XLVII Panzer Corps attack had failed even before it got started, Hausser ordered the corps to assume defensive positions along a broad front between the Vire River and Gavray. Kluge countermanded the order at once, but the resulting delay as well as inevitable confusion on the staff levels harmed the offensive purpose.

Some credit for balking the 2d Panzer Division's offensive intentions also belonged to the 2d Armored Division's CCA, which had made its weight felt on the right of the 30th Division. By noon of 28 July, when General Corlett assumed control, General Rose's combat command had already secured Villebaudon. An armored column conducting a reconnaissance in force that morning had destroyed six German armored vehicles and a Mark IV tank and had overrun about fifty soldiers to take the village. Another column reconnoitering simultaneously toward Tessy-sur-Vire, in contrast, met strong armored forces obviously belonging to the 2d Panzer Division and returned to the vicinity of le Mesnil-Herman. Ordered

---

[60] [Maj. Franklin Ferriss], Operations of 30th Infantry Division, 24 July–1 August (hereafter cited [Ferriss], Opns of 30th Div), a preliminary MS, Hist Div USFET, 1946, OCMH Files; 30th Div G–3 Jnl, entry 1955, 30 Jul; Telecon, Hobbs and Kelly, 1413, 29 Jul, 30th Div G–3 Jnl and File; 117th Inf S–3 Rpt, 30 Jul.

[61] 30th Div G–3 Jnl, entries 0540, 0910, 1342, 1347, and 1350, 29 Jul; 30th Sig Co Unit Rpt, 29 Jul; Hewitt, Story of the 30th Infantry Division, pp. 43ff. S. Sgt. J. W. Parks, who though wounded took command of a platoon after both the platoon leader and the sergeant became casualties, T. Sgt. Fred D. Steelman, who exercised heroic leadership, and S. Sgt. Frederick W. Unger were awarded the DSC for their actions.

[62] 30th Div Ltr of Instr, 30 Jul; Overlay to Accompany Verbal FO Issued 1140, 30 Jul, 30th Div G–3 Jnl and File.

to discontinue the thrust toward Tessy, directed instead to attack along the axis from le Mesnil-Herman through Ville-baudon to Percy, and strengthened by attachment of the 113th Cavalry Group, General Rose immediately reinforced his troops in Villebaudon with the cav-alry group and the 14th Armored Field Artillery Battalion.[63]

Although the route south from le Mesnil-Herman to Percy seemed clear of large German contingents, the arrival of the 2d *Panzer Division* in the Tessy-sur-Vire region threatened the CCA line of communications. The roads leading west from Tessy were excellent for sup-porting German armored thrusts toward Villebaudon and Percy. To prevent the panzer troops from cutting the north–south le Mesnil-Herman–Villebaudon–Percy road, General Rose tried to erect a barrier along his eastern boundary. He had divided CCA into three task forces, each consisting of a company of the 22d Infantry, a medium tank com-pany of the 66th Armored Regiment, a platoon of light tanks, and supporting units. Since one task force was already in Villebaudon, he sent the other two south and southeast from le Mesnil-Herman toward Moyon, giving them the eventual objective of cutting the east–west Villebaudon–Tessy highway and thereby providing flank protection for the main attack to Percy.

The task force that attacked southeast from le Mesnil-Herman on the afternoon of 28 July drove through le Mesnil-Opac and destroyed five Mark IV tanks and four antitank guns without loss. How-ever, increasingly heavy opposition from

roving tanks, infiltrating infantrymen, antitank and dual-purpose antiaircraft guns, mortars, and artillery forced the column to return to le Mesnil-Herman. The task force attacking to the south reached the village of Moyon but, unable to go farther, also returned to le Mesnil-Herman.

Meanwhile, the Germans threatened to cut the main road between le Mesnil-Herman and Villebaudon and isolate the CCA spearhead. Three enemy tanks actually moved westward from Moyon and seized a crossroads near la Denisière. Reversing one battery to fire north from Villebaudon toward la Denisière at very short range, the 14th Armored Field Artillery Battalion soon drove the three tanks away. Unable to cut the road physically, the Germans attempted to seal off Villebaudon by interdictory artillery fire along the highway. The shelling of the la Denisière intersection remained heavy, but American ammuni-tion and supply vehicles, forced to speed through the crossroads at irregular in-tervals, managed for the most part to evade damage.

On 29 July General Rose sent both task forces from le Mesnil-Herman to take the village of Moyon. Though the attempt failed, the CCA task force in Villebaudon moved south to Percy against light resistance. Percy proved untenable. The armored force with-drew to hills north of the town and awaited reinforcement. Threatening to block reinforcement, the Germans again cut the axis of communication behind the advance units near Percy. As enemy artillery interdicted the le Mesnil-Her-man–Percy highway and as enemy tanks dueled with American tank destroyers, small German detachments infiltrated

---

[63] The following account is taken largely from [Pillsbury], 2d Armored Div in Opn COBRA, pp. 32ff., and from the 2d Armored Div AAR, Jul.

across the route and set up hasty road-blocks.

The arrival of the 29th Division, while not ameliorating the situation at once, gave hope of improvement in the near future. Two of General Gerhardt's regiments—the 116th and 175th—moved into the line near Moyon and Percy to relieve the CCA task forces, which then assembled near le Mesnil-Herman. Directed to advance through Villebaudon and Percy, the third regiment, the 115th Infantry, was stopped by the German roadblocks on the highway. Although General Corlett that evening optimistically ordered an advance to Vire, the corps objective, it was obvious that he first had to eliminate the enemy bridgehead at Tessy-sur-Vire.[64]

To eliminate the bridgehead, General Corlett decided to shorten CCA's planned envelopment of Tessy. Instead of moving eastward from Percy, General Rose was to strike east from Villebaudon. If successful, the combat command might outflank the enemy's Moyon–Troisgots line. The 29th Division would then be able to proceed through Villebaudon and Percy and launch the drive toward Vire.

On the morning of 30 July, a reinforced tank battalion and an infantry company of CCA moved from le Mesnil-Herman through Villebaudon, turned east toward Tessy-sur-Vire, and immediately met firm opposition. A fire fight involving forty American tanks as well as infantry and antitank guns lasted all day. The 2d Panzer Division was tied down in the Tessy region, but the 116th Panzer Division had appeared on the scene. After being harassed and delayed

by Allied airplanes during its march across the Vire River, the 116th finally jumped off on the morning of 30 July. At once it became bogged down in a struggle for the hills around Percy, Villebaudon, and Beaucoudray. (See Map VII.)

For the Americans, the problem of taking Tessy vanished under the more pressing need to hold Villebaudon. While the 28th Division's 109th Infantry remained north of le Mesnil-Herman to constitute the corps reserve, the other two regiments of the division—the 110th and 112th—moved south of le Mesnil-Herman to back up the defense of Villebaudon. The 116th and 175th Regiments of the 29th Division exerted pressure meanwhile against Moyon and Percy, and the 30th Division placed pressure against Troisgots. As a result of this corps-wide effort and of assistance from fighter-bombers that struck Tessy-sur-Vire several times during the day, CCA retained possession of Villebaudon.[65] Meanwhile, the 29th Division's 115th Infantry, which had been blocked south of Villebaudon, finally reached the outskirts of Percy.

The 14th Armored Field Artillery Battalion played a significant part in the battle on 30 July. Ordered to move from Villebaudon to Percy that morning, the battalion had formed in a march column with the heads of the battery columns on the main road leading south. Before the move started, news of the counterattack prompted the unit to hold in place and assume firing positions. Although scattered small arms fire struck near the guns for an hour around noon,

---

[64] XIX Corps FO 9, 2330, 29 Jul.

[65] 30th Div G–3 Jnl, entries 1440 and 1539, 30 Jul.

the artillerymen accepted and fulfilled all fire missions. They marked enemy attack concentrations with red smoke to lead fighter-bombers to lucrative targets. They also engaged enemy tanks at ranges of less than 2,000 yards. Finally, when German fire became too intense, they withdrew to new positions north of Villebaudon. There the 18th and the 65th Field Artillery Battalions were attached to the 14th Armored Field Artillery Battalion, which also assumed operational control of the 44th Field Artillery Battalion through its fire direction center. Controlling the fires of four battalions of 105-mm. howitzers, the 14th also co-ordinated missions for the XIX Corps Artillery, which sent a liaison officer to the battalion for this purpose.[66]

At the end of 30 July, the XIX Corps still was seriously engaged in the Percy–Tessy-sur-Vire area. From the high ground between Percy and Tessy, the Germans shelled the American units effectively and interdicted the roads in the Villebaudon area at will.[67] Still trying to eliminate the German bridgehead at Tessy, General Corlett ordered the attack to resume on 31 July, but with a modification. From positions forming an arc from Moyon through Villebaudon to Percy, all three regiments of the 29th Division—the 116th on the left (north), the 175th in the center, and the 115th on the right (the 115th after relief near Percy by the 28th Division's 110th Infantry)—were to attack eastward toward Tessy and support another at-

tempt by CCA to destroy the bridgehead. While this attack was in progress, the 28th Division was to move south through Villebaudon to Percy to get into position for a drive south to Vire.

About noon, 31 July, two battalions—one from the 66th Armored Regiment and the other from the attached 22d Infantry—advanced eastward from Villebaudon toward Tessy-sur-Vire to spearhead a 29th Division supporting attack. Halfway to Tessy, the armored troops encountered several enemy tanks in a wood on the far side of a ravine. Unable to find a crossing site over the ravine and receiving heavy artillery fire, they halted and took cover while fighter-bombers attempted without success to dislodge the Germans. The troops of the 29th Division, like the spearhead, were unsuccessful in achieving more than limited advances.[68]

Meanwhile the 28th Division was moving south toward Percy and on that day assumed responsibility for its zone. The move was far from successful, even though the division was moving through what was essentially a rear area.[69] Displaying the usual symptoms of a unit new to combat, the troops of the 28th Division would need several days to overcome a natural hesitancy to advance under fire, to become accustomed to maneuvering in unfamiliar terrain, and to learn the techniques of advancing through hedgerow country.[70]

[66] [Pillsbury], 2d Armored Div in Opn Cobra, pp. 36–39.

[67] [Maj Franklin Ferriss], Notes on the Opns of the XIX Corps, 28 Jul 44–13 Jan 45 (hereafter cited [Ferriss], Notes), ML–2208; see Hodgson, R–58.

[68] 30th Div G–3 Jnl, entry 1440, 31 Jul.

[69] S. Sgt. Walter R. Tauchert, armed with a rifle and grenade launcher, destroyed two machine guns, routed an armored vehicle, and enabled his platoon to reach its objective. He was awarded the DSC posthumously.

[70] XIX Corps Msg, 1450, 31 Jul, 30th Div G–3 Jnl and File; 28th Div AAR, Jul.

A significant change in the situation occurred on 31 July in the 30th Division sector, where General Hobbs was trying for the fourth day to take Troisgots. For the attack on 31 July, Hobbs placed his entire attached tank battalion at the disposal of the 119th Infantry, which was to make the main effort in the center of the division front. The gesture was more impressive in theory than in fact since losses had reduced the tank battalion to thirty-four lights and mediums, of which only thirteen Shermans actually were available for front-line duty.[71] Accompanied by these tanks, the 119th Infantry was to press in on Troisgots from three sides as the other regiments supported.

An infantry battalion and a few supporting tanks managed to get into Troisgots during the afternoon and destroy by tank fire and bazooka shells several enemy tanks and self-propelled guns, the heart of the German defense. Success was in a large measure due to 1st Lt. Harry F. Hansen of the 743d Tank Battalion, who dismounted from his tank and led two infantrymen with bazookas to positions from which to fire on three hostile tanks. Two burst into flame upon direct hits, the third retired.[72] By evening the regiment was mopping up the village. The Germans had given way most reluctantly. The fall of Troisgots had been "no collapse." [73]

Capture of Troisgots occurred as news

came to the Germans that Americans in the Cotentin were threatening Granville and even Avranches (indeed, had perhaps taken them) and that British and Americans were advancing toward the town of Vire. Withdrawal became imperative. Kluge's authorization for the *Seventh Army* to pull back to a line that would still protect Granville, Tessy-sur-Vire, and Vire seemed unrealistic.[74] The forces between Percy and Tessy began to withdraw, shifting slightly westward toward Villedieu and Gavray.

Suspecting the imminent collapse of the German positions, General Corlett ordered his subordinate commanders to maintain vigorous patrolling during the night to maintain contact with the enemy. "Watch . . . and see that he does not pull out," Corlett warned.[75] If a withdrawal was discovered, the units were to pursue. Since Corlett felt that the Germans would continue to hold Tessy-sur-Vire to cover their withdrawal, he planned still another attack for 1 August. Attaching CCA to the 29th Division, he ordered General Gerhardt to drive eastward again from Villebaudon to Tessy-sur-Vire while the 30th Division pressed against Tessy from the north. The 28th Division was to move south through Percy and attack toward Vire.[76]

On the morning of 1 August, CCA spearheaded the 29th Division attack by again moving toward Tessy-sur-Vire with an armored battalion on each side of the highway. A unique armored point of five vehicles moved ahead of the force. A light tank, acting as a decoy,

[71] [Ferriss], Opns of 30th Div, pp. 31–32; 30th Div Msg, 1005, 31 Jul, 30th Div G–3 Jnl and File.

[72] Hansen was awarded the DSC.

[73] Telecon, Hobbs, 1510, 31 Jul; 30th Div G–3 Jnl, entries 0429 and 1855, 31 Jul; Hewitt, *Story of the 30th Infantry Division*, pp. 44–45; [Ferriss], Opns of 30th Div, p. 32.

[74] Telecon, 0030, 31 Jul, *AGp B KTB; AGp B* Msg, 31 Jul, *AGp B Op. Befehle*, p. 206.

[75] Telecon, Corlett and Hobbs, 1923, 31 Jul, 30th Div G–3 Jnl and File.

[76] XIX Corps Ltrs of Instr, 10 and 11, 31 Jul.

advanced along the road; two medium tanks, one hundred yards ahead of the light tank, moved along the sides of the road to flush and engage enemy tanks; and two tank destroyers, two hundred yards behind the light tank, advanced along the sides of the road, alert to reinforce the medium tanks by quick fire.

Taking advantage of ground mist, the men and vehicles of CCA crossed the ravine that had held up progress on the previous day and overran and destroyed a column of German vehicles. Although three American tanks entered the outskirts of Tessy during the morning, the Germans drove the crewmen out after all three tanks developed mechanical failures.

Earlier on 1 August General Hobbs had instructed the 120th Infantry to send a token force to participate in the capture of Tessy-sur-Vire. "We were suddenly ordered . . . to take off for Tessy," explained the commander of the rifle company selected for the mission, "so we took off." [77] Without an artillery forward observer, the company moved cross-country to within a mile of the town before an enemy machine gun and several mortars took the troops under fire. Knocking out the machine gun with grenades, the infantrymen infiltrated into the edge of Tessy. Having understood that Tessy had already been secured by CCA and that he was merely to set up roadblocks there, the company commander was disconcerted when enemy forces appeared and drove his men out helter-skelter.

CCA mounted a second attack that afternoon and penetrated Tessy. Men of the 22d Infantry cleared the center of the town and crossed the river to establish outposts. In the meantime, several CCA tanks rumbling through the northern outskirts of Tessy restored spirit to the company of the 30th Division that had earlier been driven out. "The tanks could have had wooden guns," said one of the men. Their presence alone was invigorating. Together, infantrymen and tankers cleared the northern outskirts.[78]

Getting into Tessy did not mean that the town was secure. German artillery shells continued to fall into the streets until the 35th Division of the V Corps across the river took high ground east of the town on the following day, 2 August. At that time, the 30th Division passed into XIX Corps reserve and CCA reverted to 2d Armored Division control.

The XIX Corps was still far from its post-COBRA objective. But it had contributed handsomely to the final success growing out of COBRA. By blocking for five days the German attempt to reestablish a defensive line across the Cotentin, XIX Corps had enabled troops on the First Army right to make a spectacular end run.

---

[77] Quoted in Hewitt, *Story of the 30th Infantry Division*, p. 45.

[78] Hewitt, *Story of the 30th Infantry Division*, pp. 45–46; [Ferriss], Opns of 30th Div, pp. 35–36; XIX Corps G–3 Per Rpts 54 and 55, 31 Jul and 1 Aug.

CHAPTER XVI

Breakthrough Becomes Breakout

The Outflanking Force

While General Bradley on 28 July was giving direction to the exploitation growing out of COBRA, General Collins' VII Corps still had not completed its assignment in the COBRA operation. The 1st Division, with Combat Command B of the 3d Armored Division attached, was establishing positions in the Coutances–Marigny area. The rest of the 3d Armored Division was engaged near Montpinchon. The 2d Armored Division, less CCA, was extending a line across the Cotentin from Notre-Dame-de-Cenilly to Cérences. The 4th Division, less the 22d Infantry, was hurrying to the Notre-Dame-de-Cenilly sector to reinforce the armored division. Only the 9th Division was out of contact with the enemy—needing rest, it was about to pass into corps reserve. Both the 30th Division and the 2d Armored's CCA had been transferred to the XIX Corps, and plans already were under way to redistribute some of the extra artillery provided the VII Corps for Operation COBRA.[1] (*See Maps VI and VII.*)

Still oriented to the west in accord with the COBRA plan, VII Corps would have to make a sharp turn to the south before taking part in the exploitation, a maneuver that well might delay its participation. In hope of speeding the shift and holding traffic congestion to a minimum, General Collins first ordered reorientation and attack by the units that were farthest south in the corps sector, the 2d Armored and 4th Infantry Divisions, only to see this plan disrupted by the continued pressure against the 2d Armored Division the Germans exerted in trying to escape the Roncey pocket.[2] So long as this pressure persisted, the 2d Armored Division could not assume a new mission.

Having detached the 3d Armored Division's CCB from the 1st Division in order to provide an armored reserve under his original plan, General Collins saw a solution to his problem in reuniting the combat command with its parent division and using the 3d Armored in the exploitation attack. He ordered the 3d Armored to go south early on 30 July and pass through the 2d Armored in order to attack on the right and abreast of the 4th Division. To reinforce the 4th Division, since the 22d Infantry had passed to control of the XIX Corps, Collins provided it with the 1st Division's 26th Infantry. The remainder of the 1st Division was to be in reserve, but be prepared to move south on six hours' notice. The 9th Division was to

---

[1] VII Corps Opns Memos 52 and 53, 30 and 31 Jul.

[2] VII Corps Opns Memo 51, 29 Jul (confirming oral orders issued 26 Jul).

go into bivouac for rest and reorganization.[3]

The 3d Armored and 4th Divisions were ready to take up the post-COBRA exploitation on the morning of 30 July. The two divisions were to attack southeast for seven miles from Gavray to Villedieu-les-Poëles. The infantry was to take Villedieu, an important road center in the middle of the Cotentin about half way between Granville and the town of Vire, and high ground east of Villedieu, while the armor was to seize high ground and river crossing sites west of Villedieu.

The situation seemed propitious since the Germans west of the Vire River—perhaps 16,000 men and less than three tank battalions—were in retreat. Neither reserves nor a German defensive line north of the Avranches–Tessy-sur-Vire area was in evidence.[4]

Attacking with two regiments abreast on the morning of 30 July, the 4th Division encountered little opposition until it arrived about four miles north of Villedieu-les-Poëles. Here an artillery preparation and a battalion attack during the afternoon failed to eliminate the opposition. Excellent defensive terrain and the presence of strong enemy forces, particularly on the 4th Division left on ground south of Percy, brought operations to a temporary halt.

On the 4th Division right, the two combat commands of the 3d Armored Division in the meantime had driven toward Gavray and Hambye to cross the Sienne River abreast.[5] Of the two, CCB

had less difficulty, despite poor country roads and wrecked German vehicles that had to be pushed off the roads before the columns could pass. Reaching Hambye in early afternoon of 30 July, CCB found a damaged bridge and met small arms fire from the south bank, but a small reconnaissance party supported by fire from the advance guard was sufficient to drive the Germans back. Engineers repaired the bridge by late afternoon, and the combat command continued the march south toward Villedieu-les-Poëles. Like the infantry, the armor ran into increasing resistance when nearing Villedieu. Since portions of the combat command still had to cross the Sienne before a full-scale attack could be mounted against the objective west of the town, Colonel Boudinot halted CCB and established perimeter defenses for the night.[6]

In moving to Gavray, CCA of the 3d Armored Division had been hampered by the presence of troops of other divisions. CCA's COBRA attack had brought it to, and in some places beyond, the Coutances–Lengronne highway, which had been pre-empted by, then turned over to, the VIII Corps. Since armor of the VIII Corps was driving south along this route, intermingling of VII and VIII Corps troops was inevitable. "Things were in wild disorder," General Collins later recalled. Extricating hundreds of CCA men and vehicles from what had become the adjacent corps sector was difficult work. Had CCA been able to use the main highway from Coutances through Lengronne to Gavray, its advance would have been simplified. But CCA, like

---

[3] VII Corps Opns Memo 52, 30 Jul (confirming oral orders issued 29 Jul).

[4] 3d Armd Div FO 5, 30 Jul.

[5] 3d Armd Div FO 5, 30 Jul (confirming oral orders).

[6] 3d Armd Div G–3 Per Rpt 36, 30 Jul.

CCB, had been relegated to a network of narrow, muddy, twisting roads that would have retarded movement even if hundreds of burned-out German vehicles had not blocked the way in Roncey and along the roads leading south and southeast. Furthermore, orienting CCA from west to southeast involved turning the advance guards, uncoiling columns, regrouping forces, and, as a result, much internal traffic congestion. The necessity of passing through the rear of the 2d Armored Division also added to traffic problems. Both General Collins and General Hickey had to give personal attention to traffic control at critical road intersections in order to get CCA on its way.[7]

In spite of all these difficulties, reconnaissance troops of CCA reached the Sienne River in the early afternoon of 30 July. They found the bridge to Gavray destroyed and the town, situated on the south bank, apparently held in strength. Conscious of high wooded ground across the river, where the Germans possessed good observation, concealment, and fields of fire, and acutely aware of enemy artillery, the reconnaissance troops made no effort to cross the little river before the main body of the combat command arrived.

In late afternoon the two leading task forces of CCA were in position to make an assault crossing. After two armored field artillery battalions laid down a fifteen-minute preparation and fired

counterbattery against several enemy pieces located by observation planes, the armored infantrymen waded into four feet of water to fight their way across. One task force appeared so hesitant in making its crossing that its commander, Lt. Col. Leander L. Doan, became impatient, dismounted from his tank, and personally led the assault.[8] Actually, the Germans possessed little strength. Only scattered fire bothered the infantry as they crossed. In little more than a hour the two task forces had established a consolidated bridgehead and began to prepare for a counterattack that never came. Engineers set to work building a bridge so that tanks and other vehicles could cross the following morning.

Although both attacking divisions of the VII Corps were across the Sienne by the evening of 30 July, General Collins was markedly disappointed that no more spectacular advances had been made. He therefore altered the plan of attack.

For some time General Collins had been of the opinion that the 3d Armored Division was overcautious. He had, for example, seen dismounted reconnaissance personnel searching for enemy troops while American vehicles nearby passed back and forth unmolested. He also felt that the 3d showed lack of experience and needed aggressive leadership at the top. The command did not know, for example, "how to coil up off the road or close when it was stopped." Collins had observed a "long column going off the road through one hole in a hedgerow . . . one vehicle . . . at a time . . . blocking the road to the rear for miles, holding up supplies and transpor-

---

[7] VII Corps Opns Memo 51, 29 Jul (confirming oral orders, 28 Jul); Interv by author with Gen Collins, 2 Sep 55; Talk by Gen Collins at the Armored School, Fort Knox, Ky., 19 Jan 48 (in the Library of The Armored School); Ltr, Collins to Hechler, 9 Dec 45, quoted in Hechler, VII Corps in Operation COBRA, p. 219.

[8] Colonel Doan was awarded the DSC for this action.

tation coming forward." To replace the 3d Armored Division, Collins brought the 1st Division south to take responsibility for the 3d Armored Division zone. This gave him "two exceptionally able commanders" in Generals Huebner and Barton.[9]

Attaching CCA to the 1st Division and CCB to the 4th Division—thereby reducing the 3d Armored Division headquarters to an administrative agency charged only with supplying and servicing the combat commands—Collins ordered the infantry divisions to attack abreast, each spearheaded by the attached armor. With COBRA completed, he visualized a more distant objective ten miles south of Villedieu-les-Poëles: the 4th Division was to proceed through Villedieu to St. Pois, which earlier, until the Tessy-sur-Vire battle developed, had been a XIX Corps objective; the 1st Division was to drive to Brécey and beyond, across the Sée River.[10]

The challenge of rapid advance came a day too early for the 4th Division, for the division lacked troops. Though the organic regiment that had been attached to the XIX Corps had been replaced by the 1st Division's 26th Infantry, the 26th now passed to its parent unit. Another of the 4th Division's organic regiments, the 8th Infantry, would not arrive from the Notre-Dame-de-Cenilly region until too late for the first day of renewed attack. Only one regiment, the 12th Infantry, plus the attached armor, was on hand. When the infantrymen attacked toward Villedieu-les-Poëles, they could

make only minor gains. At the same time, CCB moved eastward along the vulnerable left flank of the division and spent most of the day building bridges, reorganizing, and reducing occasional enemy roadblocks.

Not until the evening of 31 July, after the arrival of the 8th Infantry, was the 4th Division altogether ready to drive south. Calling his principal subordinates together, General Barton made it clear he had in mind rapid, sweeping advances. "We face a defeated enemy," he told his commanders, "an enemy terribly low in morale, terribly confused. I want you in the next advance to throw caution to the winds . . . destroying, capturing, or bypassing the enemy, and pressing"—he paused to find the correct word—"pressing *recklessly* on to the objective."[11] The units of the 4th Division and the attached armor took General Barton at his word when they renewed the attack on 1 August.

Meanwhile, developments had occurred even more rapidly on the corps right, where CCA spearheaded the 1st Division attack on 31 July. One task force drove quickly against scattered German forces that were employing occasional tanks and antitank guns in ineffective delaying actions. Hitting the broad side of an enemy column—light armor and personnel carriers—moving southwest from Villedieu toward Avranches, tankers of this task force disorganized and dispersed the enemy with fire at close range, though fast-falling twilight helped a large part of the column to escape. Sensing the proxi-

---

[9] Gen Collins' Talk at The Armored School; Ruppenthal Notes, ML-2185.

[10] VII Corps Opns Memo 53, 31 Jul (confirming oral orders 30 Jul).

[11] CI 30 (4th Div); see Hechler, VII Corps in Operation COBRA, pp. 236–37.

mity of stronger enemy forces, and unwilling to chance contact while his own troops were dispersed, General Hickey ordered the task force into defensive positions for the night near the village of l'Epine.

More spectacular was the thrust of another task force under Colonel Doan that cut the Villedieu-les-Poëles–Granville highway just west of Villedieu in the late afternoon of 31 July. As Doan was searching for a good place to halt, he received a message that General Collins wanted him to continue twelve miles farther to the final objective, Hill 242, south of Brécey. Doan spurred his force on. Looking ahead to a railroad embankment where he could expect opposition, he asked for fighter-bombers to fly column cover to strafe and bomb the tracks as their last mission in the fading light of day. When the ground column crossed the railway unopposed, the tankers noticed several unmanned antitank guns. Though the enemy crews later returned to their positions to oppose the infantry in wake of the armored spearhead, the effective work of the fighter-bombers had spared the armor what could have been a costly engagement.

Bypassing one of its original objectives, Hill 216 southwest of Villedieu-les-Poëles, Doan's task force barreled down the main road to Brécey during the early evening hours of 31 July. When the commander of the point had difficulty selecting the correct road at an intersection, Colonel Doan himself took over in his command tank. Making a Hollywood-type entry into Brécey, the task force commander took pot shots with his pistol at surprised German soldiers who were lounging at the curb and in houses along the main street of the town.[12]

Though the principal bridge south of Brécey had been destroyed, Doan's command prepared a hasty ford by hand-carrying rock to line the river bed. Infantrymen waded the stream and subdued scattered small arms fire. Tanks and vehicles followed. The final objective, Hill 242, lay three miles to the south, and only when his men reached a wooded area on the north slope of the hill did Doan permit a halt.

On 1 August, a week after the beginning of Operation COBRA, VII Corps was near the base of the Cotentin, more than thirty miles due south of the Périers–St. Lô highway. General Collins had reversed his field and made an extraordinary gain that outflanked the German left.

The Breakout to Avranches

In the coastal sector of the Cotentin an even more outstanding achievement was developing. Under the supervision of General Patton, the Third Army commander, VIII Corps had been demonstrating vividly just how much Operation COBRA had accomplished.

When General Bradley instructed General Patton to supervise the VIII Corps exploitation growing out of COBRA, he gave Patton charge of operations that intimately and personally concerned the Third Army commander. The quicker Patton got the VIII Corps to the threshold of Brittany, the sooner he would be able to enter battle at the head of his army.

---

[12] 3d Armd Div CCA intervs cited in Hechler, VII Corps in Operation COBRA, pp. 246–48; 3d Armd Div CCA AAR, Jul.

To enable Patton to supervise the VIII Corps, General Bradley had asked him to serve as his deputy for the forces on the right.[13] Though Patton remained in the background of command to the best of his ability, his presence was unmistakable, and his imprint on the operations that developed was as visible as his shadow on the wall of the operations tent.

The situation facing the VIII Corps on the evening of 27 July was challenging. On the one hand, the Germans were making a general withdrawal, which in effect invited the Americans to exploit. On the other hand, serious obstacles kept the Americans from making a rapid advance—the profusion of mines, wrecked vehicles, and enemy delaying forces. Furthermore, the infantry divisions that had carried the VIII Corps attack in COBRA filled the roads, and from the east came the VII Corps and the threat of congestion. As though the potential confusion between VII and VIII Corps units was not enough, a new corps, the XV, was scheduled to enter the line between the VII and the VIII as soon as the Third Army became operational.[14]

For all these drawbacks, the absence of organized German resistance on 27 July and the urge to reach the edge of Brittany exerted an overpowering influence. General Bradley, after conferring with General Patton on 27 July, had already ordered General Middleton to disregard the COBRA limit of advance north of Coutances, and infantrymen of the VIII Corps were streaming south as quickly as engineers could clear paths for them through mine fields.[15]

That evening, as orders from Bradley shifted the First Army from COBRA into exploitation, Patton manifested his influence by substituting armor for infantry. Two armored divisions were to spearhead the attack to the south.

In the COBRA attack, the lone armored division available to the VIII Corps, the 4th under Maj. Gen. John S. Wood, had been pinched out near the starting line. Located on the Carentan–Périers isthmus in corps reserve, the 4th Armored Division was behind the infantry forces completing their COBRA assignments when General Middleton ordered General Wood to move. Shortly after daylight, 28 July, Wood was to pass through the 90th Division and proceed through Périers and toward Coutances as far as Monthuchon. Expecting troops of the VII Corps to have secured Monthuchon by that time, Middleton told Wood to co-ordinate with Collins' units so that he could continue through Coutances to Cérences, twenty-two miles south of Périers and nine miles south of Coutances.[16]

The second armored force was a new unit, the 6th Armored Division under Maj. Gen. Robert W. Grow, attached from the Third Army. Middleton alerted Grow to move from his assembly area north of la Haye-du-Puits and attack on the right of the 4th Armored

[13] XV Corps G-3 Memo, Conf at Comd Post VIII Corps, 282000 Jul, 29 Jul, XV Corps G-3 Jnl and File; Pogue Interv with Bradley, Washington, 1948, Pogue Files.

[14] XV Corps G-3 Memo, Conf at Comd Post VIII Corps, 282000 Jul, 29 Jul, XV Corps G-3 Jnl and File.

[15] XV Corps G-3 Memo, Conf at G-3 Office, Hq Third U.S. Army, 281600 Jul, 29 Jul, XV Corps G-3 Jnl File.

[16] 4th Armd Div G-3 Jnl, entry 2115, 27 Jul, Overlay to Accompany FO 2, 26 Jul, and FO 3, 28 Jul; VIII Corps Msgs, 1810, 27 Jul, and 0125, 28 Jul, 4th Armd Div G-3 Jnl File.

Division down the Cotentin coast. Grow was to pass through the 79th Division, bypass Coutances on the west, and drive to Granville, twenty-eight miles south of Coutances.[17]

The plan of action for 28 July thus projected twin thrusts by the 4th and 6th Armored Divisions moving abreast through two infantry divisions, the 90th and the 79th. In the expectation that XV Corps was to be inserted on the VIII Corps left, and, anticipating that the new corps would compress the 4th Armored Division zone of advance, General Middleton intended to assign the main effort to the 6th Armored Division on the right. Followed by the 79th Division, the 6th Armored Division would subsequently drive from Granville to the base of the Cotentin near Avranches.[18]

To make possible armored operations in a corps zone jammed with infantry troops and strewn with mines, Middleton ordered the infantry divisions to intensify their demining programs and to clear the main routes. The VIII Corps Engineer, Col. William R. Winslow, hastily organized teams to teach members of the armored divisions how to remove new types of German mines.[19] To assure control and balance while the armored divisions passed to the front, General Middleton instructed the troops to halt for further orders after capturing Granville and Cérences.[20]

The 6th Armored Division reconnoitered its projected zone of advance on the afternoon of 27 July. The following morning, as the infantry divisions of the VIII Corps continued to advance against no opposition, Grow received the order to start rolling.[21] CCA (Brig. Gen. James Taylor) moved quickly to Lessay, where traffic congestion because of combat damage to the town, bridge repair, and mine fields retarded progress. Getting through Lessay was difficult, but by early afternoon CCA was moving rapidly toward Coutances. The only opposition to what resembled a road march came from an enemy roadblock two miles northwest of Coutances, where a few German infantrymen and one tank tried to delay the column. Bypassing Coutances on the west, the leading units of CCA moved a short distance down the coastal road toward Granville before halting for the night.[22]

In the left of the VIII Corps zone, the 4th Armored Division had begun to advance shortly after daybreak, 28 July, when CCB (Brig. Gen. Holmes E. Dager) moved through Périers toward

[17] 6th Armd Div AAR, Jul, and G–3 Jnl, 28 Jul.

[18] XV Corps G–3 Memo, Conf at Comd Post VIII Corps, 282000 Jul, 29 Jul, XV Corps G–3 Jnl and File.

[19] 357th Inf Jnl, entry 2220, 27 Jul; ETOUSA Engr Hist Rpt 10, Combat Engineering, p. 35.

[20] VIII Corps Msgs, 0125 and 0130, 28 Jul, to 4th and 6th Armd Divs, FUSA G–3 Jnl.

[21] VIII Corps Msg, 1600, 27 Jul, and G–3 Jnl, entries, 0113, 0200, and 1045, 28 Jul; 6th Armd Div Msg, 2210, 27 Jul, FUSA G–3 Jnl; 6th Armd Div AAR, Jul.

[22] The basic sources for the action in the VIII Corps sector described below are: G–3 Section, Combat Record of the Sixth Armored Division in the European Theater of Operations, 18 July 1944–8 May 1945, compiled under direction of Maj. Clyde J. Burk (Germany: Steinbeck-Druck Aschaffenburg, 1945) (hereafter cited as Combat Record of the Sixth Armored Division), an excellent documentary source, pp. 1–8; Capt. Kenneth Koyen, The Fourth Armored Division (Munich, Germany: Herder-Druck, 1946), pp. 7–21; F. P. Halas, VIII Corps Operations, 26–31 July 1944, a preliminary MS, Hist Div USFET (1945), OCMH Files.

KNOCKED-OUT AMERICAN TANKS OUTSIDE AVRANCHES

Coutances. Near St. Sauveur-Lendelin a dense mine field held up progress. Reconnaissance troops vainly searched side roads for alternate routes, tank dozers came forward to construct bypasses, and the main body remained in place for three hours until engineers swept and demined the main road. Under way again, CCB met scant opposition. The armor found no VII Corps troops at Monthuchon and continued to the outskirts of Coutances during the afternoon. When armored infantry dismounted and, accompanied by light tanks, entered the city on foot, German rear-guard troops fought back with artillery, mortar, and small arms fire. A sharp skirmish ensued. Supported by an artillery battalion that threaded its way forward through the stationary armored column, the armored infantry by evening had cleared Coutances of its

scattered defenders. German artillery on high ground several miles east of the city gave brief and half-hearted interdictory fire.[23]

By the end of 28 July, VIII Corps at last held Coutances, the objective that had lured the corps forward for almost a month. COBRA had accomplished what the battle of the hedgerows had not, but Coutances in the process had lost its value. More important, General Middleton had two armored divisions at the head of his troops, almost in position to pursue a withdrawing enemy—almost in position, but not quite, for although the

---

[23] 4th Armd Div G–3 Jnl, 28 Jul; VIII Corps G–3 Per Rpt 44, 29 Jul; see Abbé Georges Cadel, "Au Pays de Coutances," in Herval, *Bataille de Normandie*, I, 166–87. General Wood received the DSC for his inspiring leadership at Coutances during the engagement.

spearheads were in place, the columns were strung out and backed up through the countryside. The armor would require another day to wriggle through the infantry.

From a study of the terrain, it seemed that the Germans might try to anchor their right on Tessy-sur-Vire and withdraw their left. On this basis, the Germans might try to consolidate defenses and hold on one of three possible lines: Tessy–Coutances; Tessy–Granville; or Tessy–Villedieu-les-Poëles–Avranches.

By the end of 28 July, however, the Germans had lost Coutances and appeared incapable of stabilizing the front in the Cotentin. There was little indication of defensive preparations. The Germans seemed "completely disorganized with no sign of co-ordinated resistance." Air reconnaissance disclosed no movement of reinforcements toward the area roughly bounded by Coutances, Avranches, and Percy. On the contrary, German vehicular columns were cluttering the roads below Bréhal, Gavray, and Percy as they hurried south under punishment administered by American tactical aircraft. Destroyed and burning vehicles lined almost every main road. Trees along a 200-yard line in Coutances had been notched for felling across the highway, but were still standing when American troops arrived, clear evidence of the haste of the German withdrawal. Mines were scattered along roads and at intersections rather than in disciplined patterns. Defenders of the few isolated roadblocks that existed fought half-heartedly. Bridges were sometimes demolished, sometimes not. A small amount of light-caliber artillery fire harassed the American advance, but

the bulk of the German artillery was en route south.[24]

Convinced that German reinforcements must be on their way to the Cotentin from Brittany and from sectors east of the Vire River, American commanders hoped to overrun the potential defensive lines that remained in the Cotentin before the reinforcements could arrive. General Middleton consequently raised his immediate sights to Avranches.[25]

On a picturesque bluff 200 feet high, Avranches overlooks the bay of Mont St. Michel and the famous rock clearly visible eight miles away. Avranches fascinated the Americans, not because of the sights that have interested tourists for so long but because it is at the base of the Cotentin. For practical-minded Americans in July 1944, Avranches was the symbol of egress from the Cotentin and entrance into Brittany.

Avranches lies between two rivers, the Sée and the Sélune, which flow westward to the bay about four miles apart. The city snuggles against the Sée where two highway bridges funnel traffic from five highways arriving from the north and the east—two from Granville, one each from Coutances, Villedieu-les-Poëles, and Brécey. Below Avranches the roads are compressed into one main highway leading due south and across the Sélune River near Pontaubault, where the highway splits, the roads diverging and affording access to the east, south, and west. A bottleneck in the north–south road network, protected by water on

[24] VIII Corps G–2 Per Rpt 44, 28 Jul; FUSA Air Sec Msgs, 1800 and 2201, 28 Jul, 83d Div G–2, G–3 Jnl File, and G–2 Per Rpt 49, 29 Jul.
[25] VIII Corps Msg, 0030, 29 Jul, 83d Div G–2, G–3 Jnl and File.

three sides, situated on commanding terrain, Avranches in the summer of 1944 was a prize beyond compare.

On the evening of 28 July, armored spearheads of the VIII Corps were more than thirty miles from Avranches, but separated from the city, General Middleton believed, only by scattered opposition. He ordered the 6th Armored Division to strike swiftly through Granville to Avranches while the 4th Armored Division took Cérences, then moved southeastward to secure a crossing of the Sée River at Tirepied, several miles east of Avranches. The capture of Avranches and of crossing sites over the Sée and Sélune Rivers would make possible the commitment of the Third Army into Brittany, and to this end the 4th Armored Division was to hold open the natural bottlenèck at the base of the Cotentin and block German forces that might threaten the slender corridor from the east. Attaching forty Quartermaster trucks to the 79th and 8th Divisions, Middleton instructed each of these infantry division commanders to motorize a regimental combat team. The teams were to be ready to assist the 6th and 4th Armored Divisions, respectively.[26]

Shortly after daybreak, 29 July, the leading units of the 6th Armored Division moved southwest of Coutances to the Sienne River. At the destroyed bridge of Pont-de-la-Roque, small arms fire from the south bank stopped the advance. When reconnaissance revealed no other river crossing site in the division zone, CCA prepared a full-scale assault. The arrangements consumed most of the day. After a five-minute artillery preparation reinforced by tank

and tank destroyer fire, armored infantrymen crossed the river early in the evening against light mortar and small arms fire and dispersed the few defenders. Engineers began to construct a bridge and prepare a ford.

The ground gained was disappointing, and the loss of 3 killed and 10 wounded as against only 39 prisoners taken seemed to indicate that the division had been less than aggressive in its initial action. General Patton noted this pointedly to the division commander, as did General Middleton, who tersely commanded General Grow to "put on the heat." [27]

On the left, the 4th Armored Division was making better progress. General Wood saw that his axis of advance, the Coutances–Hyenville–Cérences highway, crossed the Sienne River in three places. Anticipating that the Germans would have destroyed the bridges, he requested permission to use, in addition, the parallel highway—the Coutances–Lengronne road—two miles to the east. Unfortunately, the road was in the VII Corps sector. After a conference at corps and army echelons and despite recognition that VII Corps troops driving westward from Montpinchon would probably overflow the highway and cause confusion and delay, the road was reassigned to the VIII Corps. General Wood then ordered CCB to use both main highways, a course of action the tankers had already initiated.[28]

Brig. Gen. Holmes E. Dager's CCB

---

[26] VIII Corps Msg, 2355, 28 Jul, VIII Corps G–3 Jnl and File.

[27] George S. Patton, Jr., *War as I Knew It* (Boston: Houghton Mifflin Company, 1947), pp. 96–97; Ltr, Grow to OCMH, 29 Mar 56.

[28] VIII Corps G–3 Jnl, entry 0250, 29 Jul; VII Corps Opns Memo 51, 29 Jul (confirming oral orders 28 Jul); 4th Armd Div G–3 Jnl, entry 0040, 29 Jul, and Overlay (Routes of CCB, 4th Armd

had worked through the night of 28 July to clear the scattered enemy troops in Coutances and just south of the city. At daybreak, 29 July, when two armored columns departed, only a few armed Germans and a profusion of mines remained in Coutances.[29] A damaged bridge immediately south of the city was quickly repaired.[30] Then, as fighter-bombers provided air cover, the armor drove forward on two routes, meeting sporadic resistance so disorganized that deployment was usually not necessary in order to overrun and eliminate it. Interference from VII Corps tanks that overflowed from the adjacent corps zone was more serious, though not fatal. The CCB columns encountered and destroyed several German tanks late in the afternoon and rolled on to the Sienne River at Cérences and south of Lengronne. There, destroyed bridges brought the advance to a halt.

In gaining about ten miles on 29 July, CCB had sustained little more than 30 casualties and had taken 125 prisoners. The problem of handling surrendering enemy threatened throughout the day to consume more time and energy than did the terrain, traffic, and spotty resistance. "Send them to the rear disarmed without guards" became a standing operating procedure.[31]

By the end of 29 July, the 4th and 6th Armored Divisions were sufficiently forward to give promise of rapid thrusts to the south on the following day. Nothing the enemy seemed capable of doing appeared strong enough to block the advance. The "disorderly withdrawal of the enemy throughout the period continued, showing no signs of slackening." German vehicular movement southward still clogged the roads south of Bréhal and Cérences. Sporadic fire from isolated self-propelled guns harassed American bridging parties along the Sienne River, but other than that the leading units of VIII Corps were out of contact with organized German defenses. To the rear of the armor, the infantry divisions had held in place and collected about a hundred prisoners. The 79th and 8th Divisions each had a motorized regimental combat team ready to reinforce the armored divisions. The corps artillery had fired only registration missions, had reconnoitered forward areas, and had displaced to the south as rapidly as possible. All seemed in readiness for a decisive thrust to Avranches.[32]

To General Middleton, the 4th Armored Division instead of the 6th now seemed in a better position to secure Avranches. The 4th was also manifesting the superiority over untested units that experienced troops generally display. Earlier in the month, to the horror of some armored experts who had protested that an armored division should not be used to hold a static front,

---

Div, East and West Elements), 1230, 29 Jul, 4th Armd Div G-3 Jnl; Interv by author with Gen Collins, Washington D.C., 2 Sep 55.

[29] 4th Armd Div G-3 Jnl, 29 Jul, and CCB S-3 Jnl, entry 0614, 29 Jul; VIII Corps G-3 Jnl, 29 Jul. Col. Louis J. Storck, the CCR commander, was killed when a mine destroyed his jeep in Coutances.

[30] Capt. William F. Pieri, who deactivated a row of mines blocking the bridge and enabled the armor to continue, was posthumously awarded the DSC.

[31] 4th Armd Div G-3 Jnl, 1825, 29 Jul, and CCB S-3 Jnl, entries 0730, 1033, and 1430, 29 Jul.

[32] FUSA Sitrep 108, 30 Jul, G-2 Per Rpt 50, 30 Jul, and Msg, 0320, 30 Jul, 83d G-2, G-3 Jnl and File; VIII Corps G-2 Weekly Rpt 6, 29 Jul, and G-3 Per Rpt 45, 30 Jul.

General Middleton had assigned the 4th a portion of the defensive line on the Carentan–Périers isthmus. There, during the week before COBRA, the division had learned enough of actual combat to acquire a confidence that was evident in its operations of 28 and 29 July. To take advantage of these factors, Middleton gave Avranches, the corps objective, to General Wood. The 6th Armored Division was to capture Bréhal and Granville.[33]

Dissatisfied with the progress of CCA, General Grow wished to get CCB (Col. George W. Read, Jr.) into action. He therefore passed CCB through the 6th Armored Division forces holding the bridgehead at Pont-de-la-Roque. Anticipating little resistance at Bréhal, Grow expected CCB, after driving through the town, to bypass Granville on the east and encircle it from the south.[34]

As expected, little besides small arms fire along the main road opposed the approach to Bréhal. CCB leapfrogged forward, firing high-explosive shells and canister into wooded areas along the road, and reached the outskirts of town, where a log roadblock with a rolling steel gate barred the way. After a flight of four P–47's made several unsuccessful passes at the obstacle, the lead tank in the column simply rammed the block, knocked down the logs, and opened a passage into the main street of Bréhal. After several random shots, a few bedraggled Germans were herded into the town square.

South of Bréhal, CCB passed a pre-

pared but undefended roadblock and drove through light artillery fire interdicting the highway to Granville. General Grow halted the advance short of the city to consolidate his gain. The division had moved about twelve miles, had taken more than 200 prisoners against 2 men killed and 10 wounded, and was demonstrating that it, too, was capable of aggressive and assured action.

Meanwhile, the 4th Armored Division was carrying the main effort of VIII Corps. As soon as General Wood had learned that he was to take Avranches, he notified the CCB commander: "Present mission cancelled—using any roads [in zone] . . . move on Avranches . . . to capture it and secure crossings east thereof." [35] For all the urgency implied in this order, the destroyed Sienne River bridges at Cérences and south of Lengronne continued to thwart advance until the afternoon of 30 July, when engineers bridged the stream. Only then could both columns of CCB cross the river and proceed to the south.

The eastern column ran into an ambush almost at once and after losing six half-tracks spent the rest of the day eradicating the resistance. Dismounted infantry, with support from artillery and a flight of fighter-bombers, attacked German positions on high ground obstructing the advance, while antitank gunners engaged and destroyed two German tanks. At the approach of darkness the Germans retired, then shelled the high ground they had vacated, apparently on the premise that American infantrymen had occupied it. But the Americans had abandoned the hill to outpost the

---

[33] VIII Corps Msg, 29 Jul, 83d Div G–2, G–3 Jnl and File.
[34] 6th Armd Div FO 3, 0300, 30 Jul.

[35] 4th Armd Div G–3 Jnl, entry 2130, 29 Jul.

tanks on the road during the night. When the skirmish ended, CCB had incurred 43 casualties and lost eight half-tracks.

The western column, under the personal command of General Dager, had better luck. Tanks moved rapidly for about ten miles through la Haye-Pesnel and Sartilly against virtually no resistance. Three and a half miles north of Avranches, the troops unknowingly passed within several hundred yards of the *Seventh Army* advance command post. General Hausser, Generalmajor Rudolf-Christoph Freiherr Gersdorff, and other general staff officers made their way to safety through the meticulously regular intervals of the column serials. On foot at first, later in commandeered vehicles, the German officers fled eastward through Brécey toward Mortain.[36]

The CCB column continued to the Sée River just north of Avranches and discovered that both highway bridges were intact. Early in the evening troops entered Avranches, an undefended city for all its prize aspects. After outposting the southern and eastern outskirts quickly, General Dager sent a small force eastward along the north bank of the Sée to secure the bridge at Tirepied, five miles away.[37]

The situation as it was known at VIII Corps headquarters on the evening of 30 July was obscure, even to the achievement at Avranches.[38] Abundant evidence indicated the complete absence of organized resistance in the corps zone. Airplane pilots reported having seen Frenchmen from Granville to Villedieu-les-Poëles "waving the Tri-Color," which obviously meant that the Germans had withdrawn south of that line. Civilians reported Germans asking the road to Mayenne, twenty-five miles to the south. Prisoners, numbering 1,200 on 30 July, consistently affirmed that German units were completely out of contact with each other and with higher headquarters.[39] Yet the experience of the 6th Armored Division in the coastal sector and the ambush of the 4th Armored Division eastern column pointed to the presence of hard-fighting enemy units. At the same time the whereabouts of the column in Avranches was unknown. If, as was rumored, troops of the 4th Armored Division's CCB had entered Avranches, then the VIII Corps left flank from Gavray to Avranches, a distance of ten miles, was wide open since the adjacent VII Corps on the evening of 30 July was crossing the Sienne River at Gavray.[40]

Unable to believe that German disorganization was as great as represented, General Middleton was hopefully cautious until he learned definitely that American troops were in Avranches. Then, late on the evening of 30 July, Middleton acted with dispatch. He ordered Wood to push through Avran-

[36] James B. Hodgson, Report of Interview [on Avranches] With General von Gersdorff, 1954, MS R-40, OCMH.

[37] Armor in the Exploitation or the 4th Armored Division Across France to the Moselle River (Ft. Knox, Ky., May, 1949), a research report prepared by Committee 13, Officers Advanced Course, p. 20; Koyen, *Fourth Armored Division*, pp. 25, 26.

[38] See, for example, VIII Corps Msg, 2030, 30 Jul, 83d Div G-2, G-3 Jnl and File.

[39] FUSA G-2 Per Rpt 51, 31 Jul; VIII Corps G-2 Jnl, 30 Jul, and Tel Msg, 1000, 30 Jul, VIII Corps G-3 Jnl.

[40] VIII Corps G-2 Jnl, 30 Jul; see above, p. 307.

ches and across the Sélune River and attached to the 4th Armored Division the motorized regimental combat team of the 8th Division that was ready to move. To prevent intermingling of the 4th and 6th Armored Divisions on the restricted road net, Middleton told Grow to take Granville and move only as far toward Avranches as the Sartilly–la Haye-Pesnel line.[41]

Appreciating the necessity for speed and on-the-spot co-ordination, General Wood delegated control of all the 4th Armored Division forces in the vicinity of Avranches to General Dager by attaching to CCB not only the infantry regiment of the 8th Division but also CCA (Col. Bruce C. Clarke), which he had already dispatched to Avranches.[42]

Taking Avranches was not enough. The narrow coastal corridor, consisting of the single main highway from Avranches to the Sélune River crossing near Pontaubault, four miles to the south, had to be made secure to allow the Third Army to pass into Brittany. The troops thus needed to hold Avranches and at the same time to seize and hold essential adjacent objectives: river crossings south and southeast of Avranches and high ground east and southeast. Part of the high ground between the Sée and Sélune Rivers—rugged terrain where several reservoirs and dams were located—was an eventual objective of the VII Corps, but responsibility for the portion south of the Sélune near the village of Ducey belonged, as did the

other tasks around Avranches, to General Dager's CCB.[43]

General Dager learned at 0200, 31 July, that he was soon to receive additional forces to help him hold Avranches, establish Sélune River crossing sites, and take Ducey. The news was opportune, less in terms of seizing the other objectives than in holding the one he had taken with such ease the afternoon before. The fact was that trouble had developed at Avranches.[44]

First indications that Avranches might not be as easy to hold as it had at first appeared had developed about two hours before midnight of 30 July. At the Sée River bridge on the main highway from Granville, men of a CCB tank company detected the approach of a large German vehicular column along the coastal road from Granville. Because the vehicles were marked with red crosses, the tankers assumed they were evacuating German wounded. They allowed the first few to pass and cross the bridge into Avranches. But when Germans in several of the trucks opened fire with rifles, the tankers returned the fire and destroyed a few vehicles, thus blocking the road. With the column halted, German soldiers piled out of their vehicles and came toward the bridge, hands high in surrender. The tank company took several hundred prisoners. Examination revealed that the vehicles were loaded with ammunition and other nonmedical supplies.

Learning from their prisoners that

---

[41] VIII Corps G-3 Jnl, 30 Jul.

[42] 4th Armd Div G-3 and CCB G-3 Jnls, 30 Jul; Halas, VIII Corps Opns, pp. 79–82; Ltr, Wood to OCMH, 24 Mar 54, OCMH Files.

[43] See VII Corps AAR, Jul.

[44] VIII Corps Msg, 0200, 31 Jul, 4th Armd Div G-3 Jnl and File; 4th Armd Div CCB S-3 Jnl. 30 and 31 Jul; see Jean Séguin, "Remous de la Lutte autour d'Avranches," in Herval, *Bataille de Normandie*, I. 208–31.

another, more heavily armed German column was also approaching down the coastal road from Granville, the men of the tank company became jittery. Small arms fire shortly after midnight announced the arrival of the second column. When an enemy shell struck an ammunition truck and set it ablaze, the tank company commander reached a quick decision. His position illuminated, lacking infantry protection for his tanks, and outnumbered by his prisoners, he ordered withdrawal. Without having lost a man or a tank, the company abandoned several hundred prisoners and the Granville road bridge to move eastward to the Sée River bridge on the Villedieu-les-Poëles road.

Over the unguarded bridge the Germans, before daylight on 31 July, entered Avranches in considerable numbers. Some emplaced several artillery pieces on the northwest edge of the Avranches bluff to dominate the bridge and the Granville road. Others in a column of trucks, horse-drawn wagons, and tracked vehicles turned eastward and disappeared into the darkness, headed toward Mortain. Still others moved toward the southern exits of Avranches, where they bumped into armored infantrymen of CCB, who were outposting the southern approaches to the city. Surprised, both American and Germans opened fire. In the confused fight, the action of one machine gunner, Pvt. William H. Whitson, was a deciding factor. Before he was killed, he destroyed nearly 50 Germans and more than 20 light vehicles with his .30-caliber gun.[45]

The Germans turned back, but only to reorganize for a second attack that came after daylight. The CCB infantrymen were ready. Using white phosphorus mortar shells effectively and supported by the providential appearance of a flight of P-47's, they held their ground. When the attack collapsed, several hundred Germans surrendered.

Meanwhile, General Dager had discovered the abandonment of the bridge on the Granville road and ordered the tank company commander to return. The company reached its former positions on 31 July, about the same time that advance units of CCA were arriving on the scene. When the German artillery pieces on the bluff opened fire on CCA, tankers engaged them while armored infantrymen crossed the river, mounted the bluff, and captured the pieces.

By the afternoon of 31 July General Dager was sure that the Germans at Avranches had actually been seeking an escape route and not attempting to recapture Avranches. Dager considered the town secure.[46] He directed CCA to move on to the other task—seizing the main bridge across the Sélune at Pontaubault, a secondary bridge at Ducey, and two dams several miles southeast of Avranches. While the bridges were of prime importance, the dams were hardly less so. If the Germans destroyed the water gates and flooded the Sélune, an immediate advance would be out of the question.

The CCA commander, Colonel Clarke, divided his troops into four task forces. He directed each to one of the

---

[45] Pvt. Whitson was posthumously awarded the DSC.

[46] For his leadership, General Dager was awarded the DSC.

ABANDONED GERMAN EQUIPMENT LITTERS A ROAD TO AVRANCHES

four objectives, which were to be secured before nightfall that day, 31 July, and ordered the forces to bypass resistance. There was no information about the enemy, nor was there time to reconnoiter. With speed the important element, the task forces planned no special tactical dispositions to provide advance or flank security. Since there was no time to obtain air support liaison parties for the individual task forces, fighter-bomber pilots without direct communication to the tankers found their own targets and kept track of progress on the ground by the bright cerise panels on the rear decks and the white painted stars on the tops of the tanks.

One task force took Ducey after several short skirmishes and outposted the bridge there. Another secured its dam objective after overcoming minor resistance. A third was well on its way to taking the other dam after plunging through a series of small roadblocks, knocking over several German motorcyclists, destroying a few enemy tanks, running a gantlet of exploding shells in a destroyed ammunition dump, and finally capturing a company of German infantrymen who walked into the task force outposts on the assumption they were German positions.

It seemed illogical to expect the Pontaubault bridge, four miles due south of Avranches, to be captured intact. If the bridges at Avranches still stood through German oversight, it was unlikely that the same mistake would be made again. American reconnaissance pilots nevertheless had reported on 30

DESTROYED ENEMY VEHICLES CLUTTERING A STREET IN AVRANCHES

July that the Pontaubault bridge was apparently in good condition and unguarded. As late as the afternoon of 31 July, pilots still failed to detect any German troops near the bridge.[47]

As a matter of fact, the Germans were trying to get into position to contest the Pontaubault bridge. They were too late. As a task force of the 4th Division's CCA swept across the bridge in the late afternoon of 31 July and outposted the important road intersections immediately south of it, enemy vehicles approached from the west. Tank and artillery fire quickly dispersed them.

The action completed by the 4th Armored Division by the morning of 1 August gave VIII Corps three crossing

sites over the Sée River (two bridges at Avranches and one at Tirepied, five miles to the east) and four over the Sélune—easily enough routes to enter Brittany. With the division in position to continue south, General Middleton ordered the 6th Armored Division, which had cleared Granville of scattered resistance and moved to the la Haye-Pensel–Sartilly line, to relieve the 4th at Avranches and Pontaubault. He also dispatched another regimental combat team of the 8th Division to the vicinity of Avranches and sent artillery and antiaircraft units to guard the critical roads and bridges.[48]

[47] VIII Corps G–3 Jnl, entries 1330 and 1430, 31 Jul.

[48] VIII Corps G–3 Jnl, entries 1525 and 1935, 31 Jul; see Charles de la Morandière, "L'Angoisse de Granville," and Mme. Paule Mortgat-Lhomer, "Les Alliés aux Portes d'Avranches," in Herval, *Bataille de Normandie*, I, 188–200, 201–07.

That little stood in the way of continued advance was clearly evident. The 4th and 6th Armored Divisions together had taken more than 4,000 prisoners on 31 July. The 79th and 8th Divisions, moving behind the armor on secondary roads, had done little more than process about 3,000 additional prisoners, all willing to be out of the war. In contrast with these figures, casualties of the VIII Corps from 28 through 31 July totaled less than 700.

Fighter-bomber pilots continued to wreak havoc on the retreating enemy columns. Destroyed enemy vehicles along the roads continued to constitute the chief obstruction to ground operations. One pilot counted seventy vehicles burning during the night of 30 July in the Vire–Laval–Rennes–Avranches region. Everywhere in the Cotentin German disorganization was rampant. Abandoned equipment and supplies—guns, tanks, and trucks—littered the countryside as German units fled south and east, and west into Brittany. So great was the destruction in the VIII Corps zone that "hundreds of dead horses, cows, and pigs [and the] stench and decay pervading" were judged "likely menaces to water points and possible bivouac areas." [49]

The facts were obvious. The German defenses in the Cotentin had crumbled and disintegrated. The Americans on the last day of July 1944 possessed and controlled the last natural defensive line before Brittany. From the German point of view, the situation had become a *"Riesensauerei"*—one hell of a mess.[50]

---

[49] VIII Corps Engineer Recon Rpt, 31 Jul, VIII Corps G–3 Jnl and File; FUSA Msgs, 31 Jul, 30th Div G–3 Jnl File and 4th Armd Div G–3 Jnl and File.

[50] Telecon, Kluge and Blumentritt, 1023, 31 Jul, *OB WEST KTB, Anlage 966.*

CHAPTER XVII

The "Incalculable" Results

The Riesensauerei

"It's a madhouse here," Kluge cried in despair as he attempted to describe the situation on the morning of 31 July.

At the *Seventh Army* command post in le Mans, Kluge for the second day was for all intents and purposes commanding the *LXXXIV Corps* and the *Seventh Army*, in addition to performing his official duties as commander of *Army Group B* and *OB WEST* .

"You can't imagine what it's like," he told General der Infanterie Guenther Blumentritt, the *OB WEST* chief of staff, on the telephone. "Commanders are completely out of contact [with their troops]. Jodl and Warlimont [Hitler's chief advisers at OKW] ought to come down and see what is taking place."

Who was to blame? The whole mess had started, it seemed to Kluge, "with Hausser's fatal decision to break out to the southeast. So far, it appears that only the spearheads of various [American] mobile units are through to Avranches. But it is perfectly clear that everything else will follow. Unless I can get infantry and antitank weapons there, the [left] wing can not hold."

Apropos of that, Blumentritt said, OKW wanted to know the locations of all the alternate and rearward defenses under construction in Normandy.

Kluge did not hide his derision. "All you can do is laugh out loud," he replied. "Don't they read our dispatches? Haven't they been oriented? They must be living on the moon."

"Of course," Blumentritt agreed smoothly.

Kluge's mood changed. "Someone has to tell the Fuehrer," he said, without designating who was to perform the unpleasant task, "that if the Americans get through at Avranches they will be out of the woods and they'll be able to do what they want."

The terrible thing, Kluge said, was that there was not much that anyone could do. "It's a crazy situation." [1]

At 0030 on 31 July, Kluge had authorized the *Seventh Army* to withdraw to a line from Granville to Troisgots.[2] Thirty minutes later he was trying to get the *LXXXIV Corps* back still farther, to the Avranches–Villedieu-les-Poëles line, but without much success—for his messages were not getting through. At this time Kluge admitted unequivocally that his left flank had collapsed.[3]

---

[1] Telecon, Kluge and Blumentritt, 1023, 31 Jul, *OB WEST KTB, Anlage 966.*

[2] *AGp B* Telecon, 0030, 31 Jul, *AGp B KTB; AGp B* Msg, 31 Jul, *AGp B Op. Befehle,* p. 206.

[3] Telecon, Kluge and Speidel, 0100, 31 Jul, *Seventh Army* Tel Jnl. This and the telephone conversations from the *Seventh Army* Telephone Journal that follow appear also in First U.S. Army. *Report of Operations,* I, 114ff.

At 0920 Kluge learned definitely that the Americans were in Avranches, but other than that the entire situation in the Avranches–Villedieu sector was "completely unclear." The only facts that could be accepted with assurance were that German losses in men and equipment were high and that U.S. fighter-bomber activity was "unprecedented." An "umbrella" of planes had covered American tanks advancing on Granville and Avranches. The responsibility for the crisis, he insisted, lay with Hausser's order for the left wing of the *LXXXIV Corps* to attack to the southeast. He had discovered that Choltitz had protested Hausser's order, and he felt that this futile protest absolved Choltitz ·from blame for the subsequent disaster. Troops under the control of the *91st Division* had established a thin line from Bréhal to Cérences as early as 28 July, but the American penetration on 31 July near Cérences had "ripped open the whole western front." The inevitable conclusion was that "Villedieu, springboard for movement east and south, is the anchorpoint for Brittany, [and] has to be held under all circumstances or else has to be recaptured." [4] But Kluge could do no more than draw conclusions; without an organized front and without adequate communications, he was powerless to influence the course of events.

Fifteen minutes later, Kluge's greatest worry was still Villedieu. He did not know nor could he find out which side held the town. Suspecting the worst, he agreed to let the *XLVII Panzer Corps* pull back the *2d* and *116th*

Panzer Divisions to the Villedieu–Percy line. He knew that east of the Vire River, in the withdrawal toward the town of Vire, the *II Parachute Corps* had lost the greater part of the *3d Parachute Division* (including the *15th Parachute Regiment* attached to it). He knew also that the *21st Panzer Division*, the last reserve division in Normandy, had been committed on the left flank of *Panzer Group West*, where the *326th Infantry Division* had been overrun by the British.[5]

Satisfied that he could do little on the front east of Avranches except hope for the best, Kluge set out to block the Americans at Avranches. At first he thought he could bring up two infantry divisions—the *84th* and *89th*—to deal with the small armored spearheads there, but he soon realized that the divisions could not possibly arrive in time.[6] He then turned to the forces in Brittany.

Since early on the morning of 31 July, when Kluge first faced the difficult and distasteful conclusion that the front was disintegrating, he had tried to get troops to hold the bridge near Pontaubault.[7] Unsuccessful in this effort, he took the drastic step of stripping the Brittany defenses by ordering Fahrmbacher, who commanded the *XXV Corps* in Brittany, to denude the St. Malo area of forces in order to prohibit the influx of Americans into Brittany. Specifically, Fahrmbacher was to send all available mobile troops to hold the Pontaubault bridge and from there to launch

---

[4] Telecon, Kluge and Speidel, 0920, 31 Jul, *Seventh Army* Tel Jnl; *Seventh Army KTB*, 28 Jul.

[5] Telecon, Kluge and Gersdorff, 0935, 31 Jul. *Seventh Army* Tel Jnl; Hodgson, R–54 and R–58.

[6] These divisions reached the Normandy front on 4 and 6 August. Hodgson, R–54.

[7] Telecon, Kluge and Zimmerman, 0210, 31 Jul, *OB WEST KTB, Anlage 952.*

a counterattack to the north to recapture Avranches.

Fahrmbacher was handicapped in two respects. Though there were many unemployed naval and air force troops in his corps sector, he could not order them to assume ground force missions because they were not under his jurisdiction. The troops directly under his control and therefore available to him were generally of two types—static troops guarding the coast line and units that had escaped from the Cotentin after taking heavy losses. Both lacked sufficient transport to make them mobile. Fahrmbacher felt that he could not perform his mission at Avranches, but he tried anyway.[8]

Fahrmbacher dispatched toward Pontaubault what remained of the *77th Division*, a unit perhaps the equivalent of a battalion in strength, reinforced by assorted paratroopers and a company of assault guns. This force, under Col. Rudolf Bacherer, the *77th Division* commander, reached the vicinity of Pontaubault in the late afternoon of 31 July, only to find the Americans already there.[9]

Hours before this took place, Kluge had reported to Hitler through Warlimont that he did not think it at all possible to stop the Americans, who had broken out of the strong static defenses that had contained them in July.[10] Hitler's "stand fast and hold" tactics, it appeared, had failed.

The Explanation

How had it happened? How had an operation designed to reach the Coutances–Caumont line been parlayed from a breakthrough into a breakout?

The explanation could be likened to a double exposure of the same subject, filmed from different points of view. The edges of the picture were slightly blurred, but the result was clearly discernible.

The Germans had astutely escaped the initial COBRA thrusts, only to fall prey to the later developments. They had been completely surprised by the COBRA bombardment and ground attack of 25 July. And yet they themselves had aggravated the consequences. That they had been outmaneuvered was soon apparent. Their communications facilities wrecked, they had found their endeavors to re-establish order marked by ignorance and inevitable frustration. Unable to keep abreast of a COBRA operation that developed remarkable speed after a slow beginning, the Germans were too late in their countermeasures. Hampered by shortages of manpower, equipment, and supplies, they were also the victims of their own mistakes. Whereas Eberbach had launched major portions of two panzer divisions in a counterattack several hours after GOODWOOD had begun and had thereby blocked British exploitation of a penetration already achieved, the Germans in the Cotentin were not able to match or even come close to Eberbach's accomplishment. A large part of the confusing and conflicting drama that had ensued in the Cotentin could in the final analysis be traced to the failure of a few men to react quickly, with deci-

[8] Telecon, Kluge and Fahrmbacher, 1000, 31 Jul, *Seventh Army* Tel Jnl; MS # 731 (Fahrmbacher).

[9] *Seventh Army* Tel Jnl, 31 Jul; *OB WEST, a Study in Command*, I, 129–30.

[10] Telecon, Kluge and Warlimont, 1045, 31 Jul, *Seventh Army* Tel Jnl.

sion, and in accord with a single purpose.[11]

At the beginning, German intelligence had failed. Radio interception had revealed significant changes in American dispositions during the week preceding COBRA, but these were not reflected in the reports that reached army group and theater headquarters. They did not even reach Hausser.[12]

More important than the lack of advance warning on COBRA and perhaps even more significant than the disparity in numbers of troops controlled by the opponents were Hausser's dispositions before COBRA, which had largely predetermined his initial reaction. From the night of 13 July, when American pressure against the LXXXIV Corps left began to diminish, Hausser was increasingly free to regroup his forces because except for minor action the fighting in the Cotentin came to an end with the fall of St. Lô on 18 July. A week of poor weather conditions before COBRA gave Hausser further respite. In all, he had about ten days to reshuffle his forces in the Cotentin. The equivalent of nearly seven infantry divisions, these forces had numbered about 21,000 combat effectives. The infantry was incapable of rapid movement, but Hausser had two panzer divisions that were highly mobile. Even though Panzer Lehr had not been at top strength (it had been unable—even with the support of its attached parachute regiment—to launch an attack east of the Vire River

to regain St. Lô), the 2d SS Panzer Division had been strong, confident, and aggressive.[13] Together, the two armored divisions comprised a force in being that could have had a serious effect on COBRA.

Kluge had suggested to Hausser that he pull his two panzer divisions out of the line, replace them with infantry, and conserve them for mobile action against American penetrations of the defensive line. Hausser, on the other hand, had been reluctant to deprive his static defense of armor. He believed that "tanks formed the backbone of the position; built into the ground, they served as antitank guns and as armored machine guns." [14] He had consequently held the armored divisions in place.

As a result, instead of having the infantry absorb the shock of the COBRA assault and having an armored reserve capable of counterattack, Hausser had so disposed his troops that the Americans knocked out one of the two panzer divisions in the COBRA bombardment— Panzer Lehr was immediately eliminated as a potential threat. The 2d SS Panzer Division, though more fortunate than Lehr in escaping bombardment, could not be extricated from the front in time for a decisive counterattack role. Once the Americans broke through, their mechanized and motorized troops easily outmaneuvered German infantrymen and paratroopers who comprised Hausser's immediate reserves, forces that were sadly deficient in transportation facilities. Without additional assembled reserves, Hausser could not close the gap

---

[11] See Hodgson, R–58; MS # B–723 (Gersdorff) is a valuable source.

[12] Seventh Army KTB, 22–24 Jul; OB WEST KTB, Anlagen Ic Anlageband II,, Feindlagekarten 1.VII.–31.XII.44, Annexes 27 and 28; MS # B–464 (Ziegelmann).

---

[13] Hechler, The Enemy Build-up Prior to Operation COBRA; MS #159 (Stueckler).

[14] MS # A–903 (Bayerlein).

that developed between the *LXXXIV* and *II Parachute Corps.*

By the very terrain his troops occupied, Hausser might have visualized his task as the maintenance of a resilient defense. He might have envisaged a gradual hard-fought withdrawal, if necessary, to the Avranches–Vire–Caen line (which Rundstedt and Rommel had discussed around the end of June), for such a withdrawal would have been in accord with the defensive concept in Normandy. Eberbach, in contrast, could not withdraw his *Panzer Group West* and retain for the forces in Normandy the same conditions of warfare. Despite the impossibility of his even considering a withdrawal and despite his lack of intention to withdraw, Eberbach had constructed alternate positions to the rear. Hausser, who could have justified a withdrawal and who could have given up ground without endangering the forces of *Army Group B*, had failed to prepare even rally points to the rear.

Though Hausser had not designated alternate positions, Choltitz was sufficiently security conscious—perhaps simply cautious enough—to do so on his own authority. Afraid to appear a defeatist in Hausser's eyes, Choltitz did not tell him of the alternate positions. The relationship between the two commanders was founded on a lack of mutual trust, co-operation, and understanding that bred confusion. When Choltitz had marked a line of defense to the rear, he had been responsible for the defense of the Cotentin from the west coast to the Vire River. After the fall of St. Lô, when the *352d Division* withdrew behind the Vire River west of St. Lô and took positions on the west bank,

Hausser allowed it to remain under the control of the *II Parachute Corps.* Thus, when Choltitz shortly after the COBRA bombardment ordered *Panzer Lehr* to man a designated line to the rear, the consequence was that *Lehr* had neither contact with the *352d* nor an anchor on the Vire River. Both units had floating flanks. When the *352d* withdrew a day later to anchor the flanks, *Panzer Lehr* had been further jostled by the COBRA exploitation and was beyond salvation.[15]

Kluge shared in the accountability for defeat. Concerned with the *Panzer Group West* sector and worried about the positions south of Caen, he had failed to note Hausser's inadequate preparations for defense. It should have been clear to him that Hausser had not grasped the role of the *Seventh Army* in the defense of Normandy.[16] Yet Kluge was preoccupied with the British threat to Falaise, and he did not remark Hausser's failure to comply with his instructions on creating armored reserves.

Kluge criticized Hausser explicitly soon after COBRA began for his employment of the *2d SS Panzer Division.* He condemned Hausser's helplessness in the face of communications difficulties. He thought that Hausser was permitting inefficiency among army staff members, particularly his chief of staff, Generalmajor Max Pemsel, who, Kluge felt, would hamper Hausser's influence on

---

[15] See MS # B-418 (Choltitz); MS # B-489 (Ziegelmann); MS # P-159 (Stueckler); MS # B-179 (Hausser); *Pz Lehr Div* FO, 23 Jul, *Pz Lehr Div Ib KTB, Allg. Anlagen,* Annex 241.

[16] See Hausser's Est of the Situation, 19 Jul, and Kluge's forwarding letter, 21 Jul, *AGp B Ia Lagebeurteilungen und Wochenmeldungen.*

the course of the battle.[17] He thought it necessary to restrain Hausser's request to withdraw, and he had insisted on withdrawal only for the purpose of gaining reserves. On the morning of 28 July he remarked that Hausser and Pemsel were obviously not masters of the situation and that he had just about decided to relieve at least Pemsel.[18] That same morning he sent his son Guenther, a lieutenant colonel who was his aide, to the *Seventh Army* sector as his personal representative.

The climax of Kluge's doubt came on the question of Coutances. Though Kluge considered closing the gap in the *Seventh Army* center vital, he felt that retention of Coutances was even more important. When Pemsel assured Kluge on 28 July that strong rear-guard action north of Coutances would keep the Americans out of the city and prevent them from launching a major effort along the coast, Kluge was certain that Hausser understood the significance of Coutances—that loss of Coutances would open the door to an American drive that might outflank the counterattack about to be launched in the army center by the *XLVII Panzer Corps*.[19] His surprise bordered on shock when he received word that evening of Hausser's plan to have the *LXXXIV Corps* in the Coutances area escape American encirclement by attacking southeast, rather than by withdrawing south along the coast. By virtually abandoning Coutances and projecting a concentration of

forces near Percy, Hausser removed opposition to an American advance down the west coast of the Cotentin.

Kluge's countermand of Hausser's order had little effect because of inadequate communication facilities. A result was that Hausser's act brought to a head Kluge's dissatisfaction with the *Seventh Army* leadership. That evening, though apparently without authority to relieve Hausser, who was one of Himmler's SS commanders, or perhaps not daring to, Kluge replaced Pemsel with Gersdorff; Choltitz, the *LXXXIV Corps* commander, with Generalleutnant Otto Elfeldt.[20] Kluge must have regretted that Hausser still commanded the *Seventh Army* on the following day, for again he countermanded Hausser's order committing the *XLVII Panzer Corps* to defense between Tessy and Gavray.

By the time that Kluge took an active part in the Cotentin operation, the battle was lost. Even though he drew upon Eberbach's *Panzer Group West* reserves in an attempt to stem the tide of events, he did so with reluctance, not because GOODWOOD had exhausted those operational reserves concentrated south of Caen, but because in the midst of the COBRA deluge he still believed that the decisive action would take place on the eastern flank near Caen. Kluge was, of course, mistaken.

German errors were only part of the story. The breakout also illustrated the magnificent ability of American commanders to take advantage of the opportunities and transform a limited envelopment in process to a breakthrough that became a breakout.

[17] Telecon, Kluge, Pemsel, and Tempelhoff, 1845, 26 Jul, *AGp B KTB*.

[18] Telecon, Kluge to Warlimont, 0925, 28 Jul, *AGp B KTB*.

[19] Telecon, Kluge and Pemsel, 1640, 28 Jul, *AGp B KTB*.

[20] Hodgson, R-40.

The abortive COBRA bombardment on 24 July had acted as a ruse. It had given the Germans a false sense of confidence and had nailed down the German main line of defense along the Périers–St. Lô highway. The real bombardment on 25 July had smashed the defense in the Marigny–St. Gilles gap. Though not at first apparent, the massed heavy and medium bomber attack had destroyed the efficiency and the initiative of the German soldier, both as an individual and as a member of the combat team, and had provided American ground troops with an initial impetus that turned out to be decisive.

To the Germans, the mere presence of unopposed aircraft overhead had been depressing, but the bombing itself had produced a temporary demoralization and a loss of will to fight or even to move about in the area under attack, a psychological effect that had given the Americans a tremendous tactical advantage. German casualties were later conservatively estimated as 10 percent of the total troops in the area. Even more important than the casualties were the confusion, the disruption of communications, and the shock effect. Some German soldiers were still deaf twenty-four hours later. Despite the bomb casualties among American troops, despite the fact that small isolated German groups had still been able to resist after the bombing, the COBRA bombardment was later judged to have been the best example in the European theater of "carpet bombing." [21]

The small and isolated German groups in the Marigny–St. Lô gap that

had been able to resist had performed so well that they had maintained a semblance of the opposition that had stopped the Americans in the battle of the hedgerows earlier in the month. Expecting the same kind of combat, American infantrymen had been afflicted with a caution that, in view of the lack of organized German defense, approached timidity.

Recognizing that the entire First Army attack depended on getting through the German defenses at once, General Collins had dissipated the hesitation marking the American ground attack on the first day of COBRA, 25 July, by committing his armor on the morning of 26 July. That act had insured COBRA's success, but the forces in the VII Corps main effort had not made the decisive thrust. Rather, the aggressiveness of General Brooks' 2d Armored Division and the single-minded leadership of General Rose had carried CCA, and with it the VII Corps, into the exploitation phase of COBRA.

Again sensing a critical moment, General Collins had ordered continued attack through the night of 26 July. It was this—in particular the activity of General Barton's 4th Division—that had rammed the COBRA attack home. Had the VIII Corps attacked during the night of 26 July, the Germans on the Cotentin west coast might not have slipped away in the dark to temporary escape.

The German miscalculations that had allowed the COBRA attack to cross the original relatively limited horizon and had made possible the post-COBRA opportunity for exploitation were quickly seized upon by General Bradley. Despite strong German forces between

---

[21] USSAFE, Intelligence Study on Effectiveness of Carpet Bombing, 21 Feb 45, Hist Sec AF File, Carpet Bombing.

Lessay and Périers and despite the ability of German forces at Marigny to keep the COBRA main effort toward Coutances from reaching fruition, General Bradley exploited and deepened a nascent disorganization of the enemy as disastrous as that caused by the heavy bombers, as compelling as the effect of the American ground attack.

With the chief COBRA premise invalidated because the Germans had eluded not only the principal COBRA envelopment to Coutances but also the subsidiary thrust, the Americans closed another trap with alacrity around Roncey. Hausser's premature anticipation of the encirclement of his west coast forces—a maneuver that was never actually completed—and his order for the troops on the left to attack toward the southeast would have had little effect on the ultimate result if American troops had not been in place to block them— in particular the 2d Armored Division and General White's CCB, which had displayed a ruthlessness in its destructive capacity. The German hold on the Cotentin west coast broken and the way thereby open not only to an encirclement of the *LXXXIV Corps* left but also to the much more serious encirclement of the entire German defensive line in France, the Americans again acted with dispatch.

With the Germans themselves having largely planted the seeds of their own destruction, "it was only necessary for the First Army to take advantage of the disorganized state of the enemy." General Bradley had not been at all hesitant about issuing his orders for the post-COBRA exploitation. "Consequently, the ensuing period, which the

[COBRA] plan had conceived [of as] . . . a holding and mopping-up period, became a vigorous attack period." [22] General Corlett's XIX Corps had blunted the enemy's planned counterattack at Tessy and had thereby destroyed German hopes of quickly re-establishing a defensive line in the Cotentin. General Collins' rapid reorganization of the VII Corps and the spectacular thrust of 3d Armored Division task forces toward St. Pois and to Brécey had denied the Germans the vital terrain about Villedieu-les-Poëles. General Patton's modification of the VIII Corps attack by inserting twin armored columns and the sensational success of General Wood's 4th Armored Division had exploded the nightmare of static warfare that had haunted the Americans so long in the Cotentin.

The British and Canadian contributions to the development of the breakout are difficult to judge. There is no doubt that General Montgomery had worried Kluge in the Caen sector. By creating uncertainty in the mind of the German field commander, Montgomery had added to and deepened the surprise that accompanied the American operation. Except for two armored divisions that had moved to the American zone to oppose the post-COBRA exploitation, Montgomery had tied down the strength of *Panzer Group West,* which still guarded the vital approaches to Falaise. Whether General Montgomery had visualized it so, or whether he was aware of the historical example, the breakout in Normandy from a larger

---

[22] First U.S. Army, *Report of Operations,* I, 106–07.

perspective resembled in the essentials of maneuver the operation in Sicily of less than a year earlier. There, too, Montgomery's forces had tied down the enemy while Patton's U.S. troops carried the main assault and made the striking gain.

Two days before COBRA, General Montgomery had suggested it might be advantageous to drop parachute troops to seize bridgeheads over the Sée and Sélune Rivers—to block a German retreat, to prevent the enemy from stabilizing his line at Avranches, and to facilitate the projected American thrust into Brittany. General Bradley had vetoed this relatively shallow drop.[23] As it turned out, an airborne operation was unnecessary.

General Eisenhower had sounded the keynote when he had written General Bradley on the eve of COBRA:

My high hopes and best wishes ride with you in your attack . . . , which is the largest ground assault yet staged in this war by American troops exclusively. Speaking as the responsible American rather than the Allied Commander, I assure you that . . . a breakthrough at this juncture will minimize the total cost [of victory]. . . . Pursue every advantage with an ardor verging on recklessness and with all your troops without fear of major counter offensive from the forces the enemy now has on his front. . . . The results will be incalculable.[24]

The results were indeed incalculable. Of the 28,000 German prisoners the First Army captured during the month of July, 20,000 were taken during the last six days. No German defensive capability was apparent in the Pontaubault–Brécey–Villedieu-les-Poëles sector. The *LXXXIV Corps* was smashed. The *II Parachute Corps* was beaten. The *Seventh Army* had been defeated. The way was open to even greater German disaster and even more incalculable results.[25]

The Allied Outlook

The action that had developed so rapidly on the First Army's right during the last few days of July was a preview of what was to come in August. Significantly, armored units had transformed the breakthrough into the breakout in all of the three corps sectors west of the Vire River. Even in the region east of the Vire, the British 11th Armoured Division had manifested the type of slashing power inherent in armored formations.

On the First Army right, the combat command had become the basic unit of advance. In the VII Corps sector, a new combination had evolved: a combat command attached to each infantry division, imparting the armored characteristics of fire power, mobility, and shock to the infantry capacity for sustained action. In all the corps sectors west of the Vire, balanced teams of tanks, tank destroyers, motorized infantry, artillery, and engineers had pushed ahead, making generous use of marching fire. The units had automatically taken crossroads, road junctions, defensible terrain features, hedgerows, and buildings under fire in order to neutralize potential resistance. All forces in the exploitation had cut German telephone wires. Leading

[23] 21 AGp Msg, 23 Jul, and FUSA Msg, 23 Jul, FUSA G-3 Jnl.

[24] Ltr, Eisenhower to Montgomery for Bradley, 24 Jul, FWD-12438, Pogue Files.

[25] FUSA G-2 Per Rpt 52, 1 Aug.

units had made a constant effort to over-run German outposts before they could relay information on American progress. The hedgerow cutter, developed to give armor mobility in the hedgerow country, was of little tactical value in the break-out, except possibly as a morale factor to the troops, since the tanks advanced on the roads, not cross-country.

Taking light casualties, U.S. troops felt their morale soar as the opposition melted. The sight of German prisoners in large numbers, "so happy to be cap-tured that all they could do was giggle," dimmed unhappy memories of the bat-tle of the hedgerows.[26] The absence of an established enemy line and the re-placement of the formerly well-prepared defensive positions with hastily dug trenches and ill-constructed emplace-ments brought exultation to American troops. The abandoned, wrecked, and disabled enemy vehicles that littered the roads were much less troublesome obstacles than well-manned strongpoints or villages and towns that had been both objectives and obstacles.[27] The 15,000 engineers who had participated in COBRA had performed with distinction their primary effort of keeping the main routes open, thereby enabling over 100,000 combat troops to pour through a gap not more than five miles wide.[28] The resulting situation had become so fluid that it had often been difficult for

headquarters to transmit their orders to subordinate units or to receive new in-structions from higher headquarters.[29]

Artillery had played a comparatively minor role. Only the armored bat-teries accompanying the advance units had been called upon to eliminate the occasional resistance that small German groups had hurriedly organized. Artil-lerymen had fired their machine guns more often than their howitzers. The question of adequate artillery ammuni-tion supplies had vanished, and even though rationing had remained in effect throughout the month, it had no effect on the small expenditures that had been necessary.[30]

Although the method of supplying the forward troops changed somewhat, General Collins later recalled "no real supply difficulties that hampered the actual operation."[31] Combat units car-ried more than their regular allowances of gasoline, usually double the amount. With kitchens left in the rear in increas-ing numbers, the combat troops for the most part ate cold K rations or heated their own 10-in-1 rations. Distances between depots and the front-line units increased. Sometimes tanks or armored cars escorted supply columns to assure their safety. Facilities for handling pris-oners had suddenly become over-burdened, and the First Army estab-lished two "holding enclosures" several miles behind the front as temporary prisoner installations until Communica-

---

[26] 83d Div G-2 Per Rpts 30 and 32, 27 and 28 Jul.

[27] 3d Armd Div CCB AAR, Jul. By 2 August, the First Army Ordnance Section possessed, in part, the following captured matériel: 75 Mark IV, 25 Mark V, and 27 Mark VI tanks; 22 77-mm., 20 76-mm., and 9 88-mm. assault guns. FUSA Ord Office, Consolidated Rpt of Captured Tanks and Assault Guns, 2 Aug, FUSA G-2 Jnl and File.

[28] CI 344-A (Engrs in the Breakthrough of VII Corps).

[29] See, for example, 1st Div G-3 Jnl, entry 2300, 28 Jul.

[30] Gen Bd USFET Rpt on Ammo Supply for FA, Study 58, File 471/1; Gen Bd Arty Rpt, App. C; VIII Corps AAR, Jul; Koyen, *Fourth Armored Division*, p. 25.

[31] Ltr, Collins to Hechler, 7 Dec 45, as cited in Hechler, VII Corps in Operation COBRA, p. 16.

tion Zone guards could march the captives to the invasion beaches for transfer to England.[32]

The wretched weather that earlier had hampered operations in Normandy had vanished. With the launching of COBRA, "the weather turned fair, and the last days of July were characterized by brilliant sunshine and warm temperatures."[33] This, perhaps as much as anything, had insured the success of the breakout, for it had permitted a most heartening development in the close and effective co-operation between the pilots of the fighter-bombers and the tankers leading the ground forces.

From 26 July through the end of the month, over 400 support missions were flown over First Army spearheads. In the VII Corps sector alone, fighter-bomber pilots claimed to have destroyed 362 tanks and self-propelled guns, damaged 216; and to have destroyed 1,337 other vehicles and damaged 380. In addition, they attacked horse-drawn wagons, gun positions, trains, warehouses, road junctions, railroad and highway bridges, troop concentrations, enemy aircraft, and one ammunition dump. In one day alone, the critical day of 26 July, fighter-bomber pilots claimed to have destroyed or damaged 85 tanks and 97 motor vehicles and to have attacked 22 gun positions. Pilots also had sought to hamper the night movement of enemy troops by dropping during the day near important crossroads—particularly near Coutances and Gavray—delayed-action bombs timed to explode during the night.[34]

From 25 through 31 July, the IX Tactical Air Command flew 9,185 sorties and dropped 2,281 tons of bombs, in addition to making 655 reconnaissance sorties. The air command's planned distribution of its resources on 28 July was representative of the distribution for the period: 7 percent of available aircraft were to provide assault area cover, 7 percent to perform offensive fighter sweeps, 7 percent to execute armed reconnaissance beyond the forward troops, 7 percent to be held in reserve to fulfill air request missions coming directly from the corps, 14 percent to attack targets as directed by the Ninth Air Force, 14 percent to fulfill close support missions requested by the First Army, 22 percent to escort medium bombers on attack missions, and 22 percent to perform armored column cover. It was later computed that from 25 through 28 July, 2,926 aircraft had dropped 5,961 tons of bombs, and 1,964 artillery pieces of all caliber (exclusive of tank guns) had fired 4,089 tons of shells on the First Army front.[35]

Armored column cover, begun on 26 July, had been a vital—and perhaps essential—factor in the American success at the end of the month. Relays of four fighter-bombers armed with bombs or rockets had flown in half-hour shifts over the head of each armored column.

[32] First U.S. Army, *Report of Operations*, I, 93–96.

[33] VIII Corps AAR, Aug.

[34] First U.S. Army, *Report of Operations*, I,

106; [George], Ninth Air Force, pp. 125, 135; Bradley, *Effect of Air Power*, p. 103; VII Corps AAR, Jul; Results of Armed Column Cover and Armed Recon in Connection with COBRA on 26 Jul. Air Opns Summary, VIII Corps G–3 Jnl and File.

[35] [George], Ninth Air Force, p. 129; FUSA and IX TAC Air Opns Summary for 28 Jul, 30th Div G–3 Jnl and File; SHAEF to Mil Mission. Moscow, S–79098, 14 Feb 45, SGS SHAEF File 380.01/1, Vol. II, Exchange of Info Between Allies and Russia.

Air support personnel riding in the forward tanks of the column maintained liaison with the pilots by means of very high frequency (VHF) radio sets installed in the tanks. The planes thus were able to act as the eyes of the ground forces, to give advance warning of impending threats and detailed information of the enemy's dispositions. They were also able to attack targets far ahead of the tank colunms. The results obtained "by the employment of the tank-air team in mobile fast moving situations," commanders later recognized, had been "an outstanding achievement in air-ground cooperation and represent[ed] the development of an unbeatable combination." [36]

Careful and detailed planning for air-ground co-operation had been necessary. Tank markings were repainted. Army liaison officers at airfields briefed pilots on air support missions to familiarize them with the situation on the ground and interrogated them upon their return from missions to secure information valuable to the ground components. An important factor that had served to bring about the "closest possible coordination" between the First Army and IX TAC staffs was that the air staff and the air representatives of the army staff were lodged under the same roof. [37]

The heart of the operation, however, lay in the radio dialogue between the pilots and the tankers. "I am receiving fire from an enemy tank nearby," a tanker would report; "can you get him?"

"I'll make a try," the pilot would reply. After making a pass, the pilot would call, "I found him. But you're too close for me to bomb safely. Back up a short distance, and I will go after him." It was simple; it was effective. The phrase "thanks a lot" frequently sounded over the radio channels. [38]

July had been a month of opposites in combat experience. Until 25 July foot troops had made slow, costly advances against stubborn hedgerow defenses; casualties had been high, and gains had been measured in yards. After 25 July armored formations had made rapid advances against a defeated, disorganized, and demoralized enemy; casualties had been light, resistance sporadic. The inception of COBRA had marked the change.

Several days after the commencement of the COBRA attack, General Marshall had requested General Eisenhower to send him information on General Bradley's offensive, which he had learned about from an unexplained radio reference to COBRA, "whatever that was." [39] By the end of July there was little question of what COBRA was or what it had done. After one week of action, U.S. troops held a line from Pontaubault eastward through Brécey and St. Pois to a point several miles north of the town of Vire. To be sure, the front line was held only by advance spearheads; the bulk of the First Army was still concentrated fifteen to twenty miles to the north. Nevertheless, the Allied forces

---

[36] First U.S. Army, *Report of Operations*, I, 121; [George], Ninth Air Force, p. 129.

[37] First U.S. Army, *Report of Operations*, I, 106, 119–20; [George], Ninth Air Force, pp. 130ff.

[38] 12th AGp Immed Rpt 38, Air Support of Ground Force Opns, 25 Aug; see 3d Armd Div CCB AAR, Action 26 Jul–31 Jul.

[39] Ltr, Marshall to Eisenhower, 31 Jul, Pogue Files.

had definitely seized the initiative, and there seemed to be no reason why they should relinquish it, particularly since the enemy disorganization was still unresolved. Brittany was at hand and Paris and the Seine had come within reach. The prospects for the future were unlimited.[40]

---

[40] Ltr, Eisenhower to Marshall, FWD–12493, 30 Jul, Pogue Files; First U.S. Army, *Report of Operations*, I, 112.

PART FOUR

BREAKOUT INTO
BRITTANY

CHAPTER XVIII

Plans, Personalities, and Problems

"From all reports," General Eisenhower wrote General Montgomery on the last day of July, "your plan continues to develop beautifully. I learn that you have a column in Avranches. This is great news and Bradley must quickly make our position there impregnable. Bradley has plenty of Infantry units to rush into forward areas to consolidate all gains and permit armor to continue thrusting. . . ." Two days later Eisenhower wrote Montgomery, "If my latest reports are correct, the enemy resistance seems to have disintegrated very materially in the Avranches region. Our armored and mobile columns will want to operate boldly against the enemy. . . ." [1]

As General Eisenhower anticipated, the bold thrust of armored columns was to characterize Allied operations during August.

In contrast with Allied optimism, the picture appeared bleak from the German side.

German Plans

Meeting on the last day of July with Jodl in the *Wolfschanze*, the Fuehrer's command post in East Prussia, Hitler faced a depressing situation. In Italy, he felt, German forces were usefully tying down numerically superior Allied troops, but elsewhere Hitler found little consolation. As he put 'it, his principal worry was defection in the Balkan area; his most anxious concern was the potential capitulation of Hungary; his most pressing military need was stability on the Eastern Front in the Baltic and Polish regions; his immediate problem was the situation in France.

Over all the situation reports and staff studies that Hitler consulted hovered the shadow of the plot that on 20 July had come close to destroying his life. Despite vigorous measures to uproot the conspiracy, he could not be sure of its extent. He suspected considerable defection within the ranks of the German generals and general staff and was certain that disloyalty to his person existed on subordinate echelons as well. Tormented by a lack of confidence in the military, Hitler decided to direct the war increasingly from his own headquarters. He himself would plan a withdrawal from France. He would have OKW issue only fragmentary orders at the proper time to insure compliance with his master plan. In that way he would not reveal the plan in its entirety to someone who might compromise its success.

Hitler's basic plan to meet the American breakout at the end of July was to secure a temporary stabilization of the

[1] Ltrs, Eisenhower to Montgomery, 31 Jul and 2 Aug, SGS SHAEF File 381, OVERLORD, 1 (a).

front while intermediate rally lines and new defensive positions were being organized in the rear. To organize new defenses in protection of Germany and to await the fruition of new production and troop training schedules, Hitler needed six weeks at the least, ten weeks at the most. To gain the time he needed, he struck two blows at the Allied logistical apparatus. He ordered all withdrawing troops to destroy transportation facilities in France—locomotives, railway lines, marshaling yards, machine shops, and bridges—a plan already abetted by Allied bombardment. And he ordered his fortress policy into effect to deny the Allies the major ports they needed and to retain for the German Navy bases for submarine warfare against Allied shipping.[2]

In 1943 OKW had designated as fortresses all the Atlantic harbors that had been extensively fortified. To each was assigned an especially dependable commander who took an oath to defend his fortress to the death. Among the fortresses were the port cities Dunkerque, Calais, Boulogne, Le Havre, Cherbourg, St. Malo, Brest, Lorient, and St. Nazaire.[3] Of these, Cherbourg had fallen in June, and at the end of July, as American troops seized Avranches and Pontaubault at the base of the Cotentin,

the principal ports of Brittany—St. Malo, Brest, Lorient, and St. Nazaire—were threatened. (*See Maps I, VIII, XII.*)

Having been vexed by the failure of the Cherbourg garrison to hold out as long as he expected, Hitler tried to make certain that his fortress commanders in Brittany and in the Pas-de-Calais would not similarly disappoint him. Hoping to deny the Allies the ports he recognized as vital to the success not only of OVERLORD but also of the entire Allied campaign in western Europe, Hitler specifically ordered the fortresses held "to the last man, to the last cartridge." Although this Hitlerian phrase was later to become trite and even farcical, it was a serious manifesto. Hitler's argument was that, since the forces guarding the fortresses were static troops, they could not be employed effectively in the war of movement the Americans were certain to initiate in August. Since they could not conduct mobile operations, they were to fight to the finish within the ports, destroying the harbors in the process. The garrison forces would thus not only destroy the base of the logistical machinery—ports of entry—that the Allies had to erect in order to wage effective war, they would also tie down Allied forces that might otherwise be used in the decisive battle inevitably to be fought on the western approaches to Germany.

At *OB WEST,* this policy was markedly unpopular. Feeling that Hitler's implementation of the fortress policy meant the inevitable loss of from 180,000 to 280,000 men and their equipment, the *OB WEST* staff believed that the static troops in the Pas-de-Calais area at least—assuming that the groups in Brittany were already lost for future operations—could be used to better advantage

[2] Hitler Conf, "*Besprechung des Fuehrers mit Generaloberst Jodl am 31.7.1944,*" in captured German documents; Jodl diary, 31 Jul; *Der Westen* (Schramm); MS # – 731 (Fahrmbacher); Pogue, *Supreme Command,* pp. 201–03; Blumenson and Hodgson, "Hitler Versus his Generals in the West," U.S. Naval Institute *Proceedings* (December, 1956). Hitler enunciated his fortress policy in Hitler Directive # 40, 23 March 1942, translated in Appendix C to Harrison, *Cross-Channel Attack,* pp. 459–63.
[3] *OB WEST, a Study in Command,* I, 22.

in reinforcing the new defensive positions to be erected in the rear of the Normandy front. But since Kluge was in command of *Army Group B* as well as of *OB WEST* and since he was in actuality giving most of his attention to tactical affairs at the army group level and below, *OB WEST* exerted no vital influence on operations. For all practical purposes it had become a message center that transmitted orders and reports up and down the chain of command. More to the point, whatever *OB WEST*'s recommendations, Hitler had already made his decision. He told Kluge to pay no attention to the U.S. forces entering Brittany.[4] Instead, Kluge was to devote his efforts to stemming the American threat eastward toward the Seine.

During the early hours of 1 August, Kluge had asked Hitler's permission to bring the *2d Parachute Division* eastward from Brest and the *319th Infantry Division* from the Channel Islands of Jersey and Guernsey to the mainland to deny the Americans entry into Brittany. Hitler refused to evacuate the Channel Islands but granted permission for Kluge to use the *2d Parachute Division*. Although the paratroopers started to move eastward, it soon became apparent that they would be too late to affect developments in Brittany. Threatened with isolation from Brest by a U.S. armored division, the paratroopers slipped back into the port city.[5]

By midmorning of 1 August, the Ger-mans learned that U.S. forces were moving freely south of Pontaubault. By noon they had reports that Americans were in Pontorson and Dol-de-Bretagne and that two batteries of a German assault gun brigade committed against the armored spearheads had been destroyed, principally, they thought, by fighter-bombers.[6] By evening there was no hope of stopping the influx of American troops into Brittany.

Although Kluge was aware of the meaning of these events, Hausser, the *Seventh Army* commander, tried to minimize the gravity of the situation by maintaining that "only armored elements have broken through [and that] so far there has been no exploitation of the breakthrough with massed forces." He admitted that several columns of American tanks, with sixty tanks in each column, had been reported near Ville-dieu-les-Poëles, and that "they must be somewhere in the area south of Avranches." Despite this, he still felt that he could stabilize his part of a front between Avranches and Caen.

Kluge evaluated the situation more realistically. Although he was talking to Hausser, he seemed to be speaking more to himself: "We have got to stop the flow [of American forces] from Avranches southward." This was his principal concern. Figuring that the *2d Parachute Division* would have to fight in Brittany and could not therefore be used to bolster the front in Normandy, Kluge turned his attention to the problem of securing additional Ger-

---

[4] *OB WEST KTB*, 1 Aug, *Anlage 1050; Der Westen* (Schramm), p. 79; *OB WEST, a Study in Command*, I, 1, 118ff.

[5] Kluge Telecon, 0230, 1 Aug, *AGp B KTB*; H. B. Ramcke, *Fallschirmjaeger, Damals und Danach* (Frankfurt: Lorch-Verlag, c. 1951), pp. 30–46; Hodgson, R–58; see below, Ch. XX.

[6] Telecons, Speidel and Gersdorff, 1020, 1 Aug, *AGp B KTB*, and Tempelhoff and Zimmerman, 1155, 1 Aug, *OB WEST KTB, Anlage 999*.

man units from other places in the west to help stabilize the Normandy front.[7]

With *OB WEST, Army Group B,* and the *Seventh Army* in no position to look after Brittany, the task devolved upon the *XXV Corps.* Designated the commander of the forces in Brittany, Fahrmbacher, the *XXV Corps* commander, was delegated the job of directing what was to become the battle of the fortresses, a campaign independent of the action developing in Normandy.[8]

Fahrmbacher, who, as the temporary *LXXXIV Corps* commander, had met the Americans in the Cotentin in June, was ill-prepared to face them again in Brittany. Of the army field forces of 100,000 troops in Brittany at the beginning of June, less than one third remained at the end of July. The others, the best-armed and best-trained units, had been sent to Normandy— the *3d* and *5th Parachute Divisions,* the *77th, 353d,* and *275th Infantry Divisions,* and two mobile kampfgruppen of regimental size (from the *265th* and *266th Divisions*). Since the *319th Division* on the Channel Islands would not see action on the mainland, the defenders of Brittany consisted of the *2d Parachute Division* and the static *343d Infantry Division* near Brest, weak elements of the static *266th Division* (perhaps in regimental strength) near Morlaix, and the remaining parts of the static *265th Division* at Lorient, St. Nazaire, and Nantes. Augmenting these troops were antiaircraft batteries, coastal artillery units, antitank

groups, engineers, and Navy and Air Force personnel.[9] To reinforce them came units and stragglers fleeing from Normandy—in particular the *77th* and *91st Divisions,* which carried with them assorted remnants of once-proud outfits. These headed for the St. Malo area, whence Fahrmbacher dispatched the *77th* toward Pontaubault and the *91st* to defend Rennes.[10]

As Fahrmbacher understood the fortress policy, the fortress commanders of St. Malo, Brest, Lorient, and St. Nazaire were to protect the submarine bases, prevent the Americans from using the ports, and contain as much of the American force as possible. Although each fortress commander had no garrison troops organized as such under his direct control, he commanded all the units and individuals of all the services within the fortress. The commanders of the field force troops had charge of activity outside the fortresses. Only after they were forced to retire within the limits of the fortresses did they come under the control of the fortress commanders.

Fortification of the port cities had begun in 1942 in response to the major threat of Allied invasion from the sea. The main construction work had at first been concentrated on the submarine installations, then on headquarters and battery positions for coastal artillery and flak, next on combat installations at possible landing points, and finally on the land front proper. So much time, effort, and concrete had gone into the

---

[7] Telecon, Kluge and Hausser, 2130, 1 Aug, *OB WEST KTB, Anlage 1015.*

[8] *OB WEST, a Study in Command,* I, 133. *LXXIV Corps* had been pulled out of Brittany on 25 July to take over a portion of the front facing the British. MS # B–722 (Gersdorff).

[9] MS # 731 (Fahrmbacher); *OB WEST KTB,* 2 Aug; Hodgson, R–34; *OB WEST, a Study in Command,* I, 40.

[10] MS # 731 (Fahrmbacher) is the basic source of this section.

Atlantic Wall installations, which, at the insistence of the Navy, had been faced toward the sea, that the land front, according to Army planners, was neglected. The fortress commanders who faced the Allied ground forces in August 1944 believed their landward defenses far from adequate.

Upon reports that the Americans had invaded the interior of Brittany and that armored columns were racing toward the port cities, Fahrmbacher and his *XXV Corps* headquarters moved on 3 August from Pontivy to Lorient. Four days later, on 7 August, when Kluge ordered Fahrmbacher to take command of Brest, Fahrmbacher did not carry out the order because land contact between Lorient and Brest had already been cut, because no preparations had been made for sea communications, and because he felt that the fortress commander of Brest was competent to conduct his own independent defense. Nor did Fahrmbacher exercise control over the action developing around St. Malo; he had no way of doing so. Though the *XXV Corps* remained nominally in control of operations in Brittany, for all practical purposes it directed only the forces in Lorient and St. Nazaire. Subordination of the St. Nazaire garrison lasted only a brief time—until U.S. troops encircled and isolated both Lorient and St. Nazaire. Reduced to a nonessential role in Lorient, Fahrmbacher and his corps headquarters found an opportunity to assume real command status when the fortress commander of Lorient was injured around 10 August by a mine. Fahrmbacher then took his place and functioned in that capacity.

Appointing Fahrmbacher commander of the forces in Brittany thus had availed the Germans little. After the first few days of August there was no unified command. All the German troops who could, abandoned the interior and scurried into the fortresses, where they awaited the inevitable opening of siege operations.

A New Army

Behind the armored spearheads pushing into German-held territory was an Allied strength on the Continent that had almost reached organizational maturity. General Crerar's First Canadian Army had become operational under the control of General Montgomery's 21 Army Group on 23 July, and it was apparent then that General Patton's Third Army would soon have to become active. The build-up was fattening the First Army almost to unreasonable proportions, and the broad scope of OVERLORD operations foreshadowed the early need of a U.S. army group. If American troops entered Brittany and drove westward as contemplated, they would diverge from British, Canadian, and other U.S. forces oriented eastward toward the Seine. An American army group in control of the American thrusts eastward and westward would simplify problems of command control and logistics.[11]

As early as mid-July, when the plans for creating an American army group still were indefinite and American forces

---

[11] SHAEF Memo, Command and Organization After D Day—OVERLORD, 21 AGp/20657/1/G (Plans), 30 May; SHAEF/17100/5/Opns (A), 1 Jun; ETOUSA Ltr, Organization and Comd of U.S. Forces, 6 Jun. All in SHAEF G-3 Opns File A 322/011/1.

were far from Brittany, the growing
number of divisions under First Army
control had prompted General Bradley
to recommend (with Montgomery's
concurrence) that the 12th Army Group
and Third Army headquarters become
operational as soon as COBRA was completed, regardless of the progress
achieved in COBRA.[12]   Anticipating
General Eisenhower's approval, Bradley
informed Generals Hodges and Patton
that the change in command would be
made during the COBRA offensive and
"without any appreciable halt in the
attack provided everything is going well;
. . . we will not halt the advance to
reorganize."[13]   General Eisenhower approved Bradley's recommendation and
authorized him to set the date for the
change.   At the same time he made
clear his desire that Montgomery continue to act as the Allied ground forces
commander until SHAEF moved to the
Continent and he, Eisenhower, assumed
personal command of the Allied ground
forces.[14]

At noon, 1 August, as armored
columns streamed beyond Pontaubault,
the 12th Army Group, under General
Bradley's command, became operational.[15]   General Hodges assumed command of the First U.S. Army, and Gen-

eral Patton's Third U.S. Army came to
life.[16]

The most flamboyant personality in
the Allied camp was without question
General Patton.   Commander of assault
troops in the North African landings in
November 1942, leader of the II Corps
in Tunisia, organizer and commander of
the Seventh U.S. Army in Sicily, Patton
had been designated the Third Army
commander in the spring of 1944.   Intensely sensitive, at times overbearing,
always temperamentally dramatic, a con-
troversial figure recognized as one of the
outstanding field commanders in the
U.S. Army, Patton was able to exert "an
extraordinary and ruthless driving
power . . . at critical moments."   He
had "demonstrated [his] ability of
getting the utmost out of soldiers in
offensive operations."[17]

Closely associated with the development of tanks and armor doctrine, a
cavalryman by temperament, tradition,
and training, and at the same time a
profound student of military history,
General Patton typified the tenets of
daring and dash.   If he seemed to be
reckless and impetuous, he was also bold
and imaginative, favoring "a good plan
violently executed *now*" rather than "a
perfect plan next week."   Like Napo-
leon, he believed that war was "a very
simple thing."   Its determining characteristics were "self-confidence, speed,
and audacity."[18]   During the month of
August, Patton and his army—whose

[12] Ltr, Bradley to Eisenhower, 19 Jul, with hand-
written endorsement by Montgomery, 20 Jul, Gen
Bd Rpts File 322/011, Box 47, Item 50.
[13] FUSA Memo, Bradley to Hodges and Patton,
21 Jul, 12th AGp File 371.3, Mil Objectives.
[14] SHAEF Ltr, Comd and Organization, U.S.
Ground Forces, 25 Jul, SHAEF/17100/5/Opns (A),
SHAEF G–3 File Opns A-322/011.1; SGS SHAEF
War Diary, 25 Jul.
[15] Chief of Staff, Maj. Gen. Leven C. Allen;
G–1, Col. Joseph J. O'Hare; G–2, Brig. Gen. Edwin
L. Sibert; G–3, Brig. Gen. A. Franklin Kibler; G–4,
Brig. Gen. Raymond G. Moses.

[16] ADSEC continued to be the direct agency of
supply for the combat forces, but Lt. Gen. John
C. H. Lee's Communication Zone headquarters
was fast getting established on the Continent.
[17] Ltrs, Eisenhower to Marshall, 29 and 30 Apr,
cited in Pogue, *Supreme Command*, p. 166.
[18] Patton, *War as I Knew It*, p. 354.

members modeled their behavior on that of their chief—were to find a situation perfectly suited to the expression of their principles of combat.[19]

Partially as a result of the personalities of the commanders, the headquarters of the First and Third Armies functioned in slightly different ways. The difference was evident only by comparison. The First Army tended to be more methodical and meticulous in staff work, and required more reports from subordinate units. More planning was committed to paper in the First Army, whereas informal briefings and conversations frequently sufficed in the Third. Yet in both armies the work of the staff members was neither underrated nor unappreciated. Long hours of patient staff work often preceded a daring decision or brought a brilliant idea to maturity and reality. The many anonymous staff officers who toiled in relative obscurity, not only on the army level but on all echelons of command, made it possible for the military leaders of World War II to direct the complex operations with such apparent ease.

To enhance the FORTITUDE deception—the Allied threat of a landing on the Pas-de-Calais—General Eisenhower forbade publicity on Patton's entrance into battle.[20] The Germans were still being tricked into keeping a considerable number of their *Fifteenth Army*

forces immobile because they were expecting Patton's appearance on the Continent outside Normandy. They could construe his unexplained absence only as signifying that another Allied invasion of western Europe would take place.[21] The Germans knew that Patton had more combat experience than Bradley; they were conscious that he outranked Bradley in grade. Respecting Patton as a dangerous opponent, they logically expected the Allies to use him to head the main U.S. forces in western Europe, which evidently had not yet appeared.[22]

The Third Army arrived on the scene in the midst of an extremely fluid situation. By taking command of VIII Corps, which on 1 August was rapidly approaching Brittany, Patton assumed control of a going concern. Behind the front, XV Corps headquarters, which had arrived in France on 15 July, and XX Corps headquarters, which had arrived on 24 July, were ready for action. The XII Corps headquarters was staging the movement of Third Army units from England to the Continent and processing them from the beach forward; part of the headquarters reached Normandy on 29 July, the remainder on 7 August.[23]

To give close air support to the Third Army, Brig. Gen. Otto P. Weyland's XIX Tactical Air Command, which had been operating as part of the IX TAC, became operational. The transfer from England to France of the headquarters of the British Second Tactical Air Force and of the U.S. Ninth Air Force—moves scheduled to be completed in the first

---

[19] The Third Army general staff consisted of Maj. Gen. Hugh J. Gaffey, chief of staff; Col. Frederick S. Matthews, G-1; Col. Oscar W. Koch, G-2; Col. Halley G. Maddox, G-3; Col. Walter J. Muller, G-4. See Hugh M. Cole, *The Lorraine Campaign*, UNITED STATES ARMY IN WORLD WAR II (Washington, 1950), Chapter I, for a detailed discussion of the Third Army command and staff.

[20] Eisenhower to Marshall, FWD-12493, 30 Jul, Pogue Files.

[21] JIC (44) 345 (O) (Final), German Appreciation of Allied Intentions in the West, 7 Aug, JIC Papers, 1944, Pogue Files.

[22] *OB WEST, a Study in Command*, pp. 55ff.

[23] TUSA AAR, I, 7, 12.

week of August—complemented the establishment on the Continent of the two army group headquarters for the ground forces. When SHAEF displaced to France and the Supreme Commander assumed direct control of ground operations, Headquarters, AEAF, was also to move in order to facilitate co-ordination of ground and air operations.[24]

The OVERLORD plan had designated Brittany the stage for the Third Army's initial operations, which were expected to begin some time between two weeks and two months after the invasion. In Normandy since the early days of July, commanders and staffs of the Third Army and its components had despaired of performing within the original OVERLORD time limits. Suddenly, less than a week before the planned limit expired, they were ordered into Brittany.

The peninsula of Brittany was important to the Allies because of its ports: St. Malo, less than fifty miles west of Avranches; Brest, on the western extremity of the peninsula; Lorient and St. Nazaire, along the southern seashore; Nantes, fifty miles east of the Loire River mouth; and the many small harbors and beaches useful for discharging cargo. If Brittany could be captured, one of the basic requirements for the success of OVERLORD would be fulfilled: a continental port capacity sufficient to support the forces deemed necessary to defeat the Germans. Without the Breton ports, the Allies, particularly the Americans, could not hope to sustain the continental build-up projected by OVERLORD. As General Eisenhower stated it,

"the ideal situation [would be] . . . to obtain the entire coastal area from Havre to Nantes, both inclusive. With such a broad avenue of entry we could [bring to the Continent] . . . every single soldier the United States could procure for us, and we would have . . . little interest in ANVIL." [25] To gain a broad avenue of entry was a major Allied objective.

Planners originally had projected the capture of Brittany in two thrusts—seizure of Nantes and St. Nazaire, and a subsequent westward drive to secure Brest and the other harbors. Logistical planners doubted that the Breton ports could be used immediately after capture. The Germans had fortified the important ones, particularly Lorient, St. Nazaire, and Brest, which were naval bases for the underwater and surface raiders that attacked Allied shipping on the Atlantic, and they were certain to defend them with determination and destroy the facilities in the process. On this assumption, the Americans had decided to construct an entirely new port on the south coast of Brittany between Lorient and St. Nazaire, where the Quiberon peninsula shelters a curving bay from the Atlantic winds. There, four ports (including the not inconsiderable harbors of Vannes and Auray), an excellent rail and road network, hard beaches with gentle gradients, and sheltered anchorages for ocean-going vessels made the area attractive. Closer to the post-OVERLORD area of operations than Cherbourg and Brest, a port complex around Quiberon would obviate com-

---

[24] AEAF Ltr, Comd and Contl of Allied Air Force, AEAF/TS 378/Air Plans, 5 Aug, Gen Bd Rpts File 322/011/1, Box 47, Item 50.

[25] Ltr, Eisenhower to Montgomery, 10 Jul, SGS SHAEF File 381, OVERLORD, I (a). ANVIL was the code name for the invasion of southern France, which was scheduled for 15 August.

plete dependence on the railway that linked Brest with the interior of France, a railroad the Germans would most probably have destroyed and one that would be difficult to repair. With the Allies in possession of Quiberon, it would not be necessary to rely so heavily on the original landing beaches in Normandy, which were expected to be useful only until autumn. Furthermore, protective bridgeheads south of the Loire River, the southern boundary of the OVERLORD lodgment area, would be needed in order to utilize Nantes and St. Nazaire, but would not be necessary for Quiberon Bay. On this basis, the Americans decided that instead of securing Nantes and St. Nazaire first, they would drive at once to seize the Quiberon area. As early as 13 May, the 1st Army Group had instructed the Third Army to prepare plans for this operation.[26]

Despite plans for using Quiberon Bay to handle large freight tonnages, the Allies were still interested in the major ports of Brittany, Brest in particular. Possession of Brest would enable personnel and vehicles coming directly from the United States to be landed there without waiting for the Quiberon complex to be built. Also, with Brest in Allied hands, convoys could sail around Brittany to the Quiberon Bay area without hindrance from German warships based at Brest. Although doubts had been expressed in July that the Allies could obtain the major ports quickly and although there appeared an increasing reluctance to undertake the complicated engineering necessary to utilize Quiberon, the Allies at the beginning of August still felt that they needed Brittany and its port facilities.[27]

Personalities and Concepts

It had long been planned to turn the VIII Corps westward into Brittany as soon as the Americans reached the base of the Cotentin at Avranches. In moving toward Rennes and St. Malo, VIII Corps was to precede other units of the Third Army, which would clear the "whole of the Brittany Peninsula."[28] General Bradley thus ordered Patton to drive south from Pontaubault to seize Rennes and Fougères, then turn westward to secure St. Malo, the Quiberon Bay area, Brest, and the remainder of Brittany, in that sequence. The Communications Zone was alerted to the task of opening and developing the ports of St. Malo, Quiberon Bay, and Brest as soon as possible after their capture.[29]

Before the invasion, it had been thought necessary to divert a sizable U.S. force to capture the Breton ports, and plans had been formed to deploy not

[26] Ruppenthal, *Logistical Support, I,* 186–88, 285–97; SHAEF/17100/35 Opns, NEPTUNE, Summary of Jt Opns Plan, Phase II, 25 Apr, SGS SHAEF File 381, OVERLORD, I (a); SHAEF/17100/35/Opns, NEPTUNE, Summary of Rev Jt Opns Plan—U.S. Forces for Phase II of Opn OVERLORD, 20 May, and SHAEF/17100/35/Opns, NEPTUNE, Summary of Third U.S. Army Outline Plan, 22 May, both in EUCOM Files, Box 3; Capt Albert Norman, The History of 12th Army Group (Third Draft), MS, Hist Br, AG Sec, 12th AGp [27 Jul 45], pp. 349–56, 12th AGp File, Box 27; Interv by Pogue with Maj Gen K. R. McLean, 11–13 Mar 47, Pogue Files.

[27] Ruppenthal, *Logistical Support, I,* 468–74.

[28] 21 AGp Dirs, M–510 and M–515, 10 and 27 Jul; Ltr, Montgomery to Bradley, Dempsey, Patton, and Crerar, M–512, 21 Jul.

[29] 12th AGp Ltr of Instrs 1, 29 Jul. The 12th Army Group orders are conveniently reproduced as Annex 4 of the 12th Army Group History and also in Annex 1 of the Third Army AAR.

GENERALS HODGES, BRADLEY, AND PATTON *discuss the drive through Brittany at General Bradley's headquarters, 17 August.*

only the VIII Corps but also the XV, and possibly even the VII and XX.[30] When German disorganization seemed so thorough, the opportunity of seizing Brittany with smaller forces became feasible.

Specifically, General Patton planned to drive southwest from Avranches through Rennes to Quiberon Bay in order to cut the Brittany peninsula near its base and prevent the reinforcement or escape of German forces thus isolated.

Next, he would clear Brittany by seizing the central plateau of the peninsula. In so doing, he would liberate a vast region of France, open interior lines of communication, and reduce the enemy defenses to isolated pockets along the coast. With the Germans penned into a few port cities, it would be relatively easy to force their capitulation. Once the ports were in American hands, the Third Army would be free to turn east, where the decisive battle of the European campaign would obviously be fought. Thus, Patton visualized his primary mission as clearing the peninsula, his incidental mission as securing Quiberon

[30] TUSA AAR, I, 13; SHAEF/17100/35/Opns, NEPTUNE, Summary of Third U.S. Army Outline Plan, 22 May, EUCOM Files, Box 3; 83d Div Min of Mtg, 0900, 30 Jul, 83d Div G-2, G-3 Jnl and File.

Bay and Brest first and the other ports later, his eventual mission as driving eastward toward Paris and the Seine.[31]

Patton's method for securing Brittany was to unleash armored columns in the peninsula. The 4th Armored Division was to drive through Rennes to Quiberon. The 6th Armored Division was to go all the way to Brest. A third column, formed by activating a provisional unit called Task Force A under the command of Brig. Gen. Herbert L. Earnest, was to advance to Brest to secure the vital railroad that follows generally the north shore.[32]

If Brest was to prove of value as a port of entry, the double-track railway linking it to Rennes had to be in good condition. Since the railroad crosses several big bridges that can not be quickly or easily replaced or repaired, Task Force A was to capture the bridges before the Germans could demolish them. That Patton considered this an important mission was clear when he requested General Grow of the 6th Armored Division also to keep an eye out for the bridges along the railroad, particularly the one at Morlaix.[33]

Unlike General Bradley, General Patton considered the capture of St. Malo incidental to the entire Brittany campaign. He did not specifically assign it as an objective to any of his forces. And he apparently influenced Bradley to the extent that Bradley agreed St. Malo could be bypassed and contained if its reduction appeared to require too many forces and too much time.[34]

What emerged was a concept quite different from that which had governed operations in the Cotentin. Patton saw his immediate objectives far in advance of the front, for his intent was to slash forward and exploit not only the mobility and striking power of his armored divisions but also the German disorganization.[35] Prone to give his subordinates free rein, Patton expected them to exercise independent judgment and tactical daring. Confident of the ability of armor to disrupt enemy rear areas and to sustain itself deep in enemy territory, and conscious of the weak and disorganized opposition, he felt that the ultimate objectives were immediately pertinent and attainable. There seemed little point in slowly reducing Brittany by carefully planned and thoroughly supervised operations unraveled in successive phases. As a result, Patton granted his subordinates a freedom of action that permitted the division commanders to be virtually independent.

With this concept of warfare that stressed taking advantage of the breaks, General Patton required constant knowledge of front-line changes. To get it,

---

[31] TUSA FO 1, 4 Aug (confirming verbal orders, 1 Aug), AAR, I, 16, and Ltr, Confirmation of Verbal Orders Issued 2 Aug 44, 4 Aug; TF A AAR and Jnl, Aug. The Third Army orders are conveniently reproduced in Annex 2 of the Third Army AAR.

[32] The principal components of Task Force A were the 15th Cavalry Group and the 6th Tank Destroyer Group, both supported by attached engineers and operating under the headquarters of the 1st Tank Destroyer Brigade. The brigade had been activated in 1942 as a tactical headquarters, but, upon its assignment to the Third Army in 1944, it had been transformed into the army tank destroyer staff section. On 1 August it was again given command status and attached to VIII Corps.

[33] 1st Tank Destroyer Brigade History, 24 Nov 42–31 Dec 44; VIII Corps FO 9, 1600, 1 Aug; TUSA

Ltr, Confirmation of Verbal Orders Issued 2 Aug, 4 Aug; TF A FO 1, 2 Aug; Interv by author with Gen Grow.

[34] 12th AGp Dir for Current Opns, 2 Aug.

[35] TUSA AAR, I, 16–18.

he renamed the 6th Cavalry Group (Col. Edward M. Fickett) the Army Information Service and transformed it into a communications unit. A varying number of reconnaissance platoons (each usually with two officers, twenty-eight men, six armored cars, and six jeeps) formed into troops under two squadrons were to report the activities of combat units down through battalion size. The reconnaissance platoons were to funnel G–2 and G–3 information through troop headquarters to squadron and group. The latter would co-ordinate and condense the information into teletype messages and send it directly to the army advance command post. Known as Patton's "Household Cavalry" and required to bypass normal communications channels, the 6th Cavalry Group was to provide a means of contact between far-flung forces engaged in diverse missions and the army command post, which was sometimes to be as much as a hundred miles behind the front.[36] It thus happened on occasion that, though corps and divisions monitored the messages, the army staff was better informed on a particular situation than the corps directing the operation.

In Brittany, the corps commander in immediate charge of operations, General Middleton, methodical and meticulous, found himself in a whirlwind that threatened to upset his ideas of orderly and controlled progress. The transfer of VIII Corps from First to Third Army brought changes in staff procedures, communications, and supply, but these were minor problems when compared to the exigencies that emerged in rapid succession as a result of the change from the positional hedgerow warfare in the Cotentin to wide-open exploitation in Brittany.

General Middleton's plans for Brittany grew out of the premises that had governed the action in the Cotentin: orderly advances were to be made to specific objectives by units developing a compact fighting front. In conformance with this manner of operation, he planned to send two columns into Brittany—two armored divisions abreast, each followed by an infantry division— the same formation employed so successfully during the post-COBRA exploitation to Avranches. The 4th Armored Division, followed by the 8th Division, was to move southwest from Pontaubault and capture Rennes; the 6th Armored Division, supported by the 79th Division, was to strike westward from Pontaubault and seize in turn Pontorson, Dol-de-Bretagne, and Dinan. Once these objectives were secured, General Middleton would send his columns on to Quiberon and St. Malo, respectively. St. Malo, Middleton believed, was his "immediate task" in Brittany.[37]

The commanders who were to lead the spearheads into Brittany regarded themselves as belonging to the Patton school of thought. They seized upon the situation of exploitation with relish. Generals Grow and Earnest, who were

---

[36] TUSA AAR, I, 5; Interv with Lt Col Samuel M. Goodwin, Executive Officer, 6th Cav Gp, Hosp Intervs, IV, GL–93 (321), ML–2235. Between 1 August and 10 October, the reconnaissance platoons lost 1 officer and 57 men. Twenty-eight were casualties of enemy action, the remaining 30 victims of traffic accidents. Montgomery used a similar communications system called *Phantom.*

[37] VIII Corps AAR, Aug, Opns Instrs, 31 Jul (confirming fragmentary verbal orders, 31 Jul), and FO 9, 1600, 1 Aug.

to pass near St. Malo, for example, made no plans to capture the city, Earnest going so far as to tell his staff, with some exaggeration, that they would go by it without even looking at it.[38]

Generals Wood and Grow in particular felt toward General Patton, who, like them, was a tank officer, an affinity they could not feel toward General Middleton, bred in the infantry. They were convinced they understood better what Patton expected. Their units had been relatively untouched by the depressing combat in the hedgerows and had not sustained the heavy losses that were normal in the Cotentin. Having thrust victoriously to Avranches in the last days of July, they believed they had accomplished what other units had not been able to do. Having led the U.S. forces from the breakthrough into the breakout, the division commanders and their units became infected with an enthusiasm and a self-confidence that were perfectly suited to exploitation but proved to be a headache to those who sought to retain a semblance of control. A naturally headstrong crew became rambunctious in Brittany.

Problems

Control was one of the major problems of the Brittany campaign, and distance added to the problem. The VIII Corps command post was located north of Avranches, and General Middleton was able to displace forward to a point several miles south of that city only on 4 August. By then the combat components of the corps were scattered, out of sight and virtually out of hearing.

Although Middleton wanted to move his command post into Brittany and closer to his far-flung units, the Third Army staff was most anxious for him not to displace the corps headquarters beyond the limited range of field telephones. Middleton complied. Communications between the army and the corps headquarters thus remained satisfactory, but this state of affairs was not duplicated below the corps level. As early as 2 August, General Middleton remarked that contact with the armored divisions was "practically nil." [39]

With the corps units stretched over a vast area and moving rapidly, signal communications broke down almost completely. "The expensive signal equipment at the disposal of the Corps," General Middleton later wrote, "was never designed apparently for a penetration and pursuit of the magnitude of the Brittany operation." [40] It was impossible to install or maintain wire communications over such distances. During the night of 3 August, the few corps signal lines to forward units that did exist were bombed out by German planes, as were the wires to the army headquarters. For about eight hours, while the lines were being repaired, the corps headquarters existed in a virtual vacuum, able to exercise only the most limited influence on operations.[41]

Although communications with both armored divisions were strained, they were particularly weak in the case of the 6th Armored Division, which had dis-

---

[38] TF A AAR and Jnl, Aug.

[39] Telecon, 6 Aug, VIII Corps G–3 Jnl; VIII Corps Sitrep, 2 Aug.
[40] VIII Corps AAR, Aug.
[41] Msg, VIII Corps Sig Officer to G–3, 0040, 4 Aug; Memo, Rpt of Evenings Activities, 4 Aug. Both in VIII Corps G–3 Jnl.

appeared in a cloud of dust on the roads to Brest. Since Signal personnel were unable to lay telephone cables fast enough and far enough, the division depended to a large extent on the high-powered SCR–399 long-distance radio, which proved unsatisfactory. As many as eight different transmitters working on the assigned corps frequency were often heard at the same time. With the corps radio communications net so jammed and signals so faint because of distance, the division had to wait for radio time. Often a code group had to be repeated six to ten times to insure accurate reception.[42]

A corps cable teletype team had been attached to the 6th Armored Division in the Cotentin, but it had been unable to keep up with the rapid advance and was replaced in Brittany by a radio teletype team using very high frequency beam antenna equipment. The new team was instructed to beam its equipment on a prominent hill near Avranches, where the corps expected to place a receiving station on 1 August. Because the enemy still was ensconced on the hill and because German planes were attacking U.S. troops and installations in the Avranches area, the corps Signal section set up its receiving station near Bréhal instead. Without knowledge of the change of location, the division radio teletype team beamed on the wrong place. Had the distance between sender and receiver been shorter, the correct location would have easily been found, but beyond fifty miles the equip-

ment was unreliable, and contact was not established for several days.[43]

With radio teletype nonoperational, with high-power radio erratic, and with wire and cable lacking, communications devolved upon messengers who traveled long distances by jeep. Sometimes a round trip between division and corps headquarters took the better part of a day. Messengers were excellent targets for bypassed enemy groups and individual snipers in the far-reaching no man's land between the corps and division command posts, and they had to have ingenuity, patience, and luck. An officer courier, Capt. Hans H. Marechal, who started from the VIII Corps command post for the 6th Armored Division headquarters about noon one day proceeded through Antrain and beyond Loudéac until French civilians warned him that several hundred Germans with a few tanks still held a town ahead. Detouring south to Pontivy, the captain met and joined a convoy of gasoline trucks going to the division. A destroyed bridge caused another change in route. At the town where the division command post had last been reported, Marechal learned from civilians that the division had moved on to another town. Eventually, he found a solitary military policeman who was awaiting the arrival of the division trains. The convoy halted, but Marechal continued alone in search of the division command post. Another reported pocket of enemy forced another detour, and then he was "off the map." Noticing tank tracks in the road, he followed them and reached the

[42] Ltr, Lt Col William J. Given to Gen Grow, 12 Jan 53, OCMH Files; 146th Armored Signal Company, *The Signal Circuit* (Luxembourg, 1945), p. 7.

[43] Interv with Col Claude E. Haswell, Third Army Sig Sec Executive Officer, 1st Lt Richard Stockton's Hosp Intervs, ML–2234.

armored division command post nine hours after he had departed the corps headquarters. Returning by the same route early the following day, Marechal discovered that Germans drifting across Brittany to find refuge in the port cities made the roads hazardous for single American vehicles. Fortunately, civilians warned him in time of hostile groups, and he regained the corps command post twenty-four hours after he had left. An enlisted man of the 6th Armored Division, who often carried messages to the corps though unable to read or write or follow a map, returned to the division on one occasion after a two-day trip—with a bullet in his back and two captured Germans on the hood of the jeep he was still driving.[44]

The hazardous journeys to supply information between corps and divisions were often futile, since situations changed so rapidly that the messages were frequently out of date by the time they were delivered.[45] The division artillery observation planes might have been used for liaison and thus have provided a faster means of communications but, in the case of the 6th Armored Division at least, most of the planes were out of action. Rough landing fields in Normandy and enemy fire had accounted for most of the casualties. The absence of landing strips in Brittany—because the fast-moving division lacked time to clear landing fields—kept the corps artillery observation planes grounded.[46]

Patton's Household Cavalry provided an additional channel of communications. One armored car with a high-powered SCR–506 radio, as well as several armored jeeps, accompanied each armored division. The radio car possessed choice and workable frequencies, and the armored jeeps, often entrusted with situation reports, were able to shoot their way through small roadblocks. Even though the cavalrymen were burdened with their own radio traffic and could absorb only a small part of the division communications, they sometimes relayed division messages.

Because of all these difficulties, the interval between the sending of a message and the receipt of its acknowledgment from the addressee usually exceeded thirty-six hours.[47] Before the end of the first week in August, the 6th Armored Division was about 150 miles west of Avranches. It was so far away from the corps that Middleton advised Patton that he had practically no control and little knowledge of the division operation, and thus virtually denied responsibility for the division activities. "This headquarters" he wrote, "has made repeated attempts to establish radio contact with the 6th Armored Division without success. A special messenger was dispatched . . . but his time of arrival cannot be stated. This headquarters will continue efforts to establish radio contact. . . ."[48]

In the face of these difficulties, confusion and misunderstanding were inevitable. Having outrun communica-

[44] Capt Marechal's Notes, 6 Aug, VIII Corps G–3 Jnl; Ltr, Given to Grow, 12 Jan 53.
[45] VIII Corps AAR, Aug.
[46] Msg, Middleton to Grow, 1715, 4 Aug.

[47] 6th Armd Div Ltr to VIII Corps, Rpts Submitted 6–7 Aug, 8 Aug, and Telephonic Msg from VIII Corps Sig Officer, 0855, 6 Aug. Both in VIII Corps G–3 Jnl.
[48] Msg, Middleton to Patton, 1700, 5 Aug.

tions in the interest of exploitation, the division commanders found it difficult to understand why their messages to corps were apparently being ignored, why they received so little assistance and guidance. Needing to react quickly to fast-changing situations, they could hardly wait for orders, which might be out of date by the time they arrived. As General Wood, the 4th Armored Division commander, later recalled, "The situation at the time was . . . extremely fluid. I had to make decisions on my own responsibility, since there were no orders from higher authority. Of course, everything went 'according to plan,' but at that time no one in the higher circles had [yet] discovered just how . . . the plan [fitted] . . . the events. . . . We were moving on our own. We could not wait for directions or objectives to be passed down from higher authority." [49]

Supplies were secured on the basis of expediency. Because of the development of the main stream of the European campaign outside Brittany, the VIII Corps was semi-independent. A tactical headquarters, it had to assume certain administrative and logistical responsibilities. Permanent supply dumps were out of the question because the breakthrough had never stopped. "Within a couple of days [we] were passing out rations like Santa Claus on his sleigh, with both giver and receiver on the move. . . . The trucks were like a band of stage-coaches making a run through Indian country. We got used to keeping the wheels going, disregarding the snipers, and hoping we wouldn't

get lost or hit." [50] Supply depots remained north of Avranches during the early part of the month, and gasoline and ammunition convoys added to traffic complications in the Avranches bottleneck. Convoys had to have armed escorts because of hostile pockets along the lines of communication in Brittany. At first, 40-mm. antiaircraft batteries were used for escort duty. Later in the month the 54th Antiaircraft Brigade assumed the task of guarding the supply routes with the aid of members of the French Forces of the Interior (FFI).

The FFI in Brittany was a sizable force numbering about 20,000 armed members.[51] During July preparations had been made in London to activate a unified command to direct this large and dispersed but potentially strong underground force. General Koenig had designated Col. Albert M. Eon as the commander of all the FFI in Brittany and had taken him to visit General Montgomery's 21 Army Group headquarters in Normandy, where the army group chief of staff, Major-General Sir Francis de Guingand, had briefed both French officers on future operations. The French leaders learned that the

---

[49] Ltr, Wood to OCMH, 24 Mar 54, OCMH Files.

[50] Interv with William M. King, 44th Armd Inf Bn, 6th Armd Div, Hosp Intervs, II, ML–2235, GL–93 (104).

[51] TUSA AAR states that the FFI membership in Brittany numbered about 30,000, but the Journal des Marches et Opérations du Commandement des F. F. I. en Bretagne (4 juillet au 10 septembre 1944) (hereafter cited as Journal des Marches) gives the figure used above. The Journal was submitted as an after action report by the commander of the FFI in Brittany, Col. Albert M. Eon, and the manuscript is in the files of the Section Historique de l'Armeé Française. Lieutenant Colonel Lugand, Maj. Jean Vial, and Capt. André Méric of the French Army historical section kindly made this source and others available to the author in the summer of 1953.

Americans planned to penetrate Brittany along two principal axes—Dinan–Brest, and Avranches–Rennes–Redon—and they hoped to be of assistance.

The Allies had planned to promote intensified FFI activities in Brittany only after trained guerrilla leaders, arms, ammunition, and supplies had been dropped into the area. This program was to have been completed about the time U.S. troops made their appearance on the peninsula, but American exploitation was so rapid that the FFI had to begin operating before the program could be fully realized.

General Bradley's 12th Army Group assumed command of the FFI in Brittany on 29 July and placed it under the control of the Third Army. Plans were made to parachute a small reconnaissance party into Brittany during the night of 2 August to establish a command post for Colonel Eon, but poor weather conditions forced cancellation of the drop. On 3 August the British Broadcasting Corporation radioed a coded message to the FFI in Brittany to begin general guerrilla activities short of open warfare. Because American troops had already sped beyond Dinan and Rennes by 4 August, General Koenig requested Colonel Eon to parachute into Brittany with his staff, take command of Resistance operations at once, and assume an initial mission of seizing and securing high ground north of Vannes in the Quiberon Bay area. Although some French officers, including Eon, had had no jump experience, the command group parachuted into Brittany during the night of 4 August. At the same time, 150 men were dropped in the Morlaix area to seize and preserve the railroad trestle bridges there. On

the following night, ten American gliders towed by British aircraft were landed between Vannes and Lorient to bring in armored jeeps, weapons, and ammunition to support local FFI troops who were ready to take the Vannes airfield. On 6 August the FFI command made contact with a U.S. armored patrol and learned that the Americans, with the assistance of local French Resistance groups, had already cleared a large part of the peninsula.[52]

The weather had turned hot and dry in August, and mechanized columns raised clouds of grit and dust as they drove over the sun-baked earth. Sun glasses became precious possessions, goggles a necessity. Overhead, the clear weather gave perfect visibility for Allied fighter-bombers.

As fluid as the situation was to become in Brittany, the immediate preliminary to it was quite the opposite. Getting troops out of Normandy and into Brittany was a difficult problem. In the coastal sector of the Cotentin there were only two main highways running southward, and debris, dead animals, and wrecked vehicles, as well as mines, obstructed traffic, while destroyed villages and damaged towns blocked it. Bulldozers had had to clear lanes through rubble in some places—particularly in Avranches — before normal military traffic could pass. Convergence of the two highways at Coutances and again at Avranches posed ad-

---

[52] Journal des Marches; 6th Armd Div Msg to VIII Corps G–2, 1410, 3 Aug; TUSA 11th Spec Force Detachment Ltr, Resistance Activities and Plans (Brittany), 4 Aug; TUSA Memo to VIII Corps. 5 Aug; Msg. Middleton to Grow, 1405, 5 Aug.

ditional difficulties. Engineers constructed a cutoff at Coutances to keep traffic moving along both routes and opened a subsidiary road from Avranches to Pontaubault. Pontaubault was the most critical traffic point of all, for through that village had to be funneled all the vehicles moving into Brittany. Establishing traffic priorities and assuring compliance with them required perseverance and patience as well as attention to detail. Task Force A was given three hours to move its 3,500 men through the Avranches–Pontaubault bottleneck; it was to arrive in Avranches "precisely at 0200, 3 August, not before" and was to clear Pontaubault exactly by 0500. "Still spending most of my time as a traffic cop," wrote a division commander. It was not unusual to see high ranking officers acting as military policemen at critical traffic points, but the payoff was the feat of getting two armored divisions into Brittany in less than forty-eight hours.[53]

Several bridges over the Seé and the Sélune Rivers, the road approaches to these crossing sites, and the dams nearby were of extreme importance. During the first few days of August the German Air Force appeared in relative strength over the Cotentin in a belated effort to block by bombardment the American entrance into Brittany. Antiaircraft

protection, a matter of small importance during July, became a vital adjunct of the breakout and exploitation. Gun crews, enthusiastic that they had an opportunity at last to participate in action against the enemy, shot down more than a score of planes around Avranches during the first week of August.

Though operations in Brittany later diminished in importance, the prospect of success at the beginning of August led to high expectations. Normandy had been slow and painful; Brittany appeared to be fast and exhilarating. Beyond the initial physical obstructions at Avranches, one fact shone brightly: the Germans had little with which to oppose the exploitation of the breakout into Brittany.[54] Confusion of purpose and method on the American side, which was to mar the breakout, stemmed from the abruptness of the change from static to mobile warfare and from the contrasting personalities of the leaders involved. With fluidity the overriding condition, the Americans broke out of the Cotentin into the relative freedom of a war of movement in Brittany, a difference that seemed to be symbolized by the man of the hour, General Patton.

---

[53] Msg, Middleton to Earnest, 2 Aug; Comments, Gen Grow to author 27 Apr 54, OCMH Files.

[54] App. A to PS SHAEF (44) 29 (First Draft), Enemy Dispositions and Possible Reaction (in Brittany), SHAEF G–3 File 24533/Opns, Future Opns; TUSA AAR, I, 16; Notes, 1 Aug, 83d Div G–2. G–3 Jnl and File.

CHAPTER XIX

Rennes, Lorient, and Nantes

On the afternoon of 1 August, General Wood's 4th Armored Division thrust southwestward from Pontaubault toward Rennes, the capital of Brittany. On the eastern edge of the province, at the base of the peninsula, and about midway between the north and south shores, Rennes is the commercial center that links Brittany to the interior of France. A city of over 80,000 inhabitants, Rennes is the hub of an extensive road network. No less than ten main highways converge there. Sixty miles southwest of Rennes are Vannes and Quiberon. Sixty miles south by southwest is St. Nazaire. Sixty miles due south is Nantes. To the southeast are Châteaubriant and Angers, towns on the roads to Orléans, Chartres, and even Paris. (*Map VIII*)

For the 4th Armored Division, Rennes was about the halfway point between Avranches and Quiberon. Whether Rennes was to be a stopover, as General Middleton, the VIII Corps commander, expected, or whether the 4th Armored Division was to continue to the southwest in a rapid drive to Quiberon, as General Patton anticipated, was not quite clear. The corps commander had instructed General Wood only to take Rennes, but when the Third Army took control, Patton ordered Wood to go beyond Rennes to Quiberon in order to seal off the entire Brittany peninsula.

With the fluid situation and precarious communication emphasizing the need for initiative on the division level, General Wood felt that he had wide latitude in interpreting and executing his assignment.[1]

From Pontaubault the 4th Armored Division's CCA raced forty miles southwest on the afternoon of 1 August, reaching the northern outskirts of Rennes by early evening. There the advance guard struck surprisingly strong opposition. An assault by a company of armored infantry supported by twenty-five Sherman tanks failed to penetrate the enemy positions, and the leading units of CCA withdrew several miles under the cover of smoke to organize a stronger attack.[2]

Two Luftwaffe companies manning 88-mm. antiaircraft guns in defense of the Rennes airport had stopped CCA. In support of the antiaircraft gunners were perhaps a hundred infantrymen with eight machine guns and three antitank guns. Elsewhere in the city were a few troops from a naval torpedo and spare parts depot and a company of infantry. Although the city had not been

---

[1] VIII Corps Opns Instrs, 31 Jul (fragmentary verbal orders), and FO 9, 1600, 1 Aug; Ltr, Wood to OCMH, 24 Mar 54, OCMH Files. Unless otherwise indicated, all messages in this chapter are from the VIII Corps G–3 Journal and File.

[2] 4th Armd Div AAR, Aug; Koyen, *Fourth Armored Division,* p. 21.

fortified as a strongpoint, the Germans recognized its value as a communications center and sought to hold it. At the same time that Fahrmbacher had sent a kampfgruppe under Bacherer toward Pontaubault to stop the American breakout, he dispatched a small force of the *91st Division* to Rennes. Under the command of a lieutenant colonel, the force reached the city just before the Americans appeared, but too late to participate in the action at the airport. Expecting a further American effort against the city, the *91st Division* troops prepared to resist. As they were doing so, two German Army replacement battalions numbering about 1,900 men reached Rennes from le Mans. Issued machine guns and *panzerfausts,* the replacement troops hastily took to the field in the northern outskirts of the city.

The German reinforcements had arrived just in time. During the evening of 1 August about thirty P–47 Thunderbolts attacked the Rennes defenses and American artillery shelled the flak positions in preparation for a full-scale assault by the combat command. In a two-hour fight, terminating shortly before midnight, the Germans held. CCA withdrew.

The defenders, who knocked out eleven American tanks and took twenty prisoners, were reinforced later that night when Koenig, the *91st Division* commander, arrived in the city with two assault guns. Taking command of the Rennes garrison, Koenig prepared for an all-out defense.[3]

Realizing on the morning of 2 August

that the defenses of Rennes were stronger than anticipated, General Wood concluded that the 4th Armored Division was not going to be able to roll through the city as it had through Avranches. On the contrary, CCA troops on high ground about five miles north of Rennes were being shelled by mortars and artillery in such volume that they expected a counterattack. With the division strung out along the fifty-mile stretch between Avranches and Rennes and short of gasoline, ammunition, and rations, Wood decided that he needed additional supplies and a seasoned infantry regimental combat team to help him take Rennes. "Want them now," he radioed Middleton, "repeat now." [4]

General Wood also wanted two more air support parties. He had not received any air support until late afternoon of 1 August, and he requested "constant air cover," specifically "dawn to dusk fighter bomber support." General Middleton promised to do his best to supply 4th Armored Division needs and ordered Wood to secure all roads leading into Rennes after he captured the city. Wood said he would do so as soon as supplies, services, and reinforcements arrived. "These urgently needed now—repeat now. Must have infantry combat team if town is to be taken." [5]

The logical support was Maj. Gen. Donald A. Stroh's 8th Division, which had followed the 4th Armored Division in the Cotentin. Ordered to be ready to reinforce the armor when necessary and relieve it from the task of eliminating major strongpoints and occupying

[3] MS # B–731 (Fahrmbacher); Zimmerman Telecon, 1925, 1 Aug, *OB WEST KTB, Anlage 1010.*

[4] Msg, Wood to Middleton, 0955, 2 Aug.

[5] Msgs, Wood to Middleton, 1525, 1 Aug, and 1100 and 1115, 2 Aug; Msgs, Middleton to Wood, 2 and 3 Aug; VIII Corps G–3 Jnl, 1–3 Aug.

critical terrain, the 8th Division was to act as a clearing force in order to prevent the 4th Armored Division from getting unnecessarily involved in action that would neutralize its mobility and striking power. On 2 August General Middleton reattached to the armored division the 13th Infantry, which had been attached to General Wood's command in Avranches but which had since reverted to parental control. To move the infantry, the corps commander also made available four Quartermaster truck companies he had secured from Third Army. Early that evening the regiment began advancing toward Rennes.[6]

Meanwhile, after the 6th Armored Division passed through Avranches and Pontaubault for its drive toward Brest, the remainder of the 4th Armored Division had moved south of Pontaubault on 2 August and assembled north of Rennes. There the whole division awaited supplies, services, and reinforcement. To keep the Germans off balance, Wood launched a series of small infantry attacks during the day.

Learning on the evening of 2 August that the 13th Infantry was en route to Rennes, General Wood conceived a spectacular idea. It already seemed evident to him that the main action in western Europe would take place not in Brittany but in central France. Few enemy forces remained in Brittany, so why proceed westward to the Atlantic ocean and a dead end? Securing Rennes was important. Blocking the base of the Brittany peninsula south of Rennes was important too. If these missions could be combined with a

maneuver that would place the 4th Armored Division in position to drive eastward rather than westward, the division would be able to make a more vital contribution to victory. Instead of being relegated to a subsidiary role in Brittany, which might become the backwash of the war, the division would join the main Allied force for the kill. The proper direction, General Wood believed, was eastward to Chartres.[7]

How best to do this was the question.

Since part of the 8th Division was coming forward from Avranches to assault Rennes, General Wood decided the 4th Armored Division should bypass the city. The armor could not bypass Rennes on the east without overstepping the corps boundary, so Wood ordered it to make a wide arc around the western edge of the city, an arc wide enough to avoid the Rennes defenses. The division would arrive south of Rennes with the heads of its columns facing eastward. Châteaubriant, thirty miles southeast of Rennes, would be the next logical objective, and forty miles east of Châteaubriant the city of Angers on the Loire River would come within armored range.

It seemed to General Wood that this maneuver still would accomplish the important parts of his mission. The initial drive would encircle Rennes and isolate it on three sides. At the end of the movement, the division would be half way between Rennes and Nantes and thus constitute a blocking force along the base of the Brittany peninsula. If the maneuver were carried through to its logical conclusion and the 4th Armored Division went to Angers, the

---

[6] 8th Div AAR, 8 Jul–4 Aug, and Msg, 2200, 2 Aug; VIII Corps Msg to Officer in Charge of Truck Co's Furnished by Third Army, 2 Aug.

[7] Ltr, Wood to OCMH, 24 Mar 54.

Brittany peninsula would be blocked at its base, not along a line from Rennes southwestward to Quiberon Bay but along a line from Rennes southeastward to Angers. This seemed to be only a slight modification of current plans even though the scheme ignored Quiberon Bay.

General Wood sent General Middleton his proposal on the morning of 3 August in the form of a hastily sketched overlay showing the planned routes of advance and a message stating that Wood "strongly" recommended that the 4th Armored Division be permitted to "push on to Angers." Anticipating no objections to his plan, Wood ordered the plan executed.[8]

General Wood's proposal, sent by messenger to General Middleton, left the division command post just before the arrival of a routine field order that VIII Corps had issued the previous evening. The corps order reiterated General Wood's mission clearly. The 4th Armored Division was to capture Rennes and establish positions from Rennes southwestward to Quiberon in order to block the movement of hostile forces into or out of Brittany. Receipt of the corps order left General Wood no alternative but to rescind his own. In a new division order he acknowledged his mission as being exactly that stated by corps. Apparently as an afterthought, he alerted the division to prepare for an advance on Châteaubriant, southeast of Rennes.[9] The afterthought was in reality the significant point, for the division had

already embarked on the wide sweep westward around Rennes.

Early on the morning of 3 August, two columns had started to outflank Rennes. CCA moved along an inner arc between fifteen and thirty miles from the center of the city. CCB swept along an outer arc. By late afternoon the heads of the columns had arrived at Bain-de-Bretagne and Derval, thirty and forty miles south of Rennes, respectively. The armor had covered somewhere between sixty and a hundred miles against almost no opposition. Tankers had dashed through small roadblocks and dispersed fragmentary enemy units. Together, the combat commands had cut seven of the ten main roads centering on Rennes. Half way between Rennes and Nantes, the columns represented a rather effective blocking force at the base of the Brittany peninsula.[10]

Even before Wood's maneuver became a *fait accompli,* Middleton accepted it, perhaps on the basis that the encirclement would cut the roads leading out of Rennes. He acknowledged the maneuver by reporting it and thereby implying approval. But the implicit approval went only so far as the first part of Wood's plan. That afternoon, Middleton instructed Wood to "Secure Rennes before you continue"— presumably before continuing toward the east.[11]

Meanwhile, Wood was reporting his progress during the afternoon of 3 August with unabating optimism. When he expected to reach Bain-de-Bretagne

[8] 4th Armd Div Plan of Attack and Routes of Advance, 3 Aug, with penciled note, and FO 5, 3 Aug; Ltr, Wood to OCMH, 24 Mar 54.

[9] VIII Corps FO 10, 2 Aug; 4th Armd Div FO 6, 0730, 3 Aug.

[10] The Armored School, Armor in the Exploitation, p. 26.

[11] VIII Corps Msg, 1000, 3 Aug; Msg, Col John P. Evans to Gen Wood, 1430, 3 Aug.

and Derval in a matter of hours, he notified Middleton that he was planning to push one column to Châteaubriant. Three hours later he reported with some exaggeration that Rennes was entirely surrounded, that the city was apparently in the process of being demolished by the Germans, and that his columns were ready to move on Châteaubriant that night. Requesting orders, he recommended Angers as his next objective. Half an hour later, he informed Middleton that he was starting to move toward Châteaubriant and might even take Angers. Suddenly, however, he acknowledged receipt of "a new mission: . . . blocking enemy retreat from Rennes." [12]

Whether receipt of Middleton's instruction to secure Rennes prompted Wood's sudden acknowledgment or not, the fact was that Wood needed Rennes before he could proceed eastward—not only to eliminate a threat to his potential left rear but also to open a supply route for his division. He therefore halted his columns and directed them to turn northeastward to block the escape routes southeast of Rennes while the attached 13th Infantry attacked the city from the north. Pushing a dozen miles or so east and northeast of Bain-de-Bretagne and Derval, the heads of the combat commands on 4 August cut the main roads southeast of Rennes and captured and destroyed some of the German units squeezed out of the city by pressure from the north. [13]

Hurrying toward Rennes during the night of 2 August, the 13th Infantry could not be in position to assault the city from the north the next day. The regimental commander therefore requested a postponement until the morning of 4 August so that he could plan and execute a co-ordinated attack together with armored elements still north of Rennes. Impatient to capture Rennes, General Wood insisted that the infantry attack on the afternoon of 3 August. In compliance, the leading infantry battalion launched the attack from route column march formation. In the face of small arms, automatic weapons, and antiaircraft fire, the battalion forced an entrance into the northeastern outskirts of Rennes. [14]

Their defensive positions penetrated, their casualties at 60 dead and 130 wounded, and the city almost encircled by U.S. armored units, the Germans prepared to depart Rennes. Hausser, the *Seventh Army* commander, gave permission at 2300 for withdrawal during the night. After burning supplies and installations, the garrison of about 2,000 Germans left at 0300, 4 August. In two march groups, both with motorized and foot troops, they moved along small roads and cross-country, reaching St. Nazaire five days later. They encountered practically no Americans because American troops were racing along the main highways. [15]

The 13th Infantry marched into Rennes on the morning of 4 August and accepted the kisses and wines of the liberated inhabitants. On the heels of the regiment came the remainder of the 8th Division, which earlier had expected to follow the 6th Armored Division to

---

[12] Msgs, Wood to Middleton, 1315, 1555, 1630, 1821, 3 Aug.

[13] The Armored School, Armor in the Exploitation. pp. 26–27.

[14] 13th Inf AAR, Aug.

[15] MS # B–731 (Fahrmbacher).

Brest. Reassuming control of the 13th
Infantry, General Stroh took responsi-
bility for providing security for Rennes.
Deployed to block all entrances into the
city, the 8th Division became the VIII
Corps reserve.[16]

Meanwhile, General Middleton had
been pondering the proper mission of
the 4th Armored Division. Though
tempted to send it eastward toward Châteaubriant, he could not ignore Quiberon Bay. Yet the entire situation—
not only in Brittany but all along the
Allied front—was in a state of flux. All
sorts of changes in the Allied plan were
being rumored, and it seemed possible
that the campaign might sweep so irresistibly eastward as to drag with it the
entire VIII Corps. With this in mind,
Middleton made a compromise decision
on the evening of 3 August. He ordered Wood to block the bridges on the
Vilaine River from Rennes to the
coast.[17] The Vilaine flows generally
southwestward from Rennes and emp-
ties into the ocean about half way between St. Nazaire and Vannes. Two
main highways cross the river—one at
Redon, the other at la Roche-Bernard.
By blocking the bridges at these towns
and elsewhere, the 4th Armored Division would seal off the Rennes–Quiberon area. At the same time the division would also be ready to continue
toward the east should that course of
action become desirable and possible.

General Wood failed to get Middleton's message. "Have received no mission repeat have received no mission,"

he radioed the corps commander during
the night of 3 August. "Reply urgent
repeat reply urgent."

Deciding that it was time to see the
division commander and make sure he
understood the situation, Middleton
drove to Wood's headquarters on 4 August.[18]

Wood threw his arms around the corps
commander in welcome.

"What's the matter?" Middleton asked
with dry humor. "Have you lost your
division?"

"No!" Wood replied. It was worse
than that. "They"—meaning the Allied
command—"they are winning the war
the wrong way."

Though Wood almost persuaded the
corps commander that he ought to be allowed to go to the east without restriction, the result of the personal conference was a compromise. Without dis-
arranging his dispositions oriented eastward, Wood agreed to block all the
roads south of Rennes, to dispatch part
of one combat command westward to
secure the Vilaine River bridges near
Redon, and to make maximum use of
reconnaissance units to secure the Vilaine River line.[19]

The same day VIII Corps issued a
list of the missions assigned to its combat components. The list confirmed
the arrangements decided upon by Middleton and Wood. Sent to the Third
Army headquarters as a routine matter,
the information did not escape the sharp
glance of Maj. Gen. Hugh J. Gaffey, the
army chief of staff. He immediately

[16] 8th Div AAR, 8 Jul–4 Aug; VIII Corps G–3
Jnl, 2–4 Aug; Msg, Evans to Wood, 2040, 3 Aug;
VIII Corps FO 9, 1600, 1 Aug; VIII Corps Msgs to
4th and 6th Armd Divs, 1645, 2 Aug.
[17] Msg, Evans to Wood, 2040, 3 Aug.

[18] Msg, Wood to Middleton, 0310, 4 Aug, and
penned notation by member of the VIII Corps
G–3 Sec on the msg.
[19] Review Panel Min, OCMH, 9 May 56; Msg,
Wood to Middleton, 1610, 4 Aug.

sent Middleton a memorandum to point out that General Patton "assumes that in addition to blocking the roads . . ., you are pushing the bulk of the [4th Armored] division to the west and southwest to the Quiberon area, including the towns of Vannes and Lorient, in accordance with the Army plan." The assumption notwithstanding, Gaffey at once ordered Patton's Household Cavalry to relay a message directly to Wood (and to Middleton for information) to the effect that the 4th Armored Division was expected to move to Vannes and Lorient, unequivocally to the west. Without comment, the corps headquarters noted the action and recorded the mission.[20]

By this time the question on the proper mission of the armored division was not the only factor affecting its movements. The division was virtually out of gas. Had the combat commands south of Rennes been obliged to move suddenly, half their vehicles would have had to remain in place.

When the combat commands had begun their wide sweep around Rennes, the division trains had been left north of that city. Supply trucks that could have carried gasoline had been sent back to Avranches to bring the 13th Infantry forward. Not until the afternoon of 4 August, after the infantry occupied Rennes, was a direct supply route opened for the armored division; gasoline then became available.[21]

The uncertainty over the mission resolved and gasoline once more plentiful,

Wood on the morning of 5 August ordered CCA to drive the seventy miles westward to Vannes. The leading units of CCA departed at 1400 and swept into Vannes seven hours later. A battalion of the FFI that had already captured the Vannes airfield guided the column to the best approaches. So swift and surprising was the advance that the Germans in the town were unable to prepare demolitions. The combat command seized the bridges and other important installations intact.[22]

Though the capture of Vannes cut the Brittany peninsula at its base, some fighting remained. On the following day, 6 August, the enemy launched a surprise counterattack from Auray and drove back CCA's outposts. A task force had to attack to re-establish the positions. To remove the root of the trouble, the task force continued to Auray, clearing the town the next morning. Thereupon the CCA commander, Colonel Clarke, sent a strong task force westward fifteen miles beyond Auray to seize a bridge at Hennebont, near Lorient. Led by light tanks, the column raced through artillery fire and found that the Germans had just destroyed the Hennebont bridge. Making a detour two miles to the north and crossing the Blavet River at Lochrist, CCA made contact with CCB near Lorient.

While CCA had taken Vannes and Auray, General Dager's CCB had driven directly toward Lorient. Reaching the outskirts of the city on the morning of 7 August and finding strong defenses, CCB detoured to the north to attack

[20] VIII Corps Msgs, 4 and 5 Aug; Memo, Gaffey to Middleton, 5 Aug; Msg, Army Info Patrol with the 4th Armd Div to VIII Corps, 5 Aug.

[21] The Armored School, Armor in the Exploitation, p. 27; Ltr, Wood to OCMH, 24 Mar 54.

[22] 4th Armd Div AAR, Aug; TUSA Info Serv Msg. 2330, 5 Aug; Koyen, *Fourth Armored Division*, pp. 22–26.

through a seemingly undefended approach from the northwest, through the village of Pont-Scorff. The move turned out to be a mistake. As the advance guard entered the village, German artillery fire fell in alarming proportions. The artillery fire killed 20 men, wounded 85, destroyed 5 half-tracks, 6 jeeps, 2 trucks, and 2 armored cars, and damaged a score of other vehicles.

The arrival of CCA in the Lorient region enabled the combat commands to establish a thin line around Lorient from Hennebont to Pont-Scorff. From positions for the most part out of range of German artillery, the division probed the Lorient defenses, trying to develop a feasible avenue of approach, but by 9 August it seemed clear that the Germans in Lorient were too strong for an armored division alone to reduce. Antitank ditches and mine fields were covered by interlocking bands of fire from what the division estimated to be 500 field pieces including antitank, anti-aircraft, coastal defense, and naval guns supplied with large stores of ammunition. Flak was so heavy that artillery planes could not get off the ground for observation. The FFI reported that the Germans had a great supply of provisions in the fortress city, including herds of cattle, and could therefore hold out for a long time. To be assured of success, an attack against Lorient would need support from the sea so that the Quiberon peninsula and Belle-Isle might first be neutralized.[23]

Concerned lest the 4th Armored Division become embroiled in static warfare at Lorient, General Wood was gratified

to receive word from Middleton to hold the armor at arm's length from the fortress. "Do not become involved in a fight for Lorient unless enemy attacks," Middleton instructed. "Take a secure position and merely watch developments." [24]

Actually, the fortress of Lorient was not as impregnable as it appeared to the Americans. The senior German commander in Lorient, Fahrmbacher, was seriously concerned lest a strong attack by the U.S. armor carry his position. Had Wood attacked between 6 and 9 August, Fahrmbacher later stated, the fortress would probably have fallen. The defenses of Lorient had not yet been organized; entire sectors were still unoccupied; many of the troops were untrained. Even the chain of command had not yet been firmly established. Preparations had been made for a garrison of 12,000 men in Lorient, but instead, there were about 25,000 Germans, plus 10,000 French civilians who constituted a potential Trojan horse and a certain drain on supplies. Rather than the 500 guns estimated by the Americans, Fahrmbacher had 197 guns in the fortress and 80 antitank pieces. By 10 August, when Fahrmbacher felt that he had erected an adequate, if provisional, defense, the American pressure decreased to the point that he no longer expected an attack.[25]

---

[23] 4th Armd Div G-3 Per Rpt 24, 9 Aug; Msg, Wood to Middleton, 2116, 8 Aug.

[24] Penned Msg, probably in Middleton's hand, on Msg, Wood to Middleton, received at the VIII Corps CP, 1145, 8 Aug.

[25] For the rest of the war, Lorient was contained, in turn by the 4th Armored Division until 15 August, by the 6th Armored Division until it was relieved in mid-September by the 94th Division, and finally by the 66th, to whom Fahrmbacher surrendered his troops and the fortress on 10 May 1945. MS # B-731 (Fahrmbacher).

The resistance marked by the intense artillery fire on 7 August at Pont-Scorff was the first that could not be bypassed since the 4th Armored Division's commitment in Brittany. At Lorient, the division was at the end of a blind alley. Having no place to go was a cruel blow to General Wood, who had not abandoned the idea of driving eastward. On the evening of 6 August General Wood had radioed a message direct to General Patton: "Dear George: Have Vannes, will have Lorient this evening. Vannes intact, hope Lorient the same. Trust we can turn around and get headed in right direction soon." [26]

Still optimistic, though somewhat subdued after CCB was halted near Lorient the following morning, Wood reported his situation to Middleton with candor:

Hoped to argue Boche into surrender of Lorient. However he still resists. Am attacking him from two sides. He may fold up. He has considerable fixed fortifications and can resist strongly if he wishes. If so, this is a job for infantry and guns. We should be allowed to reassemble and get ready to hit again in a more profitable direction, namely to Paris. Believe infantry division should be sent here at once for this job. [27]

Patton had already made the decision. "Dear John," Middleton informed Wood in a letter he signed "Troy," "George was here this P.M. and made the following decision: When you take your objective, remain in that vicinity and await orders." If Wood could not take Lorient without help, Middleton continued, he was to hold in place until a decision could be made on the amount of assistance he was to get. The reason, Middleton explained, was the obscurity that surrounded the developments not only in Brittany but on the larger front. It was possible that the American force driving toward Brest might also need help, and Patton did not want troops moved both east and west at the same time until the situation became clearer. [28]

Terribly disappointed, Wood replied, "Am being left pretty far out on this limb." Still later he grumbled, "Can achieve impossible but not yet up to miracles. Boche does not intend to fold up." He radioed his belief that at least one infantry division supported by corps artillery, additional air power, and naval forces would be required to reduce Lorient. Finally, "My division requires overhaul for further operations at similar speeds," he radioed. "Request decision. Repeat request decision." [29]

The decision that General Wood wanted was an admission by corps or army that another unit would relieve the 4th Armored Division at Lorient and an indication as to when the relief might take place. The 8th Division was supposed to have followed the 4th Armored Division into Brittany. When would it arrive at Lorient and allow Wood to get under way to the east? Why didn't the 8th come forward immediately from Rennes? Believing that the decision to move his armored division "away from the pursuit of a disorganized enemy" and toward Lorient "was one of the great mistakes of the war," and feeling certain that "a rapid

---

[26] Msg, Wood to Patton, 6 Aug.
[27] Msg, Wood to Middleton, 1000, 7 Aug.

[28] Ltr, Middleton to Wood, 6 Aug.
[29] Msgs, Wood to Middleton, 1300, 7 Aug, 0233 and 2116, 8 Aug, and Msg received at VIII Corps CP, 1100, 8 Aug.

move toward Chartres . . . would have been of immense value," he could not understand why the powerful mobile forces under his command were allowed to stand before a fortress city.[30]

What Wood did not know was that the forces in Brittany had become stepchildren. As he had expected, the main action of the European campaign was developing east of Brittany, and Patton and Middleton lacked sufficient resources to develop the Brittany operation as they wished. Yet as soon as Middleton received Wood's request for a decision on the 4th Armored Division's future course of action, he replied, both by radio and by liaison plane, instructing Wood not to get involved in a battle at Lorient.[31] At the same time he forwarded Wood's request to Patton, hoping thereby to get clarification of the entire Brittany situation and the future role of the VIII Corps.[32]

At a conference late on 8 August, Patton informed Middleton that the VIII Corps still had the job of clearing the Brittany peninsula. Securing the ports of St. Malo and Brest had priority over the capture of Lorient. Thus, Wood would have to contain Lorient until St. Malo and Brest were taken. Only then could the far-flung forces of the VIII Corps in Brittany be assembled to help Wood "take Lorient out of the picture." The difficulty was that Middleton could not do everything at the same time. Given the forces at his disposal and his widely separated objectives, he could do no more than proceed from one task to another. Wood would have

to wait until the corps got around to his particular problem.[33]

Despite this gloomy outlook, a spark of hope remained for the 4th Armored Division. Patton had told Middleton to send some troops to Nantes to relieve an American task force containing the Germans in that port city. Though Patton expected Middleton to dispatch troops from the 8th Division at Rennes, Middleton preferred to keep the 8th where it was so he could use it to reinforce the attack against St. Malo if necessary. Middleton therefore called upon the 4th Armored Division. He instructed Wood to contain Lorient and remain immobile, but he also told him to send a combat command eastward from Lorient to Nantes. An American unit was guarding Nantes, but Middleton did not know which one it was or exactly where it was. Wood was to locate and relieve the unit at Nantes. Middleton suggested that Wood send some cavalry along to enable the combat command to scout the Loire River east of St. Nazaire and Nantes and make contact with U.S. troops at Angers. The general situation, he added, looked good.[34]

Good was hardly the word for it. Wood had wanted to go to Angers five days earlier. He sent Colonel Clarke's CCA on the eighty-mile move to Nantes on the morning of 10 August. On the following day CCA relieved a battalion of the 5th Division on the outskirts of the city. That night, heavy explosions in Nantes indicated that the Germans were destroying dumps and installations.

[30] Ltr, Wood to OCMH, 24 Mar 54.

[31] Penned Msg, cited n. 24, above.

[32] Notation on Msg, Wood to Middleton, received at VIII Corps CP, 1100, 8 Aug.

[33] Memo, Middleton for Wood, 8 Aug.

[34] Memos, Patton for Gaffey, and Middleton for Wood, 8 Aug.

French civilians reported the enemy withdrawing. Clarke therefore asked Wood's permission to enter Nantes with light forces.

Earlier, when Middleton had alerted Wood for the mission of driving to Nantes, he had ordered him categorically: "Do not become involved in fight in city. Merely prevent any enemy movement to north." Four days later, with a combat command at the gates of the city, the opportunity to take Nantes easily was too tempting to resist. Wood gave Clarke permission to attack. During the afternoon of 12 August, helped by men of the FFI, who led the troops safely through mine fields, CCA stormed the city and captured it.[35]

Securing Nantes was like getting one's foot in the door. Wood's persistent efforts to drive to the east were about to succeed. A day later, on 13 August, the 4th Armored Division passed from the control of the VIII Corps, and on 15 August Wood handed over the responsibility of containing Lorient to the 6th Armored Division. By that time only a handful of 4th Armored Division troops remained at Lorient, impatient for the relief that would permit them to join the bulk of the division Wood had already sent out of Brittany. General Wood had finally gotten a mission he wanted. The 4th Armored Division was driving eastward.

During the first two weeks of August, the 4th Armored Division had displayed a constant and consistent aggressiveness. It had performed like cavalry—slashing, side-slipping, and pushing forward. It had effectively exploited a fluid situation by using speed and surprise. Having made a reputation in the Cotentin, the division expanded it in Brittany. During the first twelve days of August, the 4th Armored Division took almost 5,000 prisoners and destroyed or captured almost 250 German vehicles. Against these figures, the division lost 98 killed, 362 wounded, 11 missing; 15 tanks and 20 vehicles.[36]

Despite the impressive achievement represented by the number of the enemy destroyed and the amount of the territory liberated, the 4th Armored Division had not taken the port city assigned. Had Middleton and Wood been intent on securing Quiberon, the division might have arrived at Lorient a day or two earlier and perhaps have been in time to capture the fortress simply by smashing a way into the streets of the city; indeed, a serious effort launched immediately after the arrival of the division might still have taken the fortress.

In mid-August, as the Germans in western Europe seemed to be in the process of complete disintegration, the failure to take Lorient and Quiberon seemed less important than it would have seemed in July. By late September, Lorient and Quiberon were quite forgotten. "Looking at it with hindsight," General Middleton said many years afterward, "Wood was right, of course. But the high command at the time was absolutely right in . . . [wanting] the ports."[37] Wood's trouble was wanting to do the right thing at the wrong time.

---

[35] Evans to Wood, 8 Aug; Memo, Evans for BCT, 5th Div, 8 Aug; The Armored School, Armor in the Exploitation, p. 30; 4th Armd Div AAR, Aug.

[36] 4th Armd Div AAR, Aug; Koyen, *Fourth Armored Division*, p. 26.

[37] Min of Review Panel, OCMH, 9 May 56.

The 4th Armored Division had developed to a high degree of proficiency a reckless ardor for pursuit of a defeated enemy. The *esprit de corps* of the troops matched the supreme confidence of the division commander. It was stimulating to operate deep in enemy territory and report that over a thousand enemy soldiers were ready to surrender but that the division lacked "the time or the means to collect them." [38]   It was heady to have such assurance that men of the division could say with profound feeling of the Germans, "They've got us surrounded again, the poor bastards."[39]

On the crest of a mounting wave of optimism the 4th Armored Division turned eastward and drove out of Brittany in search of further opportunities, its commander sure at last that he was heading in the right direction.

---

[38] TUSA Memo, Situation as of 0600, 6 Aug.

[39] Koyen, *Fourth Armored Division*, p. 13.

CHAPTER XX

"Take Brest"

While the 4th Armored Division was performing its feats in Brittany, the 6th Armored Division also was executing a spectacular movement. On the afternoon of 31 July the VIII Corps commander, General Middleton, ordered General Grow's division to relieve the 4th Armored Division's CCA in the Sélune River bridgehead at Pontaubault. (*See Map VIII.*)

Convinced that exploitation beyond Pontaubault was in order, but not knowing whether Middleton intended to move at once into Brittany or to consolidate his forces first at the base of the Cotentin, Grow asked Middleton whether the 6th Armored Division was to go beyond Pontaubault immediately. The answer was no. Satisfied that a day or two would pass (while other units of the corps arrived at Avranches) before the exploitation commenced, Grow dispatched Combat Command R (CCR), commanded by Col. Harry F. Hanson, to outpost the Pontaubault bridgehead.[1]

In armored division practice, CCR was often considered more suitable for defensive than for offensive missions, primarily because it had less command tanks, radio equipment, and personnel than the other combat commands. By sending CCR ahead, General Grow indicated his intention to pass Combat Commands A and B through CCR at Pontaubault whenever he renewed the offensive. However, CCR was just moving forward when Grow received word—shortly before dawn, 1 August—to proceed at once through Pontaubault and move westward into Brittany through

Thomas A. Bruce (comdr of 128th FA Bn), 7 Jan 53. Ltrs, Gen Grow to Author, 26 and 27 Apr 54; Lt Col William J. Given (Sig Officer) to Gen Grow, 12 Jan 53; Mr. Ernest W. Mitchell (G–2) to Gen Grow, 5 Mar 53. Memo, Gen Grow to Author, n.d. Comments by Lt Col Eugene J. White, n.d. All in OCMH Files. See also, [Maj. Gen. Robert W. Grow], *Brest to Bastogne, the Story of the 6th Armored Division* (pamphlet, Stars and Stripes, Information and Education Division, Special and Information Services, ETOUSA, Paris, c. 1945); [Lt. Robert J. Burns, Jr., and Lt. John S. Dahl], *The 68th Tank Battalion in Combat* (Minden, Nebraska: Warp Publishing Co., 1945); [Lt. Elmer J. Gruber], *A History of the 212th Armored Field Artillery Battalion in the E.T.O.* (n.p., n.d.); [Maj. Samuel R. Ross, Editor-in-Chief], *Battle Book: a Combat History of Headquarters and Headquarters Battery, Division Artillery, 6th Armored Division* (Apolda, Germany: Rob. Birkner, 1945); *Overseas Pictorial History of Headquarters Battery, 231st Armored Field Artillery Battalion* (Germany, 1945).

[1] The sources for this chapter are: The invaluable msgs in the VIII Corps G–3 Jnl and File (all msgs cited are from this source unless otherwise noted). [Burk], *Combat Record of the Sixth Armored Division,* pp. 6ff. Robert W. Grow, "An Epic of Brittany," *Military Review,* XXVI, No. 11 (February, 1947), pp. 3–9. Author's Intervs with former 6th Armd Div personnel: Gen Grow 18, 19, 31 Dec 52, 3 Jan 53; Mr. Michael J. Galvin (G–3), 6 Jan 53; Col Glen C. McBride (CofS), 19 Feb 53; Col Donald G. Williams (Engr), 16 Jan 53; Lt Col

Pontorson and Dol-de-Bretagne to Dinan.[2]

Though General Grow's first impulse was to commit either CCA or CCB through CCR at once, the wreckage and rubble in Avranches and the existence of only one road to Pontaubault discouraged such action. As division military police took control of the routes through Avranches, as bulldozers worked to clear lanes for traffic, and as CCR moved to Pontaubault, Grow ordered Colonel Hanson to continue ten miles beyond Pontaubault to Pontorson. There, with the entire division through the Avranches bottleneck, Grow would pass the other combat commands through CCR for the westward advance into Brittany. Middleton visited Grow early on 1 August and approved the plans.

Several hours after Middleton's visit, as Grow was supervising the flow of traffic at a critical crossroads, General Patton arrived. Patton told Grow that he had wagered General Montgomery five pounds that U.S. troops would be in Brest "by Saturday night." Putting his hand on Grow's shoulder, Patton said, "Take Brest." To Grow's question on intermediate objectives, Patton indicated his interest in the Brest–Rennes railroad and instructed him to bypass resistance. The latter point was particularly satisfying. "That's all I want to know," Grow said. The corps objective, Dinan, was no longer valid.

To some, it might have seemed like madness to think of reaching Brest— more than two hundred miles west of

Avranches—in five days; but General Grow was delighted. He had "received a cavalry mission from a cavalryman." While serving years before as Patton's G–3, Grow had planned comparable operations for peacetime maneuvers. "It was what we had spent years studying and training for," he later recalled.

Giving armored forces seemingly impossible goals to keep commanders looking beyond the ends of their noses was not unusual for Patton. His dramatic words "Take Brest," and his ignoring of intermediate geographical objectives, clearly defined his intent to exploit through the entire length of the Brittany peninsula. The faster the exploiting force went, the greater would be its effect. If the exploitation culminated in capture of Brest, the operation would be perfect. The ultimate objective became the immediate goal. Even though it was perhaps hardly feasible to expect a solitary division to drive two hundred miles into enemy territory and single-handedly capture a fortress of unknown strength, it was exactly what General Grow set out to do.

The fragmentary corps order that Grow had received before dawn of 1 August contained a hastily sketched overlay showing a temporary boundary line between the 4th and 6th Armored Divisions and a short arrow on each side pointing hazily into the Brittany peninsula. Later that day, as Middleton changed the 6th Armored Division objective from Dinan to Brest, he indicated two general routes as a guide for the division's movement. He also gave the division the 174th Field Artillery Battalion (155-mm. self-propelled guns), which complemented the normal attach-

[2] VIII Corps Opns Instrs (confirming fragmentary verbal orders), 31 Jul; 6th Armd Div G–3 Jnl, entry 0330, 1 Aug.

PONTAUBAULT BRIDGE *over the Selune River, one of the few bridges left intact by retreating Germans.*

ments, the 603d Tank Destroyer Battalion, and the 777th Antiaircraft Artillery (Automatic Weapons) Battalion.[3]

Before General Grow could concentrate on his final objective, he had to move his division through Avranches and into Brittany and get his troops organized into two parallel columns poised for offensive action.[4]

Getting through the Avranches bottleneck was no mean achievement. On both 1 and 2 August German planes strafed the columns and tried to knock

out critical bridges, while all the combat commands and the division trains had to use the lone available highway toward Brittany. During one forty-hour period, the 777th Antiaircraft Battalion knocked out eighteen of forty enemy planes that appeared over Avranches and Pontaubault.

Beyond the bottleneck, the first terrain obstacle where the enemy might logically be expected to defend was the Couesnon River, the border of Brittany. Suspecting that the enemy would attempt to deny the crossing at Pontorson, General Grow split his division into two columns immediately south of Pontaubault, sending Hanson's CCR to Pontorson and Taylor's CCA southwestward to the Couesnon crossing at Antrain, seven miles south of Pontorson. Read's CCB followed CCR. Once across the Couesnon at Pontorson and Antrain, CCB might pass through CCR on the morning of 2 August, whereupon the 6th Armored Division would have

[3] VIII Corps Opns Instrs (fragmentary verbal orders), 31 Jul, Msg, 1 Aug, and FO 9, 1600, 1 Aug.

[4] Maj. Homer H. Hammond, The Operations of the 6th Armored Division in the Brittany Peninsula, Thesis, Officers' Advanced Course (The Infantry School, Ft. Benning, Ga., 1946–47) (hereafter cited as Hammond, 6th Armored Division); see also [Committee 9], Super Sixth in Exploitation (6th Armored Division, Normandy to Brest), Operation COBRA, Research Report, Officers' Advanced Course (The Armored School, Ft. Knox, Ky., May 1949) (hereafter cited as [Committee 9], Super Sixth), an excellent source that includes good material on logistics, intelligence, and administration.

two combat command columns ready for the westward drive along the backbone of the Brittany peninsula to Brest.

Because of the lack of contact with the enemy and the fluidity of the general situation, the 6th Armored Division G–2 hazarded no guess on enemy capabilities or intentions. He nevertheless provided an accurate enemy order of battle in Brittany: the *2d Parachute Division,* likely to be in the St. Malo area; regimental combat teams of the *265th, 266th,* and *275th Infantry Divisions,* dispersed in the peninsula; and the *343d Infantry Division,* probably in Brest. The G–2 refrained from estimating the strength of the units except to assert that they were undoubtedly below table of organization authorizations.[5]

Leading the division on 1 August, CCR drove westward toward Pontorson. Six miles beyond Pontaubault, near Brée, the advance guard—a company each of tanks and infantry and a battery of artillery, moving in that order—was almost through a defile when the enemy opened fire on the rear of the column with artillery, mortars, bazookas, and small arms from well-camouflaged positions overlooking the road. Three self-propelled artillery pieces were destroyed at once. As armored infantrymen and tanks deployed to engage the enemy, Hanson radioed Grow that he was going to attack rearward with the advance guard and squeeze the enemy against the approaching main body of CCR. Unwilling to be diverted from securing the river crossing at Pontorson, Grow radioed Hanson to keep moving, to leave the opposition entirely to the main body. The principal force of CCR

subsequently eliminated the position in a three-hour engagement, sustained seventy casualties, destroyed several pieces of German horse-drawn field artillery, knocked out an 88-mm. gun, and captured nearly a hundred prisoners. Sgt. John L. Morton of Battery A, 231st Field Artillery Battalion, alone killed thirty Germans with a carbine and submachine gun.[6]

Meanwhile, the advance guard had taken Pontorson, captured a bridge across the Couesnon intact, and established a bridgehead inside Brittany. "Mission accomplished," Hanson radioed. "Have had considerable casualties, wounded and dead. Am short of ammunition, gas, and water. Will not be able to go on without help. Am holding bridgehead for the night." Though this report revealed something less than unbridled optimism, it was enough to justify preparing CCB to pass through to continue the attack. In the meantime, Taylor's CCA had been securing the Antrain crossing uncontested.[7]

Sunrise, 2 August, found the division in the clear, "with no boundaries to worry about, no definite enemy information, in fact nothing but a map of Brittany and the knowledge that resistance was where you found it." General Grow felt he "owned *all* roads in Brittany," and he could go where he pleased as long as he drove toward Brest.

Taylor's CCA moved westward from Antrain through Combourg and Béc-

---

[5] 6th Armd Div G–2 Per Rpt 4, 31 Jul, and Jnl, entry 1125, 1 Aug.

[6] Morton was awarded the DSC.

[7] Hanson to Grow, 1832, 1 Aug, 6th Armd Div G–3 Jnl; T. Sgt. Charles D. Byrd, *The 15th Tank Battalion, a Record of Action* (Amorbach, Germany: Miltenberg, Gottlob Volkhardtsche Druckerei, 1945), (hereafter cited as Byrd, *15th Tank Battalion*) pp. 24–28.

herel almost to Quédilliac, a distance of nearly thirty-five miles. Nowhere did the command meet organized resistance. Read's CCB passed through CCR at Pontorson and avoided Dol-de-Bretagne, but ran into opposition on the outskirts of Dinan. Because a captured overlay showed the Dinan defenses to be strong, Grow instructed Read to bypass Dinan on the south and continue westward.[8] By the time Grow's message arrived, some of CCB was already fighting at Dinan. When several unexpected fighter-bombers appeared overhead, Read requested the pilots to bomb and strafe Dinan to mask a withdrawal. While the planes attacked and armored artillery fired on the town, CCB backtracked, moved southwestward, and halted for the night near Bécherel, about thirty miles west of Pontorson. In keeping with the maxim of reinforcing success, Grow had earlier switched CCR to follow CCA, which had met no resistance.

Late on the night of 2 August, General Grow conferred with his major commanders and staff to consider the problems that faced them. Though the division was well into Brittany and deployed for action, certain deficiencies already threatened continued progress. There were no well-established lines of communication or supply, and German planes over Avranches threatened to delay the division trains. The 79th Division, scheduled to follow the armor, had been diverted to the east, and no infantry was available at the moment to take its place. Though the 83d Division might eventually move into Brittany, it would require a minimum of

several days to catch up with the armored division. Finally, no one knew what to expect from the enemy, who had offered such varying opposition as the scattered resistance west of Antrain, the strong defense of Dinan, and the roadside ambush near Brée.[9] In view of these facts, the question was to determine how the 6th Armored Division might best perform its mission.

The division chief of staff cautioned against driving wildly through Brittany, recommended establishing firm bases of supply, and advised that the division should be kept consolidated and advancing in a relatively compact mass for security. General Grow dismissed these suggestions with the statement that he didn't have time to go slow—he had to get to Brest.

This announcement provoked several gasps of astonishment. Ignorant of Patton's verbal order to Grow and not yet in receipt of the corps order changing the division objective, Grow's subordinates had not thought much beyond Evran and Dinan on the Rance River, twenty-five miles west of the Couesnon. With Brest suddenly revealed as the objective, the entire operation took on new significance. The prospect of a single division driving more than two hundred miles through enemy territory was at once exciting and sobering.[10]

So pronounced was the fatigue of the

---

[8] 6th Armd Div G–3 Jnl, entry 0930, 2 Aug.

[9] 6th Armd Div G–3 Jnl, entry 2300, 2 Aug, and G–2 Per Rpts 5 and 6, 1 and 2 Aug; Msgs, Middleton to Grow, 1520, 1620, and 1645, 2 Aug; VIII Corps Sitrep 95, 2 Aug, and FO 10, 2 Aug; 79th Div G–3 Per Rpt 35, 2 Aug; Msg, Middleton to Wyche, 2 Aug.

[10] 6th Armd Div FO 5, 1 Aug. The 128th Field Artillery Battalion, organic to the 6th Armored Division, officially noted in the battalion journal at 0930, 3 August: "objective announced to be Brest."

staff officers and commanders (some fell asleep during the conference) that Grow postponed the advance until noon of 3 August. The delay not only would permit several additional hours of rest but also would enable the cavalry reconnaissance squadron to take its proper place at the front and on the flanks of the columns, a procedure impossible to this point because of the speed of the commitment into Brittany and the traffic congestion near Avranches.

The division shoved off at noon, 3 August, with the cavalry troops where they belonged. Taylor's CCA drove fifteen miles to the west, missed a turn at a crossroads, and ran into organized resistance near Mauron. Deciding that it would be more difficult to reverse direction in order to regain the correct route, Taylor attacked to eliminate an estimated enemy force of 250 men so that he could reach his original route of advance by side roads. After a three-hour fire fight, the Mauron defenses were reduced.

Meanwhile, Read's CCB drove west from Bécherel, detoured several miles to the north to avoid the tail of CCA at Mauron, and gave impetus to the attempts of a small group of Germans near Broons to flee. After having moved virtually unopposed for more than thirty miles that day, CCB received an inexplicable order to halt, an order doubly incomprehensible since Grow had that day switched CCR onto CCB's trail.

The explanation lay in word from General Middleton, who had radioed General Grow, "Do not bypass Dinan and St. Malo. Message follows by courier." [11] The messenger from corps

reached Grow, who was observing Taylor's attack at Mauron, and handed him a penciled note on a sheet of scratch paper. "Protect your front," Middleton instructed, "and concentrate so that we can move in on St. Malo tomorrow." Middleton had decided that he needed to take St. Malo at once. General Earnest's Task Force A and a portion of General Macon's 83d Division were in the St. Malo area; General Grow was to take command of these forces, add the weight of his 6th Armored Division, and launch a co-ordinated attack on the port city.[12]

General Grow's reactions were conflicting. How was he going to get to Brest by Saturday if he was diverted to Dinan and St. Malo? He first protested the corps order by radio and by officer courier and requested reconsideration of the changed mission. He then obeyed. "Mission changed," he radioed his chief of staff. CCA was to assemble near Mauron. CCB was to turn north to outflank Dinan, and CCR was to be ready to move north against Dinan.[13] Unable to reach CCB by radio, Grow pursued the combat command in his armored car. Although he toyed with the idea of letting CCB continue westward alone, he decided that this would violate the spirit of the corps order.

After stopping CCB several miles short of Loudéac, General Grow changed his scheme of maneuver. On the chance that Middleton might accede to his re-

[11] Msg, Evans to Grow, 1345, 3 Aug; 6th Armd Div G–3 Jnl, entry 1615, 3 Aug.

[12] Memo, Middleton for Grow, recorded in the 6th Armd Div G–3 Journal as having arrived "No time 3 Aug." The actual message is missing from the file. It has been reconstructed through interviews with General Grow and Colonel McBride.

[13] Msg, Grow to Middleton, 3 Aug, VIII Corps G–3 Jnl File (4 Aug); Msg, Grow to McBride, 1700, 3 Aug, 6th Armd Div G–3 Jnl.

quest and rescind the diversion to Dinan, Grow determined to keep CCB where it was, ahead of the division and on the road to Brest. Since the CCA headquarters was closer to Dinan and since an excellent highway led northward for thirty miles from Mauron to Dinan, Grow formed a special task force from CCR troops, placed Taylor's CCA headquarters in command of it, and sent it north toward the new objective.[14]

The officer courier who had gone to the corps headquarters to request reconsideration of the changed mission returned late that night and reported, "The answer was no." The disappointment at the division headquarters was so bitter that the G–3 section published the "Results of Operations" as "None."[15]

The division headquarters on the morning of 4 August was developing an attack plan for action against Dinan when, around 1100, General Patton arrived unannounced at a wheat field near Merdrignac where the headquarters was located.[16] General Grow, who had just come out of his tent, saw the army commander's jeep turn into the field and was pleasantly surprised. The division chief of staff, who was walking across the field toward General Grow, was nearby when Patton got out of his jeep. The division G–3 emerged from his operations tent in time to hear Patton's first words.

The army commander appeared to be controlling an outburst of anger with difficulty.

"What in hell are you doing setting here?" he demanded of General Grow. "I thought I told you to go to Brest."

Grow explained that his advance had been halted.

"On what authority?" Patton rasped.

"Corps order, sir," Grow said.

The division chief of staff had already put his hand into the pocket of his shirt. Grow had given him the note he had received from Middleton and had asked him to get it into the division message file. The chief of staff still had it in his pocket. He handed it to Patton.

The three officers watched Patton read Middleton's note. When he finished, he folded the paper and put it into his pants pocket. "And he was a *good* doughboy, too," Patton said quietly as though talking to himself. Then he looked at Grow. "I'll see Middleton," he said. "You go ahead where I told you to go."

One hundred miles east of the 6th Armored Division, the VIII Corps headquarters, toiling under the handicap of its communications problem with the divisions, was only vaguely aware of developments at the front.

On 2 August, when Grow had ordered his northern column (CCB) to bypass Dinan, he had notified the corps of his action. The corps noted that the armored division "pursuant to verbal orders Army Commander bypassed Dinan and is proceeding S and W." Later, news came that contingents of the division were in Dinan. Apparently on the basis of this information, the Third Army believed that the division had "passed through Dinan." When Gen-

[14] Msg, Grow to Middleton, 1910, 3 Aug.

[15] 6th Armd Div G–3 Per Rpt 7 [4 Aug]; see also Msg, Grow to Middleton, 0330, 4 Aug [Sitrep 10].

[16] On the Dinan attack details, see Ltr, no heading, 0730, 4 Aug; Grow to CO, Combat Team, 83d Div, 0525, 4 Aug, and entry 1007, 4 Aug. All in 6th Armd Div G–3 Jnl and File.

eral Earnest's Task Force A encountered
enemy tanks and infantry near Dinan
on the following morning (3 August),
it was reasonable for Middleton—who
believed that the 6th Armored Division
had been through there on the previous
evening and consequently could not be
far away—to order Grow to "assist Task
Force A at that point." As indications
of enemy build-up in the Dinan–St.
Malo region increased, Middleton began
to experience a growing uneasiness.
Though the 83d Division had begun
to advance toward Pontorson, it could
not possibly get there for another day.
Learning that the 6th Armored Division
had in reality bypassed Dinan, Middleton diverted it from its Brest run. His
explanation: "We are getting too
strung out. We must take Dinan and
St. Malo before we can proceed." [17]
What appeared unreasonable to Grow
was reasonable from Middleton's point
of view.

Later on 3 August, when the pilot of
a light artillery plane reported the locations of the 6th Armored Division columns, General Middleton realized that
the armor had advanced much farther
beyond Dinan than he had thought.
When he learned of the imminent arrival of infantry troops in the Dinan–St.
Malo sector, he changed his message to
Grow from an order to a request.
"Task Force 'A' and 83d Division will
attack St. Malo tomorrow," he radioed
Grow. "Can you participate with one
combat command . . .?" Later that

evening Middleton withdrew even this
request. "I wanted you to assist in
capture of St. Malo," he informed General Grow. "However it is apparent
that your advance precludes this . . . .
Continue your original mission." [18]

Shortly after midnight, when the
Third Army G–3 telephoned to ask
whether the 6th Armored Division had
really been diverted toward St. Malo,
the VIII Corps G–3 assured the caller
that the division was proceeding toward
Brest. The assurance was wishful.
The corps had had only the briefest of
contacts was with the division when the
division courier had arrived to transmit
General Grow's request for reconsideration of his mission. But the courier
had departed hastily without learning
that the original mission was again in
force. Since then no word had come
from the division, no acknowledgment
of the restoration of the old mission, no
information on General Grow's intentions or activities. Several hours after
daylight, 4 August, a message finally
came. "Urgently recommend no change
in division mission [toward Brest],"
General Grow had radioed the previous
evening. "Both of my commands far
beyond St. Malo. . . . would take another
day to attack Dinan from west." [19]

The corps tried again. "Proceed on
original mission toward Brest," Middleton radioed. Soon afterwards the corps
received another message from the division, but it was no acknowledgment.
"[Original] Mission changed," read the

---

[17] VIII Corps Sitrep 97, 2 Aug; Msg, Galvin to
Evans, 1630, 2 Aug; TUSA Sitrep 5, 2 Aug, and
Msg, 1845, 2 Aug; Msg, Middleton to Grow, 1110, 3
Aug; Memo, Middleton for Grow, 3 Aug, 6th Armd
Div G–3 Jnl File.

[18] VIII Corps Arty Msg, 1800, 3 Aug; Msgs, Middleton (signed Evans) to Grow, 1800, and Middleton to Grow, 2150, 3 Aug.
[19] Msg, Maddox to Evans, 0145, 4 Aug; Msg, Grow
to Middleton, 3 Aug, received at VIII Corps CP,
0700, 4 Aug.

message that General Grow had wired twelve hours earlier, "preparations being made for new mission [toward Dinan and St. Malo]." By this time, Patton's Household Cavalry was frantically trying to relay the corps order authorizing the division to continue toward Brest. Not until early that afternoon did the corps at last hear that Grow was in receipt of authority to continue on his original mission. Middleton then notified the troops in the Dinan–St. Malo sector that the armored division would not participate in the action there.[20]

Resolving the temporary confusion did not solve the problem of communications. On the contrary, as the 6th Armored Division plunged farther westward into Brittany, the problem became more acute.[21] On the night of 4 August Middleton received a clear indication of Grow's progress. The division commander requested all pertinent data on the Brest defenses, he needed a ground pilot who could guide the division into the city, and he wanted the air force to refrain from destroying the bridges between him and his objective. Later, Grow radioed that he needed additional air support and sixty feet of Bailey bridging, that members of the FFI had assured him they would clear the approaches to Brest for the division, and, finally, "We expect to be in Brest tonight." Whether Grow meant the night of 4 or of 5 August was not clear. Still later, Grow reported that he was actually moving against his objective.[22] These fragmentary pieces of information hardly gave corps headquarters a clear picture of the situation. Periodic progress reports took thirty-six hours to get from the division to the corps command post and were out of date when they arrived.

Suspense at corps was not resolved on the morning of 6 August when the next message from Grow arrived. The division commander reported simply that enemy groups in the rear were making supply operations extremely difficult. "If additional troops are not furnished to keep supply routes open," he stated, "division must live off the country which cannot furnish gasoline or ammunition. Air support essential but ground security is equally essential at once."[23]

Although Middleton restrained his intense concern regarding the whereabouts of the armor, General Patton could not. Patton asked the XIX Tactical Air Command to get some fighter-bombers over Brest and find out what was happening. Specifically, he wanted to know where the 6th Armored Division was and whether it could take Brest without assistance. Also, the pilots were to tell Grow that if there was any possibility at all of taking the port city without infantry reinforcement, he was to do so at once. At the same time, Patton instructed his Household Cavalry to get busy and tell him whether Brest had or had not been taken.[24]

[20] Msg, Middleton to Grow, 0915, 4 Aug; Msg, Grow to Middleton, 1910, 3 Aug; Msg, 6th Cav Gp to Cav Detachment with 6th Armd Div, 1040, 4 Aug; Msg, Middleton to Macon, 1348, 4 Aug.

[21] See, for example, Msg, Middleton to Grow, 1715, 4 Aug.

[22] Msg, Grow to Middleton, received by VIII Corps, 2200, 4 Aug; Msg, Grow to Middleton, 2110, 4 Aug, 6th Armd Div G–3 Jnl File, received by VIII Corps, 1205, 5 Aug; Msg, Grow to Middleton, 5 Aug.

[23] Msg, Grow to Middleton, 0535, 6 Aug.

[24] Msg, XIX TAC to 6th Armd Div, intercepted by VIII Corps, 6 Aug; TUSA Info Serv Msg, Lt Colin Satterfield to VIII Corps, 1330, 6 Aug.

It was not long before the Household Cavalry announced, "Brest is ours." Not long afterwards came the correction, "Brest was not ours," and it would "probably not fall until tomorrow."[25] His patience gone, Middleton rapped out a message to Grow. "This headquarters has no information as to your present positions," he wrote. "Radio this headquarters at once." [26]

But communications difficulties precluded the regular flow of information. Corps could only guess what was happening. Estimates of enemy intentions were vaguely optimistic but of little real value. The corps G–2 reasoned that, considering the highly disorganized state of the enemy, the disruption of German supply operations, the lack of reserves, and the growing activity of the FFI, the Germans in Brittany could do no more than offer a "spotty and sporadic [delaying action] culminating in a short token defense of the city of Brest." [27] Whether this was true or false, whether the 6th Armored Division was inside Brest or still outside, whether it was heavily engaged, in danger of being destroyed and needful of help, or having an easy time taking and securing the port were vital questions that could not be answered until word came from General Grow.

On the other hand, it seemed to corps that the strong fortifications known to exist around Brest would make the effort of a single armored division seem like the impact of an insect against the shell of a turtle. After a conference with Patton, Middleton radioed Grow to develop the situation wherever he was, whether "in front of or in Brest." If Grow could not capture and secure Brest without help, Middleton wrote,

. . . then we will reinforce you with the necessary force. As for me, I do not want you to become too involved so that you cannot take care of yourself. However, I feel that the situation at Brest should be clarified before [additional] troops are sent. Furthermore, at this time no one can say what should be sent. . . . While supply and evacuation is an Army function, yet if I can assist you in these matters do not hesitate to call.[28]

After that there was little for Middleton to do except to wait and hope for the best.

In the wheat field near Merdrignac, near noon on 4 August, Patton's unexpected arrival at the 6th Armored Division command post had virtually coincided with the receipt of corps permission for the division to continue toward Brest.[29] It did not take long for General Grow to flash the news to all subordinate commands: "Division proceeds at once on original mission to Brest. Dinan will not (repeat not) be attacked."[30] Assured that all units had received the re-orientation westward, Grow wired Middleton that he would move early that afternoon.[31] Actually, however, it took the division most of the afternoon to get ready. The effect

---

[25] TUSA Info Serv with 6th Armd Div Msg, 1120, 6 Aug; TUSA Info Serv Msg, Satterfield to VIII Corps, 1330, 6 Aug.

[26] Msg, Middleton to Grow, 1720, 6 Aug.

[27] VIII Corps G–2 Per Rpt 49, 3 Aug; see also G–2 Per Rpt 51, 5 Aug.

[28] Memo (by radio), Middleton for Grow, 6 Aug.

[29] Msgs, Evans to Grow, 0915 and 1100, 4 Aug, 6th Armd Div G–3 Jnl (Delayed Msgs due to radio silence received 4 Aug); TUSA Info Serv Detachment to 6th Armd Div, 1145, 4 Aug.

[30] Radio signed Galvin, 1125, 4 Aug.

[31] Msg, Grow to Middleton, 1230, 4 Aug.

of the abortive diversion toward Dinan was to delay the thrust on Brest almost a day.

While the division made preparations, Patton told Grow that he had come for three reasons: he had wanted to see how the unit was functioning, he had some information to impart, and he wanted to discuss supply, particularly gasoline. He admitted that he was pleasantly surprised to find the division so far into Brittany.[32] He revealed that the division would have no infantry support until later since the 83d Division would have to knock out St. Malo before proceeding to Brest. Finally, he said he was planning to send gas forward for the division on the following day and asked where Grow wanted it delivered. Looking at the map, Grow selected the town of Pontivy, twenty-five miles west of the leading division troops. The army commander was momentarily startled. Designating a supply point ahead of the combat troops rather than behind them indicated that Grow intended to advance so fast and so far that Pontivy by the following day would be a rear area suitable for a supply dump. Patton grinned. "You'll get your gas there," he promised.

Because destroyed bridges and mined fords near Loudéac and Pontivy temporarily delayed the parallel armored columns early on the evening of 4 August, General Grow took advantage of a full moon and clear weather to order a night march. There was no opposition. Members of the FFI became bolder and not only acted as guides and information agents but also harassed and hurried the departure of small German garrisons from the interior towns.

Learning from the FFI that about two thousand German paratroopers had destroyed the bridges at Carhaix and were preparing to defend there, General Grow ordered the columns to bypass that town on north and south. Avoiding entanglement there on the morning of 5 August, both columns drove toward Huelgoat, less than forty air miles from Brest. As it began to seem likely that the division would be in the port city by nightfall and win General Patton's wager with Montgomery, about five hundred Germans with artillery and tanks stopped the advance near Huelgoat. Mined defiles, heavily wooded areas, and the presence of Germans in good defensive positions forced the division into an engagement that lasted several hours.[33] The units finally cleared the enemy and prepared for what was hoped would be the final dash to Brest.

Pursuing interior routes and piloting his columns between Morlaix and Landivisiau, which he had been apprised were occupied by the Germans, General Grow pushed his troops forward on the morning of 6 August. Read's CCB moved rapidly north, then west, and struck a strong roadblock six miles south of Morlaix, obviously an outpost position. After sustaining several casualties, CCB withdrew and bypassed the resistance. That evening, when reconnaissance

---

[32] An aide who accompanied Patton later informed Grow that Patton had had to discard several maps during his trip to the division command post. Each time he ran off one map sheet onto another was an occasion for jubilant profanity.

[33] See Byrd, *15th Tank Battalion*, pp. 29–31. 2d Lt. James I. Durden of the 15th Tank Battalion, who was killed when he went forward on foot to clear a mine field under enemy fire and lead drivers along safe paths, was posthumously awarded the DSC.

troops encountered opposition at Lesneven—fifteen miles from Brest—a French
volunteer delivered a surrender ultimatum to the German garrison at Lesneven.
No reply came, and the combat command attacked, drove the enemy out,
and took possession of the town.

Taylor's CCA, in contrast, advanced
slowly over devious country lanes not
marked on maps available to the troops.
By nightfall the command was between
Morlaix and Landivisiau. Hanson's
CCR, which had switched routes near
Huelgoat to follow CCA, changed again
to reinforce the faster moving CCB.

Although the 6th Armored Division
was in the vicinity of Brest by the evening of 6 August, it was hardly in position to attack or even to demonstrate
against the objective. How strong the
city defenses were and what the Germans intended to do were yet to be
discovered.

Earlier that day an American fighter-
bomber had appeared over the division
column and the pilot had radioed Patton's request for information: "What
is situation in Brest? Where are your
forces? . . . Does 6th Armored Division
need Infantry assistance?" Grow answered that he thought Brest would be
defended and that he needed an infantry
division to support his attack on the
city. This was what had prompted the
instruction that Grow was to develop his
situation "in front of or in Brest" until
further clarification of the situation permitted sending additional troops to
Brest.[34] Until then, the 6th Armored
Division was to go it alone.

General Grow felt that he had a good
chance of taking Brest. German morale
was extremely low. The division advance had so disrupted German communications that local commanders
probably had little if any knowledge of
the situation. Because German strength
in Brittany had been drained away into
Normandy, what remained was of miscellaneous nature and low caliber.
Although the 6th Armored Division had
no accurate information on how many
Germans defended Brest, a number in
excess of 3,000 hardly seemed likely.
They were probably capable of fighting
delaying action on the radius of a fifty-
mile circle around Brest and drawing
back gradually into the fortress. Re-
membering that Granville, the first important division objective in the Cotentin, had surrendered to a tank platoon,
General Grow decided that a show of
force might satisfy the German requirements of honor and bring about the
surrender of Brest. He ordered Read's
CCB, which was closest to the city, to
move against Brest the next morning,
7 August.[35]

Attacking southwest from Lesneven,
CCB bypassed Plabennec on the north.
After destroying a large antiaircraft
warning system and observation post
near Milizac, the combat command came
under severe fire from artillery pieces in
Brest. Seven miles north of the city,
CCB had struck the hard shell of the
fortress.

Meanwhile, on 7 August, the remainder of the division arrived in the Brest
area. CCR in late afternoon reached
the vicinity of Gouesnou, about four

---

[34] Msg, Weyland to Grow, 1210, 6 Aug; Msg,
Grow to Weyland, 1250, 6 Aug; Memo (by radio),
Middleton for Grow, 6 Aug; Msg, Patton to Grow
(via plane), 1820, 6 Aug.

[35] 6th Armd Div G–2 Per Rpt 9, 6 Aug.

miles north-northeast of the center of Brest. CCA moved to the vicinity of Guipavas during the evening and night, but not as far toward Brest as Grow would have liked. Deployed in three columns and from four to seven miles from the center of the city, the 6th Armored Division was in contact with the Brest defenses.

It was apparent by this time that the Germans intended to defend and that they had adequate means to do so. Heavy artillery fire harassed the division throughout 7 August, serving notice that the element of surprise had been removed.[36] To take the fortress, the division would have to stage a full-scale attack. Needing a day to reorganize for a co-ordinated effort, Grow decided to give the German garrison one more chance to surrender. If the Germans were planning only a token defense, perhaps a surrender ultimatum might produce the desired result. While the division prepared an attack for 9 August, the G–2 and a German-speaking master sergeant drove toward the enemy line on the morning of 8 August in a jeep draped in white sheets and flying a flag of truce.

From the corps perspective, the situation appeared to be quite different: the evidence pointed to a strong defense of Brest. A hard-fought battle had developed at St. Malo. Captured overprints of the Lorient fortifications and the experience of the 4th Armored Division showed strong defenses there. Why should the Germans give only token opposition at Brest? General Middleton was certain that the reduc-

tion of each port city would be a difficult task requiring heavy artillery and a force of perhaps one armored and two infantry divisions. With only four divisions under his control, Middleton visualized protracted operations ahead, particularly since he felt that the increasing importance of developments east of Brittany might rob him of some of his resources. Proceeding with his program of reducing the German port cities one by one, with St. Malo first on the agenda, he could do little to aid his forces elsewhere; but at the same time he expected little from them.[37]

General Patton, who felt that his Household Cavalry gave him a better knowledge of what was happening in Brittany and who had received word that Grow planned to attack Brest, decided that the 6th Armored Division ought to have some reinforcement. He therefore ordered Middleton to move an infantry battalion of the 8th Division from Rennes to Brest. Early on the afternoon of 8 August, a battalion started westward to join the 6th Armored Division.[38]

Soon afterwards, a report came to army announcing that a large German force was moving toward Brest from the northeast.[39] If this were true, the 6th Armored Division was about to be squeezed and crushed between the moving force and the Brest garrison. Concern over the potential fate of the division was intensified by the inadequate communications.

[36] 6th Armd Div G–2 Per Rpt 10, 7 Aug.

[37] Memo, Evans for Maddox, 7 Aug.
[38] TUSA Info Serv Patrol Msg, received at VIII Corps CP 1156, 8 Aug; TUSA Memo to VIII Corps, 8 Aug; VIII Corps Memo to 8th Div, 8 Aug; 6th Armd Div G–3 Jnl, entry 0410, 8 Aug.
[39] TUSA Info Serv Msg, 1350, 8 Aug.

Although additional Signal equipment had been sent to the division, the presence of scattered groups of enemy soldiers in the division area delayed its use. German patrols similarly prohibited establishment of a landing strip for liaison planes. On General Grow's suggestion, a liaison plane from the corps appeared over the division command post on 7 August, and the pilot dropped a note on a panel laid out in a field. He then circled the area in a vain attempt to discover a meadow large enough to land on, for the terrain resembled the small hedgerow-enclosed fields of the Cotentin. After requesting by radio that the division bulldoze out one hedgerow to create a landing space the size of two fields, the pilot picked up a division message held aloft between lance poles, "waggled his wings, and went home with some flak on his tail." [40]

Because the hedgerowed fields were terraced, it was difficult to find two adjacent open spaces with the same floor level. After discovering a surface suitable for a landing strip, the Signal officer borrowed a bulldozer from the engineers early on 8 August and cut down a hedgerow. Shortly after he released the dozer, the area he had selected for the landing strip came under severe artillery shelling. Judging the field unsafe for a landing, he arranged another pickup and drop by the plane expected from corps. Although the shelling had ceased when the plane arrived, the pilot inspected the field from the air and decided he needed still more space for a landing. He dropped his message, se-

cured the division message, and radioed: "See you tomorrow, get a longer field."

Meanwhile, at corps headquarters, it appeared likely that the anticipated German squeeze play against the 6th Armored Division soon might develop. When radio silence, imposed by General Grow to cloak his intentions before Brest, was momentarily lifted on the evening of 8 August, a cryptic message by high-powered radio informed corps that the division command post was "under attack, codes in danger, may destroy."

At Brest, on the morning of 8 August, a four-man German patrol guided the white-draped American jeep bearing M. Sgt. Alex Castle and the 6th Armored Division G–2, Maj. Ernest W. Mitchell, toward an outpost position. At the outpost, a German lieutenant blindfolded the two emissaries before taking them into the city. When the blindfolds were removed, Mitchell and Castle found themselves in an underground command post, face to face with several German officers seated at a table.

One German raised his hand and said, "Heil Hitler." After a momentary hesitation, Mitchell saluted. Presuming the German to be the senior commander, Mitchell handed him General Grow's surrender ultimatum. When the German denied knowledge of English, Castle translated the paper aloud:

HEADQUARTERS 6TH ARMORED DIVISION, Office of the Commanding General, APO 256, US Army, 8 August 1944, MEMORANDUM TO: Officer Commanding German Forces in Brest.

1. The United States Army, Naval and Air Force troops are in position to destroy the garrison of Brest.

2. This memorandum constitutes an op-

[40] 6th Armd Div Msg, sent 2139, 6 Aug, received at VIII Corps CP, 0410, 7 Aug; Ltr, Given to Grow.

portunity for you to surrender in the face of these overwhelming forces to representatives of the United States Government and avoid the unnecessary sacrifice of lives.

3. I shall be very glad to receive your formal surrender and make the detailed arrangements any time prior to 1500 this date. The officer who brings this memorandum will be glad to guide you and necessary members of your staff, not exceeding six to my headquarters.

R. W. Grow
Major General, USA
Commanding

The German commander said he could not surrender. Mitchell asked whether he understood what that meant. The German said he did. Mitchell took back the ultimatum. The German commander heiled, Mitchell saluted. The two Americans were blindfolded and driven back to the outpost, where the bandages were removed, and Mitchell and Castle re-entered their lines and reported that the bluff had failed.[41]

With no alternative but to attack the city, General Grow requested heavy air support for the following day, 9 August. He wanted a continuous air attack for a minimum of three hours by waves of planes striking heavy guns, large oil tanks, and troop concentration areas. Planning to attack with two columns moving against the northeastern portion of the city, Grow shifted Read's CCB headquarters from the northern to the central column to take control of the troops that had been under CCR. Hanson's CCR headquarters moved to the right and assumed control of the units that had comprised Read's column.

The attack was to be made by CCB in the center and by Taylor's CCA on the left, with the four artillery battalions in position to support both columns.[42]

Chances of success apeared reasonably good. It was true that nearly every village on the outskirts of Brest was garrisoned by a few Germans with antitank guns, that the entrances into some were barred by roadblocks of steel rails, log barricades, or tetrahedrons, and in some cases concrete pillboxes, and that foxholes had been dug along all the roads leading into Brest. However, the significant facts seemed to be that the division was in contact along a line from Milizac through Gouesnou to Guipavas, apparently the outer defenses of the city, and that the enemy had only three or four thousand soldiers, augmented by an unknown number of naval forces.[43]

The attack was not to be made as scheduled. Since shortly before noon on 8 August, disturbing reports had been coming from rear outposts. Scattered enemy soldiers in stray vehicles had appeared suddenly, from nowhere it seemed. Several unit commanders complained throughout the day that troops of other commands were firing indiscriminately and endangering their men, yet investigation failed to disclose the source of the fire. The commander of the division trains, approaching Lesneven, reported that he was unable to enter the division rear area because of small arms and artillery fire, evidently from the rear of the combat commands deployed before Brest. These unaccountable reports were explained late

---

[41] Ltr, Mitchell to Grow, 5 Mar 53; *Abendmeldung*, 8 Aug, *OB WEST KTB, Anlage 1217;* the ultimatum is reproduced in Grow, "An Epic of Brittany," *Military Review*, XXVI, No. 11, p. 3.

[42] Msg, Grow to Middleton, 1500, 8 Aug, 6th Armd Div G-3 Jnl; Msg, Middleton to Grow, 0140, 9 Aug.

[43] 6th Armd Div G-2 Per Rpt 11, 8 Aug.

that afternoon when a battery of the 212th Armored Field Artillery Battalion captured Generalleutnant Karl Spang, commander of the *266th Division,* and several of his staff. From documents they carried, the 6th Armored Division learned that the *266th,* after having contributed forces to the Dinan and St. Malo garrisons, was moving from Morlaix to Brest to consolidate its remaining forces with the Brest garrison. Spang, whose capture was his first intimation that U.S. troops were "anywhere in the area," had preceded his unit in order to insure proper reception facilities for his men. By evening the situation that had been building up all day came to a head. The *266th Division,* a static unit of perhaps regimental strength, was in contact with the armored division rear.[44]

Threatened from the rear at nightfall as troops of the *266th* stumbled into the armored division's outposts, General Grow canceled the attack on Brest and instructed his subordinate commanders to leave screening forces facing the port city. Reconnaissance troops were to seal off the exits to prevent the German garrison from sallying out to meet the *266th.* The combat command columns were to reverse in place and drive generally northeast toward Plouvien in order to destroy the unsuspecting Germans, who were approaching in route march formation. Meanwhile, since the division headquarters might be overrun, several soldiers were posted at the electric code machines to destroy them with thermite canisters if necessary.

Because wires linking the division command post to subordinate units had been cut and because silence was being maintained, General Grow dispatched a handwritten field order to his subordinates by messenger. Acknowledgment returned at once from CCB and CCR, but none came from CCA. Not until later was it discovered that a message center sergeant had neglected to deliver the order to General Taylor. Fortunately, the incoming Germans did not strike CCA but blundered into the other two combat commands.

Skirmishes resulting from tentative probing contacts made during the night developed on 9 August into a full-scale engagement. Read's CCB carried the the main burden, Hanson's CCR contributed hardly less, and Taylor's CCA attacked later in the day. A group of fighter-bombers joined the action by blasting an enemy column near Lesneven. By evening the 6th Armored Division had taken almost a thousand prisoners and estimated that it had destroyed half of the enemy unit.[45]

It took another day for the division to clear the area and gather in those of the *266th* who did not manage to reach Brest by devious routes. After establishing a cordon around the landward side of Brest, the bulk of the 6th Armored Division settled down into a somewhat stable situation, beyond observed enemy artillery range. The division trains bivouacked. The infantry battalion of the 8th Division arrived. Task Force A appeared briefly near Les-

---

[44] 6th Armd Div G–2 Per Rpt 12, 0800, 9 Aug; *AGp B Sitrep,* 1715, 7 Aug, *AGp BIa Letzte Meldung, 8.v.–10.viii.44.*

[45] Msg, Grow to Middleton, 1800, 9 Aug, 6th Armd Div G–3 Jnl; Msg, Grow to Middleton, 1910, 9 Aug.

neven before proceeding on another mission. A new airfield site was cleared, and regular courier service by planes commenced. The division radio teletype team erected a double-height antenna and secured satisfactory contact with corps headquarters.

Meanwhile, General Grow still pondered how to secure Brest. It was obvious that the defenses were much stronger than he had anticipated. The outer defense line barred swift entry, and the expectation of strongpoints within the city foreshadowed vicious street fighting. Artillery positions across the bay from Brest were out of reach of an armored attack across the landward approaches. The entire Brest complex appeared beyond the capabilities of an armored division reinforced only by an infantry battalion. Yet a glimmer of hope came from the uncertainty that no one seemed to know exactly how many Germans defended the port.

If a small German force held the city, it was possible that an armored drive in strength might overwhelm the defenders. To secure a good jump-off place for an attack, Grow planned to secure the high ground near Guipavas, which seemed to be a soft spot. From the high ground, his artillery could support without displacement a division attack all the way into the city.

Efforts by CCA and the attached infantry battalion on 11 and 12 August to secure the terrain near Guipavas failed.[46] It gradually became clear that additional resources were needed: artillery to neutralize the guns in Brest and permit an advance through the outer defenses, infantry and a strong engineer attachment to attack the city proper, and fighter and medium bomber support to assist the assault troops and reduce the inner defenses. Still hoping he could eventually take Brest, General Grow requested a complement of heavy artillery. Until he received that, there was little he could do but continue to develop the outpost defenses. Enemy artillery was "much too strong" for anything more.[47]

Unfortunately for Grow's hopes, the corps' heavy artillery was engaged at St. Malo, and not until that port fell would infantry and artillery become available for an attack on Brest. The 83d or the 8th Division, perhaps both, would then move west to join the 6th Armored Division. Until then, General Middleton advised,

I believe it unwise to become too involved in a fight at Brest unless you feel reasonably sure of success. I prefer that you watch the situation and wait until an infantry division arrives. Heavy artillery will arrive with the infantry division.[48]

Any hope that General Grow had of taking Brest vanished on the evening of 12 August when he received word to contain the city with one combat command while relieving the 4th Armored Division at Lorient and Vannes with the others. Leaving CCA and the battalion of the 8th Division—about 4,000 troops—

---

[46] See Sgt. Joseph D. Buckley, *A History of the 50th Armored Infantry Battalion* (Frankfurt: Baier and Wurm, c. 1945.), pp. 24–27.

[47] Msg, Grow to Middleton, 1330, 11 Aug, received at VIII Corps CP, 1755, 11 Aug.

[48] Msg, Middleton to Grow, 2135, 11 Aug; see also, Msg, Galvin to McBride, 1400, 11 Aug, 6th Armd Div G-3 Jnl; Memo, Col. Evans to Col. Thomas J. Cross, 11 Aug.

at Brest, he completed the relief at Lorient and Vannes on 14 August.[49]

In advancing to Brest, the division had lost about 130 killed, 400 wounded, and 70 missing. Destroyed or damaged combat vehicles totaled 50, other vehicles 62, guns 11. In contrast, the division had taken 4,000 prisoners.[50]

Looking back after the war on the campaign, General Grow said he had been elated by the performance of his division in penetrating two hundred miles into Brittany, the most extended independent operation by a single division in the European theater. The 6th Armored Division had cleared the greater part of the peninsula, the proof being that before the end of the second week in August lone travelers covered long distances in the interior with no thought of danger. In addition to destroying what remained of the *266th Division* in Brittany, the 6th Armored Division had driven the other German troops in its sector into a "self-imposed prison." The division "had performed," General Grow was convinced, "the greatest cavalry-type operation of the war . . . [and] had proved the soundness of the . . . mechanized division and the hard months of training." The role of the cavalry in exploitation and the value of mobility on the battlefield, he felt, had been restored by the display of speed, initiative, and boldness that were the basic cavalry characteristics inherited by armored troops.

Disappointed, naturally, because he had not taken Brest, Grow was discouraged by the static mission of containment with which he was charged. Despite his repeated recommendations that the FFI be assigned the task of guarding the port cities so that the division might be free for more active and more compatible missions, the unit remained in Brittany for another month, guarding Brest, Lorient, and Vannes. The value of armor had been proved but was then, he felt, disregarded.

One galling question remained: Could the 6th Armored Division have taken Brest if it had arrived there sooner? Having been assured by the FFI that Brest would probably have fallen had it been attacked in strength a day or two earlier, General Grow could not forget the Dinan diversion, which had delayed the division about twenty-four hours; the slow approach of CCA into the Brest area, which had made it necessary for CCB to attack alone on 7 August; and the movement of the *266th Division* from Morlaix, which had prompted cancellation of the concerted attack planned for 9 August. With complete surprise in Grow's favor, a show of strength, he felt, might have been sufficient to persuade a vacillating commander with weak forces to capitulate.[51]

This attractive thesis was supported by the fact that only the *343d Division,* some cadre companies, relatively weak artillery, and two batteries of coastal artillery were available at the beginning of August to defend the fortress against attack from land or sea. The presence of many civilians in the city complicated the defense. The Germans could count on a garrison of only 15,000 men at max-

---

[49] Msg, Middleton to Grow, 1645, 12 Aug, received at 6th Armd Div CP, 2350, 12 Aug; Msg, Read to Grow, 2130, 13 Aug; Msg, Grow to Middleton, 2220, 14 Aug. All in 6th Armd Div G–3 Jnl.

[50] 6th Armd Div G–2 Per Rpt 15, 12 Aug.

[51] Grow, "An Epic of Brittany," *Military Review,* XXVI, No. 11, pp. 3–9; [Committee 9], Super Sixth, p. 108.

imum, many of whom were required to reinforce strongpoints already established to combat an amphibious invasion. Limited amounts of building materials and transportation facilities for defense construction were other deficiencies. Having had to consider a seaward attack of first import, the Germans felt that the landward strength of the fortress was defective. The ground fortifications were so close to the installations they protected that an attack on the defenses constituted at the same time an attack on the city's vitals—in some instances, artillery emplacements, supply depots, and military workshops were even located outside the defensive line.

Balancing these disadvantages and destroying the thesis were other factors. The old French fortifications had provided the Germans foundation for a modern defensive complex. Large, deep, artificial caves in rocky terrain afforded shellproof shelter to large numbers of the garrison. Able to resist bombardment and heavy-caliber artillery, the troops at the beginning of August were considered by the Germans to be adequate in numbers and high in morale. To the *343d Division* were soon added "splinters" of the *266th Division* and, more important, the well-trained *2d Parachute Division* (commanded by Generalleutnant Herman B. Ramcke, a devoted Nazi), the latter unit eventually forming the nucleus of the defense. After contact had been made with the 6th Armored Division near Huelgoat on 5 August, there was no longer the possibility of a surprise attack. The Germans had no doubt that an attack against Brest was imminent.[52]

The fortress commander, Col. Hans von der Mosel (not Ramcke, as the Americans had thought), had rejected General Grow's surrender ultimatum on 8 August even before the *2d Parachute Division* had joined his garrison.[53] The paratroopers had started at the beginning of August to move in two columns eastward from the Brest area toward Normandy, but Fahrmbacher, the *XXV Corps* commander, had ordered the movement halted almost at once because of the rapid American thrust into Brittany. In contact with U.S. armor near Carhaix and Huelgoat, then bypassed by the 6th Armored Division and in danger of isolation, Ramcke obeyed the OKW order that had instructed the forces in Brittany to move into the fortresses. Avoiding the Americans, the *2d Parachute Division* slipped into Brest on 9 August from the south, by way of Doualas. The division had lost, between 29 July and 12 August, about 50 dead, 200 wounded, and 100 missing, some as the result of FFI guerrilla action, some at the battle of Huelgoat. Three days after re-entering Brest, Ramcke became the fortress commander, Mosel his chief of staff.[54]

By the time General Grow was able to launch his preliminary attacks on Guipavas on 11 and 12 August, the Brest garrison numbered about 35,000 Army, Navy, and Air Force troops. But before then, even without such overwhelming strength, the Germans had made evident their decision to defend with determination. The extent of their fortifications,

---

[52] MS # B–731 (Fahrmbacher).

[53] See Ltr, Mitchell to Grow, for American belief that Ramcke had turned down the ultimatum.

[54] H. B. Ramcke, *Fallschirmjaeger, Damals und Danach* (Frankfurt: Lorch-Verlag, c. 1951), pp. 30–46.

the size of the fortress complex, and Hitler's orders to resist to the last man were more than sufficient to keep a lone armored division from taking the largest port in Brittany.[55] Even though the VIII Corps G–2 as late as 12 August estimated that only 8,000 men defended Brest, he recognized that its defenses were far stronger than he had earlier judged.[56] It should have been obvious much sooner. By mid-July, SHAEF had concluded that the Brest garrison was likely to number at minimum 17,000 troops. The numerous defensible river valleys between Morlaix and Brest, the perimeter defenses at Landivisiau, Lesneven, and Landerneau, the landward fortifications of Brest, and the numerous antiaircraft emplacements all argued against painless possession of a port that was as vital to Hitler as to the Allies.[57] Although Patton lost his five-pound bet with Montgomery, the fact was that merely in pinning the vastly superior German force at Brest against the sea, the 6th Armored Division had achieved success.

A fluid front, fast-moving columns, and a rapidly lengthening line of communication had lessened corps control, had emphasized the necessity of individual initiative and judgment, improvisation and calculated risk. With no defined front except the direction in which the division was going, the cavalry reconnaissance squadron had main-

tained a flexible screen around the front and flanks that was retracted from or deflected around resistance too strong to overcome. A forward observer traveling with the head of a column could have artillery fire on a target as soon as the self-propelled pieces could drop their ammunition trailers. Casualties were moved forward with the division until convoys could be organized for evacuation. Prisoners were also carried along until they could be turned over, against their vehement protests, to the FFI, "who seemed only too glad to accept the responsibility for their care."[58] Tanks and armored cars sometimes escorted supply vehicles, and the division band defended valiantly a supply dump near Carhaix and prevented its capture by a small German force. The army had established a gasoline dump at Pontivy, but the division had to go all the way back to Avranches for other supplies. The necessity for speed had prompted the division to disregard danger from mines; only a few times, principally at fords, had mines been encountered. In retrospect at least, the campaign seemed to have been "a routine operation" that had been aided by extremely favorable weather.[59]

Yet it was a spectacular achievement, an exhilarating accomplishment that went virtually unnoticed because of action elsewhere on a much larger scale.

---

[55] See [Committee 9], Super Sixth, p. 151.

[56] VIII Corps G–2 Weekly Per Rpt 8, 12 Aug.

[57] App. A to PS SHAEF (44) 29 (First Draft), 16 Jul, SHAEF G–3 File 24533/Opns, Future Opns.

[58] Hammond, 6th Armored Division.

[59] See Combat History of the 128th Armored Ordnance Maintenance Battalion (Wiesbaden, Germany: Wiesbaedner Kurier-Wiesbaedner Verlag, 1945) pp. 21–26.

CHAPTER XXI

St. Malo and the North Shore

The Decision at St. Malo

Anticipating quick capture of Brest, General Patton had acted to preserve the Brest–Rennes railroad as a fast means of transporting military cargo into the interior of France. The railway, running generally along the Brittany north shore, could be cut quite easily by destroying any of several important bridges. Patton had created Task Force A to secure the vital bridges before the Germans could demolish them.[1] (See Map VIII.)

Task Force A had a strength of about 3,500 men. Its headquarters, the 1st Tank Destroyer Brigade, controlled the 6th Tank Destroyer Group, the 15th Cavalry Group, and the 159th Engineer Battalion. The task force commander, General Earnest, had requested an infantry attachment, but no infantry was available during the hectic early days of August. The possibility that Task Force A would make contact with a substantial number of French Resistance forces provided hope that the FFI would perform such infantry functions as line of communications guard and command post security.

At a conference with his principal subordinates on 1 August, General Earnest announced that Patton expected Task Force A to "race to the sea" to secure the main railway bridges and incidentally help the 6th Armored Division capture Brest. Proceeding from Avranches through Dol-de-Bretagne, Dinan, Guingamp, and Morlaix, the task force was to bypass resistance except at the bridges. Three structures near St. Brieuc and two near Morlaix comprised the specific objectives. All task force units were to carry rations for six days, fuel for two hundred and fifty miles, a basic ammunition load transportable in organic vehicles, and water chlorination tablets.[2]

Through the Avranches–Pontaubault bottleneck by early 3 August, Task Force A entered Brittany and struck resistance almost immediately at a point two miles short of Dol-de-Bretagne. The cavalry commander was lost at once, his jeep later found riddled with machine gun bullets. Since the task force was supposedly following the 6th Armored Division as far as Dinan, meeting opposition was somewhat of a surprise even though General Earnest had expected that small enemy units might hit the task force's flanks. Learning from civilians that Dol was strongly defended, Earnest decided to bypass the town on

---

[1] The sources for this section are the VIII Corps G–3 Journal and File and the Task Force A After Action Report and Journal, August. Unless otherwise noted, documents referred to in this chapter are in the VIII Corps G–3 Journal and File.

[2] TF A AAR, Aug, and FO 1, 2 Aug; VIII Corps FO 9, 1 Aug, and Spec Map.

the south and continue westward. He requested VIII Corps to send infantry to reduce the bypassed Dol defenses.[3]

Interested in the strength of the St. Malo defenses, General Middleton instructed Earnest to probe northward toward St. Malo even as he drove westward toward Dinan. Beyond Dol-de-Bretagne, Earnest therefore split his column. The heads of both columns struck defensive positions about seven miles west of Dol, near Miniac. Some disorder occurred among U.S. troops engaging in combat for the first time, but Earnest quickly restored discipline and directed his cavalry to dismount and launch an infantry attack. Enemy resistance was quickly broken, but as the task force tried to push toward St. Malo, increasingly heavy resistance developed south of Châteauneuf-d'Ille-et-Vilaine.

Since the strong enemy forces defending the St. Malo–Châteauneuf–Dol area might involve Task Force A in an action that would prevent a rapid westward drive, General Earnest radioed for help. Aware that the VIII Corps had alerted the 83d Infantry Division for action in Brittany and believing that the 6th Armored Division was not far away, he called upon both the corps and the armored division in the hope that one would respond. "Please reply, need urgent," he radioed. "Rush troops." [4]

Infantrymen were in fact approaching Dol-de-Bretagne on the afternoon of 3 August, for early that morning Middleton had ordered the 83d Division to hurry a regiment to Pontorson so that

the regiment alone or the entire division, according to the way the situation developed, could follow the 6th Armored Division to Brest. The 330th Infantry reached Pontorson that afternoon and continued to Dol. Extensive defensive positions around Dol, including wire entanglements and antitank ditches, prompted the regiment to delay its attack until the morning of 4 August, but then the town was quickly secured.[5]

Although the 330th Infantry moved west beyond Dol-de-Bretagne for several miles without meeting resistance on 4 August, Task Force A pushing north that afternoon toward Châteauneuf-d'Ille-et-Vilaine encountered severe opposition, including fire from coastal guns and naval vessels in the St. Malo area.[6]

By this time a decision had to be made on St. Malo. General Bradley at first had specifically ordered the capture of St. Malo. When General Patton made no provision for its capture, Bradley had more or less acquiesced in Patton's concept of clearing the entire peninsula before getting involved in siege operations at the port cities. General Middleton, however, was becoming increasingly concerned over the large concentration of German troops in the St. Malo area. Bypassing the strongpoint in favor of more distant and alluring goals would not eliminate what might develop into a threat against the long lines of communication that would have to be established in Brittany. Allowing strong German forces to remain active at St. Malo would be like permitting a sore

[3] Ltr, Earnest to OCMH, 6 May 54, OCMH Files; Msg, Earnest to Middleton, 1030, 3 Aug.

[4] Msgs, Earnest to Middleton and Grow, 1600, 3 Aug; Msg, Earnest to Middleton, 1930, 3 Aug; TF A Jnl, entry 1255, 3 Aug.

[5] VIII Corps G–3 Sec Memo, 0630, 3 Aug; 330th Inf AAR, Aug, Telecon, Col Conrad R. Boyle and Col Evans. 0945, 4 Aug, 83d Div G–2, G–3 Jnl.

[6] TF A G–3 Sitrep 4, 1330, 4 Aug.

to develop into a cancer. Middleton favored immediate surgery.[7]

General Middleton's inability to obtain the 6th Armored Division to help Task Force A and the 330th Infantry prompted him to give the assignment of capturing St. Malo to General Macon and the 83d Division. Then Middleton learned that Patton was unwilling to let more than one regiment of the 83d participate in the attack, for Patton believed that the Germans would make only a token defense of St. Malo. Patton wanted the 83d Division to follow the 6th Armored to Brest and Task Force A to sweep the Brittany north shore.[8]

Developments in the St. Malo region on the morning of 4 August seemed to support Patton's view, since Germans manning outpost positions that comprised the outer defenses of the St. Malo fortress withdrew north toward Châteauneuf, a move that appeared to presage a show of force before capitulation. The experience of Task Force A that afternoon led to quite the opposite conclusion. The Germans had evidently withdrawn to consolidate and strengthen their defenses. Whatever the German intentions, it was obvious that the Americans needed additional troops around St. Malo.

Hoping that immediate, resolute action might achieve the desired result, Middleton ordered Macon to bring the entire 83d Division into the area to make a co-ordinated attack in conjunction with Task Force A. If St. Malo fell at once, Middleton would attach a motorized infantry battalion of the 83d Division to Task Force A and send Earnest off to fulfill his original mission.[9]

The result of the attack on 5 August proved that the reduction of St. Malo would take some time. Unwilling to hold Task Force A any longer, Middleton ordered Earnest to break contact during the night of 5 August and on the following morning to continue his mission of sweeping Brittany's north shore. In exchange for a platoon of tank destroyers that Earnest left with the 83d Division, he secured a motorized infantry battalion and a battery of 105-mm. howitzers. A medical collecting company from corps would join the task force on 8 August.[10] In the matter of time, the effect of the diversion to St. Malo on Task Force A was double that imposed on the 6th Armored Division; it delayed Earnest's westward drive about forty-eight hours.

Sweeping the North Shore

Slipping out of the St. Malo area during darkness, Task Force A bypassed Dinan on the south and moved westward on 6 August toward St. Brieuc, thirty miles from Dinan.[11] Contact was made that afternoon with FFI groups commanded by Colonel Eon, who was already in possession of St. Brieuc. Task Force A found the three bridges near the town intact, and General Earnest detailed an engineer company to guard

[7] 12th AGp Ltrs of Instr 1 and 2, 29 Jul and 3 Aug; see above, Ch. XVII. Middleton may have discussed this with Bradley when the army group commander visited the corps command post on 2 August. See Bradley, *Soldier's Story*, pp. 362–63.

[8] Msg, Middleton to Macon, 4 Aug; 83d Div G–2, G–3 Jnl, entries 1110 and 1130, 4 Aug.

[9] VIII Corps Msg, 4 Aug.

[10] Msg, Middleton to Earnest, 5 Aug; VIII Corps Msg, 2400, 5 Aug, and AAR, Aug; TF A FO 3, 1159, 5 Aug.

[11] Msg, Earnest to Middleton, 1330, 6 Aug.

them and to operate a prisoner of war enclosure.[12]

At Châtelaudren, ten miles west of St. Brieuc, Task Force A quickly overran about a company of Germans on the morning of 7 August and, accompanied by men of the French Resistance, continued five miles beyond toward Guingamp. Mine fields and antitank obstacles outside Guingamp prompted a halt. Part of the cavalry and some FFI had meanwhile made a wide detour to envelop Guingamp from the south and after infiltrating the town reported that some Germans remained but that the greater part of the garrison had withdrawn to the west. These reports and the fact that the main body of the task force had received no fire from the positions east of Guingamp encouraged General Earnest to attack despite the late hour. Against light resistance the task force took the town.[13]

The most important bridge on the double-track railway was at Morlaix, thirty miles west of Guingamp. It was an arched stone structure some thousand feet in length and two hundred feet in height, the largest railroad viaduct in France.[14] Suspecting that strong German forces would be in Morlaix, General Earnest endeavored to make contact with the 6th Armored Division so that he might call for help if necessary. "Where is Six Armored Division right flank?"

he radioed Middleton. Middleton's reply of necessity was rather vague.[15] As the task force approached Morlaix, Earnest tried without success to reach the armored division by radio.

German troops of the *266th Division* had indeed occupied Morlaix, but early on 8 August the Germans departed the town to seek refuge in Brest. Driving toward Morlaix that same morning, Task Force A encountered only about a hundred Germans deployed around a château just east of the town. Taking the strongpoint by surprise, the Americans entered Morlaix and found the railroad viaduct intact.[16]

On the following morning, 9 August, the task force took a bridge south of Morlaix, and General Earnest reported that he had completed his mission. FFI detachments guarding the main highways between Dinan and Landivisiau had extended their control over the smaller roads. Task Force A captured more than 1,200 Germans; FFI, about 300. American and French losses were small.[17]

Earnest was preparing to join the 6th Armored Division at Brest when Middleton radioed him a new mission. The task force was to return to Morlaix and proceed from there northeast to the coast to secure the beaches of the bay of St. Michel-en-Grève, where cargo arriv-

---

[12] Verbal Msg, TUSA Spec Force Detachment in contact with FFI to VIII Corps, 1625, 6 Aug; Msg, Earnest to Middleton, 2205, 6 Aug; Journal des Marches; VIII Corps AAR, Aug.

[13] Verbal Rpt of TF A Liaison Officer to VIII Corps, 7 Aug, TF A Jnl, entry 1200, 7 Aug; Msg, Earnest to Middleton, 0030, 8 Aug; TF A FO 4, 6 Aug.

[14] ETOUSA Engr Hist Rpt 10, Combat Engineering (1945).

[15] Msg, Earnest to Middleton, 2153, 6 Aug, received VIII Corps CP 0100, 7 Aug; Msg, Middleton to Earnest, 0400, 7 Aug.

[16] VIII Corps G–3 Jnl, 8 Aug; Msg, Earnest to Middleton, 2200, 8 Aug; VIII Corps AAR, Aug. One hundred and fifty special troops had been parachuted from England into Brittany during the night of 4 August to help the FFI protect the railroad bridges at Morlaix. TUSA AAR, I, 20.

[17] Msgs, Earnest to Middleton, 1352 and 1615, 9 Aug.

ing from England was to be unloaded.[18] German strongpoints had earlier commanded the beach, but only mines and angle-iron obstacles remained. Earnest's troops met no opposition as they extended their control over St. Michel-en-Grève on 11 August. Three LST's hove into sight that day and prepared to unload supplies. To insure security for supply operations, the task force patrolled the coastal region, cleared disorganized German troops from the area, and took more than a thousand prisoners; losses totaled 25.[19]

Middleton considered recalling Task Force A to St. Malo, but the FFI commander, Eon, persuaded him otherwise. A German garrison near Paimpol still held coastal forts overlooking the western approaches to the bay of St. Brieuc, thereby denying the Allies use of the St. Brieuc port and allowing the Germans to furnish the Channel Island troops with foodstuffs procured on the mainland. Eon proposed to clear the Paimpol area and requested a display of American force during his attack. Middleton gave Eon a thousand gallons of gasoline to transport about 2,500 FFI troops and instructed Earnest to send along a few armored cars, some tank destroyers, and perhaps a battery of artillery. Expecting the FFI to carry the brunt of the combat, Middleton cautioned Earnest against forming a Franco-American force under a single commander. French and Americans were to share the profits of the venture, the Americans to get the prisoners, the FFI the captured arms and equipment.[20]

The extent of the German opposition soon drew Task Force A into what developed into a four-day engagement. After reducing a strongpoint near Lézardrieux (three miles west of Paimpol) and taking 430 prisoners, the Americans and the French launched an attack against Paimpol, cleared the town by noon, 17 August, and captured more than 2,000 prisoners and much equipment. At the same time, a reinforced battalion of the 8th Division in an independent action on 15 August cleared the Cap Fréhel area, midway between Dinan and St. Brieuc, by firing a few white phosphorus rounds of 4.2-inch mortar and rounding up 300 prisoners.

The north shore had been swept clear, an achievement that belonged largely to Task Force A. The task force had secured a useable communications net between Dinan and Landivisiau. Although the railroad was of little worth because the port of Brest was not in American hands, the Task Force A operation was significant in a later context. To a large extent it made possible the logistical support for the major effort subsequently to be exerted to capture Brest.

"To the Last Stone"

When Task Force A departed the St. Malo area to sweep the Brittany north

---

[18] TF A FO 6, 2400, 8 Aug, and Jnl, entry 2100, 9 Aug; Msg, Middleton to Earnest, 1710, 9 Aug; Msg, Middleton to Earnest, 1810, 10 Aug, TF A Jnl; see 21 AGp, Dir M–515, 27 Jul.

[19] App. A to PS SHAEF (44) 29 (First Draft), 16 Jul, SHAEF G–3 File 24533/Opns, Future Opns; Memo, Evans to Earnest, 12 Aug; Roland G. Ruppenthal, *Logistical Support of the Armies, Vol. II,* UNITED STATES IN WORLD WAR II (Washington, 1959), Ch. II; TF A Opns 1 Aug–22 Sep, a preliminary MS, OCMH Files; ETOUSA Engr Hist Rpt 10.

[20] Msg, Middleton to Earnest, 1530, 14 Aug; Journal des Marches; see Memo, "JTR" [Col John R. Jeter] to Evans, 15 Aug.

shore, the 83d Division stayed to complete the task already begun. Few Americans suspected at the beginning of August that St. Malo would be difficult to take, for the rapidity of the advance into Brittany had brought a heady optimism. Yet studies made in England before the invasion indicated that there were strong defenses at the harbor, and contact with the defenders in the early days of August should have confirmed the fact that the Germans would make a determined stand there. Not until 5 August, however, did American commanders acknowledge that the Germans were capable of stubborn defense. By then, General Middleton and the VIII Corps, and particularly General Macon and the 83d Division, were aware that they had a nasty job ahead of them.[21]

Originally alerted for action against Rennes and Quiberon or against Brest, Macon had supported Task Force A at St. Malo with one regiment, hoping thereby to sweep aside the allegedly insignificant opposition at the port. The resistance that developed soon changed these plans, and by 5 August the entire division was committed there.[22] (*Map I*)

At first wanting St. Malo immediately, later agreeing to bypass and contain the port if its reduction required "too large a force and too much time," General Bradley finally decided that with American troops dispersing to the far corners of Brittany the St. Malo harbor would be valuable as an auxiliary supply port

for those forces. Used by the Germans as a naval base for coastal operations and as a supply base for the Channel Islands, St. Malo could accommodate medium-sized vessels and had facilities to unload cargo at the rate of a thousand tons a day. Although naval planners had informed General Eisenhower "that we are likely to be disappointed in its possibilities as a port," Bradley ordered St. Malo taken.[23]

To American commanders studying their maps, the Avranches–St. Malo area was much like the Normandy coastline where the OVERLORD landings had been made. The Bay of Mont St. Michel resembled in miniature the shape of the Bay of the Seine. The St. Malo peninsula appeared to be the Cotentin Peninsula seen through the wrong end of a telescope. The harbor of St. Malo was a smaller version of Cherbourg. The Rance River estuary provided a west coast for the St. Malo peninsula as the ocean did for the Cotentin. At the base of the Rance estuary, Dinan was in the same relation to St. Malo as Avranches was to Cherbourg.

A picturesque port, St. Malo was the birthplace of Jacques Cartier and the home of the privateers who had harassed English shipping for three centuries. Across the Rance River, more than a mile to the west, the beaches of Dinard had been a favorite with British tourists. The defenses protecting both towns comprised the fortress complex of St. Malo.

Although Frenchmen warned that about ten thousand German troops garrisoned the fortress, American estimates of German strength varied between three

[21] VIII Corps AAR, Aug, and G–2 Per Rpts 48, 49, and 51, dated 1, 3, and 5 Aug.

[22] VIII Corps FO's 9 and 10, 1 and 2 Aug, G–3 Memo, 0630, 3 Aug, and G–2 Rpt, Beaches South of Vannes, n.d.; Min of Mtg. 0900, 30 Jul, 83d Div G–2, G–3 Jnl.

[23] Ltr, Eisenhower to Montgomery, 10 Jul, SGS SHAEF File 381, OVERLORD, I (a).

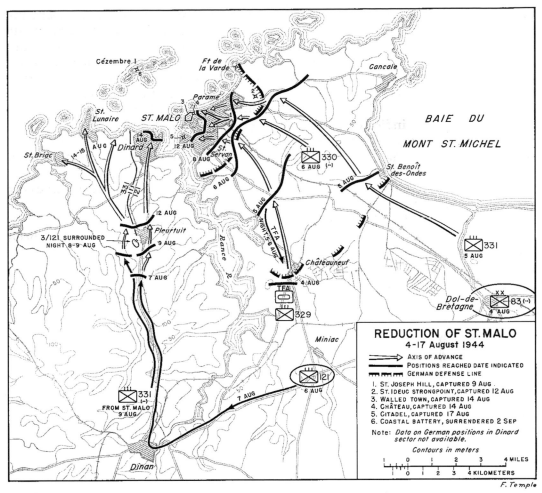

MAP 11

and six thousand. As late as 12 August VIII Corps was accepting the figure of five thousand, even though in actuality more than twelve thousand Germans occupied St. Malo and Dinard, with about two thirds of that number on the St. Malo side of the Rance.[24]

When the true numerical strength of the garrison became known after the battle, some Americans began to feel that the haste displayed in getting the Brittany exploitation under way had enabled the Germans to build up their St. Malo forces. In bypassing the port and its approaches, the Americans permitted numerous small garrisons in the surrounding countryside, as well as stragglers from the Cotentin, to take refuge in the fortress. The absence of Allied naval patrols offshore had allowed rein-

----

[24] TF A FO 2, 1159, 4 Aug; 83d Div FO's 21 and 22, 1800, 4 Aug, and 0100, 6 Aug, and Annex 1 to G-2 Per Rpt 44, 16 Aug; G-3 Per Rpt 33, 1600, 5 Aug; VIII Corps G-2 Weekly Per Rpt 8, 12 Aug.

forcement and supply to be brought into
the harbor from the Channel Islands.
The growth of the garrison, which could
not have occurred had the Americans
thrust rapidly to the port upon entering
Brittany, made reduction of the town
a major task.

Though estimates of German strength
were incorrect, American intelligence
was right in its growing realization that
the enemy in St. Malo firmly intended
to resist. The garrison commander had
rejected a proposal by French civilian
officials that he surrender in order to
save the nearby towns from damage. He
had announced that "he would defend
St. Malo to the last man even if the last
man had to be himself." [25] That he
could make a strong fight in support of
his boast soon became evident.

In early August outposts between Dol-
de-Bretagne and Dinan were withdrawn
to the Châteauneuf–St. Benôit-des-Ondes
line, which consisted of antitank obstacles and guns, roadblocks, wire entanglements, mine fields, and machine gun emplacements. Although the co-ordinated
attack, launched on 5 August by the 83d
Division and Task Force A (the latter
alone taking 655 prisoners), pierced this
line and secured Châteauneuf, the stubborn opposition gave advance notice
that the defense would stiffen as the Germans drew more closely around St.
Malo.[26]

Hoping to outflank and isolate the St.
Malo defensive complex, General Macon
on 5 August sent a battalion of the 329th
Infantry across the Rance in assault boats
to cut the Dinan–Dinard road, a move

that was to be the preliminary action for
a swift thrust to Dinard. Though the
battalion crossed the river, the men uncovered such strong resistance on the
west bank of the Rance that Macon
quickly recalled them. Adding impetus
to this decision was the discovery by the
331st Infantry, in the right of the division sector, of a much easier approach
to St. Malo. Moving north in the area
east of Châteauneuf toward Cancale, on
the east coast of the St. Malo peninsula,
the 331st encountered light covering
forces defending canals, roadblocks, and
mine fields. What the Germans were
covering was their consolidation of forces
on the main defense line of St. Malo.

That evening, 5 August, as Task Force
A prepared to slip away to fulfill its
original mission, the German commander prepared a last-ditch defense.
As part of this activity, the fortress commander abandoned Cancale, which was
occupied by the 331st Infantry on the
following morning and immediately surveyed for use as a port for landing craft.
The German commander also abandoned
Dinan, which was surrounded on the following day by FFI troops who reported
that several hundred Germans were willing to surrender, but only to Americans.[27] By then, the 83d Division was
attacking toward St. Malo with three regiments abreast—the 329th on the left,
the 330th in the center, and the 331st
on the right—and was in contact with
the main defenses of the St. Malo fortress.

On the St. Malo side of the Rance, the
fortress encompassed three communities
on the western tip of the peninsula. In

[25] 83d Div G–2 Per Rpts 32 and 33, 1800, 4
Aug, and 1600, 5 Aug.
[26] 83d Div FO 21, G–2 Per Rpt 32, 1800, 4 Aug,
and AAR, Aug.

[27] Msg, Macon (signed [Lt Col Robert W.] Hart-
man) to Middleton, 6 Aug; 83d Div G–3 Per Rpt 5,
1200, 7 Aug.

the center was the walled town of St. Malo, originally an island accessible from the mainland only at low tide. Guarding the landward entrance into town was the fifteenth century château of Anne of Brittany. Protecting the town from seaward invasion were thick ramparts of stone. East of St. Malo and adjacent to it was the relatively modern suburb of Paramé, where bourgeois homes and resort hotels lined broad boulevards. South of St. Malo and across the harbor was the fishing port of St. Servan-sur-Mer. Not really on the ocean but on the Rance River estuary, St. Servan was the ferry terminus for the regular boat runs to Dinard. Dug into a rocky promontory on a peninsula between St. Malo harbor and the port of St. Servan was a casemented fort called the Citadel, the headquarters of the German commander.

Although the Germans at St. Malo and Dinard were fighting with their backs to the sea, they had powerful support from artillery placed on the small island of Cézembre, not quite three miles offshore. The Channel islands of Jersey, Guernsey, and Alderney could furnish the St. Malo fortress supplies by water and receive German casualties.[28]

Hundreds of volunteer and impressed Todt workers had poured tons of concrete over steel for more than two years,

but the fortifications of St. Malo were not finished. Permanent coastal guns, for example, had not been installed in the Citadel, and only half a dozen field pieces, still with wheels, stood provisionally behind the firing apertures. The Germans had planned to dig an enormous antitank ditch across the St. Malo peninsula from the Rance to the sea and fill it with water, but the excavations were far from complete. Another weakness of the fortress was that it faced seaward against an expected Allied invasion from the sea. Barbed wire and other obstacles decorated the beaches.

Despite these deficiencies, the Germans were able to adjust quickly to a threat from the landward side of St. Malo. Enabling them to do so was a ring of strongpoints that barred the ground approaches. The most important were the coastal Fort la Varde, east of St. Malo; the strongpoint of St. Ideuc, on the eastern edge of Paramé; and positions on St. Joseph's Hill, in the southeast outskirts of St. Malo. The defense installations were mutually supporting, and underground wires assured telephonic communication among the principal garrisons. Stores of supplies, ammunition, water, and food, had been stockpiled in preparation against siege. As judged by *OB WEST*, the St. Malo fortifications were the most advanced of any fortress in the west.[29]

The commander of St. Malo, Col. Andreas von Aulock, was somewhat disappointed to have been relegated to a static fortress, for he would have preferred to gain striking offensive victories for his Fuehrer. Yet whether he understood the strategic importance of Hitler's

---

[28] Msgs, Macon to Middleton, 2120, 9 Aug, and 1830, 11 Aug. R. Fouque, *La Cité, Bastion de la Forteresse de Saint-Malo* (n.p., 1945) (hereafter cited as Fouque, *La Cité*), contains the best description of the St. Malo fortress, the best account of the activities of the relatively few French who remained there during the battle, and the clearest narrative of German conduct. See also Dr. Paul Aubry, *L'Agonie de Saint-Malo* (Rennes, 1945) and *La Ruée sur Saint-Malo* (Rennes, 1947) for the events that occurred within the fortress.

[29] *OB WEST, a Study in Command*, II, 9.

fortress policy or not, he prepared to do what was required of him. A veteran of Stalingrad who promised to make his defense of St. Malo "another Stalingrad," Aulock stated, "I was placed in command of this fortress. I did not request it. I will execute the orders I have received and, doing my duty as a soldier, I will fight to the last stone." [30]

Aulock, who had always been correct in his official relations with the French, could not understand why the inhabitants of St. Malo regarded him as an enemy. For their own good, he had suggested soon after the Allied landings in Normandy that the French evacuate the town, which was sure to be a battlefield. Despite Allied air bombardment on 17 July and again on 1 August, very few families had departed. The approach of U.S. ground forces prompted Aulock to clear his decks. Calling several town officials into conference on 3 August, he informed them that they were fine fellows but that he preferred to have them "in front of me rather than behind my back." Furthermore, since he wished to spare the population harm from the battle about to commence, most of the civilians had to go.

To French requests that he save historic St. Malo from destruction by declaring it an open city, Aulock answered that he had referred that question to Kluge, who had transmitted it to Hitler. Hitler had replied that in warfare there was no such thing as a historic city. "You will fight to the last man," he had ordered. As added justification to help the French comprehend Hitler's decision, Aulock explained that he commanded several small armed vessels that would have to maneuver in St. Malo waters. Since these boats constituted a legitimate military target, he could not declare the town an open city. [31]

Two days later, during the early evening of 5 August, a long line of Frenchmen, women, and children departed St. Malo in compliance with Aulock's order and entered American lines. Displaying white handkerchiefs and flags, carrying suitcases and pushing carts, most of the French population had left their homes reluctantly.

When American troops on 6 August came within range of the artillery on the island of Cézembre, German guns opened fire. One of the first shells struck the spire of the St. Malo cathedral. The steeple toppled over, a bad omen, the French believed. Later in the day fires broke out in the town. Frenchmen soon became convinced that the Germans had inadvertently spilled gasoline while burning codes and documents and that the few SS troops of the garrison with deliberate malice not only refused to permit fire fighters to put out the blaze but started others. The Americans unintentionally assisted by cutting the town's water supply in hope of encouraging German surrender, a hope concurred in by the mayor of St. Servan-sur-Mer, who had volunteered the necessary information on the location of the water valves. On the following morning, 7 August, the Germans added to the holocaust by setting off prepared demolitions that destroyed the port completely—quays, locks, breakwaters, and

---

[30] Fouque, *La Cité,* pp. 33–34; see also pp. 25, 44–45, and Plate 7.

[31] As it turned out, the few vessels were quite unimportant in the military action that developed. Fighter-bombers soon drove them from the St. Malo waters.

harbor machinery. For a week, as the town burned, a pall of smoke hovered over the St. Malo battlefield.[32]

In contact with the main defenses of the St. Malo fortress by the afternoon of 6 August, the 83d Division attacked positions forming a semicircle from the Rance to the sea. Belts of wire, large mine fields, rows of steel gates, antitank obstacles, and ditches were protected by machine gunners in pillboxes. Though the attack involved co-ordinated action by all three regiments and utilized air power and artillery, advances were markedly limited. Any last illusions that the battle might be swiftly terminated vanished.[33] To reinforce the 83d Division, General Middleton drew upon the 8th Division at Rennes for an infantry regiment (the 121st) and a medium tank company, which he attached to Macon's command; took a battalion of the corps artillery that had been attached to the 79th Division and ordered it into the St. Malo area; and requested increased air support.[34]

On 7 August the three organic regiments of the 83d Division renewed the attack toward St. Malo after a fifteen-minute artillery preparation. In the center of the division sector the German strongpoint on St. Joseph's Hill, tested on the previous day, continued to hold. Guns emplaced in a granite quarry on the hill, cavelike troop shelters hewed out of rock, and the dominating ground itself gave the German defenders such advantages that the 330th Infantry (Col.

Robert T. Foster) could not even maneuver into position for an actual assault. The only genuine hope of success rested with sustained artillery fire. While division and corps battalions delivered concentrated shelling, the infantry tried to inch up the hill. Not the infantry progress, which was infinitesimal, but constant and severe artillery and tank destroyer pounding for two days finally produced results. On 9 August more than 400 Germans on St. Joseph's Hill laid down their arms and marched out under a white flag.[35]

The elimination of St. Joseph's Hill enabled the troops on both flanks to surge forward rapidly. On the right, Colonel York's 331st Infantry drove northward through Paramé to the sea, cutting off the enemy garrisons at St. Ideuc and la Varde. On the left, Colonel Crabill's 329th Infantry moved through St. Servan to the very gates of the Citadel.

By 9 August, after five days of attack, the 83d Division had eliminated the major strongpoint on St. Joseph's Hill, had knocked out many individual bunkers and pillboxes, had captured about 3,500 prisoners, and was in possession of St. Servan and Paramé.[36] Yet for all this real achievement, resistance at St. Ideuc and la Varde, in the walled town of St. Malo itself, and fire from the Citadel continued undiminished, while supporting fires from Dinard and Cézembre rained down with telling effect.

The Reduction of Dinard

Though ground forces alone could only shell the Ile de Cézembre with ar-

---

[32] Aubrey, *L'Agonie de Saint-Malo*, pp. 49–50; 83d Div G–2, G–3 Jnl, entry 0945, 8 Jul.

[33] See 83d Div G–2 Per Rpt, 1600, 6 Aug.

[34] Msg, Middleton to Stroh, 5 Aug; Msg, Middleton to Jeter, 1260, 6 Aug; Msg, Macon to Middleton, 0035, 6 Aug; VIII Corps Msg, 6 Aug.

[35] 330th Inf G–3 Rpt, 1130, 9 Aug.

[36] Msg, Macon to Middleton, 1535, 9 Aug.

tillery, Dinard was approachable by land. On 7 August, while the 83d Division was launching its attack on St. Malo, the 121st Infantry (Col. John R. Jeter) had crossed the Rance to destroy the Dinard garrison.[37] Colonel Jeter dispatched a small force to take the surrender of the enemy force at Dinan, which had promised the FFI to capitulate to the Americans. Turning north from Dinan, the main body of the 121st Infantry soon came under heavy artillery fire.

The 121st Infantry quickly discovered that every usable road to Dinard was barred by roadblocks of concrete, rock, felled trees, and barbed wire, each covered by camouflaged strongpoints manned by from twenty to eighty men armed with a high proportion of automatic weapons. The Germans also had constructed underground pillboxes and iron rail fences, strung double-apron barbed wire and concertina entanglements, and laid extensive mine fields. The pillboxes seemed unaffected by American artillery fire. German machine gun, small arms, mortar, and artillery fire harassed every American attempt to blast passageways through the other obstacles.

The 121st Infantry's advance was painfully slow. On the afternoon of 8 August, the 3d Battalion entered the village of Pleurtuit, less than four miles from Dinard. In the process it had reduced three pillboxes by close-in engineer and infantry action. As the troops moved into the village, several German tanks came in from the flanks and cut behind the battalion. Re-establishing a previously destroyed roadblock, German infantrymen isolated the unit.

Despite the support of strong artillery, mortar, and tank destroyer fire, the rest of the 121st Infantry could not break through to the battalion. Discouragement and tragedy marked the efforts. Two artillery planes, after successfully dropping blood plasma to the 3d Battalion, locked wings and crashed, their pilots and observers killed. A third plane was shot down by enemy fire. Two other planes flying observation missions in support of the isolated unit collided and crashed.[38]

The isolation of the 121st Infantry's 3d Battalion confirmed General Macon's impression that in general the regiment's performance west of the Rance had been far from brilliant, but only on 9 August, when St. Joseph's Hill fell, was General Macon able to turn full attention to the situation. When the capitulation of St. Joseph's Hill enabled the 83d Division to occupy St. Servan and Paramé, Macon decided to reorganize his forces, reshape the battle, and give priority to the reduction of Dinard.

Eliminating the Dinard garrison, a task General Macon judged to be relatively easy, would serve four purposes: it would stop part of the effective artillery fire that came from across the Rance; it would block the possibility that German troops might escape from the St. Malo fortress westward toward Brest; it would release the isolated battalion of the 121st Infantry; and it would make possible the return of the 121st to its parent organization for possible participation in a strong attack against Brest, an operation then under discussion.

---

[37] The following account is largely from the 121st Inf AAR, Aug.

[38] VIII Corps G–2 Per Rpt 56, 2400, 10 Aug, and G–2 Weekly Rpt 8, 12 Aug; 83d Div FO 23, 2240, 6 Aug.

BEACH AT DINARD, *showing underwater obstacles planted by the Germans to prevent amphibious landings.*

To help the 121st Infantry take Dinard, General Macon first reshuffled his organic forces by replacing the 331st Infantry in the Paramé sector with the 330th and moving the 331st across the Rance to reinforce the 121st. Finally, he took personal command of the Dinard operation.[39]

On 11 August, when General Macon got a co-ordinated attack on Dinard under way, physical contact with the 3d Battalion, 121st Infantry, still had not been established. The advance through the strongly fortified and stubbornly defended area continued painfully slow. The climax of a discouraging day came in the evening when a counterattack was repulsed with difficulty. "I want Monarch 6 [General Middleton] to know," a somewhat chastened General Macon radioed to the corps headquarters, "that

the resistance we are meeting south of Dinard is more determined than I anticipated."[40]

The defense of Dinard was in the capable hands of Colonel Bacherer, who commanded a kampfgruppe composed in the main of remnants of the *77th Division,* veterans of earlier fighting in the Cotentin. Creating their own field expedients to augment the existing fortifications of the Dinard portion of the St. Malo fortress, the men fought ably. To a surrender ultimatum from General Macon, Bacherer replied defiantly: "Every house must become a fortress, every stone a hiding place, and for every stone we shall fight."[41]

Despite the excellence of the German positions and the will to resist, the Germans could not indefinitely withstand the pressure of two regiments plus the increasing power of a growing number of corps artillery battalions in support. On the afternoon of 12 August, the 331st

---

[39] 83d Div G–2, G–3 Jnl, entries 1110, 1440, and 1800, 9 Aug, and FO 24, 0200, 10 Aug. The 330th Infantry, which had detached a battalion for duty with Task Force A, took control of a battalion and an additional rifle company of the 331st; the 331st took a battalion of the 330th under its control.

[40] Msg, Macon to Evans, 1400, 11 Aug.
[41] 83d Div G–2 Per Rpt 40, 1600, 12 Aug.

Infantry broke through the German line around Pleurtuit. After destroying five bunkers by demolition and assault, knocking out an 88-mm. gun and several vehicles, and taking more than a hundred prisoners, the regiment at last made contact with the isolated battalion of the 121st.[42]

Through three days of isolation, the battalion had retained its integrity in the face of several counterattacks launched with artillery support. Surprisingly, losses were not so high as had been feared—31 killed, 106 wounded, and 16 missing. The kind of courage that had sustained the battalion was exemplified by a heroic act on 9 August, not long after the force was isolated. No sooner had an artillery shell struck the battalion command post, killing the operations and motor officers and seriously wounding the operations sergeant and a radio operator, than a German tank appeared five hundred yards away. Opening fire, the tankers killed several men. For a moment it appeared that the battalion headquarters might be annihilated. Taking matters into his own hands, Pvt. Francis A. Gardner of the Headquarters Company ran toward the tank with a bazooka. Though his first rocket missed, a 57-mm. antitank gun firing at the same time immobilized the tank by a hit on the treads. As the German crew started to abandon the disabled tank, Gardner fired a second time,

striking the turret and killing the crew.[43]

With Pleurtuit in hand, the two regiments continued their attack on 13 August, slowly and systematically reducing individual pillboxes. By the afternoon of 14 August both regiments had entered Dinard and its suburbs. The operation was completed on the following day with the clearing of Dinard and the nearby villages of St. Lunaire and St. Briac-sur-Mer. Bacherer's headquarters, located in a small fort equipped with running water, air conditioning, food, and facilities to withstand siege, was captured. Surrender of the Dinard garrison added almost four thousand prisoners, including Bacherer, to the Allied bag.

When General Middleton remarked that the 121st Infantry didn't appear to have done much, the 83d Division chief of staff explained, "It is hard to tell what they have been up against. Sometimes those things go very slow for a while then all of a sudden they break. . . ."[44] The fact was that one regiment had not been enough west of the Rance but two had been able to do the job.

Siege Operations

While General Macon had personally directed the attack on Dinard, the assistant division commander, General Ferenbaugh, had taken control of the two remaining regiments of the 83d Division. The objectives still to be reduced were the walled city of St. Malo, the Citadel, and the strongpoints of St. Ideuc and la Varde. Ferenbaugh con-

---

[42] Two members of the 121st Infantry, T. Sgt. Milford W. Wilson, who boldly diverted enemy fire to himself to cover his squad's withdrawal, and Capt. Arthur W. Kaiser, who led his company through mine fields, barbed wire, tank barriers, and artillery and machine gun fire to assault enemy positions with bayonet and grenade, were posthumously awarded the DSC.

[43] Annex 1 to 121st Inf AAR, Aug, Summary of Action of 3d Bn 121st Inf from 7 Aug to 12 Aug 44, 4 Sep.

[44] Telecon, Gen Middleton and Col Samuel V. Krauthoff, 1440, 13 Aug.

centrated first on the lesser strongholds, St. Ideuc and la Varde, which were small, mutually supporting forts. St. Ideuc in actuality was an outer defense position for la Varde, which was on the coast. German artillery at Dinard and Cézembre could fire in support.

On 9 August, while the 329th Infantry patrolled and policed the towns of St. Servan and Paramé and prepared to attack the Citadel, the two battalions under the 330th Infantry headquarters attacked toward St. Malo and St. Ideuc. For three days artillery pounded St. Ideuc and infantry and engineers operated against individual pillboxes and bunkers. In the late afternoon of 12 August, after a final burst of concentrated artillery fire and an infantry assault, the 160 surviving defenders capitulated. Without pause the assault battalion moved toward la Varde, and on the following evening, 13 August, captured the fort. Little more than a hundred Germans filed out in surrender.

Meanwhile, the other battalion under the 330th Infantry, with an additional rifle company, had been attacking toward the town of St. Malo. To gain entrance into the walled town, the troops had to secure the Paramé–St. Malo causeway. The attack thus took place across an area that funneled the troops toward the narrow causeway strip. Supported by tanks and tank destroyers, the infantrymen systematically reduced pillboxes and bunkers, measuring their progress by streets. The avenues of Paramé became thoroughfares for bullets and shells, and engineers dynamited passageways from house to house to enable the infantrymen to fight forward from one building to another.

Manned by a small garrison employing machine guns and 20-mm. pieces and overlooking the battle area was the château of St. Malo at the far end of the causeway. The thick walls of the château, designed to withstand medieval siege, proved effective against the engines of modern war.

The immediate objective of the battalion attack was the Casino at the near end of the causeway. After two days of small unit action, the battalion in the late afternoon of 11 August took the blasted and tattered Casino. The château was less than a thousand yards away, but the intervening space was as exposed as a table top.

Although guns then pummeled the château for two days, even high velocity shells from 3-inch tank destroyer guns and 8-inch shells from artillery guns and howitzers seemed to have little effect. Neither did air attack by heavy and medium bombers produce any apparent result. German machine gun fire from the château walls remained too devastating for infantry alone to cross the causeway, and mine fields prevented tanks from approaching.[45]

As the fighting had progressed, the fires within the St. Malo ramparts had become a raging inferno. Flame and smoke obscured many of the defensive positions. To allow about a thousand French civilians still inside the walls to escape the conflagration, a truce was concluded for several hours during the afternoon of 13 August. These and about five hundred hostages and internees, who had been held at a tiny French-built fort offshore, entered American lines. The blaze had no effect on the German garrison in the château, for

---

[45] 330th Inf Rpt, 1220, 12 Aug.

ARTILLERYMEN FIRING 3-INCH GUN ON GERMAN DEFENSES IN ST. MALO

the château had its own fireproof walls separating it from the burning town.

With St. Ideuc and la Varde reduced by 13 August, the entire 330th Infantry gathered to assault St. Malo on the morning of 14 August. As artillery intensified its shelling and fired smoke and high explosive against the château walls, an infantry battalion surged across the causeway, past the château and into the walled town. There were few enemy troops in the charred and still burning buildings, and these were quickly rounded up. The defenders in the château, however, still held out, and their machine guns continued to chat-

ter, discouraging engineers from placing demolition charges against the walls. Despite their virtually impregnable position, the prodding of American artillery fire and the obvious hopelessness of continued resistance finally prompted surrender that afternoon. Prisoners totaled 150.[46]

With this surrender, all organized resistance on the north shore of the St. Malo peninsula came to an end. On two small islands several hundred yards offshore, tiny forts, Fort National and

---

[46] 330th Inf S-3 Rpt, 1800, 14 Aug; 83d Div G-2, G-3 Jnl, entry 1815, 14 Aug.

STREET FIGHTING IN ST. MALO

Grand Bey, each comprising several blockhouses, had to be investigated. At low tide on 16 August a rifle company of the 329th Infantry marched across the sand to Fort National and found it unoccupied. The same company then assaulted Grand Bey. "Went in under a smoke screen, took them by surprise, tossed a few hand grenades, and they gave up." About 150 Germans surrendered.[47]

All this activity was either preliminary or tangential to the main task, reduc-

tion of the Citadel, which was supported by fire from the island of Cézembre. Although there was no longer any possibility of using the destroyed port of St. Malo, the resistance had to be eliminated to keep the Citadel and Cézembre garrisons from interfering by fire with Allied shipping to Granville and Cancale. Continued opposition from them would give courage to the small isolated German groups in Brittany that still refused to surrender, while capitulation might have the effect of softening the will to resist at Lorient and Brest. Also, complete reduction of the St. Malo com-

[47] 83d Div G-2, G-3 Jnl, entry 1555, 16 Aug; 329th Inf Msg and Sitrep, 16 Aug.

plex would free the 83d Division for employment elsewhere.[48]

The Citadel

Since reduction of Cézembre required an amphibious landing and naval support, the immediate problem facing General Macon was how to take the Citadel. Dug deeply into the ground, the Citadel was the heart of the fortress complex.[49] The rocky promontory where it was located was a natural defensive position, as indicated by remaining vestiges of fortifications built by the Gauls to protect the long since vanished village of Aleth. A French fort erected there in the mid-eighteenth century provided the foundation for extensive construction undertaken by the Germans in 1942 with Polish, Belgian, Czech, French, Dutch, Algerian, and Spanish workers laboring voluntarily or otherwise for Todt.

A casemated strongpoint of connected blockhouses, the Citadel was effective against an approach from almost any direction. Where the guns of the Citadel could not fire, pieces at Dinard and Cézembre could. Although the fire power that the fort could deliver was not overwhelmingly impressive—half a dozen field pieces (the largest of 105-mm. caliber), several mortars, and perhaps eighteen or twenty machine guns com-

prised the armament—the weapons were mutually supporting. In the event that invaders would manage somehow to scale the walls, weapons were fixed to cover the interior court. The walls shielding the defenders were of concrete, stone, and steel, so thick that they were virtually impervious to artillery and air bombardment. Inside the fort, aeration and heat ducts, a vast reservoir of water, a large amount of food and supplies, and a subterranean railroad to transport ammunition and heavy equipment facilitated the ability to withstand siege. Blocking the landward approaches were barbed wire, four lines of steel rails placed vertically in cement, and an antitank ditch. Periscopes emerging from the ground level roof of the interior fort provided observation. To improve visibility and fields of fire, the Germans had knocked down several houses in St. Servan, and only the pleading of the mayor had saved a twelfth century church from a similar fate. Personifying the strength of the Citadel was the commander, Aulock, who was determined to bring credit to himself and his forces. According to prisoners, resistance continued "only because of Colonel von Aulock."[50]

As early as 5 August, General Macon was aware that it would be difficult to take the Citadel. When the corps G–3 suggested "Why don't you take 155's and blow it off the map?" the division G–3 answered, "I don't believe we can."[51] He was speaking with more truth than he perhaps realized.

The obvious strength of the St. Malo

---

[48] Telecon, Middleton to Krauthoff, 1440, 13 Aug, 83d Div G–2, G–3 Jnl and File; VIII Corps G–2 Per Rpt 60, 2400, 13 Aug, and G–3 Per Rpt 61, 14 Aug.

[49] The best description of the Citadel is found in Fouque, La Cité, pp. 7–25. See also VIII Corps G–2 Per Rpt 56, 2400, 10 Aug, and G–2 Weekly Per Rpt 8, 12 Aug; ETOUSA Engr Hist Rpt 10, Combat Engineering (Aug, 45); [George], Ninth Air Force, pp. 203, 219.

[50] 83d Div G–2 Per Rpt 35, 1600, 7 Aug.

[51] 83d Div G–2 Per Rpt 33, 1600, 5 Aug; Telecon, Evans and Boyle, 2318, 6 Aug, 83d Div G–2, G–3 Jnl and File.

fortress, and particularly of the Citadel, prompted General Middleton to move heavy artillery of the corps into position to support the 83d Division attack. Before the battle ended, ten artillery battalions, including 8-inch guns, 8-inch howitzers, and 240-mm. howitzers, were pounding the St. Malo defenses.[52] Yet the uncertainty of ammunition hampered operations. Fire plans were often curtailed. No artillery preceded an infantry attack launched on 9 August, for example, and on the following day the stockpiles of shells were so low that only five rounds per piece were available. For several days, some of the battalions fired four rounds per gun per day. Though ammunition shortages were troublesome, the lack of apparent effect against the enemy position was depressing. The walls of the Citadel were too thick to be breached by fire, the enemy pieces too well protected by casemates to be knocked out.[53]

Air attack was similarly ineffective. Fighter-bombers gave excellent assistance when the infantry attacked smaller strongpoints, but they were unable to make an impression on the Citadel. Though two groups of medium bombers attacked the Citadel with 1,000-pound general purpose bombs, these, too, seemed to have no effect.[54] Assured by personal inspection that drastic measures were necessary to reduce the Citadel, General Middleton requested a high-level bombardment by heavy bombers in a mass attack. Unfortu-nately for Middleton, higher headquarters deemed objectives elsewhere of more importance.[55]

Since direct measures to reduce the Citadel seemed to have failed and since an all-out infantry attack would be costly, the 83d Division turned to subterfuge. A loudspeaker manned by the corps Psychological Warfare Service unit attempted without success to persuade the Germans to lay down their arms. Engineers explored the sewage system of St. Malo in the vain hope of discovering at least one conduit close enough to the Citadel to place a decisive demolition charge. A captured German chaplain was permitted to visit the Citadel to ask Aulock to give up. The chaplain returned with the report that Aulock refused to surrender because he was "a German soldier, and a German soldier does not surrender."

The mayor of St. Servan-sur-Mer suggested confidentially that a French lady who knew Aulock rather well might persuade him to lay down his arms and come out. Contact would not be difficult, he revealed, because a line still connected the Citadel and the St. Servan telephone office. Although the unorthodox nature of this suggestion at first prompted hesitation on the part of U.S. commanders, the lady rang up the Citadel anyway. Though Aulock would not come to the phone in person, he informed the lady through a subordinate that he had other things on his mind.[56]

---

[52] Memo, Evans for Maddox, 7 Aug.

[53] 83d Div G–2, G–3 Jnl, entries 0015, 9 Aug, 0935 and 1510, 10 Aug; Msg, Macon to Evans, 1400, 11 Aug.

[54] 83d Div AAR, Aug, and Msg, 1100, 6 Aug; TUSA Info Memos, 5 and 7 Aug; VIII Corps Arty (Air OP) Msg, 1350, 5 Aug.

[55] VIII Corps G–3 Jnl, entries 1030 and 1500, 10 Aug.

[56] Rpt of Maj Marcus, MC, on Mission Behind German Lines, St. Malo, n.d., 83d Div G–2, G–3 Jnl File, Aug; 83d Div AAR (7 Aug); 329th Inf AAR (10 Aug); ETOUSA Engr Hist Rpt 10; Fouque, La Cité, p. 58.

Reinforcing Aulock's indomitable will was information he had received of a major German counterattack directed through Mortain toward Avranches. If this effort succeeded, it would isolate the Americans besieging St. Malo and eventually make them loosen their grip on the city. He announced the news of the counterattack to his troops with enthusiasm and promised that the garrison would be rescued—"if everyone discharges his duty and we hold out just a little longer. . . . Anyone deserting or surrendering," he warned, "is a common dog!" When he learned that the German counterattack had stalled, he still clung to his hope of eventual relief, but his declaration to his soldiers then appeared empty. The 83d Division had by then begun to assault the Citadel.[57]

Having cleared St. Servan and reached the immediate approaches to the Citadel by 9 August, the 329th Infantry prepared an attack as follow-up to an air strike on 11 August that was "going to bomb hell out of the place." Medium bombers appeared over the Citadel on the evening of 11 August and dropped 500-pound general purpose bombs, 100-pound incendiaries, and 1,000-pound semi-armor-piercing bombs. Immediately after the air attack, a rifle company of the 329th Infantry, reinforced by several engineers and three men of the FFI, moved toward the fort to exploit breaches in the defensive works caused by the bombardment. Using Bangalore torpedoes to open passageways through the barbed wire entanglements and the antitank obstacles, the men approached the fort. While a

flame-thrower team sprayed a nearby bunker and the company established security positions, about thirty men, including the three Frenchmen, scaled the wall and reached the interior court. They saw no damage that could have been caused by the air attack, no broken concrete, no flames. Engineers dropped several pole charges through air vents and portholes without apparent effect and set off a few demolition charges without evident result. Suddenly the Germans opened a deadly cross fire with machine guns. Mortar shells began to drop around the walls and artillery shells from Cézembre fell near the fort. Having seen no real breach in the defenses, the assault group departed the fort and the rifle company withdrew.[58]

Colonel Crabill, the regimental commander who had the immediate responsibility for capture of the Citadel, next decided to form two special assault teams for close-in action against the fort. Each team was to have ninety-six infantrymen augmented by demolition groups, security groups, and a special heavy demolition group. While the teams were formed and rehearsed for action, tank destroyers assumed positions from which to deliver direct fire against the fort in the hope of demolishing enemy gun emplacements.[59]

The tank destroyers, assisted by artillery, pounded the Citadel for two days, and on 13 August medium bombers again struck the fort. Soon after the air bombardment a white flag appeared,

[57] 83d Div G–2, G–3 Jnl, entry 1415, 11 Aug, Annex 1 to G–2 Per Rpt 41, 13 Aug, and G–2 Per Rpt 38, 1600, 10 Aug; Fouque, *La Cité*, p. 50.

[58] Telecon, Lt Col Jules Deshotels and Lt Col Herbert H. Hauge, 1018, 11 Aug, 83d Div G–2, G–3 Jnl and File; 329th Inf and VIII Corps G–2 Per Rpt 58, 2400, 12 Aug; Fouque, *La Cité*, pp. 58–62.

[59] 329th Inf AAR (12 Aug)

producing a short-lived jubilation. Aulock wanted only to conclude the truce that had permitted the French civilians to depart the burning town of St. Malo.[60]

After the armistice, the artillery and tank destroyer shelling continued. Rounds expended during one 24-hour period totaled 4,103, despite threatened shortages of ammunition.[61] Again on 15 August medium bombers plastered the Citadel for thirty minutes. At the conclusion of the bomb strike, Colonel Crabill's special assault teams launched an attack, but intense machine gun fire soon drove them back.

Given no apparent alternative but to intensify the siege tactics, General Macon directed that the shelling of the Citadel continue. Two 8-inch guns of the corps artillery came to within 1,500 yards of the fort to deliver direct fire on portholes and vents. Two companies of 4.2-inch mortars that had been firing on the fort intermittently increased the proportion of white phosphorus to high explosive. Air liaison personnel at the 12th Army Group planned a bombing mission employing "gasoline jell" bombs, not only to eliminate resistance but also to experiment on the effectiveness of what later came to be known as napalm.[62] The climax of these efforts was to be an air attack projected for the afternoon of 17 August.

Forty minutes before the scheduled arrival of the planes, a white flag appeared over the Citadel. When several German soldiers emerged from the fort, an American officer went to meet them, though wary that this might be another false alarm. It was not. Aulock was indeed ready to surrender. Diverting the bombers to Cézembre, which manifested no sign of imminent capitulation, the 83d Division began to accept the surrender of four hundred Citadel defenders who emerged. Among them was Aulock, freshly-shaved, dress-uniformed, and insolent.[63]

Why had he surrendered—this commander who had sworn to defend to the last man, the last cartridge, the last stone? Still with men and cartridges, Aulock was far from having to resort to stones. His supply of food, water, and air was abundant. Allied plane attacks had hardly been felt inside the fort. The shock of impact from artillery shells had been slight. The Americans were no closer to the Citadel than they had been eight days before.

As the story emerged, it became clear that two factors had caused Aulock to renounce his vows. First, direct hits by 8-inch guns aimed singly and at specific targets at virtual point blank range had penetrated several firing apertures in the fort and had destroyed a few of the larger artillery pieces and machine gun emplacements. Second, Aulock's determination notwithstanding, American capture of the individual strongpoints of the St. Malo fortress had intensified a psychological malaise deriving from the sensation of being surrounded and trapped. Morale of the troops had deteriorated to the point where further resistance seemed senseless.

Despite his capitulation, Aulock had done his duty well. He had rendered

---

[60] 83d Div G-2, G-3 Jnl, entry 1413, 13 Aug; 329th Inf AAR, Aug.

[61] 83d Div G-2, G-3 Jnl, entry 1203, 14 Aug.

[62] Telecon, Evans and Krauthoff, 1945, 16 Aug, 83d Div G-2, G-3 Jnl and File; 329th Inf AAR (17 Aug).

[63] 329th Inf AAR (17 Aug) Fouque, *La Cité*, plate 24.

THE CITADEL AFTER IT WAS TAKEN BY U.S. TROOPS

the port of St. Malo useless to the Americans. He had held up an entire division and substantial supporting forces for almost two weeks and thus had prevented the VIII Corps from taking decisive action against the fortress ports of Lorient and Brest.

The surrender of the Citadel cleared the St. Malo–Dinard sector with the exception of the garrison on the island of Cézembre. The 83d Division had completed an impressive action. As against comparatively light losses, the division had taken more than ten thousand prisoners.[64]

[64] 83d Div Annexes 1 and 2 to G–2 Per Rpt 44, 16 Aug.

The efforts of the division during this period had nevertheless been strenuous and, as a measure of rest and rehabilitation, the troops received a different type of mission. Originally scheduled to help in the reduction of Brest as soon as St. Malo was captured, the 83d Division instead took responsibility for the "back area" of the Rennes–Brest supply line and eventually patrolled Brittany as far south as the Loire River. As the division dispersed throughout the area south of Rennes in a welcome respite after the close-in siege action, two infantry battalions of the 330th—one at Dinard and the other at St. Malo, both aided by the FFI—policed the coastline and guarded

INTERIOR OF THE CITADEL AFTER THE SURRENDER

against German infiltration from Cézembre.[65]

Cézembre

Four thousand yards offshore, the tiny island of Cézembre, half a mile long and a quarter of a mile wide, by its position opposite the mouth of the Rance River controlled the deep water channel to St. Malo and the sea approaches to Granville and Cancale. Its coastal guns had been out of range of the 83d Division artillery pieces during the early part of the battle, and its fire had been a nasty source of harassment. The division had requested the island blasted "as quickly as we can and as often as we can," and the VIII Corps had promised to "work on it from the air and naval angle." Bombers attacked the island during the night of 6 August and again on 11 August, but naval gunfire did not become available until much later. Meanwhile, the corps had brought heavy artillery into the St. Malo area, and from 9 August on the pieces shelled the island to prevent interference

---

[65] Memo, Evans for Cross, 11 Aug; Memo, Middleton for Macon, 14 Aug, 83d Div G-2, G-3 Jnl File; VIII Corps G-3 Per Rpt 61, 14 Aug, and Msg, 2300, 15 Aug; 83d Div G-2, G-3 Jnl, entries 2253, 15 Aug, 0955, 16 Aug, 1132, 16 Aug, and 2050, 17 Aug; Notes by General Ferenbaugh on Middleton-Macon conversation at St. Servan, 16 Aug, dated 17 Aug; Additional Notes from Middleton, 1000, 18 Aug.

BOMBING OF ILE DE CÉZEMBRE, OFF ST. MALO

with the ground action on the main-land.[66]

The thirty-five planes diverted to Cézembre from the attack on the Citadel on 17 August created huge columns of smoke with their napalm bombs.[67] Hoping that fires started by the bombardment would intensify the adverse effect Aulock's capitulation was sure to have on the garrison, and expecting that both factors would enlist a readiness to quit Cézembre, General Macon authorized Maj. Joseph M. Alexander and two enlisted men, as well as an accredited civilian motion picture cameraman, to demand that the Germans relinquish the island. On 18 August the party rowed across the St. Malo bay. At Cézembre, a noncommissioned officer met the boat and conducted Alexander and his interpreter to the fortress commander, a lieutenant colonel who did not give his name. Neither arrogant nor boastful, the German commander stated that the last order he had received from higher headquarters instructed him to maintain his defense. Until he received a countermanding order, he would continue to do just that. Informed that the mainland was completely under American control, he declared that he did not understand how that changed his situation. Reminded that Aulock had surrendered the day before, he countered that he had not exhausted his ammunition on Cézembre. After a courteous conversation lasting fifteen minutes, the Americans were escorted back to the beach and helped to launch their boat for the return trip.[68]

According to Alexander's observations, Cézembre was a shambles. Shelling and bombardment had demolished or badly damaged the few houses and buildings, destroyed a narrow-gauge railway designed to carry ammunition from the

[66] 83d Div G-2, G-3 Jnl, entries 1841 and 2035, 6 Aug, and 0930, 9 Aug; [George], Ninth Air Force, p. 220.

[67] 83d Div G-3 Per Rpt 45, 1600, 17 Aug; [George], Ninth Air Force, p. 174.

[68] Ltr, Alexander to Macon, Rpt of Parley on Isle de Cézembre, 18 Aug.

beach to gun positions, created large craters, and exploded an ammunition dump, scattering shells and debris throughout the island. About three hundred men comprised the garrison. From tunnels dug into rock, the men manned those coastal guns that still functioned.[69]

No further effort was made immediately against Cézembre. A week later, when preparations were being completed for a strong attack against Brest, higher headquarters decided to eliminate the nuisance of Cézembre. The 330th Infantry headquarters returned to St. Malo to direct training for an amphibious operation. Arrangements were made for assault boats and special equipment. Softening up operations commenced on 30 August when two groups of planes bombed the island. On 31 August twenty-four P–38's dropped napalm and three hundred heavy bombers struck with high explosive. Several 8-inch howitzers and guns shelled the island "day and night" with particular effort to destroy water tanks. Another parley with the island commander disclosed "that he will fight to the last drop of water." [70]

Faced with this attitude, the Allies increased their pressure on 1 September. Medium bombers of both the IX Bomber Command and the RAF Bomber Command opened an aerial assault that ended with thirty-three P–38's dropping napalm. A British warship, H.M.S. *Warspite*, fired salvos of 15-inch armor-piercing projectiles. Field artillery from the mainland fired 155-mm.,

8-inch, and 240-mm. shells at embrasures, portholes, and tunnel entrances. After this display of power, another demand for surrender was transmitted to the garrison. Again the German commander replied that he lacked permission to surrender.[71]

On the following day, 2 September, as the 330th Infantry prepared to make an amphibious assault on Cézembre, the garrison raised a white flag. The landing craft immediately conducted troops to the island and evacuated 1 German officer, 320 men, and 2 Italian officers. Although the fortifications had been severely damaged, the reason for the capitulation was a shortage of water—the distilling plant had been destroyed.[72]

So ended the battle of St. Malo, a battle that had been unexpected in its inception, in its difficulty, and in its duration. German troops, although isolated, had demonstrated convincingly the value of military discipline in carrying out the Fuehrer's will. An action of local significance by mid-August, a rear area operation more than a hundred miles behind the front, the combat nevertheless fulfilled Hitler's strategic design.

From the American point of view, the results of the Brittany campaign produced mixed reactions. August had come in like a whirlwind, gone out in a calm. The 4th Armored Division had seized Rennes by 4 August, had con-

---

[69] See 330th Inf AAR (2 Sep).

[70] Memo, Lt Col Frederick G. Cain for Col Evans, 31 Aug.

[71] 330th Inf AAR's Aug and Sep, 44; [George], Ninth Air Force, p. 174; Msg, ANCXF to SHAEF, 2215, 28 Aug, SGS SHAEF File 381, Post-OVERLORD Plng; 12th AGp Memos for Gen Kibler, 29 Aug, 12th AGp File 371.3, Mil Objectives, I.

[72] 330th Inf AAR, Sep; [George], Ninth Air Force, p. 221; 12th AGp Immed Rpt 49, Organization and Effect of Heavy Arty, 9 Sep.

ST. MALO PRISONERS MARCHING OFF TO INTERNMENT

tained 11,000 Germans in Lorient by 9 August, and had captured Nantes on 13 August. The 6th Armored Division had driven more than 200 miles down the center of the peninsula, had penned some 30,000 Germans into the fortress of Brest and had destroyed part of a German division. Task Force A had swept the northern shore of Brittany to secure the Brest–Rennes railroad and to secure the beach of St. Michel-en-Grève. In contrast with these swift exploiting thrusts, the 83d Division had besieged the fortress of St. Malo, and only after a "slugging match had slowly hammered down pillboxes, barricades, and fortified areas" was the mainland stronghold re-

duced by 17 August, the Ile de Cézembre two weeks later, by 2 September.[73]

The Brittany peninsula had been completely cut off, and a sizable segment of France, the ancient province of Brittany, had been liberated with dispatch. No organized resistance remained in the interior, for the Germans who remained in Brittany had been herded into Lorient, St. Nazaire, and Brest, where they could only escape by sea or await American siege operations.[74]

Despite these achievements, the Brittany campaign had not secured the basic strategic objectives that had motivated

[73] VIII Corps AAR, Aug.
[74] VIII Corps G–2 Est 6, 1800, 15 Aug.

it. The major ports of Brittany could not be used. St. Malo was destroyed beyond hope of immediate repair. Nantes was demolished. Brest, Lorient, and St. Nazaire were occupied by enemy forces in naturally good defensive positions bolstered by extensive fortifications. Construction of a harbor at Quiberon Bay could not be started. The logistical fruits of the action were the minor harbors of Cancale and St. Michel-en-Grève and the railway from Rennes to Morlaix. Although the VIII Corps gathered its forces for a mighty effort at Brest at the end of August, logistical planners were by then looking elsewhere for major ports of entry.

Failure to have attained the strategic goals of the operation did not appear terribly important in mid-August. Events occurring farther to the east had long since relegated the action in Brittany to secondary status. The eastern development of the breakout was overflowing Normandy into the ancient provinces of Anjou and Maine and promising to bring the campaign in western France to a climax.

PART FIVE

BREAKOUT TO THE EAST

CHAPTER XXII

Week of Decision

As operations had begun in Brittany during the early days of August, Allied and German commanders were making decisions that markedly altered the development of the campaign. The immediate consequence of the decisions on both sides decreased the importance of Brittany. Normandy remained the stage for continuing action that would soon become vital.

The German Decision

The seriousness of the German situation at the time of the American breakthrough to Avranches was not lost on Hitler.[1] The Balkans and Finland were about to be lost, and there were indications that Turkey might soon enter the war against Germany. Hitler considered these events as a kind of external defection over which he had little control. The *Putsch* of July 20th, on the other hand, was an internal defection that threatened him personally, and he was increasingly uneasy over the feeling that disloyalty had permeated the entire

German military organization even to the highest levels. Soviet advances sent his Eastern Front reeling, but because construction had been started in July on a new defense line stretching from East Prussia to the Carpathians, Hitler hoped that his forces would somehow hold. His main concern lay in the west, for he had long considered the west the vital sector of what had become, at least for the moment, a defensive war.

The breakthrough on the Western Front posed the ominous possibility that the Germans might have to withdraw from France. With France lost, the threat of Allied penetration of the German homeland would become immediate.

The Seine River, with its deep bends and twists, was difficult to defend and could be no more than a temporary rallying position, but between the Seine and the Rhine were a number of historic water obstacles where the Germans could hope to stop the Allies short of the German border. To utilize the water barriers, Jodl sketched a major defensive belt across Belgium and France (and into northern Italy) that consisted of two lines: the Somme–Marne–Saône River line, and the Albert Canal–Meuse River line, both anchored on the Vosges Mountains.

Behind these lines were the permanent fortifications of the West Wall

---

[1] The following is from: *OKW Besprechung des Fuehrers mit Generaloberst Jodl am 31.7.1944. in der Wolfschanze; Der Westen* (Schramm); Memo for Rcd, Warlimont to Eberbach, 3 Aug, *Fifth Panzer Army KTB*, Annex 248; MS # C–099c (Warlimont); Jodl Diary; *OB WEST, a Study in Command*, pp. 46–47; Bauer, Organization of the German Defenses in the West in the Fall of 1944 (1936–44), MS R–20.

(Siegfried Line), protecting the approaches to the German border. Although neglected for four years and partially dismantled, the West Wall in the summer of 1944 was not a negligible defensive factor. Late in July Jodl ordered the West Wall repaired and rearmed and the river lines in France prepared for defense. The Todt Organization was to cease work on the Atlantic Wall and commence construction of defensive positions along the newly projected lines inland. Authority was granted to impress civilians for work on roads and defenses in Belgium and France.

In addition to the erection of defensive positions, Hitler enunciated on the last day of July a two-point policy directed against Allied logistics. He ordered his forces to deny the Allies ports of entry on the Continent and, if a withdrawal from France became necessary, to destroy the transportation system there by demolishing railroads, bridges, and communications.

Though withdrawal from France was extremely undesirable, Hitler foresaw the possible necessity of it. He indicated as much by ordering the movement of some units out of the Balkans and Italy for defense of the homeland, thereby accepting the probability of losing the Balkans immediately and the calculated risk of having to withdraw in Italy to the Alps. Hitler also quickened preparations for raising a reserve force within Germany.

Stabilizing the Normandy front appeared the only alternative to withdrawal from France. On the credit side, a front line in Normandy would be the shortest and most economical of any

possible in the west. On the debit side, failure to stabilize the front in Normandy would—because of Allied air superiority—involve the German forces in mobile warfare under unfavorable conditions.

Reluctant to accept the hazards of mobile warfare in these circumstances and needing time to prepare rearward defenses, Hitler decided to take the risks and continue to fight in Normandy. Since the war in western Europe had reached a critical stage, he took responsibility for the battle upon himself. Creating a small staff taken from members of the OKW planning section (WFSt) to help him, Hitler sought to recreate the conditions of static warfare while at the same time preparing to withdraw in the event of failure. By this move, Hitler in effect assumed the functions of theater commander and filled the virtual vacuum in the chain of command that had existed since Rommel's incapacitation and Kluge's assumption of dual command of *Army Group B* and *OB WEST*. Ordering Kluge to close the gap in the left portion of the German defenses and to anchor the front on Avranches, Hitler forbade the commanders in the field to look backward toward defensive lines in the rear.

As seen by the staff of *OB WEST*, the situation in Normandy at the beginning of August, while critical, could have been worse.[2] The recent appearance on the Continent of Canadian units and other formations that had been thought to belong to Patton's army group, and the commitment in Normandy of ever-growing numbers of close-support planes indicated that a second large-scale Allied

---

[2] *OB WEST, a Study in Command*, pp. 55ff; *OB WEST KTB*, 30 Jul, and *Anlage 943*.

strategic landing in western Europe was no longer likely. Also, the Allied break-out from the limited continental lodgment and the development of mobile warfare underscored the fact that the Allies no longer needed to make another landing. The knowledge that the Germans in Normandy already faced the bulk of the Allied forces in western Europe was somewhat of a relief.

Two possibilities seemed in order. The first was the more cautious: to break off the battle in Normandy and withdraw behind delaying action to the Seine while *Army Group G* evacuated southern France. This would have the virtue of saving the main body of German troops, though admittedly at the expense of heavy losses, especially in matériel. Eberbach later claimed that, when Warlimont visited the front about 1 August, he, Eberbach, suggested an immediate withdrawal to the Seine, a recommendation Warlimont rejected as being "politically unbearable and tactically impractical." [3]

OB WEST could understand OKW's reluctance to withdraw, for pulling back to the Seine would more than likely be the first step toward retirement behind the West Wall. If the Germans did not succeed in holding the relatively short front in Normandy, then only at the West Wall—another relatively short defensive line that could be reinforced—was there a prospect of success. The consequences of such a decision would be hard to accept—surrender of France with all the political and economic implications of it, loss of long-range projectile bases along the Pas-de-Calais, unfavor-

able reaction in Italy that might lead to the loss of a region valuable to the German war economy, withdrawals on other fronts to project the homeland.

The other alternative was to stabilize the front in Normandy. To do so, the breach at Avranches would have to be closed, a step that appeared tactically feasible at the beginning of August. If the gap were not closed, there would be an unavoidable crisis on the front, for the likelihood of being able to pull back across the Seine at that late date would be slim.

As events developed, Hitler left *OB WEST* no choice. He ordered the forces in the west to continue fighting in Normandy even as Kluge was already trying to remedy the situation at Avranches.

Although all of Kluge's available forces in Normandy were committed by the first day of August, one armored and six infantry divisions were on the way to reinforce the front. The *84th* and *85th Divisions* were moving from the Pas-de-Calais toward Falaise. The *89th Division* had just crossed the Seine River, and the *331st Division* was in the process of being ferried across. Parts of the *363d Division* were already in the *Seventh Army* rear and were being committed in the *LXXXIV Corps* sector. From southern France came the *708th Division*, which was crossing the Loire River near Angers, and the *9th Panzer Division*, which was moving toward the Loire for eventual assembly near Alençon. Whether all would get to the front in time to be of use before the situation in the Avranches sector deteriorated completely was the vital question. It appeared that at least three divisions, the *363d*, the *84th*, and the *89th*, would be

[3] MS # A-922 (Eberbach)

available at Avranches during the first week in August.[4] (*Map IX*)

Except at Avranches, the situation along the front was far from desperate. Eberbach's *Panzer Group West,* which was to change its name on 5 August to the *Fifth Panzer Army,* was actively engaged only in one sector. The *LXXXVI Corps,* the *I SS Panzer Corps,* and the *LXXIV Corps* controlled quiet zones, as did the *LVIII Panzer Corps* headquarters, recently brought up from southern France. Only the *II SS Panzer Corps* was fighting hard by 2 August, having committed all three of its divisions against the British attack launched on 30 July south of Caumont toward the town of Vire.

Hausser's *Seventh Army* front, on the other hand, was hard pressed. In a narrow sector just east of the Vire River, the *II Parachute Corps* had only the *3d Parachute Division* to defend the town of Vire. West of the Vire River to the Forêt de St. Sever, the *XLVII Panzer Corps* controlled the *2d Panzer Division* (which had absorbed the *352d Division)* and the *2d SS Panzer Division* (which had absorbed the remnants of *Panzer Lehr* and the *17th SS Panzer Grenadiers).* On the left, *LXXXIV Corps* directed the *353d Division* and the *116th Panzer Division* on a front from the St. Sever forest to the Sée River. Provisional units, formed from remnants and stragglers (including the *5th Parachute Division)* and operating under the staff of the *275th Division,* covered the gap south of the Sée River and east of

Avranches, and the weak *91st Infantry Division* was at Rennes.[5]

Since the *Seventh Army* (or any other outside ground headquarters) could not exercise effective command of the *XXV Corps* in Brittany, Kluge placed the corps directly under *Army Group B* as a matter of administration. Writing off the *XXV Corps* in this manner in accordance with Hitler's orders emphasized the floating nature of the Normandy left flank. The weak forces at Rennes were obviously unable to offer sustained resistance. A large opening between the Sée and Loire Rivers invited American exploitation eastward toward the Paris–Orléans gap.[6] To cover the gap thus exposed, Kluge on 2 August ordered the *First Army* to extend its control northward from the Biscay coast of France to the Loire River, take command of the forces along the Loire, and hold bridgeheads on the north bank at the crossing sites between Nantes and Orléans. On the same day Kluge also ordered the *LXXXI Corps* headquarters to hurry south from the coastal sector between the Seine and the Somme Rivers to take control of the arriving *708th Infantry* and *9th Panzer Divisions* on a refused *Seventh Army* left flank in the Domfront–Alençon sector.[7] With these measures taken, Kluge turned his atten-

---

[4] Telecons, Kluge and Speidel, 1025, 1 Aug, Gersdorff and Helmdach, 1055, 1 Aug, Tempelhoff and Zimmerman, 1230, 1 Aug, *AGp B KTB;* Tempelhoff Telecon, 1220, 1 Aug, *AGp B KTB; OB WEST KTB,* 1 Aug.

[5] Situation Maps, 3 and 4 Aug, *LXXXI Corps Anlagen zum KTB, 1. Teil (Karten),* 2.–24.VIII.44 (CRS 61 659/9); MS # B–741 (Ziegelmann); MS # A–894 (Gersdorff); MS # B–445 (Krueger); MS # B–179 (Hausser); *AGp B KTB,* 1 Aug; Hodgson, R–54 and R–58.

[6] A corridor devoid of major natural obstacles, bounded by the Seine and the Loire Rivers.

[7] MS # B–732 (Hold); MS # B–807 (Kuntzen); Msg, *Seventh Army* to *LXXXI Corps,* 3 Aug, *LXXXI Corps Befehle H Gr u. Armee;* Telecon, Gersdorff and Wiese, 0945, 4 Aug, *LXXXI Corps KTB.*

tion to regaining Avranches as the new anchor point of the defensive line in Normandy.

If Avranches were to be regained, a counterattack had to be launched immediately. Where to get the troops for it was the problem, and Hitler provided the solution. On 2 August, in ordering a strong armored counterattack, Hitler authorized a slight withdrawal to a shorter line (Thury-Harcourt through the town of Vire to the western edge of the Forêt de St. Sever). A shortened front and the arrival of new units would give Kluge the means with which to counterattack to Avranches.[8]

Specifically, Hitler first thought of disengaging the *II SS Panzer Corps* (the *9th SS*, the *10th SS*, and the *21st Panzer Divisions*) for the counterattack, but Kluge felt this impossible because of the British pressure south of Caumont. Kluge recommended that the *XLVII Panzer Corps*, which was nearer the critical sector, make the effort with the *2d* and *2d SS Panzer Divisions* reinforced at first by the *LXXXIV Corps'* *116th Panzer Division* and later by the incoming *9th Panzer Division* (after the latter moved from Alençon to Sourdeval near Mortain). Since there was some question whether the *9th* would arrive in Alençon in time to participate, Kluge suggested that additional armor be secured by pulling the *1st SS* or the *12th SS Panzer Division* out of the Caen sector where the British appeared to have become quiet, a risk that Eberbach had agreed to accept. Jodl approved Kluge's proposals.[9]

This plan accepted, Kluge directed Hausser to launch an attack with the *XLVII Panzer Corps*, using the *2d SS,* the *2d,* and the *116th Panzer Divisions* in an initial effort and the *1st SS Panzer Division* as an exploiting force. The divisions were to be relieved from the line by 6 August through withdrawal to a shorter front.[10]

While the *LXXIV* and *II SS Panzer Corps* in the *Panzer Group West* sector prepared to withdraw during the night of 3 August in order to disengage the *1st SS Panzer Division,* Hausser planned to disengage the other three divisions from his *Seventh Army* front by executing a three-phase withdrawal. The *2d, 2d SS,* and *116th Panzer Divisions* were to be pulled out of the line in that order on three successive nights starting 3 August and assembled in the area east of Mortain by 6 August. To make this possible, the *II Parachute Corps* was to extend its responsibility to the west to take control of a regiment of the *353d Division,* and the *LXXXIV Corps* was to integrate the arriving *363d* and *84th Divisions* into its front. The *XLVII Panzer Corps,* which was to direct the attack, received the *275th* as left flank cover. With three armored divisions moving abreast in an initial assault and a fourth ready to exploit initial success, the *XLVII Panzer Corps* commander, Funck, was to attack after dark on 6 August without artillery preparation.

---

[8] *Der Westen* (Schramm), p. 79; *OB WEST KTB,* entry 2330, 2 Aug, and *Anlage 1050;* Telecon, Kluge and Buttlar-Brandenfels, 1035, 3 Aug, *AGp B KTB.*

[9] Telecons, Kluge and Buttlar-Brandenfels, 1035,

[3] Aug, Kluge and Eberbach, 1135, 3 Aug, and Kluge and Jodl, 1210, 3 Aug, *AGp B KTB.*

[10] Telecon, Kluge and Hausser, 1615, 3 Aug, *AGp B KTB;* Kluge to Jodl, 1745, 3 Aug, *OB WEST KTB,* and *Anlage 1068; AGp B Operationsbefehle,* 3 Aug.

GENERAL HAISLIP

His objective was to reach the Cotentin west coast and secure Avranches.[11]

Commitment of a Corps

While the Germans thus made their decision and laid their plans, the Americans, who were exploiting the Avranches gap, were also coming to a decision that was to alter the OVERLORD plan. The first move in the new direction of what was to be a profound change lay in the circumstances of the commitment of the XV Corps.

Commanded by Maj. Gen. Wade H. Haislip, a West Pointer who had fought in France during World War I and had

recently been the Assistant Chief of Staff, G–1, on the War Department General Staff, the XV Corps headquarters had arrived on the Continent near the middle of July as a Third Army component. Because the single mission accorded the Third Army in early planning was securing Brittany and its ports, and because XV Corps was to become operational immediately upon commitment of the Third Army, it was expected that XV Corps would share the Brittany mission with VIII Corps. Yet the situation created by COBRA raised doubt as to the need of two corps in Brittany; thus the exact role of the XV Corps remained undefined except for projected commitment near Avranches.[12]

There was even doubt about the divisions the corps would control. Though the 4th Armored Division had been tentatively assigned to XV Corps, it was well employed as part of VIII Corps. To give XV Corps an armored force, Patton promised that if the 4th could not be made available, the recently arrived and assembled 5th Armored Division would be assigned. Because the 35th and 5th Infantry Divisions, also slated to come under the XV Corps, were in the V Corps sector, far from Avranches, it seemed more convenient to use the 83d and 90th Divisions, which had been pinched out near Périers. Trying to be ready for any eventuality, General Haislip alerted the 83d and 90th Division commanders to their possible assignment to the corps while at the same time keeping a close check on

[11] Msg, *Seventh Army* to *LXXXI Corps,* 3 Aug, *LXXXI Corps KTB, Anlagen, Befehle Heeres Gruppe, Armee, usw,* containing text of Hausser's order; Telecon, Kluge and Gersdorff, 1615, 3 Aug, *AGp B KTB; Der Westen* (Schramm); *OB WEST KTB,* 4 Aug.

[12] TUSA Outline Plan, Opn OVERLORD, and Annex 1, Maps 4 and 5, TUSA AAR; 12th AGp Ltr of Instrs 1, 29 Jul; XV Corps Memo, Conf at the Office of the Asst CofS, G–3, TUSA, 281000 Jul 44, 29 Jul, XV Corps CofS's Jnl.

the 4th Armored "so that intelligent orders for it to side-slip into [the] zone of XV Corps" could be issued promptly. On 1 August Haislip learned that he was to control the 5th Armored, 83d, and 90th Divisions, but this too was to be changed.[13]

Where the XV Corps was to be employed was also somewhat a matter of conjecture. Early plans had projected a XV Corps advance along the north shore of Brittany, but at the end of July a zone on the left of VIII Corps seemed more probable. Since the immediate Third Army objective was the Rennes–Fougères area, it was reasonable to expect the XV Corps to be directed on Fougères as a preliminary for a subsequent advance to the southwest toward Quiberon. Early on 1 August, General Haislip learned that "the projected operation of the Corps toward the southwest had been cancelled, and that [a] new operation would be [started] towards the southeast."[14]

The reason for the change lay in the constriction and vulnerability of the Avranches bottleneck. To prevent German interference with American troop passage, a protective barrier was necessary. To ameliorate traffic congestion, a wider corridor was desirable. To attain these ends became the first combat mission of XV Corps, and to achieve

GENERAL EDDY

it the corps was to enter the gap between the diverging VIII and VII Corps. On 1 August the VIII Corps left flank extended almost to Rennes, while the VII Corps right flank reached for Brécey and beyond. Although the distance between Rennes and Brécey provided more than adequate room for the new corps, the few miles between Avranches and Brécey presented a problem. The approach march in particular was bound to be difficult, for units of XV Corps would have to pass through the already congested rear areas of the two adjacent corps.[15]

Although General Haislip wanted to move his armored component to the fore immediately in order to exploit German disorganization, traffic congestion was so bad that after two days the 5th Armored Division was still north of the Sée River.

---

[13] XV Corps Memos, Conf at G–3 Office, Hq Third U.S. Army, 281600 Jul, 29 Jul, and Conf at CP VIII Corps, 282000 Jul 44, 29 Jul, both in XV Corps CofS's Jnl; Telecon, Allan and Borders, 30 Jul, and Memo, Haislip to Col Pearson Menoher, 31 Jul, both in XV Corps G–3 Jnl; XV Corps AAR, Aug 44.

[14] Memo, Goldstein for Menoher, 1 Aug; XV Corps Warning Order, 1000, 1 Aug. Unless otherwise noted, all sources cited in this section are from the XV Corps G–3 Journal and File.

[15] XV Corps G–3 Memo, 2 Aug.

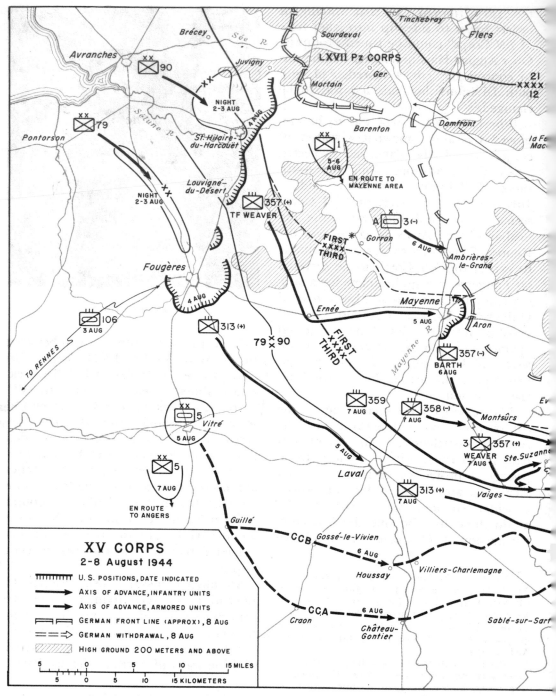

Brécey •   Sée R.   Sourdeval   Tinchebray   Flers

LXVII Pz CORPS

Avranches

Juvigny   Ger

⊠⊠ 90

NIGHT
2-3 AUG   Mortain   4 AUG

Domfront

21
XXXX
12

la Fe
Mac

⊠⊠ 79

Pontorson   Sélune R.

St-Hilaire-
du-Harcouët   Barenton

⊠⊠ 1
5-6
AUG

EN ROUTE TO
MAYENNE AREA

NIGHT
2-3 AUG   Louvigné-
du-Désert

⊠ 357 (+)
TF WEAVER   A ▭ 3 (-)

Gorron   6 AUG   Ambrières-
le-Grand

FIRST
XXXX ✱
THIRD

Fougères   4 AUG

Ernée   Mayenne   5 AUG   Aron

⊟ 106
3 AUG   TO RENNES

⊠ 313 (+)   79 ×× 90   FIRST
XXXX
THIRD   Mayenne R.   ⊠ 357 (-)
BARTH
6 AUG

Ev

⊠⊠ 5
Vitré
5 AUG   ⊠ 359
7 AUG   ⊠ 358 (-)
7 AUG   Montsûrs

3 ⊠ 357 (+)
WEAVER   Ste.Suzann
7 AUG

⊠⊠ 5
7 AUG

EN ROUTE
TO ANGERS   5 AUG   Laval   ⊠ 313 (+)
7 AUG   Vaiges

Guillé   CCB   Gossé-le-Vivien   6 AUG   Villiers-Charlemagne
Houssay

CCA   6 AUG
Craon   Château-
Gontier   Sablé-sur-Sart

XV CORPS
2-8 August 1944

⊔⊔⊔⊔⊔⊔⊔	U.S. POSITIONS, DATE INDICATED
➙	AXIS OF ADVANCE, INFANTRY UNITS
➟ ➟ ➟	AXIS OF ADVANCE, ARMORED UNITS
⊏⊏⊐	GERMAN FRONT LINE (APPROX), 8 AUG
⇛	GERMAN WITHDRAWAL, 8 AUG
▨▨▨	HIGH GROUND 200 METERS AND ABOVE

5   0   5   10   15 MILES

5   0   5   10   15 KILOMETERS

MAP 12

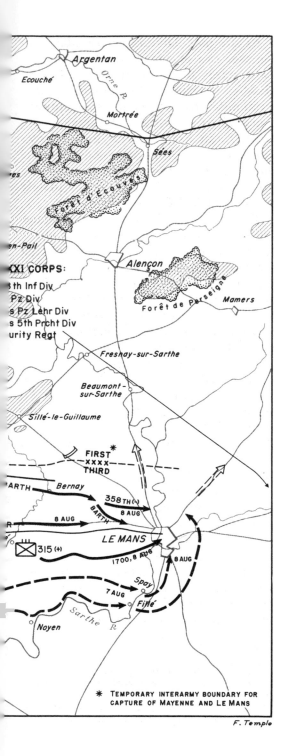

F. Temple

There, the armor was temporarily halted to conform with new instructions from the army group commander, General Bradley.[16] Fortunately, the 90th Division was able to take over the first corps assignment of moving to Avranches and eastward to take blocking positions between the Sée and the Sélune Rivers.[17] *(Map 12)*

The 90th Division's reputation at the beginning of August was still somewhat blemished. The division's part in the battle of the hedgerows during July had done little to alter the general impression that the 90th was far from being combat effective, and there had been talk of breaking it up to provide replacements for other units.[18] However, under a new commander, Brig. Gen. Raymond S. McLain, the 90th was to have another chance to make good.

General McLain's first mission was to capture St. Hilaire-du-Harcouët, a town on the Sélune River not quite fifteen air miles southeast of Avranches. Possession of a Sélune River bridgehead at St. Hilaire would widen the Avranches corridor and establish an anchor point for blocking positions east of the coastal bottleneck. With St. Hilaire in hand, McLain was to set up a defensive line north to the Sée River to block enemy movement westward between the Sée and the Sélune.[19]

---

[16] Notes taken at G–3 Mtg, XV Corps CP, 0900, 1 Aug; Telecon, Haislip and Oliver, 2345, 2 Aug; Memo, Col Menoher for Maj Gen Lunsford E. Oliver, 2245, 2 Aug; XV Corps Warning Order, 1800, 2 Aug.

[17] 90th Div Msg, 1 Aug; Memo, Menoher for VIII Corps, 1 Aug.

[18] Ltr, Lt Gen Raymond S. McLain (Ret.) to Mr. John B. Spore, ed., *Army Combat Forces Journal*, 16 Mar 54, author's extract in OCMH Files.

[19] 90th Div FO 17, 1 Aug, and AAR, Aug.

A task force under the command of Lt. Col. George B. Randolph was to screen the movement of a larger force under Lt. Col. Christian E. Clarke, Jr., that was to spearhead the division advance.[20] The leading units began to move an hour before midnight, 1 August. Although traffic was heavy and the troops had a "tough time" moving during darkness, Task Force Randolph swept aside a small number of enemy rear guards and on the morning of 2 August reached St. Hilaire. The main bridge was still intact. When Task Force Clarke arrived, the artillery took defiladed positions, other support units built up a base of fire, and an infantry skirmish line followed by light tanks charged across several hundred yards of open ground and crossed the bridge in the face of enemy shelling. The troops quickly eliminated the half-hearted resistance in the town. So rapid and aggressive had the assault been that casualties were few. With St. Hilaire in hand, General McLain brought the remainder of the 90th Division forward to a line north of the town in order to establish contact with the VII Corps at Juvigny, thus erecting a barrier against German attack from the east.[21] The performance of the division at St. Hilaire was far different from that in the Cotentin and augured well.

As the 90th Division consolidated in the area east of Avranches, General McLain received an order from General Haislip to extend his defensive line seven miles from St. Hilaire south toward Fougères to the village of Louvigné-du-Désert. In compliance, Task Forces Randolph and Clarke occupied Louvigné shortly after midnight, 2 August.[22] By this advance, the XV Corps adequately covered the VII Corps right flank.

Though the VII Corps right flank was thus protected by the advance of the XV Corps, the VIII Corps—then making the main American effort—had its left flank open between Louvigné and Rennes, a 35-mile gap covered only by patrols of the 106th Cavalry Group.[23] To remedy the situation, General Patton, just before noon on 2 August, ordered General Haislip to move the 5th Armored Division south to Fougères, the hub of an important road network. To Haislip, Patton's order not only pertained to flank protection for the VIII Corps but also indicated that XV Corps was about to embark on a campaign of exploitation.[24]

As events developed, Haislip was in for disappointment. About the same time that Patton decided to cover the exposed VIII Corps flank, General Bradley, the army group commander, was visiting General Middleton's command post. Also concerned about the corps flank, Bradley and Middleton decided to send a strong force to Fougères at once.

[20] Task Force Randolph consisted of the 90th Reconnaissance Troop and a company of light tanks of the 712th Tank Battalion. Task Force Clarke consisted of the 3d Battalion, 358th Infantry (motorized), the 344th Field Artillery Battalion (105-mm. howitzers), a platoon of the 315th Engineer Combat Battalion, a company of the 607th Tank Destroyer Battalion, and a signal detachment.

[21] Telecon, Gaffey and Menoher, 0845, 2 Aug; 90th Div AAR, Aug, FO 18, 2330, 2 Aug, and Intel Summary, 2 Aug.

[22] 90th Div Msg (Sitrep), 3 Aug.
[23] 106th Cav Gp Operational Map (3 Aug), VIII Corps G-3 Jnl and File.
[24] Ltr, Gaffey to Haislip, 2 Aug; XV Corps AAR, Aug, Warning Order, 1330, 2 Aug, and Outline Narrative, 1–14 Aug.

The only unit immediately available for this mission was the 79th Division, whose leading regiment was already at Pontorson on a projected move to follow the 6th Armored Division westward to Brest. Reversing the direction of the 79th Division "pursuant to instructions of army group commander," Middleton ordered occupation of Fougères before dark, 2 August, and establishment of contact with the 90th Division at Louvigné-du-Désert.[25] It was this set of instructions from General Bradley that prompted the halt of the 5th Armored Division north of the Sée River.[26]

Patton had acted simultaneously with Bradley to close the gap, the difference being the choice of the unit. Sending the 79th instead of the 5th Armored brought quicker action at Fougères and lessened traffic congestion around Avranches, but it also temporarily brought some complications to both the VIII and the XV Corps. The 79th Division replaced the 83d on the corps troop list, and the immediate result was some confusion: the XV Corps headquarters had "no wire to either division—90th Inf Div has no wire to anybody—79th Inf Div seems to have wire (only) to VII Corps"; and the 83d Division for a short time was simultaneously attached to two corps—VIII and XV—that were going in opposite directions.[27] Yet the shift was made with relative ease, primarily because uniformity of training and of staff procedures throughout the U.S. Army gave units flexibility. Throughout the campaign a brief telephone call was enough to set into motion an apparently complicated change.

To secure Fougères, reconnaissance troops of the 79th Division moved on the heels of a 106th Cavalry Group patrol into the town. The division occupied Fougères in force on the morning of 3 August and established contact with the 90th Division on the north.[28] As the 106th Cavalry Group (assigned to the XV Corps) continued to screen the area between Fougères and Rennes, apprehension over the VIII Corps left flank vanished.[29] The VIII Corps drove westward into Brittany, but the XV Corps, in contrast with earlier OVERLORD plans, faced to the southeast.

The orientation of XV Corps to the southeast reflected the reaction of the American high command to the changed situation brought about by the breakout. The 90th Division on the left and the 79th on the right held a defensive line from Juvigny to Fougères, facing away from Brittany, while the 5th Armored Division prepared to move south through Avranches toward the corps right flank.[30] In a sense, it was a fortuitous deployment that was to prove fortunate. For as the corps reached these positions, thinking on the higher echelons of command crystallized. The result altered a basic concept of the OVERLORD planning.

[25] VIII Corps Msg, 2 Aug, VIII Corps G-3 Jnl and File; VIII Corps FO 10, 2 Aug, and Sitrep 95, 2 Aug; XV Corps G-3 Notes, 2 Aug.

[26] TUSA Msgs, 2 Aug, XV and VIII Corps G-3 Jnls and Files.

[27] XV Corps G-3 Sec Memo and Notes of Mtg at G-3 Sec, 031400 Aug, 3 Aug; 83d Div G-2, G-3 Jnl and File, 2-3 Aug.

[28] 79th Div AAR, Aug, and Tel Msg, 1030, 3 Aug, VIII Corps G-3 Jnl and File; Wyche Diary.

[29] TUSA Msg, 1200, 3 Aug, and VIII Corps Msg, 2105, 4 Aug, VIII Corps G-3 Jnl and File; XV Corps G-3 Per Rpt 2 and Memo, 3 Aug.

[30] XV Corps G-3 Per Rpt 2, 3 Aug, and Plan of XV Corps Defense Between Fougères and La Sée River, 4 Aug.

OVERLORD Modified

In the midst of the fast-moving post-COBRA period, the utter disorganization of forces on the German left flank contrasted sharply with unexpected firmness in other parts of the German line. To exploit the collapse on the German left and to deal with continuing tenacity elsewhere, the Allied command seized upon the southeastern orientation of the XV Corps.

In the post-COBRA exploitation during the last days of July, when General Bradley had directed XIX Corps to advance along an axis projected through Tessy, Vire, and Domfront to Mayenne, Bradley thought the XV Corps might advance toward the upper reaches of the Sélune River, pinch out the VII Corps at Mortain, and meet the XIX Corps at Mayenne.[31] Unfortunately, XIX Corps had not gotten much beyond Tessy by 3 August. In contrast, XV Corps had met no "cohesive enemy front" in moving to the St. Hilaire-au-Harcouët–Fougères–Rennes line, and the 79th Division reported no enemy contact at all at Fougères.[32] To exploit this contrasting situation was tempting.

Preinvasion OVERLORD and NEPTUNE planners had expected the early Allied effort to be directed toward Brittany unless the Germans had decided to withdraw from France or were at the point of collapse, and actual operations during June and July had conformed to this concept. Since the Germans appeared on the verge of disintegration at the beginning of August, the Allies began to

consider the bolder choice offered by the planners: an immediate eastward drive toward the principal Seine ports of Le Havre and Rouen.[33]

The NEPTUNE planners had visualized the Allied right in Normandy making a wide sweep south of the *bocage* country, and as early as 10 July General Montgomery had suggested a maneuver of this kind eastward toward the successive lines Laval–Mayenne and le Mans–Alençon. Several days before COBRA and again several days after COBRA, Montgomery had reiterated this concept: he wanted the First U.S. Army to wheel eastward while the Third Army was occupied with operations in Brittany.[34]

During the latter days of July, when 21 Army Group planners considered in detail the bountiful advantages that might accrue from capture of Avranches, they were impressed by three opportunities that seemed immediately and simultaneously feasible: seize the Breton ports, destroy the German *Seventh Army* west of the Seine River, and cross the Seine before the enemy could organize the water line for defense. Thus assuming that the ground forces were about to fulfill the objectives of the OVERLORD plan, the Allies began to think seriously of post-OVERLORD operations directed toward the heart of Germany.

Occupying the OVERLORD lodgment area had always implied possession of

---

[31] XV Corps AAR, Aug, and Warning Order. 1 Aug.

[32] XV Corps G–2 Per Rpt 1, 2200, 3 Aug; 79th Div G–3 Per Rpt 37, 4 Aug.

[33] COSSAC (43) 28, Opn OVERLORD, 15 Jul 43, SHAEF File GCT 370–42/Ops 'A,' Opn OVERLORD; SHAEF/17100/35/Ops, NEPTUNE, Summary of Jt Opns Plan, Phase II, 25 Apr 44; SHAEF/17100/35/Ops, NEPTUNE, Summary of Revised Jt Opns Plan—U.S. Forces for Phase II of Opn OVERLORD, 20 May 44, EUCOM Files, Box 3.

[34] 21 AGp, Dir M–510, 10 Jul, Ltr, M–512, Montgomery to Bradley, Dempsey, Patton, and Crerar, 21 Jul, and Dir, M–515, 27 Jul.

the Breton ports, one of the most vital strategic objectives of the OVERLORD plan, before winter weather precluded further use of the invasion beaches. Now the planners were confident that a small force, one American corps of perhaps an armored division and three infantry divisions, "might take about a month to complete the conquest." The remainder of the Allied forces could turn to the other, more profitable opportunities: "round up" the Germans west of the Seine, drive them against the river, destroy them within the limits of the lodgment area, and, by seeking such distant objectives as Paris and Orléans, prepare to cross the Seine River.[35]

These speculations slighted a fundamental factor that had governed OVERLORD planning until that time: the belief that the Allies needed the Breton ports before they could move outside the confines of the lodgment area. Montgomery's planners had weighed the logistical merits of gaining Brittany against the tactical opportunities created by COBRA and by arguing for the latter presented a radically different conclusion. Until that moment the importance of the Breton ports could hardly have been exaggerated, for the very success of OVERLORD had seemed predicated on organizing Brittany as the principal American base of operations.[36]

General Eisenhower reflected the changing attitude toward the question of Brittany on 2 August. He believed that "within the next two or three days"

Bradley would "so manhandle the western flank of the enemy's forces" that the Allies would create "virtually an open [enemy] flank," and he predicted that the Allies would then be able to exercise almost complete freedom in selecting the next move. He would then "consider it unnecessary to detach any large forces for the conquest of Brittany," and would instead "devote the greater bulk of the forces to the task of completing the destruction of the German Army, at least that portion west of the Orne, and exploiting beyond that as far as [possible]." He did not mean to write off the need for the Breton ports, but securing both objectives simultaneously, he believed, would now be practical.[37]

On the same day, 2 August, General Bradley was still thinking along the lines of the original OVERLORD plan. Patton's forces then entering Brittany were still executing the American main effort, and the entire Third Army was eventually to be committed there to secure the ports. The St. Hilaire-du-Harcouët–Fougères–Rennes line, in the process of being established by the XV Corps, was no more than a shield to prevent interference with the Third Army conquest of the Brittany peninsula.[38] On the following day, 3 August, Bradley changed the entire course of the campaign by announcing that Patton was to clear Brittany with "a minimum of forces"; the primary American mission was to go to the forces in Normandy who were to drive eastward and expand the continental lodgment area.[39] Brittany had

[35] SHAEF G-3 Div, Précis of 21 AGp's Appreciation and Plan (21AGp/20748/G (Plans)), dated 29 Jul, 4 Aug, SHAEF File 18008, Post-OVERLORD Plng, G-3 Plans; see 21 AGp Dir, M-515, 27 Jul.

[36] Ruppenthal, *Logistical Support*, I, 467.

[37] Eisenhower to Marshall, S-56667, 2 Aug, Pogue Files.

[38] 12th AGp Dir for Current Opns, 2 Aug.

[39] 12th AGp Ltr of Instrs 2, 3 Aug.

become a minor prize worth the expense of only one corps. "I have turned only one American Corps westward into Brittany," General Montgomery stated on the following day, "as I feel that will be enough." [40] Had logistical planners not insisted that the ports were still needed, even fewer forces might have been committed there.[41] Several days later, when heavy resistance had been discovered at the port cities, Montgomery resisted "considerable pressure" to send more troops "into the peninsula to get the ports cleaned up quickly," for he felt that "the main business lies to the East." [42]

The new broad Allied strategy that had emerged concentrated on the possibility of swinging the Allied right flank around toward Paris. The sweeping turn would force the Germans back against the lower reaches of the Seine River, where all the bridges had been destroyed by air bombardment. Pushed against the river and unable to cross with sufficient speed to escape, the Germans west of the Seine would face potential destruction.[43]

Because the XV Corps was already around the German left and oriented generally eastward, General Haislip drew the assignment of initiating the sweep of the Allied right flank. The remaining problem was to resolve from somewhat conflicting orders the exact direction in which Haislip was to move—south, southeast, or east.[44]

"Don't Be Surprised"

Exclusive of Brittany, the mission outlined for the Third Army by General Bradley on 3 August had both offensive and defensive implications. General Patton was to secure a sixty-mile stretch of the north–south Mayenne River between Mayenne and Château-Gontier and to seize bridgeheads across the river. He also was to protect his right flank along the Loire River west of Angers, part of the southern flank of the OVERLORD lodgment area.[45]

Because this task was too great for the XV Corps alone, General Patton brought in the XX Corps to secure the Mayenne River south of Château-Gontier and to protect the Loire River flank. While the XV Corps was to drive about thirty miles southeast to the water line between Mayenne and Château-Gontier, the XX Corps was to move south toward the Loire. Although Patton assigned no further objectives, he was thinking of an eventual Third Army advance forty-five miles beyond Laval to le Mans—to the east. When, by which unit, and how this was to be done he did not say, but the obvious presumption that the XV Corps would continue eastward beyond the Mayenne River was not necessarily correct. "Don't be sur-

---

[40] Unnumbered Telg, Montgomery to CIGS (Brooke), 4 Aug, in Answers by British Historical Office to Questions by Pogue, Pogue Files.

[41] Ruppenthal, *Logistical Support, II,* 7.

[42] Telg, M–84, Montgomery to CIGS, 9 Aug, Pogue Files.

[43] 21 AGp Gen Operational Situation and Dir, M–516, 4 Aug.

[44] Compare the objectives enumerated in *Ibid;* 12th AGp Ltr of Instrs 2, 3 Aug; TUSA FO 1, 4 Aug (confirming verbal orders, 1 Aug), Ltr, Confirmation of Verbal Orders Issued 2 Aug, 4 Aug, and Ltr, Dir, 5 Aug (confirming fragmentary orders issued 4 Aug).

[45] 12th AGp Ltr of Instrs 2, 3 Aug.

prised," Patton told Haislip, if orders were issued for movement to the northeast or even to the north.[46] The implication was clear. Patton had sniffed the opportunity to encircle the Germans west of the Seine River, and he apparently liked what he smelled.

General Haislip planned to use the 106th Cavalry Group to screen the advance of the 90th Division from St. Hilaire to Mayenne and that of the 79th Division from Fougères to Laval. While the infantry divisions secured bridgeheads across the Mayenne River, the 5th Armored Division was to move south and southeast from Avranches and extend the corps front to Château-Gontier. French Resistance groups near Mayenne and Laval, numbering about 2,500 organized members, were to help by harassing the German garrisons. If the American troops met pockets of resistance, they were to go around them. "Don't stop," Patton ordered.

Sweeping through enemy territory for thirty miles and crossing a river that was a serious military obstacle was an ambitious program. The Mayenne was a steep-banked stream about one hundred feet wide and five feet deep. All the bridges except one at the town of Mayenne had been destroyed. Enemy interference was conjectural. "Nobody knows anything about the enemy," the corps G–2 stated, "because nothing can be found out about them." [47]

Air reconnaissance helped little. The reports of air reconnaissance missions filtered down to corps level too late to be of assistance. "Each day we would get a thick book from the air force," General Haislip recalled long afterwards, "and we would have to try to figure out what if anything in it applied to our little spot on the map. By the time we could figure it out, we were far away from there." [48]

Nothing could be found out about the Germans because there were hardly any Germans left. Only weak rear-echelon guard and supply detachments garrisoned Mayenne and Laval. Even though a captured American field order led the German command to expect the main American thrust to be made westward into Brittany, not eastward toward Laval and le Mans, the Germans considered that the lack of combat troops in the Laval–le Mans region still had to be remedied. The *LXXXI Corps* headquarters was moving from the Seine–Somme sector to assume responsibility for Laval and le Mans, and the *708th Infantry* and the *9th Panzer Divisions* were moving north from southern France. Because neither the corps headquarters nor the divisions had yet arrived (the leading units of the *708th* were across the Loire near Angers on 3 August), the *Seventh Army* operations officer was dispatched to the army rear command post at le Mans to organize a defense of the Mayenne–Loire area and to accelerate the movement of the arriving forces. Laval in particular was important, for its loss would threaten le Mans and Alençon, where vital German communications and supply centers were located. The army operations officer collected

---

[46] TUSA Ltr, Dir, 5 Aug (confirming fragmentary orders, 4 Aug); XV Corps Plng Paper, 2400, 4 Aug, XV Corps G–3 Jnl and File. Unless otherwise noted, all documentary sources cited in this section are from this file.

[47] XV Corps FO 1, 4 Aug, and Conf Notes, 1130, 5 Aug.

[48] Panel Conf Min, OCMH, 9 May 56.

the troops he could find—remnants, stragglers, supply personnel—and as his first measure reinforced a two-battalion security regiment performing guard duty and a flak battalion with 88-mm. guns emplaced at Laval. Despite the fact that Laval could then be considered relatively strongly held, alarming reports of troop instability and the increasing possibility of an American thrust to the east led to frantic but generally unsuccessful efforts to speed up the commitment of the incoming divisions in the Mayenne–Alençon area.[49] These forces were not in position when the XV U.S. Corps launched its attack on 5 August.

On the XV Corps left, General Mc-Lain entrusted the 90th Division advance to Mayenne to a task force under the assistant division commander, Brig. Gen. William G. Weaver.[50] Proving that facile capture of St. Hilaire had been no fluke, Weaver's force reduced several roadblocks, overran or bypassed pockets of resistance, and covered the thirty miles to the west bank of the Mayenne River in less than half a day, before noon of 5 August. Finding the highway bridge leading into the town of Mayenne still intact, but discovering also that the arrival of American troops had stirred up frenzied defensive activity, Weaver dispatched two infantry battalions to outflank the town on the south. No sooner had he done so than he became impatient and ordered the remainder of his task force to make a frontal assault by way of the bridge. The frontal attack succeeded, and even before the outflanking force had arrived in position, Mayenne had fallen. Although the Germans had mined the bridge, the 90th Division attack had forestalled demolition. While Task Force Weaver occupied Mayenne, the remainder of the division moved forward from St. Hilaire on a broader front to the Mayenne River, where engineers constructed additional bridges.[51]

To capture Laval, General Wyche built a 79th Division task force around Colonel Wood's motorized 313th Infantry and sent it along the main Fougères–Laval highway, which had previously been reconnoitered by a squadron of the 106th Cavalry Group.[52] Half way to Laval, a strong roadblock halted progress for about two hours while the leading units reduced the resistance and captured about fifty prisoners and several field guns. Additional roadblocks held up the task force briefly, and it was midnight of 5 August before American troops reached a point about two miles northwest of Laval. During the night of 5–6 August, while the remainder of the 79th Division moved forward from Fougères, patrols discovered that the German garrison had thoroughly destroyed the Mayenne River bridges but had evacuated Laval. On the following

---

[49] Telecon, Kluge and Hausser, 2130, 1 Aug, *OB WEST KTB, Anlage 1016;* MS # B–807 (Kuntzen); MS # A–918 (Gersdorff); MS # B–725 (Gersdorff); MS # B–179 (Hausser).

[50] Task Force Weaver consisted of the 90th Reconnaissance Troop, the 712th Tank Battalion, the 357th Infantry (motorized), the 343d Field Artillery Battalion, a company each of the 315th Engineer Combat Battalion and the 607th Tank Destroyer Battalion, a battery of antiaircraft artillery, and signal and military police detachments.

[51] 90th Div AAR, Aug; see 12th AGp Immed Rpt 76, Aggressive Pursuit by a Task Force, 10 Oct.

[52] Attached to the infantry regiment were the division reconnaissance troop, the 310th and 312th Field Artillery Battalions, the 749th Tank Battalion, a company each of the tank destroyer, engineer, and medical battalions, and the division air support party.

morning, against no opposition, the division crossed the river and entered Laval in force—one infantry battalion being led across a dam by French policemen, two battalions crossing the river on an engineer footbridge, another paddling across on rafts and in boats found along the west bank, and two battalions being ferried across by engineers who had rushed up assault boats. A treadway bridge spanned the river shortly after midnight, and a floating Bailey bridge was opened to traffic at noon, 7 August.[53]

Even before the capture of Laval, it had become obvious that only insignificant and disorganized forces opposed the XV Corps.[54] As soon as Mayenne fell on 5 August, Patton received permission to send the corps on to le Mans. The corps axis of advance thus changed from the southeast to the east.[55] Emphasizing that action during the next few days might be decisive for the entire campaign in western Europe, Haislip urged his commanders "to push all personnel to the limit of human endurance."[56] This was not idle talk, for the corps had a large order to fill. To take le Mans the corps, with both flanks open, would have to advance across forty-five miles of highly defensible terrain, cross a major military obstacle in the form of the Sarthe River, and capture a city of 75,000 population that the Germans presumably not only intended to defend but also had had ample time to fortify.[57]

The presumption was not altogether wrong. By this time the reconnaissance battalion of the *9th Panzer Division* and parts of the leading regiment of the *708th Infantry Division* had reached the vicinity of le Mans. Instead of holding these units and allowing the remaining portions of both divisions to assemble, the *LXXXI Corps* committed the small forces at once. The premature and, in the opinion of the Germans, disgraceful capitulation at Laval made necessary the immediate evacuation of administrative personnel from le Mans, long the location of the *Seventh Army* headquarters. With Laval lost, the Germans had to expect an American thrust along the Laval–le Mans highway and a subsequent threat to *Seventh Army* and *Army Group B* rear installations and supply dumps. Hastily trying to build up a front to deny the important center of le Mans, the *LXXXI Corps* dispatched units of the *708th Division* (arriving on foot and with horse-drawn vehicles) and the *9th Panzer Division* reconnaissance battalion west toward the Mayenne River line as soon as they arrived. These advance components were to collide with American columns near Aron and Evron in true meeting engagements.[58]

Since the 79th Division was still in the process of seizing Laval, the task of initiating the XV Corps attack to le Mans devolved upon the 90th. Accorded use of the main Laval–le Mans highway, General McLain planned to move the bulk of the division southeast from Mayenne to the highway, then eastward to le Mans behind Task Force Weaver, which was to drive along a

---

[53] 79th Div AAR, Aug.

[54] See XV Corps Rpt, 1800, 5 Aug.

[55] TUSA Dir, 5 Aug (confirming tel orders, 1640, 5 Aug); 12th AGp Ltr of Instrs 3, 6 Aug.

[56] XV Corps Dir to Div Comdrs, 1045, 6 Aug.

[57] XV Corps AAR, Aug.

[58] MS # B-807 (Kuntzen); MS # B-725 (Gersdorff).

more direct route southeast from Mayenne to the objective.[59]   General Weaver, again in command of the division
spearhead, divided his force into two
columns for an advance over parallel
roads.   One column, under his personal
command, was to proceed on the left
through the towns of Aron and Evron.[60]
The other column, commanded by Colonel Barth, was to move through Montsûrs, Ste. Suzanne, and Bernay.[61]

Barth's column on the right encountered only slight opposition on 6 August
in moving southeast from Mayenne
about twelve miles to Montsûrs, then
turning east and proceeding ten miles
farther to the hamlet of Ste. Suzanne.
There, that evening, the column struck
determined opposition and halted.

In contrast with the excellent advance
of Barth's force, Weaver's column had
hardly departed Mayenne before meeting a strong German armored and infantry force at Aron. Engaging the
enemy in a fire fight that lasted all day,
Weaver's troops were unable to advance.

Meanwhile, the remainder of the 90th
Division was approaching or crossing the
Mayenne River in two regimental
columns—the 358th (Colonel Clarke) on
the left and the 359th (under Col.
Robert L. Bacon) on the right.

Checked at Aron, Weaver on the
morning of 7 August left contingents of
the 106th Cavalry Group to contain the

enemy in the Aron–Evron sector and to
protect the division and corps left flank,
reversed the direction of his column,
and followed Barth's route of the previous day as far as Montsûrs.   Instead
of turning eastward at Montsûrs, Weaver
continued to the south.   Clarke's 358th
Infantry,   approaching   Montsûrs   in
column from the west, waited for
Weaver to clear the village before proceeding eastward toward Ste. Suzanne in
support of Barth.

Weaver, moving south, reached the
village of Vaiges on the main Laval–le
Mans highway.   There he intended to
turn east to parallel Barth's movement,
not on Barth's left as originally planned,
but on his right.   Weaver had to change
his plan when he discovered that Bacon's
359th Infantry had already entered
Vaiges from the west and was proceeding along the Laval–le Mans highway
toward the division objective, clearing
opposition that had formed around roadblocks.

Refusing to be shut out of the action,
but unwilling to risk traffic congestion
likely if his and Bacon's troops became
intermingled, Weaver led his column
northeast from Vaiges, aiming to insert
his column between Barth's and Clarke's
on the north and Bacon's on the south.
He would thus add a third column to
the eastward drive toward le Mans.
Several miles northeast of Vaiges, however, at the hamlet of Chammes between
Vaiges and Ste. Suzanne, Weaver again
was thwarted, this time by the same
enemy force opposing Barth at Ste.
Suzanne.

Barth, in the meantime, had sustained
and repelled a tank-supported counterattack launched from St. Suzanne.
American artillery fire effectively stopped

---

[59] 90th Div Mission Order, 1030, 6 Aug.

[60] This column consisted of the Reconnaissance
Troop (less a platoon), a platoon of medium tanks,
a battalion of the motorized 357th Infantry, and
an artillery battalion.

[61] Colonel Barth's column included the motorized
357th Infantry (less a battalion), two medium tank
platoons, a reconnaissance platoon, two artillery
battalions, a tank destroyer company, a platoon of
antiaircraft automatic weapons, and, as rear guard,
a battalion of the 359th Infantry.

the Germans, but in wooded terrain south of the Ste. Suzanne–Bernay road the enemy continued to resist. Soon after Weaver's arrival, however, the opposition slackened.

As enemy fires diminished and American artillery shelled the Germans, Barth rushed his motorized column past the wooded area southeast of Ste. Suzanne, passed through Bernay that night without stopping, and on the morning of 8 August struck an enemy defensive position only a few miles west of le Mans. Weaver left a small containing force at Chammes, moved south to the Laval–le Mans highway, turned east, passed through Bacon's troops, and slammed down the road, reducing small roadblocks at virtually every hamlet. Early on 8 August, Weaver, too, was only a few miles from le Mans.

As Barth and Weaver swept by the German forces in the forest southeast of Ste. Suzanne, Clarke on the north and Bacon on the south mopped up demoralized remnants and stragglers. Although the Americans had judged that only minor enemy forces had been present in the Evron area, the 90th Division took 1,200 prisoners and destroyed in large part the reconnaissance battalion of the *9th Panzer Division* and a regiment of the *708th Division*. The success of the approach march to le Mans was attributable in great measure to the aggressive persistence of General Weaver, who had not permitted his troops to be pinned down by opposition. The result left no doubt that the same 90th Division that had stumbled in the Cotentin was now a hard-hitting outfit.[62]

With both columns several miles west of le Mans by 8 August, General McLain halted the advance, terminated the task force organization, and prepared to attack the city. That night Clarke's 358th Infantry crossed the Sarthe River north of le Mans to cut the northern exits of the city. On the morning of 9 August, after shelling a German force observed escaping to the east and capturing fifty prisoners, the troops moved into the northern outskirts of the city. Barth's 357th Infantry also crossed the river during the night of 8 August, entering le Mans on the following morning.[63] Troops of the 90th Division made contact with part of the 79th Division, which had secured its portion of le Mans on the previous afternoon.

The 79th Division had started its drive east from Laval on the morning of 7 August as 106th Cavalry troops and Colonel Wood's motorized and reinforced 313th Infantry moved through the area immediately south of the main Laval–le Mans highway. Clearing small groups of Germans, the task force advanced more than half the distance to the objective. To give the attack added impetus on 8 August, General Wyche motorized Lt. Col. John A. McAleer's 315th Infantry and passed it through the 313th. The new spearhead unit surged forward, dispersing sporadic resistance, and the leading troops detrucked on the southwest outskirts of le Mans that afternoon. Concluding an outstanding exploitation effort, troops of the 79th Divi-

---

[62] For his part in transforming the division and inspiring the troops during the above action, Gen-

eral McLain was awarded the Bronze Oak Leaf Cluster to the DSC. General Eisenhower later credited General McLain with making the 90th a first-class fighting outfit. Eisenhower to Marshall, 25 Aug, cited in Cole, *Lorraine Campaign*, p. 278.

[63] 90th Div AAR, Aug; 12th AGp Immed Rpt 76, Aggressive Pursuit by a Task Force, 10 Oct.

sion crossed the Sarthe River and reached the center of le Mans, by 1700 on 8 August.[64] The *Seventh Army* headquarters troops were gone.

The 5th Armored Division had also had a hand in the advance. Commanded by Maj. Gen. Lunsford E. Oliver, the 5th Armored Division on 6 August had moved south against light resistance past Avranches and through Fougères and Vitré. At the village of Craon, opposition at a destroyed bridge temporarily halted a combat command, but quick deployment dispersed the Germans and aggressive reconnaissance secured a bypass crossing site. By evening the division was at the Mayenne River at Château-Gontier on the corps right flank. There, the division faced the serious problem of how to cross the river in the face of an acute shortage of gasoline.

Several days earlier, on 4 August, General Haislip, the corps commander, had directed the 5th Armored Division to unload fuel and lubricants from a hundred of its organic trucks so that the trucks might be used to motorize the two infantry divisions. Although Haislip had intended to return the vehicles before committing the armor, he had been compelled instead to replace them with a corps Quartermaster truck company on the night of 5 August. The division commander, General Oliver, instructed the truck company to draw gasoline at any army Class III truckhead north of Avranches and to join the armored division south of Avranches on the following morning. When the trucks failed to appear, Oliver sent an officer back to locate them. The officer

found the Quartermaster company and had the trucks loaded, but traffic congestion prevented the vehicles from getting to the division that day. Not until the early morning hours of 7 August did they arrive. Uncertain whether the Third Army could establish and maintain supply points at reasonable distances behind armored forces in deep exploitation and unwilling to risk a recurrence of the gasoline shortage, Oliver provided the division with an operational fuel reserve by attaching a platoon of the Quartermaster company to each combat command.

General Oliver need not have worried. The organic trucks of the division were released by the infantry and returned to the 5th Armored area early on 7 August. At the same time, the Third Army moved 100,000 gallons of gasoline to Cossé-le-Vivien, several miles south of Laval, whence 5th Armored Division trucks transported it across the Mayenne River to Villiers-Charlemagne. Here the division quartermaster established a Class III dump. A platoon of the division Engineer battalion protected the supply point until the division civil affairs section obtained sufficient numbers of the FFI for guard duty.

Gassed up on the morning of 7 August, the 5th Armored Division crossed the Mayenne River after eliminating the Château-Gontier garrison (about a company strong), repairing the damaged bridge there, and constructing several bridges south of Château-Gontier. General Haislip had instructed General Oliver to advance on le Mans echeloned to the right rear of the 79th Division, but had also authorized him to use all possible routes in the corps zone, providing he did not interfere with the in-

---

[64] 79th Div AAR, Aug.

fantry divisions. If the infantry encountered opposition strong enough to
retard progress seriously, the armor was
to move to the head of the corps attack.
This was not necessary. The 5th
Armored Division reached the Sarthe
River south of le Mans on the evening of
7 August and crossed during the night.
Sweeping through some opposition on
8 August, the armor bypassed le Mans
on the south, swung in a wide arc, and
moved around the eastern outskirts of
the city. By midnight of 8 August, the
converging attacks of the three divisions
had closed all exits from le Mans and infantrymen were clearing the streets of
the city.[65]

In four days, from 5 to 9 August,
General Haislip's XV Corps had moved
about seventy-five miles—from the St.
Hilaire–Fougères line to le Mans—an
extraordinarily aggressive advance at
little cost. Extremely light casualties
contrasted well with a total of several
thousand prisoners.[66] The immediately
apparent achievement of Haislip's exploitation was that the XV Corps had
frustrated German plans to organize
strong defenses at Laval and le Mans.
But soon an even more spectacular result
would become obvious.

During the first week of August the
Third Army headquarters had been serving two bodies with one head. Two
distinct fronts had been advancing in
opposite directions, moving ever farther

apart. By 8 August more than two
hundred miles separated the 6th Armored Division of the VIII Corps at the
gates of Brest and the XV Corps at le
Mans.

Less than one hundred miles east of
le Mans lay the final 12th Army Group
objective designated by the OVERLORD
plan, the eastern edge of the OVERLORD
lodgment area, an area roughly between
Paris and Orléans. With le Mans occupied so easily there seemed to be few
German forces to restrain further Third
Army advance toward its part of the objective, the Paris–Orléans gap. Yet, this
advance was not to be, for the moment
at least; a new goal appeared more desirable.

The XV Corps advance to le Mans
had in one week moved an enveloping
right flank eighty-five air miles southeast
of Avranches and was well on its way to
outflanking the German armies west of
the Seine River, or had already done so.
If the basic purpose of military operations was to close on advantageous terms
with the enemy and destroy him, and if a
favorable moment for a move of this
kind appeared, purely geographical objectives receded in importance. The opportunity for a decisive victory seemed
doubly propitious, for the Germans in
making a bid to regain the initiative in
the battle of France had played into
American hands.

General Bradley was ready to act, and
in his new decision the XV Corps had an
important role. "Don't be surprised,"
Patton had earlier warned Haislip. Instead of going farther east from le Mans,
the XV Corps turned north toward
Alençon.

---

[65] 5th Armd Div AAR, Aug.

[66] The 90th Division, for example, sustained less
than 300 casualties during the first ten days of
August and took more than 1,500 prisoners. 90th
Div AAR, Aug.

CHAPTER XXIII

Opportunities and Intentions

In contrast with the Third Army's spectacular gains during the first week of August, the First Army seemed to be standing still. The difference between the rates of progress of the two armies was easily explained. Whereas Patton's units were slashing through areas held by few German defenders, the First Army was meeting organized, stubborn resistance. Because the Third Army's achievements were more impressive, they became the side of the coin usually displayed, but the accomplishments of Hodges' First Army were no less important in determining the course of the campaign in western Europe.

The American Task

The primary intention of the Allies on 1 August was to sustain the momentum developed by COBRA. The objectives remained the same as those enunciated at the beginning of July. While the Third Army slid into Brittany, the First Army was to swing left to a north–south line facing eastward and prepare to drive to the Seine in conjunction with the British and Canadians.

The NEPTUNE planners had envisioned a rather wide wheeling movement beginning at the base of the Cotentin and clearing the OVERLORD lodgment area as far south as the Loire River. In keeping with this concept, the boundary be-

tween the First Army and the British and Canadians extended from the invasion coast southeast more than fifty miles through Bayeux and Flers, then east through Alençon and Dreux to the Eure River just short of Paris. This split the lodgment area (exclusive of Brittany) roughly into equal parts and postulated a twin drive by the 21 Army Group toward the lower Seine River (between Paris and the sea) and the 12th Army Group toward the upper Seine north of the Loire River (between Paris and Orléans). The pivot for the American turn was at a point just west of Alençon, almost sixty miles from the invasion coast.[1]

Three weeks after the invasion it had seemed obvious that pivoting on Alençon was an optimistic improbability. Also, General Montgomery preferred to anchor the British forces on the small foothold secured by the end of June rather than attempt to enlarge the space that would determine the eventual wheeling maneuver. Montgomery had therefore instructed General Bradley to secure the American left on Caumont, less than twenty miles inland, and make a shallower turning movement, describ-

---

[1] PS SHAEF (44) 13 (Final), Post-NEPTUNE Plng Forecast No. 1, 27 May, and Map "MA" attached, SGS SHAEF Post-OVERLORD Plng File, 381; SHAEF/17100/35/Ops, NEPTUNE, Summary of Revised Jt Opns Plan—US Forces for Phase II of Opn OVERLORD, 20 May, EUCOM Files, Box 3.

ing an arc through Fougères, about seventy miles north of the Loire River. This, the First Army had been unable to accomplish.

During the COBRA operation, the American left flank forces had been anchored on St. Lô. The success of COBRA and of the post-COBRA exploitation had enabled the forces on the right to sweep through the successive objectives of Laval and le Mans, about fifty miles north of the Loire. At the same time, the American pivot shifted south to the town of Vire. At the beginning of August, American and British troops were both driving to secure Vire as the point of the wheeling movement that had already started.[2]

Earlier, the Allies had believed that, before troops could move from Avranches into Brittany, it would be necessary to erect a barrier against interference from the east. This requirement partially explained Allied preoccupation with the road centers of Vire, Mortain, and Fougères. Yet before these could be seized, even as the American left remained heavily engaged near Villedieu-les-Poëles, Percy, and Tessy, the entrance into Brittany had been made. Vire, Mortain, and Fougères remained important nevertheless, for with German strength in Brittany drained to reinforce the Normandy front, a strong German threat could only come from the east or the southeast. When the Third Army assumed responsibility for taking Fougères, General Hodges concentrated upon capturing Vire and Mortain.[3]

Succeeding to the command of the First Army after having served as deputy commander, General Hodges was in demeanor and habit much like his predecessor, General Bradley. Quiet and modest, "unostentatious and retiring," General Hodges performed his duties in a workmanlike manner without fanfare. He was opposed to what he termed the "uncertain business" of "tricky maneuver." Too many units, he felt, tried to flank and skirt instead of meeting the enemy straight on, and he believed that it was "safer, sounder, and in the end quicker to keep smashing ahead." [4]

General Hodges had enlisted in the Regular Army as a private, had served in Pershing's Punitive Expedition into Mexico as an officer, and had fought in France during World War I as a battalion and a regimental commander. Commandant of the Infantry School at Fort Benning, Georgia, in 1940, Hodges had become in rapid succession Chief of Infantry, head of the Replacement and School Command of the Army Ground Forces, and Commanding General, X Corps. A lieutenant general by 1944, he assumed command of the First Army on 1 August and took control of three corps, the VII, the XIX, and the V.

By seizing Vire and Mortain, General Hodges would provide protection for the Avranches corridor while beginning the First Army turning maneuver.[5] Prospects of attaining his goals seemed favorable. The Germans were trying to stabilize their left flank, but despite counterattacks "and the belated shifting

---

[2] See 21 AGp Ltr, M–512, Montgomery to Bradley, Dempsey, Patton, and Crerar, 21 Jul; see above, Ch. III.

[3] 12th AGp Dir for Current Opns, 2 Aug.

[4] Bradley, Soldier's Story, pp. 226, 358–59; Sylvan Diary, 30 Jul.

[5] 12th AGp Ltr of Instrs 1, 29 Jul; see Msg, Eisenhower to Montgomery, FWD–12505, 31 Jul, SGS SHAEF File 381, OVERLORD, I (a).

of his reserves," the enemy appeared incapable of halting a First Army advance.[6] If eight divisions were shifted from the *Fifteenth Army,* the Germans could perhaps continue to fight along a general line from Rennes through Mortain, Falaise, and Trouville and thus prevent the emergence of Allied forces from Normandy. Otherwise, there could only be abandonment of the "no retreat" policy. Beyond that, it was possible even to foresee complete German collapse in the very near future. "Only discipline," the First Army G–2 wrote,

and habit of obedience to orders keeps the front line units fighting. It is doubtful that the German forces in NORMANDY can continue for more than four to eight weeks as a military machine. One more heavy defeat such as the recent breakthrough battle which commenced 25 July will most probably result in the collapse of the forces now at the base of the CHERBOURG Peninsula. Surrender or a disastrous retreat will be the alternative for the German forces. In the next four to eight weeks the current situation may change with dramatic suddenness into a race to reach a chaotic Germany.[7]

So optimistic an assessment, though completely warranted, was not to endure for long once the character of German resistance on the immediate First Army front was manifest.

The German Task

In planning a counterattack to regain Avranches and restabilize their Normandy defenses, the Germans had to stiffen their resistance in order to preserve the conditions under which a counterattack was possible. If the defensive

line east of Avranches were lost, regaining Avranches would avail little. At the same time, the assembly areas for the forces that were to launch the counterattack had to be protected. To accomplish these tasks was to prove difficult, for the Germans had relatively few troops in Normandy at the beginning of August. (*See Map IX.*)

Losses had been exceedingly high among the divisions in contact with the Allies during June and July. Hausser, the *Seventh Army* commander, counted eight divisions that had practically been destroyed in the Cotentin during the month of July alone: *Panzer Lehr, 5th Parachute, 17th SS Panzer Grenadier,* and *91st, 352d, 275th, 243d,* and *77th Infantry Divisions.*[8] This did not take into account the *16th Luftwaffe Field Division* and the *326th Division,* annihilated near Caen and Caumont, respectively. It did not include the divisions in Brittany and on the Channel Isles that had to be written off as far as the Normandy front was concerned: the *2d Parachute,* the *343d* and *319th Infantry Divisions,* and parts of the *265th* and *266th.* Nor did it mention that the *21st, 9th SS, 10th SS,* and *12th SS Panzer Divisions* had been badly crippled in the Caen and Caumont sectors. Only a few divisions of Eberbach's *Fifth Panzer Army,* the weak *3d Parachute* and *353d Divisions* (the latter temporarily presumed lost during COBRA and now reduced to kampfgruppe size) of Hausser's *Seventh Army,* and the armored divisions scheduled to launch the Avranches counterattack still retained combat effectiveness. Like all the troops in Normandy, these too had suffered from

---

[6] FUSA FO 3, 1 Aug.
[7] FUSA G–2 Est 13, 1 Aug.

[8] MS # B–179 (Hausser)

uninterrupted combat, inferior equipment, inadequate matériel and supplies, and Allied air superiority. Though the men were still fighting grimly, commanders were concerned lest the will to resist suddenly vanish.[9]

Two infantry divisions were scheduled to reinforce the battered units holding the Normandy left flank and also to relieve the armored divisions scheduled to counterattack. The *363d* moved through Tinchebray during the first days of August and into the Brécey–Vire line to relieve the *2d* and the *2d SS Panzer Divisions* by 5 August.[10] The *84th*, supposed to relieve the *116th Panzer Division*, was committed on 2 August in defense of the Sourdeval sector and became engaged in such violent combat that it was unable to accomplish the relief as quickly as hoped.

Despite heavy pressure exerted by the First U.S. Army, the *Seventh Army* managed, by stubborn resistance and skillful withdrawal, to retain a defensive line that, while not solid, was at least cohesive. The *XLVII Panzer Corps* headquarters gave up responsibility for the center to prepare for the counterattack, and the *II Parachute* and the *LXXXIV Corps* together fought along the Brécey–Vire line. On the right (east), the *II Parachute Corps,* controlling only the *3d Parachute Division* (reinforced by a regiment of the *5th Parachute Division)* defended the town of Vire. On the left, the *LXXXIV Corps* had the more complicated job of getting the armored divi-

sions out of the line without upsetting the precarious defensive balance. In this the corps depended heavily on the kampfgruppe of the *353d Division.* On the extreme left, under *LXXXIV Corps* control, remnants of the *5th Parachute* and *275th Divisions* held weak blocking positions south of the Sée River near Juvigny.[11]

During the first week of August, five factors gave the German commanders pause. First, they often doubted that they could prevent the counterattack assembly areas from being overrun. Second, they wondered whether the transfer of armored divisions (the *2d* and the *116th* at the end of July, and the pending transfer of the *1st SS* in August) from Eberbach's forces would so weaken the right wing that the British and Canadians would be able to effect a penetration south of Caen. Third, they were aware of the threat of encirclement by coordinated British and American drives to the town of Flers—the British by a continuation of the southeastward thrust from Caumont, the Americans by a northeastward thrust from Fougères through Domfront. Fourth, they were concerned with the threat to the *Army Group B* rear posed by American forces driving toward le Mans. Fifth, they worried that loss of high ground around Mortain—excellent terrain from which to launch offensive action—might inhibit the counterattack toward Avranches. These thoughts added to the burdens of the holding battle immediately preceding the counterattack.[12]

---

[9] MS # B–179 (Hausser); MS # B–725 (Gersdorff).

[10] On how the movement of the *363d Division* was consistently harassed by air attack, see Leigh-Mallory, "Despatch," Fourth Supplement to the *London Gazette* of December 31, 1946, p. 63.

[11] MS # B–346 (Blauensteiner); MS # B–725 (Gersdorff); MS # B–179 (Hausser).

[12] MS # B–725 (Gersdorff); MS # B–179 (Hausser); MS # B–722 (Gersdorff).

The Drive to Mortain

On the First U.S. Army right, the VII Corps had outflanked the German left by 1 August when troops of the 3d Armored Division's Combat Command A (attached to the 1st Division) pushed across the Sée River at Brécey. Between Brécey and Avranches, a distance of ten miles, yawned the gap through which the Third Army skittered toward Brittany, and since the Third Army would take responsibility for holding the Avranches corridor open, VII Corps had to move east to get out of the way. The VII Corps moved toward Mortain, a road center near commanding ground twenty miles east of Avranches between the Sée and the Sélune.[13] *(Map 13)*

General Collins, the VII Corps commander, ordered General Huebner, the 1st Division commander, "to envelop the enemy's left flank and exploit the breakthrough of his defenses" by seizing the high ground and road centers in the Mortain area. The 1st Division was to sweep southeastward across the front of and pinch out General Barton's 4th Division, which was attacking south from Villedieu through St. Pois to the Sée River, and was to make contact with General Eddy's 9th Division, which was to attack south toward Sourdeval and the high ground north of Mortain.[14]

The 1st Division turned eastward toward Mortain, the attached CCA of the 3d Armored Division acting as a spearhead while the infantry regiments mopped up. Extremely broken terrain, roads twisting and turning around hills and crossing narrow, steep-walled valleys, gave the Germans ample opportunity to ambush. Against them, the 1st Division used fire power liberally, overran elements of the *275th Division*, and took Reffuveille, le Mesnil-Adelée, Juvigny, and St. Barthélemy. On the afternoon of 3 August, the 1st Division entered Mortain after dispersing the reconnaissance battalion of the *2d Panzer Division*. General Huebner immediately outposted the high ground east of town.[15]

The relatively easy capture of Mortain contrasted with operations in the remaining portion of the VII Corps front, where the Germans manned an unbroken defensive line between St. Pois and Vire. The *84th Division* held tenaciously to Sourdeval, a scant six miles north of Mortain, but the remnants of the *Panzer Lehr Division*, which ostensibly covered Mortain, Barenton, and Passais, could not prevent patrols of the 1st Division from reaching Fougerolles-du-Plessis and Barenton, twelve miles south and seven miles southeast of Mortain, respectively.

The natural inclination to push the 1st Division along the path of least re-

---

[13] First U.S. Army, *Report of Operations, 1 August 1944–22 February 1945,* 4 Vols. (Washington, 1946), I, 3. (In footnotes throughout the remainder of the volume, all references cited as First U.S. Army, *Report of Operations,* are to the 1 August 1944–22 February 1945 report. See also footnote 15, Chapter I.); VII Corps Tactical Study of the Terrain, 17 Jul.

[14] VII Corps FO 7, 1 Aug; see 4th Div Spec Opn Rpt, St. Pois.

[15] MS # B–725 (Gersdorff); Jules et Gilles Buisson, *Mortain et sa Bataille* (Rennes, 1947), pp. 47ff. A representative action in this advance was one in which 2d Lt. Harold B. Selleck of the 26th Infantry, who had been reconnoitering an approach route for his battalion, encountered a hostile tank-infantry force, which opened fire. Selleck deployed his few troops, engaged the enemy, and captured more than a hundred prisoners, a Mark IV tank, and considerable amounts of equipment and supplies. He was awarded the DSC.

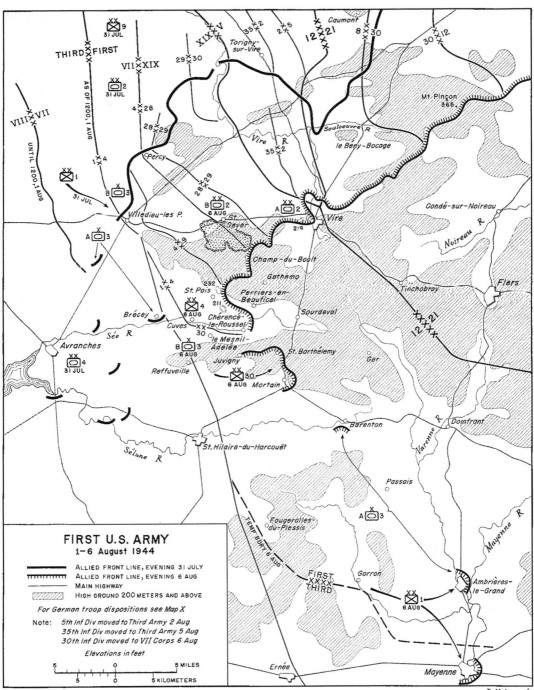

FIRST U.S. ARMY
1–6 August 1944

▬▬▬▬▬	ALLIED FRONT LINE, EVENING 31 JULY
▬ɪɪɪɪɪɪɪ	ALLIED FRONT LINE, EVENING 6 AUG
▬▬▬▬	MAIN HIGHWAY
▨	HIGH GROUND 200 METERS AND ABOVE

For German troop dispositions see Map X

Note: 5th Inf Div moved to Third Army 2 Aug
        35th Inf Div moved to Third Army 5 Aug
        30th Inf Div moved to VII Corps 6 Aug

Elevations in feet

D. Holmes, Jr.

MAP 13

TROOPS ADVANCING FROM JUVIGNY *southward toward Mortain.*

sistance, into exploitation toward the successive objectives of the Domfront–Mayenne and Alençon–le Mans lines, gave way to a more sober calculation. At Mortain the division positions formed a conspicuous salient on the German left flank and presented a potential threat to the rear of the German units fighting along the St. Pois–Vire line. Aware of the withdrawal of the *2d Panzer* and the *2d SS Panzer Divisions,* American commanders misinterpreted German troop movements as attempts to escape the threat on the flank. While other First Army units exerted pressure from the north, the 1st Division consolidated positions at Mortain to prevent enemy escape and to guard against counterattack from the north. At the same time, the division artillery took numerous targets to the north and northeast under fire, on 4 August alone firing 105

missions, of which 28 were harassing, 14 were against tanks, 15 were counterbattery, 24 were antipersonnel and antivehicular, and 5 were interdiction and preparation.[16]

As the XV Corps, on the right of the VII Corps, began to advance toward Laval and le Mans, General Hodges instructed General Collins to move to the south to cover the XV Corps north flank. In compliance, the 1st Division on 6 August displaced across the Sélune River south of Mortain to Gorron and Ambrières-le-Grand and, having met only slight interference, started to relieve the 90th Division at Mayenne.[17] To replace the 1st Division at Mortain, Hodges shifted the 30th Division from Tessy and XIX Corps control. The 1st Division was then free to exploit eastward from Mayenne toward Alençon in a drive paralleling the XV Corps thrust to le Mans.

In contrast with the 1st Division experience, the 4th Division struck determined resistance in the hills just north and northwest of St. Pois on 2 August. The 3d Armored Division's Combat Command B, attached to the 4th Division and spearheading the attack, was not far from St. Pois, but the armor awaited arrival of the infantry before resuming the attack. The rest of the division moved south from Villedieu in what appeared to resemble a gigantic traffic jam on 2 August but what was in actuality a rapid movement. General Barton had decided that "the quickest way to get them there [was to] put them all on the road at once." [18]

From the forward positions just north

---

[16] 1st Div AAR, Aug.
[17] VII Corps Opns Memo 57, 4 Aug.
[18] 4th Div Spec Opn Rpt, St. Pois.

of St. Pois, Barton had to advance about six miles and seize three objectives, each two miles apart: the town of St. Pois, Hill 211, and a bridgehead across the Sée River at Chérencé-le-Roussel.[19] Although General Collins contemplated sending the 4th Division beyond Chérencé-le-Roussel to the high ground north of Mortain in the Gathemo–Sourdeval area, the stubborn resistance in the St. Pois sector disrupted this plan.[20] The *116th Panzer Division* had been hastily withdrawn from the line near Tessy on 1 August to counter the American thrust toward Brécey, and this force had been committed in time to halt CCB and the 4th Division.[21]

Impatient to get the three objectives so that the 4th Division might go into reserve for rest as promised, General Barton applied at St. Pois a lesson learned at Villedieu. On 3 August he sent a task force of infantry and armor to bypass St. Pois on the west. Moving about five miles "without firing a shot," the task force crossed the Sée River at Cuves, four miles west of Chérencé-le-Roussel. On the following day CCB and attached infantry fought eastward from Cuves along the south bank of the Sée River, then crossed the river again at Chérencé-le-Roussel and established a bridgehead on the north bank of the Sée. While the task force was thus outflanking and enveloping the enemy, three regiments of the 4th Division attacked abreast from the northwest toward St. Pois. The 12th Infantry on the left strove to gain Hill 232, the 22d Infantry in the center attacked the town of St. Pois, and the 8th Infantry on the right drove on Hill 211. The going was difficult against the guns of the *116th Panzer Division,* and by evening the objectives were still not secured. When the attack was halted and orders given to dig in for the night, the rifle company officers of a battalion of the 8th Infantry requested and secured permission to continue as a measure of respect for their commander, Lt. Col. Erasmus H. Strickland, who had been wounded that day. The assault carried to the crest of Hill 211, and at dawn, 5 August, the regiment was ready to repel the strong but obviously final German counterattack.

Although St. Pois technically remained in German hands that morning, the town was virtually encircled. The Germans began to withdraw to the southeast to protect Sourdeval. From the hills around St. Pois, men of the 4th Division hastened the enemy's departure by bringing down artillery fire and calling in fighter-bombers to attack the columns. The cannon company of the 8th Infantry fired 3,200 shells and burned out three howitzer tubes, the 4.2-inch mortar company depleted all its ammunition stocks, and the 81-mm. mortars expended 3,000 rounds.[22]

The division mission completed by the end of 5 August, General Barton released CCB to control of the 3d Armored Division, assembled the 4th Division at St. Pois in the VII Corps reserve, and looked forward to giving his troops four

---

[19] VII Corps FO 7, 1 Aug.

[20] VII Corps Opns Memo 55, 3 Aug (confirming oral orders, 2 Aug).

[21] MS # B-725 (Gersdorff); Hosp Intervs, GL-93 (316), IV.

[22] 4th Div Spec Opn Rpt, St. Pois; 4th Div G-3 Jnl, 4-5 Aug. Pvt. Joseph J. Giordano of the 8th Infantry was awarded the DSC for heroic action on 5 August.

or five days of rest, replete with "hot showers, hot food, USO shows . . . Red Cross doughnut girls."[23]

Like the 4th Division, General Eddy's 9th Division encountered strong opposition. Moving from a rest area to assembly near Villebaudon on 1 August, the 9th Division prepared to advance twenty miles to high ground north of Mortain against what appeared to be disorganized enemy forces.[24] Two regiments abreast gained ten miles in two days, a rapid advance for the difficult terrain, but then progress slowed as they moved through hilly hedgerow terrain well defended by the *353d Division* reinforced by the remnants of the *352d Division* and a small task force of the *6th Parachute Regiment*. The 9th Division advance was tedious in the face of numerous mines and strong delaying forces at roadblocks and on critical terrain features. As the division threatened the Forêt de St. Sever, which concealed troops and semipermanent supply installations, resistance stiffened. The newly arrived *394th Assault Gun Brigade,* which had come forward to participate in the counterattack, was subordinated to the *LXXXIV Corps* to protect the Forêt de St. Sever, and the brigade's heavy artillery concentrations and antitank rockets further slowed the 9th Division attack.[25]

In order to speed the movement of the 9th Division to the Sée River and beyond to Gathemo, the immediate division objective, General Eddy secured General Collins' approval for a wide flanking attack. He sent a regiment westward through Villedieu-les-Poëles, southward through Brécey, eastward through Chérencé-le-Roussel, and then northeastward to Gathemo to encircle the German troops in the St. Pois–St. Sever-Calvados sector. Contact with the two regiments attacking south would complete a two-pronged squeeze play ending at Gathemo.[26]

Directed through the 4th and 1st Division sectors, on 5 August the 39th Infantry of the 9th Division passed through the 4th Division bridgehead held by tanks and infantry at Chérencé-le-Roussel and attacked toward the northeast. Although stiff resistance prevented progress, other contingents of the division discovered a soft spot. The 60th Infantry moved with surprising rapidity through the Forêt de St. Sever against occasional artillery and mortar fire. That afternoon, a battalion temporarily gained possession of the crossroads village of Champ-du-Boult, two miles northwest of Gathemo, though a counterattack by the *353d Division* reserve supported by the *6th Parachute Regiment* drove the battalion out.[27]

Continuing the attack on 6 August, the 9th Division regained Champ-du-Boult in the north and increased the threat to Perriers-en-Beauficel in the south. With only three miles separating the two division hooks, General Collins anticipated quick consolidation. As he began to plan the movement of the 9th to the south to cover the eastward thrust

[23] VII Corps Notes for CofS, 4 Aug, VII Corps G–3 Jnl and File; Col. Gerden F. Johnson, *History of the Twelfth Infantry Regiment in World War II* (Boston, 1947), p. 168.

[24] VII Corps FO 7, 1 Aug; 9th Div FO 15, 2 Aug, and AAR, Aug.

[25] MS # B–725 (Gersdorff); FUSA G–2 Per Rpt 49. 29 Jul.

[26] VII Corps Opns Memo 57, 4 Aug, and Notes for CofS, 4 Aug.

[27] 9th Div and 39th Inf AAR's, Aug; MS # B–725 (Gersdorff).

of the XV Corps to le Mans, the Germans counterattacked.[28]

During the first six days of August, General Collins had faced contrasting situations on his corps front. On his right, he had essentially the same opportunity for exploitation enjoyed by the Third Army's XV Corps, yet he had been bound to the First Army and its requirements and consequently was unable to capitalize on the fluid situation there. With the exception of the 1st Division, the VII Corps components had taken part in combat that resembled the earlier battle of the hedgerows. Stubborn resistance, skillful withdrawal, and effective delaying action in *bocage* terrain had resulted in a slow and hard advance. Whereas the 1st Division sustained less than 250 casualties between 2 and 7 August, the 3d Armored Division lost almost 300 men, the 4th Division 600, and the 9th Division nearly 850.[29] Although the figures hardly approached the intensity of losses in July, they indicated clearly a major difference in the character of the opposition met on different sectors of the front.

The Battle for Vire

Hard slugging characterized combat all along the remainder of the First Army front. On the immediate left of the VII Corps, the XIX Corps had been occupied for five days in smashing German attempts to re-form a defensive line from Tessy to the Cotentin west coast, but on 2 August, with Tessy finally captured, General Corlett began to drive southeastward toward the town of Vire.[30] As the 30th Division settled down at Tessy for several days of rest, the 28th and 29th Divisions, each with an attached combat command of the 2d Armored Division, attacked abreast from the Percy–Tessy line in what was hoped would be pursuit of a defeated enemy.[31]

Difficult terrain and stubborn resistance transformed the hoped-for pursuit into a protracted fight. The action of the 28th Division, which was manifesting the usual characteristics of a unit newly committed to combat, complicated the picture. On the first day of attack the division sustained almost 750 casualties, and not until the attached CCB moved to the front to lead the advance did the troops begin to move with any assurance and competence. Two days later, on 4 August, the 28th captured St. Sever-Calvados, eight miles southeast of Percy. At the same time the 29th Division, with CCA attached, reached positions northwest of the town of Vire after hard fighting.[32]

General Gerow's V Corps had also been moving toward Vire from the north. The corps objective was a line several miles north of Vire where the corps was to be pinched out by the converging advances of the adjacent forces. By 1 August the British on the left had already pinched out the 5th Division, and General Irwin prepared to join the Third Army. The two remaining divisions of the V Corps, the 35th and the 2d, crossed the Vire–Souloeuvre River line

---

[28] VII Corps Opns Memo 59, 7 Aug (confirming oral orders 6 Aug).

[29] FUSA Daily G–1 Rpts, Aug.

[30] FUSA FO 2, 28 Jul.

[31] Sgt. Harold B. Cordes of the 22d Infantry, which was still attached to the 2d Armored Division, was awarded the DSC for heroic action on 2 August.

[32] 28th and 29th Div AAR's Aug; [Ferriss]. Notes.

on 2 August and pushed south with the intent of "maintaining strong pressure against the enemy and insuring contact at all times." [33]

The Germans were withdrawing behind strong rear-guard action and were using the terrain advantageously, but General Gerow still hoped to gain enough momentum to go beyond his designated limit of advance. He requested permission from General Hodges to capture the town of Vire if the prospect became feasible. The army commander at first agreed, but on second thought refused because he was unwilling to chance the confusion that might result from intermingling XIX and V Corps forces.[34]

The 2d and 35th Divisions reached their objectives by 5 August, the former having sustained nearly 900 casualties in the process, the latter almost 600.[35] As General Baade prepared to take his 35th Division, which was no longer in contact with the enemy, out of the sector to join the Third Army, Maj. Gen. Walter M. Robertson's 2d Division established defensive positions north of the town of Vire.

The XIX Corps, according to General Bradley's post-COBRA instructions, was to have driven southeastward through Vire toward Tinchebray, thereby cutting across the V Corps front and pinching it

out. General Hodges modified these plans when increasing emphasis was placed on maintaining unrelenting pressure on the enemy. Instead of allowing the V Corps to remain idle just north of Vire, Hodges designated Tinchebray, eight miles southeast of Vire, as the next V Corps objective. To replace the departing 35th Division, he at first gave Gerow the 30th Division but, when he sent the 30th to Mortain instead, he substituted the 29th for it. After Vire was captured, the 29th Division would pass to V Corps control. Since the new V Corps sector would be narrow, Gerow was to attack with the 2d and 29th Divisions in column to capture Tinchebray. The XIX Corps would continue southward from Vire toward Domfront and Mayenne to cover the northern flank of the XV Corps (which was driving eastward toward le Mans) and also to cut off and encircle the enemy forces in the St. Pois–Gathemo area.[36] But before these plans could be put into effect, the town of Vire had to be taken. The task fell to the 29th Division and its attachment, CCA of the 2d Armored Division.

Vire, an old fortified town of 8,000 inhabitants, is built on hills dominating the Norman *bocage* and is the center of several converging roads. The town overlooks the Vire River and a tributary, the Vaux de Vire. Long a religious and artistic center, it was by virtue of its location a military prize. The townspeople in 1944 came to regard their privations of that year as a double agony. The Allied aerial bombardment of 6 June, part of the attempt to hamper German troop movements at the time of the

---

[33] FUSA FO 3, 1 Aug; V Corps FO 17, 1 Aug. Capt. William C. Miller of the 35th Division was awarded the DSC for heroic action on 2 August.

[34] *V Corps Operations in the ETO*, p. 158; Conf Notes, Gerow and Irwin, 31 Jul, 5th Div G–3 Jnl and File.

[35] FUSA Daily G–1 Rpts, Aug. Pfc. Joseph A. Elwell of the 2d Engineer Combat Battalion, who volunteered to remove mines blocking the advance, and Pfc. Lawrence Georgeatos of the 38th Infantry posthumously received the DSC.

[36] FUSA FO's 4 and 5, 4 and 5 Aug; *V Corps Operations in the ETO*, map on p. 162.

invasion, had nearly destroyed the town; the actual struggle for the town by the ground forces in August reduced the town to rubble. Late in July, as the sound of artillery came increasingly closer, the citizens were hardly reassured when German troops urged them not to be afraid. "We'll defend your town house by house," they promised.[37]

The *LXXXIV Corps'* indefatigable kampfgruppe of the *353d Division,* supported by elements of the *363d Division,* and the *II Parachute Corps' 3d Parachute Division* were responsible for the town. Roadblocks covered by antitank guns and excellent positions on dominating ground comprised the defenses.[38]

The battle for Vire started on 5 August when 29th Division tanks and infantry drove down the Tessy–Vire highway. Any hope that the Germans would abandon Vire vanished quickly, for they gave immediate notice of their intentions by striking the spearhead of the U.S. attack, the 2d Armored Division's CCA, at Martilly, less than a mile from the center of the city. A tank company assembled nineteen tanks in two fields beside the highway in preparation for crossing the Vire at a stone bridge. No sooner were the tanks assembled along the hedgerow perimeters of the fields than enemy artillery knocked out ten tanks with a disastrous concentration of fire. Although the remaining tanks moved out at once in an attempt to cross the Martilly bridge, continuing fire from dominating ground knocked out four additional tanks and prevented the crossing. Reconnaissance parties searching

for alternate sites found the ground too soft for tanks to ford the stream.

Other tanks had better luck. They secured Hill 219, west of Vire, against slight opposition and gave the Americans terrain that was extremely favorable for offensive action against the town. Since the presence of CCA tankers and infantrymen on Hill 219 constituted a serious threat to the German defense, strong counterattacks were launched from Vire throughout the day. The American positions became so precarious that General Gerhardt that evening dispatched the 116th Infantry as reinforcement.

To reach Hill 219, the 116th Infantry moved in three battalion columns, the men of each advancing single file through the hedgerowed fields, the columns about a field apart. Isolated groups of Germans concealed in scattered farmhouses and foxholes and along the hedges were quickly eliminated. The regiment reached the crest of Hill 219 late on the night of 5 August. By the following morning it was evident that this was the best jump-off point for an assault against Vire.

By that time General Corlett had reached the conclusion that it would be unprofitable to continue to employ the 2d Armored Division's combat commands to spearhead the infantry division's attacks. The broken terrain and the lack of a good road net made the area basically unsuitable for armored operations. The corps commander felt that the tanks could add little to infantry capabilities, in fact they actually clogged the few available roads and impeded the infantry advance. Furthermore, during the five days between 1 and 6 August, the combat commands had sustained

[37] André Letondot, "La Double Agonie de Vire," in Herval, *Bataille de Normandie,* I, 288.

[38] MS # B–725 (Gersdorff); MS # B–346 (Blauensteiner).

about 450 casualties, a large number for armored troops and not commensurate with the gains.[39] Feeling that the armored division could be employed better elsewhere, General Corlett instructed General Brooks to move the 2d Armored Division off the roads in order to let the 28th and 29th Divisions pass through. The armored division—with the exception of CCA on Hill 219, designated now as the XIX Corps reserve—assembled and prepared to move into the VII Corps zone. Meanwhile, the 28th Division made ready to continue southeastward to Gathemo and beyond, and the 29th Division completed preliminary consolidation for the assault on Vire.

Just before dark on 6 August, the 116th Infantry descended the steep east slope of Hill 219. The men moved in single file through dense underbrush and over thick outcroppings into a narrow ravine at the bottom of the hill. They were more interested in speed than in concealment, for the Germans did not wait long before beginning to shell the route of advance. Protected to a degree by the sharp angle of declivity and the narrowness of the gully, the assault troops crossed a shallow stream at the bottom of the hill and climbed the opposite wall of the ravine. Rushing in small groups across a shell-pocked secondary road, the troops ran up a gently sloping hill and into the town of Vire.

Buildings set ablaze by artillery threw a pall of smoke over the town, and piles of rubble blocked the streets. The exercise of command even at company level was difficult during the street fighting, but men of the 116th Infantry dis-

played individual initiative and judgment and worked efficiently in small groups to clear the town. Prisoners constituted a problem in the darkness, and many escaped after capture. By dawn of 7 August the regiment had secured Vire and had set up blocking positions on five roads leading east and south from the town. The 29th Division officially reported the capture of Vire, as the Germans systematically began to shell the town.

The 29th Division sustained nearly a thousand casualties while advancing the ten miles from Tessy through Vire, in the process achieving its third major victory in less than a month: St. Lô, Tessy, and Vire.[40] Yet the gain of twenty miles from St. Lô to Vire must have seemed to the troops hardly fair compensation for so much weariness and pain.

The First Army achievements during the first six days of August were somewhat inconclusive even though the objectives deemed essential for continued operations—Mortain and Vire—were in American possession and even though undiminished pressure had forced a withdrawal that the enemy, by his determined resistance, had demonstrated he was unwilling to make. By capturing the Forêt de St. Sever the Americans denied the Germans excellent observation and cover and came into control of an extensive road net.[41]

Despite these accomplishments, the First Army was still short of its objectives in the Sourdeval area, and a twenty-mile gap lay open in the right portion of

---

[39] FUSA Daily G–1 Rpts, Aug.

[40] FUSA Daily G–1 Rpts, Aug.
[41] See V Corps G–2 Tactical Study of the Terrain, 30 Jul, V Corps G–3 Jnl and File.

CLEARING OPERATIONS IN VIRE

the army front between the 1st Division at Ambrières-le-Grand and the 30th Division at Mortain. Stubborn resistance in the Sourdeval–Gathemo salient despite a developing American threat of encirclement perplexed American commanders. General Hodges on 4 August thought there might be some German strength coming west toward the salient and in order "to stop them as short as possible" he had approved a suggestion made by General Collins. In view of the slow XIX Corps advance south from Tessy, Collins proposed to push the VII Corps almost due east to Gathemo and thus intrude on the XIX Corps zone. However, the VII Corps continued to have difficulties in its own zone, the XIX Corps rate of advance improved, and the original boundaries remained in effect.

Determined enemy resistance in the center, evidence of increasing strength among German forces, and the gap in the VII Corps zone promoted caution on the part of the First Army. It was this that had kept the First Army from exploiting the fluid situation on the German left "with impunity" as had the Third.[42]

The failure to eliminate the opposi-

---

[42] FUSA Rpt of Opns, p. 4; Sylvan Diary, 4 Aug.

tion that had crystalized around Sourdeval was like an ominous cloud mar-
ring an otherwise clear summer sky.
Optimism obscured some of the cloud's
meaning. The cloud actually foreshadowed a storm.

Montgomery's Intentions

British troops had also threatened the
town of Vire during the first week in
August as the 8 Corps of the Second
British Army right flank continued the
drive south begun from Caumont on 30
July. Although patrols of the 11th
Armoured Division had reached a point
a little more than a mile north of Vire
on 2 August, antitank fire by the *3d
Parachute Division* forced a withdrawal.
On the following day paratroopers,
aided by parts of the *9th* and *10th SS
Panzer Divisions* under *II SS Panzer
Corps* control, counterattacked exposed
British flanks and encircled a small
armored force, causing the armor to halt
temporarily.[43]   The 11th Armoured
then resumed the attack toward the
southeast and advanced through le Bény-
Bocage, across the Vire–Condé-sur-
Noireau road, and into position to
threaten Tinchebray and Flers by 6
August. (*See Map IX.*)

The 30 British Corps, in the center of
General Dempsey's army, had struck
southeast on 30 July from the vicinity
of Villers-Bocage toward Thury-Harcourt and the Orne River. Stubborn
resistance and rugged terrain centering
on the thousand-foot height of Mt. Pincon denied rapid advance, but the Brit-

ish nevertheless secured a foothold on
the slopes of the high ground. On 5
August Dempsey broadened his attack,
and two days later the 12 Corps crossed
the Orne River between Mt. Pinçon and
Caen, securing a shallow bridgehead.

Meanwhile, the 2d Canadian Corps
of the First Canadian Army had
mounted several holding attacks in the
Caen sector to prevent the Germans
from shifting reinforcements to other
sectors under Allied attack. Even as
General Crerar thus sought to divert the
Germans, his main concern was to prepare a major effort to be launched south
of Caen toward Falaise.[44]

Plans for a major attack from Caen
toward Falaise revealed the development
of General Montgomery's intentions.
The strategic decision reached by the
Allies early in August involved a drive
to the Seine, but the first step toward the
Seine was the clearance of the area west
of the Orne. General Eisenhower had
pointed this out as early as 31 July when
he wrote: "With the Canadian Army
fighting intensively to prevent enemy
movement away from the Caen area,
Dempsey's attack coupled with Bradley's
will clean up the area west of the Orne
once and for all." [45]

Several days later, General Montgomery was thinking beyond the Orne.
By 4 August he felt that the enemy front
was "in such a state that it could be
made to disintegrate completely." He
had concluded that "the only hope" the
Germans had of saving their armies was
a "staged withdrawal to the Seine." By
swinging the Allied right flank "round

---

[43] MS # B–346 (Blauensteiner); MS # B–840
(Eberbach); Answers by the CG, 11th Armd Div,
to Questions by Hist Sec USFET, 6 Nov 45, ML–
2251.

[44] Montgomery, *Normandy to the Baltic*, pp.
140–50; Stacey, *Canadian Army*, p. 195.
[45] Ltr, Eisenhower to Montgomery, FWD–12505,
31 Jul, SGS SHAEF File 381, OVERLORD, I (a).

towards Paris," Montgomery could hasten and disrupt the withdrawal and force the Germans back against the Seine and its destroyed bridges.

If the Germans withdrew to the Seine, as Montgomery thought they must, their immediate move logically would be to positions east of the Orne River, generally along a line between Caen and Flers. If Montgomery could act quickly enough, a drive to the south from Caen to Falaise would place troops behind the preliminary German withdrawal to the Orne. If Crerar's troops secured Falaise, if Dempsey's troops reached Condé-sur-Noireau, and if enemy forces remained in between, the Germans would be "in a very awkward situation."

Thus, although the broader Allied strategy was an intent to pin the Germans back against the Seine, the immediate opportunity was present to "cut off the enemy now facing Second Army and render their withdrawing east difficult—if not impossible." Destroying enemy personnel and equipment would be but the beginning of a "wide exploitation of success," presumably meaning exploitation on a wide front toward the Seine. The main instrument of destruction was to be the First Canadian Army making ready to attack toward Falaise *as early as possible and in any case not later than 8 August."* [46]

Two days after stating these plans, General Montgomery explained his intentions more specifically. As Montgomery saw the situation on 6 August, the Germans faced dismal alternatives in making the withdrawal that seemed to Montgomery the only course open to them. If they tried to utilize a series of delaying positions between the Caen–Vire line and the Seine, they would be unable to hold any long front in strength. With relatively few troops available, it would be impossible for the Germans to retain a pivot point at Caen for the withdrawal and simultaneously to restore the crumbled left flank. In the absence of established alternate lines in the rear, the Germans could not let go both ends of the line. If the Germans persisted in holding Caen, they offered the Allies the opportunity of swinging completely around their left and cutting off their escape. If they endeavored to buttress their encircled left flank and thereby weakened their pivot point, they gave the Allies access to the shortest route to the Seine. In either case, the Germans invited destruction of their forces west of the Seine River.

General Montgomery accepted the invitation with alacrity, announcing his intention to destroy the enemy forces within the boundaries of the OVERLORD lodgment area. He planned to pivot the Allied armies on the left, swing hard with the right toward Paris, drive the Germans against the Seine, and crush them before they could repair the destroyed bridges to evacuate their retreating forces.

Judging that the Germans would try to escape the COBRA consequences by accepting the lesser evil and pivoting on the Caen area as they fell back, Montgomery planned to unhinge the Germans' withdrawal by robbing them of their pivot point, Caen. General Crerar was to accomplish this by driving to Falaise, then attacking to the Seine along the Lisieux–Rouen axis. As a com-

[46] 21 AGp Gen Operational Situation and Dir, M–516, 4 Aug; Montgomery, *Normandy to the Baltic*, pp. 150–51.

plementary maneuver, General Dempsey
was to push out in an arc, swinging
southeast and then east, putting the
main weight on the right flank. After
moving through Argentan and Laigle,
the British were to drive through the
Dreux–Evreux area and prepare to cross
the Seine between Mantes-Gassicourt
and les Andelys. On the right, General
Bradley's 12th Army Group was to make
the main effort on the right flank, thrusting rapidly east and northeast toward
Paris.

Speed, General Montgomery indicated, was the overwhelming requisite
for success. Commanders were therefore to press forward boldly and take
great risks. Destroying the enemy forces
west of the Seine might be so damaging
a blow, he thought, as to hasten the end
of the war.[47]

In brief, General Montgomery's intentions were postulated on the belief
that the Germans had no alternative but
to withdraw to and across the Seine.
On this premise he sought to disorganize, harass, and pursue them, transform
their retreat into a rout, and destroy
their forces in detail. The maneuver
he ordered would swing three Allied
armies into the German forces while the
fourth Allied army would catapult forward to outrun them.[48]

General Bradley was not entirely convinced of the irresistible logic of Montgomery's interpretation. He ordered
Patton to move toward le Mans and
eventually toward the Paris–Orléans
gap, and he ordered Hodges to seize the
Domfront–Ambrières-le-Grand area as a

preliminary for a drive toward Alençon.
But he was concerned by the fact that
the Germans might turn and leap.
They were capable, Bradley judged, of
assembling strong armored forces in the
vicinity of Domfront, and from there
they might attack westward toward Avranches.[49]

Like Bradley, Hodges felt that because
the German left flank was still "floating,"
it was reasonable to expect a German
counterattack aimed at arresting American momentum.[50] Similarly, but more
specifically, Haislip had pointed out that
a German counterattack toward Avranches with the purpose of separating
American forces north and south of the
Sée and Sélune Rivers was "a distinct
capability."[51]

Despite these warnings, commanders
were in no mood to listen to what
seemed to be prophets of gloom. Without worrying about what the Germans
might do, the Allies pursued their own
offensive plans. While Crerar prepared
to jump off toward Falaise, while Dempsey made ready to push southeast toward
Argentan, while Hodges displaced part
of his forces southward to take up the
pursuit toward Alençon, and while Patton was sending the XV Corps eastward
toward le Mans, the Germans disregarded Montgomery's logic. In their
first large-scale counterattack since the
invasion two months earlier, the Germans turned and sprang westward toward Avranches.

---

[47] 21 AGp Gen Operational Situation and Dir,
M–517, 6 Aug.

[48] See Eisenhower to Marshall, FWD–12674, 7
Aug, Pogue Files.

[49] 12th AGp Ltr of Instrs 3, 6 Aug. Bradley later
made no claim to anticipating a German counterattack. Bradley, *Soldier's Story*, p. 371.

[50] FUSA FO 4, 4 Aug.

[51] XV Corps Plan for XV Corps Defense Between
Fougères and La Sée River, 4 Aug, XV Corps G–3
Jnl and File.

CHAPTER XXIV

The Mortain Counterattack

German Intentions

The attack launched toward Avranches during the early hours of 7 August was the product of a curious lack of empathy between Hitler and Kluge. Hitler had issued the attack order on 2 August, and Kluge had carried out the planning, but by 6 August Hitler had developed his original concept into a grandiose scheme that Kluge had not even imagined.

The original goal of the counterattack was to regain Avranches and thereby re-establish a continuous defensive line in Normandy and restore the conditions that had made possible the static warfare of June and July. According to General der Panzertruppen Adolf Kuntzen, commander of the *LXXXI Corps* who was briefed by Kluge on 3 August, Kluge from the beginning felt that the counterattack could not fundamentally change the situation. The sole advantage, from Kluge's point of view, an advantage he was sure Hitler appreciated, was that the counterattack might facilitate a general withdrawal from Normandy to a new line of defense.[1] Denied by Hitler the freedom to look backward, Kluge could only hope that OKW was in the process of organizing defenses in the rear.

As late as 6 August, the day before the attack, Kluge's misgivings were reflected in his attempts to make last-minute changes in the plan. He was dissatisfied with the strength of the attacking force as constituted under the *XLVII Panzer Corps*, and he tried vainly to find additional units for reinforcement. The *LXXXI Corps*, in the vicinity of Alençon, was the only nearby force, and Kluge wanted it to commit the *9th Panzer Division* in a thrust to St. Hilaire-du-Harcouët once the division arrived in the area. In contrast, Hausser desired the *LXXXI Corps* to send the armored division in an attack toward Mayenne. The controversy soon entered the realm of academic discussion, for it quickly became evident that the divisions slated for the *LXXXI Corps*—the *9th Panzer* and the *708th Infantry*—would arrive from southern France too late to affect significantly the operations around either Avranches or Mayenne.

Unable to increase the striking power of the attack force either by additional units or by commitment of the *LXXXI Corps*, Kluge began to think that the *XLVII Panzer Corps* ought not to make the main effort north of Mortain as planned—between that town and the Sée River—but instead southwest through Mortain. *Seventh Army* staff planners, who had formulated the attack plan, had early pointed out that an axis of attack

[1] MS # B–807 (Kuntzen); *AGp B KTB*, 3 Aug.

south of Mortain—between the town and St. Hilaire—would not only broaden the front and tend to dissipate the limited forces available but would also commit the armored assault force to a poor road net. The best route to Avranches, they argued, was the most direct route, since it had the added advantage of keeping the attackers on the dominating terrain north of Mortain. Despite the completion of the attack preparations, it took the persuasion of Hausser's chief of staff, Gersdorff, to reassure Kluge that the plans about to be executed were probably the better, particularly since a thrust toward St. Hilaire would more than likely result in road congestion.[2]

It was a late hour to be thinking of altering plans, for the preattack situation was becoming increasingly dangerous, and an immediate effort was necessary to bolster the left flank before the lines there disintegrated completely. Even though the front had been contracted to the Chérencé-le-Roussel–Champ-du-Boult–Vire line, there was no telling how much longer the *LXXXIV Corps* could successfully hold on to the designated assembly areas and the high ground around Mortain. American occupation of Mortain was a serious setback that threatened to nullify these important attack prerequisites, and the American capture of Laval on 6 August endangered the supply bases near Alençon and le Mans.

Despite the disadvantages and diffi-

culties, some commanders felt that the tactical situation between 4 and 6 August had actually developed more favorably than might have been expected. The *II SS Panzer Corps* and the *II Parachute Corps* had eased, at least temporarily, the crisis along the army boundary near Vire. Although Hausser had to keep the *116th Panzer Division* committed defensively, he had pulled the *2d SS* and *2d Panzer Divisions* out of the line without breaking the connected front between the Sée River and Vire. The German field commanders nevertheless agreed that the attack had to be launched as soon as possible in order to regain operational initiative before new developments further complicated the situation.

Accepting the tactical necessity of executing the plans at once as scheduled, Kluge was rather disconcerted by several calls from Hitler on 6 August. Since 2 August, when Hitler had issued the original order, there had been neither instruction nor interference from higher headquarters. Kluge had interpreted his conversation with Jodl on 3 August as authority to command all the German forces in the west (including the Navy and the Air Force) and as clearance for attacking as he wished. Accepting the responsibility along with the freedom granted to deal with the American breakout and enjoying the implicit confidence thus accorded him, Kluge had arranged to have an advance command post set up west of Alençon so that he could personally supervise the attack. Suddenly however, on 6 August just a few hours before the attack was to begin, when Kluge was already committed to launching the effort that night, Hitler

[2] Telecon, Gersdorff and Kuntzen, 1115, 6 Aug, *LXXXI Corps KTB;* Telecons, Gersdorff and Kluge, 1025 and 1045, 6 Aug, *AGp B KTB;* MS # B–179 (Hausser) ; MS # B–725 (Gersdorff). The two latter documents and Hodgson, R–58, are basic sources for this chapter.

called *OB WEST* for a report on the progress of the planning.[3]

Not only did Hitler want a report on Kluge's intentions and plans by that evening, he also placed additional strength at Kluge's disposal. He made available sixty Panther tanks still held in reserve east of Paris and released to Kluge eighty Mark IV tanks and all the armored cars of the *11th Panzer Division,* which was moving northward from southern France toward Normandy. These troops were to reinforce the counterattack.[4] It was rather late to be getting additional forces, but they were a positive contribution. Later that afternoon, after Hitler received preliminary reports on the counterattack during his customary daily briefing at the Wolf's Lair headquarters, Jodl called *OB WEST* to inform Kluge that Hitler wanted some changes made. The most important was that Hitler did not wish Funck, the *XLVII Panzer Corps* commander, to lead the attack; instead, he wanted Eberbach, commander of the *Fifth Panzer Army.*[5]

This telephone conversation revealed clearly that Hitler and Kluge were not tuned to the same wave length; they were not thinking of the same kind of operation. Kluge was ready to attack, whereas OKW was apparently only in the preliminary stages of planning. Kluge intended only to regain Avranches and restore the defensive line, while Hitler evidently thought in terms

ARTILLERY OBSERVATION POST *near Barenton.*

of a big offensive to be launched by several corps under Eberbach.

To accede to Hitler's wishes meant postponing the attack at least twenty-four hours to await the concentration of stronger forces and also disregarding the developments around le Mans. In view of the precarious tactical situation, any delay seemed unreasonable. The northern front at the Sée River might disintegrate, and the deep south flank of *Army Group B* might be so enveloped that contact between the combat troops and the supply complex based on Alençon would be impossible. Already that evening Barenton (seven miles southeast of Mortain) was being threatened, and the weakness of the *275th Division's* defenses at the village made obvious the distinct menace to the southern flank. Furthermore, Radio Calais, a German

[3] Telecons, 1445 and 1500, 6 Aug, *OB WEST KTB;* Telecon, Kluge and Jodl, 1210, 3 Aug, *AGp B KTB;* MS # B-723 (Gersdorff).

[4] Telecon, 1510, 6 Aug, *OB WEST KTB; Telecon,* 1516, 6 Aug, *AGp B KTB.*

[5] Telecon, Jodl and Blumentritt, 1525, 6 Aug, *OB WEST KTB.*

intelligence agency, informed Kluge that the Allies had recognized the shift of his troops for what it was. Uncertain of the ability of the German defenses to hold much longer and fearing that the Allies would bomb his assemblies out of existence, Kluge persuaded Hitler to let the attack go as planned even though it meant that he could not use the additional armor Hitler had made available.[6]

Only with great reluctance did Hitler permit the attack to be launched. Desiring the most massive blow that could be assembled, he was not convinced that the counterattacking force was as strong as it could have been. He accepted Kluge's recommendation nevertheless, and issued specific instructions for the conduct of operations once Avranches was captured. He directed that Eberbach take command from Hausser at Avranches and swing from there to the northeast into the First U.S. Army flank, thereby disrupting and nullifying the American breakout. To insure compliance, Hitler dispatched the chief of the OKW Army staff, General der Infanterie Walter Buhle, to the west by plane.[7]

Hitler's intention, which had crystallized too late to affect the initial attack, was clear in the order he issued on the following day, 7 August, after the attack was under way. "The decision in the Battle of France," he wrote, "depends on the success of the [Avranches] attack. . . . The C-in-C West has a unique opportunity, which will never

return, to drive into an extremely exposed enemy area and thereby to change the situation completely."[8] The Avranches counterattack, as the Germans called it, was to be the decisive blow sought since the invasion, the master stroke of strategic significance that was to destroy Operation OVERLORD. The first step in that direction was to divide the First and Third U.S. Armies at Avranches. Once this was accomplished, further measures were to roll up the Allied front. Choltitz, the former LXXXIV Corps commander who was being briefed by Hitler for a new assignment, recalled later that Hitler expected the offensive to throw the Allies back "into the sea."[9]

The field commanders did not share Hitler's conviction. Kluge had not suspected that Hitler anticipated such exalted results. Hausser, who considered the task of regaining Avranches relatively easy, felt that holding Avranches after taking it would be the difficult part of the assignment, to say nothing of launching a further attack to the northeast. The result of the conflicting intentions was what became known to the Americans as the Mortain counterattack, a drive launched in some uncertainty but with Avranches clearly defined as the objective. (*Map X*)

The Attack

The first echelon of the attacking force was to be composed of three armored divisions moving westward abreast toward an initial objective along

[6] Telecons, Kluge and Blumentritt, 1600, 6 Aug, Kluge and Buttlar-Brandenfels, 1650, 6 Aug, and Zimmerman and Templehoff, 1905, 6 Aug, *AGp B KTB*; Telecon Jodl and Zimmerman, 1900, 6 Aug, *OB WEST KTB*.
[7] *Der Westen* (Schramm), p. 83.

[8] Quoted in Msg, *AGp B* to *Fifth Pz A*, 7 Aug. *Fifth Pz A KTB*, *Anlage 275*; *OB WEST KTB*, 7 Aug, and *Anlage 1176*.
[9] Choltitz, *Soldat unter Soldaten*, pp. 222–23.

the Brécey–St. Hilaire road. The *116th Panzer Division* on the right was to attack without prior assembly and strike along the north bank of the Sée River toward Chérencé; it was to be echeloned to the right rear to protect the north flank. Making the main effort in the center, the *2d Panzer Division* (reinforced by a panzer battalion each from the *1st SS* and the *116th Panzer Divisions*) was to thrust along the south bank of the Sée, using the St. Barthélemy–Reffuveille road as its principal axis of advance. The *2d SS Panzer Division* (reinforced by the *17th SS Panzer Grenadiers*, a division reduced by combat to regimental strength) was to attack on both sides of Mortain; it was to be echeloned to the left to cover the open south flank. Following the first echelon closely, the *1st SS Panzer Division* (less an armored infantry regiment and a tank battalion, which remained with the *Fifth Panzer Army*) was to exploit initial success and capture Avranches. The reconnaissance battalion of *Panzer Lehr* was to patrol the deep south flank. The *LXXXI Corps* was to block a possible American thrust toward Alençon.

The situation on the evening of 6 August was judged favorable. With regard to weather, a vital factor, forecasters had predicted fog for the following morning, a desirable condition for the attack. If the fog cleared later in the day, the Luftwaffe was prepared to furnish aerial support in strength. The commander of the fighter plane contingent in the west had visited the *Seventh Army* command post on 6 August to inform the ground troops that three hundred operational planes in France had been gathered to provide cover for the counterattack the next day. Ground opposition seemed weak, for only elements of two U.S. divisions, the 3d Armored and the 30th Infantry, had been identified in the attack zone, as was the actual case. Against them were concentrated between 120 and 190 German tanks poised for the surprise attack. Once Avranches was captured, a newly arriving infantry division, the *331st* (scheduled to be at Tinchebray by 9 August), would be committed between the *XLVII Panzer Corps* and the *LXXXIV Corps* in order to regain Brécey.[10]

On the debit side of the ledger, the assembly of the counterattack forces had been made in great haste, at night, and with great difficulty. Units had assembled while in almost constant contact with Allied forces. In some instances, they had been compelled to fight their way to assembly points while in danger of being encircled. There was no distinct boundary between moving into position and jumping off in attack. Many units had already taken heavy losses before the attack started. In contrast with the usual daily personnel losses that averaged about 3 percent of those units in contact, German casualty reports for 6 August inexplicably attained heights of 30 and 40 percent. The meaning of the casualty figures was obscure to the Germans, for although it indicated the urgent necessity of getting the counterattack under way before attrition sapped the strength of their forces in Normandy, the fact that the *353d Division* (kampfgruppe size) and *363d Division* had together knocked out 28 American tanks on 6 August indicated that the German units, though

---

[10] See MS # C–017 (Speidel).

severely reduced, were still combat effective.[11]

At H Hour–2200, 6 August–Hausser received a phone call from Funck, the *XLVII Panzer Corps* commander, who wanted the attack postponed. Two factors, Funck felt, made this necessary. First, the advance elements of the *1st SS Panzer Division* (the exploiting force) were only beginning to reach Tinchebray, even though the division commander had promised to be ready to cross the line of departure in strength a good six miles farther west around 2300. Obviously, the division would not be able to reach its assigned position in time. Nor would it be able to detach an armored battalion in time to reinforce the *2d Panzer Division* as planned. The reasons for the delay in arrival were several: the *89th Division* had been slow in relieving the *1st SS* on the *Fifth Panzer Army* front; traffic congestion and Allied air attacks had harassed the approach march; and finally, a piece of pure bad luck, the panzer battalion hurrying toward the *2d Panzer Division* had been moving through a defile in close formation when a crashing Allied fighter-bomber fell on the lead tank, blocked the entire battalion, and forced the tanks to back up and turn around in constricted space.

The second factor that Funck brought to Hausser's attention was the attitude of the commander of the *116th Panzer Division*, Generalleutnant Gerhard Graf von Schwerin, who had not dispatched the tank battalion he was supposed to furnish the *2d Panzer Division*. This was not the first time, Funck explained,

that the commander of the *116th* had failed to comply with orders. He requested that Schwerin be relieved.

Hausser was inclined to agree with Funck that the news of both incidents was serious, but he was unwilling to postpone the attack. Hausser's only concession was to delay the jump-off until midnight to give the *1st SS Panzer Division* two more hours to come forward. He did nothing about Schwerin.[12]

The attack started shortly after midnight without an artillery preparation. The *2d SS Panzer Division* on the left attacked in two columns, overran Mortain from both sides and captured the town, then advanced toward high ground west of Mortain and to the southwest toward St. Hilaire. There was no significant American opposition, and by noon of 7 August *2d SS Panzer* troops held blocking positions about half way between Mortain and St. Hilaire, thereby protecting the southern flank of the attack. A thrust to St. Hilaire and a direct threat to Avranches from the southeast seemed simple except for the 2d Battalion, 120th Infantry, ensconced and encircled on Hill 317 immediately east of Mortain. This contingent, with unexcelled observation of the *2d SS Panzer* zone south and west of Mortain, called for artillery fire on the division and thus pinned the troops down, preventing further advance.[13]

The *2d Panzer Division*, making the

---

[11] Telecon, Gersdorff and Lt Col Guenther von Kluge, 2100, 6 Aug, *Seventh Army* Tel Msgs.

[12] Telecons, Wisch and Gersdorff, 1630, 6 Aug. and Funck and Hausser, 2200, 6 Aug, *Seventh Army* Tel Msgs; MS # B–017 (Voigtsberger); MS # A–918 (Gersdorff).

[13] Telecon, Gersdorff and Speidel, 1515, 7 Aug, and Gersdorff Telecon, 1200, 7 Aug, *AGp B KTB*; MS # P–159 (Sueckler); see Jules and Gilles Buisson. *Mortain et sa Bataille*, pp. 74ff.

main effort in the center, got only half of its troops off during the early hours of 7 August, the column on the right moving along the south bank of the Sée. Despite the failure of a tank battalion of the *116th Panzer Division* to appear for attachment, the armored column moved off, achieved surprise, and rolled through le Mesnil-Tôve to le Mesnil-Adelée. There, some elements turned north to protect the flank against a possible thrust from Chérencé, while the main body continued west toward the Brécey–St. Hilaire road. Shortly after daybreak, 7 August, just west of le Mesnil-Adelée and three miles short of the initial objective, the column encountered resistance that forced a halt.

The left column of the *2d Panzer Division* delayed attacking until dawn of 7 August, when the panzer battalion of the *1st SS* finally joined and completed the assault formation. The column then advanced easily through Bellefontaine. Strong antitank fire at St. Barthélemy made an organized effort necessary in order to reduce the opposition. The advance then continued almost to Juvigny before being stopped.

With the *2d Panzer Division* bogged down short of the initial objective, Funck committed the *1st SS Panzer Division* through the *2d Panzer* units in midmorning, hoping thereby at least to gain Juvigny. The restricted road net, limited maneuver room, and American resistance on the ground and in the air balked further progress. With tank losses skyrocketing, Funck halted the attack around noon and instructed the troops to dig in.

Because both columns of the *2d Panzer Division* and the reinforcing column of the *1st SS Panzer Division* had

attacked on exceedingly narrow fronts, their spearhead wedges in unfavorable positions at le Mesnil-Adelée and east of Juvigny were especially vulnerable to counterattack. American artillery and antitank pieces located north and south of the Sée River struck the points of the German columns and kept the units immobile for the rest of the day.[14]

The north flank along the Sée was open, and it gave the German command particular cause for concern because the *116th Panzer Division* had failed to attack. Schwerin had been threatened with encirclement by American attacks toward Gathemo and Chérencé, and he had simply withheld the attack order from his subordinates. He had no confidence in the ability of the *84th Division*, which was relieving him, to hold against the American pressure, and consequently felt that he could neither detach a tank battalion to the *2d Panzer Division* nor launch the attack toward Avranches. Also, Schwerin had apparently lost hope for victory. Involved in the conspiracy of July 20th, he was one of the field commanders who were to have negotiated with the Allies for an armistice. No matter whether tactical or political factors were more important to Schwerin, his failure to participate in the Avranches counterattack was a flagrant case of disobedience. At 1600, 7 August, Hausser and Funck relieved him of command and replaced him with Funck's chief of staff, Col. Walter Reinhard. Thirty minutes later the division

---

[14] Telecons, Ziegelmann and Lt Col Guenther von Kluge, 0430, 7 Aug, Gersdorff Telecon, 0915, 7 Aug, and Gersdorff and Speidel, 1515, 7 Aug, *AGp B KTB*; MS # A-904 (Luettwitz) ; MS # A-918 (Gersdorff)

finally jumped off. The troops made no progress.[15]

Instead of a well-massed, co-ordinated effort, only three of the six assault columns—the *2d SS Panzer Division* and one column of the *2d Panzer Division*—had jumped off on time. The attack had achieved surprise, and the armored troops had rolled forward about six miles. When the day dawned clear, without the anticipated fog, the ground troops, who were experienced in Normandy and knew what to expect from Allied air superiority, began to dig in. At that moment the advance came to a halt, and the commitment of the *1st SS Panzer Division* availed nothing. Heavy American artillery fires indicated that surprise was already gone. When Allied planes came out in force to bomb and strafe the armored columns, the troops were already under cover, their vehicles under camouflage, but British Hurricanes and Typhoons firing rockets nevertheless struck awe into the German formations. As for the mighty German air effort promised, the fighter planes that got off the ground near Paris did not get much beyond their airfields. Allied squadrons engaged them at once, and not a single German plane reached Mortain that day.[16]

By late afternoon, 7 August, it appeared to Hitler that Kluge had displayed poor judgment in allowing the

commitment of the *1st SS Panzer Division* north of Mortain rather than southwest toward St. Hilaire, where American opposition had been absent. It also seemed to him that the attack had been launched prematurely, hastily, and carelessly. If Kluge had waited until the *9th SS, 10th SS,* and *9th Panzer Divisions* had been assembled for a truly massive effort, Hitler felt, the attack more than likely would have brought better results. Deciding that he could no longer entirely rely upon Kluge, he took a more direct role in the operations.

Still under the impression that the situation offered him a unique opportunity for disrupting the Allied breakout and eventually destroying the Allied beachhead, Hitler determined to continue the attack to Avranches. "I command the attack be prosecuted daringly and recklessly to the sea," he wrote that afternoon. He ordered that, "regardless of the risk," the *II SS Panzer Corps* (with the *9th SS* and the *10th SS Panzer Divisions* and either the *12th SS* or *21st Panzer Division*) be withdrawn from the *Fifth Panzer Army* line and committed in the Avranches sector "to bring about the collapse of the Normandy front by a thrust into the deep flank and rear of the enemy facing Seventh Army." To consummate what to him had become the master stroke of the western campaign, "Greatest daring, determination, imagination must give wings to all echelons of command. Each and every man must believe in victory. Cleaning up in rear areas and in Brittany can wait until later." [17]

[15] Telecons, Funck and Hausser, 2200, 6 Aug, Gersdorff and Reinhard, 1800, 7 Aug, Gersdorff and Hausser, 1540, 7 Aug, Gersdorff and Speidel, 1940, 7 Aug, *Seventh Army* Tel Msgs; Gersdorff and Speidel, 1515, 7 Aug, Kluge and Hausser, 2150, 7 Aug, *AGp B KTB*; MS # B–017 (Voigtsberger); ETHINT 17 (interview with Schwerin); MS # C–017 (Speidel); MS # B–721 (Speidel).

[16] Telecon, Blumentritt and Gersdorff, 1940, 7 Aug, *Seventh Army* Tel Msgs; MS # P–169 (Stueckler); see Pogue, *Supreme Command,* p. 208, n. 43.

[17] Quoted in Msg, *AGp B* to *Fifth Pz A,* 7 Aug, *Fifth Pz A KTB, Anlage 275; Der Westen* (Schramm), p. 83; *OB WEST KTB,* 7 Aug, and *Anlage 1176;* see also MS # A–918 (Gersdorff).

Kluge had already concluded that the attack had failed. His judgment was as much influenced by developments on the northern and southern flanks of the *Seventh Army* as by the progress of the attack itself. American pressure had not ceased, and renewed threats from the north at Gathemo and from the south at Barenton posed unpleasant thoughts that the *Seventh Army* spearheads directed toward Avranches might be encircled and destroyed. The wiser course of action, he began to think, might be to withdraw.[18]

A call from Eberbach on the afternoon of 7 August added to Kluge's concern. It also reinforced his feeling that withdrawal from Mortain might be in order. Eberbach was troubled by the weakness of his thinned-out defense—lines covering the approaches to Falaise—and asked for reinforcement. Kluge diverted the incoming *331st Division* toward the *Fifth Panzer Army* front and was considering sending units from the *Seventh Army* when Hitler's order arrived to announce that the effort toward Avranches was to continue. Kluge virtually apologized when he phoned Eberbach to tell him that Eberbach not only would get no additional strength but would lose two panzer divisions at once and a third armored division eventually. "I foresee that the failure of this [continued] attack [to Avranches]," he told Eberbach, "can lead to collapse of the entire Normandy front, but the order [from Hitler] is so unequivocal that it must be obeyed."[19]

Transmitting Hitler's order to Hausser, Kluge informed him that the *10th SS and 12th SS Panzer Divisions* were to arrive in the *Seventh Army* sector on 8 August and be committed soon afterwards toward Avranches under the *LVIII Panzer Corps* headquarters, which had recently come up from southern France. As soon as the corps assembled its two SS panzer divisions, the *Seventh Army* would continue the attack without regard to the northern and southern flanks. Until the new attack was ready, the positions reached by the forward elements were to be held. The last remaining elements of the *1st SS Panzer Division* (including twenty-five assault guns), which had become available for use that evening, moved into a line that had suddenly, if only temporarily, changed from offense to defense.

Hausser, too, admitted failure on 7 August. He ascribed the causes to the Allied air superiority, the immobility of the *116th Panzer Division*, and a stronger than expected American resistance. Although additional striking forces augmented the chances of regaining Avranches, continuing threats to the army's flanks increased the chances of disaster. But since Hitler felt that the outcome of the war depended on another attack toward Avranches, there was no choice.[20]

The American Reaction

To the Americans who felt the force of the counterattack toward Avranches, there was little impression that the Germans had been clumsy in launching

[18] See, for example, Telecon, Kluge and Kuntzen, 0730, 7 Aug, *LXXXI KTB*.

[19] Telecon, Kluge and Eberbach, 2140, 7 Aug, *Fifth Panzer Army KTB*; *AGp B* Forward CP Tel Log (entry 2000, 7 Aug), *AGp B KTB*.

[20] *Seventh Army* Tel Jnl, entry 2200, 7 Aug; see *OB WEST KTB*, 7 Aug, and *Anlage 1184*.

their effort. Accompanied by surprise, the attack raised the specter of catastrophe. Loss of Mortain was a serious blow.

A town of 1,600 inhabitants, Mortain is at the foot of a rocky hill rising just to the east—Hill 317. The hill is the southern spur of wooded highland, convulsed and broken terrrain around Sourdeval called by tourist bureaus "la Suisse normande" (Norman Switzerland). Near the juncture of the ancient provinces of Normandy, Brittany, and Maine, Hill 317 provides a magnificent view of the flat tableland to the south and west—the Sélune River plain, which is crossed by ribbons of road and stream. Domfront, fifteen miles eastward, and the bay of Mont St. Michel, twenty miles to the west, are visible on clear days. After the 1st Division had entered Mortain without difficulty on 3 August, the VII Corps commander, General Collins, inspected the positions and pointed to the high ground east of Mortain. "Ralph," he told the 1st Division commander, "be sure to get Hill 317." "Joe," General Huebner replied, "I already have it." [21]

On 6 August the 30th Division occupied Mortain to free the 1st Division and its attached CCA of the 3d Armored Division for displacement south to Mayenne and exploitation east toward Alençon. Although the 1st Division was then rather far from VII Corps supply dumps (too long a run, General Collins thought, for effective supply),

Collins, who like the entire Allied command at the time was thinking in terms of the offensive, expected to move the corps beyond Mortain in short order. While the 4th Division remained in corps reserve near St. Pois, the 9th Division was to attack through Gathemo and Sourdeval, and the 30th Division was to push east toward Barenton and Domfront. There was no intimation that a German counterattack would upset these plans. [22]

Questions had been raised a week earlier—"Will the enemy counterattack against the VII Corps south of the Sée River? . . . Will the enemy counterattack against the left flank of the Corps? . . . Where and in what strength will the VII Corps encounter organized resistance?" But the answers were as anticlimactic as they appeared obvious. The corps G–2 estimated 5,400 combat effectives in opposition; a parachute division and an infantry division, each with 1,000 combat effectives, were the strongest units he believed to be on the corps front. [23] The Germans could hardly offer serious resistance. The stubborn opposition in the Villedieu-les-Poëles and Gathemo sectors during the first days of August was apparently nothing more than rear-guard action covering a general withdrawal.

The 30th Division, because of traffic snarls, did not reach Mortain until six or seven hours after the planned time, and General Hobbs took responsibility for the sector at 2000, 6 August, four hours before the German counterattack started. His primary mission was to de-

[21] Collins' Talk at the Armored School, 19 Jan 48. The last German in Mortain trying to escape was killed by a French policeman armed with a nineteenth century rifle and one bullet. Jules and Gilles Buisson, "Les Combats de Mortain," in Herval, *Bataille de Normandie,* I. 229.

[22] VII Corps Notes for CofS, 6 Aug, Opns Memo 59, 7 Aug (confirming oral orders, 6 Aug), and G–2 Summary, 1800, 6 Aug.

[23] VII Corps FO 7, 1 Aug, and Incl 3.

fend the front from St. Barthélemy through Mortain to Barenton. Since the first two villages were in American hands, he set out to take the third. Because a small task force (attached tanks from CCA of the 3d Armored Division) of the 1st Division was to have taken Barenton that evening, Hobbs sent an infantry battalion (less one company but augmented by a company of medium tanks and a reconnaissance platoon) to relieve the armor at Barenton. Soon after this force departed Mortain, enemy aircraft strafed the column, destroyed several trucks, caused twenty-five casualties, and delayed the advance for an hour. Being attacked by German planes was a rather rare occurrence, but it did not necessarily signal portentous events; the column continued. When the men of the 30th Division made contact with CCA near Barenton, they learned that the armored troops had held the village but briefly before being expelled. Joining forces, the two units prepared to attack Barenton on the following morning, the 7th.[24]

General Hobbs was also to attack toward Domfront, and he planned to send a reinforced infantry regiment there on 7 August. His G–2 also raised questions: Would the Germans defend high ground north of Barenton, high ground east and north of Domfront, or the road to Domfront? Would the Germans counterattack between Chérencé-le-Roussel and Mortain?[25] The questions came somewhat late.

Around midnight of 6 August, the VII Corps disseminated a warning that the Germans might counterattack near Mortain within the next twelve hours. Pilots had seen concentrations of German armor north and east of Sourdeval, forces thought to belong to the *1st SS, 2d,* and *116th Panzer Divisions.* If these units made a westward thrust to Avranches, they would cut the communications of those American forces operating south of the Sélune River. Until the threat either developed or vanished, the 30th Division was to postpone sending a regiment to Domfront; Hobbs was to move a battalion south of the Sélune to protect communications with the 1st Division; he was also to reinforce his troops on Hill 317 east of Mortain.[26] This, too, came too late.

Activity on 7 August opened in the 1st Division zone near Mayenne during the early minutes of the day. Reconnaissance troops of the *9th Panzer Division* launched an attack that seemed for a few hours as though it might develop into something serious. Though Americans later connected this with the Mortain counterattack, the action around Mayenne was local in nature and unrelated, except perhaps most tenuously, to the major effort around Mortain.

The German forces attacking at Mortain entered the 1st Division sector southeast of Barenton four and a half hours afterwards, about 0430, when six tanks and supporting infantry of the *2d SS Panzer Division* broke through a screen maintained by the 4th Cavalry Reconnaissance Squadron attached to

---

[24] 30th Div G–3 Per Rpt 54, 0200, 7 Aug; see Hewitt, *Story of 30th Division,* pp. 56–57; Sylvan Diary, 6 Aug.

[25] 30th Div FO 2, 0030, 7 Aug, and Intel Summary, 0400. 7 Aug.

[26] Telecon, Collins with Huebner and Hobbs, 0038, 7 Aug; see VII Corps AAR, Aug; Hewitt, *Story of 30th Division,* p. 54.

NORTH OF MORTAIN. *Enemy vehicles wrecked during the German counter-attack to Avranches.*

the 1st Division. The consequences were not important. The cavalry withdrew several miles, consolidated forces, and established new lines.

Throughout the rest of the day the 1st Division, outside the critical German attack zone, remained in spotty contact with the enemy. Extensive patrolling to protect Mayenne and the corps lines of communication established a pattern of activity that was to be characteristic for several days. Meanwhile, the division waited for "orders to continue

the exploitation" eastward toward Alençon.[27]

It was Lt. Col. Van H. Bond's 39th Infantry, 9th Division, that was first seriously threatened near the Sée River during the early hours of the German attack. Separated from the main body

[27] 1st Div AAR, Aug, and G–3 Per Rpts 63 and 64, 7 and 8 Aug; 4th Cav Recon Sq S–3 Rpt 1, 2400, 7 Aug; 3d Armd Div G–3 Per Rpt 44, 7 Aug. 2d Lt. Joseph Gorniak, Jr., of the 1st Medical Battalion was awarded the DSC for his heroic leadership of medical personnel during a chance encounter with a German patrol.

of the division, the regiment was attacking northeastward from Chérencé to make contact with the 47th and 60th Regiments pushing southeastward in the Gathemo area. At midnight, 6 August, the Germans still held the intervening ground about Perriers-en-Beauficel.

Shortly after midnight a forward observer of the 26th Field Artillery Battalion, which was supporting the 39th Infantry, heard tanks moving westward along the road between St. Barthélemy and Chérencé. The tank motors did not sound like Shermans. After establishing the fact that no American tanks were operating there, the artillery battalion, upon data furnished by the observer, began to fire at a range of five thousand yards but soon reduced it to only a thousand. By 0150, 7 August, not only the artillery battalion but also the infantry regiment was sure that a German armored column was moving west toward le Mesnil-Tôve.

A platoon of the regimental cannon company in le Mesnil-Tôve concluded that the Germans were already too close for effective defense. Dismantling their guns and disabling their vehicles, the troops abandoned the village and rejoined the infantry. So that German activity might be reported accurately, the platoon leader stayed behind. After verifying the fact that at least twenty enemy tracked vehicles were moving westward, he reported thirty-five more vehicles in the vicinity, including personnel carriers from which infantrymen were unloading. At the same time, word came from the regimental switchboard at le Mesnil-Tôve that the village was under machine gun fire, that all American troops had departed, and that

field trains and ammunition dumps nearby had been overrun and set afire.

The regimental commander had taken his first action at 0250, 7 August, when he instructed one of the infantry battalions to switch its antitank defenses toward the south to protect the rear. Thirty minutes later he directed his reserve (an infantry company and several tank destroyers) to attack south from Chérencé to le Mesnil-Tôve in order to cut behind the German spearhead. When the attack made no headway out of Chérencé, it became apparent that the Germans had cut directly across the regimental axis of communication. All three infantry battalions were north of the German penetration. The regimental command post, the cannon company (less one platoon), the antitank company (less two gun platoons), and the firing batteries of the 26th Field Artillery Battalion were south of the German column.[28]

The German attack struck the 30th Division more directly. The *2d SS Panzer Division* surged through Mortain, knocked out roadblocks manned by Col. Hammond D. Birks's 120th Infantry north and south of the village, overran the 2d Battalion command post in Mortain and drove the staff into hiding, and isolated the rifle battalion on Hill 317. The battalion, reinforced by a company of the 3d Battalion, had split a rifle company three ways to establish two roadblocks north of Mortain and one south of the village. One roadblock north of Mortain, augmented by a few antitank guns, remained in action and accounted for over forty enemy vehicles and tanks

---

[28] 39th Inf and 9th Div AAR's, Aug; Hewitt, *Story of 30th Division*, p. 57.

during the next few days. Two roadblocks were destroyed at once, the survivors making their way to the surrounded hilltop to join the three rifle
companies, the heavy weapons company,
and the several antitank pieces that occupied the most important terrain in
the Mortain sector.

Near St. Barthélemy, the Germans
overran two companies of Lt. Col. Walter M. Johnson's 117th Infantry, surrounded a battalion headquarters, and
threatened the regimental command
post four hundred yards away. A patrol checking the outpost defenses of the
regimental headquarters had suddenly
been confronted by about fifty Germans.
T. Sgt. Harold V. Sterling engaged the
enemy while four companions maneuvered to safety. Then all five men conducted a fire fight for one hour until
reinforcement arrived and the German
group withdrew. In the belief that
moving the regimental headquarters
might have an adverse effect on morale,
Colonel Johnson stayed to direct the
battle in his sector, although he was
virtually encircled.[29]

Despite these initial blows, the 30th
Division made no report to higher headquarters of the counterattack until 0315,
7 August, when German tanks were already in possession of Mortain and had
reached a point four miles west of St.
Barthélemy near le Mesnil-Tôve. Still
the division G–3 was "not yet greatly
concerned," even though he admitted
that the Germans had cut behind the
39th Infantry in the Chérencé–Gathemo

sector, penetrated four miles behind the
30th Division front, threatened to drive
uncontested to Avranches, and might
attain St. Hilaire and Ducey without
interference. Unperturbed an hour
and a half later, he promised that the
penetration would be cleaned up at the
first light of day. Passing these reports
to the First Army, a staff officer at the
VII Corps headquarters added that the
penetrations appeared to have been
made by "uncoordinated units attempting to escape rather than aggressive
action." Everyone on the lower echelons, it appeared, was confident that the
attacks "would be rapidly taken care
of." The army headquarters was under
the impression that the disturbance was
a local infantry counterattack that was
repulsed without difficulty. Not until
the coming of dawn was it obvious that
the German effort was serious, "heavier
than was first thought, but . . . under
control."[30]

At daybreak on 7 August, Generals
Hodges and Collins were highly conscious of the fact that the German counterattack at the least threatened the VII
Corps, at the most menaced the entire
bridgehead south of the Sélune. If the
German forces north of Mortain thrust
northward across the Sée River, they
might run riot through the corps rear
area, destroying supply installations and
nullifying in great part the exploitation
of COBRA.[31]

Fortunately the 4th Division, in corps
reserve and anticipating several days of
rest and recreation, had reacted in a
positive manner during the early morn-

[29] CI 96 (30th Div, 6–12 Aug). Sergeant Sterling
received the DSC, as did Pfc. Clifford W. Buzzard
and Pvt. Frank D. Joseph, Jr., who destroyed two
enemy tanks with a bazooka and two rounds of
ammunition.

[30] 30th Div Msgs, VII Corps G–3 Jnl and File;
Telecons, 0400, 0520, and 0700, 7 Aug, FUSA G–2
Jnl and File; Sylvan Diary, 6 Aug.
[31] VII Corps AAR, Aug.

ing hours. The 4th Division Artillery was placing a large volume of fire on German movements south of the Sée, and General Barton had assembled his troops for immediate commitment. By 0530 Barton was able to assure the corps commander that the Germans did not seem to be trying to go north of the Sée and that if they did, the 4th Division was ready.[32]

Though reassured about the situation along the Sée River, General Collins was far from satisfied with the southern portion of the corps zone, that part along the Sélune River. There was little to arrest German movement between St. Hilaire and Barenton, and the enemy was already established in that area. Only two men of the 120th Infantry Intelligence and Reconnaissance Platoon had returned from an ambush near Romagny, just southwest of Mortain. If Collins recalled the 1st Division from Mayenne to close the St. Hilaire gap, he would create a similar opening at Mayenne. In quest of additional forces to plug the hole, which was inviting the Germans to drive to Ducey and wrest the vital Pontaubault bridgehead from American control, he called upon CCB of the 3d Armored Division (relieved the previous afternoon from attachment to the 4th Division and assembled south of the Sée River in the 30th Division rear). He attached the combat command to the 30th Division and told General Hobbs "to handle the situation S W of Mortain with it."[33] The more immediate necessity of meeting the German main effort north of Mortain and along the south bank of the Sée, however,

forced Hobbs to commit CCB in that area.

By chance, an extra unit seemed to materialize out of thin air. The 2d Armored Division (less CCA, which remained near Vire) had departed the XIX Corps sector shortly after midnight, 6 August, leaving St. Sever-Calvados and moving to Villedieu-les-Poëles, then south through St. Pois toward Chérencé-le-Roussel and Mayenne with the intention of supporting or accompanying the 1st Division in an advance toward Alençon. As the leading units of the armored column approached Chérencé on the morning of 7 August, they began to receive artillery fire from across the Sée. The column stopped, but not for long, for General Collins seized upon the troops to plug the hole on the corps right.[34] Meanwhile, the armor had provided temporary stability for the 39th Infantry of the 9th Division at the Sée River.

Backtracking from Chérencé, the armored column moved west several miles to get out of range of the enemy shelling, crossed the Sée, marched to St. Hilaire, and that night took positions near Barenton. So that "one man would be in command of everything at Barenton," General Brooks, the 2d Armored Division commander, assumed control over the troops of the 30th Division and of the 3d Armored Division's CCA, which had unsuccessfully tried to secure the village that day.[35]

Because the 2d Armored Division could not alone close the gap, General

[32] 4th Div AAR, Aug.

[33] Telecon, Collins and Hobbs, 0755, 7 Aug, 30th Div G-3 Jnl and File.

[34] Msg, Collins to Hobbs, 0042, 7 Aug, 30th Div G-3 Jnl and File; FUSA Sitrep 125, 7 Aug.

[35] Telecons, Collins and Hobbs, 1720, 7 Aug, Collins and Brooks, 2125, 7 Aug, 30th Div G-3 Jnl and File.

Bradley gave General Collins the 35th Division, recently released from the V Corps to join the XX Corps of the Third Army in the Fougères–Vitré area. While still under XX Corps control and with some understandable confusion of orders and plans, the 35th Division, having planned to attack south with the Third Army, advanced that evening northeast toward St. Hilaire with the eventual objective the Mortain–Barenton road south of Hill 317.[36]

Thus, less than twenty-four hours after the Germans attacked, the VII Corps had a strength of seven divisions—five infantry and two armored (less one combat command).[37] Still another was alerted for possible shift from the Third Army should the Germans effect a more serious penetration.

Meanwhile, the 30th Division was battling desperately at some disadvantage. Before coming to Mortain, the 30th was to have become part of the V Corps, and plans and reconnaissance had been made toward that end. When the division was abruptly shifted into the VII Corps sector, there was no time for real reconnaissance. With little knowledge of where neighboring units were located and practically no information on enemy dispositions, the 30th hastily took over the positions held by the 1st Division. Shallow foxholes and field artillery emplacements far forward in offensive formation were adequate to accommodate a unit pausing temporarily but were less suitable for defense. Large-scale maps showing the terrain in detail did not become generally available until several days later, and for the most part the lower echelons used crumpled maps that 1st Division men had pulled out of their pockets and off their map boards and passed along before departing. The 30th took over the telephone wire nets left in place and found it so difficult to repair breaks in the unfamiliar system that the division eventually laid its own wire. Although the defensive positions could have been better, the main drawback was that the division had not had sufficient time to become properly oriented. Nor was the division at full strength in meeting the counterattack. Nearly eight hundred replacements, which had joined only a few days before, were hardly assimilated. Two of the nine infantry battalions were absent: one had been dispatched to Barenton on the evening of 6 August, the other had been attached to the 2d Armored Division near Vire. The men of the remaining seven battalions were tired after their march from Tessy to Mortain on 6 August and soon reached a condition "of extreme battle weariness." [38]

General Hobbs at first tended to minimize the importance of what seemed to him to be only a German demonstration. He was concerned somewhat about a possible breakthrough southwest of Mortain to St. Hilaire, but the corps commander, who was making arrangements to block the gap there, directed Hobbs to the more immediate problem in the Juvigny area. Collins ordered Hobbs to

---

[36] 35th Div AAR, Aug, and FO 13, 2000, 7 Aug (issued verbally 1845, 7 Aug) ; Notes for General Hobbs, 1249, 7 Aug, and Telecon, Collins and Hobbs, 1550, 7 Aug, 30th Div G–3 Jnl and File.

[37] The 35th Division remained officially under XX Corps control until midnight, 8 August, but tactically its action was an integral part of the VII Corps operation.

[38] Telecon, Hobbs, Stephens, and Col Robert G. McKee, 1805, 9 Aug; Hewitt, *Story of 30th Division*, pp. 54–55; Ruppenthal Notes, ML–2185.

furnish four medium tanks to protect the corps wire teams so that telephone lines could remain operative and the corps be kept informed of developments as they occurred. He instructed Hobbs to report hourly on the situation at Juvigny, by radio if other communications were not functioning.

Apparently feeling that Hobbs did not fully appreciate the implications of the attack, Collins told him to take the counterattack seriously. Hobbs protested that he already had committed all his infantry and engineers and was without a reserve, surely indication enough that he was serious. Yet when Collins attached a regiment of the 4th Division to the 30th, Hobbs said he didn't think he needed it, everything was going fine. Surprised, Collins decided to "play it safe" and give Hobbs the regiment "anyway" as an immediate reserve.[39]

By noon of 7 August, intelligence officers estimated that the German forces behind American lines consisted of five battalions of infantry, four of artillery, and two or three of tanks. There seemed no question but that the Germans had "launched a major counterattack to separate First and Third Armies."[40] Stopping the attack depended substantially on the 30th Division.

Hobbs had three main problems: cutting off the penetration northwest of Mortain, blocking the thrust southwest

of Mortain toward St. Hilaire, and recapturing Mortain to re-establish contact with the isolated and surrounded battalion. Against the penetration north and northwest of Mortain, Hobbs ordered Col. Truman E. Boudinot's CCB of the 3d Armored Division (attached to the 30th Division) and Col. Edwin M. Sutherland's 119 Infantry to drive northeast and northwest from Reffuveille and Juvigny, respectively, toward le Mesnil-Adelée. He instructed the 117th Infantry to take St. Barthélemy then drive northwest to le Mesnil-Tôve. The two infantry regiments and the combat command, working closely together, established a cohesive front on 7 August and commenced attacking generally north toward the Sée River. To close off the opening that led to St. Hilaire, Hobbs could do little except hope that the 35th Division would arrive quickly. The 120th Infantry launched repeated company attacks in efforts to regain Romagny and cut the roads leading southwest, but the Germans were unwilling to relinquish their positions. Until the 35th Division exerted additional force and drove the Germans from the southwestern outskirts of Mortain, the isolated battalion on Hill 317 would remain encircled.

Meanwhile, the battle raged in the 30th Division sector. The most serious factor was the disorganization and isolation of small units. Communication throughout the division zone was precarious; wires were cut or shot out, and infiltrating German troops and enemy raiding parties menaced messengers and command posts. The 823d Tank Destroyer Battalion destroyed 14 enemy tanks, 2 trucks, a half-track, 3 full-tracked vehicles, 2 motorcycles, a staff car, and a

---

[39] Telecons and Msgs, 30th Div G-3 Jnl and File, 7 Aug, in particular Hobbs and Lewis, 0900, Collins, and Hobbs, 1140, 1150, 1550, 1600; 105th Engr C Bn S-3 Rpt, 7 Aug; VII Corps Msg (signed Lt Col Bergin V. Dickey), 7 Aug, VII Corps G-3 Jnl and File.

[40] FUSA G-2 Per Rpt 59, 8 Aug; Collins to Huebner, 1745, 7 Aug, VII Corps G-3 Jnl and File.

machine gun position before being overrun by enemy infantry and losing 13
wounded, 3 killed, 91 missing, and 11 of
its 3-inch guns and prime movers.
"There were many heroes today," the
battalion commander reported, "both
living and dead." One battalion of the
117th Infantry lost 350 men on 7 August,
and enemy infiltrators were behind the
regimental lines "at several different
points." But at the end of the day, even
though the troops were "very fatigued,
supply problems not solved, defensive
sector penetrated," the regimental commander could state: "however key terrain feature still held." [41] The 30th Division lost more than 600 men and much
equipment on 7 August, but after the
initial shock of the counterattack, the
troops held firm.

The situation was similar throughout
the corps zone. The 4th Division reacted effectively with artillery fire, destroying during the afternoon of 7 August a German column that tried to move
across its front. The division, besides
releasing a regiment for attachment to
the 30th Division, moved a second regiment to Chérencé in support of the 39th
Infantry, which had been split in two by
the initial penetration. Despite the precarious situation of the 39th Infantry,
Colonel Bond in the early afternoon of
7 August moved those elements that were
south of the German thrust around and
through the 4th Division sector to rejoin
the infantry battalions on the north bank
of the Sée. The regimental line at the

end of the day was generally the same as
on 6 August. A few miles to the northeast, the other two regiments of the 9th
Division failed to make contact with the
39th, but they gained excellent hilltop
positions to assure the integrity of the
corps left. That evening General Collins attached the 39th Infantry to the 4th
Division, which was in contact with the
regiment and able to support it.[42]

American artillery had responded to
the attack with liberal expenditures of
ammunition, operating on the premise
that it was better to waste shells than
miss a possible target. The weather was
excellent throughout the day, and in addition to the artillery observation planes
that pinpointed targets, fighter-bombers
roamed the area at will, destroying
enemy matériel and morale. Ten squadrons of Typhoons of the RAF 2d Tactical
Air Force operating from airfields in
France flew 294 sorties in the Mortain
area. Of seventy enemy tanks estimated
to have made the original penetration,
only thirty were judged to be in operation at the close of the day. On the
morning of 8 August, the estimate was reduced to twenty-five still remaining behind American lines. Prisoners taken
by the corps on 7 August numbered
350.[43]

Chance had played an important role
in the American reaction. The German
decision to make the main effort north
of Mortain rather than south of it was
vital. The 4th Division was in the right
place from which to bring flanking fire

---

[41] 823d TD Bn Unit Rpt, 7 Aug; 117th Inf Unit
Rpt, 7 Aug. Lt. Col. Robert E. Frankland, commander of a battalion that destroyed more than
fifteen German tanks, was awarded the DSC. A
soldier of that battalion, Pvt. Peter Preslipsky, also
received the DSC for destroying two tanks by
bazooka fire.

[42] 39th Inf, 9th Div, and 4th Div AAR's, Aug.
[43] Telecon, Hobbs, and Lewis, 1715, 7 Aug, 30th
Div G–3 Jnl and File; FUSA Sitrep 127, 8 Aug;
39th Inf, 30th Div, VII Corps AAR's, Aug; Leigh-
Mallory, "Despatch," Fourth Supplement to the
London Gazette of December 31, 1946, p. 66.

on the main effort. CCB of the 3d Armored Division, assembled near Reffuveille, a few miles from the deepest point of the penetration, was able to attack the German spearheads immediately. The accidental appearance of the 2d Armored Division near Chérencé brought comfort to the 39th Infantry, and the fact that the armor was not needed elsewhere and could therefore be inserted into the battle was a happy circumstance. The location of the 35th Division was another lucky break. The capricious factor of weather also was favorable for the Allies. It was fortunate, finally, that officers of good judgment had seen to it that American troops occupied Hill 317, "the key to the whole area."

There was more than chance involved.

The reaction to the counterattack demonstrated a flexibility and a rapidity of reflex that was most clearly illustrated by the fact that British planes operated effectively on the American front.

The forward motion of the Mortain counterattack had come to a halt soon after daylight on 7 August, when the Germans drove their tanks off the roads into the fields and hastily threw camouflage nets over them to escape detection from the ground and air. Although the Germans failed that day to regain the momentum that had enabled them to make a serious penetration of the American lines, they held stubbornly to their forward positions and awaited reinforcement for a renewed thrust toward Avranches. Meanwhile, the battle at Mortain continued.

PART SIX

ENCIRCLEMENT AND THE DRIVE
TO THE SEINE

CHAPTER XXV

Encirclement

Envelopment from the North

Twenty-four hours after the Germans counterattacked toward Avranches, the First Canadian Army, from positions three miles south of Caen, launched a massive attack southeast toward Falaise. The timing was accidental, but it could hardly have been more fortunate.

The Canadian attack had been in preparation for almost a week, its object at the least to wear down enemy units, at the most to unhinge the German withdrawal to the Seine that General Montgomery expected.[1] The German thrust toward Avranches, changing the situation, widened Montgomery's perspective on the role of the Canadian effort. The Canadian attack now became his main instrument of destruction.

The Canadians were to "break through the German positions astride the road Caen–Falaise," and advance toward Falaise, twenty-one miles southeast of Caen.[2] For the first fifteen miles the road was "arrow-straight," rising "gradually, sometimes almost imperceptibly, but steadily," from little more than sea level to more than six hundred feet in height. "Up this long, smooth, dangerous slope the Canadians were to fight," across acres of waving wheat broken by an occasional village, a patch of woods, an occasional orchard—through an area where only an infrequent hedgerow or belt of trees lined the side roads.[3]

The ground was good for employing armor, but solidly built villages and the woods provided defenders excellent natural centers of resistance. Three German divisions—the *272d* and *89th Infantry* and the *12th SS Panzer*—manned two defensive lines in depth. Fifty 88-mm. antiaircraft pieces, sited for antitank action, supplemented about sixty dug-in tanks and self-propelled guns.

To overcome these strong defenses, General Crerar decided to combine overwhelming air support with ground penetration under the cover of darkness. After a strike by heavy bombers, tanks were to lead the attack. Infantrymen riding in armored personnel carriers (self-propelled gun carriages specially converted for troop transport by Lt. Gen. G. G. Simonds, the corps commander, and later called Kangaroos), were to follow the tanks and detruck at appropriate points to mop up.

[1] 21 AGp Operational Situation and Dir, M–516, 4 Aug; see above, Ch. XXII.

[2] British Army of the Rhine, *Battlefield Tour: Operation TOTALIZE, 2 Canadian Corps Operations Astride the Road Caen–Falaise: 7–8 August 1944* (Germany: Printing and Stationery Service, Control Commission for Germany, 1947) (hereafter cited as British Army of the Rhine, *Operation TOTALIZE*), p. 9. The following account, except as otherwise noted, is taken from this source, which gives a detailed report of plans, preparations, intelligence, and execution, and includes excellent maps; see also Stacey, *Canadian Army*, pp. 188ff.; and Montgomery, *Normandy to the Baltic*, pp. 154ff.

[3] Stacey, *Canadian Army*, p. 188.

An hour before midnight, 7 August, more than a thousand RAF planes were ready to blast bomb zones flanking the projected ground assault area, and fighter-bombers were prepared to loose more than 5,000 tons of bombs on the assault area. Even though darkness, weather, smoke, and dust made visibility so poor that only two thirds of the planes dropped their loads, the bombardment was more effective than that in Operation GOODWOOD, less than three weeks earlier.[4] On the ground, 720 artillery pieces were available to shell the enemy and light the battlefield with flares. While Bofors fired tracer bullets to mark the direction of the attack and searchlights provided "artificial moonlight," two divisions moved out shortly before midnight. Preceded by tanks with flailing mechanisms to detonate enemy mines and by engineers who were to establish routes through German mine fields, eight columns of armor (each with four vehicles abreast) moved toward Falaise.

Dense clouds of dust mixed with ground mist obscured vision. Although the assault troops crawled in low gear at one hundred yards a minute, collisions occurred and units lost their way. Yet the confusion that enveloped the attackers was less than that covering the defenders. By dawn of 8 August the Canadians had gained their first objectives; they had penetrated the German lines for a distance of three miles.

Off to a good start, the attack bogged down as the Canadians struck a solid line of defense, a "lay-back position."[5] To

break through, the Canadians committed two fresh but inexperienced armored divisions, one of which was the 1st Polish Armored Division.[6] At that point everything seemed to go wrong. The new divisions displayed the usual shortcomings of green units. An air attack, delivered by bombers flying across the front and moving progressively forward like a creeping barrage, killed 25 men and wounded 131 (including a division commander), mostly Polish troops. Although the ground attack continued through 8 and 9 August for a gain of five more miles, momentum then ceased. The attack had carried the Canadian Army eight miles forward, but the same distance still separated it from Falaise.[7]

Meanwhile, the Second British Army, attacking since 30 June from positions south of Caumont, continued to exert pressure while turning between Thury-Harcourt and Vire southeastward toward Falaise and Flers. The original idea of the offensive was to pivot the line in order to keep pace with the Americans; later the purpose was changed to deny the enemy time to organize a withdrawal to the Seine; and finally, after the Mortain counterattack, to crush the German forces that were trying to hold the north flank of the counterattack toward Avranches.

---

[4] *AAF III*, p. 252; Telecon, Kluge and Eberbach, 2200, 8 Aug, *Fifth Panzer Army KTB;* Leigh-Mallory, "Despatch," Fourth Supplement to the *London Gazette* of December 31, 1946.

[5] Montgomery, *Normandy to the Baltic,* p. 157.

[6] Many Poles had been equipped and trained in England with British aid. They were troops that had escaped Poland after the defeat in 1939 and had reached England by way of Norway, Hungary, France, and other lands, or volunteer units (formed in France and the Middle East), which after the French surrender in 1940 escaped to England in a variety of ways. See F. C. Anstruther, *Poland's Part in the War* (Glasgow: The Polish Library, 1944), a pamphlet, 39 pp.

[7] *AAF III*, pp. 250–51; [Ackerman], Employment of Strategic Bombers in a Tactical Role, pp. 86–88; Wilmot, *Struggle for Europe,* pp. 410ff.

Despite the changing purpose of the offensive, the attack itself continued relentlessly, grinding down the *LXXIV Corps* and making necessary its reinforcement by elements of the *II SS Panzer Corps*. British forces pushed through a region not particularly suited for offense, an area of rough terrain devoid of good roads. It was a slow, hard advance, destitute of glamor and newspaper headlines, but it was inexorable, and it increased German concern over the way the situation was developing.[8]

The German Dilemma

The aerial bombardment on the night of 7 August and the estimate that six hundred Canadian tanks were attacking toward Falaise alarmed the German command in Normandy:

"We didn't expect this to come so soon," Kluge told Eberbach, "but I can imagine that it was no surprise to you."

"No," Eberbach said, "I have always awaited it and looked toward the morrow with a heavy heart." [9]

The moment was particularly dark because Kluge, in compliance with Hitler's order for a second and stronger attack toward Avranches, had started to move three armored divisions out of the *Fifth Panzer Army* sector toward the Mortain area. The *10th SS Panzer Division* was already on the move, but orders for the *9th SS* and *12th SS Panzer Divisions* were canceled. The latter remained south of Caen to help stop the Canadians. Units of the newly arriving *85th Division*, instead of being assembled at Tinchebray for eventual commitment near Brécey, were diverted immediately to the Falaise sector. The Panther tank battalion of the *9th Panzer Division* and a rocket brigade, also scheduled to participate in the attack toward Avranches, joined the defenses north of Falaise.[10]

The second attack toward Avranches was scheduled for the evening of 9 August but, on the basis of the Canadian threat, Kluge that afternoon postponed it. Developments on the American front contributed to Kluge's decision. Attacks on 8 August by the V and XIX Corps between Vire and Sourdeval had strained the *II Parachute* and *LXXXIV Corps* and had ripped the *363d Division* to such an extent that the *Seventh Army* was trying to accelerate the arrival of the *331st Division* into the line. Perhaps worse, U.S. pressure had compelled the *XLVII Panzer Corps* during the night of 8 August to pull back slightly the *2d Panzer Division's* most advanced wedge of the counterattack forces near le Mesnil-Tôve and Chérencé. Even more threatening was the attack of the 2d Armored Division against the deep southern flank of the *2d SS Panzer Division* at Barenton. Finally, the capture of le Mans and the possibility of an American attack northward to Alençon tied down the *LXXXI Corps* and prevented the *9th Panzer Division* from

---

[8] Second British Army Opns, 21 Jul–9 Sep 44, a chronological rcd submitted to Hist Sec USFET by Maj. D. P. Draycott, G (Ops) Rcds, Hq BAOR, 2 Nov 45, and Info furnished Hist Sec USFET by 21 AGp, 9 Aug 45, ML–2251; MS # B–840 (Eberbach).

[9] Telecon, Kluge and Eberbach, 2100, 8 Aug, *Fifth Pz A KTB*; see also, Account by Brigadefuhrer Kurt Meyer, Commander, *12th SS Panzer Division*, in British Army of the Rhine, *Operation TOTALIZE*, p. 101.

[10] *OB WEST, AGp B*, and *Fifth Pz A KTB's*, 8 and 9 Aug.

adding its strength to the second attempt to gain Avranches.[11]

The second effort was to have been made over the same terrain as the first, but this time with two corps moving abreast: the *XLVII Panzer Corps* (with four armored divisions—*1st SS, 2d SS, 2d,* and *116th*) and the *LVIII Panzer Corps* (with the *9th SS and 10th SS Panzer Divisions,* as well as the Panther tank battalion of the *9th Panzer Division*). The attacking corps were to have been supported by two rocket brigades and reinforced later by the *12th SS Panzer* and *85th Infantry Divisions.*[12] Continued Allied pressure and the threats to the flanks made it necessary to divert an increasing number of elements designated for the attack to defensive missions. The *116th, 2d SS,* and remnants of *Panzer Lehr* moved to the *LXXXIV Corps* to support the *363d* and *353d Divisions* between Vire and Sourdeval; the *LVIII Corps* (with the *10th SS Panzer Division)* was inserted at Barenton to relieve the weak *275th Division* (which moved to the *Fifteenth Army* area for reconstitution) and protect the long *2d SS Panzer Division* flank. The emphasis turned unmistakably to defense.

Despite postponement of the second attempt to drive toward Avranches and despite the fact that the *XLVII Panzer*

Corps, basically the striking force, retained control over the *1st SS* and *2d Panzer Divisions,* the German commanders in Normandy felt that a renewed effort might still succeed if certain conditions were met: if the positions north of Falaise remained stable, if a strong defense could be established north of Alençon to protect the ammunition and gasoline dumps nearby, if the Panther battalion and a rocket brigade newly made available could be moved quickly to the *Seventh Army* sector, and if Eberbach, designated by Hitler to take command of the renewed effort toward Avranches, could have a few days in which to unscramble the assault forces and reassemble them for the attack.[13]

Hitler, who issued a new order that day, 9 August, was convinced that Eberbach could achieve success if he avoided the mistakes of the first attack, which Hitler considered to have been launched "too early, too weak, and in unfavorable weather." To insure proper timing, Hitler reserved for himself the designation of H Hour. Meanwhile, Eberbach was to prepare to attack southwest from the vicinity of Domfront, then northwest to the ultimate objective, Avranches. To protect Eberbach's left flank, *LXXXI Corps* was to follow the two assault corps echeloned to the left rear. Recognizing that Allied pressure had to be resisted particularly at Falaise, Hitler ordered sufficient antitank weapons, tanks, and assault guns, which were

---

[11] MS # B-179 (Hausser) and MS # B-725 (Gersdorff) are basic sources for the following section. For a vivid account of the movement of the *331st Division* from the Pas-de-Calais—movement made difficult by Allied air attacks on rail lines—see Leigh-Mallory, "Despatch," Fourth Supplement to the *London Gazette* of December 31, 1946, p. 63.

[12] *Seventh Army Order, Ia Nr. 640/44,* 9 Aug, *LXXXI Corps Befehle H Gr u Armee;* Speidel's Est of the Situation, 1000, 9 Aug, *AGp B Operationsbefehle.*

[13] Telecons, Kluge and Jodl, 1500, 9 Aug, and Buhle and Jodl, 2210, 9 Aug, *AGp B KTB;* Telecons Kluge and Gersdorff, 1520, 9 Aug, and Tempelhoff, Speidel, and Gersdorff, 1250, 9 Aug, *Seventh Army* Tel Msgs; *Seventh Army* Est of the Situation, 10 Aug, Msg, *AGp B* to *OB WEST,* 0200, 11 Aug, *AGp B Op. Befehle,* pp. 412-13; MS # B-445 (Krueger).

coming from the *Fifteenth Army* sector, diverted to the *I SS Panzer Corps* for a strong stand at Falaise. Elsewhere along the front, Hitler prohibited local counterattacks that might lead to serious personnel losses; he also authorized withdrawals to neutralize any penetrations the Allies might effect.[14]

Although some commanders later called Hitler's order "pure utopia" and not in keeping with the situation on the ground, the situation in the air, and the supply situation—"the apex of conduct by a command [OKW] ignorant of front line conditions, taking upon itself the right to judge the situation from East Prussia"—the commanders facing the crisis in Normandy reorganized for a renewed attempt.[15] They planned to have the *LXXXIV Corps* pull the *116th Panzer Division* out of the front for assembly; they hoped to withdraw the *84th Division* to a shorter line east of Perriers-en-Beauficel; they instructed the *XLVII Panzer Corps* to withdraw the *2d Panzer Division* somewhat and pull out the *1st SS Panzer Division* for assembly. The *1st SS* and *116th Panzer Divisions* were then to be concentrated in forward assembly areas under *LVIII Panzer Corps* to provide impetus for the new attack. The *Seventh Army* also expected to receive the *9th Panzer Division*'s Panther battalion and two mortar *(werfer)* brigades to bolster the second effort. The new attack was to be launched, as Hitler wished, under Eberbach's command and from the Mortain–Domfront area toward St. Hilaire and eventually Avranches.

Leaving command of the *Fifth Panzer Army* to Panzergeneraloberst Josef (Sepp) Dietrich, formerly the commander of the *I SS Panzer Corps*, Eberbach, somewhat against his will, took command of *Panzer Group Eberbach*. His headquarters, formed for the express purpose of making the second attack to Avranches on 11 August, was directly under *Army Group B*. Eberbach assembled a skeleton staff of great ability that included Lt. Col. Guenther von Kluge, the field marshal's son, as chief of staff, and Maj. Arthur von Eckesparre, formerly Rommel's G–4, as operations officer. The command was nevertheless deficient in personnel and equipment and could function only with the aid of the *Seventh Army* staff or a corps headquarters. Despite these handicaps and the additional one of Eberbach's pessimism, the provisional headquarters began to plan the attack in detail.[16]

It did not take Eberbach long to conclude that he could not attack on 11 August. He felt that he would probably have to commit part of his attack forces to protect his assembly areas and thus would not be able to assemble his troops by that date. Judging that only 77 Mark IV and 47 Panther tanks were available for the attack, he wanted more. He also requested vehicle replacements and additional ammunition and POL supplies. All this would take time. Most important, however, Eberbach believed that because of Allied air superiority he could attack only after dark and in early morning when ground fog might provide concealment. At best, his movements would be restricted to the six

[14] Telecon, Jodl and Blumentritt, 1745, 9 Aug, *OB WEST KTB;* Hitler Order, 2300, 9 Aug *(WFSt/Op. Nr. 77280/44 g.Kdos. Chefs.),* quoted in Msg from *AGp B* to the armies, 1130, 10 Aug, *AGp B Fuehrer Befehle.*

[15] Quote is from MS # B–725 (Gersdorff) .

[16] Msg, *AGp B* to *OB WEST* and *Seventh Army,* 1815, 9 Aug, *AGp B KTB;* see *OB WEST, a Study in Command,* p. 132; MS # A–922 (Eberbach) .

hours between 0400 and 1000. If his assault forces failed to reach their objective during that period, the events at Mortain would be repeated—his troops would be smashed by Allied air and artillery. To attack after nightfall, he needed the light of the waning moon, not to be had until 20 August. At that time also, according to meteorologists, the weather would change and become unfavorable for aerial activity. Thus 20 August, not 11 August, in Eberbach's estimation, was the best date for launching the new attack toward Avranches.[17]

While Eberbach was coming to his conclusions, a new threat developed. Just as it appeared that the Canadian attack on the north flank was halted, the Americans on the south flank "unmistakably swerved" north from le Mans toward Alençon. As Kluge evaluated the situation on the evening of 10 August, if the changed direction of the XV Corps drive was connected with the Canadian effort toward Falaise, he faced the threat of double envelopment. Furthermore, the weak forces of the LXXXI Corps could not possibly protect the army group on the southern flank. Nor could the LXXXI Corps keep the vital Alençon–Flers line open. Instead of continuing the attack toward Avranches, Kluge thought it "worth considering whether the spearheads of the enemy columns driving north should not be smashed by a . . . swiftly executed panzer thrust." He requested Jodl to get a decision on this matter from Hitler.[18]

Hitler replied with queries. He wanted clarification on why Eberbach could not mount his attack toward Avranches before 20 August. He wanted to know what Funck, the commander of the XLVII Panzer Corps, thought of resuming that attack. Hitler interpreted Kluge's suggestion as meaning an attack to regain le Mans and asked when, with what forces, and from where such an attack could be launched. Finally, he asked when the 11th Panzer Division, if he ordered it moved from southern France, could reach the Loire River near Tours so that it could support an attack on le Mans—for if another attack toward Avranches could not be mounted before 20 August, Hitler conceded, an attack against the U.S. XV Corps "must perforce be carried out before that time." [19]

Before he answered Hitler's questions, Kluge phoned Eberbach. The commanders were in agreement that a new attempt to gain Avranches was out of the question, at least for the moment. The obstacles to a renewed drive toward Avranches were not only the strong opposition at Mortain and the unrelaxed pressure elsewhere along the front but also the uncomfortable thought that the Canadians attacking south toward Falaise and the Americans attacking north toward Alençon seemed to be converging on a common point. If the Allied forces joined, the major part of the German forces would be encircled. The Canadian and American spearheads had to be blunted immediately, and since the Canadians were apparently stopped, action ought to be taken against the Ameri-

---

[17] Pz Gp Eberbach Ltr, Ia Nr. 2/44 g.Kdos., 10 Aug, OB WEST, Anlagen, Incl to Annex 1458.
[18] Kluge to Jodl, 10 Aug, AGp B Lagebeurteilungen, Wochenmeldungen.

[19] Telecon, Blumentritt and Speidel, 0200, 11 Aug, AGp B KTB.

cans, who threatened the vital supply installations around Alençon.[20]

Kluge informed Hitler to this effect an hour and a half later. All commanders agreed, Kluge said, that the prospect of continuing the attack to Avranches was unfavorable because the enemy had reinforced, surprise had been lost, and the attacking force needed time to bring forward more troops, tanks, gasoline, and ammunition, and required certain weather conditions. There was no possibility of fulfilling the necessary preattack requirements within a few days. As for an attack against the XV Corps, Kluge would need at least two of the best panzer divisions, which he envisioned attacking from the vicinity of Alençon. The direction of the attack would depend on developments. He hoped to make his approach march during the night of 11 August and attack on 13 August with the hope of completing the operation three days later. The *11th Panzer Division* in southern France could not reach the area of operations in time to lend support.[21]

Kluge was again in touch with Hitler's headquarters at noon on 11 August. He had conferred with Hausser and Eberbach, and all three commanders were convinced that an attack on Avranches had no prospect of success. The situation on the extreme southern flank of the army group was deteriorating so rapidly—the *9th Panzer Division*, for example, was fighting near Alençon with its back close to vital supply installations—that immediate measures had to

be taken in that area. Kluge needed more armor there. The only practical way to get armor was to pull three divisions out of the line—the *116th* that night, the *1st SS* and *2d Panzer Divisions* during the following night. These units could be released only if the *Seventh Army* salient at Mortain were reduced by withdrawal to the east. This meant abandoning hope of a breakthrough to the sea at Avranches. A clear-cut decision had to be made at once. In Kluge's mind, the decision could be only one thing: attack the XV Corps in the vicinity of Alençon with panzer divisions pulled out of the line and bring additional infantry divisions forward to launch an attack against the XV Corps from east to west, thus stabilizing the situation on the army group left flank.[22]

After further discussion with Jodl in midafternoon, Kluge issued a written report to Hitler and disseminated it to his subordinate commands, probably as a warning order subject to Hitler's approval. In this report, Kluge projected the following actions. The *Seventh Army* was to withdraw its Mortain salient that night. An attack force—composed of the *XLVII Panzer* and *LXXXI Corps* headquarters, the *1st SS*, *2d*, and *116th Panzer Divisions*, two *werfer* brigades, and possibly an additional panzer division—was to assemble in the Carrouges area and prepare to attack during the early morning hours of 14 August, one day later than Kluge had originally contemplated. The attack, with three divisions abreast, was to be launched in a southeasterly direction

[20] Telecon, Kluge and Eberbach, 0315, 11 Aug, *AGp B KTB*; Kluge's Est of the Situation, 10 Aug. *AGp B Lagebeurteilungen, Wochenmeldungen.*

[21] Telecon, Kluge and Jodl, 0445, 11 Aug, *AGp B Lagebeurteilungen, Wochenmeldungen.*

[22] Telecon, Kluge and Jodl, 11 Aug, *AGp B Lagebeurteilungen, Wochenmeldungen.*

along the Lalacelle–la Hutte axis—generally a thrust starting northwest of Alençon and cutting across the le Mans—Alençon road.[23]

Hitler's response to Kluge's report reached *Army Group B* headquarters late that evening. Acknowledging the new set of circumstances that had come into being, Hitler, though reiterating his intention to attack westward to the sea (this time by way of Mayenne), admitted that "the serious threat to the deep southern flank" of the army group required quick action. He therefore approved Kluge's plan to have Eberbach launch an attack with an armored corps from the vicinity of Carrouges. But instead of an effort envisaged by Kluge as an attempt to destroy the American spearheads driving north toward Alençon, Hitler envisioned an attack against the deep west flank of the U.S. XV Corps, the axis of the thrust passing in a more southerly direction across the Sillé-le-Guillaume–Beaumont road. In order to disengage the necessary forces, Hitler agreed to "a minor withdrawal of the front between Sourdeval and Mortain." He retained the *11th Panzer Division* in southern France as the only mobile reserve in the *Nineteenth Army* sector because Kluge assured him that it could not reach the Normandy front in time to attack near Alençon, and perhaps because he was apprehensive over the imminent Allied invasion of southern France.[24]

Thus, while the Germans awaited reinforcements and favorable weather for another try at Avranches in compliance with Hitler's wishes, Eberbach was to make an effort to eradicate the American threat to Alençon. To make this possible, the *Seventh Army* during the night of 11 August began to withdraw eastward from Mortain.[25]

The Battle at Mortain

The German withdrawal from Mortain on the night of 11 August brought the battle that had been raging there to an end. Until that time, although the Americans could mark an increasing improvement in their situation about Mortain, no decisive result had been achieved.

General Hobbs, for example, had been variously elated and depressed. "We are holding and getting in better shape all the time," he informed General Collins on 8 August. "It was precarious for a while . . . [but] we are doing everything in God's power to hold." Yet on the following day, when Hobbs wondered aloud whether his positions might be "practically untenable," Collins flared in exasperation: "Stop talking about untenable." [26]

Essentially, the battle was small unit combat, "infiltration and counter infiltration," close-range fighting by splinter groups maneuvering to outflank, and in turn being outflanked, "a seesawing activity consisting of minor penetrations by both sides," operations characterized by ambush and surprise and fought on a level often no higher than that of the

---

[23] Msg, Kluge to Jodl (info to subordinate comds), 1745, 11 Aug, *AGp B Lagebeurteilungen, Wochenmeldungen.*

[24] Hitler Order, *WFSt/Op. Nr.* 772830/44, g.Kdos. *Chefs.,* 11 Aug, quoted in *AGp B* Msg to the armies, 0030, 12 Aug, *AGp B Fuehrer Befehle.*

[25] See MS # A–918 (Gersdorff); *OB WEST, a Study in Command,* p. 57.

[26] Telecons, Collins and Hobbs, 1220, 8 Aug, and 2307, 9 Aug, 30th Div G–3 Jnl and File.

individual soldier. "What does the situation look like down there?" the 30th Division G-3 asked a regimental officer. "Looks like hell," came the reply. "We are just mingled in one big mess, our CP is getting all kinds of fire, tanks within 500 yards of us." [27]

Though the Germans had been stopped on the first day of their attack, their retention of the ground gained represented a distinct challenge, particularly to the 30th Division, to expel them. In General Hobbs's words, it was a matter of "trying to plug up these rat holes." [28] The rats were dangerous, as was indicated by the fact that the division's lines changed but little for four days.

The first improvement occurred on 8 August, when the attached CCB of the 3d Armored Division and the 119th Infantry, after combining forces, made physical contact with the 4th Division several miles west of Chérencé and thereby blocked the possibility of unopposed further westward movement by the Germans along the south bank of the Sée. The death of Col. William W. Cornog, Jr., a CCB task force commander killed by an enemy shell on 9 August, temporarily disrupted efforts to eject the Germans from le Mesnil-Tôve, but after hard fighting on 10 and 11 August the armor and infantry regained the village and re-established contact with the 39th Infantry at Chérencé. On 12 August the 117th Infantry, on the immediate right, re-entered the

SCURRYING ALONG A HEDGEROW *in the Mortain area.*

smoking pile of rubble that was St. Barthélemy. The American lines north of Mortain were thus restored to the positions held before the counterattack.

In the sector south of Mortain, the 35th Division had had a difficult assignment in advancing through St. Hilaire to the Mortain–Barenton road. Two regiments had initially attacked abreast, but small counterattacks split unit formations repeatedly. General Baade, the division commander, committed his reserve regiment on 9 August, and all three attacking abreast made liberal use of tank and artillery fire. Unit commanders also formed "killing parties" to clear Germans out of the paths of advance. Still Baade was not satisfied with the progress, and though he exerted pressure to get the division moving for-

---

[27] FUSA G-2 Jnl, entries 0215, 9 Aug, and 1700, 11 Aug; Hassenfelt Telecon, 0520, 8 Aug, 30th Div G-3 Jnl and File.

[28] Telecon, Collins and Hobbs, 1044, 9 Aug, 30th Div G-3 Jnl and File; see also 30th Div Ltr of Instrs, 2230, 9 Aug.

ANTIAIRCRAFT POSITION *near St. Hilaire.*

ward aggressively, it took the 35th Division four days and more than seven hundred casualties to cover eight miles.[29]

The Germans withdrew from their positions southwest of Mortain and released their hold on Romagny on 11 August as the 35th Division reached the Mortain–Barenton road. General Baade then prepared to assault the south slope of Hill 317 to relieve the isolated battalion of the 30th Division on the crest. At noon, 12 August, after having moved up the south slope of the hill, troops of the 35th Division made contact with the battalion. Minutes later, the 120th In-

fantry, 30th Division, re-entered Mortain and relieved the men on the hill.[30]

The fact that the 2d Battalion, 120th Infantry, had retained possession of the top of Hill 317 during the battle of Mortain was one of the outstanding small unit achievements in the course of the campaign in western Europe. The battalion command post in Mortain had been overrun early on 7 August, and the command group had been captured on the following morning as the officers endeavored to reach their troops on the hill. Under the leadership of Capt. Reynold C. Erichson, who assumed command of the surrounded force, the troops on the hill for five days denied the Germans possession of terrain that would have given them observation over the major part of the VII Corps sector. Like Erichson, Capt. Delmont K. Byrn, who directed the heavy weapons company, and 1st Lts. Ralph A. Kerley, Joseph C. Reaser, and Ronal E. Woody, Jr., who commanded the rifle companies, refused to surrender.[31] They were fortunate in having with them two forward observers of the 230th Field Artillery Battalion, 1st Lt. Charles A. Barts and 2d Lt. Robert L. Weiss, who brought accurate fire not only on the Germans assaulting the hill positions but also on other German units within sight of the crest.[32]

Under almost constant attack (the regimental-sized *17th SS Panzer Grenadier Division* under control of the *2d SS*

[29] 35th Div AAR, Aug, and G–3 Per Rpt 55, 8 Aug; VII Corps Msg, 8 Aug (recording 35th Div Radio Msg, 1517, 8 Aug); Telecons, Hobbs and Baade, 2225, 11 Aug, and 1255, 12 Aug, and Gen Hobbs, Col Howard S. Searle, and Gen Collins, 1021, 8 Aug, 30th Div G–3 Jnl and File; FUSA Daily G–1 Estimated Losses, Aug.

[30] On the damage to Mortain, see Leon Blouet, *Mortain en Flammes* (Mortain, 1951).

[31] Erichson, Byrn, Kerley, Reaser, and Woody received the DSC for their leadership on Hill 317.

[32] Hewitt, *Story of 30th Division*, pp. 70–71; *History of the 120th Infantry Regiment* (Washington: Infantry Journal Press, 1947), pp. 46–56.

Panzer Division had had the mission of seizing Hill 317), the troops on the hill had captured several prisoners; though they needed radio batteries, food, and medical supplies, they were "Not too worried about situation as long as [friendly] artillery fire continues." After two days of isolation, they still "didn't seem to be worried." [33] If the men were not overly concerned about their situation, General Hobbs was. While waiting for the 35th Division to advance and relieve the pressure, he maintained a ring of artillery fire around the hill.[34]

It was not long before the 30th Division did more. On 9 August, two light artillery planes tried to drop supplies by parachute, but German flak drove them away. C–47 cargo planes did somewhat better on the afternoon of 10 August, dropping two days supply of food and ammunition, though half fell outside the defensive perimeter. Another drop on the following day was less successful.[35]

Meanwhile, Lt. Col. Lewis D. Vieman, commander of the 230th Field Artillery Battalion, conceived the idea of sending supplies by shell. Using smoke shell cases normally employed for propaganda leaflets, the battalion fired bandages, adhesive tape, morphine, and other medical supplies onto the hill. The first of the supply shoots occurred on the evening of 10 August, and eventually

THROUGH THE RUBBLE OF MORTAIN

105-mm. assault guns of the 743d Tank Battalion and 155-mm. howitzers of the 113th Field Artillery Battalion participated in the effort. Although it was impossible to propel blood plasma, which was badly needed on the hill, the other supplies helped morale considerably.[36]

Fed by French farmers who shared with the soldiers their chickens, vegetables, and the common danger, nearly seven hundred men held out.[37] By 12 August three hundred men had been killed or wounded, but more than three hundred walked off the hill unharmed. During the battle of Mortain they had been a "thorn in the flesh" that had

[33] Telecon, Hobbs and Ellis, 2135, 9 Aug, and entry 2246, 8 Aug, 30th Div G–3 Jnl and File; MS # B–725 (Gersdorff).

[34] See Telecon, Collins and Hobbs, 2307, 9 Aug, 30th Div G–3 Jnl and File.

[35] Maj. William K. C. Collonan of the First Army G–4 Section had reconnoitered Hill 317 as a passenger in a light plane on 9 August in order to arrange for cargo drops. The plane was struck by flak, and Major Collonan parachuted and fell into enemy lines. He was awarded the DSC.

[36] See Hewitt, *Story of 30th Division*, pp. 69-75, for a detailed account.

[37] See Jules and Gilles Buisson, *Mortain et sa Bataille;* also their "Les Combats de Mortain," in Herval, *Bataille de Normandie*, I, 219-42.

paralyzed all German movements in the area.[38]

The 2d Armored Division had made a similar contribution by attacking northeast from Barenton toward Ger into the German left flank and rear. Employing the small task force of the 3d Armored Division's CCA and the battalion of the 30th Division already near Barenton, the 2d Armored Division had attacked on 8 August and advanced three miles into the broken terrain of the Mortain forest. Although stiffening opposition had prevented capture of Ger, the armored division had kept a spear sticking into the enemy flank for four more days, a constant threat hampering German communications between Tinchebray and Sourdeval, disrupting forward assembly areas between Sourdeval and Ger, and forcing commitment of the *10th SS Panzer Division* elsewhere than toward Avranches.[39]

On 12 August, with the 35th Division beyond the Mortain–Barenton road and the 30th Division again in possession of St. Barthélemy and Mortain, the costly battle came to an end. The 30th Division alone had lost almost two thousand men in six days. The 9th Division, fighting on the fringe of the Mortain action, had sustained nearly a thousand casualties in closing the gap that had separated the division from the 39th Infantry. In protecting the Sée River line, the 4th Division, which had contributed a regiment each to the 9th and 30th

Divisions, had sustained about six hundred casualties.[40]

As heavy as American casualties were, German losses were greater. The effect of artillery and air power had been particularly telling. One regiment of the *2d Panzer Division* had been annihilated near le Mesnil-Tôve. The *1st SS Panzer Division* had had especially heavy tank losses. The *2d SS Panzer Division* had been slashed by artillery fire called from Hill 317, by tank fire from the 2d Armored Division near Barenton, and by air attacks that had seemed particularly effective in its sector. Allied tactical aircraft, somewhat hampered by early morning haze, flew from midmorning to darkness, while Brig. Gen. James M. Lewis, the 30th Division Artillery commander, alone massed more than twelve battalions of artillery to achieve devasting results. Between 1900 and 2000, 9 August, the 30th Division Artillery, for example, fired thirty observed and fully adjusted counterbattery missions, an imposing total for an hour's activity and one that was later claimed as a record. Observation was excellent from both the ground and the air, and artillerymen and pilots "just plaster [ed the enemy] . . . all along the line." Close to a hundred German tanks lay abandoned in the Mortain sector at the close of the battle.[41]

---

[38] MS # B–445 (Krueger).

[39] For heroism on 8 August, 2d Lt. Glenn H. Warren of the 82d Armored Reconnaissance Battalion received the DSC. Capt. Thomas F. Carothers and Pvt. William J. Draper of the 41st Armored Infantry Regiment received the DSC for heroism from 9 to 14 August and on 11 August, respectively.

[40] VII Corps, 2d Armd Div, 4th, 9th, and 30th Div AAR's, Aug; Msgs, Brooks to Collins, 0830 and 0907, 8 Aug, VII Corps G–3 Jnl and File; VII Corps Opns Memo 60, 8 Aug (confirming oral orders, 7 Aug); Collins' Talk at the Armored School, 19 Jan 48.

[41] CI 96, 30th Div, 6–12 Aug; 30th Div FO 22, 1230, 9 Aug; Telecons, Gen Hobbs and Col Otto Ellis, 0823, 8 Aug, and Hobbs and Lewis, 1715, 7 Aug, 30th Div G–3 Jnl and File; Hewitt, *Story of 30th Division*, p. 77; MS # B–725 (Gersdorff).

WRECKED GERMAN ARMOR IN THE SOURDEVAL AREA

At the outset of the attack, American officers had estimated that the enemy seemed capable of driving a wedge to Avranches "to rupture" the front and make the position of the forces south of Avranches "logistically untenable." It was not long, however, before the "potential threat of a major counterattack" vanished. The enemy had very quickly "been forced to abandon his ambitious effort . . . because of heavy tank casualties from allied air attacks . . . and artillery fire." As early as 8 August, intelligence officers were optimistically considering what the Germans might do after the current attack was defeated or contained.[42]

The only effect of the Mortain counterattack was that it had "practically stopped the VII Corps advance." Beyond that, it had prompted some readjustment of forces in the Mortain–Avranches area, but the rearrangement of units had no more than local significance. What the counterattack might have accomplished seemed in retrospect to have been its only merit. Even had it succeeded in cutting the supply lines to the Allied forces south of Avranches, SHAEF was prepared to supply those forces with two thousand tons per day by air.[43]

Taken by surprise in newly occupied

[42] TUSA G–2 Per Rpt 59, 9 Aug; FUSA G–2 Per Rpts 60, 61, and 64, 9, 10, and 13 Aug, and G–2 Est 14, 8 Aug; VII Corps G–2 Per Rpt 64, 8 Aug.

[43] VII Corps and FUSA AAR's, Aug; Lt. Gen. Walter Bedell Smith, "Eisenhower's Six Great Decisions," *Saturday Evening Post*, Vol. 218, No. 50 (June 15, 1946), 18.

positions, the 30th Division had stood its ground and fought as hard as any unit was to fight in the European theater. "It isn't very easy," a staff officer wrote, "to tell the man in the front lines that the battle is going well when he's still up against that old combination of machine guns, burp guns, mortars, 88s, artillery, tanks—and terrain. . . . [But] the battle is going well; [and] it's worth saying." [44]

The battle had indeed gone well, not only at Mortain but elsewhere on the First Army front. On the VII Corps left, XIX Corps, after having attacked in the Sourdeval–Gathemo area (with the 28th and 29th Divisions and CCA of the 2d Armored Division) and having sustained more than 1,200 casualties in three days of heavy fighting, finally moved forward with relative ease on 11 August, and on the following day made contact with the 30th Division north of Mortain and pinched out the 4th and 9th Divisions. On the First Army left the V Corps, which had held on firmly to the town of Vire with the 2d Infantry Division while exerting pressure toward the southeast, noted diminishing German pressure on 12 August. [45]

By that date, the Allies were maneuvering to trap the Germans who had plunged unsuccessfully toward Avranches.

Concepts of Encirclement

As early as 8 August, General Bradley was confident that the reinforced VII Corps would hold at Mortain. He felt

that the Mortain counterattack had "apparently been contained." As he studied the situation, he came to the further conclusion that the Germans by attacking had "incurred the risk of encirclement from the South and North," and he acted at once to capitalize on the opportunity. [46]

In the presence of General Eisenhower who was visiting his headquarters on 8 August, General Bradley telephoned General Montgomery and secured approval for a bold course of action designed to encircle the German forces west of Argentan and Falaise. [47] What he proposed was a radical change—a 90-degree turn—in the 12th Army Group offensive axis. Instead of driving eastward toward the Seine, the First and Third Armies would wheel to the north and attack toward the army group boundary, specifically toward the towns of Flers and Argentan. (*Map 14*) Since the towns were within the 21 Army Group zone, the American armies would advance only to the boundary, the east–west line generally from Mortain through Domfront and Carrouges to Sées. There, the American forces would be in a position to act as the southern jaw of a vise. Approaching the same line from the north, the British and Canadian forces between Tinchebray and Falaise would, in effect, form the other jaw. Closing the jaws on the

[44] 30th Div G-2 Notes for Co Comdrs, 10 Aug, 30th Div G-3 Jnl and File.

[45] *V Corps Operations in the ETO*, pp. 163ff.; CI 85 (the Battle for Vire) ; [Ferriss], Notes.

[46] 12th AGp Ltr of Instrs 4, 8 Aug.

[47] Bradley, *Soldier's Story* pp. 372, 374–75; Montgomery, *Normandy to the Baltic*, p. 158; Eisenhower, *Crusade in Europe*, p. 275; Butcher, *My Three Years With Eisenhower*, p. 636. For an interesting speculative account of the command decisions at Mortain, see O. G. Haywood, Jr., "Military Decision and Game Theory," *Journal of the Operations Research Society of America*, II, No. 4 (November, 1954) , 371–85.

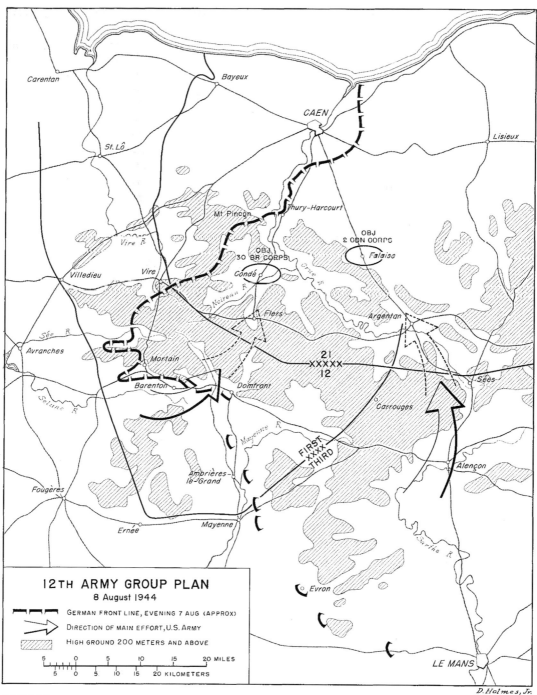

12TH ARMY GROUP PLAN
8 August 1944

▬▬▬ GERMAN FRONT LINE, EVENING 7 AUG (APPROX)

➤ DIRECTION OF MAIN EFFORT, U.S. ARMY

▨ HIGH GROUND 200 METERS AND ABOVE

```
5    0    5    10    15    20 MILES
5    0    5    10    15    20 KILOMETERS
```

MAP 14

D. Holmes, Jr.

army group boundary would entrap and crush the Germans in between.

Specifically, General Bradley ordered General Patton to "advance on the axis Alençon–Sées to the line Sées–Carrouges prepared for further action against the enemy flank and rear in the direction of Argentan." This meant turning the XV Corps north from le Mans, and for this purpose Bradley gave Patton another armored division. He also ordered the 35th Division, involved in the battle around Mortain, to revert to the Third Army "without delay," but the division was still needed by the VII Corps, and Bradley soon revoked this part of this order.

General Bradley instructed General Hodges to pivot on Mortain, advance to the Barenton–Domfront line, and be ready to take further action northeast in the direction of Flers. Hodges was also to eliminate the German salient in the Vire–Mortain–Ger area.[48]

General Hodges issued his order the day after Bradley's instructions. To eliminate the German salient around Mortain, Hodges set up a converging attack by the VII and XIX Corps. VII Corps, attacking generally eastward along an axis through Mortain (south of a new temporary boundary with XIX Corps), was eventually to be pinched out by the advance of XIX Corps, which was attacking to the south through Sourdeval and Ger. This would wipe out the German salient. XIX Corps was then to assume control over its original zone and some of the forces of VII Corps and continue the attack east and northeast toward Flers. VII Corps was to concentrate its strength in the area south

and southeast of Domfront and, together with its forces near Mayenne, it was to launch an attack northeast in the direction of Argentan. Meanwhile, V Corps was to attack from the Vire area southeastward to Tinchebray. The effect of these moves would be to push the German forces opposing First Army to the army group boundary. According to the erroneous interpretion of enemy intentions by the First Army G–2, who was two days ahead of events, the Germans by 9 August were already "pulling back to avoid entrapment." [49]

As for the Third Army, General Patton felt that since the "purpose of the operation is to surround and destroy the German army west of the Seine," he had first to surround the Germans so that their destruction would be inescapable. He envisioned forces cutting through the German rear on a relatively narrow front and encircling the enemy by making contact with the Canadians on the opposite Allied flank. This was the task he gave XV Corps.[50]

On 11 August—a day after XV Corps attacked north from le Mans, the same day that Kluge decided the Mortain salient had to be reduced, and a day before the First Army began its new attack—General Montgomery made known his concept of encirclement. He based his concept on the estimate that the bulk of the enemy forces were west of a north–south line passing from Caen through Falaise, Argentan, and Alençon to le Mans. As the Canadians attacked

[48] 12th AGp Ltr of Instrs 4, 8 Aug.

[49] FUSA FO 6 and G–2 Est 14, 9 Aug.

[50] Memo, Patton for Gaffey, 8 Aug, VIII Corps G–3 Jnl and File; TUSA Ltr of Instrs, Patton to Haislip, 8 Aug, XV Corps G–3 Jnl and File, and Dir, 10 Aug (confirming fragmentary orders, 8 Aug).

toward Falaise and the XV U.S. Corps attacked toward Alençon, the gap, through which must come all German supplies and reinforcement from the east, would narrow. "Obviously," General Montgomery stated, "if we can close the gap completely, we shall have put the enemy in the most awkard predicament." (Map 15)

As the gap narrowed, the enemy was likely to react in one of two ways. He might bring up additional divisions from the east; or, more probably, he would try to move his armored and mobile forces eastward through the gap toward ammunition and gasoline supplies. If the Germans chose the latter course of action, they would probably operate in the general Domfront, Argentan, Alençon area in order "to have the benefit of the difficult 'bocage' country." Their purpose would be to hold off the Americans and withdraw on the Falaise–Vire line.

Expecting the Germans to mass stronger forces in defense of Alençon than of Falaise, Montgomery concluded that it would be easier for the Canadians to reach Argentan from the north than it would be for the Americans to get there from the south. He therefore ordered the First Canadian Army to continue its effort to capture Falaise, stating that it was "vital that it should be done quickly." The Canadians were then to drive south from Falaise to take Argentan. On the Canadian right, the Second British Army, turning to the left, was also to drive toward Falaise by pushing forward its left wing. At the conclusion of the advance, the British would occupy a north–south line between Falaise and Argentan, the right bound-

ary of the Canadian army sector. Meanwhile, the XV U.S. Corps was to advance north from le Mans through Alençon to the army group boundary, which was several miles south of Argentan along a line between Carrouges and Sées.

The projected result would be a meeting of Canadian and American forces just south of Argentan to encircle the Germans who had concentrated the bulk of their forces west of the Orne and a sweeping advance by the British to herd the Germans into the Canadian and American lines. The First U.S. Army, inferentially, would drive the Germans in its zone into the path of the British advance. "It begins to look," General Montgomery wrote, "as if the enemy intends to fight it out between the Seine and the Loire. This will suit us very well. . . . Clearly our intention must be to destroy the enemy forces between the Seine and the Loire." Yet Montgomery did not overlook the possibility that the enemy might successfully evade encirclement at Argentan. In that case, the Allies were to be ready to institute the wider encirclement earlier projected to the Seine.[51]

What seemed perfectly apparent to all was that Allied occupation of Falaise and Alençon would narrow to thirty-five miles the gap between the two flanks of the German defensive positions. Since the bulk of the German forces were west of the gap and facing complete encirclement, capture of the two towns would cut two of the three main east–west roads still in German hands and force the Germans to escape eastward, if they

---

[51] 21 AGp Gen Operational Situation and Dir, M–518, 11 Aug.

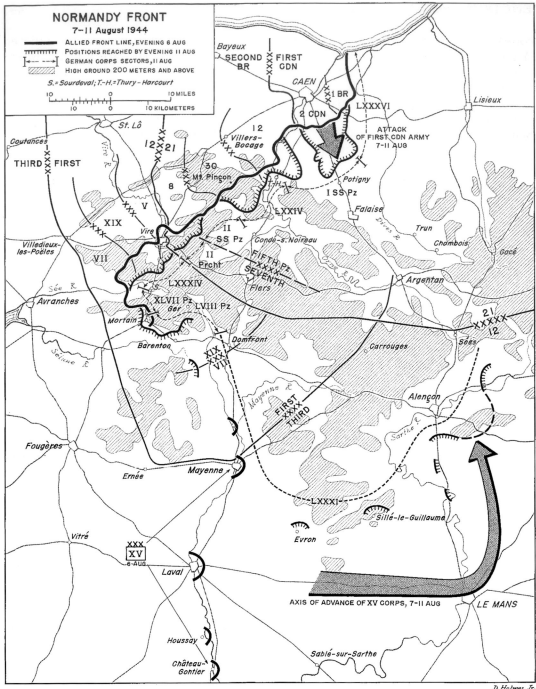

NORMANDY FRONT
7–11 August 1944

▬▬▬	ALLIED FRONT LINE, EVENING 6 AUG
┬┬┬┬	POSITIONS REACHED BY EVENING 11 AUG
⊢--→	GERMAN CORPS SECTORS, 11 AUG
░░░	HIGH GROUND 200 METERS AND ABOVE

S. = Sourdeval; T.-H.= Thury - Harcourt

10   0   10 MILES
10   0   10 KILOMETERS

Bayeux

SECOND   FIRST
BR   CDN

CAEN

1 BR

2 CDN

LXXXVI

Lisieux

ATTACK
OF FIRST CDN ARMY
7–11 AUG

Coutances

THIRD   FIRST

St. Lô

12   21

12
Villers-
Bocage

30
Mt. Pinçon

8

Potigny

T.-H.

I SS Pz

Falaise

Dives R.

Trun

Chambois

Gacé

V

XIX

Vire

II
SS Pz

LXXIV

Condé-s. Noireau

Villedieux-
les-Poêles

VII

II
Prcht

FIFTH Pz.
SEVENTH

Flers

Argentan

Orne R.

Sée R.

Avranches

LXXXIV

XLVII Pz
Ger.

LVIII Pz

Mortain

Barenton

Domfront

Carrouges

Sées

21
12

XIX
VII

Sélune R.

Mayenne R.

FIRST
THIRD

Alençon

Sarthe R.

Fougères

Ernée

Mayenne

LXXXI

Sillé-le-Guillaume

Vitré

XXX
XV
6-AUG.

Laval

Evron

AXIS OF ADVANCE OF XV CORPS, 7–11 AUG

LE MANS

Houssay

Château-
Gontier

Sablé-sur-Sarthe

D. Holmes, Jr.

MAP 15

could, along the axis of the Vire—Flers—Argentan highway.[52]

It seemed not altogether unlikely that the opinion General Montgomery had ventured in mid-June—that the Allies might defeat the Germans between the Seine and the Loire—was about to be realized.[53]

Envelopment from the South

General Haislip's XV Corps had taken le Mans on 8 August with the 5th Armored and the 79th and 90th Infantry Divisions, and soon afterwards it was ready to drive north. The initial corps objective, thirty miles north of le Mans, was the town of Alençon—the great cross-roads of the Rouen–Bordeaux and Rennes–Paris highways. The final objective was eleven miles beyond Alençon, a fifteen-mile stretch of the east–west road connecting the towns of Carrouges and Sées.

In driving north along the le Mans–Alençon–Argentan axis, XV Corps would have both flanks open. On the right, elements of the 106th Cavalry Group during the following few days would roam almost at will and meet only the slightest resistance. On the left, a gap of about twenty-five miles would separate the corps from the closest American units at Mayenne.[54] (Map 16)

To increase the striking power of the XV Corps, Patton gave Haislip the 2d

French Armored Division and ordered Haislip to lead with his armor, which would mean the 5th U.S. and the 2d French Armored Divisions. Much was expected of the French troops, for they were experienced in combat and eager to liberate their country. Commanded by Maj. Gen. Jacques Philippe Leclerc, the division had fought in Africa before being brought to England in the spring of 1944 expressly to represent French forces in Operation OVERLORD. Re-equipped with American matériel, the division arrived on the Continent and assembled just south of Avranches during the early days of August. It had been alerted briefly for possible employment at Mortain before being ordered to le Mans where, on 9 August, it was attached to the XV Corps.[55]

To protect the XV Corps deep left and rear, General Patton drew upon the 80th Division, newly arrived on the Continent and under the command of Maj. Gen. Horace L. McBride. The 80th Division was to clear the Evron area, where General Weaver's 90th Division task force had uncovered considerable resistance while driving on le Mans. Few Germans remained, and the 80th carried out its assignment without much trouble. The few difficulties came mainly from the fluid situation prevailing on that part of the front. For several days the divi-

---

[52] 30th Div G–2 Notes for Co Comdrs, 11 Aug, 30th Div G–3 Jnl and File.

[53] 21 AGp Dir, M–502, 18 Jun.

[54] XV Corps FO 3, 9 Aug; TUSA Ltr of Instrs, Patton to Haislip, 8 Aug; 12th AGp Ltr of Instrs 4, 8 Aug; XV Corps Outline Narrative, 1–14 Aug; see Xavier Rousseau, ed., La Bataille de Normandie au Pays d'Argentan (Argentan, 1945–47) (hereafter cited as Rousseau, Bataille de Normandie), p. 19.

[55] Principal sources for the operational activity of the French division are Capitaine Even, "La 2e D.B. de son Débarquement en Normandie à la Libération de Paris," Revue Historique de l'Armée, I (March 1952) (hereafter cited as Even, La 2e D.B.), 107–32; and 2d French Armd Div G–3 Rpt, Opérations de la 2ème D.B. Depuis le Jour 'J' Jusqu'a la Prise de Strasbourg, ML–1051. See Cole, Lorraine Campaign, p. 187 and n. 4, same page. Leclerc was the nom de guerre of Philippe François Marie de Hauteclocque.

sion oscillated between attachment to the XX and to the XV Corps, and such matters as corps control, boundaries, and objectives were rather vague.[56]

The road net between le Mans and Argentan determined the XV Corps zone of attack. Haislip committed the 2d French Armored Division, followed by the 90th Division, on the left and directed the two units to move along an axis through Alençon to Carrouges; the 5th Armored Division, followed by the 79th, was to move through Mamers to Sées. No cohesive front faced the corps. Intelligence was lacking.[57]

While the French force was entering the corps zone on 9 August, the 5th Armored Division in compliance with Haislip's orders, was securing the line of departure for the attack to the north and clearing initial assembly areas for the French. The corps engineers were constructing two bridges over the Sarthe near le Mans to facilitate entry of the French troops into their zone of advance. Early on 10 August all was in readiness for the attack.

The German decision to commit *Panzer Group Eberbach* in the Alençon area was not to be made for another day, and thus on 10 August the *LXXXI Corps* was defending the le Mans–Alençon axis. The corps had two divisions in the line: the *708th*, with most of its strength west of the Sarthe River (where it had been badly hurt by the 90th Division), seemed "doomed to failure" by its poor fighting quality; the *9th Panzer* (less its Panther battalion, diverted to the Falaise defenses) deployed its well-trained troops

---

[56] Interv with Col Harry D. McHugh, Stockton's Hosp Intervs, Vol. III, GL–93 (235).

[57] XV Corps AAR, Aug, and G–2 Per Rpt 8, 0300, 11 Aug.

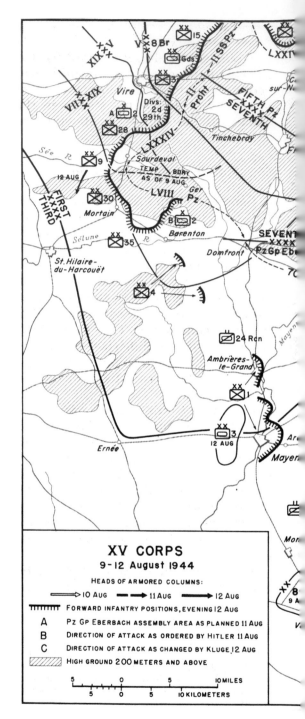

XV CORPS
9-12 August 1944

HEADS OF ARMORED COLUMNS:
⟹ 10 Aug ━▶ 11 Aug ━━▶ 12 Aug
ⅢⅢⅢ FORWARD INFANTRY POSITIONS, EVENING 12 AUG
A PZ GP EBERBACH ASSEMBLY AREA AS PLANNED 11 AUG
B DIRECTION OF ATTACK AS ORDERED BY HITLER 11 AUG
C DIRECTION OF ATTACK AS CHANGED BY KLUGE 12 AUG
▨ HIGH GROUND 200 METERS AND ABOVE

5   0   5   10 MILES
5 0   5   10 KILOMETERS

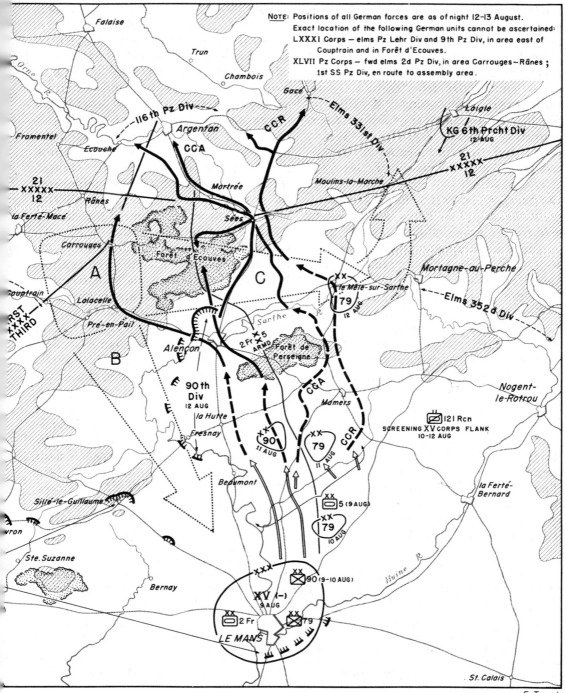

NOTE: Positions of all German forces are as of night 12-13 August.
Exact location of the following German units cannot be ascertained:
LXXXI Corps — elms Pz Lehr Div and 9th Pz Div, in area east of
Couptrain and in Forêt d'Ecouves.
XLVII Pz Corps — fwd elms 2d Pz Div, in area Carrouges—Rânes;
1st SS Pz Div, en route to assembly area.

F. Temple

more directly in the path of the American advance but had some elements committed west of the Sarthe and was to have difficulty concentrating for employment as an entity. On the east flank, the corps commander felt "there were no units worth mentioning." Backing up the line were remnants of *Panzer Lehr,* consisting almost entirely of supply forces and thus of "negligible combat strength," and remnants of the *352d Division,* which had been pulled out of the *Seventh Army* line for wholesale reconstitution. The corps was about to acquire a regimental-sized kampfgruppe of the *6th Parachute Division,* moving west from central France, but the unit could not reach the sector in time to meet the initial American thrust.[58]

The two armored divisions of XV Corps jumped off abreast for a day of action characterized by sharp tank skirmishes, harassing enemy artillery fire, and traffic congestion. Taking relatively light casualties (though the *9th Panzer* and *352d Divisions* together claimed to have knocked out thirty-six tanks), the Americans outflanked the *9th Panzer Division* and moved forward about fifteen miles, or about halfway to Alençon. The command posts of the *9th Panzer* and *Panzer Lehr Divisions* at Fresnay-sur-Sarthe came under fire. Both units withdrew to the north.[59]

The Forêt de Perseigne, a densely wooded area extending almost ten miles across the corps front between Alençon and Mamers, had seemed to SHAEF to offer excellent concealment for at least two German divisions and extensive supply installations, and intelligence officers warned the XV Corps of this possibility. More frequent roadblocks, utilizing tanks rather than antitank guns, and concentrated artillery fire encountered by the corps on 11 August appeared to bear out this concern, prompting Haislip to order his armored divisions to bypass the forest on both sides.[60] To cover the resultant separation of his columns, Haislip ordered three artillery battalions to interdict the exits from the forest and requested an air strike on the forest with incendiary oil bombs to burn and smoke out enemy forces. As it turned out, the Germans had evacuated the woods. French and American armor bypassed the area without undue interference.[61]

On 11 August the Germans were coming to their decision to have *Panzer Group Eberbach* launch a massive counterattack against the XV Corps left flank with armored divisions pulled out of the Mortain salient. The *LXXXI Corps,* its main forces the *9th Panzer* and *708th Divisions,* was to protect the assembly area for the projected attack. Eberbach

---

[58] The basic German sources are MS # B-807 (Kuntzen); MS # B-445 (Krueger); MS # B-725 (Gersdorff); MS # B-179 (Hausser); MS # A-922 (Eberbach).

[59] Lt. Col. William A. Hamberg of the 10th Tank Battalion got his tank across a bridge raked by enemy fire that had already destroyed two American tanks. Reaching an infantry company disorganized by the death of the company commander, Colonel Hamberg dismounted and organized a tank-infantry attack. He was awarded the DSC.

[60] When Pfc. Charles P. McGuire of the 47th Armored Infantry, who was driving the leading vehicle of a motorized column, was halted by enemy fire, he dismounted and advanced alone to destroy the hostile machine gun position. He then returned to his vehicle to lead the column again until he was killed by an 88-mm. shell. He was posthumously awarded the DSC.

[61] Principal sources for American action are the XV Corps and 5th Armd Div AAR's, Aug; see Telecon, Oliver and Menoher, 1540, 11 Aug, XV Corps CofS Jnl and File.

MAMERS, *where American forces met little resistance.*

visited Alençon that afternoon and found the sector in confusion. The *LXXXI Corps* command post was threatened by the American advance. Rear area service troops were fleeing northward to the accompaniment of nearby blasts from the guns of American tanks. Burning vehicles, knocked out by Allied planes and tanks, littered the countryside. The *9th Panzer Division* had been reduced to the point where Eberbach estimated it consisted of only a battalion of infantry, a battalion of artillery, and perhaps a dozen tanks. A bakery company was taking defensive positions at Sées.

The splinter units of the *LXXXI Corps* directly in the path of the XV Corps advance were evidently incapable of stopping the XV U.S. Corps. If the

116th Panzer Division, the first to be pulled out of the line near Mortain, arrived near Argentan in time to stop the Americans, Eberbach's armored attack could perhaps be launched. Meanwhile, Eberbach ordered antiaircraft batteries at Argentan to prepare immediately for defensive ground action.

French and American troops took advantage of German confusion to press forward. Even though the terrain impeded armored mobility, General Leclerc reminded his units that speed, maneuver, and daring must mark their operations. In an audacious thrust that night, a French task force drove to the Sarthe River at Alençon and early on 12 August captured the bridges there intact. The town was not defended.[62] That same morning, after having bypassed Alençon on the east and rushed through Mamers against slight resistance, General Oliver's 5th Armored Division secured the town of Sées.

Patton's instructions to Haislip on 8 August had directed the XV Corps to drive to the Carrouges–Sées line and prepare for a further advance northward. On the basis of the "further advance" inferentially authorized, General Haislip, on the evening of 11 August, established Argentan as the new corps objective. While the 5th Armored Division turned to the northwest from Sées to secure Argentan, the 2d French Armored Division was to take Carrouges, close on a line between Carrouges and Argentan, and face generally northwest. If the Canadians reached Argentan as instructed, the Germans west of the Falaise–Argentan–Alençon line would be

---

[62] See Commandant Richard Mouton, "Libération d'Alençon," in Herval, *Bataille de Normandie,* II, 9–14.

encircled, and XV Corps, with two armored divisions in the line and two infantry divisions (the 79th and 90th, which were following) in support, would hold a strong shoulder between Alençon and Argentan.[63]

There seemed to be one serious obstacle that might hinder the maneuver: the Forêt d'Ecouves blocked the southern approaches to Argentan. If the Germans were to prevent encirclement, they had to keep a gap open between Falaise and Alençon so that their troops might withdraw eastward toward Dreux and Paris. It was plausible then to expect the Germans to try to hold this prominent terrain feature on the southern shoulder of the gap.[64]

General Haislip had instructed Leclerc to pass west of the forest. But Leclerc decided to send one combat command east of the woods, while another went through the forest and the third bypassed it on the west. He envisioned all three columns converging at Ecouché, a town five miles southwest of Argentan on the final Carrouges–Argentan objective line. There was one drawback to this plan: the combat command bypassing the Forêt d'Ecouves on the right (east) would trespass on the main highway from Alençon to Argentan through Sées, which had been reserved for the 5th U.S. Armored Division. Leclerc nevertheless disregarded his division boundary and Haislip's order and ex-

ecuted his plan. The three French combat commands partially cleared the forest and fought their way to within sight of Ecouché and the Carrouges–Argentan line.

When French troops usurped the Alençon–Sées–Argentan highway on 12 August, the 5th Armored Division, fortunately, had already taken Sées. Unfortunately, a 5th Armored Division combat command north of Sées—at Mortrée, five miles southeast of Argentan—had to postpone its attack toward Argentan for six hours. Only after the French column cleared the road could gasoline trucks blocked south of Sées come forward to refuel the command. The attack did not jump off until late afternoon, and by then the Germans had interposed a new unit between the armor and Argentan. The attack, which if launched six hours earlier might have resulted in capture of Argentan, made little progress.

That day, 12 August, *Panzer Group Eberbach* assumed command in the Argentan sector. The *XLVII Panzer Corps* headquarters, having turned over its responsibility at Mortain to the *LVIII Panzer Corps*, arrived at Argentan. Since the *LXXXI Corps* headquarters had been severed from its divisions in the Argentan sector by the American attack and was out of contact with them, the *XLVII Panzer Corps* took control of the remnants of the *9th Panzer Division* in the Ecouves forest. When a strong infantry battalion of the *116th Panzer Division*, which was moving from the Mortain sector, became available early in the afternoon, the *XLVII Panzer Corps* sent it toward Sées. The battalion reached Mortrée in time to block the 5th Armored Division attack.

[63] XV Corps Opns Instrs, 2200, 11 Aug, cited in XV Corps Narrative Outline, 1–14 Aug; Notes of Mtg, 0730, 12 Aug, XV Corps CofS Jnl and File.

[64] XV Corps G–2 Per Rpt 9, 0300, 12 Aug; Capitaine Jean Maigne, "Les Forces Françaises et la Jonction 'OVERLORD-DRAGOON,'" *Revue d'Historie de la Deuxième Guerre Mondiale*, No. 19 (July 1955), 17–33.

The entire *116th Panzer Division* moved to Argentan during the night of 12 August, and the *XLVII Panzer Corps* committed it piecemeal to build up a thin line of defense south of Argentan. The *708th Division,* "literally pulverized," was to be transferred on 13 August to the *Seventh Army.* The *LXXXI Corps,* which had only radio contact with the remnants of the *352d Division* (sent to the Chartres area for rehabilitation), with the newly arriving *331st Division,* and with the kampfgruppe of the *6th Parachute Division,* was placed under control of the *Fifth Panzer Army* with the mission of covering Eberbach's east flank and blocking an American drive into the center of France along a potential front of about one hundred miles.[65]

Loss of Alençon and Sées completely changed the situation for the Germans. Kluge had suggested an attack against the XV Corps spearheads. Hitler had wanted Eberbach to attack well behind the spearheads. Either attack, if launched, might well have dealt the U.S. corps a crippling blow. Instead, Eberbach on 12 August had to commit the *116th Panzer Division* in defense, and because of continuing American pressure he was virtually certain he would have to do likewise with the *1st SS* and *2d Panzer Divisions,* scheduled to become available the following day, 13 August. Not only was the American advance upsetting German offensive plans, it had already deprived the *Seventh Army* of its supply

base, thereby making Hausser's forces entirely dependent for logistical support on the *Fifth Panzer Army.* The ammunition and fuel supply situation, as a consequence, was "dreadfully serious." Only three main roads were available for supply and troop movements. Even these the Germans could use only at night because of Allied aircraft and excellent flying weather. All the roads were so congested that vehicular traffic moved at a walk. Some committed divisions existed in name alone, and all were far below authorized strengths. On 12 August the French and American armored divisions claimed almost a hundred tanks destroyed and nearly fifteen hundred prisoners taken. Most alarming, the Germans could no longer disregard the fact that if the Canadians reached Falaise and the Americans reached Argentan, only thirteen miles would separate them from achieving a literal encirclement of the German forces on the western front. With this menace a distinct possibility, Eberbach redoubled his efforts to establish a stable defense at Argentan.[66]

Eberbach had another reason for redoubling his efforts. Kluge was still planning to launch an attack in the Alençon sector, but because the relentless advance of the XV Corps created a new situation, he modified his plan for the attack scheduled now to begin on 14 August. In an order issued on the evening of 12 August, Kluge shifted the axis of attack from the southeast to a due east direction toward le Mêle-sur-Sarthe. Upon reaching le Mêle-sur-

---

[65] *OB WEST. a Study in Command,* p. 129; Telecons, Kluge and Eberbach, 2345, 12 Aug, and Blumentritt and Speidel (reporting telecon, Blumentritt and Jodl), 1510, 12 Aug, *AGp B KTB;* Telecon, Eberbach and Wiese, 0630, 13 Aug, *LXXXI Corps KTB.*

[66] Telecons, Eberbach and Kluge, 1750 and 2345, 12 Aug, and Blumentritt and Speidel, 1510, 12 Aug, *AGp B KTB.*

Sarthe–Mortagne area, Eberbach was to turn north and complete the destruction of the American forces. Kluge thought it possible that the XV Corps would be beyond (north of) the Argentan–Laigle line before the beginning of the attack, but Eberbach was to execute his mission nevertheless. Eberbach's forces were initially to include the *1st SS, 2d,* and *116th Panzer Divisions* and elements of the *9th Panzer Division,* two *werfer* brigades, and a heavy artillery battalion—these to be reinforced by the *10th SS Panzer Division.*[67]

Meanwhile, south of Argentan General Haislip on 12 August was still motivated by his desire to have XV Corps make contact with the Canadians. About to reach the line he had been instructed to secure, he assigned the 2d French Armored Division the objective of Argentan and instructed General Oliver to assemble his 5th Armored Division southeast of that town. He then notified General Patton rather pointedly that he was about to capture the last objective given by the army commander. Should Patton authorize the XV Corps to proceed north of Argentan, Haislip would be ready to move the American armored division through the French division in Argentan for a drive north to meet the Canadians. Haislip recommended he receive additional troops so he could also block all the east–west roads north of Alençon.[68]

Haislip did not have long to wait for a reply. Very early on 13 August he received word from Patton to "push on

slowly in the direction of Falaise." The axis of advance and the left boundary were both to be the Argentan–Falaise road. When the XV Corps reached Falaise, Haislip was to "continue to push on slowly until . . . contact [with] our Allies" was made.[69] Meanwhile, Patton was searching for additional forces he could attach to the corps.

With a definite mission to keep moving, Haislip was pleased when the 2d French Armored Division on 13 August finished encircling and clearing the Forêt d'Ecouves. Leclerc took Carrouges and Ecouché, then built up a line between Carrouges and Argentan. A French patrol entered Argentan that afternoon and reached the center of the town, bringing the inhabitants short-lived hope of liberation, but German tanks soon forced the patrol to retire. That same morning the 5th Armored Division tried to advance north toward Falaise, but all efforts to get to Argentan or around its eastern outskirts failed. German guns well sited and skillfully concealed on dominating ground north of Argentan wrought a surprising amount of damage on the French and American attack formations.[70]

Elements of the *1st SS* and *2d Panzer Divisions* had reached the Argentan sector early on 13 August despite road congestion, air raids, fuel shortages, and communications troubles. The artillery of the *1st SS* arrived first without infantry protection, then came the Signal

---

[67] Kluge Order, 2100, 12 Aug, *AGp B Lagebeurteilungen, Wochenmeldungen.*

[68] Msgs, Haislip to Leclerc and Oliver, 1845, 12 Aug, and Haislip to Patton, 2130, 12 Aug, XV Corps CofS Jnl and File.

[69] Msg, Gaffey to Haislip, 0040, 13 Aug, XV Corps CofS Jnl and File.

[70] XV Corps G–2 Per Rpt 11, 0300, 14 Aug; see Rousseau, *Bataille de Normandie,* pp. 40, 43–44; Even, *La 2e D.B.,* pp. 110–11; Maigne, Les Forces Françaises et la Jonction 'OVERLORD–DRAGOON,' pp. 18–19.

battalion, later, tanks; the infantry would not arrive until the following day. The *2d Panzer Division* arrived in better condition, but only at half strength; the other half was to require an additional day for the road march. With the *116th Panzer Division* holding well at Argentan, Eberbach directed the *2d* into the Ecouché area and committed the *1st SS* in defense of the ground between Carrouges and la Ferté-Macé. Although these dispositions might have seemed adequate on paper, their actual strength was slight. Eberbach estimated that the *1st SS* had thirty tanks, the *2d* twenty-five, and the *116th* fifteen. The *9th Panzer Division* had been practically destroyed in the Forêt d'Ecouves.[71]

Thus, developments had forced Eberbach to commit piecemeal the panzer units that were earmarked as his striking force in the more urgent task of bolstering the badly shattered southern flank of *Army Group B*. On 13 August events canceled Kluge's plan to inflict a crushing blow on the U.S. XV Corps.

It was clearly apparent to the German command that three weak panzer divisions would not be able to maintain for long, if at all, the slender defensive line established to oppose the XV Corps. On the morning of 13 August Dietrich, the *Fifth Panzer Army* commander, stated officially for the first time what in retrospect all commanders later claimed to have thought—that it was time to be-

gin to escape the Allied encirclement. "If the front held by the [Fifth] Panzer Army and the Seventh Army is not withdrawn immediately," he warned,

and if every effort is not made to move the forces toward the east and out of the threatened encirclement, the army group will have to write off both armies. Within a very short time resupplying the troops with ammunition and fuel will no longer be possible. Therefore, immediate measures are necessary to move to the east before such movement is definitely too late. It will soon be possible for the enemy to fire into the pocket with artillery from all sides.[72]

Yet, contrary to expectations, the defensive line at Argentan did hold. It held not because of German strength but because of a cessation of the American attack. Early in the afternoon of 13 August the XV Corps attack came to an abrupt and suprising halt. General Bradley stopped further movement to the north. Patton had to inform Haislip not to go beyond Argentan. Haislip was to recall any elements that might be "in the vicinity of Falaise or to the north of Argentan." Instead of pressing the attack toward the Canadians, the XV Corps was to assemble and prepare for further operations in another direction.[73]

---

[71] Friedel Telecons, 1230 and 2140, 13 Aug, *AGp B KTB*.

[72] Telecon, Speidel, Wiese, Gause, and Dietrich, 1035, 13 Aug, *AGp B KTB*.

[73] Msg, Gaffey to Haislip (received at XV Corps CP, 1415, 13 Aug), XV Corps CofS Jnl and File; Memo, Patton to Haislip, 13 Aug; TUSA Dir, 13 Aug.

CHAPTER XXVI

The Argentan-Falaise Pocket

Bradley's Decision

When General Bradley halted the XV Corps just south of Argentan on 13 August, the Canadian army was still several miles north of Falaise. The stretch of terrain—less than twenty-five miles—that separated Canadian and American forces became known as the Argentan–Falaise Gap. Why Bradley did not allow Patton to try to close the gap and seal the Argentan–Falaise pocket later became the subject of a considerable polemic.

Rumor soon after the event ascribed the halt to warnings by the Allied air forces that planes had dropped time bombs along the highways in the Argentan–Falaise area to harass German movements; further northward movement by the XV Corps would have exposed American troops to this hazard. Whether this had a part in shaping Bradley's decision or not, the fact was that fighter-bomber pilots had sown delayed-action explosives over a wide area between 10 and 13 August, though the bombs were fused for a maximum of twelve hours delay and thus could not have endangered the troops.[1]

Perhaps more to the point was General Bradley's later explanation that a head-on meeting of Canadians and Amer-icans would have been a "dangerous and uncontrollable maneuver" that (in General Eisenhower's words) might have caused a "calamitous battle between friends."[2] Yet General Bradley himself afterwards offered two solutions that might have been applied to co-ordinate the artillery fires of the forces coming together: a distinctive terrain feature or conspicuous landmark could have been selected as the place of juncture, or the Canadian or American axis of advance could have been shifted several miles east or west to provide a double (and stronger) barrier across the German escape routes without the danger of a head-on meeting.[3]

A disadvantage of bringing Canadians and Americans closer together was that it would have hampered artillery and particularly air operations. Close support missions would have become increasingly restricted and the danger of bombing error greater. As it was, the extremely fluid front necessitated considerable shifting of bomb lines to protect the ground troops and made the work of the Allied pilots a delicate mat-

[1] Stacey, *Canadian Army*, p. 204, n. 9; Patton, *War As I Knew It*, p. 105; *AAF III*, pp. 257–58.

[2] Bradley, *Soldier's Story*, p. 377; Eisenhower, *Crusade in Europe*, pp. 278–79; see also, Butcher, *My Three Years With Eisenhower*, p. 641. It would also have disarranged plans to "get the U.S. and British forces lined up and started together going east." Answers by Generals Smith and Bull to questions by Hist Sec, ETOUSA, 14–15 Sep 45.

[3] Bradley, *Soldier's Story*, p. 377.

ter. Yet for all the hazards of error, Allied aircraft operated in the Argentan–Falaise area with excellent effect until 17 August, when the bomb line in that sector was removed and close air support, at least officially, ceased.[4]

Another reason contributing to General Bradley's reluctance to send American troops beyond Argentan was his preference, as he later said, for "a solid shoulder at Argentan to a broken neck at Falaise." Although he afterwards stated that he had not doubted the ability of the XV Corps to close the gap (despite increasing resistance on the morning of 13 August), he had questioned the ability of the corps to keep the gap closed. Incorrectly believing that elements of nineteen German divisions were already stampeding eastward through the gap, he thought it conceivable that they would trample the thin line of American troops.[5]

Holding the XV Corps at Argentan conformed with General Bradley's concept of destroying the enemy by closing two jaws, for at Argentan the XV Corps formed the lower front teeth of a not yet solid mandible.[6] Actually, the XV Corps was already in an exposed position. Both flanks were open. There were no German forces to speak of to threaten the right flank, but the situation was quite the opposite on the left.

American intelligence officers did not seem aware of Eberbach's mission to launch a massive attack against the deep XV Corps left flank, yet if Eberbach had been able to get it off, the attack would have struck exactly through a gap in the American line. Between the 1st Division troops firmly ensconced at Mayenne and French forces at Carrouges there was a gap of about twenty-five miles. American troops started to close the gap on the morning of 13 August, but until they actually did, a XV Corps advance beyond Argentan to close the Falaise gap would have extended the Mayenne gap. Although General Bradley did not mention this fact in his later account, it was reasonable for him to be concerned at the time with the exposed position of the XV Corps.

These reasons were sufficient to justify General Bradley's decision, but he may also have felt he could not let the XV Corps go to and beyond Argentan without exceeding his authority. Near Argentan the American troops were already across the army group boundary and impinging on the 21 Army Group zone. Since General Montgomery commanded the ground forces in France, Bradley needed his consent to go farther. Although Montgomery did not prohibit American advance beyond the boundary, neither did Bradley propose it.[7]

General Montgomery did not take the initiative, probably because he thought the Canadians would close the gap from

---

[4] *AAF III*, pp. 253–54; 12th AGp Memo for Rcd (Kibler), 18 Aug, ML–205. Leigh-Mallory (in his "Despatch," Fourth Supplement to the *London Gazette* of December 31, 1946, p. 66) stated that he opposed the fixing of any bomb lines at all, for he felt they restricted close air support, denied fighter-bombers excellent targets, and allowed many enemy troops to escape. He would have preferred a less cautious policy, which would have permitted fighter-bombers to attack identified targets at will.

[5] Bradley, *Soldier's Story*, p. 377.

[6] See above, Ch. XXV.

[7] Kibler, the 12th Army Group G–3, recollected long afterward that Bradley had telephoned Montgomery to ask permission to go beyond Argentan and that Montgomery had refused (Answers to Questions by Lt Col Hugh M. Cole, 29 May 45, ML–501), but Bradley denied ever asking (Bradley, *Soldier's Story*, p. 376).

the north. Early in August he had planned to have Patton's Third Army make a wide envelopment to the Seine. Instead, Bradley had reacted to the Mortain counterattack by suggesting and securing approval for a shorter envelopment—the right hook thrust by the XV Corps to Argentan. The virtue of this maneuver was that it took advantage of the Canadian attack on 8 August toward Falaise, an attack launched out of an entirely different context. Juncture of the two forces was implicit. Yet the Americans were at that time much farther from Argentan than the Canadians. Montgomery, estimating that the Germans would shift their defensive strength to protect their southern flank against the Americans, consequently felt that the Canadians, attacking from the opposite flank, could cover the shorter distance to Argentan more quickly.[8]

Halting the XV Corps at Argentan seemed in retrospect to many commanders, Allied and German, to have been a tactical error, a failure to take full advantage of German vulnerability.[9] General Bradley, too, seemed afterwards to consider the halt a mistake, and he sought to refute criticism by placing the responsibility for the halt on Montgomery. In that connection, he recalled that he and Patton had doubted "Monty's ability to close the gap at Argentan" from the north, and had "waited impatiently" for word to continue northward. While waiting, Bradley wrote, he and Patton saw the Germans reinforce the shoulders of the Argentan–Falaise gap and watched the enemy pour troops and matériel eastward to escape out of the unsealed pocket. It seemed to him and Patton, Bradley remembered, that Dempsey's British army by driving from the northwest was accelerating German movement eastward and facilitating German escape, actually pushing the Germans out of the open end of the pocket, like squeezing a tube of tooth paste. "If Monty's tactics mystified me," Bradley later wrote, "they dismayed Eisenhower even more. And . . . a shocked Third Army looked on helplessly as its quarry fled [while] Patton raged at Montgomery's blunder."[10]

It was true that the Germans were building up the shoulders of the gap by 13 August, but by that date they were not fleeing eastward to escape encirclement. Either Bradley and Patton were anticipating what was soon to occur or General Bradley's memory was faulty by several days. If Patton, in a subordinate role, could only rage, and if Bradley thought he might offend a sensitive Montgomery, Eisenhower, who was in France and following combat developments, might have resolved the situation had he thought it necessary to do so. Yet General Eisenhower did not intervene. Interfering with a tactical decision made by a commander who was in closer contact with the situation was not Eisenhower's method of exercising command. Long after the event, General Eisenhower implied that the gap might have been closed, which, he thought,

---

[8] See 21 AGp Dir, M–518, 11 Aug; see above, Ch. XXV. On Montgomery's overly optimistic estimate of the speed with which the Canadians would get to Falaise, see Wilmot, *Struggle for Europe*, p. 417.

[9] See, for example, Patton, *War As I Knew It*, p. 105, and MS # B–807 (Kuntzen).

[10] Bradley, *Soldier's Story*, p. 377.

"might have won us a complete battle of annihilation." [11]

If this had been clear to Bradley at the time, he probably would have picked up the telephone and proposed to Montgomery that the XV Corps proceed beyond the army group boundary to make contact with the Canadians. Yet to propose was, in effect, to recommend, particularly in a situation where Montgomery and Bradley were both army group commanders and where one was British, the other American. Because sending the XV Corps through and beyond Argentan was risky, Bradley probably felt he could not in good conscience recommend such a course of action without reservation. Because Montgomery, not Bradley, was the ground force commander and thus the responsible commander, Bradley, by so proposing, would be saddling Montgomery with responsibility for a course of action that Bradley himself was, apparently, unwilling to recommend wholeheartedly. For Montgomery would, more than likely, have felt impelled to accept the recommendation, given the circumstances of the command setup. Where the assumption of risk was involved, finesse, good manners, and the subtleties of coalition warfare required the responsible commander to make the responsible decision without prompting, and this only Montgomery—or Eisenhower—could have done.

What might have seemed clear to commanders from the perspective of a later vantage point was not so clear at the moment of decision. Bradley himself made the decision to halt, probably on the basis of five tactical considerations: (1) Montgomery, the ground force commander, had not moved the army group boundary, nor did he seem about to do so, and thus he appeared not to favor further American advance. (2) On the evidence of the increasing resistance to the XV Corps on the morning of 13 August, there was no certainty that American troops could move through or around Argentan and beyond. (3) Since the XV Corps was already in an exposed position by virtue of the vacuums on both flanks, there was no point in closing the Argentan–Falaise gap at the expense of further exposing the corps, particularly by enlarging the gap on the left. (4) Intelligence estimates inclined to the incorrect view that the bulk of the German forces had already escaped the pocket. (5) The Canadians were about to launch their second attack to Falaise, an effort that, it was hoped, would get troops beyond Falaise to Argentan and preclude further American advance into the 21 Army Group sector.

The Canadians at Falaise

Despite Montgomery's injunction for speed in getting to Falaise and beyond from the north, General Crerar, whose Canadian army had been stopped in the Caen–Falaise corridor by 9 August, was unable to mount a full-scale operation at once.[12] While Crerar regrouped his

---

[11] Eisenhower, *Crusade in Europe*, pp. 278–79; Pogue, *Supreme Command*, p. 214. Montgomery's chief of staff, Major-General Sir Francis de Guingand, believed that the Falaise gap might have been closed if Montgomery had not restricted the Americans by means of the existing army group boundary. "The Americans felt this [restriction]," he wrote. Guingand, *Operation Victory*, p. 407.

[12] Wilmot (*Struggle for Europe*, pp. 424–25) notes, "the evidence suggests that the thrust from the north was not pressed with sufficient speed and strength."

forces and arranged for air support, he launched a diversionary action on his right on 12 August in division strength, hoping thereby to outflank German positions along the Caen–Falaise road. On 14 August, as the diversion continued into its third day of difficult fighting without substantial advance, he kicked off his main effort.

The main effort was "a concentrated, very heavy blow on a decidedly narrow front," much like the first attack seven days earlier, but it dispensed with artillery preparation to gain surprise, used smoke to provide cover, and employed a "short fierce stroke by medium bombers." [13] Smoke and dust made it difficult for armor and infantry to maintain proper orientation toward the objective, but two armored columns bypassed the resistance astride the main road and approached the objective from the northeast. More than 800 heavy bombers of the RAF and RCAF then dropped 3,700 tons of bombs in the area. [14] Although several bomb loads fell short of their targets and inflicted almost 400 casualties and heavy equipment losses, on Canadian and Polish units, the attack advanced to within three miles of Falaise on the first day.

With the Germans off balance, Canadian troops entered Falaise from the northwest on 16 August and cleared the town by the end of the following day. Artillery shells and air bombardment had transformed the town of William the Conqueror into a pile of rubble. Bulldozer operators, trying to open

routes for traffic, could hardly determine where the streets had been. [15]

Though the Canadians had finally reached Falaise, U.S. troops were still just south of Argentan. The gap had been narrowed, but fifteen miles still separated the Allies. "Due to the extraordinary measures taken by the enemy north of Falaise," General Eisenhower wrote to Marshall, ". . . it is possible that our total bag of prisoners will not be so great as I first anticipated." [16]

The Pocket Tightened

The task of filling the hole on the XV Corps left flank belonged to the First U.S. Army, specifically to the VII Corps. While the V and XIX Corps on the north exerted pressure on the Germans by attacking, respectively, toward Tinchebray and Flers, the VII Corps on the south was to drive from Mayenne to the northeast toward Fromental to cover the XV Corps left flank. In the case of each corps, the objective was the army group boundary, which corresponded with the right flank boundary of the Second British Army. In advancing to the southeast, the British troops would pass in turn across the fronts of all three First Army corps. *(Map 17)*

General Hodges had ordered the First Army to attack as early as 9 August, but not until the *Seventh Army* withdrew from Mortain did the operation get under way. On 12 August the V and XIX Corps initiated the attack. The VII Corps needed an additional day for

[13] Stacey, *Canadian Army*, p. 201.

[14] Leigh-Mallory, "Despatch," Fourth Supplement to the London *Gazette* of December 31, 1946, p. 65.

[15] Stacey, *Canadian Army*, pp. 201–03; Jean Boulle and Léonce Macary, "Falaise n'est Plus," in Herval. *Bataille de Normandie*, I, 368–95.

[16] Msg, Eisenhower to Marshall. CPA 9–0228. 17 Aug, Pogue Files.

displacement south of Mortain to Mayenne.

In Gerow's V Corps sector, the 29th and 2d Divisions attacked abreast through a narrow sector of rough terrain lacking good roads, and three days later captured Tinchebray and high ground south of the town. With the corps front facing eastward and the troops out of contact with the enemy, the advance came to a halt. Hodges had hoped to trap a considerable number of Germans, but the prisoners taken during the four day attack came to the disappointing total of 1,200, less than the number of casualties sustained by the V Corps.[17]

From positions near Sourdeval, Corlett's XIX Corps had attacked with the 28th Division. In hope of improving the division's performance, which he considered unsatisfactory, Corlett on 12 August provided the division a new commander, Brig. Gen. James E. Wharton, formerly assistant commander of the 9th Division.[18] Several hours later General Wharton was mortally wounded, and the next day General Cota came from the 29th Division to take command of the 28th.

On 13 and 14 August, respectively, the 2d Armored and 30th Divisions, earlier part of the VII Corps, augmented the XIX Corps. Pivoting on Ger, the corps moved eastward against light resistance and seized Domfront, which was garrisoned by a battalion composed of stragglers, depot personnel, and soldiers recovering from minor wounds—many of whom were intoxicated when the Americans arrived. On 15 August the

corps made contact with the British several miles west of Flers, and on the following day British forces swept southward across the XIX Corps front, as they had across the V Corps front. Although the advance had been relatively rapid and casualties comparatively light, few Germans had been trapped.[19]

The VII Corps commenced its effort on 13 August after Collins released the 35th Division to the Third Army, reunited the combat commands of the 3d Armored Division under a new commander, Maj. Gen. Maurice Rose, brought the 9th Division to join the 1st at Mayenne, and placed the 4th Division in reserve south of Barenton.[20] Against an estimated 7,600 combat effectives, the 1st Division on the left and the 3d Armored Division on the right drove more than twenty miles northeastward from Mayenne on the first day. Fairly heavy fighting occurred on the following day around Rânes as resistance stiffened in defense of the highway between Flers and Argentan. Though the 9th Division moved into the center to strengthen the corps attack, strong opposition slowed the advance. Montgomery approved a request to cross the army group boundary, and at the end of 17 August the corps made contact with British troops at several points along its

---

[17] V Corps Operations in the ETO, pp. 163–80.

[18] On 28th Division problems, see, for example, CI 72 and the 109th Inf Jnl, 6–9 August.

[19] [Ferriss], Notes; FUSA G–2 Jnl and File, 12 and 13 Aug; 30th Div AAR, Aug, and FO 24, 2300, 13 Aug; MS # B–807 (Kuntzen). See G. Hubert, A. Paillette, and A. Timothée, "Un Enjeu Féodal: Domfront," in Herval, Bataille de Normandie, I, 317–42, for an excellent account of how civilians helped the American troops liberate Domfront without bombardment.

[20] General Watson, relieved from command of the 3d Armored Division and reduced to the grade of colonel, became assistant division commander of the 29th Division, where he served with distinction and was later promoted to brigadier general.

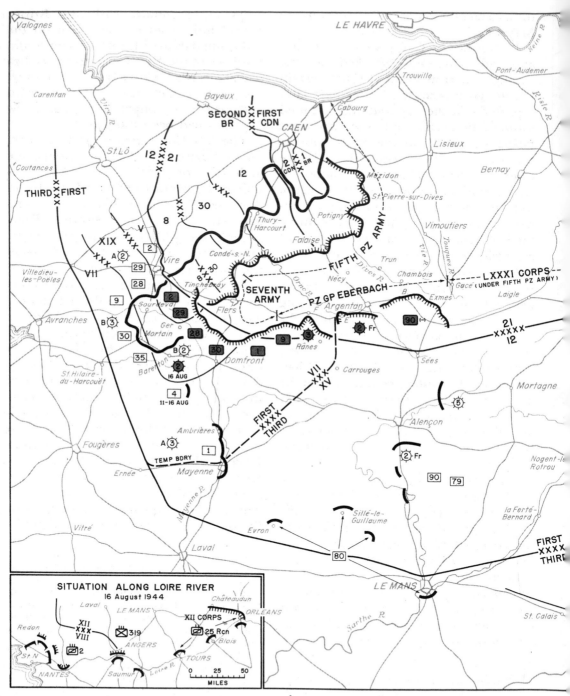

Valognes

LE HAVRE

Carentan

Bayeux

Trouville

Pont-Audemer

SECOND
BR
XX
FIRST
CDN

CAEN

Lisieux

Bernay

Coutances

St.Lô

12 XXX 21

Mézidon

2
CDN
XXX
1
BR

St.Pierre-sur-Dives

THIRD XXX FIRST

XXX

30

Thury-
Harcourt

Patigny

FIFTH PZ ARMY

Vimoutiers

8

Villedieu-
les-Poêles

XIX
A②
V
XXX
2
29
28

Vire

Condé-s.-N.

Falaise

Trun

VII
XXX
8
30
Tinchebray

Nécy
SEVENTH
ARMY

Dives R.

Chambois

LXXXI CORPS
(UNDER FIFTH PZ ARMY)

Laigle

9
B③
30
Sourdeval
2
29

Flers

Orne R.

PZ GP EBERBACH
F

Argentan
2 Fr

90

Exmes

21
XXXXX
12

Avranches

B②
35
Barenton
28
30
Ger
Mortain
1

Domfront
9
Rânes

Carrouges
Sées

Mortagne

St.Hilaire-
du-Harcouët
2
16 AUG

4
11-16 AUG

VII
XXX
XV

5
Alençon

Ambrières

FIRST
XXXX
THIRD

Fougères

A③
1

Nogent-le-
Rotrou

Ernée

TEMP BDRY

Mayenne

2 Fr

90
79

la Ferté-
Bernard

Vitré

Mayenne R.

Evron

Sillé-le-
Guillaume

Laval

80

FIRST
XXXX
THIRD

LE MANS

Sarthe R.

St.Calais

SITUATION ALONG LOIRE RIVER
16 August 1944

Laval   LE MANS

Châteaudun

ORLEANS

Redon

XII
XXX
VIII

319

XII CORPS

25 Rcn

St.N.
2

ANGERS

Blois

NANTES

Saumur

Loire R.

TOURS

0   25   50
MILES

MAP 17

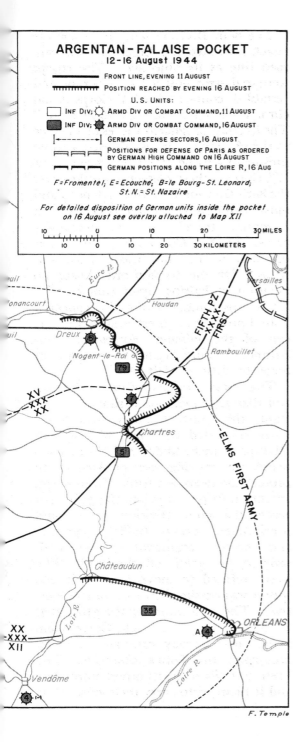

ARGENTAN - FALAISE POCKET
12-16 August 1944

────── FRONT LINE, EVENING 11 AUGUST
ⲧⲧⲧⲧⲧⲧⲧⲧ POSITION REACHED BY EVENING 16 AUGUST
U.S. UNITS:
☐ INF DIV; ○ ARMD DIV OR COMBAT COMMAND, 11 AUGUST
■ INF DIV; ● ARMD DIV OR COMBAT COMMAND, 16 AUGUST
|◄------►| GERMAN DEFENSE SECTORS, 16 AUGUST
⊏⊐ ⊏⊐ ⊏⊐ POSITIONS FOR DEFENSE OF PARIS AS ORDERED
            BY GERMAN HIGH COMMAND ON 16 AUGUST
⊏⊐ ⊏⊐ ⊏⊐ GERMAN POSITIONS ALONG THE LOIRE R, 16 AUG

F=Fromentel; E=Ecouché; B=le Bourg-St. Leonard;
St. N.=St. Nazaire

For detailed disposition of German units inside the pocket
on 16 August see overlay attached to Map XII

F. Temple

front. In the five-day action, the VII Corps had closed the gap on the XV Corps left flank, had taken more than 3,000 prisoners, and had destroyed a considerable amount of enemy equipment.[21]

Though VII Corps had been well on its way on 13 August to closing the gap on the XV Corps left, the XX Corps, recently committed under Third Army command, had also been involved.[22] The fluid situation had prompted some confusion. Events outran decisions, and communications conveyed outdated missions. The result was a comedy of errors.

The beginning of the story occurred on 8 August, when Patton had ordered Haislip's XV Corps to advance north from le Mans to secure the Sées–Carrouges line. He also alerted the XX Corps to the possibility of its commitment beside the XV—but on which side of the XV Corps the XX would eventually operate, the Third Army could not yet tell.[23] Three days later Third Army instructed XX Corps to assemble on the Mayenne–le Mans line for an attack to the northeast to secure the Sées–Carrouges line, the objective previously assigned to the XV Corps.[24] Apparently, Third Army had decided to commit the XX Corps on the XV Corps left. The only unit immediately avail-

[21] VII Corps AAR, FO 8 (and Incl 2 to Annex 2), 13 Aug (confirming oral orders, 12 Aug), Opns Memo 63, 11 Aug (confirming oral orders, 10 Aug), and Opns Memo 65, 13 Aug (confirming oral orders, 12 Aug); SHAEF G–3 Div, GCT/006.71/Ops (A), Ltr, Press Info—Falaise Gap, 20 Jun 45, SGS SHAEF File 000.7, Vol. II; Ltr, Bradley to Eisenhower, 10 Sep, Pogue Files.
[22] For the commitment of the XX Corps, see below, Ch. XXVIII.
[23] TUSA Ltr of Instr, Patton to Haislip, 8 Aug.
[24] Dir, Gaffey to Walker, 11 Aug.

able to XX Corps was the 80th Division, which had been clearing the Evron area.

A day later, on 12 August, after telephone conversations between staff officers of both headquarters, Third Army, confirming the previous attack order, changed the corps objective. The XX Corps was to advance only until it came in contact with the XV Corps around Alençon (taken by the XV Corps that morning) or farther north, there to await further orders.[25] Completion of this mission would sweep clear the XV Corps left flank.

The XX Corps issued its field order close to midnight. In an area between VII Corps on its left and XV Corps on its right, XX Corps designated zones of advance for two divisions to attack abreast, the 80th on the right, the 7th Armored (recently arrived on the Continent and hurrying toward le Mans) on the left. Because the armored division would not arrive in the area until the afternoon of 13 August, XX Corps ordered the 80th Division to initiate the attack at 0800, 13 August; the armor was to follow, pass through the 80th, and take the lead. With two regiments abreast, the 80th was to attack from the Evron–Sillé-le-Guillaume area to capture the Argentan–Sées line. The northeasterly route of advance thus projected cut directly across roads being used by the XV Corps going north from Alençon toward Argentan. Evidently through oversight, the XX Corps field order made no mention of the Third Army instruction to hold the advance upon establishing contact with the XV Corps in the vicinity of Alençon or farther north.[26]

The 80th Division field order for the attack indicated the Argentan–Sées railroad line as its objective. The troops were to destroy hostile forces in zone and "establish contact with XV Corps Armd elms, when same cross Division front." The overlay designated routes of advance to the objective. It also showed a route presumably to be taken by "Armd elms XV Corps"—these elements would enter the 80th Division zone from Alençon and move through the Forêt d'Ecouves to Argentan, thereby cutting diagonally across the XX Corps zone, which was oriented to the northeast. Like the corps order, the division order made no mention of halting upon contact with XV Corps forces. Quite the contrary, "rapid progress . . . is essential to the success of the mission. Forces . . . will advance without regard to progress of forces to right and left." [27]

The attack jumped off on 13 August, and that afternoon the regiment on the right, the 318th Infantry, was hopelessly entangled with part of the 90th Division, which, under XV Corps command, was moving west of Alençon to protect the deep left flank of the corps. Intent on its own mission, the 318th cut across the 90th Division routes and precipitated serious traffic congestion and heated argument. The 90th ordered the 318th off the road. The 318th refused to move because it was sure it was on the right road to its objective. The 90th informed the 318th that another unit (under XV Corps command) had already captured and was occupying the 80th's objective. The 318th was adamant; its orders were clear and it planned to carry them out. The

[25] Dir, Gaffey to Walker, 12 Aug.

[26] XX Corps FO 2, 2345, 12 Aug.

[27] 80th Div FO 4, 0400, 13 Aug.

90th radioed XV Corps headquarters. The 318th radioed 80th Division headquarters. The XV Corps commander sent an officer down to tell the 318th to "get the hell off the road." The 318th retorted that it was under XX Corps jurisdiction, then dispatched a cub plane to division headquarters for help. Elements of the French armored division arrived on the scene and compounded the confusion.[28]

The regimental commander of the 318th Infantry finally got a radio message through to the 80th Division headquarters. He informed General McBride that the XV Corps had ordered him off the road, then said: "My mission requires speed. What is decision?"[29] What he did not know was that his mission had become outdated by the rapid development of events. The VII Corps had started to close the gap on the XV Corps left that morning, and General Bradley had decided to halt the XV Corps short of Argentan. The commitment of the XX Corps on the XV Corps left proved unnecessary. Instructed to regroup, the XX Corps at 1300 had ordered the 80th Division to concentrate in the Laval–Evron area.[30] General McBride therefore radioed the 318th—and the 317th Infantry as well—to "halt in place, clear road, bivouac present position for night . . . and await further orders."[31]

This did not quite end the confusion. The regiment went into bivouac, but

the area turned out also to be in the path of the 90th Division advance. More argument ensued until the regimental commander wearily chose another bivouac. On the following morning General McBride went forward and personally ordered both regiments back to the Laval–Evron area.[32]

By then the V, XIX, and VII Corps of the First Army were closing firmly to the army group boundary. When they completed their moves, the Allied front resembled an irregular horseshoe virtually encircling the major part of the German forces in Normandy. Allied troops held a line from the Canadian positions at Falaise westward to the British near Flers, then eastward to Argentan, thereby forming the Argentan–Falaise pocket. Yet the Argentan–Falaise gap still existed, and through the fifteen-mile opening the Germans were to try to escape complete encirclement.

The German Decision To Withdraw

Pulling the German armored divisions out of the Mortain sector to augment *Panzer Group Eberbach* near Argentan left the *Seventh Army* in a drastically weakened condition. Corps strove to maintain more than precarious contact with adjacent units, plugging holes in the line with scanty local reserves from splinter divisions. Despite desperate efforts to hold the line, the "undiminished violence" of the V and XIX U.S. Corps attacks on 12 August forced the *Seventh Army* to continue the withdrawal it had started from Mortain the previous night.

---

[28] 80th Div AAR, Aug; XV Corps Memo, 13 Aug, 80th Div G–3 Jnl File; Interv with McHugh, Stockton's Hosp Intervs, III, GL–93 (235).

[29] Msg, 318th Inf to 80th Div G–3, 1754, 13 Aug (received 1825), 80th Div G–3 Jnl.

[30] XX Corps FO 3, 1300, 13 Aug.

[31] Msgs, McBride to 317th and 318th Inf Regts, 1845, 13 Aug, 80th Div G–3 Jnl.

[32] Interv with McHugh, Stockton's Hosp Intervs. Vol. III, GL–93 (235).

Yet since Hitler was still obsessed with the thought of attacking again toward Avranches, Kluge could not order an unequivocal withdrawal eastward to escape the threatening Allied encirclement.[33]

Combat on the *Seventh Army* front assumed the character of delaying action. The units fought only to gain time and avoid annihilation. By their tactics they sought to lure the Allies into time-consuming reconnaissance and deployment for attack, then they retired to the next position, usually during the night. The *Seventh Army* continued to resist in this way, withdrawing rapidly weakening units slowly but steadily through successively shrinking fronts. On 13 August the destruction of telephone wires by bombs and artillery intensified feelings of insecurity, for throughout the day the *Seventh Army* was out of communication with *Panzer Group Eberbach*. For twenty-four hours personnel at the *Seventh Army* headquarters wondered whether they were already cut off and isolated.

Panzer Group Eberbach was also drastically reduced in strength by 13 August. The *9th Panzer Division* had only 260 men, 12 tanks, and a few artillery pieces. The *1st SS Panzer Division* had 352 men, 8 self-propelled assault guns, and 14 Mark IV and 7 Mark V tanks. The *2d Panzer Division*, which had had 2,220 men, 5 self-propelled assault guns, and 9 Mark IV and 3 Mark V tanks on 11 September, was considerably diminished two days later.[34]

While these were extreme cases, the over-all strength of *Army Group B* had declined markedly during the two months following the Allied invasion. By 14 August the Germans in the west had lost 3,630 officers, more than 151,000 enlisted men, and 3,800 *Osttruppen*—a total of almost 160,000 troops. On the surface, this compared favorably with the Allied battle casualties of approximately 180,000 by that date. The difference, however, was more than offset by the increasing number of Allied units arriving on the Continent and by the constant influx of Allied replacements. For the Germans, only 30,000 men had arrived to replace losses in the west; only 10,000 more were on their way to the front.[35] On the basis of this alone, the German situation was hardly promising. Added to this was the increasing threat of Allied encirclement.

An order from Hitler arrived in the west early on 14 August, and according to him, "The present situation in the rear of the army group is the result of the failure of the first attack on Avranches." Alluding to what seemed to the Germans to be a change in the direction of the XV U.S. Corps thrust from the north to the west, Hitler advised of the "danger that Panzer Group Eberbach, which was committed much too far to the north, will again become involved in a sterile frontal fight." What he wanted was an attack in Eberbach's sector, "in the Alençon–Carrouges area," in order to destroy the great part of the

[33] Principal sources are Hodgson MS R–58, and MS # B–179 (Hausser), MS # B–346 (Blauensteiner). MS # A–918 (Gersdorff), MS # B–807 (Kuntzen), MS # A–922 and MS # B–840 (Eberbach), MS # B–445 (Krueger).

[34] *Mittagmeldung*, 15 Aug, *OB WEST KTB, Anlagen*, p. 1403.

[35] *OB WEST KTB Lagebeurteilung*, 14 Aug, *Anlagen*, p. 1379. The Allied figure has been estimated from the 12th Army Group, G–3 Report 71, 2300, 15 August, and from the British Army of the Rhine, *Notes on the Operations of the 21 Army Group* (Germany, October 1945).

XV U.S. Corps. The *9th and 10th SS Panzer Divisions* and the *21st Panzer Division*, he instructed, "can and must be employed for this purpose." This time the reinforced *Panzer Group Eberbach* had to be committed far enough to the south to strike the deep left flank of the enemy and thus deny him the possibility of launching a counterthrust into the right flank of the panzer group as he had done before. In order to free the three designated panzer divisions for the attack, Hitler admitted that contraction of the salient west of Flers could not be avoided. Yet he warned Kluge that as the front west of Flers was withdrawn to a shorter line, the enemy would bring strong pressure to bear against the south flank between Domfront and Alençon. The speed and the extent of the withdrawal to the shorter line near Flers, therefore, should depend on the amount of Allied pressure. Concerned also by "anticipated landings" on the coast of southern France (actually to take place on the following day), Hitler advised Kluge that "destruction of the enemy near Alençon" was the immediate *OB WEST* mission and that all further directives from Hitler would depend on the course of the battle there.[36]

If Hitler's order failed to bring comfort, it at least had the virtue of being positive. It authorized further withdrawal, and Kluge ordered the westernmost forces to start a retrograde movement that was to take place in two stages (two nights) to a shorter line roughly through Flers. Kluge instructed Dietrich to disengage the *II SS Panzer Corps*, with the *9th SS* and *21st Panzer Divisions*, in the course of the withdrawal and to transfer those forces to Eberbach. Then, during the evening of 14 August, Kluge departed his *Army Group B* command post and went forward to see how further compliance with Hitler's order could best be carried out.[37]

Meanwhile, what had seemed like the beginning of stabilization on 13 August had deteriorated by the end of the next day. The "great offensive" the Germans had expected on the Canadian front materialized. On a nine-mile front the Canadians made a breach in the German defenses astride the Caen–Falaise road for a depth of five to six miles. On other parts of the front other penetrations occurred, the "most unpleasant" being the pressure of American forces around Domfront. Ammunition and gasoline shortages were getting more critical by the hour.[38]

As Kluge drove toward Dietrich's *Fifth Panzer Army* headquarters on the evening of 14 August, he found the roads clogged with traffic and dispirited troops. When he reached Dietrich's command post, he learned firsthand that the depleted divisions of the panzer army were too weak to react effectively to the second Canadian attack toward Falaise. In view of the gravity of the situation on the *I SS Panzer Corps* front, the *21st Panzer Division* had to be diverted to

---

[36] Quoted in Msg, *OB WEST* to *AGp B*, 0445, 14 Aug, *AGp B Fuehrer Befehle*. In a letter to Jodl written five days later, on 19 August, Blumentritt stated that Kluge had been depressed by Hitler's order, which by its detailed instructions seemed to imply a lack of confidence in Kluge's ability to handle the situation. Blumentritt's letter is extracted in *OKW/222*, 25 Aug.

[37] Telecons, Speidel and Blumentritt, 1110, 14 Aug, and Kluge and Speidel, 2330, 14 Aug, *AGp B KTB*; Kluge's Order, 1810, 14 Aug, *OB WEST KTB, Anlagen*, p. 1380.

[38] *AGp B Tagesmeldung*, 0200, 15 Aug, *OB WEST KTB, Anlagen*.

SIGNAL CORPS TROOPS *in Domfront repair wires cut by the Germans.*

Falaise in order to prevent a complete collapse of the German defenses in that critical sector. Word from the southern sector was scarcely better. Having judged it impossible to attack because of a shortage of tanks, gasoline, and ammunition and because of the constant activity of Allied planes over the battlefield, Eberbach had ordered all his troops to "pass to the defensive." The *10th SS Panzer Division* had become involved with hard-pressing American forces who were endangering the *Seventh Army* left flank north of Domfront. Thus, of the three panzer divisions designated by Hitler to reinforce Eberbach, only the *9th SS* for the moment was available.

The prospect was grim. If Dietrich could not hold the Canadians, and if Eberbach could not launch a strong at-

tack in the very near future south of Argentan, the only alternative would be to break out as quickly as possible from the threatened encirclement by moving east and northeast through the Argentan–Falaise gap. Delay could very well mean the loss of all the forces in the pocket.[39]

Kluge left Dietrich's headquarters early on 15 August to confer with Hausser and Eberbach at the village of Nécy. Four hours later Kluge and his small party had vanished from sight and sound. When radio contact could not be re-established, a frantic search to find Kluge ensued.

While the search proceeded, the situation in the pocket worsened. Allied attacks continued, with Falaise, Domfront, and Argentan the critical points of pressure. Astride the Caen–Falaise road, the *12th SS Panzer Division* met the continued Canadian attacks with its last strength, while several miles to the west (near Condé-sur-Noireau) the *21st Panzer Division* had to be committed to seal off a penetration. Near Domfront, as the *Seventh Army* executed the second stage of its withdrawal to Flers, American troops threatened to overrun the thin rear-guard line of resistance. Near Argentan, *Panzer Group Eberbach* lost possession of Ecouché.

In addition to these developments, a new difficulty arose, this one outside the pocket. On the *Army Group B* right, in the *Fifth Panzer Army* sector, an Allied attack launched along the boundary line between the *I SS Panzer* and *LXXXVI Corps* broke through the German defenses, and Allied spearheads

---

[39] Telecon, Kluge and Speidel, 2330, 14 Aug, *AGp B KTB;* see *Der Westen* (Schramm), pp. 353–58.

reached the Dives River near Mézidon and St. Pierre. An immediate decision was required, and with Kluge still missing Dietrich ordered a withdrawal to positions behind the Dives River.[40]

Meanwhile, there was still no word on Kluge's whereabouts by 1830, when Blumentritt, Kluge's chief of staff at *OB WEST*, was talking to Jodl on the telephone. "The situation west of Argentan," Blumentritt declared, "is worsening by the hour." Implying that withdrawal from the pocket was becoming increasingly necessary, Blumentritt passed on the insistence of Dietrich, Hausser, and Eberbach that "an over-all decision has to be made."

"If such a decision has to be made as a last resort," Jodl replied, "it could only be to attack toward Sées to gain room so that other intentions can be carried out."

"I am duty bound," Blumentritt said, "to point out the state of the armored units." All suffered from a great shortage of gasoline because of the difficulty of transporting supplies westward into the pocket.

Jodl did not see the logic of this thinking. In order to break out of the encircling Allied forces, one had to attack.

"We must speak frankly," Blumentritt said. If Jodl had in mind an attack with all available forces in order to bring out of the pocket—if at all possible—at least part of the forces, this was a sound decision. But if the intention was to carry out some other operation, such was no longer feasible.

Jodl was not convinced.

"I must emphatically state," Blumentritt said, "that I am in a difficult position as chief of staff when Kluge is not here. I have the most urgent request. As long as Kluge is absent, someone must be appointed by the Fuehrer to take charge. It could only be Hausser, Dietrich, or Eberbach."

Jodl seemed to incline toward Hausser.

"I'll be most grateful," Blumentritt said, "for the quickest possible decision. As far as I am concerned, I am cool as a cucumber. But I must say that the responsible people on the front contemplate the situation as being extremely tense."

Jodl stressed once more the essential prerequisite for any possible action in the future: an attack by Eberbach. "But," he added with a touch of sarcasm, "the only reports we receive are that he is unable to do anything."

Blumentritt overlooked the remark. "If a new commander in the field is appointed by the Fuehrer," he reminded Jodl, "he must be given a clearly stated limited mission without any strings attached." Only then would he be able to estimate reasonably how he could expect to come out of the situation. Otherwise, the Germans would probably lose the best divisions they had. Time was short—"it is five minutes before twelve." [41]

An hour later Hitler placed Hausser in temporary command of the forces under *Army Group B*.[42] Later that night

---

[40] *Tagesmeldung*, 0230, 16 Aug, and Gause Telecon, 1915, 15 Aug, *AGp B KTB*. Dietrich also discreetly suggested his availability to command the army group if Kluge did not turn up.

[41] Telecon, Blumentritt and Jodl, 1830, 15 Aug, *OB WEST KTB, Anlagen*, p. 1420.

[42] Though clearly the impetus for Hausser's appointment came originally from Blumentritt, some individuals on higher military and political echelons apparently connected Kluge's disappearance with the Allied invasion of southern France, which occurred the same day. Since the

Hitler telephoned Generalfeldmarschall Walter Model and Generalfeldmarschall Albert Kesselring for advice on a successor to Kluge should such an appointment become necessary.[43]

Hausser's immediate mission as acting commander of *Army Group B* was to destroy the American forces near Sées "which threaten all three armies with encirclement." To achieve this, he was to attack with *Panzer Group Eberbach* from the west. The *LXXXI Corps*, stretched on a 70-mile front from Gacé to Chartres, was to lend its dubious support from the northeast. The *Fifth Panzer Army* was to stand fast north of Falaise, and the *Seventh Army* was to protect Eberbach's rear.[44]

Before Hitler's order reached Hausser on the evening of 15 August, Kluge turned up. What had caused him to vanish was not in the least mysterious. An Allied plane had strafed his party and knocked out his radio. The presence of Allied aircraft overhead had prevented him from reaching his rendezvous point until late in the day.[45]

Whether Hitler's order could be carried out was a moot point because the

situation in the southern sector on the evening of 15 August was discouraging. Furthermore, in the west the *Seventh Army* was in the process of withdrawing to a line east of Flers. The *10th SS Panzer Division* was unable to disengage, not only because of its involvement in battle near Domfront but also because it lacked fuel to move anywhere else for offensive commitment. The long *Panzer Group Eberbach* front from Briouze through Rânes and Ecouché to east of Argentan, with the *1st SS*, *2d*, and *116th Panzer Divisions* on line facing south, was being hammered. Though the Rânes, Carrouges, and Ecouché areas seemed to the Allies to be "crawling" with Germans, the fact was that the *LVIII Panzer Corps* was being squeezed and this in turn was endangering the *LXXXIV Corps*.[46] Of the two panzer divisions earmarked for Eberbach's attack, the *2d SS* was in assembly area northeast of Argentan and ready for employment, but the *9th SS*, delayed in its relief by a shortage of gasoline, was still west of the Orne River. Not much could be expected from the *LXXXI Corps*, which held its overextended sector with an equivalent of about two divisions—the newly arrived *331st Division* and a regimental-sized kampfgruppe of the *6th Parachute Division* on the right from Gacé to Verneuil, remnants of the *352d Division* with some security elements attached on the left from Dreux to Chartres. An improvised kampfgruppe under a Captain Wahl covered the twenty-mile gap in the middle—two understrength battalions of the *2d SS Panzer Division* and twenty Panther tanks of

Gestapo had uncovered allegations but no proof that Kluge had been involved in the July 20th conspiracy, it seemed to some that Kluge might have been trying to make contact with the Allies to arrange a negotiated peace. A detailed bibliography of the case against Kluge may be found in Hodgson, R–58; see also FitzGibbon, *20 July*.

[43] *Der Westen* (Schramm); *OB WEST KTB*, 15 Aug, and *Anlage*, p. 1624.

[44] Msg, *AGp B* to *Fifth Pz* and *Seventh Armies*, 2315, 15 Aug, quoting Hitler Order, *WFSt/Op. Nr. 772887*, 1930, 15 Aug, *AGp B Fuehrer Befehle*.

[45] Zimmerman Telecon, 0450, 16 Aug, repeating radio Msg from *Pz Gp Eberbach*, 2200, 15 Aug, intercepted by *II Fighter Corps*, in *OB WEST KTB*, *Anlage 1444*; *Der Westen* (Schramm), pp. 367–68; *Fifth Pz A KTB Nr. 2, Anlagen*; *AGp B KTB*, 15 Aug, and *Op. Befehle*, p. 308.

[46] For an Allied assessment, see 2d French Armd Div G–3 Rpt, Opns.

the *9th SS Panzer Division*, which had been moving behind the front toward the east before being intercepted by the *331st Division* and put to use by the corps. Despite these discouraging conditions, Jodl, who telephoned shortly before midnight to inquire about Kluge's whereabouts, held the opinion that no matter how bad the situation seemed, it was necessary to attack to the east to broaden the open end of the pocket—"because it is impossible to get two armies out the end of an intestine." [47]

Jodl could not see what was happening in the *Panzer Group Eberbach* sector. The roads were virtually impassable; units were intermingled; movements were frequently made under the muzzles of long-range Allied artillery pieces; tanks were repeatedly immobilized for lack of fuel; ammunition supplies arrived erratically; the troops were hungry and exhausted; communication was almost nonexistent, except by radio. Signs of disintegration appeared in certain formations, and straggler lines picked up many more than the usual number of men. Divisions consisted of "a miserable handful of troops" that "never before fought so miserably." [48] An *Army Group B* staff officer, alluding to the retreat from Moscow in 1812, described the situation on the roads as having "a Napoleonic aspect"; since the army group had no means with which to bring matters under control, could *OB WEST* help? [49]

Kluge's reappearance on the evening of 15 August brought hope that a weighty decision would be made. After conferring with Hausser and Eberbach, Kluge returned to Dietrich's command post where telephone communication was better. There he remained during the night and the next day, in touch with Jodl, Blumentritt, and Speidel.

His first act was to send a message to Jodl. At 0200, 16 August, Kluge informed Jodl that in his judgment—and he was supported by the army commanders—all the available armored forces together were insufficient for a large-scale attack to improve the situation in the army group rear. He felt that scanty POL supplies were a "decisive" factor. He was discouraged by the "increasingly critical" south flank. He therefore recommended immediate evacuation of the western salient through the still existing Argentan–Falaise gap. Hesitation in accepting his recommendation, Kluge warned Jodl, would result in "unforeseeable developments." [50]

Kluge then waited for the decision from Hitler on whether or not to withdraw. At 1135, 16 August, he telephoned Generalleutnant Hans Speidel, his chief of staff at *Army Group B*, to be brought up to date on messages received by the headquarters. Not long afterwards he talked on the telephone with Blumentritt, who informed him of the Allied landings in southern France. Blumentritt suggested that Kluge request OKW for a free hand in directing the withdrawal operation out of the

---

[47] Telecon, Jodl and Speidel, 2310, 15 Aug, *AGp B KTB*. See also *Seventh Army Abendmeldung*, 15 Aug, and Addenda, *OB WEST KTB, Anlagen*, p. 1415.

[48] MS # B–807 (Kuntzen).

[49] Telecon, 1202, 15 Aug, *OB WEST KTB, Anlagen*, p. 1402.

[50] Msg, Kluge to Jodl, signed 0200, 16 Aug, intercepted by *II Fighter Corps* at 1145, 16 Aug, *AGp B Op. Befehle*, pp. 308–09.

pocket that had obviously become necessary.[51]

At 1245 Kluge telephoned Jodl and again set forth his estimate of the situation. Unquestionably, Jodl admitted, the armies had to be withdrawn eastward. But it seemed to him that a withdrawal was feasible only if the escape opening were enlarged, and this could be done only by an attack to the southeast.

Kluge was direct and to the point. He believed it impossible to comply with Hitler's wish as expressed in Hitler's directive to Hausser. An attack southeastward through Argentan and Sées was out of the question. "No matter how many orders are issued," Kluge said, "the troops cannot, are not able to, are not strong enough to defeat the enemy. It would be a fateful error to succumb to a hope that cannot be fulfilled, and no power in this world [can accomplish its will simply] through an order it may give. That is the situation."

Jodl assured Kluge that he understood perfectly. A concise and clear directive from the Fuehrer, he said, would be sent to Kluge in the shortest possible time.[52]

Twenty minutes later Speidel telephoned Kluge to report information to the effect that a directive from Hitler would shortly arrive in the field. Presumably it would give Kluge full freedom of action. Since Jodl had agreed that withdrawal was necessary, Kluge directed Speidel to prepare immediately the draft of a withdrawal order for *Seventh Army*. The *Seventh Army* was to begin withdrawing on the following morning. Hausser was to pull two divisions out of the front at once and dispatch them to the *Fifth Panzer Army*, which had lost two divisions in two days of fierce combat. The *II SS Panzer Corps* headquarters was to be made subordinate to *Panzer Group Eberbach* so that Eberbach could exercise better control over the many splinter units assigned to him. How to get the *Seventh Army* back across the Orne was the most troublesome problem of the withdrawal. The movement of supplies westward into the pocket was already virtually impossible. Tanks were being abandoned for lack of fuel. The bridges over the Orne were not suitable for heavy traffic. Because antiaircraft protection was generally inadequate, Allied air attacks on massed vehicles at the Orne River crossing sites could create insurmountable difficulties. For these reasons it was necessary to provide for the strict regulation of traffic during the withdrawal. The *Seventh Army* was to be charged with this job. Since the most difficult part of the withdrawal would be across the Orne River itself, Kluge wanted a corps headquarters that had no other assignment to take charge of traffic control over the Orne; he designated the *LVIII Panzer Corps* for the task.[53]

An hour and a half later, at 1439,

---

[51] Telecon, Kluge and Speidel, 1135, 16 Aug, *AGp B KTB*; Telecon, Kluge and Blumentritt, 1155, 16 Aug, *OB WEST KTB, Anlagen*, p. 1450. Blumentritt and Speidel spoke on the telephone around noon and speculated on the withdrawal movement. Speidel expressed the opinion, and Blumentritt was apparently in agreement, that the withdrawal had to be carried out to the Dives River–Laigle line. Telecon, Blumentritt and Speidel, 1210, 16 Aug, *AGp B KTB*.

[52] Telecon, Kluge and Jodl, 1245, 16 Aug, *Fifth Pz A KTB, Anlage 24*.

[53] Telecon, Kluge and Speidel, 1305, 16 Aug, *AGp B KTB*.

though Hitler's directive had still not arrived in the west, Kluge issued his withdrawal order. The armies were to withdraw behind the Orne River during two
successive nights, starting that night.
Two divisions of the *Seventh Army* were
to be disengaged and dispatched to the
Fifth Panzer Army as rapidly as possible
to assist in the Falaise area. *Panzer
Group Eberbach* was to cover the withdrawal by launching attacks in the Argentan area. Eberbach was to be ready
to send two panzer divisions under *II SS
Panzer Corps* eastward to the Vimoutiers
area, where it was to remain at the disposal of the army group.[54]

Two hours afterwards, Hitler's order
arrived. It authorized *Army Group B*
to withdraw its forces that were west of
the Dives River. The movement eastward was to be made in two stages:
across the Orne River, then across the
Dives. Junction with the *LXXXI Corps*
was to be made near Gacé. Hitler emphasized two requirements: Falaise had
to be strongly held as a "corner pillar,"
and the Argentan–Falaise gap had to be
enlarged by an attack launched by *Panzer Group Eberbach* toward the southeast.[55]

There was nothing in Hitler's order
that had not previously been considered
and discussed more than once in the
headquarters along the chain of command. Withdrawal behind the Dives

River had been contemplated, and the
necessity of holding the Falaise shoulder
of the gap was self-evident. While
Jodl's concept of enlarging the escape
corridor by Eberbach's attack to the
southeast was theoretically sound, no
means existed to carry out the attack.
Yet Hitler and Jodl both refused to accept this hard fact despite irrefutable
evidence presented by the commanders
in the field. By 16 August, with the
loss of Falaise that day the most dramatic
illustration of the shrinking pocket, the
commanders found themselves not only
virtually surrounded by a contracting
enclosure but also threatened with being
engulfed by crumbling walls. Furthermore, their only escape route was in imminent danger of being blocked.

The decision to withdraw having finally been made, the Germans began to
pull out of the pocket after dark on 16
August.

The Allied Decision to Close the Pocket

Having halted the XV Corps just
south of Argentan on 13 August, General Bradley made another decision on
the following day. Without consulting
General Montgomery, he decided to retain only part of the XV Corps at Argentan while sending the rest to the east toward the Seine River (and across it if
possible), with Dreux the first objective.

The reasons for Bradley's action were
clear. The apparent scarcity of enemy
forces between Argentan and the Seine
seemed to warrant a thrust to the eastern
boundary of the OVERLORD lodgment
area. There seemed no need to retain
a large force at Argentan, for "due to the
delay in closing the gap between Argen-

---

[54] *AGp B* Order, 1439, 16 Aug, *AGp B Op.
Befehle.* Because it seemed that the large number
of divisions could not be brought across the few
available Orne River bridges in two days' time,
Kluge later amended his order to allow a third day
if necessary. Telecon, Kluge and Speidel, 1700,
16 Aug, *AGp B KTB.*

[55] Telecon, Blumentritt and Speidel, 1645, 16 Aug,
AGp B KTB, Hitler Order, 1555 (?), 16 Aug,
OB WEST KTB, Anlagen, p. 1457.

tan and Falaise"—by implication the fault of the Canadians who had not reached the army group boundary as the Americans had—it appeared that "many of the German divisions which were in the pocket have now escaped." On the basis of Montgomery's directive of 11 August, which had stated that the wider envelopment to the Seine would be in order if the Germans evaded encirclement at Argentan and Falaise, an eastward drive seemed justifiable. It was true that the Mayenne gap on the left of the XV Corps appeared to be well on its way to elimination, and the XV Corps could have therefore attacked northward through Argentan with greater security on 14 August. But since Montgomery had had twenty-four hours to order a resumption of the XV Corps advance to Argentan and farther north and had not done so, Bradley felt he need not hold all his forces in place. He decided to keep two divisions of the XV Corps at Argentan and to reinforce them with the 80th Division. These units, "together with the VII Corps," he thought, "will be sufficient for the southern jaw of the trap." [56]

Patton received word of the decision by telephone, and on 14 August instructed General Haislip to go eastward with part of his XV Corps. Haislip alerted his two divisions on the right— the 5th Armored and 79th Infantry—for the movement. The 79th Division, assembled between Alencon and Mortagne, had been out of contact with the enemy since moving north from le Mans in the wake of the 5th Armored Di-

vision—though on 14 August a small part of the 79th hunted down and destroyed about fifty German tracked vehicles trying to escape eastward from the Forêt d'Ecouves toward Mortagne. The division made ready to depart the area on the following day. To free the 5th Armored Division, the 2d French Armored Division extended its lines eastward to cover the southern exits from Argentan, and the 90th, which had followed the French from le Mans to Alençon, took positions east of Argentan along the le Bourg-St.-Léonard–Exmes road.

On 15 August the two departing divisions drove toward Dreux, followed by the XV Corps headquarters and artillery. A skeleton corps staff remained at Alençon to conduct the holding operation that had devolved upon the 2d French Armored, the 90th, and the 80th Divisions.[57]

Deployed along the Ecouché–Exmes line, the 2d French Armored and 90th Infantry Divisions held the southern shoulder of the Argentan–Falaise gap, while the 80th Division prepared to move north from the Evron area to bolster them. The two divisions on line kept the east–west roads through Argentan under constant interdiction fire and shelled particularly the Argentan–Laigle highway, a vital traffic artery toward Paris and the Seine. Argentan itself, burning since 13 August, remained in German hands.[58]

[56] 12th AGp Dir for Current Opns, 15 Aug (the quotations above are from this document) ; Bradley, *Soldier's Story*, pp. 378–79; 21 AGp Dir, M–518, 11 Aug.

[57] TUSA Dir to XV Corps (signed Brig. Gen. Hobart R. Gay) , 14 Aug, and Dir, 15 Aug (confirming oral orders, 14 Aug) ; Telecon, Gaffey and Menoher, 2145, 14 Aug, XV Corps CofS Jnl and File; XV Corps and 79th and 90th Div AAR's, Aug.

[58] Rousseau, *Bataille de Normandie*, pp. 40 and 12 (the latter "new pages") ; see also Xavier Rousseau, "Souffrances d'Argentan," in Herval, *Bataille*

As though confirming American estimates that most of the Germans had already escaped the Argentan–Falaise pocket, contact along the Ecouché–Exmes line slackened on 15 August.[59] Patton on the following day ordered the 90th Division commander, General McLain, to dispatch a force to the town of Gacé on 17 August to find out what was there. Sixteen miles east of Argentan, Gacé would give the 90th Division control of a hill mass dominating the terrain to the north and northeast and would deny the Germans an important road center on the escape routes north to Lisieux and northeast to Bernay and Rouen. But before the 90th Division could act, the Germans broke the comparative calm that had existed. Contingents of the *2d SS* and *116th Panzer Divisions* launched an attack on the afternoon of 16 August against 90th Division roadblocks at the village of le Bourg-St.-Léonard.[60]

Six miles east of Argentan, little more than three miles south of Chambois, and at the southeastern edge of the Forêt de Gouffern, le Bourg-St.-Léonard is on the crest of the ridge forming the watershed between the Orne and the Dives River valleys. A narrow belt of woods running along the ridge line from Falaise to le Bourg-St.-Léonard offered the retreating Germans good concealment and a staging area for an attempt to break out of encirclement. But the Argentan plain to the southwest and the Dives River valley to the northeast, over which the German troops had to move on their way out of the pocket, was open land almost devoid of cover. The dominating terrain near le Bourg-St.-Léonard provided excellent observation over a large part of the Dives River valley, where the last battle of the Argentan–Falaise pocket was to be fought.

The attack against the 90th Division opened Kluge's planned withdrawal to the Seine, and it drove the 90th off the ridge. Though American infantry supported by tanks retook both le Bourg-St.-Léonard and the ridge after dark, action there had not yet ended. The fight for possession of this tactically important terrain feature was to continue for another twenty-four hours.

The German attack was something new, something quite different from the rather disorganized forces the 90th Division had scattered and destroyed during the preceding days. It became apparent, contrary to earlier intelligence estimates, that a large proportion of the German forces still remained in the Argentan–Falaise pocket.[61] Closing the gap by the joint effort of Canadian and American forces thus became even more urgent than before.[62]

Closing the gap on 16 August was bound to be more difficult, not only because of the German withdrawal of the Mortain salient and the concentration of German troops at the shoulders but also because of the reduction of forces at Argentan in favor of the drive to the

---

de Normandie, I, 396–411; XV and 5th Armd Div AAR's, Aug; Interv with Capt Ernest Rothemberger, Stockton's Hosp Intervs, ML–2234.

[59] See, for example, XV Corps G–2 Per Rpt 12, 0300, 15 Aug, and 90th Div AAR, Aug.

[60] 90th Div AAR, Aug; MS # B–179 (Hausser).

[61] See Magna Bauer, Major Shifts of Divisions Made by the Germans to and Within the German Normandy Front Between 30 July and 25 August 1944, and the Significance of These Movements in View of Allied Strategy, R–33, OCMH Files.

[62] Eisenhower to Marshall, CPA 9–0228, 17 Aug, Pogue Files.

·Le Bourg-St.-Léonard *and the terrain across which the Germans ultimately withdrew from the Argentan-Falaise pocket.*

Seine. Four divisions and twenty-two battalions of artillery had been in the vicinity of Argentan on 14 August, but two divisions and fifteen artillery battalions had departed on the following day.[63] On 16 August, when the Germans began their withdrawal across the length of the American front, it was doubtful that the American forces around Argentan were strong enough to hold the shoulder. Two divisions and seven artillery battalions were on the Ecouché–Exmes line; the 80th Division was still southwest of Alençon, a considerable distance away.

Yet on that day Montgomery phoned Bradley to suggest a meeting of Canadians and Americans, not somewhere between Falaise and Argentan, but seven miles northeast of Argentan, near Trun and Chambois.[64]

In compliance with Montgomery's suggestion, Bradley ordered Patton to launch a drive northeastward from the Ecouché–Exmes line to seize Chambois and Trun and make contact with the Canadians. The departure of the XV Corps meant the absence of a headquarters in the Argentan area to co-ordinate the divisions on the southern shoulder of the gap. Earlier that day, Patton had alerted McBride, the 80th Division commander and the senior officer in the area,

to be ready to take command if necessary in a defensive situation. But this was hardly practical for the offensive action ordered by Bradley. Patton thus directed McBride to move the 80th forward to join the 90th Division and the 2d French Armored Division.[65] He then created a provisional corps under command of his chief of staff, Maj. Gen. Hugh J. Gaffey, for the purpose of getting the drive under way at once.[66]

With four officers comprising his staff, General Gaffey arrived near Alençon on 16 August, set up a command post, established communications with the three divisions comprising his command, and soon after midnight issued an attack order. He directed the 2d French Armored Division to send one combat command west of Argentan to cut the Argentan–Falaise road; the 90th Division to take Chambois and establish a bridgehead over the Dives River there; the French to pass another combat command through the 90th to capture Trun; the 80th Division to move to an assembly area south of Argentan.[67]

All units were to be ready to attack by 1000, 17 August. But before they jumped off, a new corps commander arrived on the scene. The attack did not get under way as scheduled.

---

[63] Royce L. Thompson, A Statistical Study of the Artillery Battalions at the Argentan–Falaise Pocket (hereafter cited as Thompson, Arty Study), OCMH Files.

[64] Bradley, Soldier's Story, p. 379. The date of the telephone call has been inferred from internal evidence; see also Patton, War as I Knew It, p. 109, and Pogue, Supreme Command, p. 214.

[65] Earlier that day the 80th Division had been alerted for movement southeast to Châteaudun, not far from Orléans, there to become the Third Army reserve. 80th Div FO 5, 0200, 16 Aug.

[66] TUSA Ltr, Provisional Corps, 16 Aug.

[67] Third Army Provisional Corps Opns Order 1, 17 Aug; see [1st Lt. Hollis Alpert], Notes on the Closing of the Chambois Gap (hereafter cited as [Alpert], Notes), OCMH Files.

CHAPTER XXVII

Closing the Pocket

The Beginning of the End

When the Germans began their withdrawal on the night of 16 August, the bulk of the depleted forces of *Army Group B* were west of the Dives River and inside the Argentan–Falaise pocket. Elements of the *Fifth Panzer* and *Seventh Armies* and of *Panzer Group Eberbach*—comprising four panzer corps, two army corps, and one parachute corps—seemed about to be trapped. (*Map XI*)

Only two army corps, both under the *Fifth Panzer Army*, were outside the pocket, and they held the rest of the army group front, to the north and east of the pocket. On the north and facing generally west was the *LXXXVI Corps* (with three infantry divisions), deployed east of the Dives River on a 25-mile front from the coast to a point south of St. Pierre-sur-Dives; its left flank, badly shattered by Canadian Army attacks during the past few days, had no contact with the *I SS Panzer Corps*. East of the pocket and facing generally south was the *LXXXI Corps* (with two infantry divisions on the flanks and an improvised kampfgruppe in the center), stretched along a 70-mile front from Gacé to Rambouillet.

The pocket itself was shaped like an elongated letter U lying on its side, the open part on the Dives River, the curvature near Flers. The shortest possible road distance from the westernmost part of the pocket near Flers to the town of Trun, near the center of the gap on the east, was close to 40 miles. The width of the corridor averaged somewhere between 11 and 15 miles, which meant that most of the ground inside the pocket was within range of Allied artillery fire.

The Germans judged they needed three nights to get the westernmost forces across the Orne River, one more night to complete the withdrawal behind the Dives. Thus the outcome of the withdrawal operation would depend on whether the crumbling shoulders of the gap could be held and the exit kept open for four days.

The withdrawal started quietly after dark on 16 August. That night the westernmost forces moved back to the Orne River. The Allies interfered very little, and the movement was orderly. The troops then prepared to start crossing the Orne on the following night, the *II Parachute* and *LXXXIV Corps* making ready to defend the river line and cover the withdrawal of the *1st SS* and *2d Panzer Divisions* of *Panzer Group Eberbach*.

The comparative calm accompanying the beginning of the withdrawal did not last, for events on 17 August hastened the deterioration of the German situation. On that day Montgomery telephoned Crerar's First Canadian Army to direct increased pressure on the pocket from the north. Among other instructions Montgomery relayed to Crerar's chief of staff by telephone was a specific order: "It is absolutely essential that both armoured divisions of the 2d Canadian Corps, i.e. 4th Canadian Armoured Division and 1st Polish Armoured Division, close the gap between First Canadian Army and Third U.S. Army. 1st Polish Armoured Division must thrust on past Trun to Chambois at all costs, and as quickly as possible." [1]

Three things happened as a result. First, east of the Dives, part of the *LXXXVI Corps* left flank was forced back behind the Viette River. Second, the two armored divisions of the 2d Canadian Corps, the 4th Canadian on the right, the 1st Polish on the left, struck the weakened *I SS Panzer Corps*. Advancing roughly parallel to the Dives River, the armored divisions broke through the German line and reached positions little more than a mile from the Trun–Vimoutiers highway, less than two miles north of Trun. Third, another penetration southwest of Falaise presented a potential threat to the *Seventh Army* right rear.

To deal with these developments, elements of the *2d SS* and *9th SS Panzer Divisions* of the *II SS Panzer Corps*, moving to Vimoutiers in army group reserve, were committed against the Allied penetration at Trun, and the *Seventh Army* was ordered to accelerate its withdrawal across the Orne River.

The departure of the *II SS Panzer*

Corps had already created a precarious situation on the German southern flank, where the *116th Panzer Division* and elements of the *2d SS Panzer Division* (the latter at le Bourg-St.-Léonard) were holding the gap open. Units of both German divisions had attacked and taken le Bourg-St.-Léonard on the previous day, only to be pushed off the ridge. But at dawn of 17 August they attacked again with infantry, armor, and artillery well massed. Again they drove 90th Division troops from the village and ridge. Heavy fighting continued throughout the day, this time the Germans retaining possession of the high ground.

The situation there might have been quite different had General Gaffey's provisional corps launched its attack to seize Chambois. But before Gaffey's operation could get under way, another officer appeared on the scene with authority to take command of the forces on the Argentan–Exmes line. He was General Gerow, commander of the V Corps.

The V Corps, under First Army command, had been pinched out near Tinchebray on 15 August and had no further immediate combat mission. When General Montgomery made known by telephone on the following day his intention to close the pocket at Trun and Chambois, the availability of the V Corps headquarters made it an obvious choice to take charge of the divisions around Argentan. General Bradley therefore ordered General Hodges to send General Gerow to the southern shoulder of the gap. General Patton, apparently not informed of this arrangement, had meanwhile sent General Gaffey to the area.

Gerow, on the evening of 16 August, had received a telephone call instructing

[1] Canadian Mil Hq Hist Sec Rpt No. 146, Opns of the First Canadian Army in North-West Europe, 31 Jul–1 Oct 44 (hereafter cited as Canadian Opns), ML-2250.

him to report immediately, with several key officers, to First Army headquarters. He took eight officers with him. Traveling in three jeeps, they reached their destination shortly after midnight and found the tent that housed the war room a beehive of activity.

Hodges and his chief of staff, Maj. Gen. William B. Kean, informed Gerow that he (Gerow) was to assume command at once of three divisions near Argentan and to close the Argentan–Falaise gap. "Where are those divisions?" Gerow asked. No one knew exactly. Nor could anyone tell him anything about the enemy situation there.

Shortly after midnight, in the midst of a heavy rain, Gerow and his staff departed in search of the three divisions. By daybreak on 17 August Gerow was in his new area. He set up a command post in the Hôtel de France at Alençon and located General Gaffey. Messages to the First and Third Armies soon clarified the matter of command. Bradley shifted the army boundary to place Trun and Chambois in the First Army zone of advance. The provisional corps headquarters was disbanded. Because the V Corps Artillery was moving from Tinchebray to the Argentan area on 17 August, Gerow postponed the attack toward Chambois and Trun until the following morning.

For this attack General Gerow wanted the le Bourg-St.-Léonard ridge as the line of departure. Though General McLain proposed to recapture the village and ridge as part of his effort on 18 August, Gerow insisted on having the high ground before the attack. In compliance, the 90th Division attacked after dark, re-entered the village at midnight,

and secured the jump-off positions Gerow wanted.[2]

The German situation on the southern shoulder of the gap was further aggravated that evening of 17 August, for the *116th Panzer Division* received orders to relieve the *2d SS Panzer Division* troops near le Bourg-St.-Léonard so the latter could rejoin the *II SS Panzer Corps* at Vimoutiers. The relief was accomplished during the night by committing the last *116th Panzer Division* reserve—a reconnaissance battalion about eighty men strong.

Meanwhile, Kluge had outlined and made known his future intentions in a warning order to his army commanders. The armies, after crossing the Orne River, were to fall back without delay to the Dives River–Morteaux–Trun–Gacé–Laigle line. There *Panzer Group Eberbach* was to be disbanded. The *Seventh Army* was to assume responsibility for the front between the seacoast and Laigle. The *Fifth Panzer Army*, with Eberbach again in command, was to take the sector from Laigle to the vicinity of the Eure River just west of Paris.[3]

Kluge was not to remain in command much longer. Model arrived on the

2 Interv by Col S. L. A. Marshall with Lt Gen Leonard T. Gerow, 12 Sep 45, quoted in [Alpert], Notes; *V Corps Operations in the ETO,* pp. 181–86; 12th AGp Ltr and Ltr of Instrs, both 17 Aug; Msg, Col James H. Hagan to Gen Haislip, 0750, 17 Aug, and Memo, Hagan for Menoher, 0025, 17 Aug, XV Corps CofS Jnl and File; Sylvan Diary, 16 Aug. For their inspiring and heroic leadership at le Bourg-St.-Léonard, Brig. Gen. William G. Weaver and Maj. Leroy R. Pond were awarded the Oak Leaf Cluster to the DSC, and Maj. Robert H. Schulz and Lt. Col. George B. Randolph were awarded the DSC, the latter posthumously.

3 Kluge to Dietrich, Hausser, and Eberbach, 1430, 17 Aug, *AGp B Op. Befehle.*

17th with instructions from Hitler to relieve Kluge and become *OB WEST* and *Army Group B* commander as soon as he was familiar with the situation. Model's arrival in the west was not altogether surprising. Hitler had not granted Kluge the free hand that Jodl had seemed to promise. Furthermore, Hitler had advised Kluge to stay personally out of the pocket. While this could have reflected perhaps nothing more than concern for Kluge's well-being, it could also be interpreted as virtual confinement to quarters, an attempt to keep the commander in chief in the west away from the temptation of making contact with the Allied command for the purpose of arranging an armistice.[4]

Developments on higher command levels were of little concern to the western-most German troops in the pocket, who continued their withdrawal during the night of 17 August. In the face of light Allied pressure from the west, the bulk of the units crossed the Orne River that night in good order despite road congestion, Allied artillery fire, and diminishing supplies. Gasoline shortages prompted the destruction and abandonment of some tanks and self-propelled guns. Few supplies were reaching the troops by road transport, but an air delivery on the evening of 17 August by 45 Heinkels (bombers modified to cargo carriers) brought some relief.[5] Behind the Orne River, the forces prepared to move on the following night to the high

FIELD MARSHAL MODEL

ground immediately east of the Falaise–Argentan highway.

The retreat across the Orne was a creditable achievement. Many divisions were by then only weak groups unable to hold a connected front. The *85th Division,* for example, had reported as its strength on 15 August a battalion and a half of infantry and two guns. The *LXXIV Corps* had lost contact with the adjacent *I SS Panzer Corps* on its right flank. Yet special bridge commanders had regulated traffic strictly. Troops moved well in widely dispersed formations. Despite steep river banks, heavy Allied artillery fire, and daylight surveillance by "countless numbers" of

---

[4] *OB WEST KTB,* 17 Aug; *OB WEST, a Study in Command,* pp. 152–53; Ltr, Blumentritt to Jodl, 19 Aug, extracted in *OKW/222; AGp B KTB,* entry 1815, 17 Aug; Telecon, Speidel and Blumentritt, 2135, 17 Aug, *AGp B KTB.*

[5] See Telecons, 0020 and 1050, 18 Aug, *AGp B KTB.*

Allied planes that pursued even individual vehicles, the *Seventh Army* maintained discipline. Two circumstances, German commanders recalled later, aided them in their river crossing: in their opinion, the British "did not follow up very vigorously from the west," and Allied planes concentrated their attacks on Trun, Chambois, and Vimoutiers rather than farther to the west over the Orne.[6]

Enter Model, Exit Kluge

Early on 18 August, at 0600, Field Marshal Model, the *OB WEST* and *Army Group B* commander-designate, drove to the *Fifth Panzer Army* command post near Lisieux to confer with Dietrich, Eberbach, and Hausser. Since Hausser was unwilling to leave his troops at that critical time, his chief of staff, Generalmajor Rudolf-Christoph Freiherr von Gersdorff, represented him at the conference. All the conferees were in general agreement on the measures that needed to be taken.

Above all, a front had to be re-established, either one west of the Seine River or one along it, according to the way the situation developed. The first attempt to stabilize the front was to be made along the Touques River. The *Seventh Army*, with *Panzer Group Eberbach* subordinated to it for the withdrawal operation, was to get out of the pocket as quickly as possible. The *Seventh Army* had to be behind the Dives River on 20 August and behind the Touques two days later. *Panzer Group Eberbach* was to be responsible for protecting the

northern flank with the *II SS Panzer Corps (2d SS, 9th SS, 12th SS, and 21st Panzer Divisions)* and the southern flank with the *XLVII Panzer Corps (2d and 116th Panzer Divisions).*[7]

Returning to his headquarters that afternoon, Model reported his views to Jodl and requested their immediate referral to the Fuehrer. Model's appraisal of the situation and discussion with his commanders led him to make four main points. First, the outcome of the withdrawal operation and the prospect of supplying the troops depended heavily on reducing the absolute air supremacy of the Allies for the next few days. Second, hard fighting on the ground would be necessary during the withdrawal, but Model hoped to accomplish the withdrawal according to the following timetable: during the night of 18 August, to the Falaise–Argentan road; during the night of 19 August, behind the Dives River; during the night of 20 August, to the Touques River–Laigle line. He hoped also to be able to release certain armored units and headquarters for assembly near the Seine. Third, upon completion of the withdrawal, the *Seventh Army* was to take command of the sector from the sea to Laigle, inclusive; the *Fifth Panzer Army*, under Eberbach, was to assume responsibility for the sector between Laigle and Paris. The *First Army*, moving northeastward from the Atlantic coast of France, was to take charge of the Paris sector and the upper Seine River. Fourth, the troops were spent; no combat performance of any kind could be

---

[6] MS # B–727 (Gersdorff) and MS # A–922 (Eberbach).

[7] Min of Conf, 18 Aug, *Fifth Pz Army KTB*, *Anlage 34;* Tempelhoff Telecon, 1050, 18 Aug, *AGp B KTB.*

expected from them unless certain minimum requirements were fulfilled.

Model listed the minimum requirements. He needed without delay 20 replacement battalions—4 for panzer divisions, 6 for SS panzer divisions, and 10 for infantry divisions—plus 5 army engineer battalions. As an example of how depleted his units were, he planned to form four kampfgruppen from remnants of ten divisions—one kampfgruppe consisting of what remained of the *84th, 85th, 89th,* and *271st Divisions* and comprising 1,200 men and 8 artillery batteries; another kampfgruppe consisting of the *276th, 277th, 326th,* and *363d Divisions* and totaling 1,300 men and 8 batteries; a third of the *3d Parachute Division,* 1,500 men and 8 batteries; and a fourth of the *353d Division,* 2,000 men and 6 batteries.

He also needed immediate matériel replacements: at least 270 tanks or assault guns to provide each armored division with about 30; 9 artillery battalions of 108-mm. howitzers to replace guns lost by the panzer divisions; and as many 180-mm. howitzers as possible. He required a 9,000-ton capacity transportation facility to expedite the delivery of essential supplies and the movement of reserve units to the front. And, finally, he requested that 6 panzer brigades in the process of activation in Germany be dispatched to the Western Front.[8]

Meanwhile, the situation on the *Army Group B* front had again deteriorated on 18 August. The army group reported the left flank of the *LXXXVI Corps* pushed behind the Vie River, still out of contact with the *I SS Panzer*

Corps. Deep penetrations had occurred east and west of the Dives. East of the river the Canadians were in possession of Trun and had advanced to the vicinity of St. Lambert, while a British thrust along the Falaise–Argentan highway reached a point about halfway between the two towns. The pressure from the south was generally contained, but along the eastern edge of the woodland east of Argentan American forces had unhinged the southern shoulder and threatened Chambois. By the end of the day, the gap on the eastern end of the pocket appeared closed, though presumably as yet only with weak forces.[9]

The most significant development had occurred on the north flank in the zone of the 2d Canadian Corps. The 4th Canadian Armoured Division took Trun, and reconnaissance elements advanced to the edge of St. Lambert. Beside it, the Polish division secured the area around Hordouseaux and Hills 258 and 137, while a reinforced reconnaissance troop probed to within half a mile north of Chambois. The result denied the Germans one of their two main escape routes.[10]

On the southern shoulder of the gap, General Gerow's V Corps had launched its attack on 18 August. Gerow had instructed the 2d French Armored Division on the left to hold firmly to the Ecouché–Argentan line, in order to

[8] Model's Rpt to Jodl, 18 Aug, *OB WEST KTB, Anlagen,* p. 1513.

[9] *AGp B Tagesmeldung,* dated 19 Aug, *AGp B KTB.*

[10] Two main sources have been used for the action on the northern flank: Canadian Opns; *1. Dywizja Pancerna w Walce (The First Armored Division in Battle)* (Brussels: La Colonne, Ltd., 1947) (hereafter cited as *1st Polish Armored Division*), pp. 67–70, 91–103. Mr. Wsevolod Aglaimoff kindly made available the information published in the Polish language.

prevent the Germans from breaking out of the impending trap, and assist the corps attack by fire. In the center, between Argentan and le Bourg-St.-Léonard, the 80th Division was to commit the 318th Infantry in a thrust designed to bypass Argentan on the east, cut the Argentan–Trun road, and enter Argentan from the northeast.[11] On the right, from a line between le Bourg-St.-Léonard and Exmes, the 90th Division was to drive north to capture high ground near Chambois. Fifteen artillery battalions were to lend support.[12]

The 318th Infantry, 80th Division, made no progress against strong German resistance. Occupying rising ground and possessing superior observation, the Germans knocked out four Sherman tanks with their first few antitank shells. Their artillery and machine gun fire inflicted severe casualties on the infantry. General McBride called off the attack and requested the artillery fire of seven supporting battalions in an attempt to reduce the German defenses before trying to advance again.[13]

The 90th Division had more, but not complete, success. Moving cross-country, American infantrymen outflanked resistance astride the le Bourg-St.-Léonard–Chambois road, then cut the road about half way to Chambois.[14] Morn-

ing mist rising from patches of damp and densely thicketed forests hampered the troops at first. Later, thick smoke from smoldering timber set afire by white phosphorus shells obscured their vision. This, plus German fire (particularly of the *8th Werfer* (Rocket) *Brigade*) and defensive action by the *116th Panzer Division,* prevented the 90th from attaining its objective.

The gap on the eastern end of the pocket remained open, and through it that night German headquarters and units escaped. The *116th Panzer Division,* for example, sent trains and artillery through the Trun–Chambois gap. The *LVIII Panzer Corps* headquarters, having fulfilled its mission of regulating traffic over the Orne bridges, moved across the Dives to safety.

Yet the Germans had ample cause for concern. The pocket had been further compressed. "Practically speaking," according to German commanders, "the pocket was closed." With the exception of a narrow belt of woodland running along the watershed between the Orne and Dives River valleys, the terrain offered little cover. The roads were like chalk marks on a billiard table, in plain view of Allied aircraft and artillery observers. During the night of 18 August intense artillery fire suddenly descended on the pocket from all sides in unprecedented volume, and it continued throughout the following day.[15]

Outside the *Army Group B* perspec-

---

[11] Only one other regiment of the 80th Division, the 317th, was available to Gerow, and he kept it as his corps reserve. The third regiment, the 319th, was on a separate mission near the Loire River.

[12] V Corps FO 20, 1800, 17 Aug; V Corps Ltr of Instr (Gerow to Leclerc) 18 Aug; Thompson, Arty Study.

[13] 80th Div AAR, Aug; Interv with McHugh, Stockton's Hosp Intervs, Vol. III, GL–93 (235).

[14] Lt. Col. Christian H. Clarke, Jr., though suffering a painful and partially disabling wound, manifested heroic leadership and was awarded the DSC.

[15] MS # A–919 (Gersdorff); see Telecon, Gersdorff and Speidel, 2020, 20 Aug, *AGp B KTB;* Commandant Richard Mouton, "Le Piège se Referme à Chambois," in Herval, *Bataille de Normandie,* I, 416; Leigh-Mallory, "Despatch," Fourth Supplement to the *London Gazette* of December 31, 1946, p. 67.

tive, events in the west were also having their effect on higher levels, and on 18 August Hitler issued an order to amplify his instructions of the 16th, instructions that applied to the situation in southern France. On 16 August, a day after the Allied invasion of southern France, Hitler had ordered all noncombat troops of *Army Group G* west of the line Orléans–Clermont-Ferrand–Montpellier to begin moving northeastward to the Seine–Yonne River line. This order affected neither the combat troops of the *Nineteenth Army* opposing the Allied Mediterranean landings nor the fortress troops on the Atlantic coast. On 18 August, because developments in the *Army Group B* sector foreshadowed the possibility that the *Nineteenth Army* might be cut off in the near future, Hitler ordered *Army Group G* to disengage its forces in southern France—with the exception of troops at Toulon and Marseille. *Army Group G* was to move to gain contact with the southern flank of *Army Group B* and begin at once to organize a rallying position along a line from Sens through Dijon to the Swiss border. Firm rear-guard action on predetermined lines of resistance was to insure the orderly withdrawal of all troops from southeastern France. The *11th Panzer Division* was to be left in the Rhône River valley as protection against Allied airborne landings and later was to form the rear guard of the *Nineteenth Army*. The progress of pursuing Allied forces was to be impeded to the utmost by demolition and destruction—"not one locomotive, bridge, power station, or repair shop shall fall into enemy hands undestroyed." Fortress areas on the Atlantic and Mediterranean coasts of France were to be defended to the last man,

Marseille and Toulon by a division each.[16]

With *Army Groups B* and *G* withdrawing from northwest and southern France by 18 August, Model at midnight, after a day of inspection and conference in the west, assumed command of *OB WEST* and *Army Group B*.[17] His predecessor, Kluge, departed for Germany by automobile.

Shortly before Model's arrival in the west, Kluge had told a colleague, "You may rest assured that I shall talk with him [Hitler] again tonight without mincing any words. Something has to happen. I owe this to the troops and to the German people. One way or another."[18] Relieved of command before he could do so, Kluge nevertheless fulfilled his promise by writing a frank letter to Hitler before his departure. On the road to Metz he then committed suicide, taking potassium cyanide. Hitler at first repressed news of Kluge's death, but soon after he received Kluge's letter he informed important party officials and military authorities of Kluge's suicide.[19] Hitler also advised them that Kluge had admitted his guilt for the defeat in the west. Kluge was buried quietly at home without the public acclamation later accorded Rommel, who, unlike Kluge, was to be forced to take his own life.

---

[16] Hitler Order, *OKW/WFSt/Op*, 16 Aug, received by *OB WEST* at 0320, 17 Aug, *OB WEST KTB, Anlagen*, p. 252; Hitler Order, 18 Aug, *OB WEST KTB, Anlagen*, p. 1499.

[17] *Fifth Pz A KTB, Anlage 40*.

[18] MS # B–807 (Kuntzen) .

[19] Telecon, 1710, 20 Aug, *AGp B KTB*. Speidel reported that Kluge had complained on several occasions of dizziness and also that Kluge had seemed deeply affected by the critical situation of the encircled troops and by the fact that his son was among them.

Kluge's letter to Hitler contained neither bitterness nor reproach:

When you receive these lines, I shall be no more. I cannot bear the accusation that I sealed the fate of the West by taking wrong measures. . . . I have never feared death. Life for me, who am already included on the list of war criminals to be surrendered, has no more meaning.

. . . .

I have been relieved of command. . . . The evident reason is the failure of the armored units in their push to Avranches and the consequent impossibility of closing the gap to the sea. As responsible commander, my "guilt" is thereby affirmed. Allow me, my Fuehrer, to state my position in all deference.

Because of previous combat, Kluge declared, the armored units that had launched the attack toward Avranches had been far too weak to assure success, and even with increased striking power, they would never have regained the sea. Assuming, nevertheless, that Avranches had through some miracle been recaptured, the danger to the army group would have only been postponed, not eliminated. The order to drive to the north from Avranches in an attempt to change the strategic situation in the west had been *"completely* out of the question. . . . Your order, therefore, presupposed a state of affairs that did not exist." The grand and daring operational concept enunciated by Hitler, unfortunately, had been impracticable in execution.

Conceding that it probably would have been better to delay the attack for one day, Kluge contended that such a postponement would not have basically changed the course of events. The units in the west had been forced to become self-sufficient in men and matériel because the crisis on the Eastern Front had not permitted adequate replacement. Not the failure of the Avranches counterattack but the rapid decline in the number of available tanks and antitank weapons, the insufficient supplies and equipment, and personnel attrition had produced the situation that had culminated in the Argentan–Falaise pocket.

Both Rommel and I, and probably all the leaders here in the West, who have experienced the struggle with the English and Americans and [witnessed] their wealth in matériel, foresaw the development that has now appeared. . . . Our views were *not* dictated by pessimism but by sober recognition of the facts.

Hoping that Model would master the situation, Kluge concluded:

Should the new weapons in which you place so much hope, especially those of the air force, not bring success—then, my Fuehrer, make up your mind to end the war. The German people have suffered so unspeakably that it is time to bring the horror to a close.

I have steadfastly stood in awe of your greatness, your bearing in this gigantic struggle, and your iron will. . . . If Fate is stronger than your will and your genius, that is Destiny. You have made an honorable and tremendous fight. History will testify this for you. Show now that greatness that will be necessary if it comes to the point of ending a struggle which has become hopeless.

I depart from you, my Fuehrer, having stood closer to you in spirit than you perhaps dreamed, in the consciousness of having done my duty to the utmost.[20]

[20] Ltr, Kluge to Hitler, 18 Aug, translated by MIRS London, 28 May 45, CRS Files, EAP 21–X/15; Kluge's Farewell to Hitler, 18 Aug, M.I.-14/7, OCMH Files; see Hodgson's translation in R–58; see also Bormann File on Kluge in OCMH Files. Eberbach believed later that Kluge might have

Neither the letter nor Kluge's suicide affected the course of events. Nor did they bring comfort to Hitler, whose forces in the west were undergoing the destruction incident to defeat.

The Pocket Closed

During the night of 18 August and throughout the next day the *Seventh Army*, with *Panzer Group Eberbach* attached, fell back behind the railroad east of the Falaise–Argentan highway. The pocket was then approximately six miles deep and seven miles wide. Inside were the headquarters of the *Seventh Army, Panzer Group Eberbach,* and the *LXXIV* and *LXXXIV Corps,* the *II Parachute* and *XLVII Panzer Corps;* the remnants of six infantry divisions still operating as entities: the *84th, 276th, 277th, 326th, 353d,* and *363d;* one parachute division, the *3d;* three panzer divisions, the *12th SS, 2d,* and *116th;* perhaps two more panzer divisions, the *1st SS* and *10th SS;* a number of splinter groups of divisions that had ceased to exist as tactical units and that had been absorbed by other divisions or amalgamated into kampfgruppen; and a mass of stragglers, service elements, and trains—all compressed within an area that lay entirely under the watchful eye and effective fire of Allied artillery and air.[21]

Getting across the Dives River was the next step in the withdrawal operation, but with the exit from the pocket in imminent danger of being closed by Allied pincers at Trun and Chambois, Hausser, the *Seventh Army* commander, came to the conclusion that he would have to fight his way across the Dives and out of the pocket that night—not an easy matter.[22] Daylight movements were extremely costly. All the roads leading to the Dives were clogged with the wreckage of vehicles and armament of every kind. Though distances separating headquarters were short, chaotic conditions made communications precarious. For example, the *LXXIV Corps,* which was holding the northwestern sector of the pocket, was out of touch with army headquarters. At 1130 on 19 August the corps dispatched a radio message reporting its dispositions, requesting urgently information on the general situation and its own combat mission, and stating that it was out of contact with two of its divisions (the *84th* and *363d,* still west of the railroad early that morning, about six miles from the corps command post). This message reached the army headquarters by some roundabout way two hours later, even though the straight-line distance between the corps and army command posts was little

---

averted the defeat in August by disobeying Hitler and withdrawing to the Seine at the beginning of the month, but Eberbach conceded that Kluge was being watched so closely after the July 20th *Putsch* that a false step would have resulted in his immediate relief and the substitution of a more manageable commander. MS # A–922 (Eberbach).

[21] The *LVIII Panzer Corps* headquarters was near Vimoutiers. (Radio Msg, *LVIII Pz Corps* to *Seventh Army,* 0330, 19 Aug, *Seventh Army KTB, Anlagen.*) Eberbach himself was at the *II SS Pan-*

zer *Corps* command post in the Vimoutiers area. The *I SS Panzer Corps,* split in two by the attacks of the Canadian and Polish armored divisions, was trying to hold the line north of the Allied penetration with what remained of its units east of the Dives River.

[22] Sources for the German action include MS # B–824 (Straube), MS # B–610 (Viebig), MS # B–526 (Badinski), MS # P–179 (Nettmann), MS # P–169 (Fiebig), MS # B–163 (Dettling), MS # A–968 (Elfeldt), MS # B–784 (Criegern), MS # A–985 (Mahlmann), MS # P–164 (Meyer).

more than three miles.[23] Handicapped by communications difficulties, Hausser tried to give his instructions on the forthcoming operation personally to his corps commanders. On that day he was able to visit three of his four corps headquarters.

The Dives River itself was not considered a serious obstacle, but the main Allied opposition was expected to be met along the east bank. According to fragmentary intelligence available inside the pocket, a small opening on the eastern edge of the pocket was supposed to exist along the river south of Trun; farther south toward Chambois the situation was not at all clear.

Hausser intended to break out of the encirclement by means of a two-corps attack. The *II Parachute Corps* was to thrust across the Dives River south of Trun, the *XLVII Panzer Corps* to cross farther south near Chambois. The *II SS Panzer Corps* was to render assistance from outside the pocket by launching a supporting attack with two divisions from Vimoutiers toward the Trun–Chambois area, thereby opening a path for the *Seventh Army* escape. The *II SS Panzer Corps* attack had originally been planned for 19 August, but Allied fighter-bombers prevented the air delivery of necessary supplies, and the attack was postponed until the morning of 20 August.[24] Thus Hausser's forces would be on their own in the initial stage of the breakout scheduled for the night of 19 August.

The preparations for the effort took

[23] Msg, 1130, 19 Aug, *Seventh Army KTB, Anlagen.*

[24] *AGp B Tagesmeldung,* 19 Aug, dated 0215, 20 Aug, and Telecon, *II Fighter Corps* CofS and *AGp B Ia/F,* 1500, 19 Aug, *AGp B KTB.*

all day. About 0700 that morning Hausser had arrived at the *II Parachute Corps* headquarters. Meindl, the corps commander, interpreted such an early visit as a bad omen, and he greeted Hausser with: "I presume the lid is on [the kettle—the German word for pocket in the military sense] and we shall probably have to try to break out." Hausser replied that that indeed was the matter he had come to discuss.

After Hausser indicated his ideas, Meindl formulated his *II Parachute Corps* plan. With his two divisions, the *3d Parachute* and *353d,* he proposed to break through the Allied lines between Trun and Chambois, secure the Mt. Ormel hill mass three to four miles the other side of the Dives, turn about on that dominating ground, and, facing west, keep the breach open for troops following. From a line of departure near la Londe and starting at 2230, the four regiments of the *3d Parachute Division* were to advance cross-country on compass azimuths toward Coudehard and the Mt. Ormel hill mass, seven miles away. The paratroopers were to move on two axes, with two regiments on the left, one on the right, and the fourth covering the rear. They were to cross the Dives south of Magny, then move to seize the northern part of the Ormel ridge. Exploiting the cover of darkness to the utmost, the paratroopers were to advance "Indian fashion," as noiselessly as possible. No fire was to be opened before dawn. Because of gasoline shortages, artillerymen were to expend their remaining ammunition during the day, then destroy their pieces. A few antitank and 88-mm. antiaircraft guns, provided with gasoline, were to accompany the troops. Similarly, the *353d Division*

GENERAL MEINDL

on the right was to break out across the Dives near St. Lambert and Chambois, then seize the southern portion of Mt. Ormel.

Hausser approved Meindl's plan. He also issued his order for the *XLVII Panzer Corps* attack. To give the *II Parachute Corps'* penetration by stealth a better chance of success, Hausser instructed the *XLVII Panzer Corps* to start its attack no earlier than midnight—this would serve to keep from arousing prematurely Allied vigilance and countermeasures. The *XLVII Panzer Corps* was to assemble the *1st SS* and *2d Panzer Divisions* (perhaps also remnants of the *10th SS Panzer Division*) in the Forêt de Gouffern, and break out in the St. Lambert–Chambois area. The *116th*

Panzer Division, holding the line along the Argentan–Chambois road, was to cover the rear and, on order, follow the other divisions out.[25]

The *LXXIV Corps,* holding the northwestern part of the pocket perimeter with five divisions (the *277th, 276th, 326th, 84th,* and *363d*—the latter two still west of the railroad), had the mission of protecting the rear of the breakout operation in its sector. The corps was then to move through the breach and out.

The *LXXXIV Corps,* having passed its last division, the *353d,* to the control of the *II Parachute Corps* on the previous

---

[25] Hausser to Model, 0930, 19 Aug, *Seventh Army KTB, Anlagen;* MS # A–923 (Meindl) ; see also MS # A–904 (Luettwitz) and MS # B–162 (Mueller) .

day, had neither units nor a mission on the morning of 19 August. Shortly before noon Elfeldt, the corps commander, received the order to break through the Allied lines near Trun with the few remaining elements of the *12th SS Panzer* and *277th Divisions,* which were to be pulled out of the front. Convinced that unfavorable terrain and strong concentrations of Allied forces around Trun precluded success, Elfeldt, with Meindl's support, obtained a change in mission. With remnants of only the *12th SS Panzer Division* under his command, he was to protect the north flank of Meindl's *II Parachute Corps,* then move behind the paratroopers across the Dives River. The *LXXIV Corps* was to follow.

Because of communications difficulties, it took the better part of the day, and in some instances most of the night, for all orders to reach subordinate units.

As darkness fell on 19 August, the pocket contracted still more. The units along the railroad pulled back to the forests of Feuillet and Gouffern. The *84th* and *363d Divisions,* which had held the most western positions during the day, moved through the new rear-guard outposts and into the Bois de Feuillet, there to assemble and make ready to follow the forces charged with making the breakout.

Meanwhile, British troops crossed the Orne River and moved eastward to within a few miles of the Falaise–Argentan highway.

While the Germans inside the pocket readied themselves for what was to be the last act of the Argentan–Falaise drama, the deterioration of the situation on the *Fifth Panzer Army* front approached a climax on 19 August. The *LXXXVI Corps* line was breached in two places, and Livarot on the extreme left flank was lost. Farther south, that part of the greatly weakened *I SS Panzer Corps* still east of the Dives River was unable to check the advance of the two armored divisions of the 2d Canadian Corps.

These divisions, one Canadian, the other Polish, continued to raise havoc with the Germans. Some elements of the 4th Canadian Armoured Division at Trun crossed to the west bank of the Dives River. In the northeastern part of St. Lambert, a small force of about 175 men, 15 tanks, and 4 self-propelled antitank guns held doggedly against repeated attacks by German units that tried desperately to keep the escape route through St. Lambert open. Reconnaissance elements advanced to the vicinity of Moissy, and an armored brigade was present in the Hordouseaux–Ecorches area.

To strengthen the northern jaw of the closing pincers, the 3d Canadian Infantry Division deployed along the eastern bank of the Dives River between Beauvais and Trun, while an infantry brigade of the 4th Armoured Division closed to the Trun–Vimoutiers highway between Trun and Hordouseaux.

Meanwhile, the 1st Polish Armored Division was advancing on two axes over difficult tank terrain infested with enemy troops. The bulk of the division, on the left, moved from the area around Hill 258 toward Mt. Ormel. This prominent ridge about two miles long straddles the Chambois–Vimoutiers highway and dominates the countryside for miles. By noon of 19 August the forward units were approaching the northern extremity of the ridge, Hill 262. After a short fight they occupied it.

Moving southward along the ridge, Polish tanks surprised a long column of German vehicles and armor moving bumper to bumper on the Chambois–Vimoutiers highway. The Poles opened fire and destroyed the column. Dense smoke from the burning vehicles spread over a large area in the dusk and reduced visibility to such an extent that further advance that day to the next objective—another Hill 262 on the southern end of the ridge—was impossible. By midnight two Polish armored regiments and three battalions of motorized infantry were concentrated on the northern end of the Mt. Ormel ridge and were making ready to resume the advance the next morning. Thus, when Meindl's breakout attack got under way, an important part of his objective was already in Polish hands.

On the Polish right, two armored regiments reinforced with a troop of antitank guns had started about 1100 from the vicinity of Ecorches toward Chambois. After reaching a hill less than a mile north of Chambois, and after being joined in the afternoon by the division reconnaissance regiment, the group launched an attack on the town from the northeast—astride the Vimoutiers–Chambois highway. The approaches to Chambois were littered and the streets literally choked by the debris of German wreckage, which proved a greater obstruction to progress than did enemy resistance. A small detachment working its way into Chambois from the south finally reached the main intersection of the town late in the afternoon. There it met Company G of the 90th Division's 359th Infantry, which had entered the town from the southwest.

The American troops had reached Chambois on the second day of Gerow's V Corps attack on the southern shoulder of the gap between Argentan and Exmes. General Gerow had released his corps reserve, the 317th Infantry, to its parent unit, the 80th Division, and General McBride had committed it with the 318th. Though still unable to enter Argentan, 80th Division troops cut the Argentan–Trun road. On the corps right General McLain's 90th Division, reinforced by French tankers, continued to drive toward Chambois, an objective reached in late afternoon. The village was in flames, and everywhere there was an unbearable stench of death and burned flesh, an unbelievable clutter of dead Germans, dead horses, and destroyed equipment.[26]

While Americans and Poles cleaned out the last defenders of Chambois, commanders of the Polish group and the American 2d Battalion, 359th Infantry, met and worked out a plan for the common defense of the town. The Poles handed over to the Americans about 1,300 prisoners as well as their own wounded because they lacked facilities for them. Tired, short of ammunition and supplies, the Polish units in Chambois were cut off from their rear.

Thus the long-sought juncture of Allied forces to close the pocket occurred. The closure, however, was of the most tenuous sort. Trun and Chambois were both firmly in Allied hands, and a small Canadian force held part of

---

[26] Msg, Gerow to Hodges, 2005, 19 Aug; [Alpert], Notes. For his part in the capture of Chambois, Capt. Edward R. Lienhart was awarded the DSC. Pfc. George J. Caldwell and Pfc. Walter C. Giebelstein, working together as a bazooka team, destroyed four tanks with five rounds of ammunition, and were also awarded the DSC.

A POLISH SOLDIER *(left) and an American officer confer near Chambois.*

St. Lambert, almost midway between Trun and Chambois, but the rest of the river line between Trun and Chambois was covered only by a few outposts and some roving patrols of Canadian and Polish reconnaissance units.

Two main highways run to the northeast from the river, one from Trun, the other from Chambois—both leading to Vimoutiers. The highway from Trun was definitely in Allied hands. The other, from Chambois across the Mt. Ormel ridge, was blocked by Allied troops at two places—at Chambois and at Mt. Ormel. Between the highways coming together at Vimoutiers are many smaller roads and country lanes. Several of these secondary routes converge near Coudehard, a village on the western slope of Mt. Ormel.

Not far from Coudehard, on the north-

ern eminence of Mt. Ormel, is the fifteenth-century Château Boisjos, which had witnessed a decisive battle during the Hundred Years' War.[27] It was about to witness the climactic action in the battle of Normandy.

The German Breakout

Hausser, *Seventh Army* commander and in charge of the encircled forces, arrived with a small staff after dark on 19 August at the *II Parachute Corps* command post.[28] There Meindl, the corps commander, was making his final preparations for the breakout. In order to be able to handle the situation promptly as it developed, Meindl chose his place behind the forward elements of the left column of the *3d Parachute Division.* Hausser also elected to break out with the paratroopers.

Unit commanders and noncommissioned officers of the division had been thoroughly briefed. The men had slept for a few hours and had eaten. No one underestimated the difficulty of the undertaking, but weariness seemed to have vanished and the troops appeared in good spirits.

The forward elements moved from the line of departure at la Londe at 2230. Forty-five minutes later Meindl's column drew fire from a tank near the Trun–Argentan highway. Two more encounters with Allied outposts occurred before the paratroopers, around 0030 on 20

---

[27] See Rousseau, *Bataille de Normandie,* p. 131.

[28] The scarcity of official German records has made it necessary to depend almost entirely on the recollections, as noted below, of some of the German commanders who were participants and who later tried to reconstruct the sequence of events of the breakout.

August, reached the Dives River. Because the division commander, General-leutnant Richard Schimpf, was seriously wounded in the last encounter, Meindl himself assumed command of the *3d Parachute Division.*[29]

Bypassing Allied-held points had delayed progress and broken contact among units and along the chain of command. Thus when Meindl reached the Dives somewhere between Magny and St. Lambert, he had with him only twenty paratroopers and Hausser's small command group. As he searched for a suitable crossing site, Meindl came upon one of his regimental commanders, who told him of a ford, about a mile southeast of Magny, where the water was about five feet deep.

To move a large body of men across the river and maintain silence in close proximity to enemy forces was no easy task. The opposite bank was covered with dense underbrush, and it rose steeply toward a hill, where three enemy tanks stood silhouetted against the sky. There was no time to lose if the troops were to get out of the pocket before daylight. Having gathered a larger group about him, Meindl took the lead and set off to the southeast, crossed the river about half a mile downstream from St. Lambert, went around the hill

crowned by tanks, and ran head on into machine gun fire from a concealed tank thirty yards away. Meindl and the few men around him hit the ground, while those in the immediate rear rushed to the protection of the dead angle of the hill. Aroused by the commotion, other tanks in the vicinity opened fire. Trajectories were high, and none of the paratroopers was hurt. At about the same time wild musketry fire flared up on the right rear near St. Lambert, where the *353d Division* was supposed to be crossing the river.

According to Meindl, the liberal use of tracer bullets by the Allies was quite helpful in revealing gaps in their lines through which the paratroopers were able to infiltrate. On the other hand, the Very lights were a great nuisance. Drifting leisurely to the ground, they illuminated large areas, froze all movement, and delayed progress considerably.

Meindl's group, reduced to about fifteen men, worked its way out of the field of tank fire by crawling along a furrow in the ground. The men continued eastward, deflected from time to time by hostile tanks. As the sky began to pale, they were still only half way to their objective, the hill mass of Mt. Ormel near Coudehard. The fire fight at St. Lambert had subsided, but another broke out in the left rear, in the direction of Neauphe-sur-Dives, where Meindl thought his rear-guard regiment was likely to be. A drizzling rain set in. The dim diffused morning light seemed oppressive. The exertion of the past hours suddenly began to tell. The men felt very tired.

They continued nevertheless to work their way eastward, picking up strag-

[29] On 14 August Schimpf had issued a message to his paratroopers as follows: "False rumors are the same as bad odors—both come from the rear. . . . contrary to all rumors . . . there is no need to worry that the division might be encircled and cut off from its supply lines. . . . Even if the enemy should ever succeed temporarily in interrupting our supply routes, this would be no reason for a paratrooper, who is specially trained to jump into the midst of the enemy, to feel depressed. . . . He who thinks or talks otherwise will be slapped across the mouth." VII Corps G–2 Per Rpt 79, 23 Aug.

glers and small groups of men along the way. By the time there was enough light to distinguish the main features of the landscape, they found themselves less than a mile west of the northern hill of the Mt. Ormel ridge. This was Meindl's objective, but it was not long before he realized that it was already in Allied hands and that the encircling ring was much deeper than he had anticipated.[30]

The Allied troops on Mt. Ormel were that part of the 1st Polish Armored Division that had advanced to the ridge on 19 August and by nightfall had occupied a defensive perimeter on the northern extremity, Hill 262 just north of the Chambois–Vimoutiers highway.[31] Two infantry battalions and a tank regiment deployed along the ridge line facing westward; the third infantry battalion and the other tank regiment guarded the approaches to the hill from the north and east. There were about 1,500 infantrymen, approximately 80 tanks.

No supplies had reached the Poles by evening of 19 August and at 0200, 20 August, it was established that Germans were astride the roads to their rear. Throughout the night they heard the rumble of traffic moving toward Vimoutiers; reconnaissance reported Germans digging in along the Chambois–Vimoutiers road. Nevertheless, apart from a few concentrations of harassing mortar fire on the southern part of the perimeter, the night passed uneventfully.

In the morning a task force moved out to secure the southern part of the Ormel ridge, a move that soon had to be canceled as heavy enemy pressure began to develop against the northern sector of the Polish perimeter.

When the morning mist lifted, almost the whole plain to the west came into Polish view. The ground was covered with German columns moving to the northeast in dispersed formations on the roads and cross-country.

While Polish guns were taking profitable targets under fire, a German attack, the first of several that day, struck the northeastern part of the perimeter at 0900. The attack was beaten off by 1030. In the meantime, German tanks had been observed around 1000 moving from the direction of Champosoult toward Hill 239, less than two miles north of the Polish perimeter. A detachment dispatched to deny the Germans possession of the hill, from which they could enfilade the Polish position, was unable to accomplish its mission. About an hour later gun fire from the direction of Hill 239 struck the Poles on Hill 262. Very quickly the Poles lost five tanks and a number of killed and wounded.

The German units involved in both of these actions belonged to the *2d SS Panzer Division* of the *II SS Panzer Corps*. The mission of the corps, which had earlier assembled in the Vimoutiers area, was to assist the *Seventh Army* breakout by an attack with two divisions in a southeasterly direction toward the Trun–Chambois line. The *9th SS Panzer Division* on the right advanced toward Trun, the *2d SS* on the left toward Chambois. Both divisions had been "utterly torn asunder" by previous night marches and air attacks. Together they had perhaps twenty tanks; their infantry

---

[30] MS # A–923 (Meindl).
[31] The account of Polish action is based on the *1st Polish Armored Division*, pp. 110–16.

consisted of about the equivalent of three battalions. They had few communications facilities. Roads were "so packed with burned out vehicles" that tanks had "to clear an alley before passing." Yet Allied aircraft were not overhead, for the weather was bad, just as the meteorologists had predicted for this day, the date that Eberbach so long ago had thought he could attack again toward Avranches. The *9th SS Panzer Division* bogged down near Champosoult and played a passive role for the rest of the day, but the *2d SS* actively engaged the Poles on Mt. Ormel and thereby made a significant contribution to the *Seventh Army* breakout.[32]

When the first German attack struck the Polish perimeter, Meindl was northwest of Coudehard, not far from the place he had reached at dawn. He was immobilized there for a considerable time, first by an encounter with Polish tanks, later by a heavy concentration of Allied fire on the entire Coudehard area. Around 0900, Meindl saw behind him a paratroop unit charging headlong into Polish fire from Hill 262. He stopped the attack, admonished the captain in command for his reckless behavior, oriented him on the situation around Hill 262, and pointed out the possibility of outflanking the hill from the north. Learning from the captain the whereabouts of Hausser, Meindl turned over to the captain's command the men who had joined him during the night, a considerable number by then, and set out to find Hausser.

Retracing his steps to the west, then turning south, then east, chased by artillery fire part of the way, Meindl found the army commander southwest of Coudehard about noontime. In an old bomb crater—the area was under artillery fire—they discussed the situation. Meindl reported his intention of attacking Hill 262 from the north and learned from Hausser that a panzer division had reached the Mt. Ormel area and was preparing to attack the ridge. Hausser intended to join this division for the final breakout. He told Meindl to make every effort to open the way for the remaining divisions. Despite the extreme exhaustion of his men, Meindl expressed confidence that they would make it, though probably not before evening. By this time a large number of troops and two tanks had joined his attack force.

While Meindl was conferring with Hausser, an impressive volume of German artillery and mortar fire, especially the latter, began to fall on the Polish positions on Mt. Ormel. About two hours later the Germans launched a series of determined, but apparently unco-ordinated, attacks against the perimeter. Lasting through the afternoon, the attacks struck for the most part against the northern and southern sectors of the Polish positions. The climax of the battle came about 1700, when German infantry supported by tanks broke into the northeastern part of the perimeter. The attack was finally beaten off by the combined efforts of infantrymen, tankers, and men of a mortar platoon acting as riflemen after they had expended their mortar ammunition. Another deep penetration occurred at the junction of two Polish infantry bat-

---

[32] MS # P–162 (Harzer); MS # P–159 (Stueckler and Wisliceny); MS # A–922 (Eberbach); see also *AGp B Tagesmeldung*, 20 Aug, dated 0155, 21 Aug, *AGp B KTB*.

talions near the Chambois–Vimoutiers highway. Not until about 1900 was this last German thrust contained and the penetration sealed off.

These attacks, by elements of the *2d SS Panzer Division,* Meindl's paratroopers, and unidentifiable units, had the apparent effect by late afternoon of 20 August of compressing the Polish perimeter to the extent where the Poles were no longer able to control some of the vital German escape roads in the vicinity of Hill 262.[33]

With the road to Champosoult opened, Meindl's next concern was to get the seriously wounded to safety. He organized a column of vehicles loaded with wounded and marked with Red Cross flags. To make the appearance of this column conspicuous and to convey his intention to the Allies, Meindl stopped all traffic on the road for fifteen minutes. Then the vehicles carrying the wounded moved out in close formation. The Allies understood the message. As the Red Cross convoy emerged on the road all artillery fire ceased. "Not a shot was fired on the column," Meindl wrote later, "and I can openly acknowledge the feeling of gratitude to the chivalrous enemy. . . ." Half an hour later, after the Red Cross flags had disappeared into the distance, traffic resumed and Allied artillery fire opened up once more.

News of the breakthrough at Coudehard spread to the rear like wildfire

and a multitude of stragglers poured through the opening until late into the night. Meindl established a command post near a crossroad on the Coudehard–Champosoult road, not far from the nose of Hill 262. Shortly after midnight part of the rear-guard regiment of the *3d Parachute Division* arrived, and Meindl passed to the regimental commander the other elements of the division nearby. Meanwhile, a heavy rain had begun to fall. Traffic on the road gradually thinned out, then ceased completely. Finally, an armored reconnaissance battalion, the rear guard of a panzer division, came by and reported nothing was following behind it.

Estimating that he could not keep the breach open during the coming day, Meindl decided to start before dawn of 21 August. Anxious to insure movement at the proper time, he kept vigil while his exhausted men slept despite the heavy rainfall—except a few outposts that Meindl thought "could also have been asleep."

After the fury of the German attacks had subsided, the Poles remained in firm control of Hill 262, but their situation was serious. Shortages of ammunition and gasoline were becoming acute. About 300 wounded were lying in the open under enemy fire without adequate medical care. The presence of some 800 prisoners inside the small perimeter was a problem. Hope that 4th Canadian Armoured Division elements would bring badly needed supplies and open the road to the rear so that the wounded and prisoners could be evacuated was not fulfilled. The Canadians themselves were busily engaged a few miles to the northwest. No help reached the Poles

---

[33] Meindl states that the attack on the "hill east of Coudehard had succeeded" by 1630 and that by 1700 German vehicles had begun to roll along the "curving road from Coudehard to the east." These times correspond quite well with the time of the full-scale German attack described in the Polish narrative.

that day, and when night came their perimeter formed a small island in a broad stream of escaping Germans.

Escape

Meindl's leadership was without doubt one of the significant actions of the German breakout, perhaps the focal incident. Other commanders and other units had also contributed to the final, though only partially successful, outcome of the operation. Their activities during the twenty-four hours following the arrival of darkness on 19 August were diverse, illustrating clearly the nature and the complexity of the event.

The *353d Division,* under Generalleutnant Paul Mahlmann, had also executed a breakout attack as part of the *II Parachute Corps* effort. Assembled on the evening of 19 August in woods near Vorché, six miles west of the Dives, the division started its movement at nightfall. Meindl had instructed Mahlmann to make his main effort at St. Lambert on the left, while sending his vehicles through Chambois. A little later Mahlmann received information that both localities were in Allied hands. He therefore decided to make his main thrust across the Dives in the Chambois area to try to save his vehicles.

At Tournai-sur-Dives, about halfway to the river, the division came to a halt. The village was burning and its streets were blocked by wrecked vehicles, dead horses, and abandoned tanks. The terrain around Tournai did not permit bypassing the village, so a passage had to be cleared. This took three hours. Though the area lay under harassing artillery fire, the division suffered no losses from it.

Shortly before dawn Mahlmann, in the column on the right, was approaching Chambois. He made contact with a group of tanks, which, according to the officer in charge, had the mission of cleaning the enemy out of the Chambois area. But because this appeared impossible, the tank commander decided to cross the Dives River at Moissy. The tanks moved out around daybreak. Mahlmann and his column, along with stragglers from other units who had joined, followed them closely across the river. The tanks continued through Moissy and disappeared into the distance. Shortly afterward Allied tanks appeared in the vicinity and closed the gap. Their appearance was followed by an intense concentration of Allied artillery fire on the village jammed with German troops. Losses were high, and all semblance of organization vanished.

Mahlmann finally succeeded in bringing some order out of chaos. He organized a breakout attempt with the help of two stray tanks found in the village. The tanks had barely left the village when Allied fire knocked them out. Again, disorganization and apathy set in—spent, dispirited, resigned to their fate, men huddled under whatever cover they could find.

Taking a dozen stouthearted fellows, Mahlmann reconnoitered a concealed road leading to the east, receiving a light head wound in the process. The road enabled Mahlmann to get at least part of the men in Moissy out. Most of the wounded had to be left. All guns and vehicles, except two or three amphibious jeeps, along with part of the division staff, were lost.

Mahlmann headed for the southern eminence of Mt. Ormel, and that after-

noon he and those who accompanied
him began to climb the western slope
of the hill. The whole area seemed
covered with an amorphous mass of
German soldiers hastening toward the
ridge. An American observation plane
circled leisurely, seeming to hang in the
sky, as it directed artillery fire on the retreating troops.

As he approached his objective, Mahlmann faced a situation quite different
from that which had confronted the *3d
Parachute Division* on his left. German pressure on the northern part of
Ormel had forced the Poles to call off
their advance to Hill 262 (south) in
the morning. Thus Mahlmann was
able to occupy his objective without
opposition.

There Mahlmann organized three
combat groups and deployed them
along the ridge line facing west, one
composed of SS men on the right,
another of men of his own division on
the left, and the third of paratroopers
in reserve. His efforts to establish contact with units on the flanks and with
higher headquarters were unsuccessful.

Late in the afternoon, when the SS
group reported hostile reconnaissance
units on the north flank, Mahlmann decided to fall back three miles to the east
to a new line behind the Vie River.
He accomplished his withdrawal without
undue interference, and that evening infantrymen and paratroopers occupied
the new position. The SS group, disobeying orders, continued to move eastward and vanished.

Soon afterward Mahlmann made personal contact with *Seventh Army* headquarters and received instructions to remain on the Vie until the next day,

when his division would be pulled back
and sent to the rear for rehabilitation.[34]

Like Meindl's paratroop corps for the
north flank, the *XLVII Panzer Corps*
had the task of opening the way for the
surrounded forces on the southern
flank.[35] Funck's *XLVII Panzer Corps*
had the *1st SS* and *2d Panzer Divisions*
(probably the *10th SS Panzer Division*
also) assembled in the Forêt de Gouffern,
the *116th Panzer Division* holding a long
thin line practically from Argentan to
the Dives. The corps was to cross the
river in the St. Lambert–Chambois area,
with the *116th* covering the rear.

The corps breakout order did not
reach the *2d Panzer Division* commander, Generalleutnant Freiherr Heinrich von Luettwitz, until around 1900,
19 August. Because reconnaissance
revealed the roads so clogged with wreckage as to make night movement impossible, Luettwitz decided to hold off his
attack until 0400, 20 August. He placed
all of his tanks (about fifteen) and his
armored vehicles at the head of his
column, left an infantry regiment reinforced with several antitank guns as a
rear guard, and ordered what remained
of his artillery to support his advance.

A dense fog hung over the area that
morning, and the *2d Panzer Division*
was not the only unit moving toward St.
Lambert. Columns composed of all
sorts of components streamed through
the fog, sometimes eight abreast. When
the fog lifted, a "hurricane" of Allied artillery fire descended. Vehicles dashed
toward the Dives, Luettwitz later re-

---

[34] MS # A–985 (Mahlmann).
[35] There is a scarcity of information regarding
the activities of this corps.

membered, "turned around, circled, got entangled, stopped, and were destroyed. Tall pillars of flame from burning gasoline tanks leaped into the sky, ammunition exploded, and wild horses, some severely wounded, raced" in aimless terror. Effective control was impossible.

Only the armored elements and part of an armored infantry regiment reached St. Lambert in an orderly manner about 1000. Luettwitz led an attack across the river into the village. Incredibly, the bridge across the Dives still stood despite the bombs and shells that had fallen nearby. "The crossing of the Dives bridge," Luettwitz recalled later, "was particularly horrible, the bodies of killed men, dead horses, vehicles, and other equipment having been hurled from the bridge into the river to form there a gruesome tangled mass."

On the east bank of the river, Luettwitz organized and dispatched combat troops for passage through the hail of Allied fire. Wounded that afternoon, he finally departed around 2100, reaching Orville and safety early on 21 August.[36]

Meanwhile the *XLVII Panzer Corps* headquarters and the *1st SS Panzer Division* had probably fought across the Dives River in the St. Lambert–Chambois area early on the morning of 20 August. More than likely they completed their breakout that afternoon.[37]

Covering the *XLVII Panzer Corps* rear, the *116th Panzer Division* had deployed in two groups on the evening of 19 August. One was in the Argentan area, the other north of the Forêt de Gouffern near Bon-Ménil. About 0900, 20 August, the division lost radio communication with the corps headquarters. In the afternoon, when heavy Allied pressure developed against the Argentan group, it pulled back to positions north of the forest.

The pressure was exerted by the 80th Division, which finally took Argentan that day.[38] On the same day British troops approaching from the west moved to the Falaise–Argentan road.

Both groups of the *116th Panzer Division* remained in place during the rest of the day. When the division commander, Col. Gerhard Mueller, learned around 1800 that the corps headquarters was east of the Dives, he prepared to break out during the night at St. Lambert.

Mueller sent a reconnaissance party to St. Lambert after nightfall. Allied artillery fire on the village indicated it was not yet in Allied hands. After strenuous efforts, the troops cleared a narrow passage through the wreckage in the streets. During a two-hour period around midnight, 20 August, the division staff, remnants of the infantry regiment, 5 artillery pieces, and about 50 combat vehicles passed through the village without significant losses. They continued to Coudehard, then to Orville and safety. The Argentan group—about 8 tanks, 10 20-mm. antiaircraft guns, and about 80 Engineer troops—lost its way in the darkness, tried to break out near Trun, and was taken prisoner.[39]

Hausser's breakout attack by the *II*

---

[36] MS # A–904 (Luettwitz).

[37] No information is available from corps and division sources. The above has been deduced from statements by Blauensteiner, *II Parachute Corps* chief of staff, and from incidents described by Mahlmann, Meindl, and Lt. Col. Hubert Meyer.

[38] For singlehandedly destroying a machine gun position that had halted his company, Pfc. Earl G. Goins was awarded the DSC.

[39] MS # B–162 (Mueller).

Parachute and *XLVII Panzer Corps* had thus succeeded in large measure. But success did not make it possible for the rest of the troops simply to follow out of the pocket. They too had to fight to get across the Dives River.

The missions of the two remaining corps, the *LXXXIV* and the *LXXIV*, were to cover, respectively, the northern flank and the rear of the breakout operation. Both were then to move across the Dives in the wake of the paratroopers and tankers.

The *LXXXIV Corps* had only remnants of the *12th SS Panzer Division* under its command. Because of the chaotic conditions on the roads and the complete disruption of communications, the division organized its units into two groups for better control. The motorized elements, including what remained of the artillery and the division radio section, were to follow the *1st SS Panzer Division* across the river at Chambois. The rest of the division, mostly infantry, subdivided into task forces for independent action if necessary, was to follow the *3d Parachute Division* through St. Lambert. Four or five tanks or tank destroyers were to cover the rear. General Elfeldt, the corps commander, and Lt. Col. Hubert Meyer, the division commander, accompanied the infantry group.

Around midnight of 19 August, Meyer sent a liaison patrol to the *3d Parachute Division* to obtain word on the outcome of the breakout. The patrol did not return. As all remained quiet along the Dives River, Meyer assumed that the paratroopers' penetration by stealth had succeeded. Therefore, in the very early

hours of 20 August, he ordered the infantry group to move out.

At daybreak the group came into contact with several tanks of the *1st SS Panzer Division* preparing to attack through Chambois. The armored infantrymen joined the tanks, but intense Allied artillery, tank, and antitank fire from high ground south of Chambois soon stalled the attack. Because the German armor was drawing the Allied fire, the infantry detached itself and in small groups began to cross the river between Chambois and St. Lambert. Some troops of other units were advancing toward the Allied positions and waving white handkerchiefs and flags.[40]

The two commanders became separated. Elfeldt and his staff took part in an action near St. Lambert with a hastily assembled group of soldiers. Meeting strong opposition and "having literally spent his last cartridge," Elfeldt, the *LXXXIV Corps* commander, surrendered. Meyer, having crossed the Dives, took command of a group of soldiers and led them on foot across the plain toward the southern spur of Mt. Ormel. Using whatever natural concealment was available, they reached safety. Some of the motorized elements of the *12th SS Panzer Division* also escaped that afternoon. Most of the artillery was lost.

The *LXXIV Corps,* designated the covering force in the rear of the breakout attack, had, on 19 August, three of its five infantry divisions (*276th, 277th,* and *326th*) along the northwestern perimeter of the pocket, the other two (*84th* and *363d*) assembled in the Bois de

---

[40] MS # A–968 (Elfeldt), MS # B–784 (Criegern), MS # P–164 (Meyer).

Feuillet. The two latter divisions were ready to cross the Dives River in the wake of the *LXXXIV Corps,* the other three were to follow on order.

Communications were practically non-existent. Orders from corps to division could be transmitted only by staff officers. There was no liaison with the *II Parachute Corps*—General der Infanterie Erich Straube, the *LXXIV Corps* commander, had no knowledge of the time set for the breakout attack. All efforts to establish contact with the *Seventh Army* failed.[41]

The state of affairs in the *LXXIV Corps* sector was therefore somewhat chaotic. The *277th Division* on the corps right was in contact with two corps headquarters, its own and the *LXXXIV,* and for a while received contradictory orders from both. The two divisions farther to the south, the *276th* and *326th,* were out of touch with corps headquarters throughout the day, and both division commanders pondered the problem of whether they should continue to wait for orders or act on their own initiative.

In the early hours of 20 August, after the *12th SS Panzer Division* pulled out of the line on the *277th Division* right, the *277th* fell back to a position along a curved line facing west and northwest—about one and a half miles from Villedieu-lès-Bailleul. There the division remained for the rest of the day. Around 2300, still without orders from the corps, his men exhausted, and short ammunition even for the infantry weapons, the division commander, Colonel Wilhelm Viebig, decided to break out that night. The remnants of the divi-sion, about 900 men, moved from their positions to a previously reconnoitered crossing site on the Dives northwest of St. Lambert. The noise of the crossing brought Allied artillery and machine gun fire, and in the ensuing confusion Viebig lost control. Nevertheless, small groups screened by heavy rain continued to move, and what remained of the division reached the *II SS Panzer Corps* lines on the morning of 21 August. A few days later, when Viebig assembled his command—combat units, administrative elements, stragglers, hospital returnees— he had about 2,500 men, of whom approximately 1,000 were combat troops.[42]

Generalleutnant Curt Badinski's *276th Division,* on the *277th* left, received its first order from corps about 0300, 20 August: the division was to fall back, apparently in conjunction with the *277th* withdrawal, to a line just west of Vorché and on the Trun–Occagnes road. Not long after carrying out this move, Badinski received his second and last order from the corps. He was to break out of the pocket south of Trun, starting from his positions at 0830, 20 August.

Soon after his units got under way, it appeared to Badinski that an attempt to break out in broad daylight was bound to fail. Every movement was detected by Allied observation planes and im-mediately subjected to a heavy concen-tration of artillery fire. Badinski therefore halted the movement, hoping to renew the attempt after darkness, but before the day was over his command post on the edge of the Forêt de Gouf-fern was surrounded by Allied tanks, and Badinski and his small staff were taken prisoner. Most of the division

---

[41] MS # B–824 (Straube).

[42] MS # B–610 (Viebig).

remnants shared their fate. Only a few men escaped during the stormy night.[43]

The *326th Division* received its order to break out during the night of 19 August. The division was to assemble at nightfall, 20 August, near St. Lambert, from there to make its way to Coudehard. Learning that an improvised group of infantry and tanks of the *1st* and *10th SS Panzer Divisions* had crossed successfully at St. Lambert during the afternoon of 20 August, the *326th Division* arranged with elements of the *116th Panzer Division* to make a concerted break that night. The plan worked well. The armor crossed the St. Lambert bridge, miraculously still intact despite the continuous and heavy shelling, and the infantry went over an emergency footbridge nearby. From the river the men marched in a seemingly endless single file column on azimuth toward Coudehard. Despite some inevitable confusion and an occasional burst of fire from Allied outposts, the column reached a road near Coudehard, where the tanks were waiting. Closing behind the tanks, the infantry resumed its advance and, bypassing Coudehard, reached the positions of the *2d SS Panzer Division* at dawn.[44]

The other two divisions under *LXXIV Corps,* the *84th* and *363d,* had been assembled in the Bois de Feuillet ready to follow the *LXXXIV Corps* across the Dives. The *84th Division* commander, Generalleutnant Irwin Menny, was captured; elements of at least one regiment apparently escaped through St. Lambert on 20 August.[45]

The *363d Division* had had its mission changed early on 20 August by what turned out to be its last order from *LXXIV Corps.* Instead of following the *LXXXIV Corps* across the Dives, the *363d* was to occupy and hold a line from Bailleul to Bon-Ménil, north of the Forêt de Gouffern. Generalleutnant Augustus Dettling, the commander, carried out the order but, subjected to heavy Allied pressure during the day, was forced to give up some ground With no instructions from corps, Dettling decided to break out at nightfall. Organized into three kampfgruppen, the division was across the Dives at St. Lambert by 2200, then moved on azimuth toward Coudehard. It sustained considerable losses in killed, wounded, and captured; it lost the bulk of its heavy weapons, all of its artillery, and most of its vehicles. About 2,500 men reached Champosoult and safety the next morning.[46]

The commander of the *LXXIV Corps,* Straube, and part of his staff crossed the Dives during the afternoon of 20 August at St. Lambert, where Straube met Luettwitz, who commanded the *2d Panzer Division.* Together, they worked out measures for holding the crossing site open and organized the men of all arms converging on St. Lambert into kampfgruppen for the completion of the breakout. In the evening Straube departed with one such group of several hundred men and a few tanks. He reached Meindl's command post near Coudehard around midnight, then completed his breakout with the paratroopers.[47]

[43] MS # B–326 (Badiński) .

[44] MS # P–179 (Nettmann)

[45] Information is scanty; see MS # P–169 (Fiebig) .

[46] MS # B–163 (Dettling) .

[47] MS # B–824 (Straube) .

While the battle had raged around the Poles on Mt. Ormel, the Polish and American troops in Chambois were also subjected to considerable pressure. Desperate German efforts launched against Chambois on 20 August to open an escape route through the town made the situation so tense that there were moments when Poles and Americans wondered whether they could retain possession of the town.

For the Polish armored group, it was the second day of heavy action without resupply. That evening American supplies came forward, and the Poles received a share of the ammunition, gasoline, and rations.[48]

On that day the 90th Division Artillery was operating with observation later described as an "artilleryman's dream." Five battalions pulverized columns driving toward the Dives. American soldiers cheered when German horses, carts, trucks, volkswagens, tanks, vehicles, and weapons went flying into the air, disintegrating in flashes of fire and puffs of smoke.[49]

Near Chambois several German tanks and perhaps a company of infantrymen would have escaped but for Sgt. John D. Hawk of the 359th Infantry, who manned a light machine gun. A tank shell disabled Hawk's gun and wounded him, but he secured a bazooka and with a companion kept the tanks in a small wood until two American tank destroyers arrived. Their shelling was ineffective until Hawk climbed to an exposed position to act as a human aiming stake. The subsequent fire of the tank destroyers knocked out two German tanks and forced the remaining Germans into the open to surrender.[50]

The heavy rain that set in around midnight of 20 August helped thousands of Germans to escape to safety. At 0230, 21 August, Meindl began to wake up the men around him near Coudehard. It took some time to get a man on his feet and make him understand what was going on. By 0345, Meindl's troops were assembled along the road in march formation, and the head of the column started to move eastward in the drenching rain. Meindl himself, with two tanks and a small group as the rear guard, departed around 0500. Two hours afterwards, they were within the lines of the *2d SS Panzer Division* near Champosoult.

Later that day Meindl learned that some of his paratroopers had escaped by a route southeast of Coudehard, that a tank unit had brought the seriously wounded *Seventh Army* commander, Hausser, safely out of the pocket, and that he, Meindl, was to move his *II Parachute Corps* to the Seine River south of Rouen. He estimated that between 2,500 and 3,500 paratroopers had escaped; their combat strength did not exceed 600. Of the two regiments of the *353d Division* that broke out at St. Lambert, only remnants of one later rejoined

---

[48] 90th Div G-3 Per Rpt, 21 Aug. According to the Polish narrative: "The fraternity of arms displayed by the Americans during our common battle deserves special recognition. The Americans shared with us their rations, ammunition, gasoline, and were very generous with their cigarettes. It will be difficult to forget the supply officer of the American regiment, Major Miller, who, being short of working hands, helped personally to load ammunition boxes on our trucks." *1st Polish Armored Division*, pp. 104-05.

[49] *V Corps Operations in the ETO*, p. 190; Interv with Capt M. H. Smith, Hosp Intervs, Vol. III, GL-93 (249); [Alpert], Notes.

[50] Hawk was awarded the Medal of Honor.

TRUCKLOADS OF PRISONERS HEADED FOR PRISONER OF WAR CAMPS

the division, the rear-guard regiment having been completely lost.

Only small isolated groups were able to slip across the Dives during the early morning hours of 21 August. Fighting along the river subsided gradually, and by noon, with all of St. Lambert firmly in Canadian hands, the escape route was closed. Rounding up the remnants of the *Seventh Army* trapped west of the Dives began. Allied troops accepted German surrenders, in mass and in small groups, and gathered up stragglers "who had been living in holes in the ground in the forest since separating from their units." It was not uncommon for an

Allied division to collect prisoners from as many as twenty divisional units in a single day. "We very much enjoyed going into the woods," a regimental commander later recalled. "One of my lieutenants and I got nineteen [prisoners] on one trip." [51]

Meanwhile, a sizable number of men and vehicles, the tail end of the forces that had succeeded in getting across the Dives during the night, were still moving toward the Mt. Ormel ridge on the

---

[51] Quotes are from VII Corps AAR, Aug, and McHugh Interv, Stockton's Hosp Intervs, III, GL–93 (235); see also V Corps G–2 Est of Enemy Situation 7, 2400, 23 Aug.

morning of 21 August. Shortly before noon the Poles on Hill 262 had their hands full repelling German attacks on the southwestern part of their perimeter, that part closest to the Chambois–Vimoutiers road. The culmination came around noon with a suicidal attack of German infantry straight up the hill from the area around the Coudehard church. The massed fires of Polish machine guns smashed it.

Canadian troops advanced and finally made contact with the Polish perimeter that afternoon. Supplies arrived about 1400; evacuation of the wounded and the prisoners began. About that time enemy activity ceased, and what the Poles called the Battle of Maczuga came to an end. Having captured approximately 1,000 Germans, the Poles had lost about 350 men; 11 tanks were damaged or destroyed.[52]

Beyond Mt. Ormel, German soldiers, singly and in groups, had continued to pass through the lines of the *II SS Panzer Corps* throughout the morning of 21 August. The movement thinned out in the afternoon and by 1600 ceased altogether. At dusk the corps moved back its two divisions to an assembly area near Orbec, thirteen miles northeast of Vimoutiers.

Army Group B praised the action of the *II SS Panzer Corps* in the highest terms, for it considered the corps had been a major factor making possible the escape of much of the *Seventh Army*.[53] In reality, the corps contribution to the breakout operation, though noteworthy considering its skeleton forces, was not so spectacular as the army group believed. The *II SS Panzer Corps* had accomplished three things: it tied up elements of Canadian and Polish armor on the outer edge of the encircling ring; it helped to open the Coudehard–Champosoult road; and it provided a rallying position for troops that were able to escape the pocket. The major factor deciding the outcome of the breakout operation was the determination and the will to fight of the units inside the pocket.

The Results

How many Germans escaped? No one knew. At the end of 20 August *Army Group B* reported that "approximately from 40 to 50 percent of the encircled units succeeded in breaking out and joining hands with the II SS Panzer Corps." This was an optimistic assessment. By the end of the following day, the strength of six of seven armored divisions that had escaped the pocket totaled, as reported at that time, no more than 2,000 men, 62 tanks, and 26 artillery pieces.[54]

Later estimates of the total number of Germans escaping varied between 20,000 and 40,000 men, but combat troops formed by far the smaller proportion of these troops. The average combat strength of divisions was no more than a few hundred men, even

---

[52] *Maczuga* is the Polish word for cudgel, which seemed to match the shape of the Mt. Ormel ridge. See *1st Polish Armored Division*, pp. 116–17.

[53] *AGp B Tagesmeldung*, 21 Aug, dated 0100, 22 Aug.

[54] *AGp B Tagesmeldungen*, 20 Aug, dated 0155, 21 Aug, and 21 Aug, dated 2000, 21 Aug, *AGp B KTB*. Hitler on 23 August ordered *OB WEST* to submit a report on strengths and losses pertaining both to the divisions that had escaped from the pocket and to those that had not been involved, but this report, if submitted, has not been located. *AGp B KTB, Anlagen*, 21–23 Aug, p. 1626.

THE POCKET DESERTED

though the over-all strength of some divisions came close to 3,000. The explanation lay in the fact that a partial exodus had begun at least two or three days before the breakout attack—when shortages of ammunition, gasoline, and other supplies had already become acute.[55]

Some divisions acting on their own initiative, others with the approval of corps, had started to send to the rear, in some instances as far east as the Seine River, all nonessential personnel and vehicles, as well as artillery pieces that could not be supplied with ammunition. Ironically, on 18 August, the day after the *271st Division* ceased to exist as a fighting unit, the division commander, Generalleutnant Paul Danhauser, discovered large stocks of artillery ammunition of all calibers in the Bois de Feuillet, stocks that had been forgotten, overlooked, or simply abandoned. "The

shock of this discovery," Danhauser later wrote, "brought tears to the eyes of the commander of the artillery regiment whose batteries had expended their last rounds some days ago." [56]

The few batteries sent out of the pocket before the final few days were saved. The rest of the artillery, heavy weapons, and other equipment remaining inside the pocket was almost completely lost—destroyed by Allied fire, by the Germans themselves, or abandoned. One commander estimated, probably with some exaggeration, that not many more than 50 artillery pieces and perhaps that many tanks reached safety. Radios, vehicles, trains, supplies were lost; "even the number of rescued machine guns was insignificant." [57] "The losses in material are very high," *Army Group B* reported, ". . . set on fire by enemy fighter-bombers . . . and by

[55] See MS # B–526 (Badinski); MS # P–179 (Nettmann)

[56] MS # P–177 (Danhauser).
[57] MS # A–922 (Eberbach).

massed fires of heavy artillery. All radio stations were silenced, and the army was deprived of its means of command. Yet the performance of the men who fought the breakout battle in the face of overwhelming odds merits the highest praise." [58]

The severe ordeal to which the Germans were subjected for many days—constant air and artillery pounding, exhausting night marches on clogged roads after a day's fighting, shortages of ammunition and supplies—could not be endured indefinitely without affecting troop morale. Many "unpretty pictures" were witnessed by German commanders—incredible disorder on the roads where often the right of the strongest prevailed (tankers and paratroopers being the chief offenders); the panic, men with hands up surrendering in droves; at least one case of outright mutiny when a sergeant shot and killed his commanding officer because the commander refused to consent to surrender.

But the units that were under the firm control of their commanders fought to the limit of their physical and moral endurance and thereby made the escape of a sizable part of the encircled troops possible. One such unit, a paratroop outfit, made quite an impression on men of an SS panzer division when, emerging from the pocket, the paratroopers passed through the tankers smartly, in road formation, singing.[59]

Behind the men who had fought their way out of the pocket lay an inferno of destruction.

The carnage wrought during the final days as the artillery of two Allied armies and the massed air forces pounded the ever-shrinking pocket was perhaps the greatest of the war. The roads and fields were littered with thousands of enemy dead and wounded, wrecked and burning vehicles, smashed artillery pieces, carts laden with the loot of France overturned and smoldering, dead horses and cattle swelling in the summer's heat.[60]

Of the higher staffs, only the *LXXXIV Corps* headquarters was missing. Most of the higher commanders, including Hausser, were wounded. When Hausser was evacuated, Funck, the *XLVII Panzer Corps* commander, took temporary command of the *Seventh Army*, which was subordinated to the *Fifth Panzer Army*.[61]

The Allies did not know exactly how many prisoners they took. From 13 through 17 August it was possible to count them accurately—British and Canadians reported daily figures in excess of a total of 6,000, the First U.S. Army 2,500 for 15 August alone. After 17 August the figures were approximate—for example, the First Army estimated more than 9,000 on 21 August.[62] All together, the Americans probably took about 25,000 prisoners, British and Canadians an equal number. Among the captives were three general officers. In addition to the 50,000 men captured,

---

[58] *AGp B Tagesmeldung*, 20 Aug, *AGp B KTB*.
[59] MS # P-159 (Stueckler); MS # B-526 (Badinski); MS # P-179 (Nettmann).

[60] First U.S. Army, *Report of Operations*, I, 18; see *V Corps Operations in the ETO*, p. 188, and 90th Div AAR, Aug. Guingand, *Operation Victory*, page 410, has a vivid description of the destruction.
[61] Telecons, 1335 and 1355, 21 Aug, *AGp B KTB*. Dietrich remained in command of the *Fifth Panzer Army* and apparently Eberbach several days later took command of the *Seventh Army*. See *AGp B Tagesmeldung*, 31 Aug.
[62] FUSA G-2 Telecon, 1730, 18 Aug, FUSA G-2 Jnl and File, and AAR, Aug.

approximately 10,000 dead were found on the field.[63]

As examples of the extent of German losses, the 2d French Armored Division captured 8,800 prisoners and claimed the destruction or capture of more than 100 tanks, over 100 artillery pieces, and 700 vehicles. The 90th Division in four days took over 13,000 prisoners and 1,000 horses; an incomplete inventory of destruction revealed that in addition to 1,800 horses that were dead, 220 tanks, 160 self-propelled artillery pieces, 700 towed artillery pieces, 130 antiaircraft guns, 130 half-track vehicles, 5,000 motor vehicles, and 2,000 wagons had been destroyed or damaged; high-power radio and cryptographic sets, mobile ordnance shops, medical laboratories, and surgical installations had been abandoned.[64]

An officer who had observed the destruction of the Aisne–Marne, St. Mihiel, and Meuse–Argonne battlefields in World War I and had seen the destruction in London and at St. Lô in World War II, wrote:

None of these compared in the effect upon the imagination with what I saw yesterday southwest of Trun. . . . The grass and trees were vividly green as in all Normandy and a surprising number of houses [were] . . . untouched. That rather peaceful setting framed a picture of destruction so great that it cannot be described. It was as if an avenging angel had swept the area bent on destroying all things German. . . .

I stood on a lane, surrounded by 20 or 30 dead horses or parts of horses, most of them still hitched to their wagons and carts. . . . As far as my eye could reach (about 200 yards) on every line of sight, there were . . . vehicles, wagons, tanks, guns, prime movers, sedans, rolling kitchens, etc., in various stages of destruction. . . .

I stepped over hundreds of rifles in the mud and saw hundreds more stacked along sheds. . . . I walked through a mile or more of lanes where the vehicles had been caught closely packed. . . . I saw probably 300 field pieces and tanks, mounting large caliber guns, that were apparently undamaged.

I saw no foxholes or any other type of shelter or field fortifications. The Germans were trying to run and had no place to run. They were probably too exhausted to dig. . . . They were probably too tired even to surrender.

I left this area rather regretting I'd seen it. . . . Under such conditions there are no supermen—all men become rabbits looking for a hole.[65]

Despite the devastating defeat the Germans had suffered, a surprising number of troops had escaped the pocket. Yet those who had escaped had still to reckon with another crisis—this one at the Seine.

---

[63] V Corps G–2 Est of Enemy Situation 7, 23 Aug; FUSA AAR, Aug; B. H. Liddell Hart, *Strategy, The Indirect Approach,* p. 317; Sylvan Diary, 20 Aug.

[64] 2d French Armd Div G–3 Rpt, Opns; 90th Div AAR, Aug.

[65] 12th AGp WD Observers Bd Ltr, AGF Bd Rpt, ETO, No. 208, Visit to Falaise Pocket, 31 Aug.

CHAPTER XXVIII

The Drive to the Seine

While the XV Corps left part of its forces at Argentan and started the wider envelopment to the Seine on 15 August, other components of the Third Army farther to the south were also driving to the Seine, sweeping clear the vast area north of the Loire River. The advance to the Seine fulfilled a prophecy made a week earlier—that "the battle of Normandy is rapidly developing into the Battle of Western France." [1]

South to the Loire

The drive to the Seine had actually begun on 3 August, when General Bradley instructed General Patton to secure the north–south line of the Mayenne River, clear the area west of the Mayenne River as far south as the Loire, and protect the 12th Army Group south flank with minimum forces. [2] Since the VIII Corps was driving southwest toward Rennes and the XV Corps was about to move southeast toward Mayenne, Patton oriented the XX Corps south toward Nantes and Angers. As the main American effort veered eastward in accordance with the modified OVERLORD plan and the XV Corps drove toward Laval and le Mans, Patton ordered the XX Corps to cross the Mayenne River in a parallel drive to protect the XV Corps south flank. [3]

Bradley approved Patton's eastward orientation and even furthered it by designating the Paris–Orléans gap as the ultimate Third Army objective. Yet he specified once more the additional mission of protecting the south flank along the Loire River to guard against possible German incursion from the south. Angers and Nantes would therefore have to be captured. [4] (*See Maps 12 and 17.*)

The demands of this dual mission became the responsibility of Maj. Gen. Walton H. Walker, a West Pointer who had served in France during World War I, who had been an infantryman and artilleryman before turning to armor, and who had commanded the IV Armored Corps, later redesignated the XX Corps, in training.

Early plans for XX Corps to control the 2d French Armored and the 5th and 35th Infantry Divisions went awry when the 35th became involved in the Mortain counterattack and when the French division, after a brief alert for possible action at Mortain, joined the XV Corps. The 5th Division thus remained the sole instrument available for the XX Corps initial commitment.

---

[1] 30th Div G–2 Notes for Unit Comdrs, 8 Aug.
[2] 12th AGp Ltr of Instrs 2, 3 Aug.

[3] TUSA Dir, 5 Aug (confirming fragmentary orders, 4 Aug).
[4] 12th AGp Ltr of Instrs 3, 6 Aug; 21 AGp Operational Situation and Dir, M–517, 6 Aug.

11TH INFANTRYMEN *meet resistance in the drive to Angers.*

Having fought with the V Corps before being pinched out on the First Army left flank near Vire, General Irwin's 5th Division received instructions an hour before dawn on 4 August to join the XX Corps by moving immediately through Villedieu and Avranches to an assembly area near Vitré, forty miles south of Avranches. The suddenness of the call precluded advance planning, and General Irwin felt handicapped by a lack of definite knowledge of his next combat mission and the terrain in which he would fight. With no inkling that this manner of operating would

soon be normal, General Irwin began at once to march from one American flank to the other.[5]

On the road for three days in a march hampered by traffic congestion, the 5th Division reached Vitré on 7 August. On that day Patton orally instructed Walker to move a regiment of the 5th Division to seize Angers, fifty-five miles southeast of Vitré; an infantry battalion

---

[5] General Irwin's Official Diary of the Div Comdr; XV Corps G-3 Memo, Conflict with XX Corps, 5 Aug, XV Corps G-3 Jnl and File. The quotations in this section, unless otherwise noted, are from General Irwin's diary.

to capture Nantes, sixty-five miles southwest of Vitré; and the rest of the division to Segré, twenty-two miles northwest of Angers. Gaffey, Third Army chief of staff, arrived at Irwin's command post at noon that day to transmit the mission for quick compliance. Though tired from their long hours on the road, the 5th was to move at once. Perhaps Gaffey was not explicit, perhaps Irwin misinterpreted. In any event, Irwin felt that the fifty-mile distance between Nantes and Angers, as well as the distance of both towns from Vitré, made it impractical for him to take both objectives at the same time. The development of the major operations to the east and Patton's instructions for Walker to reach the Mayenne River south of Château-Gontier seemed to give Angers priority over Nantes.[6]

Information on the enemy in the area south and east of Vitré was scant, but "a general withdrawal by the Germans, extent and destination not yet clear," was presumed. Actually, there were scarcely any Germans between Vitré and the Loire River. The *First Army* in southwest France had been charged on 2 August with protecting the crossing sites along the Loire River, its northern boundary. Two days later the *LXXX Corps* artillery commander brought a measure of unified leadership to the troops along the river line from St. Nazaire to Saumur—security formations, naval personnel, antiaircraft units, and the like. On 8 August, the *16th Division* (formed by consolidating the *158th Reserve Division*—which was intended originally to furnish replacements to the units committed in Normandy—and the

16th Luftwaffe Field Division) assumed responsibility for defending the Loire along a front that eventually extended from Nantes to Orléans. The *16th Division* was short of equipment but was well trained and well led.[7] Part of this force, with some few elements that had come from Normandy, met the 5th U.S. Division at Angers, a city of 95,000 inhabitants located just south of the point where the Mayenne and Sarthe merge to become the Maine River. The Maine, only six miles long, flows through Angers before joining the Loire. Three miles south of Angers, a highway bridge crosses the Loire at les Ponts-de-Cé.

From Vitré, General Irwin dispatched Col. Charles W. Yuill's 11th Infantry through Candé in a direct approach to Angers from the west. He sent a company-sized task force on a more devious route to cross the Mayenne and Sarthe Rivers, outflank Angers on the east, cut the main highway south of the city, and capture the bridge across the Loire.[8] The small task force soon discovered that all bridges across the Sarthe and Mayenne in the division zone were demolished and that few Germans were between Château-Gontier and the Loire. The force then retraced its steps and rejoined the division, which in the meantime had displaced to Angers behind the 11th Infantry. The 11th had encountered no serious resistance until reaching a point two miles west of Angers on the evening of 7 August. General Irwin

---

[6] TUSA AAR, I, p. 22; 5th Div AAR, Aug.

[7] MS # B-245 (Haeckel); MS # B-034 (Schramm).

[8] See *The Fifth Division in France* (Metz, France: Imprimerie du Journal de Lorraine, 1944), pp. 9-13; *The Fifth Infantry Division in the ETO* (Atlanta, Georgia: Albert Love Enterprises, 1945), no pagination.

had then moved the remainder of the division south from Vitré.

Impatient, General Walker phoned Irwin at noon, 8 August. Walker wanted Angers quickly, but he also wanted a reinforced infantry battalion sent to Nantes. If German activity at Lorient, Brest, and St. Malo indicated a pattern of behavior likely to be encountered at all the ports, it was reasonable to assume that strong and determined German forces held Nantes. Although his available troops permitted him only to contain the enemy in the area, Walker desired at least a token force to block the northern exits of Nantes and prevent the Germans from sallying forth unnoticed against American communications.

Irwin, who was already involved at Angers, his major objective, wanted to keep his units well consolidated so he could deal with any emergencies. Operating in what he considered a vacuum of information, he was uneasy because his "mission, zone of action, and adjacent forces [were] not clear," even though he was "using every agency" to find out what his neighbors were doing. Nevertheless, when he learned at the end of the afternoon of 8 August that Walker was "much exercised" because no troops were on the way to Nantes, Irwin sent out a call for trucks. They arrived early on 9 August, and a reinforced infantry battalion motored to Nantes. Encountering no opposition until reaching the outskirts of the city, the battalion destroyed a telephone center and a radio station, then set up blocking positions along the city's northern exits.

Meanwhile, the 11th Infantry on 8 August had captured intact a railroad bridge southwest of Angers, and this gave direct access into the city. General Irwin funneled Col. Robert P. Bell's 10th Infantry across the bridge on 9 August and prepared a co-ordinated two-regiment attack for the following day.

General Walker visited the division and was satisfied with the preparations, but he characteristically "urged more speed in attack." Launched on 10 August, the drive carried American troops into the city, and, by the morning of 11 August, the 5th Division had almost two thousand prisoners and was in control of Angers. American aircraft destroyed the highway bridge south of the city by bombardment, thus isolating Angers from the south.[9]

Developments elsewhere had their effect on the XX Corps. On the basis of information that German reinforcements were moving into the le Mans–Alençon–Sées area, Third Army on 11 August directed Walker to assemble on the Mayenne–le Mans line three of the four divisions then assigned to him. With the 7th Armored, 35th, and 80th Divisions, he was to attack promptly from the Mayenne–le Mans line to the northeast to secure the Carrouges–Sées line. The intention apparently was to eliminate a potential German threat from the west against the exposed left and rear of the

---

[9] *The XX Corps, Its History and Service in World War II* (Osaka, Japan: The Mainichi Publishing Co., Ltd., 1951) (hereafter cited as *XX Corps*), pp. 74–77. On 8 August the Reconnaissance Troop supply section was transporting fuel and rations forward in convoy when the leading armored vehicle performing escort duty struck a mine and was destroyed. Hostile troops nearby opened fire. For braving the fire to rescue several wounded and unconscious soldiers who were lying in the road, S. Sgt. Wardie Barnett and T/5 Vincent Hughes were awarded the DSC.

XV Corps, which was driving north toward Argentan. In addition, Walker was directed to move the 5th Division, less a regiment to be left at Angers, northeast along the Loir River about fifty miles from Angers to a line generally between le Mans and Tours, there, as Patton put it, "to guard against a very doubtful attack on our [south] flank." [10]

The 7th Armored Division, which had recently landed at OMAHA Beach and was hurrying toward le Mans, was not immediately available, nor was the 35th Division, engaged at Mortain. But so urgent was the need to cover the exposed left flank of the XV Corps that Walker, directed again on 12 August to attack, initiated action on the 13th with the two regiments of the 80th Division at hand. Though the attack made good progress and swept away scattered German resistance, it ended in embarrassment as the 80th Division troops collided with XV Corps units moving across their attack zone. [11]

Meanwhile, the 5th Division was moving northeast from Angers. To General Irwin, who was less than fully informed on the big picture, "sudden and unexpected changes cause[d] considerable confusion in arrangements, transportation, and plans," particularly since there was "no indication of reasons for orders." His bewilderment increased during the next few days when orders "made no sense at all" and prompted "great confusion."

Between 12 and 16 August, Irwin received conflicting orders that indicated not much more than changing directions of march. Strained communications, sketchy information, and a surprising absence of German opposition characterized his division's movements, and he could only guess that his ultimate objective might be Dreux, Châteaudun, or Orléans. In time, General Walker told him to remain south of the Chartres–Etampes highway. Finally Walker advised him to stand fast just south of Chartres. Irwin then assumed that he was "heading south of Paris to the east," but he hoped for a few days rest so that his troops could take care of long-needed mechanical maintenance.

Meanwhile, a 4th Armored Division combat command had relieved the battalion of the 5th Division at Nantes, and the 319th Infantry of the 80th Division had replaced Colonel Roffe's 2d Infantry, which Irwin had temporarily left at Angers. As these components joined the division near Chartres, Irwin again had a complete unit, and he would soon get a definite mission. [12]

The Drive to the East

Despite Irwin's bewilderment as to the meaning of his apparently uncharted and aimless peregrinations, a well-defined course of action was emerging. Although the strands of significance were often improvised and tangled, they reflected a pattern of activity designed to exploit the German disorganization in western France. The general area of operations for those units not engaged at the Argentan–Falaise pocket lay between the Seine and Loire Rivers, an

[10] Memo, Patton for Gaffey, 8 Aug, XV Corps G–3 Jnl and File; see also TUSA AAR, I, 26, and Annex 2.
[11] See above, Ch. XXVI.

[12] Ltr, Patton to Walker, 11 Aug, and Msg, Patton to Walker, 12 Aug, XV Corps G–3 Jnl and File; Memo, 15 Aug, VIII Corps G–3 Jnl and File.

open, level plain ideally suited for armored operations. The chalk plateaus in the Evreux, Dreux, Chartres, and Châteaudun areas provided excellent airfield sites capable of insuring satisfactory air support for post-OVERLORD operations east of the Seine. Since securing this ground was an essential preliminary to breaking out of the lodgment area, the operations of the Third Army were oriented toward this goal.[13]

Depending on further developments in the fast changing situation, the most likely objectives toward which the Third Army could next direct its efforts were closing the Argentan–Falaise gap, cutting off at the Seine the Germans escaping from the pocket, and securing the Paris–Orléans gap. Accordingly, Patton on 13 August ordered his forces to assume flexible dispositions. The XV Corps at Argentan was already in position to secure the Argentan–Falaise gap. Patton gave the XX Corps the 7th Armored Division and instructed Walker to secure Dreux as the initial step in blocking German escape across the lower Seine. The XII Corps, with newly assigned subordinate units, was to concentrate in the area southeast of le Mans to be in position for an advance to the Paris–Orléans gap. Because of the fluid situation, Patton instructed all three corps commanders to be prepared to operate to the north, northeast, or east.[14]

The XII Corps headquarters had virtually completed the administrative task of landing and assembling the Third

Army units coming from England and dispatching them to the front. Although the corps headquarters had been scheduled to take control of the 7th Armored and 80th Infantry Divisions, neither proved available; the 80th was involved at Argentan, and the 7th Armored was moving toward Dreux. Fortunately, the 35th Division was about to complete its mission near Mortain, and Patton gave it, as well as the 4th Armored Division (coming from Brittany and VIII Corps control), to XII Corps. With these forces, XII Corps, in addition to protecting the south flank of the army, could advance toward the Paris–Orléans gap or, if necessary, support the XX Corps drive to the lower Seine.[15]

After Bradley halted the XV Corps at Argentan and after Patton ordered Haislip to split the corps and move two divisions eastward, Patton found himself on 15 August, for all practical purposes and exclusive of the VIII Corps in Brittany, in command of four corps of two divisions each. Half of the XV Corps (2d French Armored and 90th Infantry Divisions) was facing north in the Argentan area, while the XV Corps headquarters with the other half (5th Armored and 79th Infantry Divisions) was heading generally eastward, as were the XX Corps (7th Armored and 5th Divisions) and the XII Corps (4th Armored and 35th Divisions). On 15 August Patton directed the XII Corps to seize Châteaudun and Orléans and protect the army right flank along the Loire. He changed the objective of the XX Corps—instead of taking Dreux, the corps was to establish a bridgehead across

[13] PS SHAEF (44) 11 (Final), SHAEF Plng Staff, Post-NEPTUNE Courses of Action After Capture of the Lodgment Area, Sec. II: Method of Conducting the Campaign, 30 May, SGS SHAEF File 381, Post-OVERLORD Plng.

[14] See TUSA Dir, 13 Aug.

[15] TUSA AAR, Aug; Memo, Maddox for Evans, 13 Aug.

the Eure River at Chartres. He instructed the XV Corps to establish a bridgehead over the Eure at Dreux. Thus evolved the Third Army three-corps drive eastward to the Seine.[16] (*Map XII*)

Though General Patton alerted his corps commanders for advances beyond these objectives, General Bradley exerted a restraining influence. Bradley was concerned with the strain that the rapid advance was imposing on supply and communications facilities. In accord with OVERLORD planning, Bradley wanted to give the logistical apparatus time to develop installations that would provide a secure base for post-OVERLORD operations beyond the Seine. He therefore restricted Patton to Dreux, Chartres, and Orléans so that he, Bradley, could there regroup his forces and readjust the army boundaries.[17]

To secure Orléans was the mission of Maj. Gen. Gilbert R. Cook, a West Pointer who had fought in France during World War I, who had commanded XII Corps since 1943, and who in addition was deputy commander of the Third Army. To perform his first combat mission as corps commander, General Cook set up his headquarters at le Mans on 13 August and awaited the arrival of his widely separated units—the 4th Armored Division coming out of Brittany

and the 35th Division on the road from Mortain.

Since Patton had told him to "get started as soon as possible," Cook formed an armored-infantry column composed of elements from both divisions and headed the column down the main road from le Mans to Orléans on 15 August.[18] The 4th Armored Division's CCA under Colonel Clarke had driven from Nantes to St. Calais—more than a hundred miles—in one day, but after a short halt for refueling, the tankers moved on toward Orléans. Immediately behind came a 35th Division regimental task force, Col. Robert Sears's 137th Infantry. The armor was eventually attached to the infantry, and both units then operated under General Sebree, the 35th's assistant division commander.

There was little knowledge of enemy strength or dispositions save vague reports that the Germans were assembling forces to defend Châteaudun and Orléans. As a result of conflicting intelligence, Cook later received contrary messages from Patton advising him to proceed directly to Orléans and also to go by way of Châteaudun. To resolve the matter, Cook ordered Sebree to take Orléans if quick capture appeared feasible without reinforcement and if it appeared possible to hold the city with light forces after its capture.

With very few maps, without prior reconnaissance, lacking information of enemy dispositions, and ignorant of the natural obstacles of the region, tankers

---

[16] TUSA Dir, 15 Aug (confirming verbal orders, 14 Aug); 12th AGp Dir for Current Opns, 15 Aug; Telecon, Gay to Menoher, 1845, 15 Aug, XV Corps CofS Jnl and File; XV Corps AAR, Aug; Bradley, *Soldier's Story*, p. 379.

[17] Telecons, Gen Gaffey and Maj Gen Gilbert R. Cook, 1740, 15 Aug, and Gaffey and Hagan, 1540, 16 Aug; Memos, Gaffey for Haislip and for Walker, 15 Aug. All in XV Corps CofS Jnl and File. Ruppenthal, *Logistical Support*, I, 484–88.

[18] This account is from the XII Corps, 4th Armd Div, and 35th Div AAR's; Extracts from Cook's Diary and XII Corps Historical Officer's Notes, CI 354, GL–140; Maj Randolph Leigh's XII Corps, Hosp Intervs, IV, GL–93 (319); and Koyen, *Fourth Armored Division*, pp. 27ff.

and infantrymen plunged boldly toward Orléans. Though all the bridges between St. Calais and Orléans had been destroyed, energetic reconnaissance revealed crossing sites. By dark of 15 August, the large Orléans airport, which had been strongly fortified with antiaircraft and antitank guns but left virtually undefended, was captured, and American troops were at the outskirts of the city.

About that time, because of changing plans on higher levels of command, Patton directed Cook to halt the advance on Orléans and secure Châteaudun. Cook objected, saying he could take both. Patton gave no immediate answer but called back later and authorized continuation of the attack on Orléans with the forces already committed. Cook again objected, this time to the restriction on employing his forces. Patton finally told him to go ahead and use his own judgment.

After meeting with Baade, Sebree, Clarke, and Sears on the morning of 16 August, Cook directed the attack to Orléans continued. While two columns of armor attacked the city from the north and northeast, the 137th Infantry assaulted Orléans from the west. The converging attacks crushed slight opposition, and that night the city of Joan of Arc was in American hands.

Meanwhile, Cook had also directed Baade to capture Châteaudun. General Baade sent Col. Bernard A. Byrne's 320th Infantry, and after an all-night march and a short sharp engagement against several hundred Germans with a few tanks, the regiment took the town by noon of 17 August.[19] Concentrating his

forces in the Châteaudun–Orléans area, General Cook awaited further instructions.

The speed of the XII Corps advance to Orléans dashed German hopes of organizing a defense of the Paris–Orléans gap. The *First Army* and the *LXXX Corps* headquarters had displaced from the Bay of Biscay region to Fontainebleau and Reims, respectively, on 10 August to form a line west of the upper Seine that would tie in with the *Seventh Army* and *Fifth Panzer Army* defenses west of the lower Seine. Developments at Argentan and Falaise and the lack of combat units for immediate attachment to the *First Army*, however, prevented more than a cursory defensive effort along the upper Seine south of Paris. The *LXXX Corps* instead built up defensive positions along the Marne River. The troops that had met the Americans at Orléans and Châteaudun had been miscellaneous rear-guard elements reinforced by remnants of the *708th Division* and hastily assembled antiaircraft and antitank units, all under the control of local commanders who had been instructed to prepare defensive positions with the aid of impressed French inhabitants. The *First Army*, for all practical purposes, commanded local strongpoints "of doubtful combat value." [20]

The loss of Orléans on 16 August, the weakness of the *First Army*, developments at Argentan and Falaise in Normandy, and the Allied invasion of south-

---

[19] Interv with 1st Lt Donald E Severance, Hosp

Intervs, ML–2234; information made available to the author by Generals Cook and Baade.

[20] *First Army* FO 2, 16 Aug, translated and reproduced in Annex 1 to TUSA G–2 Per Rpt 69, 19 Aug; principal German sources are MS # A–911 (Emmerich), MS # B–728 (Emmerich), and MS # B–034 (Schramm).

ern France on 15 August prompted OKW and *OB WEST* to relinquish southwest France. Anticipating an Allied drive up the Rhône River valley and a continued eastward advance from Orléans, the Germans could foresee the eventual meeting between the DRAGOON (southern France) and OVERLORD forces. They therefore tried to avert the isolation of their own forces in southwest France. As the Germans in Normandy began their definite withdrawal out of the Argentan–Falaise pocket, a general withdrawal from the Bay of Biscay to Dijon started under the supervision of the *LXIV Corps*. The *16th Division* was assigned the task along the Loire of covering the northern flank of the withdrawal movement. Spread rather thin, the division garrisoned the towns at the Loire crossing sites with the exception of Nantes, Angers, and Orléans, which were in American possession. Perhaps a thousand infantrymen reinforced by some artillery pieces, a few antitank weapons, and a handful of tanks, guarded the Loire crossings at Saumur, Tours, and Blois.

The withdrawal from southwest France got under way as approximately 100,000 men moved northeastward, mostly on foot. The great majority had engaged in agricultural, construction, and security operations, and very few combat troops were among them. Their movement stimulated the FFI to activity that increased from relatively minor nuisance raids to major harassing action, including intensified FFI operations along the Loire River. At the same time, American pressure along the north bank of the Loire, both on the ground and in the air, increased.[21]

The American units that had swept from St. Calais directly to Orléans and Châteaudun had not come near the Loire River except at Orléans, although the need to capture Orléans had not eliminated General Cook's mission to protect the south flank of the 12th Army Group along the Loire. Since the American sweep to Orléans had followed routes along the north bank of the Loir River, a tributary of the Sarthe that parallels the Loire for about seventy miles, a buffer zone about twenty-five miles wide existed between the Loire and the Loir—a sort of no man's land inhabited by American and German patrols and by the FFI.

Contrary to later legend, General Patton appreciated the possibility that the German troops at the Loire might make sorties against the underbelly of the Third Army (and 12th Army Group) and become nuisances to U.S. lines of communication. He therefore requested General Weyland to have the XIX Tactical Air Command patrol the Loire River valley constantly. For the 24-hour coverage that was subsequently provided, a squadron of night fighters augmented the daylight operations of the XIX TAC fighter-bombers. Similarly, General Cook directed General Baade to keep artillery observation planes of the 35th Division over the Loir River valley.[22]

Despite these efforts, aerial surveillance could not take the place of ground action. Unless American troops destroyed the bridges across the Loire.

[21] MS # B-245 (Haeckel).

[22] XII Corps G-2 Per Rpts, 15-23 Aug, and AAR, Aug; Patton, *War As I Knew It*, p. 384; Memo, Patton for Gaffey, 8 Aug; [Taylor], Development of Night Air Operations, 1941-1952, p. 27.

the Germans would be able to raid U.S. lines of communication. General Cook therefore instructed the 4th Armored Division to sweep the north bank of the Loire between Tours and Blois. General Wood gave the mission to General Dager's CCB, which was moving from Lorient toward Orléans. CCB was to clear the north bank and destroy the bridges but was not to become involved in action that might delay its progress. In compliance, as CCB drove the 250 miles from Lorient to Vendôme (forty miles west of Orléans) in thirty-four hours, General Dager dispatched patrols to the river. These were sufficient to cause the Germans, already harassed by the FFI, to demolish the bridges themselves and withdraw to the south bank between Tours and Blois. A XII Corps task force composed of the 1117th Engineer Group and an attached artillery battalion performed the same function for the bridges between Blois and Orléans. With all the bridges destroyed, aircraft keeping the Loire River valley under surveillance, patrols guarding the buffer zone between the Loir and the Loire from Angers to Orléans, and the Germans manifesting little hostile intent, the southern flank of the 12th Army Group appeared secure. General Cook had accomplished his mission. His first assignment as XII Corps commander was also his last. In poor health for some time, he finally gave in to doctors' orders and relinquished his command.

The XX Corps mission to take Chartres had evolved out of a fluid situation that bred some confusion. After having attacked on the left of XV Corps on 13 August toward the Carrouges–Sées line, the same objective given to XV

Corps, and having collided with XV Corps units, XX Corps received new orders sending it to Dreux. General Walker's field order, issued on the morning of 14 August, directed an attack "on the axis le Mans–Nogent-le-Rotrou–Dreux–Mantes-Gassicourt to seize the line of the Seine between Meulan–Vernon." [23] As far as Dreux was concerned, this projected an advance to the northeast. But XV Corps on the XX Corps left was preparing on the same day to advance to the east, also on Dreux, with the two divisions departing the Argentan area. If the two corps converged on a single point, in this case Dreux, a confusion of major proportions was inevitable. During the evening of 14 August, therefore, Walker received a new mission—Chartres became the new XX Corps objective.

As a result of these changes, the initial commitment of the 7th Armored Division was fraught with haste and potential disorder. Having almost been sent into attack on the XV Corps left as it was hurrying from its recent unloading at OMAHA Beach toward le Mans, the 7th Armored Division on the afternoon of 13 August received orders to pass through le Mans, clear the roads to enable the 35th Division to advance on Orléans, and assemble near la Ferté-Bernard, fifty miles southwest of Dreux. While the division was assembling near la Ferté-Bernard, General Walker arrived at the command post at noon, 14 August. He ordered the division commander, Maj. Gen. Lindsay McD. Silvester, to begin his attack at once—toward Dreux and Mantes-Gassicourt.

---

[23] XX Corps FO, 14 Aug.

GENERAL WALKER HOLDING ROADSIDE CONFERENCE *with General Silvester.*

Though some division components were still coming from the beaches, Silvester had three armored columns advancing toward Dreux that afternoon.[24]

The columns encountered scattered resistance and advanced about fifteen miles to Nogent-le-Rotrou by evening. At that time Silvester received word of the change in objective. He was to move instead to Chartres.[25] Silvester immediately notified his subordinate commands of the change in direction, and by the morning of 15 August the forces had shifted and consolidated into two columns.[26] The excellent road net, the sparseness of enemy opposition, and good command control had facilitated a difficult readjustment made during the hours of darkness. Yet, despite the shift of armored columns, considerable traffic intermingling occurred on 15 August between the 7th Armored and the 79th Divisions on the approaches to Nogent-le-Roi.

Still mindful of driving to the Seine, General Silvester sent Col. Dwight A. Rosebaum's CCA and Lt. Col. James W. Newberry's CCR north of Chartres and

---

[24] This account is taken from the XX Corps, 7th Armd Div, and 5th Div AAR's, Aug; *XX Corps,* p. 79; CI 285; Irwin Diary; personal documents loaned to the author by General Silvester.

[25] Telecon, Walker and Silvester, 2145, 14 Aug, 7th Armd Div G-3 Jnl.

[26] 7th Armd Div G-3 Jnl, entry 2255, 14 Aug.

into the area between Chartres and Dreux; he dispatched Brig. Gen. John B. Thompson's CCB to take the new objective. At the outskirts of Chartres by the evening of 15 August, CCB attacked with two forces. One force entered the town from the northwest; the other sought to enter from the southwest. The latter met determined opposition that came somewhat as a surprise because of the relatively light resistance encountered earlier. At a disadvantage in the failing light, the troops withdrew.

Meanwhile, the 5th Division, which had moved from Angers, was arriving at an area about eight miles southwest of Chartres.

Like the Americans, the Germans were surprised by the effectiveness of the Chartres defenses. The *First Army,* in command of the area between Chartres and the Loire, had designated Chartres as an "absorption point," where remnants of units (among them the *17th SS Panzer Grenadier* and *352d Divisions*) and stragglers from the Normandy battlefield were to be reorganized. As at Châteaudun and Orléans, a local commander was in charge of assembling these and rear-area troops (among them students of an antiaircraft training center at Chartres) into a coherent force. On the afternoon of 15 August, as the 7th U.S. Armored Division was approaching, General der Infanterie Kurt von der Chevallerie, the *First Army* commander, was holding a conference in the town to plan how newly arriving units that Hitler had ordered there—the *48th Division* from northern France and the *338th Division* from southern France—might best reinforce the defenses west of the Seine in general and the defenses of

Chartres in particular. Before the fight for Chartres terminated, regimental-sized portions of both new divisions (the *338th* tied to the artillery of the vanished *708th Division*) were committed there.[27]

CCB of the 7th Armored Division attacked Chartres again on 16 August and extended a precarious hold over part of the objective despite active resistance inside the town and the arrival of increasing numbers of new troops in wooded areas just south of the town.[28] Corps artillery, cautioned to be careful of the historic town and its cathedral, commenced to fire on 17 August in support of CCB, which encircled Chartres and fought to clear German troops from the town. Since the Germans continued to defend stubbornly, and because tanks were at a disadvantage in the narrow streets, General Walker ordered the 5th Division to aid the armor.

General Irwin, still not altogether informed on the broad picture, wished he had more information on the American armored dispositions, felt that the XX Corps was overextended, and believed that security against enemy infiltration was insufficient. He dispatched the 11th Infantry just as General Walker made his usual telephone call to urge speed. The 11th Infantry attacked toward Chartres on 18 August, and, despite stiff opposition that included tanks and artil-

[27] Hitler Order, *WFST/Op.Nr. 772830/44 g.Kdos. Chefs,* 11 Aug, quoted in Msg, *AGp B* to the armies, 0030, 12 Aug, *AGp B Fuehrer Befehle;* MS # B–732 (Hold), MS # B–003 (Hoehne), MS # B–728 (Emmerich), MS # P–166 (Casper); *First Army* FO 2, 16 Aug, translated and reproduced in Annex 1 to TUSA G–2 Per Rpt 69, 19 Aug.

[28] Col. Welborn B. Griffith, Jr., the XX Corps G–3 who was killed at Chartres, and 1st Lt. Mario J. Fortuna of the 38th Armored Infantry Battalion, who led an assault party in the capture of a nearby village, were awarded the DSC.

ARMORED BIVOUAC AREA *near Chartres. The cathedral can be seen in the background.*

lery, the combined efforts of armor and infantry succeeded in clearing and securing the remainder of the town.[29] More than two thousand prisoners were taken, a large German Air Force installation (including airport, warehouses, depots, a bomb assembly plant, and fifty planes) was captured, and the XX Corps was in possession of a historic gateway to Paris, only fifty miles away.

At the same time, the XV Corps was making its sixty-mile advance from Argentan: the 79th Division toward Nogent-le-Roi, and the 5th Armored Division toward Dreux. The 5th Armored met only a few Germans at lightly defended roadblocks. Although German jamming of radios interfered with communications between unit commanders and the heads of their columns, the troops crossed the Eure River on the morning of 16 August, encircled Dreux, fired at some German troops fleeing eastward, and took the town that afternoon. Nine artillery pieces, six destroyed tanks, and a little more than two hundred

[29] S. Sgt. Clarence E. White of the 11th Infantry was instrumental in the success, establishing and maintaining an exposed artillery observation post. Though wounded, White adjusted fire until he collapsed from loss of blood. He was awarded the DSC.

prisoners were captured. The motorized 79th Division, advancing toward Nogent-le-Roi, met hardly a German and on 16 August established a bridgehead on the east bank of the Eure River, thirty-seven miles from Paris.[30]

Although capture of Orléans and Chartres had placed the XII and XX Corps within striking distance of Paris, the approach to the French capital from Dreux was shorter and considered better. Five bridges across the Eure and a good road net afforded more than adequate accommodations for military movement.[31] Despite the attractiveness and the importance of Paris—the most vital communications center in France—the Seine River, not the city, became the foremost Allied objective.

To the Seine and Across

General Bradley had limited General Patton to Dreux, Chartres, and Orléans primarily because of logistical problems. The essential difficulty was that the supply services did not have enough transportation to keep up with the breakout from the Cotentin and the spectacular momentum of the Allied advance.[32] It was obvious after the first week in August that the combat gains were outstripping the capacity of the Communications Zone to keep the units adequately supplied. Because of the rapidity of troop movement and the relative paucity of targets, ammunition was less a problem than were gasoline and rations.[33] Gasoline consumption, which skyrocketed, and ration requirements, which remained constant, threatened to bring operations to a halt.

In order to keep the troops moving, Allied commanders looked to air supply.[34] Nevertheless, only small amounts of supplies actually arrived on the Continent by air in early August, primarily because transport planes were being held in readiness for possible airborne operations at Orléans and Chartres. Once the two cities were captured, use of the transports was less restricted. On 19 August twenty-one C-47's landed forty-seven tons of rations near le Mans in the first delivery of what was to become a daily emergency airlift to the Third Army.[35]

Although this emergency measure hardly promised to make up all shortages, the temptation to take advantage of the weak enemy opposition at Dreux, Chartres, and Orléans (despite the local resistance at Chartres) was irresistible. After meeting with Hodges and Patton to discuss "spheres of influence" and "zones of action," Bradley on 17 August removed his restriction on going beyond the confines of the OVERLORD lodgment area to the Seine. Since the main enemy forces were concentrated west of the lower Seine (north of Paris), Allied troops advancing to the Seine would in

---

[30] XV Corps, 79th Div, 5th Armd Div AAR's, Aug; Wyche Diary; Notes of Mtg, 2000, 16 Aug, XV Corps CofS Jnl and File.

[31] Notes of Mtg, 2000, 16 Aug, XV Corps CofS Jnl and File.

[32] For detailed discussion, see Ch. XXXI, below.

[33] The Gen Bd, USFET, Rpt on Ammo Supply for FA, Study No. 58, File 471/1, p. 19.

[34] Ltr, Eisenhower to Montgomery, 2 Aug, SGS SHAEF File 381, OVERLORD I (a); SHAEF Msg S-57489, 12 Aug, Msgs, EXFOR Main to SHAEF, MGA-2, 14 Aug, SHAEF to EXFOR Main, FWD-12901, 15 Aug, and 12th AGp to SHAEF, Q-2050, 11 Aug, SGS SHAEF File 373/2.

[35] Bradley, *Soldier's Story*, p. 385; Bradley, *Effect of Air Power*, p. 71; Huston, *Biography of A Battalion*, pp. 370-72; TUSA AAR, Aug.

GERMAN REMOVING BOOBYTRAP *under the eyes of a U.S. soldier.*

effect be extending to the river the lower jaw of the Allied trap, which already stretched from Argentan through Chambois to Dreux.[36]

To conserve gasoline and other supplies, Patton held the XII Corps at Orléans. He instructed the XX Corps to complete the capture of Chartres and at the same time to assume responsibility for Dreux. He directed the XV Corps to drive twenty-five miles northeast from Dreux to the Seine at Mantes-Gassicourt, a town thirty miles northwest of Paris. At Mantes, the XV Corps was to interdict the roads east of the river and disrupt German ferrying operations.[37]

The 5th Armored and 79th Infantry

Divisions of the XV Corps, relieved at Dreux and Nogent-le-Roi by the 7th Armored Division, moved easily to Mantes-Gassicourt on 18 August, set up roadblocks to collect German stragglers, and placed interdictory artillery fire on the river-crossing sites. On the following day a task force of the 79th entered Mantes-Gassicourt and found the Germans gone.

On 19 August, while the XV Corps was discovering that no effective obstacle save the river itself barred a crossing of the Seine, the top Allied commanders were reaching agreement to modify further the OVERLORD planning. Instead of halting at the Seine to reorganize and build up a supply base west of the Seine, the Allied command decided to move immediately into post-OVERLORD operations directed toward Germany.[38]

To drive across the upper Seine south of Paris and the lower Seine north of Paris would be a comparatively simple maneuver, but the presence of a considerable number of Germans between the Argentan–Falaise pocket and the lower Seine presented an opportunity to complete the destruction of the forces that had escaped the pocket. The Allies estimated that 75,000 enemy troops and 250 tanks could still be encircled west of the Seine.[39] If American troops drove down the west bank of the Seine from Mantes-Gassicourt, they might cut German escape routes, push the Germans toward the mouth of the Seine, where the river is wider and more diffi-

[36] 12th AGp Ltr and Ltr of Instrs 5, 17 Aug; see also XV Corps G–2 Per Rpt 15, 0300, 18 Aug, and Sylvan Diary, 17 Aug.

[37] TUSA Dirs, 17 and 18 Aug; Patton to Haislip, 17 Aug, XV Corps G–3 Jnl and File.

[38] 12th AGp Memo for Rcd, 19 Aug, ML–205. For a detailed discussion of this decision, see Ch. XXX, below.

[39] Notes of Mtg, 2000, 19 Aug, XV Corps CofS Jnl and File.

cult to cross, and fashion another en-circlement inside Normandy.

The major difficulty of a maneuver such as this was the same that had in-hibited American activity north of Argentan. At Mantes, the XV Corps was again beyond the zone assigned to the 12th Army Group. Further ad-vance toward the mouth of the Seine would place the corps across the pro-jected routes of advance of the British and Canadian armies and would surely result in "an administrative headache."[40]

Although General Bradley offered to lend trucks to transport British troops to Mantes-Gassicourt and suggested that the British move units through the American zone to launch the attack down the west bank of the river, General Dempsey de-clined with thanks on the basis that his logistical organization could not support such a move. For the Allies then to take advantage of the alluring possibilities at the Seine—disrupting the German with-drawal, bagging additional prisoners among the escapees from the Argentan–Falaise pocket, removing Germans from the British zone, and thus allowing Dempsey to move to the Seine against "almost negligible resistance"—General Montgomery would have to permit further intrusion of American troops into the British sector and accept in ad-vance the administrative consequences. He, Bradley, and Dempsey decided to chance the headache.[41]

Having decided to send part of Pat-ton's force down the west bank of the Seine, the Allied commanders saw a coincident opportunity to seize a bridge-head on the east bank of the river as a springboard for future operations. The XV Corps thus drew a double mission—the 5th Armored was to attack down the west bank while the 79th established a bridgehead on the east bank. In his order issued on 20 August, Montgomery cautioned: "This is no time to relax, or to sit back and congratulate ourselves. . . . Let us finish off the business in rec-ord time."[42] By then, American troops were already across the Seine.

General Wyche had received a tele-phone call at 2135, 19 August, from General Haislip, who ordered him to cross the Seine that night.[43] The 79th was to get foot troops on the east bank at once, build a bridge for vehicles, tanks, and heavy equipment, and gain ground in sufficient depth (four to six miles) to protect the crossing sites at Mantes from medium artillery fire.

In a situation that was "too fluid to define an enemy front line," General Wyche anticipated little resistance. His 79th Division had that day engaged only scattered German groups in flight, had captured nineteen vehicles and a Mark IV tank, and had received only sporadic machine gun fire from across the Seine. The river itself was the main problem, for near Mantes it varied in width from five hundred to eight hundred feet.

[42] 21 AGp Gen Operational Situation and Dir, M–519, 20 Aug.
[43] The following account is taken from the XV Corps and 79th Div AAR's, Aug; Wyche Diary; XV Corps FO 6, 2330, 19 Aug, and G–2 Per Rpt 17, 0300, 20 Aug; Telecons, Menoher and Wyche, 2135, 19 Aug, and Col Menoher and Col Kramer Thomas, 1000, 20 Aug; Haislip Memo, 2100, 19 Aug; Notes of Mtg, 2000, 19 Aug; 314th Infantry Regi-ment, *Through Combat*, pp 27–30; *History of the 313th Infantry in World War II* (Washington, 1947), pp. 95–99; Interv with Capt Ernest Rothem-berg, Hosp Intervs, ML–2234.

Fortunately, a dam nearby offered a narrow foot path across it, and Engineer assault boats and rafts could transport other troops and light equipment. For the bridge he was to build, Wyche secured seven hundred feet of treadway from the 5th Armored Division.

While a torrential rain fell during the night of 19 August, men of the 313th Infantry walked across the dam in single file, each man touching the one ahead to keep from falling into the water. At daybreak, 20 August, as the 314th Infantry paddled across the river, the division engineers began to install the treadway. In the afternoon, as soon as the bridge was ready, the 315th Infantry crossed in trucks. By nightfall, 20 August, the bulk of the division, including tanks, artillery, and tank destroyers, was on the east bank. The following day battalions of the XV Corps Artillery crossed. Antiaircraft units hurriedly emplaced their pieces around the bridge, arriving in time to shoot down about a dozen enemy planes on the first day and to amass a total of almost fifty claimed in four days. To supplement the treadway, engineers constructed a Bailey bridge that was opened to traffic on 23 August. On the east bank, the 79th not only extended and improved the bridgehead, repelled counterattacks, and interdicted highways, ferry routes, and barge traffic lanes, but also dramatically pointed out to the Germans their critical situation by capturing the *Army Group B* command post at la Roche-Guyon and sending the German headquarters troops scurrying eastward to Soissons.[44]

The Second Encirclement Attempt

Hitler was wrong on 20 August when he surmised that the Allies intended to capture Paris at once. Yet he guessed correctly that they would try to destroy the forces of *Army Group B* in the area between Argentan and the lower Seine, primarily by thrusting downstream along the west bank of the river. Hitler did not say how this was to be prevented, but he instructed Model to establish a defensive line at the Touques River with the admittedly "badly battered" *Fifth Panzer* and *Seventh Armies*. If Model found a defense at the Touques unfeasible, he was authorized to withdraw for a stand at the Seine. In this case, the *Fifth Panzer Army* was to provide reception facilities on the east bank of the Seine, protect crossings for the *Seventh Army,* and at the same time make contact with the *First Army*, which was to defend the Paris–Orléans gap and prevent an Allied advance toward Dijon.[45]

Hitler obviously did not appreciate the extent of *Fifth Panzer Army* exhaustion, *Seventh Army* disorganization, and *First Army* weakness. Perhaps he was deluded by self-imposed blindness. Possibly he was the victim of the patently false reports and briefings that were later to become common practice. Perhaps he overestimated the effect of a not inconsiderable number of divisions that had been moving toward the battle zone in Normandy since the Mortain counterattack—the *6th Parachute,* the *17th* and *18th Luftwaffe Field,* the *344th, 331st, 48th,* and *338th Infantry*—their purpose

---

[44] ETHINT 18 (Schwerin); *AGp B KTB,* 19 Aug.

[45] Hitler Order, 20 Aug, Msg, *FHQu.* 20 Aug, *OKW/WFSt/Op. Nr. 772956/44, OKW/175.*

to cover Paris and the *Army Group B* rear. In any event, though Hitler hoped to stop the Allies at the Touques or at the Seine, he was already preparing to organize the Somme–Marne River line for defense.[46]

Model on 20 August subordinated the *Seventh Army* to the *Fifth Panzer Army* (perhaps because Hausser had been wounded and was evacuated), thereby giving Dietrich command of the entire area from the coast to the *First Army* boundary (Chartres–Rambouillet–northwest outskirts of Paris). On 21 August he spelled out Dietrich's mission. The *Fifth Panzer Army* was to occupy and hold during the night of 21 August the Touques River – Lisieux – Orbec – Laigle line. Because it was "of paramount importance" to bolster the eastern flank in the Eure sector, Model ordered Dietrich to move all the armored units fit for combat (except those of the *II SS Panzer Corps*) to the vicinity of Evreux, the area Model considered most threatened. The eventual task of these forces was to regain contact with the Paris defenses of the *First Army*. Because a firm hold on the Seine River between Vernon and the army boundary was a prerequisite to successful defense in that area, a corps headquarters was to be charged with building defenses there; the arrival of the *49th Division* at the Seine was to be accelerated by all available means. "I am stressing in particular," Model stated, "the importance of

the sector between the Eure and the Seine River where an enemy breakthrough attempt to Louviers can be expected." The *Fifth Panzer Army* was to absorb all the *Seventh Army* headquarters. The armored units of the *Seventh Army* unfit for combat were to be sent to the Beauvais–Senlis area for rehabilitation under the *LVIII Panzer Corps* headquarters. Other units of the *Seventh Army* temporarily unfit for combat were to be dispatched across the Seine for rehabilitation, construction of fortifications along the Seine, and defense of the river line.[47]

In another order issued the same day, Model informed Dietrich that if the development of the situation required withdrawal behind the Seine, the withdrawal was to be carried out in four steps, through a series of three intermediate positions.[48]

On that date Dietrich organized his army front into three corps sectors, with the *LXXXVI* on the coast, the *II SS Panzer* in the center, and the *LXXXI* on the left. In compliance with Model's directive, he dispatched an armored group to the Evreux area—the remnants of the *2d*, *1st SS*, and *12th SS Panzer Divisions* under *I SS Panzer Corps*.[49]

Despite the orderly appearance of troop dispositions and unit boundaries on a map, the forces were weak. The *Seventh Army* could not even begin to

[46] *OB WEST KTB*, 8 Aug, *Anlagen 1218* and *1220*; Telecons, Tempelhoff and Metzke, 1150 and 1220, 8 Aug, *AGp B KTB*; MS # B–727 (Gersdorff); MS # B–807 (Kuntzen); Hitler Order, *WFSt/Op. Nr. 772830/44 g.Kdos. Chefs*, 11 Aug, quoted in Msg, *AGp B* to the armies, 0030, 12 Aug, *AGp B Fuehrer Befehle; OB WEST, a Study in Command*, p. 139.

[47] Model Order to Dietrich (No. 6376/44), 21 Aug, *Fifth Pz Army KTB, Anlage 37.*

[48] Model to Dietrich (No. 6353/44), 21 Aug, *Fifth Pz Army KTB, Anlage 38.* Whether this preceded or followed the order cited immediately above is not clear. Though the numbering of the *Anlagen* suggests that it follows, the numbers on the documents suggest otherwise.

[49] Dietrich Order, 21 Aug, *Fifth Pz Army KTB, Anlagen.*

prepare an accurate strength report, but Dietrich on 21 August instructed two corps of his army to count their men, tanks, and artillery pieces. The count was discouraging. The *I SS Panzer Corps* reported that the *10th SS Panzer Division* had only a weak infantry battalion (perhaps 300 men), no tanks, no guns; the *12th SS Panzer Division* had 300 men, 10 tanks, no artillery; the *1st SS Panzer Division* was unable to give any figures. The *II SS Panzer Corps* reported that the *2d SS Panzer Division* had 450 men, 15 tanks, 6 guns; the *9th SS Panzer Division* had 460 men, 20 to 25 tanks, and 20 guns; the *116th Panzer Division* had one battalion of infantry (perhaps 500 or 600 men), 12 tanks, and no artillery.

A week later the strength of these divisions, plus that of the *21st Panzer Division*—all that remained of Model's armored forces—totaled 1,300 men, 24 tanks, and 60 artillery pieces.[50]

In that intervening week the Allies were driving toward the Seine.

When the XV Corps had been ordered to thrust downstream along the west bank of the Seine from Mantes-Gassicourt and clear the area between the Eure and Seine Rivers, General Hodges (after a conference with Generals Bradley and Montgomery) had been instructed to assist with the First U.S. Army. Hodges was to use the XIX Corps, which had been pinched out of the western portion (upper jaw) of the Argentan–Falaise pocket. In the same kind of displacement from the upper to the lower jaw that the V Corps headquarters had made from Tinchebray to Argentan, the XIX Corps and its divisions were to displace more than a hundred miles in a large and complicated troop movement from the vicinity of Flers to cover the gap between the V and XV Corps—from Gacé to Dreux. The corps moved and by 19 August was concentrated (with the 2d Armored, 28th, and 30th Divisions) in the Mortagne–Brezolles area. From there the XIX Corps was to attack north toward the Seine. The XIX and XV Corps would thus fashion a two-corps drive straddling the Eure River, with the divisions of the XIX on the left attacking to Elbeuf and XV (5th Armored Division) on the right attacking to Louviers.[51]

The *LXXXI Corps*, which since 16 August had had the difficult mission of screening the south flank of both German armies in Normandy from Gacé to Paris, was scheduled to defend the Eure River line. When parts of the *344th Division* (a static division released by the *Fifteenth Army*) arrived near Gacé on 17 August, conglomerate forces under the headquarters of *Panzer Lehr* were pulled out of the line and sent east of the Seine for rehabilitation. Soon afterwards, portions of the *6th Parachute* and *331st Divisions* came into the sector and were committed on the *344th* left (east). The *17th Luftwaffe Field Division*, previously employed at Le Havre as a static division, took positions near Dreux so hastily that its commitment could not be executed in an orderly or unified manner. These units were far from im-

---

[50] Telecon, Rotbers and Tempelhoff, 1545, 21 Aug, and *Fifth Pz Army* Rpt, 0650, 28 Aug, *AGp B KTB*.

[51] 12th AGp Ltr of Instrs 5, 17 Aug, Addenda to Ltr of Instrs 5, 19 Aug, and Memos for Rcd, 18 and 19 Aug; Telecon, Patton to Haislip, 19 Aug, XV Corps G–3 Jnl and File; Sylvan Diary, 19 Aug.

pressive; besides being understrength, they were poorly trained. Yet an SS captain named Wahl, the trains commander of the *17th SS Panzer Grenadier Division,* had on his own initiative been gathering tanks from all sources (for the most part from the *2d SS, 9th SS,* and *2d Panzer Divisions*), principally replacement tanks on their way to units; Wahl assembled these to protect the Seine crossing sites. On 19 August combat remnants of the *17th SS Panzer Grenadiers* under Fick joined Wahl. Two days later contingents of the *1st SS Panzer Division* provided further reinforcement between the Eure and the Seine, and the whole improvised formation became known as *Kampfgruppe Mohnke.*[52]

While the 79th Division started across the Seine on the evening of 19 August, a 5th Armored Division liaison officer was carrying from the corps headquarters to the division command post the order to drive downstream. Rain and a black night prevented him from reaching the division until shortly before dawn, 20 August. A few hours later armored units were moving. Referring not only to the celerity of execution of the corps order but also to the Seine crossing, General Haislip declared, "What we did last night was a Lulu."[53] There was no doubt about it.

The object of the armored drive down the Seine was to force the Germans as close to the mouth of the river as possible. Between Mantes-Gassicourt and Rouen, the Seine, averaging some five hundred feet in width, was suitable in many places for bridging and had many ferry slips. North of Rouen, the width of one thousand to twelve hundred feet and the tidal range would present the Germans with more hazardous and difficult crossings.[54]

The first objective of the attack between the Eure and the Seine was to cut the German escape routes leading to the Seine River crossings between Vernon and Pont de l'Arche. Though Montgomery's order issued on 20 August directed an advance "to Louviers, and Elbeuf, and beyond," Patton on the previous evening had instructed Haislip to drive on Louviers and Elbeuf, the latter forty miles from Mantes, until relieved by elements of the XIX Corps; the 5th Armored Division was then to return to Mantes-Gassicourt. A day later Patton limited Haislip and told him to deny the Germans the use of crossing sites as far north as Louviers until relieved by XIX Corps on his left. Haislip designated Louviers, thirty miles from Mantes, as the final objective, and Maj. Gen. Lunsford E. Oliver, the division commander, indicated intermediate objectives at Vernon and at the loop of the Seine near les Andelys, ten and twenty miles from Mantes, respectively.[55]

[52] MS # B–741 (Ziegelman); MS # B–680 (Hoecker); MS # B–727 (Gersdorff); *17th SS Engineer Battalion KTB;* LXXXI Corps KTB (17 Aug), and *Anlagen;* Msg, *17th Luftwaffen Feld Div* to *LXXXI Corps,* 2040, 19 Aug, *LXXXI Corps Tagesmeldungen;* Order of Battle Annex 2, *17 Luftwaffen Feld Div* (Air Force Field Division), 18 Aug, attached to XV Corps G–2 Per Rpt 16, 0300, 19 Aug. Principal German sources for this section are MS # B–034 (Schramm), MS # B–807 (Kuntzen), MS # B–445 (Krueger); see also 5th Armd Div G–2 Per Rpts, 20–25 Aug.
[53] Notes of Mtg, 0900, 20 Aug, XV Corps CofS Jnl and File.

[54] SHAEF G–3 Div Note on Assault Across the River Seine, 3 Jul, 12th AGp Mil Objs, 11.
[55] Patton to Haislip, 1830, 19 Aug, XV Corps G–3 Jnl and File; TUSA Dir, 20 Aug; XV Corps FO 6, 2230, 19 Aug; 5th Armd Div AAR, Aug; 21 AGp Dir, M–519, 20 Aug.

Almost immediately after leaving their positions about eight miles northwest of Mantes on 20 August, the 5th Armored Division ran into strong opposition from the kampfgruppe of panzer elements commanded successively by Wahl, Fick, and Col. Wilhelm Mohnke. The Germans fought skillfully, using to good advantage terrain features favorable for defense, numerous ravines and woods in particular. Fog and rain that continued for several days provided additional cover for German ambush parties using *Panzerfausts* and antitank grenades against American tanks. It took the armored division five days of hard fighting to advance about twenty miles and accomplish its mission.

At 0600, 24 August, XV Corps passed from the control of Third Army to that of First Army. On that day General Hodges informed General Haislip that, starting on the following morning, Second British Army elements (belonging largely to the 30 Corps) were to cross the American zone north of the Pacy-sur-Eure–Mantes-Gassicourt highway and close to the Seine. Haislip was to move the 5th Armored Division south of the British area by 0800, 25 August, leaving reconnaissance troops along the Seine until British relief.[56]

This order also affected the XIX Corps on the XV Corps left. The XIX Corps had assembled its three divisions in the Mortagne–Brezolles area and on 20 August attacked with two divisions abreast—the 2d Armored on the left to advance on the Verneuil–Elbeuf axis, the 30th on the right to attack through Nonan-

court to Autheuil on the Eure River. General Corlett echeloned the 28th Division to the left rear to protect the corps west flank.[57]

General Brooks's 2d Armored Division forced crossings over the Avre River, bypassed Verneuil, leaving its reduction to the 28th Division, and continued toward Breteuil. Despite rain, mud, and poor visibility, the armor continued to advance rapidly, bypassing Breteuil, leaving it also to the 28th, and rushed headlong through Conches and le Neubourg toward the Seine. Opposition from the *17th Luftwaffe Field Division* and the *344th* and *331st Divisions* just melted away. Small pockets of infantrymen were easily swept into prisoner of war cages, and jammed columns of motorized and horse-drawn vehicles were smashed, burned, or captured.[58] A counterattack launched by the *LXXXI Corps* with elements of the *1st SS, 2d SS, 2d,* and *116th Panzer Divisions* had little effect; German troops manifested a stronger inclination to get to the Seine ferries than to fight.

By 24 August 2d Armored Division spearheads were at the southern outskirts of Elbeuf. There they struck stubborn resistance.

From the beginning of the American attack west of the Seine on 20 August, Model and Dietrich had focused their attention on developments occurring on

---

[56] XV Corps and 5th Armd Div AAR's, Aug; XV Corps G–2 Per Rpt 20, 0200, 23 Aug; FUSA Ltr of Instr, 24 Aug.

[57] FUSA Ltrs of Instrs, Hodges to Gerow, 17 Aug (confirming verbal orders, 16 Aug), and Hodges to Corlett, 18 Aug; XIX Corps FO 16, 2030, 19 Aug; [Ferriss], Notes.

[58] Telecon, Gause and Schneider, 0430, 23 Aug, *LXXXI Corps KTB.* Pvt. Bennie F. Boatright of the Medical Detachment, 41st Armored Infantry, was killed as he courageously went to the aid of wounded soldiers. He was posthumously awarded the DSC.

the *Fifth Panzer Army* south flank. The relentless pressure exerted by the XIX and XV Corps during four days rolled up the panzer army left flank for almost half the length of the army front. Model's plan, outlined on 21 August, for an orderly retrograde movement in four successive phases, came to naught, and the units on the northern flank of the army, those facing the British, had to accelerate their withdrawal.

All desperate efforts to check the American advance by the weak remnants of panzer divisions, some of which had to be pulled from other parts of the front where they were also badly needed, were to no avail. On 24 August, when American spearheads were approaching Elbeuf, the German commanders foresaw the danger that the remainder of the army might be cut off from the Seine crossings. They therefore deployed the battered splinters of eight panzer divisions along the southern part of the front, between the Risle and Seine Rivers.[59]

This force, representing the concentration of armored units on the southern flank of the German bridgehead west of the Seine—with part under the *II SS Panzer Corps* and part under the *116th Panzer Division* (once again commanded by Schwerin)—had the mission of protecting the Seine crossings to Rouen. It defended Elbeuf, but not for long.

On 25 August CCA of the 2d Armored Division, reinforced by a combat team of General Cota's 28th Division, launched a co-ordinated attack on Elbeuf and entered the town. The troops secured Elbeuf on the following day, then turned it over to Canadians arriving from the west.[60]

Meanwhile, General Hobbs' 30th Division on the XIX Corps right had advanced against sporadic resistance and on 23 August, without opposition, occupied Evreux, bypassed by the 2d Armored Division. The 30th remained in its positions and in corps reserve on 24 August. On the following day, upon corps order, two regiments moved north to ground west and south of Louviers, thereby cutting the roads into town from the west. Patrols found Louviers abandoned by the Germans.[61]

While the XIX and XV Corps were clearing the Eure area from Mantes-Gassicourt to Elbeuf, British and Canadian troops were approaching the Seine from the west. The First Canadian Army had been attacking eastward since 16 August, when units crossed the Dives River in the coastal sector near Mézidon. British airborne troops under Canadian control broadened the offensive by attacking in the marshes near Cabourg. Progress against the German forces that had not been involved in the Argentan–Falaise action was slow, for the withdrawal by the German units outside the pocket was well planned and orderly, with demolitions, obstacles, and mines left in wake of the rear guards. The Canadian army did not reach and cross the Touques River until 22 August, when the 1st Belgian Infantry Brigade,

---

[60] ETHINT 18 (Schwerin); 2d Armd and 28th Div AAR's, Aug; see Charles Brisson, "La Libération d'Elbeuf et la Bataille dans la Vallée de la Seine," and André Bourlet, "Combats á Elbeuf," in Herval, *Bataille de Normandie*, II, 167–83 and 184–88.

[61] 30th Div AAR, Aug; [Ferriss], Notes; see J. L. Cailly, "Louviers Libéré," in Herval, *Bataille de Normandie*, II, 160–61.

---

[59] See *Fifth Pz Army KTB*, 24 Aug.

moving along the coast, arrived at Deauville. On that day Montgomery released the 2d Canadian Corps for an advance to the Seine. Two days later units breached the Touques defenses at Lisieux. Bypassing the city, the Canadians drove on toward Bernay to maintain contact as the German withdrawal to the Seine began to accelerate. On 26 August Canadian forces were at Bourgtheroulde, where they relieved the XIX U.S. Corps of responsibility for Elbeuf. On the following day other Canadian forces in the coastal sector, among them the Royal Netherlands (Princess Irene's) Brigade, approached the mouth of the Seine.

Meanwhile, the Second British Army was also moving east, on the route through Bernay toward les Andelys and Louviers and along the highway through Gacé and Laigle toward Mantes-Gassicourt and Vernon. Little opposed the advance, and British troops met American forces of the XIX Corps at the Risle River.[62]

During the last week of August the British and Canadians closed to the lower Seine from Vernon to the coast. In accordance with arrangements made on 24 August, Americans of the XIX and XV Corps withdrew along the west bank of the Seine south across the army group boundary. British and American columns alternately used crossroads and completed the transfer of territory with relative ease. The administrative head-

ache earlier envisioned never developed.[63]

While the Americans were turning over part of the Seine's west bank to the British and Canadians, the Germans were trying desperately to maintain a semblance of order in what remained of their contracting bridgehead west of the Seine. Between 20 and 24 August, the Germans got about 25,000 vehicles to the east bank. But pressed against the west bank, the German units were fast being compressed into the wooded peninsular pieces of land formed by the loops of the river north of Elbeuf and Bourgtheroulde. As Allied artillery fire fell into this area, destroying vehicles and personnel jammed at entrances to river crossings, the Germans fought to maintain defensive lines and keep their escape facilities operating.

With I SS Panzer Corps in command of the 49th Infantry and 18th Luftwaffe Field Divisions on the east bank of the Seine generally south of Louviers, Dietrich on 24 August proposed a reorganization of command for those forces still west of the river—the LXXXVI and LXXXI Corps were to assume control of all the infantry divisions, the II SS Panzer Corps of all the armored divisions. On the following day he put it into effect. He drew his corps boundaries so that the LXXXVI controlled the units on the Fifth Panzer Army right,

---

[62] Montgomery, *Normandy to the Baltic*, pp. 173, 176–77; Second Br Army Opns, 21 Jul–9 Sep, BAOR, 2 Nov 45, and Info furnished by 21 AGp to Hist Sec USFET, 9 Aug 45, ML–2251; Intentions Second British Army and First Canadian Army, 19, 20, 21, and 23 Aug, 12th AGp File 371.3 Mil Ops, Vol. I.

[63] FUSA Ltr of Instrs, Hodges to Haislip and Corlett, 24 Aug; XV Corps CofS Jnl and File, 23–26 Aug; First U.S. Army *Report of Operations*, I, 20; [Ferriss], Notes. Events during the month had moved so fast that defining the changing army group boundaries had proved to be a virtually impossible task until 21 August. See 21 AGp to SHAEF, 21 Aug, SHAEF File GCT 384–1/Ops (A), Boundaries of Armies and AGps.

the *LXXXI* those in the center, and the *I SS Panzer* (on the east bank) those on the left. The armored units under the *II SS Panzer Corps* and concentrated on the southern flank of the German bridgehead west of the Seine had no designated sector of their own. Though thousands of troops—estimated by the Second British Army between forty and fifty thousand—were still west of the Seine, the Germans were hoping to organize a coherent front on the east bank. There the *Fifth Panzer Army* would operate in a sector between the *Fifteenth Army* (in the coastal area south to Le Havre) and the *First Army* (covering Paris and the rest of the *Army Group B* front).[64]

Model on 25 August instructed Dietrich to withdraw the few units still west of the Risle River across the river that night, and all the forces in the Seine River bridgehead behind the Seine in one bound on the following night. Once across the Seine, the army was to organize and reinforce positions in such a manner as to assure successful defense of the river line. In addition, the remnants of the armored units were to be formed into two reserve groups—one to be located northeast of Rouen, the other near Beauvais. The *II Parachute Corps* headquarters was to move to Nancy for rehabilitation under control of the *First Parachute Army*. The *Seventh Army* was to move the remnants of eleven divisions unfit for combat—the *3d Parachute*, the *84th, 85th, 89th, 243d, 272d, 276th, 277th, 326th, 363d,* and *708th Infantry,* plus other splinter units—to the Somme River–St. Quentin area in the rear for

rehabilitation. In addition, all elements of these units that could be spared were to construct fortifications along the Somme.[65]

Thus, though the Germans were preparing to defend along the Seine, the plans seemed impossible of execution. According to one estimate—probably too low—of the battle strength of the *Fifth Panzer Army* on 25 August, 18,000 infantrymen, 314 artillery pieces, and 42 tanks and self-propelled guns were arrayed against the Allies who, in addition to their overwhelming superiority in the air, in ammunition, and in gasoline supplies, were estimated to have more than 100,000 infantry in line and 90,000 in immediate reserve, 1,300 artillery pieces deployed and 1,100 in reserve, 1,900 tanks in operation on the front and 2,000 more in reserve.[66] Holding at the Seine appeared a slim prospect. The Somme River line seemed to offer the only possible position for the next stand.

Before any stand could be made, the troops jammed against the west bank of the Seine had to be extricated and brought across the river. They were virtually trapped. Three days had been necessary in July and early August to move two divisions abreast westward across the Seine toward the front; it was therefore obvious that a crossing in reverse under the unfavorable conditions of late August would allow little more than personnel to get to the east bank. The approaches to the ferries were inadequate, and the remnants of the *Seventh Army* congested the approaches. By 25 August eighteen major ferries and several smaller ones were still operating

---

[64] *Fifth Pz Army KTB,* 24 and 25 Aug; Second Br Army Intel Summary 81, 2400, 24 Aug; see also *AGp B KTB,* 21 and 25 Aug.

[65] Model Order to Dietrich, 25 Aug, *AGp B KTB, Anlage 46.*

[66] *Fifth Pz Army KTB, Anlage 50.*

in the Rouen area; miscellaneous boats and rafts made hazardous trips; one small bridge to Rouen was still intact. These facilities were hardly adequate for the thousands of troops who in some instances fought among themselves for transportation across the river. Orderly movement was difficult if not impossible. Though it was generally agreed that tanks were to be saved first, SS formations often insisted that they had priority over all other units, and it was sometimes necessary for high-ranking commanders to resort to the use of force or at least the threat of force in order to carry out the semblance of an orderly procedure. Some "unpleasant scenes" took place at the Seine.[67]

Despite some disorder and panic, the Germans managed to get a surprisingly large number of troops to the east bank of the Seine, mostly on 26 and 27 August. To the Germans, it seemed that the British and Canadians did not push as hard as they might have. Neither did the Allied air forces seem as active as usual during the critical days of the withdrawal. The Seine ferries that remained in service operated even during daylight hours.[68]

This achievement was rather hollow. There was no longer any option of defending at the Seine or even hoping for an orderly withdrawal east of the river. The escaping units were weak and close to exhaustion.

[67] *LXXXI Corps KTB, Anlagen, Karen;* Telecon, Blumentritt, Speidel, Jodl, 1045, 25 Aug, *AGp B KTB;* MS # B–758 (Kuntzen) and MS # B–807 (Kuntzen); Montgomery, *Normandy to the Baltic,* p. 176; Second Br Army Intel Summary 81, 2400, 24 Aug; *AGp B KTB,* 21 and 25 Aug.

[68] *OB WEST, a Study in Command,* p. 162; see Leigh-Mallory, "Despatch," Fourth Supplement to the *London Gazette* of December 31, 1946, p. 67, for an opposite point of view.

In contrast, the Allies, having closed to the lower Seine north of Paris and being in possession of a bridgehead held by the 79th Division, were ready to undertake post-OVERLORD operations east of the Seine.

Through the Paris–Orléans Gap

A day after operations along the lower Seine had started, those directed toward the upper Seine south of Paris began. On 21 August the XX Corps attacked eastward from Dreux and Chartres, the XII Corps from Châteaudun and Orléans. The objective of the two corps, moving abreast, was the Paris–Orléans gap—the Seine River line south of Paris.[69]

Confronting the two corps was the German *First Army,* commanded now by General de Panzertruppen Otto von Knobelsdorff, who was trying to gather forces to defend the upper Seine and a line southward through Nemours, Montargis, Gien, and Orléans. His immediate task was to delay the Americans by blocking the main roads until new divisions promised for the Western Front could be brought up to defend the line of the Seine. The only delaying forces available were security troops, local garrisons, antiaircraft detachments, and stragglers from scattered units, all with hopelessly inadequate equipment.

Those portions of the *48th* and *338th Divisions* that had met the Americans at Chartres fell back to the Seine to join other newly arriving and as yet uncommitted portions that gathered at Melun, Fontainebleau, and Montereau. These were far from impressive forces—the *48th*

[69] 12th AGp Memo for Rcd, 19 Aug, including additional notes of conf, Bradley and Patton, 1730, 19 Aug, ML–205; TUSA Dir, 20 Aug.

was without combat experience, inadequately trained, and deficient in equipment; the *338th* lacked organic transportation and became partially mobile only after commandeering French vehicles. At Montargis, which Hitler had ordered strongly defended, were assembled the erstwhile defenders of Orléans—fragments of the *708th Division* and the usual quota of security troops and supply personnel. The *348th Division* and the *18th Luftwaffe Field Division* were on the way from northern France to the *First Army* but were diverted later toward the Seine north of Paris.[70]

On the American side, General Eddy, former commander of the 9th Division, took General Cook's place in command of XII Corps and was given the mission of driving to the Yonne River at Sens, seventy miles east of Orléans.[71] After attaching the 137th Infantry, 35th Division, to the 4th Armored Division, General Eddy on 20 August ordered General Wood to attack. CCA (with a battalion of attached infantry) pushed off in a drive that gathered speed as it progressed. Though the tankers found Montargis defended and the bridge over the Loing River at the town destroyed, reconnaissance troops located a damaged but usable bridge at Souppes-sur-Loing, fifteen miles north of Montargis. Ignoring Montargis, CCA dashed to Souppes-sur-Loing on 21 August, crossed the river, and, against occasional small arms

fire, raced to Sens. Spearheads entered the city that afternoon and took the German garrison so by surprise that some officers were strolling in the streets in dress uniform—tourists who had missed the last truck home. Having captured the city, CCA established a bridgehead on the east bank of the Yonne by the morning of 22 August.

To eliminate those Germans concentrated at Montargis, the 35th Division pushed to the western outskirts of the city while CCB of the 4th Armored, which had also crossed the Loing River at Souppes, turned south to outflank the defenses. A co-ordinated attack crushed the resistance and liberated the town on 24 August. After clearing Montargis, armor and infantry proceeded to sweep the area eastward to Sens.

From Sens, CCA of the 4th Armored Division drove forty miles to the outskirts of Troyes on the morning of 25 August. There the bulk of the command launched a frontal attack in desert-spread formation. With tanks approximately a hundred yards apart and tankers firing their weapons continuously, the troops charged across three miles of open ground sloping down toward the city. Inside Troyes, the Germans fought back. Though street fighting continued through the night, the Americans were in possession of the greater part of the city by nightfall. That evening a column crossed the Seine a few miles north of the city. Not until the following morning, when this column drove into the rear of the German garrison, did the battle come to an end.[72]

---

[70] MS # B–003 (Hoehne); MS # B–728 (Emmerich); MS # B–732 (Hold); *First Army* FO 2, 16 Aug, translated and reproduced in Annex 1 to TUSA G–2 Per Rpt 69, 19 Aug. MS # P–166 (Casper) is the principal German source.

[71] The following account is taken from the XII Corps, 4th Armd Div, and 35th Div AAR's, Aug; CI 354.

[72] Col. Bruce C. Clarke, the CCA commander, and Maj. Arthur L. West, Jr., who led the armored attack, were awarded the DSC.

FERRYING JEEPS ACROSS THE SEINE IN THE EARLY MORNING FOG

Meanwhile, the 35th Division pushed through Joigny to St. Florentin, thereby protecting the corps right flank east of Orléans.

Armor and infantry had worked together smoothly. Crossing their columns west of Montargis, the divisions had performed a difficult maneuver efficiently. Casualties were extremely light, prisoners numerous.

While advancing to the Seine, Eddy had also protected the army group south flank. Patton had relieved him of guarding the Loire River west of Orléans by assigning that task to the VIII Corps. East of Orléans, part of the 35th Division, CCR of the 4th Armored, and cavalry troops patrolled a line from Orléans through Gien to Joigny until the 319th Infantry of the 80th Division

moved from Angers to relieve them.[73] The other regiments of the 80th Division (attached to the XII Corps) marched from Argentan to assemble near Orléans.

On the left of XII Corps, when General Walker received word to take XX Corps eastward and secure Seine River bridgeheads between Melun and Montereau, reconnaissance patrols of the 7th Armored Division had already moved to Rambouillet and the Seine River. The virtual absence of enemy forces convinced American commanders that little would oppose the advance.[74]

---

[73] Msg, Middleton to Patton, 19 Aug, VIII Corps G–3 Jnl and File.

[74] The following is taken from the 5th Div AAR, Aug; Irwin Diary; *XX Corps*, pp. 84–89; *Fifth Infantry Division in the ETO*.

In driving from Chartres to Fontainebleau and Montereau (fifteen miles
apart), General Irwin's 5th Division
would cross a wide plateau cut by narrow
valleys and two rivers, the Essonne and
the Loing, which afforded the Germans
outpost positions for Seine River defenses. With Fontainebleau as the primary objective, Irwin committed two
regiments abreast on 21 August. The
10th Infantry, on the right, moved to
Malesherbes, reduced unexpectedly
heavy local opposition, crossed the
Essonne River on two bridges still intact, and continued three miles before
stopping for the night. The 2d Infantry, on the left, met a strong garrison at
Etampes. Unable to reduce the resistance, the regiment encircled the town,
isolated the garrison, and set about in-
vesting the town systematically. Unwilling to be delayed, General Irwin
committed his reserve, the 11th Infantry,
in the center. The 11th skirted
Etampes on the south and crossed the
Essonne River, which proved to be no
major obstacle. The 5th Division thus
had advanced about forty miles during
the day and still had two regiments
abreast for a final thrust to the objectives.

On 22 August the 10th Infantry encountered increasing resistance while
attacking from Malesherbes toward la
Chapelle, which fell that evening.
There, the regiment was in position
either to reinforce the attack on Fontainebleau or to continue to Montereau.
For a while it appeared that reinforcement of the 11th Infantry drive toward
Fontainebleau would be necessary, for
that regiment had advanced barely five
miles on 22 August before running into
a counterattack. Early the next morn-

ing, 23 August, the resistance faded, enabling the 11th Infantry to move the
twelve miles to Fontainebleau before
noon.

At the Seine, Lt. Col. Kelley B. Lemmon, Jr., a battalion commander, discovered the bridge destroyed. He swam
the river, found five small boats on the
east bank, tied them together, and
paddled them back for the troops to use
to establish a bridgehead. Meanwhile,
Capt. Jack S. Gerrie, a company commander, and T. Sgt. Dupe A. Willingham, a platoon sergeant, had found a
canoe, and they paddled across the Seine
to reconnoiter the east bank. Detected
by Germans, Gerrie covered Willingham
while the sergeant swam back to organize a firing line on the west bank.
Under cover of this fire, Gerrie also
swam back.[75]

After a short fire fight with elements
of the *48th Division,* riflemen began to
cross the Seine in random boats found
along the bank. By the following day,
24 August, a battalion had paddled
across, engineers had installed a treadway bridge, and the entire 11th Infantry
was east of the Seine River.

When it had become apparent on 23
August that the defenders of Fontainebleau were about to melt away, Irwin
had sent the 10th Infantry on to Montereau. Men of the 10th forded the
Loing River not far from its juncture
with the Seine, and vehicles crossed at
Nemours, already liberated by the FFI.
On 24 August, the regiment cleared
Montereau. That evening, after engineers brought assault boats to the
river, the infantrymen established a

---

[75] All three received the DSC.

ADVANCING UNDER FIRE TOWARD FONTAINEBLEAU

bridgehead on the east bank of the Seine. In the face of a feeble counterattack by the *48th Division* on the following morning, the entire 10th Infantry crossed the river.[76]

The 2d Infantry, meanwhile, had taken Etampes on 22 August. When it was clear that these troops would not be needed to reinforce the other regiments, they crossed the Yonne River between Montereau and Sens.

The 5th Division had moved rapidly and aggressively almost seventy miles to Montereau and almost sixty miles to Fontainebleau. The attack displayed good command judgment and flexibility of maneuver.

On the left at Dreux, General Silvester's 7th Armored Division had received the mission of driving to Melun and crossing the Seine there, ten miles north of Fontainebleau and twenty-five miles south of Paris.[77] Straddling the Seine at the apex of a long, V-shaped bend, the town of Melun is divided by the river into three parts. The principal portion is on the right (east) bank; the modern part is on the left; the third section is on an island in the center of the river, the site of a Roman camp dating from the time of Caesar's Gallic

---

[76] Pvt. Harold A. Garman of the 5th Medical Battalion was later awarded the Medal of Honor for having, under fire, rescued from drowning wounded men being evacuated across the river.

[77] The following is taken from the XX Corps and 7th Armd Div AAR's, Aug; CI 285, GL–165; *XX Corps*, pp. 84–89; and personal papers of General Silvester.

wars. A highway bridge, still intact, joined the three parts of town.

The problem of taking Melun was not simple since the Seine is 250 to 300 feet wide there. Twisting and turning between steep banks, it presents a serious natural obstacle. The *48th Division* occupied a defensive sector fifty miles long between Montereau and Corbeil; at Melun and in possession of dominating ground along the right bank of the Seine was a reinforced infantry regiment.

General Silvester suspected that Melun would be strongly held and doubted that the Germans would permit the bridge across the Seine there to remain intact for long. Charged still with maintaining security at Dreux and mindful of the proximity of Paris, he retained CCB at Dreux. He sent CCR on 21 August directly to Melun to seize the bridge and take the town by frontal assault if possible, to perform a holding mission if not. At the same time, he dispatched CCA in the main effort to cross the river several miles north of Melun and threaten the town from the rear.

CCA on the left and CCR on the right gained thirty miles on 21 August despite rather difficult terrain—steep hills and narrow valleys, thick woods (including the great forest of Rambouillet), and innumerable villages that afforded the enemy excellent opportunities for roadblocks, mine fields, and ambush. On 22 August, though artillery fire near Arpajon delayed CCA, CCR reached the railway embankment on the outskirts of Melun. The bridge across the Seine was still standing and in good condition.

Hoping to take the enemy by surprise, General Silvester ordered CCR to attack at once without an artillery preparation. When the combat command did so, Ger-

man artillery, automatic weapons, and small arms fire soon halted the attack. Another assault the same evening, this time after an air attack and a twenty-minute preparation by three battalions of artillery, was also unsuccessful. The troops then took defiladed positions and prepared to make a third attack on the following day.

Before the combat command could attack on the morning of 23 August, the Germans destroyed the bridge. Recognizing that CCR, which lacked assault boats, could then perform only a diversionary and holding action at Melun, General Silvester canceled the attack the combat command had scheduled, then turned his attention to CCA, held up near Arpajon.

Prodded forward on 23 August, CCA late that afternoon reached the Seine near the village of Ponthierry, about seven miles downstream from Melun. Since the bridge at Ponthierry was destroyed, armored infantrymen crossed the river in assault boats several hundred yards to the north at the hamlet of Tilly and established a slender bridgehead that evening. Division engineers worked through the night to bridge the river.

Meanwhile, the corps commander, General Walker, had appeared at the CCR command post near Melun late on the morning of 23 August. Dissatisfied with what he considered the idleness of CCR, he ordered an immediate attack. That afternoon armored infantrymen of CCR advanced to the river. Enough of the bridge structure remained to give foot soldiers passage to the island in the middle of the stream. While Walker virtually took control of the local operation, an infantry company scrambled across the wreckage of the bridge and secured the island.[78] The only result of this success was the liberation from a prison on the island of several hundred French felons who fled to the west bank, where civil affairs personnel, military police, and civilian authorities took them into custody. Heavy fire from the east bank of the Seine inflicted numerous casualties on CCR units. The action appeared stalemated.

Downstream at Tilly, however, engineers completed a treadway bridge on the morning of 24 August, and tankers and artillerymen of CCA crossed at once to reinforce the bridgehead and establish blocking positions to the north and east.

---

[78] General Walker received the DSC, as did his aide-de-camp, 1st Lt. David W. Allard, who swam across the Seine River under enemy fire to get information for the corps commander.

Immediately behind came CCB, relieved of its duty at Dreux. Across the river and on the east bank, CCB turned south and drove toward Melun. Hasty mine fields and small roadblocks slowed the advance, but early on 25 August armored columns of CCB entered Melun from the northeast and dispersed the defenders.

As the result of the action by the XII and XX Corps between 20 and 25 August, the Third Army had four bridgeheads across the upper Seine River south of Paris between Melun and Troyes. North of Paris along the lower Seine, the First Army had another bridgehead at Mantes Gassicourt. And on 25 August, in the most dramatic act of liberation to take place in France, the Allies were securing still another bridgehead across the Seine at Paris.

CHAPTER XXIX

The Liberation of Paris

Allied Plans

As American troops neared Paris, soldiers recalled the "fanciful tales of their fathers in the AEF" and began to dream of entering the city themselves.[1] Despite their hopes, despite the political, psychological, and military significance of the city, and even though any one of three corps had been capable of liberating Paris since mid-August, the Allied command had long before decided to defer liberation on the basis of tactics, logistics, and politics.

Before the cross-Channel attack, Allied planners had thought it likely that the Germans would hold on firmly to Paris. With two potential switch lines in the Marne and Oise Rivers, the Germans would possess not only favorable defensive positions but also a most suitable base for a counteroffensive. To attack Paris directly would therefore probably involve the Allies in prolonged street fighting, undesirable both because of the delay imposed on operations toward Germany and because of the possibility of destroying the French capital. Yet the Allies would need to reduce the German defenses at Paris before they could initiate action beyond the Seine River. The best way to take the capital, the planners indicated, would be to by-pass and encircle it, then await the inevitable capitulation of the isolated garrison.[2]

Staff officers responsible for supply favored this course. Because the Combined Chiefs of Staff had advised the Supreme Commander that he was to distribute relief supplies to liberated areas if he could do so "without hindrance . . . to the logistical administrative support required to sustain the forces allocated . . . for the defeat of Germany," the logisticians saw Paris in terms of a liability. The Allied civil affairs commitment there could not help but drain supplies from the combat units and adversely affect military operations.[3]

The civil affairs commitment seemed particularly large in August because Allied bombing and French sabotage directed against German transport had virtually isolated the capital from the provinces. A famine of food, coal, gas, and electricity threatened the city. Planners estimated that four thousand tons of supplies per day would be required, which, if converted to gasoline

---

[1] Bradley, *Soldier's Story,* p 384.

[2] PS SHAEF (44) 11 (Final), SHAEF Plng Staff, Post-NEPTUNE, Courses of Action After Capture of the Lodgment Area, Sec. II: Method of Conducting the Campaign, 30 May, SGS SHAEF File 381, Post-OVERLORD Plng.

[3] CCS to Eisenhower, W–42278, 27 May, SGS SHAEF File 014.1, Civil Affairs in Northwest Europe, I; PS SHAEF (44) 11 (Second Preliminary Draft), Post-NEPTUNE Opns, 22 Jul, SHAEF File 18008, Post-OVERLORD Plng, G–3 Plans.

for the combat troops, was "enough for a three days' motor march toward the German border." In view of the disintegration of the German forces in Normandy, which invited immediate Allied pursuit operations toward Germany, the necessity of diverting troops and supplies to Paris on humanitarian grounds, though difficult to reject, seemed unwarranted, particularly since the military supply lines were already strained and since continued military pressure east of Paris might bring the war to a quick end. The Allies felt that the Germans in Paris could only delay the Allied advance, and because the Allies would soon have other crossing sites over the Seine, an unnecessary challenge might provoke the Germans into destroying the city.[4]

The political factor working against immediate liberation stemmed from the aspirations of General Charles de Gaulle, chief of the Free French movement. Though Marshal Henri Pétain headed the government in France, de Gaulle several days before the invasion had proclaimed his own National Committee of Liberation the provisional government of the French Republic. By making possible de Gaulle's entry into Paris and thus unavoidably intervening in the internal affairs of France, General Eisenhower "foresaw possible embarrassment."

The result might be the imposition of a government on France that the French people might not want.[5]

These logistical and political factors played a part in the Allied decision to postpone the liberation, despite recognition that "Paris will be tempting bait, and for political and morale reasons strong pressure will doubtless be exerted to capture it early."[6] The circumstances were such as to give full play to the desire to spare Paris and its two million inhabitants devastation and injury. Ever since the preliminary phases of Operation OVERLORD when Allied planes had attempted to destroy the German communications network in France, pilots had attacked railroad marshaling yards outside Paris rather than terminals inside the city, and in August the same motivation applied in the decision to swing ground troops around the capital rather than through it.

German Hopes

The German high command had long had "grave worries" that loss of Paris to the Allies would publicize the extent of the German reverses. Because of this and because of Hitler's tactical plans, the Germans decided at the beginning of August to hold the French capital.[7]

At the same time that Hitler had conceived the Mortain counterattack, he had had to consider seriously the possible eventuality of withdrawing his forces from Normandy, perhaps from

---

[4] Msg, Eisenhower to Koenig, SGS SHAEF War Diary, 5 Aug; Adrien Dansette, *L'Histoire de la Libération de Paris* (Paris, c. 1946) (hereafter cited as Dansette, *Libération de Paris*), pp. 70–78. Dansette is a basic source for this chapter. Eisenhower, *Crusade in Europe*, p. 296; Bradley, *Soldier's Story*, pp. 384–87; 21 AGp Gen Operational Situation and Dir, M–519, 20 Aug; Montgomery, *Normandy to the Baltic*, p. 176; PS SHAEF (44) 11, Post-NEPTUNE Opns (First Draft), 12 Aug, Final, 17 Aug, SHAEF File 18008, G–3 Plans.

[5] Pogue, *Supreme Command*, p. 241, and Ltr, Pogue to author, 28 Nov 54, OCMH Files.

[6] PS SHAEF (44) 11 (Second Preliminary Draft), Post-NEPTUNE Opns, 22 Jul, SHAEF File 18008, Post-OVERLORD Plng, G–3 Plans.

[7] *OB WEST, a Study in Command* (pp. 136, 138, 142ff., and 155) is a useful source.

France. To cover the withdrawal, OKW on 2 August ordered General der Flieger Karl Kitzinger, Military Governor of France, to construct and organize defensive positions along the line of the Somme, Marne, and Saône Rivers, to which the forces then in Normandy would retire. To insure a successful withdrawal to the Seine and Marne, Hitler directed OKH to establish a special command at Paris under *Army Group B*, and on 7 August he appointed Choltitz, former commander of the *LXXXIV Corps* in the Cotentin, Commanding General and Military Commander of Greater Paris.[8]

Choltitz's mission at first was to make Paris "the terror of all who are not honest helpers and servants of the front." [9] He was to inactivate or evacuate all superfluous military services in Paris, dispatch all rear-area personnel able to bear arms to front-line units, restore discipline among troops accustomed to easy living, and maintain order among the civilian population. Several days later Choltitz received the prerogatives of a fortress commander—unqualified command of the troops of all services in the area and full authority over the civilian inhabitants. Paris was to be defended to the last man. All the seventy-odd bridges within the city limits were to be prepared for demolition. The troops were to battle outside the city as well as inside in order to block the Allies at the Seine.[10]

Choltitz's predecessor in Paris, Generalleutnant Hans Freiherr von Boineburg-Lengsfeld, whose mission had been merely to maintain "peace and order," had on his own initiative constructed an "obstacle line" west and southwest of Paris, which he felt could be defended successfully with the troops at his disposal. He believed that fighting inside Paris would be an act of complete irresponsibility because of the almost certain destruction of irreplaceable art treasures. He judged that his forces—twenty-five to thirty thousand men of the *325th Security Division,* armed with light infantry weapons for guard duty—would be able to delay the Allies outside the city and west of the Seine. Just before Choltitz' arrival, antiaircraft and security elements occupied these positions to block the main highway approaches to the capital.[11]

The forces west and southwest of Paris soon grew in strength in response to Hitler's desire for additional antitank weapons west of the Seine. Antitank companies from units in the *Army Group G* sector and from the *6th Parachute* and *48th* and *338th Infantry Divisions* (all of which were soon to become at least partially involved in the defense of Paris) were to move to the Paris–Orléans gap, screen the capital, and knock out American reconnaissance columns and armored spearheads that were moving eastward from le Mans. Col. Hermann Oehmichen, an antitank expert, arrived from Germany to teach local units the technique of antitank

---

[8] MS # B–034 (Schramm) and Choltitz, *Soldat unter Soldaten,* pp. 219–73, are basic sources; see also MS # A–967 (Boineburg-Lengsfeld), MS # B–611 (Hesse), and MS # B–741 (Ziegelmann).

[9] Msg, Hitler to Choltitz, *OB WEST KTB, Anlage 1219; OB WEST KTB,* 8 Aug.

[10] *OB WEST KTB,* 11 Aug; MS # B–732 (Hold); MS # B–728 (Emmerich); Interrogation of Col

Paul Krause, Mil Comdr East Paris, FUSA PWI Rpt 12, 29 Aug (hereafter cited as Krause Interrogation), FUSA (Tactical Echelon) G–3 File.

[11] MS # B–015 (Boineburg); *OB WEST KTB,* 8 Aug.

protection. With him he brought a cadre of instructors trained in antitank defense and demolition, a reconnaissance battalion, a column of light trucks, and a supply of *Panzerfaeuste*. Although Oehmichen's program was not completed in time to halt the American drive toward the Paris–Orléans gap, some of his antitank elements reinforced the Paris defenses.[12]

By 16 August the defenses west of Paris included twenty batteries of 88-mm. antiaircraft guns, security troops of the *325th Division*, provisional units consisting of surplus personnel from all branches of the Wehrmacht, and stragglers from Normandy. The remnants of the *352d Division* were soon to join them. These troops, all together numbering about 20,000 men, were neither of high quality nor well balanced for combat. Upon the approach of American forces, Choltitz recommended that Lt. Col. Hubertus von Aulock (brother of the St. Malo defender) be placed in command of the perimeter defense west and southwest of Paris. Kluge, still in command of *OB WEST* and *Army Group B*, promoted Aulock to the rank of major general, gave him authority, under Choltitz, to reorganize the defenses, and assigned him Oehmichen to co-ordinate the antitank measures. Choltitz, with about 5,000 men and 50 pieces of light and medium artillery inside Paris and about 60 planes based at le Bourget, remained the fortress commander under the nominal control of the *First Army*.[13]

When Kluge visited Choltitz around 15 August, the two officers agreed that the capital could not be defended for any length of time with the forces available. In addition, should the city be besieged, the supply problem would be insurmountable. Thus, house-to-house fighting, even assuming the then questionable presence of adequate troops, would serve no useful purpose. Destroying the bridges as ordered, even if sufficient explosives were on hand, was against the best German interest because the Germans could cross the Seine by bridge only at Paris. The better course of action was to defend the outer ring of Paris and block the great arterial highways with obstacles and antitank weapons.

Jodl probably informed Hitler of at least some of this discussion, for on 19 August Hitler agreed that destruction of the Paris bridges would be an error and ordered additional *Flak* units moved to the French capital to protect them. Impressed with the need to retain the city in order to guarantee contact between the *Fifth Panzer* and *First Armies*, Hitler also instructed Jodl to inform the troops that it was mandatory to stop the Allies west and southwest of Paris.[14]

Since the Americans had of their own accord stopped short of the gates of Paris, the defenders outside the city improved their positions and waited. Inside the

---

[12] *OB WEST KTB, Anlagen 1241, 1298 (OB WEST* Msg, 2115, 11 Aug), *1322 (OB WEST* Msg, 1140, 12 Aug), and *1323 (OB WEST* ltr, 12 Aug); Hitler Order, *WFSt/Op. Nr. 772830/44, g.Kdos., Chefs,* 11 Aug, quoted in Msg, *AGp B* to the armies, 0030, 12 Aug, *AGp B Fuehrer Befehle.*

[13] Danke Telecon, 1400, 16 Aug, *OB WEST KTB;* Msg, *OB WEST* to OKW, roem Ia Nr. 6946/44 gen.Kdos., 0400, 17 Aug, *OB WEST KTB, Anlage 1483;* MS # B–732 (Hold); MS # B–728 (Emmerich); Kluge Msg, 1230, 17 Aug, and Speidel Msg, 1945, 18 Aug, *AGp B Op. Befehle,* folios 321 and 336; *OB WEST KTB, Anlage 1628.*

[14] MS # B–034 (Schramm).

capital the garrison had a sufficient number of tanks and machine guns to command the respect of the civil populace and thereby insure the security of German communications and the rear.[15]

French Aims

Though the liberation of Paris was not an immediate major military goal to the Allies, to Frenchmen it meant the liberation of France. More than the spiritual capital, Paris was the only place from which the country could be effectively governed. It was the hub of national administration and politics and the center of the railway system, the communication lines, and the highways. Control of the city was particularly important in August 1944, because Paris was the prize of an intramural contest for power within the French Resistance movement.

The fundamental aim of the Resistance—to rid France of the Germans—cemented together men of conflicting philosophies and interests but did not entirely hide the cleavage between the patriots within occupied France and those outside the country—groups in mutual contact only by secret radios and underground messengers.[16] Outside France the Resistance had developed a politically homogeneous character under de Gaulle, who had established a political headquarters in Algiers and a military staff in London, and had proclaimed just before the cross-Channel attack that he headed a provisional government. Inside France, although it was freely acknowledged that de Gaulle had symbolically inspired anti-German resistance, heterogeneous groups had formed spontaneously into small, autonomous organizations existing in a precarious and clandestine status.[17] In 1943 political supporters of de Gaulle inside and outside France were instrumental in creating a supreme co-ordinating Resistance agency within the country that, while not eradicating factionalism, had the effect of providing a common direction to Resistance activity and increasing de Gaulle's strength and authority in Allied eyes.

Although political lines were not yet sharply drawn, a large, vociferous, and increasingly influential contingent of the left contested de Gaulle's leadership inside France. This group clamored for arms, ammunition, and military supplies, the more to harass the Germans. Some few in 1943 hoped in this small way to create the second front demanded by the Soviet Union. The de Gaullists outside the country were not anxious to have large amounts of military stores parachuted into France, and the matériel supplied was dropped in rural areas rather than near urban centers, not only to escape German detection but also to inhibit the development of a strong left-wing opposition.[18]

Early in 1944 the de Gaullists suc-

---

[15] See XII Corps G–2 Per Rpt, 19 Aug, XII Corps AAR, Aug.

[16] The following account is from Dansette, *Libération de Paris*, and Participation of the French Forces of the Interior in the Liberation of France, a MS prepared by French Resistance Unit, ETOUSA Hist Sec, 1944 and 1945, OCMH Files, Pt II, Ch. II, Sec. 6, The Liberation of Paris (hereafter cited as Resistance Unit, Liberation of Paris).

[17] See App. A to Annex Rpt, French Resistance. 19 Apr, JIC Papers, Pogue Files.

[18] See studies, Ltrs, and Msgs in SGS SHAEF File 373/2, Employment of Airborne Forces in Opn OVERLOOK, particularly those dated 21 and 23 Jun, 15 and 23 Jul, and 2 Aug.

ceeded in establishing the entire Resistance movement as the handmaiden of
the Allied liberating armies. The
Resistance groups inside France became
an adjunct of OVERLORD. French Resistance members, instead of launching independent operations against the Germans, were primarily to furnish information and render assistance to the Allied
military forces. To co-ordinate this
activity with the Allied operations, a
military organization of Resistance members was formed shortly before the cross-
Channel attack: the French Forces of the
Interior. SHAEF formally recognized
the FFI as a regular armed force and
accepted the organization as a component
of the OVERLORD forces. General
Koenig (whose headquarters was in
London), the military chief of the Free
French armed forces already under
SHAEF, became the FFI commander.
When the Allies landed on French soil,
the FFI (except those units engaged in
operations not directly connected with
the OVERLORD front—primarily those in
the south, which were oriented toward
the forthcoming ANVIL landing on the
Mediterranean coast) came under the
command of SHAEF and thus under de
Gaulle's control.[19]

News in July of unrest in Paris and
intimations that there was agitation for
an unaided liberation of the city by the
Resistance led General Koenig to order

immediate cessation of activities that
might cause social and political convul-
sion.[20] Since Allied plans did not envision the immediate liberation of the
capital, a revolt might provoke bloody
suppression on the part of the Germans,
a successful insurrection might place de
Gaullist opponents in the seat of political power, civil disorder might burgeon
into full-scale revolution.

Despite Koenig's order, the decrease
in the German garrison in August, the
approach of American troops, and the
disintegration of the Pétain government
promoted an atmosphere charged with
patriotic excitement. By 18 August
more than half the railway workers were
on strike and virtually all the policemen
in the capital had disappeared from the
streets for the same reason. Public anti-
German demonstrations occurred frequently. Armed FFI members moved
through the streets quite openly.
Resistance posters appeared calling for a
general strike, for mobilization, for insurrection.

The German reaction to these mani-
festations of brewing revolt seemed so
feeble that on 19 August small local FFI
groups, without central direction or discipline, forcibly took possession of police
stations, town halls, national ministries,
newspaper buildings, and the seat of the
municipal government, the Hôtel de
Ville. The military component of the
French Resistance, the FFI, thus dis-
obeyed orders and directly challenged
Choltitz.

The Critical Days

The challenge, although serious, was
far from formidable. Perhaps 20,000

---

[19] SHAEF/17245/6.5/20ps (A), Operational Dir
to CG FFI, 15 Jun, SHAEF File G–5/702, Dirs,
France; Notes of Decisions Made at a Mtg Held at
SHAEF, 10 Jul; Min of Mtg, 14 Jul; Gen Eisen-
hower to Brig Gen William J. Donovan, FWD–
12464, 26 Jul; AFHQ, Comd and Operational
Employment of the FFI, 29 Jul; Etat Major des
Forces Françaises de l'Intérieur, Twelfth Monthly
Progress Rpt to SHAEF Aug 44, 10 Sep. Last five
in SGS SHAEF File 322, FFI. SGS SHAEF War
Diary, 15 Jul.

[20] Min of Mtg, 14 Jul, SGS SHAEF File 322, FFI.

men in the Paris area belonged to the FFI, but few actually had weapons since the Allies had parachuted only small quantities of military goods to them. While the Resistance had been able to carry on a somewhat systematic program of sabotage and harassment—destroying road signs, planting devices designed to puncture automobile tires, cutting communications lines, burning gasoline depots, and attacking isolated Germans—for the FFI to engage German armed forces in open warfare was quite another matter.[21]

The leaders of the Resistance in Paris, recognizing the havoc that German guns could bring to an overtly insubordinate civilian population and fearing widespread and bloody reprisals, sought to avert open hostilities. They were fortunate in securing the good offices of Mr. Raoul Nordling, the Swedish consul general, who volunteered to negotiate with Choltitz. Nordling had that very day succeeded in persuading Choltitz not to deport but to release from detention camps, hospitals, and prisons several thousand political prisoners. The agreement, which "represented the first capitulation of Germany," was a matter of considerable import that "was not lost either on the Resistance or on the people of Paris."[22] Having established a personal relationship with Choltitz that

promised to be valuable, Nordling was able to learn on the evening of 19 August that Choltitz was willing to discuss conditions of a truce with the Resistance. That night an armistice was arranged, at first to last only a few hours, later extended by mutual consent for an indefinite period.

Without even a date of expiration, the arrangement was nebulous. Choltitz agreed to treat Resistance members as soldiers and to regard certain parts of the city as Resistance territory. In return, he secured Resistance admission that certain sections of Paris were to be free for German use, for the unhampered passage of German troops. Yet no boundaries were drawn, and neither Germans nor French were certain of their respective sectors. Thus, an uneasy noninterference obtained.[23]

The advantages for both parties were clear. The French Resistance leaders were uncertain when Allied troops would arrive, anxious to prevent German repressive measures, aware of Resistance weakness to the extent of doubting their own ability to defend the public buildings seized, and finally hopeful of preserving the capital from physical damage.

For the Germans, the cessation of hostilities per se fulfilled Choltitz' mission of maintaining order within the capital and enabled him to attend to his primary mission of blocking the approaches to the city. Having known for a long time of the attempts to subordinate the Resistance to the Allied military command, the Germans guessed that sabotage directly unrelated to Allied military operations was "mainly the work

---

[21] See SHAEF/17245/6/5/2/Ops (A), Operational Dir to CG FFI, 15 Jun, SHAEF File G–5/702, Dirs, France.

[22] Resistance Unit, Liberation of Paris, p. 1244 (see pp. 1242–44, and Dansette, Libération de Paris, pp. 139–46 for detailed account) ; Ministerial Counselor Eckelmann's Rpt to OKW/Abwicklungsstab/Rudolfsstadt, 31 Jan 45, Rpt D–32 (hereafter cited as Eckelmann, Rpt to OKW), OCMH Files. Eckelmann assisted Choltitz in Paris, was taken prisoner during the liberation, and was apparently released and repatriated.

[23] Krause Interrogation.

of communist groups." [24]   It was therefore reasonable for Choltitz to assume that the disorder in Paris on 19 August, which had no apparent connection with developments on the front, was the work of a few extremists.   Since part of his mission was to keep order among the population and since the police were no longer performing their duties, Choltitz felt that the simplest way of restoring order was to halt the gunfire in the streets.   To prevent what might develop into indiscriminate rioting, he was willing to come to an informal truce, "an understanding," as he termed it." [25]

A more subtle reason also lay behind Choltitz' action.   Aware of the factionalism in the French Resistance movement, he tried to play one group off against the other to simplify his problem of control. [26]   Choltitz believed that since the insurrectionists directed their immediate efforts toward seizing government buildings and communications facilities, the insurrection was at least in part the opening of an undisguised struggle for political power within France.   The Pétain government no longer functioned in Paris (Pétainist officials with whom the Germans were accustomed to work no longer answered their telephones), and in this vacuum there was bound to be a struggle for power among the Resistance factions. "The Resistance had reason to fear," a German official wrote not long afterwards, "that the Communists would take possession of the city before the Americans arrived." [27]   By concluding a truce, Choltitz hoped to destroy the cement that held the various French groups together against their common enemy and thus leave them free to destroy themselves.

That Choltitz felt it necessary to use these means rather than force to suppress the insurrection indicated one of two things—either he was unwilling to endanger the lives of women and children or he no longer had the strength to cope with the Resistance.   He later admitted to both.   In any event, French underground activities had become so annoying that Choltitz' staff had planned a coordinated attack on widely dispersed Resistance headquarters for the very day the insurrection broke out, but Choltitz himself had suddenly prohibited the action.   Instead of resorting to force, he listened to representations in favor of peace from the neutral Swedish and Swiss consulates.   Meanwhile, should civil disturbance become worse, Choltitz gathered provisional units to augment his strength, securing, among other units, a tank company of *Panzer Lehr*. [28]

Choltitz apparently informed Model, the new chief of *OB WEST* and *Army Group B*, of his weakness, for when Hitler on 20 August advised Model that Paris was to become the bastion of the Seine–Yonne River line, Model replied that the plan was not feasible.   Although Model had arranged to move the *348th Division* to Paris, he did not think these troops could arrive quickly enough

[24] See Rundstedt's Est of the Situation, 25 Oct 43; *Der Oberbefehlshaber West, Ia Nr. 550/43 g.Kdos, Chefs, 28.10.43, Beurteilung der Lage Ob. West am 25.10.1943*, Sec. K, *Innere Lage*, in Bavarian State Archives, Munich, Germany.

[25] Choltitz, *Soldat unter Soldaten*, p. 252.

[26] Choltitz Rpt, cited in *OB WEST KTB*, 23 Aug, *Anlage 1646*.

[27] Eckelmann, Rpt to OKW.

[28] Krause Interrogation; Telecon, 1900, 20 Aug, *AGp B KTB*; Telecons, 21–24 Aug, *AGp B KTB*, particularly Blumentritt and Tempelhoff, 1745, 21 Aug; Choltitz, *Soldat unter Soldaten*, pp. 252–53.

to hold the city against the external Allied threat and the internal Resistance disturbance.   Apparently having misunderstood Hitler's desire, Model decided that the Seine was more important than Paris.   Since the Seine flows through the city, defending at the river would necessitate a main line of resistance inside the capital.   With the civil populace in a state of hardly disguised revolt, he did not believe Choltitz could keep civil order and at the same time defend against an Allied attack with the strength at hand.   Model therefore revealed to OKW that he had ordered an alternate line of defense to be reconnoitered north and east of Paris.[29]

Model's action seemed inexcusable since the order to create a fortress city implied that Paris was important enough in Hitler's judgment to warrant a defense to the last man.   Furthermore, Hitler had explicitly stated on 20 August, "If necessary, the fighting in and around Paris will be conducted without regard to the destruction of the city." Jodl therefore repeated Hitler's instructions and ordered Model to defend at Paris, not east of it, even if the defense brought devastation to the capital and its people.[30]

Hitler himself left no doubt as to his wishes when he issued his famous "field of ruins" order:

The defense of the Paris bridgehead is of decisive military and political importance. Its loss dislodges the entire coastal front north of the Seine and removes the base for the V-weapons attacks against England.

In history the loss of Paris always means the loss of France. Therefore the Fuehrer repeats his order to hold the defense zone in advance [west] of the city. . . .

Within the city every sign of incipient revolt must be countered by the sharpest means . . . [including] public execution of ringleaders. . . .

The Seine bridges will be prepared for demolition. Paris must not fall into the hands of the enemy except as a field of ruins.[31]

The French Point of View

Resistance leaders in Paris had meanwhile radioed the exterior Resistance for help, thereby alarming Frenchmen outside Paris by reports, perhaps exaggerated, of disorder in the city and by urgent pleas that military forces enter the capital at once.[32]   De Gaulle and his provisional government had long been worried that extremist agitation not only might bring violent German reaction but also might place unreliable Resistance elements in the capital in political power.   The parties of the left were particularly influential in the Paris Resistance movement, to the extent that the FFI commander of Paris belonged to one of them.   Conscious of the dictum that he who holds Paris holds France and sensitive to the tradition of Paris as a crucible of revolution, its population ever ready to respond to the

---

[29] Hitler Order, 20 Aug; Msg, *FHQu*, 20 Aug, *OKW/WFSt/Op. Nr. 772956/44*, in *OKW/175*; Msg, Model to Jodl, 1800, 21 Aug, *AGp B Fuehrerbefehle*; MS # B–034 (Schramm).

[30] Hitler Order, 20 Aug; *OB WEST* and *AGp B KTB's*, 21 Aug.

[31] Hitler Msg, quoted in full in Msg, *OB WEST* to *AGp B*, 1100, 23 Aug, *AGp B Fuehrerbefehle*. Choltitz *(Soldat unter Soldaten*, pp. 255–59) and Schramm (MS # B–034) date Hitler's order as 22 August, and it is possible that some commanders received the substance of the message before the official reception and recording of it. The *AGp B KTB* reports the order in an entry at 1030, 23 August.

[32] See Resistance Unit, Liberation of Paris, *passim* and annexes, for Resistance messages from Paris to the exterior.

cry *"Aux barricades!"* the French commanders within the OVERLORD framework advocated sending aid to Paris immediately.[33] Their argument was that if riot became revolution, Paris might become a needless battleground pulling Allied troops from other operations.

An immediate hope lay in parachuting arms and ammunition into the city. This would enable the FFI to resist more effectively and perhaps permit the Resistance to seize tactically important points that would facilitate Allied entry. Despite a natural reluctance to arm urban people and SHAEF's concern that the heavy antiaircraft defenses of Paris might make an air mission costly, an airdrop of military equipment was scheduled for 22 August. When a thick fog that day covered all British airfields, the drop was postponed. On the following day, when the British radio made a premature announcement that Paris had already been liberated, SHAEF canceled the operation.[34]

The decisive solution obviously lay in getting Allied troops into the capital, for which provision had been made in Allied plans as early as 1943. SHAEF had agreed to include a French division on the OVERLORD troop list "primarily so that there may be an important French formation present at the re-occupation of Paris."[35] The 2d French Armored Division had been selected. Just before the cross-Channel attack and again early in August, the French military chief, General Koenig, had reminded General Eisenhower of the Allied promise to use that unit to liberate Paris. Its entry into the capital would be a symbolic restoration of French pride as well as the preparation for de Gaulle's personal entry into Paris, symbolic climax of the French Resistance.[36] When the situation seemed propitious for these events to take place, General Leclerc's armored division was at Argentan, more than a hundred miles away, while American troops were less than twenty-five miles from the center of the capital. If the French could persuade General Eisenhower to liberate Paris at once, would he be able to honor his promise to employ Leclerc?

General Eisenhower had no intention of changing the plan to bypass Paris, as Generals de Gaulle and Koenig discovered when they conferred with him on 21 August, but he repeated his promise to use Leclerc's division at the liberation. Although the French had agreed to abide by General Eisenhower's decisions on the conduct of the war in return for Allied recognition of a *de facto* government headed by de Gaulle, General Alphonse Juin that same day, 21 August, carried a letter from de Gaulle to the Supreme Commander to threaten politely that if General Eisenhower did not send troops to Paris at once, de Gaulle might have to do so himself.[37] The threat was important, for de

---

[33] See Rousseau, *Bataille de Normandie,* pp. 204–05 for an account of French pressure on Eisenhower.

[34] Detailed accounts are found in Dansette, *Libération de Paris,* pp. 320–24, and in Resistance Unit, Liberation of Paris, pp. 1251, 1255.

[35] Ltr, Gen Morgan (Deputy Chief of Staff, SHAEF) to French Forces in London, 7 Mar, quoted in Resistance Unit, Liberation of Paris, p. 1236; Pogue, *Supreme Command,* p. 239; SH/3244/Sec, Employment of French Forces in Continental Opns, 19 Jan, one of many documents on this matter in SGS SHAEF File 381, French, I.

[36] Even, La 2e D.B., p. 114, n. 9.

[37] Ltr, de Gaulle to Eisenhower, 21 Aug, SGS SHAEF File 092, French Relations; Pogue, *Supreme Command,* p. 240; Interv by Pogue with de Gaulle, 14 Jan 47, and Butcher Diary, 11 Jul, Pogue Files.

Gaulle was the potential head of the French government and would theoretically stand above the Supreme Commander on the same level with President Roosevelt and Prime Minister Churchill.

Leclerc, who was conscious of the historic mission reserved for him, had long been impatient for orders to move to Paris. As early as 14 August, when he learned that Patton was sending part of the XV Corps (but not the 2d French Armored Division) eastward from Argentan, Leclerc had requested the corps commander to query the Third Army commander as to when the French division was to go to Paris. Leclerc's explanation—"It is political"—availed little, for the army chief of staff bluntly ordered that Leclerc was to remain where he was. Two days later Leclerc wrote Patton suggesting that since the situation at Argentan had become quiet, the 2d French Armored Division might commence to assemble for its projected march on Paris.[38] That evening he visited Patton's headquarters, where he saw Bradley as well as Patton, and gained cordial assurance from both that he would have the honor of liberating the capital. Patton laughingly turned to General Wood, who was also present and who had been pressing for permission to lead his 4th Armored Division to Paris. "You see, Wood," Patton supposedly said, "he [Leclerc] is a bigger pain in the neck than you are." [39] Patton nevertheless announced his intention of moving Leclerc to Dreux as soon as possible.[40]

Unfortunately for Leclerc's hopes, the last stage of operations to close the Argentan–Falaise pocket had started, and his armored division found itself again engaged, eventually under the control of the First U.S. Army and General Gerow's V Corps. Although Leclerc was not told, Bradley and Patton on 19 August agreed once more that only the French division would "be allowed to go into Paris," probably under First Army control.[41] Leclerc fretted and bombarded V Corps headquarters with requests premised on the expectation of a momentary call to Paris—for example, he attempted to secure the release of the French combat command attached to the 90th Division. For his part, General Gerow saw no reason to employ the French division any differently from his American units, for Paris was no specific concern of his.[42]

Invited by General Hodges to lunch on 20 August, Leclerc seized upon the occasion for "arguments, which he presented incessantly," that roads and traffic and plans notwithstanding, his division should run for Paris at once. He said he needed no maintenance, equipment, or personnel, but a few minutes later admitted that he needed all three. General Hodges "was not impressed with him or his arguments, and let him understand that he was to stay put" until he received orders to move.[43]

When British troops on 21 August moved across the V Corps front and V

---

[38] Telecon, Gaffey and Menoher, 1715, 14 Aug, and Ltr, Leclerc to Patton [16 Aug], XV Corps CofS Jnl and File.

[39] Quoted in Dansette, *Libération de Paris*, p. 310.

[40] Notes [16 or 17 Aug], XV Corps CofS Jnl and File.

[41] 12th AGp Memo for Rcd, 19 Aug, ML–205.

[42] Ltr, Leclerc to Gerow [20 Aug]; Msgs, Gerow to Leclerc, 2045, 20 Aug, 1400, 21 Aug; V Corps Dir, 21 Aug, and Ltrs of Instrs, 21 and 22 Aug. All in V Corps G–3 Jnl and File. Unless otherwise noted, documents hereafter cited in this chapter are in the V Corps G–3 Jnl and File.

[43] Sylvan Diary, 20 Aug.

Corps divisions began to withdraw to assembly areas south of Argentan, Leclerc saw no justification for remaining so far distant from his ultimate objective. "We shall not stop," he had said in 1941, "until the French flag flies over Strasbourg and Metz," and along the route to these capitals of Alsace and Lorraine, Paris was a holy place.[44] He persuaded himself that Gerow was sympathetic to his wishes, and though the corps commander was powerless to authorize Leclerc's march on Paris, Leclerc convinced himself that as the sole commander of French regular military forces in Operation OVERLORD, he was entitled to certain prerogatives involving national considerations.[45] Furthermore, since Koenig, who anticipated that the 2d Armored would liberate Paris sooner or later, had appointed Leclerc provisional military governor of the capital, Leclerc felt that this gave him authority to act.[46]

With at least an arguable basis for moving on Paris, Leclerc on the evening of 21 August (the same day that Eisenhower had rejected de Gaulle's request) dispatched a small force of about 150 men—ten light tanks, ten armored cars, ten personnel carriers—under a Major Guillebon toward the capital. Guillebon ostensibly was to reconnoiter routes to Paris, but should the Allies decide to enter the city without the 2d French Armored Division, Guillebon was to accompany the liberating troops as the representative of the provisional government and the French Army.[47] Writing to de Gaulle that evening, Leclerc explained, "Unfortunately, I cannot do the same thing for the bulk of my division because of matters of food and fuels" (furnished by the U.S. Army) and because of respect for the "rules of military subordination."[48]

Knowing that Guillebon could not reach Paris undetected, Leclerc sent his G–2, Maj. Philippe H. Repiton, to Gerow on the morning of 22 August to explain his act on the following basis: insurrection in the capital made it necessary for an advance military detachment to be there to maintain order until the arrival of regular French political authorities. Guillebon's absence, Leclerc pointed out, did not compromise the ability of the division to fulfill any combat mission assigned by the corps. Gerow, who was thoroughly a soldier and who had received a peremptory message from the Third Army asking what French troops were doing outside their sector, saw only Leclerc's breach of discipline. "I desire to make it clear to you," Gerow wrote Leclerc in a letter he handed personally to Repiton, "that the 2d Armored Division (French) is under my command for all purposes and no part of it will be employed by you except in the execution of missions assigned by this headquarters." He directed Leclerc to recall Guillebon.[49]

Unwilling to comply, Leclerc sought

[44] Quoted in Dansette, *Libération de Paris*, pp. 211–12.

[45] See Rousseau, *Bataille de Normandie*, pp. 204–05.

[46] Ltr, Koenig to Leclerc, # 2039, 11 Aug, cited in Even, La 2e D.B., p. 114, n. 9.

[47] Even, La 2e D.B., pp. 114–16; Etat Major des Forces Françaises de l'Interieur, Twelfth Monthly Progress Rpt to SHAEF Aug 44, 10 Sep 44, SGS SHAEF File 322, FFI.

[48] Quoted in Dansette, *Libération de Paris*, p. 313.

[49] Dir, Gerow to Leclerc, 22 Aug, with handwritten note; Even, La 2e D.B., p. 116; Dansette, *Libération de Paris*, p. 314; Ltr, Gerow to OCMH, 22 Sep 54.

higher authority by taking a plane to the First Army headquarters. There he learned that General Bradley was conferring with General Eisenhower on the question of Paris. Leclerc decided to await the outcome of the conference.

Eisenhower's Decision

Reflecting on Choltitz' behavior after the truce arrangement, Resistance members were somewhat puzzled. They began to interpret his amenity as a special kind of weakness, a weakness for the physical beauty as well as the historical and cultural importance of Paris. They figured that Choltitz was appalled by the destruction he had the power to unleash, and they wondered whether he worried that fate had apparently selected him to be known in history as the man who had ravaged the capital.[50] How else could one explain his feigned ignorance of the Resistance, his calling the insurrection only acts of violence committed by terrorists who had infiltrated into the city and who were attempting to incite a peaceful population to revolt, his pretense that he had no authority over French civilians (despite his plenary power from Hitler to administer Paris), his acceptance of Nordling's explanation that the Resistance members were not terrorists or ruffians but patriotic Frenchmen, and his willingness to agree to a truce? Either that or he felt that the German cause was hopeless. His offhand but perhaps studied remark to Nordling that he could of course not be expected to surrender to irregular troops

such as the FFI seemed a clear enough indication that to salve his honor and protect his family in Germany he had at least to make a pretense of fighting before capitulating to superior forces. He apparently would surrender to regular Allied troops after a show of arms.

To convince the Allied command of the need for regular forces in Paris at once while Choltitz vacillated between desire and duty, Resistance emissaries, official and unofficial, departed the city to seek Allied commanders.[51] Nordling's brother Rolf and several others in a small group reached the Allied lines on 23 August and made their way up the echelons to the Third Army headquarters. Patton, who was disappointed in being denied the liberation of Paris, was contemptuous of their efforts. Deciding that "they simply wanted to get a suspension of hostilities in order to save Paris, and probably save the Germans," he "sent them to General Bradley, who"—he imagined incorrectly—"arrested them." [52]

Nordling's group reached Bradley's command post too late to affect the course of events, but another envoy, Resistance Major Gaullois (pseudonym of a M. Cocteau), the chief of staff of the Paris FFI commander, had left Paris on 20 August and had reached Bradley's headquarters on the morning of 22 August.[53] He may have had some influence, for he spoke at some length with Brig. Gen. A. Franklin Kibler, the 12th Army Group G–3, who displayed interest in the information that Choltitz would surrender his entire garrison as soon as

---

[50] This is Dansette's thesis (see *Libération de Paris*, pp. 138–39, 293–94) ; see also Resistance Unit, Liberation of Paris.

[51] See, for example, V Corps G–2 Jnl, entries 2100, 20 Aug, and 2100, 1 Aug.

[52] Patton, *War as I Knew It*, pp. 115, 117.

[53] Bradley, *Solder's Story*, pp. 390–91, is in error because of an incorrect time sequence.

Allied troops took his headquarters—the Hôtel Meurice on the rue de Rivoli.[54]

It so happened that General Eisenhower had on the evening of 21 August (after his conference with de Gaulle) begun to reconsider his decision to delay the liberation of Paris. In this connection he requested Bradley to meet with him on the morning of 22 August. De Gaulle's letter, delivered by Juin, had had its effect, and Eisenhower had jotted down that he would probably "be compelled to go into Paris."[55] The Combined Chiefs of Staff had informed him on 16 August that they had no objection to de Gaulle's entry into the capital, certainly strong evidence of Allied intentions to recognize his government, and it was becoming increasingly clear that the majority of French people approved of de Gaulle and thereby reinforced his claim to legality.[56] Koenig's deputy, a British officer who reflected the British point of view of favoring (apparently more so than the United States) de Gaulle's political aspirations, also urged the immediate liberation of the capital.[57] Pressed on all sides, General Eisenhower set forth his dilemma in a letter to General Marshall:

Because of the additional supply commitment incurred in the occupation of Paris, it would be desirable, from that viewpoint, to defer the capture of the city until the important matter of destroying the remaining enemy forces up to include the Pas de Calais area. I do not believe this is possible. If the enemy tries to hold Paris with any real strength he would be a constant menace to our flank. If he largely concedes the place, it falls into our hands whether we like it or not.[58]

The dilemma had another aspect. If liberating Paris only fulfilled a political need, then the Supreme Commander's position of conducting operations on military grounds alone would not allow him in good conscience to change his mind—unless he turned Leclerc and the French loose to liberate the capital as they wished. If he could not approve such a politically motivated diversion of part of his forces, or if he felt he could not afford to lose control of the French division, he had to have a military basis for an Allied liberation. Yet how could he initiate action that might damage the city? The only solution seemed to be that if the Germans were ready to quit the city without giving battle, the Allies ought to enter—for the prestige involved, to maintain order in the capital, to satisfy French requests, and also to secure the important Seine crossing sites there.

Much indicated to General Eisenhower that the Germans were ready to abandon Paris. De Gaulle thought that a few cannon shots would disperse the Germans. Bradley had told Eisenhower that he, Bradley, agreed with his G–2, who thought "we can and must walk in." Bradley had even suggested, facetiously, that the large number of civilian newspapermen accredited to his headquarters comprised a force strong enough to take the city "any time you want to," and that

---

[54] Resistance Unit, Liberation of Paris, p. 1253.

[55] Handwritten note by General Eisenhower on Ltr, de Gaulle to Eisenhower, 21 Aug, SGS SHAEF File 092, French Relations; see Pogue, *Supreme Command*, p. 240, and V Corps G–3 Memo, 21 Aug.

[56] Pogue, *Supreme Command*, pp. 239, 241.

[57] Resistance Unit, Liberation of Paris, p. 1250; Pogue, *Supreme Command*, p. 231.

[58] Ltr, Eisenhower to Marshall, CPA–90235, 22 Aug, SHAEF G–3 File Ops A 322.011/1, Comd and Contl of U.S./Br Forces.

if they did, they would "spare us a lot of trouble." [59]

In the midst of conflicting rumors that Choltitz was ready to capitulate and that the Germans were ready to destroy the city with a secret weapon, the Resistance envoys appeared. They brought a great deal of plausible, though incorrect, information. They assured the Allied command that the FFI controlled most of the city and all the bridges, that the bulk of the Germans had already departed, that enemy troops deployed on the western outskirts were only small detachments manning a few roadblocks. They argued that the Germans had agreed to the armistice because the German forces were so feeble they needed the truce in order to evacuate the city without fighting their way through the streets. The envoys stated both that the armistice expired at noon, 23 August, and that neither side respected the agreement. Since the FFI had few supplies and little ammunition and was holding the city on bluff and nerve, the Resistance leaders feared that the Germans were gathering strength to regain control of the city and bring destruction to it upon the termination of the truce. To avoid bloodshed, it was essential that Allied soldiers enter the city promptly at noon, 23 August. [60]

Unaware that the reports were not entirely accurate, the Allied command reached the conclusion that if the Allies moved into Paris promptly, before guerrilla warfare was resumed, Choltitz would withdraw, and thus the destruction of the bridges and historic monuments that would ensue if he had to fight either the Resistance or the Allies would be avoided. [61] Since the available "information indicated that no great battle would take place," General Eisenhower changed his mind and decided to send reinforcement to the FFI in order to repay that military organization, as he later said, for "their great assistance," which had been "of inestimable value in the campaign." [62] Reinforcement, a legitimate military action, thus, in Eisenhower's mind, transferred the liberation of Paris from the political to the military realm and made it acceptable.

To make certain that Choltitz understood his role in the liberation of Paris, an intelligence officer of the " 'Economic Branch' of the U.S. Service" was dispatched to confirm with Choltitz the "arrangement" that was to save the city from damage. The Allies expected Choltitz to evacuate Paris at the same time that Allied troops entered, "provided that he did not become too much involved in fighting the French uprising." The time selected for the simultaneous departure and entry was the supposed time the truce expired—noon, 23 August. [63]

---

[59] Ltr, de Gaulle to Eisenhower, 21 Auf (and handwritten note) ; Bradley, *Soldier's Story*, p. 386; Pogue, *Supreme Command*, p. 240; Dansette, *Libération de Paris*, p. 316.

[60] Memo dictated by Bradley for Hodges, 22 Aug, transmitted by Hodges to Haislip and Gerow, XV Corps CofS Jnl and File. The memo is also Incl 1 of V Corps FO 21, 23 Aug, and a photostatic copy appears in *V Corps Operations in the ETO*, p. 200. This document contains all the information then known by the Allied command on the situation in Paris.

[61] Ltr, Bradley to OCMH, 7 Jan 55, OCMH Files; Interv by Pogue with Gen Bradley, 6 Nov 46, Washington, D.C., Pogue Files.

[62] Eisenhower, *Crusade in Europe*, p. 296.

[63] Ltr, Bradley to OCMH, 7 Jan 55; FUSA Memo, Info [to be] Elicited from the German Commandant of Paris, 31 Aug, FUSA G-2 Jnl and File; Ltr, Pogue to author, 27 Sep 54, OCMH Files; Dansette, *Libération de Paris*, pp. 138–39.

ALLIED AIRLIFT, *planned on 22 August, began delivery of food and fuel to the people of Paris on 27 August.*

Since a civil affairs commitment was an inescapable corollary of the decision to liberate Paris, General Eisenhower ordered 23,000 tons of food and 3,000 tons of coal dispatched to the city immediately. General Bradley requested SHAEF to prepare to send 3,000 tons of these supplies by air. The British also made plans to fulfill their part of the responsibility.[64]

The decision made, Bradley flew to Hodges' First Army headquarters late in the afternoon of 22 August to get the action started. Finding Leclerc awaiting him at the airstrip with an account of his differences with Gerow over Guillebon's movement to Paris, Bradley informed Leclerc that General Eisenhower had just decided to send the French armored division to liberate Paris at once. Off the hook of disobedience, Leclerc hastened to his command post, where his joyous shout to the division G–3, "Gribius, . . . mouvement immédiat sur Paris!" announced that a four-year dream was finally about to come true.[65]

---

[64] *V Corps Operations in the ETO*, p. 198; Bradley, *Soldier's Story*, p. 387; 21 AGp/5541/2/Q (Plans), Development of British Advance Base in Area Havre–Rouen–Dieppe, 22 Aug, 12th AGp File, Mil Objs, II.

[65] [Lt.-Col. Repiton-Préneuf *et al.*], *La 2e DB, Général Leclerc, Combattants et Combats en France* (Paris: Aux Editions Arts et Métiers Graphiques, 1945), p. 45.

On to Paris

"For the honor of first entry," General Eisenhower later wrote, "General Bradley selected General Leclerc's French 2d Division." And General Bradley explained, "Any number of American divisions could more easily have spearheaded our march into Paris. But to help the French recapture their pride after four years of occupation, I chose a French force with the tricolor on their Shermans." Yet the fact was that SHAEF was already committed to this decision. Neither Eisenhower nor Bradley could do anything else except violate a promise, an intention neither contemplated. Perhaps the presence and availability of the French division made it such an obvious choice for the assignment that the prior agreement was unimportant, possibly forgotten. Both American commanders wanted to do the right thing. Even General Hodges had independently decided about a week earlier that if he received the mission to liberate Paris he would include French troops among the liberation force.[66]

Suddenly General Bradley was at the First Army headquarters on the afternoon of 22 August with "momentous news that demanded instantaneous action." Since 20 August, he told General Hodges, Paris had been under the control of the FFI, which had seized the principal buildings of the city and made a temporary armistice with the Germans that expired at noon, 23 August. Higher headquarters had decided that

Paris could no longer be bypassed. The entry of military forces was necessary at once to prevent possible bloodshed among the civilian population. What troops could Hodges dispatch without delay?

General Hodges said that V Corps had completed its assignment at Argentan and was ready for a new job. From Argentan the corps could move quickly to the French capital with Leclerc's 2d French Armored and Barton's 4th Infantry Divisions. It would be fair for General Gerow, the corps commander, to have the task of liberating Paris because he and Collins had been the two American D-Day commanders and Collins had had the honor of taking Cherbourg.

Bradley accepted Hodges' recommendation, and the V Corps was alerted for immediate movement to the east. Then frantic phone calls were put in to locate General Gerow. He was found at the 12th Army Group headquarters and instructed to report to the army command post with key members of his staff. Late that afternoon, as Gerow and his principal assistants gathered in the army war room, a scene that had taken place a week earlier was repeated. Maps were hastily assembled, movement orders hurriedly written, march routes and tables determined, and careful instructions prepared for the French, "who have a casual manner of doing almost exactly what they please, regardless of orders." [67]

General Gerow learned that General Eisenhower had decided to send troops

---

[66] Eisenhower, *Crusade in Europe*, p. 296; Bradley, *Soldier's Story*, p. 391; Ltr, Eisenhower to Marshall, CPA–90235, 22 Aug. SHAEF G–3 File Ops A 322.011/1, Comd and Contl of U.S./Br Forces; Sylvan Diary, 22 Aug.

[67] Sylvan Diary, 22 Aug; see Telecons, Gen Kean and Brig Gen Henry J. Matchett, 1720 and 1730, 22 Aug; V Corps G–3 Jnl, entries 1743 and 1745, 22 Aug; *V Corps Operations in the ETO*, pp. 197ff.

to Paris to "take over from the Resistance Group, reinforce them, and act in such mobile reserve as . . . may be needed." The Allies were to enter Paris as soon as possible after noon of 23 August. The Supreme Commander had emphasized that "no advance must be made into Paris until the expiration of the Armistice and that Paris was to be entered only in case the degree of the fighting was such as could be overcome by light forces." In other words, General Eisenhower did not "want a severe fight in Paris at this time," nor did he "want any bombing or artillery fire on the city if it can possibly be avoided."[68]

A truly Allied force was to liberate the city: the 2d French Armored Division, the 4th U.S. Infantry Division, an American cavalry reconnaissance group, a 12th Army Group technical intelligence unit, and a contingent of British troops. The French division, accompanied by American cavalry and British troops, all displaying their national flags, was to enter the city while the 4th Division seized Seine River crossings south of Paris and constituted a reserve for the French. Leclerc was to have the honor of liberating Paris, but he was to do so within the framework of the Allied command and under direct American control.[69]

The leader of the expedition, General Gerow, had been characterized by General Eisenhower as having demonstrated "all the qualities of vigor, determination, reliability, and skill that we are looking for."[70] Further, he had had the experience needed for a mission fraught with political implications. Serving with the War Plans Division of the War Department from 1936 to 1939, he was chief of that division during the critical year of 1941. He was thus no stranger to situations involving the interrelationship of military strategy and national policy. Yet he had not been informed of the political considerations involved, and his instructions to liberate Paris were of a military nature.[71]

Acting in advance on General Hodges' orders to be issued on 23 August to "force your way into the city this afternoon," Gerow telephoned Leclerc on the evening of 22 August and told him to start marching immediately. The 38th Cavalry Squadron was to accompany Leclerc to "display the [American] flag upon entering Paris." [72] According to the formal corps order issued later, the only information available was that the Germans were withdrawing from Paris in accordance with the terms of the armistice. The rumor that the Germans had mined the sewers and subways was important only in spurring the Allies to occupy the city in order to prevent damage. No serious opposition was expected. If the troops did, however, encounter strong resistance, they were to assume the defensive.[73]

---

[68] Memo dictated by Bradley to Hodges, 22 Aug, XV Corps CofS Jnl and File.

[69] See Montgomery, *Normandy to the Baltic,* p. 176; Notes of Mtg, 0900, 23 Aug, XV Corps CofS Jnl and File; VII Corps Opns Memo 73, 23 Aug (confirming oral orders, 22 Aug).

[70] Eisenhower to Marshall, FWD–12428, 22 Jul. Pogue Files.

[71] Interv, author with Gen Gerow, Maj Gen Charles G. Helmick (formerly V Corps Arty Comdr), and Brig Gen John G. Hill (formerly V Corps G–3), 15 Oct 54, OCMH Files; Ltr, Gerow to OCMH, 22 Sep 54.

[72] Gerow Memo for Rcd, 25 Aug.

[73] V Corps Ltr of Instrs, Gerow to Leclerc, 22 Aug, and Dir, Gerow to 102d Cav Recon Gp (Mecz), 23 Aug; Ltr, Gerow to OCMH, 22 Sep 54, OCMH Files.

Despite the anticipated absence of opposition, Gerow commanded a large force that was to move on two routes—Sées, Mortagne, Château-en-Thymerais, Maintenon, Rambouillet, Versailles; and Alençon, Nogent-le-Rotrou, Chartres, Limours, Palaiseau. The northern column—the bulk of the French division, the attached American troops, a U.S. engineer group (controlling three combat battalions, a treadway bridge company, a light equipment platoon, and a water supply platoon), the V Corps Artillery (with four firing battalions and an observation battalion), in that order of march—had an estimated time length of fourteen hours and twenty-five minutes. The southern column—a French combat command, the bulk of the American cavalry, the V Corps headquarters, the 4th Division (reinforced by two tank destroyer battalions, an antiaircraft battalion, two tank battalions), in that order—had a time length of twenty-two hours and forty minutes. For some unexplained reason the British force, despite General Eisenhower's explicit desire for British participation, failed to appear. To make certain that the French troops, which led both columns, respected the truce in the capital, Gerow ordered that no troops were to cross the Versailles–Palaiseau line before noon, 23 August.[74] (Map XIII)

Although Gerow had ordered Leclerc to start to Paris immediately on the evening of 22 August, the division did not commence its march until the morning of 23 August. By evening of 23 August the head of the northern column was several miles beyond Rambouillet on the road to Versailles; the southern column had reached Limours. At both points, the French met opposition.

Within Paris, before receiving Hitler's order to leave the city to the Allies only as a "field of ruins," Choltitz had had no intention of doing anything but his duty. His handling of the insurrection was sufficient evidence of that. When Aulock, who commanded the perimeter defenses west of the city, requested permission to withdraw on 22 August because he felt he could not stop an Allied advance, Choltitz said no. But after receiving Hitler's order and realizing that he was expected to die among the ruins, Choltitz began to reconsider. About the same time he learned that the *348th Division*, which was moving from northern France to strengthen the Paris defenses, was instead to be committed north of the capital along the lower Seine.[75] At that moment he became rather cynical. "Ever since our enemies have refused to listen to and obey our Fuehrer," he supposedly remarked at dinner one evening, "the whole war has gone badly."[76]

One of Choltitz' first reactions to Hitler's "field of ruins" order was to phone Model and protest that the German high command was out of tune with reality. The city could not be defended. Paris was in revolt. The French held important administrative buildings. German forces were inadequate to the task of preserving order. Coal was short. The rations available would last the

[74] V Corps Ltr of Instrs, Gerow to Leclerc, 22 Aug, and FO 21, 23 Aug.

[75] Choltitz, *Soldat unter Soldaten*, p. 259; MS # B-728 (Emmerich).

[76] Quoted in Dansette, *Libération de Paris*, pp. 293–94.

troops only two more days.[77] But Choltitz was unable to secure a satisfactory alternative from Model, so he phoned Speidel, Model's chief of staff at *Army Group B*. After sarcastically thanking Speidel for the lovely order from Hitler, Choltitz said that he had complied by placing three tons of explosive in the cathedral of Notre Dame, two tons in the Invalides, and one in the Palais Bourbon (the Chamber of Deputies), that he was ready to level the Arc de Triomphe to clear a field of fire, that he was prepared to destroy the Opéra and the Madeleine, and that he was planning to dynamite the Tour Eiffel and use it as a wire entanglement to block the Seine. Incidentally, he advised Speidel, he found it impossible to destroy the seventy-odd bridges.[78]

Speidel, who had received Hitler's order from OKW and had realized that the destruction of the bridges meant destroying monuments and residential quarters, later claimed that he had not transmitted the order forward and that Choltitz had received it directly from *OB WEST*. Yet, since Gestapo agents were monitoring Speidel's telephone to prove his complicity in the July 20th plot, Speidel later recalled that he urged Choltitz—as diplomatically and as obliquely as he knew how—not to destroy the French capital.[79]

Choltitz had no intention of destroying Paris. Whether he was motivated by a generous desire to spare human life and a great cultural center, or simply by his lack of technical means to do so—both of which he later claimed—the fact was that representatives of the neutral powers in Paris were also exerting pressure on him to evacuate Paris in order to avoid a battle there.[80] Yet Choltitz refused to depart. Whether he was playing a double game or not, his willingness to avoid fighting inside Paris did not change his determination to defend Paris outside the city limits—a defense that eventually included orders to demolish the Seine River bridges, three rejections of Allied ultimatums to surrender, and refusal of an Allied offer to provide an opportunity for him to withdraw.[81]

The field fortifications on the western and southern approaches to the city formed a solid perimeter that was more effective than Aulock judged. Obviously, 20,000 troops dispersed over a large area could not hold back the Allies for long, but they could make a strong defense. Artillery, tanks, and antiaircraft guns sited for antitank fire supported strongpoints at Trappes, Guyancourt, Châteaufort, Saclay, Massy, Wissous, and Villeneuve-le-Roi. The roads to Versailles were well blocked, and

---

[77] Telecon, Choltitz and Model, 1200, 23 Aug, *AGp B KTB*. His mention of the shortage of rations contrasts with his later statement that he had Eckelmann distribute army food to the French populace. Choltitz, *Soldat unter Soldaten*, p. 245.

[78] Telecon, Choltitz and Speidel, 2215, 23 Aug, *AGp B KTB*; Choltitz, *Soldat unter Soldaten*, pp. 256–57.

[79] MS # C–017 (Speidel).

[80] Marcelle Adler-Bresse, "Von Choltitz, a-t-il Changé d'Avis?" (a review of Choltitz' *Brennt Paris? Tatsachenbericht des letzten deutschen Befehlshabers in Paris* (Mannheim: Weltbucherei, 1950) and his *Soldat unter Soldaten*) and notice of an article in the East Berlin newspaper *Tagliche Rundschau*, December 28, 1954, both in *Revue d'Histoire de la Deuxième Guerre Mondiale*, No. 19 (July, 1955), p. 116; Dietrich von Choltitz, "Pourquoi en 1944, je n'ai pas détruit Paris," *Le Figaro*, October 4, 1949; Telecon, Choltitz and Speidel, 2225, 24 Aug, *AGp B KTB*.

[81] Telecon, Choltitz and Speidel, 1100, 25 Aug. *AGp B KTB*; Eckelmann, Rpt to OKW.

forward outposts at Marcoussis and Montlhéry as well as strong combat outposts at Palaiseau and Longjumeau covered the approaches to the positions guarding the highway north from Arpajon.[82]

On the Allied side, there was practically no information on the actual situation inside Paris and on its approaches. When General Leclerc arrived in Rambouillet with a small detachment around noon 23 August, well ahead of his division, he learned for the first time from his reconnaissance elements and from French civilians that there appeared to be a solid defense line along the western and southwestern suburbs of Paris, a line reinforced by tanks, antitank weapons, and mines. This meant that a major effort by the whole division would be necessary to open the way into the city proper.

Eager though he was to come to the rescue of the FFI in Paris, which he thought might have by this time liberated the interior of the city, General Leclerc had to postpone his attack. He had to wait until the following morning because the main body of his division could not reach the Rambouillet area before evening of the 23d.[83]

The Liberation

Leclerc's plan of attack departed from Gerow's instructions. Two combat commands, Colonel de Langlade's and

Colonel Dio's, in that order, were advancing toward Rambouillet on the northern route; Col. Pierre Billotte's combat command was on the south. Instead of making the main effort from the west through Rambouillet and Versailles, Leclerc decided to bring his major weight to bear on Paris from the south, from Arpajon. He directed Billotte to go from Limours to Arpajon, turn north there, and attack toward the southern part of Paris. He switched Dio to the southern route in direct support of Billotte. CCR was to stage a diversionary attack toward St. Cyr, while Langlade, skirting Versailles on the south, was to push through Chevreuse and Villacoublay to Sèvres. When Leclerc showed his operations order to General de Gaulle, who was at Rambouillet that evening, de Gaulle said merely that Leclerc was lucky to have the opportunity of liberating Paris, and thereby, by inference at least, approved.[84]

Not so the Americans, who years later could not understand Leclerc's reasons for disregarding the V Corps instructions. Was Leclerc reluctant to attack through Versailles because he did not want to endanger that national monument? Was he concerned about securing the right flank protection afforded by the Seine River and the destroyed bridges between Corbeil and Paris? Though he had cautioned his troops to avoid the large traffic arteries, was he attracted nevertheless to the wide Orléans–Paris highway, which passes through Arpajon? Did he want to display his independence and his resent-

---

[82] MS # B–741 (Ziegelmann), including Sketch # 2b; Eckelmann, Rpt to OKW; Even, La 2e D.B., p. 118; V Corps Operations in the ETO, pp. 200–202; CI 32 (4th Div); 2d French Armored Division G–3 Report, Operations, is a basic source for the military activity of the division.

[83] Ltr, Leclerc to de Gaulle, 1330, 23 Aug, reproduced in Even, La 2e D.B., facing p. 118.

[84] 2d Fr Armd Div Opns Order, 1800 [23 Aug]; see Even, La 2e D.B., pp. 117–18, and Dansette, Libération de Paris, pp. 329, 336.

GENERAL LECLERC AT RAMBOUILLET, ON THE ROAD TO PARIS

ment of American control in a matter that seemed to him to be strictly French? Perhaps he had not even seen Gerow's instructions.[85]

Actually, the military basis of Leclerc's decision was his estimate that the opposition along the Arpajon–Paris axis seemed "less robust" than in the Rambouillet–Versailles area.[86] Guillebon's detachment on the previous day had encountered German outposts near Arpajon.

These were weak when compared to the positions in the Rambouillet area, where American troops of the XX Corps had swept aside the outposts and laid bare the main line of resistance. By deciding to make his main effort at Arpajon, Leclerc inadvertently selected as his point of intended penetration the place where the German defense was in greatest depth.

There were other unfortunate results. By directing his southern column to go from Limours to Arpajon, he impinged on the sector of the 4th Division. By switching his principal effort from Versailles to the southern axis through

---

[85] Interv with Gerow, Helmick, and Hill, 15 Oct 54, OCMH Files; see Even, La 2e D.B., p. 118.
[86] 2d Fr Armd Div G–2 Rpt, Opns; Even, La 2e D.B., p. 118.

FRENCH SOLDIERS ATTACK TOWARD CHÂTEAUFORT

Arpajon, he placed his main attack outside the range of the V Corps Artillery.[87]

When Gerow received Leclerc's operations order on the morning of 24 August, he immediately warned General Barton, the 4th Division commander, of French encroachment but instructed Barton to continue on his mission "without regard to movements of French troops." After informing General Hodges, the army commander, of Leclerc's activity, Gerow drove to Rambouillet to see Leclerc and straighten out the matter. He discovered that Leclerc had gone forward from Rambouillet. Gerow followed until traffic congestion forced him to return to his command post.[88]

Meanwhile, Leclerc had launched his attack toward Paris at dawn, 24 August, in a downpour of rain that later diminished to a drizzle. On the left, CCR made a diversionary attack to block off St. Cyr, and Langlade moved toward Châteaufort and Toussus-le-Noble. The armored columns quickly encountered mines and artillery fire, but after a four-hour fire fight at close range, the French knocked out three of eight tanks and penetrated the German defensive line. With only slight enemy interference, Langlade's combat command then swept toward the Pont de Sèvres, the greatest obstruction being the enthusiastic welcome of civilians, who swarmed about the combat vehicles, pressing flowers,

[87] See V Corps Arty Jnl, entry 0700, 23 Aug.

[88] Msg, Gerow to Barton, 0840, 24 Aug; V Corps Operations in the ETO, p. 203; Dansette, Libération

de Paris, p. 401; Msg, Hodges to Gerow, 1240, 24 Aug; Interv with Gerow, Helmick, and Hill, 15 Oct 54, OCMH Files.

kisses, and wine on their liberators and luring some from duty. "Sure we love you," the more conscientious soldiers cried, "but let us through." At Sèvres by evening, Langlade found the bridge still intact and unmined. He quickly sent several tanks across the Seine and established a bridgehead in the suburb immediately southwest of Paris. French troops had almost, but not quite, reached the capital.

Billotte's combat command in the main effort north from Arpajon had a much more difficult time. Encountering resistance at once, the troops had to turn to a dogged advance through a succession of German outposts, roadblocks, and well-positioned strongpoints supported by numerous antiaircraft guns sited for antitank fire. Narrow, crooked roads through a densely populated region of small stone villages further frustrated rapid progress. It took two full-scale assaults to capture Massy, and costly street fighting was necessary to take heavily defended Fresnes that evening. American tactical air suport could not assist because of the rainy weather.[89]

Whereas Langlade had moved fifteen miles, had tanks across the Seine, and was almost touching Paris, Billotte, after advancing thirteen bitter miles, was still five miles from the Porte d'Orléans (the closest point of entry into the city proper), seven miles from the Pantheon (his objective), and eight miles from Ile de la Cité, the center of the capital. The easy entrance the Allies had expected had not materialized.

To the American commanders following French progress on the midafternoon of 24 August, it was incredible that

Leclerc had not yet liberated Paris. Since they expected the Germans to withdraw, Leclerc's slow progress seemed like procrastination. That the French had failed to move immediately from Argentan and to reach their designated line of departure by noon, 23 August, seemed to substantiate this feeling. If Leclerc's inability to move more rapidly on 24 August was due to his unwillingness to "jeopardize French lives and property by the use of means necessary to speed the advance," that too was insubordination, for Leclerc had been instructed that restrictions on bombing and shelling Paris did not apply to the suburbs.[90]

It seemed to Bradley, as he recalled later, that the French troops had "stumbled reluctantly through a Gallic wall as townsfolk along the line of march slowed the French advance with wine and celebration."[91] Gerow substantiated the impression. It appeared to him that the resistance was slight and the attack halfhearted, that the French were fighting on a one-tank front and were not only unwilling to maneuver around obstacles but also were reluctant to fire into buildings.[92]

Exasperated because Leclerc was disregarding "all orders to take more aggressive action and speed up his advance," General Gerow requested authority to send the 4th Division into Paris. Permission might be enough, he thought, to shame Leclerc into greater activity and increased effort. Agreeing

---

[89] See V Corps G-3 Jnl, entry 1520, 24 Aug.

[90] Ltr, Gerow to OCMH, 22 Sep 54.

[91] Bradley, *Soldier's Story*, p. 392.

[92] Interv with Gerow, Helmick, and Hill, 15 Oct 54. General Gerow was also troubled by reports that French troops were stopping in towns along the way to celebrate with the inhabitants. Sylvan Diary, 23 Aug.

that he could not wait for the French "to dance their way to Paris," Bradley exclaimed, "To hell with prestige, tell the 4th to slam on in and take the liberation." [93]

Actually, Leclerc had all the incentive he could possibly need to enter Paris quickly. He was quite conscious of the prestige involved for French arms and aware of the personal distinction that awaited him as the hero of the liberation. He had heard conflicting and exaggerated reports of the German threats, reprisals, and destruction that only the entrance of regular troops could prevent. He knew that de Gaulle expected him to be in Paris on 24 August to resolve the internecine struggle for power in the capital—"Tomorrow," de Gaulle had written the previous evening, "Tomorrow will be decisive in the sense that we wish." [94]

Four factors had retarded Leclerc: faulty attack dispositions; the reluctance of his troops to damage French property; the real problem posed by the enthusiastic welcome of the French population; and the German opposition, which had been stronger than anticipated.

The 4th Division staff understood that the American division was being ordered into Paris as a normal procedure of reinforcing a unit that was having unexpected difficulty with an enemy who was not withdrawing, but instead strengthening his defenses. A British intelligence agency reported no evidence that the

French were moving too slowly and declared: ". . . the French Armored Division is moving into Paris at high speed. Those enemy elements . . . in the way . . . have been very roughly handled indeed." Finally, French losses in the battle toward Paris did not indicate an absence of opposition; 71 killed, 225 wounded, 21 missing, and 35 tanks, 6 self-propelled guns, and 111 vehicles destroyed totaled rather heavy casualties for an armored division. [95]

The American commanders, however, were less interested in reasons than in results. Ordered to liberate Paris and dissatisfied with Leclerc's progress, they committed the 4th U.S. Infantry Division without regard to preserving the glory of the initial entry for the French. "If von Choltitz was to deliver the city," General Bradley wrote, "we had a compact to fulfill." [96]

Advised by Hodges that it was "imperative" for Allied troops to be in Paris without delay and that considerations of precedence in favor of the French no longer applied, Gerow ordered Leclerc: "Push your advance vigorously this afternoon and continue advance tonight." He notified General Barton that he was still to secure a Seine River bridgehead near Corbeil, but now he was to shift his main effort from east to north and use all the means at his disposal "to force a way into the city as rapidly as possible." When Barton said that he would start north from Villeneuve-le-Roi two hours

[93] Ltr, Gerow to OCMH, 22 Sep 54, and Interv with Gerow, Helmick, and Hill; Msg, Gerow to Leclerc, 24 Aug. Quote is from Bradley, *Soldier's Story*, p. 392.

[94] Ltr, Gen de Gaulle to M. Luizet, 2230, 23 Aug, quoted in Even, La 2e D.B., p., 121; Dansette, *Libération de Paris*, pp. 329–30.

[95] CI 32 (4th Div); Resistance Unit, Liberation of Paris, p. 1252; 21 AGp Phantom Sitrep, U.S. Armies, 2400, 24 Aug; Even La 2e D.B., p. 131. The losses are through 29 August, but most occurred on 24 August.

[96] Bradley, *Soldier's Story*, p. 392; Ltr, Bradley to OCMH, 7 Jan 55, OCMH Files.

after midnight, Gerow informed Leclerc that Barton would help the French and that Leclerc was to render assistance to Barton "in every way." [97]

Leclerc decided to make one more effort that night. Although Langlade was practically inside the city at Sèvres and faced no opposition, Leclerc could get no word to him, for, as the French admitted, "liaison between the columns for all practical purposes no longer exists." [98] For that reason, Leclerc called on Billotte to dispatch a small detachment of tanks and half-tracks to infiltrate into the city. A small force under a Captain Dronne rolled along side roads and back streets, through the southern suburbs. Civilians pushed aside trees they had felled along the routes to hamper the Germans, repaved streets they had torn up to build barricades, and guided Dronne into the capital by way of the Porte de Gentilly (between the Porte d'Orléans and the Porte d'Italie). Following small streets, Dronne crossed the Seine by the Pont d'Austerlitz, drove along the quays of the right bank, and reached the Hôtel de Ville shortly before midnight, 24 August. [99]

Although the Germans had resisted effectively on 24 August, their defenses melted away during the night as Choltitz ordered Aulock to withdraw behind the Seine. [100] General Barton, who had as-sembled the 4th Division near Arpajon, selected the 12th Infantry—which was closest to Paris and had lost over 1,000 casualties while attached to the 30th Division at Mortain and needed a boost to morale—to lead the division into Paris on 25 August. Motorized, the regiment started to take the road through Athis-Mons and Villeneuve-le-Roi, but gunfire from the east bank of the Seine deflected the movement away from the river. Without encountering resistance, the troops, screened by the 102d Cavalry Group, reached Notre Dame cathedral before noon, 25 August, "the only check . . . being the enormous crowd of Parisians in the streets welcoming the troops." Units of the regiment occupied the railroad stations of Austerlitz, Lyon, and Vincennes, and reconnaissance elements pushed northeast and east to the outskirts of the city. [101] (Map 18)

While American troops secured the eastern half of Paris, the French took the western part. Langlade's command advanced to the Arc de Triomphe, Billotte's to Place du Châtelet, the spear-heads of both columns meeting later at Rond Point des Champs Elysées. Dio's troops, split into two task forces, moved to the Ecole Militaire and to the Palais Bourbon. Several sharp engagements took place with Germans entrenched in public buildings, some of them of great historic value—Luxembourg, Quai d'Orsay, Palais Bourbon, Hôtel des Invalides, and Ecole Militaire among

---

[97] Msg, Gerow to Leclerc, 24 Aug; Gerow Memo for Rcd, 24 Aug; Ltr, Gerow to Leclerc, 2345, 24 Aug; Interv by author with Gen Barton, 10 Jun 54, OCMH Files.

[98] 2d Fr Armd Div G-3, Rpt, Opns.

[99] Even, La 2e D.B., pp. 122–23; Dansette, Libéra-tion de Paris, pp. 334–39; 2d Fr Armd Div G-3 Rpt, Opns; Telecon, Choltitz and Speidel, 2225, 24 Aug, AGp B KTB.

[100] Telecons, Choltitz and Speidel, 2225, 24 Aug, and 1100, 25 Aug, AGp B KTB.

[101] CI 32 (4th Div); A Short History of the 38th Cavalry Reconnaissance Squadron (Mechanized) (Prestice, Czechoslovakia, 1945), pp. 15–18; Johnson, History of the Twelfth Infantry Regiment in World War II, pp. 168–71; 4th Div AAR, Aug, and FO 24, 0800, 25 Aug (confirming oral orders, 2400, 24 Aug).

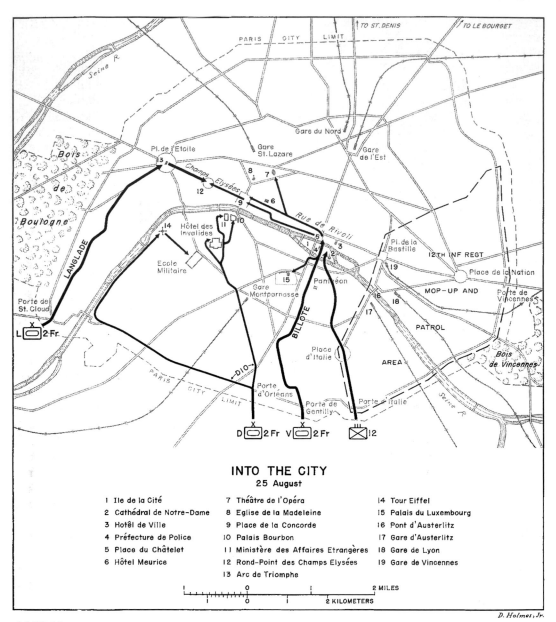

INTO THE CITY
25 August

1	Ile de la Cité	7	Théâtre de l'Opéra	14	Tour Eiffel
2	Cathédral de Notre-Dame	8	Eglise de la Madeleine	15	Palais du Luxembourg
3	Hotêl de Ville	9	Place de la Concorde	16	Pont d'Austerlitz
4	Préfecture de Police	10	Palais Bourbon	17	Gare d'Austerlitz
5	Place du Châtelet	11	Ministère des Affaires Etrangères	18	Gare de Lyon
6	Hôtel Meurice	12	Rond-Point des Champs Elysées	19	Gare de Vincennes
		13	Arc de Triomphe		

D. Holmes, Jr.

MAP 18

others. About two thousand Germans remained in the Bois de Boulogne.

To avoid a fanatic last-ditch struggle that might irreparably damage the city, Choltitz' formal surrender was necessary. Though Nordling presented him with an ultimatum from Billotte, Choltitz refused to capitulate.

In the Rue de Rivoli, 25 *August*.

The end came after French tankers surrounded the Hôtel Meurice shortly after noon, set several German vehicles under the rue de Rivoli arcades on fire, and threw smoke grenades into the halls of the hotel. A young French officer suddenly burst into Choltitz' room and in his excitement shouted, "Do you speak German?" "Probably better than you," Choltitz replied coolly and allowed himself to be taken prisoner.[102]

Leclerc had installed his command post in the Montparnasse railway station, but he himself went to the Prefecture of Police. Barton, who was in Paris and wanted to co-ordinate the dispositions of the divisions with Leclerc, located him there having lunch. Holding his napkin and appearing annoyed at being disturbed, Leclerc came outside to talk with Barton. Without inviting him to lunch, Leclerc suggested that Barton go to the Montparnasse station. Barton, who was hungry as well as irritated by Leclerc's attitude, finally said, "I'm not in Paris because I wanted to be here but because I was ordered to be here." Leclerc shrugged his shoulders. "We're both soldiers," he said. Barton then drove to the Gare Montparnasse, where he found General Gerow already taking charge of the enormous responsibility of Paris.[103]

Instead of taking Choltitz to Montparnasse, which would have been normal procedure, his French captors took him to the Prefecture of Police, where Leclerc was waiting. There Choltitz signed a formal act of capitulation in the presence of Leclerc and the commander of the Paris FFI, who together as equals

---

[102] Choltitz, *Soldat Unter Soldaten*, p. 264.

[103] Interv with Barton, 10 Jun 54

accepted Choltitz' surrender—not as representatives of the Supreme Commander, Allied Expeditionary Force, but in the name of the Provisional Government of France.[104] Copies of the document were quickly reproduced and circulated by special teams of French and German officers to scattered enemy groups still in the city. All surrendered (including a large force of 700 men with several tanks in the Luxembourg gardens) except the troops in the Bois de Boulogne.[105] The V Corps took about 10,000 prisoners in the city and received a "staggering amount of information . . . from FFI sources." Choltitz made certain that the Allies understood that "he could have destroyed bridges and public buildings but despite pressure from above would not give [the] order" to do so.[106]

Choltitz insisted that only the arrival of military forces had "saved Paris from going up in smoke." He stated that neither mines nor booby traps had been placed in the city. He said that he had concluded long before his capitulation that it "was hopeless" to defend the city; and he had thus "taken no great steps to do so." He asserted that the war among the French political factions had "surpassed all his expectations." He emphasized that "he was damn glad to get rid of the job of policing both Paris and the Frenchmen, both of which he apparently detests." [107]

As for the internecine struggle for political power inside the capital, the de Gaullists had proved more astute and better disciplined than their opponents. Taking advantage of the insurrection on 19 August, they had quickly seized the seat of government and taken the reins of political control.

The Aftermath

Paris was liberated, but one more scene was required—the appearance of General de Gaulle. He arrived unannounced in the city on the afternoon of 25 August to an enthusiastic reception by deliriously cheering Parisians. The demonstration persuaded him to make an official entry to strengthen an uneasy political unity that prevailed and to display his personal power. He therefore requested Leclerc to furnish part of the 2d French Armored Division for a parade from the Etoile to the Place de la Concorde; and through General Koenig, who was also in the capital as the de Gaullist-appointed military governor, de Gaulle invited Gerow and his staff to participate, together with one American officer and twenty men and a like number of British.[108]

Gerow was hardly ready to comply. Although the situation was "quiet in main Paris area except some sniping," groups of isolated Germans southwest of Paris near Meudon and Clamart, in the eastern part near Vincennes and Montreuil, and north of Paris near Montmorency and le Bourget claimed exemption from Choltitz' surrender terms. In addition to these forces, another group still held the Bois de Bou-

[104] The surrender document is reproduced in *V Corps Operations in the ETO*, p. 204.

[105] Even, La 2e D.B., pp. 126–29; Dansette, *Libération de Paris*, pp. 349–73; Telecons, Emmerich and Tempelhoff, 2225, 25 Aug, and Feyerband and Speidel, 0810, 26 Aug, *AGp B KTB*.

[106] FUSA Rpt, 2055, 26 Aug; 4th Div G–2 Per Rpt, 2000, 26 Aug; FUSA AAR, Aug.

[107] Sylvan Diary, 29 Aug.

[108] V Corps G–3 Jnl and File, 26 Aug.

GENERAL VON CHOLTITZ *shortly after his capitulation (above); high-ranking German prisoners in the Hôtel Majestic (below).*

logne. Furthermore, Paris posed serious problems of control, both with regard to the civilian population and to the troops, particularly because of the danger that the liberation hysteria might spread to the soldiers. The thought of a German air attack on a city with unenforced blackout rules and inadequate antiaircraft defenses hardly added to Gerow's peace of mind. The Germans north and east of the city were capable of counterattacking. Feeling that the city was still not properly secure, anticipating trouble if ceremonial formations were held, and wishing the troops combat-ready for any emergency, Gerow ordered Leclerc to maintain contact and pursue the Germans north of the capital.[109]

Leclerc replied that he could do so only with part of his forces, for he was furnishing troops for de Gaulle's official entry. Acknowledging Gerow as his military chief, Leclerc explained that de Gaulle was the head of the French state.[110] Profoundly disturbed because the de Gaulle-Leclerc chain of command ignored the Allied command structure, Gerow wrote Leclerc a sharp note:

You are operating under my direct command and will not accept orders from any other source. I understand you have been directed by General de Gaulle to parade your troops this afternoon at 1400 hours. You will disregard those orders and continue on the present mission assigned you of clearing up all resistance in Paris and environs within your zone of action.

Your command will not participate in the parade this afternoon or at any other time except on orders signed by me personally.

To keep the record straight, Gerow informed Hodges that he had "directed General Leclerc to disregard those orders [of de Gaulle] and carry out his assigned mission of clearing the Paris area."[111]

Some members of Leclerc's staff were purportedly "furious at being diverted from operations but say Le Clerq has been given orders and [there is] nothing they can do about [it]." They were sure that the parade would "get the French Division so tangled up that they will be useless for an emergency operation for at least 12 hours if not more."[112]

Torn by conflicting loyalties, Leclerc appealed to de Gaulle for a decision. To an American present, de Gaulle supposedly said, "I have given you LeClerc; surely I can have him back for a moment, can't I?"[113]

Although Barton suggested that Gerow might cut off Leclerc's gasoline, supplies, and money, Gerow felt that it would have been unwise, as he later wrote, "to attempt to stop the parade by the use of U.S. troops, so the only action I took was to direct that all U.S. troops be taken off the streets and held in readiness to put down any disturbance should one occur."[114]

Gerow's concern was not farfetched. When Hitler learned that Allied troops were entering the French capital, he asked whether Paris was burning,

---

[109] V Corps G–2 Msg, 1303, 26 Aug; Gerow to Hodges, 0010, 26 Aug; V Corps AAR, Aug; Ltr, Gerow to OCMH, 22 Sep 54, and Ltr and attachments, Maj Gen Harold W. Blakeley to author, 30 Sep 55, extracts in OCMH Files; Dansette, Libération de Paris, p. 420.

[110] 2d Fr Armd Div Msg, 26 Aug.

[111] Gerow to Leclerc, Orders, 26 Aug; Msg, Gerow to Hodges, 1302, 26 Aug.

[112] Msg, 26 Aug, probably from V Corps liaison officer with the French division.

[113] Quoted in Dansette, Libération de Paris, p. 403; see Ltr, Gerow to OCMH, 22 Sep 54.

[114] Ltr, Gerow to OCMH, 22 Sep 54; Interv with Barton, 10 Jun 54.

"Brennt Paris?" Answered in the negative, Hitler ordered long-range artillery, V-weapons, and air to destroy the city. Supposedly contrary to Model's wish, Speidel and Choltitz later claimed to have hampered the execution of this order.[115]

Scattered shooting and some disorder accompanied de Gaulle's triumphal entry of 26 August. Whether German soldiers and sympathizers, overzealous FFI members, or careless French troops were responsible was unknown, but Gerow curtly ordered Leclerc to "stop indiscriminate firing now occurring on streets of Paris." Ten minutes later, Leclerc ordered all individual arms taken from his enlisted men and placed under strict guard. Shortly thereafter, in an unrelated act, 2,600 Germans came out of the Bois de Boulogne with their hands up. They might have instead shelled the city during the parade. Frightened by what might have happened, de Gaulle and Koenig later expressed regrets for having insisted on a parade and agreed to cooperate in the future with the American command.[116]

Meanwhile, part of Leclerc's division had, in compliance with Gerow's instructions, pushed toward Aubervilliers and St. Denis on 26 August, and two days later, after a three-hour battle with elements of the *348th Division* (recently arrived from the Pas-de-Calais), the French took le Bourget and the airfield. Some French units seized Montmorency

GENERAL DE GAULLE. *At his left is General Koenig, behind them, General Leclerc.*

on 29 August, while others cleared the loop of the Seine west of Paris from Versailles to Gennevilliers and took into custody isolated enemy groups that had refused to surrender to the FFI.[117]

At the same time, the 4th Division had established Seine River bridgeheads near Corbeil on 25 August, had cleared the eastern part of Paris, and after assembling in the Bois de Vincennes, began on the afternoon of 27 August to advance toward the northeast. Two days later the troops were far beyond the outermost limits of Paris.[118]

All the corps objectives, in fact, had been reached "well outside Paris limits" by 27 August.[119] To continue its at-

---

[115] MS # C–017 (Speidel); Choltitz, *Soldat Unter Soldaten*, p. 256.

[116] Gerow to Leclerc, 1710, 26 Aug; Leclerc to his subordinate officers, 1720, 26 Aug; V Corps AAR, Aug; Msg, Vissering to SHAEF, 26 Aug, SGS SHAEF File 092, French Relations; Pogue, *Supreme Command*, p. 242.

[117] Even, La 2e D.B., pp. 129–30; Gerow to Leclerc, 0750, 27 Aug, 1020, 28 Aug; V Corps Dirs, 29 Aug.

[118] 4th Div AAR, Aug; CI 32 (4th Div).

[119] V Corps AAR, Aug.

tack eastward, V Corps released the French division, retained command of the 4th Division, and received the 28th Infantry and 5th Armored Divisions.

Developments leading to the release of the French division began on 26 August, when General de Gaulle wrote General Eisenhower to thank him for assigning Leclerc the mission of liberating Paris. He also mentioned that although Paris was "in the best possible order after all that has happened," he considered it "absolutely necessary to leave [the division] here for the moment." [120] Planning a visit to Paris on 27 August to confer with de Gaulle on this and other matters and "to show that the Allies had taken part in the liberation," General Eisenhower invited General Montgomery to accompany him. When Montgomery declined on the ground that he was too busy, Eisenhower and Bradley went to Paris without him. [121] At that time de Gaulle "expressed anxiety about conditions in Paris" and asked that two U.S. divisions be put at his disposal to give a show of force and establish his position. Since General Gerow had recommended that Leclerc be retained in Paris to maintain order, General Eisenhower, who earlier had thought of using Leclerc's division for occupation duty in the capital, agreed to station the French division in Paris "for the time being." To give de Gaulle his show of force and at the same time make clear that de Gaulle had received Paris by the grace of God and the strength of Allied arms, Eisenhower

planned to parade an American division in combat formation through Paris on its way to the front. [122]

Ostensibly a ceremony but in reality a tactical maneuver designed as a march to the front, the parade would exhibit American strength in the French capital and get the division through the city—a serious problem because of traffic congestion—to relieve Leclerc's division. [123] While the 5th Armored Division assembled near Versailles for its forthcoming commitment, General Cota led the 28th Division down the Champs Elysées on 29 August and through the city to the northern outskirts and beyond in a splendid parade reviewed by Bradley, Gerow, de Gaulle, Koenig, and Leclerc from an improvised stand, a Bailey bridge upside down. [124]

The motives behind de Gaulle's request for Leclerc's division to remain in Paris were two, possibly three. He may have wanted simply to remove friction between Leclerc and Gerow by diplomatically securing Leclerc's transfer back to Patton's Third Army. More to the point, he revealed a lack of confidence in his basic position vis-à-vis the French people. Although he had been assured on 23 August by one of his chief political advisers that "the authority of the Provisional Government of the Republic

---

[120] Msg, de Gaulle to Eisenhower, 1915, 26 Aug, SGS SHAEF File 092, French Relations.

[121] Pogue, *Supreme Command*, pp. 242–43; Eisenhower to Montgomery, 26 Aug, and Montgomery to Eisenhower, 0336, 27 Aug, Pogue Files.

[122] Butcher Diary, entry 26 Aug, and Ltrs, Eisenhower to Marshall, 22 and 31 Aug, Pogue Files; Eisenhower to de Gaulle, FWD–13336, 28 Aug. SGS SHAEF File 014.1, France; Gerow to Hodges, 0010, 26 Aug; *V Corps Operations in the ETO*, p. 205; Ltr, Pogue to author, 27 Sep 54, OCMH Files.

[123] V Corps AAR, Aug; Interv by author with General Barton; Ltr and attachments from General Blakeley to author; Interv with Gerow, Helmick, and Hill, 15 Oct 54. American engineers eventually opened five express routes through the city.

[124] *V Corps Operations in the ETO*, pp. 208, 211; Sylvan Diary, 29 Aug.

FRENCH RESISTANCE FIGHTERS *march in a Paris liberation parade.*

is recognized by the whole population," he gave at least one observer the impression that he was not entirely sure of himself politically.[125] Finally, de Gaulle did not seem to know "what to do with the F.F.I. or how best to use or control them," for since the FFI had been permitted to retain its arms, it seemed immediately after the liberation to be the "worst danger in Paris." [126]

Staffed by men of courage who had helped their country in one of the darkest periods of its history, the FFI was the single avenue for unifying all the Resistance movements and was perhaps the greatest moral force in France at the time of the liberation. Yet active resistance through the FFI had appealed to the reckless as well as to the daring. With the arrival of Leclerc's soldiers, the FFI in the capital became "a band of forgotten men." Certain more responsible members, feeling their presence no

[125] Ltrs, Luizet to de Gaulle, 1800, 23 Aug, de Gaulle to Luizet, 2230, 23 Aug, quoted in Even, La 2e D.B., pp. 118-21; Butcher Diary, entry 26 Aug (written by Lt.-Col. James Frederic Gault); see Resistance Unit, Liberation of Paris, p. 1253; Pogue, *Supreme Command*, p. 242, n. 32; Interv by Pogue with Gen de Gaulle, 14 Jan 47, Pogue Files.
[126] Butcher Diary, entry 26 Aug; Msg, Vissering

to SHAEF, 28 Aug, SHAEF File 014.1, France, II; Msg, 12th AGp to SHAEF, Q–20323, 12 Aug, and SHAEF Msg, 13070, 21 Aug, SGS SHAEF File 322, FFI

longer required, disappeared and resumed their normal pursuits. Others sought to exploit their weapons for personal ends. Disturbing incidents took place in the capital and the provinces, some simple disorders, others, such as the proclamation of local soviets in isolated areas, politically inspired.[127]

Koenig, anxious to relieve the situation by placing disturbing elements in uniform and thus under military discipline, asked SHAEF to furnish uniforms and equipment for 15,000 men. SHAEF complied immediately. SHAEF had earlier recognized that legal status for the FFI required the enrollment of its members in the French Army in order to provide them with a distinctive form of military dress that would distinguish them from irregular forces not entitled to the privileges and guarantees of military custom and law.[128] Using this as a lever, Koenig projected the policy by announcing that FFI members, "because of the magnificent patriotic zeal which they evinced in particular [ly] difficult circumstances, are naturally indicated to constitute the frame of our future Armies."[129]

Such tactful circumspection was not de Gaulle's forte. Three days after the liberation of Paris, he ordered that, "beginning the 29 August 1944, the high command of the underground forces in Paris are inactivated, dissolved, and their duties will be carried out by the Commanding Generals of the different military regions." Those Resistance members liable for military service were to be regularly drafted into the Army.[130] The French War Department implemented the decision by issuing the regulations "to be applied concerning integration of the FFI's into the Army."[131] Despite criticism by extremists of the left, who declared that the action restricted the growth of a "national popular and democratic army," the Provisional Government in September passed decrees placing the FFI under French military law.[132]

Although de Gaulle had wanted the 2d French Armored Division in Paris immediately after the liberation, Leclerc protested occupation duty. The division nevertheless stayed in the capital to clear the few remaining Germans and to guard bridges, military stores, and installations.[133] On 3 September, after de Gaulle apparently was satisfied with the order in the capital and the solidity of his political position, he requested General Eisenhower to remove the division from the capital for use in active operations. Five days later, the division rejoined the Third Army.[134]

[127] Psychological Warfare Div AEF, Spec Rpt (France) No. 10, FFI, S.824R/I.S. 204, 9 Oct, SGS SHAEF File 322, FFI.

[128] Msg, Vissering to SHAEF, 28 Aug, SHAEF File 014.1, France, II; SHAEF/17245/6/5/Ops (C), French Forces of the Interior 22 Jul, SGS SHAEF File 322, FFI; SGS SHAEF War Diary, 22 Jul.

[129] Spec Mil Staff of the Supreme Comd of French Forces in Great Britain, Organization of the French Forces of the Resistance, 2.051 EMP/DM, 11 Aug, SGS SHAEF File 322, FFI.

[130] Gen de Gaulle, Decision, Ref No. 7 CAB-Mil/PA, 28 Aug, SGS SHAEF File 322, FFI.

[131] War Dept, Cabinet, Provisional Govt of the Republic, Memo for the Dept of the Chief of the General Staff, Ref No. 14/CAB, 28 Aug, SGS SHAEF File 322, FFI.

[132] Office of the Secretary of War, Decrees of 19 and 20 Sep 44, concerning the Organization of the FFI . . ., excerpts from the "Journal Officiel" of the French Republic, No. 81, 23 Sep, SGS SHAEF File 322, FFI.

[133] V Corps Dir, Gerow to Leclerc, 29 Aug, FO 23, 1100, 28 Aug, and AAR, Aug.

[134] Pogue, Supreme Command, pp. 242–43; V Corps Operations in the ETO, p. 210.

The climax of deteriorating Franco-American relations in regard to Paris occurred when General Gerow turned Paris over to the French administration. Gerow had understood that, as the senior military commander in Paris, he had responsibility for exercising control over the city during the military phase of the liberation and that he was eventually to transfer his power to General Koenig, the military governor of Paris. Yet Gerow found his authority constantly challenged by de Gaulle, Koenig, and Leclerc, to the extent that he felt impelled to request SHAEF to clarify "how far their authority extends."[135]

On the second day after the liberation, General Gerow stormed into the First Army headquarters and, in the absence of the army commander, made known his troubles to General Kean, the chief of staff. "Who the devil is the boss in Paris?" he asked. "The Frenchmen are shooting at each other, each party is at each other's throat. Is Koenig the boss . . . De Gaulle . . . or am I the senior commander of troops in charge?" Assured that he was in charge, General Gerow said "All right. . . . There will be repercussions, mind you. You will have plenty of kicks—and kicks from important people, but I have a military job to do. I don't give a damn about these politicians and [I mean] to carry out my job."[136]

There were other irritations. General Gerow was surprised to find a Communications Zone representative, Brig. Gen. Pleas B. Rogers, in the city almost immediately. He also learned that an international agreement had been made for the control of Paris, an agreement of which he had not been informed.[137] Furthermore, Koenig had arrived in Paris on 25 August and had immediately taken over civil affairs without checking with Gerow as a matter of courtesy. "So long as there was no interference on his part with tactical operations," Gerow wrote later, "I raised no objections to his action."[138]

Judging the city militarily secure on 28 August, Gerow formally turned the capital over to Koenig, who flatly informed him, "The French authorities alone have handled the administration of the city of Paris since its liberation. . . . Acting as the military governor of Paris since my arrival, I assumed the responsibilities . . . the 25th of August 1944.[139] Koenig probably felt that he could not make the slightest sign that might be interpreted as admitting French dependence on the Americans. "We shouldn't blame them," General Eisenhower wrote with charity, "for being a bit hysterical." [140]

Gerow turned U.S. military control in the city over to the Seine Base Section of the Communications Zone. During the early days of September, the large COMZ-ETOUSA headquarters moved from the Cotentin to Paris, a central location where adequate facilities, in contrast to those of the Cotentin, per-

---

[135] Msg, Vissering to SHAEF, 26 Aug, SGS SHAEF File 014.1, France; see also *V Corps Operations in the ETO*, p. 198; Ltr, Gerow to OCMH, 22 Sep 54; V Corps AAR, Aug, and G–5 Sec Staff Rpt.

[136] Sylvan Diary, 26 Aug.

[137] Ltr and attachments, Blakely to author, 30 Sep 55, OCMH Files.

[138] Ltr. Gerow to OCMH, 22 Sep 54; see Gerow to Hodges, 0010, 26 Aug.

[139] The letters are reproduced in *V Corps Operations in the ETO*, p. 209.

[140] Msg, Eisenhower to Marshall, 31 Aug, Pogue Files.

mitted more efficient operation. Occurring when transportation was so critical as to immobilize some combat units, the move came at an unfortunate time. Also, long before the liberation, General Eisenhower had reserved the city and its hotels, in his mind at least, for the use of combat troops on furlough. "Field forces in combat have always begrudged the supply services their rear-echelon comforts," General Bradley later wrote. "But when the infantry learned that Com Z's comforts had been multiplied by the charms of Paris, the injustice rankled all the deeper and festered there throughout the war."[141] Though Eisenhower tried to reduce the number of rear-echelon troops in the city, the military population of Paris nevertheless swelled to what seemed like unreasonable proportions.[142]

One of the first impressions the liberators of Paris received was that the population appeared "healthy and full of vigor." Yet at the time of liberation only one day's supply of food was on hand for civil population.[143] "The food situation is serious," de Gaulle had wired. "The lack of coal is grave. Thanks in advance for what you can do to remedy this." "You may depend on us to do everything consistent with the military situation," the Supreme Commander replied. "Every effort is being

made to rush food and coal to Paris."[144] A tremendous relief program was already under way.

The greatest problem in organizing relief for Paris was transport. Bombing and sabotage had disrupted railroads, rolling stock was in short quantity, bridges had been destroyed, heavy military traffic had damaged roads. The requirements of the breakout had placed a heavy strain on motor vehicles, and gasoline was in such short supply that combat operations were about to come to a halt.[145] So serious was the lack of transport that at least one Liberty ship with food for Paris could not be accepted for discharge on the Continent.[146]

To overcome these deficiencies, General Eisenhower ordered carrier planes to supplement rail and road movements. On 27 August airplanes began delivering 3,000 tons of food, medical items, and soap from the United Kingdom at the rate of 500 tons a day. General Bradley authorized a daily allocation of 60,000 gallons of fuel—gasoline or diesel—and 6,000 gallons of lubricants for vehicles delivering supplies to Paris. He also allotted 1,000 gallons of fuel oil for collective kitchens in the capital. All transportation that could possibly be spared from military requirements was made available. Two ships departed the United Kingdom on 27 August carrying 179 3/4-ton trucks, each with a trailer, to be used to get supplies to the French.

Although every effort was made to get

---

[141] Bradley, *Soldier's Story*, pp. 405–06.

[142] Eisenhower to Lee, FWD–15033, 16 Sep, SHAEF File G–3 Ops A, 312.1–2, Dirs to AGps; Pogue, *Supreme Command*, pp. 320–33; Interv by Pogue with Maj Gen Walter Bedell Smith, Washington, 13 May 47, Pogue Files; see also Ruppenthal, *Logistical Support, II*, 31–32.

[143] V Corps G–5 Staff Sec Rpt, and AAR, Aug; *V Corps Operations in the ETO*, p. 206; Msg, Vissering to SHAEF, 27 Aug, SGS SHAEF File 014.1, France.

[144] De Gaulle to Eisenhower, 1915, 26 Aug, SGS SHAEF File 092, French Relations; Eisenhower to de Gaulle, FWD–133336, 28 Aug, SGS SHAEF File 014.1, France.

[145] See below, Ch. XXXII, for a detailed discussion.

[146] Msg, EXFOR Rear Movements to COMZ, QM–430, 30 Aug, SGS SHAEF File 014.1, France.

PARISIANS' WELCOME TO GENERAL DE GAULLE

coal into the city for essential utilities, its importation was an especially difficult problem because railroad service was lacking and because all the trucks in service were carrying food. Military vehicles rushed 1,000 tons of supplies per day from British and American continental stockpiles provided for that purpose. French and captured German trucks moved several hundred tons of nearby indigenous stocks into the capital daily. Ships brought cargo from the United Kingdom for relief distribution. To offset the diminishing military stockpiles, American agricultural specialist officers were assigned to help French officials locate supplies in surplus pro-ducing areas and arrange for their delivery to the city. The French began to move cattle on the hoof to Paris.

Half the daily relief supplies provided by the Americans and 800 tons of coal per day were moved at the expense of the military effort. Representatives of the two army groups and the Communications Zone co-ordinated the flow within Paris, while French authorities arranged local distribution. More than a month and a half after the liberation of Paris, French relief was still a consequential Allied military responsibility.[147]

[147] Msg, Gen Eisenhower to Asst Secy of War John J. McCloy, FWD–13308, 27 Aug; Gen Bradley to Maj Gen Frank F. Scowden, Q–10373, 27 Aug;

In retrospect, the liberation of Paris was as much a Franco-American conflict as an Allied-German struggle. The French secured almost all they wanted by convincing a reluctant, but in the end amenable, Allied command to do their bidding. The restoration of French dignity, implicit in the liberation, had come about largely through French efforts sustained by Allied complaisance. If the Allies somewhat spoiled the liberation for the French by forcing the French to share it with American troops, their motives were as pure as their impatience was typical. Regarding the prestige inherent in the liberation as small repayment for the dead Allied soldiers lost between the beaches of Normandy and the gates of the capital, the Americans were astonished when the expected French gratitude for assistance became instead a resentment and insubordination that could not be dissipated by relief supplies. Interestingly enough, the British, whether by accident or design, refrained from participating in the liberation and the ceremonies, perhaps because they regarded the liberation as primarily a French matter, possibly because they were aware of an undercurrent of anti-British feeling as a result of the destruction of the French fleet. It was unfortunate also that the man in the street confused the name of the American commander, Gerow, with that of General Henri Giraud, one of de Gaulle's political opponents, and that so overwhelmingly a de Gaullist victory in the capital could have been blemished by a simple phonetic similarity. Over the entire experience hovered the shadowy figure of Choltitz, who sought to satisfy all masters and who in the end could say that he saved Paris from destruction and could be a hero to all. No wonder, with the complications that threatened to rip the fabric of the façade of the liberation—that wonderful joy and delight of the liberated people and of civilized people everywhere, the flowers, the kisses, the songs, and the wine—no wonder it seemed cruel to expose the intrigue and bickering behind the scenes. Certainly it was simpler to believe the legend that emerged afterwards: the French Resistance in Paris had liberated the capital without outside help.[148]

Msg, Gen Eisenhower to Maj Gen John H. Hilldring, S–58600, 28 Aug; SHAEF to 12th AGp (Rear), FWD–13340, 28 Aug; Lee to Scowden, JX–13369, 27 Aug; 12th AGp to SHAEF G–5, Q–10443, 30 Aug; SHAEF Msg, FWD–13411, 30 Aug. All in SGS SHAEF File 014.1, France, II. See also V Corps G–5 Sec Staff Rpt, V Corps AAR, Aug.

[148] Adrien Dansette, "Du 19 au 25 août 1944: Paris se Libéré," *Miroir de l'Histoire*, No. 55 (August, 1954), 151–60; see also Pierre Billotte "10e Anniversaire de la Libération de Paris," *Le Monde*, Année 11, # 2980 (25 August 1954).

PART SEVEN

PURSUIT

CHAPTER XXX

The Battle for Brest

The Post-OVERLORD Decision

Near the end of August the Allies could consider Operation OVERLORD virtually complete. They had secured a continental lodgment area from which to mount an assault against the heart of Germany. The next step, according to plans, was to transform the lodgment into a continental base to support the blow that was to lay the enemy prostrate and allow Allied troops to overrun the German homeland.

To prepare for the final attack toward Germany, the Allies had intended, even as late as mid-August, to halt for several weeks at the Seine.[1] But developments on the battle front during the second half of August—the partial destruction of two German armies in Normandy and the landings in southern France—had prompted German withdrawal along the entire front. This made it imperative for the Allies to deny the enemy the chance to recover and make a stand at any of several terrain features along the path of retreat that were favorable for defense. Logistical considerations notwithstanding, pursuit operations had to be undertaken at once. (*See Maps I, VIII, XII.*)

When the Allies reached the Seine, the logistical situation was far from satisfactory. With the exception of Cherbourg, the Allies had no major ports. Preinvasion planners had assumed that the conclusion of OVERLORD would find the Americans in possession of the Breton ports of St. Malo, Brest, Quiberon Bay, and Nantes, and the British in position to take Rouen and Le Havre.[2] Although by mid-August the British could anticipate quick capture of the Seine ports and even the Channel ports, the Americans possessed only Cherbourg and the destroyed and useless harbor facilities at St. Malo. Strong German garrisons still held Brest, Lorient (and the Quiberon peninsula), and St. Nazarie (which barred the mouth of the Loire River and therefore access to Nantes). All Allied supplies were still coming across the beaches, with the exception of inconsequential quantities arriving through such minor ports as Isigny, Granville, and Cancale, and somewhat larger amounts discharged at Cherbourg. Although the tonnage landed with such limited facilities exceeded all expectations, the approach of autumn weather cast a shadow on future prospects.

The logistical apparatus on the Con-

---

[1] PS SHAEF (44) 11, Post-NEPTUNE Opns, First Draft, 12 Aug. Final, 17 Aug. SHAEF File 18008, G-3 Plans.

[2] Of the many papers and studies that echo this premise, see, for example, SHAEF Plng Staff, Post-NEPTUNE Courses of Action After Capture of Lodgment Area, 3 May, SGS SHAEF File 381, Post-OVERLORD Plng.

tinent was also deficient.[3] The spectacular nature of the breakout from the cramped pre-COBRA beachhead had made it impossible for supply installations to keep up with the combat units, supply distances having suddenly changed from tens of miles to hundreds. The First Army had relinquished logistical responsibilities to the Communications Zone at the end of July, just when the demands of the static battle of the hedgerows were giving way to the different requirements of mobile warfare. The Communications Zone, instead of expanding the depot system as planned, had to assume the more pressing task of delivering supplies directly to the consumers. The result was not the most secure logistical base from which to launch post-OVERLORD operations.

Despite his awareness of the logistical flaws, General Eisenhower on 17 August felt that "the beating" the Allies were administering the enemy in Normandy would enable the Allies to "dash across the Seine." Two days later he decided to cross the Seine in strength.[4] On 20 August, while the 79th Division was securing the first Allied bridgehead over the Seine, the Allied command was giving serious consideration to the next goal—the Rhine River, more than two hundred and fifty miles to the east.[5]

The decision to cross the Seine necessitated little soul searching. The example of McClellan at Antietam was too well known. Pursuit of a defeated enemy was axiomatic.

General Eisenhower's decision to pursue the enemy across the Seine changed neither the port development plans nor the prevalent feeling that the Breton ports were vital for the development of the campaign.[6] According to the Allied troop dispositions and the plans for post-OVERLORD operations, the 21 Army Group would advance up the Channel coast while the 12th Army Group drove eastward away from the coast and across northern France. By liberating and opening the Seine and Channel ports, which had been reserved in the OVERLORD planning for British and Canadian logistical operations, the 21 Army Group would ease its supply problems. In contrast, the American forces would be moving away from the coast and lengthening their supply lines. Since in August Cherbourg was still handling less cargo than anticipated and since the gales of September might disrupt and even terminate the beach operations on the invasion coast, sheltered waters and port unloading facilities in Brittany, despite their increasing distance from the front, remained objectives of vital importance.

"We are promised greatly accelerated shipments of American divisions directly from the United States," General Eisenhower explained to General Montgomery as he set forth his thoughts on pursuit

[3] See Ruppenthal, *Logistical Support*, I, 483ff; The Gen Bd USFET, Rpt on Ammo Supply for FA, Study 58, p. 18, File 471/1.

[4] Msg, Eisenhower to Marshall, CPA–90228, 17 Aug, Pogue Files; Ltr, Eisenhower to Montgomery, 19 Aug, SGS SHAEF File 381, Post-OVERLORD Plng; 12th AGp Memo for Rcd (Additional Notes of Bradley-Patton Conf, 1730, 19 Aug), 19 Aug, 12th AGp File 371.3, Mil Obs, I.

[5] 21 AGp Operational Situation and Dir, M–519, 20 Aug, SGS SHAEF File 381, Post-OVERLORD Plng; 12th AGp Operational Plan, 20 Aug, 12th AGp

Ltrs of Instrs; 12th AGp G–4 Jnl, 20 Aug, 12th AGp File 371.3, Mil Obs, I; Maj Gen Manton S. Eddy's Diary, entry 22 Aug.

[6] Ruppenthal, *Logistical Support*, I, 470–74, and II, Ch. II; see ANCXF to SHAEF, 15 Aug, SGS SHAEF File 373/2.

operations beyond the Seine, "and it is mandatory that we capture and prepare ports and communications to receive them. This has an importance second only to the destruction of the remaining enemy forces on our front." The speed of Bradley's advance east of Paris, General Eisenhower felt, would be governed by the speed with which the Breton ports could be secured and the supply situation improved.[7]

The opening attack on the most important of the Breton ports, Brest, coincided on 25 August with the start of the pursuit beyond the Seine. Generals Eisenhower, Bradley, and Patton anticipated quick success on both fronts, and the Supreme Commander talked of sending the VIII Corps to secure Bordeaux very soon—as soon as the Breton ports fell.[8]

A fortress city of 80,000 people situated on the northern shore of an excellent landlocked roadstead of ninety square miles, Brest had been a major base of the French Navy. Because it was primarily a naval base and remote from the industrial centers of France, Brest had never attained commercial importance. In World War I, the American Expeditionary Force had used it as the principal port for the direct movement of troops from the United States to France. Though the cargo-handling facilities were not as good as at other French ports, Brest offered the Allies an excellent deep water harbor. The railroad from Brest to Rennes, along the north shore of Brittany, had been captured in good condition, and supplies discharged at Brest could easily be transported to the troops in the interior of France.[9]

Conscious of the deficiency of unloading equipment at Brest and of the probability that the Germans would destroy all facilities before letting the port fall into Allied hands, the Allies had drawn plans for constructing a port complex at Quiberon Bay. Yet in order to use not only Quiberon but also Lorient, St. Nazaire, and Nantes, the Allies first had to clear the sea lanes around the Brittany tip—that is, eliminate the German naval base at Brest and seize the submarine pens there.[10]

In the same way that the Allies thought the fall of St. Malo would weaken the German will to resist at the other port cities, they hoped that the reduction of Brest would affect the morale of the garrisons at Lorient and St. Nazaire. After Brest, the Allies intended to attack Lorient "if it was still holding out."[11]

Thus it came about that as the Allies plunged into pursuit of the retreating enemy east of the Seine, more than fifty thousand U.S. troops became involved in siege operations against the fortress of Brest, three hundred miles west of the front.

[7] Ltr, Eisenhower to Montgomery, 19 Aug, SGS SHAEF File 381, Post-OVERLORD Plng; Eisenhower to CCS, CPA-90235, 22 Aug, SHAEF G-3 Ops A 322.011/1, Comd and Contl of U.S./Br Forces; see 12th AGp Ltr, Rpt of Staff Visit . . . to Hq VIII Corps, 16 Aug (Bradley-Middleton conf), ML-205.

[8] 12th AGp Memo for Rcd, 19 Aug, ML-205.

[9] See above, Ch. XXII.

[10] Ruppenthal, *Logistical Support*, II, Ch. II; 12th AGp Ltr of Instrs 6, 25 Aug. The VIII Corps AAR's of August and September give excellent accounts of the action at Brest and have been used throughout the chapter as the basic sources; see also Kenneth Edwards, *Operation NEPTUNE* (London: Collins, 1946), pp. 264-69.

[11] Middleton-Macon Conf Notes, 17 Aug; VIII G-2 Est 6, 15 Aug. All documents in this chapter, unless otherwise noted, are in the VIII Corps G-3 Journal and File.

The Problems at Brest

Brittany had become the province of General Middleton and the VIII Corps when they entered the peninsula by way of Avranches on the first day of August. Before the first week was over, the majority of the Germans had fled the interior portions and taken refuge in ports designated by Hitler as fortresses: St. Malo, Brest, Lorient, and St. Nazaire. The only enemy forces in the interior were small detachments that hid by day and attempted to reach a fortress port by night.

Though the Germans inside the fortresses displayed little penchant for sallying forth, they had to be contained until means to eliminate them became available. Excluding those at St. Malo and a small force at Paimpol, Middleton estimated that approximately 35,000 Germans (about 10,000 field forces and 25,000 naval, marine, and miscellaneous garrison troops) remained in Brittany. He judged that about 16,000 troops (half of which were field forces) garrisoned Brest, 9,500 the Lorient area (including Concarneau and Belle-Isle), and 9,500 St. Nazaire.[12] (*See Map VIII.*)

Middleton's primary mission, after the fall of St. Malo, would be the capture of Brest, but the forces then available to him were insufficient for this and his other tasks. The whirlpool that was sucking Allied forces eastward to the Seine and beyond left the VIII Corps with responsibility for a widening gap between its forces in Brittany and the southern flank of the Third Army. Eventually Middleton guarded a south-

ern flank two hundred and fifty miles long. When he received, because of a typographical error, a telegram intended for the VII Corps, telling him to "take over the Melun bridgehead" on the Seine, he replied, "Can't do it; stretched too far already."[13]

Having lost the 4th Armored Division to the XII Corps, Middleton covered the Nantes–Angers area with the 2d Cavalry Group and a regiment of the 80th Division. He had the bulk of the 6th Armored Division at Lorient, a small combat command of the 6th and a few 8th Division troops at Brest. With Task Force A clearing the Paimpol area, the 83d Division heavily engaged at St. Malo, and the 8th Division protecting Rennes, the capture of Brest and the protection of an ever-extending front along the Loire River were beyond the capacities of the corps. To permit the 83d Division (upon the reduction of St. Malo) to assume the less wearing mission of patrolling the Loire River, and to reinforce the 8th Division and Task Force A scheduled for action at Brest (several thousand FFI members under Colonel Eon were also available for action on the periphery of Brest), Bradley transferred from the First Army to Middleton the 2d and 29th Divisions, which had been pinched out near Tinchebray during the reduction of the Argentan–Falaise pocket, and two Ranger battalions, which had been performing rear-area guard duty.[14]

[12] VIII Corps G–2 Est 6, 1800, 15 Aug; 12th AGp Plng Sec Memo, 20 Aug.

[13] XX Corps Msg, 25 Aug, and reply, VIII Corps G–3 Jnl.
[14] 2d Cav Gp Unit Rpt 1, 15 Aug; 319th RCT FO 5, 15 Aug; Memos, Maddox for Evans and Evans for Maddox, 25 Aug; Memos, Gaffey for Middleton, 14 Aug, and Middleton for Patton, 14, 15, and 19 Aug; Bradley to Hodges and Patton, 18

At Lorient General Grow, the 6th Armored Division commander, chafed under his static containment mission and wrote Middleton "a plea for the characteristics of the Division to be exploited to the maximum at the earliest practicable date."[15] Middleton appreciated Grow's eagerness to get into the main operational stream outside Brittany, but considered the presence of an armored reserve essential. Grow then went to see Patton, who told Grow to move a combat command to Orléans; on the way, the troops were to clear small German groups that were still a nuisance along the Loire River. At least part of the 6th Armored Division would thus be closer to the main body of the Third Army and more quickly available to Patton. CCB started out of Brittany on 28 August, forced a small group of Germans on the north bank to evacuate to Saumur, found no other enemy forces north of the Loire River, and eventually moved to Montargis.[16]

Meanwhile forces gathered for the attack on Brest. The Communications Zone headquarters took responsibility for Rennes and relieved the 8th Division, which reached Plabennec by 18 August. The 2d Division arrived at Landerneau on 19 August, and the 29th Division assembled just south of Lannilis four days later. With Task Force A and contingents of the FFI also nearby, Middleton was ready to commence his operation against Brest as soon as adequate supplies could be stocked. (*Map XV*)

Adequate supplies were as much a problem for Middleton as they were for the commanders driving east from the Seine. By far the most serious shortage for the siege-type action about to take place at Brest was in artillery ammunition. The shortage was already plaguing the corps at St. Malo, and on 10 August Middleton had warned the Third Army that he foresaw heavy ammunition expenditures at Brest. Patton promised that even though the Third Army might be rationed in ammunition, he would see to it that the VIII Corps was supplied.[17] When the army requested formal estimates of the Brest requirements, Middleton based his reply on the St. Malo experience and on the expectation of using an armored division and three infantry divisions supported by thirteen battalions of corps artillery. He requested an initial stock of 8,700 tons of ammunition, plus a replenishment allowance of 11,600 tons for the first three days.

The Third Army staff considered the request excessive on two grounds. It anticipated that only two divisions and ten corps artillery battalions would take part in the operation against Brest, and it believed that the corps had overestimated the strength of the enemy garrison and its will to resist. Setting 1 September as the target date for the fall of Brest, Third Army allotted only about 5,000 tons for the entire operation—less than

---

Aug; TUSA Dir, 17 Aug, and Msg, 23 Aug; 12th AGp Ltr and Ltr of Instrs 5, 17 Aug; Journal des Marches.

[15] Grow to Middleton, 20 Aug.

[16] Memos, Middleton for Patton, JTR for Evans, 15 Aug, Middleton for Grow, 18 and 21 Aug; 6th Armd Div FO 14, 28 Aug; TUSA Operational Dir, 27 Aug; Patton to Middleton, 2 Sep; Read to Grow. 30 Aug, 6th Armd Div CCB Unit Jnl.

[17] VIII Corps G-3 Jnl, entry 13 Aug; Ruppenthal, *Logistical Support, I*, 528ff. is an excellent account of the logistical difficulties at Brest. See also *Conquer, the Story of the Ninth Army, 1944-1945* (Washington: Infantry Journal Press, 1947) (hereafter cited as *Story of Ninth Army*), pp. 53ff.

a quarter of what Middleton considered essential for the first three days. As it turned out, three divisions and a separate task force supported by eighteen corps artillery battalions—division artillery and tank destroyer battalions brought the total to thirty-four battalions—were eventually to take part in the battle, a force that further emphasized the discrepancy between requirements and stocks.

Third Army's unwillingness to send more than 5,000 tons of ammunition to the VIII Corps reflected the critical nature of supply transportation for the main Third Army drive to the east. In addition, co-ordination between Third Army and VIII Corps was difficult because of the growing distance between the two headquarters. On 25 August the army and corps command posts were two hundred and seventy miles apart. Hoping to alleviate the difficulties, Third Army arranged to have the Brittany Base Section of the Communications Zone provide direct administrative support to VIII Corps. A slight increase in ammunition stocks resulted.

When Generals Bradley and Patton visited the VIII Corps headquarters on 23 August, General Middleton convinced them he needed more ammunition. They immediately authorized 8,000 tons, which they thought would be sufficient for six days, the length of time they considered reasonable for the operation. Expecting the ammunition to be delivered, Middleton launched his attack on 25 August. When all the authorized supplies did not arrive, he had to suspend operations. Three days later he learned that what he had regarded as minimum, Bradley and Patton had considered adequate.

As a result of better co-ordination, better arrangements for ship and rail transportation to the Brest area were made on 29 August. Still, not until 7 September did the corps have enough ammunition stocks to permit resumption of a sustained full-scale attack. Even then, so many agencies were involved that no one knew the exact status of supply or what was en route or on order. Hoping nevertheless that a steady flow of ammunition had been established, Middleton launched another attack on 8 September. He was not disappointed. By 10 September Bradley had assigned the Brest operation first priority on supply. When the operation finally terminated, 25,000 tons of ammunition were in the corps supply point, much of which was later reshipped to the active front, hundreds of miles away.[18]

The difficulties in fulfilling the VIII Corps requirements had come from intense competition among the armies engaged in the pursuit for the severely limited overland transport available. Ammunition shortages in Brittany occurred at the same time that gasoline crises affected the pursuit. The VIII Corps used the beach of St. Michel-en-Grève (near Morlaix) to receive LST-shipped items, but the seaborne cargo was not adequate to supply all needs, and trains and trucks had to bring most of the supplies to Brest from Normandy. An airfield near Morlaix was used to bring in emergency supplies and to evacuate wounded.[19]   Poor communica-

---

[18] 12th AGp Ltr of Instrs 8, 10 Sep.

[19] 12th AGp Ltr, Rpt of Staff Visit, 16 Aug, ML–205; Ruppenthal, *Logistical Support, I,* 532; Bradley, *Effect of Air Power,* pp. 70–71; ETOUSA Engr Hist Rpt 10, Combat Engineering, is a useful source and has been used extensively in this chapter.

SUPPLIES FOR BREST.   *Trucks leaving LST near Morlaix for Brest.*

tions, long distances, and weather contributed their adverse effects, but at the bottom of the difficulties was improper co-ordination for the Brest operation at all the echelons of higher command due to the optimistic initial belief that Brest would fall quickly.

Another headquarters became involved in the Brest operation on 10 September, when VIII Corps passed from Third Army control to Lt. Gen. William H. Simpson's Ninth U.S. Army, operational five days earlier at Rennes. The Ninth Army assumed responsibility for protecting the southern flank of the 12th Army Group and for conducting opera-

tions in Brittany. In addition it had the task of receiving, processing, and training units arriving in France. General Bradley had thought of inserting the Ninth Army into the line during the pursuit east of Paris, but the speed of the advance and logistical difficulties prompted him to assign it to Brittany. To permit Middleton to give undivided attention to Brest, General Simpson placed the 6th Armored and 83d Divisions, which were not involved at Brest, directly under his own control. Almost immediately afterwards, when Bradley called for troops to augment the forces in the pursuit, Simpson accelerated the movement into Brittany of the 94th Division, commanded by Maj. Gen. Harry J. Malony, in order to release the 6th Armored Division. Around the middle of September, after the newly arrived division assumed the job of guarding Lorient, the 6th Armored Division finally moved eastward to rejoin the Third Army.[20]

The problems of getting the operation started and keeping it in motion were matched by the task of reducing the defensive complex of the fortress of Brest.[21] (*Map XIV*) The city itself, originally on the slopes of hills on both sides of the Penfeld River, spread over several neighboring communities, among them Recouvrance and St. Pierre-Quilbignan on the west, Lambézellec on the north, St. Marc on the east. The city proper and the small commerical port area are east of the river; the western side, known as Recouvrance, includes the naval base, with extensive repair shops, drydocks, quays, barracks, storehouses, and U-boat shelter pens.

The countryside around Brest, a gently rolling plateau, presents a pattern of small hills and low ridges separated in some places by narrow deep-cut valleys, the whole criss-crossed by numerous streams. The Germans used these terrain features to good advantage and organized a system of positions of various kinds and in varying strengths to establish a defense in depth.

The defensive works ranged from simple trenches to concrete pillboxes, casemates, and gun emplacements. Ob-

stacles included barbed wire entanglements, mine fields, and antitank ditches. The Germans incorporated into their defensive system a number of old French forts, built before the Franco-Prussian War and located in the western and northwestern suburbs of the city. Even the high ramparts of an ancient fortress at the mouth of the Penfeld, a work constructed by Vauban in the seventeenth century, had a role in the defense scheme—in some places thirty-five feet high, fifteen feet thick, and protected by a moat, overgrown with grass, vines, and flowers, and serving as a promenade for Sunday strollers, the walls sheltered gun emplacements.

The Germans integrated into their land defenses dual-purpose antiaircraft guns and guns stripped from ships sunk in the harbor by Allied planes. Batteries of coastal and field artillery on the Daoulas promontory and the Quelern peninsula provided additional fire support. Heavy guns near le Conquet, intended primarily to protect the sea approaches to Brest, could also help the landward defenses. Although the Germans considered their twelve batteries of Army field artillery and eighteen batteries of Navy *Flak* inadequate for the task of defending Brest, the Americans were to find them more than troublesome.[22]

Approximately thirty thousand troops defended Brest, nearly twice the number estimated by the Americans. The core of the defense was the *2d Paratroop Division*, composed of tough young soldiers. Their commander, Ramcke, who had gained prominence in the German air-

[20] *Story of Ninth Army*, pp. 21, 28–39, 45–46; 12th AGp Memo for Rcd, 19 Aug, ML–205; 12th AGp Ltr of Instrs 7, 5 Sep.
[21] See Albert Vulliez, *Brest au Combat, 1939–1944* (Paris, c. 1950), map facing p. 154.

[22] MS # B–731 (Fahrmbacher); 12th AGp Immed Rpt 49, German Defenses at Brest, 9 Sep.

ANCIENT WALL AND MOAT *on land side, inner fortress at Brest.*

borne attack on Crete in 1940, was also the fortress commander. His chief of staff was Colonel von der Mosel who, before Ramcke's appointment, had commanded the fortress. Generalmajor Josef Rauch, the commander of the *343d (Static) Division*, was charged with the Daoulas and Crozon sectors.[23]

Ordered by Hitler to hold to the last man, Ramcke was determined to do so. If he needed to justify resistance that could count victory only in the number of days the garrison held out, Ramcke could feel that the Allied forces he tied down at Brest and the ammunition he caused the Allies to expend there would constitute just that much less that could be brought to bear on the German homeland. Having evacuated all the French civilians who might encumber his defense, Ramcke used his paratroopers as nuclei to stiffen the defense of strongpoints held by the miscellaneous naval and static personnel of the garrison.[24]

Between 13 August, when the 6th Armored Division had started to displace from Brest to Lorient, and 18 August, when the bulk of the 8th Division began to arrive near Brest, the presence of little more than a combat command of Allied troops near Brest led the German garrison to make raids on the countryside.[25] These came to an end as U.S. forces gathered. On 18 August the VIII Corps command post moved one hundred and twenty miles to Lesneven, fifteen miles from Brest, to undertake the siege of the

---

[23] MS # B-427 (Kogard); Vulliez, *Brest au Combat*, pp. 224-25 has a good description of Ramcke.

[24] Ramcke, *Fallschirmjager, Damals und Danach*, pp. 46-48, 51; CI 14 (2d Div).
[25] Journal des Marches.

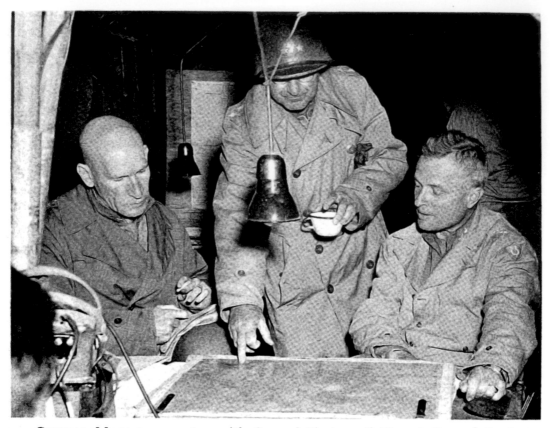

GENERAL MIDDLETON *confers with General Simpson (left) and General Stroh (right) near Brest.*

fortress. Though Bradley and Patton thought the Germans would soon capitulate, Middleton figured that Brest would be little different from St. Malo. Several days before the operation began, planners at the 12th Army Group also concluded that the Brest garrison would probably fight to the last man.[26]

The Fight for Brest

Even before the arrival of all his forces in the Brest area, General Middleton launched a preliminary operation designed to protect his flanks, isolate his objective, prevent the escape of the garrison across the harbor, and secure observation points on the promontory between Brest and Daoulas.[27] Combining the 2d Division's 38th Infantry, plus additional units, with General Earnest's long-standing Task Force A, General Middleton created a unit called Task

---

[26] *Story of Ninth Army,* p. 24; 12th AGp Plng Sec Memo, 20 Aug.

[27] Ninth U.S. Army Operations, I, Brest–Crozon, USFET Hist Div. MS (1946), OCMH Files, is a valuable source.

Force B under Brig. Gen. James A. Van Fleet, the assistant commander of the 2d Division.[28] He instructed Van Fleet to attack from Landernau to Hill 154, a dominating feature on the approaches to Brest south of the Elorn River. *(See Map VIII.)*

Task Force B jumped off on 21 August and advanced rapidly for several miles until stopped by a massive volume of fire from positions on Hill 154 and from artillery north of the Elorn. The defenders, soldiers of the *353d Division*, were well dug in on a strong position that included a network of trenches around the crest of the hill, eight steel and concrete reinforced pillboxes, and barbed wire entanglements. They had more than twenty-five machine guns, several antitank weapons, and mortars. The strength of the position and the fire power allocated to its defense indicated the importance the Germans attached to its possession.

Supported by tank destroyer and artillery fire, a battalion of the 38th Infantry assaulted on 23 August over rocky terrain that afforded scant cover and concealment. Success was in large part attributable to the action of Staff Sgt. Alvin P. Casey, who though mortally wounded destroyed a pillbox with grenades.[29] Against a total loss of 7 dead and 28 wounded, Task Force B took 143 prisoners and counted about a hundred German bodies on the crest of the hill.[30]

Having deprived the Germans of an excellent observation post on the eastern approaches to Brest, Task Force B pushed forward to clear the remainder of the promontory. By forcing the Germans to demolish the reinforced concrete bridge over the Elorn River and thereby cut land communication between the promontory and Brest, the force secured Middleton's left flank. The task force used flame throwers, demolitions, and tank destroyer and artillery fire to destroy pillboxes and emplacements. It cleared the entire peninsula by the last day of August and took 2,700 prisoners. Characterizing the action an "outstanding success," Middleton dissolved the task force, sending the 38th Infantry to rejoin the 2d Division, Task Force A to guard the approaches to the Crozon peninsula, and the 50th Armored Infantry Battalion to Lorient to rejoin the 6th Armored Division.[31]

Because the Daoulas promontory juts out into the roadstead southeast of Brest, it provided excellent artillery positions. Middleton dispatched a corps artillery group there to take under fire the rear of the landward defenses around Brest and also German positions on the Crozon peninsula. On the basis of plans drawn by Task Force B, Middleton formed a

---

[28] Other components were: three field artillery battalions (from the 2d Division), the 50th Armored Infantry Battalion, a company each of the 68th Tank Battalion and the 603d Tank Destroyer Battalion, and a battery of the 777th AAA AW SP Battalion (from the 6th Armored Division). The components of Task Force A were: the 1st Tank Destroyer Brigade, controlling the 6th Tank Destroyer Group, the 705th Tank Destroyer Battalion, a battalion of the 330th Infantry (83d Division), the 15th Cavalry Group, and an engineer combat battalion. VIII Corps G-3 Msg, 21 Aug. The 38th Infantry headquarters acted in a dual capacity—for the regiment and for Task Force B. Ltr, Zwicker to OCMH, 14 Mar 56.

[29] Casey was awarded the Medal of Honor.

[30] Memos, Van Fleet for Earnest, 21 Aug, and Evans for Middleton, 28 Aug.

[31] CI 15 (2d Div); Buckley, *History of the 50th Armored Infantry Battalion*, pp. 27-28. Other 6th Armored Division elements rejoined the division early in September.

provisional battalion of fifty-seven machine guns, twelve tank destroyers, and
eight 40-mm. Bofors guns to provide
security for the artillery group and to
engage targets of opportunity in and
around Brest.[32]

The success of Task Force B led to
the formation of a similar unit for action
on the right flank. Known as Task
Force S and commanded by Col. Leroy
H. Watson, the assistant commander of
the 29th Division, the regimental-sized
force was to clear the tip of Brittany,
specifically the coastal area between
Brest and le Conquet.[33] Cutting the
Brest–le Conquet highway on 27 August,
the troops moved westward to the coast,
captured the small fort at Pointe de
Corsen (an important radar station) and
isolated le Conquet and the nearby important artillery batteries at Lochrist
(dual-purpose 88-mm. guns and four 280-
mm. pieces in open pits). Siege action
against the defenses of le Conquet and
Lochrist came to an end on 9 September
after a four-man patrol led by 1st Lt.
Robert Edlin entered the main position
of the Lochrist fort and burst into the
commandant's office. Pulling the pin of
a hand grenade he carried, Edlin called
for surrender or death. The commandant surrendered his forts and more

than a thousand men.[34] Task Force S
was then dissolved.

After several postponements because
of the difficulties of securing ammunition
and of co-ordinating air, naval, and
ground forces, General Middleton set
the date of the main attack against Brest
for the afternoon of 25 August. He
planned to attack the city with three infantry divisions abreast, the 29th Division on the right, the 8th Division in the
center (the main effort), and the 2d Division on the left. By then the divisions
were in contact with the forward edge of
the German defense perimeter, which
formed a rough semicircle four to six
miles around the mouth of the Penfeld
River. In that area were two defense
belts. The outer line consisted of field
fortifications developed in depth and reinforced with antitank obstacles, concrete works, and emplacements, most of
which were built during the few previous
months. The inner belt, about four
miles wide but only 3,000 yards deep,
strongly fortified throughout with field
works and permanent-type defenses, had
been built long before the Allied landings in Normandy for close-in protection
of the naval base. Because of the shallowness of the defense area, the outer
belt was the main battle ground on
which the Germans had to fight the
battle of Brest. (*See Map XIV.*)

Middleton arranged to have heavy and
medium bombers attack targets in the
city as well as on the peninsulas of the
Brest complex and obtained enough
fighter-bombers (some with 5-inch rockets, some with jellied gasoline bombs)

---

[32] 12th AGp Immed Rpt 69, Supporting Fires at
Brest, 28 Aug; Ltr, Zwicker to OCMH, 14 Mar 56.
[33] Task Force S had a variable composition but in
general consisted of a battalion of the 116th Infantry, the 2d and 5th Ranger Battalions, the 224th
Field Artillery Battalion, parts of the 86th Cavalry
Reconnaissance Squadron, the 29th Division Reconnaissance Troop, and a company each of engineers, antiaircraft artillery, and 4.2-inch mortars.
The task force was aided by two hundred Russians
who had deserted the German Army. See Ninth
U.S. Army Opns, I, Brest–Crozon, and Vulliez,
Brest au Combat. pp. 206–08.

[34] Edlin received the DSC.

for a constant four-plane air alert in support of each division. In addition, Middleton secured the assistance of the British battleship H.M.S. *Warspite* for a 15-inch-gun bombardment of the heavy coastal batteries, particularly those near le Conquet.[35]

Part of the bombing program had to be canceled because of adverse weather conditions, but seven groups of medium bombers and 150 Flying Fortresses struck Brest and started a large fire in Recouvrance, west of the Penfeld River. The *Warspite* hurled some three hundred shells into the coastal batteries near le Conquet and after scoring several direct hits shifted to forts in Recouvrance. Fifteen medium and heavy battalions of the corps artillery were also active. Fighter-bombers strafed and bombed, and sank several ships in the harbor near the Crozon peninsula.[36] Despite this heavy volume of preparatory fire, the well-co-ordinated ground attack of the three divisions made little progress.

Attempting to soften the will to resist, RAF heavy bombers struck Brest around midnight of 25 August, and on the following morning American and RAF heavies blasted targets again. The resumption of the ground attack on 26 August, however, brought little change. The German garrison remained firm.[37]

The attack on 26 August displayed the kind of combat that was to predominate during the siege of Brest. Because ammunition stocks were low, the artillery reduced its activity to direct support missions. As the Americans came to a full realization of the strength of the German opposition, and as the pattern of the enemy defense system emerged, commanders on all echelons saw the necessity of changing their own tactics. The units turned to more detailed study of their tactical problems with the purpose of reaching intermediate objectives. The nature of the battle changed from a simultaneous grand effort to a large-scale nibbling—a series of actions dictated by the local problems of each sector commander.[38]

The divisions began to probe to locate and systematically destroy pillboxes, emplacements, fortifications, and weapons, moving ahead where weak spots were found, overwhelming pillboxes with flame throwers and demolitions after patient maneuver and fire. Small sneak attacks, the repulse of surprise counterattacks, mine field clearance, and the use of smoke characterized the slow squeeze of American pressure. Fog, rain, and wind squalls during the remainder of August restricted air support, while continued shortages of ammunition curtailed the artillery. Yet on 28 August, a regiment of the 29th Division bounded toward Brest on the le Conquet highway for almost two miles against virtually no resistance. On the following day, the 8th Division gained on one front, but the Germans cut off two leading companies

---

[35] SHAEF Msg, 25 Aug, SGS SHAEF File 381, Post-OVERLORD Plng; Bradley to Middleton and Middleton to Bradley, 24 Aug; 12th AGp Immed Rpt 44, Air Ground Opns in Attack on Brest, 31 Aug; VIII Corps FO 11, 22 Aug. Vulliez, *Brest au Combat*, pp. 225ff., gives an interesting account of the battle from the point of view of the civilian population.

[36] Bradley, *Effect of Air Power*, pp. 128ff.

[37] 2d Lt. Earl O. Hall of the 13th Infantry, who participated in vicious fighting for trenches and concrete emplacements until killed by artillery fire, was posthumously awarded the DSC.

[38] 2d Div FO 10, 23 Aug, and Ltr of Instrs, 2030, 26 Aug; MS # B–731 (Fahrmbacher); Brest Fortress Comdr Rpt, 12 Aug, *OB WEST KTB, Anlage 1330*.

of infantry and marched them into Brest as prisoners. In the 2d Division sector, the troops were in the midst of dogged fighting to reduce strong positions. Typical of the fighting was the action of Lt. Col. H. K. Wesson of the 9th Infantry, who reorganized a rifle company reduced to forty-six men, then led the unit in an assault across hedgerowed terrain, destroyed a machine gun position, and took fourteen German paratroopers prisoner.[39]

On 1 September, the expected completion date of the siege, as ammunition prospects seemed momentarily improved and with the divisions in the main German defenses, General Middleton again launched a co-ordinated attack after a strike by medium bombers and a forty-five-minute preparation by the division artillery pieces and nine corps artillery battalions. Although the VIII Corps Artillery fired 750 missions, including 136 counterbattery, in twenty-four hours, and although single pieces, batteries, and sometimes battalions kept known enemy gun positions under continuous fire, the only apparent result of the attack was a gain of several hundred yards by the 8th Division. Even this small gain was almost immediately lost to counterattack.[40]

Discouraged, General Middleton wrote "a rather pessimistic letter" to General Bradley. He reported that his troops were "none too good," that replacement arrivals were behind schedule, that ammunition supply was poor though improving, and that air support "left much to be desired." The Germans had "no intention to fold up right away,

having shown no signs of weakening." Middleton requested more 4.2-inch mortars, more artillery, and more and better air support. General Bradley talked to Maj. Gen. Hoyt S. Vandenberg, the commander of the Ninth Air Force, in an attempt to improve the air support, and several days later General Eisenhower authorized Vandenberg to "utilize maximum number of aircraft which can be effectively employed in support of this operation." [41]

Middleton's letter was like the darkness before dawn. The first real break occurred on 2 September when the 2d Division captured Hill 105 southwest of Guipavas. A month earlier the 6th Armored Division commander, General Grow, had recognized the hill as a key terrain feature in the defense of Brest, one of two hills dominating the eastern approaches to the city. As the Germans fell back from Hill 105 several hundred yards in the center of the corps zone, the 8th Division advanced and took another of the fortified hills in the outer defense ring. Yet the 29th Division, facing Hill 103 east of the village of Plouzané, had no such success.

For five more days the divisions continued their individual efforts. While medium and heavy bombers attacked Brest every day save one, local ground attacks inched the front toward the port. By the end of the first week in Septem-

[39] Colonel Wesson was posthumously awarded the DSC.
[40] See TUSA AAR, Sep.

[41] Memo, Kibler for Swift, Brest, 2 Sep, ML-205; Leigh-Mallory to Vandenberg, Smith to Vandenberg, and Eisenhower to Vandenberg 4, 6, and 7 Sep, SGS SHAEF File 381. General Middleton also sought landing craft for local amphibious operations against Brest, but his request was denied by naval authorities on the ground that no plan had been developed for such action. SHAEF to ANCXF, FWD-13554, 2 Sep, SGS SHAEF File 381, Post-OVERLORD Plng.

2D DIVISION TROOPS *move through a devastated area near Brest.*

ber, the grip around the Brest garrison had tightened. The 2d Division was within reach of Hill 92 (the second hill dominating the northeastern approaches); the 8th Division was on the approaches to the village of Lambézellec (the gateway to Brest from the north); and the 29th Division, still denied Hill 103 ("we're on it, but so are the Jerries"), stood before Fort de Mengant, five miles west of the Penfeld River.[42] By then the besieged area was so small that heavy bombers could no longer attack without endangering the American ground troops.

On 7 September Middleton judged that he had enough ammunition on hand (and assurance of more to come) to sus-

tain another effort on the whole front. Securing six planes per division for constant air alert, he launched a co-ordinated attack on 8 September after a strong artillery preparation. The weight of all three divisions carried a number of positions that previously had been denied. The 2d Division captured strongly fortified Hill 92; the 8th Division—to a great extent because of the actions of Pfc. Ernest W. Prussman, who was virtually the leading man in the attack—advanced two regiments several hundred yards toward Lambézellec and Hill 82; and the 29th Division finally took an important strongpoint at Kergonant, just north of the village of Penfeld.[43]   Prisoners totaled close to one

---

[42] 29th Div G-3 Jnl, 30 Aug.

[43] See S. L. A. Marshall and John Westover, Capture of Kergonant Strong Point During the Brest

GUN CREW FIRING *into the German-held section of the port of Brest.*

thousand men; American casualties numbered two hundred and fifty.

With that achievement on 8 September and the arrival of eight LST's and two trainloads of ammunition that night, the corps commander was optimistic for the first time since the beginning of the operation. Furnished at last with adequate artillery support on the following day, the 2d Division reached the streets of Brest, the 8th Division, after securing Lambézellec, launched a two-regiment attack and entered the city also, and the

Campaign (hereafter cited as Marshall and Westover, Kergonant Strong Point), ETOUSA Hist Sec, Bn and Small Unit Study 3, n.d. Pfc. Prussman was posthumously awarded the Medal of Honor. S. Sgt. George T. Scanlon of the 121st Infantry, who led an assault on enemy dugouts, was awarded the DSC.

29th Division secured the village of Penfeld. Prisoners that day totaled more than 2,500.

As the numbers of prisoners rose, hopes of victory quickened. The battle for Brest entered its final but most painful stage. The 2d and 8th Division became involved in street fighting against troops who seemed to contest every street, every building, every square. Machine gun and antitank fire from well-concealed positions made advances along the thoroughfares suicidal, and attackers had to move from house to house by blasting holes in the building walls, clearing the adjacent houses, and repeating the process to the end of the street. Squads, and in some instances platoons, fought little battles characterized by General Robertson, the 2d Division com-

TROOPS FIGHTING THEIR WAY THROUGH THE STREETS OF BREST

mander, as "a corporal's war." [44] A typical obstruction was a concrete reinforced dugout no higher than ten inches above ground, which was built on a street corner with an opening for a heavy machine gun at street level. Eight men (with two flame throwers, a bazooka, and two BAR's) made a wide detour, neutralized several small nests of resistance, came up behind the pillbox, and flamed the position until thirteen Germans surrendered.[45]

Because the 2d Division had a larger section of the city to reduce before reaching the old wall, the 8th Division completed its street fighting and arrived at

the fortified city wall first, at Fort Bougen on 10 September. An infantry assault, preceded by an artillery preparation, failed to breach the wall, which was 25 to 35 feet high and behind a dry moat 15 to 25 feet deep. General Stroh prepared an attack for the following day, but after direct fire from heavy-caliber corps artillery pieces tore gaps in the upper portion of the wall without effect on the lower sections, it was obvious that an infantry assault would be costly and of doubtful success. Since the converging movement on the city compressed the division fronts and deprived the divisions of sufficient maneuver room, General Middleton decided to withdraw the 8th Division. This took place in several stages. Two battalions assumed part of the 29th Division front

---

[44] VIII Corps AAR, Sep; see *Story of Ninth Army*, pp. 32ff.

[45] CI 15 (2d Div).

REMAINS OF FORT KERANROUX

west of the Penfeld around midnight, 10 September. On the following night the 2d Division relieved the 8th Division east of the Penfeld. Two days later the advance of the 29th Division pinched out the two battalions still in line, and the 8th Division, no longer in contact with the enemy, began to move to Crozon to secure the peninsula, to eliminate the guns there that fired on the troops attacking Brest, and to prevent escape of the Brest garrison across the harbor.[46]

The change proved beneficial. General Gerhardt attacked at midnight, 11 September (in part to cover the displacement of the 8th). Crossing an antitank ditch near the village of St. Pierre, men of the 29th on 12 September advanced toward Hill 97 from the north and west and toward two old French fortifications, Forts Keranroux and Montbarey. While the 2d Division still was involved in vicious street fighting, the 29th Division faced the necessity of reducing these and other forts.

Hoping that the Germans might be ready to surrender, General Middleton sent a proposal to Ramcke while guns remained silent on the morning of 13 September. When Ramcke declined, Middleton published the letters of parley

[46] *Story of Ninth Army*, pp. 32–33; 8th Div AAR, Sep.

FORT MONTBAREY

for distribution to his troops. "Take the Germans apart," he told his men.[47]

Fort Keranroux was the first objective on the 29th Division's list. A battalion of the 175th Infantry, which for three days had been denied a close approach because of strong outer works, attacked again on the afternoon of 13 September. Staff Sgt. Sherwood H. Hallman leaped over a hedgerow and eliminated a German machine gun emplacement by grenades and rifle fire that killed several men and forced the surrender of twelve others. About seventy-five nearby Germans, who had until then defended the

approaches, followed suit.[48] The entire battalion advanced two thousand yards to Fort Keranroux, which was under bombardment from planes and artillery and covered by smoke shells. Two infantry companies, crossing the open ground immediately in front of the fort, lost but ten men and gained the entrance in fifteen minutes. A hundred Germans surrendered. The fort had been so blasted by bombs and shells that the original outlines of the main emplacements were no longer recognizable.

Fort Montbarey was more difficult. An old French casemated fort with earth-filled masonry walls some twenty-five

---

[47] VIII Corps G-3 Jnl and File, 13 Sep; Captured German Documents, Brest (Middleton-Ramcke correspondence), OCMH Files.

[48] Hallman received the Medal of Honor.

GENERALMAJOR HANS VON DER MOSEL
*and other German officers surrender
at Brest.*

feet thick, surrounded by a dry moat
fifty feet in width, and garrisoned by
about a hundred and fifty men, Montbarey was protected by outlying positions
that included riflemen and 20-mm. guns
covering a mine field of 300-pound naval
shells equipped with pressure igniters.
Even the preliminary task of approaching the fort seemed impossible. The
VIII Corps engineer, Colonel Winslow,
had early recognized the difficulties posed
by the forts and had requested a detachment of flame-throwing tanks. The aid
came in the form of a squadron of the
141st Regiment, Royal Armoured Corps,
which was attached to the 116th Infantry, the regiment charged with capturing Montbarey. The British unit had
fifteen Crocodiles—a Churchill tank
mounting a flame gun in place of a machine gun and towing a trailer with
flame-throwing fuel. Their function

was to scorch the firing positions of the
outer wall of the fort and cover engineers who were to place charges to breach
the wall in advance of an infantry assault.

On 14 September, after men of the
121st Engineer Combat Battalion cleared
a path through the mine fields under the
cover of artillery high-explosive and
smoke shells, four Crocodiles advanced
in file toward the fort. When two tanks
wandered from the path and struck
mines and another was destroyed by
enemy fire, the attack was suspended.
For the rest of the day and the next,
artillery, tank destroyers, and mortars
pounded the fort. Although eight
fighter-bombers assigned to work with
the 29th Division were grounded by
weather, they were able to give support
when the infantry resumed the attack on
the following day.

Meanwhile, Engineer troops, working
at night, improved the path through the
heavily mined and shell-pitted fields.
At dawn on 16 September, the Crocodiles
advanced to within eighty-five yards of
the fort. After an intensive artillery
preparation, smoke shells were placed to
cover the outer wall. Concealed by
the smoke, three Crocodiles advanced,
reached the moat surrounding the wall,
and flamed the apertures. At the same
time, engineers placed 2,500 pounds of
explosive at the base of the wall and
tank destroyers and a 105-mm. howitzer
of the regimental cannon company
hurled shells against the main gate from
a distance of two hundred yards. A
breach was torn in the main gate, and
the engineer demolition charge opened
a hole in the fortress wall large enough
for infantry assault. Battered by almost
constant fire from the ground and the

GENERAL RAMCKE *after his capture at Brest.*

air for several days, and dazed by the shock of the explosion, the surviving eighty members of the German garrison surrendered. The assault battalion of infantry had sustained about eighty casualties during the preparatory stage of the attack but took none in the final assault.[49]

With Fort Montbarey in friendly hands, the main Recouvrance defenses were open. Before dark on 16 September, combat patrols were over the wall and in the old city. Resistance disintegrated. Over a ten-day period the 5th Ranger Battalion, in a series of actions that came to be known as the battle of the forts, had captured the fort at Pointe du Petit Minou and Forts de Mengant

and de Dellec and thereby cleared the western shoreline of the harbor of Brest.[50] By the end of 17 September only the submarine pens and Fort du Portzic remained in enemy hands. The groups holding these capitulated on the following morning.

Meanwhile, the 2d Division had fought through the streets of Brest to reach the city wall on 16 September. After a strongpoint near the railroad station was eliminated, and after a patrol exploited an unguarded railroad tunnel through the wall into the inner city, troops climbed the wall and swept the remaining half mile to the water's edge.

As the battle for Brest had been fought in two sectors separated by the Penfeld River, so the German capitulation occurred in two parts, both on 18 September. Von der Mosel surrendered all the troops in Recouvrance to the 29th Division; Col. Erich Pietzonka of the *7th Parachute Regiment* surrendered the eastern portion of the city to the 2d Division, appropriately enough in President Wilson Square. Nearly ten thousand prisoners, who had prepared for capitulation by shaving, washing, donning clean uniforms, and packing suitcases, presented a strange contrast to the dirty, tired, unkempt, but victorious American troops.[51] Ramcke, however, escaped across the harbor to the Crozon peninsula.

A cavalry squadron of Task Force A had cut the base of the Crozon peninsula on 27 August and patrolled there until Task Force B completed the Daoulas operation. Task Force A then moved onto Crozon. General Earnest took Hill

---

[49] 12th AGp Immed Rpt 46, Employment of Crocodile (Flame Throwing) Tanks Near Brest, 27 Sep; Action at Fort Montbarey, ETOUSA Hist Sec, Bn and Small Unit Study 2, n.d.

[50] For a detailed account, see CI 88 (29th Div).
[51] 29th Div AAR, Sep; CI 14 (2d Div); Ninth U.S. Army Opns, Brest–Crozon.

330, the dominating terrain near the base, then contented himself with patrolling since he knew he could expect no assistance from the forces in the main battle at Brest.[52]

When the 8th Division, pinched out before Brest, arrived on Crozon in mid-September, General Stroh (supported by the attachment of Task Force A and the 2d Ranger Battalion) directed an attack that overran a defensive line maintained by the *343d Division.* The German division commander, Rauch, surrendered on 17 September, a day before the garrison in the city of Brest capitulated. The final action on Crozon occurred on 19 September when troops scaled the wall across the throat of the Quélern and pushed to the Pointe des Espagnols. Only a group of diehards about Ramcke remained. That Ramcke too was ready to surrender was obvious when he sent a message asking Brig. Gen. Charles D. W. Canham, the 8th Division's assistant commander, for his credentials. Canham replied that his troops served to identify him. Claiming later to have fired the last shell from his remaining 75-mm. assault gun, Ramcke surrendered during the afternoon of 19 September.[53]

The action on Crozon had been far from easy. In taking 7,638 prisoners on the peninsula, for example, the 8th Division between 15 and 19 September incurred casualties of 72 killed and 415 wounded.

The final action occurred on 20 September when Task Force A drove down to Douarnenez to demand the surrender of an isolated group of three hundred Germans. Though they refused at first

to surrender, a few artillery rounds and the threatening presence of a single fighter-bomber overhead proved sufficient persuasion.

The operations against Brest had been a series of actions against approximately seventy-five strongpoints. The heavy-walled forts of massive stonework were for the most part pivots of resistance rather than bastions of a line, their real importance coming from their dominating sites. The Americans had generally advanced after probing for weak spots, moving against open flanks, turning those flanks, and finally reducing outer works by fire before destroying the individual strongpoints at close range. Local actions, often seemingly unrelated—"At one time we had three separate wars going in the division," General Gerhardt later stated—produced an over-all pressure that was hammered home by increasing amounts of artillery fire and by air attacks. The actual conquest of the garrison had come as the result of action by the combined arms— heavy artillery fire, infantry assault, engineer blasting operations, and the use of flame throwers. Bunkers and pillboxes of reinforced concrete, sometimes nine feet thick, did not always require close-in action toward the last because in many instances the constant pounding of bombs and shells had prepared the Germans mentally for capitulation.[54]

Air support normally did not directly aid the advance of small units in the same way that close support artillery, mortars,

[52] TF A Opns, 1 Aug–22 Sep.

[53] Ramcke, *Fallschirmjaeger, Damals und Danach,* p. 67; Ninth U.S. Army Opns, Brest–Crozon.

[54] Marshall and Westover, Kergonant Strong Point; CI 14 (2d Div); 2d Div Ltr of Instrs, 2000, 14 Sep; Interv with Capt Robert E. Garcia, Hosp Intervs, ML–2234; Ltr, Gerhardt to OCMH, 26 Apr 56; 29th Div AAR, Sep.

and machine guns did. The principal function of the planes was to destroy or neutralize strongpoints a thousand yards or more behind the enemy front, though the immediate effect weakened morale among the Germans in close contact. Air also restricted enemy movement, (particularly of reserves), kept gun crews under cover and away from firing positions, and limited hostile observation.[55]

From 25 August through 19 September, the VIII Corps received continuous air support except during periods of inclement weather. Fighter-bombers on alert status alone flew approximately 430 separate missions involving more than 3,200 sorties. Fighter-bombers of the IX and XIX Tactical Air Commands also attacked fifty targets on planned missions between 4 and 7 September. Medium and heavy bombers of the Eighth and Ninth Air Forces and of the Royal Air Force attacked coastal and heavy antiaircraft batteries, forts, blockhouses, strongpoints, and defensive installations in the inner ring of the Brest defenses.[56]

Despite the impressive amount of air power employed at Brest, difficulties had ensued because of inadequate communications and because the corps was conducting an independent operation hundreds of miles from the main front. Aircraft had to be diverted to Brest, and good weather on one front did not always signify the same for the other. The heavy and medium bomber effort had been less effective than expected because the planes were sometimes assigned tasks beyond their capabilities. Yet if certain selected targets proved invulnerable to bombardment and shelling, the effect of tons of explosives dropped from the air and the expenditure of almost 500,000 rounds of artillery had lent authority to the tightening grip around the city.

American casualties totaled 9,831; prisoners numbered 38,000, of which more than 20,000 were combat troops. The 2d Division had advanced approximately eight miles at a cost of 2,314 casualties. It had expended more than 1,750,000 rounds of small arms ammunition, 218,000 rounds of heavy caliber, had requested 97 air missions—fulfilled by 705 fighter-bombers, which dropped 360 tons of bombs. The 29th Division, expending a similar amount of ammunition, had lost 329 killed and 2,317 wounded. Casualties of the 8th Division for the month of September were close to 1,500.[57]

The VIII Corps turned over the captured fortress of Brest and the prisoners to the Brittany Base Section of the Communications Zone on the evening of 19 September, and the combat troops moved into assembly areas to rest, receive winter clothing, and repair armament and transport. Task Force A was soon dissolved. The 29th Division departed on 24 September to rejoin the First Army, and on 26 September the VIII Corps headquarters and the 2d and 8th Divisions began to move by rail and motor to Belgium and Luxembourg for

---

[55] CI 87 (29th Div), Air Support at Brest; Bradley, *Effect of Air Power*, 128ff.; 12th AGp Immed Rpt 65, Close Air Support of Ground Forces Around Brest, 26 Sep.

[56] Air Chief Marshal Harris suggests *(Bomber Offensive*, p. 214) that without heavy bombers the Allies would have been able to capture Brest (and other fortified ports) only after much more prolonged siege warfare.

[57] VIII Corps G–1 Per Rpt, 19 Sep; CI 16 (2d Div); Ninth U.S. Army Opns, Brest–Crozon; 8th Div AAR, Sep.

DRYDOCK DESTRUCTION AT BREST

commitment in a new zone, still under Ninth Army control.[58]

In an unrelated action occurring at the same time as the capture of Brest, the 83d Division, which was protecting the Third Army south flank, had accepted a mass German surrender at the Loire River. Allied successes in Normandy and on the Mediterranean shores of France had prompted German forces in southern France to withdraw. The German prisoners taken at the Loire were from the rearmost portion of troops that

had been withdrawing from southwest France since mid-August, a group, mostly noncombatant military personnel, under Generalmajor Botho H. Elster, formerly commandant of Biarritz. When the Germans lost contact with a screening force that was to have provided escort to Dijon, they became increasingly harassed by Allied planes and the FFI. By 5 September, Elster's columns stretched virtually unprotected more than thirty miles along the roads generally between Poitiers and Châteauroux. The commander of twenty-four men of the Intelligence and Reconnaissance Platoon, 329th Infantry, 1st Lt. Samuel W. Magill, displayed initiative and daring by taking his unit south of the Loire to make con-

[58] *Story of Ninth Army*, pp. 53–55. Some heavy equipment was moved by water transport through the English Channel. Edwards, *Operation NEPTUNE*, p. 269.

tact with Elster on 8 September. Two days later Elster surrendered to General Macon, the 83d Division commander. Elster conducted his force—754 officers, 18,850 men, and 10 women, plus 400 civilian automobiles, 500 trucks, and 1,000 horse-drawn wagons—in three columns across the Loire at Orléans, Beaugency, and Mer into hastily constructed prisoner of war enclosures.[59]

The Best Laid Plans

The capture of Brest gave the Allies a totally destroyed city and a thoroughly demolished port. The desolation was appalling. The Germans had wrecked everything that might be of any use to the Americans, Ramcke later boasting that he had done so "in good time."[60] Twisted bridge structures blocked the Penfeld River channel. The wharves, drydocks, cranes along the waterfront, even the breakwaters enclosing the naval basin and the commercial port, had been ruined. Scuttled ships lay in the harbor.

The American operation had also contributed to the destruction. Bombs and shells from air and ground, including white phosphorus and jellied gasoline, had burned and gutted practically every building in the downtown section of Brest as well as in Recouvrance. Demolished houses had tumbled into the streets, filling thoroughfares with rubble. Even after bulldozers cut paths through the piles of brick and masonry, weak-ened and collapsing walls made passage hazardous. The French inhabitants who had been evacuated before the siege returned to find their city virtually obliterated.[61]

The vast amount of reconstruction and repair necessary to rehabilitate the port led the Allies to confirm a decision already made—that use of Brest was not necessary. The difficult operation at Brest had contrasted bleakly with the triumph of the pursuit, and Allied commanders had been as disappointed by the siege of Brest as they had been elated by the surge toward the Rhine. Interest in the geographically remote ports of Brittany had begun to wane toward the end of August as unabashed Allied optimism raised hopes that the Channel ports, including even Rotterdam and Amsterdam, would soon come within reach.[62]

On 3 September SHAEF planners recommended the abandonment of plans to use the ports of Lorient, Quiberon Bay, St. Nazaire, and Nantes, a recommendation SHAEF accepted four days later. Had the battle of Brest not been in progress, the planners might well have withdrawn their approval of Brest also, a conclusion they finally reached on 14 September, even before capture of the city. Yet only a day before, General Eisenhower had said that since no one could predict with certainty when the Channel ports would be taken and opened, he still felt that he needed Brest to receive newly arriving troops and their organizational equipment that were scheduled to come directly from the

---

[59] Inside German-Occupied France, September 1944; 329th Inf AAR, Sep; 83d Div AAR, Sep; *Story of Ninth Army*, pp. 47–50.

[60] Ramcke, *Fallschirmjaeger, Damals und Danach*, p. 65.

[61] See Alix de Carbonnières and Antoine Coste, *L'Assaut de Brest* (Brest: P. le Bris, 1951), *passim*.

[62] See Remarks of Lt Col William Wihe, 26 Sep, CI 87 (29th Div).

United States.[63] Thus the continuing idea of taking Brest was like insurance that everyone hoped he would not have to collect.

Whatever the actual value of Brest in retrospect, it appeared with certainty at the end of August that Brest and the other ports were needed to supplement the far from adequate port capacity of Cherbourg and the minor harbors of Normandy. Yet soon afterwards, port plans for Lorient and St. Nazaire were scrapped, and the 15,000-man German force at Lorient and the 12,000-man force at St. Nazaire, together with a small pocket northwest of Bordeaux, were contained until the end of the war.[64]

Since the Breton ports, on which the Allies had counted so heavily, were not put to use, what had been accomplished by the siege of Brest? The immediate result was the elimination of a strong German garrison of aggressive, first-rate soldiers. Containment of the Brest garrison, according to General Bradley, would have required "more troops than we could spare on an inactive front." According to Patton, he and Bradley agreed that Brest was useless, but they felt that "when the American Army had once put its hand to the plow, it should not let go."[65] In any event, comple-

tion of the operation freed VIII Corps for action in the operations directed toward Germany. The charge was later made that the employment of three divisions and valuable transport and supplies at Brest adversely affected pursuit operations, for just at that time troops, vehicles, and supplies were desperately needed on the main Allied front. Yet the resources used at Brest, slender when compared to the total effort, could hardly have altered the pattern of a pursuit that was destined to run a limited course.[66]

The serious Allied problem of port capacity had prompted the Brest operation. The Allied commanders who had initiated the operation had not been able to foretell exactly when and to what extent the Channel ports would alleviate the situation. Thus they looked upon Brest as a port in reserve. The fact that capture of neither the destroyed harbor of Brest nor the Channel ports proved to be an immediate solution did not vitiate their wisdom and vision. For, as it turned out, the problem persisted. Not until November, when Antwerp was opened, was the problem of port capacity finally solved.

If it seemed in retrospect that the commanders erred in starting the siege of Brest, they did so on the side of caution, preferring to be safe rather than sorry. If they displayed any recklessness at all, it was in the pursuit beyond the Seine, where that kind of behavior was understandable.

---

[63] Msg, Eisenhower to Bradley, FWD–14066, 7 Sep, SHAEF File Eisenhower's Ltrs and Dirs; Msg, Eisenhower to Bradley, FWD–14764, 13 Sep, 12th AGp Incoming Cables; see Msg, Eisenhower to CCS, FWD–14376, 9 Sep, SGS SHAEF File 381.

[64] Story of Ninth Army, pp. 39–49; MS # B–731 (Fahrmbacher).

[65] Bradley, Soldier's Story, p. 367; Patton, War as I Knew It, p. 128.

---

[66] See Pogue, Supreme Command, pp. 259–60, and Ruppenthal, Logistical Support, I, 535–36.

CHAPTER XXXI

The Drive Beyond the Seine

The Framework of the Pursuit

The implications of the essentially simple decision on 19 August to cross the Seine were far reaching. Once across the Seine, the Allies would be heading toward the Rhine River and Germany. Where they were to make their main effort and how far they were to go occasioned much debate.

The basic directive of the Combined Chiefs of Staff governing Allied operations in western Europe pointed the Allies merely to "the heart of Germany." The Combined Chiefs had very likely chosen such a vague objective in the expectation that changing circumstances would offer the Supreme Commander a variety of goals. The Allied strategic planners perceived Berlin as the most significant political objective, but they were also conscious of its great distance from Europe's western shore. Closer and within striking distance from France was the Ruhr, the heart that pumped industrial lifeblood to the German military forces, the goal selected by SHAEF planners as the most practical for post-OVERLORD operations. An Allied attack on the Ruhr would compel the Germans to commit a considerable number of forces in its defense, thus enabling the Allies to close with and destroy a sizable part of the hostile army.

There were four routes from northern France to the Ruhr: by way of the flat-lands of easily flooded Flanders; via Amiens, Maubeuge, and Liège along the northern edge of the Ardennes; through the hilly woodland of the Ardennes; and, less direct, south of the Ardennes through Metz, the Saar, and Frankfurt. Having eliminated Flanders and the Ardennes on the basis of terrain considerations, the planners recommended that the Allies advance north and south of the Ardennes with mutually supporting forces on a broad front oriented on Liège and on Metz. Initially, they had ruled out this dual concept because of the disadvantages of maintaining forces on two widely separated lines of communication, but they came to believe that success would force the Germans to withdraw in both areas, thus permitting adequate lateral communication.

Of the two recommended axes—northeast from the lower Seine through Liège, and east from the upper Seine through Metz—the planners indicated that the main effort should be made northeastward along the direct route to the Ruhr. Historically the most traveled invasion road between France and Germany, the route offered the most advantages: the best facilities for military traffic, a left flank protected by the sea, the Channel ports of Antwerp and Rotterdam, excellent airfield sites, a combat zone within range of light and medium bombers based in England, liberation of Belgium and part of the Netherlands, and seizure of the V-weapon launching sites.

The route of a complementary thrust through Metz was less advantageous. More difficult for tank warfare and having fewer airfield sites, it did not lead directly to the Ruhr but to the Saar Basin, which had a much smaller industrial capacity than the Ruhr. Nevertheless, twin drives on a broad front would stretch the enemy and allow the Allies to shift the main weight of their attack if necessary.[1] Applied to the troop dispositions in August, the planners' recommendations meant that the 21 Army Group would strike northeast through Amiens, Maubeuge, and Liège in the main effort; the 12th Army Group would go east toward Metz in a subsidiary thrust.

When General Eisenhower decided on 19 August to cross the Seine, the Allied forces were destroying those enemy units still west of the river. The fact that the bulk of the enemy troops could escape only across the lower Seine emphasized the reasonableness of making the principal Allied effort in the coastal region. Pressing on the heels of the retreating *Fifth Panzer* and *Seventh Armies,* the Allied forces would also unhinge the *Fifteenth Army* from its positions along the Channel coast. To support the

drive, General Eisenhower proposed to reinforce the 21 Army Group with the First Allied Airborne Army (activated on 2 August under the command of Lt. Gen. Lewis H. Brereton) and perhaps also with a "minimum" of U.S. ground units. At the same time that the 21 Army Group thrust northeastward, the 12th Army Group would move eastward into the interior of France in order, among other aims, to sever lines of communication between *Army Group G* in southern France and *Army Group B.*[2]

A day before, on 18 August, General Montgomery had concluded that the 21 and 12th Army Groups should keep together in a solid mass of some forty divisions, a force so strong that it need fear nothing. This steamroller, in Montgomery's estimation, should move northeast from the Seine to clear the Channel coast, the Pas-de-Calais, and west Flanders, and also to secure Antwerp. The initial objectives would be the destruction of German forces on the coast, the establishment of air bases in Belgium, the seizure of the V-weapon sites, and the opening of ports. Montgomery had not yet discussed his conception with Eisenhower, but he did so with Bradley, who, according to Montgomery, seemed impressed with the cogency of Montgomery's thought.[3] Bradley and Patton about this time were talking informally of sending three U.S. corps toward the Rhine near Karlsruhe, Mannheim, and Wiesbaden.[4]

---

[1] PS SHAEF (44) 11, Post-NEPTUNE Courses of Action After Capture of Lodgment Area, 3 and 30 May, SGS SHAEF File 381, Post-OVERLORD Plng; SHAEF Memo on V-1 and V-2, 12 Aug, SHAEF File 18008, G-3 Plans; Cole, *Lorraine Campaign,* pp. 8-10; Pogue, *Supreme Command,* pp. 249-50; Ruppenthal, *Logistical Support, I,* 485. An excellent discussion is found in T. Dodson Stamps and Vincent J. Esposito, *A Military History of World War II, I, Operations in the European Theaters* (West Point, N.Y.; U.S. Military Academy, Department of Military Art and Engineering, 1953), pp. 432-34.

[2] Ltr, Eisenhower to Montgomery, 12 Aug, SGS SHAEF File 381, Post-OVERLORD Plng.
[3] Telg, Montgomery to CIGS, M-99, 1830, 18 Aug, in Answers by Br Hist Sec to Questions by Pogue, OCMH Files.
[4] Interv by Harrison and Pogue with Bonesteel, 18 Jun 47, Pogue Files. See Pogue, *Supreme Command,* p. 250; Patton, *War As I Knew It,* p. 114; and Bradley, *Soldier's Story,* p. 398.

Montgomery had still not talked with Eisenhower when Bradley informed Montgomery two days later that the Supreme Commander inclined toward the idea of splitting the Allied force, sending half east toward Nancy. Since no firm decision had been reached, Montgomery resolved to try to change the Supreme Commander's mind. Meanwhile, he tentatively alerted the 21 Army Group for movement to the northeast, the 12th Army Group for two possible movements: either a dual thrust northeast toward Brussels and east to the Saar or a concentrated drive to the northeast on the 21 Army Group right flank.[5]

General Eisenhower, although still basically reflecting the planners' recommendations, made an alteration on 22 August. As before, the 21 Army Group (reinforced by the Allied airborne army and other units) was to go northeast from the Seine toward the Ruhr in the main effort north of the Ardennes, and the 12th Army Group was to go eastward in a subsidiary drive. But now, despite a general orientation eastward south of the Ardennes, the 12th Army Group, he thought, might shift its direction of advance from east to northeast toward the coastal region and Belgium and the Netherlands if it became necessary to bolster the main thrust.[6]

After General Montgomery saw the Supreme Commander on 23 August and presented his concept for a concentrated thrust north of the Ardennes, General Eisenhower modified his plans again.[7] "For a very considerable time," he confided to General Marshall, "I was of the belief that we could carry out the operation to the northeast simultaneously with a thrust east, but later have concluded that due to the tremendous importance of the objectives in the northeast we must first concentrate on that movement." [8]

For his main effort, General Montgomery requested not only reinforcement by the airborne army but also by the First U.S. Army. Despite General Bradley's feeling that a corps would be sufficient and General Eisenhower's belief that Montgomery was being overly cautious, the Supreme Commander acceded. Instead of driving eastward to pass south of the Ardennes, General Hodges was to go northeast from the Seine—north of the Ardennes—in support of the 21 Army Group. General Eisenhower then allocated the bulk of the 12th Army Group stocks of gasoline to Hodges, thereby depriving Patton of adequate supplies for a long strike toward the Saar. Since the more important objectives lay to the northeast— the V-weapon sites, airfields, the Channel ports, and the Ruhr—the subsidiary effort was curtailed. Yet since Patton had about a week's supply of fuel on hand, he would be able to initiate an advance beyond the Seine. "I cannot tell you," Eisenhower wrote Marshall, "how anxious I am to get the forces accumulated for starting the thrust east from Paris. I have no slightest doubt that we can quickly get to the former French-Ger-

---

[5] Ltr, Montgomery to ACIGS, 20 Aug, in Answers by Br Hist Sec; 21 AGp Gen Operational Situation and Dir, M–519, 20 Aug.

[6] Msg, Eisenhower to Marshall, CPA–90235, 22 Aug, SHAEF G–3 Ops A 322/011.1, Comd and Contl of U.S./Br Forces.

[7] See Montgomery, *Normandy to the Baltic*, p. 192.

[8] Msg, Eisenhower to Marshall, 24 Aug, Pogue Files.

man boundary but there is no point in getting there until we are in a position to do something about it." [9]

Thus three armies were to drive northeast from the lower Seine—the First Canadian, the Second British, and the First U.S.—in the Allied main effort north of the Ardennes and directly toward the Ruhr. The Third U.S. Army, alone, was to make the subsidiary thrust east from the upper Seine and pass south of the Ardennes. Although the First U.S. Army was to perform a supporting role, it had the most direct and best route to the Ruhr—the Maubeuge–Liège axis. The Second British Army, designated to make the main effort of the principal thrust, and the First Canadian Army on its left, were to move through the water-crossed flatlands of Flanders, passing over the old battlefields of World War I.

Specifically, according to Montgomery's instructions, Crerar's Canadian Army was to clear the Channel coast, including the Pas-de-Calais; Dempsey's British army was to drive into northwest Belgium, west of a boundary from Mantes-Gassicourt generally through Beauvais, Amiens, Lille, and Ghent to the southern bank of the Schelde estuary; Hodges' First Army was to move generally northeast along the Paris–Brussels axis to the Maastricht, Liège, Charleroi, and Namur areas east and south of Brussels. Simultaneously, Bradley would send Patton toward the Rhine River between Koblenz and Mannheim.[10]

Montgomery had drawn the boundary between the army groups along a line from Mantes-Gassicourt to a point just east of Antwerp.[11] The 21 Army Group thus had a zone that ended at the Schelde—the Canadian and British armies at the conclusion of their advance would be facing the estuary. Looking all the way to the Rhine, Bradley suggested that Montgomery curve the boundary northeastward at Tournai to allow the British army to wheel through Antwerp toward the Rhine and the Ruhr, and thereby cover the First Army left flank.[12]

Though very much aware of the Ruhr as the goal, Montgomery had his eyes fixed on the immediate objectives assigned by Eisenhower—capture of the Channel ports, destruction of the *Fifteenth Army,* and seizure of the V-weapon sites. He foresaw that the Canadians would have to drop elements off to deal with the fortified port cities as they moved northward along the coast. He was also uncomfortably aware that British logistical deficiencies dictated a reduction in combat forces for the initial drive east of the Seine. With limited forces, Montgomery had limited his sights. His primary concern was to destroy the *Fifteenth Army,* the last uncommitted German force in France and Belgium, by pinning that army against the Schelde estuary. With this force eliminated, the V-bomb launching sites overrun, and airfields secured, the Allies, it appeared, would face virtually no opposition, and after taking Antwerp could

[9] *Ibid.;* Ltr, Eisenhower to Montgomery, 24 Aug, SGS SHAEF File 381, Post-OVERLORD Plng, I; Pogue *Supreme Command,* pp. 251–52.

[10] 21 AGp Dir, M–520, 26 Aug, SGS SHAEF File 381, Post-OVERLORD Plng, I; 12th AGp Ltr of Instrs 6, 25 Aug, and Memo, Future Opns, 25 Aug (the latter in ML–205).

[11] Montgomery, *Normandy to the Baltic,* map, p. 210.

[12] Ltr, Bradley to Montgomery, 26 Aug, 12th AGp File 371.3, Mil Objs, I; Bradley, *Soldier's Story,* pp. 398ff.

go where they pleased.[13] Since changing the boundary at Tournai would have no effect on these initial goals, and since the change would facilitate an airborne operation near Tournai that was being planned for early September, Montgomery readily acquiesced in Bradley's suggestion.[14]

The objectives disclosed no basic difference between the two men insofar as they judged the future course of the campaign. Both were optimistic, and they accepted the prophesies that were common that the end of the war was "within sight, almost within reach." There was "no clue yet as to the enemy's final intentions," but it seemed that "events may move too fast for him."[15] The Germans were thought to have lost the equivalent of thirty divisions since D Day, and the Allies judged that only four or five divisions of the once-powerful *Fifteenth Army* still remained uncommitted east of the Seine. The forces that had fought in Normandy and that were rapidly retreating east of the river seemed to comprise two weak groups north and south of Paris. "The enemy forces are very stretched and disorganized," Montgomery observed; "they are in no fit condition to stand and fight us."

The time had come to "cripple his power to continue in the war."[16]

The German situation was every bit as bad as the Allies thought. Hitler and Jodl had been concerned with rearward lines of defense since the end of July, and at the beginning of August the military governor of France, Kitzinger, had been charged with responsibility, under OKW, for erecting field fortifications along the Somme, Marne, and Saône Rivers to the Jura Mountains of the Franco-Swiss border. With the Seine River forming a potential outpost line and the terrain around Amiens–Compiègne–Soissons sector forming the center of the Kitzinger line, the Germans hoped to stablize a withdrawing front far west of Germany.[17]

Unequivocal German withdrawal in the west had begun on 16 August in three separate movements. *Army Group B* comprised the main body, with fourteen battered infantry divisions, nine fresh but incompletely trained divisions along the Channel coast in reserve, the remnants of fourteen divisions released from the Normandy front for rehabilitation, and nine mangled armored divisions providing a sort of cavalry screen. *Army Group G* was withdrawing five divisions of the *Nineteenth Army* northward up the Rhône River valley in a rapid but orderly movement. Its *LXIV Corps,* with two divisions encumbered by noncombatants, was retiring from southwest France through a hostile country infested with FFI guer-

[13] Montgomery, *Normandy to the Baltic,* pp. 196ff; Ltr, Eisenhower to Montgomery, 24 Aug, and 21 AGp Dir, M–520, 26 Aug, SGS SHAEF File 381, Post-OVERLORD Plng, I.

[14] Montgomery, *Normandy to the Baltic,* pp. 200, 208.

[15] Montgomery statement reported in TUSA Briefing of G–3 Liaison Sec and Liaison Officers, 22 Aug, and Second [British] Army Intel Summary 81, 2400, 24 Aug, XV Corps G–3 Jnl and File; SHAEF Weekly Intel Summaries, 23, 24, 26 Aug, SHAEF G–2 File; Pogue, *Supreme Command,* pp. 244–45; Montgomery, *Normandy to the Baltic,* p. 192; First U.S. Army *Report of Operations,* I, 31.

[16] TUSA G–2 Rpt, 26 Aug; Montgomery, *Normandy to the Baltic,* p. 171; 21 AGp Operational Situation and Dir, M–520, 26 Aug.

[17] *OB WEST, a Study in Command,* p. 155, Bauer, R–20; *OB WEST* Ltr Order 1000, 4 Aug. *OB WEST KTB, Anlage 1098.*

rilla bands. All three groups headed for the Kitzinger line.[18]

Work on the line did not progress far. Kitzinger did not have enough engineer units to supervise the preparation of tank obstacles, mine fields, and the like. Organization Todt, which had been ordered to stop construction on the Atlantic Wall—except at the V-weapon sites—in order to work for Kitzinger, was slow in responding and short of matériel and equipment; even under optimum conditions it could not have furnished enough workers to build a defensive position of the proper length and depth in the time required. Impressed civilian labor did little good, for unlike the Germans in East Prussia, who willingly dug trenches to try to stop the Russians, the French in France were hardly enthusiastic about working at a task that would only postpone their own liberation.[19]

Warned on 22 August that the Kitzinger line seemed hardly begun, Jodl consulted with Hitler and on the following day placed Kitzinger under *Army Group B* control. Putting Model in charge of the construction had little effect—it was already too late. The Seine River line had already been breached at Mantes-Gassicourt, and heavy American pressure on the approaches to several crossing sites along the Seine indicated that the Seine River position concept might soon, perhaps in a matter of hours, be hopelessly compromised. This meant that time for building up the Somme–Marne defense line, roughly seventy miles from the

Seine, was extremely short. Even though Model assured Jodl on 28 August that he was getting nearby French civilians to do nothing but dig, dig, dig, he did not believe it possible to stop the Allies short of the western approaches to the Rhine River. Only on German soil could the German Army count on civilians to help construct effective fortifications.[20]

Model needed troops, and he asked for fifteen additional divisions in the Troyes, Dijon, and Jura Mountains area; four army headquarters, twelve corps headquarters, thirty or thirty-five divisions for front-line duty, plus a panzer army, four panzer corps, and twelve panzer divisions as a mobile hard-hitting reserve for the Kitzinger line. With these, he thought he could meet with some degree of equality the fifty Allied divisions that he expected to be facing on 1 September.[21]

Though Hitler had been making arrangements to get new units to the west, he hardly could fulfill Model's request. In mid-July Hitler had ordered approximately one hundred fortress battalions, then being used in rear areas, to be transformed into replacement battalions for the front, and of these approximately eighty would eventually reach the west. In mid-August he had ordered twenty-five *Volks Grenadier* divisions organized in Germany as a general reserve, and four became available for the west almost immediately. The *3d* and *15th Panzer Grenadier Divisions*, experienced troops,

---

[18] *OKW/WFSt Daily Operationskarten*, 10–31 Aug.

[19] Telecon, Model and Speidel, 1250, 28 Aug, *AGp B KTB*.

[20] Telecons, Blumentritt and Jodl, 2300, 22 Aug, Model and Jodl, 1920, 28 Aug, and Telecon, 1515, 23 Aug, transmitting Friedel Telecon to *OB WEST, AGp B KTB; OB WEST KTB*, 24 Aug.

[21] Msg, Model to Jodl, 2300, 24 Aug, *AGp B Wochenmeldungen und Lagebeurteilungen*.

were traveling from Italy for commitment in France. Two "shadow divisions" (filler troops trained to restore veteran units reduced to cadre strength) and two panzer brigades (tank-infantry task forces designed to defend critical positions) were also slated for *OB WEST*. These forces would not become available until the end of August or early September, nor would they give Model his desired strength. Meanwhile, the front was disintegrating.[22]

Logistical matters seemed somewhat less discouraging. The difficulties of transporting supplies to the front in July and early August had diminished as distances shrank—the reverse of the Allied situation. Summertime had provided the Germans with insufficient hours of darkness for supply movements to the Normandy coast, and their railroad trains and motor convoys, forced to travel in daylight, had attracted Allied fighter-bombers. Wrecked and plundered trucks, wagons, and freight cars littering the countryside attested to the extent of losses. The Germans had attempted to ameliorate the situation by assigning mobile *Flak* units to guard railroads and highways. Barges on the Seine had supplemented overland traffic. As the front withdrew eastward, though the problems were by no means solved, the combat troops came closer to three supply complexes that had been established on 25 July just east of the Meuse River—one in Luxembourg near Arlon, another in the Nancy and Toul area, and the third around Belfort.[23]

The location of the supply bases appeared fortunate. With the Kitzinger line practically invalidated by the speed of the Allied advance and by its incomplete state of construction, the Germans looked toward the next natural rearward obstacle that might halt the Allied drive toward Germany. The Schelde estuary, the Albert Canal, and the Meuse River formed a continuous water line. Perhaps the armies could make a successful stand there.[24]

Since 21 August *LVIII Panzer Corps* had supervised the rehabilitation of the *Fifth Panzer* and *Seventh Armies'* fragmentary panzer divisions in "refreshing areas" immediately east of the Seine, but Model soon realized that "a smooth and efficient refreshing of the divisions was out of the question." He ordered the panzer divisions to move behind the Somme and the Marne. With the Seine River crossings intolerably congested by 25 August, he instructed the *Seventh Army*—commanded by Eberbach after Hausser was wounded in the Argentan–Falaise pocket—to reconstitute its divisions behind the Somme also, while the *Fifth Panzer Army,* commanded by Dietrich, was to cover the withdrawal. Whether the troops could get back to the Somme before the Allies arrived was a matter of grave conjecture. The *First Army* forces along the upper Seine were so few that whether or not they reached the Marne was really of little importance. By 29 August Model frankly admitted that the Allies had "attained absolute tactical superiority" in both mobility and weapons, and he judged them capable of sweeping through the still uncompleted Kitzinger line and

[22] *OB WEST KTB,* 21–28 Aug; Pogue, *Supreme Command,* p. 303; Cole, *Lorraine Campaign,* p. 50.
[23] *OQu West KTB, Anlage 101;* Hodgson, R–58, pp. 162ff.

[24] *OB WEST, a Study in Command,* p. 166.

destroying the German military forces in the west.[25]

Patton's Advance to the Meuse

Holding Seine River bridgeheads south of Paris, General Patton faced a dilemma. Eastward lay Metz, an objective that had fascinated him for a long time.[26] Yet an equally glowing opportunity existed to make a third envelopment according to the pattern established at Argentan and Elbeuf. If after moving south and east of Paris the Third Army wheeled north toward Beauvais, Patton would stick armored spearheads into the flank of those German forces that had escaped across the Seine River. To some commanders it seemed that the maneuver was the old Schlieffen plan in reverse, with the same weakness on the right. The maneuver would also place the Third Army athwart the routes of advance of the other armies and probably delay a drive toward the German border. Nevertheless, Patton prepared to execute both plans—a drive to Metz and an envelopment—until Bradley pointed him unequivocally eastward, toward the upper Rhine, two hundred and fifty miles away.[27]

A series of water barriers lies between the upper Seine and the Rhine. To the northeast is the Marne, a semicircular tiara ornamented by Château-Thierry, Epernay, Châlons-sur-Marne, Vitry-le-François, and St. Dizier. Beyond is the Vesle River and the cathedral city of Reims. Cutting across the army zone of advance next in succession come the Aisne, the Meuse (flowing through the familiar World War I towns of Verdun, St. Mihiel, and Commercy), and the Moselle (flowing through Metz and Nancy). Farther east, one hundred miles away, is the Rhine River itself, the objective of the Third Army pursuit.

Though the water obstacles offered excellent defensive opportunities, the Americans did not believe the Germans capable of organizing serious resistance.[28] They were right. Although the *First Army* knew of the two possible routes the Third U.S. Army might take, so few German forces were on hand that little could be done to prevent Patton from moving freely. Losses in vehicles and signal equipment, which had been extremely heavy, intensified the problem of deploying inadequate numbers of troops to threatened sectors. Knobelsdorff tried to protect the *First Army* left flank along the Seine east of Montereau by committing the *17th SS Panzer Grenadier Division*—which had been restored to nearly full strength by two newly arrived panzer grenadier regiments composed mostly of school personnel with no unit training—and remnants of the *9th Panzer Division*—consisting of a battalion of armored infantry, four or five tanks and assault guns, and one battery of artillery. To oppose a Third Army drive toward Reims, Knobelsdorff counted on the *LXXX Corps*, which had organized absorption points along the

---

[25] Msgs, Model to Jodl, 1250, 28 Aug, and 2400, 29 Aug, *AGp B KTB; OB WEST KTB*, 21 and 25 Aug; MS # B–157 (Dingler); MS # C–017 (Speidel).

[26] Interv, author with Brig Gen Oscar Koch, formerly TUSA G–2, Washington, Oct 54.

[27] TUSA Plans for Opns, 23 Aug, and Msg, 24 Aug; 12th AGp Ltr of Instrs 6, 25 Aug; Eddy Diary, entry 24 Aug; Answers by Gen Kibler to Questions by Col Hugh M. Cole, 29 May 46, ML–501.

[28] See TUSA G–2 Per Rpts, 26 Aug–2 Sep.

DEMOLISHED BRIDGE AT CHÂLONS-SUR-MARNE

Marne from Melun via Château-Thierry to Châlons and, with organic remnants fleshed out by stragglers, had established a thin but coherent line from Soissons through Epernay to Châlons. Security troops, provisional units, and stationary antiaircraft detachments supplemented the combat forces in the *First Army* sector.[29]

Although it was true that the German opposition posed no great problem, the distance from the upper Seine to the Rhine, the frontage to be covered, and the wide-open right flank were serious matters. The strength of the Third

Army south of Paris and the status of supply might not be equal to the task.

The Third Army south of Paris consisted of two corps, the XII and the XX, standing abreast, each with one armored and one infantry division—contrary to general belief, far from "top heavy" in armor. To flesh out the corps, Patton added one infantry division to each, the 90th going from Argentan to XX Corps, the 8th from Orléans to XII. The VIII Corps was not available for the eastward drive since it was engaged in Brittany, but the XV Corps, which was holding the Mantes-Gassicourt bridgehead in the First U.S. Army zone, was soon to revert to Patton's command. Patton hoped to match the XV, the XX, and the XII Corps with his three immediate

[29] MS # B–222 (Knobelsdorff); MS # B–728 (Emmerich); MS # B–732 (Hold); MS # B–003 (Hoehne).

objectives, Reims, Châlons, and Vitry-le-François, but the XV Corps did not become available as soon as expected, and since only two corps were south of Paris, objectives had to be juggled.[30] As it turned out, the XII and XX Corps were adequate.

The problem of supplies was more serious. No appreciable ration reserves had been accumulated, clothing and individual equipment needed replacement, shortages of medical and signal supplies were becoming critical, and gasoline stocks were dangerously low. With the exception of clothing and individual equipment—which had top priority for the rest of the month—stocks were replenished by emergency measures and by good fortune. On 25 August two hundred and seven air transports landed at Orléans with 507 tons of supplies, mostly rations, and on the following day 80 tons of medical supplies were airlifted in. Ten tons of medical equipment were captured at Orléans, fifteen tons at Dreux, and twenty at Fontainebleau. Three hundred miles of German telephone wire found in a cave near Chartres replaced to a certain extent the innumerable reels of wire unraveled across the countryside. Other signal supplies arrived from England with a shipment of four truck companies to the Third Army. When Third Army gasoline receipts on 23 August fell short of daily expenditures, the Communications Zone established a special trucking service from the beaches. This, however, could not remedy the situation at once, for the XII Corps, which estimated that it used between 200,000 and 300,000 gallons of gasoline to move fifty miles, found only 31,000 gallons on hand on 24 August and 75,000 gallons on the following day. Only the capture of thirty-seven carloads of German gasoline and oil at Sens restored stocks somewhat and made possible at least the commencement of operations east of the Seine bridgeheads.[31]

Before moving his forces beyond the Seine, Patton relinquished to the First U.S. Army the Melun bridgehead, which had been secured by the XX Corps. He also relieved XII Corps of the duty of guarding the Loire River west of Orléans by extending VIII Corps responsibility.[32] With these details attended to, he ordered XX Corps to advance from Fontainebleau and Montereau to Nogent-sur-Seine, then to Reims; he instructed XII Corps to drive from Troyes to Châlons-sur-Marne. (Map XV)

In the XII Corps zone, CCA of the 4th Armored Division was capturing Troyes on 25 August. The German garrison of security troops and miscellaneous remnants resisted surprisingly well. Not until noon of the following day did the battle come to an end, with the Americans in possession not only of the town but of 500 prisoners and with Allied fighter-bombers harassing a small group of fleeing Germans.

While CCB swept the corps zone without encountering any resistance to speak of, and while the 35th Division protected the right flank from Orléans to Troyes, CCA on 28 August sped fifty miles from

---

[30] 12th AGp Ltr of Instrs 6, 25 Aug, and corrected copy, 29 Aug; TUSA Plans for Opns, 23 Aug, Operational Dir, 25 Aug, and Msgs, 26 Aug.

[31] TUSA AAR, Aug.
[32] TUSA Memo to VIII Corps and Operational Dir, 25 Aug.

Troyes to Vitry-le-François without difficulty and crossed the Marne. As the 80th Division attacked from Troyes toward Châlons on the west bank of the Marne, CCA moved down the east bank. By noon of 29 August the squeeze play had netted Châlons.

By then XII Corps was virtually out of gasoline. Fortunately, more than 100,000 gallons of German fuel were captured, mostly at Châlons. By careful restrictions of vehicular movement, the corps could continue toward Commercy and the Meuse River.[33]

CCA of the 4th Armored turned southeast from Châlons and entered St. Dizier, which had earlier been captured by the 2d Cavalry Group, and on the morning of 31 August, in a heavy rain, the combat command drove toward the Meuse. A light company in advance of the main body surprised enemy outposts at Commercy, neutralized artillery emplacements by shooting the gun crews before they could so much as remove their breechblock covers, seized the bridge across the Meuse intact, and took possession of high ground immediately to the east.

On the same day, while the 35th Division guarded the corps right flank, CCB advanced across the Marne near Joinville. A day later, on 1 September, CCB took Vaucouleurs and seized high ground east of the Meuse. The 80th Division moved through Bar-le-Duc, took over the bridgehead at Commercy, and established another Meuse bridgehead at St. Mihiel.[34]

Much the same thing was happening in the XX Corps sector. The corps lacked positive knowledge of the forces in opposition, but it was not long before the 7th Armored Division, attacking east from Melun on 25 August, encountered troops of the *48th* and *338th Division,* horse-drawn artillery of the *708th Division,* and tank elements of the *17th SS Panzer Grenadier.* The 5th Division attacked east from Montereau on 26 August and met somewhat less opposition as it seized Nogent-sur-Seine and Romilly.

To free the 7th Armored Division for a quick thrust northeast to Reims, Walker instructed the 5th Division to clear Provins. Then, as the 5th Division followed on the right and the 90th followed on the left, the 7th Armored spearheaded the attack toward Reims on 28 August with two combat commands abreast—a total of six columns driving ahead to fulfill General Silvester's hope that one or two at least would capture bridges over the Marne intact. Advancing against small pockets of resistance, in actuality the disintegrating panzer grenadiers, the armored division reached Epernay and came into contact with the *LXXX Corps'* Marne River defenders. Two platoons of American armored infantry got across a still-intact bridge near Dormans before the Germans demolished it. Though most of the bridges were already destroyed, engineers quickly threw treadways across the river during the night. From Epernay, CCB drove north toward the Aisne, bypassing Reims on the east. Meanwhile, CCA and CCR on the left jumped ahead to Château-Thierry, overran roadblocks on the out-

---

[33] TUSA AAR, Aug, and Operational Dir, 30 Aug (confirming orders, 29 Aug) ; XII Corps AAR, Aug; Eddy Diary, entry 29 Aug.

[34] XII Corps, 4th Armd, 80th, and 35th Div AAR's, Aug; CI 384 (XII Corps) ; Koyen, *Fourth Armored Division,* pp. 29-34; Cole, *Lorraine Campaign,* p. 57.

skirts of the city, and seized several Marne River bridges. Continuing through Fismes to the Aisne on 29 August, CCA and CCR wheeled eastward and cut the roads north of Reims. The 5th Division then liberated Reims on 30 August without difficulty.

That afternoon XX Corps drove eastward in a column of divisions toward Verdun, seventy miles away. Difficult terrain such as the Argonne Forest, increasing but still scattered resistance, and the necessity of conserving gasoline slowed the advance. The Germans had installed mines to destroy the Meuse River bridge at Verdun, but the FFI prevented demolition. By noon on 31 August, 7th Armored Division tanks were in town and across the river, and on the first day of September, despite German air attacks that vainly tried to destroy the bridge, XX Corps was across the Meuse in strength.[35]

The Third Army's eastward advance during the last week in August had been a spectacularly fast movement against disorganized opposition—pursuit warfare at its best, a headlong, pell-mell rush that swept Allied troops irresistibly toward the German border. By its nature opportunistic and relatively uncontrolled, it was also exciting. Units sought the enemy for battles of maneuver and surprise, and reconnaissance detachments and advance points had occasional nasty engagements. It was a motorized advance, everybody riding on tanks, trucks, trailers, and jeeps. It was a frantic search for bridges or fords. The Americans had the exhilaration of striking to-

ward distant objectives and maintaining an incredibly rapid movement to deny the enemy the ability to organize and defend natural terrain obstacles. It was an immense clearing operation that liberated thousands of square miles.

Pursuit warfare meant capture of exciting booty such as the thirty-four carloads of German freight that contained parachutes (the silk was excellent for scarves and as gifts), tinned food, margarine (rumored from Indianapolis), powdered milk, sardines (supposedly from California), liver paste (allegedly from New York), and plenty of wine and cognac (indubitably French). It was also a time of hysterical happiness for liberated Frenchmen.

It was a period of confusion, when a jeepload of soldiers who had missed a turn in the road might capture a village, when an antiaircraft battery or a few Quartermaster truck drivers might inadvertently take a hundred Germans prisoner, when a single officer might go way ahead of his unit only to find that another outfit had already seized his assigned objective.

It was also a time of anxiety for commanders, of worry that gasoline supplies might be inadequate to allow continuation of a virtually unimpeded advance, of reflection that the tyranny of logistics might be more baleful than the opposition of the enemy. It was not clear then whether the reason was a shortage of gasoline on the Continent or an inability to get it forward from the beaches. The ever present possibility of a lack of fuel supplies hung like Damocles' sword, threatening to cut the triumphant Third Army movement toward the Rhine. Yet Patton remained cheerful, the most optimistic man in the world, unwilling

[35] XX Corps, 5th and 90th Divs, AAR's, Aug; CI 285 (7th Armd Div); Irwin Diary; *XX Corps*, pp. 94–104.

to be concerned, at least outwardly. Patton was also, it seemed, the luckiest man in the world, for captured stocks of fuel had helped him get across the Meuse.[36]

In possession of Meuse River bridgeheads between Verdun and Commercy, Patton was in position to attack toward the Moselle between Metz and Nancy, and from there the Rhine River was barely a hundred miles away.[37] This was his intention, but by then his supply lines were drawn to the breaking point. Soldiers in the forward echelons needed shoes, heavy underwear, and socks, and these items could not move fast enough to reach the advancing spearheads. The mechanical beasts of burden needed spare parts and maintenance. Still the most critical shortage was gasoline. The 12th Army Group on 30 August had notified the Third Army that no appreciable gasoline stocks would be forthcoming until at least 3 September, and, sure enough, the army received no gasoline on the last day of the month.[38]

By then the army was virtually bone dry. Individual tanks were dropping out of combat formations for lack of gasoline. The chance of a speedy resumption of the pursuit east of the Meuse, a hope that depended on motorized columns, appeared nil. To glum commanders whose units had swept across France only to immobility at the Meuse, the Biblical quotation, "But what shall it profit a man . . . ," seemed apt. "It seems strange to me," General Eddy confided to his diary, "that we should be

sitting here. . . . I am convinced that if we could obtain the necessary fuel this war might be over in a matter of a few weeks." He forgot that the Third Army drive toward Metz was only the subsidiary Allied effort, and the disappointment of halting an exhilarating drive was doubly galling because he thought that the other Allied armies were still "forging ahead, evidently with everything that is needed." [39]

Although General Eddy's reflection mirrored a feeling prevalent throughout the Third Army at the beginning of September, the other armies were not getting everything they needed. Nor would a plentiful supply of gasoline for the Third Army have won the war.[40] When gasoline became available in the first week of September and General Patton's troops attacked eastward toward the Moselle, they discovered that strong and organized German forces opposed them. Although it might have seemed to the Third Army that its brief halt had allowed enemy units to gather, the German defenders did not spring from Hitler's head full grown and fully armed as did Athena from Zeus'.

It was true that the advance east of the Seine had almost immediately eliminated the newly reconstituted *17th SS Panzer Grenadier Division* and had reduced the *48th* and *338th Divisions* to small kampfgruppen, but it was also true that the American drive that threatened Dijon, toward which the German troops in southern France were withdrawing, forced the German high command to allocate the most immediately available reinforcements to the *First Army*. By

[36] Stockton's Hosp Intervs (in particular with Col McHugh), III, GL–93 (235) ; Eddy Diary.

[37] TUSA Operational Dir, 30 Aug (confirming orders, 29 Aug).

[38] TUSA AAR, Aug.

[39] Eddy Diary, entry 2 Sep; Irwin Diary.

[40] See TUSA AAR, Sep.

29 August the large gap on the *First Army* left, which left open the road to the Saar by way of Vitry-le-François, Verdun, and Metz, caused OKW to assign to the *First Army,* in addition to the two panzer grenadier divisions coming from Italy, four *Volks Grenadier* divisions, two panzer brigades, and eventually several divisions that had fought in Normandy. With these forces, the *First Army* received the mission of defending the exposed German border between Luxembourg and Nancy and of preventing the potential encirclement of *Army Group B* by fighting at Moselle River.[41]

The Germans had shown no evidence of rout or mass collapse. On the contrary, German military government officers and OKH inspectors had manifested considerable individual initiative in scraping together provisional units and trying to slow the Americans by forcing spearheads to deploy off the roads or by destroying an occasional bridge, and by fighting wherever possible. Despite serious losses, the Germans had extricated fighting men of good quality. It was the security troops, the antiaircraft personnel, and the supply forces who filled the American prisoner of war cages, not the combat soldiers, and American intelligence officers recognized that the enemy was preparing a defensive line "known only to himself." Although the Germans were wholly on the defensive, they were trading earth for time in the hope that worsening weather conditions, bringing poor visibility and mud, would ground Allied airplanes and immobilize Allied tanks.[42]

If Patton's troops had not met stiffened resistance at the Moselle, they would have encountered it at the Rhine. In either case, the rugged warfare that awaited the Third Army was to bring disturbing memories of the hedgerows. The Lorraine campaign was to prove that the August pursuit was a finite experience. Adequate gasoline at the end of the month would probably not have sustained the dream of an unlimited pursuit terminating in quick victory.[43]

The Main Effort

The Allied pursuit launched across the lower Seine and from the Melun bridgehead exhibited the same characteristics displayed by the pursuit beyond the upper Seine. "The enemy has not the troops to hold any strong position," General Montgomery had advised.

The proper tactics now are for strong armored and mobile columns to bypass enemy centers of resistance and push boldly ahead, creating alarm and despondency in enemy rear areas. Enemy bypassed will be dealt with by infantry columns coming on later. I rely on commanders of every rank and grade to "drive" ahead with the utmost energy; any tendency to be "sticky" or cautious must be stamped on ruthlessly.[44]

More German forces than had opposed the Third Army were in the Allied path of advance nearer the coast, but

---

[41] *OB WEST KTB,* 29 and 31 Aug, *Anlagen 1800* and *1829;* MS # B–034 (Schramm) ; MS # B–214 (Mantey) ; *OB WEST, a Study in Command,* p. 139; Cole, *Lorraine Campaign,* p. 50.

[42] TUSA G–2 Est 9, 28 Aug; XX Corps G–2 Per Rpt 19, 0700, 29 Aug; XX Corps Annex 1 to FO 9, 30 Aug; TUSA Per Assessments of German Capabilities, 26 Aug–2 Sep.

[43] See Cole, *Lorraine Campaign.*

[44] 21 AGp Gen Operational Situation and Dir. M–520, 26 Aug, SGS SHAEF File 381, Post-OVERLORD Plng.

they were in bad straits. Road congestion added to the problems of German commanders who sought with little success to preserve a semblance of order in the flight to the Somme River. With artillery and antitank guns lost, staffs and technical services dispersed, command and communication virtually nonexistent, and rumors spreading among the troops that everyone was heading back to Germany, the *Fifth Panzer* and *Seventh Armies* found it impossible to conduct controlled operations. There had been no over-all planning early enough to make the withdrawal beyond the Seine an orderly procedure, and after a brief attempt by some units to make a stand, all fell back to the Somme.

The *LXVII Corps,* under the control of the *Fifteenth Army* and responsible for the coastal area between the Seine and the Somme, had received no orders to direct the river crossings of the troops streaming eastward, but did so anyway. Co-ordinating with the *Fifth Panzer Army* traffic control staff, the *LXVII Corps* tried to collect troops, allocate them to assembly areas, and secure supplies for them—a hopeless task that came to an end on 27 or 28 August when the *Fifteenth Army* ordered the corps to withdraw behind the Somme.[45]

The *LVIII Panzer Corps* had appointed about one hundred officers to block the roads and stop the beginnings of a panic-stricken retreat toward Reims and points east. Under the control of the *First Army,* the corps tried to form a defensive line between the Oise and the Seine, positions generally northeast of Paris, from Beaumont to Meaux—with panzer remnants; with the *348th Division,* which was arriving in a dilatory fashion from northern France too late to strengthen the Paris defenses as intended; and with fragments of the *18th Luftwaffe Field Division* and the *6th Parachute Division.* When news came that the *First Army* was falling back from the upper Seine toward Reims, *Army Group B* assigned the *LVIII Panzer Corps* to the *Fifth Panzer Army.* Lacking communications with army, without even knowledge of where the army command post was located, the corps decided to withdraw toward Compiègne.[46]

The *LXXXI Corps,* directed to hold the area around Vernon, tried to cling to wooded terrain near Mantes with several straggler battalions and panzer troops formerly belonging to the *II SS Panzer Corps.* Allied attacks as well as the general climate of retreat soon dissipated combat strength, and, without units capable of battle and without supplies, the *LXXXI Corps* withdrew toward the Somme.[47]

As the German forces rushed rearward, a vast undefended gap opened between the weak forces of the *First Army* and the conglomerate masses of the *Fifth Panzer* and *Seventh Armies* seeking refuge in the Pas-de-Calais area, which was defended by the *Fifteenth Army.* Into the gap came the First U.S. Army.

General Hodges was to support the British by advancing in a northeasterly direction from the Mantes-Gassicourt–Melun line to Péronne–Laon, more than

---

[45] MS # B-596 (Gerber); MS # B-236 (Sponheimer).

[46] MS # B-157 (Dingler); MS # B-728 (Emmerich).

[47] MS # B-807 (Kuntzen); MS # B-728 (Emmerich).

eighty-five miles away. Then, after driving about fifty miles to Mons–Sedan, the army was to turn gradually to the east and advance a hundred and twenty-five miles through Liège–Arlon, the duchy of Luxembourg, and across the Rhine River between Cologne and Koblenz to the southern fringe of the Ruhr.[48]

The terrain, the best invasion route to Germany, posed no special problems. The army would generally follow the Oise River valley to Landrecies, the Sambre River valley from Maubeuge to Namur, the Meuse River valley to Liège. Only in the right side of the zone were there several obstacles—the Marne, the Aisne, and the Meuse Rivers crossed the routes of advance in succession, and later the Ardennes interposed its rugged terrain. But if the army could move quickly, and there seemed no reason why it should not, it would forestall effective opposition on these terrain features. In the left part of the army zone, where General Hodges was to make his main effort to support the British, no major waterways or terrain obstacles intervened. Enemy resistance was expected to be ineffective along the whole army front.

Hodges had four corps, only two of which were immediately available. Gerow's V Corps in the center was liberating Paris. Haislip's XV Corps headquarters, commanding the forces in the Mantes-Gassicourt bridgehead, was to rejoin the Third Army after being replaced by Corlett's XIX Corps headquarters. Collins' VII Corps was to take over the Melun bridgehead. With Corlett on the left and Collins on the

right, Hodges would launch a twin pursuit to encircle Paris and drive to Péronne and Laon. Heavy artillery was to remain west of the Seine for the time being. Supplies for the pursuing troops seemed adequate.[49]

Collins' VII Corps attacked to the northeast from Melun on 26 August and quickly unhinged the *LVIII Panzer Corps* line near Meaux. Dispersing the defenders and passing within a mile of the *First Army* command post near Fontenay-Trésigny, American tankers sped through Château-Thierry and Soissons on 28 August, reaching Laon two days later. On the last day of the month armored troops were at Rethel and Montcornet, a hundred miles beyond the Seine. General Rose, who had developed the 3d Armored Division "into a marvelous thing, . . . built up morale, taught the division how to . . . fight," led the advance, with the 9th Division (commanded now by Maj. Gen. Louis A. Craig) and Huebner's 1st Division clearing the corps zone behind the armor.[50]

Until the XIX Corps headquarters took over the Mantes-Gassicourt bridgehead, XV Corps continued in command. Hobbs' 30th Division reinforced Wyche's 79th (which had held the bridgehead for a week with the help of extensive artillery support and a "big program of harassing and interdicting fires") on 27 August, and Brooks' 2d Armored Divi-

---

[48] 12th AGp Ltr of Instrs 6, 25 Aug, and Memo, Future Opns, 25 Aug, ML–205.

[49] FUSA Ltr, FA and TD's, 27 Aug, FUSA G–2 Jnl and File, L–379 (56).

[50] Collins' Talk, 19 Jan 48; VI Corps AAR, Aug, FO 9, 26 Aug, and Opns Memo 76, 26 Aug; 9th and 1st Div AAR's, Aug; MS # B–728 (Emmerich). S. Sgt. Lafayette G. Pool of the 32d Armored Regiment, who commanded the lead tank of an armored column for three days and alone accounted for four German tanks, three antitank guns, and approximately fifty vehicles, was awarded the DSC.

sion crossed the Seine on 28 August to protect the left flank of the bridgehead. The 79th and 30th began to expand their hold on the east bank by seizing and securing badly broken and heavily wooded ground. Thirty-five artillery battalions fired "a generous amount of ammunition" in support.[51]

At noon, 29 August, as Haislip's XV Corps headquarters started to move to an assembly area southeast of Paris and eventual Third Army assignment, Corlett's XIX Corps took command of the three divisions east of the Seine. Since the troops were emerging on terrain favorable for rapid advance and since the organized resistance of the *LXXXI Corps* had disintegrated, Corlett moved the 2d Armored Division into the lead, and the corps drove forward against virtually no opposition. Two days later the corps was fifty miles to the east, on a line between Beauvais and Compiègne.[52]

Gerow's V Corps joined the pursuit on 29 August in the army center when Cota's 28th Division, after parading in Paris, joined Barton's 4th. Two days later Oliver's 5th Armored Division passed through both infantry divisions to move into the lead. In five columns, with three combat commands abreast,

the armor dashed to the Forêt de Compiègne, hampered only occasionally by hastily erected roadblocks. There, the troops met units under control of the *LVIII Panzer Corps*. Bogged down in poor terrain, hindered by some confusion of communications, the tankers let 4th Division infantry pass through to clear the forest and take the city of Compiègne, forty-five miles northeast of Paris. In the early morning hours of 1 September, contingents of the corps got across the Aisne River between Compiègne and Soissons.[53]

For the soldiers, the countryside had become a monotonous blur of changing scenery. Their eyes bloodshot and tear-filled from sun, wind, dust, and weariness, they followed a blinding road all day long and at night strained to keep the cat eyes of the vehicle ahead in sight.[54] Little seemed spectacular except the lack of opposition and the growing feeling that they would soon reach Germany. "Unfortunately," it often seemed, "the Germans pulled out of the town before we arrived."[55] Those infantrymen who clung to the tanks of the advance units were grateful that the "tank-riding detail" got them "first into the towns, with first shot at the cheers, the cognac, and the kisses."[56]

There were exhilarating moments such as the one in the little village of Braine (on the Vesle River ten miles east of Soissons). When the French stationmaster informed American tankers

---

[51] Notes of Msgs, 0900, 23, 26, 27, and 28 Aug, Notes of Hodges-Haislip Conf, 1130, 1330, 26 Aug, XV Corps CofS Memo, 2015, 27 Aug, Opns Instrs 8, 2100, 27 Aug, XV Corps CofS Jnl and File; [Ferriss], Notes; XV Corps and 79th Div AAR's, Aug. 1st Lt. Alfred P. McPeters of the 315th Infantry was posthumously awarded the DSC for heroic action that day.

[52] TUSA Operational Dir to XV Corps, 26 Aug; XV Corps CofS Memos, 27 and 28 Aug; Hodges to Menoher, 28 Aug; First U.S. Army, *Report of Operations*, I, 30. 1st Lt. James L. Mosby of the 120th Infantry, who singlehandedly destroyed an antitank position on 29 August, was awarded the DSC.

[53] *V Corps History of Operations in the ETO*, pp. 213ff; 5th Armd, 4th, and 28th Div AAR's, Aug and Sep; CI 32 (4th Div).

[54] 3d Armored Division, *Spearhead in the West* (with G-3 Supplement) (n.p., n.d.), p. 81.

[55] 1st Lt. C. A. Wollmer, Hosp Intervs, IV, GL-93 (316).

[56] 314th Infantry, *Through Combat*, p. 32.

passing through that a German train coming from Paris was due in fifteen minutes, no one was interested, no one except Sgt. Hollis Butler, who commanded a gun section of the 468th Antiaircraft Artillery Automatic Weapons Battalion (self-propelled). German planes had been virtually nonexistent east of the Seine, and his men had not fired for several days. Although a train was bound to be less exciting than a plane, Sergeant Butler pulled his carriage mounting a 37-mm. gun and dual .50-caliber machine guns out the column and covered the railroad so that his men could shoot a few rounds. When the train appeared, the crew quickly disabled the locomotive and raked the cars with machine gun fire. Turning themselves for the moment into infantrymen, the artillerymen advanced in squad formation with marching fire, captured thirty-six cars (among them machine shops for tank repair) and seventy prisoners. Local FFI members were on hand to take the prisoners, and the Americans got into their vehicles and rejoined the column. Because the train blocked the tracks, it was easy for men of the 54th Armored Field Artillery Battalion to capture a second train thirty minutes later.[57]

While the First Army was having such easy success, the 21 Army Group was also getting across the Seine and toward the Somme, some seventy miles distant. The First Canadian Army, instructed to drive up the Channel coast with the main weight on the right for pursuit purposes and at the same time to develop right hooks to secure the

Channel ports, faced a more difficult problem in getting across the Seine. Not only was the river wider between Rouen and the sea, German troops had been deflected downstream by the American drive down the west bank and were fighting with desperation to maintain escape routes across the river. Canadian forces neverthless secured five bridgeheads—two in the Elbeuf–Rouen area, three between Rouen and the coast—and on 30 August, against slight opposition, entered and liberated Rouen, the capital of Normandy and the second largest port in France.

The Second British Army, beset by logistical difficulties, retained one corps west of the Seine and used its transportation facilities to support the two corps making assault crossings near Vernon and Louviers. Armored forces departed the Vernon bridgehead on 29 August, but weather, scattered mine fields, and small German pockets of resistance kept the advance to a mere twenty miles. On the afternoon of the following day, as the weather improved and resistance diminished, British tankers drove forward with increasing speed. After continuing to advance through the night, they reached Amiens early on 31 August and, with FFI assistance, secured the city and took several bridges over the Somme intact. Eberbach, the *Seventh Army* commander who had just signed an order for the defense of the Somme River line, was captured.[58]

With the capture of Amiens, the last sector of the German Somme–Marne defense line fell into Allied hands, a line earlier penetrated by the Third Army

---

[57] VII Corps AAR, Aug; 3d Armored Division, *Spearhead in the West*, pp. 84–85.

[58] Montgomery, *Normandy to the Baltic*, pp. 201ff; Stacey, *Canadian Army*, pp. 207ff.

capture of Châlons and the First Army advance northeast of Paris. With the exception of the Albert Canal and Meuse River water line, which appeared undefended, virtually no obstacles seemed to lie between the armies making the main Allied effort and the western approaches to the Rhine.

CHAPTER XXXII

Toward the Heart of Germany

The Mons Pocket

At the end of August 1944 the Allied armies were like knights of old who set out in quest of the Holy Grail but were not averse to slaying dragons and rescuing damsels in distress along the way. The Allies desired the Channel ports to assuage their logistical aches; the Pas-de-Calais coastal area to neutralize the German V-weapons; the liberation of northwest France, Belgium, and the Netherlands; and the destruction of the enemy forces remaining between the Seine and Germany. But their fundamental objective was the Rhine River.[1] (*See Map XV.*)

Some Allied commanders believed that an immediate crossing of the Rhine would lead to quick capture of the Ruhr. The apparently disintegrating German military organization then would collapse and carry with it a tottering German political structure. That would be the end of the war.[2] As the First Army G–2 put it:

Critical situations on the Western and Eastern front, in the Balkans, in Finland, and in German industry, particularly oil, must deprive any sane German of the last vestiges of hope. The only important question is how long it will take the vast majority of Germans in and out of the military forces, who can accept surrender to the Allies without fear of death or dishonor, to overthrow the elaborate and powerful system of control exercised by the relatively few for whom surrender means death as criminals and who will naturally choose to fight so long as there is one brave or fanatical German soldier between them and the enemy.[3]

Threatened also by the Soviet advance in the east, which had come to within one hundred and fifty miles of the German border, the Germans no longer seemed to have sufficient forces to make a stand anywhere short of the West Wall—or Siegfried Line, as the Allies called it. A complex of permanent-type fortifications of varying strength and depth along the western frontier of Germany, the West Wall extended from the Dutch border near Kleve to Switzerland north of Basle. To the Allies, the only sound military strategy for the Germans seemed to be to rush repairs on these fortifications and immediately withdraw from France to them, using delaying action to retard the Allied advance.[4]

---

[1] See Ltr, Eisenhower to Bradley, 29 Aug, 12th AGp File Mil Objs, I; 12th AGp Memo, Future Opns, 25 Aug, ML–205. The RAF Bomber Command alone had dropped 24,000 tons of bombs per month for the past two and a half months on the V-weapon launching sites in the Pas-de-Calais without decisive effect. Harris, *Bomber Offensive*, p. 236.

[2] See Montgomery, *Normandy to the Baltic*, p. 200. and Guingand, *Operation Victory*, p. 414.

---

[3] FUSA Weekly Intel Summary 4, 29 Aug.

[4] *Ibid.* The name Siegfried Line originated in World War I, when the Germans applied the code name *SIEGFRIEDSTELLUNG* to a rear de-

On the basis of this estimate, the overriding Allied goal became the desire to reach the Rhine before the Germans could organize an effective defense at the West Wall. The West Wall was no longer the impressive shield it had once been. The Germans had neglected and partially dismantled it after their victories in 1940. They had stripped most of its armament for use at the Atlantic Wall. Its works had fallen into disrepair, and no appreciable number of troops manned the line in the summer of 1944. Yet the West Wall remained an important psychological barrier for both the Germans and the Allies.[5] If the Allies could reach it before the Germans could man it (either with troops retreating from Normandy or with others already in Germany), the Allies would probably be able to get through to the Rhine with little difficulty. The pursuit east of the Seine was thus to display some of the aspects of a race.[6]

Though the Albert Canal and Meuse River formed a natural obstacle favorable for defense far in front of the West Wall, it hardly seemed possible that the remnants of the *Seventh Army*, the de-

feated *Fifth Panzer Army*, and the shrunken *Fifteenth Army*, all located in the northwest portion of France, in Belgium, and in the Netherlands, could re-establish a stable front short of the German border. Only the overstrained Allied supply lines might stop a rapid Allied advance. In the face of the glowing opportunity for continued pursuit of disorganized forces, the Allies decided to keep moving as long as possible. The armies were to "go as far as practicable," General Bradley announced, "and then wait until the supply system in rear will permit further advance."[7] The hope was to get at least through the West Wall to the Rhine.

If the German high command had anything to be thankful for, as *OB WEST* staff members later recalled, it was that the Allies failed to conduct an immediate and ruthless exploitation of the Seine River crossing at Mantes-Gassicourt by an enveloping movement along the east bank of the Seine to Le Havre. That kind of maneuver, the Germans thought, would have led to the complete destruction of the *Fifth Panzer* and *Seventh Armies* and would have created an irreparable gap between the *Fifteenth* and *First Armies*. The path to the northeast—to Germany—would have been undefended, and further resistance in France would have been futile. Since the Allies had not elected this course, the Germans continued to fall back toward the Schelde estuary, the Albert Canal, and the Meuse River, trying to maintain a fairly orderly withdrawal in the hope that a continuous front might be re-established there. The ports of

---

fensive position established in 1916 behind the central portion of the Western Front. Extending from St. Laurent, just east of Arras, through St. Quentin to Missy-sur-Aisne, four miles east of Soissons, the line played an important role as the battle front fluctuated during the last two years of the war. The Germans fell back on it in the early spring of 1917, and from there launched their last great offensive in France in March 1918. They withdrew to the same position in September and were finally dislodged from it by the Allied counteroffensive in October.

[5] CI 361–A (XIX Corps); Charles B. MacDonald, *The Siegfried Line Campaign,* UNITED STATES ARMY IN WORLD WAR II (Washington, 1961); Cole, *Lorraine Campaign,* p. 194.

[6] See Montgomery, *Normandy to the Baltic,* pp. 198–99.

[7] 12th AGp Admin Instrs 13, 27 Aug; The Siegfried Line, TSFET Hist Sec MS, 1946, OCMH Files, Ch. 4, p. 1.

Calais, Boulogne, and Dunkerque, about to be isolated, were to be held in compliance with Hitler's fortress policy directed against Allied logistics.

If the Germans could maintain a defensive line at the Schelde, Albert, and Meuse, they would retain the Netherlands and its naval bases, air warning service, and food and war production; they would deny the Allies the port of Antwerp, preserve the territorial integrity of Germany, and protect the Saar and the Ruhr. Most important, they would gain time to repair and rearm the West Wall.[8]

The troops extricated from Normandy west of the Seine and those in the Pas-de-Calais tried to maintain a cohesive front close to the northern coast of France. Screening their landward flank with mobile units, they hoped by delaying action to blunt Allied spearheads thrusting into that flank and thereby to gain time to reach the Schelde–Albert–Meuse line. German commanders insisted that the Allied pursuit was hesitant and that orderly resistance could be successful despite inferiority in strength and resources. Yet congested roads, traffic bottlenecks, an insufficient number of bridges and ferries, the fatigue of continuous movement, Allied strafing from the air, and the lack of information on the general situation created a depressing feeling of defeat.[9]

Model was no longer master of the *Army Group B* situation. With hope of holding at the Somme–Marne River line shattered, he found himself issuing futile orders that were out of date before the disorganized units received them. The *Fifteenth Army*, in precarious command of the Channel ports, was in danger of being cut off and isolated. The *Fifth Panzer Army*, which had moved inland to take command of the bulk of the remaining armor, was unable to hold around Soissons. The *Seventh Army* had scarcely begun to resurrect its ghost divisions at the Somme when it lost its commander, Eberbach, who was taken prisoner on 31 August. Unable to form a cohesive battle line, Model by 3 September saw no course open except withdrawal to the West Wall. The Germans had been routed and whatever resistance occurred was to a large extent the product of individual initiative on the lower echelons.[10]

Whether the Germans in northwest France could withdraw more quickly than the Allies could advance was the important question. To the Allies, the answer seemed negative on the basis of comparative motorization alone. More precise indications were also available. The XIX Corps on the First Army left seemed to have outraced enemy forces that were apparently moving eastward in an attempt to block the Allied pursuit.[11] Various Resistance groups in northern France were of the opinion that the Germans did not have enough men, matériel, and mobility to establish and hold a strong defensive line anywhere short of the West Wall.[12] Despite

[8] *OB WEST, a Study in Command*, pp. 160–61, 175.

[9] Among the many personal documents see, for example, MS # B–236 (Sponheimer) and MS # B–596 (Gerber)

[10] See Hitler Msg, 0530, 3 Sep, *AGp Fuehrerbefehle; AGp B Tagesmeldungen,* 1 Sep; First U.S. Army, *Report of Operations,* I, 31–32.

[11] 30th Div G–2 Per Rpt 72, 30 Aug; 28th Div G–2 Rpt, 1 Sep; VII Corps G–2 Memo for VII Corps CofS, 31 Aug, VII Corps G–2 Jnl and File.

[12] XIX Corps Mil Intel Team Rpt 101, 30 Aug, FUSA G–2 (Comd Echelon) Jnl and File.

weather conditions that prevented extensive air reconnaissance during the last days of August, Allied pilots noted large German groups in various stages of disorganization drifting east and northeast across the First U.S. Army front—more than a hundred enemy armored vehicles near St. Quentin, more than three hundred miscellaneous vehicles clogging the road net northeast of Amiens. By 1 September only a few German tanks remained on the Second British Army front.[13]

Recognizing that the Germans could hope to organize resistance only at the Albert–Meuse line, General Bradley temporarily shifted his sights from the Rhine River in favor of a maneuver to block the German retreat and eliminate the major part of the German forces in France. To accomplish this, Bradley decided to turn the army from a northeasterly direction to the north. Hodges' troops, by racing across the Franco-Belgian border to cut the Lille–Brussels highway, might sever the escape routes of approximately two panzer and eight to ten infantry divisions that appeared to be west of a north–south line from Laon to Mons, Belgium.[14]

This projected advance resembled the third envelopment that earlier Patton had tentatively planned east of the Seine. In effect the maneuver would reinstate the earlier boundary line that had been drawn by Montgomery and then changed at Bradley's request. At the conclusion of its northward drive, the First U.S. Army would have compressed the British and Canadians into a narrow zone ending at the Schelde estuary. The British and Canadians would then be facing out toward the sea. Apparently without consulting higher headquarters, General Bradley ordered General Hodges to execute the maneuver.

The most important objective of the shift in direction was the city of Tournai, Belgium, and during the afternoon of 31 August the First Army G–3, Brig. Gen. Truman C. Thorson, arrived at Corlett's XIX Corps headquarters to outline the new plan. Instead of driving through Montdidier and Péronne and turning gently eastward toward Mons, Corlett was to go north beyond Péronne to Tournai, a hundred miles ahead of the corps' leading units, and then north to Ghent, forty miles farther. The immediate objective, Tournai, was to be taken within forty-eight hours—at the latest by midnight, 2 September.[15]

The precise deadline for reaching Tournai reflected additional motives. General Bradley thought that the British would advance less rapidly than the Americans and that the Germans holding Tournai would consequently constitute a threat to the First Army left flank. More important, an airborne operation was scheduled to take place at Tournai against General Bradley's wishes. Bradley had consistently opposed the use of airborne troops during the pursuit because he believed that ground forces alone could gain distant objectives and

[13] VII Corps G–2 Rpt 87, 31 Aug; Telecon, FUSA G–2 Air and FUSA G–2, 2305, 31 Aug, FUSA G–2 (Comd Echelon) Jnl and File; Telecon, FUSA and V Corps, 0545, 1 Sep, and FUSA G–2 Air to V Corps G–2, 1915, 1 Sep, V Corps G–3 Jnl; Second Br Army G–2 to XIX Corps G–2, 1710, 1 Sep, XIX Corps G–2 Jnl.

[14] XIX Corps G–2 Est, Possible Lines of Action Open to the Germans, 1200, 28 Aug; FUSA G–2 Est 23, 31 Aug; First U.S. Army, *Report of Operations*, I, 33ff; see Cole, *Lorraine Campaign*, p. 12.

[15] [Ferriss], Notes.

because he felt that available aircraft would be better employed to bring supplies to the ground units rather than to transport airborne troops. Overruled by Eisenhower, Bradley had warned that ground units would secure the Tournai drop zones before airborne troops could land there. To insure the correctness of his prediction, he ordered General Hodges to get the XIX Corps to Tournai despite the fact that Tournai was within the British army zone.[16]

General Hodges was under another impression. He thought that the reason why Bradley wanted additional speed on the different axis was his desire to link up with the paratroopers scheduled to drop on 3 September.[17]

To get to the Belgian border in the short time allowed, Corlett used all his available trucks, chiefly of artillery and antiaircraft units, to motorize two regiments of the 79th Division and one of the 30th—this in addition to the organic transportation that enabled each infantry division to motorize one regimental combat team. With the 2d Armored Division leading two almost completely motorized infantry divisions, the XIX Corps set forth to bypass resistance and make night marches if necessary in order to reach Tournai at the appointed hour. "Get a good night's sleep and don't worry," the armored commander, General Brooks, advised Corlett, "it's in the bag." Nearby, the excited corps chief of staff exclaimed, "Hot pursuit!" [18]

Col. John H. Collier's CCA of the 2d

Armored Division crossed the Somme early on 1 September after bypassing a pocket of resistance at Montdidier, which the 79th Division soon eliminated, and on 2 September—two hours before the midnight deadline—reached Tournai. While a regiment of the 30th took the city, both infantry divisions assembled in the objective area around midnight. General White's CCB arrived after a two and a half hour engagement with an enemy column that resulted in the destruction of 96 German vehicles and 28 guns. The Reserve had just enough gasoline to reach the objective but instead assembled about ten miles short of it to keep a small supply of fuel on hand for emergencies. Except for these two instances of resistance, the corps had advanced against only the faintest kind of opposition.[19] Even destroyed bridges had failed to slow the rate of advance. In keeping with procedure that had become standard, engineers laid a treadway bridge first, then built a Bailey bridge nearby. When the Bailey was completed, the traffic was diverted to it, and the treadway was pulled up for the next crossing.

American incursion into the British zone had begun to look like a habit, and one of General Montgomery's aides visited Corlett on the afternoon of 2 September to protest. Montgomery wanted XIX Corps halted short of Tournai so that American troops would not interfere with the British advance, but it was too late to stop the columns. When Hodges informed Corlett later in the evening that a change in plans made

[16] Bradley, *Soldier's Story*, pp. 401–02; 12th AGp Memo for Rcd, 2 Sep, ML–205; Ltr, Bradley to OCMH, 7 Jan 55, OCMH Files.

[17] Sylvan Diary, 31 Aug.

[18] Telecon, Corlett and Brooks, 2015, 31 Aug, XIX Corps G–3 Jnl and File; Wyche Diary.

[19] XIX Corps and 2d Armd, 79th, and 30th Divs AAR's, Aug and Sep.

a halt necessary, the leading troops were virtually on the objective.[20]

The XIX Corps halted at Tournai, as much because the units were out of gasoline as because of orders. While British troops, who had reached the vicinity of Tournai shortly after the Americans, swept beyond, XIX Corps processed a disappointing total of only 1,300 prisoners. A small captured barge loaded with German gasoline enabled reconnaissance units to mop up the area. Meanwhile, Corlett waited for further instructions and gasoline supplies.

The Tournai airborne operation had in the meantime been canceled. Awakened at daybreak on 3 September by a complaint from Montgomery that American troops were blocking the roads at Tournai, Bradley was satisfied that they had also blocked the airborne drop.[21] General Eisenhower had tentatively decided on 2 September to cancel the operation on the announced theory that the purpose of the drop—to bar German escape routes to the east—had been achieved by ground action. After conferring with Montgomery, the Supreme Commander confirmed his decision. In the meantime, the commander of the First Allied Airborne Army, General Brereton, had announced poor weather conditions as the official reason for canceling the drop.[22]

Like XIX Corps, V Corps had received instructions to advance north. It was to cut the Lille–Brussels highway at Leuze (ten miles east of Tournai) and Ath. Using artillery, tank destroyer, antiaircraft, and engineer transportation facilities, General Gerow formed provisional truck companies to motorize his infantry.[23] With the 4th Division, reinforced by a 5th Armored Division combat command, in the lead, and the remainder of the armor and the 28th Division following, V Corps accelerated its pace on the evening of 31 August. The corps advanced continuously until the morning of 2 September when, in the vicinity of Landrecies, about twenty miles short of the border, most of the units ran out of gasoline. Gerow received word from Hodges later in the day to remain on the Cambrai–Landrecies line, but his order to halt did not reach all the elements of the 5th Armored Division. By afternoon of the 3d, CCB was about eight miles south of Leuze, and its reconnaissance elements were on the final objective. The only resistance, encountered near Landrecies, had been overcome without difficulty. Relatively few prisoners were taken.[24]

Although most bridges in the V Corps zone had been destroyed by the Germans, a few had been seized intact and

---

[20] Corlett to Hodges, 1645, 2 Sep, XIX Corps G–3 Jnl and File; First U.S. Army, *Report of Operations*, I; Ltr, Corlett to OCMH, 2 Sep 53.

[21] Bradley, *Soldier's Story*, p. 403.

[22] 12th AGp Memo for Rcd, 2 Sep, ML–205; Huston, Airborne Operations, Ch. VII, p. 19; SHAEF 24500/3/Ops (Airborne), Employment of Airborne Forces [26] Aug, SHAEF File 24533/Ops; 21 AGp Dir, M–522, 29 Aug, Pogue Files. "In the 40 days since the formation of the First Allied Airborne Army," General Brereton wrote on 16 September, "we have planned 18 different operations, some of which were scrubbed because our armies moved too fast and others because Troop Carriers were engaged in air supply." Brereton, *Diaries*, p. 343. See also AEAF Ltr, Airborne Opns to Further OVERLORD, 6 Jul, SGS SHAEF File 373/2, Employment of Airborne Forces in Opn OVERLORD; SHAEF Msg to AGWAR, FWD–12907, 16 Aug, SHAEF Msg File, Plans and Opns.

[23] V Corps Ltr of Instrs, 31 Aug.

[24] *V Corps History of Operations in the ETO*, pp. 216ff.; Gerow to Oliver, 2 Sep, V Corps G–3 Jnl and File; First U.S. Army, *Report of Operations*, I, 30ff.

a few had been saved by FFI action. Piles of destroyed German equipment along the roads attested to the accurate fire from Allied aircraft. Ground troops sometimes had to use bulldozers to clear paths through the wreckage and the dead horses, from which hungry civilians had already cut steaks.[25]

The VII Corps, on the army right, had also received orders on 31 August to change direction. Instead of driving northeastward from Montcornet and Rethel toward Namur and Liège, Collins was ordered to turn north and drive through the towns of Avesnes, Maubeuge, and Mons. General Collins' first concern was for the gap that would develop on the right between his corps and the Third Army. When he asked Hodges who was to fill the gap, he learned that that was his own problem. Though Collins thought at first that he would have to leave a division behind for the purpose, he decided instead to cover the gap with the 4th Cavalry Group, reinforced by a battalion each of light tanks, motorized artillery, tank destroyers, and infantry, three Engineer companies, and a platoon of a Medical collecting company. Even though he had been diverted to the north to trap Germans, Collins still had his eyes fixed on the West Wall. Anxious to continue northeastward across the Meuse, he instructed the 4th Cavalry not only to maintain contact with Patton but also to seize a Meuse bridgehead near Mézières. Meanwhile, he swerved the 3d Armored Division—which was moving toward Sedan and Charleville—onto new roads to the north toward Hirson and Vervins.

The 9th Division was to protect the right flank; the 1st Division was to come up on the left to reinforce the armor.[26]

The 3d Armored Division drove due north on the highway through Vervins, and by nightfall of 2 September spearheads were approaching Mons. Hodges, who had notified Corlett and Gerow on 1 September that there was talk of swinging eastward again toward the Rhine, was unable to reach Collins by telephone that day. Thus, he did not transmit news that might have acted as a brake on the VII Corps drive to the north. On 2 September Hodges received instructions to "curl up" the VII Corps short of Mons and hold because of gasoline shortages. But again he was unable to get word to the leading elements of the corps. On the morning of 3 September the 3d Armored Division took firm possession of Mons. Yet armored columns were strung out for twenty-five miles behind, as far back as Avesnes. By that time the 9th Division on the east flank had moved to Charleroi, and 1st Division units were pushing into Avesnes, on the tail of the armored units.[27]

The apparent absence of enemy forces in the Avesnes–Mons area was deceptive. In reality the First Army maneuver initiated on the last day of August had not been in vain. Though the comparatively few prisoners taken by XIX and V Corps indicated that the Germans had escaped those northward thrusts, in-

---

[25] CI 32 (4th Div) ; 3d Armored Division, *Spearhead in the West*, p. 78.

[26] 12th AGp Immed Rpt 73, Cavalry as a Task Force, 8 Oct; Interv by author with General Collins, 2 Sep 55; VII Corps Opns Memos 79 and 81, 30 Aug and 1 Sep (confirming oral orders, 30 and 31 Aug) ; VII Corps G–3 Per Rpt 86, 1 Sep.

[27] VII Corps Sitrep, 3 Sep; 3d Armd, 1st, and 9th Div AAR's, Aug and Sep; Sylvan Diary, 1 and 2 Sep.

creasing contact with German troops along the Avesnes–Mons line indicated that many Germans had not evaded VII Corps.

Thousands of Germans were in fact moving into the area southwest of Mons, generally along the axis of the Amiens–Cambrai–Mons highway. While the 3d Armored Division set up a line of north-south roadblocks along the Avesnes–Mons road to cut further German movement toward the northeast, the 1st Division attacked northwest from Avesnes into a confused and milling mass of retreating enemy. Blocked on the east by the 3d Armored Division, pushed on the west by the XIX Corps near Valenciennes, hemmed in on the south from Cambrai to Landrecies by the V Corps, about to be cut off on the north by the British advance beyond Tournai, and jabbed on the southeast by the 1st Division, a large, amorphous enemy group was pocketed.

Many of the troops trapped near Mons belonged to three corps—the *LVIII Panzer*, the *II SS*, and the *LXXIV*—that had earlier been under the control of *Fifth Panzer Army*. Near St. Quentin on the last day of August, the three corps headquarters had been out of contact with any higher command. Without instructions from above, the three commanders conferred and decided to form a provisional army among themselves. Straube, the *LXXIV Corps* commander, assumed command of the other two corps, while his staff began to function as the provisional army headquarters.

Straube was completely in the dark on what was happening outside his immediate area but, from Allied radio broadcasts and from meager reports occasionally delivered by subordinate headquar-

ters, he estimated that the provisional army was in imminent danger of encirclement. Deciding to withdraw to an area that was naturally suited to a defensive effort, he chose the canal and marsh region near Mons. Since he realized that the faster-moving Americans still might encircle the troops of the three corps, who for the most part traveled on foot, he started an immediate well-planned and well-organized movement.

The main units that Straube controlled were remnants of the *3d Parachute Division*, "almost insignificant in numbers"; the *6th Parachute Division*, which had a strength of about two infantry battalions plus a few heavy-caliber weapons; the *18th Luftwaffe Field Division*, in one-battalion strength; and two infantry divisions that were "hardly useful." Around these forces had gathered fragmentary units, stragglers, depot personnel, and a host of miscellaneous troops. Harassed from the air, ambushed by Resistance groups, attacked by Allied spearheads, finally encircled near Mons, the provisional army, with little ammunition, fuel, or communications, blundered into American roadblocks and upon contact was thrown into confusion.[28]

During the night, for example, a German half-tracked vehicle stumbled on a Sherman tank installed as a road obstacle. Other American tanks nearby opened fire down a straight stretch of road. When an early round set a German vehicle ablaze, illuminating others, it was "like shooting sitting pigeons." At daybreak tankers of the 3d Armored Division discovered that they had destroyed a column a mile long. During the ensuing confusion, when Medical Corps

---

[28] MS # B–157 (Dingler).

personnel captured a German general, it "did not seem at all unusual." [29]   Pfc. Gino J. Merli of the 18th Infantry, who feigned death when his machine gun section was overrun, remained at this weapon throughout the night; at dawn more than fifty enemy dead were found nearby.[30]   The encircled Germans, who had been thinking of flight, were in no mood to fight, and only a few, including headquarters personnel of the *LVIII Panzer* and *II SS Corps*, escaped.   On the afternoon of 3 September alone, the 3d Armored and 1st Divisions took between 7,500 and 9,000 prisoners.   The IX Tactical Air Command claimed the destruction of 851 motor vehicles, 50 armored vehicles, 652 horse-drawn vehicles, and 485 persons.[31]   In three days about 25,000 prisoners were taken, remnants of twenty disorganized divisions.   These potential defenders of the West Wall were thus swept off the field of battle.[32]

The head-on encounter at Mons was, from the tactical point of view, a surprise for both sides.   Neither Americans nor Germans had been aware of the approach of the other, and both had stumbled into an unforeseen meeting that resulted in a short, impromptu battle.[33]

[29] Interv with 1st Lt. C. A. Wollmer, Hosp Intervs, IV, GL–93 (316).

[30] Merli was awarded the Medal of Honor.

[31] VII Corps G–3 Per Rpt 89, 4 Sep. S. Sgt. Edward A. Patyniski and Pfc. Roy V. Craft of the 18th Infantry and Pvt. Melvin V. Pardee of the 18th Field Artillery Battalion were awarded the DSC for distinguished action, the latter two posthumously.

[32] MS # B–346 (Blauensteiner); First U.S. Army, *Report of Operations*, I, 30ff.; Pfc. Arnold J. Heidenheimer, *Vanguard to Victory, History of the 18th Infantry, 1776–1954* (Aschaffenburg, Germany, 1954), pp. 24–25.

[33] Bradley, *Soldier's Story*, p. 408; FUSA AAR, Sep; Interv by author with General Collins. General Montgomery later was under the impression that

While American troops were sweeping Germans into prisoner of war compounds, the plans for future action were again being changed.   Part of the reason was the desire to correct a hundred-mile gap between the First and Third Armies, but the underlying basis for the change was a belief that practically no external conditions would interfere with an Allied drive to and across the Rhine.

Broad Front versus Narrow

On 1 September, at the height of the accelerated American pursuit, SHAEF became operational on the Continent with headquarters in the Cotentin near Granville.   General Eisenhower, in addition to exercising the Supreme Command, assumed personal command of the ground forces, thereby replacing the pro tem commander, Field Marshal Montgomery.[34]   The change in the command structure brought the Allied organization to full flower.   The British Second Tactical Air Force, with headquarters on the Continent, was from this point on to be associated with the 21 Army Group. The Ninth U.S. Air Force, also established on the Continent, was to assist the 12th Army Group, as well as the 6th Army Group in southern France, which was to become operational under the control of SHAEF two weeks later.[35]

the pocket had centered on the Forêt de Compiègne. Montgomery, *Normandy to the Baltic*, p. 213.

[34] A detailed account may be found in Pogue, *Supreme Command*, pp. 261ff. Montgomery was promoted to the rank of field marshal, effective 1 September.

[35] See SHAEF Msg, FWD–13188, 24 Aug, in SHAEF G–3 Ops A 322.011/1. As the German air defense and "early warning system" seemed about to be "crumbled to pieces," increasing numbers of Allied Air Force ground stations began to be moved to the Continent. Harris, *Bomber Offensive*, pp. 229–30.

The alteration in the command of the ground forces had long been planned. In anticipation that General Eisenhower would take control of the land warfare beyond the Seine, General Montgomery had made his plans for the advance beyond the Seine on the basis that he would direct only those forces on the routes north of the Ardennes.[36]   General Bradley had done the same for Patton's subsidiary drive south of the Ardennes.

Though General Eisenhower sought to take effective control of all ground action, it was difficult to accomplish, not only because SHAEF was far from the front but also because signal facilities were in short supply.   General Eisenhower had foreseen the problem as early as 19 August, when he had dictated for the record:

Obviously, communications from the senior fighting commanders to their divisions on the front took precedence over the establishment of communications for SHAEF headquarters. Our woeful insufficiency in Signal troops has made it impossible, as yet, to provide for me on the Continent a headquarters which would permit me to discharge all the responsibilities devolving upon me and at the same time take over the broad operational coordination necessary between Army Groups. Even now, with all available US signal units allocated to Bradley, his communications with Patton are ordinarily limited to radio telephone or laborious code, and to his rear they are no better. . . .
. . . the very signal units I need have had to be given to Bradley so that he could keep in even sketchy contact with the rapidly changing situation.

Some time ago I ordered my staff to be ready to function on the Continent September 1st. I still hope to make that date,

although it is much earlier than any of the technicians believed it could be done.[37]

It was nevertheless done although, during the next few weeks, it would seem that immediate and firm direction and control were sometimes lacking.

To SHAEF at this time the hostile army appeared to be "no longer a cohesive force but a number of fugitive battle groups, disorganized and even demoralized, short of equipment and arms." The German strategic situation presented signs of so much deterioration that recovery no longer seemed possible. Political upheaval within Germany or insurrection within the Army seemed likely to hasten the end of the war.[38]

The success of the subsidiary Allied invasion of western Europe by way of southern France underscored the apparent hopelessness of the German situation.   The DRAGOON forces, primarily American and French, had had little difficulty in landing in southern France west of Cannes on 15 August and in driving up the Rhône valley.   SHAEF had estimated that DRAGOON would have no direct effect on OVERLORD until the forces from the Mediterranean moved well over three hundred miles to Dijon, and that this was hardly to be expected before November.[39]   Yet at the end of August, in addition to having captured the major port of Marseille, the Allied forces in southern France were approach-

---

[36] See 21 AGp Dirs, M–519 and M–520, 20 and 26 Aug, SGS SHAEF File 381, Post-OVERLORD Plng. I.

[37] Butcher Diary, entry 19 Aug; see Eisenhower to Marshall, 24 Aug, Pogue Files, and Memo, Eisenhower for Bedell Smith, Comd Organization, 22 Aug, SGS SHAEF File 381, Post-OVERLORD Plng, I.
[38] SHAEF Weekly Intel Summary 23, 2 Sep, SHAEF G–2 File; FUSA G–2 Est 24, 3 Sep; TUSA G–2 Est 9, 28 Aug; see Pogue, Supreme Command, pp. 244–45.
[39] PS SHAEF (44) 11 (Final), Post-NEPTUNE Opns, 17 Aug, SHAEF File 18008, G–3 Plans.

ing Lyon, little more than a hundred miles short of Dijon.[40] Since German withdrawal all along the Western Front made the juncture of OVERLORD and DRAGOON forces foreseeable in the near future, an Allied *coup de grâce* seemed in order. How to deliver the coup became the subject of much discussion in early September.

The discussion was an outgrowth of differences apparent as early as 19 August, when General Eisenhower had decided to cross the Seine and initiate pursuit operations without waiting for a more secure logistical basis. He had then thought of following the preinvasion plan of splitting his forces equally to make a dual thrust toward the Ruhr by routes north and south of the Ardennes. General Montgomery, in contrast, had favored a single drive north of the Ardennes directly toward the Ruhr. The result in late August had been a compromise that leaned toward Montgomery's point of view. Three armies carried the main effort north of the Ardennes, while Patton's Third Army, making the subsidiary effort, had had its gasoline supplies curtailed.[41]

On 2 September, as Eisenhower met with Bradley, Hodges, and Patton, he reinstituted what later came to be called the broad-front strategy. Hoping to keep the enemy stretched so that he would be unable to organize an effective defense at the West Wall, General Eisenhower allocated gasoline stocks to the Third Army just as Hodges' First Army was running out of gas at the Belgian

border and sent both U.S. armies toward the Rhine. Patton was to advance toward Mannheim and Frankfurt; Hodges was to shift from his northward course—which pointed across the British routes of advance in Belgium—to an eastward axis toward Koblenz and Cologne. To cover the gap that had opened between the First and Third Armies, Hodges was to send one corps through the Ardennes, a route not recommended by the preinvasion planners.[42]

At this particular moment, Dempsey's Second British Army was in the midst of a spectacular advance. Having crossed the Somme River at Amiens on 31 August and again between Amiens and Abbeville on 1 September against disorganized resistance, British armor drove into the industrial region of northern France. Outflanking Arras, bypassing Lille, moving through Douai and Tournai, armored spearheads swept across the Belgian border and took Brussels, Antwerp, and Ghent on 3, 4, and 5 September, respectively. With three armored divisions in the lead and with infantry mopping up, the British advanced 250 miles in six days to the Albert Canal between Antwerp and Hasselt.

Crerar's First Canadian Army had similar success. Moving out of the Rouen bridgehead on the last day of August, armor began pursuit action while infantry turned to the ports. Infantrymen took Dieppe and le Tréport on 1 September and St. Valery-en-Caux the following day. While the 1 British Corps swung toward Le Havre, the 2d

[40] See Robert Ross Smith, The Riviera to the Rhine, a volume in preparation for the series UNITED STATES ARMY IN WORLD WAR II.

[41] See Ltr, Eisenhower to Bradley, 29 Aug, 12th AGp File Mil Objs, ML–205.

[42] 12th AGp Memo for Rcd, 2 Sep, ML–205; see Eisenhower Msg, SHAEF FWD–13765, 4 Sep, 12th AGp File 371/3, Mil Objs, I. A detailed account of the high-level discussion is found in Pogue, *Supreme Command*, pp. 252–55.

Canadian Corps moved through the coastal belt, invested Boulogne, Calais, and Dunkerque, and took Ostend by 9 September. Armored troops had meanwhile crossed the Somme River near Abbeville on 2 September and driven toward Belgium. Held up briefly by resistance near Bruges, the mobile elements were at the Belgian-Dutch border and within striking distance of the Schelde estuary by the second week in September. The Canadians had overrun the flying bomb launching sites in the Pas-de-Calais by 6 September, although the Germans began two days later to fire V-weapons from the Netherlands and continued to do so until almost the end of the war.[43]

Impressed by the development of the pursuit and particularly by the capture of Brussels and Antwerp on 3 and 4 September, Field Marshal Montgomery began to believe that the Germans in the west were so weak as to be incapable of withstanding a major Allied effort. He concluded that the war could be ended at once by a thrust launched immediately to Berlin via the Ruhr. He proposed to the Supreme Commander on 4 September that all the Allied resources available on the Continent be allocated for this drive, a strong single thrust that General Eisenhower later misunderstood to be "pencillike."[44]

General Eisenhower, who had two days earlier made it possible for Patton to resume operations and who had thereby instituted a broad-front movement, justified his course of action, which was more cautious than Montgomery's, by a reasoned statement. Eisenhower did not believe that the Allies could support a drive to Berlin, and he thought that the Allies first needed to attain the successive objectives of breaching the West Wall, crossing the Rhine on a wide front, and seizing the Ruhr and the Saar. An advance on the entire front, he argued, would compel the Germans to stretch their meager forces to the breaking point and would imperil the rear of the *Army Group G* forces retreating from southern France. He also thought it desirable to keep Patton moving because he wanted the Allies to take advantage of all existing lines of communication. If, however, Montgomery needed additional assistance, Eisenhower was willing to give him SHAEF's strategic reserve, the Allied airborne army, which could help Montgomery seize crossings over the Rhine, help him make a deep advance into the Ruhr, and enable him even to threaten Berlin. The only factor, he said, that limited optimism for future operations and ruled out what he interpreted as Montgomery's proposal for a thin thrust to Berlin was logistics, already "stretched to the limit."[45]

It was just the logistical situation that made Montgomery feel that the Allies could afford only one effort. He wanted it to be a strong effort, and he believed that it should be aimed through the Ruhr and toward Berlin.[46]

---

[43] The last flying bomb was launched from the Pas-de-Calais on 3 September. Harris, *Bomber Offensive*, p. 236. Between 13 June and 1 September the Germans had launched an average of 102 V–1 bombs daily, of which 2,340 reached London. Helfers, Employment of V-weapons by the Germans During World War II, p. 34.

[44] Montgomery to Eisenhower, M–160, 4 Sep. Pogue Files.

[45] Eisenhower to Montgomery, FWD–13889, 5 Sep, and Eisenhower Memo for Rcd, 5 Sep, Pogue Files. Wilmot, *Struggle for Europe*, pages 466 and 468 suggests that the Americans perhaps thought Montgomery too timid to direct pursuit operations.

[46] Montgomery to Eisenhower, 7 Sep, Pogue Files.

Yet SHAEF judged Montgomery's suggestion too optimistic. Eisenhower provided him additional support, particularly in locomotives and rolling stock, but he refused to allay Montgomery's basic dissatisfaction over what Montgomery considered an unrealistic Allied dispersion of effort. During early September Eisenhower continued to allocate fuel supplies on a broad-front basis. Bradley managed to keep an uneasy gasoline balance between the two U.S. armies, his principal motive apparently the desire to keep Patton moving. With Hodges oriented toward Cologne, Bonn, and Koblenz, and Patton toward Mannheim and Mainz, and, if possible, Karlsruhe, it was clear that General Eisenhower preferred to use all the routes toward Germany, good and bad alike.[47]

The Nature of the Pursuit

The Allied advance toward the West Wall was spectacularly fast and fluid. It operated with a minimum of control and a maximum reliance on subordinate commanders. Unit dislocations, changing routes of advance, and an overriding fluidity resulted. When gasoline stocks permitted, the pursuit resembled a stampede of wild horses. The dust that was kicked up did not obscure the fact that a mass Allied movement east of the Seine took place, a gigantic and sometimes haphazard closing action of all available forces toward Germany in which a frantic search for a bridge still

intact was often the most significant detail. "There have been so many changes in the First Army direction," an observer wrote, "that indeed it seems at times as if those 'on top' did not have an altogether clear and consistent conception of the direction from which they wish to cross the German frontier." [48]

Thinly spread, both laterally and in depth, the armies overran and liberated northern France, most of Belgium and Luxembourg, and parts of the Netherlands. Reconnaissance units and cavalry swept far and wide, clearing great areas, particularly on the flanks, to free infantry and armor for advance along the main highways. Various patriotic groups were helpful.[49] Local Resistance members usually appeared soon after the arrival of American troops in a town, and they quickly formed into units and marched out to clear the countryside of German stragglers and to guard bridges and lines of communication. Individuals sometimes accompanied Allied reconnaissance units. Civilians cleared a number of obstacles, in at least one case repairing a destroyed bridge before the arrival of Engineer troops. Engineer support platoons often accompanied cavalry ahead of the main body of troops to remove obstacles before they could delay the advance. The artillery was usually unable to displace fast enough to get into action, and even the light artillery did comparatively little firing.[50]

---

[47] Bradley, *Soldier's Story*, pp. 410–14; 12th AGp Ltr of Instrs 8, 10 Sep (confirming oral orders); see also the provocative discussion in Wilmot, *Struggle for Europe*, pp. 458ff. and 482ff.

[48] Sylvan Diary, 2 Sep.

[49] See David Ryelandt, "The Resistance Movement," in Jan Albert Goris, ed. and translator, *Belgium under Occupation* (New York: Moretus Press for the Belgian Government Information Center, 1947), pp. 191ff.

[50] CI 32 (4th Div); 4th Div AAR, Sep; First U.S. Army, *Report of Operations*, I, 35.

There was only sporadic contact with the enemy along the fronts of the on-rushing armies. Only in a few instances did the Germans try to make a stand, usually at river-crossing sites. The inadequacy of the German forces, their lack of communications, their drastic shortages of equipment, and what seemed to be command confusion on the lower levels led to the abandonment of any pretense of re-establishing a line anywhere except at the West Wall. Occasional roadblocks (usually no more than several felled trees), a few destroyed bridges, and feeble rear-guard action characterized the opposition. A typical rear guard was composed of a small group of infantry and perhaps one or two tanks or mobile guns stationed at a town or road center until direct pressure or an outflanking move prompted withdrawal. Resistance was spotty and without consistent plan. Many bridges were abandoned intact. Few cities or towns were defended. Inadequate and haphazard strongpoints, frequently placed at illogical locations and often undefended, did little to slow the Allied advance. Road marches punctuated by occasional skirmishes of short duration and involving a company or at most a battalion for only several hours characterized the action.

Although the enemy could do little to hinder, shortages of supplies markedly slowed the advance. Since 3 August, when the Allies had turned eastward toward the Seine, logistical considerations had been subordinated to prospects of immediate tactical advantage.[51] Push-

LIBERATED. *French girls knock down German headquarters sign.*

ing the advance in a gamble for quick victory had entailed a ruthless disregard for an orderly development of the logistical structure. The normal logistical structure based on a depot system could not be established under the pressure of supplying forward units on a day-to-day basis during the war of movement. The result was that 90 to 95 percent of all the supplies on the Continent at the end of August lay in depots near the original invasion beaches. Virtually no supplies existed between these stocks and the army dumps three hundred miles away. With supply loads being carried increasingly farther forward and carriers requiring more and more time to complete longer round trips, the deliveries to the armies dwindled during the last

[51] The following is taken from Ruppenthal, *Logistical Support*, I, 483ff., 499ff., 544ff., 553ff., 562–63, 572ff.

few days of August to several thousand tons per day.

The planners had intended to rely on the excellent French railways for long-distance hauling, but Allied air attacks and French sabotage had virtually demolished the railroad system. The reconstruction of damaged rail lines, which required repair of choke points, rail centers and junctions, bridges, tunnels, viaducts, roundhouses, machine shops, and rolling stock, could not keep pace with the advancing forces. As early as June, when it had become apparent that paralyzing German mobility by destroying the transportation system would mean similar paralysis later for the Allies, supply chiefs had begun to request that facilities be spared and had started to hope in earnest that the Germans would not destroy them in retreat. Though the rail lines east of Paris were in better shape, the hub of the system around the French capital had been heavily damaged. By 30 August two main railroads were open as far as the capital, but the mutilated rail yards of Paris and the destroyed Seine River bridges prohibited through traffic. Small tonnages could be routed forward through Paris only after 4 September. Not until mid-September, although bottlenecks around Paris and the shortage of rolling stock still inhibited railway traffic, would the railroads begin to assume their hoped-for importance as long-distance carriers. By then the pursuit would be over.

Motor transport played a much larger role on the Continent than had been planned, and consequently theater facilities were neither well suited nor well prepared for extensive operations be-

cause of shortages of vehicles and properly trained drivers. One of the most dramatic logistical developments was the organization by the Communications Zone of the Red Ball Express, a long-distance through-highway system inaugurated late in August. Designed as an emergency expedient to support the Seine crossings by getting 82,000 tons of supplies to the Chartres–Dreux area by 1 September, the Red Ball Express became an institution that lasted until November and operated east of the Seine as well. On 25 August Red Ball convoys began to use two parallel one-way round-trip routes from which all other traffic was excluded, and before long more than a hundred truck companies were involved. On 29 August, for example, 132 truck companies—6,000 vehicles—moved more than 12,000 tons of supplies. Operating day and night and without blackout precautions, the Express delivered 135,000 tons of supplies to army service areas by mid-September.

The cost of this achievement was high—mounting strain on personnel and equipment, continual use of vehicles without proper maintenance, rapid deterioration of equipment and roads, abuse of vehicles by overloading and speeding, a large number of accidents caused by driver fatigue. The Red Ball fostered the habit of poor road discipline, offered opportunity for malingering, sabotage, and black marketeering, and tempted combat units to hijack and otherwise divert supplies. Haste contributed to poor documentation of shipments and concomitant sparse information on the status of supply. "Red Ball was part of a gamble, part and parcel of the tactical decision to cross the Seine and exploit to the full the existing tactical advantage." [52]

Because the Communications Zone refrained from moving its depots forward in the interests of conserving transportation facilities, the armies took over much of the hauling. Their supply vehicles sometimes had to make round trips of up to three hundred miles. Bradley had instructed Patton and Hodges to leave their heavy artillery west of the Seine so that artillery cargo trucks could be used to transport supplies, and Hodges, for example, formed between ten and twenty provisional truck companies from these vehicles to help his forty-three Quartermaster truck companies.

The Allies also transported supplies by air, though the advantages of speed and freedom of movement were often offset by low volume and tonnage capacity, uncertainty of available aircraft, inadequate ground facilities at loading and landing sites, the possibility of enemy interference, and the hazard of weather. As a result, air supply could only be regarded as an emergency measure. However, under the direction of the Combined Air Transport Operations Room (CATOR), a special AEAF staff section that acted as a regulating station for all air supply missions, small shipments to ground forces began in June, medical evacuation commenced in July, and on 19 August more extensive air shipments started. By 25 August over 4,000 tons of supplies had been delivered to forward ground units, mainly whole blood and such signal equipment as field wire and radio parts. At the end of August, competing demands of the various armies, the civil relief program for Paris, and

planned airborne operations reduced air deliveries to a trickle, but an enlarged airlift was resumed on 6 September. From 19 August to mid-September, American planes carried a total of 20,000 tons of supplies, of which about 13,000 tons were delivered to the 12th Army Group.[53]

By far the most important requirement of the pursuit was gasoline. During the week of 20 August, when most of the units of both U.S. armies were for the first time engaged in a war of movement, the daily consumption of gasoline ran well over 800,000 gallons. By 28 August the Communications Zone transportation resources were spread so thin and the lines of communication extended so far that daily deliveries could no longer be relied on. Increasing gasoline demands were due not only to the requirements of the combat forces but also to the ever-growing requirements of the carriers—Red Ball trucks alone consumed more than 300,000 gallons per day.

Gasoline was only one of many requirements. The troops of a single division ate about thirty-five tons of field rations a day, besides expending ammunition and wearing out clothing and equipment. Fortunately, captured German items sometimes alleviated shortages. A German dump in Namur, Belgium, for example, provided beef and canned plums and cherries; a candy factory yielded flour and sugar; a warehouse full of salt was worth its weight in gold. Yet captured stocks hardly fulfilled requirements and exactly when

---

[52] Ruppenthal, *Logistical Support*, I, 572.

[53] See Leigh-Mallory, "Despatch," Fourth Supplement to the *London Gazette* of December 31, 1946, pp. 83–84.

dwindling supplies would finally bring the pursuit to a halt was a painful question that troubled all commanders.

The port capacity problem was still with the Allies, despite optimism in early September stemming from capture of Rouen on 31 August, seizure of Antwerp on 4 September, the rapid liberation of the minor Channel ports of Dieppe and Ostend, the quick investiture of Le Havre, Boulogne, Calais, and Dunkerque, and the not so remote possibility of taking Rotterdam and Amsterdam. The capacity of most of the ports was small, even when they were captured intact, and Le Havre, taken on 12 September, was far behind the front. Most important of all, British seizure of Antwerp—the greatest port in continental Europe, one close to the fighting front—had failed to prompt the Germans to relinquish the banks of the Schelde estuary along the sixty miles between Antwerp and the sea. Until the Schelde could be cleared, Antwerp was useless. It would be more than two months before the complex port problem would be solved.[54]

To the West Wall

The reorientation of First Army on 3 September from a northward to an eastward direction involved some complications. Gerow's V Corps in the center, virtually pinched out by the converging advances of the corps on its flanks, was to move across the rear of Collins' VII Corps to a new zone on the army right. Corlett's XIX Corps and Collins' VII Corps, turning to the right, were to ad-

vance, respectively, on the left and in the center of the army zone.[55] Since Meuse River crossings were the most urgent objective, Hodges diverted available gasoline supplies to the V and VII Corps, which were closer to the Meuse and which were to strike at once toward the river between Sedan and Namur. The XIX Corps thus remained inactive for several days.

Ordered to move through the Ardennes to fill the gap between the First and Third Armies, Gerow designated an assembly area in his new zone. Some units assembled there before marching eastward, others moved at once because of an absence of opposition. While the 4th Division on 4 September cleared some slight resistance near St. Quentin in the old zone, the 102d Cavalry Group and the 5th Armored Division abreast, the latter particularly troubled by gasoline shortages, started toward the Meuse. By 5 September they had crossed the river without difficulty. As the 4th Division followed the cavalry and the 28th Division trailed the armor, V Corps began to move through the Ardennes. A rugged wooded plateau, the Ardennes extends in a northeasterly direction across the Meuse River valley in France, through Belgium and north Luxembourg, almost to the Rhine. The corps was to sweep the region, maintain contact with the Third Army, and eventually support Patton's projected Rhine River crossings.

Spread thin over a fifty-mile front, the corps moved through southern Belgium

---

[54] For the port story, see Ruppenthal, *Logistical Support, II,* Chs. III and IV, and MacDonald, *The Siegfried Line Campaign.*

[55] Hodges to the corps commanders, 3 Sep, FUSA G-2 (Comd Echelon) Jnl and File; VII Corps FO 10, 3 Sep; Hodges to Gerow, 1727, 3 Sep, V Corps G-3 Jnl and File; see Answers by Gen Kibler to Questions by Col Cole, 29 May 46.

and Luxembourg in a dozen or more parallel battalion columns several miles apart. The troops encountered only the most perfunctory resistance and advanced as rapidly as their limited transportation permitted. When the 5th Armored Division ran out of gas on 7 September, Gerow passed the 28th through and diverted his meager supplies of gasoline to the infantry, which consumed less than armor. The 4th and 28th both moved steadily forward on foot and by motor.

On 8 September Gerow looked ahead to the West Wall, prepared an attack against it for 10 September, and designated Koblenz as the objective. Choosing to make his main effort on the left,[56] he shifted his infantry to the north and aimed at Pruem in an approach to Koblenz. Conducting a virtually independent operation, his cavalry screens maintaining only light contact with units on his flanks, yet instructed to support a Third Army crossing of the Rhine, Gerow nevertheless turned toward closer contact with the First Army. If he concentrated the bulk of his strength at Trier, he would be forty miles from the closest Third Army forces at Metz. Perhaps recognizing the significance of the stable defenses the Germans seemed to have erected at the Moselle, Gerow turned the 4th and 28th Divisions northeastward into a narrowing zone of advance that led to the juncture of the borders of Belgium, Luxembourg, and Germany.

Meanwhile, the 5th Armored Division, with an infantry regiment attached, refueled on 9 September, passed through the 28th Division, and entered Luxembourg. On the following day, as the inhabitants of Luxembourg gave an enthusiastic welcome, the armored troops entered and liberated the capital unopposed. With them came Prince Felix, consort of the Grand Duchess and at the time a brigadier in the British Army. East of the city, American tankers came into contact with some enemy forces. His troops extended over a sector about thirty miles wide, General Oliver halted his advance briefly to await instructions concerning the West Wall.

That afternoon General Gerow ordered his divisions to close the next day into assembly areas previously designated on the St. Vith–Echternach line. From there they were to probe the West Wall positions.

Although the Rhine River was only fifty miles away and the end of the war seemed at hand, General Hodges was about to postpone a co-ordinated attack on the fortifications for a day or two until sufficient artillery ammunition for an attack on the fortified line could be moved forward. Obscured by the prevailing optimism, the pause turned out to be a significant event—it marked the end of the pursuit.[57]

On the evening of 3 September, the three divisions of Collins' VII Corps were deployed on a 20-mile front from Mons to a point south of Charleroi. The 3d Armored and 1st Divisions were around Mons, the 9th was at Philippeville. Screening the right flank of the corps along the Meuse River, the 4th Cavalry Group was at Mézières and

---

[56] V Corps FO 26, 1830, 8 Sep; V Corps Memo for Rcd, 10 Sep, V Corps G–3 Jnl and File.

[57] V Corps Operations in the ETO, pp. 229ff.; TSFET, Siegfried Line.

Rocroi. Instructed to move eastward through Liège and Aachen to the Rhine near Bonn, Collins ordered the 9th Division to seize a Meuse River bridgehead near Dinant. The division moved out, hoping to be across the Meuse within twenty-four hours.[58]

An unexpectedly large number of roadblocks slowed the advance. At the river between Givet and Namar, the division discovered that Germans held the east bank in some strength. Two regiments established shallow bridgeheads north and south of Dinant, but success was far from certain. With excellent observation of the crossing sites and the bridgeheads, German troops counterattacked while their artillery shelled supply parties and potential bridge sites. One American battalion, partially surrounded, lost over two hundred men.

The German stand at Dinant was the first attempt to defend a water line since the Seine, and to the American troops it was a surprising divergence from the pattern of the pursuit. Veteran elements of the *2d SS* and *12th SS Panzer Divisions,* under *I SS Panzer Corps* control, forced the 9th Division to cling grimly for thirty-six tense hours to footholds on the east bank. The Americans were unable to reinforce the bridgeheads properly, expand and consolidate them, or construct bridges for armor and supply vehicles. During the evening of 6 September, an American company commander on the east bank reported the approach of an unidentified tank column from the east, exclaiming, "We are either the luckiest people in the army or

we are all going to be *kaput."* They were lucky. The tanks were part of a task force dispatched on Collins' order by the 3d Armored Division, which had crossed the Meuse farther north. The task force soon broke the German defenses. Infantrymen took Dinant on the morning of 7 September without opposition and that afternoon began to advance rapidly eastward.[59]

The 3d Armored Division, immobilized at Mons twenty-four hours for lack of gasoline (the troops took more than 2,500 prisoners while waiting— "Hunting was excellent"), began a forty-mile march to Namur on 4 September. Tanks moved on both sides of the Sambre River; infantrymen crossed the Meuse on a damaged bridge and dispersed light German forces defending Namur. By morning of 6 September tanks were rolling over the river on a 505-foot floating treadway bridge. While an armored task force moved south to help the 9th Division, the remainder of the division again found itself out of gasoline. Meanwhile, the 1st Division had cleaned up the Mons pocket, and the infantry moved up to sweep the corps left.

When gasoline was again available, the armor advanced east of Namur astride the Meuse River, reached the town of Huy that evening, and captured the bridges there intact. On the afternoon of 7 September, after another short halt while gasoline was brought up, the 3d Armored Division moved the fifteen remaining miles to Liège practically unopposed. The Liège bridges were destroyed, but enemy opposition was

---

[58] 9th Div FO's 30 and 31, 0230, 3 Sep, and 2230, 4 Sep.

[59] 9th Div AAR, Sep; TSFET, Siegfried Line; MS # P-164 (Meyer); MS # P-159 (Stueckler).

weak. Hindered somewhat by the enthusiastic welcome of the inhabitants, the troops completed routine mopping up. One of the participants later remarked:

Our chief difficulty was the fact that there were so many civilians trying to get out of town. We carried on a battle anyway, firing over their heads. At one point my tank ran over four of them as we backed up . . . . several civilians crawled up on the tank and begged for guns. We had none for them. We entered the town and our tanks went up parallel streets cleaning out Ger mans. This took us all afternoon and we suffered no casualties.[60]

In the slightly bored tone that indicated that they had become accustomed to this sort of thing, the troops reported, "Once again cognac, champagne, and pretty girls." [61]

Advancing on the Liège–Aachen axis, the best invasion route into Germany, the VII Corps took Verviers and Eupen on 9 and 11 September, respectively. Although resistance was still sporadic, it seemed to be increasing. There were no more V-for-Victory signs, no more flowers, no more shouts of *Vive l'Amérique*. Instead, a sullen border populace showed hatred, and occasional snipers fired into the columns.[62]

By the end of 10 September the VII Corps was deployed along a front extending from Malmédy through Verviers to Herve, eleven miles east of Liège. The 9th Division had lost contact with the enemy, and it appeared that the Germans were disengaging to take positions in the West Wall. With German soil within reach, pursuit came to an end for the VII Corps too. Ahead lay the task of breaching the West Wall.[63]

Corlett's XIX Corps—which remained temporarily out of action near Tournai awaiting gasoline—trained, rested, and incidentally gathered almost nine hundred prisoners. The 79th Division departed the corps to rejoin the Third Army.[64] By the time gasoline arrived and the corps was ready to move, the Allied forces on both sides had already outflanked the Germans in the new zone of advance leading east toward the Albert Canal and Meuse River between Hasselt and Liège. Bypassing or overrunning ineffectual rear-guard detachments, the 113th Cavalry Group rushed past the historic battlefields near Waterloo and reached the canal line on 7 September. The 2d Armored and 30th Divisions followed as rapidly as fuel supplies permitted, the infantry marching a good part of the way on foot. The units closed to the water barrier by 10 September.

Cavalrymen had meanwhile explored the situation along the water line and discovered all bridges destroyed and apparently strong German detachments dug in on the east bank. Since the British on his left already had a bridgehead across the Albert Canal and the VII Corps on his right was beyond both the Albert Canal and the Meuse, Corlett saw no reason for his corps to stage what

---

[60] Interv with 1st Lt Robert A. Annin, Hosp Intervs, ML–2234. Maj. Gen. Maurice Rose, the 3d Armored Division commander, was awarded the DSC for his leadership 6–9 September.

[61] 3d Armored Division, *Spearhead in the West*, p. 91.

[62] *Ibid*, p. 93. Colonel Gibney, commander of the 60th Infantry, was awarded the DSC for heroic leadership on 9 September.

[63] 3d Armd Div AAR, Sep; CI 259 (3d Armd Div) ; 9th Div AAR, Sep.

[64] See Ltr, Corlett to OCMH, 2 Sep 53.

would probably be a costly assault crossing. While General Corlett made arrangements with his neighbors to use their bridges across the water obstacles, XIX Corps, like V and VII Corps, paused briefly.[65]

No one knew it yet, but the pursuit was over. The troops were soon to discard the "carnival garlands, ribbons, and souvenirs gathered during the liberation parade" through northern France, Belgium, and Luxembourg and become caught up again in hard fighting.[66] Patton's Third Army was already immersed in the difficulties of the Lorraine campaign. Immobilized by lack of gasoline for several days, the army attacked on 5 September to gain Moselle River bridgeheads near Metz and Nancy. Five days later, though some troops had seized Toul in the Moselle bend, others had been repulsed at Pont-à-Mousson, and the army was fighting furiously for bridgeheads in the Metz and Nancy areas. Hodges' First Army was soon to be involved in problems of similar difficulty at the West Wall.[67] The war of movement set in motion by Operation COBRA in the last days of July was merging imperceptibly into a war of position.

The End of the Line

Though it was not to become obvious for a week or so, the Allied troops were tired. The pursuit had been wearing on men and equipment. Casualties had not been heavy at any one place, but their cumulative effect reduced the strength of all combat units. Tanks and vehicles had gone so long and so far without proper maintenance and repair that in one armored division less than a third of the authorized number of medium tanks were actually fit for combat.[68] Another had had so many tanks fall out of column because of mechanical failure or lack of gasoline that its equipment was spread over the countryside between Valenciennes and Luxembourg, more than a hundred miles. Since the gasoline shortage prevented transferring vehicles for repair, mobile crews performed on-the-spot adjustments when they were able, but those tanks that needed shop treatment had long to wait.[69] Tank engines had passed the time limit of efficient operation but were hard to replace. Of 190 reserve engines considered necessary for effective combat, one armored division had had only 30 available at the beginning of the pursuit. Replacement tracks were particularly difficult to come by. Ceaseless driving caused vehicles literally to fall apart, and serious shortages of spare parts could not be remedied in the near future.[70]

Transportation facilities were unable to maintain an adequate flow of supplies to the front. By 6 September, for example, daily deliveries to the First Army were 1,500 tons (almost one third) below normal daily requirements. With income below operating expenses, the army began to live on its capital; basic loads vanished, reserve stocks virtually disappeared. Although a diminishing arrival of everyday necessities had not

---

[65] XIX Corps FO 22, 1730, 7 Sep; [Ferriss], Notes.

[66] Quote from 3d Armd Div CCA AAR, Sep.

[67] See Cole, *The Lorraine Campaign*, and MacDonald, *The Siegfried Line Campaign*.

[68] 3d Armd Div AAR, Sep.

[69] 5th Armd Div AAR, Sep.

[70] See XV Corps AAR, Aug.

actually stopped the sustained drive, the day of reckoning was not far away. The Allies needed no soothsayers to know that an economy of famine awaited them as they moved onto German soil.

Yet it seemed as though the Allies only partly appreciated the implications of these conditions, for no admission was made that the pursuit had come to an end. Instead, optimism in most quarters continued, "tempered only by exasperation over supply shortages." The first train arrived in Soissons on 6 September, bringing hope that shortages might soon cease to exist. On that day the regrouping of the First Army forces had been almost completed, and American leaders had expected the drive to the Rhine to gather speed. With ten days of good weather, General Hodges said, he thought the war might well be over as far as organized resistance was concerned. Four days later, however, despite promises that shortages would be only temporary, Hodges admitted, as he awaited shipments of artillery, that the supply situation would undoubtedly delay, at least slightly, a concentrated attack on the Siegfried Line.[71]

Hodges' feeling actually mirrored concern with a question that was beginning to trouble some Allied commanders: Was the pursuit going to peter out before the Allies got through the West Wall and across the Rhine? Certain signs, though not to become clear until later, indicated that this might happen. The Allied forces were overextended along a 200-mile front between Antwerp and Switzerland, the troops exhausted, their equipment badly worn. Continental ports of entry were inadequate, and

transportation on the Continent was unequal to the demands placed upon it. As the Allies approached the German border, opposition seemed to stiffen, and the existence of the West Wall had its psychological effects. To insure the establishment of at least one bridgehead beyond the Rhine, General Eisenhower on 10 September approved employment by Field Marshal Montgomery of the Allied strategic reserve, the First Allied Airborne Army, which Montgomery was to use like seven-league boots in an attempt to get across the lower Rhine in the Netherlands.[72]

Whether Eisenhower drew upon SHAEF's strategic reserve to exploit the success of the pursuit or to propel a dying advance across the Rhine, the act, while perhaps subconsciously admitting the weariness of the Allied troops, sought to take advantage of German disorganization before the Germans could re-form a cohesive line. As the dispersed though optimistic Allied forces approached the West Wall, vague symptoms appeared that the Germans might achieve what they would later call the "Miracle of the West." *Army Group B,* despite the Mons pocket, managed to get what remained of its units east to the West Wall, and *Army Group G* (the *Nineteenth Army* and the *LXIV Corps*) escaped from southern and southwest France with the major part of its combat elements. By 10 September the juncture of *Army Groups B* and *G* was accomplished, and the front formed a continuous, if not solid, line from the North Sea to the Swiss border.[73] Considering the shortages of men, arms, equipment,

---

[71] Ruppenthal, *Logistical Support, I,* 583; Sylvan Diary, 6 and 10 Sep.

[72] For an account of this operation, see MacDonald, *The Siegfried Line Campaign.*

[73] *OB WEST, a Study in Command,* p. 166.

DRAGON'S TEETH, THE SIEGFRIED LINE

and supplies, the condition of the West Wall, and the immensity of the defeat suffered, the German recuperation would later appear incredible.

During the first few days of September there had been no coherent German defense. Panic infected rear areas. Supply installations were destroyed without orders, fuel depots demolished, ammunition dumps abandoned, ration and supply installations looted by troops and civilians, and reports on the status of supply nonexistent.[74] The retreating units had hardly any heavy weapons. Few of the panzer divisions had more than five to ten tanks in working order. The morale of the troops was depressed by Allied control of the air and by the abundance of Allied matériel, as compared with the inadequate German supplies. On 4 September Model stated that, in order to prop up the entire Western Front before it gave way completely, he needed a minimum of twenty-five fresh infantry divisions and at least five or six panzer divisions.[75]

Hitler, for his part, showed little appreciation of the difficulties facing *OB WEST* and some lack of knowledge of the situation. Since 28 August, on Hitler's order, *OB WEST* had been planning a counterattack against the southern Allied flank, a strike north in the Troyes area between the Seine and Marne Rivers. On 3 September Hitler

---

[74] MS # B-596 (Gerber).

[75] *AGp B Lagebeurteilungen, Ia;* MS # B-730 (Brandenberger); MS # B-623 (Keppler); MS # C-048 (Kraemer).

instructed *OB WEST* to launch an attack from the Nancy–Langres area toward Reims to roll up the Third Army right flank, to prevent junction of the OVERLORD and DRAGOON forces, and to cut American lines of communication. Reinforcements arriving piecemeal and committed defensively prevented the attack from ever getting under way. As late as 9 September, several days after the Americans had crossed the Meuse and the day after the British had crossed the Albert Canal, Hitler ordered the *Seventh Army* to "continue to fight a delaying action forward of the West Wall, especially [at] the mighty obstacles of the Meuse and the canal west of Maastricht." [76] He continued to hope that German counterattacks would cut off Allied armored spearheads and stabilize the front. He felt that the West Wall was at least potentially impregnable. And he guessed that the Allies were outrunning their supplies and would soon have to halt.

Perhaps the most critical day for the Germans had been 4 September. On that day, as the *Fifteenth Army* withdrew along the French coast generally to the north and as the *Fifth Panzer* and *Seventh Armies* retired generally to the northeast, the Second British Army plunged into the gap between the two forces and captured Antwerp. The news brought consternation to Hitler's headquarters in East Prussia. The possibility that Antwerp would solve the Allied port deficiency was bad enough, but far worse was the fact that only replacement and rear echelon units held the line along the entire Albert Canal

from Antwerp to Maastricht. Unless blocked quickly, "the door to northwestern Germany stood open." [77]

Hitler immediately ordered headquarters of the *First Parachute Army* and Generaloberst Kurt Student, commander of the German parachute troops, to move to the Netherlands and defend the canal lines. *OB WEST*, which had intended to commit the *First Parachute Army* in the Nancy–Langres area in a counterattack against the right flank and rear of Patton's Third Army, ordered Dietrich's *Fifth Panzer Army* headquarters to Nancy for the purpose. Dietrich departed at once, transferring his troops to the *Seventh Army*, newly commanded by General der Panzertruppen Erich Brandenberger.[78] Model ordered the *Fifteenth Army*, cut off by the British thrust to Antwerp, to withdraw part of its troops to the banks of the Schelde estuary (the sixty-mile water entrance to Antwerp); another part to the fortresses of Boulogne, Dunkerque, and Calais for a last-ditch defense; and a third portion to attempt to break through toward the east.[79] Though the latter quickly proved impossible, the presence of German troops in the Channel ports and along the Schelde would prove a headache to the Allies for weeks to come.[80] Meanwhile Student was forming a defense of the Albert Canal as "an improvisation on the grandest scale," and in a few days he succeeded in organizing the semblance of a defensive line by borrowing and

---

[76] *AGp B* to *Seventh Army*, transmitting Hitler Order, 9 Sep, *AGp B KTB, Op. Befehle;* see Pogue, *Supreme Command*, p. 304.

[77] MS # B–034 (Schramm).

[78] *OB WEST KTB*, 3 and 4 Sep.

[79] *AGp B* to *OB WEST*, 0115, 5 Sep, *AGp B Tagesmeldungen.*

[80] See Lucian Heichler, German Defense of the Gateway to Antwerp, OCMH MS R–22, and The Germans Opposite the XIX Corps, OCMH MS R–21.

confiscating staffs, troops, and matériel from retreating units.[81]

Hitler on 5 September also recalled Rundstedt whom he had relieved at the beginning of July. While Model remained the *Army Group B* commander, Rundstedt assumed his old post, Commander-in-Chief, West. Though Rundstedt was every bit as pessimistic as Model and canceled plans for counterattacks, his reappearance at *OB WEST* brought a resurgence of morale. Rundstedt was able to direct his attention to the whole Western Front, which Model in his preoccupation with *Army Group B* had been unable to do, and for the first time since 18 July, when Kluge had assumed Rommel's duties in addition to his own, a theater commander was present to co-ordinate the entire defensive effort in the west.

Counting his forces, Rundstedt found that *Army Groups B* and *G* consisted of forty-eight infantry and fifteen panzer-type divisions, of which only one quarter could be considered anywhere near full combat strength. He judged their effectiveness to be the equivalent of twenty-seven infantry and six or seven panzer divisions at the most. He estimated that the Allies had sixty in opposition. The silver lining in this dark cloud was the fact that although few units were up to authorized strength, the staffs of all higher headquarters were for the most part intact and able to function. Discipline and reorganization soon revealed that the fabric of command, though stretched and worn, could be made serviceable. By 11 September most of the German units that had been battered, outflanked, encircled, and ap-

parently destroyed had reappeared, in name at least, and were making an honest effort to protect the German border in the west.[82]

That they were able to accomplish even this much was miraculous in view of earlier German casualties. During June, July, and August the Germans had lost a minimum of 1,200,000 troops killed, wounded, missing, and captured, casualties of which approximately two thirds had been incurred in the east, where larger masses of men were employed.[83] The *OB WEST* staff later estimated that the campaign in the west, from the invasion to the West Wall, and including southern France, had cost Germany about 500,000 troops, of which about 200,000 had been lost in the coastal fortresses. Matériel losses were impossible to estimate; in addition to battle losses, all equipment permanently installed or lacking mobility was gone.[84]

In contrast, the Allies had landed more than 2,100,000 men and 460,000 vehicles on the Continent by 11 September, a combat force of forty-nine divisions.[85] Excluding the forces in southern France, where losses were light, Allied casualties from 6 June to 11 September numbered almost 40,000 killed, 164,000 wounded, and 20,000 missing—a total of 224,000, which was less than half the German casualties in the west.[86]

No wonder Rundstedt warned on 10 September that he needed at least five

---

[81] MS # B–717 (Student); see MacDonald, *The Siegfried Line Campaign.*

[82] *OB WEST, a Study in Command,* pp. 175ff., 188; see Charles V. P. von Luttichau, The Ardennes Offensive: Germany's Situation in the Fall of 1944, Pt. III, The Military Situation, OCMH MS R–19.

[83] See Cole, *Lorraine Campaign,* pp. 29–43, for a detailed examination of German manpower and equipment losses.

[84] *OB WEST, a Study in Command,* pp. 192ff.

[85] SHAEF G–3 War Room Summary 99.

[86] SHAEF G–3 War Room Summary 102.

or six weeks to restore the West Wall and characterized his situation on 11 September as "continued reduction in combat strength and lack of ammunition."[87] SHAEF had observed that the Germans did not seem to have enough men to hold the West Wall, and despite the increasing deterioration of Allied logistics, commanders on all echelons were quite certain that the end of the war was at hand.[88] The troops that had fought in the battle of the hedgerows remembered with some surprise how St. Lô had "seemed months away and Germany itself almost unattainable."[89]

There was a quality of madness about the whole debacle of Germany's forces in the West. . . . Isolated garrisons fought as viciously as before, but the central planning and coordination . . . were missing. . . . it looked very much as though Adolf Hitler . . . might be forced into surrender long before American and British units reached the Rhine. That was the avowed opinion of allied soldiers on the western front, and German prisoners were of the same mind, often stating that it couldn't last for another week.[90]

The fact that the Third Army had met increasing resistance in Lorraine hardly seemed as important as the fact that the enemy was in headlong flight before the First U.S. Army. Other developments bolstered this point of view:

While it is highly unlikely that Hitler, while he holds the reins of Government in Germany, will ever permit a capitulation of her Army, his position as head of government is becoming daily more unstable, and

interior unrest and dissension coupled with the gradual loss of Germany's satellites makes her position less and less stable. This indicates an early end of Herr Hitler.[91]

Most officers believed that the West Wall was only a bluff and that, since the Germans had hardly any troops left, it would take the Allies three days at the most to get through the fortifications. After that, there would remain only the task of mopping up scattered demoralized units inside Germany.[92]

The Siegfried Line . . . although a strong natural position, is not what it was ballyhooed to be by the Germans. . . . it will not be too difficult to break. . . . the great expenditure of money, materiel, and time the Germans made on the Siegfried Line is as great a waste as the French Maginot Line proved to be.[93]

General Bradley reported that Hodges was "quite optimistic about his ability to push through the Siegfried Line and on to the Rhine," and that the "situation in front of Patton looks very hopeful."[94] Field Marshal Montgomery was still thinking of getting on to Berlin. And General Eisenhower, though he may have had reservations, began to consider objectives beyond the Rhine—as far distant as Berlin.[95]

In most respects, optimism seemed justifiable. Turkey had broken diplomatic relations with Germany in August, and Rumania, Bulgaria, and Finland were negotiating for peace. A repetition of the autumn of 1918, when Bulgaria had defected, and Turkey and

---

[87] *OB WEST KTB*, 11 Sep; *AGp B* Sitrep, 11 Sep, *AGp B KTB*.

[88] SHAEF Weekly Intel Summary 25, 9 Sep, SHAEF G–2 File; see Pogue, *Supreme Command*, p. 283.

[89] Hewitt, *Story of the 30th Infantry Division*, p. 22.

[90] 3d Armored Division, *Spearhead in the West*, p. 81.

[91] VII Corps Annex 2 to FO 9. 27 Aug.

[92] See CI 32 (4th Div).

[93] 5th Armd Div AAR, Sep.

[94] Bradley to Eisenhower, 14 Sep, 12th AGp File Mil Objs, II.

[95] See, for example, Eisenhower to Bradley. 15 Sep, SHAEF File GCT 370–31/Plans.

Austria had collapsed, appeared at hand. The Allies in September 1944 were beyond the Ghent–Mons–Mézières–Sedan–Pont-à-Mousson line that the Allies in 1918 had reached by 11 November. To some observers it seemed that the Allies were closer to victory after the pursuit in 1944 than after Marshal Ferdinand Foch's grand autumn offensive, which had preceded German surrender in World War I.

Everywhere the Allies looked in early September of 1944, they saw success. The Germans in Italy were retreating northward. The Russians were about to enter Germany in the east. In the Pacific the two main lines of Allied advance were converging on the Philippines and landings were about to take place that would immediately precede the invasion of Leyte in October. About the same time that the Japanese in northern India were being driven across the border into Burma, the Allies captured the Burmese city of Myitkyina. At the Quebec conference (OCTAGON) in mid-September, Allied leaders displayed great optimism as they discussed the probability of an immediate occupation of the German satellites, of the Axis-occupied countries, and of Germany itself.[96]

The end of the war in Europe seemed just around the corner, and General Marshall considered that "the push on the West Wall is of major importance in the conduct of global war at the moment."[97] Allied forces in southern France on 10 September were about to capture Dijon, and that evening the first meeting occurred between reconnaissance troops of the OVERLORD and ANVIL-DRAGOON forces. When Lt. Gen. Jacob L. Devers' 6th Army Group became operational under SHAEF control on 15 September, General Eisenhower would command forces along a continuous front from the Netherlands to Switzerland, with three army groups ready to enter Germany. No one seemed to remember Marshal Foch's reply in November 1918, when asked how long it would take to drive the Germans back to the Rhine if they refused the armistice terms, "Maybe three, maybe four or five months, who knows?"[98]

Twenty-six years later, on 10 September 1944, General Bradley designated six critical terrain features on the Rhine River—rather evenly spaced corps objective areas across the 12th Army Group front—as suitable bridgehead sites.[99] Not even the most pessimistic prophet, if a pessimist could have been found in early September, would have ventured the prediction that it would take the Allies much longer than "three, maybe four or five months" to gain these objectives. Yet it would be March 1945 before the Allies got across the Rhine River. A cycle similar in some respects to that which had occurred during the period of the breakout and pursuit would have to be repeated before final victory came in Europe.

---

[96] See Ray S. Cline, *Washington Command Post: The Operations Division* (Washington, 1951), pp. 330, 340, and Maurice Matloff, *Strategic Planning for Coalition Warfare: 1943–1944* (Washington, 1959), Ch. XXIII, both volumes in the UNITED STATES ARMY IN WORLD WAR II series.

[97] Marshall to Eisenhower, W–25528. 5 Sep. Pogue Files.

[98] Quoted in B. H. Liddell Hart, *A History of the World War, 1914–1918* (London: Faber & Faber, 1934), p. 490.

[99] 12th AGp Ltr of Instrs 8, 10 Sep; Answers by Gen Kibler to Questions by Col Cole, 29 May 46. ML–501.

Appendix A

TABLE OF EQUIVALENT RANKS

U.S. Army	German Army and Air Force	German Waffen-SS
None	Reichsmarschall	None
General of the Army	Generalfeldmarschall	Reichsfuehrer-SS
General	Generaloberst	Oberstgruppenfuehrer
Lieutenant General	General der Infanterie	Obergruppenfuehrer
	Artillerie	
	Gebirgstruppen	
	Kavallerie	
	Nachrichtentruppen	
	Panzertruppen	
	Pioniere	
	Luftwaffe	
	Flieger	
	Fallschirmtruppen	
	Flakartillerie	
	Luftnachrichtentruppen	
Major General	Generalleutnant	Gruppenfuehrer
Brigadier General	Generalmajor	Brigadefuehrer
None	None	Oberfuehrer
Colonel	Oberst	Standartenfuehrer
Lieutenant Colonel	Oberstleutnant	Obersturmbannfuehrer
Major	Major	Sturmbannfuehrer
Captain	Hauptmann	Hauptsturmfuehrer
Captain (Cavalry)	Rittmeister	
First Lieutenant	Oberleutnant	Obersturmfuehrer
Second Lieutenant	Leutnant	Untersturmfuehrer

Appendix B

Recipients of the Distinguished Service Cross

All pertinent Army records have been scrutinized in an effort to include in the following list the name of every soldier who received the DSC for his part in the operations recounted in this volume. Inasmuch as no complete listing of DSC awards is maintained in any single Army file, it is possible that some names may inadvertently have been omitted. (P) indicates a posthumous award; * indicates that the Bronze Oak Leaf Cluster was awarded to a DSC previously ordered; # indicates that both the DSC and the Bronze Oak Leaf Cluster were awarded to the individual for separate actions during the operations narrated in this volume.

1st Lt. David W. Allard
Capt. James D. Allgood
Capt. Benjamin W. Anderson (P)
T/Sgt. Joe M. Barnett
S/Sgt. Wardie Barnett
Lt. Col. Jacob W. Bealke, Jr.
Pvt. Anthony J. Blazus, Jr.
Pvt. Bennie F. Boatright (P)
S/Sgt. Thomas R. Brazil
Pfc. Buster E. Brown
1st Sgt. Virgil L. Brown (P)
Cpl. Richard S. Butterfield
Pfc. Clifford W. Buzzard
Capt. Delmont K. Byrn
Pfc. George J. Caldwell
Pfc. Alfred A. Cannon
T/Sgt. Lawrence Cappeletti
Capt. Thomas F. Carothers
T/Sgt. Wilson R. Carr
Capt. Phillip H. Carroll
S/Sgt. Ignacio H. Castro
Sgt. Wilbur Caton
S/Sgt. James J. Cermak
Capt. Graham V. Chamblee
Col. Bruce C. Clarke
Lt. Col. Christian H. Clarke, Jr.
S/Sgt. Gayln Clay
Capt. Richard T. Clemens
Capt. Cameron A. Clough
Sgt. Peter A. Cocossa (P)
Lt. Col. Wilson D. Coleman (P)
Maj. William K. C. Collonan (Missing)
T/Sgt. Irvin F. Conley (P)
Sgt. Harold B. Cordes
Pfc. Roy V. Craft (P)
Pfc. Clifford L. Curry
Brig. Gen. Holmes E. Dager
1st Lt. Anthony V. Danna

Sgt. Samuel C. Davis (P)
Capt. Mario T. De Felice
Pfc. William A. Delmont (P)
Lt. Col. Leander L. Doan
Pvt. William J. Draper
2d Lt. James I. Durden (P)
1st Lt. Robert Edlin
Pvt. Leonard L. Eggleston
Pfc. Joseph A. Elwell (P)
Capt. Reynold C. Erichson
Pfc. Louis Ferrari (P)
Col. Harry A. Flint (P) *
Pfc. Milo J. Flynn
Pvt. Thomas T. Flynn
Cpl. Clarence E. Follis
1st Lt. Mario J. Fortuna
Lt. Col. Robert E. Frankland
S/Sgt. Carl J. Frantz
Lt. Col. Arthur H. Fuller
T/Sgt. Joseph P. Fuller
Pfc. James L. Geach
Capt. Harry L. Gentry
Pfc. Lawrence Georgeatos (P)
Capt. Jack S. Gerrie
Pfc. Walter C. Giebelstein
Col. Jesse L. Gibney
Pvt. Jack Gill (P)
Pfc. Joseph J. Giordano
Capt. Hamilton F. Glover (P)
Pfc. Earl G. Goins
Capt. Richard G. Gooley
2d Lt. Joseph Gorniak, Jr.
1st Lt. John R. Greene (P)
Col. Wilborn B. Griffith, Jr. (P)
S/Sgt. Konstanty Gugala
S/Sgt. Stanley P. Gull
S/Sgt. Lawrence W. Gunderson (P)
2d Lt. Earl O. Hall (P)

Lt. Col. William A. Hamberg
1st Lt. Harry F. Hansen
Pfc. Earl W. Harrington (P)
Brig. Gen. William K. Harrison, Jr.
2d Lt. Frank A. Heberstreit, Jr. (P)
Pfc. Ted Hefley
S/Sgt. Richard F. Heinzelman
2d Lt. Robert J. Henglein
1st Lt. William J. Henry
Lt. Col. Lindsay C. Herkness, Jr.
2d Lt. John F. Hermanspan, Jr. (P)
Lt. Col. William M. Hernandez (P)
Col. Chester J. Hirschfelder
Pvt. Eugene Hix (P)
T/5 Vincent J. Hughes
Capt. Howard H. Ingling
S/Sgt. George E. Jackson
1st Lt. George E. Jenkins
Pvt. Frank D. Joseph, Jr.
Capt. Arthur W. Kaiser (P)
Sgt. Robert F. Kee (P)
1st Lt. Robert J. Kemp
1st Lt. Ralph A. Kerley
Pfc. Frank Kielbasa (P)
Pvt. Thomas E. King (P)
2d Lt. Richard A. Kirsting (P)
S/Sgt. William B. Kolosky
2d Lt. Edward F. Koritzke (P)
T/3 Henry J. Kucharski
S/Sgt. Edward J. Land
S/Sgt. Martin J. Lavelle
Pfc. Amijan O. Lazar (P)
Lt. Col. Kelley B. Lemmon, Jr.
Capt. Edward R. Lienhart
2d Lt. Richard H. Lininger (P)
Lt. Col. Frederick H. Loomis
S/Sgt. Edward V. Maloney (P)
Lt. Col. Raymond B. Marlin
Capt. John W. Marsh (P)
Lt. Col. Paul W. McCollum (P)
Pfc. Charles P. McGuire (P)
Brig. Gen. Raymond S. McLain*
1st Lt. Alfred P. McPeters (P)
Cpl. Raymond H. Milanowski
1st Lt. Arthur J. Miller
1st Lt. Hubert G. Miller
Capt. William C. Miller
Capt. John S. Milligan, Jr. (P)
1st Lt. George R. Mitchell
1st Lt. Richard J. Monihan
1st Sgt. John R. Morton

1st Lt. James L. Mosby
Pvt. Arden Nystrom (P)
Cpl. Franklin D. Owen (P)
Pvt. Melvin V. Pardee (P)
S/Sgt. J. W. Parks
Cpl. Clarence Patton (P)
S/Sgt. Edward A. Patynski
T/Sgt. Lloyd N. Peterson
1st Lt. Vernon W. Pickett (P)
Capt. William F. Pieri (P)
S/Sgt. Joseph S. Pomber (P)
Maj. Leroy R. Pond#
S/Sgt. Lafayette G. Pool
Pfc. Henry N. Powell (P)
T/5 John G. Prentice (P)
Pvt. Peter Preslipsky
Pvt. Barney H. Prosser
1st Lt. William L. Pryor (PW)
Pfc. Joseph S. Przasnyski
Maj. Lloyd J. Ptak
1st Lt. Murray S. Pulver
Pfc. Mike S. Rabago (P)
Lt. Col. George B. Randolph (P)
1st Lt. Joseph C. Reaser
1st Lt. Delbert G. Reck
Cpl. Leonard V. Reppart
T/5 Frank F. Reyna
Pfc. Frederick S. Richardson
1st Lt. David S. Rinehart
Maj. Gen. Maurice Rose
Pfc. Hoyt T. Rowell
Pfc. Dominick J. Salvemini (P)
S/Sgt. George T. Scanlon
Maj. Robert H. Schulz
2d Lt. Harold B. Selleck
Pfc. Edward J. Sharkey (P)
Capt. Naubert O. Simard, Jr. (P)
Sgt. William T. Sipola (P)
2d Lt. Ewell L. Smith, Jr.
T/Sgt. Harold D. Snyder
1st Lt. William F. Squire (P)
Capt. George T. Stallings
Sgt. Edward L. Stannard (P)
Capt. Charles D. Stapleton (P)
T/Sgt. Fred D. Steelman (P)
T/Sgt. Harold V. Sterling
Pfc. Leo D. Stroup
S/Sgt. Walter R. Tauchert (P)
Pvt. Floyd Taylor
Pfc. William Thurston
T/Sgt. John Tokarchek
T/Sgt. Howard W. Trego

S/Sgt. Frederick W. Unger
Pfc. Richard Von Patten
Pfc. Theodore G. Wagner
1st Lt. George E. Wagoner
Brig. Gen. Nelson M. Walker (P)
Maj. Gen. Walton H. Walker
Pfc. Walter S. Wanielista (P)
2d Lt. Frank Warnock
2d Lt. Glenn H. Warren
Brig. Gen. William G. Weaver*
Pfc. Alfred B. Weiner (P)
Sgt. Harry Weiss (P)

Lt. Col. H. K. Wesson (P)
Maj. Arthur L. West, Jr.
S/Sgt. Clarence E. White
Pvt. William H. Whitson (P)
S/Sgt. Mark D. Wilcox
Capt. Leonard S. Wilds
Capt. Robert C. Wiley (P)
T/Sgt. Dupe A. Willingham (P)
T/Sgt. Milford W. Wilson (P)
Maj. Gen. John S. Wood
1st Lt. Ronal E. Woody, Jr.
Pfc. Leo Zingale

Bibliographical Note

The official records of U.S. units in the field provide the documentary basis of *Breakout and Pursuit*. These consist of monthly narrative After Action Reports accompanied by supporting papers (journals, periodic reports, messages, staff section reports, and overlays), as well as administrative records, originating in each headquarters down through regiment and separate battalion. Without this collection of primary source material, in the possession of the World War II Records Division, National Archives and Records Service (NARS), it would have been impossible to write a detailed history of operations. All else has been supplementary.

The unit records naturally vary in quantity and quality. Some are so sketchy that they are historical in form only. Others are so complete that they could well have been motivated by a passion for history. Among those headquarters that preserved records of exceptional completeness and thereby lightened the task of the historian are the VIII and XV Corps and the 90th and 9th Divisions. Particular mention must be made of the valuable records of telephone conversations in the papers of the 2d, 29th, 30th, and 83d Divisions.

The U.S. Air Force Historical Section made available from its records primary source material on Operation Cobra. The Historical Sections of the French Army and Navy made available published and manuscript accounts to the author during his brief visit to France in the summer of 1953.

Certain headquarters consolidated their After Action Reports after the war and published official histories. In this category are the 12th Army Group *Report of Operations* (in fourteen volumes, which detail the work of the staff sections), the First U.S. Army *Report of Operations* (two separate series: one in seven volumes covering the period 20 October 1943 to 1 August 1944, the other in four volumes, covering the period from 1 August 1944 to 22 February 1945), the two-volume Third Army *After Action Report* (of which most of the official supporting documents seem to have vanished), and the *V Corps Operations in the ETO*.

Other headquarters published unofficial histories. Many of these tend to be little more than mementos for members of the command, strong on photographs, personal anecdotes, and a well-earned pride of unit accomplishment. Notable exceptions are the *Combat Record* of the 6th Armored Division, the 314th Infantry Regiment's *Through Combat,* the 3d Armored Division's *Spearhead in the West,* Robert L. Hewitt's *Work Horse of the Western Front: the Story of the 30th Division,* and *Conquer, the Story of the Ninth U.S. Army, 1944-1945.*

Combat interviews secured shortly after action by members of Information and Historical detachments assigned to the field armies provide detailed accounts of activity on the individual, squad, platoon, and company levels. Among other things, they illustrate graphically the meaning of morale, the significance of leadership, the value of a foxhole, and the fragmentary nature of the information usually possessed by the individual soldier on the battlefield. The interviews sometimes give glimpses into the operations of a headquarters and occasionally note personal conferences and statements by key commanders. Particular mention must be made of the valuable material recorded in Maj. Franklin Ferriss' Notes on XIX Corps Operations and of the 4th Division interviews conducted under the direction of Lt. Col. William Gayle. James A. Huston's *Biography of a Battalion,* an independent work, presents a vivid picture of how a battalion staff worked. Hospital Interviews, made in the United Kingdom and collected into four typescript volumes, are transcriptions of conversations rather than recorded replies to searching questions and therefore are of variable value, their historical worth primarily being an occasional significant detail.

After the war, some of the combat historians were assigned to the U.S. Forces European Theater Historical Section to prepare a series of preliminary manuscript studies on the operations. Written during parts of 1945 and 1946, these accounts suggested an organizational basis for part of *Breakout and Pursuit* at the least and in some instances presented rather complete stories of segments of the campaign. Their deficiency in general is their lack of knowledge of decisions made on the higher echelons of command. Consequently, the writers were usually limited to a day-by-day presentation of events. The manuscripts used in this volume were written by Hollis Alpert, Franklin Ferriss, David Garth, George Halas, Kenneth Hechler, Monroe Ludden, and Jose Topete.

A growing body of published historical literature throws increasing light on the period. The volumes in the European subseries of the UNITED STATES ARMY IN WORLD WAR II by Hugh Cole, Forrest C. Pogue, Gordon Harrison, Charles B. MacDonald, and Roland G. Ruppenthal have all been most helpful, as the frequency of their appearance in the footnotes will attest. Stacey's *The Canadian Army, 1939–1945* has served as the principal source on Canadian operations; Montgomery's *Normandy to the Baltic* on British operations. Wilmot's *The Struggle for Europe* has been helpful for both Canadian and British activities. No single source has been used for the operations of the 2d French Armored Division, but Even's account in the *Revue Historique de l'Armée* has been most satisfactory. *St. Lô,* in the Army's American Forces in Action Series, has been used extensively. *Europe: Argument to V-E Day,* a volume in the series THE ARMY AIR FORCES IN WORLD WAR II, has proved valuable. Also helpful were the Reports of Generals Marshall and Eisenhower and the Despatches of Air Marshal Leigh-Mallory and Admiral Sir Bertram H. Ramsay. The British Army of the Rhine in 1947 compiled a series of books as the basis for battlefield tours; excellent accounts of key actions, the titles applicable to this volume are *GOOD-WOOD, BLUECOAT, TOTALIZE,* and *NEPTUNE*—the code names of the operations covered. Dansette's *Histoire de la Libération de Paris* is a superb account of that subject.

Memoirs have furnished insights into the activities as well as the personalities of important personnages. The published accounts by Generals Eisenhower, Bradley, Patton, de Guingand, and Air Marshal Harris are well known. The Brereton *Diaries* fall into the category of memoirs rather than of primary source material. On the German side the published recollections of Speidel, Choltitz, and Ramcke have been consulted, as has Blumentritt's description of Rundstedt, a memoir rather than a biography.

Herval's two-volume *Bataille de Normandie* offers an interesting collection of scenes of warfare as remembered by inhabitants of the terrain over which the battles were fought. Some of these reminiscences that detail the hazards of civilian life during a bombardment or attack were compressed from book-length manuscripts; others were later expanded into published volumes. Among the best are accounts by J. and G. Buisson (on Mortain) and by Commandant Richard Mouton (on Argentan–Falaise). In the same category of personal or community adventure is the collection edited by Xavier Rousseau, who was interested in the region around Argentan. Other local historians have written narratives of the battles around their towns, among the better ones the volume by R. Fouque on St. Malo. Such material has value to the military historian as a reminder that warfare does not take place on an abstract sand-table level. It also serves to explain vividly such matters as liberation. Witness the exclamation of a Frenchman who has just come into contact with an American soldier for the first time: "Oh! I beg your pardon. Excuse me. How quite joyful we are to be delivered . . . Rule Britannia . . . Yankee Doodle . . . Oh!" (Rousseau, *La Bataille de Normandie au Pays d'Argentan*, p. 30).

The Pogue Files, OCMH, mentioned so frequently throughout the volume, belongs in a special classification. Dr. Forrest C. Pogue collected a vast amount of material while preparing his volume, *The Supreme Command.* One part consists of interviews and letters that Dr. Pogue obtained after World War II from important participants. Another part includes papers, journals, and letters written by key participants during the war. Dr. Pogue kindly opened much of his collection to the author, making available in some instances original papers, transcripts, and photostats, in other instances his own notes of interviews or of papers. Much of the material in the Pogue Files is not available elsewhere, though some documents that have been cited as in the Pogue Files exist in SHAEF or 12th Army Group files as well.

Principal research on the German operations of the period was performed by Mr. James B. Hodgson, who wrote several manuscripts (in OCMH Files) more or less attuned to the organization of *Breakout and Pursuit.* These manuscripts are based principally on German documentary sources, the most important being the daily war diaries of operations, *Kriegstagebuecher (KTB)*, maintained by the forward echelons of all commands, together with supporting documents in annexes *(Anlagen).* The captured German records seized by the U.S. Army during and immediately after World War II are in the custody of the World War II Records Division, NARS.

Though many of the German military records have been lost, enough are extant to give a remarkably clear picture of operations. The details are vivid, primarily because of the small size of the German staffs. Stenographic notes of commanders' conferences were more frequently preserved than not. All the diaries contain reasons for commanders' decisions. The after action reports were approved by the chief of staff or comparable officer of the unit who obviously was aware of the scrutiny that later historians would give them.

Details on Hitler's planning are in the Fuehrer Fragments—remnants of notes of Hitler's conferences—found in the published U.S. Office of Naval Intelligence (ONI) *Fuehrer Conferences* and, partially, in Gilbert's *Hitler Directs His War.* The ONI *Fuehrer Directives* (in two volumes) and the International Military Tribunal *Documents* (in forty-odd volumes) include most of the important policy papers on Hitler's strategy. Hitler's field orders for operations on the Western Front may be found in the *OB WEST KTB Anlagen* and in the *Army Group B Fuehrerbefehle.*

The daily situation reports on which OKW based its knowledge of the war in the west are collected in the OKM war diary, which is also useful as an index to Hitler's strategic thought. The Jodl diary, actually Jodl's memo book, is helpful. The most important document on the OKW level is the *OKW/WFSt KTB, Der Westen,* written from his own notes by Maj. Percy Schramm in the spring of 1945 (referred to in the volume both as *Der Westen* (Schramm) and as MS # B–034 (Schramm). Though the supporting documents of this manuscript have been destroyed and though it is sometimes difficult to check obvious errors and inconsistencies, *Der Westen* is the only source that reflects Hitler's day-to-day planning.

The *OB WEST KTB* is principally useful as an index to select supporting documents, which present much material on OKW intentions and sometimes the reasons for decisions both strategic and tactical. The *OB WEST KTB Anlagen,* in the custody of the German Bundesarchiv in Bonn, became available for consultation only after completion of *Breakout and Pursuit* and were used primarily to check information already secured from other sources.

The *Army Group B* records are by far the best of any echelon, the war diary opening each day with a description of events and following with a chronological listing of telephone conversations, conferences, and notes. Supporting documents, collected according to category and not indexed to the text, include the *Fuehrerbefehle,* field orders, and periodic reports.

The *Seventh Army KTB* is wordy and less useful than its telephone journal. Though no *Seventh Army* field orders for July have survived, the telephone notes, as well as command conference minutes in the supporting documents of other war diaries, provide a rather complete picture. The *Fifth Panzer Army (Panzer Group West)* records are quite short, while those of the *LXXXI Corps,* the only corps that has left a record, are detailed and excellent.

Few, if any, division war diaries survived the war. The operations of *Panzer Lehr* are reflected to a small extent in the division rear echelon *Ib Kriegstagebuch,* which preserved some messages and field orders. The *352d Division* diary, which was not available, seems to have been the basis of a manuscript written by Lt. Col. Fritz Ziegelmann, the *Ia.* The diaries of the 155-mm. howitzer battalion of the *353d Division* and of the *17th SS Engineer Battalion* are exceptional survivals.

Some after action reports (through 15 July 1944) appear in a collection of documents entitled *AGp B KTB Anlagen.* A few others were collected by the OKH *Abwicklungsstab Rudolstadt,* which had the task of completing the administrative affairs of deactivated units.

Rear echelon headquarters under the *Ib* or *OQu* of the command also maintained diaries that detailed the activities of administrative and technical services. The *Oberquartiermeister West KTB* and the *AGp B Versorgungsabteilung KTB (Ib KTB)* reflect most of the German logistical difficulties in the west.

Maps of the changing situation are mostly on the OKW level and often represent the cumulative errors of reporting dispositions through the multitude of headquarters.

The officers' personnel files of the OKH (in OCMH Files) provide much personal history of important participants, as does Josef Foltmann and Hanns Moeller-Witten, *Opfergang der Generale* (Berlin, 1952).

Immediately after World War II, the USFET Historical Section was responsible for organizing a project wherein high-ranking German officers wrote accounts of their experiences. This work still continues under the supervision of the USAREUR Historical Section. The *Guide to Foreign Military Studies 1945–54, Catalogue and Index,* published in 1954, indicates the broad scope of the more than a thousand studies. It is difficult to evaluate the manuscripts. Those based on contemporary material are in the small minority. The bulk, written from memory, must be accepted with caution. Many officers indulge in apologetics. Most seem to hold Hitler responsible for their own tactical errors. Yet all give details that are to be found nowhere else.

Glossary

AAA	Antiaircraft artillery
AAF	Army Air Forces
AAR	After action report
Abn	Airborne
ACIGS	Assistant Chief, Imperial General Staff
Admin	Administrative
ADSEC	Advance Section
AEAF	Allied Expeditionary Air Force
AEF	Allied Expeditionary Force
AF	Air Force
AFA	American Forces in Action
AGF	Army Ground Forces
AGp	Army Group
AGWAR	Adjutant General, War Department
Ammo	Ammunition
ANCXF	Allied Naval Commander Expeditionary Force
Anlage(n)	Appendix or annex
ANVIL	The plan for the Allied invasion of southern France
Armd	Armored
Arty	Artillery
Avn	Aviation
AW	Automatic weapons
BAOR	British Army Operations Records
BAR	Browning automatic rifle
BCT	Battalion combat team
Bd	Board
BLUECOAT	British Second Army attack south from Caumont, beginning on 29 July 1944
Bn	Battalion
Br	Branch; British
C	Combat
Cav	Cavalry
CB	Combat battalion
CCA	Combat Command A
CCB	Combat Command B
CCR	Combat Command R
CCS	Combined Chiefs of Staff
CG	Commanding General
CI	Combat Interviews

CIGS	*Chief, Imperial General Staff*
CinC	Commander in Chief
Circ	Circulation
Cml	Chemical
CO	Commanding Officer
Co	Company
COBRA	First Army plan and operation to penetrate the German defenses in the Cotentin by the combination of concentrated power on the ground and overwhelming bombardment from the air; the breakthrough starting 25 July
CofS	Chief of Staff
Comd	Command
Comdr	Commander
COMZ	Communications Zone
Conf	Conference
Contl	Control
COSSAC	Chief of Staff to the Supreme Allied Commander (designate)
CP	Command post
CROSSBOW	The Allied air attacks by heavy bombers on the launching sites for the German V–1 weapons
Dept	Department
Dir	Directive
Div	Division
Doc	Document
DRAGOON	The plan for the Allied invasion of southern France, code name that replaced ANVIL
DSC	Distinguished Service Cross
ECB	Engineer combat battalion
Engr	Engineer
ESB	Engineer special brigade
Est	Estimate
ETHINT	European Theater Historical Interview of former German military personnel
ETOUSA	European Theater of Operations, U.S. Army
EUCOM	European Command
FA	Field artillery
FFI	*Forces Françaises de l'Intérieur* (French Forces of the Interior)
Flak	Antiaircraft
Fld	Field
FO	Field Order

FORTITUDE	Allied deception operations designed to convince the Germans of an invasion of western Europe in the Pas-de-Calais area
FUSA	First U.S. Army
G–1	Personnel section of division or higher staff
G–2	Intelligence section of division or higher staff
G–3	Operations section of division or higher staff
G–4	Logistics and Supply section of division or higher staff
Gen	General
GOODWOOD	British Second Army plan and operation, south of Caen, 18 July 1944
Gp	Group
HE	High-explosive
Hist	Historical
Hosp	Hospital
Hq	Headquarters
IG	Inspector General
Immed	Immediate
Incl	Inclosure
Inf	Infantry
Info	Information
Instr	Instruction
Intel	Intelligence
Interv	Interview
I.S.I.S.	Inter-Service Information Series
Jnl	Journal
JPS	Joint Staff Planners
Jt	Joint
King Tigers	German heavy tanks
KTB	*Kriegstagebuch* (war dairy)
Ltr	Letter
LVT (1)	Landing Vehicle, Tracked, Unarmored (Mark I) "Alligator"
MC	Medical Corps
Mecz	Mechanized
Mil	Military
Min	Minutes
MIRS	Military Intelligence Research Section
MLR	Main line of resistance
Msg	Message
Mtg	Meeting
NCWTF	Naval Commander Western Task Force
Nebelwerfer	Rocket projector or chemical mortar

NEPTUNE	The plan for the invasion of western Europe, used for security reasons after September 1943 in place of OVERLORD
OB WEST *Oberbefehlshaber West*	*Oberbefehlshaber West* Highest ground headquarters of the Western Front
Oberster Befehlshaber *der Deutschen* *Wehrmacht*	Supreme Commander in Chief of the Armed Forces
Objs	Objectives
Obs	Observation
OCMH	Office of the Chief of Military History
OKH	*Oberkommando des Heeres* (Army High Command)
OKL	*Oberkommando der Luftwaffe* (Air Force High Command)
OKM	*Oberkommando der Kriegsmarine* (Navy High Command)
OKW	*Oberkommando der Wehrmacht* (Armed Forces High Command)
OMAHA	The Normandy beach assaulted by the U.S. V Corps on 6 June 1944
ONI	Office of Naval Intelligence
OP	Observation post
Opn (s)	Operation (s)
Ord	Ordnance
OVERLORD	Plan for the invasion of western Europe in 1944 designed to secure for the Allies the lodgment area bounded by the Seine, Eure, and Loire Rivers
Panther	German Mark V tank
Panzerfaust	Recoilless German antitank rocket, hand-carried
Per	Periodic
Plng	Planning
POL	Petrol, oil, and lubricants
Prog	Progress
PS	Planning staff
PWI	Prisoner of war interrogation
Pz	*Panzer*
QMG	Quartermaster General
RAF	Royal Air Force
Rcd	Record
RCT	Regimental combat team
Recon	Reconnaissance
Regt	Regiment
Rev	Revised

Rhinos	Rhinoceros attachments to cut hedgerows
Rpt	Report
S–3	Operations and training section of a unit not having a general staff
SC	Supreme Commander
SCAEF	Supreme Commander, Allied Expeditionary Force
SCR	Signal Corps radio
Sec	Section
Secy	Secretary
Serv	Service
SGS	Secretary, General Staff
SHAEF	Supreme Headquarters, Allied Expeditionary Force
Sig	Signal
Sitrep	Situation report
SOP	Standing operating procedure
SP	Self-propelled
Spec	Special
Sq	Squadron
SS	*Shutzstaffel* (Elite Guard)
TAC	Tactical Air Command
TD	Tank destroyer
Tel	Telephone
Telecon	Telephone conversation
Telg	Telegram
TF	Task force
Tiger	German Mark VI (heavy tank)
Tk	Tank
Totalize	First Canadian Army attack toward Falaise, 8 August 1944
TSFET	Theater Service Forces European Theater
TUSA	Third U.S. Army
USAF	U.S. Air Force
USAFET	U.S. Army Forces, European Theater
USFET	U.S. Forces in the European Theater
USSAFE	U.S. Strategic Air Forces in Europe
USSTAF	U.S. Strategic Air Forces
Utah	The Normandy beach assaulted by the U.S. VII Corps on 6 June 1944
V–1	*Vergeltungswaffe* (Vengeance weapon)
V–2	Supersonic rockets
VHF	Very high frequency
Waffen SS	Combat arm of the SS
Wehrmacht	Armed Forces
Wehrmachtbefehlshaber	Armed Forces Commander
Werfer	Mortar, rocket launcher

WFSt	*Wehrmachtfuehrungsstab* (Armed Forces Operations Staff)
WP	White phosphorus

Basic Military Map Symbols*

Symbols within a rectangle indicate a military unit, within
a triangle an observation post, and within a circle a supply
point.

Military Units—Identification

Antiaircraft Artillery . . . .

Armored Command . . . .

Army Air Forces . . . .

Artillery, except Antiaircraft and Coast Artillery . . . .

Cavalry, Horse . . . .

Cavalry, Mechanized . . . .

Chemical Warfare Service . . . .

Coast Artillery . . . .

Engineers . . . .

Infantry . . . .

Medical Corps . . . .

Ordnance Department . . . .

Quartermaster Corps . . . .

Signal Corps . . . .

Tank Destroyer . . . .

Transportation Corps . . . .

Veterinary Corps . . . .

Airborne units are designated by combining a gull wing
symbol with the arm or service symbol:

Airborne Artillery . . . .

Airborne Infantry . . . .

*For complete listing of symbols in use during the World War II period, see
FM 21–30, dated October 1943, from which these are taken.

Size Symbols

The following symbols placed either in boundary lines or above the rectangle, triangle, or circle inclosing the identifying arm or service symbol indicate the size of military organization:

Squad . . . . •

Section. . . . . ••

Platoon . . . . •••

Company, troop, battery, Air Force flight I

Battalion, cavalry squadron, or Air Force squadron II

Regiment or group; combat team (with abbreviation CT following identifying numeral) III

Brigade, Combat Command of Armored Division, or Air Force Wing. X

Division or Command of an Air Force. XX

Corps or Air Force XXX

Army. XXXX

Group of Armies. XXXXX

EXAMPLES

The letter or number to the left of the symbol indicates the unit designation; that to the right, the designation of the parent unit to which it belongs. Letters or numbers above or below boundary lines designate the units separated by the lines:

Company A, 137th Infantry . . . . A ⊠ 137

8th Field Artillery Battalion. . . . . ⊡ 8

Combat Command A, 1st Armored Division. . . . . A ⬭ I

Observation Post, 23d Infantry. . . . . ⧊ 23

Command Post, 5th Infantry Division . . . . ⊠ 5

Boundary between 137th and 138th Infantry . . . . —¦¦¦— with 137 above and 138 below

Weapons

Machine gun . . . . •→

Gun. . . . . •

Gun battery . . . . ⊔⊔⊔

Howitzer or Mortar . . . . ◆

Tank . . . . ◇

Self-propelled gun . . . . ⬭•

Index